# THE OXFORD INDIA

The Oxford India Collection is a series which brings together
writings of enduring value published by OUP.

Other titles include

*The Oxford India Ghalib*
*The Oxford India Ramanujan*
*The Oxford India Illustrated Corbett*

THE OXFORD INDIA
# PREMCHAND

with an introduction by
FRANCESCA ORSINI

**OXFORD**
UNIVERSITY PRESS

# OXFORD
UNIVERSITY PRESS

YMCA Library Building, Jai Singh Road, New Delhi 110 001

Oxford University Press is a department of the University of Oxford. It furthers the
University's objective of excellence in research, scholarship, and education
by publishing worldwide in

Oxford   New York
Auckland   Cape Town   Dar es Salaam   Hong Kong   Karachi   Kuala Lumpur
Madrid   Melbourne   Mexico City   Nairobi   New Delhi   Shanghai   Taipei   Toronto

With offices in
Argentina   Austria   Brazil   Chile   Czech Republic   France   Greece   Guatemala
Hungary   Italy   Japan   Poland   Portugal   Singapore   South Korea   Switzerland
Thailand   Turkey   Ukraine   Vietnam

Oxford is a registered trademark of Oxford University Press
in the UK and in certain other countries

Published in India
by Oxford University Press, New Delhi

© Oxford University Press 2004

ISBN-13: 978-0-19-566501-7
ISBN-10: 0-19-566501-5

Printed in India by De-Unique, New Delhi 110 018
Published by Oxford University Press
YMCA Library Building, Jai Singh Road, New Delhi 110 001

# Contents

PART II: NOVELS

Nirmala (translated by Alok Rai)

Gaban: The Stolen Jewels (translated by Christopher R. King)

*Appendix: The Aim of Literature* by Francesca Orsini

# *Introduction*

To be labelled a 'classic' can be a double-edged sword. On the one hand, everybody knows a classic and encounters it at least once in a lifetime, either at school or elsewhere. On the other hand, a classic comes packaged with a number of definitions already stamped all over it. Moreover, readers approach a classic with such high expectations that more often than not they are disappointed on actually reading it. Above all, what often gets lost in reading a classic is the sense of surprise, of bold discovery, of unexpected ideas. All this is true of Premchand, Hindi and Urdu's 'classic' writer of the early twentieth century. He comes packaged with all the right definitions: realist, humanist, secularist, social reformer, politically engaged, etc. And yet there is often little sense that by reading his novels and stories one will *discover* anything new or valuable for oneself *now*.

Everybody in India reads at least one of Premchand's stories at school, but most people never read him again. Why? The story that one is most likely to encounter in school textbooks is 'Idgah', a story which taps into village and childhood nostalgia, celebrates the victory of renunciation over selfish temptation, and presents a picture of communal harmony. Like all other village children, five-year-old Hamid is looking forward to the Eid fair in town after Ramadan, but he is an orphan and his old grandmother can only give him three paisas to spend. When he tours the fair he greedily eyes the stalls selling clay toys and sweets, but when taunted by his friends he finds fault with each and every one of them. Instead, he uses his pocket money to buy iron tongs for his grandmother so that she will no longer burn her fingers when picking up chapattis from the ironplate. On the way back, the children are divided into those who look down upon the humble tongs—what kind of a plaything is that?—and those who, led by Hamid, see them as a new and original toy. At the end of the story, the clay toys are all broken into pieces while only the tongs survive. And in the emotional climax the old grandmother is moved to tears by Hamid's love and his spirit of renunciation. It is a moving story, the high moral values cleverly offset by Hamid's sophistry, an obvious case of sour grapes. But what schoolchild would like the suggestion that he or she should forfeit toys for something as plain and useful and boring as a pair of tongs, no matter how much the imagination may turn them into a plaything? What stays in mind is the moral demand and the sentimental ending, which makes the story apiece with the didactic stories that abound in most Hindi school readers. What child would want to read more Premchand after that?

And yet one only has to read Premchand's contemporaries to see how staggeringly different he was from *all* of them, what an enormous stretch of ground he covered in his comparatively short life, and how refreshingly able he was to pick up his pen and create characters who spoke and felt like human beings. Half of his characters were women, itself a huge novelty, and they, too, spoke vehemently, powerfully, convincingly at a time when women were just entering the public sphere. As Alok Rai has pointed out, Premchand's apparent 'organicity', the way in which he came to crystallize and symbolize an entire zone of social consciousness in the decades from the 1910s to the 1930s, masks a remarkable story of self-fashioning as an intellectual and a teller of tales.

## The Extraordinary, Ordinary Man

Dhanpat Rai was born to an ordinary Kayastha family in 1880 in village Lamhi, a few miles from Banaras. His early childhood in Lamhi was perhaps the only sustained experience of village life he had, but the enduring connection with Lamhi made sure that when he, alone among the Hindi and Urdu writers of his generation, turned to write about village life, characters and politics, he did so without the distanced objectivity of an urban outsider. His father was a postal clerk and held one of those transferrable jobs rightly indicated by Benedict Anderson as contributing to the formation of a supra-regional political consciousness. Young Dhanpat, called Nawab at home, began his schooling in Urdu and Persian in the typical Kayastha mould of the times, but he also attended Mission and government schools, and soon developed a taste for reading fiction. His early family life was also ordinarily tragic: his mother died when he was seven and when his father remarried the relationship with his stepmother was not affectionate; moreover, his first, arranged, marriage proved to be with an incompatible girl, with whom young Premchand refused to co-habit. His father's death in 1897 brought a sudden, but by no means unusual, burden of responsibilities, and though for a while Premchand tried to keep studying he had to turn to teaching for a living. Teaching at the time was a respectable profession but a poorly paid one: Premchand's first salary in 1899 was Rs 18 per month. Teacher Training College seemed a way out of this dead end, and after graduating in 1904 his career prospects improved. He ended up as a sub-deputy inspector of schools, in other words, an officer in the education department, a somewhat powerful position which could command local influence and a side-income in the form of bribes from headmasters and textbook publishers. The temptations and the gap between the investment in and high expectations of education, the pitiful salary of a government clerk or civil servant, and the demands of social status, crop up regularly in Premchand's fiction, often leading to disastrous consequences.

As a matter of fact, about a third of Hindi and Urdu writers in this period were teachers and, as for them, Premchand's lifeline to the world of letters and of public opinion were journals, in his case the prestigious Urdu journal *Zamana*, edited in Kanpur by Munshi Dayanarayan Nigam. In the period between 1905 and 1920 Premchand contributed to *Zamana* articles on literary and political matters and his first short stories; in 1915 his stories also started appearing in the prestigious Hindi journal *Sarasvati*. Premchand's first collection of short stories, *Lament for the Motherland* (*Soz-e vatan*, published in Urdu in 1908) attracted unfavourable attention from the authorities—Premchand was reprimanded for its seditious content, changed his penname from Nawab Rai to Premchand, and started toying with the idea of leaving his government job to become a full-time editor or to work in non-government 'national' schools. In 1906 he married Shivrani Devi, a child-widow, who would prove to be the right companion for him and eventually took up writing herself. By 1918 Premchand realized that publishing in Hindi gave more opportunities and meant reaching out to a larger number of readers, and from then on his novels appeared earlier in Hindi than in Urdu, though he was careful always to see them in print in Urdu, too. The exact dynamics of the switch are still slightly unclear; the possibility being that for some time Premchand continued to write in Urdu shorthand and either himself copied or had his texts copied out in Devanagari by someone else; this involved also substituting suitable (Sanskritic) Hindi terms for the abstract Persian and Arabic words. By the 1920s Premchand's stories were actively sought by all the major Hindi literary journals of the day, and in particular he wrote many of his women-centred stories for the radical woman's journal *Chand*.

In 1921, like other ordinary people answering Gandhi's call for non-cooperation, Premchand took the plunge and resigned from his government job, a 41 year-old man with two young children. From then on writing became his only steady source of income while he held a succession of teaching and editing jobs and invested most of his money in his own publishing and editing ventures: the Saraswati Press, the literary monthly *Hans* (1930) and the political weekly *Jagaran* (1932). In the 1930s he even tried scriptwriting for a film company in Bombay but with little satisfaction. When in 1930, Hindi editor Banarsidas Chaturvedi asked him in an interview how much he had earned from his literary writing, Premchand's reply was between Rs 50 and 80 per month. This seems like meagre earnings, but actually Premchand was the most successful Hindi and Urdu writer of his day. For over twenty years he wrote roughly a story a month and was payed up to Rs 20 per form; in the 1920s he earned Rs 200 per month as editor of the prestigious Hindi monthly *Madhuri*, and in 1925 he received as much as Rs 1800 for his novel *Rangbhumi* (*The Field of Action*). No other writer in Hindi earned that much. But, as his biographers have pointed out, all of his earnings went to pay for his journals and printing press. The aspiration Premchand shared with so many writers of his generation to have his own journal did not automatically entail sound business know-how, and that, compounded by his preference for

simple living, has contributed to the image of Premchand as the quintessentially poor Hindi writer.

As Premchand's fame rose, he was translated into other Indian languages and even abroad, and became actively engaged as an intellectual on the national stage. In 1934 he toured South India, where he gave a speech on how only a gradual, inclusive and consensual process could really make Hindi become the 'national language' of India, and in his final years he actively campaigned in favour of Hindustani in the Hindi–Hindustani controversy. A few days before his untimely death in 1936 at the age of 56, in his presidential address at the first meeting of the Progressive Writers' Association in Lucknow, entitled 'The Aim of Literature' (*Sahitya ka uddeshya*), he spelt out many of his ideas regarding literature, its need to 'mirror the truths of life' and to develop a 'new sense of beauty'. These were the ideals that supported the socially and politically engaged literature that he contributed to create in Hindi and Urdu.[1]

## The Most Valuable Thing in the World

In order to appreciate the novelty and originality of Premchand's fiction it is necessary to grasp its point of departure. At the time when he started reading and writing in the last decade of the nineteenth century and the first of the twentieth, fiction in Urdu and Hindi consisted largely of old and new stories (*qissas* and *fasanas*) of adventure, romance and magic (*tilism*) and of detective and historical novels (translations from Bengali as well as original compositions). Among English novels, it was those by the popular and sensationalist Victorian writers like WGD Reynolds of *Mysteries of London* fame that were translated. Besides them, there was a first crop of 'education' novels like those by Deputy Nazir Ahmad in Urdu and Pandit Gauridatt in Hindi, and various hybrid experiments. Particularly successful among these had been Pandit Ratan Nath Sarshar's *Fasana-e Azad* (1878-9) and the novels by Mirza Hadi Rusva, including his fictional 'autobiography' of a Lucknow courtesan, *Umrao Jan Ada* (1899) and the rags-to-riches tale of a reformed aristocrat, *Sharifzada*. As his biographer tells

---

[1] Premchand, 'Sahitya ka uddeshya', in *Kuch vichar*, Allahabad, Sarasvati Press 1982, see Appendix here.

us, Premchand was an avid and eclectic reader of all these genres, and echoes can be found in his first attempts at writing.

'The most valuable thing in the world' (*Duniya ka sabse anmol ratna*, 1907), Premchand's first story, turns the familiar motifs of the Arabo-Persian romantic-magic quest (a princess asks her suitors to bring her 'the most valuable thing in the world' in order to win her hand) into a quest for *new* values. What is the most valuable thing in the world, wonders the puzzled lover. He first thinks he has found the answer when he sees a young widow ready to become a *sati*. The act is heavily romanticized ('pure feelings', 'sacred flames', the husband and wife are called 'lovers', *premi* and *premika*), and the protagonist is positive that the ashes from the pyre will surely be the most valuable thing in the world. But no, the princess, though impressed, is not convinced, and the lover resumes his quest, directed this time towards the 'sacred land' of Hindustan. Here he encounters a horrific scene, a battlefield strewn with corpses and a mighty and dying Rajput hero, who exhales his last breath with the cry 'Bharatmata ki jay', 'Victory to Mother India', on his lips. The protagonist takes the last drop of his blood back to the princess and is finally rewarded: truly 'that last drop of blood shed to defend one's country (*vatan*) is the most valuable thing in the world', she agrees. Patriotism is made to fit into the familiar romantic quest. That Premchand was looking far and wide for new inspiring sources is evidenced by another story in his first collection, where 'Joseph' Mazzini is presented as torn between worldly love and patriotic love. His self-sacrifice for the sake of total devotion to the patriotic cause is shown to subsume the human love between him and Magdalene: in a structure of feeling that would be repeated in many a romantic-nationalist story, true human love does not require consummation, indeed it flourishes in renunciation. Letters and perhaps even a single meeting are enough to bear witness to that love, whose energy can then be channelled towards a higher aim. In this collection, then, we see Premchand treading familiar narrative paths while busily re-aligning their implicit values. Then, quite suddenly after this collection, his formula changed: in place of romantic and/or patriotic story-lines, the focus is on ordinary practices, values and characters in society. These are then shown to be highly problematic, and the crisis that they inevitably produce can be resolved only through a change of perspective, which usually involves a 'change of heart' on the part of one or more characters.

## Towards Social Realism

Premchand's new formula can be summed up as 'social realism', evident in his focus on social and political issues and on power relations, and in his new, complex, view of character which combined social type, commonsense beliefs and a new attention to psychological states and inner conflicts. As we shall see, it was a formula that brought together realistic descriptions of setting, character and social relations with melodramatic features such as virtue misrecognized, the use of chance, intense emotional and ethical dilemmas and strong scenes.[2] Premchand drew creatively upon the heterogeneous narrative strategies of realism and the melodramatic in order to convey the 'truths of life' as well as deep emotional truths.

The first instance of Premchand's new formula appears in a slim story from 1910, 'Rich daughter-in-law' ('Bare ghar ki beti'), purportedly one of Premchand's own favourites. With a few, sure strokes the narrator presents the socio-economic context and the psycho-social characteristics of each character. The girl's father, a once-rich zamindar, has dissipated all his wealth in lawyers and outward show. Anandi, one of his seven daughters, talented and well-loved, is consequently forced to marry into a much humbler family, but she adjusts gracefully to her new circumstances. Her husband is a typical middle-class product of modern education, a clerk who commutes and mediates between town and village and who, despite his BA, is not anglicized but rather takes part in Hindi literary–religious activities and has rather conservative views on women. His brother, by contrast, is a simple and uneducated youth who spends all his time wrestling. In a pattern that will be repeated in most of his stories, Premchand takes a common, everyday occurrence or a familiar social practice and shows its critical consequences while, at the same time, taking in turn the points of view of all involved. Here Anandi has a heated exchange with her brother-in-law, her husband takes her side, and a rift is created in the family. Everybody is 'right', everybody has reasons with which the reader can identify, but the result is a crisis nonetheless. The only way out of the stalemate is when one of the characters, in this case Anandi, has a 'change of heart' and sets things on a different, conciliatory course.

[2] The classic study of melodrama and fiction is Peter Brooks, *The Melodramatic Imagination*, New Haven, Yale University Press, 1976.

The result is that the commonsensical meaning of the title, a saying which implies that a rich and therefore haughty daughter-in-law will create trouble in the family, is completely reversed: a rich daughter-in-law is judicious and knows what is best.

Such, in Premchand's view, is the power and the mission of fiction: to present familiar social evils and suggest ways out of the destructive cycle. It is easy to take this formula for granted, and even to laugh at such a high call. Can literature really change society? Should it even try? Is the attempt going to force narratives into unseemly acrobatics between so-called realistic depiction, idealistic characters and improbable resolutions? ('idealistic realism' is how this formula of Premchand's is usually termed). Once again, contextualizing Premchand's efforts will help recover the sense of experimentation.

One of the consequences of intensified British colonial presence in nineteenth-century north India, especially after the upheaval of 1857, was a profound sense of revaluation and reconsideration of cultural values among Indian intellectuals. Treasured poetic traditions, whether in Urdu or in Braj Bhasa, were now seen as complicit in the general decline of the country, part of an enfeebled aristocratic culture, and new literary languages and forms were deemed necessary in order to instil the values and tastes essential for national regeneration. This period of modern literary history is sometimes called the 'age of prose', but in fact it was poetry, the genre with the highest cultural capital, or drama, the form seen as possessing the greatest potential for disseminating ideas and values, that were involved first. Prose only meant non-fictional, discursive prose in order to spread useful knowledge and new, patriotic ideas through journals and textbooks. Fiction, whether of the old, magical–adventure type, or the new, sensational novels, was only the butt of criticism. It was therefore the task of novelists like Premchand to convince the critics, first, that fiction was a serious enterprise and, second, that it could contribute to the project of cultural and social reform. Even though Premchand, much like contemporary readers, appreciated and enjoyed the adventurous fiction of Sarshar and Reynolds, he was clear in his mind that the kind of fiction he wanted to write was based on different premises.

The difference between a *fasana* and a *navil*, he wrote as early as 1909, is that the latter draws 'a clear picture of the period it narrates, it throws light on its customs, habits and behaviour and it gives no place to supernatural events, or even if it does, it is with such skill that ordinary readers will consider them to be true.'[3] Rather than telling the reader about a character or a situation, the narrator should show them in action in a way that induces empathy in the reader. Announcing the purpose of the novel on the front page is therefore the mark of an inferior kind of novel: 'drawing pictures of the feelings and conditions of human beings, of natural sights or of the wonders of the world is itself a conclusion or a purpose', he continued, and humour can achieve more than many sermons. Characters in a novel comprise both individual characters endowed with unique features (what we call 'three-dimensional characters') and social types. A later essay, written in 1922 after his first major novels, set out to justify and describe the novel in more comprehensive terms: 'Novel writing is considered 'light literature' because it entertains a reader, but it takes as much mental toil for a novelist to write a novel as for a philosopher to write a book on philosophy.'[4] He listed subject, plot, and 'spice' (*masala*) as the novel's constitutive elements. Simplicity, originality, and interest are the marks of a good plot; *masala* includes experience, self-study, insight, curiosity, observation and, when the novelist has no direct experience of a milieu, imagination. One of the six possible kinds of plot was 'social and political reform'. While in the earlier essay he was taking a position against the first wave of didactic novels, in the one written in 1922 he addressed those critics who had started to argue for 'art for art's sake' and criticized literature with an aim. Combining entertainment and message (*upadesh*, literally 'sermon' or 'teaching') was possible in novels, he argued, and 'the seed for so many social reforms in the West has been sown by novels'.

While the 1909 article can be read as a declaration of intent, with social realism presented in the guise of anthropological interest ('the customs, habits and behaviour' of a certain period), the later article shows Premchand already set on an ambitious course that was to map onto Hindi and Urdu fiction the social structure, public debates, private behaviour and contemporary political events of north India in the 1920s and 1930s for the first time. While his regular stream of stories delivered social and political vignettes, his novels, after the first

---

[3] Premchand, 'Sharar aur sarshar', *Vividh Prasang*, Allahabad, Hans Prakashan, 1962, vol. 1, p. 60, originally published in *Urdu-e moalla*, 1909.

[4] Premchand, 'Upanyas rachna', in *Madhuri*, October 1922, p. 354.

attempts, developed complex architectures with a broad range of characters, attitudes, situations and relationships revolving usually around a single main topic. In *Seva-sadan* (1919) it was the place of women in public space, zamindari families and peasant exploitation and resistance in *Premashram* (1921), civil disobedience in *Rangabhumi* (1925), mismatched marriages in *Nirmala* (1927), and the whole span of rural society and urban elites in *Godan* (1936). This set Premchand apart from all his contemporaries, popular and successful writers like Sudarshan, Vishvambharnath Kaushik, J.P. Srivastava, Dhaniram Prem, Pandey Bechan Sharma Ugra, Bhagavaticharan Varma, etc., who combined to various degrees contemporary settings, social types and strong plots. The architectural layout of Premchand's novels produced a high degree of dynamism and yet interconnectedness among characters and closure in story-lines: every new event or a decision deep in a character's heart set things on a new course and produced one of many possible outcomes in the overall combinatory scheme. The fact that he wrote nine substantial novels, three of which are included in this volume, and over 150 short stories in seventeen years bears witness to how productive and flexible the formula could be.

## Many Layers, New Ground

Let me bring out the complex architecture of Premchand's novels with some examples. In *Premashram*, the range of social characters and relations is introduced through the well-known device of the family plot and through two parallel plotlines, one following the events related to a zamindar family in Banaras and its connections to the police service, the bureaucracy and the law, and the other related to some villagers who are also the zamindars' tenants in a village a few miles outside the city. Differentiation within the zamindar family is laid out in the beginning, when the family is first introduced. It is generational as well as related to individual attitudes. The older generation believed in decorum; their attitude towards their tenants was one of benevolent paternalism, and expressions of loyal subjection could be sure to guarantee pardon and protection. The new generation, formally educated, is split between one brother who wants to salvage and administer whatever is left of the property with managerial ruthlessness (which does not exclude violence and elaborate deceit), and the other brother who, after a stint abroad, has come back full of ideals of reform, sets up a model cooperative farm and supports peasants' demands, though he falls short of going against his brother. The range is further extended through the towering figure of the grand *taluqdar* to whom the family is related by marriage, and who provides an example of princely grandeur. In the village, the peasants are pitted against the excesses of the zamindars' agent, his violent henchmen, and the occasional extortion of civil servants on tour. The village plotline charts their gradual path towards united action as the ruthless zamindar embroils them in one court suit after another, involving mass arrests, false witnesses and other forms of intimidation: detailed court scenes here make their first appearance in a Hindi novel, echoing contemporary newspaper reports of nationalist trials.[5] Villagers, too, include a variety of social types and attitudes. Within a single family, the father is prone to private outbursts of defiance but humbly appeals to the zamindars' paternalism in public, while his son is literate and articulate, reads the radical nationalist newspaper *Pratap* and believes in the power of collective resistance.

Apparently schematic, this structure is greatly complicated by the psychological presentation of characters, and of their actions, speech and motives. This takes place along two sets of contrasts. The first is the contrast between the fact that all characters speak and act in accordance with what they perceive is the acceptable and 'right thing to say', and what we readers know to be their true motives or feelings behind what they say or do. The result is an elaborate and never-ending game in which all characters are involved, and a peculiar triangular relationship between the narrator, the character and the reader, in which the narrator asks the reader both to believe and disbelieve the character's statements. On the one hand common sense and morality govern all the characters' utterances: desires in particular are taboo, even to the characters themselves, who resort to denial and

---

[5] The villagers' verdict on the educated classes is no less scathing: 'The whole world speaks highly of education and knowledge. To us it seems that after studying man becomes even more crooked and deceitful'. Premchand, *Premashram*, Chapter 30, Allahabad 1963 (1921) p. 335. For a fascinating study of the parallelisms between debates about peasants and the land question in Hindi journals, the peasant movement in Avadh in 1920–1, and this novel, see V.B. Talwar, *Kisan, rashtriya andolan aur Premchand: 1918–22*, New Delhi, Northern Book Centre, 1990.

to elaborate self-explanations. The only, occasional, exception to this rule are quarrels, but even then characters often cover up their true feelings with acceptable expressions. Thus, Jalpa in *Gaban* can never *say* that she wants that special necklace, because expressing that desire would not be acceptable: even when quarrelling with her husband she vehemently protests that she is 'not like those women who would plunge the whole household into difficulties just to wear jewels' (p. 46). Pandit Totaram's sudden realization in *Nirmala* that the age difference between himself and his young wife can never be bridged, turns him against his adolescent son: in a psychologically shrewd scene of parental envy, the father suddenly takes an interest in his son's studies and questions him, but the more his son answers him well the more Totaram feels annoyed. Finally he decides to send his son away to the hostel, but while the son confusedly senses the decision to be a sort of banishment, Totaram insists on phrasing it in terms of parental concern for his studies (Chapter 7, pp. 56–8). On the other hand, while 'acceptable words' are the way in which all characters express themselves, desires which are sometimes secret to the characters themselves are revealed to us readers by way of our access to their inner feelings and of revealing clues whose real meaning we, unlike the other characters, are privy to.

This first contrast is modulated by Premchand to produce different meanings: in the case of the stories about Pandit Moteram Shastri, the result is an attack against religious figures of authority and the superstitious religiosity that sustains their authority. In the case of Jalpa's husband, Ramanath, the meaning is a combined social and individual critique: as the son of a low-ranking clerk whose honesty is like a curse, he is trapped between the social demands of his class and caste (expressed through the marriage arrangements), as well as his personal ambition, and the reality of his economic condition: there is no way in which he can match his middle-class status unless by deceit. In Nirmala's case, her attraction for Totaram's son is an 'unutterable truth' even to herself: only once, after tragedy has happened, does she confess it to her sister Krishna. We feel that if Nirmala and Mansaram were to acknowledge their mutual attraction, their sense of self would be shattered: such sense of a (moral) self is predicated upon the denial of desire, though of course the novel precisely grants readers access to those desires. For the rest of the novel, Totaram's suspicion is portrayed as a venomous and self-blinding force that unfairly misrepresents Nirmala's relations with Mansaram: she is the melodramatic heroine whose virtue is misrecognized.

The second contrast is between Premchand's valorization of renunciation and self-sacrifice in line with Gandhian ideals, and the acknowledgement in his fiction that harbouring desires is only too human and that every human being is weak. So, moments of self-sacrifice for others or for a good cause are marked as heroic moments, and a supernatural energy (*tejas*) comes to fill the character and strengthen their resolve (this is particularly true of his nationalist stories). Women in particular are valorized as icons of *tyag*, and Premchand sings the same paeans to motherhood that one heard everywhere in nationalist discourse at that time. At the same time, the weaknesses and desires present in all his characters define, rather than undermine, their 'humanity': even if society does not like it, all human beings feel desires and strive to fulfil them, Premchand suggests. In fact, their very weaknesses and desires unite heroes and villains, victims and oppressors, undercutting the moral gulf that separates them. The result is a fluctuating and morally complex universe, where one person's reasonable desire is the next person's undoing, and where principled action leads to moral approbation and disaster at the same time (witness Hori's fate in *Godan*).

*Nirmala* is exemplary in this respect. Genealogically, its roots are in the reformist discourse about mismatched marriages that rests on the social ill of dowry: young brides are married to old bridegrooms who either request no dowry or even pay the girl's parents; they, in turn, unable to provide a girl with dowry, find a way out of the social and ritual opprobrium of keeping a post-pubescent daughter unmarried. The way in which popular narratives of social reform viewed this question is suggested by the cartoon from *Chand* which appeared in the same women's journal in which *Nirmala* was serialized: the young bride, who cannot love her decrepit husband, feels attracted to the young male in the house, gets pregnant and, once cruelly abandoned by her lover and the family, has no alternative but to become a prostitute.[6] *Nirmala* treads instead a delicate line. Although Premchand is anxious to state at several points in the novel that the root of her

---

[6] A similar plotline is found in Premchand's story 'Naya vivah' (*Sarasvati*, May 1932).

(1) The old bridegroom thinks
nothing of the age difference and
marries a young bride.

(2) Attraction is natural between the
'young-blooded' stepmother and
stepson.

(3) The old man 'finally goes
to hell'.

(4) Once the obstacle is removed,
passion overtakes the two young
bereaved, who think nothing of the
possible consequences.

Illustration 4.3 (1), (2), (3), (4), (5), (6), (7), (8). This unusually long cartoon on
the subject of 'mismatched marriages' was accompanied by a verse commentary
by *Chāṁd*'s house-poet, Ānandīprasād Śrivāstava.

(5) Soon enough, the stepmother is pregnant and the son denies any responsibility.

(6) The stepmother is thrown out of the house and taken to a place of pilgrimage, where a priest takes advantage of her.

(7) Abandoned yet again, the woman falls prey to a procuress.

(8) Finally, 'Now that she is a prostitute all respect her. Those who threw her out are crazy after her now.'

Source: *Chāṁd*, VII, pt. 1, 3, February 1929, pp. 501–8.

misfortune is the *social practice* of mismatched marriages and dowry, yet his attention to the *psychology* of characters takes the novel along quite a different path and elides the difference between victims and oppressors to the point that all become victims of their own passions and of circumstances: Totaram's sister is hostile to Nirmala and initially turns the children against her because she fears, rightly in fact, for her position in the household. Totaram is a victim of his own misguided romantic–erotic aspirations, then of visceral and destructive jealousy towards his own son Mansaram, and is unable to accept Nirmala's offer of dutiful wifely devotion, the second-best thing to love. Mansaram is a victim of the unspoken games and cross-messages that pit the three adults in the family against each other. Nirmala, the most obvious victim, harbours her own unconfessable desires (notice her feelings at meeting the man who would have been her husband, in Chapter 16) and turns into a mean-spirited shrew (Chapter 21). The contrast between voiced arguments and unspoken intentions and between the valorization of self-sacrifice and the acceptance of human desires and weaknesses is brought out to the surface in several melodramatic scenes: the quarrels between Nirmala and her sister-in-law, the terrible misunderstanding when Totaram sees Nirmala coming out of Mansaram's room at night (Chapter 8), Mansaram's final reconciliation with Nirmala just before his death. Only melodrama could bring out the emotional intensity and psychological complexity of the equation, and the apparent 'inconsistency' (see Alok Rai's Afterword) can be seen in fact as symptomatic of this complexity and of Premchand's desire to withhold at every stage any simple deterministic solution such as that offered by the cartoon. The forcible identification of the reader with each and every character produces horror and stirs up strong emotions, while indeterminacy keeps the reader on tenterhooks. Together, they make *Nirmala* a compelling and satisfying novel, and a prime example of Premchand's combination of social realism and melodrama.

## Premchand's Women

The first striking thing about Premchand's women characters is how many of them there are! It is only with Premchand that we have in Hindi and Urdu literature a sense that women make up half of society, and that they are as varied in character and social position as men, with whom they are shown as constantly interacting.[7] In Premchand's early stories, women feature mostly as figures of romantic love (with, we have seen, a new patriotic twist), as heroic warriors, *viranganas*, or as objects of sympathy and of reformist zeal (see 'Anath larki/ The Orphan girl', 1914). Consistent with the nationalist valorization of Indian woman as emblem of self-sacrifice and service (*tyag* and *seva*), such traits in a woman character acquire immediately an iconic quality, and she dazzles the narrator, male character and reader with her supernatural glow. This, I would add, is about as far as any other popular male Hindi writer of the period would go. But, while holding on to this vision of service and self-sacrifice as intrinsic womanly virtues, Premchand also explored the social and psychological conditions of an unprecedented range of women characters: widows, wronged or adjusting wives, political activists and sympathizers, actresses and prostitutes, educated women and female labourers, superstitious wives and troubled reformers, women against women and women against men. Many of these stories were published in the foremost and most radical women's journal of the period, *Chand*, established by Ramrakh Singh Sahgal in Allahabad in 1922, and echo several of the campaigns, arguments and voices that were heard in that journal.[8] As editor of the journals *Madhuri* (1927–31), *Hans* (1930–) and *Jagaran* (1932–), Premchand himself reported regularly on news and debates concerning women, supported reform bills like the Sharda Bill (about widows' rights to their husbands' property) and the Gaur Bill (for divorce), and insisting on the need for men and women to have equal rights.[9]

These fictional narratives give flesh to the discursive messages of social reform by embodying them in verisimilar human characters and familiar conflicts. For example, in 'Widow with Sons', 'The Funeral Feast' and 'A Desperate Case', all included here, the reader is forced to

---

[7] In this respect, Premchand's narratives differ from woman-centred didactic novels such as those of Deputy Nazir Ahmad's.

[8] 'Dhikkar/Reproach' (*Mansarovar*, vol. 1), 'Narak ka marg/The Path to Hell' (*Chand*, March 1925) and 'Shudra' (*Chand*, January 1926, *Mansarovar*, vol. 2) come straight from the lurid stories of sexual mesalliances that featured as real and fictional letters in *Chand*. Similarly, his stories about 'good-hearted' actresses and prostitutes follow well-set patterns; see my *The Hindi Public Sphere: Language and Literature in the Age of Nationalism*, Delhi, Oxford University Press, 2002, pp. 274–95.

[9] See Amrit Rai, ed.,*Vividh Prasang*, vol. 3, Allahabad, Hans Prakashan, 1962.

recognize and confront domestic cruelty face to face. In these stories the patriarchal family is the arena and also the main culprit, especially for its treatment of widows and its inequality towards daughters. Predictably, commonsense opinions objectifying women feature prominently in these stories, juxtaposed to the suffering of individual women characters and often leading to melodramatic confrontations or equally melodramatic self-annihilations.

The same strategy of embodiment appears in Premchand's stories about the nationalist movements, written especially around the mass campaigns of 1920 and 1930. Here, by lending discursive arguments and patriotic resolve to his women characters and, at the same time, addressing women readers as political actors, Premchand suggested that women readers, too, could exercise agency and produce the desired change in their own homes (as in 'Wife into Husband'). Finally, 'Mandir/Temple' (*Chand*, May 1927, *Mansarovar*, vol. 5) belongs, like 'Deliverance' (1931), to a handful of stories thematizing the cruelty of caste and religious intolerance against dalits; but whereas in 'Deliverance' the rage is contained and offset by the narrator's sarcasm directed at the (un)godly Pandit, in 'Mandir/Temple' and 'Ghasvali/ The Grasscutter' (*Madhuri*, October 1929, *Mansarovar*, vol. 1) the two powerful figures of lower-caste and lower-class women deliver damning indictments of caste society and male power. As in 'The Power of a Curse' (an early story written in 1911), the only weapon the weak have is a curse, a public invocation of divine retribution that tears apart the complacency of caste commonsense.

It is interesting that while the burgeoning voices of Hindi women writers in this period like Mahadevi Varma and Subhadra Kumari Chauhan preferred the character of the silently suffering woman, attracting the reader's pity for her unjust predicament, and left it to the narrator to express rage on her behalf, a male writer like Premchand chose women characters to voice the strongest arguments, complaints and feelings.[10]

In 'Widow with Sons',

Phulmati's entire soul screamed as though struck by a thunderbolt and the words issued from her mouth like blazing sparks:

[10] In Mahadevi's sketches about women characters, for example, the narrator is full of indignation for the unjust treatment meted out on them by their families, but the characters themselves say nothing.

'I made this home, I saved up its wealth, I gave birth to you and reared you, and now I'm an outsider in this house? It's the law of Manu and you want to go by it? Fine, take your house and the lot, but I won't agree to live here as your dependent. I'd rather die. Congratulations for the outrage you're committing! I planted the tree and I'm not allowed to stand in its shade. If that's the law, then let it be burned.' (*Widows, Wives and Other Heroines*, p. 14)

While Premchand's critique of patriarchy is beyond dispute, the family as an institution remained for him an ideal, as the story 'Divided Hearths' testifies. This may go some way towards explaining a feature which feminist critics have already commented upon, that is Premchand's evident ambivalence, to say the least, about educated and westernized women, whom he depicted as hopelessly devoted to self-gratification and detached from the true values of Indian womanhood, service and self-sacrifice, and also, most significantly, from the family.[11] Miss Padma in the eponymous story and Miss Malti in *Godan* are stereotypical in that western education, professional employment (one is a lawyer, the other a doctor), liberal ideas, flirting and 'free love' all come as part of a single package. It is also significant that the psychological complexity and social acumen of Premchand's other stories is absent here, as if he could not bring himself to take their predicament and their subjectivity seriously. True, in both cases the women are shown to suffer from the free love relationship since men take it as a passport to withhold commitment and to carry on multiple affairs. And in the sad (but not tragic) ending Miss Padma, now a mother, throws out her obnoxious lover and father of her child—is it motherhood that gives her strength and a new sense of purpose?

## What is Still Left to Translate

I started out this introduction by asking: why read Premchand the Hindi/Urdu 'classic' now? This anthology of translations is a good place to begin answering that question as it will open up Premchand's work to new readers and new readings. It is in fact astounding that until recently only part of Premchand's substantial opus was translated

[11] See Charu Gupta, 'Portrayal of Women in Premchand's Stories: A Critique', in *Social Scientist*, vol. 19, nos. 5–6, May–June 1991, pp. 88–113; and Geetanjali Pandey, *Between Two Worlds: An Intellectual Biography of Premchand*, New Delhi, Manohar, 1989.

into English. To date, most of his novels remain untranslated, and the same is true of his essays, editorials, letters and reviews, which together run into five large volumes. These reveal Premchand the engaged intellectual, taking an active part in all the debates of the day and commenting on issues like the national language, Hindi, Urdu and Hindustani, Congress, the nationalist movement and British rule, *shuddhi* campaigns and Hindu–Muslim relations, peasant activism and socialism, the war in Europe and untouchability, citizenship and local government, education and the Urdu and Hindi literary fields.

Uniquely among Hindi intellectuals of his time, Premchand shared neither their deep allegiance to the 'glorious Aryan past' nor their consequent alienation from the history of Indo-Muslim rule. Nor were his literary tastes rooted in the Braj Bhasa poetic tradition, like many of his contemporaries. His negative judgement of Indo-Islamic aristo-cratic culture stemmed rather from his belief in the new social role of literature, which he expressed in his speech at the first meeting of the Progressive Writers' Association. Consequently he felt little attach-ment to that side of religious and courtly culture. His strong social conscience and radical politics, which brought him closer and closer to socialism, were rooted in an utterly secular and inclusive view of the Indian nation, which makes him a particularly valuable and rare rôle-model these days. 'Soldier of the pen' was how Amrit Rai, his biogra-pher and son and himself a distinguished writer and engaged intellectual, called Premchand, and reading his notes and editorials one really has the sense of a man busy shaping the nation with the only weapon he had at hand, his pen.

University of Cambridge                      FRANCESCA ORSINI
2003

# PREMCHAND'S
## Short Stories

PART I

# *Introduction to* The World of Premchand

The blossoming of Hindi fiction in the second half of the twentieth century, with writers of such psychological subtlety and satirical brilliance as Shrilal Shukla, Mohan Rakesh, Nirmal Verma and Mudrarakshasa, to name only a few, was made possible in large part by the novels and short stories of Premchand. When his works began to be published around 1905, fiction in Hindi and Urdu consisted primarily of romantic chronicles of a historical or fantastic nature, or didactic tales. By the time his last stories and novels appeared in the nineteen thirties the realistic psychological novel had been firmly established in these languages and set the standard as well as the social themes and character studies that typified the accomplished fiction by the younger writers who followed.

Dhanpat Rai, known from 1910 on by the pen-name of 'Premchand,' was born in the village of Lamhi, near Varanasi, in 1880, in humble circumstances but with access to a good education in Persian and Urdu letters, as might be expected in a literate family of the Kayasth community, so well-known for producing men of letters, teachers and lawyers. Some of the difficulties of his early years are described in the autobiographical sketches that conclude this volume.

From the time he began writing, near the beginning of the twentieth century, Premchand's life was extraordinarily active. When he died in 1936 Premchand left fourteen published novels, about three hundred short stories, countless letters, editorials and essays, several plays and screen plays, and a number of translations from English and adaptations of European novels. He also had a busy career as editor and publisher. A passionate advocate of both the Independence movement and Hindu–Muslim harmony, he devoted many editorials to India's political and communal problems and played an active role in the movement for Hindustani as a national language. He was a generous critic as well and championed the work of younger writers such as Jayshankar Prasad and

3

Jainendra Kumar. His productivity is all the more astonishing when one learns that he suffered from poor health throughout much of his life.

From the early to the late fiction there is a steady and readily perceptible growth in Premchand's mastery of the short story. The first stories, written often with a patriotic or nationalistic bias, tend toward romantic and melodramatic evocations of heroic exploits from legend or Indian history. Turning to the past also provided Premchand, along with some of his contemporaries such as Prasad and Nirala, an opportunity to criticize foreign oppression without naming the British, although this did not save his first collection of stories from being banned and burned in 1909. The plots of most of these early tales, full of chivalric idealism and noble sacrifice, disguises and amazing adventures, show the influence of the Urdu *dastans,* the favourite reading of his youth.

Like most of his work until about 1916, these stories were written originally in Urdu — not so much a language distinct from Hindi as a phase of the same language, with a different alphabet but sharing with Hindi its basic grammatical system and a major proportion of the working vocabulary. Although in the popular imagination Urdu is associated with Muslims and Hindi with Hindus, in fact educated Hindus of Uttar Pradesh — one thinks of Pandit Nehru — were likely to be more at home in Urdu, and the literary Hindi of current fiction draws freely and constantly on Urdu vocabulary. Premchand described his own background as deriving more from Muslim culture (particularly Persian and Urdu litera- ture) and indignantly rejected as a myth the idea that Urdu was for Muslims and Hindi for Hindus. From early in his career he frequently prepared Hindi editions of his Urdu writings and con- tinued to do so, sometimes with collaborators, and later super- vised Urdu versions of works originally written in Hindi.

The principal reasons for Premchand's turning from Urdu to Hindi were the dearth of Urdu publishers willing to publish his work, his lack of sympathy for the elaborate Urdu style fashionable at the time, and his belief that writing in Hindi would reach a wider audience. But it should be noted here, since it is often overlooked, that Premchand never gave up writing original works in Urdu — 'Hindi in the morning, Urdu in the afternoon,' as he once put it. Although in the latter part of his life Hindi versions of his work were the first to be published, we often cannot establish, in the case of the short stories, which language they had originally been written in; and where there are considerable variations in the two texts it is difficult to decide when Premchand himself is responsible for particular omissions and additions or changes in the vocabulary.

Premchand very soon turned for his inspiration to the village world, which would become the richest subject for his best work. The villages and small towns of eastern Uttar Pradesh, specifically the rural districts around Allahabad and Varanasi, apparently perfectly ordered according to mechanically exact social regulations that had functioned more or less unchanged and unquestioned for centuries, offered Premchand an endlessly fascinating stage for the interplay of diverse personalities at every stage of evolution, operating within a rigid, efficient, and often cruel social structure. Caste snobbery (though it is much more than snobbery, since caste operates as a religious imperative), crushing poverty and brutal exploitation by landowners, moneylenders and parasitical Brahmins; the overwhelming desire for sons to carry on the family and perform the rituals; the terror at the possibility of disgrace, loss of face and ostracism; the shame of widowhood; the proverbial conservatism and cunning of the peasant — these are recurring strands in the fabric of Premchand's portrayal of village life. From the early stories on, his compassion, humour and psychological understanding of the villagers are apparent. In the earlier stories there is a tendency toward editorializing, as well as hyperbole and occasional redundancy. Maupassant's influence may be seen in Premchand's preoccupation with the structure of his plots and the occasional trick endings. The best stories of the late twenties and thirties are more often than not free of these characteristics, but many of the early stories as well, 'The Power of a Curse,' for example, move past such limitations and achieve a high degree of success when measured by Western standards of that era.

Influenced by Dickens, Tolstoy, Chekhov and Marx, Premchand very early directed his fiction toward social reform. The inhumanity of caste hierarchies and the plight of women stirred his indignation and remained constant themes throughout his work. The romantic heroism of the earliest tales is later supplanted by realistic studies of character and an idealistic view of the agitation against British oppression, with cutting satire on those Indians (as in 'A Little Trick' and 'A Moral Victory') who set their personal

5.

interests above the freedom movement. From Gandhi, and perhaps also from George Eliot's *Silas Marner,* which he freely paraphrased in a Hindi version, he derived his idealistic concept of the potential regeneration of character through the experience of the sacrifice and goodness of others. (Gandhi's call in 1921 for non-cooperation was at least partly responsible for Premchand's resignation from his government post as a school teacher.) Although with his maturing as a writer Premchand's narration will become increasingly dramatic and (at least on the surface) objective, and the presentation of character immeasurably subtler than in the early works, didactic and reformist impulses remain strong in his writing. The range of his later fiction expands beyond the village to an India changing in what one of his characters calls 'the new light,' where young intellectuals and emancipated women are now faced with problems very different from those of uneducated villagers. Though they are still preoccupied with social problems naturalistically observed, the tone and technique of the stories following the First World War move closer to Chekhov, while melodrama gives way to tragicomedy, and explicit moralizing to moral fable. In 'My Big Brother' a potentially ludicrous situation is developed with pathos, although the touch remains light and the story is genuinely comic; in 'The Shroud,' one of Premchand's last stories and one of his two most famous, the intolerable grimness of the characters' lives becomes the subject of grotesque comedy, with the reader left free to draw his own conclusions. 'The Chess Players' (1924), probably the most famous of all Premchand's short stories, set in Lucknow at the time of the British annexation, portrays in terms of absurdist tragedy the moral vacuity and madness of the city's aristocracy in counterpoint against the background of a historical crisis.

More than half a century after Indian independence one cannot say that Premchand's world no longer exists. Here and there the surface of things has changed but, outside the big towns and cities, it would be premature to conclude that there has been a radical transformation in the conditions of everyday life in most rural districts. What may strike a Western reader as melodramatic or exaggerated in some of these stories is still commonplace in India, as a perusal of today's Indian newspapers will confirm. No matter how much they are officially discouraged, in the countryside caste restrictions remain a grim reality, and the alarming resurgence of religious fundamentalism does not encourage hope for improvement; dowries determine marriages, and the often perilous status of women is still a major concern; farmers are apt to resort to traditional high-interest moneylenders instead of government banks which offer low-interest loans; the break-up of the great landed estates still has the peasantry at the mercy of the former landowners for marketing their produce; and above all, death may come swiftly and unexpectedly but is accepted with resignation — such are still some of the basic elements which constitute life in the Indian villages.

Premchand's indignation and his very choice of subject matter tend somewhat to set him apart from the Hindi fiction writers who came into prominence immediately after him. Though some writers (Ashk, Renu and Nagarjun, for example) continued to treat social problems and village life, for the most part middle-class experience in urban settings becomes the focus for fiction in the middle decades of the century, with an emphasis on psychological and philosophical questions rather than social reform. This is apparent in the novels and short stories of Jainendra Kumar (a close friend of Premchand) and Agyeya (S. H. Vatsyayan). In the next generation, the writers of *nayi kahani*, or 'new story,' who came into prominence in the fifties and sixties — Nirmal Verma, Mohan Rakesh and Gyanranjan, for example — continued the emphasis on psychological themes, injected now with social satire; for instance, the narrative in Rakesh's portraits of *nouveau riche* Delhi society is now tinged with existentialist angst. Even the city is no longer seen naturalistically but rather as a reflection of the restricted, desperate world of the writer's psyche, turned away from the epic horizons of Premchand's multifarious vision. More recently, however, Shrilal Shukla in *Rāg Darbārī*, Mudrarakshasa in *Daṇḍavidhān*, two of the finest novels in Hindi since Premchand's *Godan,* have returned to the villages of northeastern India for the subject of their work; and although Premchand's idealism is missing (as indeed it was in stories like 'The Shroud'), he is recalled in the implicit passionate indignation that informs their work.

In the matter of style, recent Hindi narrative, mostly preoccupied as it is with the lives of city dwellers, has tended inevitably to dispense with Premchand's inexhaustible fund of humble similes and proverbs while gaining in complexity as it has moved

7

toward a more symbolic representation of experience. In one respect, nevertheless, most contemporary fiction writers have continued to follow Premchand's example: they employ a vocabulary strongly influenced by colloquial speech rather than the highly Sanskritized and artificial vocabulary propagated by many officials and academics — a Hindi satirically dubbed 'sarkari,' i.e. governmental. Colloquial speech has retained a great number of words of Arabic or Persian origin, classified by purists as 'Urdu,' and many writers, like Mohan Rakesh, have sensibly claimed that Hindi and Urdu, except in the hands of academics and fanatical politicians, are in truth one language with two alphabets. Premchand himself, like Gandhi, was a proponent of 'Hindustani,' a blend of colloquial Urdu and Hindi. While conceding that Hindustani was not a 'literary language,' he declared (writing in English), 'I believe in our literary expression coming as close as possible to spoken speech.' His own Hindi style draws heavily on Urdu as well as a vocabulary derived from Sanskrit, and depends on the judicious blending of the two linguistic streams for much of its colour and force.

It is characteristic of the great writer that the significance of his work will extend far beyond his own era and its purely local or immediate context (although, as noted above, many of the social problems of Premchand's time continue to persist long after India achieved independence). I believe he continues to interest us today because of the originality and clarity of his vision and his ability to dramatize universal human problems. His validity as a critic of society stems in part from the fact that he himself had his roots in that society and never set himself above it; in confirmation of his integrity, his criticism remains inseparable from his love and is never tinged with spite. In this he is markedly distinct from some of the new breed of Indian nay-sayers — essayists and novelists born away from the subcontinent or electing to live abroad in exile, and who have made the ferocious denunciation of Indian culture and Indian values something of a fashion.

Although to date The World of Premchand is the only English translation of the author's stories to be published outside India, since its original publication several more such collections have been published in his homeland. Nevertheless, despite the great fascination he has never ceased to exert over the minds of his countrymen, at this moment there is no critical edition of his work.

Such an edition is badly needed because of the frequent unreliability of the various printings of his writing and the many divergences among them.

In presenting these stories here my division into three groups is, in part, arbitrary. Stories like 'A Day in the Life of a Debt Collector' and 'A Car Splashing' might well be considered scenes from village life, though it seemed to me that there is a certain urban sensibility in both, and in one the very presence of the automobile suggests the larger sphere of the town. The stories in the third division are more involved with problems of individuality and growing awareness, while 'The Shroud' and 'Deliverance,' though very clearly village stories, transcend the limitations of the earlier rural tales and attain to a greater universality of statement. The thirty stories collected here have been culled from the collections titled *Kafan, Solāh Aprāpya Kahāniyāṅ*, the eight volumes of *Mānasarovar* and the two volumes of *Gupta Dhan*.

## Acknowledgements

I would like to express my appreciation and gratitude to Mrs Bonnie R. Crown, who as Director of the Asian Literature Program of the Asia Society encouraged and assisted in the original publication of this book; to the late Sripat Rai, Premchand's son, for generously giving permission to publish my translations; to Mrs Shaista Rahman of Brooklyn College, Edith Irwin, Neil Gross, and the late Gordon Roadarmel; to Frances Pritchett and Susham Bedi of Columbia University, for many valuable suggestions and comments; to my students who have taught me so much while we studied many of these stories together; to Robert O. Swan, and particularly Ainslie Embree and the late Barbara Miller for their encouragement and support; and finally, to the American Institute of Indian Studies for the fellowship which made this undertaking possible.

# Introduction to Widows, Wives and Other Heroines

I t was more or less fortuitous that a theme for this collection of Premchand's short stories emerged and suggested its title. In the course of translating those stories I had selected I realized that with one exception all of them had women as their central characters and, for the most part, the particular virtues he felt they embody. The initial aim of this undertaking, however, had been simply to translate some of Premchand's best stories that, I feel, had been unjustly neglected. Previous collections have drawn upon a fairly narrow range of his short fiction, overlooking many of the best stories from the vast selection—there are over 300—and I have chosen some of those for this sampling. In keeping with the general theme which evolved for this collection, I have also included a few less significant stories (e.g., 'Desire') for what they add to our knowledge of Premchand's understanding of women and their specific problems in the context of Indian tradition and changing social values.

It may be difficult for the present-day reader to realize how radical these stories were in their time. It has often been noted that Premchand (1880-1936) revolutionized the Hindi novel and short story by lifting it from the realm of fantasy and romance to the level of modern realism. In his own evolution as a writer one sees a steady progression from the kind of Hindi fiction current at the beginning of this century to a more realistic standard, marked at first (some would say marred) by moralizing and propaganda for social and political causes. In the last stories, such as 'The Secret' and 'Second Marriage,' the moralizing diminishes or disappears, making way for a more naturalistic (and consequently mostly darker) portrait of universal human problems. In this respect too Premchand was a pioneer in Hindi literature. But no matter how much his technical skill grew and his subject matter expanded, no matter how the very last stories become more and more

10

pessimistic, his idealism never deserted him; even in despair he is not cynical.

His admiration and idealization of women is so pervasive that one finds heroines in almost every one of his stories. Mothers and daughters, wives and widows, whores and sometimes even the usually dreaded mother-in-law of Indian folklore—these are the characters who most often represent both compassion and common sense (and argue vociferously for it) in the face of cruel, repressive and, to the secular mind, lunatic traditions. In the stories it is men who usually make terrible mistakes and women who redeem them or die in the attempt. One could easily find scores of other stories, many still untranslated, to present further galleries of varied portraits of women (and I hope others will do this). The selection for a single volume must necessarily be largely arbitrary. I have chosen for the most part stories which have not appeared before in translation, at least not in book form, or which have been represented by freely paraphrased (or 'transcreated') versions.

When dealing with sexual matters Premchand is usually extremely oblique. In a society of marriages planned according to caste and astrological calculations, the sexual equilibrium of a couple's life should be assumed automatically to be ideal in every way. That this was not true in innumerable marriages was perfectly obvious, to be sure, but not something to be discussed. Like Hindi films of the present day, fiction before Indian independence generally avoided such questions and wallowed instead in improbable romance, replete with supernatural happenings. Premchand made a great advance merely by treating such subjects as infidelity, prostitution and double standards in the man-woman relationship. The role of financial considerations in planning marriages, concealed behind a hypocritical demand for religious conformity, is a frequent theme. Premchand never tires of dramatizing the situation of defenceless women, whether wives, widows or prostitutes, exploited and even terrorized by society with the sanction of religion. Refreshingly, not all his heroines remain victims. In 'The Actress', though the protagonist's sense of realism prevents her from marrying the Kunwar Sahib, she makes it clear in her letter that she will return after he has been respectably wed to reclaim his love. In 'Second Marriage', the resourceful young wife of the elderly Dangamal lays the groundwork for a love affair, and Premchand gives all his sympathy to the soon-to-be adulterers. When the protagonist of 'The Secret', a surprisingly Jamesian or Prufrockian character, remains crippled by sexual fear, Manjula quits her job and we next see her, at the end of the story, enjoying life in Mussoorie with a presumably

11

satisfactory lover. Though such subjects are treated objectively in Hindi fiction today, they were novel and, to many, shocking at the time Premchand died in 1936.

Dhanpat Rai, known after 1920 by his pen-name Premchand, was born in 1880 in Lamhi, a village near Banaras in the United Provinces (today Uttar Pradesh), the state where he spent most of his life, residing at various times in Allahabad, Lucknow and Banaras, leaving only in 1933 to write for a film company in Bombay, or to make brief visits to other cities for literary conferences.

He belonged to the Kayasth community, which was noted for its teachers and lawyers. Despite his family's limited resources he had a good education in Persian and Urdu. He began writing early and had a novel serialized in a Banaras journal from 1903 to 1905. (It should be noted that dating Premchand's early work is often problematical; the author himself made several conflicting statements about his first publications). In 1905 he embarked on a career as a teacher.

Patriotism and romantic love are the dominant themes in Premchand's first short story collection, published in 1908. Because of government censorship the writer never mentions England or the British in the patriotic tales, choosing instead to set his plots in medieval times or foreign history in order to disguise his pro-independence sentiments in attacks on past oppressors or glorifying other independence movements. All the same, his story collection was banned in 1909 and the unsold copies burned. Though continuing to write, in 1909 he accepted a government position as Sub-Deputy Inspector of Schools, a post he held until 1921 when, in response to Gandhi's call for non-cooperation with the British, he resigned. Following his resignation, and for the rest of his life until he died in 1936, Premchand was beset with financial problems and chronic ill health.

Along with his short stories, Premchand wrote fourteen novels. In the early stage of his career he wrote in Urdu, switching to Hindi in later works, which then began to appear in both languages. But he also continued to write in Urdu and made or supervised at least some of the translations of his work from one language to the other. In addition to fiction, his *oeuvre* includes plays, screen-plays, criticism and translations (Galsworthy, George Eliot and Anatole France, among others). He was also a noted journalist and magazine editor.

The Russian realists and the other European writers he translated helped to direct him towards social questions—religious intolerance, nationalism, the position of women, political corruption and, above all, poverty—which would become the main themes of his fiction. His entire career coincided with the most significant years of Mahatma Gandhi's agitation for Indian independence, and many of Gandhi's principles are reflected in his novels and stories, especially the concept of *satyāgraha*, 'holding firmly to the truth,' as the basis for non-violent non-cooperation. Implicit in the idea of satyāgraha is the belief that by practising it people can awaken the best instincts in their adversaries and bring about a transformation for the good in their character. From all we know of Premchand himself, he was one of those who, without benefit of theory or doctrine, held firmly to the truth with remarkable consistency.

As has often been the case with writers of voluminous fiction for publication in newspapers or journals, there are occasional errors or confusions in Premchand's narrative. For example, in 'Widow With Sons' we are first told that all four brothers are married, but later we learn that Sitanath, the youngest, is not and does not plan to marry. In 'The Prostitute' it is said that Singar Singh, a Sikh, has cut his long hair (which constitutes a violation of his religion), but later we are told that his 'long hair is loose,' but that he is without moustache or beard (another violation). In such cases I have amended the text as seemed necessary.

In many of the stories the dialogue will often include long, highly emotional and hyperbolic speeches which seem like virtual operatic arias. If this technique appears historically dated, it is important to see it in its Indian context. Hyperbolic expression of intense emotion has been an accepted aesthetic tradition in Indian imaginative literature since its beginnings. But beyond this, I believe Premchand resorted to that tradition as a means to emphasize the significance and validity of his social ideas, new and no doubt troubling for many of his readers in the twenties and thirties. The predicaments of his characters, victims of caste, class and gender prejudice, were so common and had been accepted for so long, that society needed a violent jolt to be awakened to their horror; rhetorical exaggeration was one of Premchand's most effective instruments to provide that jolt.

Because Hindi narrative prose frequently falls into a pattern of short, rather choppy sentences with little subordination beyond the ubiquitous 'to', I have sometimes combined sentences and merged paragraphs, occasionally introducing a subordinating conjunction. But in general I have kept to the original paragraphing and sentence sequences as much as possible without losing coherence and clarity.

For the most part, the translation is as literal as comprehensible translation will allow. In some cases a Hindi idiom is easily transferable to English. To cite one example, where in English one may speak of 'digging up something [unpleasant, usually] from the past', Hindi has digging up 'from the grave'. In such an instance, I will make a literal translation to convey something of the original tone and colour. Other idioms have no transferable context; the Hindi *'peṭ meṁ ḍāl lenā,'* literally, to throw into the belly, means (in the particular context of the story where it occurs) for a person to keep something (a secret, gossip, etc.) to himself. In such cases, which occur on every page, obviously a substitute for literal translation must be found. In another instance, in 'The Funeral Feast,' I have replaced an idiomatic passage with a variation on an English proverb in order to avoid laborious footnoting. One of the characters tells a woman she need not worry about her children's future because God will contrive some scheme to help them; to this counsel he appends the Urdu expression, *'hīle rozī, bahāne maut,'* literally, 'schemes (or pretexts)—livelihood, excuses—death,' i.e. 'God or fate or perhaps ourselves will contrive schemes [for] livelihood, death finds its own excuses'. After giving up looking for a graceful and conversational way to express this in English I suggest instead, 'Life proposes, death disposes',which is admittedly not the same thing.

Hindi does not typically employ indirect discourse, with the result that narrative often represents the thoughts of characters in the immediate present in a kind of interior monologue, frequently resorting to series of rhetorical questions. In several instances I have rendered these passages in the standard manner of indirect discourse.

In the matter of dialogue, especially in earlier stories, Premchand often uses a dramatic format, simply giving the speaker's name followed by a dash. When possible I have omitted the name or, when necessary for clarity, replaced the dash with a simple 'said'. I have also occasionally treated dialogue with some freedom in an effort to find English equivalents that are as idiomatic as the Hindi. Conversational Hindi, particularly as spoken in villages, tends to be elliptical, allusive and understated, but perfectly clear because of the extraordinary comprehensiveness of established manners and traditional codes of interaction among people of various stations and relationships. Furthermore, many Hindi speakers, even when not literate, know by heart a vast amount of traditional poetry and *bhajans*, religious songs from the works of Sur, Tulsi and Kabir, and may allude to them with a word or phrase so resonant that it is immediately clear without explication.

14

Among village people (and many traditional people in cities as well) it is also customary for titles to be preferred to names. Women who follow the old way, for example, do not address (or mention) their husbands by name but rather, most often, as 'voh', 'he', with plural honorific verb forms. The titles used are themselves sometimes ambiguous. 'Dādā', for instance, may mean grandfather, uncle, father, or elder brother, or any older acquaintance; when the context is not specific the translator must decide for himself which is the most likely. In 'Divided Hearths', Panna is called 'Kākī' by her own children and her stepson; though 'Kākī' specifically designates a maternal aunt, this use in the story is not unusual; and it may also serve as a form of respectful address for any older woman.

Those Hindi, Urdu or Sanskrit words, 'dhotī' or 'panchāyat', for example, which are now found in most standard English dictionaries (e.g., Websters' New World) are retained in the translation, without footnoting. In the case of certain foods (such as 'amritī', 'rasgullā',) no attempt to provide laborious descriptions has been made. I have in a few instances added a word or phrase in apposition to clarify what might otherwise mystify a reader unfamiliar with Indian traditions and rituals.

A word frequently encountered is *birādarī*, literally 'brotherhood'. It has two general meanings, one, all the members of a family (down to the most distant cousins), has the sense of 'the gathered kinsmen' or 'kinfolk'; and two, in the sense in which Premchand most often uses it in these stories, the 'caste community', i.e. all the members of a particular caste or sub-caste. I have generally translated it simply as 'community'. In a story like 'The Funeral Feast' it will be seen that the community, through the direction of its council of five elders, the 'panchāyat', disposes of tremendous power and, when corrupt, can violate civil law with impunity on the pretext of preserving certain traditions and religious customs peculiar to that particular 'birādarī'.

As of this writing, stories previously translated and published in book form in other collections are: 'The Actress' and 'Second Marriage'.

Some of the stories are followed by a note in which, in many cases, hoping to keep footnotes to a minimum, I have incorporated explanations for certain terms. Some readers may want to glance at the concluding note before reading the story. The titles are generally direct translations of the original; when this is not the case, there is a note to that effect. The stories have been drawn from the eight volumes titled *Mansarovar*, or *Kafan*, Premchand's final collection.

15

Indian literature in the modern regional languages remains under-represented in readable translations. The study of these languages in the United States and the Commonwealth has been mainly directed towards doing fieldwork in the social sciences. The critic Indranath Chaudhuri observes in a newspaper article from 1993* that in Western universities when Indian literature is studied it is with a socio-anthropological interest, without regard to universal values or the importance of understanding the continuity of the Indian literary tradition and what is specifically Indian in the aesthetics of a given work.

With this in mind, this collection is offered in the hope of stimulating greater interest among Western readers in Indian literature in general and Hindi literature and language in particular.

Here I would like to acknowledge gratefully the encouragement and good counsel regarding Hindi/Urdu idiomatic usage given to me by Professor Frances Pritchett, Shamsur Rahman Farooqi and most particularly Professor Susham Bedi.

New York, December 1995

---

* Indranath Chaudhuri, 'Videśom mem hindī śikṣan', Navbharat Times, 10 October 1993, p. 2ff.

# THE VILLAGE

# The Road to Salvation

The pride the peasant takes in seeing his field flourishing is like the soldier's in his red turban, the coquette's in her jewels or the doctor's in the patients seated before him. Whenever Jhingur looked at his cane fields a sort of intoxication came over him. He had three *bighas* of land which would earn him an easy 600 rupees. And if God saw to it that the rates went up, then who could complain? Both his bullocks were old so he'd buy a new pair at the Batesar fair. If he could hook on to another two *bighas*, so much the better. Why should he worry about money? The merchants were already beginning to fawn on him. He was convinced that nobody was as good as himself — and so there was scarcely anyone in the village he hadn't quarrelled with.

One evening when he was sitting with his son in his lap, shelling peas, he saw a flock of sheep coming towards him. He said to himself, 'The sheep path doesn't come that way. Can't those sheep go along the bank? What's the idea, coming over here? They'll trample and gobble up the crop and who'll make good for it? I bet it's Buddhu the shepherd — just look at his nerve! He can see me here but he won't drive his sheep back. What good will it do me to put up with *this*? If I try to buy a ram from him he actually asks for five rupees, and everybody sells blankets for four rupees but he won't settle for less than five.'

By now the sheep were close to the cane-field. Jhingur yelled, '*Arrey*, where do you think you're taking those sheep, you?'

Buddhu said meekly, 'Chief, they're coming by way of the boundary embankment. If I take them back around it will mean a couple of miles extra.'

'And I'm supposed to let you trample my field to save you a detour? Why didn't you take them by way of some other boundary path? Do you think I'm some bull-skinning nobody or has your money turned your head? Turn 'em back!'

'Chief, just let them through today. If I ever come back this way again you can punish me any way you want.'

19

'I told you to get them out. If just one of them crosses the line you're going to be in a pack of trouble.'

'Chief,' Buddhu said, 'if even one blade of grass gets under my sheeps' feet you can call me anything you want.'

Although Buddhu was still speaking meekly he had decided that it would be a loss of face to turn back. 'If I drive the flock back for a few little threats,' he thought, 'how will I graze my sheep? Turn back today and tomorrow I won't find anybody willing to let me through, they'll all start bullying me.'

And Buddhu was a tough man too. He owned 240 sheep and he was able to get eight *annas* per night to leave them in people's fields to manure them, and he sold their milk as well and made blankets from their wool. He thought, 'Why's he getting so angry? What can he do to me? I'm not his servant.'

When the sheep got a whiff of the green leaves they became restless and they broke into the field. Beating them with his stick Buddhu tried to push them back across the boundary line but they just broke in somewhere else. In a fury Jhingur said, 'You're trying to force your way through here but I'll teach you a lesson!'

Buddhu said, 'It's seeing you that's scared them. If you just get out of the way I'll clear them all out of the field.'

But Jhingur put down his son and grabbing up his cudgel he began to whack the sheep. Not even a washerman would have beaten his donkey so cruelly. He smashed legs and backs and while they bleated Buddhu stood silent watching the destruction of his army. He didn't yell at the sheep and he didn't say anything to Jhingur, no, he just watched the show. In just about two minutes, with the prowess of an epic hero, Jhingur had routed the enemy forces. After this carnage among the host of sheep Jhingur said with the pride of victory, 'Now move on straight! And don't ever think about coming this way again.'

Looking at his wounded sheep, Buddhu said, 'Jhingur, you've done a dirty job. You're going to regret it.'

*

To take vengeance on a farmer is easier than slicing a banana. Whatever wealth he has is in his fields or barns. The produce get into the house only after innumerable afflictions of nature and the gods. And if it happens that a human enemy joins in alliance with

20

those afflictions the poor farmer is apt to be left nowhere. When Jhingur came home and told his family about the battle, they started to give him advice.

'Jhingur, you've got yourself into real trouble! You knew what to do but you acted as though you didn't. Don't you realize what a tough customer Buddhu is? Even now it's not too late — go and make peace, otherwise the whole village will come to grief along with you.'

Jhingur thought it over. He began to regret that he'd stopped Buddhu at all. If the sheep had eaten up a little of his crop it wouldn't have ruined him. The fact is, a farmer's prosperity comes precisely from being humble — God doesn't like it when a peasant walks with his head high. Jhingur didn't enjoy the idea of going to Buddhu's house but urged on by the others he set out. It was the dead of winter, foggy, with the darkness settling in everywhere. He had just come out of the village when suddenly he was astonished to see a fire blazing over in the direction of his cane-field. His heart started to hammer. A field had caught fire! He ran wildly, hoping it wasn't his own field, but as he got closer this deluded hope died. He'd been struck by the very misfortune he'd set out to avert. The bastard had started the fire and was ruining the whole village because of him. As he ran it seemed to him that today his field was a lot nearer than it used to be, as though the fallow land between had ceased to exist.

When he finally reached his field the fire had assumed dreadful proportions. Jhingur began to wail. The villagers were running and ripping up stalks of millet to beat the fire. A terrible battle between man and nature went on for several hours, each side winning in turn. The flames would subside and almost vanish only to strike back again with redoubled vigour like battle-crazed warriors. Among the men Buddhu was the most valiant fighter; with his *dhoti* tucked up around his waist he leapt into the fiery gulfs as though ready to subdue the enemy or die, and he'd emerge after many a narrow escape. In the end it was the men who triumphed, but the triumph amounted to defeat. The whole village's sugar-cane crop was burned to ashes and with the cane all their hopes as well.

*

21

It was no secret who had started the fire. But no one dared say anything about it. There was no proof and what was the point of a case without any evidence? As for Jhingur, it had become difficult for him to show himself out of his house. Wherever he went he had to listen to abuse. People said right to his face, 'You were the cause of the fire! You ruined us. You were so stuck up your feet didn't touch the dirt! You yourself were ruined and you dragged the whole village down with you. If you hadn't fought with Buddhu would all this have happened?'

Jhingur was even more grieved by these taunts than by the destruction of his crop, and he would stay in his house the whole day.

Winter drew on. Where before the cane-press had turned all night and the fragrance of the crushed sugar filled the air and fires were lit with people sitting around them smoking their *hookas*, all was desolation now. Because of the cold people cursed Jhingur and, drawing their doors shut, went to bed as soon as it was dark. Sugarcane isn't only the farmers' wealth; their whole way of life depends on it. With the help of the cane they get through the winter. They drink the cane juice, warm themselves from fires made of its leaves and feed their livestock on the cuttings. All the village dogs that used to sleep in the warm ash of the fires died from the cold and many of the livestock too from lack of fodder. The cold was excessive and everybody in the village was seized with coughs and fevers. And it was Jhingur who'd brought about the whole catastrophe, that cursed, murdering Jhingur.

Jhingur thought and thought and decided that Buddhu had to be put in a situation exactly like his own. Buddhu had ruined him and he was wallowing in comfort, so Jhingur would ruin Buddhu too.

Since the day of their terrible quarrel Buddhu had ceased to come by Jhingur's. Jhingur decided to cultivate an intimacy with him; he wanted to show him he had no suspicion at all that Buddhu started the fire. One day, on the pretext of getting a blanket, he went to Buddhu, who greeted him with every courtesy and honour — for a man offers the *hooka* even to an enemy and won't let him depart without making him drink milk and syrup.

These days Jhingur was earning a living by working in a jute-wrapping mill. Usually he got several days' wages at once. Only by means of Buddhu's help could he meet his daily expenses between times. So it was that Jhingur re-established a friendly footing between them.

22

One day Buddhu asked, 'Say Jhingur, what would you do if you caught the man who burned your cane-field? Tell me the truth.'

Solemnly Jhingur said, 'I'd tell him, "Brother, what you did was good. You put an end to my pride, you made me into a decent man."'

'If I were in your place,' Buddhu said, 'I wouldn't settle for any-thing less than burning down his house.'

'But what's the good of stirring up hatred in a life that lasts such a little while in all? I've been ruined already, what could I get out of ruining him?'

'Right, that's the way of a decent, religious man,' Buddhu said, 'but when a fellow's in the grip of anger all his sense gets jumbled up.'

*

Spring came and the peasants were getting the fields ready for planting cane. Buddhu was doing a fine business. Everybody wanted his sheep. There were always a half dozen men at his door fawning on him, and he lorded it over everybody. He doubled the price of hiring out his sheep to manure the field; if anybody objected he'd say bluntly, 'Look, brother, I'm not shoving my sheep on you. If you don't want them, don't take them. But I can't let you have them for a pice less then I said.' The result was that everybody swarmed around him, despite his rudeness, just like priests after some pilgrim.

Lakshmi, goddess of wealth, is of no great size; she can, accord-ing to the occasion, shrink or expand, to such a degree that some-times she can contract her most magnificent manifestation into the form of a few small figures printed on paper. There are times when she makes some man's tongue her throne and her size is reduced to nothing. But just the same she needs a lot of elbowroom for her permanent living quarters. If she comes into somebody's house, the house should grow accordingly, she can't put up with a small one. Buddhu's house also began to grow. A veranda was built in front of the door, six rooms replaced the former two. In short, the house was done over from top to bottom. Buddhu got the wood from a peasant, from another the cowdung cakes for the kiln fuel to make the tiles; somebody else gave him the bamboo and reeds for the mats. He had to pay for having the walls put up but he

23

didn't give any cash even for this, he gave some lambs. Such is the power of Lakshmi: the whole job — and it was quite a good house, all in all — was put up for nothing. They began to prepare for a house-warming.

Jhingur was still labouring all day without getting enough to half fill his belly, while gold was raining on Buddhu's house. If Jhingur was angry, who could blame him? Nobody could put up with such injustice.

One day Jhingur went out walking in the direction of the untouchable tanners' settlement. He called for Harihar, who came out, greeting him with *'Ram Ram!'* and filled the *hooka*. They began to smoke. Harihar, the leader of the tanners, was a mean fellow and there wasn't a peasant who didn't tremble at the sight of him.

After smoking a bit, Jhingur said, 'No singing for the spring festival these days? We haven't heard you.'

'What festival? The belly can't take a holiday. Tell me, how are you getting on lately?'

'Getting by,' Jhingur said. 'Hard times mean a hard life. If I work all day in the mill there's a fire in my stove. But these days only Buddhu's making money. He doesn't have room to store it! He's built a new house, bought more sheep. Now there's a big fuss about his house-warming. He's sent *paan* to the headmen of all the seven villages around to invite everybody to it.'

'When Mother Lakshmi comes men don't see so clearly,' Harihar said. 'And if you see him, he's not walking on the same ground as you or me. If he talks, it's only to brag.'

'Why shouldn't he brag? Who in the village can equal him? But friend, I'm not going to put up with injustice. When God gives I bow my head and accept it. It's not that I think nobody's equal to me but when I hear *him* bragging it's as though my body starts to burn. "A cheat yesterday, a banker today." He's stepped on us to get ahead. Only yesterday he was hiring himself out in the fields with just a loincloth on to chase crows and today his lamp's burning in the skies.'

'Speak,' Harihar said, 'Is there something I can do?'

'What can you do? He doesn't keep any cows or buffaloes just because he's afraid somebody will do something to them to get at him.'

'But he keeps sheep, doesn't he?'

24

'You mean, "hunt a heron and get a grouse?"'

'Think about it again.'

'It's got to be a plan that will keep him from ever getting rich again.'

Then they began to whisper. It's a mystery why there's just as much love among the wicked as malice among the good. Scholars, holy men and poets sizzle with jealousy when they see other scholars, holy men and poets. But a gambler sympathizes with another gambler and helps him, and it's the same with drunkards and thieves. Now, if a Brahman Pandit stumbles in the dark and falls then another Pandit, instead of giving him a hand, will give him a couple of kicks so he won't be able to get up. But when a thief finds another thief in distress he helps him. Everybody's united in hating evil so the wicked have to love one another; while everybody praises virtue so the virtuous are jealous of each other. What does a thief get by killing another thief? Contempt. A scholar who slanders another scholar attains to glory.

Jhingur and Harihar consulted, plotting their course of action — the method, the time and all the steps. When Jhingur left he was strutting — he'd already overcome his enemy, there was no way for Buddhu to escape now.

On his way to work the next day he stopped by Buddhu's house. Buddhu asked him, 'Aren't you working today?'

'I'm on my way, but I came by to ask you if you wouldn't let my calf graze with your sheep. The poor thing's dying tied up to the post while I'm away all day, she doesn't get enough grass and fodder to eat.'

'Brother, I don't keep cows and buffaloes. You know the tanners, they're all killers. That Harihar killed my two cows, I don't know what he fed them. Since then I've vowed never again to keep cattle. But your's is just a calf, there'd be no profit to anyone in harming her. Bring her over whenever you want.'

Then he began to show Jhingur the arrangements for the house-warming. *Ghee*, sugar, flour and vegetables were all on hand. All they were waiting for was the Satyanarayan ceremony. Jhingur's eyes were popping.

When he came home after work the first thing he did was bring his calf to Buddhu's house. That night the ceremony was performed and a feast offered to the Brahmans. The whole night passed in lavishing hospitality on the priests. Buddhu had no opportunity to go to look after his flock of sheep.

The feasting went on until morning. Buddhu had just got up and had his breakfast when a man came and said, 'Buddhu, while you've been sitting around here, out there in your flock the calf has died. You're a fine one! The rope was still around its neck.'

When Buddhu heard this it was as though he'd been punched. Jhingur, who was there having some breakfast too, said, 'Oh God, my calf! Come on, I want to see her! But listen, I never tied her with a rope. I brought her to the flock of sheep and went back home. When did you have her tied with a rope, Buddhu?'

'God's my witness, I never touched any rope! I haven't been back to my sheep since then.'

'If you didn't, then who put the rope on her?' Jhingur said. 'You must have done it and forgotten it.'

'And it was in your flock,' one of the Brahmans said. 'People are going to say that whoever tied the rope, that heifer died because of Buddhu's negligence.'

Harihar came along just then and said, 'I saw him tying the rope around the calf's neck last night.'

'Me?' Buddhu said.

'Wasn't that you with your stick over your shoulder tying up the heifer?'

'And you're an honest fellow, I suppose!' Buddhu said. 'You saw me tying her up?'

'Why get angry with me, brother? Let's just say you didn't tie her up, if that's what you want.'

'We will have to decide about it,' one of the Brahmans said. 'A cow slaughterer should be stoned — it's no laughing matter.'

'Maharaj,' Jhingur said, 'the killing was accidental.'

'What's that got to do with it?' the Brahman said. 'It's set down that no cow is ever to be done to death in any way.'

'That's right,' Jhingur said. 'Just to tie a cow up is a fiendish act.'

'In the Scriptures it's called the greatest sin,' the Brahman said. 'Killing a cow is no less than killing a Brahman.'

'That's right,' Jhingur said. 'The cow's got a high place, that's why we respect her, isn't it? The cow is like a mother. But Maharaj, it was an accident — figure out something to get the poor fellow off.'

Buddhu stood listening while the charge of murder was brought against him like the simplest thing in the world. He had no doubt it was Jhingur's plotting, but if he said a thousand times that he

26

hadn't put the rope on the calf nobody would pay any attention to it. They'd say he was trying to escape the penance.

The Brahman, that divinity, also stood to profit from the imposition of a penance. Naturally, he was not one to neglect an opportunity like this. The outcome was that Buddhu was charged with the death of a cow; the Brahman had got very incensed about it too and he determined the manner of compensation. The punishment consisted of three months of begging in the streets, then a pilgrimage to the seven holy places, and in addition the price for five cows and feeding 500 Brahmans. Stunned, Buddhu listened to it. He began to weep, and after that the period of begging was reduced by one month. Apart from this he received no favour. There was no one to appeal to, no one to complain to. He had to accept the punishment.

He gave up his sheep to God's care. His children were young and all by herself what could his wife do? The poor fellow would stand in one door after another hiding his face and saying, 'Even the gods are banished for cow-slaughter!' He received alms but along with them he had to listen to bitter insults. Whatever he picked up during the day he'd cook in the evening under some tree and then go to sleep right there. He did not mind the hardship, for he was used to wandering all day with his sheep and sleeping beneath trees, and his food at home hadn't been much better than this, but he was ashamed of having to beg, especially when some harridan would taunt him with, 'You've found a fine way to earn your bread!' That sort of thing hurt him profoundly, but what could he do?

He came home after two months. His hair was long, and he was as weak as though he were sixty years old. He had to arrange for the money for his pilgrimage, and where's the money-lender who loans to shepherds? You couldn't depend on sheep. Sometimes there are epidemics and you're cleaned out of the whole flock in one night. Furthermore, it was the middle of the hot weather when there was no hope of profit from the sheep. There was an oil-dealer who was willing to loan him money at an interest of two *annas* per rupee — in eight months the interest would equal the principal. Buddhu didn't dare borrow on such terms. During the two months many of his sheep had been stolen. When the children took them to graze the other villagers would hide one or two sheep away in a field or hut and afterwards slaughter them and eat them. The boys, poor lads, couldn't catch a single one of them, and even when they saw, how could they fight? The whole village was banded together. It was an awful dilemma. Helpless, Buddhu sent for a butcher and sold the whole flock to him for 500 rupees. He took 200 rupees and started out on his pilgrimage. The rest of the money he set aside for feeding the Brahmans.

When Buddhu left, his house was burgled twice, but by good fortune the family woke up and the money was saved.

It was *Savan*, the month of rains, with everything green. Jhingur, who had no bullocks now, had rented out his field to sharecroppers. Buddhu had been freed from his penitential obligations and along with them his delusions about wealth. Neither one of them had anything left; neither could be angry with the other — there was nothing left to be angry about.

Because the jute mill had closed down Jhingur went to work with pick and shovel in town where a very large rest house for pilgrims was being built. There were a thousand labourers on the job. Every seventh day Jhingur would take his pay home and after spending the night there go back the next morning.

Buddhu came to the same place looking for work. The foreman saw that he was a skinny little fellow who wouldn't be able to do any heavy work so he had him take mortar to the labourers. Once when Buddhu was going with a shallow pan on his head to get mortar Jhingur saw him. '*Ram Ram*' they said to one another and Jhingur filled the pan. Buddhu picked it up. For the rest of the day they went about their work in silence.

At the end of the day Jhingur asked, 'Are you going to cook something?'

'How can I eat if I don't?' Buddhu said.

'I eat solid food only once a day,' Jhingur said. 'I get by just drinking water with ground meal in it in the evenings. Why fuss?'

'Pick up some of those sticks lying around,' Buddhu said. 'I brought some flour from home. I had it ground there — it costs a lot here in town. I'll knead it on the flat side of this rock. Since you won't eat food I cook I'll get it ready and you cook it.'

'But there's no frying pan.'

'There are lots of frying pans,' Buddhu said. 'I'll scour out one of these mortar trays.'

The fire was lit, the flour kneaded. Jhingur cooked the *chapatties*, Buddhu brought the water. They both ate the bread with salt

28

and red pepper. Then they filled the bowl of the *hooka*. They both lay down on the stony ground and smoked.

Buddhu said, 'I was the one who set fire to your cane field.'

Jhingur said light-heartedly, 'I know.'

After a little while he said, 'I tied up the heifer and Harihar fed it something.'

In the same light-hearted tone Buddhu said, 'I know.'

Then the two of them went to sleep.

# A Feast for the Holy Man

A wandering holy man appeared in the doorway of Ramdhan the farmer and said: 'May you prosper, child — and show your reverence for a holy man.'

Ramdhan went to his wife and said, 'A *sadhu's* at the door, we have to give him something.'

His wife had been scouring pots, all the while worrying about what they were going to eat that day, for there wasn't even a speck of grain in the house. It was the first month of spring but even at noon the skies were clouded over. The crops had been cleaned out of the barn; the money-lender had taken half, the landowner's agents had collected the other half, and the chaff had been sold to get the ox-trader off their backs — and that was all. For themselves they had saved one small sack. By threshing it over and over again they had managed to get scarcely one maund of grain out of it. Somehow or other they had got into spring, but God knew how they would go on or what the oxen would eat or even the people in the house. But a holy man had come to their door — how could they send him away disappointed, what would he think in his heart? She said: 'What can I give him when there's nothing at all left?'

Ramdhan said, 'Go look in the clay jug, if there's any flour left bring it.'

'Yesterday I used whatever I could scrape out of it — do you expect a miracle?'

'I'm not going to be heard telling the *baba* there's nothing in the house. Borrow something from one of the neighbours.'

'Look what I've already borrowed without ever being able to pay anything back! What kind of a face can I show them now?'

'Isn't there something set aside for an offering to the gods?' Ramdhan said. 'Get it and I'll give it to him.'

'Then where will we get anything to offer the gods?'

'Hasn't a god come a-begging? If you've got something to give, you give. If you haven't, you don't.'

30

'And I suppose you think we've got ten or twenty pounds of meal set aside for them! With luck there's about a pound. After that's gone what if another *sadhu* comes? You'll have to send him about his business.'

'We'll take care of this problem first, and then we'll see.'

Grumbling, she got up and picked up a small clay pot in which there was scarcely a pound. With the greatest difficulty it had been kept aside as an offering to the gods. Ramdhan stood reflecting a moment. Then he put the flour in a bowl, went outside and poured it into the *sadhu's* sack.

*

When he had taken the flour the *mahatma* said, 'My child, for today we intend to rest here. Give me just a little *dal* and then the *sadhu's* offering will be complete.'

Ramdhan went in again and told his wife. By chance there was some *dal* left in the house. Ramdhan took it, along with some salt and some cowdung cakes for fuel. Then he fetched water from the well. Methodically the holy man shaped the flour into cakes, cooked the *dal*, and took some potatoes from his sack and mashed them. When all the food was ready he said to Ramdhan, 'Child, for a proper offering to the Lord we need just a spoonful of *ghee*. If the food is not prepared according to the ritual, then what kind of an offering will it be?'

'*Babaji,*' Ramdhan said, 'there's no *ghee* in the house.'

'Child, don't say such things. God has given you much!'

'Maharaj, I have no cows or buffaloes, so how should I have *ghee*?'

'Child, in God's storerooms there's a little of everything — so just go and ask the mistress of the house.'

Ramdhan went back in and said to his wife, 'He's asking for *ghee* — he's a beggar who begs his way but he can't get one bite down without *ghee*!'

'Then take some of this *dal* and take it to the banya. After everything else, why make him angry with us just for this?'

They got the *ghee*. The holy man took out a handful of food as an offering to the Lord, rang a little bell and sat down to enjoy the meal offered to himself.

He ate his fill, then rubbing his belly lay down on the threshold.

Ramdhan brought the *sadhu's* plate, pot and ladle into the house to scour them.

That night nothing was cooked in Ramdhan's house. They just warmed up plain *dal* and drank it.

When he lay down to sleep, Ramdhan said to himself, 'Well, he's a better man than I am!'

# The Power of a Curse

Munshi Ramsevak came out of his house frowning and said, 'Death would be better than living like this.' Death gets quite a few invitations of this sort: if she accepted them all the whole world would be depopulated by now.

In the village of Chandpur Munshi Ramsevak was a very rich man and he was full of all the special qualities of very rich men. The foibles of human nature provided the foundation of his living. He could be seen every day seated on a broken bench under a *neem* tree within the precincts of the open-air small-pleas court, his satchel crammed with papers opened up in front of him. Nobody had ever seen him presenting a brief before the tribunal or arguing a case; but everyone called him 'attorney'. It might blow up a storm, rain or hail, but the attorney could not be budged from his bench. Whenever he made his way to the open court the villagers crowded after him. He was regarded by everyone with respect and trust, and he was renowned for possessing the eloquence of the divine Saraswati herself. Call it an attorneyship or a legal practice, but it was only maintaining a family tradition. He had no very great income; people might talk about silver coins but even copper coins rarely came his way. Though there was no doubt about Ramsevak's legal knowledge, he was compelled by complications to forego a real lawyer's job. Anyway, whatever it was, his profession was kept up only for the sake of continuing the family tradition. In actual fact his real means of livelihood was provided by widows without family but rich in the good things of life and by old men with lots of money and little sense. The widows handed over their money to him for safe-keeping and old men who feared their wastrel sons entrusted their wealth to him. But once any money went into his fist it forgot the way to come out again. When the need arose he himself would borrow — after all, without borrowing whose work would make any headway? He borrowed in the morning to give back by evening, but the evening never came. In brief, Munshi Ramsevak knew how to borrow but not to give. This

33

too was the family tradition.

All these matters frequently presented obstacles to Ramsevak's peace and quiet, but he had not the least fear of law and justice. To oppose him in this sort of business was like tackling a crocodile in the water. And still whenever any wretch did tangle with him, cast aspersions on his honesty or insulted him, Ramsevak was deeply hurt. And this sort of unfortunate incident kept on happening; there were shallow creatures everywhere who took delight in demeaning others. Egged on by such people, petty fellows would sometimes slander him. Otherwise, to take one example, how would an insignificant green-grocer's widow have the audacity to march right into his courtyard and curse him? He'd been an old customer of hers, for years he'd got vegetables from her. If he didn't pay, the woman ought to have been content —sooner or later she would have received it. But the foul-mouthed bean-monger went to pieces about it after only a couple of years and for a matter of a few pice tried to disgrace an established gentleman. Munshi Ramsevak got so irritated he was ready to do away with himself — he was not to blame for any of it.

*

In the same village lived a Brahman widow named Munga. Her husband had been a sergeant in the native Indian battalion in Burma and had died in battle there. In view of his fine service, the government had bestowed a sum of rupees 500 on her. Being a widow and times being hard, the poor creature entrusted all her money to Ramsevak, and begging back tiny sums every month she managed to eke out a living.

Munshiji had carried out his duty for several years now with full honesty. But when Munga had grown old without any sign of dying and he realized that perhaps from the whole amount she did not intend to leave even half to pay for her funeral expenses, he said to her one day, 'Munga, are you going to die or aren't you? Or just say straight out that you'll look after your own funeral fees.' That day Munga's eyes were opened, her dream dispelled, and she said, 'Give me back the full amount!' The account book was ready: not a pice of it remained according to the book. She violently grabbed his hand and said, 'You've made off with 250 rupees of mine but I won't let you keep a pice of it!'

34

But a poor widow's anger is just the sound of a blank bullet that may scare a child but has no real effect at all. She didn't have any influence in the courts, she couldn't read or write or keep accounts. To be sure, there was some hope in the panchayat, the village council. The panchayat met, people gathered from several villages. Munshi Ramsevak was ready and agreeable; he stood up in the council and addressed the members: 'Friends! You are all noble and devoted to the truth. I bow to you all. I am grateful to the core to you for your generosity and mercy, your charity and love. Do you people think I really made off with the money of this unfortunate widow?'

With one voice the councillors said, 'No, no! You couldn't do such a thing!'

Munshiji said, 'If you all agree that I've stolen her money, then there'll be nothing left for me except to drown myself. I'm not a rich man, nor can I take pride in being munificent. But thanks to my pen and to your kindness I cannot call myself needy. Am I so petty as to embezzle a widow's money?'

The councillors were unanimous. 'No, no, you couldn't do such a thing!'

They had had a taste of his money and that was that. The council acquitted him and adjourned.

Munga heaved a sigh and, making the most of it, said to herself, 'If I'm not to get it here, then all right, I won't, but I'll get it back in heaven.'

*

There was nobody now to help Munga or listen to her grieving. Whatever woes poverty bestowed she had to bear them all. She was strong of body and if she had wanted she could have worked hard. But from the day the panchayat gave its judgment she swore she wouldn't work. Now she was obsessed with the thought of her money. All day and all night, walking or sitting, she had only one idea: to inveigh against Munshi Ramsevak. Seated day and night at the door of her hut she fervently cursed him. For the most part in her pronouncements she employed poetic speech and metaphors so that people who heard her were astonished.

Gradually her mind gave way. Bare-headed, bare-bodied, with a little hatchet in her hand, she would sit in desolate places. She

35

abandoned her hut and was seen wandering around the ruins in a cremation *ghat* along the river — dishevelled, red-eyed, grimacing crazily, her arms and legs emaciated. When they saw her like this people were frightened. Now no one teased her even for fun. Whenever she came out in the village, women shut the doors of their houses, men slunk away and children ran off screeching. But there was one child who didn't run away and that was Munshiji's son Ramgulam. Whatever defect had been omitted in the father was to be found in the son, and he was always getting the other boys into trouble too. The village one-eyed and lame men hated the sight of him. And he enjoyed insults as much as though they were compliments. He would keep after Munga, clapping his hands and taking the village dogs with him, until the poor woman, utterly bewildered, would flee the hamlet. Having lost her mind along with her money she had earned the title of the local mad-woman. She would sit alone, talking to herself for hours, express-ing her intense desire to eat, smash, pinch and tear Ramsevak's flesh, bones, eyes, liver and the like, and when her hatred reached its climax she would turn her face toward Ramsevak's house and shriek the terrible words, 'I'll drink your blood!'

Women were frightened when they heard her howling voice in the stillness of the night. But more terrible than her words was her wild laughter. In the imagined pleasure of drinking Munshiji's blood she would burst into laughter that resounded with such demoniacal violence, such bestial ferocity that when people heard it in the night their blood was chilled. It seemed as though hundreds of owls were hooting together. Munshiji was a man of great courage and tenacity, not one to be afraid of a madwoman any more than of the courts, but when he heard Munga's awful words he was scared. We may not be afraid of human justice but the fear of God's justice resides by nature in every man's heart — Munga's dreadful night-wanderings sometimes inspired such reflections in Ramsevak's mind, and even more in his wife's.

Nagin, who was pregnant now, was a very shrewd woman. She advised her husband about all his business dealings. The people who said Munshiji possessed the eloquence of Goddess Saraswati were mistaken: this virtue really belonged to his wife. She was as brilliant in speech as he in writing. And these two, husband and wife, would now consult together on what to do about this situa-tion in which they found themselves powerless.

One midnight when Munshiji, according to his regular custom, had banished his troubles with a few swallows of liquor and gone to sleep, suddenly Munga let out a shriek right on his door-step and howled, 'I'll drink your blood!'

Munshiji was electrified by her horrible peals of laughter. His legs shook with fear, his heart thumped. Gathering up his courage with a great effort he opened the door and woke Nagin. Peevishly she said, 'What's the matter?' Munshiji whispered, 'She's standing on the door-step.'

Nagin sat up. 'What's she saying?'

'Don't be stupid, what do you think she's saying?'

'You mean she's right at the door?'

'Yes, can't you hear her?'

Nagin was not afraid of Munga but she was very much afraid of the misdeed she symbolized; still, she believed she could get the best of her by talking. 'Just let me talk to her,' she said but Munshiji forbade her.

The two of them tiptoed to the threshold and peeking from the door they saw Munga's dim figure lying on the ground, they heard her panting. In her hungering for Munshiji's flesh and blood she had completely used up her own: even a child could have knocked her down — and yet she could make the whole town tremble.

The night passed. The door was shut but Ramsevak and Nagin spent the hours sitting up. Munga could not get inside but who could stop her voice? Her voice was the most terrible thing about her.

At dawn, Munshiji went outside and said to her, 'Why are you lying there?'

'I'll drink your blood,' Munga said.

Rearing up, Nagin said, 'I'll knock your head right off!'

But Nagin's venomous tone had no effect on Munga, who shrieked with laughter.

Disconcerted, Nagin fell silent before that laughter. Then Munshiji spoke again: 'Get up!'

'I won't!'

'Just how long do you think you're going to lie here?'

'I'll go when I've drunk you blood!'

In these straits Munshiji's pungent pen was of no use and Nagin's fiery eloquence grew cold. They went inside to consult on how to put an end to this calamitous situation.

When the Goddess comes she has a drink of goat's blood and goes on her way, but this witch came to drink human blood, the very blood which, if even a drop of it was spilled while Munshiji was sharpening a pen nib, was lamented throughout the household for weeks and months while the event was related from house to house in the village. Would Munga's shrivelled body become young again from drinking that blood?

The news got around the village that Munga was squatting on Munshiji's doorstep. The villagers took great delight in his embarrassment and loss of face. Whole flocks of people gathered around at once. Little Ramgulam didn't like this crowd and he got so angry with Munga that if he had had the power he would have flung her into a well. As soon as an idea like this struck him he would be so tickled that he could hardly control his laughter. Oh, what fun it would be to dump her into a well! But the bitch wouldn't get away from the door, what could you do? Munshiji kept a cow, which was very well fed with oilseed cake, grain and straw; but all of it went to her bones and her frame became ever more robust. Ramgulam collected the dung of this cow in a pot and flung it at the poor woman. Some of it splashed on the onlookers too. Munga was completely covered and the people hastily retreated, saying, 'This is Munshi Ramgulam's door where you can expect such fine manners! Get away quickly or there'll be some even greater show of courtesy.' While the crowd dispersed Ramgulam went into the house and had a good laugh and clapped his hands. Munshiji congratulated his son on this ingenious and appealing way of getting rid of that good-for-nothing crowd. The whole mob finally disappeared, but Munga went on lying there exactly as before.

Noontime came. Munga ate nothing. Then it was evening. Even after a barrage of threats and abuse she refused to eat. The village headman came and coaxed her, and Munshiji even begged her with folded hands, but she would not agree. Finally he got up and went inside. He said that hunger alone could overcome so fierce a hatred.

That night Munga neither ate nor drank anything and once again Munshiji and Nagin lay awake until morning. By now Munga's howling and laughing were heard much less frequently. The people of the household assumed that the worst was over. As soon as it was daylight Munshiji opened the door and saw Munga lying motionless. Flies were already buzzing around her mouth; her breathing had stopped. She had come just to die at his door. To the man who'd taken her life savings she had entrusted her corpse as well, she was making him a gift of the very clay of her body.

It is impossible to describe the sensation this event produced in the village and the extent of Ramsevak's disgrace. As much of a commotion as there can be in such a tiny village over such an extraordinary event, well, it was even greater than that, and Munshiji's dishonour was not a whit less than it ought to have been. Whatever prestige he'd been able to maintain vanished. Now not even the leather-tanners would have accepted water from him or touched him. If a cow in somebody's household dies while tied to a peg, then that man goes around for months begging from door to door; no barber will shave him, no water-carrier bring him water, nor anyone touch him; such is the penance for cow-slaughter. The punishment for the murder of a Brahman is even stiffer and the disgrace immeasurable. Knowing this, Munga had come to die on his doorstep. She knew she could not accomplish much alive but dead she could do a great deal.

*

Munshi Ramsevak was versed in law: according to the law he was innocent. Munga had not died according to any legal instance, no example of it could be found in the Indian Penal Code. Therefore those people who wished to impose a penance on him were entirely mistaken. There was no great harm so far as he was concerned: if the water-carrier did not want to draw his water, Munshiji would draw it himself — anyway, what was wrong with doing such little chores for yourself? And what if the barber wouldn't shave him? — what's the use of getting shaved? The beard's a lovely thing, the very glory and embellishment of man. And then if later you get fed up with the beard, you can always buy a razor for a paltry sum. He wasn't worried when the *dhobi* refused to wash his clothes. In any street in town there was nothing cheaper than soap. With just one cake a whole pile of clothes could be made clean as a duck's feathers. How could the *dhobi* make clothes that clean? He whips them on the stones until they're in tatters. He wears your clothes, rents them out to others, throws them into his boiling cauldron and steeps them in fuller's earth. And of course

39

they're ruined. That's why shirts don't last more than two or three years. If that hadn't been the case grandfather would have got along with having only two jackets and two shirts made every fifth year. Throughout the day Munshiji and his wife consoled themselves with such reasoning. But as soon as it was evening their rationalizing petered out.

Fear took hold of them when darkness fell. As the hour turned late this fear grew all the stronger. They'd left the front door open by mistake and not one of them was daring enough to get up and shut it. Finally Nagin took a lamp, Munshiji his axe and Ramgulam the sickle, and the three of them, quaking and shrinking, went to the door. There Munshiji boldly tackled the problem: he made a valiant attempt to go outside. Trembling but with a loud voice he said to Nagin, 'You're frightened for nothing. Do you think she's sitting out there?' But his loving Nagin pulled him back inside and said angrily, 'You're wicked to joke about it.' Having won this tilt the three of them went into the kitchen and began to cook something.

But Munga had got under their skins. Seeing their own shadow they'd jump, sure it was Munga. It seemed to them that she was sitting in every dark corner. That emaciated body and scattered hair, the mad look, the horrible eyes — it was Munga to a tee!

In the kitchen they had set several large clay pots for flour and pulse and there were some old rags lying around too. Driven by hunger a mouse came out looking for the grain which those pots in fact had never had a taste of — but it was well-known in the village that in this house the mice had to be resourceful thieves.

The mouse crept under the rags with a rustling sound. The way those rags were spread out they looked exactly like Munga's skinny legs. When she saw them Nagin jumped and let out a shriek. Losing his head completely Munshiji sprang for the door and Ramgulam started running and got entangled in his father's legs. Just then the mouse emerged and when they saw it they recovered their wits. Ramsevak walked boldly toward the pot. 'Leave it alone,' Nagin said. 'We've seen how brave you are.'

Her contempt made Munshiji very angry. 'Do you think I was afraid?' he said. 'What was there to be afraid of? Munga's dead, so how could she be there? Didn't I go outside yesterday? You tried to stop me but I didn't pay any attention.'

This argument silenced Nagin. Yesterday it had been no ordinary deed to go outside the door or even to try to. Whoever had shown such evidence of bravery could not be called a coward by anybody. Nagin was just being perverse.

After they'd eaten the three of them came into the bedroom. But even there Munga did not leave them alone. They were talking, enjoying themselves. Nagin told the tale of Raja Hardaul and Rani Sarandha, Munshiji recounted the circumstances of several criminal cases. But even in these diversions Munga's image refused to leave their minds. The very slightest tap would startle them. If there was a rustling of leaves the hair would stand up on all three of them. Several times a low voice reached them from within the earth: 'I'll drink your blood . . .'

At midnight Nagin was startled from her sleep. It seemed to her that Munga, with her red eyes and sharp pointed teeth, was sitting on her chest. Nagin screamed. She started running toward the courtyard like a madwoman, and suddenly she fell senseless to the ground, sweating all over. Munshiji had been awakened by her yell but he was so frightened he didn't open his eyes. Like a blind man he felt his way to the door. After a long while he found it and came into the courtyard. Nagin was lying on the ground writhing. He lifted her up and brought her inside, but she didn't open her eyes the whole night. Toward dawn she began to rave incoherently. In a little while her fever rose, her body turned hot as a griddle. By evening she was in a delirium and at midnight when all the world was plunged in silence she took her leave of it forever. Fear of Munga had killed her. While Munga lived she had always feared Nagin's hissing. But sacrificing her own life, she could now take Nagin's.

The night passed, day drew on, but not one person in the village showed up to bear Nagin's corpse away. Munshiji went from house to house, but no one answered the door. After all, who will go to a murderer's house? Who will do honour to the corpse of an assassin? This time Munshiji's prestige, his genius at law and the fear of his mighty pen were of no use to him at all. Rejected everywhere, he turned back to his house. Here everything appeared to him as gloomy as possible. He came as far as his door but he didn't set foot inside. Outside was Munga, inside Nagin. Mustering his courage, he finally entered the house reciting passages from the 'Holy Acts of God Hanuman'. Only he knew what was passing in his mind. There was the corpse: no one of the earlier generation was

41

left, no one from the coming except his son. To be sure, he might marry again. This last spring he'd only reached fifty. But where could he find a worthy and sweet-tongued wife? What a loss! Who was there now to cope with dunning creditors, who could silence them? Who could keep the accounts of all his transactions so well? Whose sharp voice could shoot out like an arrow to pierce the hearts of his creditors? There was no compensation for such a loss. The next day Munshiji loaded the body on to a wheel-barrow and went toward holy Ganges.

*

The number of people attending the cremation was not large. There was Munshiji himself and one other, his dear son Ramgulam. Even Munga's corpse had not had to suffer such humiliation.

Having done away with Nagin, Munga was not going to leave Munshiji alone. At every moment her image remained before his eyes. Wherever he might be his mind always harked back to her. If he could have devised any little diversion perhaps he might not have been so nervous, but not even the village scarecrows would give him a nod. The poor man had to draw his own water and even wash the pots. No mind can remain stable with only worry, anger, anxiety and fear before it, especially this mind that had been preoccupied every day with the disputes of law.

Like a prisoner in solitary confinement, somehow or other he managed to get through the next ten or twelve days. At the end of two weeks, his mourning over, Munshiji changed his clothes and with his mat and satchel went to the open court. Today his expression was a little brighter. Today, he thought, his clients would flock around him, they'd condole with him and he'd shed a few tears. Then there would be an abundance of foreclosures, settlements and mortgages and he'd be rolling in money. In the evening he would celebrate a little with some liquor — giving *that* up had increased his depression. Full of these thoughts he reached the court.

But there, instead of the abundance of mortgages and the flood of foreclosures and the merry greetings of clients, he encountered the sandy wastes of disappointment. He sat for hours with his satchel open but nobody came near him, or even inquired about how he was. Not only were there no new clients but very old ones,

42

whose business Munshiji's family had handled for generations, today hid their faces from him. That incompetent and loutish Ramzan, whom Munshiji used to laugh at and who could not even write properly, today he was as mobbed as Krishna among the milkmaids. It was all a matter of fate. The clients walked around with their faces averted as though they didn't know him. After wasting his whole day at the court Munshiji went home, sunk in worry and disappointment. As soon as he came close to the house Munga's image rose before him. He was so nervous that when on opening the door two dogs, shut in by Ramgulam, came rushing out he completely lost his wits, let out a shriek and fell senseless to the ground.

What happened to Munshiji after this is not known. For several days people saw him go to the court and come back drooping. It was his duty to go to the court and although there was a dearth of clients there this was now the only trick left to keep the creditors off his back and inspire confidence in them. After that he went off to the shrine of Badrinath and was not seen for several months.

One day a *sadhu* came to the village — on his forehead ashes, locks long and matted, a clay waterpot in his hand. His countenance closely resembled Ramsevak's and his speech also was not much different. He sat in meditation beneath a tree. That night smoke rose from Ramsevak's house, the glow of a fire was visible and then a burst of flame. All the villagers came running — not to put the fire out but to see the fun.

As for Ramgulam, when Munshiji disappeared he went off to live with an uncle and stayed there a while, but no one there could put up with his ways.

One day he was digging up radishes in somebody's field. The owner gave him a few slaps. This made him so angry that he went into the man's granary and set it on fire. It burned down completely and thousands of rupees went up in smoke. The police investigated and Ramgulam was arrested. For this offence he is at present in the reformatory at Chunar.

# A Catastrophe

In Banaras district there is a village called Bira in which an old, childless widow used to live. She was a *Gond* woman named Bhungi and she didn't own either a scrap of land or a house to live in. The only source of her livelihood was a parching oven. The village folk customarily have one meal a day of parched grains, so there was always a crowd around Bhungi's oven. Whatever grain she was paid for parching she would grind or fry and eat it. She slept in a corner of the same little shack that sheltered the oven. As soon as it was light she'd get up and go out to gather dry leaves from all around to make her fire. She would stack the leaves right next to the oven and, after twelve o'clock, light the fire. But when, according to custom, she did not start her fire on such fast days as the eleventh of the month and the day of the full moon, or on the days when she had to parch grain for Pandit Udaybhan Pandey, the owner of the village, on those days she went to bed hungry. She was not only obliged to work without pay for Pandit Udaybhan but she also had to fetch the water for his house. And, for this reason, from time to time the oven was not lit. She lived in the Pandit's village, therefore he had full authority to make her do any sort of odd job. It couldn't be called an injustice; it would have been an injustice only if he'd paid her for it. In his opinion if she received food for working for him, how could it be considered as work done without pay? The peasant has a full right to tether his bulls without feeding them after they've worked a full day in the fields. If he doesn't do this, it's not from any kindness of his but only concern for his profit. Panditji did not have this worry because Bhungi wasn't going to drop dead after staying hungry for a couple of days. And if by chance she should die, then some other *Gond* could very easily be found to fill her place. He was doing her a favour, as a matter of fact, by letting her live in the village at all.

\*

It was spring, the sun was moving into a new sign of the zodiac, a day on which the fresh grain was fried and eaten and given as a gift. No fire was lit in the houses. Bhungi's oven was being put to good use today. There was a crowd worthy of a village fair around her. She had scarcely opportunity to draw a breath. Because of the customers' impatience squabbles kept breaking out. Then two servants arrived, each carrying a heaped basket of grain from Pandit Udaybhan with the order to parch it right away. When Bhungi saw the two baskets she was very alarmed. It was already after twelve and even by sunset she would not have time to parch so much grain. With one or two hours more she could have earned enough food for a whole week. But God had not seen fit to allow it, instead he had sent these two messengers from Hell. Now she would have to stay at the oven parching until after dark for no payment. In despair she took the two baskets.

One of the flunkeys said menacingly, 'Don't waste any time or you'll be sorry.'

'Sit here and wait,' she said, 'and when it's parched take it and go. Cut off my hand if I touch anybody else's grain.'

'Who's got time to sit around and wait? Just have it done by sundown.'

With this command the servants went away and Bhungi began to parch the grain. It's no laughing matter to parch a whole *maund* of grain. She had to keep stopping from the parching in order to keep the oven fire going. So by sundown not even half the work was done. She was afraid Panditji's men would be coming and as soon as they'd arrived insult and beat her. She began to move her hands all the more frantically. She would look toward the road and go on throwing sand into the trough until the sand got cold and the grain began to come out only half-roasted. She couldn't figure out what to do — she couldn't parch and she couldn't stop, and she began to realize what a catastrophe it was. What sort of bread did Panditji give her for her work? He wasn't one to wipe her tears! If she worked herself to the bone it was to earn some kind of food, but as soon as Panditji caught sight of her he'd threaten her, and just because she occupied four inches of his land. So high a price for so little land? And so many plots in the village lying fallow, so many cottages deserted. Saffron didn't grow in those empty fields, why should he be after her every hour of the day? When anything happened he'd threaten to dig up her oven and ruin it. If only she

45

had a man to protect her she wouldn't have to put up with this.

While she was caught up in these gloomy thoughts the servants returned and said, 'Well, is the grain parched?'

Feeling bold, Bhungi said, 'Can't you see? I'm parching it now.'

'The whole day's gone and you haven't finished any more grain than this? Have you been roasting it or spoiling it? This is completely uncooked! How's it going to be used for food? It's the ruin of us! You'll see what Panditji does to you for this.'

The result was that that night the oven was dug up and Bhungi was left without a means of livelihood.

*

Bhungi now had no means of support. The villagers suffered a good deal too from the destruction of the oven. In many houses even at noon cooked cereal was no longer available. People went to Panditji and asked him to give the order for the old woman's oven to be rebuilt and the fire once more lighted, but he paid no attention to them. He could not suffer a loss of face. A few people who wished her well urged her to move to another village. But her heart would not accept this suggestion. She had spent her fifty miserable years in this village and she loved every leaf on every tree. Here she had known the sorrows and pleasures of life; she could not give it up now in the last days. The very idea of moving distressed her. Sorrow in this village was preferable to happiness in another.

A month went by. Very early one morning Pandit Udaybhan, taking his little band of servants with him, went out to collect his rents — he didn't have any confidence in estate agents. He wouldn't allow any other person to share in his dues, his fines and his fees for religious services. Now when he looked toward the old woman's oven he fell into a violent rage: it was being resurrected. Bhungi was energetically rebuilding it with balls of clay. Most likely she'd spent the night at this work and wanted to finish it before the sun was high. She did not in the least doubt that she was going against the Pandit's wishes, but she had no conception of how long-lasting anger can be, she could not realize that such a great person could have so much hatred for a pathetic old woman. She naturally assumed that human character had somehow to be loftier than that. But alas, the poor creature had grown old without

46

growing wise.

Suddenly Panditji shouted, 'By whose order?'

Bewildered, Bhungi saw that he was standing before her.

He demanded once again, 'By whose order are you building it?'

In a fright she said, 'Everybody said I should build it and so I'm building it.'

'I'll have it smashed again.' With this he kicked the oven. The wet clay collapsed in a heap. He kicked at the trough again but she ran in front of it and took the kick in her side. Rubbing her ribs she said, 'Maharaj, you're not afraid of anybody but you ought to fear God. What good does it do you to ruin me like this? Do you think gold is going to grow out of this foot of ground? For your own good, I'm telling you, don't torment poor people, don't be the death of me.'

'You're not going to build any oven here again.'

'If I don't how am I going to be able to eat?'

'I'm not responsible for your belly.'

'But if I do nothing except chores for you where will I go for food?'

'If you're going to stay in the village you'll have to do my chores.'

'I'll do them when I've built my oven. I can't do your work just for the sake of staying in the village.'

'Then don't, just get out of the village.'

'How can I? After twelve years of working a field the tenant earns a share in it. I've grown old in this hut. My in-laws and their grandparents lived in this same hut. Except for Yama, king of death, nobody's going to force me out of it now.'

'Excellent, now you're quoting Scripture!' Pandit Udaybhan said. 'If you'd worked hard I might have let you stay, but after this I won't rest until I've had you thrown out.' To his attendants he said, 'Go get a pile of leaves right away and set fire to the whole thing; we'll show her how to make an oven.'

*

In a moment there was a tremendous racket. The flames leapt toward the sky, the blaze spread wildly in all directions. The people of the whole village came clustering around this mountain of fire. Hopelessly, Bhungi stood by her oven watching the conflagra-

47

tion. Suddenly, with a violent dash, she hurled herself into the flames. They came running from everywhere but no one had the courage to go into the mouth of the blaze. In a matter of seconds her withered body was completely consumed.

At that moment the wind rose with a gust. The liberated flames began to race toward the east. There were some peasants' huts near the oven which were engulfed by the fierce flames. Fed in this way, the blaze spread even further. Panditji's barn was in its path and it pounced upon it. By now the whole village was in a panic. They began to band together to put out the fire but the sprinkle of water acted like oil on it and the flames kept mounting higher. Pandit Udaybhan's splendid mansion was swallowed up; while he watched, it tossed like a ship amid wild waves and disappeared in the sea of fire. The sound of lamentation that broke out amidst the ashes was even more pitiful than Bhungi's grievous cries.

# January Night

Halku came in and said to his wife, 'The landlord's come! Get the rupees you set aside, I'll give him the money and somehow or other we'll get along without it.'

Munni had been sweeping. She turned around and said, 'But there's only three rupees. If you give them to him where's the blanket going to come from? How are you going to get through these January nights in the fields? Tell him we'll pay him after the harvest, not right now.'

For a moment Halku stood hesitating. January was on top of them. Without a blanket he couldn't possibly sleep in the fields at night. But the landlord wouldn't be put off, he'd threaten and insult him, so what did it matter if they died in the cold weather as long as they could just take care of this calamity right now? As he thought this he moved his heavy body (that gave the lie to his name)*and came close to his wife. Trying to coax her he said, 'Come on, give it to me. I'll figure out some other plan.'

Munni drew away from him. Her eyes angry, she said, 'You've already tried "Some other plan" You just tell me what other plan can be found. Is somebody going to give you a blanket? God knows how many debts are always left over that we can't pay off. What I say is, give up this tenant farming! The work's killing you, whatever you harvest goes to pay up the arrears, so why not finish with it? Were we born just to keep paying off debts? Earn some money for your own belly, give up that kind of farming. I won't give you the money, I won't!'

Sadly Halku said, 'Then I'll have to put up with his abuse.' Losing her temper, Munni said, 'Why should he abuse you — is this his kingdom?'

But as she said it her brows relaxed from the frown. The bitter truth in Halku's words came charging at her like a wild beast.

---

* Halku is derived from *halka*; meaning 'light'.

She went to the niche in the wall, took out the rupees and handed them over to Halku. Then she said, 'Give up farming this time. If you work as a hired labourer you'll at least get enough food to eat from it. No one will be yelling insults at you. Fine work, farming someone else's land! Whatever you earn you throw back into it and get insulted in the bargain.'

Halku took the money and went outside looking as though he were tearing his heart out and giving it away. He'd saved the rupees from his work, pice by pice, for his blanket. Today he was going to throw it away. With every step his head sank lower under the burden of his poverty.

*

A dark January night. In the sky even the stars seemed to be shivering. At the edge of his field, underneath a shelter of cane leaves, Halku lay on a bamboo cot wrapped up in his old burlap shawl, shivering. Underneath the cot his friend, Jabra the dog, was whimpering with his muzzle pressed into his belly. Neither one of them was able to sleep.

Halku curled up drawing his knees close against his chin and said, 'Cold, Jabra? Didn't I tell you, in the house you could lie in the paddy straw? So why did you come out here? Now you'll have to bear the cold, there's nothing I can do. You thought I was coming out here to eat *puris* and sweets and you came running on ahead of me. Now you can moan all you want.'

Jabra wagged his tail without getting up, protracted his whimpering into a long yawn, and was silent. Perhaps in his canine wisdom he guessed that his whimpering was keeping his master awake.

Halku reached out his hand and patted Jabra's cold back. 'From tomorrow on stop coming with me or the cold will get you. This bitch of a west wind comes from nobody knows where bringing the icy cold with it. Let me get up and fill my pipe. I've smoked eight pipefuls already but we'll get through the night somehow. This is the reward you get for farming. Some lucky fellows are lying in houses where if the cold comes after them the heat just drives it away. A good thick quilt, warm covers, a blanket! Just let the winter cold try to get them! Fortune's arranged everything very well. While we do the hard work somebody else gets the joy of it.'

50

He got up, took some embers from the pit and filled his pipe. Jabra got up too.

Smoking, Halku said. 'If you smoke the cold's just as bad, but at least you feel a little better.'

Jabra looked at him with eyes overflowing with love.

'You have to put up with just one more cold night. Tomorrow I'll spread some straw. When you bed down in that you won't feel the cold.'

Jabra put his paws on Halku's knees and brought his muzzle close. Halku felt his warm breath.

After he finished smoking Halku lay down and made up his mind that however things were he would sleep now. But in only one minute his heart began to pound. He turned from side to side, but like some kind of witch the cold weather continued to torment him.

When he could no longer bear it he gently picked Jabra up and, patting his head, got him to fall asleep in his lap. The dog's body gave off some kind of stink but Halku, hugging him tight, experienced a happiness he hadn't felt for months. Jabra probably thought he was in heaven, and in Halku's innocent heart there was no resentment of his smell. He embraced him with the very same affection he would have felt for a brother or a friend. He was not crippled by the poverty which had reduced him to these straits at present. Rather it was as though this singular friendship had opened all the doors to his heart and brilliantly illuminated every atom of it.

Suddenly Jabra picked up the noise of some animal. This special intimacy had produced a new alertness in him that disdained the onslaught of the wind. Springing up, he ran out of the shelter and began to bark. Halku whistled and called him several times. But Jabra would not come back to him. He went on barking while he ran around through the furrows of the field. He would come back for a moment, then dash off again at once. The sense of duty had taken possession of him as though it were desire.

*

Another hour passed. The night fanned up the cold with the wind. Halku sat up and bringing both knees tight against his chest hid his face between them, but the cold was just as biting. It seemed as

51

though all his blood had frozen, that ice rather than blood filled his veins. He leaned back to look at the skies. How much of the night was still left! The Dipper had not yet climbed half the sky. By the time it was overhead it would probably be morning. Night was not even three hours gone.

Only a stone's throw from Halku's field there was a mango grove. The leaves had begun to fall and they were heaped in the grove. Halku thought, 'If I go and get a pile of leaves I can make a fire of them and keep warm. If anybody sees me gathering the leaves in the dead of night they'll think it's a ghost. Of course there's a chance some animal's hidden in my field waiting, but I can't stand sitting here any longer.'

He ripped up some stalks from a nearby field, made a broom out of them and picking up a lighted cowdung cake went toward the grove. Jabra watched him coming and ran to him wagging his tail.

Halku said, 'I couldn't stand it any more, Jabra. Come along, let's go into the orchard and gather leaves to warm up with. When we're toasted we'll come back and sleep. The night's still far from over.'

Jabra barked his agreement and trotted on toward the orchard. Under the trees it was pitch dark and in the darkness the bitter wind blew, buffeting the leaves, and drops of dew dripped from the branches.

Suddenly a gust carried the scent of henna blossoms to him. 'Where's that sweet smell coming from, Jabra? Or can't your nose make out anything as fragrant as this?'

Jabra had found a bone lying somewhere and he was chewing on it. Halku set his fire down on the ground and began to gather the leaves. In a little while he had a great heap. His hands were frozen, his bare feet numb. But he'd piled up a regular mountain of the leaves and by making a fire out of them he'd burn away the cold.

In a little while the fire was burning merrily. The flames leapt upward licking at the overhanging branches. In the flickering light the immense trees of the grove looked as though they were carrying the vast darkness on their heads. In the blissful sea of darkness the firelight seemed to pitch and toss like a boat.

Halku sat before the fire and let it warm him. After a while he took off his shawl and tucked it behind him, then he spread out both feet as though challenging the cold to do its worst. Victorious over the immense power of the winter, he could not repress his

52

pride in his triumph.

He said to Jabra, 'Well, Jabra, you're not cold now, are you?'

Jabra barked as though to say, 'How could I feel cold now?'

'We should have thought of this plan before, then we'd never have become so chilled.' Jabra wagged his tail. 'Fine, now what do you say we jump over the fire? Let's see how we manage it. But if you get scorched I've got no medicine for you.'

Jabra looked fearfully at the fire.

'We mustn't tell Munni tomorrow or there'll be a row.'

With that he jumped up and cleared the fire in one leap. He got his legs singed but he didn't care. Jabra ran around the fire and came up to him. Halku said, 'Go on, no more of this, jump over the fire!' He leaped again and came back to the other side.

*

The leaves were all burned up. Darkness covered the orchard again. Under the ashes a few embers smouldered and when a gust of wind blew over them they stirred up briefly, then flickered out again.

Halku wrapped himself up in his shawl again and sat by the warm ashes humming a tune. The fire had warmed him through but as the cold began to spread he felt drowsy.

Jabra gave a loud bark and ran toward the field. Halku realized that this meant a pack of wild animals had probably broken into the field. They might be nilgai. He distinctly heard the noise of their moving around. Then it seemed to him they must be grazing; he began to hear the sound of nibbling.

He thought, 'No, with Jabra around no animal can get into the field, he'd rip it to shreds. I must have been mistaken. Now there's no sound at all. How could I have been mistaken?'

He shouted, 'Jabra! Jabra!'

Jabra went on barking and did not come to him.

Then again there was the sound of munching and crunching in the field. He could not have been mistaken this time. It really hurt to think about getting up from where he was. It was so comfortable there that it seemed intolerable to go to the field in this cold and chase after animals. He didn't stir.

He shouted at the top of his lungs, 'Hillo! Hillo! Hillo!'

Jabra started barking again. There were animals eating his field just when the crop was ready. What a fine crop it was! And these cursed animals were destroying it. With a firm resolve he got up and took a few steps. But suddenly a blast of wind pierced him with a sting like a scorpion's so that he went back and sat again by the extinguished fire and stirred up the ashes to warm his chilled body. Jabra was barking his lungs out, the nilgai were devastating his field and Halku went on sitting peacefully near the warm ashes. His drowsiness held him motionless as though with ropes. Wrapped in his shawl he fell asleep on the warmed ground near the ashes.

When he woke in the morning the sun was high and Munni was saying, 'Do you think you're going to sleep all day? You came out here and had a fine time while the whole field was being flattened!'

Halku got up and said, 'Then you've just come from the field?'

'Yes, it's all ruined. And you could sleep like that! Why did you bother to put up the shelter anyway?'

Halku sought an excuse. 'I nearly died and just managed to get through the night and you worry about your crop. I had such a pain in my belly I can't describe it.'

Then the two of them walked to the edge of their land. He looked: the whole field had been trampled and Jabra was stretched out underneath the shelter as though he were dead.

They continued to stare at the ruined field. Munni's face was shadowed with grief but Halku was content.

Munni said, 'Now you'll have to hire yourself out to earn some money to pay off the rent and taxes.'

With a contented smile Halku said, 'But I won't have to sleep nights out here in the cold.'

# Neyur

In the sky silver mountains raced along and bumped together. As though the sun and clouds were battling sometimes it was overcast, then again there was the glitter of dazzling sunshine. These were monsoon days that had turned sultry, the wind had died.

Outside the village several workmen were setting up a dike between two fields. Bare-bodied, drenched in sweat, *dhotis* tucked up tight around their hips, they were all busy shovelling the rain-softened earth into line.

Gobar rolled his blind eye and said, 'Brother, my hands won't move. By now they must have fired the signal gun. Let's have something to eat.'

'Finish the dike,' Neyur said, laughing, 'and then have your food. I started work even before you.'

Deena said, putting the basket on his head, 'The amount of *ghee* you ate up in your youth, Brother Neyur, why you don't even get that much water these days.'

Neyur was a short, husky, dark, nimble fellow of about fifty. But the strongest young fellows could not match him in working. Two or three years ago he was still wrestling; he'd given it up when his cow died.

'How can you go on without smoking a pipe, Brother Neyur?' Gobar asked. 'I can manage if I don't get any bread but I can't stand to be without tobacco.'

'And when you go home,' Deena said, 'will you have to cook your own supper? Doesn't your old woman do anything? I wouldn't put up for a day with a little wife like that.'

Neyur's wrinkled face with its tangled moustaches flashed a smiling line of laughter that lent a certain beauty to his ugliness. He said, 'Her young days have gone, son, she can't do any work these days — what can I do?'

'You've spoiled her,' Gobar said, 'otherwise why wouldn't she work? She has a fine time lying on her cot smoking her pipe and fighting with the whole village. You've grown old but she's stayed young right up to now.'

Deena said, 'She tries to give young women a run for their money. All she thinks about is cinnabar, make-up and jasmine for her hair. You never see her without a fancy coloured *sari* and what's more she can't live without jewels. You're a donkey and go on taking care of her. Otherwise why should you put up with scolding and slaps all the time?'

Gobar said, 'It makes me mad the way she fusses about dressing up. She won't do any work. But she has to dress up and eat the best.'

'What do you know about it, son?' said Neyur. 'When she came I had enough land under cultivation for seven plows. She would lie around like a queen. The times have changed now but what's happened to her? Her heart is still the same. If she sits for half-an-hour in front of the hearth her eyes get red and her head starts to pound. I can't stand looking at that. A man gets married for times like these, otherwise why should he get involved at all in the worries of running a household? When I go home I make some bread, bring the water and she'll eat a couple of bites — if it weren't for that, well, I'd do the way you do and gobble down some scraps and a jug of water. Ever since the daughter died she's been a lot sadder, it was a very great blow to her. What do you and I know about the way a mother feels, son? Before, I used to scold her once in a while but how could I scold her now?'

Deena said, 'Why did you climb up the tree yesterday — are the figs ripe already?'

Neyur said, 'I was breaking off some leaves for the goat — we got her to have milk for our daughter. She's old now but she gives a little milk. My old woman lives just on bread and that goat's milk.'

After he got home Neyur had just taken a pot and the well cord to go and wash when his wife, lying on her cot, said, 'Why do you always come home so late? A man shouldn't sacrifice all his life for work. When everybody gets the same pay what's the use of killing yourself working?'

Neyur's heart melted with tenderness — in his wife's devotion to him, he told himself, there wasn't even a hint of selfishness. How much love there was! Who else cared about his comfort, about whether he lived or died? And that was why he would have given his life for her. He said, 'You must have been a goddess in another life, Budhiya, it's true!'

'All right, stop the flattering. Who's sitting here listening to us

56

now that you should talk so fine?'

His heart bursting with pleasure, he went off to bathe. When he came back she was making thick *chapatties* and she'd put potatoes to roast in the fire. He mashed them, then they sat down to eat.

Budhiya said, 'You haven't had any happiness from marrying me. I lie around and eat and I worry and upset you. It would be much better if God took me off your hands.'

'If god comes, I'll tell him, Take me first! If he didn't I'd be left alone in this empty hut.'

'If you're not here what will it be like for me? Just to think about it makes my sight go dim. I must have done something very good to get you. Who else would put up with me?'

For just such sweet satisfaction Neyur was ready to do anything. Lazy, greedy, selfish Budhiya, just by sweetening her tongue the way a sportsman baits the hook, kept on making Neyur dance.

This was not their first conversation on the subject of who would die first. Many times before this the question had come up and been dropped in just the same way. But for some reason or another Neyur had come to the conclusion that he would be the first to go. For so long as Budhiya might survive him she was to live in comfort and not have to hold out her hand to anyone. It was precisely for this that he worked like a dog trying to scrape a few pice together. The hardest work, the work nobody else would do, Neyur would do it. After working the whole day with spade and hoe, during the sugar cane season he would press cane or guard the fields at night. But the days were slipping by and whatever he earned, that too was slipping away. Life for him without Budhiya would — but he couldn't even imagine that.

But this talk with her terrified Neyur today. Like one drop of dye in water the fear began to spread through his mind. In the village there was no shortage of work for Neyur. He got the same wages he'd always got, but in this time of depression those wages didn't go very far.

Unexpectedly a *sadhu* came wandering into the village from somewhere and lit his ceremonial fire in the shade of the *peepul* tree right in front of Neyur's hut. The villagers took it as a stroke of good luck and they all gathered together to do reverence and honour to *Babaji*. They brought wood, spread out blankets, gave him flour and *dal*. Having nothing at home to give him, Neyur took on the job of making his meals. Intoxicating *charas* weed was

57

brought and the holy man began to smoke.

In just two or three days the *sadhu's* fame had spread around. What an enlightened soul he was, he could tell the past and future and everything! And he was entirely without attachment to the world — he would not touch money with his hands, he scarcely ate anything. Throughout a whole day he would eat only a couple of pieces of bread. But his face shone like a lamp and how sweetly he spoke! Simple-hearted Neyur became the holy man's greatest devotee. If by some chance *Babaji* should take pity on him then he would find enlightenment, all his troubles would disappear.

The devotees had all gone home. The night was bitingly cold. Only Neyur was there, rubbing *Babaji's* feet.

*Babaji* said, 'Child, the world is an illusion — why are you caught in its snares?'

'I'm an ignorant man, Maharaj,' Neyur said, bowing his head. 'What shall I do? There's my wife — how could I leave her?'

'You think *you're* taking care of her?'

'Who else is there to help her, *Babaji?*'

'So God is nothing and you're everything?'

It was like a revelation to Neyur. How puffed up you've been, he told himself, how proud! You spend your life labouring and you think you're everything for Budhiya. You think you can meddle in the work of the Lord, who holds the whole world in his keeping. With the full sense of faith springing up in his simple villager's heart he reproached himself. He said, 'I'm an ignorant man, Maharaj.'

He could say no more than this. Tears of remorse fell from his eyes.

The holy man said majestically, 'You are about to learn the wonders of the Lord. If he wanted he could make you a millionaire in a second. In one second he could take away all your worries. I am merely a lowly servant of his like the humble crow of the Puranas, but in me too there's enough power to make you rich. You're a pure-hearted, true and honest man, and I feel compassion for you. I've observed everybody in this village most carefully. There's no strength or faith in any of them. But in you I've found a devoted heart. Do you possess any silver?'

It seemed to Neyur that he stood before the gate of heaven.

' I must have about a half dozen rupees, Maharaj.'

' Haven't you got any old broken silver jewellery?'

' My wife has a little jewellery.'

' Tomorrow night bring me as much silver as you can find and see the greatness of God. Right in front of you I'll put the silver in a pot and set it in the fire. Come early in the morning and take the pot out of the fire, but be sure to remember that if you spend any of the gold sovereigns you get in drinking or gambling or any wicked deeds you'll become a leper. Go home to bed now, but just one word more: don't talk about this to anyone, not even your wife.'

Neyur went home as happy as if God's hand had touched his head and he could not sleep all night. In the morning he borrowed two or three rupees from each of various people and got fifty rupees together. People trusted him — he'd never done anybody out of a pice, he was a man of his word, a man of good will. It was not hard for him to get the fifty rupees. But how could he take Budhiya's jewellery? He played a trick. 'Your jewellery's become very dirty,' he told her. 'It ought to be cleaned with lemon juice. If it's left in the lemon juice overnight it'll be just like new.' So Budhiya put the ornaments in a pot and left them to soak. When she had gone to sleep that night Neyur put the money in the same pot and went to *Babaji. Babaji* recited a few spells. He set the pot in the ashes of his fire and after blessing Neyur sent him home.

The whole night Neyur tossed and turned and at the crack of dawn he went to pay a visit to the holy man. But there was no sign of *Babaji.* Alarmed, Neyur searched with his fingers through the burned-out ashes: the pot had disappeared. He beat his chest and desperately started out to look for the saint. Making his way toward the market he reached the edge of the pond. Ten minutes he waited, twenty, a half hour, but not a sign of the saint.

The devotees began to arrive, asking where *Babaji* had gone. Not even his blanket, not even his pots were there.

One man said, 'These wandering saints never stay for long —here today, there tomorrow. If they stayed in one place would they be saints? They might make friends with people and get trapped by worldly attachments.'

'He was enlightened,' another said.

'He had no lust for worldly things.'

'Where's Neyur? The saint was very kind to him — he must have told Neyur.'

They began to look for Neyur, but there wasn't a trace of him. Meanwhile Budhiya came out of the house calling for him. Then

59

what a commotion! — Budhiya weeping and reviling Neyur.

Neyur was running along the boundary dikes between the fields as though he wanted to get clean out of this sinful world.

Somebody said, 'Yesterday Neyur borrowed five rupees from me. He said he'd give them back tonight.'

'He took two from me and promised to bring them back.'

Budhiya wept. 'The good-for-nothing took my jewellery. We'd saved twenty-five rupees and and he took them too.'

People understood that the saint was some kind of fraud and that he'd deceived Neyur. Lord, the cheats there are in the world! Nobody suspected Neyur of anything like that. The poor fellow was honest and he'd been tricked. He was probably hiding somewhere right now because of shame.

*

Three months passed.

In Jhansi district on the banks of the Dhasan there's a quite small village called Kashipur. The river banks are high ridges, and on one of them, for some time now, a *sadhu* had taken up his abode. A short, dark, well-knit fellow — Neyur, dressed up as a *sadhu* to deceive people, the same simple ingenuous Neyur who never looked at what belonged to somebody else, who was happy to earn his bread by his own hard labouring. He hadn't for a second ever forgotten his house, his village and Budhiya. After a few more days of this life he intended to go back and then he'd live happily with his little worries and his little hopes, laughing and playing in the village world. When he came home after the day's work bringing a bit of grain or a few pice, then with what tender affection Budhiya would welcome him. It was as though all his toil and fatigue were sweetened in that sweetness of hers. Alas, when would those days come again? He had no idea of how Budhiya was getting along. Who would treat her kindly? Who would cook for her and feed her? He'd left no money in the house, he'd lost even her jewellery. Then his rage rekindled and he wished he could get his hands on that saint. Alas, greed, greed!

Among Neyur's unquestioning devotees there was a beautiful young woman whose husband had abandoned her. Her father, who lived from an army pension, had married her to an educated man, but the fellow was under his mother's thumb and the girl could not get along with her mother-in-law..The girl wanted to live with her husband apart from his mother, but he would not agree to this. In a huff she'd walked out of the house. In the three years since this had happened the father-in-law's house had not once sent for her, nor had the husband even come to see her. The girl wanted to win control over her husband by any means — surely it could not be difficult for holy men to work a change in someone's heart if only they were compassionate!

One day she was alone with the saint describing her misfortune. It seemed to Neyur that he had found the prey he'd been stalking. He said solemnly, 'Daughter, I am not an enlightened man nor a mahatma, nor do I get involved in worldly problems, but when I see your faith and love I feel compassion for you. If God wishes, then your wish will be fulfilled.'

'You can bring it about, I have faith in you.'

'Whatever God wishes will come to pass.'

'Only you can bring the little boat of an unhappy woman like me safe across to the other shore.'

'Trust in the Lord.'

'You alone are my Lord.'

As though moved by religious scruple Neyur said, 'But daughter, to accomplish what you want a big ritual must be performed and the ceremony costs hundreds, thousands. I can't say if it will succeed in fulfilling your wish. I'll do what I can. But everything's in the Lord's keeping. I don't touch money with my hands, but I can't bear to watch your suffering.'

That night she brought her gold jewellery in a basket and set it down at the saint's feet. With trembling hands he opened the basket and looked at the jewellery gleaming in the moonlight. He blinked. All this wealth was his! The girl was standing in front of him with folded hands. 'Accept it,' she said. There was nothing else for him to do, just take the basket and put it on the ground where he slept and send the girl off with a blessing. She would come early in the morning and he would be as far away as his legs could carry him. This was the luck he'd longed for! To go back to his village with bags full of rupees and to set them down before Budhiya. Oh! He couldn't have imagined a greater happiness than this.

But for some reason or other he could not bring himself to do the little he had to. He couldn't pick up the basket to stow it beneath his blanket. It was a trifle but he couldn't see how to do it, he could

61

not even stretch out his hand toward the basket, he had no control over his hands. But if his hands were useless he still had a tongue, there would have been nothing world-shaking in saying, 'Daughter, pick it up and put it under my blanket,' his tongue would not be cut off for that. But it seemed to him now that he had no control even over his tongue. He could get what he wanted done with just a look, but now even his eyes refused to obey him. The master of his spirit, despite all its allies and ministers, was without power and without will. A hundred thousand rupees might be set before him, the naked sword might be in his hand and the cow tied with a strong rope but he could never bring that sword down on her neck. Even if someone were to kill him for it he could never do it. This abandoned woman was like such a cow to him. Finding the opportunity he'd been seeking for three months his soul was shaken. Greed, like some jungle beast eager for its prey, was chained, its claws drooped, its teeth lost their power.

With tears in his eyes he said, 'Daughter, pick up the basket and go. I was only testing you. Your wish will be fulfilled.'

On the far side of the river the moon had set in the bosom of the trees. Neyur got up slowly and after bathing in the Dhasan started on his way. He had come to loathe the cowdung ashes and sandalwood smeared on his forehead for his masquerade. He was astonished that he had ever gone out of his village. Just the fear of a little derision! He began to experience a strange elation, as though he had freed himself from his chains and won a great victory.

*

Neyur reached his village on the eighth day. Children came running, springing and jumping, to welcome him and took the stick out of his hand.

One boy said, 'Auntie's died, uncle.'

It was as though Neyur had been paralyzed. The corners of his mouth fell, his eyes were stricken. He couldn't ask anything, he couldn't even speak. He stood for a second spellbound, then he ran furiously toward his hut. The swarm of children ran after him, but their meanness and mischief had left them. The hut lay open. Budhiya's cot was right where it had always been. Her pipe was set where it always was. In one corner were a few clay and brass pots. The children stood outside, not daring to go in, for Budhiya's ghost was there.

There was a great commotion in the village. Uncle Neyur had come back! A crowd collected at the door of the hut, everyone was asking questions. 'Where have you been all these days? She died on the third day after you went away. Night and day she cursed you. Even while she was dying she kept up abusing you. When we came on the third day, she was lying dead. Where have you been all this time?'

Neyur did not answer. He just looked at them with pitiable, desperate eyes, as though he had lost the power of speech. From that day on no one ever knew him to speak or cry or laugh.

A half mile from town there is a surfaced road, and a lot of people travel along it. Very early mornings Neyur goes and sits beneath a tree at the edge of the road. He asks for nothing from anybody. But travellers give him a little something — parched grain or wheat or small change. At evening he comes back to the hut, lights a lamp, makes supper, eats, and lies down on the same cot. The moving force of his life has vanished, he merely exists.

How profound humanity is! The plague came to the village; people abandoned their homes and fled. No one bothered about Neyur now; nobody feared him and nobody loved him. When the whole town ran away, Neyur did not leave his hut. Then Holi came, everyone made merry, but Neyur did not come out of his hut. And even today he can still be seen sitting silent, still, lifeless, beneath the tree at the edge of the road.

# The Story of Two Bullocks

The jackass is held to be the most stupid of animals. Whenever we want to call somebody a first-class fool we call him a jackass. Whether the jackass really is a fool, or his meek submissiveness has earned him this title, is something not easy to determine. Cows strike with their horns, and one who's just calved will spontaneously take on the aspect of a lioness. The dog, too, is a fairly pitiable creature, but sometimes even he will go into a rage. But an angry jackass has never been seen or heard. No matter how much you may beat the poor fellow, no matter what sort of rotten straw you fling down in front of him, not even a flicker of discontent will pass over his features. He may possibly prance around once or twice in spring, but we've never seen him happy. He's never been known to change whether in joy or sorrow, winning or losing, or in any condition whatsoever. Whatever virtues the sages and holy men may possess, all have reached their culmination in the jackass; yet people call him a fool. Such disrespect for virtue has never been seen before. Perhaps simplicity is not suitable for this world. Just look now, why are the Indians living in Africa in such a wretched state? Why aren't they allowed to slip into America? The poor fellows don't drink liquor, they put aside a little money for a rainy day, break their backs working, don't quarrel with anybody, suffer insults in silence. All the same, they have a bad reputation. It's said they lower the standard of living. If they learned to fight back, well, maybe people would begin to call them civilized. The example of Japan is before us — a single victory has caused them to be ranked among the civilized peoples of the world.

But the jackass has a younger brother who is scarcely less asinine, and that's the bullock. We use the expression 'the calf's uncle' in more or less the same way we say 'jackass.' There are some people who would probably call the bullock supreme among fools, but we have a rather different opinion. The bullock from time to time *will* strike back, and even a rebellious bullock has been observed occasionally. And it also has several other ways of expressing its discontent, so it cannot be ranked with the jackass.

Jhuri the vegetable farmer had two bullocks named Hira and Moti. Both were of fine Pachai stock, of great stature, beautiful to behold, and diligent at their labours. The two had lived together for a very long time and become sworn brothers. Face to face or side by side they would hold discussions in their silent language. How each understood the other's thoughts we cannot say, but they certainly possessed some mysterious power (denied to man who claims to be supreme among living creatures). They would express their love by licking and sniffing one another, and sometimes they would even lock horns — not from hostility but rather out of friendship and a sense of fun, the way friends as soon as they become intimate slap and pummel one another; any friendship lacking such displays seems rather superficial and insipid and not to be trusted. Whenever they were yoked together for plowing or pulling the wagon and stepped along swinging their necks each would attempt to take most of the burden on his own shoulders. When they were released from the yoke after their day's work at noon or in the evening they would lick and nuzzle one another to ease their fatigue. When the oilseed cake and straw was tossed into the manger they would stand up together, thrust their muzzles into the trough together, and sit down side by side. When one withdrew his mouth the other would do so too.

It came about that on one occasion Jhuri sent the pair to his father-in-law's. How could the bullocks know why they were being sent away? They assumed that the master had sold them. Whether it bothered them or not to be sold like this no one can say, but Jhuri's brother-in-law Gaya had to sweat through his teeth to take the two bullocks away. When he drove them from behind they'd run right or left; if he caught up the tether and dragged them forward they'd pull back violently. When he beat them, both would lower their horns and bellow. If God had given them speech, they would have asked Jhuri, 'Why are you throwing us poor wretches out? We've done everything possible to serve you well. If working as hard as we did couldn't get the job done, you could have made us work still harder. We were willing to die labouring for you. We never complained about the food, whatever you gave us to eat we bowed our heads and ate it, so why did you sell us into the hands of this tyrant?'

At evening the two bullocks reached their new place, hungry after a whole day without food, but when they were brought to the manger, neither so much as stuck his mouth in. Their hearts were heavy; they were separated from the home they had thought was their own. New house, new village, new people, all seemed alien to them.

They consulted in their mute language, glancing at one another out of the corners of their eyes, and lay down. When the village was deep in sleep the two of them pulled hard, broke their tether and set out for home. That tether was very tough, no one could have guessed that any bullock could break it; but a redoubled power had entered into them and the ropes snapped with one violent jerk.

When he got up early in the morning Jhuri saw that his two bullocks were standing at the trough, half a tether dangling from each of their necks. Their legs were muddied up to the knees and resentful love gleamed in their eyes.

When Jhuri saw the bullocks he was overwhelmed with affection for them. He ran and threw his arms around their necks, and very pleasant was the spectacle of that loving embrace and kissing.

The children of the household and the village boys gathered, clapping their hands in welcome. Although such an incident was not without precedent in the village it was nevertheless a great event. The gathering of boys decided they ought to present official congratulations. From their houses they brought bread, molasses, bran and chaff.

One boy said, 'Nobody has bullocks like these,' and another agreed, 'They came back from so far all by themselves,' while a third said, 'They're not bullocks, in an earlier life they were men.' And nobody dared disagree with this.

But when Jhuri's wife saw the bullocks at the gate she got angry and said, 'What loafers these oxen are, they didn't work at my father's place for one day before they ran away!'

Jhuri could not listen to his bullocks being slandered like this. 'Loafers, are they? At your father's they must not have fed them so what were they to do?'

In her overbearing way his wife said, 'Oh sure, you're the only one who knows how to feed bullocks while everybody else gives them nothing but water.'

Jhuri railed at her, 'If they'd been fed why would they run off?'

Aggravated, she said, 'They ran away just because those people don't make fools of themselves spoiling them like you. They feed them but they also make them work hard. These two are real lazy-bones and they ran away. Let's see them get oilseed and bran now!

I'll give them nothing but dry straw, they can eat it or drop dead.'

So it came about. The hired hand was given strict orders to feed them nothing but dry straw.

When the bullocks put their faces in the trough they found it insipid. No savour, no juice — how could they eat it? With eyes full of hope they began to stare toward the door.

Jhuri said to the hired hand, 'Why the devil don't you throw in a little oilseed?'

'The mistress would surely kill me.'

'Then do it on the sly.'

'Oh no, boss, afterwards you'll side with her.'

*

The next day Jhuri's brother-in-law came again and took the bullocks away. This time he yoked them to the wagon.

A couple of times Moti wanted to knock the wagon into the ditch but Hira, who was more tolerant, held him back.

When they reached the house, Gaya tied them with thick ropes and paid them back for yesterday's mischief. Again he threw down the same dry straw. To his own bullocks he gave oilseed cake, ground lentils, everything.

The two bullocks had never suffered such an insult. Jhuri wouldn't strike them even with a flower stem. The two of them would rise up at a click of his tongue, while here they were beaten. Along with the pain of injured pride they had to put up with dry straw. They didn't even bother to look in the trough.

The next day Gaya yoked them to the plow, but it was as though the two of them had sworn an oath not to lift a foot — he grew tired beating them but not one foot would they lift. One time when the cruel fellow delivered a sharp blow on Hira's nostrils Moti's anger went out of control and he took to his heels with the plow. Plough-share, rope, yoke, harness, all were smashed to pieces. Had there not been strong ropes around their necks it would have been impossible to catch the two of them.

Hira said in his silent language, 'It's useless to run away.'

Moti answered, 'But he was going to kill you.'

'We'll really get beaten now.'

'So what? We were born bullocks, how can we escape beating?'

'Gaya's coming on the run with a couple of men and they're both

67

carrying sticks.'

Moti said. 'Just say the word and I'll show them a little fun. Here he comes with his stick!'

'No, brother!' Hira cautioned. 'Just stand still.'

'If he beats me I'll knock one or two of them down.'

'No, that's not the *dharma* of our community.'

Moti could only stand, protesting violently in his heart. Gaya arrived, caught them and took them away. Fortunately he didn't beat them this time, for if he had Moti would have struck back. When they saw his fierce look Gaya and his helpers concluded that this time it would be best to put it off.

This day again the same dry straw was brought to them. They stood in silence. In the house the people were eating dinner. Just then a quite young girl came out carrying a couple of pieces of bread. She fed the two of them and went away. How could a piece of bread still their hunger? But in their hearts they felt as though they had been fed a full meal. Here too was the dwelling of some gentle folk. The girl was Bhairo's daughter; her mother was dead and her stepmother beat her often, so that she felt a kind of sympathy for the bullocks.

The two were yoked all day, took a lot of beatings, got stubborn. In the evening they were tied up in their stall, and at night the same little girl would come out and feed some bread to each of them. The happy result of this communion of love was that even though they ate only a few mouthfuls of the dry straw they did not grow weak; still their eyes and every cell of their bodies filled with rebelliousness.

One day Moti said in his silent language, 'I can't stand it any longer, Hira.'

'What do you want to do?'

'Catch a few of them on my horns and toss them.'

'But you know, that sweet girl who feeds us bread is the daughter of the master of this house. Won't the poor girl become an orphan?'

'Then what if I toss the mistress? After all, she beats the girl.'

'But you're forgetting, it's forbidden to use your horns against womankind.'

'You're leaving me no way out! So what do you say, tonight we'll break the ropes and run away?'

'Yes, I'll agree to that, but how can we break such a thick rope?'

'There *is* a way. First gnaw the rope a bit, then it will snap with

68

one jerk.'

At night when the girl had fed them and gone off the two began to gnaw their ropes, but the thick cord wouldn't fit in their mouths. The poor fellows tried hard over and over again without any luck.

Suddenly the door of the house opened and the same girl came out; the bullocks lowered their heads and began to lick her hand. Their tails stood up while she stroked their foreheads, and then she said, 'I'm going to let you go. Be very quiet and run away or these people will kill you. In the house today they were talking about putting rings in your noses.'

She untied the rope, but the two stood silent.

'Well, let's go,' said Hira, 'only tomorrow this orphan's going to be in a lot of trouble. Everybody in the house will suspect her.'

Suddenly the girl yelled, 'Uncle's bullocks are running away! Daddy, daddy, come quick, they're running away!'

Gaya came rushing out of the house to catch the bullocks. They were running now, with Gaya fast behind them. They ran even faster and Gaya set up a shout. Then he turned back to fetch some men of the village. This was the chance for the two friends to make good their escape, and they ran straight ahead, no longer aware by now just where they were. There was no trace of the familiar road they'd come by. They were coming to villages they'd never seen. Then the two of them halted at the edge of a field and began to think about what they ought to do now.

Hira said, 'It appears we've lost our way.'

'You took to your heels without thinking. We should have knocked him down dead right on the spot.'

'If we'd killed him what would the world say? He abandoned his *dharma*, but we stuck to ours.'

They were dizzy with hunger. Peas were growing in the field and they began to browse, stopping occasionally to listen for anyone coming.

When they had eaten their fill the two of them were exhilarated with the experience of freedom and began to spring and leap. First they belched, then locked horns and began to shove one another around. Moti pushed Hira back several steps until he fell into the ditch. Then even Hira finally got angry. He managed to get up and then clashed with Moti. Moti could see that their game was on the verge of getting serious so he drew aside.

*

But what's this? A bull is coming along bellowing. Yes, it really is a bull, and he's heading right their way. The two friends look around anxiously for a way out. This bull is a regular elephant, you'll risk your very life if you try to take him on, but even if you don't fight him it looks as though you won't save your life either. And he's coming straight for them. What a terrifying sight!

'We're in for it now,' said Moti. 'Can we get out of it alive? Think up something to do.'

Worried, Hira observed, 'He's gone crazy with pride. He'd never listen to our pleas.'

'Then why don't we run for it?'

'Running away is cowardly.'

'In that case — die here! But your humble servant just wants to get away.'

'But what if he chases us?'

'Then think up something quick!'

'The plan is this, the two of us must attack at once. I'll strike from in front, you from behind, and when he gets it from both sides he'll take to his heels. When he turns on me gore him sideways in the belly. We may not come out of it alive, but there's no other way.'

Risking everything, the two friends made their attack. The bull had no experience doing battle with a united enemy. He was accustomed to fighting one enemy at a time. As soon as Hira pounced on him Moti charged from behind. When the bull turned to face him Hira attacked. The bull wanted to take them on one at a time and knock them down, but the two were masters of the art and gave him no chance. At one moment when the bull became so enraged that he moved to make an end of Hira once and for all Moti struck from the side and gored his belly. When the bull wheeled around in a fury Hira gored him from the other side. Finally the poor fellow ran off wounded, and the two friends pursued him for some distance until the bull collapsed out of breath. Then they left him.

The two friends went along swaying from side to side in the intoxication of victory.

In his symbolic language Moti said, 'I really felt like killing the bastard.'

Hira scolded, 'One ought not to turn one's horn on a fallen enemy.'

'That's all hypocrisy. You ought to strike the enemy down so he doesn't get up again.'

'But how are we going to get home now? — just think about *that*.'

'First let's eat something, and think afterwards.'

A pea field was right there in front of them. Moti went crashing in; Hira kept on warning him, but to no avail. He had scarcely eaten a couple of mouthfuls when two men with sticks came running and surrounded the two friends. Hira was on the embankment and slipped away, but Moti was down in the soggy field. His hooves were so deep in mud that he couldn't run, and he was caught. When Hira saw his comrade in trouble he dashed back. If they were going to be trapped, then they'd be trapped together. So the watchmen caught him too.

Early in the morning the two friends were shut up in a village pound.

*

The two friends had never in all their life had such an experience — the whole day went by and they weren't given even a single wisp of straw to eat. They couldn't understand what kind of master this could be. Even Gaya was a lot better than this. There were several water buffaloes here, nanny-goats, horses and donkeys. But no food was set before any of them; all were lying on the ground like corpses. Several were so weak that they couldn't even stand up. The whole day the two friends kept their eyes glued to the gate. But nobody appeared with food. Then they began to lick the salty clay of the wall, but what satisfaction could they get from that?

When they got no food in the evening either, the flame of rebellion began to blaze in Hira's heart. He said to Moti, 'I can't stand this any more, Moti.'

With his head hanging down Moti answered, 'I feel as though I'm dying.'

'Don't give up so quickly, brother! We've got to think up some plan to get out of here.'

'All right, let's smash the wall down.'

'I'm not up to that now.'

'What do you mean, weren't you just bragging about your strength?'

'All the bragging has gone out of me!'

The wall of the enclosure was a crude earthen construction. Hira was very strong indeed; when he thrust his pointed horn against the

71

wall and struck hard a little chunk of clay came loose. With that his spirits rose. Running again and again he crashed against the wall and with every blow he knocked off a little of the clay.

At this very moment the pound watchman came out with his lantern to take count of the animals. When he caught sight of Hira's mischief he paid him back with several blows of his stick and tied him up with a thick rope.

From where he lay Moti said, 'So all you got was a beating after all!'

'At least I used my strength as best I could.'

'What good was it struggling so hard when you just got tied up all the more securely?'

'Nevertheless, I'm going to keep on struggling no matter how much they tie me up.'

'Then you'll end up paying with your life.'

'I don't give a damn. Being like this is the same thing as dying. Just think, if the wall were knocked down how many creatures would be saved. How many of our brothers are shut up here! There's no life left in any of their bodies. If it goes on like this for a few more days they'll all die.'

'That's for sure. All right then, I'll give it a good try.'

Moti struck with his horn at the same place in the wall. A little clay tumbled down and his courage grew. Again he drove his horn against the wall with such violence that he might have been battling with a living enemy. Finally, after a couple of hours of violent probing, the top of the wall gave way, lowering it about a foot. When he struck again with redoubled power half the wall crumbled.

When the wall was about to fall the animals who were lying around half dead revived. Three mares took off at a gallop, then the nanny-goats dashed out, and after that the buffaloes also slipped away. But the donkeys were still lying just as they had been before.

Hira asked them, 'Why aren't you two running away?'

One of the jackasses said, 'What if we get caught again?'

'What does that matter? Now's your chance to escape.'

'But we're scared! We'll just stay put right here.'

It was already past midnight. The two donkeys were standing there, wondering whether to run away or not, while Moti was busy trying to break his friend's rope. When he gave it up Hira said, 'You go, just let me stay here. Maybe somewhere we'll meet again.'

With tears in his eyes Moti said, 'Do you think I'm that selfish,

Hira? You and I have been together for such a long time! If you're in trouble today, can I just go off and leave you?'

Hira said, 'You'll get a real beating — they'll realize this is your mischief.'

Moti said proudly, 'If I get beaten for the same offence that got you tied up with a rope around your neck, what do I care? At the very least a dozen or so creatures have been saved from death. All of them will surely bless us.'

After he'd said this, Moti thrust at the two donkeys with his horns and drove them out of the enclosure; then he came up close beside his friend and went to sleep.

It's scarcely necessary to describe the hullaballoo set up by the clerk, the watchman and the other officials as soon as it was light. Sufficient to say that Moti got a terrific drubbing and he too was tied up with a thick rope.

*

The two friends stayed tied up there for a week. No one gave them so much as a bit of hay. True, water *was* given to them once. This was all their nourishment. They got so weak that they could not even stand up, and their ribs were sticking out.

One day someone beat a drum outside the enclosure and towards noon about fifty or sixty people gathered there. Then the two friends were brought out and the inspection began. People came and studied their appearance and went away disappointed. Who would buy bullocks that looked like corpses?

Suddenly there came a bearded man with red eyes and a cruel face; he dug his fingers into the haunches of the bullocks and began to talk with the clerk. When they saw his expression the hearts of the two friends grew weak from what their intuition told them. They had no doubt at all as to who he was and why he felt them with his hands. They looked at one another with frightened eyes and lowered their heads.

Hira said, 'We ran away from Gaya's house in vain. We won't survive this.'

Without much faith Moti answered, 'They say God has mercy on everybody. Why isn't He being merciful to us?'

'To God it's all the same whether we live or die. Don't worry, it's not so bad, for a little while we'll be with Him. Once He saved us in

73

the shape of that little girl, so won't He save us now?'

'This man is going to cut our throats. Just watch.'

'So why worry? Every bit of us, flesh, hide, horns and bones, will be used for something or the other.'

When the auction was over the friends went off with that bearded man. Every bit of their bodies was trembling. They could scarcely lift their feet, but they were so frightened they managed to keep stumbling along — for if they slowed down the least bit they'd get a good whack from the stick.

Along the way they saw a herd of cows and bullocks grazing in a verdant meadow. All the animals were happy, sleek and supple. Some were leaping about, others lying down contentedly chewing their cud What a happy life was theirs! Yet how selfish they all were. Not one of them cared about how their two brothers must be suffering after falling into the hands of the butcher.

Suddenly it seemed to them that the road was familiar. Yes, this was the road by which Gaya had taken them away. They were coming to the same fields and orchards, the same villages. At every instant their pace quickened. All their fatigue and weakness disappeared. Oh, just look, here was their own meadow, here was the same well where they had worked the winch to pull up the bucket, yes, it was the same well.

Moti said, 'Our house is close by!'

'It's God's mercy!' said Hira.

'As for me, I'm making a run for home!'

'Will he let us go?'

'I'll knock him down and kill him.'

'No, no, run and make it to our stalls, and we won't budge from there.'

As though they'd gone crazy, joyfully kicking up their heels like calves, they made off for the house. There was their stall! They ran and stood by it while the bearded man came dashing after them.

Jhuri was sitting in his doorway sunning himself. As soon as he saw the bullocks he ran and embraced them over and over again. Tears of joy flowed from the two friends' eyes, and one of them licked Jhuri's hand.

The bearded man came up and grabbed their tethers.

'These are my bullocks,' said Jhuri.

'How can they be? I just bought them at auction at the cattle pound.'

74

'I'll bet you stole them,' said Jhuri. 'Just shut up and leave. They're *my* bullocks. They'll be sold only when *I* sell them. Who has the right to auction off my bullocks?'

Said the bearded man, 'I'll go to the police station and make a complaint.'

'They're my bullocks, the proof is they came and stood at my door.'

In a rage the bearded man stepped forward to drag the bullocks away. This is when Moti lowered his horns. The bearded man stepped back. Moti charged and the man took to his heels, with Moti after him, and stopped only at the outskirts of the village where he took his stand guarding the road. The butcher stopped at some distance, yelled back threats and insults and threw stones. And Moti stood blocking his path like a victorious hero. The villagers came out to watch the entertainment and had a good laugh.

When the bearded man acknowledged defeat and went away Moti came back strutting.

Hira said, 'I was afraid you'd get so mad you'd go and kill him.'

'If he'd caught me I wouldn't have given up before I'd killed him.'

'Won't he come back now?'

'If he does I'll take care of him long before he gets here. Let's just see him take us away!'

'What if he has us shot?'

'Then I'll be dead, but I'll be of no use to him.'

'Nobody thinks of the life we have as being a life.'

'Only because we're so simple . . .'

In a little while their trough was filled with oilseed cake, hay, bran and grain, and the two friends began to eat. Jhuri stood by and stroked them while a couple of dozen boys watched the show.

Excitement seemed to have spread through the whole village.

At this moment the mistress of the house came out and kissed each of the bullocks on the forehead.

# Ramlila

For some time now I haven't gone to see the Ramlila. I find it absurd to watch men running around with crude monkey masks, short pants and black high-collared shirts, and grunting — I don't enjoy all that. The Ramlila of Banaras, now, is world-famous; they tell me people come from far away to see it. Once I also eagerly went to see it, but I could find no difference between that Lila and one in some remote village. Though I admit that in the Ramnagar performance some of the costumes were good. The demons and monkeys had masks of brass, their maces were of brass too; possibly the crowns worn by the exiled brothers were genuine. But apart from the costumes, in Ramnagar too there was nothing but the same grunting. And still, hundreds of thousands of people crowded to see it.

But there was a time when I too delighted in the Ramlila. Delight, though, is much too mild a word. That delight was nothing less than intoxicating. As it happened, in those days the Ramlila ground was not at all far from my house, and the house that was filled with the costumes and make-up of the Lila characters was also close by. The putting on of the make-up began at two o'clock. I would already be sitting there from twelve on, and the enthusiasm with which I ran about doing little jobs —well, it was more than I feel today when I cash my pension cheque. In one room the princes would be getting their make-up on. Ochre was ground and applied all over their bodies, powder daubed on their faces, and over the powder they put little spots of red, green and blue. Forehead, brows, cheeks, chin, all were covered with these spots. One particular man was an expert at this job and he would make up each of the three chief characters in turn. My job was to bring them water in the pots of dye, grind the ochre, and fan them. When, after these preparations, the chariot came forth and I mounted on it behind Rama, the pleasure, the pride, the thrill was such as now I don't get even from sitting in a chair at the Viceroy's grand durbar. Once when the home-member accepted a proposal of mine in the legislature I experienced something of that pleasure, pride and thrill, and when my eldest son was

76

nominated to the post of deputy tax-collector then too similar emotions stirred in my heart. But there is a great difference between those occasions and the childhood excitement. Then it seemed to me that I was enthroned in the very heavens.

It was the day when Guha the ferryman would take Rama across the Ganges. Falling in with three or four boys I had joined them to play stick-ball; thus led astray on this day, I failed to go to see the costuming. The chariot made its sortie and still I did not give up playing. For me to give up my turn at bat there would have to be a much greater need for self-sacrifice than that. Had I been fielding I would have dashed away long before; but being on the winning side is quite a different matter. Well, I finished off my turn. If I'd wanted, then by cheating I could have had another few minutes at bat, I was quite capable of that. But now was not the occasion, so I ran straight for the little river. The chariot had already reached the bank. From far off I saw the boatman bringing the boat out. I ran, but it was hard to move fast in the crowd. When finally I pushed through the mob at risk of life and limb and got all the way to the river bank, Guha had already pushed off in his boat.

How much faith I had in Rama then! Without worrying about my own studies, I'd been coaching him so he wouldn't fail. Although he was older then me he was studying in a lower grade. But this same Ramchandra now seated in the boat turned his head away as though he didn't even know me. Even in acting some hint or other of the truth can emerge. Why after all should one who always casts a severe look on his devotees bestow any grace on me? Agitated, I began to jump like a calf feeling the yoke on its neck for the first time. First I would leap forward toward the river, then spring back looking for someone to help me, but everybody was completely engrossed in their own excitement. My yells were noticed by nobody. In later times I was to suffer many disastrous moments, but what I suffered in that instant I have never since experienced.

I decided that from now on I would never speak to Ramchandra again, nor ever bring him anything to eat. But as soon as he'd crossed the stream and turned back toward the bridge, I ran and jumped on to his chariot and was as happy as though nothing at all had happened.

*

77

The Ramlila had reached its final act: Rama was to be installed on his throne. But for some reason there was a delay. Perhaps the contributions for the performance had fallen short. At that stage no one was bothering to look after Ramchandra. He neither got leave to go home nor was any arrangement made for his meals. At about three every afternoon a light snack was sent over from the house of Chaudhri Sahib, the village headman. But for the rest of the day not even a sip of water was provided. But my veneration for Ramchandra still remained unchanged. In my eyes he even now was Lord Rama. Whenever I got something to eat at home I would take it and give it to him. I found more happiness in feeding him than I myself ever got from eating. As soon as I got some fruit or sweets I would dash headlong for the village meeting hall. If I didn't find him there I'd hunt high and low for him and have no rest until I'd given it to him.

So — the day of Rama's coronation was here. A big awning, beautifully decorated, was suspended over the Ramlila ground. A crowd of prostitutes also came on to the scene. In the evening Ramchandra's procession would be taken out and at every door the *aarti* — the ritual of the lighted lamps — would be performed. According to his faith each man would give either rupees or more ·pice. My father was in the police force — and that explains why he performed the lamp ceremony without giving anything at all. I can't describe how ashamed I was at this. By chance I had a rupee: before Dassehra my uncle had come to visit and given it to me; that rupee I'd saved and not been able to to spend it even during the Dassehra holiday. I immediately took it out and threw it down on the *aarti* tray. My father could only stare angrily at me, though he never spoke a word. But his expression said clearly enough that by this impudence of mine I had disgraced him.

While ten was still striking the ceremony was completed. The tray was full of rupee notes and coins. I can't say precisely but my guess is there couldn't have been less than four or five hundred rupees. Now, Chaudhri Sahib had already spent quite a bit more than that. He was very concerned that he should somehow or other collect no less than another two hundred rupees, and the best plan for accomplishing this seemed to be to use the prostitutes to take up a collection at a grand party. When people had come and sat and the party really got going, Abadijan, one of the girls, was to catch hold of the wrist of each of those fine gentlemen and use such blandishments that even though they were terribly embarrassed they would throw down something or other. When Abadijan and Chaudhri Sahib began to confer, by chance I could hear what both of them were saying. Chaudhri Sahib must have assumed that a brat like me could understand nothing, but by God's grace I was a sharp kid, and I understood the whole plot.

'Listen, Abadijan,' Chaudhri Sahib was saying 'you're being very high-handed. In the past we've never had any business together, but God willing, you'll be able to keep coming to the village. Now, the contributions this time have fallen short, otherwise I wouldn't be putting the pressure on you.'

'But why are you trying out these big shot's tricks with me?' said Abadijan. 'You won't get anywhere, believe me. Bravo! I'm to collect the cash while you take it easy. A fine way you've figured out to make money! This way you'll become a maharajah in no time at all. Compared to you a zamindar won't amount to anything. Why, you'll be able to open a brothel tomorrow morning! God's oath, you'll be rolling in money.'

'You're making jokes while I'm in a tight spot.'

'And still you're trying to cheat me! Look, I make fools of sharpers like you every day.'

'All right, once and for all, what are you after?'

'Whatever I take in, half is yours, half is mine,' said Abadijan. 'Come on, give me your hand on it.'

'Agreed.'

'Fine, but first count out a hundred rupees for me in case you decide to welsh on the deal afterwards.'

'Wonderful! You'll take this, then you'll pocket the rest!'

'Well, did you expect me to give up my wages? Oh, aren't you clever though ! Okay: what's wrong my way? You're a sensible man but you talk nonsense.'

'So you're resolved to get paid double?'

'Even if you object a hundred times, yes. Or else my hundred rupees might just disappear somewhere. Do you think I've been bitten by a mad dog to go around sticking my own hand in people's pockets?'

Chaudhri got nowhere: he was obliged to give way to Abadijan. And now the party began. Abadijan was a flirt of the highest order. For one thing, she was very young, and in the bargain beautiful. Her charms were so remarkable that even I was overwhelmed. And she was also not lacking in skill in understanding the qualities of men. She got something or other from everyone she sat down in front of. Probably nobody was giving anything less than five rupees. She came and sat down in front of Father too. I could have died of shame, and when she caught hold of his wrist I was close to panic. I'd believed that Father would shove her hand away and maybe even rebuke her, but what happened? Oh God! my eyes didn't deceive me. Father was laughing through his moustache. Never before had I seen such a tender smile on his face. His eyes were alight with passion, he was positively ecstatic. But God would preserve my honour, for just look: gently he freed his wrist from Abadi's tender hands. *Arrey!* What next? Abadi flung her arms around his neck. Surely now Father would strike her. The witch was completely shameless.

One gentleman smiled and said, 'You're wasting your time with him, Abadijan, knock on some other door.'

He'd said just what I was thinking, and said it most properly. But for some reason Father held his head high and looked at him with angry eyes without saying a word. But the expression of his face cried out angrily, 'You merchant you! How can you presume to understand me? At a moment like this I'm ready to lay down my very life. What does mere money mean? If you feel up to it, see what *you* can do. If I don't give at least twice as much as you, let me hide my face forever!' Astonishment all around! What a scandal! Earth, why don't you open, sky why don't you shatter!

Why doesn't death claim me! Father thrusts his hand into his pocket, draws out something and after flourishing it at the merchant hands it over to Abadijan. A gold sovereign! Applause on all sides. I couldn't determine whether Father had come out a loser, I only saw that he had taken out a gold sovereign and given it to Abadijan. At this moment his eyes shone with pride as though he had shown himself the most generous man in the world. This is the same Father who when he saw me give a rupee at the *aarti* stared at me as though he would tear me apart. He had been hurt in his prestige by my decent act while this time he could scarcely control his pleasure in this disgusting business.

*

Abadijan *salaamed* Father with a charming smile and moved on. But I couldn't stand sitting there any longer. My head was bowed with shame; if I had not seen this with my own eyes I wouldn't have believed it. Usually I told my mother about whatever I'd seen or heard away from the house. But I hid this business from her, for I knew how much it would have hurt her to learn about it.

The singing went on all night. I kept hearing the beat of the drums. I was tempted to go and watch but I didn't have the courage, for how could I show my face to anyone? If someone happened to mention my father slightingly, what could I have done?

In the early morning hours Ramchandra was to take his leave. As soon as I got up from my *charpoy*, still rubbing my eyes, I went running off to the village meeting hall. I was afraid Ramchandra might already have left. When I got there I saw that the prostitutes' carriages were ready to leave. A score of men were crowding around them, their expressions full of longing. I scarcely gave them even a glance but made straight for Ramchandra. Lakshman and Sita were sitting there crying and Ramchandra standing by, his jug and string swung over his shoulder, trying to console them. Except for me there was no one else there. My voice choking, I asked him, 'Have you already said your good-byes?'

'Yes, already,' said Ramchandra. 'But can you call it a good-bye? Chaudhri Sahib just said, "Leave now, go away."'

'But didn't you get any going-away money and clothes?'

'Haven't got them yet! Chaudhri Sahib says, "Right now there's no money left over. Come again some time and get it."'

'You didn't get anything?'

'Not a pice. He just says, "There's nothing left over." I'd been thinking if I got a few rupees why then I'd buy myself some books for studying. But I got nothing, not even expenses for the trip. He says, "It's not far, is it? You can make it on shank's mare."'

I was so angry I wanted to go to Chaudhri Sahib and tell him off. Rupees for the whores, carriages, everything. But for poor Ramchandra and his companions nothing at all! The people who squandered ten and twenty rupees apiece on Abadijan didn't have even two or three rupees for the players. Father gave a gold sovereign to Abadijan. Well — let's see what he'll give to them. I went running to him. He was just about to go off somewhere on an investigation. When he saw me he said, 'Where are you wandering off to? Is this your idea to go loafing when it's time to study?'

I said, 'I've just been to the assembly hall. Ramchandra's about to leave but Chaudhri Sahib's given him nothing.'

'And just what business is that of yours?'

'How can they go off like that? They don't even have expenses for the road.'

'What, not even expenses? That *is* very unfair of Chaudhri Sahib.'

'If you'll just give a couple of rupees, I'll pass them on to them. Maybe that will be enough for them to get home.'

Father gave me a sharp look. 'Get along,' he said, 'back to your books. I don't have any money on me.'

With that, he rode off on his horse.

From that day on, my faith in my father was finished. I never again took his scolding seriously. My heart said, 'You have no right to give me advice.' I was angered just by the sight of him. Whatever he told me to do, I'd do the opposite. It may have been to my detriment, but at that time my heart was full of revolutionary ideas.

By luck I had just two *annas* left. I took the coins and, though I was terribly embarrassed, went back to Ramchandra and gave them to him. I was completely unprepared for Ramchandra's joy when he saw those coins. He pounced on them as a thirsty man goes for water.

The three players took the two *anna* pieces and set out on their way. I was the only one who saw them off, as far as the edge of the village.

After I said good-bye to them and came back my eyes were full of tears; but my heart was overflowing with happiness.

# The Thakur's Well

Jokhu brought the *lota* to his mouth but the water smelled foul. He·
said to Gangi, 'What kind of water is this? It stinks so much I can't
drink it! My throat's burning and you give me water that's turned
bad.'

Every evening Gangi filled the water jugs. The well was a long
way off and it was hard for her to make several trips. She'd brought
this water yesterday and there'd been no bad smell at all to it then.
How could it be there now? She lifted the *lota* to her nostrils and it
certainly smelt foul. Surely some animal must have fallen into the
well and died. But she didn't know where else she could get any
water.

No one would let her walk up to the Thakur's well. Even while
she was far off people would start yelling at her. At the other end of
the village the shopkeeper had a well but even there they wouldn't
let her draw any water. For people like herself there wasn't any well
in the village.

Jokhu, who'd been sick for several days, held back his thirst for a
little while. Then he said, 'I'm so thirsty I can't stand it. Bring me the
water, I'll hold my nose and drink a little.'

Gangi did not give it to him. His sickness would get worse from
drinking bad water — that much she knew. But she didn't know that
by boiling the water it would be made safe. She said, 'How can you
drink it? Who knows what kind of beast has died in it? I'll go and get
you some water from the well.'

Surprised, Jokhu stared at her. 'Where can you get more water?'

'The Thakur and the shopkeeper both have wells. Won't they let
me fill just one *lota*?'

'You'll come back with your arms and legs broken, that's all.
You'd better just sit down and keep quiet. The Brahman will give a
curse, the Thakur will beat you with a stick and that money-lending
shopkeeper takes five for every one he gives. Who cares what people like us go through? Whatever they say about giving some help,
we can just die and nobody will even come to this door to have a

83

look. Do you think people like that are going to let you draw water from their well.'

The harsh truth was in these words and Gangi could not deny it. But she wouldn't let him drink that stinking water.

*

By nine o'clock at night the dead-tired field hands were fast asleep but a half dozen or so idlers were gathered at the Thakur's door. These were not the times — nor were there any occasions — for valour in the field; valour in the courtroom was the topic of the day. How cleverly the Thakur had bribed the local police chief in a certain case and come off scot-free! With what skill he'd managed to get his hands on a copy of the dossier in an important lawsuit. The clerks and magistrates had all said it was impossible to get a copy. One had demanded fifty for it, another a hundred, but for no money at all a copy had come flying. You had to know the right way to operate in these matters.

At this moment Gangi reached the Thakur's property to get water from his well.

The dim glow of a small oil lamp lit up the well. Gangi sat hidden behind the wall and began to wait for the right moment. Everybody in the village drank the water from this well. It was closed to nobody, only those unlucky ones like herself could not fill their buckets here.

Gangi's resentful heart cried out against the restraints and bars of the custom. Why was she so low and those others so high? Because they wore a thread around their necks? There wasn't one of them in the village who wasn't rotten. They stole, they cheated, they lied in court. That very day the Thakur had stolen a sheep from the poor shepherd, then killed and eaten it. They gambled in the priest's house all twelve months of the year. The shopkeeper mixed oil with the *ghee* before he sold it. They'd get you to do their work but they wouldn't pay wages for it to save their lives. Just how were they so high and mighty? It was only a matter of words. No, Gangi thought, *we* don't go around shouting that we're better. Whenever she came into the village they looked at her with eyes full of lust, they were on fire with lust, every one of them, but they bragged that they were better than people like her.

She heard people coming to the well and her heart began to

84

pound. If anybody saw her there'd be the devil to pay and she'd get an awful kicking out of it. She grabbed her bucket and rope and crept away to hide in the dark shadows of a tree. When had these people ever had pity on anybody? They beat poor Mahngu so hard that he spat blood for months, and the only reason was that he refused to work in the forced labour gang. Was this what made such people consider themselves better than everybody else?

Two women had come to draw water and they were talking. One said: 'There they were eating and they order *us* to get more water. There's no money for a jug.'

'The men folk get jealous if they think they see us sitting around taking it easy.'

'That's right, and you'll never see them pick up the pitcher and fetch it themselves. They just order us to get it as though we were slaves.'

'If you're not a slave, what are you? You work for food and clothes and even to get nothing more than five or six rupees you have to snatch it on the sly. What's that if it isn't being a slave?'

'Don't shame me, sister! All I do is long for just a second's rest. If I did this much work for somebody else's family I'd have an easier time, and they might even be grateful. But here you could drop dead from overwork and they'd all just frown.'

When the two of them had filled their buckets and gone away Gangi came out from the shadow of the tree and drew close to the well platform. The idlers had left, the Thakur had shut his door and gone inside to the courtyard to sleep. Gangi took a moment to sigh with relief. On every side the field was clear. Even the prince who set out to steal nectar from the gods could not have moved more warily. Gangi tiptoed up on to the well platform. Never before had she felt such a sense of triumph.

She looped the rope around the bucket. Like some soldier steal-ing into the enemy's fortress at night she peered cautiously on every side. If she were caught now there was not the slightest hope of mercy or leniency. Finally, with a prayer to the gods, she mustered her courage and cast the bucket into the well.

Slowly, slowly it sank in the water. There was not the slightest sound. Gangi yanked it back up with all her might to the rim of the well. No strong-armed athlete could have dragged it up more swiftly.

'She had just stooped to catch it and set it on the wall when suddenly the Thakur's door opened. The jaws of a tiger could not have terrified her more.

The rope escaped from her hand. With a crash the bucket fell into the water, the rope after it, and for a few seconds there were sounds of splashing.

Yelling 'Who's there? Who's there?' The Thakur came toward the well and Gangi jumped from the platform and ran away as fast as she could.

. When she reached home, Jokhu, with the *lota* at his mouth, was drinking that filthy, stinking water.

# A Desperate Case

Some men are angry with their wives for giving birth to one daughter after another but never a son. They know it's not the wives' fault, or if it is, then no more than their own, but just the same whenever you see them they're vexed with their wives, call them unlucky and continue to torment them. Nirupma was one of these unlucky women and Ghamandi Lal Tripathi one of those cruel husbands. Nirupma had had three daughters in a row and everyone in the household gave her unkind looks. Her mother-in-law's and father-in-law's displeasure did not concern her particularly —they were old-fashioned people who considered daughters an unpleasant responsibility, the result of sins in earlier incarnations. But it was her husband's disaffection that grieved her, especially since even the fact that he was an educated man did not restrain him from speaking nastily to her. Far from loving her, he never spoke to her without getting angry; for days at a time he would not even come into the house and when he did he was so on edge that she trembled with fear lest there be a row. Although there was no lack of money in the family Nirupma never dared express a wish for even the most trivial object. She thought, 'I really am ill-omened — otherwise would God have created only girls in my womb?' She longed for a gentle smile from her husband, a tender word, to the point where she hesitated to show affection to her daughters lest people say, 'She's certainly making a lot of fuss over trifles!' When it was time for her husband to come home she would on one pretext or another keep the girls out of his sight. The greatest calamity was that Tripathi had threatened, if she had another girl next time, to leave the house forever rather than tolerate such hell for another second. Nirupma worried constantly about this too.

She fasted on Tuesdays, on Sundays, on the eleventh of the month of *Jeth* and at countless other times. She was always performing rituals, but no ritual had fulfilled her wish. Continually putting up with disdain, insults, scolding and contempt, she had become disgusted with the world. It was inevitable that she should be disheartened in a house where, longing for a tender word, a friendly glance, a loving embrace, no one so much as bothered with her.

One day, feeling absolutely desperate, she wrote a letter to her elder brother's wife; every word of it cost her an intolerable pain. Her sister-in-law replied: Your brother is coming to fetch you right away. Recently a genuine saint has come to the village and his blessing has never been known to fail. Several childless women have had sons after his blessing. We have every hope that with you as well it will have the desired effect.

Nirupma showed this letter to her husband. Sadly he said, 'Saints have nothing to do with procreation and conception, it's God's business.'

'Yes, but saints can attain to special powers.'

'Maybe so, but visiting them won't do any good.'

'Still, I'll go and visit this one.'

'Go if you want to.'

'If barren women have had sons, am I any less worthy than they?'

'Didn't I tell you to go? When you do you'll find out. But it seems to me that it's not in our fate to see a son's face.'

*

A few days later Nirupma went with her brother to her father's house. She took the three girls with her. Sukeshi, her sister-in-law, embraced her affectionately and said, 'The people of your house are very cruel — to curse fate for having three such darlings! They must be heavy for you, give them to me.'

When, after dinner, with Sukeshi and the younger brother's wife, they were going to bed Nirupma asked, 'Where does this saint live?'

'Why such haste?' Sukeshi said. 'I'll tell you in good time.'

'It's close by, isn't it?'

'Very close. When you want, I'll send for him.'

'He's very fond of you people, is he?'

'He eats here twice a day. He lives right here.'

'Then why suffer when the doctor's already in the house? I want to see him right away.'

'What will you give me?'

'What is there I could give you?' Nirupma said.

'Give me your youngest girl.'

'Go on, you're making fun of me.'

88

'All right, but you'll have to let him hug you just once.'

'Sister, if you laugh at me I'll go away!'

'This saint's very fond of pretty women.'

'Then he can go to the devil,' Nirupma said. 'He must be a scoundrel.'

'But that's the payment he demands for his blessings. He doesn't accept any other award.'

'The way you talk anybody would think you were working for him.'

'Well, he arranges everything through me. I take the offerings, I also give the blessings, I also make the food for him,' Sukeshi said.

'So you made all this up, admit it, just to get me here!'

'No, not at all, I'm going to tell you of a plan that will allow you to live in peace in your own home.'

Then the two of them began to whisper. When Sukeshi had finished talking, Nirupma said, 'And what if it should be a girl again, after all?'

'So what? You'll have spent a little while in peace and quiet anyway. No one will be able to take those days away from you. If you have a son, then all will be fine; if it's a daughter then some new plan will have to be worked out. With the idiots you've got in your house what else can we do except resort to tricks like this?'

'I feel a little nervous about it.'

'In a couple of days write to Tripathi to tell him you've seen the saint and that he's told you he'll grant your wish. God willing, from that day on you'll be treated with a lot more respect. Tripathi'll come on the run ready to sacrifice his life for you. For at least a year you'll have a pleasant time of it. After that, we'll see.'

'But won't it be a sin to lie to my husband?'

'To pull the wool over the eyes of a selfish fellow like him is a virtue!'

\*

After three or four months Nirupma went home. Ghamandi Lal came to get her. Sukeshi was very detailed in her description of the saint. She said, 'It's never been known that a holy man gave a blessing like that without producing results. But of course, some people are so unlucky there's nothing to be done for them.'

Ghamandi Lal openly expressed his contempt for blessings and promises; he seemed ashamed to give credence to such things in this day and age, but there was no doubt that he was impressed.

Nirupma was welcomed back. When she became pregnant everyone's hearts thrilled with new hopes. The mother-in-law, who before had never done anything but revile her, treated her like a guest. 'Daughter, let it be, I'll make the supper, you'll get a headache.' Whenever Nirupma began to take out the water jug to fill it or to move a cot, then the mother-in-law would run to her. 'Daughter, leave it, I'm here, you mustn't lift anything heavy.' If she had been going to have a girl none of this would have had any effect on the child, but boys, even while they're still in the womb, begin to sit up and be proud. Now Nirupma was made to eat quantities of milk pudding so the boy would be robust and fair. Ghamandi Lal made a habit of getting clothes and jewellery for her, every month he would bring something new. Even when she'd been a new bride Nirupma had not led so pleasant an existence.

The months began to slip by. According to signs and omens she recognized Nirupma began to be convinced that it would be a girl this time too. But she kept this heretical opinion to herself. She would think, 'It's like a monsoon sunshine — how can you trust it? Enjoy it while you can, the rain-clouds are going to cover it all.' She was jumpy about every little thing. She had never been particularly temperamental, but no one in the house would make the slightest noise lest she be upset and thus produce an ill effect upon the boy. Sometimes just to torment the family Nirupma would carry out a religious fast, and she found pleasure in tormenting them. She would think, 'The more I torment you selfish ones the better. You honour me, don't you, only because I'm going to give birth to a child who'll carry on your name. I'm nothing, the child alone is everything; I have no importance, everything hinges on your child. And this is my husband: at first how much he loved me, he wasn't worldly and greedy then. Now his love is a little trick to satisfy his selfishness. I'm an animal to be stuffed with fodder and water for the sake of my milk. If that's the way it is, fine, but now I can control you all. I'll make you give me as many jewels as I can, you won't be able to take them back.'

And so the nine months came to an end. Nirupma's two sisters-in-law were sent for from her father's house. Golden ornaments had already been made for the child; a fine milch-cow was purchased for his milk and Ghamandi Lal brought a little pram to take him on walks. On the day the labour pains started the astrologer was summoned to the door to cast the horoscope. A huntsman had been called to fire off the shotgun and women were gathered together to strike up a hymn. Everyone wanted details of what was happening inside the house. The woman doctor had been sent for. The musicians sat waiting for the word; the village singer with his fiddle was ready to sound the strains of 'Let the mother be proud, Lord Krishna.' All the preparations, all the hopes, all the jubilation was hanging on one word only. With every moment of delay the impatience grew. To hide his excitement Ghamandi Lal was reading a newspaper, just as though it were all one whether it was a boy or a girl. But his old father was not so controlled. He could not restrain his exuberance, he talked to everybody and laughed and kept rattling a bag full of coins.

The huntsman said, 'I'll take a turban and scarf from the master.'

Delighted, the old man said, 'Go on, how many turbans will you take? I'll give you such an expensive one every hair on your head will fall out.'

The singer said, 'And I'll accept something to live on from the master.'

'And how much will you eat? We'll feed you till your belly bursts.'

Suddenly a housemaid came out looking flustered. Before she had managed to say anything the huntsman fired off the shotgun and immediately afterwards the pipes struck up a tune and the singer, hitching up his *dhoti*, sprang up to dance.

The maid shouted, 'Are you all drunk on *bhang*, you people?'

'What's happened?' the huntsman said.

'What's happened? It's a girl again, that's what's happened.'

'A girl?' the old man said, and with that he threw up his arms and sat down as though hit by a thunderbolt. Ghamandi Lal came out of his room and said, 'Go and ask the lady doctor — you just came running out here without really seeing anything.'

'Babuji,' the maid said, 'I saw with my own eyes.'

'And it's really a girl?'

'Such is our fate,' his father said. 'Go, everybody, get along. If it's written in your fate that you're not going to have something, then how can you ever get it? Go, run! Hundreds of rupees thrown away, all our preparations ruined!'

Ghamandi Lal said, 'We'll have to talk to this saint. I'll go today to make inquiries about the bastard.'

91

'He's a fraud, a fraud!' his father said.

'I'll expose all his cheating,' Ghamandi Lal went on. 'If I don't crack his skull then I'll eat my words. He's some kind of swindler. Because of him I've thrown away hundreds of rupees. The pram, the cow, the swing, the golden ornaments — whose head can I throw them at? Think how many he must have cheated like this! If the score is paid off for once, then it will be some satisfaction.'

'Son, it's not his fault, it's the fault of fate.'

'Why did he claim this wouldn't happen? How much money women must have squandered on the cheat! He's got to be made to cough it all up, otherwise I'll report him to the police. The law has punishments for swindling too. From the very first I was afraid it might be a fraud. But my brother-in-law's wife fooled me — if she hadn't I'd never have been caught in such a swindler's trap. He's just a pig.'

'Be patient,' his father said. 'What God has wished he has wrought. Both girls and boys are gifts of God. And where there's three you can be sure there'll be another.'

Father and son went on talking. The singer, the huntsman and the others picked up their staffs and set out on their way. The house seemed to have gone into mourning. The lady doctor had also taken leave, and apart from the mother and the midwife there was no one in the lying-in room. The old mother was so disconsolate that she'd taken to her bed.

When the child's twelfth-day ceremony had been performed Ghamandi Lal went to his wife for the first time and said angrily, 'So it's a girl again!'

'What could I do,' Nirupma said, 'it's not in my control.'

'That wretched swindler really cheated us.'

'What can I say now? If he were a swindler, why would all those women keep going to the saint day and night? It's not in my fate. If he'd taken anything from anybody then I'd say he was a fraud, but I take an oath that I never gave a pice to him.'

'Whether he took anything or not I've spent a fortune. We've learned that it's our destiny not to have a son. If the family line is coming to an end, then what does it matter if it happens now or in ten years? I'll go away somewhere, there's no joy left in this household.'

For a long time he stayed on bemoaning his fate; but Nirupma did not even lift her head.

The calamity had fallen on her once again, and again the same reproaches, the same insults and snubs, and no one cared whether she ate or not, whether she was sick, whether she was happy. Ghamandi Lal did not go away but the threat was almost always in Nirupma's mind. In this way several months passed and then once again Nirupma wrote Sukeshi to tell her she had put her in a more wretched situation than before, and now nobody even cared whether she lived or died. If this state of affairs went on, then whether her husband renounced the world and became an ascetic or not, she herself would certainly leave the world in a different way.

When she read this letter Sukeshi understood how things were. This time she did not invite Nirupma, knowing that they would not let her come, so she herself went, taking her husband along. She was a very lively, clever and fun-loving woman. As soon as she arrived she saw the baby girl in Nirupma's lap and said, '*Arrey!* what's that?'

'It's fate — what else?' said Nirupma's mother-in-law.

'What do you mean fate? You must have made some mistake in following the saint's instructions. It's not possible that whatever he's promised should fail to come about. Now tell me, did you fast on Tuesdays?'

'Without fail, I didn't skip one fast,' Nirupma said.

'And did you feed five Brahmans on Tuesdays also?'

'But he didn't tell me to do that.'

'Don't you tell me, I remember perfectly, he said it right in front of me and with a lot of emphasis too. You must have thought, "What's the point of feeding the Brahmans?" You didn't understand that unless you fulfilled every part of the ritual it wouldn't come out the way he said.'

'She never said anything about it,' the mother-in-law said. 'And why five? We would have fed ten Brahmans — we're not lacking in religion, after all.'

'Of course not, she just forgot, that's obvious. There's no possibility of getting a son this way. Great devotion and piety are necessary and you were confused by just one Tuesday fast?'

'She's unlucky, what else?' said the mother-in-law.

Ghamandi Lal said, 'How could anybody not remember what he made such a fuss about saying? She's just trying to upset us all.'

'And I ask you,' his mother said, 'how the saint's words could fail

93

to be fulfilled. For seven years I've lit the lamp and made offerings to the Goddess of the *tulsi* plant to get a grandson.'

'And she thought it was going to be easy as eating rice,' Ghamandi Lal said.

'Well,' Sukeshi said, 'what's happened has happened. Tomorrow's Tuesday, fast again and give a dinner to seven Brahmans. We'll see whether or not the saint's promise will be fulfilled.'

'It's useless,' Ghamandi Lal said, 'nothing will come of doing it.'

'Babuji,' Sukeshi said, 'you're educated, but with your learning how much your heart has shrunk! How old are you right now? How many sons would you like to have? If you don't have so many you're fed up with them I'll eat my words.'

The mother-in-law said, 'Daughter, how can anyone have that many sons?'

'If God wills,' Sukeshi said, 'then you'll get your wish. I got mine.'

'Are you listening, my dear?' Ghamandi Lal said. 'Don't make any mistake this time. Make sure you understand everything sister-in-law tells you.'

'You can be sure,' Sukeshi said, 'I'll remind you. How to prepare the feast, how to go about everything, how to perform the ablutions, I'll write it all down for you and Mother, and no more than eighteen months from today I'll claim a fat reward from you.'

Sukeshi stayed a week and after giving careful instructions to Nirupma she went back home.

*

Nirupma's star shone again; Ghamandi Lal was consoled with the thought that the future would redeem the past. Again Nirupma went from slave to queen, the mother-in-law treated her with the highest consideration, and everybody paid her the greatest attention.

The days passed. Nirupma would sometimes say, 'Mother, last night I dreamed that an old woman came to me and called out and gave me a coconut. She said, "This is what I've given you."' And sometimes she would say, 'Mother, I don't know why but a great joy has sprung up in my heart, I long to hear beautiful singing, to bathe in the river. It's almost like being intoxicated.' When the mother-in-law heard these things she would smile and say, 'Daughter, these are good omens.'

Nirupma had *bhang* brought to her on the sly and ate it, because red and drunk-looking eyes meant a son, and then looking at Ghamandi Lal with her drowsy eyes she would say, 'Are my eyes red?'

'It seems as though you were actually drunk,' he would observe contentedly. 'This is a good omen.'

Nirupma had never been especially fond of perfume but now she was ready to give her life for a fragrant garland.

Before going to bed Ghamandi Lal now made a habit of reading heroic stories to her out of the *Mahabharata*; sometimes he would describe the glorious deeds of Guru Govind Singh. Nirupma was very fond of the story of Abhimanyu. Ghamandi Lal wanted to ensure that his unborn son would be a hero.

One day Nirupma said to him, 'What name will you give him?'

'I'm sure you've already picked one out. I haven't thought about it at all. It has to be a name associated with valour and glory. You think of a name.'

The two of them began to discuss names. They went through every name from Harishchandra to Zoravar Lal but they couldn't pick one out for this extraordinary boy. Finally Ghamandi Lal said, 'What do you think of Teg Bahadur?'

'That's fine, I like it.'

'It's a splendid name. You've heard about the great deeds of Teg Bahadur. The name has a tremendous influence on the person.'

'The name is really everything,' Nirupma said. 'Whether it's Damri, Chhakauri, Ghurhu, or Katvaru, whenever you look at somebody's name you find, "As the name, so the man." Our child's name will be Teg Bahadur — the warrior's sword.'

*

The time for the delivery came. Nirupma knew what was about to happen. But outside everything was ready for the celebration. This time nobody had the slightest doubt. Everything had been made ready for the singing and dancing. A canopy had been put up and a throng of friends sat under it chatting. The sweets-maker took *puris* and sweets out of his boiling pan. Several sacks had been filled with grain so that as soon as the good tidings had been received it could be distributed among the beggars. To avoid all delay the sacks had already been opened.

But with every second Nirupma's heart sank. What would happen now? She had got through three years by some sort of deceit, and

95

they'd been happy years, but now disaster was hovering over her head. Alas, she thought, what a victim she was. To be punished this way without guilt! If it was God's wish that no sons should ever be born from her womb, what fault was it of hers? But who listened? She was really an unlucky woman, she ought to be abandoned, she was ill-omened, and that was why she was a victim. What was going to happen? In a second all the joy and jubilation would collapse in lamentation. They would begin to revile her, curse her inside and out. She was not afraid of her mother and father-in-law, but her husband might once again cease to look at her, in his disappointment he might renounce his house and home. There was nothing but evil fortune on every side. 'Why should I live to see the misery of my family?' she said to herself. 'The trick is done with, there's no hope to be had from it any more. There used to be such longings in my heart; to bring up my darling girls, to get them married and see their children would have been happiness. But it's all finished now. Lord, be their father, look after them, but I'm going now.'

The woman doctor said, 'Well, it's a girl again.'

Inside and outside there were sounds of lamentation. Ghamandi Lal said, 'A curse on such a life, I'm ready for death!'

His father said, 'She's ill-omened, damned ill-omened.'

The beggars said, 'Weep your destiny, we're going to look for some other door!'

The noise had not died down when the doctor said, 'There's no hope for the mother, we can't save her — her heart has stopped.'

# THE TOWN

# A Day in the Life of a Debt-Collector

Seth Chetaram bathed, poured water in sacrifice to Shiva, chewed two peppercorns, drank two pots of water and taking his stick went out to dun the people who owed him money.

Sethji was some fifty years old. The hair had fallen from his head and his skull was as clean as a sandy field. His eyes were small but absolutely round. Right under his head was his belly and beneath his belly his legs looking like two pegs stuck in a barrel. This barrel, by the way, wasn't empty. It was chock full of energy and vitality. The way it jiggled and danced when Sethji was putting the pressure on some defaulting debtor would have shamed an acrobat. He would glare so fiercely and roar so loudly that a regular mob would gather to watch him. But you couldn't call him a miser because, when he was in his shop, he threw down a pice to every beggar. Of course, at those times his frown was so severe and his eyes so terrible and his nose so wrinkled that the beggar would never go by his shop again.

He was absolutely dedicated to the theory that persistent dunning was the way to prosper. From right after breakfast until evening he was constantly occupied in dunning. In the course of his visits he would find a lunch set aside in one house, in another he would partake — at his debtor's expense — of milk, *puris*, sweets and other dishes. A free meal is nothing to be sneezed at. Save just one *anna* per meal and then for this one item in his thirty years of money-lending he would have saved some 800 rupees. Then when he came back a second time he could get milk, curds, oil, vegetables, and cowdung cakes or other fuel. Generally he didn't have to get his own dinner in the evening either. So he never failed to go out on his dunning expeditions. The heavens could burst asunder, fire rain down, a tornado strike, but Sethji, as though obeying an immutable law of nature, was sure to go out to collect his debts.

This morning his wife asked, 'Lunch?'

'No!' Sethji thundered.

'Supper?'

99

'We'll see when I get back.'

There was a farmer who owed Sethji five rupees. For six months the rogue had paid neither principal nor interest, he hadn't even come around with some little offering. His house was at least three miles away and therefore Sethji had put off going. He decided that he would go today and not leave without getting his money from the rascal no matter how much he might squirm and moan. But it was most unpleasant to make such a long journey on foot. People might say, 'A big name but a poor show! He wants to be called a Seth but he hops it on foot.' So he ambled along at a leisurely gait looking here and there and chatting with people he met so it would be understood that he was just out for a stroll.

Suddenly he met an *ekka* coming his way. The *ekka* driver, who was Muslim, asked, 'Where do you have to go, Lala?'

'I don't have to go anywhere,' Sethji said. 'It's just two steps more. However, I suppose I might as well have a seat.'

The *ekka* driver gave Sethji a piercing look, and Sethji stared back with his fierce red eyes. Both of them understood that the other was going to prove a slippery proposition.

The *ekka* started to roll. Sethji made the first move. 'Where is your house, my good man?'

'Excellency, my house is wherever I lie down. When I had a house — well, then I had it. But now I'm houseless, homeless and, worst of all, wingless. Fate has clipped my wings, cut off my tail and abandoned me. My grandfather was a revenue collector for the Nawab, excellency, the master of seven districts. Anybody he wanted shot was shot and if he wanted somebody hanged, he had him hanged. Even before the sun came up thousands and thousands of purses appeared before him. The Nawab treated him like a brother. That was how it was then but now we're forced to work for people like you. Times change.'

Sethji realized that he was up against a tough opponent, a regular champion. It wasn't going to be easy to get the better of him, but since the challenge had been offered he'd have to take it up. He said, 'But surely you belong to the Imperial household? Your very appearance bears witness to that. Times change, brother, not every day turns out the same. At home we say that Lakshmi is fickle, she doesn't always act the same: today she comes to my house, tomorrow to yours. Your father must have left you a regular pile of rupees?'

100

'*Arrey*, Sethji, there was no counting that wealth. I don't know how many cellars it filled. The gold and silver were piled up by the boxful and there were baskets jammed full of jewels. Every single gem was worth half a million. The glitter was so great it put lamps to shame. But fate was still around to be reckoned with. One day Grand-daddy passed away and then we lost our connection with the Nawab. The whole treasure was looted. Peple loaded trucks with the jewels and carted them off. Even then, enough was left in the house for Daddy to live out his days in luxury — the luxury a fool would live in. He used to go out in a palanquin carried by sixteen attendants. There were mace-bearers scurrying both in front and behind. And still he left enough for me to live on. If I'd lived sensibly I'd be well off today. But a rich man's son has got to live like a rich man. I used to get out of bed clutching a bottle of booze. All night long there'd be wild parties with whores dancing. How'd I know I'd have to suffer for it one day?'

Sethji said, 'Brother, thank Almighty God that you can look after your family honestly. Just think of how many of our brothers, on the other hand, tread the paths of wickedness day and night — nevertheless they stay as poor as templemice. You've got to keep to religion, without religion you just live out your days — and what's the difference if you spend them eating fine things or chewing a dry crust? Religion's the big thing. As soon as I saw your face I knew you were a man of principle and integrity. When people are dishonest it's written all over their faces.'

'Sethji, what you say is true. You've got to keep up religion, it's everything. When I get four pice from you people I use it in feeding my children. *Huzoor*, just look at other *ekka* drivers — why, everyone of them is given up to bad habits, every one of them is. But I've taken the pledge. Why should you do something that just brings on misfortune? I have a big family, *huzoor*, my mother, my children, several dependent widows, and all my earnings come from this *ekka*. Still, somehow or other the good Lord looks after us.'

'He's the author of all things, Khan Sahib. May there always be abundance in your earnings.'

'That depends on the generosity of people like you.'

'It depends on the generosity of God. And you've turned out fine. I've had a lot of trouble from *ekka* drivers but now it seems that everywhere there are good and bad alike. I've never before met a man as honest and decent as you. What a fine nature you've got, I congratulate you!'

When the *ekka* man heard this fulsome praise he understood that the gentleman was a champion talker. He wouldn't have praised him, he thought, unless he intended to cheat him. So the *ekka* man decided he'd have to use some other angle to get what he wanted. It was going to be hard to get anything on the basis of generosity, so maybe he'd give if he was scared. The *ekka* driver said, 'But don't assume, Lalaji, that I'm as nice and honest as I look. I'm honest with the honest but with the bad ones I'm a regular son of a bitch. So just tell me, if you want me to shine your shoes I will. But when it comes to the fee I don't do any favours for anybody. If I did, how would I eat?'

Sethji had been convinced that once he did battle with the *ekka* man he'd finish his journey without so much as a pice in payment. But after this speech his ears pricked up. 'Brother,' he said, 'I don't do anybody any favours either when it's a matter of money. But there are times when it's a matter of friendship and then one's more or less obliged to give in. You too will have to make sacrifices from time to time. There should be no sharp dealings and harsh treatment from friends.'

The *ekka* man observed dourly, 'I'm not kind to anybody. No teacher taught *me* lessons in kindness. I'm about as kind as a rat. Who'd dare hold back a penny from me? I don't let even my wife get away with a penny, so how should I act with others? Other *ekka* drivers flatter their moneylenders, they hang around their doors. But I kick the moneylenders out. Everybody wails when they hear my name. When I get my hands on some money, I gobble it up plain and simple. Just see, friend, what you can get out of me, you can cart off anything I've got in my house —if you can.'

Sethji felt he was coming down with fever. He thought, 'This devil won't let me off without getting his money. If I'd known this calamity was in the offing I wouldn't have got into his *ekka* for anything. Whoever wore his feet out from such a little walk? If I had to fork over money like this every day business would be ruined.'

Sethji was a pious soul. He had sacrificed to Shiva from the time he'd reached the age of reason and never once neglected the ceremony. Surely Shiva the Benevolent Lord would not fail to come to his aid on this occasion. Concentrating on the Lord, he said, 'Khan Sahib, extort from somebody else, but you'll have to cope with the police too, they don't show favouritism to anybody.'

The *ekka* driver burst out laughing. 'On the contrary,' he said, 'they pay *me*. Whenever I find a victim I invite him in at once for a low rate and set out for the police station. I get my fare and I get a reward too. Who dares protest? I don't even have a license but I drive my *ekka* merrily right through the market. No bastard can touch me. I do best where there's the biggest crowd. I pick up the finest people and take them to the police station. Who comes out on top at the police station? There are twenty excuses to hold people. If it's a man they say it's suspected that he went chasing after a certain woman or if it's a woman they say that she's run away in a huff from her father-in-law's house. Then who can say anything? The police inspector may want to get out of it but even he can't leave. Don't think I'm honest. I'm a son of a bitch. When passengers don't agree on the fare I take them to the police station and get two for one. If they even make a squeak, I roll up my sleeves and get ready to take care of them — then there's nobody who can stand up to me.'

Sethji was aghast. True, he held his staff in his hand but he felt too weak to use it. He'd really got himself into a mess —there was no telling what evil omens had marked his leaving the house. If he fell foul of this wretch he might be laid up for a week or more. From now on he'd have to use his wits and get down and away as well as he could. Humble as a wet cat he said, 'Very well, Khan Sahib, stop now, we've reached my village. Tell me, how much do I owe you?'

The *ekka* man whipped the horse all the more and said roughly, 'Consider how much I've earned, brother. If you hadn't got on I could have taken three passengers. I would have been paid four *annas* from each one of them, which makes twelve. I'll just ask you for eight.'

Sethji was thunderstruck. In his whole life he'd never paid so much for a ride. Under no circumstances could he pay such a fare for a distance like this. In every man's life there are occasions when he takes no heed of the consequences; for Sethji this was such an occasion. If it had been a matter of one or two *annas* then (though they would have been like drops of his own blood) he would have given them. But for eight *annas* — why, it was half a rupee — he was ready not only for an argument but even a scuffle. Fully resolved, he sat firmly in his place.

At this moment they reached a hut at the edge of the road. The *ekka* stopped, Sethji stepped down, took a two-*anna* coin from the knot in his *dhoti* and reached to give it to the *ekka* driver, who scowled back at him, accepting the fact that he'd lost this round. The savour of the struggle had gone sour, it set his teeth on edge. Souring it for Sethji as well was the only consolation. Gently he said, 'Take it as a gift from me to buy your kids some candy. Allah keep you in safety.'

Sethji took out another *anna* and said, 'Enough, now wag your tongue all you like, I won't give a pice more.'

'No, master, as you yourself would say, how are we poor people going to feed our children? We people are human too, *huzoor*.'

In the meantime a woman had come from inside the hut. She wore a pink sari and was chewing on *paan*. She said, 'You took a long time this morning.' Then she looked at Sethji. 'Fine, today you got a high-class passenger, so I suppose you're in a mood for some mischief. You must have hooked on a coin — hand it over this minute.'

With this she came up to Sethji and said, 'Sit down on our *charpoy* and rest, Lala. It's great luck that we've got a glimpse of you so early in the morning.'

A languorous fragrance came from her clothes. Sethji was all attention and he leered at her. The woman was graceful, saucy, mettlesome and tempting. The image of his wife rose before his eyes: lumpish, flabby, clumsy, her clothes musty. Sethji was not in the least of an amorous disposition but this time his eyes were overwhelmed. Trying not to stare at her he took a seat on the *charpoy*. He was still a mile off from his destination but he didn't so much as think of that.

The woman picked up a small fan and began to wave it over Sethji. With every motion of her hand a whiff of fragrance hit him and intoxicated him. He'd never experienced such bliss. He was used to looking at everything with disgust, but now his very body was drunk. He tried to take the fan out of her hand.

'It's too much trouble for you, let me do the fanning.'

'Nonsense, Lalaji, you're in our home. Won't you let me take even this little trouble over you? What else would be fitting for us to do? Do you have far to go? It's late now — where are you headed for?'

Sethji turned his old sinner's eyes away and restrained his wicked thoughts. He said, 'There's a village I have to go to, not far from here. I'll be coming back right past here this evening.'

Delighted she said, 'So you'll be here again today! And where would you be going in the evening? For once you ought to have a little fun away from your house. Who knows when we'll meet again!' The *ekka* man came in and said in Sethji's ear, 'Get your money out and I'll buy some snacks.'

Silently Sethji took out an eight *anna* coin and gave it to him.

Then the driver asked, 'Shall I fetch some sweets for you? We can find some here worthy of you, they'll sweeten your mouth.'

Sethji said, 'No need to get me anything. Now this four-*anna* piece is for getting something nice for the children.'

Taking out the four-*anna* coin, Sethji threw it down with as much bold assurance as if he attached no value to it, but he wanted to see the expression on the woman's face, yet he was afraid lest she think that he was giving the coin as though he were paying somebody.

The *ekka* driver picked up the coin and was already leaving when his wife said, 'Give that four-*anna* bit back to Sethji! Aren't you ashamed of snatching it up like that? Take this rupee from me and go get eight *annas* worth of sweets.'

She took out a rupee and flung it down. Sethji was embarrassed — that a poor wife of an *ekka* driver who wasn't worth a brass farthing should show so much hospitality that she would dig out a whole rupee, well, how could he stand for that? 'No, no,' he said, 'I won't permit it. Take back your rupee.' His delighted eyes gobbled her up. 'I'll give a rupee, take this and get eight *annas* worth.'

The *ekka* man went off then to see to the sweets and snacks, and his wife said to Sethji, 'It's going to take him some time —while he's gone have some *paan*.'

Sethji looked around him, for he could not take *paan* made by these people. 'But there's no *paan* shop around here,' he said.

'What,' she said, giving him a teasing glance, 'won't the *paan* I make be as good as what you get from a shop?'

Embarrassed, Sethji said, 'No, no, I didn't mean that. But aren't you Muslim?'

Playfully insistent she said, 'God's oath, for saying that, I'll feed you *paan* and then leave you.'

Then she took a betel leaf from a *paan* box and walked towards Sethji. For a moment he hemmed and hawed, then stretched out with both hands trying to push her away and shut his lips tight, but when she would in no wise accept his refusal Sethji made a mad dash to escape. He left his staff on the *charpoy*. After he'd run about twenty steps he stopped, panting, and said, 'Look, you shouldn't go

105

against somebody's religion like that. If we people take food you've touched we're defiled.'

Then she began to chase him. He ran again. He hadn't had to run like this for fifty years. His *dhoti* came undone and started to fall off but there was no time to tie it up again. The poor fellow was veritably flying on the wings of religion. At some moment or other his moneybag slipped from the knot at his waist. When he stopped after another ten yards to pull up his *dhoti* he no longer had the purse. He turned back and looked. The *ekka* man's wife showed him the purse in her hand and beckoned to him to come back. But religion meant even more than money to Sethji. He went another few steps, but then he stopped again.

Suddenly his piety asserted itself. Could he throw religion over for a few rupees? He'd get plenty more rupees but where would he get another soul?

With these thoughts he took his way like a dog mauled in a dogfight, his tail drooping, and every so often he stopped to turn back and see whether those devils were coming after him.

## A Car-Splashing

Well, it's like this: early in the morning I finish off my bath and my prayers, paint a vermillion circle on my forehead, get into my yellow robe and wooden sandals, tuck my astrological charts under my arm, grab hold of my stick — a regular skull-cracker — and start out for a client's house. I was supposed to settle the right day for a wedding; it was going to earn me at least a rupee. Over and above the breakfast. And my breakfast is no ordinary breakfast. Common clerks don't have the courage to invite me to a meal. A whole month of breakfasts for them is just one day's meal for me. In this connection I fully appreciate rich gentlemen and bankers — how they feed you, how they feed you! So generously that you feel happy all over! After I get an idea of the generosity of the client I accept his invitation. If somebody puts on a long face when it's time to feed me I lose my appetite. How can anybody feed you if he's weeping? I can't digest a meal like that at all. I like a client who hails me with, 'Hey Shastriji, have some sweets!' whom I can answer, 'No, friend — not yet.'

It had rained a lot during the night. There were puddles everywhere on the road. I was walking along all wrapped up in my thoughts when a car came along splashing through the puddles. My face got spattered. And then what do I see but my *dhoti* looking as though somebody mixed up a mess of mud and flung it all over it. My clothes were ruined; apart from that, I was filthy, to say nothing of the money lost. If I'd caught those people in the car I'd have done a job on them they wouldn't forget. I stood there, helpless. I couldn't go to a client's house in this state and my own house was at least a full mile away. The people in the street were all clapping to ridicule me. I never was in such a mess. Well, old heart, what are you going to do now? If you go home what will the wife say?

I decided in a trice what my duty was. I got together about a dozen stones from all around and waited for the next car. I'd show them a Brahman's power.

It wasn't even ten minutes before a car came into sight. Oh no! It was the same car. He'd probably gone to get the master from the station and was returning home. As soon as it got close I let fly a rock, I shot it out with all my strength. The gentleman's cap went flying and landed on the side of the road. The car slowed down. I fired again. The window-pane smashed to pieces and one piece even landed on the fine gentleman's cheek drawing blood. The car stopped and the gentleman got out and came toward me, gave me a punch and said, 'You swine, I'll take you to the police!' I'd scarcely heard him when, throwing my books down on the ground, I grabbed him by the waist, tripped him and he fell with a smack in the mud. I jumped on top of him at once and gave him a good twenty punches one after the other until he got dizzy. In the meantime his wife got out. High-heeled shoes, silk sari, powdered cheeks, lipstick, mascara. She began to poke at me with her umbrella. I left the husband and wielding my stick said, 'Lady, don't meddle in men's business or you may get a whack and a bruise and I'd be very sorry about that.'

The gentleman found the occasion to pick himself up and give me a kick with his booted feet. I got a real knock in the knee. Losing patience, I struck out with my stick, getting him in the legs. He fell like a tree when you chop it down. Memsahib came running brandishing her umbrella. I took it away from her without any trouble and threw it away. The driver had been sitting in the car all this time. Now he got out too and came rushing at me with a cane. I brought my stick down on him too and he fell flat. A whole mob had gathered to see the fun. Still lying on the ground the sahib said, 'You rogue, we'll hand you over to the police!'

I wielded my stick again and wanted to thump him on the skull but he folded his hands and said, 'No, no, *baba*, we won't go to the police. Forgive me.'

I said, 'All right, leave the police out of it or I'll crack you over the skull. I'd get six months at the most for it but I'd break you of the habit. You drive along and splash up mud and you're blind with conceit. You don't give a damn who's in front of you or alongside of you.'

One of the onlookers said, '*Arrey*, Maharaj! These drivers know perfectly well they're splashing and when some man gets drenched they think it's great fun and laugh at him. You did well to give one of them a lesson.'

'You hear what the people are saying?' I shouted at the sahib. He gave a dirty look toward the man who'd spoken and said to him, 'You're lying, it's a complete lie.'

'You're still just as rude, are you! Shall I have another go at you with the stick?'

'No, *baba*,' he said humbly. 'It's true, it's true. Now are you satisfied?'

Another bystander said, 'He'll tell you what you want to hear now but as soon as he's back in his automobile he'll start the same old business all over again. Just put 'em in their cars and they all think they're related to the maharaja.'

'Tell him to admit he's wrong,' said another.

'No, no, make him hold on to his ears and do kneebends.'

'And what about the driver? They're all rogues. If a rich man's puffed up, that's one thing, but what are you drivers so conceited about? They take hold of the wheel and they can't see straight any more.'

I accepted the suggestion that master and driver hold on to their ears and do kneebends, the way you punish little children, while Memsahib counted. 'Listen, Memsahib,' I said, 'you've got to count a whole hundred bends, not one less but as many over as you like.'

Two men drew the master up by his hands, two others that gentleman-driver. The poor driver's leg was bruised but he began to do the knee-bends. The master was still pretty cocky; he lay down and began to spew out gibberish. I was furious and swore in my heart that I wouldn't let him go without doing a hundred knee-bends. I ordered four men to shove the car off the edge of the road.

They set to work at once. Instead of four, fifty men crowded around and began to shove the car. The road was built up very high with the land below it on either side. If the car had slid down it would have smashed to pieces. The car had already reached the edge of the road when the sahib let out a groan and stood up and said, '*Baba*, don't wreck my car, we'll do the knee-bends.'

I ordered the men to stand off. But they were all enjoying themselves and nobody paid any attention to me. But when I lifted up the stick and ran for them they all abandoned the car and the sahib, shutting his eyes, began to do the knee-bends.

After ten of them I said to the Memsahib, 'How many has he done?'

Very snooty, she said, 'I wasn't counting.'

'Then sahib's going to be groaning and moaning all day long, I won't let him go. If you want to take him home in good health count the knee-bends, then I'll let him go.'

The sahib saw that without his punishment he wouldn't get away with his life, so he began the knee-bends again. One, two, three, four, five . . .

Suddenly another car came into view. Sahib saw it and said very humbly, 'Panditji, take pity on me, you are my father. Take pity on me and I won't sit in a car again.'

I felt merciful and said, 'No, I don't forbid you to sit in your car, I just want you to treat men like men when you're in it.'

The second car was speeding along. I gave a signal. All the men picked up rocks. The owner of this car was doing the driving himself. Slowing down he tried to creep through us gradually when I advanced and caught him by the ears, shook him violently and after giving him a slap on both cheeks, said, 'Don't splash with the car, understand? Move along politely.' But he began to gabble until he saw a hundred men carrying rocks, then without any more fuss he went on his way.

A minute after he left another car came along. I ordered fifty men to bar the road; the car stopped. I gave him a few slaps too but the poor fellow was a gentleman. He took them as though he enjoyed them and continued his journey.

Suddenly a man said, 'The police are coming.'

And everybody took to his heels. I too came down off the road and sidling into a little lane I disappeared.

# From Both Sides

Pandit Shyamsarup was a young lawyer of Patna. He was not like those elderly young men who often appear in polite society these days, all of whose physical and intellectual strength, understanding and sense, outer and inner resources, resides in their tongue. Not at all, our Panditji did not belong to that class of elderly young men. He was one of those joyous fellows who used the tongue less, heart and brain, hand and foot more. Once a principle had become established in his heart he followed it completely. One of his great virtues was that he did not take on many different cases all at once. Those people who surrounded him pleading, their hands stretched out, got nothing at all. If simple people hope for some practical help from a person who is the secretary of a dozen associations and the president of half a dozen societies, well let them. But nobody sensible would, for all that poor fellow's strength is dissipated via his overworked tongue. Panditji no doubt understood this subtle point.

He had established a little society for the uplift of Untouchables and devoted his leisure time and a small part of his income to this charitable enterprise. Evenings when he left the court he would have a light meal, then take his bicycle and ride to the villages close outside the city. There he would sometimes sit to chat with the tanners, sometimes among the scavengers to converse with them in their unsophisticated speech concerning morals and behaviour. He would take their children on his lap, treat them affectionately, and on Sundays, or when it was a holiday, he would go and show magic lantern shows for them. Throughout the year his company and his sympathy did much for the improvement of the Untouchables of his district. The eating of dead cattle was completely stopped. And if the consumption of liquor did not altogether cease, nevertheless Hamid Khan, the police inspector, was much displeased no doubt from the decrease in the fights and rows that liquor had formerly caused every day.

Gradually Panditji's sympathy developed a fraternal relationship

111

with the Untouchables. In his district there were 300 villages and the number of low-caste people was no less than 6,000. Panditji had a friendly, brotherly affection for all of them. He attended their weddings and behaved with them according to their customs. If there was some altercation among them very often a petition for judgment would be brought to Panditji. It was not possible for him to hear of one of them being ill without his going to find out about the nature of the man's sickness. In Indian medicine he had acquired a little skill; he would attend the sick man and if he found him in difficult straits would help him along with money. But for the most part his love and sympathy were sufficient in themselves. For such achievements money was not so necessary as disinterested humanitarianism and the zeal for social service. After a whole year of his enthusiastic and unflaggingly sympathetic endeavours, a sort of revolution had been produced in this community. Their houses and huts, their eating and drinking habits, their rituals and customs, all seemed to have undergone some reform, and the most important thing was that these people had learned to respect them. Formerly two or three ignorant *zamindars* had caused them trouble but when they saw that these people had acquired a different spirit they left them alone. A few silly people wanted to institute proceedings with the police in this matter; Inspector Hamid Khan himself was also on the look-out for a little profit, but what did these scavengers and tanners possess which could make it worth his while? Panditji's ties with them went on growing even stronger, reaching such a point that at last, at the wedding of the tanner community's headman's daughter, he sat down and ate with them.

*

Pandit Shyamsarup's wife was named Kolesari Devi. Like the general run of Indian women she loved her husband with all her heart and soul. She had only a very limited knowledge of reading and writing, but through living with Panditji she had become somewhat acquainted with community and cultural problems. But —whether you call it a human weakness or a natural reaction — she could not tolerate anyone else's criticism. She herself was not sharp-tongued nor did she get involved in arguments. But any stinging word, any heart-searing taunt produced something like an ulcerous wound on her heart. She listened only to hear and had

112

never learned at all to give an answer, but in her heart she was accustomed to suffer anguish. Panditji was acquainted with this peculiarity of hers, so he never uttered a word that might wound her.

Several years ago at the time Panditji had just begun his law practice they had something of a struggle to make ends meet. On the first day of a new sign of the zodiac, Kolesari had observed the occasion with a bit of charity, distributing five rupees worth of *kichri* to the poor. Panditji returned empty-handed from court after a day of profitless labour and, finding out what she had done, became furious. He said angrily, 'I have to break my back for every pice and you waste the household money. If that's the sort of person you are you ought to have told your father to marry you to some Maharaja!' Kolesari listened with her head bowed, made no answer, neither protested nor wept, but for a full six months she suffered from fever and weakness of the liver, and Panditji learnt a lesson to last him his whole life.

Well, when Panditji returned from eating at Ramphal Chaudhri's house the news spread like wildfire throughout the city. The next day — it may have been Somvari Amavas — Kolesari went to take a ritual dip in the Ganges. Women from other wealthy families of the city had also come to bathe. When they saw Kolesari they began to whisper among themselves. One woman, who appeared to be of some aristocratic family, said to the woman next to her, 'Just look at the fine lady there — her husband goes around eating with Untouchables and she comes to bathe in the Ganges!' Kolesari heard her, as it was intended she should. In just the way the potter's thread is sucked into the tender clay the harsh remark penetrated her heart. She grew agitated, she felt as though she had been stabbed with a knife. She forgot all about bathing and hastily made her way back home. The serpent's poison had seeped into every one of her veins. She cooked the morning meal for Panditji and served it to him. He set out for court — a wealthy client was in trouble. In his good spirits about this he had not even noticed his wife's frowning countenance. When he came back elated in the afternoon he found her lying down with her face covered. Alarmed, he said, 'Kola, why are you lying down? You never do at this hour. Are you ill?' Kolesari sat up and said, 'I'm perfectly all right, I just felt like lying down.' But this answer was not sufficient to reassure Panditji. If she was feeling well, then why was there no red from

113

*paan* on her lips, why was her hair dishevelled and her face sad, and why hadn't ice been ordered for him? These were the thoughts that came rushing all together into Panditji's head. He changed clothes, had a snack, talked about this and that, even told her a few anecdotes. But the snake's poison was not drawn out by these spells. Kolesari still said nothing except an occasional 'Hm' or 'Uh.' The poison had closed up her ears.

It was now evening, time for Panditji's ride; he took out his bicycle and rode off. But the thought of Kolesari's apathy continued to trouble him. Today there was a wedding among the low-caste Pasis of Manjh village. When he arrived there the wedding procession had come from some distance away. The groom's people had insisted on liquor and the bride's had rejected the idea completely. The groom's people demanded that the women, according to a custom, should dance in the doorways. The bridal party said they no longer had any such custom. Panditji had been successful in Manjh village, but wedding parties were outside his sphere of influence. Both sides were disputing these points when Panditji arrived. He reasoned with them until they calmed down. On occasions like this he usually didn't return home until ten o'clock because his advice would produce a lot of heated discussion. But today his heart was not in his work. Kolesari's face, overcast with sadness, kept appearing before his eyes. He kept wondering if he could have said anything unpleasant to her but could not imagine that he had. Her depression, though, was not without a cause, there had to be something the matter. Troubled by these worries he returned home at seven o'clock.

*

Pandit Shyamsarup had his supper and went to bed. This time too Kolesari had eaten nothing. She still appeared downcast. Finally Panditji asked her, 'Kola, why are you sad?'

'I'm not sad,' she said.

'Aren't you feeling well?'

'Why shouldn't I be? Surely you can see I look perfectly healthy.'

'I don't agree,' said Panditji. 'There has to be some reason or other for you to be so sad. Don't you think I have the right to ask you about it?'

'You are the lord of my heart and soul. If you don't have the right,

114

who does?'

'Then why this secrecy? I never hide my feelings from you.'

Lowering her eyes, Kolesari said, 'Am I hiding things?'

'Until now, no, but today you certainly are. Look at me, look into my eyes. People say that women can often gauge a man's love in one glance. But maybe before now you've never sounded the depths of my love. Believe me when I say that your low spirits today have really upset me. If you won't tell me even now, I'll think you have no faith in me.'

Kolesari's eyes filled with tears. She looked at Panditji and said, 'And will you pull out the thorn that's piercing my heart?'

Shyamsarup's hair stood on end. Distressed, he got up and with a trembling voice said, 'Kola! How unfair it is for you to ask me such a question. I'm ready to sacrifice myself and everything I have for you. You ought not to have such thoughts where I'm concerned.'

Kolesari had expected him to say something quite different. 'My God knows,' she said, 'that I have never doubted your love. I only asked you this question because I thought you would probably laugh at me when you heard why I was depressed. I knew that whatever I said, I shouldn't say it. I also knew that it would be painful for you to agree with me. So I wanted to hide it from you. That was all it was. It would have been forgotten in two or three months. But the way you've scolded me obliges me to tell you. The day you think I no longer have faith in you, well, you know that could only mean I'm dead. So now you're making me tell you.'

'Then tell me without being afraid, I'm on pins and needles to know.'

Said Kolesari, 'I want you to stop associating and eating with Untouchables.'

Just as the innocent prisoner sighs when he hears the sentence of punishment from the judge, so now Panditji drew a deep breath and, remaining silent for some time, went to lie down. Then he got up and said, 'Very well, I shall carry out your command. It's a violation of my feelings, quite true, but I won't object. Only tell me at least, did something happen to cause you to ask this of me or did it just occur to you for no special reason?'

'The women have been insulting me and I can't bear it. I've no right to ask them to stop talking, they're free to say whatever they want. It's from you that I can claim that right, and so I've asked you.'

115

'Very well, and so it will be.'

'Now I have yet one more request to make. Men are not worried by taunts and mockery, but women are weak, our hearts are weak,. we're easily wounded by cutting remarks. But you're not to think about that at all. You mustn't violate your own feelings to spare me some insulting remarks. I'll listen to their taunts, and if I find it too painful I'll just stop going out and having anything to do with those women.'

Shyamsarup embraced Kolesari and said, 'Kola, I'll never agree to let you suffer insults on my account. I won't let any taunting wound your tender heart. Just be happy, and sing me one of your favourite songs.'

Kolesari was content. Her face brightened. She picked up the harmonium and began to sing in sweet soft tones:

'To meet with the beloved is painful, oh mad one . . ...'

*

A week passed and Panditji did not go out to the villages. He had accepted as his life's mission the establishment of fraternal relations with his Untouchable brothers, making them able to understand themselves as human beings, drawing them out of the toils of ignorance and falsehood; and when he found an obstacle in the path of this work it is hardly surprising that he became troubled and melancholy. Man finds pleasure in life so long as he continues to believe that he is performing his duty. In the world there are numerous creatures of God who do not know what their individual or community duty is. But it's a mistake to call such people human Those people who have an irresistible urge to do evil, knowing what they do is bad, cannot desist from doing it, and if they don't find the suitable occasion to do it they will profit from occasions even less suitable. The gambler, no matter how much you explain and threaten, cannot leave off gambling. Even if you shut the alcoholic in a cage, as soon as he is free he will head straight for the tavern. Such is the intoxication of doing wrong. All day Panditji was involved with his work, but in the evening, which was the special time for his pleasant recreation, he became very restless, and to sacrifice his social commitment for a personal obligation had to go violently against his feelings. When he would sit in his garden alone and argue about this with himself at times he became irri-

116

tated at his weakness and feel like going to Kolesari and saying flatly that he would not give up his duty for personal caste pride. He wanted to tell her, 'I can do anything so you'll be pleased with me, only not this one thing.' But alas, what effect could these words have on Kola? Poor dear crazy noble Kola! he thought, wouldn't her love for me suffer? No, Kola, dearer than my life, how stupid I'd be if I considered myself unlucky after finding someone as precious as you. For your happiness I could endure anything. I believe that if you knew right now how troubled I am, I'm sure you'd consider enduring insults a mere nothing, you'd be ready to be slandered by the whole world. What do I have to match your unique love? One's duty to society is no doubt a very lofty obligation. But sometimes and in particular conditions one must abandon one's civic duty for considerations of caste. King Rama's duty was to stay in Ayodhya and mete out justice and increase the prosperity of his subjects, but he regarded this patriotic duty as nothing in comparison with honoring his father's oath, which was his private and personal duty. It was King Dasharatha's patriotic duty to hand over his throne to Rama because he knew that Rama was adored by the populace of Ayodhya. But he sacrificed that responsibility so he could honor his oath, which was a private obligation.

But Panditji's mistake was to think that Kolesari did not understand his emotional turmoil. From that night when they had had that conversation not a moment passed when her heart was not stricken with the thought that she had acted very unjustly toward him. She no longer saw on his face that radiance which is the gift of a contented heart. He no longer enjoyed his meals. When he spoke it was as though his thoughts were elsewhere; if he laughed it seemed that he was merely imitating laughter. In every word one could sense his attempt to conceal his emotions. To Kolesari his feelings were as clear as though reflected in a mirror. Time and time again she reproached herself. 'How selfish I am! How mean, how petty — because I gave way before the insults of an ill-tempered woman I have been so unjust to him. For my sake he has done so much violence to himself — but I couldn't stand the hurt from an insult.' As she thought this she wanted to free him from the obligation she'd imposed on him, but Panditji would never give her the least occasion for doing so.

*

For a week Pandit Shyamsarup's Untouchable brothers were patient. They thought he might be ill or busy pleading a case or perhaps he had gone out of town. With such thoughts they consoled themselves. But after a week they could bear it no longer. A whole crowd of them, in homespun jackets, white turbans on their heads, leather shoes on their feet and wooden staves over their shoulders, came to his house to ask if he was all right. There was no way out for Panditji but to invent some pretext to explain his breach of duty, and his pretext was that his wife was ill. From evening until morning the line of people was unbroken. When people from one village left, those from another would arrive and Panditji was obliged to make the same excuse to all of them. What else was he to tell them?

A second week passed, but the illness lingered in Panditji's house. One evening he was sitting in his doorway when Ramdin the Pasi, Phallu the head man and Gobari came bringing Hakim Nadirali Khan Sahib the basketmaker with them. Hakim Sahib was the Bu Ali Sena* of his time. As Satan fled from Bu Ali Sena's incantations so did illness as soon as it spotted Hakimji, no matter how long-lasting and chronic it was, take to its heels. And generally along with the illness the sick man also passed away. As soon as Panditji saw Hakim Sahib he became flustered. My game is up, he thought, what's my next move? Where did those wretched people get the idea to bring this fellow with them to confront me? A fellow who can't be put off but will come straight to the heart of the matter. But time was urgent, there was no leisure for further reflection. At that moment in Panditji's heart, despite loving Kolesari more than a thousand lives, the thought occurred: 'Would that God could give her just a touch of fever only for a little while.' That way somehow or other he'd get out of this fix. But when does death ever come simply because you call it?

Racking his brains, coughing, shifting from side to side and bowing his head, Panditji said, 'Well, it's one of those illnesses that women have but now, thank you very much, her condition is improving. At present she's taking medicine prescribed by the English lady doctor. You know, this is the age of English civilization, people have more confidence in English remedies and the patient gets well with the help of the doctor or hakim he has confidence

---

* A renowned Persian physician and astrologer.

118

in. And that's why I didn't trouble you.'

'What you say is true,' Hakim Sahib agreed. 'Which lady doctor is treating her?' Panditji scratched his head once again and looking all about him said, 'Miss Bogan.'

At this moment Pandit Shyamsarup was obliged to call his legal skills into play. For today when he rose he surely had glimpsed the face of some inauspicious person. Circumstances, instead of improving, were steadily getting worse because while they'd been talking Kallu Chaudhri, Hardas the farmer and Jugga the washerman came into view and with them Miss Bogan herself, riding along on horseback. Panditji turned deathly pale. Silently he cursed Miss Bogan roundly — what had brought this wretched sister-in-law of Satan here at just this moment? But it was no time to fret. He immediately rose from his chair, shook hands with Miss Bogan and without giving her any chance to ask anything seized her hand, drew her into the women's drawing-room, and made her sit in a chair. Then he went at once to Kolesari and said, 'We're in a sticky situation just now. I've been telling those people you were ill as an excuse to get them off my back somehow or other, but today they've brought Hakim Nadirali Khan and Miss Bogan and got me in a corner. I've just left Miss Sahiba in the drawing-room. Tell me — what am I to do?'

Kolesari said, 'Well, I'll just get sick, that's all.'

Panditji laughed. 'I wish illness only on your enemies.'

'Their being sick won't be much use right now. Go and bring her in. I'll wrap myself up in a blanket and lie down.'

So Panditji went out to fetch Miss Bogan, Kolesari wrapped herself up from head to toe in the blanket and feigned moaning. Miss Bogan looked at her tongue, took her temperature and, looking worried, said, 'The illness is well entrenched. It's a case of hysteria. There's no superficial fever, but there's fever in her liver. You have a headache, don't you?'

'My head's splitting,' said Kolesari.

'And I don't imagine you feel hungry?'

'I don't even want to look at food.'

Miss Bogan had completed her diagnosis. She wrote a prescription and took her leave. Hakim Nadirali Khan regarded it as useless to wait any longer; in any case, he had taken a fee in advance.

119

Panditji came out and said to his well-wishers, 'I'm afraid you people have been put to this trouble for nothing. My wife's health is really improving now. Anyway, I'm most grateful to you.'

When the visitors had gone Panditji came inside and had a good laugh; when he'd finished laughing he began to think that today he'd had to do what he shouldn't have done. At least, would his wife relent now? But Kolesari did not laugh.

*

Pandit Shyamsarup ate his dinner and lay down to sleep, but sleep did not come to Kolesari. She tossed and turned, sometimes got up and sat or wandered around the room, sometimes opened a book and sat beside the lamp, but nothing appealed to her. In the way the moonbeams danced beneath the trees swaying in the breeze, so did her reflections go on troubling her. She thought of what a wrong she had done to her husband. 'Alas, how he must have suffered today!' she thought. 'Because of me, he who had never uttered a lie in his life, was forced to invent and weave a web of lies. If he had been disposed to tell lies, today the vast estate of Didarganj would have been under our control. I've forced this wretched predicament on a man who would be ready to die for the sake of truth. And only because I am the partner of his destiny. My job is to show him sympathy, help him in virtuous undertakings and console him. But instead of all these obligations I've forced him into a web of lies. God forgive me for my sin.'

'My duty was to share with him and help him in his charitable works. How decent, how honest, how well-intentioned, how generous these village people are! And I stopped my husband from serving these noble souls, only because a foul-mouthed woman insulted me, and not content with that I've now compelled him to tell lies as well. Despite this petty high-handedness of mine my husband, more virtuous than virtuous, nobler than noble, compassionate and pure-souled, has kept his heart exactly as before. He thinks I'm a fool, ignorant, weak, stubborn, and hide these weaknesses in the bosom of his vast love. How mean I am! I'm not worthy even to wash his feet! How he laughed today when Miss Bogan left. How pure his laughter, and only to reassure me, only to dispel my distress. My darling! I'm bad from head to toe, I'm vile. In your love for me keep thinking of me as a crazy slave-girl.'

120

While she reflected she looked once at Pandit Shyamsarup's· face; a pleasant dream had made it bloom, a slight smile played on his lips. When she observed this Kolesari's heart seemed to mount on a wave of love. Just as the tide rises from the sea, so at times a tide of love rises in the human heart. At this moment a river of love began to flow in Kolesari's eyes. Restless with this love she snuggled close to her husband's chest, which was the shelter of her love. Just as a thief freely plunders the treasure of a sleeping householder, so did Kolesari unrestrainedly plunder the treasure of her sleeping husband's love, and just as the thief fears that the master of the house may waken, so did Kolesari's heart pound lest he might wake. A woman's love is not easily seen with the eyes; modesty and shame incline her not to lift up her eyes. She fears that this passion may be taken for show or affectation so she, as it were, puts fetters on the feet of her love. At this moment Kolesari was free of such inhibiting thoughts.

When the tide rises in the sea pieces of wreckage from sunken ships and shells are thrown up on the shore. This tide rising from Kolesari's heart drew out the thorn that had been tormenting her.

\*

The next day when Panditji came home from court he said to Kolesari, 'I've been asked to go out of town for two or three days.'

'Why, where will you go?' Kolesari asked him.

'I've taken a case out in one of the country districts. I'm going to Bhagalpur.'

'Are you leaving right now?'

'It's arranged for tomorrow.'

Panditji set out for Bhagalpur on the mail coach at six that evening and was busy pleading his case for the next four days. He'd promised to be gone only three days but it took four. Finally, on the fifth day he was free. He got back to Patna at three in the afternoon and walked to his house. When he entered his quarter he met Satpat Chaudhri of Manjh village. Panditji said, 'Chaudhriji, where are you rushing off to?'

Startled, Chaudhri looked up and said, 'Your honor, you were supposed to be back yesterday. Why were you delayed?'

'I couldn't get back yesterday. Is everything all right here?'

'Everything's fine, thank you. But today there are big doings at your house.'

'At my house?' Panditji asked, surprised. 'What's going on?'

'The mistress of the house has called a meeting. All our women got an invitation.'

Panditji was delighted. As he walked on he saw a hundred friendly faces coming toward him from all directions, as if a village wedding party was marching along. He greeted everyone, and when he reached his door it looked as though a festival was in full swing. A hundred men were sitting on the carpet smoking *hookahs*. They had come with the women Kolesari had invited. Panditji went straight to his own quarters. After he'd changed his clothes he said to the servant 'Don't let them know I'm back,' and began to watch the spectacle from the window of his study.

A white carpet had been spread in the courtyard. On it were sitting three or four hundred women dressed up in their village finery. Some were laughing, others chatting, and Kolesari was carrying around a tray of *paan*. She was giving sweets and toys to the children and fondling them affectionately. When the *paan* had all been distributed the singing began. Today Kolesari was also wearing a coarse sari and had taken off her jewels. She sat down with a drum and began to sing with the women.

Sitting at the window, Panditji watched all this. His heart swelled with an excess of joy. He longed to go to Kolesari and embrace her. After the singing had ended Kolesari, in straightforward language, gave the women counsel for fifteen minutes, and then the gathering broke up. Kolesari embraced the women as she saw them off. Among them was one extremely old woman. When she stepped forward to embrace Kolesari, Kolesari bowed down, touched the woman's feet with the hem of her sari and then touched her own forehead with it. When he observed this humble courtesy, Panditji sprang up for joy and jumped three times; he could not control himself. He left his study and walked into the courtyard. He signalled to Kolesari to come inside and there he embraced her. She began to ask about how he felt and why he had been delayed. She said, 'If you hadn't come today I would have gone to you myself.' But Panditji had no time to listen to such things. He hugged her again and again, his spirit unsatisfied, and so too his love. Embarrassed, Kolesari said, 'Enough, you're going to squander all your love in one day!'

'What can I say? I can't get enough. I long to love you to the limit

122

of my love for you. You're a goddess, really!'

If Panditji had been given — well, not a kingdom but some district — he would not have been by any means so exuberant. When he had done pouring out his love he said to the women standing in the courtyard, 'Sisters, Kolesari wasn't sick. She had forbidden me to meet you, but today she herself has invited you and established a bond of sisterhood. You can't imagine how happy I am at this moment. Because of this joy I feel, I'm going to open banking houses for lending money in ten villages with one thousand rupees each and there you people can take out loans interest free. When you borrow money from the mahajans you're forced to pay one or two *annas* on the rupee. As soon as these banks are opened you'll be free from your bondage to the money-lenders, and the banks will be under the supervision of the one who invited you here today.'

All the women lifted up their arms and began to pray for his long life and prosperity. Kolesari said, 'Hurrah! he's thrown this botheration on me!'

Panditji smiled. 'When you've stuck your foot in the water you'll learn to swim.'

'Well, I do know something about keeping books,' said Kolesari.

'And the rest will come by itself,' said Panditji. 'But when did you learn to give advice? You used to be shy of talking to women. Only two weeks ago you forbade me to meet these people, today you consider them your sisters. Then it was your turn to make a move, and now its mine.'

Kolesari laughed. 'You spread a net to trap me.'

'The net,' said Panditji, 'was cast from both sides.'

# A Moral Victory

His Excellency the Viceroy was coming to Banaras. Government officials both high and low prepared to welcome him. In the meantime, the members of the Congress Party had given notice that they would call a general strike. This produced great consternation among the officials. On the other hand, they had set flags along the streets, cleaned everything up and raised a reception dais, on the other, police and soldiers with drawn bayonets were drilling in every street and alley. The officials were desperately trying to ensure that the strike would not occur, while the Congress was determined that it should. The officials might be able to count on brute strength but the Congress had the assurance of moral power. This time let there be a test to see which one would control the field.

From morning to night the magistrate rode out to threaten the shopkeepers that he'd put them in jail, that he'd have their shops looted, that he'd do this and do that. Folding their hands the shopkeepers would say, 'Your Lordship is a king, you can do whatever you want. But what are we to do? Those Congress people won't leave us alive. They'll have a sit-down strike on our doorsteps, they'll jump into wells, they'll fast — who knows, if a few of them give up their lives we'll be disgraced forever. If your Lordship can explain it to these Congress people we'll be very much obliged. It won't be any loss to us if we don't have to close our shops. The most important men in the country will be coming and if our shops are open we'll sell the most expensive merchandise and get double the price. But what can we do? We have no control over those devils.'

Even more disturbed than the officials were Rai Haranandan Sahib, Raja Lalchand and Khan Bahadur Maulvi Mahmud Ali. They did their utmost along with the magistrate and on their own as well. They summoned the shopkeepers to their homes, cajoled and threatened them, bullied the cart and buggy drivers, flattered the labourers. But they were so scared by that handful of Congress workers that not one of them paid any attention to these gentlemen, and it reached the point where a neighbourhood greengrocer's wife boldly said, 'Your Lordships, you can have us all killed but we won't open the shops! We don't intend to get ourselves dishonoured.'

The biggest worry was that the workmen making the dais — carpenters, smiths and the like — might strike. If they did it would be a calamity. Rai Sahib said: 'Gentlemen, let's invite merchants from other cities to open a separate market here.'

Khan Sahib said, 'There's not enough time left to arrange for another market. Let's arrest the Congress agitators and confiscate their property — then see whether or not we control them!'

'If we start making arrests,' Raja Lalchand said, 'the towns-people will be even more aroused. If your Lordship tells Congress that if they call off the strike they'll all get government jobs, why — since most of them are unemployed — as soon as they hear your offer they'll be wild with joy.'

But the magistrate accepted none of these proposals. And so it went on until there were only three days left before the Viceroy's visit.

*

Finally Raja Lalchand had an inspiration: why shouldn't they too resort to moral pressure? After all, Congress had made a great show in the name of religion and morality. The government ought to imitate them, beat the tiger at its own tricks. They would have to find a man who would go on a hunger strike, even fasting unto death, until the shops opened. Such a man would have to be a Brahman and someone the citizens respected and would pay attention to. Raja Sahib's colleagues thought it was a fine idea, they jumped with enthusiasm. Rai Sahib said, 'That's it, we've cracked their front! Fine, now which Brahman shall it be —Pandit Gadadhar Sharma?'

'Certainly not,' said Raja Lalchand. 'Who pays any attention to him? He only writes for the newspapers. What do the people of Banaras know about him?'

'Then would Damri Ojha be our man?' Rai Sahib suggested.

'Not at all,' Raja Sahib said. 'Who knows him except for the College students?'

125

'How about Pandit Moteram Shastri?'

'That's it, that's it!' Raja Sahib said. 'You've hit it on the head, he's certainly the man for us! We must send for him. He's learned, he's pious and — he's shrewd. If he's willing to help then we've won our game.'

Raja Sahib immediately despatched a message to Pandit Moteram. At that moment Shastriji was at his prayers. He no sooner heard this providential summons than he cut short his morning ritual and prepared to go. If Raja Sahib had summoned him, then what a windfall it might be! To his good wife he said, 'Today the moon's auspicious! Bring my clothes and I'll find out why they've sent for me.'

'Your food's ready,' his wife said. 'Go and eat — you don't know when you'll get back.'

But Shastriji did not think it proper to keep a man waiting so long. He put on his long green broadcloth jacket with the red fringe, wound a gold-embroidered scarf around his neck, then set a Banaras gold silk turban on his head. He put on a silk *dhoti* with a wide red border and stepped into his pattens. His Brahmanic glory radiated from his countenance. From a long way off it was plain that some great holy personage was approaching. People who met him on the road bowed their heads and many shopkeepers stood up to greet him. Today the very name of Banaras, it seemed, was illustrious only because of him, there was nobody else at all worth taking note of. And what a gentle soul, pausing to say a few words to the children! It was in this style that Panditji made his way to Raja Sahib's house. The three friends rose and greeted him. Khan Sahib said, 'Tell us, Panditji, how have you been feeling? By God, you're worthy of being put on display! You must weigh a good ten *maunds.*'

Rai Sahib said, 'For one *maund* of learning you need ten *maunds* of intellect. According to this rule, for every *maund* of intellect you need ten of flesh, otherwise who could lift up the burden?'

'You people don't understand,' Raja Sahib said, 'wisdom is like a cold: if it doesn't affect the head, it goes down into the body.'

Khan Sahib, said, 'But I've heard the great ones say that a fat man's the enemy of wisdom.'

'Your reckoning was wrong,' Rai Sahib said, 'otherwise you would surely have understood that if the ratio of mind to body is

126

one to ten then the fatter the man the bigger the intellect.'

'From which it is proven,' Raja Sahib said, 'that the fatter the man the fatter the head.'

Pandit Moteram said, 'If I've been summoned to your noble presence because of my fat head, then why should I bother to bring my sharp wits too?'

After this exchange of pleasantries, Raja Sahib explained the present problem to Panditji as well as the plan for solving it which he had conceived. He said, 'So there it is. Just understand that this time your future prosperity is in your own hands. Probably nobody has ever had so magnificent an opportunity to decide his fortune. If there's no general strike, for the rest of your life you won't have to ask for anything from anybody. So you must resolve on such a fast that the whole town is shaken. Congress has gained its power by hiding behind a screen of religious piety — so you must manage to shock the religious sensibilities of the people.'

Gravely Moteram replied, 'This is not such a difficult job. I can perform ceremonies that bring the rain down from the skies, I can calm the small pox fever, I can raise or lower the price of grain. So it's no great matter to take care of those Congress people. Great British dignitaries who can read and write think no one can do the work I do. But they have no knowledge of the occult sciences.'

'Well then, sir,' said Khan Sahib, 'one must declare you a second God! Had we known the powers you have we wouldn't have worried for such a long time.'

'Sir,' Moteram said, 'I can locate hidden treasures, summon the dead — all I need is customers to appreciate my powers. It's not virtues that are lacking in the world but connoisseurs — that is to say, virtuous people — to appreciate them. As the Bhojpuri proverb has it, "Good things galore but a dearth of good folk."'

'Fine,' Raja Lalchand said. 'Now how much will you want for this ceremony?'

'Whatever your faith in me suggests.'

'Well, can you tell us just what sort of a ceremony you're going to perform?'

'It will be a total fast, during which I'll recite spells and prayers. If I don't cause a sensation in the city my name isn't Moteram.'

'And when will you start?'

'I can start right away. But first you might give me just a few rupees to offer in my invocations to the gods . . .'

And to be sure there was no shortage of rupees. Panditji took his money and set out for home in high spirits. But when he told the news to his wife, she looked worried and said, 'It was silly to get yourself into this mess! Since when can you tolerate being hungry? You'll be the laughing stock of the whole town, they'll die laughing. Better give them back their rupees.'

Moteram reassured her. 'Who says I can't stand being hungry? I'm not such a fool as to do this on an empty stomach. First of all, prepare a meal for me. Go out and get some pastry and fudge and *rasgoolas.* I'll simply stuff myself. Then I'll eat a pound of cream with almonds. Whatever room is left I'll fill with butter curds. Then we'll see how hungry I get! For three days I won't be able to draw a breath so who's going to be hungry! Our luck is on the upswing, we'd regret it if we hesitated now. If the market doesn't close, think of how rich I'll be. If it does, well, it's no money out of my pocket. I've already got my hands on a hundred rupees.'

While she set about preparing his meal, Pandit Moteram sent out the town crier with the news that that evening Moteram Shastri was going to discuss the country's political problems in the square before the Town Hall. People surely would come. Panditji had always stayed out of political matters; if he was to speak about them today everyone would be extremely curious to hear him for he had a great reputation in the city. At the appointed time a crowd of several thousand gathered. After all the proper preparations Panditji arrived from home. His belly was so stuffed that he could scarcely walk. As soon as he reached the square the audience stood up and bowed right to the ground in greeting.

Moteram said, 'Citizens, merchants, bankers and moneylenders! I've heard that after listening to the Congress people you have decided to close your shops on the occasion of the auspicious visit of the British Viceroy. What sort of ingratitude is this? Why, if he wanted the Viceroy could have you all shot out of cannons this very minute and the whole city plowed under as well. It's no joke, this man is a king! He overlooks your mistakes and takes pity on your poverty and you're ready to go out like sheep to the slaughter. If the Viceroy wishes he can close down the railway and the post offices and shut off all your supplies. Tell me, what could you do then? If he wanted, he could put everybody in Banaras in jail — tell me, what would you do then? Can you run away from him? Is there any place where you could find shelter? Therefore, if you have to remain in this country as his subjects why do you contrive all this mischief? Remember, your lives are in his power. If you let the rabble take over the town, then the whole city will be laid low with grief. Do you think you can stop a hurricane with a broom? Beware, anybody who closes up his shop! If anybody does, I tell you, I'll fast at this very spot until I die.'

One skeptic shouted, 'Sir, it will take you at least a full month of fasting to die — what can happen in three days?'

Moteram roared back, 'The breath of life doesn't reside in the body but in the head. If I want, I can escape this life this very minute by my yogic powers. I have warned you, now you know and your way is plain. Heed my words and you will prosper. Heed them not and you will be destroyed, you'll never be able to show your faces anywhere in the world. Enough! Understand this, here I take my seat.'

*

When they heard the news the town people were stunned. This latest trick of the officials left them bewildered. The Congress leaders at once pronounced it hypocritical. The Government supporters had given the Pandit some money and got up the whole fraud. When every other means — army, police and courts — had failed, they had devised this new trick. It was nothing else than political bankruptcy. Since when had Moteram Shastri been such a patriot that, concerned about the condition of the country, he would take a fast upon himself for it? Let him die of hunger indeed — in two days he'd give up. This new stratagem had to be nipped in the bud lest it actually succeed — imagine what it would be like if the government got its hands on a new weapon like this and used it all the time. The ordinary people were not so sophisticated that they would understand these mysteries, they would let themselves be bullied.

But the city merchants and money-lenders were most of them so under the thumb of their religion that these remonstrations had not the slightest effect on them. They said, 'Gentlemen, because of you people the Government has turned against us, they're ready to take action, put us out of business. How many will go bankrupt and not even be able to show their faces to the officials? When we used to go to them before the officials would say, "Come in, Sethji" and treat us with respect, but now they shove us around in the railway carriages and no one pays any attention. Whether you have an income or not, they glance at our account books and raise the taxes. We have borne all this and will go on bearing it, but we cannot accept leadership in religious matters from you people. When a noble, learned and pious Brahman renounces food and water because of us, then how can we eat and sleep with a quiet conscience? If he should die, what answer would we have ready for the Lord?'

The upshot of the matter was that not one of them heeded the Congress. At nine o'clock a deputation of merchants set out to attend on Panditji.

Now, today Panditji had eaten as much as he could, but eating as much as he could was no uncommon occurrence for him. About twenty days of every month he managed to get himself invited out to dine, and over-eating is natural when you're invited out. Seeing one's fellow-diners one is inclined to rivalry and to demonstrating one's appreciation to the host, and above all because of the excellence of the food itself one consumes more than an ordinary amount. Panditji's appetite had never failed to meet these challenges successfully. So at this moment, at the arrival of the dinner hour, his resolution somewhat wavered. Not that he was actually beset by hunger, but at meal times if his stomach was not absolutely crammed then in his imagination he began to suffer the pangs of appetite. Such was the condition of Shastriji at this moment. He was tempted to call some street vendor and help himself to a few sweets, but the officials had posted several soldiers around for his protection. They would not hear of withdrawing. Panditji's vast wisdom was now busy with the problem of how to get rid of those kill-joys. What reason was there to post the louts there? Was he a prisoner, were they afraid he'd run away?

It was possible the authorities had put him in this situation because they feared the Congress people might try to use force to remove him. Nobody knew the tricks they might try, and of course it was the duty of the authorities to protect Panditji from any such disgraceful underhanded conduct.

Panditji was sunk in these reflections when the merchants' deputation arrived. He was reclining comfortably, propped up on his elbows. The leaders touched his feet in greeting and said, 'Maharaj, why have you brought this wrath down upon us? We shall respectfully do whatever you command. Rise up and take food and drink. We didn't know you really were going to take this vow or we would have begged you not to before you did. Be gracious to us. It's long past dinner time now. We will never disregard what you tell us.'

'These Congress people will ruin you,' Panditji said. 'They're already sinking and they'll take you with them. If the market's closed, it will be your loss alone. What does the Government care? You'll starve to death if you go on strike. Does the Government care? You'll go to jail and hard labour. The Government doesn't care! I don't know what crazy idea's got into your skulls to cut off your own noses to spite others. Don't listen to those rogues. Why do you want to shut up the shops?'

'Maharaj,' a merchant answered, 'so long as the whole city's agreed on it how can we oppose them? If the Congress gives the order to have us looted, who'll help us? Rise up and take food! Tomorrow we'll hold a meeting and let you know whatever happens.'

'So go and have your meeting and then come back,' Moteram said.

As the disappointed deputation was about to leave, Panditji said, 'Would any of you happen to have a pinch of snuff?'

One gentleman took out his snuff box and gave it to him.

When they were gone Moteram said to the policemen, 'What are you standing around here for?'

'It's the magistrate's order,' one of them answered. 'What can we do?'

'Get moving,' Panditji said.

'Can we go on your say-so? If we do we'll be dismissed tomorrow — will you feed us?'

'I'm telling you to go away. If you don't, then I will myself. Am I some kind of prisoner to have you surrounding me?'

'Just go then,' the policemen said. 'If you think you can.'

'Why shouldn't I be able to? Have I committed any crime?'

'So, go,' the policeman said, 'and then we'll see what happens.'

Panditji leapt up in all his Brahmanical splendour and slapped the policeman so hard that he fell back several steps. The others lost their nerve — they'd all assumed he was a flabby weakling, but when they saw how fierce he was they silently slipped away.

Moteram now sat gazing here and there to see if some food vendor was in sight so that he could get something from him. But

131

then he reflected that if such a person said a word to anyone people would begin to clap their hands in derision. Decidedly, he would have to operate so deftly that not a soul would suspect a thing. These were predicaments that tested one's wits. He went on struggling for a moment with this thorny problem.

By chance at that instant a peddler appeared. Eleven o'clock had just struck, there was complete stillness on all sides. 'Peddler!' Panditji called out, 'Oh, peddler!'

The peddler said, 'Tell me — what shall I give you? You're hungry, aren't you? Giving up food and water is work for holy men, not for the likes of you and me.'

'What the devil are you talking about?' said Panditji. 'Am I less than any holy man? If I want, why I can go for months without feeling hungry or thirsty. I called you only because I want you to give me your oil lamp. I just wanted to see what was crawling around — I was afraid it was a snake.'

The peddler handed his oil lamp to Panditji, who had begun to scan the ground about him. Suddenly the lamp fell from his grasp and went out. The oil overflowed and he gave it another knock so that whatever oil was left spilled out too.

Shaking the lamp the peddler said, 'Maharaj, there's no oil left in it at all. I'd have sold another four pice worth of goods tonight if you hadn't put me out of business.'

'Brother, it's only the hand — because I dropped the lamp do you want me to cut off my hand? Take these pice and go somewhere and fill your lamp with oil.'

The peddler took the coins. 'After I've got it filled why should I come back here?'

'Just set your basket down and go and get your oil quickly. Otherwise, a snake might bite me and then my death will be on your head. There's some animal around for sure. See, it's crawling! Now it's disappeared. Run, lad, and come back with the oil, I'll look after your basket. If you're afraid, take your money with you.'

The vendor fell into a quandary. If he took his money from the basket then he feared lest Panditji think ill of him, believing that he considered the Brahman dishonourable. But if he left it who could say what Panditji intended? Nobody's intentions remained honourable all the time. Finally he decided that he would leave the basket there and let fate take its course. He set out in the direction of the market, leaving Panditji staring at the basket and feeling

132

rather desperate. There were very few sweets left. There were some five or six bags but from each he could extract no more than two pieces. He was afraid his secret would become known. He thought, 'But what if I ate them? My hunger would only get worse, I'd be like a tiger smelling blood. There wouldn't be much fun in a sin like that.' He sat back in his place. But after a moment his hunger grew stronger. 'Still, it would be nice,' he thought. 'No matter how insignificant the amount of food, it's still food.' He got up, took out the sweets. But just as he was about to stick the very first piece of fudge into his mouth he saw the peddler hastening toward him with his lamp lit. He had to finish off the sweets before he arrived. He put two pieces together into his mouth and was still chewing them when that devil of a peddler had come another ten steps. Panditji stuffed four pieces into his mouth and swallowed them half-chewed. There were still six pieces left and by now the peddler had gone as far as the gate. Panditji thrust all that was left into his mouth. Now he could neither chew it nor spit it out. That demon was charging him like an automobile with his lamp blazing away. When he was right in front of him Panditji swiftly swallowed all the sweets. But after all he was a man and not a crocodile: his eyes filled with water, he choked, he shuddered, coughed violently. Holding out his lamp the vendor said, 'Take this and look around, though if you're ready to fast to death why are you afraid of dying from snakebite? Why worry? If you die the Government will look after your kids, won't it?'

Panditji was so angry that he determined to scold this vulgar troublemaker, but he was unable to produce a sound. He silently took the lamp and after pretending to look around handed it back.

The peddler said, 'Whatever possessed you to take the side of the Government anyway? If they're going to meet all day tomorrow they'll hardly make a decision until nightfall. By that time you'll be feeling pretty dizzy.'

With this he went away and Panditji, after coughing a little while, fell asleep.

*

The next day as soon as it was light the merchants began to discuss the problem, and there was a regular commotion among the Congress Party leaders as well. The Vigilance Committee officials also pricked up their ears. They'd devised a splendid plan to intimidate those simple-minded baniyas. The Association of Brahmans held a separate meeting and decided that Pandit Moteram had no right at all to meddle in political affairs. What did Brahmans have to do with politics? In short, the whole day was passed in debating the pros and cons, and nobody paid any attention to Panditji. People said openly that he'd been given a thousand rupees by the government for taking this fast on himself. Poor Panditji had passed the night tossing about and when he rose his body felt stiff as a corpse's. When he stood up he saw stars before his eyes, his head began to spin. His stomach felt as though someone were scraping it. He kept his eyes glued on the road to see if anybody would come to conciliate him or not. He was still full of this expectation when the time of evening prayer went by. At this hour it had always been his custom to eat a snack after the ritual. Today he had not even had a sip of water. Who could say when the happy moment might arrive? Then he began to feel a great anger against his wife. She must have slept the whole night with her belly full. At this moment she would have just finished a good meal but hadn't even come here to have a look to see whether he was alive or dead. Couldn't she, under some pretext or other, bring him just a little bit of fruit pastry? But why should she care about that? She'd taken the rupees and kept them and whatever else he got she would keep as well and make a regular jackass out of him.

At any rate, Panditji waited the whole day through and no conciliator appeared. They were reluctant to come because of the suspicion in their hearts that Panditji, overcome by his own selfishness, had become involved in some fraudulent bargain and was only putting on a show.

*

At nine o'clock that evening Seth Bhondumal, the leader of the merchants' association, said decisively, 'I suppose Panditji is going through this performance only for his own profit, but since he's only a mere mortal it's none the less painful for him to go without food and water. It's against religion for a Brahman to renounce food and water while we sleep peacefully with full stomachs. If he's conducted himself against religion then he will have to suffer for it. But why do we turn away from our duty?'

The Congress Secretary was not enthusiastic. 'I've said what I had to say. You people are the leaders of society. Whatever you decide we will accept, act and we'll move with you. I also have my share of religious feeling. But listen to one request: will you people let me go there before you? I want to talk with him alone for ten minutes. You can be waiting at the gate. When I return, then you can go to him. What objection can anybody have to this?' They granted his request.

The Secretary had spent a considerable time in the police department and knew something of the weaknesses of human character. He went straight to the market and bought four rupees' worth of sweets, taking care to select a large quantity of the most fragrant. He had them wrapped in tinfoil and went off to make his offering to the sulky Brahman. He also took a jug of cold scented water. Waves of delicious scent emanated from both the bag and the jug. The power of scent is such that it can make a man hungry even when he's not hungry — and how much more a really hungry man?

At this time Panditji was lying on the ground dozing. He'd eaten nothing during the night — for of what account were a half dozen or so pygmy-sized sweets? And he'd had nothing at noon. Now once again meal time had slipped by. He no longer felt the restlessness of the expectation of food but the very chill of desperation. All his limbs were slack, he could not even open his eyes. He tried several times but they closed automatically. His lips were dry. If he gave any sign of life it was only a very low moaning. He had never before been in such a fix. A couple of times a month he suffered from indigestion, which he would assuage with myrobolans and other medicines. But he'd never suffered indigestion so acutely that he'd given up eating. He whole-heartedly cursed the inhabitants of the city, the Vigilance Committee, the Government, God, the Congress Party and his own true wife. There was nothing to be hoped for from any of them. Now he was no longer strong enough even to stand up and go to the market. He was convinced that by tonight his spirit would have taken flight. For he knew that the thread of life is not some string that won't break no matter how much it's pulled.

'Shastriji!' the Secretary called.

Still lying down Moteram opened his eyes. They were as full of self-pity as those of a child whose candy's been snatched from his hand by a crow.

The Secretary set the bag of sweets down before him and the pot of water with a cup on it. Then he said casually, 'How long are you going to go on lying here?'

The aroma put Panditji's faculties back into operation. He sat up and said, 'Until an agreement has been reached.'

'But there's not going to be any agreement. The Council met all day without settling it. Anyway, tomorrow evening the Viceroy will be here. Do you have any idea of what kind of shape you'll be in by then? Your face has already turned pale!'

'If I'm fated to die here, who can avert his fate? Are those *rasgoolas* in that bag?'

'Yes, all kinds of sweets. They were made specially to be sent to one of my relatives for a ceremony.'

'That's why they smell so good. Open up the bag a little, will you?'

Smiling, the Secretary opened the bag and Panditji began to devour the sweets with his eyes. A blind man whose sight has been restored would not gaze upon the world with greedier eyes. Moteram's mouth watered. The Secretary said, 'If you hadn't taken a vow, I'd give you a taste of them. They cost two-and-a-half rupees a pound.'

'They must be magnificent! I haven't had any *rasgoolas* for several days.'

'And you've got yourself into a pickle for nothing! If you don't survive, of what use is the money?'

'What can I do? I'm trapped!' Panditji said. 'I might have made a meal of this many sweets.' He delicately touched them. 'They must be from Bhola's shop.'

'Just try a couple of them.'

'How can I? I'd be breaking a sacred oath.'

'Come on, taste them! The pleasure they'll give you right now couldn't be bought for thousands of rupees. Who's going to know about it anyway?'

'Who am I afraid of?' Moteram said. 'Here I am dying of thirst and hunger and nobody cares in the least. So why be afraid? Bring it here, hand me the bag. Go on, tell everybody, Shastriji's broken his vow. To hell with business and the market! I don't care about anybody. When there's no religion left in the world, why should I bother to take it on myself alone?'

136

With this Panditji drew the bag toward himself and steadily applied his hand with the result that in a flash the bag was half empty.
By this time the merchants had reached the gate and were standing
there. Going to them, the Secretary said, 'Come a little closer and
see the fun. You people won't have to open your bazaar; nor will
you have to toady to anybody. I've solved the whole problem. This
is the Congress spirit!'

Moonlight filled the square. They came closer and saw Panditji
engaged in doing away with the sweets with the profound absorption of a holy man in a trance.

Bhondumal said, 'I touch Panditji's feet in reverence. We were all
coming, why didn't you wait? We had devised a plan so that you
would have accomplished your purpose without breaking your
vow.'

But Moteram said, 'I *have* accomplished my purpose. This is a
divine joy that can't be obtained for any amount of money. If you
have any respect for me, then order some more sweets exactly like
this from the same shop!'

# Man's Highest Duty

One Holi morning Pandit Moteram Shastri — that devotee of pastries and lover of sweets — sat on a broken cot in his yard, his head hanging low, the very image of care and melancholy. His faithful spouse sat nearby watching him anxiously and trying in her gentle voice to wheedle him out of his depression.

After he had remained plunged in gloomy reflections for some time Panditji said sadly, 'My good luck has gone the devil knows where. Even on Holi it deserts me.'

'Evil days have come upon us,' his wife said. 'Ever since you told me to, I pray to the Sun God twice a day, morning and evening, to get an invitation sent to you from somewhere. I've lit hundreds of lamps to Mother *Tulsi*, but the fact is, they've all deserted you. Not one of them will come to help you through these hard times.'

'The Gods and Goddesses have nothing to do with it,' said Moteram. 'When they come and help us through our difficulties then we can start talking about Gods and Goddesses but there are an awful lot of people sitting around gobbling up pancakes and *halva* without paying for them.'

'But isn't there one single gentleman left in this whole town? Have they all died?'

'They've all died — or rather, they've all gone rotten. There may be five or ten of them but in a whole year only a couple of them show their generosity even once. And when they do, they give you only five or six pounds of sweets to eat. If I had my way, I'd send the whole lot of them off to hard labour. It's all the work of those Arya Samaj religious reformers.'

'But you just sit around the house! Even these days there must be some generous person who'd invite you out. Some time or other you ought to go out and offer sermons and blessings.'

'How do you know I haven't? If any such gentlemen existed in this town, I wouldn't give him a blessing when I went to see him. But who the devil is around to listen to me? Everybody's wrapped up in his own business.'

In the meantime Pandit Chintamani had put in an appearance. This was Moteram's best friend. To be sure, he was a little younger than Moteram and accordingly his paunch had not attained the splendid proportions of the latter's.

'Tell me, friend,' Moteram said, 'what news? Do you know of any good opportunities?'

'No opportunities,' Chintamani said, 'just my own luck and now even that's run out.'

'Then you must have just come from home?'

'Brother, let's become wandering *sadhus.* When there's not the slightest pleasure left in life, what's a man to do? Now tell me, if you don't get something decent to eat even on a day like this, how's a body to keep going?'

'Yes, brother, what you say is true.'

'Then you can't think of anything to do now either? Say it straight out and then we'll renounce the world.'

'No, friend, don't despair. Don't you know, without dying you can't get into heaven? For obtaining dainty morsels you have to undergo strict austerities. My opinion is that we should act, go right away to the banks of the Ganges and give a talk. Who knows, we may stir the heart of some gentle soul.'

'A fine idea,' said Chintamani. 'Let's get going.'

The two gentlemen got up and made their way toward the Ganges. It was still early morning. Hundreds of people were bathing there or reading scriptures aloud or thronging the steps and applying the auspicious vermillion to their foreheads. Some were already setting out for home, their *dhotis* still wet from the river.

As soon as the two gentlemen appeared they were greeted on all sides with the cries of 'Reverence! Blessings!' After replying to these salutations the two friends went to the edge of the river and busied themselves in the ritual of bathing. After this they climbed up the steps and began to sing a hymn. This was so remarkable an occurrence that hundreds of curious people gathered around. When the audience was several hundreds strong Pandit Moteram said with great dignity: 'Good people, you know that when Brahma created this unprofitable world he made the Brahmans from his mouth. Is there anyone who doubts this?'

'No, maharaj,' they said, 'what you say is true — who can deny it?'

'So the Brahman emerged from the mouth of the god Brahma,

this is certain. Therefore, the mouth is the most sublime part of the human body. Thus the highest duty of any living creature is to afford delight to the mouth. Is this true or isn't it? Does anyone deny it? Let him come forward! We can prove our theory by the scriptures.'

'Maharaj, you are a learned man — who would dare refute you?'

'Very well, then, now that it's been determined that to delight the mouth is man's highest duty, is it difficult to see that people who do not contribute to the mouth are creatures of sorrow — will anyone deny this?'

'Maharaj, you are blessed, a teacher of the true scriptures.'

'Now the question arises, how shall we delight the mouth? We say: according to your faith and according to your capacity. There are different ways. To sing the glories of the Gods, to offer prayers to the Lord, to converse with holy men and avoid wicked speech. From all these things the mouth will derive pleasure. But the highest, the most sublime and effective way is something different: Can any of you say what it is? Let him speak.'

'Maharaj,' they said, 'who can open his mouth in your presence? Please tell us.'

'Very well, I'll shout it out and sing it to the skies. Its greatness is as the full moon's light compared to all the other lunar phases.'

'Do not delay, tell us the way you mean.'

'Listen, then, pay attention: the way is this — to feast the mouth with the finest foods, to feed it the very best dishes. Does anyone deny this? Let him speak and we shall call scripture to witness.'

There was a sceptic among the crowd. 'I can't understand how the mouth can obtain greater pleasure in eating fine foods than in speaking truth.'

Several others agreed with him. 'We doubt it too. Maharaj, remove our doubt.'

'Does anyone else disbelieve? I shall be delighted to refute you. Good people, you ask how there can be greater pleasure in eating than in speaking truth. My answer is that the first way is visible and substantial, while the second is invisible. To illustrate, just imagine that I have committed a crime. If the judge summoned me and explained gently that what I had done was bad, unbefitting for me, such treatment would not succeed in setting me on the right path. Gentlemen, I'm not a saint. I'm a poor mortal caught in the toils of worldliness and delusion. Such a punishment would not have any effect on me. As soon as I'd left the judge's presence I'd begin again on the evil path. Have you understood me? Does anyone deny it?'

'Maharaj! You are an ocean of knowledge, a pearl among the Pandits — may you prosper!'

'Now let's turn back to the illustration I gave. If the judge had summoned me, promptly thrown me in jail and there subjected me to various hardships, then when I left prison I would remember those sufferings for years, and of course I would renounce the path of evil. You will ask why this is so — since both are forms of punishment why should one have an effect and the other none! The reason is that the form of one is visible and the other's hidden. Do you understand this?'

'May you prosper for your kindness! God has bestowed great sense and wisdom on you!'

'Very well, now your question will naturally be what kind of food is best. I will explain. Just as God created different kinds of colours for the gratification of the eyes, so he created diverse flavours for the mouth. But of all these flavours which is finest? This is according to each one's taste, but according to the Vedas and Shastras the taste of sweetness is the most esteemed. The gods become intoxicated with sweetness to the point where even the omnipotent, all-encompassing supreme deity himself prefers sweet foods above all. Can anyone name a god who takes salty food? Can anybody name even one such deity? There's not one. None of the gods therefore hanker after foods that are sour, tart, acid or pungent.'

'Maharaj, your wisdom has no limits!'

'Thus I have proven that of all foods, sweet foods are the best. Now again you will ask a question: will all sweet foods afford the mouth equal pleasure? If I said yes, you would all set up a cry that Panditji has gone mad. Therefore, I will say no and say it over and over again. Not all sweets have equal savour. There's a lot of difference between refined sugar and the cane. So our first duty is to see that we eat and serve only the best of sweets. In my opinion, for a feast fit for God, you should fill a plate with Jaunpur 'nectars,' Agra 'pearl-drops,' Mathura creams, *rasgoolas* from Lucknow, rose-apple candy from Ayodhya and Delhi *halva*. The gods would go wild over such a dish. And the enterprising and noble soul who gets together such a tasty dish for the Brahmans — he will find an abode in heaven in his own corporeal form! If you have faith, then we urge

141

you emphatically to fulfill your religious obligations — for otherwise you cannot consider yourselves men.'

Pandit Moteram's speech was over. People applauded. Some gentlemen, overwhelmed by the sermon and display of knowledge, showered flowers upon him. Then Pandit Chintamani began his own flowery discourse: 'Good people, you have heard the powerful utterance of my best friend Pandit Moteram and there was no need for me to be standing by. However, although I am in agreement with him on almost every question, I hold a different doctrine on one point. In my opinion if he put only Jaunpur 'nectars' on the plate, it would be far tastier, far more delicious than five different kinds of sweets. And I can prove my point by reference to the scriptures.'

Flaring up, Moteram said, 'Your idea is utterly wrong. Jaunpur 'nectars' are not fit to be compared with 'pearl-drops' from Agra and Delhi *halva*.'

'Prove it!' Chintamani shouted.

'Visibly and substantially?'

'That shows how stupid you are!'

'All your life you've been gobbling down everything in sight,' Moteram said, 'but you don't know a thing about food.'

In reply Chintamani flung his prayer-mat at Pandit Moteram, who dodged the blow and charged Chintamani like a wild elephant. But at this moment the people gathered around and separated the two mahatmas.

# A Lesson in the Holy Life

Domestic squabbles and a dearth of invitations led Pandit Chinta-mani to consider renouncing the world and when he vowed to become a wandering ascetic his best friend, Pandit Moteram Shastri, gave him this advice.

'Friend, I've been intimately acquainted with a good many first-class mahatmas. Now, when they arrive at some well-to-do citizen's door they don't fall in a heap and hold out their hands and call down hypocritical blessings such as "God keep you in body and soul, may you always be happy." Such is the way of beggars. As soon as a holy man reaches the door he lets out his war-cry in a regular yell so that everybody inside the house is astonished and comes running to see what's happened. I know two or three of these slogans — you can use any you like. Gudri *Baba* used to say, "If anybody dies five will die!" When they heard this battle-cry people would fall right at his feet. Siddh Bhagat had a fine slogan: "Eat, drink and be merry but watch out for the holy man's stick." Nanga *Baba* would say, "Give to me, feed me, let me drink, let me sleep." Just remember, your prestige depends a good deal on your slogan. What else can I tell you? Don't forget, you and I have been friends for a long time, we've enjoyed the same free dinners hundreds of times. Whenever we were at the same banquet we used to compete to eat up one dish more than the other. I'm going to miss you! May God give you a happy life.'

Chintamani wasn't pleased with any of the slogans. He said, 'Think up some special cry for me.'

'All right — how's this one: "If you don't give to me I'll run you into the ground."'

'Yes, I like that one, but if you'll allow me, I'll shorten it.'

'Go right ahead.'

'Then how about this: "Give or I'll run you into the ground."'

Moteram leaped up. 'By the Lord above, that's absolutely unique! Devotion has illuminated you. Splendid! Now try it out just once and we'll see how you do it.'

143

Chintamani stuck his fingers in his ears and yelled with all his might. 'Give or I'll run you into the ground!' The noise was so thunderous that even Moteram was startled. The bats flew out of the trees in dismay and dogs began to bark.

Moteram said, 'Friend, hearing your cry I was stirred to the depths of my heart. Such a cry has never been heard before, it was like the roar of a lion. Now your slogan has been decided, I have a few other things to tell you, so pay attention. The language of holy men is quite distinct from our ordinary way of speaking. We say "Sir," for example, to some people, and just "you" to others. But the holy man says "thou" to everybody, important or insignificant, rich or poor, old or young; however, go on treating old people with respect. Also remember never to talk plain Hindi. Otherwise the secret will be out that you're an ordinary Brahman and not a real holy man. Make your language fancy. To say, for example, "My good woman, give me something to eat" is not the style of the holy man. A genuine mahatma will say it like this: "Woman, spread a feast before me, and you will be walking in the paths of righteousness."'

'Friend,' Chintamani said, 'how can I praise you enough? You've helped me beyond measure.'

Having given this advice, Moteram took his leave. Chintamani set out and what should he see right away but a crowd of holy men sitting in front of a *bhang* and hashish shop smoking hashish. When they saw Chintamani one of the holy men pronounced his slogan:

> *Move along, move along,*
> *Otherwise, I'll prove you wrong.'*

Another holy man proclaimed:

> *Fee fi fo fum*
> *We holy men have finally come,*
> *From now on only fun.'*

While these syllables were still echoing in the skies a third mahatma roared out:

> *Here and there*
> *down and up*
> *Hurry up and fill my cup.'*

Chintamani could not restrain himself. He burst out with 'Give or I'll run you into the ground!'

As soon as they heard this the holy men greeted him. The bowl

144

of the *hookah* was refilled at once and the task of lighting it was assigned to Pandit Chintamani. He thought, if I don't accept the pipe my secret will be out. Nervously he took it. Now anyone who has never smoked hashish can try and try without being able to make the pipe draw. Closing his eyes Chintamani inhaled with all his might. The pipe fell from his hands, his eyes popped, he foamed at the mouth but not the least bit of smoke came from his lips nor was there any sign that the pipe was kindled. This lack of know-how was quite enough to ruin his standing in the society of holy men. A couple of them advanced angrily and roughly catching him by the hands, pulled him up.

'A curse on you,' one said, and another, 'Aren't you ashamed of pretending to be a mahatma?'

Humiliated, Panditji went and sat down near a sweets shop and the holy men, striking tambourines, began to sing this hymn:

> *'Illusion is the world, beloved, the world is an illusion.*
> *Both sin and holiness are lies — there's the philosophical*
> *solution.*
> *The world is all illusion.*
> *A curse on those who forbid us bhang and hashish,*
> *Krishna, lover, all the world's illusion.'*

# A Little Trick

Whenever Seth Chandumal took a look at his shop and warehouse crammed full with goods he would heave a long sigh. How could he sell them? The bank interest was going up, the shop rent was climbing, the clerks' wages had to come out of whatever was left. He had to provide all this money out of his own pocket. If this situation lasted a few more days there would be no alternative to bankruptcy. And still those Congress boycotters kept after him like devils.

Seth Chandumal's shop was in Chandni Chowk in Delhi and he also had some shops out in the provinces. When the city Congress Committee tried to get him to sign the pledge not to deal in English cloth he didn't so much as consider the possibility. Then several wholesale dealers in the market, following his example, refused to put their signatures to the pledge letter. Chandumal, who had never attained any eminence as a leader, won it now without even trying. He was sympathetic to the Government. At various times he would offer a little contribution to the official bigshots. He was also chummy with the police and he belonged to the municipal council as well. As an opponent of the Congress programme for action he had become the treasurer of the Peace Council, which supported cooperation with the British —this was the reward for his collaboration. The officals had purchased 24,000 rupees worth of cloth for the welcome prepared for the Prince of Wales. Why should so powerful a man fear the Congress? What was their importance anyway? The police encouraged him too: 'Never sign their pledge! Just see what those people are doing. You can blame us if we don't put every one of them in jail.' So Sethji's courage grew and he determined to do battle with the Congress. The result of this was that for three months Congress volunteers blockaded his shop from nine in the morning until dark. The police squad fired at them several times and several times beat them up, while Sethji himself often showered volleys of abuse on them. But the boycotters could not be budged; on the contrary,

146

because of these outbreaks of violence Chandumal's business fell off still more. From the provinces his storekeepers kept on sending even more desperate news. It was a complicated problem, he saw no way out of the impasse. He had observed that the people who'd signed the pledge went right on selling foreign cloth on the sly — there were no boycott demonstrators in front of *their* shops. He was forced to bear the full brunt of the disaster alone.

He reflected, 'What advantage has my friendship with the police and judges brought me? *They* can't get rid of these demonstrators! Customers won't come at the command of soldiers. If only the boycott can be stopped somehow or other the business might still be saved.'

Meantime his chief accountant said, 'Lalaji, just look, a few traders were coming over our way. Those boycotters told them some kind of nonsense and now they've all gone away.'

'I'd be perfectly satisfied if those sinners were all shot,' Chandumal said. 'They won't give up until they destroy me.'

'If you signed the pledge — it would be a disgrace, of course — but then they'd lift the boycott and somehow or other we'd sell off everything.'

'I've considered that too,' Chandumal said. 'But think how great the loss of face would be. After putting up such a front I can't give in, I'd lose all my prestige with the judges and they'd taunt me for backing down. "Just an idiot fighting the Congress!" After a defeat like that my pride would be crushed. How would I look asking for help from the people I struck and had beaten and insulted and ridiculed? But there might be a way out. If a little trick could work then we'd be out of the soup. The thing is to kill the snake without breaking the stick! If I can just lift the boycott without toadying up to anybody . . .'

*

At nine in the morning Chandumal had come back from a ritual dip in the Jumna and reclining, propped up by his bolster, he began to read through some letters. The managers of his other shops all related the same tale of woe. With each letter he read Sethji's anger mounted. In the meantime two volunteers came with banners to stand guard outside his shop.

Sethji shouted, 'Get away from my shop, you!'

147

'Maharaj,' one of the volunteers answered, 'we're on the road —do you want us to stay out of the road too?'

'I don't want to have to look at your faces,' Sethji said.

'Then be good enough to write to the Congress Committee. We got our orders from them to come and stand guard here.'

A constable came along and said, 'What's the matter, Sethji, is this fellow talking back to you?'

Chandumal said, 'I told him to get away from in front of my shop but he says he won't leave. Just look at the way they persecute me!'

The constable said to the volunteers, 'Both of you get moving or I'll come and pin back your ears.'

'We're on the road,' the volunteer said, 'not in his shop.'

The constable was eager to show his efficiency. He also hoped for some little compensation if he did Sethji a favour. He yelled at the volunteers and when they paid no attention he struck one of them such a blow that the poor fellow fell flat on the ground. Several demonstrators came clustering from here and there, and a number of policeman gathered too. Idle onlookers enjoy nothing more than an incident like this and they flocked around as well. Someone shouted, 'Long live Mahatma Gandhi!' and everyone chimed in, and in a twinkling there was a regular mob.

One onlooker said, 'What's up, Chandumal? Can you have these poor people treated so barbarously in front of your shop without being ashamed? Have you no fear of God?'

Sethji said, 'I give you my oath I never said a word to any police-man. These people came out of nowhere after the poor fellows. You're slandering me without any cause.'

'But Lalaji,' the constable protested, 'you yourself said these two volunteers were scaring off your customers. Are you trying to slip out of that now?'

'A lie, a complete lie, a hundred percent lie!' Sethji said. 'You people started a fight with them just to show how good you are at your work. These poor fellows were standing way off from my shop, they weren't talking to anybody or causing any trouble. Then you started after them. Is my business selling or fighting with people?'

'Lalaji,' said another constable, 'Be sensible now. You got us worked up and then you kept out of it. If you hadn't told us to, why would we have hit these people? And the Inspector ordered us to pay special attention to Seth Chandumal's shop. "Don't let any volunteers gather there!" he said, So we came to protect your shop. If you hadn't made the request why should the Inspector have given us this assignment?'

'The Inspector must have wanted to show how efficient he is, I suppose,' Chandumal said. 'Why should I ask him for anything? Everybody's against Congress anyway, but the police go all to pieces just to hear them mentioned. Do you mean you do your duty only if I make a complaint?'

In the meantime somebody had informed the police station that violence had broken out between police and volunteers in front of Lala Chandumal's shop. The news got to the Congress office too. In a little while the captain of the armed police and the Inspector arrived, and a whole force of Congress officials came on the run. The crowd was enormous. Shouts of victory rang out occasionally. The police and Congress leaders began to argue. The result of it all was that the police arrested the two volunteers and marched them off toward the police station.

After the police officials had gone Sethji said to the Congress president, 'I've learned today how brutally those people treat the volunteers.'

'Then those two volunteers weren't arrested in vain,' the president said. 'You don't have any doubts about this matter now, do you? Have you really learned how violent and destructive they are?'

'Yes indeed, I really have learned.'

'But the police will surely ask you to testify.'

'Let them ask,' Chandumal said. 'I'll just tell the truth straight out, whether it ruins me or not. From now on there's not going to be any police brutality in front of my door. I hadn't understood at all.'

'The police will put a lot of pressure on you,' the Congress secretary said.

'Let them do their utmost, I'll never lie. The Government's not going to get off in the *real* courthouse,' and Chandumal looked heavenward for an instant.

'Now our honour is in your hands,' the secretary said.

'You won't find me an enemy of my country,' Chandumal said.

Afterwards when the president and other officials were about to leave the secretary said, 'The man appears truthful.'

Dubiously the president observed, 'By tomorrow we'll have the proof of it.'

*

In the evening the Police Inspector called Lala Chandumal to the station and said, 'You'll have to testify and we're counting on your collaboration.'

'I'm ready,' said Chandumal.

'Did the volunteers insult the constables?'

'I didn't hear any insults.'

'Whether you heard any or not, that's not the point. You'll have to say that they kept customers away by hitting them, that there were scuffles, that they threatened to kill — you'll have to say all this.' To the sub-inspector he said, 'Copy this description which I've taken down at Sethji's dictation.'

'You won't hear *me* lying in a packed courtroom,' Seth Chandumal said. 'There'll be thousands in court who know me. How could I show my face to anybody, where could I go?'

'These are all personal matters,' the Inspector said. 'In politics nobody worries about truth and falsehood or honour and shame.'

'But I'd be dishonoured,' Sethji said.

'In the eyes of the Government your prestige would be four times as great.'

Chandumal reflected. 'No,' he said, 'I can't testify. Get some other witness.'

'You'd better think about it, now! This could ruin you completely.'

'If it does, then so be it.'

'Your rank as treasurer of the Peace Council will be taken away from you.'

'Well,' Chandumal said, 'that's not what pays my bills.'

'You'll forfeit your license to carry a gun.'

'So I'll forfeit it — who cares?'

'And then there'll be an income tax investigation.'

'Investigate by all means — it will be to my advantage, the way business is.'

'You won't have a chair left to sit in!'

'I'm going bankrupt anyway — what good is a chair?'

'All right then. You may go now. But one of these days we'll take care of you!'

\*

At this time the next day in the Congress office a programme was decided on for the morrow. The president said, 'Send a couple of volunteers to blockade Chandumal's shop.'

'In my opinion,' said the secretary, 'there's no need to now.'

'Why? He still hasn't signed the pledge letter, has he?'

'He didn't sign but he's certainly on our side now. He's made this plain by refusing to testify on behalf of the police. You can imagine how the officials will be after him for that. Moral courage like this can't come without a transformation of his ideas as well.'

'Yes, certainly there's been some change in his ideas.'

'No sir, it's a total revolution,' the secretary said. 'You know what it means to scorn the authorities in such matters — it's like a declaration of treason. It means just as much as a vow of renunciation for an ascetic. Now every judge in the district will be positively thirsting for his blood. It wouldn't be surprising if the governor himself was informed about this.'

'Then there's nothing else but for him to sign the pledge if only as a matter of form. Somehow or other get him over here and let's settle the matter.'

'He's very proud, he'll never come. On the contrary, if he sees that we don't trust him he's liable to try to go back over to the other side.'

'Very well then, if we're to trust him let's take the volunteers away from his shop. But still I say that you'll have to keep an eye on him by finding some pretext for going to see him.'

'You really don't have to be so suspicious,' said the secretary.

When Sethji came to his shop at nine o' clock he didn't see a single volunteer. He broke into a grin. 'We won the toss,' he said to the accountant.

'So it seems — not one of those gentlemen's put in an appearance.'

'And they're not going to. The game is in our hands now. We gambled and we got everything. Aren't you convinced? How quickly I made them my friends. Just ask me to and I'll send for 'em and make 'em lick my boots! They're not anybody's friends and nobody's enemies, they're just slaves of money. Tell the truth now, what did you think of my little trick?'

'I could go right down on my knees to you for it! The snake is dead and the stick didn't break. But those Congress fellows will be keeping an eye on you.'

151

'I'm ready for 'em, I can match wits with them and give them tit for tat. There are people coming, so get out a bale of the English cloth and start giving it to the traders. In a week we'll be out of the woods!'

# Penalty

Scarcely a month ever went by without Alarakkhi having some fine deducted from her pay. Once in a while she would actually get five of her six rupees; but though she put up with just about anything she had managed not to let Khan Sahib put his hands on her. Munshi Khairat Ali Khan was the Inspector of Sanitation and hundreds of sweeper women depended on him. He was good-hearted and well thought of — not the sort who cut their pay, scolded them or fined them. But he went on regularly rebuking and punishing Alarakkhi. She was not a shirker, nor saucy or slovenly; she was also not at all bad-looking. During these chilly days she would be out with her broom before it was light and go on assiduously sweeping the road until nine. But all the same, she would be penalized. Huseni, her husband, would help her with the work too when he found the chance, but it was in Alarakkhi's fate that she was going to be fined. For others pay-day was an occasion to celebrate, for Alarakkhi it was a time to weep. On that day it was as though her heart had broken. Who could tell how much would be deducted? Like students awaiting the results of their examinations, over and over again she would speculate on the amount of the deduction.

Whenever she got so tired that she'd sit down a moment to catch her breath, precisely then the Inspector would arrive riding in his *ekka*. No matter how much she'd say, 'Please, Excellency, I'll go back to work again,' he would jot her name down in his book without listening. A few days later the very same thing would happen again. If she bought a few cents worth of candy from the sweets-vendor and started to eat it, just at that moment the Inspector would drop on her from the devil knew where and once more write her name down in his book. Where could he have been hiding? The minute she began to rest the least bit he was upon her like an evil spirit. If he wrote her name down on only two days, how much would the penalty be then? God knew. More than eight *annas*? If only it weren't a whole rupee! With her head bowed she'd go to collect her pay and find even more deducted than she'd estimated. Taking her money with trembling hands she'd go home, her eyes full of tears. There was no one to turn to, no one who'd listen, where the Inspector was concerned.

Today was pay-day again. The past month her unweaned daughter had suffered from coughing and fever. The weather had been exceptionally cold. Partly because of the cold, partly because of the little girl's crying she was kept awake the whole night. Several times she'd come to work late. Khan Sahib had noted down her name, and this time she would be fined half her pay. But if it were only half it would be a blessing. It was impossible to say how much might be deducted. Early in the morning she picked up the baby, took her broom and went to the street. But the naughty creature wouldn't let herself be put down. Time after time Alarakkhi would threaten her with the arrival of the Inspector. 'He's on his way and he'll beat me and as for you, he'll cut off your nose and ears!' The child was willing to to sacrifice her nose and ears but not to be put down. At last, when Alarakkhi had failed to get rid of her with threats and coaxing alike, she set her down and left her crying and wailing while she started to sweep. But the little wretch wouldn't sit in one place to cry her heart out; she crawled after her mother time and time again, caught her sari, clung to her legs, then wallowed around on the ground and a moment later sat up to start crying again.

'Shut up!' Alarakkhi said, brandishing the broom. 'If you don't, I'll hit you with the broom and that'll be the end of you. That bastard of an Inspector's going to show up at any moment.'

She had hardly got the words out of her mouth when Inspector Khairat Ali Khan dismounted from his bicycle directly in front of her. She turned pale, her heart began to thump. 'Oh God, may my head fall off if he heard me! Right in front of me and I didn't see him. Who could tell he'd come on his bicycle today? He's always come in his *ekka.*' The blood froze in her veins, she stood holding the broom as though paralyzed.

Angrily the Inspector said, 'Why do you drag the kid after you to work? Why didn't you leave it at home?'

'She's sick, Excellency,' Alarakkhi said timidly. 'Who's at home to leave her with?'

'What's the matter with her?'

'She has a fever, *Huzoor.*'

154

'And you make her cry by leaving her? Don't you care if she lives or dies?'

'How can I do my work if I carry her?'

'Why don't you ask for leave?'

'If my pay is cut, *Huzoor*, what will we have to live on?'

'Pick her up and take her home. When Huseni comes back send him here to finish the sweeping.'

She picked up the baby and was about to go when he asked, 'Why were you abusing me?'

Alarakkhi felt all her breath knocked out of her. If you'd cut her there wouldn't have been any blood. Trembling she said, 'No, *Huzoor*, may my head fall off if I was abusing you.'

And she burst into tears.

*

In the evening Huseni and Alarakkhi went to collect her pay. She was very downcast.

'Why so sad?' Huseni tried to console her. 'The pay's going to be cut, so let them cut it. I swear on your life from now on I won't touch another drop of booze or toddy.'

'I'm afraid I'm fired. Damn my tongue! How could I . . ..'

'If you're fired, then you're fired, but let Allah be merciful to *him*. Why go on crying about it?'

'You've made me come for nothing. Everyone of those women will laugh at me.'

'If he's fired you, won't we ask on what grounds? And who heard you abuse him? Can there be so much injustice that he can fire anyone he pleases? If I'm not heard I'll complain to the panchayat, I'll beat my head on the headman's gate — '

'If our people stuck together like that would Khan Sahib ever dare fine us so much?'

'No matter how serious the sickness there's a medicine for it, silly.'

But Alarakkhi was not set at rest. Dejection covered her face like a cloud. When the Inspector heard her abuse him why didn't he even scold her? Why didn't he fire her on the spot? She wasn't able to work it out, he actually seemed kind. She couldn't manage to understand this mystery and not understanding it she was afraid. If he meant only to fine her he would have written her name in his book. He had decided to fire her — that must have been why he was so nice. She'd heard that a man about to be hanged is given a fine last meal, they have to give him anything he wants — so surely the Inspector was going to dismiss her.

They reached the municipal office building. Thousands of sweeper women were gathered there, all made up and wearing their brightest clothes and jewelry. The *paan* and cigarette vendors had also come, along with the sweets peddlers. A swarm of Pathan money-lenders were on hand to collect money from those who owed them. Huseni and Alarakkhi went and stood with the others.

They began to distribute the pay. The sweeper women were first. Whoever's name was called would go running and taking her money call down undeserved blessings on the Inspector and go away. Alarakkhi's name was always called after Champa's. Today she was passed over. After Champa, Jahuran's name was called, and she always followed Alarakkhi.

In despair she looked at Huseni. The women were watching her and beginning to whisper. She longed just to be able to go home, she couldn't bear this derision. She wished the earth would open and swallow her up.

One after another the names were called and Alarakkhi went on looking at the trees across the way. Now she no longer cared whose name was called, who went, and who stared at her and who was laughing at her.

Suddenly startled, she heard her name. Slowly she stood up and walked ahead with the slow tread of a new bride. The paymaster put the full amount of six rupees in her hand.

She was stupefied. Surely the paymaster was mistaken! In these three years she had never once got her full pay. And now to get even half would have been a windfall. She stood there for a second in case the paymaster should ask for the money back. When he asked her, 'Why are you standing here now, why don't you move along?' she said softly, 'But it's the full amount.'

Puzzled the paymaster looked at her and said, 'What else do you want — do you want to get less?'

'There's no penalty deducted?'

'No, today there aren't any deductions.'

She came away but in her heart she was not content. She was full of remorse for having abused the Inspector.

156

# The Writer

Early in the morning Mr. Pravin prepared a cup of tea boiled twenty times over and drank it without sugar and milk. This was his breakfast. For months he had not had sweetened tea with milk — for him milk and sugar were not among the necessities of life. To be sure, he did go into the bedroom to wake his wife and ask for some money; but when he saw her fast asleep in the torn, soiled quilt he did not want to wake her. He thought that because of the cold the poor woman might not have fallen asleep all night and had only a moment ago managed to shut her eyes. It wasn't right to wake someone who'd just fallen asleep. Silently he came away.

After he drank his tea he arranged his pen and inkwell and became absorbed in writing that book which in his opinion would be the greatest creation of the century and which, when published, would take him out of his anonymity and launch him into the empyrean of fame and glory.

A half hour later his wife came in, rubbing her eyes, and said, 'Have you already had your tea?'

With a smile on his face Pravin said, 'Yes, already. It turned out very well.'

'But where did you get the milk and sugar?'

'I haven't had milk and sugar for a long time now. These days plain tea tastes better to me. Mixing in milk and sugar spoils the taste. The doctors also maintain that you ought to drink tea plain. In Europe, you know, the custom is not to use milk at all. It's really just the invention of our local sweet-toothed aristocrats.'

'I don't know how you can like unsweetened tea! Why didn't you wake me? There was some money set aside.'

Mr. Pravin began to write again. Right from his early years this disease had afflicted him, and he had been feeding it now for twenty years. His body had wasted away in this sickness, his health had declined, and at forty, old age had set in; but the illness was incurable. From sunrise until midnight he was immersed in the inner universe of a worshipper of literature, his face turned away

157

from all the rest of the world while he went on offering as oblation the flower of his heart. But in India the worship of Saraswati is an offence to Lakshmi. With only one spirit how could you delight both goddesses, how could the vessel of sacrifice be made one? And this disfavour of Lakshmi's did not manifest itself only in the form of impoverishment. Her cruelest joke was that newspaper editors and book publishers did not offer any heart-felt sympathy either. Could it be that the entire world had conspired against him? It had reached the point where this constant indigence seemed to have crushed his self-confidence. Possibly he was now beginning to realize that in his works there was no substance, no genius, and the feeling tore at his heart. This human life, so difficult to attain, had been destroyed all for nothing! He did not even have the consolation that though the world had not honoured him, yet his lifetime of work was not so insignificant after all. The constant doing without basic necessities had finally surpassed the bounds of asceticism. If there was any satisfaction it was that his life's companion was two steps ahead of him in renunciation and auster- ity. And Sumitra was happy in this situation. Pravin might have some complaints against the world, but like an air-filled cushion Sumitra kept protecting him from the shocks of the outside world. There was no question of her bemoaning her fate, and no frown ever appeared on the brow of this goddess.

Picking up the teacup, Sumitra said, 'Then why don't you go and take a walk for an hour or two? When you know that nothing at all has come of devoting your whole life to this work why torment yourself for nothing?'

Pravin, without looking up from his paper and still moving his pen, said, 'From writing at least I have the satisfaction that I'm doing something. Going out for a walk seems to me just a waste of time.'

'Still, so many of these educated men go out to enjoy a stroll — are they just wasting their time?'

'But most of those people don't suffer any decrease in their income when they go out for a stroll, they're mostly government servants who get a monthly salary or have a profession that people respect. But I'm just a mill worker. Have you ever seen a mill worker taking a stroll? The only people who need to take walks are those who don't lack for food. Anyone too broke to get enough to eat doesn't go for walks. When people are happy and enjoying life they need health and life enhancement. But for me life is a burden, and I have no wish to keep this burden any longer on my head.'

When Sumitra heard these words so full of despair her eyes filled with tears and she went inside. Her heart told her that one day surely glory and fame would reward these sacrifices even if Lakshmi remained unfavourable. But Pravin had now reached that limit of despair from which no glimmer of any hopeful dawn could be seen rising in the hostile sky.

*

There's a celebration at some nobleman's house, and he sends an invitation to Mr. Pravin. Today Pravin's mind is flying on the winged horse of happiness. He has been deep in dreams about it the whole day. What words will the Raja use to welcome him, what will he say to thank him, what will they converse about, and with what famous people will he become acquainted — all day Pravin has been enjoying dreaming about such things. For this occasion he has also composed a poem in which he compares life to a garden. He put aside all his own strong principles this time because he did not want to wound the feelings of the aristocrats.

By noon he had already begun his preparations. He shaved, bathed with soap, applied oil to his hair. The problem was what to wear. A long time had passed since he'd had his jacket made, and its condition had deteriorated very much like his own. Just as from the slightest chilly spell he caught cold or a headache when it turned warm, in much the same way the jacket too had suffered a decline. He took it out and brushed it.

Sumitra said, 'It was pointless for you to accept that invitation. You should have written that you weren't feeling well. To go in such rags is really bad.'

Pravin said with philosophical gravity, 'Those to whom God has given heart and discrimination don't look at people's clothes, but at their virtues and character. After all, it's something that the Raja's invited me. I don't hold any official position, I don't have any estates or property, I'm not a contractor, I'm just a simple writer. A writer's value lies in his works. Since I believe this I don't have any more cause to feel ashamed than would any other writer.'

Filled with pity for his simplicity, Sumitra said, 'By living so long in a world of dreams you've become cut off from the real world.

159

I'm telling you, at the Raja's people will be looking most of all at what everybody's wearing. It's a fine thing to be simple, certainly, but that doesn't mean one has to look down at heel.'

Pravin felt that there was some sense in this. In the way of scholarly people he had no hesitation in acknowledging his mistakes. He said, 'I understand, I'll go after the lamps are lit.'

'But I ask you, why go at all?'

'How can I explain to you now that in every being there's a hunger for honour and respect? You'll ask, why is there this hunger? Because it's a stage in our self-development. We're a minute part of that great reality which pervades the whole universe, so it's inevitable that the qualities of the whole be present in the part. Therefore, our natural inclination lies in the direction of fame and respect, self-advancement and knowledge. I don't regard this desire as wrong.'

To make an end of it, Sumitra said, 'Very well, my dear, then go. I'm not arguing with you, but do make some provision for tomorrow, for I've only one *anna* left. I've already borrowed from the people I can borrow from and I've had no opportunity to pay them back. At this point I can't think of anything at all to do.'

Pravin said after a moment, 'There's money coming to me from a few magazines for some of my articles. Maybe it will come by tomorrow. And if we have to fast tomorrow, what does it matter? Our *dharma* is to work. We work and do it with all our heart and soul. If despite all that we have to fast, it's not my fault. So — I can only die. People like us die by the hundreds of thousands every day and the world keeps going on just the way it was before. So why grieve if we die of hunger? Death is nothing to fear. I accept the practice of those followers of Kabir who carry off the bier with music and song. I'm not afraid of it. You tell me, is it beyond my powers or not to do anything more than I'm doing? The whole world can sleep peacefully but I continue to sit with my pen. People go on enjoying pleasures and amusements, but all that's forbidden to me. For months I scarcely have occasion to laugh, even on Holi I didn't take any time off. Even when I'm ill all I'm concerned with is writing. Remember, you were sick and I couldn't find time to go to the doctor. If the world doesn't appreciate it — so what? It's only the world's loss, but no loss for me. The lamp's duty is to burn away — it's not concerned with whether its light is shed or something blocks it.

'And do I have any friends either, any acquaintances or relations, to whom I'm not indebted? I'm ashamed now just to go out of the house. The only satisfaction is that people don't think me dishonest. They may not be able to give me any more help but they surely sympathize with me. It's enough for my happiness that today the opportunity's come for a nobleman to honour me!'

Then suddenly he became as though intoxicated. Proudly he said, 'No, I won't go at night after all. My poverty has now reached the point of being a disgrace. It's futile to conceal it. I'll go this very moment. A man invited by noblemen and rajas can't be of such little account. Those aristocrats aren't just ordinary nobles, they're among the nobles of India, not just this town. Anyone who still thinks of me as worthless is worthless himself.'

*

It was evening. Pravin put on his old thread-bare jacket, worn-out shoes and shabby hat, and left the house, looking rather like a rustic or a burglar. Had he been prepossessing in build and looks, then even dressed like this he might have created an imposing effect, since a robust physique is of itself impressive. But there is an opposition between physical well-being and literature. If some literary personage is robust and over-sized then you may assume that there's no tenderness in him, no sweetness, no heart. The lamp's business is to burn away; the lamp full to the brim is one that doesn't want to burn. Nevertheless, he marched along with confidence, his whole presence radiated pride.

Now, usually when he left the house he slipped through the back alleys to evade the shopkeepers. But today he walked right in front of them with his head high, today he was ready to give a crushing reply to their demands for payment. But it was evening, there were shoppers sitting on all the shop platforms and no one looked his way. The sums which he, in his poverty, considered shameful, in the eyes of the shopkeepers were not of such importance that they would take an acquaintance to task about them in front of everybody, particularly when today he appeared to be on his way to meet someone.

Pravin had already made the circuit of the whole market but he was not satisfied. He walked through it again, and again was unsuccessful. This time he went straight to Hafiz Samad's shop and stood

161

there. Hafiz was a general merchant from whose shop Pravin had taken an umbrella a good while back and had not yet been able to finish paying for it. When he saw Pravin he said, 'My dear sir, you still haven't paid for the umbrella. If I had a hundred or so customers like you I'd go bankrupt! It really has been a long time.'

Pravin was delighted, his heart's desire fulfilled. 'I haven't forgotten, Hafizji,' he said, 'but these days I've had so much work that I could hardly leave the house. But, if I may say so, I've no shortage of admirers. There are quite a few people always hanging around. Right now in fact the Raja Sahib — you know, the one who lives in the mansion on the corner — I'm on my way to his place to a banquet. Something like this keeps coming up every day.'

Impressed, Hafiz Samad said, 'Excellent! You're on your way to the Raja's. Naturally, only the nobles can appreciate geniuses like you, who else can? Praise God, you're unique in this age of ours! Now, should the opportunity come about, then don't forget us poor people. If the Raja Sahib were disposed to look upon me with favour, what more could I ask? Why, he must require a whole shopful of goods. His yearly income's two hundred and fifty or three hundred thousand.'

The amount seemed trivial to Pravin. The tongue's a spend-thrift, so what harm in saying a million or two? He said, 'Two hundred and fifty or three hundred thousand! You're insulting him. His income's no less than a million. One gentleman estimates it at two million. He has estates, buildings, shops, contracts, trust funds and then, he's in the good graces of the most important people in the government.'

Hafiz said very humbly, 'Sir, this shop is yours, such is my desire! *Arrey*, Muradi!' (he called to his servant), 'just go and have two paisa's worth of the best *paan* made up and bring it for the gentleman. Come now, have a seat for a few minutes, if there's anything you'd like, let me show it to you. My business is at your disposal.'

Pravin took the *paan* and said, 'But now forgive me, I'll be late, I'll come back some other time.'

He got up and stopped in front of a cloth merchant's shop belonging to one Manohar Das. When he saw Pravin, hope revived in him. The poor fellow had been bewailing his name, thinking he might even have left town. Now he assumed he had come to pay him. He said, 'Dear Mr. Pravin, I haven't had the good fortune to see you for quite some time. I sent notes to you on several occasions, but my servant was unable to locate you.' To his accountant he said, 'Just have a look and see what the gentleman owes us.'

Pravin's spirits were suffocated by his debts; but today he stood there as though he were wearing armour which no weapon could pierce to wound him. He said, 'I'm in a hurry just now, I'll stop if I may on my way back from the Raja Sahib's and then I can sit down with you without worrying, but I'm in a hurry now.'

The Raja Sahib owed Manohar Das several thousand rupees. Still, the merchant had not given up on him, he would get back three for every one. He placed Pravin in a very high rank as one whose profession was to plunder the aristocrats. He said, 'Do come and take some *paan*, sir. The Raja Sahib's only for a day, but my dear sir, we are for all the year round. If you need some clothes, then come and take them. Holi will soon be upon us. If you find the opportunity won't you please remind the Raja's treasurer that his old account has not been paid for a very long time, so why not clear it up now! When somebody doesn't pay bills for two years at a time what kind of profit can we expect?'

Pravin said, 'Please let me pass up the *paan* for now, brother. I'm going to be late. When the Raja's so keen to meet me and does me such a great honour, then it's my obligation not to cause him any inconvenience. We writers aren't hungry for wealth you see, we want people to appreciate our quality. If anyone will do us honour, we're his slaves. If somebody is conceited about his worldly power, we don't care a straw about him.'

\*

When Pravin arrived before the Raja Sahib's vast mansion the lamps had already been lit. The motorcars of the rich and noble were lined up, uniformed doormen stood at the gates. One gentleman was greeting each of the guests. When he saw Pravinji he felt rather uncertain. Then, looking him up and down, he said, 'Do you have an invitation?'

Pravin had the invitation in his pocket, but he was angered by this discrimination. Why was he being asked to show his invitation? Why aren't the others being asked? He said, 'No, I don't have the invitation. If you ask these other gentlemen for theirs I can show you one as well. But if not, I regard this singling-out as an insult. Tell the Raja Sahib Pravinji came to his door and returned home.'

'No, no, sir, come along inside. We'd never been introduced, so please forgive my rudeness. Our gatherings take their lustre only from distinguished men like yourself. God has bestowed eloquence upon you such as cannot be described!'

This personage had never seen Pravin before. But what he said he could say just as well about any literary man, and we trust that no literary man could scorn the praise.

When Pravin proceeded on he saw electric lanterns casting their glow over the spacious decorated lawn before the summer house. In the centre was a pool, with the marble figure of a nymph from whose head a fountain sprayed jets of water which appeared in the glimmer of the coloured lanterns as though a rainbow had melted and rained down on them. Tables were set up all round the pool, with bright bouquets on the white tablecloths.

As soon as he saw Pravin the Raja Sahib welcomed him: 'Come along, come along! I was thrilled when I read your piece in *Hans.** Quite astonished, really. I had no idea that a real find like you was hidden away in this town.'

Then he began to introduce him to the gentlemen who were there. 'You surely have heard the name of Mr. Pravin. Now here he is in person! What sweetness and power, what feeling and language, what inventiveness and style, what a wonder! Bravo! My heart feels as though it's about to dance!'

One gentleman, dressed in an English suit, looked at Pravin as though he were some creature in a zoo and said, 'Have you also made a study of the English poets? Byron, Shelley, Keats, and so on?'

Pravin said curtly, 'Yes, of course, I've read a bit of them.'

'If you were to translate the works of one of these great poets you would be rendering an inestimable service to the Hindi language.'

Pravin considered himself not a whit less than Byron, Shelley and the others. They were English poets, their language, style, subjects and significance, all were according to English taste. He did not think it a matter of pride for him to translate them any more than they would have thought it a matter of pride to translate him. He said, 'We are not so lacking in intellectual worth that we have to go begging from the foreign poets. In my opinion, in this subject at

* An important literary magazine begun in 1930 and published from Lucknow. Premchand, its first editor, published many of his late stories in *Hans.*

164

least India can teach the West something.'

At this absurd statement the Anglophile gentleman decided Pravin was crazy.

The Raja Sahib looked at Pravin as though to say, Please remember where you are when you speak! He said, 'But how can we criticize English literature? In poetry no one can rival them.'

Regarding Pravin arrogantly, the Anglophile gentlemen said, 'Our poets have never yet even understood the meaning of poetry. Until the present our poetry has consisted of pathetic descriptions of separated lovers and catalogues of women's charms.'*

Pravin gave as good as he got. 'I believe you haven't studied our present-day poets, or if you have, then only superficially.'

The Raja Sahib had now decided to shut Pravin up. 'This is Mr. Paranjpe, Pravinji! His articles are printed in the English papers and he is regarded with the greatest respect.'

Which meant, Now stop talking nonsense.

Pravin understood; he was supposed to look insignificant before Paranjpe.

It was intolerable to Pravin that despite being devoted to foreign dress and customs and language and hostile to his own people, this fellow should be treated with such respect. But what could one do?

Another gentleman of the same stamp came on the scene and was cordially greeted by the Raja Sahib. 'Welcome, Dr. Chaddha, how are you?'

The doctor shook hands with the Raja and then looking with curiosity at Pravin asked, 'May I know your good name, sir?'

The Raja Sahib introduced Pravin, adding, 'A fine poet and writer in Hindi.'

The doctor said with a peculiar tone, 'I see, you're a poet!' and without asking anything walked along.

Then another gentleman of the same sort put in an appearance, a well known barrister, to whom the Raja Sahib also introduced Pravin. He said in the same peculiar manner, 'I see, you're a poet!' and walked on. The same performance was repeated several times. And each time Pravin received the identical praise: 'I see, you're a poet!'

Every time these words inflicted a new wound on Pravin's heart.

---

* The stock-in-trade of poets writing in *Braj* before Premchand's time.

165

He understood very well the sentiment behind them. The plain meaning was, 'If you want to waste your time cooking up such nonsense, go ahead. What use is it to you? But how can you be so foolhardy as to blunder into cultured society like ours?'

In his inmost heart Pravin was angry with himself. He had considered himself terribly lucky when he got the invitation but on realizing how much he had been insulted when he came here, his own contented little house was heaven. He reproached himself: This is the punishment for those greedy for prestige. But now your eyes have been opened as to just how worthy of respect you are! You're utterly useless in this selfish world. Why should attorneys and barristers honour you? You can't be one of their clients, nor can they hope to get any law-suits from you. And why should doctors honour you? They have no wish to visit your house without collecting a fee for it. You were born to write, so go and write. That's the sum, you're of no other use in the world.

Suddenly there was great excitement among the gathering: tonight's guest of honor had arrived. This gentleman had just been appointed as judge in the High Court, for which achievement the festivities had been organized. The Raja Sahib rushed to him, shook his hand, and said to Pravinji: 'I imagine you've brought your poem?'

Pravin said, 'I wrote no poem.'

'Truly? But how perfectly dreadful of you! Come, my good man, dash off something right away. Just a few lines will do, that's all. It's quite imperative for a poem to be written on such an occasion as this.'

'I can't write anything as quickly as that.'

'Have I then wasted my time introducing you to all these people?'

'You have indeed wasted your time.'

'*Arrey*, my dear fellow, then recite something by some ancient poet, who among these people would know the difference?'

'Certainly not — it you will forgive me. I'm no minstrel or street-side story-teller.'

Saying this, Pravin immediately took his departure. When he arrived home he was smiling.

Delighted, Sumitra asked, 'Why have you come home so early?'

'I wasn't needed there.'

'Come now, you're all smiles, you must have been highly

166

honoured.'

'Oh yes, I was honoured in a way I hadn't hoped for.'

'And you're very happy!'

'Only because tonight I learned a lesson for all time. I'm a lamp and I was created to burn. Today I forgot that principle. But the good Lord didn't let me stray for long. This wretched dwelling of mine is heaven for me. Tonight I understood the truth that the service of literature demands complete sacrifice.'

# A Coward

The boy's name was Keshav, the girl's Prema. They went to the same college, they were in the same class. Keshav believed in new ways and was opposed to the old caste customs. Prema adhered to the old order and fully accepted the traditions. But all the same there was a strong attachment between them and the whole college was aware of it. Although he was a Brahman Keshav regarded marriage with this Baniya girl as the culmination of his life. He didn't care a straw about his father and mother. Caste traditions he considered a fraud. If anything embodied the truth for him it was Prema. But for Prema it was impossible to take one step in opposition to the dictates of caste and family.

One evening the two of them met in a secluded corner of Victoria Park and sat down on the grass facing one another. The strollers had gone off one by one but these two lingered on. They had got into a discussion it was impossible to end.

Keshav said angrily, 'All it means is that you don't care about me.'

Prema tried to calm him down. 'You're being unjust to me, Keshav. It's only that I don't know how I can bring it up at home without upsetting them. They're devoted to the old traditions. If they hear anything about a matter like this from me can't you imagine how distressed they'll be?'

'And aren't you a slave of those old traditions too then?' Keshav asked her sharply.

'No, I'm not,' Prema said, her eyes tender, 'but what my mother and father want is more important to me than anything.'

'And you yourself don't count at all?'

'If that's how you want to understand it.'

'I used to think those old ways were just for silly hypocrites but now it seems that educated girls like you knuckle under to them too. Since I'm ready to give up everything for you I expect the same thing from you.'

In silence Prema wondered what authority she had over her own life. She had no right to go in any way against the mother and father

168

who had created her from their own blood and reared her with love. To Keshav she said humbly, 'Can love be considered only in terms of husband and wife and not friendship? I think of love as an attachment of the soul.'

'You'll drive me crazy with your rationalizations,' Keshav said harshly. 'Just understand this — if I'm disappointed I can't go on living. I'm a materialist and it's not possible for me to be satisfied with some intangible happiness in the world of the imagination.'

He caught Prema's hand and tried to draw her toward him, but she broke away and said, 'I told you I'm not free. Don't ask me to do something I have no right to do.'

If she'd spoken harshly he would not have been so hurt. For an instant he restrained himself, then he stood up and said sadly, 'Just as you wish,' and slowly walked away. Prema, in tears, continued to sit there.

*

When after supper that night Prema lay down in her mother's room she could not sleep. Keshav had said things to her that shadowed her heart like reflections in unquiet waters, changing at every moment, and she could not calm them. How could she talk to her mother about such things? Embarrassment kept her silent. She thought, 'If I don't marry Keshav what's left for me in life?' While she thought about it over and over again her mind was made up about just one thing — if she did not marry Keshav she would marry no one.

Her mother said, 'Still not sleeping? I've told you so many times you ought to do a little work around the house. But you can never take any time off from your books. In a little while you'll be going to some strange house and who knows what sort of place it will be? If you don't get accustomed to doing housework, how are you going to manage?'

Naively Prema asked, 'Why will I be going to a strange house?'

Smiling, her mother said, 'For a girl it's the greatest calamity, daughter. After being sheltered at home, as soon as she's grown up off she goes to live with others. If she gets a good husband her days pass happily, otherwise she has to go through life weeping. It all depends on fate. But in our community there's no family that appeals to me. There's no proper regard for girls anywhere. But we have to stay within our caste. Who knows how long caste marriages

169

are going to go on?'

Frightened Prema said, 'But here and there they're beginning to have marriages outside the caste.' She'd said it for the sake of talking but she trembled lest her mother might guess something.

Surprised, her mother asked, 'You don't mean among Hindus?' Then she answered herself. 'If this has happened in a few places, then what's come of it?'

Prema did not reply. She was afraid her mother had understood her meaning. She saw her future in that moment before her like a great dark tunnel opening its mouth to swallow her up. It was a long time before she could fall asleep.

*

When she got up early in the morning Prema was aware of a strange new courage. We all make important decisions on the spur of the moment as though some divine power impelled us toward them, and so it was with Prema. Until yesterday she'd considered her parents' ideas as unchallengeable, but facing the problem courage was born in her, much in the way a quiet breeze coming against a mountain sweeps over the summit in a violent gust. Prema thought, 'Agreed, this body is my mother's and father's but whatever my own self, my soul, is to get must be got in this body. To hesitate now would not only be unfitting, it would be fatal. Why sacrifice your life for false principle? If a marriage isn't founded on love then it's just a business bargain with the body. Could you give yourself without love?' And she rebelled against the idea that she could be married off to somebody she had never seen.

After breakfast she had started to read when her father called her affectionately. 'Yesterday I went to see your principal and he had a lot of praise for you.'

'You're only saying that!'

'No, it's true.' Then he opened a drawer of his desk and took out a picture set in a velvet frame. He showed it to her and said, 'This boy came out first in the Civil Service examinations. You must have heard of him.'

He had brought up the subject in such a way as not to give away his intention, but it was clear to Prema, she saw through it at once. Without looking at the picture she said, 'No, I don't know who he is.'

170

With feigned surprise her father said, 'What? You haven't even heard his name? His picture and an article about him are in today's paper.'

'Suppose they are?' Prema said. 'The examinations don't mean anything to me. I always assumed that people who took those exams must be terribly conceited. After all, what do they aim for except to lord it over their wretched, penniless brothers? — And pile up a fortune doing it. That's no great career to aspire to.'

The objection was spiteful, unjust. Her father had assumed that after his eulogy she would be interested. When he'd listened to her answer he said sharply, 'You talk as though money and power mean nothing to you.'

'That's right,' she said, 'they don't mean a thing to me. I look for self-sacrifice in a man. I know some boys who wouldn't accept that kind of position even if you tried to force it on them.'

'Well, I've learned something new today!' he said sarcastically 'And still I see people swarming around trying to get the meanest little jobs — I'd just like to see the face of one of these fellows capable of such self-sacrifice. If I did I'd get down on my knees to him.'

Perhaps if she'd heard these words on another occasion Prema might have hung her head in shame. But this time, like a soldier with a dark tunnel behind him, there was no way for her to go except forward. Scarcely controlling her anger, her eyes full of indignation, she went to her room and from among several pictures of Keshav picked out the one she considered the worst and brought it back and set it down in front of her father. He wanted to give it no more than a casual glance, but at the first glimpse he was drawn to it. Keshav was tall and even though thin one recognized a strength and discipline about him; he was not particularly handsome but his face reflected such intelligence that one felt confidence in him.

While he looked at it her father said, 'Who is he?'

Prema, bowing her head, said hesitantly, 'He's in my class.'

'Is he of our community?'

Prema's face clouded over: her destiny was to be decided on the answer. She realised that it was useless to have brought out the picture. The firmness she had had for an instant weakened before this simple question. In a low voice she said, 'No, he's not, he's a Brahman.' And even while she was saying it, agitated she left the

171

room as though the atmosphere there were suffocating her, and on the other side of the wall she began to cry.

Her father's anger was so great at first that he wanted to call her out again and tell her plainly it was impossible. He got as far as the door, but seeing Prema crying his anger softened. He was aware of what Prema felt for this boy and he believed in education for women but he intended to maintain the family traditions. He would have sacrificed all his property for a suitable bridegroom of his own caste. But outside the limits of his community he could not conceive of any bridegroom worthy or noble enough; he could not imagine any disgrace greater than going beyond them.

'From today on you'll stop going to college,' he said with a harsh tone. 'If education teaches you to disregard our traditions, then education is wicked.'

Timidly Prema said, 'But it's almost time for the examinations.'

'Forget about them.'

Then he went into his room and pondered a long time.

*

One day six months later Prema's father came home and called Vriddha, his wife, for a private talk.

'As far as I know,' he said, 'Keshav's a well-brought-up and brilliant boy. I'm afraid that Prema's grieving to the point where she might take her life. You and I have tried to explain and so have others but nobody has had the slightest effect on her. What are we going to do about it?'

Anxiously his wife said, 'Let her, but if she has her way how can you face the dishonour? How could I ever have borne a wicked girl like that?'

He frowned and said with a tone of reproach, 'I've heard that a thousand times. But just how long can we moan about this caste tradition business? You're mistaken if you think the bird's going to stay hopping at home once it's spread its wings. I've thought about the problem objectively and I've come to the conclusion that we're obliged to face the emergency. I can't watch Prema die in the name of caste rules. Let people laugh but the time is not far off when all these old restrictions will be broken. Even today there have been hundreds of marriages outside the caste limitations. If the aim of marriage is a happy life for a man and a woman together we can't

172

oppose Prema.'

Vriddha was angry. 'If that's your intention then why ask me?' she said. 'But I say that I won't have anything to do with this marriage, and I'll never look at that girl's face again, I'll consider her as dead as our sons who died.'

'Well then, what else can you suggest?'

'What if we do let her marry this boy? He'll take his civil service examinations in two years and with what he has to offer it will be a great deal if he becomes a clerk in some office.'

'But what if Prema should kill herself?'

'Then let her — you've encouraged her, haven't you? If she doesn't care about us why should we blacken our name for her? Anyway, suicide's no game — it's only a threat. The heart's like a wild horse — until it's broken and bridled nobody can touch it. If her heart stays like that who's to say that she'll stick with Keshav for a whole life-time? The way she's in love with him today, well, she can be in love with somebody else just as much tomorrow. And because of this you're ready to be disgraced?'

Her husband gave her a questioning look. 'And if tomorrow she should go and marry Keshav, then what will you do? Then how much of your honour will be left? Out of shyness or consideration for us she may not have done anything yet, but if she decides to be stubborn there's nothing you or I can do.'

It had never occurred to Vriddha that the problem could have such a dreadful ending. His meaning struck her with the violence of a bullet. She sat silent for a moment as though the shock had scattered her wits. Then backing down, she said, 'What wild ideas you have! Until today I've never heard of a decent girl marrying according to her own wish.'

'You may not have heard of it but I have, I've seen it and it's entirely possible.'

'The day it happens will be my last!'

'But if it has to be this way isn't it preferable that we make the proper arrangements? If we're to be disgraced we may as well be efficient about it. Send for Keshav tomorrow and see what he has to say.'

*

Keshav's father lived off a government pension. By nature he was ill-tempered and miserly; he found satisfaction only in religious ostentation. He was totally without imagination and unable to respect the personal feelings of anybody else. At present he was still living in the same world in which he had passed his childhood and youth. The rising tide of progress he called ruination and hoped to save at least his own family from it by any means available to him. Therefore when one day Prema's father came to him and broached the prospect of her marrying Keshav, old Panditji could not control himself. Staring through eyes dim with anger he said, 'Are you drunk? Whatever this relationship may be it's not marriage. It appears that you too have had your head turned by the new ideas.'

'I don't like this sort of connection either,' Prema's father said gently. 'My ideas about it are just the same as yours. But the thing is that, being helpless, I had to come to see you. You're aware too of how willful today's youngsters have become. It's getting hard for us old-timers to defend our theories. I'm afraid that if these two become desperate they may take their lives.'

Old Panditji brought his foot down with a bang and shouted, 'What are you saying, Sir! Aren't you ashamed? We're Brahmans and even among Brahmans we're of high rank. No matter how low a Brahman may fall he can never be so degraded that he can countenance a marriage with a shop-keeping Baniya's daughter. The day noble Brahmans run out of daughters we can discuss the problem. I say you have a fantastic nerve even to bring this matter up with me.'

He was every bit as furious as Prema's father was humble, and the latter, unable to bear the humiliation any longer, went off cursing his luck.

Just then Keshav returned from college. Panditji sent for him at once and said severely, 'I've heard that you're betrothed to some Baniya girl. How far has this actually gone?'

Pretending ignorance, Keshav said, 'Who told you this?'

'Somebody. I'm asking you, is it true or not? If it's true and you've decided to go against your caste, then there's no more room for you in this house. You won't get one pice of my money. Whatever is in this house I've earned, and it's my right to give it to whoever I want. If you're guilty of this wicked conduct, you won't be permitted to put your foot inside my house.'

174

Keshav was familiar with his father's temper. He loved Prema and he intended to marry her in secret. His father wouldn't always be alive and he counted on his mother's affection; sustained by that love he felt that he was ready to suffer any hardship. But Keshav was like a faint-hearted soldier who loses his courage at the sight of a gun and turns back.

Like any average young fellow he would argue his theories with a passion and demonstrate his devotion with his tongue. But to suffer for them was beyond his capacity. If he persisted and his father refused to weaken he didn't know where he would turn, his life would be ruined.

In a low voice he said, 'Whoever told you that is a complete liar and nothing else.' Staring at him, Panditji said, 'So my information is entirely wrong?'

Yes, entirely wrong.'

'Then you'll write a letter to that shopkeeper this very moment and remember that if there's any more of this gossip he can regard you as his greatest enemy. Enough, go.'

Keshav could say no more. He walked away but it seemed to him that his legs were utterly numb.

*

The next day Prema sent this letter to Keshav.

Dearest Keshav,

I was terribly upset when I heard about the rude and callous way your father treated mine. Perhaps he's threatened you too, in which case I wait anxiously to hear what your decision is. I'm ready to undergo any kind of hardship with you. I'm aware of your father's wealth but all I need is your love to content me. Come tonight and have dinner with us. My mother and father are both eager to meet you.

I'm caught up in the dream of when the two of us will be joined by that bond that cannot be broken, that remains strong no matter how great the difficulties.

Your Prema

By evening there had been no reply to this letter. Prema's mother asked over and over again, 'Isn't Keshav coming?' And her father kept his eyes glued on the door. By nine o'clock there was still no sign of Keshav nor any letter.

In Prema's mind all sorts of fears and hopes revolved. Perhaps Keshav had had no chance to write a letter, no chance to come today so that tomorrow he would surely come. She read over again the love letters he'd written her earlier. How steeped in love was every word, how much emotion, anxiety and acute desire! Then she remembered the words he'd said a hundred times and how often he'd wept before her. It was impossible to despair with so many proofs, but all the same throughout the night she was tormented by anxiety.

Early in the morning Keshav's answer came. Prema took the letter with trembling hands and read it. The letter fell from her hands. It seemed to her that her blood had ceased to flow. He had written:

I'm in a terrible quandary about how to answer you. I've been desperate trying to figure out what to do and I've come to the conclusion that for the present it would be impossible for me to go against my father's orders. Don't think I'm a coward. I'm not being selfish either. But I don't have the strength to overcome the obstacles facing me. Forget what I told you before. At that time I had no idea of how hard it was going to be.

Prema drew a long, painful breath, then she tore up the letter and threw it away. Her eyes filled with tears. She had never had the slightest expectation that the Keshav she had taken into her heart of hearts as her husband could be so cruel. It was as though until now she'd been watching a golden vision but on opening her eyes it had vanished completely. All her hope had disappeared and she was left in darkness.

'What did Keshav write?' her mother asked.

Prema looked at the floor and said, 'He's not feeling well.' What else was there to say? She could not have borne the shame of revealing Keshav's brutal disloyalty.

She spent the whole day working around the house, as though there was nothing wrong. She made dinner for everyone that evening and ate with them, then until quite late she played the harmonium and sang.

In the morning they found her lying dead in her room at a moment when the golden rays of dawn bestowed on her face the illusory splendour of life.

# THE WORLD

# A Servant of the Nation

The servant of the nation said, 'There is only one way to redeem the country and that is to treat the low as brothers, the outcastes as equals. In the world all are brothers: no one is high, no one is low.'

The world cheered. 'How sublime a vision, how compassionate a heart!'

His beautiful daughter Indira heard and was plunged into a sea of care.

The servant of the people embraced a young man of low caste.

The world said, 'He is an angel, an apostle, the pilot of the ship of state!'

Indira watched and her eyes began to glow.

The servant of the people brought the young man of low caste inside the temple into the presence of God and said, 'Our God is in poverty, in misfortune and in degradation.'

The world said, 'How pure in heart he is! How wise!'

Indira looked and smiled.

Indira went to the servant of the people and said, 'Respected father, I wish to marry Mohan.'

The servant of the people looked at her with loving eyes and asked, 'Who is Mohan?'

Indira said joyously, 'Mohan is the honest, brave and good young man you embraced and brought into the temple.'

The servant of the people looked at her with the eyes of doom and turned away.

# The Chess Players

It was the era of Wajid Ali Shah*. Lucknow was plunged deep in luxurious living. Exalted and humble, rich and poor, all were sunk in luxury. While one might arrange parties for dancing and singing another would find enjoyment only in the drowsy ecstasy of opium. In every sphere of life pleasure and merry-making ruled supreme. Indulgence in luxury pervaded the government, the literary world, the social order, arts and crafts, industry, cuisine, absolutely every-where. The bureaucrats were steeped in gross sensuality, poets in describing lovers and the sufferings of separation, artisans in creat-ing intricate patterns of gold and silver thread and embroidery, merchants in selling eye-shadow, perfumes, unguents and coloring for the teeth. All eyes were dimmed with the intoxication of luxury. No one had any awareness of what was going on in the world. There were quail fights, betting on matches between fighting par-tridges, here the cloth for *causar*** spread out, there shouts of 'What luck, I've made an ace and twelve!' and elsewhere a fierce chess battle getting under way.

From king to beggar all were swept with the same antic spirit, to the point where when beggars were given money they spent it not on bread but on opium or *madak****. By playing chess, cards or *ganjifa***** the wits were sharpened, the process of thought was developed, one became accustomed to solving complex problems — arguments of this sort were presented with great vehemence. (The world is not free even today of people of this persuasion!). So if Mirza Sajjad Ali and Mir Raushan Ali spent most of their time sharpening their wits, what reasonable person could object? Both of them were masters of hereditary estates and had no worry about their income, so they could lounge around at home enjoying their

---

* The last king of Oudh (Avadh); the story takes place in 1856.
** A game of dice.
*** An intoxicant prepared from opium.
**** A type of card game.

idleness. After all, what else was there to do? Early in the morning, after breakfast, they would sit down, set out the board, arrange the chessmen, and warlike stratagems would begin. From then on they were quite unaware of when it was noon or afternoon or evening. Time and time again word would be sent from the kitchen that dinner was ready and the answer would come back: Get on with it, we're coming, set the table. It would reach the point where the cook, desperate, would serve their meal right in their chamber and the two friends would go on with both activities, eating and playing simultaneously.

In Mirza Sajjad Ali's household there was no elder, so the games took place in his drawing room. But this is not to say that the other people of Mirza's household were happy with these goings-on. And not only the members of his household but the neighbours and even the servants were constantly making malicious comments. 'The game's ill-omened! It's destroying the family. Heaven forbid that anybody should become addicted to it, he'd be utterly useless to God or man, at home or in the world! It's a dreadful sickness, that's what.' Even Mirza's wife, the Begam Sahiba, hated it so much that she sought every possible occasion to scold him. But she hardly ever found the chance, for the game would have begun before she woke and in the evening Mirzaji would be likely to appear in the bedroom only after she had gone to sleep. But the servants of course felt the full force of her rage. 'He's asked for *paan*, has he? Well, tell him to come and get it himself! He hasn't got time for his dinner? Then go and dump it on his head, he can eat it or give it to the dogs!' But to his face she could not say anything at all. She was not so angry with him as with Mir Sahib, whom she referred to as 'Mir the Troublemaker.' Possibly it was Mirzaji who laid all the blame on Mir in order to excuse himself.

One day the Begam Sahiba had a headache. She said to the maid, 'Go and call Mirza Sahib and have him get some medicine from the doctor. Be quick about it, run!' When the maid went to him Mirzaji said, 'Get along with you, I'll come in a moment or two.' The Begam Sahiba's temper flared at this. Who could put up with a husband playing chess while she had a headache? Her face turned scarlet. She said to the maid, 'Go and tell him that if he doesn't go at once I'll go out to the doctor myself *.' Mirzaji was immersed in a very

---

* For an aristocatic lady in *purdab* this would be inappropriate.

interesting game, in two more moves he would checkmate Mir Sahib. Irritated, he said, 'She's not on her deathbed, is she? Can't she be just a little patient?'

'Come now,' said Mir, 'go and see what she has to say. Women can be touchy, you know.'

'To be sure,' said Mirza, 'why shouldn't I go? You'll be check-mated in two moves.'

'My dear fellow, better not count on it. I've thought of a move that will checkmate you with all your pieces still on the board. But go on now, listen to her, why make her feel hurt for no reason at all?'

'I'll go only after I've checkmated you.'

'Then I won't play. Do go and hear her out.'

'I'll have to go to the doctor's, old man. It's not just a mere headache, it's an excuse to bother me.'

'Whatever it is, you really must indulge her.'

'Very well, but let me make just one more move.'

'Absolutely not, until you've gone to her I won't so much as touch a piece.'

When Mirza Sahib felt compelled to go to his wife the Begam Sahiba was frowning, but she said with a moan, 'You love your wretched chess so much that even if somebody were dying you wouldn't think of leaving it! Heaven forbid there should ever be another man like you!'

Mirza said, 'What can I tell you? Mir Sahib simply wouldn't agree. I had a most difficult time of it putting him off so I could come.'

'Does he think everybody is just as worthless as himself? Doesn't he have children too or has he just let them go to the dogs?'

'He's utterly mad about chess,' said Mirza. 'Whenever he comes I'm compelled to play with him.'

'Why don't you tell him off?'

'He's my equal in age and a couple of steps above me in rank, I'm obliged to be courteous with him.'

'In that case, *I'll* tell him off! If he gets angry, let him. Is he supporting us, after all? As they say, "If the queen sulks, she'll only hurt herself." Hiriya!' she called her maid, 'Go out and take up the chessboard, and say to Mir Sahib, "The master won't play now, pray be good enough to take your leave."'

'For heaven's sake, don't do anything so outrageous!' said Mirza. 'Do you want to disgrace me? Wait, Hiriya, where are you going?'

'Why don't you let her go? Anybody who stops her will be simply killing me! Very well, then, stop her, but see if you can stop me.'

Saying this, the Begam Sahiba headed for the drawing room in high dudgeon. Poor Mirza turned pale. He began to implore his wife: 'For God's sake, in the name of the holy Prophet Husain! If you go to him it will be like seeing me laid out!' But the Begam did not pay the slightest attention to him. But when she reached the door of the drawing room all of a sudden, finding herself about to appear before a man not of her household, her legs felt as though paralyzed. She peeked inside, and as it happened, the room was empty. Mir Sahib had done a little shifting of the chess pieces and was now strolling outside in order to demonstrate his innocence. The next thing that happened was that the Begam went inside, knocked over the chessboard, flung some of the pieces under the sofa and others outside, then clapped the double doors shut and locked them. Mir Sahib was just outside the door. When he saw the chessmen being tossed out and the jingling of bangles reached his ears he realized that the Begam Sahiba was in a rage. Silently he took his way home.

Mirza said, 'You have committed an outrage!'

She answered, 'If Mir Sahib comes back here I'll have him kicked out straightaway. If you devoted such fervour to God you'd be a saint. You're to play chess while I slave away looking after this household? Are you going to the doctor's or are you still putting it off?'

When he came out of his house Mirza, instead of going to the doctor's, went to Mir Sahib's and told him the whole story. Mir Sahib said, 'So I guessed when I saw the chess pieces sailing outside. I took off at once. She seems to be quick to fly off the handle. But you've spoiled her too much, and that's not at all the way to do things. What concern is it of hers what you do away from her part of the house? Her work is to look after the home. What business does she have with anything else?'

'Well, tell me, where are we going to meet now?'

'No problem, we have this whole big house, so that's settled, we'll meet here.'

'But how am I going to placate the Begam Sahiba? She was furious when I sat down to play at home, so if I play here it could cost me my life.'

'Let her babble, in a few days she'll be all right. But of course you ought to show a little backbone yourself.'

*

For some unknown reason Mir Sahib's Begam considered it most fitting for her husband to stay far away from home. For this reason she had never before criticized his chess-playing, but on the contrary, if he was late in going she reminded him. For these reasons Mir Sahib had been deluded into thinking his wife was extremely serious and humble. But when they began to set up the chess board in the drawing room and Mir Sahib was at home all day the Begam Sahiba was very distressed. This was a hindrance to her freedom, and all day long she would yearn to be at the door looking out.

Meantime, the servants had begun to gossip. Formerly they had lain around all day in idleness, if someone came to the house, if someone left, it was no business of theirs. Now they were living in fear all twenty-four hours of the day. Orders would come for *paan*, then for sweets. And, like some lover's heart, the *hookah* had to be kept burning constantly. They would go to the mistress and say, 'The master's chess games are giving us a lot of trouble. We're getting blisters on our feet from running all day. What kind of a game is it that starts at dawn and goes on till evening? Diversion for an hour or two, that's enough for any game. Of course we're not complaining, we're your slaves, whatever you command naturally we'll do it; but this game is positively sinister! Whoever plays it never prospers, and surely some disaster will befall his home. It can reach the point where one neighbourhood after another's been known to go to rack and ruin. Everybody in this part of town is gossiping about it. We have eaten your salt, we're grieved to hear bad things about the master, but what can we do?'

Hearing this, the Begam Sahiba would say, 'I don't like it myself, but he won't listen to anybody, so what can be done?'

In their quarter there were also a few people from an earlier generation who began to imagine all sorts of disasters: 'There's no hope now. If our nobles are like this, then God help the country! This chess playing will be the ruin of the kingdom. The omens are bad.'

186

The entire realm was in an uproar. Subjects were robbed in broad daylight and nobody was there to hear their appeals. All the wealth of the countryside had been drawn into Lucknow to be squandered on whores, clowns and the satisfaction of every kind of vice. The debt to the East India Company kept on growing day by day, and day by day the general misery was getting harder to bear. Throughout the land, because of the wretched conditions, the yearly taxes were no longer collected. Time and again the British resident warned them, but everyone in Lucknow was so drowned in the intoxication of sensual indulgence that not a soul gave any heed.

Well then, the chess games continued in Mir Sahib's drawing room over the course of several months. Newer strategies were devised, new defences organized, and ever new battle formations planned. From time to time quarrels broke out as they played, and they even reached the point of exchanging vulgar insults; but peace was quickly restored between the two friends. At times the game would come to a halt and Mirzaji would return home in a huff and Mir Sahib would go and sit in his own chamber. But with a good night's sleep all the bad feelings would be calmed; early in the morning the two friends would arrive in the drawing room.

One day when they sat engrossed in thorny chess problems an officer of the royal army arrived on horseback and inquired for Mir Sahib. Mir Sahib panicked, wondering what disaster was about to come down on his head. Why had he been summoned? The case appeared desperate. To the servants he said, 'Tell him I'm not at home.'

'If he's not at home where is he?' the horseman demanded. The servant said he didn't know — what was this all about? 'How can I tell *you* what it's about?' said the officer. 'Maybe soldiers are being levied for the army. It's no joke, being the master of rent-free estates. When he has to go to the front lines he'll find out what it's all about.'

'Very well, go along, he'll be informed.'

'It's not just a matter of informing him. I'll come back tomorrow, I have orders to take him back with me.'

The horseman left. Mir Sahib was shaking with terror. He said to Mirzaji, 'Tell me, sir, what's going to happen now?'

'It's a great misfortune! What if I'm summoned too?'

'The bastard said he was coming back tomorrow.'

'It's a calamity, no doubt of it. If we have to go to the front we'll

187

die before our time.'

'Now listen, there's one way out: we won't meet here at the house any more. Starting tomorrow we'll have our game in some deserted place out on the banks of the Gomti. Who could find us there? When that fine fellow comes for me he'll have to go back without us.'

'By Allah, that's a splendid idea! That's certainly the best way.'

In the meantime, Mir Sahib's Begam was saying to that cavalry officer, 'You've got them out of the way very nicely,' and he answered, 'I'm used to making such jackasses dance to my tune. Chess has robbed them of all their common sense and courage. After this they won't stay at home, whatever happens.'

*

From the next day on the two friends would set out from the house at the crack of dawn, carrying with them a rather small carpet and a box of prepared *paan*, and go to the other side of the Gomti river to an old ruined mosque which had probably been built in the time of Nawab Asafuddaula *. Along the way they would   pick   up tobacco, a pipe and some wine, and spread their carpet in the mosque, fill the *hookah* and sit down to play. After that they had no care for this world or the next. Apart from 'check' and 'checkmate,' not another word came out of their mouths. No *yogi* could have been more profoundly plunged in trance. At noon when they felt hungry they would go to some baker's shop and eat something, smoke a pipeful, and then return to engage once more in battle. At times they would even forget all about eating.

Meantime, the political situation in the country was becoming desperate. The East India Company's armies were advancing on Lucknow. There was commotion in the city. People were taking their children and fleeing to the countryside. But our two players were not in the least concerned about it. When they left home they took to the narrow alleyways, fearing lest some government official might catch a glimpse of them and have them forced into military service. They wanted to enjoy the thousands in income from their estates without giving anything in return.

---

*'Ruler of Oudh, 1775-97; his reign was noted both for debauchery and for the construction of many buildings, especially mosques.

One day the two friends were sitting in the ruined mosque playing chess. Mirza's game was rather weak and Mir Sahib was checking him at every move. At the same time the Company's soldiers could be seen approaching. This was an army of Europeans on their way to impose their rule on Lucknow.

Mir Sahib said, 'The British army's coming. God save us!'

Mirza said, 'Let them come, but now get out of check.'

'Maybe we ought to have a look, let's stand here where we can't be seen.'

'You can look later, what's the rush? Check again.'

'They have artillery too. There must be about five thousand men. What odd-looking soldiers! They've got red faces, just like monkeys, it's really frightening.'

'Don't try to get out of it, sir! Use these tricks on somebody else. Checkmate!'

'What a strange fellow you are! Here we have the city struck with calamity and you can only think of ways to checkmate. Do you have any idea how we're going to get home if the city's surrounded?'

'When it's time to go home we'll see about it then. This is checkmate, your king's finished now.'

The army had marched by. It was now ten in the morning. A new game was set up.

Mirza said, 'What are we going to do about food today?'

'Well, today's a fast day — are you feeling hungrier than usual?'

'Not in the least. But I wonder what's happening in the city.'

'Nothing at all's happening in the city. People are eating their dinner and settling down comfortably for an afternoon nap. The King's in his harem, no doubt.'

By the time they sat down to play again it was three. This time Mirzaji's game was weak. Four o'clock had just struck when the army was heard marching back. Nawab Wajid Ali had been taken prisoner and the army was conducting him to some unknown destination. In the city there was no commotion, no massacre, not a drop of blood was spilled. Until now no king of an independent country could ever have been overthrown so peacefully, without the least bloodshed. This was not that non-violence which delights the gods, but rather the sort of cowardice which makes even great cowards shed tears. The king of the vast country of Oudh was leaving it a captive, and Lucknow remained deep in its sensual slumber. This was the final stage of political decadence.

189

Mirzaji said, 'Those tyrants have imprisoned His Majesty.'

'I suppose so. Look here — check.'

'Just a moment, sir, I don't feel in the mood now. The poor King must be weeping tears of blood at this moment.'

'I'm sure he is — what luxuries will he enjoy as a prisoner? Checkmate!'

'Everybody has to suffer some change in his fortunes,' said Mirza. 'But what a painful situation!'

'True, that's the way things are. Look, checkmate! That does it, you can't get out of it now.'

'God's oath, you're hard-hearted. You can watch a great catastrophe like this and feel no grief. Alas, poor Wajid Ali Shah!'

'First save your own king, then you can mourn for His Majesty. It's checkmate now. Your hand on it!'

The army passed by, taking the King with them. As soon as they were gone Mirza again set up the chess pieces. The sting of defeat is bitter. Mir said, 'Come now, let us compose an elegy for His Majesty.' But Mirza's patriotism had vanished with his defeat. He was eager for vengeance.

*

It was evening. In the ruins the swallows were returning and settling in their nests, the bats began to chitter. But the players were still at it, like two blood-thirsty warriors doing battle together. Mirzaji had lost three games in a row; the outlook for this fourth game was not good either. He played each move carefully, firmly resolved to win, but one move after the other turned out to be so ill-conceived that his game kept deteriorating. For his part, Mir Sahib was singing a *gazal* and snapping his fingers from sheer high spirits, as though he had come upon some hidden treasure. Listening to him, Mirzaji was furious, but praised him in order to conceal his exasperation. But as his game worsened his patience began to slip out of control until he reached the point of getting angry at everything Mir said.

'Don't change your move, sir,' he would say. 'How can you go back on a move? Whatever move is to be made, make it just once. Why is your hand on that piece? Leave it alone! Until you figure out your move don't so much as touch your piece! You're taking half-an-hour for every move, that's against the rules. Anyone who takes

190

more than five minutes for a move may be understood to be checkmated. You changed your move again! Just be quiet and put that piece back there.'

Mir Sahib's queen was in danger. He said, 'But when did I make my move?'

'You've already made it. Put the piece right there, in that same square.'

'Why should I put it in that square? When did I take my hand off the piece?'

'If you wait till doomsday to make your move, you'll still have to make it.'

'You're the one who's cheating! Victory and defeat depend on fate, you can't win by cheating.'

'Then it's settled, you've lost this game.'

'How have I lost it?'

'Then put the piece back in the same square where it was.'

'Why should I put it there? I won't!'

'Why should you put it there? You *have* to put it there.'

The quarrel was getting worse. Each stuck to his position, neither one would give an inch. Their words began to move to irrelevant matters. Mirza said, 'If anybody in your family had ever played chess then you might be familiar with the rules. But they were just grass-cutters. So how can you be expected to play chess? Real aristocracy is quite another thing. Nobody can become a noble just by having had some rent-free estates given to him.'

'What! Your own father must have cut grass! My people have been playing chess for generations.'

'Come off it, you spent your whole life working as a cook in Gaziuddin Haidar's house and now you're going around posing as an aristocrat.'

'Why are you defaming your own ancestors?' said Mir. 'They must all have been cooks. My people have always dined at the King's own table.'

'You grass-cutter you! Stop your bragging.'

'You check your tongue or you'll be sorry! I won't stand for talk like that. I put out the eyes of anybody who frowns at me. Do you have the courage?'

'So you want to find out how brave I am! Come on then, let's have it out, whatever the consequences.'

Said Mir, 'And who do you think is going to let you push them

191

around!'

The two friends drew the swords from their belts. It was a chivalric age when everybody went around carrying swords, daggers, poniards and the like. Both of them were sensualists but not cowards. They were politically debased, so why should they die for king or kingdom? But they did not lack personal courage. They challenged one another formally, the swords flashed, there was a sound of clanging. Both fell wounded, and both writhed and expired on the spot. They had not shed a single tear for their king but gave up their lives to protect a chess queen.

Darkness was coming on. The chess game had been set up. The two kings each on his throne sat there as though lamenting the death of these two heroes.

Silence spread over all. The broken archways of the ruins, the crumbling walls and dusty minarets looked down on the corpses and mourned.

# The Road to Hell

I don't know when I fell asleep last night. For a long time I was reading the 'Lives of the Holy Men.' What great souls they were, caring only for the love of God, completely intoxicated with it! Devotion like that can come only from strict spiritual discipline. Wouldn't I be capable of such discipline? What other joy is left for me in this life? There may be some who love jewels, God knows, but as for me jewels are a torment to my eyes; some might give up their life for wealth but for me just to hear it mentioned starts a fever in me. Yesterday that crazy Sushila had a wonderful time helping me to make myself beautiful — no matter how much I tried to stop her, she wouldn't listen. Then what I'd most feared finally happened. For every minute I laughed with her I was to cry all the more. Is there any other woman in the world whose husband goes into a violent rage when he sees her? Any other woman who hears her husband say, 'You're destroying my hopes for the other world and nothing else, the way you're made up makes that plain,' without wanting to take poison? Finally I went downstairs and began to read the 'Lives.' Now I shall worship only Lord Krishna in Brinda-ban, I shall show him my beauty, and when he sees it he will not grow angry for he will know what is in my heart.

*

Lord! How can I say what is in my heart? You dwell within me, you know all that is most secret in me. I wish I could tell him my desires, serve him as a wife should, move only at his bidding, I wish he might never feel the slightest pain from anything I do or anything concerning me. It's not his fault — whatever was in my stars has come to pass. But even knowing all this when I see him coming then my heart sinks, I grow deathly pale, I feel dizzy, I long not to see him, not even to have to talk to him. No one could ever feel so miserable even seeing his worst enemy. The moment I see him coming my heart starts to pound. Whenever he goes away for a day

193

or two it's as though a weight is lifted off my heart. I talk, I even laugh, a little happiness starts to come into my life, but at the first news that he's come back everything grows dark around me. I don't know why I should feel this way, but it seems to me that in an earlier birth we were enemies, and to take vengeance for this old hatred he married me — that former existence is still living in our hearts. Otherwise why would he be angry whenever he sees me and why would the sight of him disgust me? No marriage is meant to be like this! How much happier I was at home. Perhaps I might have stayed there and been happy. But because of the accursed custom it's felt to be inevitable that every unfortunate girl must be tied to the neck of some man or other. They don't know how many tender hearts shaken with longings are trampled under its foot. The sweetest imaginings — whatever is best in man, most sublime and beautiful, its living image rises up and appears before one as soon as the word is mentioned. But what is that word for me? A spear to stab the heart, a mote in the eye, an arrow of bitterness piercing the breast. I always see Sushila laughing. She never complains about being poor. She has no jewels, no clothes, she lives in a tiny rented house, she does all the housework with her own hands, but all the same I've never seen her cry. If I had my way, I'd exchange my wealth for whatever she has today. When she sees her husband coming home smiling, all the shabbiness of her life disappears, her heart is a yard wide with joy. In his embrace there's a happiness I'd sacrifice the wealth of the three worlds for.

*

Today I couldn't control myself and I asked him, 'Why did you marry me?' The question's been in my mind for months but I'd held it back. The cup spilled over today. When he heard the question he looked confused and irritated, shrugged and said, 'To look after the house, to take the job of managing it, not for anything else. Did you think it was to have a good time?' So without a housekeeper the place would have seemed like a deserted house to you? Servants would have wasted the household money, and if something fell on the floor it would have stayed there, no one would bother to pick it up. So it seemed that I was brought to this house to keep it in order! I was supposed to maintain it and be grateful to him that everything in it belonged to me. The money's the big thing and I'm just here to

194

look after it. A house like this ought to be set on fire at once! Until now, without knowing it, I've been the chief housekeeper, not of course as good a one as he thought I should be but according to my own capacity, surely. I swear that from today on I won't touch anything under any circumstances. I know this: no man marries to get himself a housekeeper and he said what he said out of spite. But Sushila spoke true, without a wife his house would have been as empty for him as a cage without a bird. This is the fate of us women!

*

I don't know why he's so suspicious of me. From the time fate brought me to this house I've seen him glare at me suspiciously. Why? If I just put a flower in my hair he begins to scowl. I never go anywhere, never talk to anybody, and still he's suspicious! It's intolerable to be treated so shabbily. As though I didn't have any pride of my own. Why does he think I'm so vile? — isn't he ashamed of being suspicious of me? If a one-eyed man sees anybody laugh he thinks people are laughing at him. Maybe he's got the notion that I'm mocking him. Perhaps this is what happens to your mind when you try to do something beyond your powers. A beggar sitting on a king's throne can't sleep in peace; one enemy after another seems to appear on every side. I think this must be the state of any old man who marries.

Today I was going out to see the temple decorations for Krishna's birthday — Sushila had told me about it. Any man of average intelligence can understand that going out dressed like some old peasant woman is a way of making a fool of yourself, but suddenly he popped up from I don't know where and frowning at me said, 'What are you getting dressed up for?'

I told him I was just going out for a little to see the celebrations at the temple. As soon as he heard this he frowned and said, 'There's no need for you to go. For a woman who can't serve her husband properly it's not a virtue, it's a sin to go to the temple. You want to get away from me — I know women's tricks.'

I got so angry that I couldn't say a thing. I went right away to change my clothes and swore I'd never go to the temple again. Is there no limit to his distrust? I don't know what I was thinking that held me back, I ought to have answered him that I'd leave the house that instant without being afraid of anything he might do

195

about it.

He's surprised that I'm always sad and depressed, in his heart he feels I'm ungrateful. Maybe he thinks he conferred a great privilege on me by marrying me. I was supposed to be overwhelmed with joy at becoming the mistress of such vast property and wealth, I was expected to sing his praises on every mountain-top.

But I don't do anything of the sort, instead I mope around with a long face. Still, there are times when I actually feel sorry for the poor man. He doesn't understand that there's something in a woman's life which can't be lost without heaven itself turning into hell.

*

He's been sick for three days. The doctor says it's pneumonia and there's no hope of saving him. But somehow I don't feel any distress. I didn't used to be so hard-hearted, I don't know where my kindness has gone. Whenever I saw a sick person my heart used to grow faint with pity; I could never bear to hear anyone cry.

But for three days I've been listening to him groaning on his bed in the next room and I haven't gone to see him. How could I possibly even shed a tear? It seems to me as though there's no relationship between us at all. I don't care if anybody calls me a monster or a bitch, but I haven't the slightest hesitation in saying that I feel a kind of spiteful pleasure in his illness. He's kept me here in a prison — I won't give it the pure name of marriage, it's just been a prison. I'm not so big-hearted that I can revere someone who's kept me a prisoner or that I'll kiss the feet that kicked me. It occurred to me that God is punishing him for his wickedness. A woman doesn't become a man's wife just by being chained to him. For a marriage to be a marriage the heart has to be stirred at least once by love.

I can hear my husband cursing me over and over again while he lies in his room, blaming me entirely for his illness, but I don't care at all. Whoever wants his property and his money can take it, it's of no use to me.

*

I've been a widow now for three months, at least that's what people say. Anyone who wants to can say it, but I consider myself the very same as before. I didn't break my wedding bangles — why should I? Even before I didn't streak the part in my hair with cinnabar like other married women and I don't do it now. The grown-up son from the first marriage saw to the old man's funeral rites, I stayed out of it. Everyone in the house has his own way of criticizing me. If anybody sees me with a flower in my hair they screw up their faces, if they see me wearing jewellery they glare, but it doesn't bother me in the least. To irk them I wear bright saris and lots of jewels and I don't feel the slightest sorrow. I've been freed from captivity. A few days ago I went to Sushila's house. It's a tiny house, there's nothing fancy and no furniture, there are not even *charpoys*, but how happily Sushila lives in it. When I see her joy all kinds of imaginings begin to rise in my heart — why should I call them nasty when I don't really think they are? How much pleasure there is in their lives, their eyes are always smiling, tender smiles play on their lips, a stream of love seems to flow in their words. With this happiness — no matter how momentary it may be — their lives are a success, no one can mistake it, the memory of it suffices for all time, it's a plectrum to stir the heart forever with sweet music.

One day I said to Sushila, 'If your husband went somewhere far away would you just weep and die?'

Sushila answered gravely, 'No, sister, I wouldn't die. His memory would always be fresh, even if he spent years away.'

That is the love I want, my heart goes on trembling for the awakening of that music, I also want such memories as will make my heart vibrate always, an intoxication that will engulf me forever.

\*

I sobbed all through the night. I don't know why my heart was so full. My life seemed to lie spread before me like a desert where there was nothing green but a few scrubby weeds. The whole house was ready to gobble me up, I was becoming so jumpy I couldn't keep still. These days I feel no impulse to look at the religious books, I have no wish to go walking anywhere. I don't know myself what I want. Yet what I don't know my body knows, I am the living embodiment of my desires, every one of my limbs cries out with the anguish inside me.

The restlessness of my mind has reached that final stage where I feel neither shame nor fear of people's contempt. For the greedy, selfish father and mother who threw me into the pit, for the heartless creature who hypocritically took the marriage vows with me, for all of them I feel an endless hatred, I want to see them shamed. I want to disgrace them by disgracing myself. By giving up my life I want to see them die. My womanliness has vanished. In my heart a wild fire has begun to blaze.

Everyone in the house was sleeping. Silently I went downstairs, opened the door and left the house, as someone overcome by the heat might go out and run toward any open place. I'd been suffocating in that house.

On the road the shops were closed, all was still. Suddenly an old woman appeared, startling me as though she'd been a ghost. She came close to me and looked me up and down and said, 'What road are you looking for?'

Bitterly I said, 'The road to death.'

The old woman said, 'In your fate it is written that your life holds many joys in store. The dark night is over, the light of dawn is in the skies.'

Laughing, I said, 'Are your eyes so sharp that even in the dark you can read the writing of the fates?'

'I don't read with my eyes, child,' the old woman said, 'I read with the mind — I haven't grown old without learning something. Your evil days are past and the good ones are coming. Don't laugh, child, I've been doing this work for a long time.

Because of this old woman many a girl who was about to throw herself into the river sleeps on a bed of flowers, and some who were ready to drink a cup of poison are drinking milk. And so I come out late of nights to see if by my help some unfortunate girl may be saved. I ask nothing in return — I have everything I need from the Lord — my desire is only to do some kindness to others in so far as I can — money for those who want money, children for those who want children, what else shall I say? I can recite the spell which will fulfill anyone's desires.'

I said, 'I want neither wealth nor children. What I want is not in your power to give.'

She laughed. 'Daughter, I know what you want, you want that thing which can make a heaven of this earth and which gives greater bliss than the blessings of the gods, the flower of heaven, the new moon, the rarest thing. But in my spells is the power to provide even this destiny. You thirst for love, and I can set you on a ship to bear you over the sea of love, tossed about by the very waves of love.'

Becoming curious, I asked, 'Mother, where is your house?'

'Very close, daughter, come along and I'll bring you there —trust me.'

She seemed to me to be a goddess come down from heaven. I went along with her.

\*

Alas, that old woman I took for a goddess was a witch from hell. I looked for nectar and found poison; I longed for a chaste love and I fell into a foul, poisonous ditch. I did not find what was not to be found. I desired a bliss like Sushila's, not the sensual wallowing of a whore. But once in your life a step's been taken on the wrong road it's hard to come back on the right one.

Still, the responsibility for my ruin is not on my head but on my mother and father and that old man who wanted to be my husband. I would not write these lines except with the idea that people who read this history of my soul may have their eyes opened. I say again, for your daughters do not look for wealth, property or prestige, look only for a husband. If you can't find the right one then let your daughter remain a spinster or poison her, strangle her, but don't marry her to an ugly old man. A woman can bear the most agonizing grief, the greatest afflictions, anything, but she cannot bear the trampling down of the longings of her youth.

As for me, there is no hope left in this life. I would not exchange even this vile existence for the one I've left behind.

## Miss Padma

After she had achieved success as a lawyer Miss Padma discovered a new experience: the emptiness of life. Considering marriage an unnatural bond, she had decided that she would remain independent and enjoy life. When she had got her M. A. and Law degrees she began her practice. She was young, beautiful, soft-spoken, and also extremely intelligent. There was nothing to stand in her way. Quick as a flash she left her young male colleagues far behind as she forged ahead and by now her salary was at times more than a thousand a month. Now there was no longer much need for hard work and racking her brains; most of her cases were of a kind she was already familiar with so that there seemed to be no necessity for any kind of preparation. She had acquired considerable confidence in her powers. She had learned the formulas by which one triumphs at the bar; consequently she now found she had a great deal of leisure time, which she spent reading romances, strolling, going to the cinema and visiting friends. Holding that some minor vice was absolutely necessary to make life happy, she became addicted to gardening. She would order all sorts of seeds and enjoy watching them sprout and bloom and bear fruit. But all the same she continued to experience the emptiness of life.

It was not that she was indifferent to men; on the contrary, she had no shortage of lovers. Had she possessed nothing but youth and beauty she still would have suffered no lack of worshippers, but in her case youth and beauty were joined to wealth as well, so how could there fail to be a flock of admirers? Padma was not averse to sexual enjoyment; what she detested was dependence and making marriage the chief occupation of life. So long as she could remain free and savour sensual pleasure why shouldn't she? She saw no moral obstacle to enjoyment since she considered it merely an appetite of the body. This appetite could be appeased by any neat, clean shop, and Padma was always looking for a shop like that. The customer takes from the shop the things he likes. So also Padma. Therefore she had dozens of lovers — lawyers, professors,

doctors, noblemen. But they were every one of them mere sensualists — the kind who like bees unconcernedly drank the nectar and
flew away. There was not even one she felt she could rely on. This
was the moment when she realized that her heart demanded not
just physical enjoyment but something more as well: a total self-
dedication, and this she had not found.

Among her lovers there was a certain Mr. Prasad — a handsome
man, and learned. He was a professor in a local college, and also a
worshipper of the ideal of free love. Padma became infatuated with
him and wanted to keep him attached to her, to make him completely her own; but Prasad did not fall into her clutches.

One evening Padma was about to go out for a walk when Prasad
arrived. The walk was postponed. There was far more pleasure in
chatting than in strolling, and today Miss Padma was on the point of
speaking of her deeper feelings to Prasad. She had, in fact, decided,
after much soul-searching, to speak frankly.

With her gaze fixed on Prasad's intoxicating eyes she said, 'Why
don't you come and stay here in my bungalow?'

'Oh,' said Prasad with malicious amusement, 'the result of that
would only be that in two or three months we wouldn't even be
talking to one another.'

'I fail to get your point,' said Padma.

'The point is simply what I'm saying.'

'But after all, why?'

'I don't want to lose my independence,' said Prasad, 'you don't
want to lose yours. If your lovers come to you I'll be jealous, and
vice versa. Ill feeling will spring up, then hostility and you'll kick
me out of the house. The house is yours! If this ends up hurting me,
how can our friendship continue?'

The two of them were silent for a moment. Prasad had set forth
the situation in such clear, straightforward, blunt words that they
could find nothing to say.

Finally, it was Prasad who thought of a new approach. He said,
'Until we take an oath that from this day forward I am yours and you
are mine there's no way that we can live together.'

'Will you take such an oath?'

'First tell me that you will.'

'I will,' said Padma.

'Then so will I.'

'But except for this one thing I'll remain free in every other matter.'

'And I except for this one thing will remain free too.'

'Agreed.'

'Agreed!'

'When do we start?'

'Whenever you say.'

'Then I say, right from tomorrow on.'

'It's a deal. But if you don't behave in accordance with the oath, then what?'

'And what about you?' said Padma.

'*You* can throw me out of the house; but how could I punish you?'

'You'd just give me up, what else could you do?'

'Not at all, that wouldn't satisfy me in the least. If it came to that, I'd want to debase you, even kill you.'

'How cruel you are, Prasad!'

'So long as we're both free, neither of us has the right to criticize the other. But once we're bound by the oath I won't be able to stand any disregard of that oath, nor will you. You have the means to punish me, but I have none to punish you. The law gives me no rights. I could enforce the oath only by my brute strength, but how could I alone do anything in front of all these servants of yours?'

'But you're looking only at the dark side of the picture. While I'm yours, then this house, these servants and property, everything is yours. We both of us know that there's no greater social sin than envy. I can't say whether you love me or not, but I'm ready to do, to bear, anything for your sake.'

'Are you really sincere, Padma?'

'With all my heart.'

'But somehow or other I can't quite believe you.'

'But I believe you completely.'

'But understand this, I'm not going to stay on in your house as a guest. I'll stay only as master.'

'You shall stay as master not only of the house but of me as well. And I shall be your mistress.'

*

Professor Prasad and Miss Padma live together and are happy. For both of them the ideal of life they had set for themselves has become true. Prasad earns a salary of only two hundred, but now it doesn't bother him to spend twice that. Formerly he drank liquor only occasionally, but now he's drunk day and night. Now he has his own private car, his own private servants, he goes on ordering every sort of expensive item and Padma happily tolerates all his extravagances. Rather, there's no question of toleration, she herself is delighted to dress him in fine suits and set him up in the most luxurious style. Now probably the grandest noblemen of the city don't have a watch to match Professor Prasad's. The more Padma gives way to him, the more he abuses her generosity. At times indeed he seems intolerable to her but for some incomprehensible reason she finds herself under his thumb. If she sees Prasad the least bit moody or worried, her heart is troubled. On top of this, he begins saying sarcastic things to her. Those who were her former lovers also try to provoke her and make her dissatisfied but as soon as she goes to Prasad she forgets everything. Prasad has acquired complete domination over her, and he's well aware of it. Prasad has read her profoundly and come to understand her perfectly.

But just as in politics authority tends to be abused, in the same way in love as well it is abused, and the one who's weaker must be made to pay. Padma, so proud of herself, was now Prasad's whore and why should Prasad fail to profit from her weakness? In analyzing her he had hit the nail on the head and gradually he was driving it in deeper every day, to the point where nights he began to come home late. He would not take Padma with him; he would make some excuse, such as a headache, not to go out with her, then when she'd left for a stroll he'd take his car out and dash off.

By now two years had passed and Padma was pregnant; she had also begun to get fat. The freshness and charm her looks had had were now no more. She was like, as it were, a once rare commodity no longer prized from over-availability.

So it was that one day when Padma returned home Prasad had disappeared. She became extremely irritated. For some time now she'd been observing Prasad's mood changing, and today she'd got up the courage to speak plainly to him. Ten o'clock struck, then eleven, then midnight, and Padma continued to sit up waiting for him. Dinner got cold, the servants went to bed. Time and time again she would get up, go to the door and scan the street. Some time between twelve and one Prasad came home.

Padma had screwed up her courage, but as soon as she stood

before Prasad she became aware of the weakness of her position. Nevertheless she asked him in a fairly firm voice, 'Where were you so late? Do you have any idea how late it is?'

At this instant she appeared to Prasad like the image of ugliness. He had gone to the cinema with a woman student from his college. He said, 'You ought to have gone to sleep. In your condition you ought to get as much rest as possible.'

Padma's courage mounted. She said, 'Answer my question even if it finishes me off.'

'Then you can finish me off too,' said Prasad.

'For some time now I've watched your feelings change.'

'Your eyesight must have gained considerably in acuteness.'

'You've been cheating on me, I can see *that* plainly enough.'

'I didn't sell myself to you. If you're really fed up with me I'm ready to leave right now.'

'How can you threaten to leave? You gave up nothing when you came here.'

'I didn't give up anything? You have the nerve to say that! I can see you're turning vicious. You think you've clipped my wings, but at this point I'm ready to shake you off. Right now!'

Padma's courage seemed to have been extinguished. Prasad was already taking out his suitcase. Humbly she said to him, 'I haven't said anything for you to get so angry. I was only asking you where you were. Don't you even want me to have *that* much right? I never do anything against your wishes and yet you scold me for anything and everything. You don't feel the slightest pity for me! I ought to get a little sympathy from you. Haven't I always been ready to do anything for you? And now, when I'm in this condition, you turn away from me . . .'

She choked up and, laying her head on the table, began to sob.

Prasad had achieved total victory.

*

Motherhood was now a very unpopular topic with Padma. One concern alone hovered over her. At times she would tremble with fear and regret. Prasad's lack of restraint got worse every day. What should she do, what should she not do? She had reached the final stage of her pregnancy and no longer went to court but sat at home alone the whole day. Prasad would come home in the evening, have his tea and then fly off again and not come back before eleven or midnight. Nor did he conceal from her where he went. It was as though he had come to hate the very sight of her. Pregnant, sallow, troubled, suspicious, depressed —nevertheless, she did not cease to try to tie Prasad to her with make-up and jewellery. But the more she tried the more Prasad was put off. In her condition, cosmetics made her seem even uglier.

The labour pains began. Prasad was not aware. A nurse and a woman doctor were standing by, but Prasad's absence made Padma's labour all the more terrible. When she saw the child beside her she felt a wave of happiness; but then, not finding Prasad with her, she turned her face away from the child, as though she'd found a worm in a sweet fruit.

When after five days she left the lying-in room, as though getting out of jail, she had turned into a naked sword. Having become a mother she experienced a strange power in herself.

She gave a check to the servant and sent him to the bank. She had to settle some bills rising from her delivery. He came back empty-handed.

'The money?' Padma asked.

He said, 'The teller told me that Prasad Babu took all the money out.'

Padma felt as though she'd been shot. She had saved up 20,000 rupees as though it had been her life's blood. For this child! Alas! On leaving the maternity room she learned that Prasad had taken a girl from the college and gone off to England to tour. Furious, she went into the house, picked up Prasad's picture, dashed it to the ground and stamped on it. Whatever he had left behind she gathered together, put a match to it and spat on his name.

A month went by. Padma was standing at the gate of her bungalow holding her child. Her rage had finally turned to grief and despair. Sometimes she felt sorry for the child, sometimes affection, sometimes hatred. On the road she saw a European woman going along with her husband pushing a perambulator with their child in it. She watched the lucky couple wistfully and her eyes filled with tears.

# My Big Brother

My big brother was five years older than me but only three grades ahead. He'd begun his studies at the same age I had but he didn't like the idea of moving hastily in an important matter like education. He wanted to lay a firm foundation for that great edifice, so he took two years to do one year's work; sometimes he even took three. If the foundations weren't well-made, how could the edifice endure?

I was the younger, he the elder — I was nine, he was fourteen. He had full right by seniority to supervise and instruct me. And I was expected to accept every order of his as law.

By nature he was very studious. He was always sitting with a book open. And perhaps to rest his brain he would sometimes draw pictures of birds, dogs and cats in the margin of his notebook. Occasionally he would write a name, a word or a sentence ten or twenty times. He might copy a couplet out several times in beautiful letters or create new words which made no rhyme or reason. Once, for example, I saw the following: Special Amina brothers and brothers, in reality brother-brother, Radheshyam, Mr Radheshyam, for one hour. Following this was the sketch of a man's face. I tried very hard to make some sense out of this rigmarole but I didn't succeed and I didn't dare ask him. He was in the ninth grade, I was in the sixth. To understand his creation was beyond my powers.

I wasn't really very keen about studying. To pick up a book and sit with it for an hour was a tremendous effort. As soon as I found a chance I'd leave the hostel and go to the field and play marbles or fly paper kites or sometimes just meet a chum — what could be more fun? Sometimes we'd climb on to the courtyard walls and jump down or straddle the gate and ride it back and forth, enjoying it as though it were an automobile. But as soon as I came back into the room and saw my brother's scowling face I was petrified. His first question would be, 'Where were you?' Always this question, always asked in the same tone and the only answer I had was silence. I don't know why I couldn't manage to say that I'd just been outside playing. My silence was an acknowledgement of guilt and my brother's only remedy for this was to greet me with indignant words.

'If you study English this way you'll be studying your whole life and you won't get one word right! Studying English is no laughing matter that anyone who wants to can learn. Otherwise everybody and his cousin would be regular experts in English. You've got to wear out your eyes morning and night and use every ounce of energy, then maybe you'll master the subject. And even then it's just to say you have a smattering of it. Even great scholars can't write proper English, to say nothing of being able to speak it. And I ask you, how much of a blockhead are you that you can't learn a lesson from looking at me? You've seen with your own eyes how much I grind, and if you haven't seen it, there's something wrong with your eyes and with your wits as well. No matter how many shows and carnivals there may be have you ever seen me going to watch them? Every day there are cricket and hockey matches but I don't go near them. I keep on studying all the time, and even so it takes me two years or even three for one grade. So how do you expect to pass when you waste your time playing like this? If it takes me two or even three years, you'll fritter your whole life away studying in one grade. If you waste your time like this, it would be better if you just went home and played stick-ball to your heart's content. Why waste our dad's hard-earned money?'

Hearing a dressing-down like this I'd start to cry. What could I answer? I was guilty but who could endure a scolding like that? My brother was an expert in the art of giving advice. He'd say such sarcastic words, overwhelm me with such good counsel that my spirits would collapse, my courage disappear. I couldn't find in myself the power to toil so desperately, and in despair for a little while I'd think, 'Why *don't* I run away from school and go back home? Why should I spoil my life fiddling with work that's beyond my capacity?' I was willing to remain a fool, but I just got dizzy from so much work. But after an hour or two the cloud of despair would dissipate and I'd resolve to study with all my might. I'd draw up a schedule on the spot. How could I start work without first making an outline, working out a plan? In my timetable the heading of play was entirely absent. Get up at the crack of dawn, wash hands and face at six, eat a snack, sit down and study. From six to eight English, eight to nine arithmetic, nine to nine-thirty history, then mealtime and afterwards off to school. A half hour's rest at 3.30 when I got back from school, geography from four to five, grammar from five to six, then a half hour's walk in front of the hostel, six-thirty to seven English composition, then supper, translation from eight to nine, Hindi from nine to ten, from ten to eleven miscellaneous, then to bed.

But it's one thing to draw up a schedule, another to follow it. It began to be neglected from the very first day. The inviting green expanse of the playground, the balmy winds, the commotion on the football field, the exciting stratagems of prisoner's-base, the speed and flurries of volley ball would all draw me mysteriously and irresistibly. As soon as I was there I forgot everything: the life-destroying schedule, the books that strained your eyes — I couldn't remember them at all. And then my big brother would have an occasion for sermons and scoldings. I would stay well out of his way, try to keep out of his sight, come into the room on tiptoe so he wouldn't know. But if he spotted me I'd just about die. It seemed that a naked sword was always swinging over my head. But just as in the midst of death and catastrophe a man may remain caught in the snares of illusion, so I, though I suffered reproaches and threats, could not renounce fun and games.

*

The yearly exams came round: my brother failed, I passed and was first in my class. Only two year's difference was left between him and me. It occurred to me to taunt him. 'What was the good of all your horrible self-punishment? Look at me, I went on playing and having a good time and I'm at the head of my class.' But he was so sad and depressed that I felt genuinely sorry for him and it seemed shameful to me to pour salt on his wounds. But now I could be a little proud of myself and indeed my ego expanded. My brother's sway over me was over. I began to take part freely in the games, my spirits were running high. If he gave me another sermon, then I'd say straight out, 'With all your grinding what kind of marks did you get? Playing and having fun I ended up first in my class.' Although I didn't have the courage to say anything so outrageous it was plain from my behaviour that my brother's power over me was gone. He guessed it — his intuition was sharp and one day when I'd spent the whole morning playing stick-ball and came back exactly at meal time, he said, with all the air of pulling out a sword to rush at me:

'I see you've passed this year and you're first in your class, and you've got stuck up about it. But my dear brother, even great men live to regret their pride, and who are you compared to them? You must have read about what happened to Ravan. Didn't you learn anything from his story or did you just read it without paying any attention? Just to pass an exam isn't anything, the real thing is to develop your mind. Understand the significance of what you read. Ravan was master of the earth. Such kings are called 'Rulers of the World'. These days the extent of the British Empire is vast, but their kings can't be called 'Ruler of the World' — many countries in the world don't accept British rule, they're completely independent. But Ravan was a Ruler of the World, all the kings of the earth paid taxes to him. Great divinities were his slaves, even the gods of fire and water. But what happened to him in the end? Pride completely finished him off, destroying even his name. There wasn't anybody left to perform all his funeral rites properly. A man can commit any sin he wants but he'd better not be proud, nor give himself airs. When he turns proud he loses both this world and the next. You must have read about what happened to Satan too. He was so proud that he thought there was no truer devotee of God than himself. Finally it came about that he got shoved out of heaven into hell. Once the king of Turkey became very stuck-up too; he died begging for alms. You've just been promoted one grade and your head's turned by it — you've gone way up in the world! Understand this, you didn't pass through your own efforts but just stumbled on it by luck, like a blind man who catches hold of a quail. But you can catch a quail only once like that, no more. Sometimes in stick-ball too a lucky shot in the dark hits the goal, but nobody gets to be a good player from it, the kind who never misses a shot.

'Don't assume that because I failed I'm stupid and you're smart. When you reach my class you'll sweat right through you teeth when you have to bite into algebra and geometry and study English history — it's not easy to memorize these king's names. There were eight Henrys — do you think it's easy to remember all the things that happened in each Henry's time? If you write Henry the Eighth instead of Henry the Seventh you get a zero. A complete flunk! You won't get zero not even zero. What kind of idea do you have about it anyway? There were dozens of Jameses, dozens of Williams and scores of Charleses! You get dizzy with them, your mind's in a whirl.

209

Those poor fellows didn't have names enough to go around. After every name they have to put second, third, fourth and fifth. If anybody'd asked me I could have reeled off thousands of names. And as for geometry, well, God help you! If you write *a c b* instead of *a b c* your whole answer is marked wrong. Nobody ever asks those hard-hearted examiners what is the difference, after all, between *a b c* and *a c b* or why they waste their time torturing the students with it. Does it make any difference if you eat lentils, boiled rice and bread or boiled rice, lentils and bread? But what do those examiners care? They see only what they've written in their books. They expect us to learn it word for word. And this kind of parroting they call teaching! And in the long run what's the point of learning all this nonsense? If you bring this perpendicular line down on that line it will be twice the base line. I ask you, what's the point of that? If it isn't twice as long it's four times as long or half as long, what the devil do I care? But you've got to pass so you've got to memorize all this garbage.

'They say, "Write an essay on punctuality no less than four pages long." So now you open up your notebook in front of you, take your pen and curse the whole business. Who doesn't know that punctuality's a very good thing? A man's life is organized according to it, others love him for it and his business prospers from it. How can you write four pages on something so trifling? Do I need four pages for what I can describe in one sentence? So I consider it stupidity. It's not economizing time, it's wasting it to cram it with such nonsense. We want a man to say what he has to say quickly and then get moving. But no, you've got to drag it out to four pages, whatever you write, and they're foolscap pages too. If this isn't an outrage on the students, what is it? It's a contradiction for them to ask us to write concisely. Write a concise essay on punctuality in no less than four pages. All right! If four pages is concise then maybe otherwise they'd ask us to write one or two hundred pages. Run fast and walk slow at the same time. Is that all mixed up or isn't it? We students can understand that much but those teachers don't have the sense — and despite that they claim they're teachers. When you get into my class, old man, then you'll really take a beating, and then you'll find out what's what. Just because you got a first division this time you're all puffed up — so pay attention to what I say. What if I failed, I'm still older than you, I have more experience of the world. Take what I say to heart or you'll be sorry.'

210

It was almost time for school, otherwise I don't know when this medley of sermons would have ended. I didn't have much appetite that day. If I got a scolding like this when I passed, maybe if I'd failed I would have had to pay with my life. My brother's terrible description of studying in the ninth grade really scared me. I'm surprised I didn't run away from school and go home. But even a scolding like this didn't change my distaste for books a bit. I didn't miss one chance to play. I also studied, but much less. Well, any-way, just enough to complete the day's assignment and not be disgraced in class. But the confidence I'd gained in myself disappeared and then I began to lead a life like a thief's.

*

Then it was the yearly exams again and it so happened that once more I passed and my brother failed again. I hadn't done much work; but somehow or other I was in the first division. I myself was astonished. My brother had just about killed himself with work, memorizing every word in the course, studying till ten at night and starting again at four in the morning, and from six until 9.30 before going to school. He'd grown pale. But the poor fellow failed again and I felt sorry for him. When he heard the results he broke down and cried, and so did I. My pleasure in passing was cut by half. If I'd failed my brother couldn't have felt so bad. But who can escape his fate?

There was only one grade left between my brother and me. The insidious thought crossed my mind that if he failed just once more I'd be at the same level as him and then what grounds would he have for lecturing me? But I violently rejected this unworthy idea. After all, he'd scolded me only with the intention of helping me. At the time it was really obnoxious, but maybe it was only as a result of his advice that I 'd passed so easily and with such good marks.

Now my brother had become much gentler toward me. Several times when he found occasion to scold me he did it without losing his temper. Perhaps he himself was beginning to understand that he no longer had the right to tell me off or at least not so much as before. My independence grew. I began to take unfair advantage of his toleration, I half started to imagine that I'd pass next time whether I studied or not, my luck was high. As a result, the little I'd studied before because of my brother, even that ceased. I found a new pleasure in flying kites and now I spent all my time at the sport. Still, I minded my manners with my brother and concealed my kite-flying from him. In preparation for the kite tournament I was secretly busy solving such problems as how best to secure the string and how to apply the paste mixed with ground glass in it to cut the other fellows' kites off their strings. I didn't want to let my brother suspect that my respect for him had in any way diminished.

One day, far from the hostel, I was running along like mad trying to grab hold of a kite. My eyes were on the heavens and that high-flying traveller in the skies that glided smoothly down like some soul emerging from paradise free of worldly attachments to be incarnated in a new life. A whole army of boys came racing out to welcome it with long, thick bamboo rods. Nobody was aware who was in front or in back of him. It was as though every one of them was flying along with that kite in the sky where everything is level, without cars or trams or trains.

Suddenly I collided with my brother, who was probably coming back from the market. He grabbed my hand and said angrily, 'Aren't you ashamed to be running with these ragamuffins after a one-paisa kite? Have you forgotten that you're not in a low grade any more? You're in the eighth now, one behind me. A man's got to have some regard for his position, after all. There was a time when by passing the eighth grade people became assistant revenue collectors. I know a whole lot of men who finished only the middle grades and today are first degree deputy magistrates or superintendents. How many eighth-grade graduates today are our leaders and newspaper editors? Great scholars work under their supervision but when you get into this same eighth grade you run around with hoodlums!

'I'm sorry to see you have so little sense. You're smart, there's no doubt of that, but what use is it if it destroys your self-respect? You must have assumed, "I'm just one grade behind my brother so now he doesn't have any right to say anything to me." But you're mistaken. I'm five years older than you and even if you come into my grade today — and the examiners being what they are there's no doubt that next year you'll be on an equal footing with me and maybe a year later you'll even get ahead of me — but that difference of five years between us not even God — to say nothing of you — can remove. I'm five years older than you and I always will be. The experience I have of life and the world you can never catch up

212

with even if you get an M.A. and a D.Litt. and even a Ph. D. Understanding doesn't come from reading books. Our mother never passed any grade and Dad probably never went beyond the fifth, but even if we studied the wisdom of the whole world mother and father would always have the right to explain to us and to correct us. Not just because they're our parents but because they'll always have more experience of the world. Maybe they don't know what kind of government they've got in America or how many constellations there are in the sky, but there are a thousand things they know more about than you or me. God forbid, but if I should fall sick today then you'd be in a pickle. You wouldn't be able to think of anything except sending a telegram to Dad. But in your place *he* wouldn't send anybody a telegram or get upset or be all flustered. First of all he'd diagnose the disease himself and try the remedy; then if it didn't work he'd call some doctor. And sickness is a serious matter. But you and I don't even know how to make our allowance last through the month. We spend what father sends us and then we're penniless again. We cut our breakfast, we have to hide from the barber and washerman. But as much as you and I spend today, Dad's maintained himself honourably and in good reputation the greater part of his life and brought up a family with seven children on half of it. Just look at our headmaster. Does he have an M.A. or doesn't he? And not from here either, but from Oxford. He gets a thousand rupees, but who runs his house? His old mother. There his degrees are useless. He used to manage the house himself, but he couldn't make both ends meet, he had to borrow. But since his mother has taken over it's as though Lakshmi had come into his house. So brother, don't be so proud of having almost caught up with me and being independent now. I'll see that you don't go off the track. If you don't mind, then' (showing me his fist) 'I can use this too. I know you don't like hearing all this.'

I was thoroughly shamed by this new approach of his. I had truly come to know my own insignificance and a new respect for my brother was born in my heart. With tears in my eyes, I said, 'No, no, what you say is completely true and you have the right to say it.'

My brother embraced me and said, 'I don't forbid you to fly kites. I'd like to too. But what can I do? If I go off the track myself then how can I watch out for you? That's my responsibility.'

Just then by chance a kite that had been cut loose passed over us with its string dangling down. A crowd of boys were chasing after it.

My brother is very tall and leaping up he caught hold of the string and ran at top speed toward the hostel and I ran close behind him.

# Intoxication

Ishwari's father was a rich landowner, mine an impecunious clerk who had no wealth beyond his working wages. There was a continual debate between us. I was forever attacking the *zamindars*, calling them jungle beasts, blood-sucking leeches, the flowering parasitic growth at the top of the trees. He took the side of the *zamindars* but of course his position was somewhat weak because he could present no real argument in their defense. It's a weak argument to say that not all men are equal, that there'd always been rich and poor and there always would be. It was difficult to prove the justness of such a system by humanitarian or moral principles. In the heat of these discussions I would often become angry and sarcastic, but even when he was defeated Ishwari would go on smiling. I never saw him lose his temper. Perhaps it was because he understood the weakness of his position. He certainly had his share of the harshness and arrogance of the rich. He never addressed a decent word to the servants. If they were the least bit late in making the bed, if the milk was by chance too hot or too cold, if his bicycle hadn't been properly cleaned, then he was beside himself. He wouldn't tolerate the least laziness or insolence. But with his friends, and particularly with me, he was always exceptionally cordial and sympathetic. Perhaps if I'd been in his place the same harshness might have sprung up in me as well, for my love of the people was not the result of conviction but rather of my personal circumstances. But perhaps if he'd been in my shoes he would have kept up the same high style, for by nature he was fond of luxury and good things.

I had decided not to go home for the coming Dassehra holidays. I didn't have the fare nor did I want to impose the burden for it on my parents — I knew that what they were giving me already was far beyond their resources. And on top of that I was concerned about exams. I had a lot left to study and who can do any studying when he goes home? But then I didn't want to stay on alone like a ghost in the hostel either, so when Ishwari invited me home with him I accepted without any urging. I could prepare for exams very well with Ishwari since he was not only rich but also bright and industrious.

When he invited me he also said, 'But pay attention to one thing, friend. If you attack the *zamindars* in my house there'll be a row and my folks won't like it. They rule over their tenants with the claim that God created those tenants just to serve them. And the tenants feel the same way — if they ever got it into their heads that there's no basic difference between *zamindars* and themselves, that would be the end of the *zamindars.*'

I said, 'Do you expect me to go there and not be myself?'

'Yes, that's just what I expect.'

'You'll be disappointed!'

Ishwari didn't answer. Perhaps he was leaving it to my discretion and he was right to. If he'd insisted then I might have been stubborn about it.

*

Second class? Why, I'd never even travelled inter-class before and now I had the good luck to be travelling in second. The train arrived at nine at night but in our eagerness we went to the station as soon as it was dark. After wandering around here and there for a while we went and had a meal in the refreshment room. After one look at my clothes and manners it didn't take the stewards long to figure out who was the master and who the hanger-on, but I don't know why I was annoyed by their impudence. The money came out of Ishwari's pocket — probably he gave them more in tips than my father earned in a month. When we left he alone tipped them — eight *annas*. Nevertheless I expected from them the same attentiveness and politeness they gave to him. Why should they all run when he gave them an order and show less alacrity when I asked for something? I didn't enjoy my supper. This discrimination completely occupied my thoughts.

The train arrived and we got in. The stewards bowed farewell to Ishwari; they didn't so much as look at me.

'How well-mannered they all are,' Ishwari said. 'Not one of our servants has such good manners.'

Sourly I observed, 'If you treated your servants to eight-*anna* tips like these you'd find them better-mannered.'

'Do you mean you think they're polite just because they're expecting a tip?'

'Of course not! Fine manners and etiquette are doubtless in their blood.'

The train, a mail express, started. After leaving Prayag station it stopped first at Pratapgarh. A man opened the door of our compartment. I let out a yell at once: 'This is second class!' and afterwards I shouted it in English too.

The traveller came into the compartment and looking at me with singular contempt said, 'Yes, your humble servant is perfectly aware of that,' and sat down on a lower berth. I can't describe how embarrassed I was.

By morning we reached Moradabad. At the station several people were waiting to welcome us. Two of them were gentlemen of the household, five of them servants. The latter picked up our luggage and the two gentlemen walked behind. One was a Muslim named Riyasat Ali, the other a Brahman named Ramharakh. Both of them looked at me as though I struck them as outlandish. 'You're a crow,' those looks seemed to say, 'what are you doing with the swans?'

Riyasat Ali asked Ishwari, 'Is this other young gentleman studying with you?'

'Yes,' Ishwari said, 'we study together and we live together as well. I might add that it's only because of him that I stay on in Allahabad, otherwise I would have moved on to Lucknow long ago. This time I've dragged him along with me. Several telegrams came from his home but I persuaded him to refuse them. The last telegram was marked urgent at four *annas* per word but I got him to turn that one down too.'

Both gentlemen stared at me in astonishment. They appeared to be trying to look impressed.

In a slightly suspicious tone Riyasat Ali said, 'But he seems to be very plainly dressed.'

Ishwari dispelled his doubts. 'He's a follower of Mahatma Gandhi, sir! He won't wear anything except the native homespun cotton. He's burned all his former clothes. Actually, he's practically a maharaja — he has an income of 250,000 a year, but to look at him you'd think he'd been picked up in some orphanage.'

Ramharakh said, 'One sees very few rich people with natures like that! No one would ever guess.'

'If you'd ever seen the Maharaja of Changli,' Riyasat Ali corroborated, 'you would have swallowed your teeth. He used to go wandering around the market dressed in a coarse cotton vest and wearing village-made shoes. They say that once he was snapped up to work in a labour gang — and he was the man who founded a college with a million rupees.'

I found all this very embarrassing, and I don't know why the whole lie didn't simply strike me as ridiculous. It was as though with each sentence I was coming closer and closer to this imaginary· glory.

I'm not a particularly good horseman. To be sure, when I was a child I'd several times ridden on old cart horses. I now saw that two smartly fitted out horses were standing ready for us. I was desperate. I mounted, trembling, but I managed to hide my fear. I steered the horse in back of Ishwari. It was lucky that he didn't gallop his, otherwise I might have gone back with broken arms and legs. It's possible he knew just how much of an equestrian I was.

*

Ishwari's house was a regular castle if it was anything. A gate like a mosque's, watchmen stationed at the entrance, servants beyond the counting, and an elephant tied up in the courtyard. Ishwari introduced me to his father and uncles and all the rest of his family with the same exaggerated stories. I can't tell you what a romance he invented. Not only the servants but all the people of the family as well regarded me with respect. They were landed gentry with an income of thousands, and yet the sort of people who regarded even a police constable as an officer. Several gentlemen there even called me 'Excellency'.

When we were finally alone I said to Ishwari, 'My friend, you're being a regular devil — why are you trying to get me into a jam?'

With a forced smile Ishwari said, 'The trick was necessary in front of those idiots, otherwise they wouldn't have had a decent word for you.'

In a short while the barber came to massage our feet: the young lords had just come from the station, they must be tired. Pointing to me Ishwari said, 'First massage the prince's feet.'

I was lying down on the *charpoy*. It had hardly ever happened to me in my whole life before to have someone massage my feet. I'd mocked Ishwari in the past for the follies of the rich, the fatuity of the gentry and the oppression by the big shots and I don't know what all else, and today I was caught right in the middle of it posing as a rich gentleman's offspring.

By this time it was ten o'clock. The household followed the old leisurely and courtly ways; the light of the new order had managed to reach only the highest places. The call for dinner came from the women's part of the house. We went to bathe. I had always washed out my own *dhoti*, but now I followed Ishwari's example and left it there — I would have been ashamed to wash my *dhoti* with my own hands. We went in to dine. In the hostel we sat down at the table with our shoes on but here we had to have our feet washed. A servant was standing there with water. Ishwari stretched out his foot and the servant washed it. I also stretched out my foot and the servant washed it too. I have no idea where my earlier notions had flown to.

*

I had thought that out here in the country I'd be able to concentrate on my studies in earnest. But I spent the whole day in walks and excursions. We'd drift on the river in a houseboat or fish or hunt birds or go to watch the village wrestling matches or get together for a game of chess. Ishwari would have a lot of eggs brought and make omelettes on the English stove in his room. There was always a crowd of servants gathered round. No need to stir hand or foot, you just had to stir your tongue. If you sat down to bathe they were on the spot to wash you, if you lay down there were two to keep the fan going.

Mahatma Gandhi's rich young disciple had become famous. His renown spread through the whole estate. They made sure there wasn't the slightest delay in serving his breakfast lest the 'prince' be angry, and the bed was ready right on time when he wanted to go to sleep. I was even touchier than Ishwari, or felt obliged to become so. Ishwari made his own bed but the prince, as a guest — well, how could he make his bed with his own hands? It was beneath his dignity.

One day the following incident actually took place. Ishwari was in the women's part of the house where he had probably tried to talk with his mother. Ten o'clock struck. I was so sleepy I could hardly keep my eyes open. But how could I set out the bedding?

219

Not a prince like me! At around 11.30 a bearer came in, a rather over-familiar fellow. In his various household chores he'd forgotten to make my bed and remembering only now he came on the run. I gave him a tongue-lashing he wasn't apt to forget.

Hearing my tirade, Ishwari came along and said, 'You've done well. All these lazy fellows deserve a scolding like that.'

It happened that one day Ishwari had gone somewhere to a party. When evening came the lamp was not lit. It was on the table and there were matches there too, but Ishwari never lit the lamp so how was the prince to light it? I was exasperated. The newspaper had been set out; I was longing to read it but the lamp wasn't lit! By chance Riyasat Ali happened to come in just then. I blew up and gave him such a scolding that the poor fellow was speechless. 'You people don't bother at all to see that the lamp is lit!' I said. 'I don't know how such lazy wretches are tolerated here. They wouldn't be kept on an hour in my house.' With trembling hands Riyasat Ali lit the lamp.

There was a Thakur who often used to come to Ishwari's house. He was a very enterprising fellow and a devoted follower of Gandhi. Believing me to be a disciple of Gandhiji he was very deferential to me. But he was hesitant about asking me for anything.

One day when he saw me alone he came to me and, folding his hands, said, 'Sir, you're a follower of Gandhi Baba, aren't you? People say that when we have Independence there won't be any more of those landowners.'

Pompously I said, 'What need will there be for the landowners? What do they do except suck the blood of the poor?'

Then the Thakur asked, 'Do you mean that the land will be taken away from all the *zamindars*?'

I said, 'But a lot of them will give it gladly. The ones who won't will have to have their land taken away from them. We people in my family are all set. The minute Independence comes we'll make over all our land and villages to the tenants.'

I was sprawled in a chair with my legs stuck out. The Thakur started to squeeze my feet and then he said, 'The landowners are very cruel these days, master! If your honour would give me just a tiny bit of land on your estate then I'd move there and work for you.'

'I have no authority over the land now, my friend, but as soon as I get control of it I'll send for you first thing. I'll have you taught how

220

to drive a car and you can be my chauffeur.'

That day, I heard later, the Thakur drank a good deal of *bhang*, gave his wife a good beating and was all set to fight with the village moneylender.

\*

So in this way the vacation drew to a close and we set out for Allahabad again. A lot of the people of the village came to see us off and the Thakur came with us to the station. I played my part to perfection too and stamped on every heart the image of my aristocratic refinement and magnanimity. I really longed to give each one of the servants a good tip but didn't have the where-withal. I already had my return ticket, I had only to get into the train. But when it came it was jam-packed with people coming home from the Durga-puja holidays. In second class there wasn't room to squeeze a stick and it was even worse in the inter. But this was the last train and we absolutely had to get on it. With the greatest difficulty we found room in third class. Our splendid get-up made a great impression there. But it really vexed me to be stuck in third. We'd come lying down the whole way in comfort and we were going back all twisted up — there wasn't even room to turn from one side to the other.

There were several educated people there too. Among themselves they were praising British rule. One gentleman remarked, 'No such justice has ever been seen in another government. Great and small, all are equal. If he wrongs anybody even the king will have to account to a court for it.'

'*Arrey*, sahib,' another man confirmed, 'you can bring a suit against the Emperor himself, the Emperor can be sentenced in court.'

There was one man going to Calcutta who had a big bundle tied to his back. He couldn't find any place to set it down. Uncomfortable with the thing on his back he frequently stood up by the door. I was sitting right next to the door so that each time he moved the bundle rubbed against my face. I didn't like it. For one thing, there was almost no air, and then this lout was just about suffocating me by crowding it into my face. I put up with it for some time, then suddenly I got mad. I caught hold of him and gave him a shove around and hit him two good slaps.

With a threatening look he said, 'Why are you hitting me, Babuji?

221

I also paid my fare.'

I stood up and hit him two or three more times.

There was an uproar in the compartment; everyone began yelling at me from all sides.

'If you're so delicate why didn't you sit in first class?'

'He's some bigshot in his own backyard, but he's not there now. If he hit *me* like that I'd show him.'

'What did the poor man do wrong? There's no room to breathe in here and he just wanted to get a breath of fresh air at the window and this fellow goes into a rage! When a man's got money does he completely lose his human-kindness?'

'This is British rule too — the very thing you were raving about.'

A villager said, 'He wouldn't try anything like that in front of those Englishmen — why's he acting so high and mighty here?'

In English Ishwari said, 'What an idiot you are!'

And it seemed to me that at this moment my intoxication began to clear a little.

# The Price of Milk

In the big cities these days you can find midwives, nurses and 'lady doctors,' as they call the female obstetricians. But in the villages it's still the untouchable sweeper women who preside over the delivery rooms, and there is little hope of any change in this situation in the near future.

Babu Maheshnath was the *zamindar* of his village, an educated man and aware of the need for reform in the way babies were delivered, but he saw no way to overcome the obstacles to such reform. No nurse would agree to go out to the villages, or if after a lot of persuasion one agreed then she'd demand such a fantastic fee that Babu Sahib could do nothing but come away with his head abjectly bowed. As for the lady doctors, he did not dare approach them; to pay one of them he might have had to sell half his property. And so when, after three daughters, his fourth child, a son, was born, once again he sent word to Gudar the sweeper and his wife. Children being apt to be born most often at night, it happened that one midnight a servant from Babu Sahib's house set up such a shout at Gudar's door that he woke up the whole neighbourhood. It was no girl this time for him to whisper the news.

For months they had been preparing in Gudar's house for this happy occasion. Their only fear was that it would once again turn out to be a girl, in which case they'd get nothing more out of it than the usual rupee and a sari. A great many times husband and wife had quarrelled and made bets about this matter. Bhungi, Gudar's wife, would say, 'If it isn't a son this time I'll hide my face in shame. That's right, I'll hide my face — but all the signs are for a son.' And Gudar would say, 'But can't you see it's going to be a girl? It's plain as day! If it's a son I'll shave off my moustache, that's right, I'll shave it off!' Gudar may have felt that if in this way he strengthened his wife's determination that it should be a son it would help to assure its actually coming about.

Bhungi said, 'You can shave it off right now, you old cheat. I said it was going to be a son but instead of listening you just went on talking. I'll shave it off myself and won't leave even a bristle.'

'There's my good old woman! It'll grow again, won't it? After three days take a look, it'll be just the way it was before. And anyway, I'll claim half of whatever you get, I'm telling you now.'

Bhungi made a contemptuous gesture with her thumb. Then, handing her three-month-old son to Gudar, started out with the messenger.

'*Ari*!' Gudar called. 'Where are you running off to? I'll have to go to play the music for the celebration. Who's going to look after the baby?'

Without coming back Bhungi said, 'Get him to sleep and put him down right there on the ground, then I'll come back and nurse him.''

*

At Maheshnath's house Bhungi was warmly welcomed now. She got fruits and vegetables in the morning, *puris* and *halva* at noon, and the same things again in the afternoon and at night. And Gudar got plenty to eat as well. Since Bhungi was not able to nurse her own baby more than once or twice each day extra milk was arranged for him. It was Babu Sahib's lucky little boy who drank Bhungi's milk. And even after the twelfth-day naming ceremony* the arrangement was not stopped. The mistress of the household was a strong, healthy woman, but this time for some reason or other she had no milk. The times she'd had the three daughters she gave so much milk that they got indigestion. This time there wasn't a drop. So Bhungi was not only the midwife but the wet-nurse as well.

The mistress would say, 'Bhungi, if you take good care of my baby you'll be able to just sit around eating as long as you live. I'll see that you're given five *bighas* rent-free. You'll live at ease right down to your grandchildren's time.'

And Bhungi's darling, unable to digest the alien milk, would throw up frequently and went on getting skinnier day by day.

Bhungi would say, 'When your son has his tonsure ceremony, I'll take some bracelets, I'll insist on that.'

---

* When a child is born, the mother is considered impure until the twelfth-day naming; hence there is nothing amiss in her being attended by an untouchable woman like Bhungi.

'Of course, my dear,' the mistress would answer. 'Why that threatening tone? Which do you want, silver or gold?'

'Oh mistress! If I wore silver bracelets who could I show my face to — and who would they make fun of?'

'Very well, my dear, I promise you gold.'

'And when your son is married I'll take a necklace and, for my husband, silver wrist-bands.'

'You shall have them — God grant we see that day!'

In the household Bhungi reigned, second only to the mistress. The cook, the maids, all the various servants paid heed to her; it reached the point where even the mistress gave way to her. Once she even scolded Maheshnath himself, and he let it go with a laugh. There had been some talk about Untouchables. 'Whatever may happen in the world,' Maheshnath had said, 'sweepers will remain nothing but sweepers. It's too hard to make civilized people out of them.'

To this Bhungi had said, 'Master, it's the sweepers who make it possible for the high-caste people to be civilized. Just let somebody do the same for us!'

In any other circumstances could Bhungi have got away with this insolence without having every hair of her head yanked out? But this time Babu Sahib chuckled and said, 'Bhungi always has something wise to say.'

*

The period of Bhungi's rule could not continue beyond a year. The Brahmans objected to the child's being nursed with an Untouchable's milk, and Moteram Shastri even enjoined a penance. So the nursing was abandoned but the matter of a penance was laughed away. To taunt the Brahman Maheshnath said, 'A penance, Shastriji? Very sensible! Until yesterday the child was nourished by the blood of this same Untouchable, so he must already be contaminated. My my, that's a great religion you've got!'

Shaking his topknot violently Shastriji said, 'In truth, the child was nourished on her blood until yesterday, and indeed on flesh as well — since she is an eater of meat. But today's business for today, let yesterday take care of itself. At the Jagannath temple at Puri Untouchables sit down to eat together with Brahmans — but they can't do it here. When we're ill we sit at our meals all dressed, we eat highly spiced stews, but Babuji, upon recovering we must once again eat according to the rules of morality. The regulations for emergencies are strange indeed!'

'So the meaning of this then is that morality changes — sometimes one thing, sometimes another?'

'What else! There's one morality for the king, another for the subject, one for the poor, another for the rich. Kings and princes can eat when they want, with whom they want, they can marry anybody they want, there are no restrictions for them! Those people have the power. Restrictions are for ordinary folk.'

So there was no penance, but Bhungi was obliged to step down from her eminence. But anyway she received so much in the way of gifts and tips that she couldn't take it away by herself, and she got the gold bracelets as well, and instead of one, two beautiful new saris, not just plain muslin like the ones when the daughters were born.

*

This same year there was a severe outbreak of the plague and Gudar was the first to fall victim. Bhungi was left alone, but she continued to live just as before. People kept an eye out to see if she'd go away now. There was talk with a certain sweeper, a certain headman paid a call, but Bhungi didn't go anywhere, she was still there five years later when her boy Mangal, despite being skinny and nearly always sick, was starting to run around. Next to Maheshnath's Suresh he looked like a dwarf.

One day Bhungi was cleaning a drain at Maheshnath's house. It was clogged with several months' accumulation of sludge so that the water had begun to form pools in the courtyard. Bhungi thrust a long stout bamboo pole into the drain and shook it vigorously. She had stuck her right arm inside the drain up to the elbow when suddenly she let out a shriek and drew her arm back out. At almost the same moment a black snake came slithering out of the drain. People came running and killed it. But they could not save Bhungi. They assumed it was a harmless water snake, so at first they took no precautions for her. It was only when the poison had spread through her body and she was seized by convulsions that they realized it was not a water snake but a venomous corn snake.

Mangal was now an orphan. He made a habit of hanging around

Maheshnath's door all through the day. There was so much leftover food in the house that they might have fed a dozen such children. There was thus no shortage of food but all the same it made him feel bad when the food was dropped down from above into his clay bowls. Everybody ate from fine plates, and clay bowls for him!

He might not have been aware at all of this discrimination but the village boys constantly shouted abuse at him. There was no one who would ask him to play with them, and even the piece of canvas he slept on was untouchable. There was a *neem* tree in front of the house. Mangal made his home directly under it with his piece of torn canvas, two clay bowls and a *dhoti* passed on from Suresh. The spot was equally comfortable in every season, winter, summer and the rains. In the scorching June winds, the freezing cold and the drenching rains lucky little Mangal stayed alive and was actually a lot healthier than he'd been before. And there was even someone he could call his own, a village dog which, fed up with being picked on by his fellows in the pack, had taken refuge with him. They both ate the same food, slept on the same canvas and even had the same temperament and understood one another's moods. There was never once a quarrel between them.

The pious people of the village were surprised at this generosity of Babu Sahib's. For Mangal to loiter and sleep right in front of his door — it couldn't have been fifty feet — seemed to them contrary to genuine religion. Disgusting! If this sort of thing continued, you could be sure that religion was finished once and for all. God created the Untouchables too, we know that, to be sure, and who isn't aware that one ought not to commit any injustice against them? — after all, God is known as the redeemer of the lowly. But the traditions of society have to be considered too! One would feel embarrassed just to approach that door. Maheshnath might be the master of the village, one would be obliged to go there, but let it be understood that it was odious.

Mangal and Tommy, the dog, had become fast friends. Mangal would say, 'Look, Tommy, move over a little and go to sleep. Where do you expect me to lie? You're spread over the whole canvas.'

Tommy would whimper, wag his tail and instead of sliding over would crowd closer and begin to lick Mangal's face.

Every evening he would go to look at his house and cry a little while. The first year the thatched roof fell in, the second one the wall collapsed and now only half the walls were standing, all jagged at the top. This was the treasure of affection he had found. The memories, the yearning and the love together drew him to this ruin, and Tommy always came with him. Mangal would sit on the jagged wall and dream of his past life and the future while Tommy time and time again would try unsuccessfully to leap up into his lap.

*

One day several boys were playing and Mangal too came along, though he stood far apart. It's not certain whether Suresh took pity on him or whether the players needed someone to pair off, but in any case he decided that today Mangal should take part in the game — who was going to come along and see them here?

'Hey Mangal,' he said , 'how about playing!'

'No, brother,' Mangal said, 'What if the master should see? I'd get my hide skinned off, but as for you, you'd get away with it.'

'Who's going to see us here, you idiot? Come on, we're playing horse-and-rider. You'll be the horse and the rest of us will climb on you and ride.'

Sceptically Mangal asked, 'Will I always be the horse or will I get to be a rider, tell me that.'

This was a complicated question. Nobody had considered it. After a moment's reflection Suresh said, 'Who'd let you get on his back? Think of that! After all, are you a sweeper or not?'

But Mangal too stood his ground. 'When did I ever say I wasn't a sweeper? But it was my own mother who brought you up and fed you with her milk. So long as I'm not going to get to be a rider I won't be the horse. You people are pretty smart! You want to enjoy being riders and I'm supposed to stay just a horse.'

'You've got to be the horse!' Suresh scolded and ran to catch him. Mangal ran off with Suresh after him. Mangal quickened his step and Suresh too put on more steam. But from being so overfed he'd turned flabby and he was already panting from running.

Finally he stopped and said, 'Come and be the horse, Mangal, otherwise whenever I do get my hands on you I'll really beat you up!'

'Then you'll have to be a horse too.'

'All right, we'll be horses too.'

'You ride afterwards. Be the horse first, then I will after I've ridden.'

Suresh, in fact, wanted to play a trick. When he heard this proposal of Mangal's he said to his companions, 'Just look at the little stinker's nerve! There's a sweeper for you.'

The three of them surrounded Mangal and forced him down on all fours. Suresh jumped on his back at once and straddled him. He made a clicking sound with his tongue and said, 'Giddyup, horse, giddyup!'

Mangal moved along for a little while but he felt as though his back would break from the burden. Slowly he flattened his back and slipped out from under Suresh's thighs. Master Suresh fell with a thud and began to sound his horn.

His mother heard him crying somewhere. Wherever Suresh might be crying her sharp ears picked it up, and his crying was really quite peculiar, like the whistle on a narrow-gauge engine.

She said to the maid, 'Go look, Suresh is crying somewhere, find out if anybody's hit him.'

In the meantime Suresh himself came, rubbing his eyes. Whenever he found an opportunity to cry he was sure to come complaining to his mother and she would wipe his eyes and give him sweets and dried fruit. It's true, he was eight years old but he was a complete blockhead. Excessive affection had done to his wits what excessive eating had done to his body.

His mother asked, 'Why are you crying, Suresh? Did someone hit you?'

Still crying Suresh said, 'Mangal touched me.'

She could not believe it. Mangal was so self-effacing that she would not have credited any mischief to him. But when Suresh began to swear it was true she was obliged to believe him. She sent for Mangal and scolded him. 'What's going on, Mangal, now you're dreaming up all sorts of mischief! I told you you were never to touch Suresh. Do you remember or not? Speak up!'

In a low voice Mangal said, 'How could I forget?'

'Then why did you touch him?'

'I didn't touch him.'

'If you didn't touch him why was he crying?'

'He fell, that's why.'

'Stubborn and lying too!' Madam broke off, grinding her teeth. If she beat him she would have to take a purificatory bath that very moment. Even if she just took a cane in her hand the lightning current of contact would be conducted through the cane to course through her body. And so she heaped as much abuse on him as she could and ordered him to get out at once. If he ever appeared at their door again she'd drink his blood. Though they gave him all that free food he dreamed up nasty tricks, etc. etc.

Mangal was not likely to feel humiliation, but he could feel fear. Quietly he picked up his pots, tucked the piece of canvas under his arm, put the *dhoti* over his shoulder and set out weeping. He would never come back there again. The result would be that he would die of hunger. What harm in that? What good was there in living like this? Where was there any other shelter for him in the village? Who would take in a sweeper? He went off toward the ruins of his house where memories of the happy days might dry his tears, and cried his heart out.

At that moment Tommy came looking for him, and then the two of them forgot their grief.

*

But as daylight faded Mangal's despair also began to disappear, while the hunger that had gnawed at his childhood and consumed his body had now become all the more intense. His eyes turned constantly toward his bowls. Up at the house he would be getting Suresh's left over sweets by now, but here — not a scrap to eat. He consulted with Tommy: 'What are you going to eat? I'm just going to go to bed hungry.'

Tommy whimpered as though to say, 'You just have to put up with this sort of insult throughout life. But if you lose heart, how can you keep going? Just consider my case now, sometimes somebody beats me with a stick and yells after me, then in a little while I go back to him with my tail wagging. That's the way you and I are made, my friend.'

Mangal said, 'Get along now, eat anything you find, don't worry about me.'

In his dog language Tommy said, 'I won't go alone, I'll take you with me.'

'But I'm not going.'

'Then I won't go either.'

'You'll die of starvation.'

'Do you think you'll stay alive then?'

'But there's nobody around to cry over me.'

230

I'm in the same fix, friend — that bitch I was in love with last fall has been unfaithful, she's with Kallu now. Luckily she took her pups off with her, otherwise my existence would have been miserable. Who'd look after five puppies?'

After another moment hunger produced another plan.

'The mistress must be looking for us, don't you think so, Tommy?'

'What else? Babuji and Suresh must have finished eating by now. The servant must have taken out the leftovers, he's probably calling us.'

'A lot of *ghee* will be left in Babuji's and Suresh's plates and best of all, cream!

'And every bit of it's going to be thrown into the garbage.'

'Let's see if someone's looking for us.'

'Who's going to come looking for us? Do you think they're priests who'll chant our name? They'll call "Mangal, Mangal!" just once and that's it, the food will be dumped into the drain.'

'All right then, let's get going. But I'll stay hidden if anybody calls out my name, then I'll come back — understand?'

They both started out and when they got to Maheshnath's door stayed crouching in the shadows. But how could Tommy be patient? Slowly he found his way into the house. He saw that Maheshnath and Suresh were seated at their dinner. Quietly he settled down on the verandah but all the time he was afraid somebody might come along and whack him with a stick.

The servants were chatting. One said, 'Nobody's seen hide nor hair of that Mangal today. The mistress bawled him out so maybe he's run away.'

Another answered, 'If they threw him out it's a good thing. Who wants to have to look a sweeper in the face every single morning?'

Mangal shrank back even further into the shadows. All his hopes sank deeper than the depths of the sea.

Maheshnath stood up. A servant washed his hands. Now he would smoke his *hooka* and fall asleep. Suresh would sit with his mother and listen to some story or other until he fell asleep. Who was there to worry about poor Mangal? He thought. It was so late now that there was no chance anyone would call for him, even by force of habit.

He lingered on for some time, disappointed, then, sighing, he was just on the point of going when a bearer appeared carrying a plate of leftovers.

Mangal came out from the darkness into the light. How could he resist now?

The servant said, 'Where the devil were you? We thought you must have gone off somewhere. Here, eat this — I was just about to dump it out.'

Humbly Mangal said, 'But I've been waiting here a long time.'

'Then why didn't you speak out?'

'Because . . . I was afraid.'

'Well, take this and eat it.'

He lifted up the leaf dish and dropped it into Mangal's out-stretched hands. The eyes which Mangal turned to him were full of humble gratitude.

Tommy came out from inside too. The two of them began to eat from the leaf right there under the *neem* tree.

Patting Tommy's head with one hand, Mangal said, 'Just think, we were so hungry that if we hadn't at least got this bread they've thrown away what would we have done?'

Tommy wagged his tail.

'It was my mother who nursed Suresh.'

Tommy wagged his tail again.

'They say nobody can ever really pay the price of milk, and this is the payment I'm getting.'

And once more Tommy wagged his tail.

# The Shroud

Father and son sat in silence at the door of their hut before a burnt-out fire and inside Budhiya, the son's young wife, lay fainting in the throes of child-birth. From time to time such an agonizing cry came out of her that their hearts skipped a beat. It was a winter night, all was silent, and the whole village was obliterated in the darkness.

Ghisu said, 'It looks as though she won't make it. You spent the whole day running around — just go in and have a look.'

Annoyed, Madhav said, 'If she's going to die why doesn't she get it over with? What can I do by looking?'

'You're pretty hard-hearted, aren't you? You live at your ease with somebody all year and then you don't give a damn about her.'

'But I couldn't stand looking at her writhing and thrashing.'

They were a family of Untouchable leather-workers and had a bad name throughout the whole village. If Ghisu worked one day he'd take three off. Madhav was such a loafer that whenever he worked for a half hour he'd stop and smoke his pipe for an hour. So they couldn't get work anywhere. If there was even a handful of grain in the house then the two of them swore off work. After a couple of days fasting Ghisu would climb up a tree and break off branches for firewood and Madhav would bring it to the market to sell. And so long as they had any of the money they got for it they'd both wander around in idleness. There was no shortage of heavy work in the village. It was a village of farmers and there were any number of chores for a hard-working man. But whenever you called these two you had to be satisfied with paying them both for doing one man's work between them. If the two of them had been wandering ascetics there would have been absolutely no need for them to practice. This was their nature. A strange life theirs was! They owned nothing except for some clay pots; a few torn rags was all that covered their nakedness. They were free of worldly cares! They were loaded with debts, people abused them, beat them, but they didn't suffer. People would loan them a little something even though they were so poor there was no hope of getting it back. At the time of the potato and pea harvest they would go into other people's fields and dig up potatoes and gather peas and roast them or they'd pick sugarcane to suck at night. Ghisu had reached the age of sixty living this hand-to-mouth existence, and like a good son Madhav was following in his father's footsteps in every way, and if anything he was adding lustre to his father's fame. The two of them were sitting before the fire now roasting potatoes they'd dug up in some field. Ghisu's wife had died a long time ago. Madhav had been married last year. Since his wife had come she'd established order in the family and kept those two good-for-nothings' bellies filled. And since her arrival they'd become more sluggish than ever. In fact, they'd begun to let it go to their heads. If someone sent for them to do a job, they'd bare-facedly ask for twice the wages. This same woman was dying today in child-birth and it was as though they were only waiting for her to die so they could go to sleep in peace and quiet.

Ghisu took a potato and while he peeled it said, 'Go and look, see how she is. She must be possessed by some ghost, what else? But the village exorcist wants a rupee for a visit.'

Madhav was afraid that if he went into the hut Ghisu would do away with most of the potatoes. He said, 'I'm scared to go in there.'

'What are you afraid of? I'll be right here.'

'Then why don't you go and look?'

'When my woman died I didn't stir from her side for three days. And then she'd be ashamed if I saw her bare like that when I've never even seen her face before. Won't she be worried about her modesty? If she sees me she won't feel free to thrash around.'

'I've been thinking, if there's a baby what's going to happen? There's nothing we're supposed to have in the house — ginger, sugar, oil.'

'Everything's going to be all right, God will provide. The very people who wouldn't even give us a pice before will send for us tomorrow and give us rupees. I had nine kids and there was never a thing in the house but somehow or other the Lord got us through.'

In a society where the condition of people who toiled day and night was not much better than theirs and where, on the other hand, those who knew how to profit from the weaknesses of the peasants were infinitely richer, it's no wonder they felt like this. We could even say that Ghisu was much smarter than the peasants and instead of being one of the horde of empty-headed toilers he'd found a place for himself in the disreputable society of idle gossip-mongers. Only he didn't have the ability to stick to the rules and code of such idlers. So while others of his crowd had made themselves chiefs and bosses of the village, the whole community pointed at him in contempt. Nevertheless, there was the consolation that although he was miserably poor at least he didn't have to do the back-breaking labour the farmers did, and other people weren't able to take unfair advantage of his simplicity and lack of ambition.

They ate the potatoes piping hot. Since yesterday they'd eaten nothing and they didn't have the patience to let them cool. Several times they burned their tongues. When they were peeled the outside of the potatoes didn't seem very hot but as soon as they bit into them the inside burned their palates, tongues and throats. Rather than keep these burning coals in their mouths it was a lot safer to drop them down into their bellies, where there was plenty of equipment to cool them. So they swallowed them quickly, even though the attempt brought tears to their eyes.

At this moment Ghisu recalled the Thakur's wedding, which he'd attended twenty years before. The way the feast had gratified him was something to remember all his life, and the memory was still vivid today. He said, 'I won't forget that feast. Since then I've never seen food like it or filled my belly so well. The bride's people crammed everybody with *puris*, everybody! Bigshots and nobodies all ate *puris* fried in real *ghee*. Relishes and curds with spices, three kinds of dried vegetables, a tasty curry, sweets — how can I describe how delicious that food was? There was nothing to hold you back, you just asked for anything you wanted and as much as you wanted. We ate so much that nobody had any room left for water. The people serving just kept on handing out hot, round, mouth-watering savouries on leaves. And we'd say, 'Stop, you mustn't,' and put our hands over the plates to stop them but they kept right on handing it out. And when everybody had rinsed his mouth we got *paan* and cardamom too. But how could I take any *paan*? I couldn't even stand up. I just went and lay down in my blanket right away. That's how generous that Thakur was!'

Relishing the banquet in his imagination Madhav said, 'Nobody feeds us like that now.'

'Who'd feed us like that today? That was another age. Now everybody thinks about saving his money. Don't spend for weddings, don't spend for funerals! I ask you, if they keep on hoarding the wealth they've squeezed out of the poor, where are they going to put it? But they keep on hoarding. When it comes to spending any money they say they have to economize.'

'You must have eaten a good twenty *puris?*'

'I ate more than twenty.'

'I would have eaten fifty!'

'I couldn't have eaten any less than fifty. I was a husky lad in those days. You're not half so big.'

After finishing the potatoes they drank some water and right there in front of the fire they wrapped themselves up in their *dhotis* and pulling up their knees they fell asleep — just like two enormous coiled pythons.

And Budhiya was still moaning.

*

In the morning Madhav went inside the hut and saw that his wife had turned cold. Flies were buzzing around her mouth. Her stony eyes stared upwards. Her whole body was covered with dust. The child had died in her womb.

Madhav ran to get Ghisu. Then they both began to moan wildly and beat their chests. When they heard the wailing the neighbours came running and according to the old tradition began to console the bereaved.

But there was not much time for moaning and chest-beating. There was the worry about a shroud and wood for the pyre. The money in the house had disappeared like carrion in a kite's nest.

Father and son went weeping to the village *zamindar*. He hated the sight of the two of them and several times he'd thrashed them with his own hands for stealing or for not coming to do the work they'd promised to do. He asked, 'What is it, little Ghisu, what are you crying about? You don't show yourself much these days. It seems as though you don't want to live in this village.'

Ghisu bowed his head all the way to the ground, his eyes full of tears, and said, 'Excellency, an awful thing's happened to me. Madhav's woman passed away last night. She was in agony the whole time. The two of us never once left her side. We did whatever we could, gave her medicine — but to make a long story short, she gave us the slip. And now there's nobody left even to give us a piece of bread, master. We're ruined! My house has been destroyed! I'm your slave — except for you who is there to see that she's given a decent funeral? Whatever we had we spent on medicine. If your excellency is merciful, then she'll have a good funeral. Whose door can we go to except yours?'

The *zamindar* was soft-hearted. But to be kind to Ghisu was like trying to dye a black blanket. He was tempted to say, 'Get out and don't come back! When we send for you, you don't show up but today when you're in a jam you come and flatter me. You're a sponging bastard!' But this was not the occasion for anger or scolding. Exasperated, he took out a couple of rupees and threw them on the ground. But he didn't utter a word of consolation. He didn't even look at Ghisu. It was as though he'd shoved a load off his head.

When the *zamindar* had given two rupees how could the shop-keepers and moneylenders of the village refuse? Ghisu knew how to trumpet the *zamindar's* name around. Somebody gave him a couple of *annas*, somebody else four. Within an hour Ghisu had harvested a tidy sum of five rupees. He got grain at one place, wood from somewhere else. And at noon Ghisu and Madhav went to the market to get a shroud. There were people already cutting the bamboo to make a litter for the corpse.

The tender-hearted women of the village came and looked at the dead woman, shed a few tears over her forlorn state and went away.

*

When they reached the market Ghisu said, 'We have enough wood to burn her up completely, haven't we, Madhav?'

'Yes, there's plenty of wood, now we need the shroud.'

'That's right, come along and we'll pick up a cheap one.'

'Of course, what else? By the time we move the corpse it will be night — who can see a shroud at night?'

'What a rotten custom it is that somebody who didn't even have rags to cover herself while she was alive has to have a new shroud when she dies!'

'The shroud just burns right up with the body.'

'And what's left? If we'd had these five rupees before then we could have got some medicine.'

237

Each of them guessed what was in the other's mind. They went on wandering through the market, stopping at one cloth-merchant's shop after another. They looked at different kinds of cloth, silk and cotton, but nothing met with their approval. This went on until evening. Then the two of them, by some divine inspiration or other, found themselves in front of a liquor shop, and as though according to a previous agreement they went inside. For a little while they stood there, hesitant. Then Ghisu went up to where the tavern-keeper sat and said, 'Sahuji, give us a bottle too.'

Then some snacks arrived, fried fish was brought and they sat on the verandah and tranquilly began to drink.

After drinking several cups in a row they began to feel tipsy. Ghisu said, 'What's the point of throwing a shroud over her? In the end it just burns up. She can't take anything with her.'

Madhav looked toward heaven and said, as though calling on the gods to witness his innocence, 'It's the way things are done in the world, otherwise why would people throw thousands of rupees away on Brahmans? Who can tell if anybody gets it in the next world or not?'

'The bigshots have lots of money to squander so let them squander it, but what have we got to squander?'

'But how will you explain it to people? Won't they ask, "Where's the shroud?"'

Ghisu laughed. 'So what? We'll say the money fell out of the knot in our *dhotis* and we looked and looked but couldn't find it. They won't believe it but they'll give the money again.'

Madhav laughed too over this unexpected stroke of luck. He said, 'She was good to us, that poor girl — even dying she got us fine things to eat and drink.'

They'd gone through more than half a bottle. Ghisu ordered four pounds of *puris*. Then relish, pickle, livers. There was a shop right across from the tavern. Madhav brought everything back in a trice on a couple of leaf-platters. He'd spent one and a half rupees; only a few pice were left.

The two of them sat eating their *puris* in the lordly manner of tigers enjoying their kill in the jungle. They felt neither fear of being called to account nor concern for a bad reputation. They had overcome those sensibilities long before.

Ghisu said philosophically, 'If our souls are content won't it be credited to her in heaven as a good deed?'

Respectfully Madhav bowed his head and confirmed, 'Absolutely will! Lord, you know all secrets. Bring her to paradise — we bless her from our hearts . . . the way we've eaten today we've never eaten before in our whole lives.'

A moment later a doubt rose in his mind. He said, 'What about us, are we going to get there some day too?'

Ghisu gave no answer to this artless question. He didn't want to dampen his pleasure by thinking about the other world.

'But if she asks us there, "Why didn't you people give me a shroud?" What will you say?'

'That's a stupid question!'

'But surely she'll ask!'

'How do you know she won't get a shroud? Do you think I'm such a jackass? Have I been wasting my time in this world for sixty years? She'll have a shroud and a good one too.'

Madhav was not convinced. He said, 'Who'll give it? You've eaten up all the money. But she'll ask me. I was the one who put the cinnabar in her hair at the wedding.'

Getting angry, Ghisu said, 'I tell you she'll have a shroud, aren't you listening?'

'But why don't you tell me who's going to give it?'

'The same people who gave before will give the money again —well, not the money this time but the stuff we need.'

As the darkness spread and the stars began to glitter the gaiety of the tavern also increased steadily. People sang, bragged, embraced their companions, lifted the jug to the lips of friends. All was intoxication, the very air was tipsy. Anybody who came in got drunk in an instant from just a few drops, the air of the place turned their heads more than the liquor. The sufferings of their lives drew them all there and after a little while they were no longer aware if they were alive or dead, not alive or not dead.

And father and son went on slopping it up with zest. Everyone was staring at them. How lucky the two of them were, they had a whole bottle between themselves.

When he was crammed full Madhav handed the leftover *puris* on a leaf to a beggar who was standing watching them with famished eyes. And for the first time in his life he experienced the pride, the happiness and the pleasure of giving.

Ghisu said, 'Take it, eat it and say a blessing — the one who earned it is — well, she's dead. But surely your blessing will reach

239

her. Bless her from your heart, that food's the wages for very hard labour.'

Madhav looked heavenward again and said, 'She'll go to heaven, *Dada*, she'll be a queen in heaven.'

Ghisu stood up and as though bathing in waves of bliss he said, 'Yes, son, she'll go to heaven. She didn't torment anybody, she didn't oppress anybody. At the moment she died she fulfilled the deepest wish of all our lives. If she doesn't go to heaven then will those big fat people go who rob the poor with both hands and swim in the Ganges and offer holy water in the temples to wash away their sins?'

Their mood of credulity suddenly changed. Volatility is the special characteristic of drunkenness. Now was the turn for grief and despair.

'But *Dada*,' Madhav said, 'the poor girl suffered so much in this life! How much pain she had when she died.'

He put his hands over his eyes and began to cry, he burst into sobs.

Ghisu consoled him. 'Why weep, son? Be glad she's slipped out of this maze of illusion and left the whole mess behind her. She was very lucky to escape the bonds of the world's illusion so quickly.'

And the two of them stood up and began to sing.

*'Deceitful world, why do you dazzle us with your eyes?*
*Deceitful world!'*

The eyes of all the drunkards were glued on them and the two of them became inebriated in their hearts. Then they started to dance, they jumped and sprang, fell back, twisted, they gesticulated, they mimed their feelings, and finally they collapsed dead drunk right there.

# Deliverance

Dukhi the tanner was sweeping in front of his door while Jhuriya, his wife, plastered the floor with cow-dung. When they both found a moment to rest from their work Jhuriya said, 'Aren't you going to the Brahman to ask him to come? If you don't he's likely to go off somewhere.'

'Yes, I'm going,' Dukhi said, 'But we have to think about what he's going to sit on.'

'Can't we find a cot somewhere? You could borrow one from the village headman's wife.'

'Sometimes the things you say are really aggravating! The people in the headman's house give me a cot? They won't even let a coal out of their house to light your fire with, so are they going to give me a cot? Even when they're where I can go and talk to them if I ask for a pot of water I won't get it, so who'll give me a cot? A cot isn't like the things we've got — cow-dung fuel or chaff or wood that anybody who wants can pick up and carry off. You'd better wash our own cot and set it out — in this hot weather it ought to be dry by the time he comes.'

'He won't sit on our cot,' Jhuriya said. 'You know what a stickler he is about religion and doing things according to the rule.'

A little worried, Dukhi said, 'Yes, that's true. I'll break off some *mohwa* leaves and make a mat for him, that will be the thing. Great gentlemen eat off *mohwa* leaves, they're holy. Hand me my stick and I'll break some off.'

'I'll make the mat, you go to him. But we'll have to offer him some food he can take home and cook, won't we? I'll put it in my dish —'

'Don't commit any such sacrilege!' Dukhi said. 'If you do, the offering will be wasted and the dish broken. *Baba* will just pick up the dish and dump it. He flies off the handle very fast, and when he's in a rage he doesn't even spare his wife, and he beat his son so badly that even now the boy goes around with a broken hand. So we'll put the offering on a leaf too. Just don't touch it. Take Jhuri the

241

*Gond's* daughter to the village merchant and bring back all the things we need. Let it be a complete offering — a full two pounds of flour, a half of rice, a quarter of gram, an eighth of *ghee*, salt, turmeric, and four *annas* at the edge of the leaf. If you don't find the *Gond* girl then get the woman who runs the parching oven, beg her to go if you have to. Just don't touch anything because that will be a great wrong.'

After these instructions Dukhi picked up his stick, took a big bundle of grass and went to make his request to the Pandit. He couldn't go empty-handed to ask a favour of the Pandit; he had nothing except the grass for a present. If Panditji ever saw him coming without an offering, he'd shout abuse at him from far away.

*

Pandit Ghasiram was completely devoted to God. As soon as he awoke he would busy himself with his rituals. After washing his hands and feet at eight o' clock, he would begin the real ceremony of worship, the first part of which consisted of the preparation of *bhang*. After that he would grind sandalwood paste for half-an-hour, then with a straw he would apply it to his forehead before the mirror. Between two lines of sandalwood paste he would draw a red dot. Then on his chest and arms he would draw designs of perfect circles. After this he would take out the image of the Lord, bathe it, apply the sandalwood to it, deck it with flowers, perform the ceremony of lighting the lamp before it and ringing a little bell. At ten o'clock he'd rise from his devotions and after a drink of the *bhang* go outside where a few clients would have gathered: such was the reward for his piety; this was his crop to harvest.

Today when he came from the shrine in his house he saw Dukhi the Untouchable tanner sitting there with a bundle of grass. As soon as he caught sight of him Dukhi stood up, prostrated himself on the ground, stood up again and folded his hands. Seeing the Pandit's glorious figure his heart was filled with reverence. How godly a sight! — a rather short, roly-poly fellow with a bald, shiny skull, chubby cheeks and eyes aglow with brahmanical energy. The sandalwood markings bestowed on him the aspect of the gods. At the sight of Dukhi he intoned, 'What brings you here today, little Dukhi?'

Bowing his head, Dukhi said, 'I'm arranging Bitiya's betrothal.

242

Will your worship help us to fix an auspicious date? When can you find the time?'

'I have no time today,' Panditji said. 'But still, I'll manage to come toward evening.'

'No, maharaj, please come soon. I've arranged everything for you. Where shall I set this grass down?'

'Put it down in front of the cow and if you'll just pick up that broom sweep it clean in front of the door,' Panditji said. 'Then the floor of the sitting room hasn't been plastered for several days so plaster it with cowdung. While you're doing that I'll be having my lunch, then I'll rest a bit and after that I'll come. Oh yes, you can split that wood too, and in the storeroom there's a little pile of hay — just take it out and put it into the fodder bin.'

Dukhi began at once to carry out the orders. He swept the doorstep, he plastered the floor. This took until noon. Panditji went off to have his lunch. Dukhi, who had eaten nothing since morning, was terribly hungry. But there was no way he could eat here. His house was a mile away — if he went to eat there Panditji would be angry. The poor fellow suppressed his hunger and began to split the wood. It was a fairly thick tree trunk on which a great many devotees had previously tried their strength and it was ready to match iron with iron in any fight. Dukhi, who was used to cutting grass and bringing it to the market, had no experience with cutting wood. The grass would bow its head before his sickle but now even when he bought the axe down with all his strength it didn't make a mark on the trunk. The axe just glanced off. He was drenched in sweat, panting, he sat down exhausted and got up again. He could scarcely lift his hands, his legs were unsteady, he couldn't straighten out his back. Then his vision blurred, he saw spots, he felt dizzy, but still he went on trying. He thought that if he could get a pipeful of tobacco to smoke then perhaps he might feel refreshed. This was a Brahman village, and Brahmans didn't smoke tobacco at all like the low castes and Untouchables. Suddenly he remembered that there was a *Gond* living in the village too, surely he would have a pipeful. He set off at a run for the man's house at once, and he was in luck. The *Gond* gave him both pipe and tobacco, but he had no fire to light it with. Dukhi said, 'Don't worry about the fire, brother, I'll go to Panditji's house and ask him for a light, they're still cooking there.'

With this he took the pipe and came back and stood on the

verandah of the Brahman's house, and he said, 'Master, if I could get just a little bit of light I'll smoke this pipeful.'

Panditji was eating and his wife said, 'Who's that man asking for a light?'

'It's only that damned little Dukhi the tanner. I told him to cut some wood. The fire's lit, so go give him his light.'

Frowning, the Panditayin said, 'You've become so wrapped up in your books and astrological charts that you've forgotten all about caste rules. If there's a tanner or a washerman or a birdcatcher why he can just come walking right into the house as though he owned it. You'd think it was an inn and not a decent Hindu's house. Tell that good-for-nothing to get out or I'll scorch his face with a firebrand.'

Trying to calm her down, Panditji said, 'He's come inside — so what? Nothing that belongs to you has been stolen. The floor is clean, it hasn't been desecrated. Why not just let him have his light — he's doing our work, isn't he? You'd have to pay at least four *annas* if you hired some labourer to split it.'

Losing her temper, the Panditayin said, 'What does he mean coming into this house!'

'It was the son of a bitch's bad luck, what else?' the Pandit said.

'It's all right,' she said, 'This time I'll give him his fire but if he ever comes into the house again like that I'll give him the coals in his face.'

Fragments of this conversation reached Dukhi's ears. He repented: it was a mistake to come. She was speaking the truth —how could a tanner ever come into a Brahman's house? These people were clean and holy, that was why the whole world worshipped and respected them. A mere tanner was absolutely nothing. He had lived all his life in the village without understanding this before.

Therefore when the Pandit's wife came out bringing coals it was like a miracle from heaven. Folding his hands and touching his forehead to the ground he said, 'Panditayin, Mother, it was very wrong of me to come inside your house. Tanners don't have much sense — if we weren't such fools why would we get kicked so much?'

The Panditayin had brought the coals in a pair of tongs. From a few feet away, with her veil drawn over her face, she flung the coals toward Dukhi. Big sparks fell on his head and drawing back hastily

244

he shook them out of his hair. To himself he said, 'This is what comes of dirtying a clean Brahman's house. How quickly God pays you back for it! That's why everybody's afraid of Pandits. Everybody else gives up his money and never gets it back but who ever got any money out of a Brahman? Anybody who tried would have his whole family destroyed and his legs would turn leprous.'

He went outside and smoked his pipe, then took up the axe and started to work again.

Because the sparks had fallen on him the Pandit's wife felt some pity for him. When the Pandit got up from his meal she said to him, 'Give this tanner something to eat, the poor fellow's been working for a long time, he must be hungry.'

Panditji considered this proposal entirely outside of the behaviour expected of him. He asked, 'Is there any bread?'

'There are a couple of pieces left over.'

'What's the good of two or three pieces for a tanner? Those people need at least a good two pounds.'

His wife put her hands over her ears. 'My, my, a good two pounds! Then let's forget about it.'

Majestically Panditji said, 'If there's some bran and husks mix them in flour and make a couple of pancakes. That'll fill the bastard's belly up. You can never fill up these low-caste people with good bread. Plain millet is what they need.'

'Let's forget the whole thing,' the Panditayin said, 'I'm not going to kill myself cooking in weather like this.'

*

When he took up the axe again after smoking his pipe, Dukhi found that with his rest the strength had to some extent come back into his arms. He swung the axe for about half-an-hour, then out of breath he sat down right there with his head in his hands.

In the meantime the *Gond* came. He said, 'Why are you wearing yourself out, old friend? You can whack it all you like but you won't split this trunk. You're killing yourself for nothing.'

Wiping the sweat from his forehead Dukhi said, 'I've still got to cart off a whole wagon-load of hay, brother.'

'Have you had anything to eat? Or are they just making you work without feeding you? Why don't you ask them from something?'

'How can you expect me to digest a Brahman's food, Chikhuri?'

245

'Digesting it is no problem, you have to get it first. He sits in there and eats like a king and then has a nice little nap after he tells you you have to split his wood. The government officials may force you to work for them but they pay you something for it, no matter how little. This fellow's gone one better, calling himself a holy man.'

'Speak softly, brother, if they hear you we'll be in trouble.'

With that Dukhi went back to work and began to swing the axe. Chikhuri felt so sorry for him that he came and took the axe out of Dukhi's hands and worked with it for a good half hour. But there was not even a crack in the wood. Then he threw the axe down and said, 'Whack it all you like but you won't split it, you're just killing yourself,' and he went away.

Dukhi began to think, 'Where did the *Baba* get hold of this trunk that can't be split? There's not even a crack in it so far. How long can I keep smashing into it? I've got a hundred things to do at home by now. In a house like mine there's no end to the work, something's always left over. But he doesn't worry about that. I'll just bring him his hay and tell him, '*Baba*, the wood didn't split. I'll come and finish it tomorrow.'

He lifted up the basket and began to bring the hay. From the storeroom to the fodder bin was no less than a quarter of a mile. If he'd really filled up the basket the work would have been quickly finished, but then who could have hoisted up the basket on his head? He couldn't raise a fully loaded basket, so he took just a little each time. It was four o'clock by the time he'd finished with the hay. At this time Pandit Ghasiram woke up, washed his hands and face, took some *paan* and came outside. He saw Dukhi asleep with the basket still on his head. He shouted, '*Arrey*, Dukhiya, sleeping? The wood's lying there just the way it was. What's taken you so long? You've used up the whole day just to bring in a little fistful of hay and then gone and fallen asleep! Pick up the axe and split that wood. You haven't even made a dent in it. So if you don't find an auspicious day for your daughter's marriage, don't blame me. This is why they say that as soon as an Untouchable gets a little food in his house he can't be bothered with you any more.'

Dukhi picked up the axe again. He completely forgot what he'd been thinking about before. His stomach was pasted against his backbone — he hadn't so much as eaten breakfast that morning, there wasn't any time. Just to stand up seemed an impossible task. His spirit flagged, but only for a moment. This was the Pandit, if he didn't fix an auspicious day the marriage would be a total failure. And that was why everybody respected the Pandits — everything depended on getting the right day set. He could ruin anybody he wanted to. Panditji came close to the log and standing there began to goad him. 'That's right, give it a real hard stroke, a real hard one. Come on now, really hit it! Don't you have any strength in your arm? Smash it, what's the point of standing there thinking about it? That's it, it's going to split, there's a crack in it.'

Dukhi was in a delirium some kind of hidden power seemed to have come into his hands. It was as though fatigue, hunger, weakness, all had left him. He was astonished at his own strength. The axe-strokes descended one after another like lightning. He went on driving the axe in this state of intoxication until finally the log split down the middle. And Dukhi's hands let the axe drop. At the same moment, overcome with dizziness, he fell, the hungry, thirsty, exhausted body gave up.

Panditji called, 'Get up, just two or three more strokes. I want it in small bits.' Dukhi did not get up. It didn't seem proper to Pandit Ghasiram to insist now. He went inside, drank some *bhang*, emptied his bowels, bathed and came forth attired in full Pandit regalia. Dukhi was still lying on the ground. Panditji shouted, 'Well, Dukhi, are you going to just stay lying here? Let's go, I'm on my way to your house! Everything's set, isn't it?' But still Dukhi did not get up.

A little alarmed, Panditji drew closer and saw that Dukhi was absolutely stiff. Startled half out of his wits he ran into the house and said to his wife, 'Little Dukhi looks as though he's dead.'

Thrown into confusion Panditayin said, 'But hasn't he just been chopping wood?'

'He died right while he was splitting it. What's going to happen?'

Calmer, the Panditayin said, 'What do you mean what's going to happen? Send word to the tanners settlement so they can come and take the corpse away.'

In a moment the whole village knew about it. It happened that except for the *Gond* house everyone who lived there was Brahman. People stayed off the road that went there. The only path to the well passed that way — how were they to get water? Who would come to draw water with a tanner's corpse nearby? One old woman said to Panditji, 'Why don't you have this body thrown away? Is anybody in the village going to be able to drink water or not?'

The *Gond* went from the village to the tanners' settlement and told everyone the story. 'Careful now!' he said. 'Don't go to get the body. There'll be a police investigation yet. It's no joke that somebody killed this poor fellow. The somebody may be a pandit, but just in his own house. If you move the body you'll get arrested too.'

Right after this Panditji arrived. But there was nobody in the settlement ready to carry the corpse away. To be sure, Dukhi's wife and daughter both went moaning to Panditji's door and tore their hair and wept. About a dozen other women went with them, and they wept too and they consoled them, but there was no man with them to bear up the body. Panditji threatened the tanners, he tried to wheedle them, but they were very mindful of the police and not one of them stirred. Finally Panditji went home disappointed.

*

At midnight the weeping and lamentation were still going on. It was hard for the Brahmans to fall asleep. But no tanner came to get the corpse, and how could a Brahman lift up an Untouchable's body? It was expressly forbidden in the scriptures and no one could deny it.

Angrily the Panditayin said, 'Those witches are driving me out of my mind. And they're not even hoarse yet!'

'Let the hags cry as long as they want. When he was alive nobody cared a straw about him. Now that he's dead everybody in the village is making a fuss about him.'

'The wailing of tanners is bad luck,' the Panditayin said.

'Yes, very bad luck.'

'And it's beginning to stink already.'

'Wasn't that bastard a tanner? Those people eat anything, clean or not, without worrying about it.'

'No sort of food disgusts them!'

'They're all polluted!'

Somehow or other they got through the night. But even in the morning no tanner came. They could still hear the wailing of the women. The stench was beginning to spread quite a bit.

Panditji got out a rope. He made a noose and managed to get it over the dead man's feet and drew it tight. Morning mist still clouded the air. Panditji grabbed the rope and began to drag it, and he dragged it until it was out of the village. When he got back home he bathed immediately, read out prayers to Durga for purification, and sprinkled Ganges water around the house.

248

Out there in the field the jackals and kites, dogs and crows were picking at Dukhi's body. This was the reward of a whole life of devotion, service and faith.

# Two Autobiographical Sketches

My life is a level plain. There are pits here and there but no cliffs, mountains, jungles, deep ravines or desert wastes. Those good people who have a taste for mountaineering will be disappointed here.

I was born in 1880. My father was a postal employee, my mother an ailing woman. I also had an older sister. At the time of my birth my father was earning about twenty rupees a month; by the time he died his salary was forty. He had been a very thoughtful man, moving through life with his eyes wide open but in his last days he had stumbled and even fallen and brought me down with him: when I was fifteen he had me married. And scarcely a year after the marriage he died. At that time I was studying in the ninth grade. In the house were my wife, my step-mother, her two children and myself, and there was not a pice of income. Whatever savings we'd had were used up in my father's six-month illness and funeral expenses. And my ambition was to get an M.A. and become a lawyer. In those days jobs were just as hard to get as now. With a great effort you might find some post with a salary of ten or twelve rupees a month. But I insisted on going on with my studies. The chains on my ankles were not just iron but of all the metals together and I wanted to walk on the mountain tops!

I had no shoes and no decent clothes, and there were the high prices — barley was half-a-rupee for ten pounds. I was studying in the High School of Queens College in Banaras, where the headmaster had waived the fees. The exams were coming up soon. When I left school at half-past three I would go to the part of town known as Bamboo Gate to teach a boy there. I'd get there at four and tutor until six, then leave for my house, which was five miles away in the country. Even walking very fast, I could not get there before eight o'clock. And I had to leave the house at eight sharp in the morning, otherwise I couldn't get to school on time. At night after supper I studied by the light of the oil lamp. I don't know when I slept. Nevertheless I was determined.

Somehow or other I passed my matriculation exams. But I made only second division and there was no hope left of being admitted to Queens College since fees could be remitted only for the first division. By chance Hindu College opened up the same year. I decided to study in this new institution. A Mr. Richardson was the principal. I went to his house and found him in full Indian dress — *kurta* and *dhoti* — sitting on the floor writing something. But it had not been so easy for him to change his personality — after listening to me only long enough for me to get half my request out he said he didn't discuss College business in his house and I should go to the College. Fine, I went to the College and he saw me there but our meeting was a disappointment. He could not remit the fees. What could I do next? If I presented suitable recommendations then perhaps he might consider my request. But who in the city would know a country boy?

Everyday, I set out from home to try to get a recommendation from somewhere, and after an arduous twelve miles return in the evening. Who was there to ask? Nobody was concerned about me.

But after several days I found someone to recommend me, Thakur Indranarayan Singh of the board of directors of Hindu College. I had gone to him and wept, and taking pity on me he'd given me a letter of recommendation. In that instant my happiness knew no bounds. Blissful, I returned home. I intended to go see the Principal the next day, but as soon as I reached home, I came down with a fever. I couldn't get rid of it for a week. I kept drinking concoctions made from *neem* leaves until I could barely stand it. One day I was sitting at the door when my old family priest came along. Seeing my state, he asked for details and then immediately went off into the fields. He dug up a root and when he brought it back washed it and ground it in with seven grains of black pepper and made me drink it. It had a magical effect. After no more than an hour the fever broke. It was as if the herb had taken it by the neck and throttled it. I asked Panditji many times for the name of the root but he wouldn't tell me. He said that if he did its effectiveness would vanish.

After a month I went again to see Mr. Richardson and showed him the letter of recommendation. Giving me a sharp look he said, 'Where were you all this time?'

'I was ill.'

'What was wrong with you?'

251

I wasn't ready for the question. If I told him it was a fever perhaps the Sahib would think I was lying. In my estimation a fever was a very light matter, insufficient to explain so long an absence. I felt I should name some disease which by its gravity would draw his sympathy. At the moment I could think of the name of none. When I'd gone to Thakur Singh he'd mentioned that he suffered from palpitations of the heart. And that was the word I thought of. I said in English, 'Palpitation of heart, sir.'

Astonished, the Principal looked at me and said, 'Are you completely well now?'

'Yes, sir.'

'Very well, fill out the entrance application form.'

I assumed that the worst was over. I took the form, filled it out and brought it back. At that môment the Principal was in one of his classes. At three o'clock I got the form back. Written on it was: 'Look into his ability.'

Here was a new problem. My heart sank. I could hope to pass no subject except English; I shivered at the thought of algebra and geometry. Whatever I'd learned I'd completely forgotten. But what else was there to do? Trusting to luck, I went to class and presented my application. The Professor, a Bengali, was teaching English; the subject was Washington Irving's *Rip van Winkle*. I took a seat in the back row. In a few minutes I saw that the professor was competent in his subject. When the hour was over he questioned me about the day's lesson and then wrote on my form 'Satisfactory.'

The next hour was algebra. The teacher here was also a Bengali; I showed him the form. Most often the students who came to a new school have not been able to find admittance elsewhere, and that was the case here; the classes were full of incompetent students. Whoever came in the first rush had been enrolled — to the hungry the meanest gruel tastes good. But now the stomach was full and students were chosen only after careful selection. This professor examined me in mathematics and I failed; in the box marked 'maths' on the form he wrote 'Unsatisfactory.'

I was so disappointed that I didn't bring the application back to the Principal. I went straight home. For me mathematics was the peak of mount Everest, I could never reach it. In Intermediate College I'd already failed it a couple of times and, discouraged, gave up taking the exam. Ten years later when it was made optional I took another subject and passed easily. Until that time who knows how many young people's aspirations have been finished off by mathematics! Anyway, I went home disappointed, but the desire for learning was still strong. What could I do sitting at home? How to improve my maths and get enrolled in college was the problem. For this I would have to live in town.

By luck I got a post tutoring a lawyer's sons with a salary of five rupees. I decided to live on two rupees and give the other three to my family. Above the advocate's stable there was a rather small, unfinished room. I got permission to stay there. A piece of canvas was spread out for my bed, I got a very small lamp from the market and began my life in town. I also brought some pots from home. Once a day I cooked *khichri* and after washing and scouring the pots I'd set out for the library —maths was the pretext, but I would read novels and the like. In those days I read Pandit Ratannath Dar's *Fasana-e-Azad* (*The Romance of Azad*) as well as *Chandra-kanta Santati* (*Chandrakanta's Children*), and I read everything of Bankim Chatterji's that I could find in Urdu translation in the library.

The brother-in-law of the advocate's sons had been a fellow student of mine for the matriculation. It was on his recommendation that I'd got this post. We were very good friends, so when I needed money I'd borrow from him and settle the account when I got my pay. Sometimes I'd have only two or three rupees left, sometimes three. On the day when I had two from my pay I'd lose all restraint — a craving for sweets would draw me towards the candy shop. I'd eat up two or three *annas* worth at once. On the same day I'd go home and give my family the two or two-and-a-half rupees. The next day I'd begin to borrow again. But there were times when I was embarrassed about borrowing and day after day I'd fast.

In this way four or five months went by. Meantime I had taken two-and-a-half rupees worth of clothes from a draper on credit. Every day I used to walk by his place — he had complete confidence in me. When after a couple of months I hadn't been able to pay him I gave up going that way and took a detour. It was three years before I could pay off this debt. In those days a labouring man who made his home in the back of the advocate's house used to come to me to learn a little Hindi. He was always saying, 'Know this, little brother!' and we had all come to call him that by way of nickname. One day I borrowed eight *annas* from him too. Five years later he came to my house in the village and collected that half-a-rupee from me.

I still longed to study, but everyday I grew more and more despondent. I wanted to find a job somewhere but I had no idea of how and where to find one.

That winter I hadn't a pice left. I had spent a few days eating a piçe worth of the cheapest cereal each day. Either the moneylenders had refused to loan me anything or from embarrassment I couldn't ask. One evening, just at dusk, I went to a bookseller to sell a book — 'The Key to Chakravarti's Mathematics,' which I had bought two years before. I had held on to it until now with great difficulty but today in complete despair I decided to sell it. Although it had cost me two rupees I settled for one. Taking my rupee I was just about to leave the shop when a gentleman with big moustaches who had been sitting there asked me, 'Where are you studying?'

I said, 'I'm not studying anywhere but I hope to enroll somewhere.'

'Did you pass your matric exams? Then don't you want a job?'

'I can't find a job anywhere at all.'

This gentleman was the headmaster of a small school, and he needed an assistant teacher. He offered me a salary of eighteen rupees; I accepted. Eighteen rupees at that time was beyond the highest flight of my pessimistic imagination. I arranged to meet him the next day and left with my head in the clouds. I was ready to cope with any circumstances and if mathematics didn't stop me I would certainly get ahead. But the most difficult obstacle was the university's total lack of understanding, which then and for several years afterwards led it to treat everybody in the manner of that thief who made everybody, tall and short, fit one bed.

*

I began to write stories for the first time in 1907. I had read Tagore's stories in English and had Urdu translations published in the Urdu newspapers. But as early as 1901, I had begun to write novels. In 1902 one of my novels came out and a second in 1904, but until 1907 I had not written one short story. The title of my first story was 'The Most Precious Jewel in the World,' published in Zamana in 1907. After this I wrote another four or five stories. In 1909 a collection of five stories was published with the title 'Sufferings of the

*Motherland.*' At this time the partition of Bengal had taken place; in the Congress the radical faction had developed. In these five stories I praised devotion to the country.

At that time I was a deputy inspector in the department of education in Hamirpur district. One evening, six months after the stories had been published, while I sat in my tent I received a summons to go at once to see the District Collector, who was then on his winter tour. I harnessed the bullock-cart and travelled between thirty and forty miles through the night and reached him the next day. In front of him was placed a copy of my book. My head began to throb. At that time I was writing under the name of Navabrai. I had had some indication that the secret police were looking for the author of this book. I realized they must have traced me and that I was being called to account.

The Collector asked me, 'Did you write this book?'

I told him I had. He asked for the theme of each one of the stories and finally losing his temper said, 'Your stories are full of sedition. It's fortunate for you that this is a British government. If it were the Mughal Empire, then both your hands would be cut off Your stories are one-sided, you've insulted the British government.' The judgment was that I should give all copies of the book into the custody of the government and that I should not ever write anything else without the permission of the Collector. I felt I'd got off lightly. Of the thousand copies printed hardly three hundred had been sold. The remaining seven hundred I sent for from the *Zamana* office and had them delivered over to the Collector.

I assumed the danger was past. But the authorities could not be satisfied so easily. Afterwards I learned that the Collector had discussed the matter with the other officials of the district. The Superintendent of Police, two deputy collectors and the deputy inspector — whose subordinate I was — sat to consider what my fate should be. One of the deputy collectors, using quotations from the stories, asserted that in them there was nothing but sedition from beginning to end, and not just ordinary sedition but a contagious variety. The demi-god of the police said, 'So dangerous a man ought to be severely punished.' The deputy inspector was very fond of me. Afraid lest the affair be long drawn out he made the suggestion that in a friendly way he would sound out my political opinions and present a report to this committee. His idea was to explain to me and to write in his report that the writer was violent only with his

255

pen and had nothing whatever to do with any political disturbance. The committee accepted his suggestion, although the police chief even at this moment was still blustering and threatening. Suddenly the Collector asked the deputy inspector, 'Do you expect that he'll tell you what he really thinks?'

'Yes, I'm intimate with him.'

'By pretending to be friendly you want to find out his secret views? But that's spying! I consider it vile.'

Losing his wits the deputy inspector stammered, 'But I . . . Your Excellency's order . . .'

'No,' the Collector interrupted, 'that's not my order. I had no intention of giving any such order. If the author's sedition can be proven from his book, then he should be put on trial in an open court, otherwise dismiss the case with a warning. I don't like the idea of a smile on the face and a knife in the hand.'

When the deputy inspector himself told me this story several days later, I asked him, 'Would you really have done this spying?'

He laughed. 'Impossible. Even if he'd given several hundred thousand rupees I wouldn't have done it. I just wanted to stop any legal proceedings, and they've been stopped. If there'd been a court case, you would definitely have been sentenced. You would have found no one to plead your cause. But the Collector is a noble gentleman.'

'Very noble indeed ,' I said.

256

# Notes to the Stories

## 1  The Road to Salvation

Original title: *Mukti-Marg, 'Salvation Road'*. First published in 1924. One of Premchand's finest stories of village life for its sympathy and objectivity and the mock epic humour of its battle scenes and satire.

The 'Satyanarayan' ceremony, held to honour auspicious occasions like house-warmings, consists of special prayers, the recitation of the exploits of Lord Vishnu, specially consecrated foods and banquets for the Brahmans.

The conclusion of the story makes it clear that Buddhu is of a lower social community than Jhingur. The higher caste may not eat food prepared by the lower unless, as in this case, the actual cooking is done by the higher-ranking man, since fire purifies everything it touches.

## 2  A Feast for the Holy Man

Original title: *Babaji Ka Bhog, 'The Pleasure of the Holy Man'*. Throughout the story *bhog* is used ironically in its double sense of pleasure, enjoyment, and a ritual offering of food sacrificed to the Gods. Ramdhan is described as an *Ahir*, a community associated with cow-herding — another ironic element in the story, since he has no cattle but only plough oxen. Although in his catalogue Amrit Rai gives no date for this story, it is a fine example of the compression and absence of editorial comment which characterize Premchand's last stories.

## 3  The Power of a Curse

Original title: *Garib Ki Hay, 'The Lament of the Poor'*. First published in 1911. In this quite early story there is a good deal of the moralizing that so often characterized the earlier work and considerable redundancy as well. I have cut this where it seemed in the interests of the story.

It is worth nothing that in this tale Munshi Ramsevak is ostracized not because he is a wicked man — which everyone has accepted throughout his career — but because he is technically the cause of a Brahman's death. Premchand's attitude toward the villagers is no less critical than it is toward Munshiji.

The name *'Nagin'* suggests *'nag'*, a cobra, hence the reference to her hissing, rearing up, etc.

257

## 4  A Catastrophe

Original title: *Vidhuvans*, '*Destruction*'. Written in the early twenties. Though usually designating a tribal community, in eastern Uttar Pradesh *Gond* indicates a person of a very low-ranking social group who are privileged, according to the complicated rules regulating the preparation of food, to handle food for high-caste groups. Cf. '*Deliverance*'

## 5  January Night

Original title: *Pus Ki Raat*, '*A Night in the Month of Pus*', ( *Pus*, a month in the Hindu solar calendar corresponding to December-January). First published in 1930.

## 6  Neyur

Original title: *Neyur*. First published in 1933. The name Neyur is a peasant name, a dialect derivation from '*neola*,' mongoose. In the Urdu version of the story Premchand omitted the last two paragraphs, replacing them simply with his sentence: 'But he does his work exactly the way he used to and takes only a few crusts of bread for wages.'

## 7  The Story of Two Bullocks

Original title: *Do Bailon Ki Katha*, '*The Story of Two Bullocks*'. First published in 1931. The bullocks of the tale are endowed with not only a human but a specifically Hindu character, such as the belief in reincarnation and the importance of *dharma*. The political implications of this little fable today has only a slight historical interest, but the story has not lost its poignant charm, revealing Premchand's profound sympathy for abused non-human animals as well as the oppressed people of his country. The Hindi style, disarmingly simple but carefully controlled, is virtually impossible to reproduce in translation.

## 8  Ramlila

Original title: *Ramlila*. First published in 1926.
   Every autumn in villages and cities throughout North India Ramlilas are performed — dramatizations with music of episodes from the epic of Rama, which may take several days to complete, culminating with Rama's return from exile with Sita, his wife, and his brother Lakshman, and triumphant coronation. Some are great spectacles, such as the famous Ramlila of Ramnagar, Varanasi; others, like the one described here, are much simpler performances with only a few characters. In this story the players are given no names beyond those of the roles they play —Rama (Ramchandra), Sita and Lakshman.

## 9  The Thakur's Well

Original title: *Thakur Ka Kuan*, *'The Thakur's Well'*. 'Thakur' is a title of Rajputs, members of the second highest caste and thus 'twice-born,' entitled to wear the sacred thread Gangi refers to contemptuously.

'Thakur' is also used to refer to the supreme deity. Whether Premchand meant it ironically is not certain, but the idea is reinforced by the irony of the protagonist's name, Gangi, with its inevitable suggestion of Ganga, the Ganges, whose water is the holiest in the world.

This is a late story (1932) and a fine example of Premchand's later simplicity and his rejection of the editorial comment that sometimes mars earlier stories.

## 10  A Desperate Case

Original title: *Nairashya*, *'Despair' or 'Disappointment'*. First published 1924.

## 11  A Day in the Life of a Debt-Collector

Original title: *Tagada*, *'Dunning'*. A story from the early thirties.

## 12  A Car-Splashing

Original title: *Motor Ke Chinte*, *'Splashing from a Car'*. A late story. Though Indian commentators have paid little attention to this story, it is interesting for a number of reasons: the title is not an abstraction (such are comparatively rare), the villain is allowed to talk for himself — unlike the other heavy-eating pandits of the stories — and it pictures sudden, irrational violence erupting, in this case provoked by hostility to the westernized rich.

## 13  From Both Sides

Original title: *Donon Taraf Se*. First published in 1911 in Urdu, this story was not reprinted until 1983 in Sripat Rai's collection *Solah Aprapya Kahaniyan* in the original Urdu but in Devanagari script. Premchand apparently never prepared a Hindi version.

## 14  A Moral Victory

Original title: *Satyagrah*, the Gandhian term for an act of civil disobedience. First published in 1923.

This is one of the more elaborate episodes in the cycle of Moteram Shastri stories. Premchand obviously enjoyed the fat rogue's shrewdness, cheek, garbled eloquence and unabashed wickedness, and most of the stories about him share a vitality of narration that is not matched by structure and direction.

### 15 Man's Highest Duty

Original title: *Manusya Ka Param Dharm, 'Man's Supreme Religious Obligation'.* First published in 1920.

### 16 A Lesson in The Holy Life

Original title: *Guru-Mantra, The Precepts of the Teacher'.* Written in the twenties. In this sketch, which is a part of the satirical saga of Moteram Shastri, the slogans are half nonsensical and the concluding hymn highly ironical. The hashish is *ganja* commonly smoked by *sadhus*, particularly in Banaras.

### 17 A Little Trick

Original title: *Chakma, 'A Trick'.* First published in 1922. This is one of about a dozen stories by Premchand that dealt with the boycott of British cloth as a part of the Congress drive for independence.

### 18 Penalty

Original title: *Jurmana, 'Penalty'.* A late story. The story hinges on a point that may be obscure — the fact that the Inspector is persecuting Alarakkhi because she has rejected his advances. The Inspector's return to decency is a favourite theme of Premchand's and, in view of what we know of the character, not so surprising as it may at first appear. His one conversation with Alarakkhi is a kind of precis of the dialectics of poverty, developed in similar though much longer dialogues in the novels and other stories. Premchand's affinity with the Russian novelists is clear here in the affecting way he brings out the simplicity and humility of the poor.

### 19 The Writer

Original Title: *Lekhak, 'The Writer'.* First published in 1931. Though the story is uneven it provides an interesting satirical glimpse of provincial urban society (probably Allahabad, because of the mention of the High Court) where Premchand spent much of his professional life, and sharply defines, with some hyperbole, the author's quarrel with the philistines who dominated that society. Typical of many stories is his pairing of the avaricious Muslim merchant with an equally avaricious Hindu shopkeeper, with which he no doubt intended to emphasize his anti-communalism.

### 20 A Coward

Original title: *Kayar, 'Coward'* or *'Cowards'* — ironic and ambiguous in either case. First published in 1933.

## 21 A Servant of the Nation

Original title: 'Rastra Ka Sevak'.

## 22 The Chess Players

Original title: *Satranj Ke Khilari*, The Chess Players. Perhaps Premchand's best-known story, though not his best; like *Sadgati* (Deliverance), it has been made into a film by Satyajit Ray. As with a great many of Premchand's stories, there are versions in both Hindi and Urdu. The Chess Players was first published in 1924, in Hindi; the Urdu version, *Satranj Ki Bazi* (The Chess Game) appeared some time before 1928. Earlier publication does not always establish the priority of a version, though in this case, in view of the priority in publication, the Hindi may be the original one. In the preparation of the alternate version of his stories Premchand sometimes employed collaborators, so the question of the author's language is thorny and requires detailed investigation. The Hindi *Satranj Ke Khilari* is spare and abstract in its delineation of Lucknow society, while the Urdu *Satranj Ki Bazi* is more detailed and moralized explicitly at the conclusion. In making this translation I have followed the Hindi version throughout.

## 23 The Road to Hell

Original title: *Narak Ka Marg*, 'The Path of Hell'. First published in 1925.

## 24 Miss Padma

Original title: *Miss Padma*. Amrit Rai, Premchand's son, does not include this in his list of his father's short stories; it appears to be a late work, probably from the early thirties.

## 25 My Big Brother

Original title: *Bare Bhai Sahab*. First published 1934.

## 26 Intoxication

Original title: *Nasa*, 'Intoxication'. First published in 1934.

## 27 The Price of Milk

Original title: *Dudh Ka Dam*, 'The Price of Milk'. A late story, first published in 1934. This is representative of Premchand's best work, objective, compassionate and free of editorializing, the scene of Mangal's departure from his home under the *neem* tree is one of the finest in all Premchand. Lest it be considered in the least sentimental, it should be pointed out that, sentimentality being an expression of emotion in excess of what is warranted by the situation, the emotion of the story is, on the contrary, beautifully banked. Nowhere else has Premchand so well dramatized the plight of the sweeper (i.e. untouchable). In his biographical study of his father Amrit Rai justly observes that in these late stories the anger of the earlier works has given way to anguish. It seems scarcely possible to do justice to Premchand's style in translation, for obviously no exact equivalent can be found for Bhungi's earthy conversation, Moteram's inflated rhetoric (complicated humorously by provincial pronunciation) or the idiomatic ellipses of Mangal's speech. In this dark story the ironic significance of Mangal's name — auspicious, fortunate — should be kept in mind.

## 28 The Shroud

Original title: *Kafan, 'The Shroud'*. First published in 1936.

## 29 Deliverance

Original title: *Sadgati 'Deliverance'*, implying a death in a state of bliss or grace. First published 1931.

Dukhi is a *Chamar*, an untouchable who works with skins and hides and hence particularly objectionable to a Brahman 'Dukhi' means sorrowful — such names are common in villages and are usually bestowed to discourage or avert the envy of the gods; in this case, of course, it is ironic. The *Gonds* are a community of low standing but considerably above the *Chamars*. Cf. 'A Catastrophe.'

## 30 Two Autobiographical Sketches

Original title: *Jivan-Sar, 'The Substance of Life'*. In the original there is a third sketch which deals mainly with Premchand's deteriorating health. His father's 'stumbling' and 'fall,' refer apparently to the father's second marriage late in life and his early marrying of his son.

In the second sketch, the sentence Premchand would most probably have received if his case had been brought into court, was banishment to Burma. The final line is ambiguous: Indian interpreters feel that Premchand is being ironic, and irony is certainly there, but for all that he represented British oppression the Collector's sense of fairness doubtless was respected by Premchand, who makes a point of similar anomalies elsewhere in his work.

## 21  A Servant of the Nation

Original title: *'Rastra Ka Sevak'.*

## 22  The Chess Players

Original title: *Satranj Ke Khilari*, The Chess Players. Perhaps Premchand's best-known story, though not his best; like *Sadgati* (Deliverance), it has been made into a film by Satyajit Ray. As with a great many of Premchand's stories, there are versions in both Hindi and Urdu. The Chess Players was first published in 1924, in Hindi; the Urdu version, *Satranj Ki Bazi* (The Chess Game) appeared some time before 1928. Earlier publication does not always establish the priority of a version, though in this case, in view of the priority in publication, the Hindi may be the original one. In the preparation of the alternate version of his stories Premchand sometimes employed collaborators, so the question of the author's language is thorny and requires detailed investigation. The Hindi *Satranj Ke Khilari* is spare and abstract in its delineation of Lucknow society, while the Urdu *Satranj Ki Bazi* is more detailed and moralized explicitly at the conclusion. In making this translation I have followed the Hindi version throughout.

## 23  The Road to Hell

Original title: *Narak Ka Marg*, 'The Path of Hell'. First published in 1925.

## 24  Miss Padma

Original title: *Miss Padma.* Amrit Rai, Premchand's son, does not include this in his list of his father's short stories; it appears to be a late work, probably from the early thirties.

## 25  My Big Brother

Original title: *Bare Bhai Sahab.* First published 1934.

## 26  Intoxication

Original title: *Nasa*, 'Intoxication'. First published in 1934.

## 27  The Price of Milk

Original title: *Dudh Ka Dam*, 'The Price of Milk'. A late story, first published in 1934. This is representative of Premchand's best work, objective, compassionate and free of editorializing, the scene of Mangal's departure from his home under the *neem* tree is one of the finest in all Premchand. Lest it be considered in the least sentimental, it should be pointed out that, sentimentality being an expression of emotion in excess of what is warranted by the situation, the emotion of the story is, on the contrary,

263

beautifully banked. Nowhere else has Premchand so well dramatized the plight of the sweeper (i.e. untouchable). In his biographical study of his father Amrit Rai justly observes that in these late stories the anger of the earlier works has given way to anguish. It seems scarcely possible to do justice to Premchand's style in translation, for obviously no exact equivalent can be found for Bhungi's earthy conversation, Moteram's inflated rhetoric (complicated humorously by provincial pronunciation) or the idiomatic ellipses of Mangal's speech. In this dark story the ironic significance of Mangal's name — auspicious, fortunate — should be kept in mind.

## 28 The Shroud

Original title: *Kafan, 'The Shroud'*. First published in 1936.

## 29 Deliverance

Original title: *Sadgati 'Deliverance'*, implying a death in a state of bliss or grace. First published 1931.

Dukhi is a *Chamar*, an untouchable who works with skins and hides and hence particularly objectionable to a Brahman 'Dukhi' means sorrowful — such names are common in villages and are usually bestowed to discourage or avert the envy of the gods; in this case, of course, it is ironic. The *Gonds* are a community of low standing but considerably above the *Chamars*. Cf. 'A Catastrophe.'

## 30 Two Autobiographical Sketches

Original title: *Jivan-Sar, 'The Substance of Life'*. In the original there is a third sketch which deals mainly with Premchand's deteriorating health. His father's 'stumbling' and 'fall,' refer apparently to the father's second marriage late in life and his early marrying of his son.

In the second sketch, the sentence Premchand would most probably have received if his case had been brought into court, was banishment to Burma. The final line is ambiguous: Indian interpreters feel that Premchand is being ironic, and irony is certainly there, but for all that he represented British oppression the Collector's sense of fairness doubtless was respected by Premchand, who makes a point of similar anomalies elsewhere in his work.

# WIDOWS, WIVES AND OTHER HEROINES

# Widow with Sons

W hen Pandit Ayodhyanath died everybody said, 'God give every man such a death!'*

He left four young sons and a daughter. Three of the boys were married; Kumud, the daughter, was still single. He had also bequeathed considerable wealth: a proper brick house, two orchards, several thousands in jewels and twenty thousand in hard cash. Phulmati, his widow, grieved for him, and was distraught for several days but found consolation when she gazed at her four sons, each one so courteous, and the wives of the three older ones, each more obedient than the other. Before she slept her daughters-in-law would take turns in massaging her feet, and in the mornings when she got up and had her bath they'd put out her sari. The whole household was run at Phulmati's command—she was mistress of her home, even though the keys were in the keeping of the eldest daughter-in-law, for in her old age she had no love of authority which so often makes old people bitter and quarrelsome; nevertheless, not one of the children could get even a sweet without her permission.

The eldest son, Kamta, earned fifty rupees working in an office; Umanath, the second son, had obtained a doctor's degree and was considering opening a clinic somewhere. Dayanath had failed his BA and earned a little writing articles for newspapers; and Sitanath, the youngest boy and also the sharpest and most promising, having passed his BA in the first division, was preparing for his MA exams. In none of the four was there any of that tendency to dissipation, foppishness or extravagance which could anger their parents and bring dishonour to their family.

One evening, twelve days after the pandit had died, preparations were being made for the thirteenth day ritual.** There would be a

*A common expression, implying a peaceful death.
**Final rites in honour of the dead.

feast for the Brahmans, and all their caste brethren had been invited. Sitting in her room, Phulmati watched the porters bring in the sacks of flour. Tins of ghee, baskets of greens and vegetables, bags of sugar and pots of curd were on their way, along with gifts for the officiating priest—cooking vessels, clothes, beds and bedding, umbrellas, shoes, canes, lanterns and the like. But nothing was being brought to Phulmati. According to the usual arrangement, all these things should have been shown to her. She would look at each item, approve it and decide whether it was too much or too little; everything would then be placed in the storeroom. She could not understand why on this occasion it was thought unnecessary to show her these things and get her opinion. And why in the world were there only three sacks of flour? She had definitely ordered five. And only five canisters of ghee had come instead of the ten she'd asked for. Then she discovered that the quantity of sugar, vegetables and all the rest had been similarly reduced. She could not imagine who on earth had interfered with her arrangements and assumed the authority to change the quantities she'd settled on.

For forty years Phulmati's word concerning all household matters had been honoured by everyone. If she said a hundred rupees were to be spent, a hundred were spent, if she said one it would be one. Even Pandit Ayodhyanath himself would never oppose her wishes. But today every single order she'd given was being countered before her very eyes.

She held herself in check for a little while but finally could stand it no longer. Independent rule had become ingrained in her. Bursting with anger she went to Kamtanath and said:

'Were only three sacks of flour brought? But I ordered five. And five tins of ghee when I asked for ten canisters! Don't you remember, I ordered ten? I'm certainly in favour of economizing, but how shameful if the soul of the man who laboured to dig this well of our prosperity should long for water!'

Kamtanath neither asked for her forgiveness, nor acknowledged his error. He stood there for a moment, rebellion on his face, before he said, 'We all decided that only three bags of flour were needed, and for three bags five canisters of ghee would be sufficient. And by this reckoning all the other items were reduced as well.'

Phulmati was furious. She said, 'And just whose decision was that?'

'I told you, all of us.'

'So my opinion doesn't count for anything?'

'Of course it does. But the rest of us also know how to look out for our own interests.'

Stupefied, Phulmati stared into his eyes. She could not grasp the meaning of his words. 'Our own interests!' In this family she herself had been responsible for guarding all their interests, everything to do with profit and loss. No one, not even the sons she had brought into the world, had any right to interfere in her management. But this brat was talking back at her so insolently you'd think the house was his and he had killed himself working on its behalf, while she was just an outsider. What arrogance!

Flushed with anger, she said, 'You are not responsible for *my* interests. I have the authority to do as I see fit. Go at once and bring another two bags of flour and five more canisters of ghee, and after this, just be careful and see to it that no one goes against my orders.'

In her opinion she had scolded him enough. Perhaps such severity had not even been called for, and she was already regretting her fierceness. He was only a boy, he'd probably assumed some economizing was necessary, and hadn't consulted her since his Amma was always practising thrift in everything she did. If he'd realized frugality in such a matter as this would displease her he never would have dared to go over her head. So, although Kamtanath was still confronting her and it was apparent from his expression that he was not in the least eager to honour her command, Phulmati retired to her room with her mind at peace. The possibility that anyone should be capable of going against her orders after such a scolding never even occurred to her.

But as time gradually passed it began to dawn on her that she no longer enjoyed the status which only till a week or two ago had been hers. When the gifts of sugar, sweets, curd, pickles and the like began arriving with the invited kinfolk, Bari Bahu* took charge of them quite in the manner of the mistress of the house. No one bothered to ask Phulmati about her wishes, and if the people of the clan asked anyone about anything, it was always Kamtanath or Bari Bahu.

Phulmati observed and reflected that Kamtanath had recently been acting the big shot, lying about night and day drinking *bhang*, absenting himself from his office no less than fifteen days in the month, leaving the office to get along somehow or other. Actually, the boss is just showing his respect to his father otherwise long before now they would have thrown him out. 'And what does a slovenly woman like Bari Bahu understand about these things?' Phulmati wondered. 'Even if she tried she couldn't look after those rags of her's which she calls clothes and

*Kamtanath's wife, the eldest daughter-in-law.

269

now she's trying to run the whole house! They'll be disgraced, nothing less, all of them together will dishonour the family. In time they'll be short of one thing or another, for you need great experience in these matters and the stocks of food will be so depleted that it will reach the point where some guests will find food set before them while others will be served an empty plate. What in the world has happened to them all? And what possessed Bari Bahu to open the strongbox? Who the devil was she to open the strongbox without my orders? Of course she does have the key but that strongbox has never been opened except when I've asked for money to be taken out. But now she opens it as though I were nothing at all. I won't stand for it!'

She sprang up and went directly to Bari Bahu. 'Why did you open the strongbox, Bahu?' she said sternly. 'I didn't tell you to.'

Without any hesitation Bari Bahu answered, 'Supplies have come from the market, so are we not to pay for them?'

'I know nothing about any supplies, or how much, or how they've come. Until the account book's been checked how can any money be paid out?'

'The account book has been checked.'

'By whom?'

'How do I know who did it? Go and ask the men. I got the order: "Get out the money and pay up," so I'm taking the money to pay for the supplies.'

Phulmati was speechless with rage. But this was no occasion to start a row, with the house full of men and women who'd come as guests. If she took her sons to task right now people would say that discord had broken out in his family as soon as Panditji had died. With the weight of a stone on her heart Phulmati retired once again to her room. As soon as the guests departed she would dress down her boys one by one. Then she'd see who'd oppose her and what he'd dare to say. None of them would be able to make any excuses then.

But her mind was not idle while she sat in her room; she cast an eagle eye over the entire situation as she pondered what rules of hospitality had been violated and where decorum was forgotten. By now the feast had begun, with all the relatives seated together in a row. The courtyard could scarcely accommodate two hundred people, so how were they going to manage some five hundred guests? If they seated two rows instead of one, would there be any harm ? Doing it this way would mean that the feast would end at two instead of midnight even though these people were all in a hurry to go to bed. Could they somehow avoid this calamity and go peacefully to sleep? People were sitting so close together that nobody could move, and the leaf-plates were being piled one on top of another. The puris were cold, guests were demanding hot ones. When puris get cold they also get tough—how could anybody eat them? Who could explain why the cook had been taken away from his griddle? Everything was an absolute disgrace.

Suddenly people were complaining loudly: no salt in the vegetables! Bari Bahu made haste to start grinding salt. Phulmati chewed her lips with anger but for the moment she kept her mouth shut. Finally the salt was ground and sprinkled over the food on the leaf plates. Meanwhile, the guests became even more restless: the water was warm, they wanted cold water. But no one seemed to have cold water on hand, nor had any ice even been ordered. A servant was hustled off to the market, but of course at this hour of the night there was no ice to be had and he returned empty-handed. The guests were obliged to settle for the warm water from the tap. If Phulmati had had her way she would have pinched her sons' noses good and hard. Her family had never suffered such humiliation. They were all dying to become masters of the house—and they hadn't remembered even to ask for something so essential as ice! How could they have been so forgetful? They certainly had plenty of time to gossip and chatter. What would the guests be thinking privately, having come for a feast for the whole clan and not even finding ice in the house!

But listen, there's yet another commotion, the guests are rising up from their places. What could be the matter now? Phulmati could not remain indifferent. She came out of her room, walked out to the veranda, and asked Kamtanath, 'What's going on, my dear? Why are people getting up from their meal?'

Kamtanath turned and slipped away without answering her, leaving her fuming. At that moment one of the serving women came out and she asked her the same question. It appeared that one of the guests had found a dead mouse in his food. Phulmati stood there dumbfounded. Inside she was fuming so much that she felt like knocking her head against the wall. Those wretches had dared take charge of the feast! Was there any limit to their grossness? How many of the guests had had their religious purity utterly defiled! So of course they were springing up from their places. Who would let his *dharma* be polluted by witnessing something so vile? Oh, everything planned was ruined, hundreds of rupees thrown away, to say nothing of the disgrace.

By now the guests had all left. The food lay on their leaf plates just as they left them. Phulmati's four sons were standing shamefaced out in the courtyard, each one blaming the other. Bari Bahu was furious with her sisters-in-law, and all of them were laying the blame on Phulmati's daughter, Kumud, while the girl stood by in tears. At this moment Phulmati came to them and said angrily, 'Well, have you all dishonoured yourselves enough or not? Or is there still something you could do to make it worse? After such a disgrace you should all go and drown yourselves. You're no longer fit to show your faces in town.'

Not one of her sons said anything in answer.

Growing ever fiercer, Phulmati went on, 'What's the matter with you people? Have you no shame at all? The soul of the man who spent his life preserving the honour of this house, must be weeping. And you've gone and fouled his spirit like this! In town they'll have nothing but contempt for you, there's nobody who'll even come to piss at your door.'

Kamtanath had listened all this while in silence, but finally his anger boiled over and he said, 'All right, now you shut up, Amma. A mistake was made, we all agree, a terrible mistake, but are you going to murder us all for it? Everybody makes mistakes. Man repents and goes on. Nobody's going to be killed for it.'

Bari Bahu defended herself. 'How could any of us know that Kumud Bibi wouldn't be able to handle so much work? She ought to have put the vegetables into the cauldrons carefully, but she just tilted the basket and threw them in. Is that our fault?'

'It's not Kumud's fault,' Kamtanath rebuked her. 'It's not yours either, nor mine. Just a matter of fate—if disgrace is written in it, there is no escaping it. So at a feast as big as this the vegetables weren't thrown into the pots one piece at a time but one basket after another. Accidents like that happen from time to time. Why should we be ridiculed or disgraced for that? You're just rubbing salt in the wound.'

Grinding her teeth, Phulmati said, 'You're not even ashamed! You just go on saying rude, perverse things.'

Without hesitating, Kamtanath answered, 'Why should I be ashamed? Was anybody robbed? Nobody saw ants in the sugar or weevils in the flour. But we failed to discover that mouse and everything was spoiled. If we had we could have pulled it out and thrown it away—nobody would have been the wiser.'

Phulmati was astonished. 'What, you mean you would have fed them food defiled by a dead mouse and polluted their religious purity?'

Kamtanath laughed. 'What a lot of old-fashioned talk you're spouting, Amma. Does religion have anything to do with things like that? As for all those pious people who jumped up from their dinner, do you think there's even one of them who hasn't gorged himself on mutton and goat? They don't even abstain from turtle and snails from the pond. So what's wrong with a bit of mouse?'

At this moment Phulmati felt that it would not be long before the end of the world. When educated people could start accepting such sinful ideas then the Lord would surely come again to save the sacred order of the world. Distressed, she could only walk away.

One evening a couple of months later the four boys were sitting in a room talking after their day's work. Bari Bahu was also present to take part in the plotting. The subject was Kumud's marriage.

Leaning back against a bolster, Kamtanath said, 'Father's plan for her died with him. True, Murari Pandit might be both learned and of good family—but any man who sells his learning and good name for money is low. Now we couldn't marry Kumud to the son of such a low creature without paying plenty, at least five thousand. So tell him the deal is off and start looking for another bridegroom. Altogether all we have is twenty thousand, and that means a share of five thousand for each one of us. If we give five thousand for a dowry and another five thousand wasted in gifts and feasts for the groom's party, our business plans will be ruined.'

Umanath said, 'I'll need at least five thousand to open my own dispensary. So I won't be able to contribute one pice from my share. And then when I open up I'll no longer have any salary and I'll have to live at home for at least another year.'

Dayanath had been reading a newspaper. Taking off his glasses, he said, 'I'm thinking of starting a paper. The press and newsprint will require a capital of at least ten thousand. If I have five thousand of my own I'll find some partner for the other five thousand. I can't get by just by writing articles for the papers.'

Kamtanath shook his head. 'Good Lord—they won't even print your articles for nothing—who in the world would pay you for them?'

'That's not true!' Dayanath countered. 'Of course I wouldn't dream of writing without getting an advance.'

Kamta tried to take back what he'd said. 'I wasn't referring to you, brother. You always do manage to come up with some money, but not everybody else does.'

Bari Bahu piously offered, 'If the girl is lucky she can be happy in a poor home, if she's unlucky then she'll be miserable in a palace. These matters are all the work of fate.'

Kamtanath gazed admiringly at his wife. 'And then,' he said, 'we also have to get Sita married this year.'

While Sitanath, the youngest, listened to his brothers' selfish words he became impatient to say something. As soon as he heard his name, he spoke:

'Don't worry about getting me married. So long as I haven't found some profession I won't dream of marrying. And to tell the truth, I don't want to get married. The country doesn't need children these days, it needs people who can work. You can use my share of the money for Kumud's wedding. After everything was settled with Pandit Murarilal it's not right to break it off.'

Umanath said sharply, 'And where's ten thousand going to come from?'

Startled, Sitanath said, 'I was talking about just contributing my share.'

'And what about the rest?'

'Tell Murarilal there'll be some decrease in the dowry. He's not so greedy that he wouldn't be ready to take a little less on an occasion like this. If he's content with three thousand the wedding can be arranged for five.'

Uma turned to Kamtanath. 'Do you hear what he's saying, Bhai Sahib?'

'What harm's in it for you?' Dayanath burst out. 'He's just giving *his* money, so take it and use it. There's no enmity between us and Murari Pandit. It makes me happy that there's at least one among us ready to make some sacrifice. He won't need his money right now, he's going to get a government scholarship. Once he's got his degree he'll find a job somewhere or other, but we don't have an option like that.'

Kamtanath showed his farsightedness. 'You said only one thing of possible harm. Well, if one of us is in trouble are the others just going to look on without helping? He's still a kid, how does he know if some day a single rupee is going to be as useful as a thousand? Who knows, in the future he may get a government scholarship and go abroad to study, or find a job in the Civil Service. Then he'll need four or five thousand to prepare for the trip. Then who can he go around holding out his palm to? I don't want his life ruined for the sake of a dowry.'

This reasoning effectively stopped Sitanath. A little embarrassed, he said, 'Well, yes, if anything like that *did* happen then I suppose I'd need the money.'

'Do you mean you think it's impossible for it to happen?'

'Oh, I don't think it's impossible. But it's certainly a long shot. The ones who have recommendations get the scholarships. Who cares about me?'

274

'Sometimes the recommendations don't do any good and the ones who didn't get them win the prize.'

'Well . . . whatever you think is right. But as far as I'm concerned, even if I don't go to England I want Kumud to marry into a decent family.'

With an expression of loyalty, Kamtanath said, 'My dear little brother, a dowry doesn't assure a decent family. As your *Bhābhī*\* said, this is all a matter of fate. I want us to break off with Murarilal and search for a family that will settle for very little. I can't spend any more than one thousand for this marriage. How about Pandit Dindayal?'

Umanath was delighted. 'A very fine man! An MA, not just a BA, and a good income from his clients.'

Dayanath objected. 'But we ought to ask Amma for her opinion too.'

Kamtanath saw no necessity for this. 'Her mind's pretty well shot by now, you know. And she does go on about the old ways. She's hoping and hoping for Murarilal because she doesn't understand that his time has come and gone. As far as she's concerned Kumud is to go to Murari Pandit even if it ruins us all.'

Uma expressed his doubt. 'But Amma means to give all her jewels to Kumud, you'll see, so we have to consider her.'

Kamtanath's selfishness was not strong enough to go against morality. 'She has full right over her jewellery, that's her property as a woman. She can give it to anyone she wants.'

Uma said, 'But even if it's her property can she just throw it away? After all, it actually came from Father's earnings, didn't it?'

'Wherever it came from, she still has full authority over it.'

'That's just legal obfuscation. We have to share twenty thousand while Amma can hold on to ten thousand in jewellery! Just consider, with that money we could marry Kumud into Murari Pandit's family.'

Umanath, accomplished in the art of fraud, wasn't one to easily let go of such a great sum. He intended to devise some ruse to take every bit of the jewellery away from his mother. Until now he hadn't thought it a good idea to get Phulmati all riled up with talk about Kumud's marriage.

Kamtanath shook his head. 'Brother,' he said, 'I don't like these tricks.'

'Brother,' Uma said, annoyed, 'that jewellery must be worth at least ten thousand.'

\*Sister-in-law.

275

Kamtanath said resolutely, 'Whatever they may be worth, I don't want to have a hand in anything unethical.'

'So then stay out of it! Just don't get in my way.'

'Oh, I'll stay out of it.'

'And you, Sita?'

'So will I.'

But when Dayanath was asked the same question, he declared himself ready to cooperate with Uma. Out of the ten thousand he was to get a share of two and a half. For such a great amount if a little trickery was necessary it was surely pardonable.

After her dinner Phulmati had just gone to bed when Uma and Daya came in and sat down beside her. The expression on their faces suggested that a great calamity had just occurred. Suspicious, Phulmati said, 'You both look upset?'

Uma scratched his head. 'Writing articles for the newspapers is a very dangerous job, Amma. No matter how much you can get away with, somehow or other they finally catch you. Because of an article he wrote Dayanath has been hit with a fine of five thousand. If he can't pay it by tomorrow he'll be arrested and sentenced to ten years in jail.'

Phulmati struck her head and said, 'But why do you write such things, son? Don't you know that right now is an unlucky time for us? How can we pay that fine?'

Looking guilty, Dayanath answered, 'I didn't write anything to warrant a fine, Amma. But what can I do if it's my fate? I've tried as much as I possibly could, but the district magistrate is so strict he won't make the slightest concession.'

'But haven't you asked Kamtanath to arrange for the payment?'

Umanath scowled. 'You know what he's like, Amma, money is dearer to him than life itself. Even if Daya has to do hard labour in the Andamans Kamta won't give a pice.'

In corroboration, Daya said, 'So I haven't even mentioned the matter to him.'

Rising from her charpoy, Phulmati said, 'Go on now, I tell you he'll surely give it. Don't we have money for a day like this or is it just to be buried and forgotten?'

'No, Amma,' Umanath interrupted her, 'don't say anything to him. He will not only refuse to give the money, but will also cause a lot of trouble. He'll get worried about his job and he won't even let Daya go on living in this house. I wouldn't be surprised if he went to the authorities and informed on him.'

Helpless, Phulmati said, 'But then, how are you going to arrange for the money? I don't have any, but—there are my jewels. So take them and pawn them somewhere and pay the fine. Now put your hands on your ears and promise me that from this day you won't write a word for any newspaper.'

Dayanath put his hands over his ears and said, 'It cannot be, Amma, I can't save my life by taking your jewels. I'll just go to jail, even if it means five or ten years imprisonment. Anyway, what use am I just sitting around here?'

Striking her breast, Phulmati said, 'What nonsense you're talking, son! As long as I live no one will be able to arrest you. If anybody tries I'll gouge his eyes out. These jewels are for now, not for some other day. If you're not here then I might as well take them and throw them into the fire.'

She picked up a little wicker basket and set it down before them.

Daya looked at Uma as though appealing for help and said, 'What's your opinion, Bhai Sahib? This is exactly why I said we shouldn't tell Amma about it. So it can only be jail and nothing else.'

As though after long deliberation, Uma said, 'How could we *not* tell Amma about such a terrible misfortune? I couldn't very well keep it to myself. But as for what to do now, I really can't decide. It doesn't seem right that you should go to jail, nor does it seem right that Amma's jewels should be pawned.'

Her voice thick with emotion, Phulmati asked, 'You don't mean you think my jewels are dearer to me than you? But I'd sacrifice my very life for you, so what are jewels to me?'

Daya said firmly, 'Amma, I will not take your jewels no matter what happens to me. Until this very day, I've never been any help at all to you; how can I deprive you of your jewellery? You should never have brought forth such an unworthy son from your womb. I've never given you anything but trouble.'

Just as firmly Phulmati said, 'If you won't take them, do you think I won't go and pawn them on my own and then go to the district magistrate and pay your fine? If you like, you can put me to the test. After I die only God knows what will be, but so long as I live no one will be able to look at you with disapproval.'

Gazing at his mother as though with gratitude, Umanath said, 'Well, Daya, there's nothing else for us to do. It's all right, take them, but remember: as soon as you get hold of some money of your own, redeem those jewels. It's true what they say, motherhood's an endless sacrifice. Who but a mother can show such affection? We're wretches because we don't give her one hundredth part of the devotion we ought to.'

Then the two of them, looking as though still troubled by qualms of an ethical nature, finally picked up the little wicker basket and went off. Their mother watched them with loving eyes and longed to gather them to her bosom as if to bless them with all her soul. Today, after so many months, her mother's broken heart was achieving, as it were, the pinnacle of bliss through giving. Her powerful imagination had been searching for a road to some such renunciation like this, an offering of herself. In her there was not a single trace of possessiveness or greed or attachment; renunciation alone was her happiness, renunciation alone her privilege. Recovering her lost authority today, through offering her very life for the ideal she had created, she was gratified.

Three more months went by. Having made off with their mother's jewellery, the four brothers began to enjoy their spoils; they also consoled their wives with the thought that they had not caused Phulmati any grief. Moreover, if her soul was comforted by a little polite attention, what was the harm in that? All four did exactly as they pleased, but would first ask their mother's advice or trick the simple woman into going along with them and agreeing to all their ploys. She thought it was a terrible idea to sell the orchard, but the four of them made up such lies about it that she finally agreed. But they could reach no unanimity in the matter of Kumud's marriage. Phulmati insisted on Murari Pandit, her sons held out for Dindayal. One day they quarrelled openly about it. Phulmati said:

'A daughter has a share in her parents' earnings. You inherited an orchard worth sixteen thousand and a house worth twenty-five. Out of twenty thousand in cash doesn't Kumud have a share of five?'

'Amma,' said Kamta humbly, 'Kumud is your daughter, and then— she's our sister. In three or four years or so you'll be leaving us, but our connection with her will go on for a long time. So to the best of our abilities we must be sure to do nothing that would be unfavourable to her. But when you speak of Kumud's share—she doesn't have any. When Father was alive it was a different matter. He could spend as much as he liked for her marriage, and no one had the right to stop him. But now each one of us will be obliged to economize. What would be the sense of spending five thousand when one would do the trick?'

By way of emphasizing the point, Uma offered, 'Why five thousand, you might as well say ten.'

Kamtanath frowned. 'Not so. I would say no more than five. But five thousand's not within our means.'

'She's going to marry Murarilal's son,' Phulmati insisted, 'whether it costs five thousand or ten. My hard work earned that money, and I wore myself out saving it up. I'll spend whatever I want. Didn't I give birth to all of you? Well, I gave birth to Kumud too, and in my eyes every one of you is equal. I don't ask anything from anybody. You can sit around and enjoy the show while I arrange it all. Five thousand of that twenty belongs to Kumud!'

For Kamtanath there was now no other path but to take refuge in the bitter truth. 'Amma,' he said, 'you're talking rubbish. That money you claim to be yours is not, it's ours! Without our permission you can't spend a pice of it.'

Phulmati felt as though bitten by a snake. 'What did you say? Just say that again? I can't spend my own money that I've saved!

'It's not your money, it's become ours.'

'Perhaps it will be yours, but only after I die!'

'No, it became ours as soon as Father died.'

Umanath said roughly, 'Amma doesn't understand legal matters, she's just babbling for nothing.'

Her head spinning with anger, Phulmati said, 'To hell with your law! Laws like that mean nothing to me. Your father was no rich merchant. If I hadn't slaved and gone hungry you wouldn't be able to sit around loafing today. So long as I'm alive you can't touch my money. I spent ten thousand for each of you three to marry and I'll spend the same for Kumud.'

By now Kamtanath was losing his temper too. 'You have no right to spend anything at all!'

'Bhai Sahib,' Uma rebuked him, 'it's foolish to argue with Amma. Simply write to Murarilal that there's to be no marriage with Kumud. That's it, it's done. Amma knows nothing of the law so there's no point in arguing with her.'

Controlling herself, Phulmati said, 'Very well, what is the law, let me hear about it.'

'The law is this,' Uma said with an air of impartiality. 'When a father dies his property goes to his sons. A mother has a right only to food and clothing.'

'And just who made this law?' Phulmati demanded, uneasy.

'Our rishis,' said Uma quietly, 'Lord Manu, who else?'

For a moment Phulmati was speechless. Then she said in a hurt voice, 'So then, in this house I'm to depend on your rags and scraps?'

'Whatever you want to call it,' said Umanath in the heartless tone of a judge.

279

Phulmati's entire soul screamed as though struck by a thunderbolt and the words issued from her mouth like blazing sparks:

'I made this home, I saved up its wealth, I gave birth to you and reared you, and now I'm an outsider in this house? It's the law of Manu and you want to go by it? Fine, take your house and the lot, but I won't agree to live here as your dependent. I'd rather die. Congratulations for the outrage you're committing! I planted the tree and I'm not allowed to stand in its shade. If that's the law, then let it be burned.'

The anger and panic of the mother had no effect on the four young men. They were safe from these darts, protected by the steel armour of the law.

After some time Phulmati got up and went away. Now, for the first time in her life, her blind affection fo her sons had become a curse to afflict her. The motherhood she had considered the great crown of her life, counting it a blessing for which she could sacrifice all her desires and hopes, now seemed to her a fiery pit in which her life was being consumed and turned to ash.

Day turned to evening. At the door a neem tree stood without a leaf stirring, head bowed, as though distressed by the doings of the world. Towards the west the God of light and life, like Phulmati's motherhood, was dying in a blazing pyre.

When Phulmati went to her room and lay down she felt as though her back had been broken. That her sons would become her enemies within days of her husband's death was beyond her wildest imaginings. The boys she had nourished with her own heart's blood had now inflicted such a blow to that same heart! Her own house was now a bed of thorns for her. It was intolerable to her proud nature that she should be maintained like an orphan in a house where she was not appreciated or respected.

But she saw no way out. If she lived separately from her sons who would be disgraced? If the world spat upon her, so what? And if it spat upon her sons, so what? For the disgrace would be hers alone. People would say that though she had four sons the old woman was forced to live apart and get by as best she could. People she'd always looked down upon would be laughing at her. No, that disgrace was far more heart-breaking than this dishonour. Now the only thing to be done was to screen herself and her family from outsiders. But she would have to make herself over according to the new circumstances. Times had changed. Till now she had lived as the mistress of the house, now she would have to live like a scullery maid. If this was God's will there was consolation that these were the insults and blows of her children, not the insults and blows of outsiders.

For a long time she covered her mouth and wept. She passed the whole night in this anguish of the soul. The autumn light stole from the bosom of Usha, the goddess of dawn, as might some prisoner stealthily making his escape from prison. According to her custom, this morning Phulmati rose at first light; but in the course of the night her entire outlook had been transformed. While the whole house still slept she took a broom and began to sweep the courtyard. The dew-wet brick stung her bare feet like thorns. Panditji never let her rise so early, for the winter cold was dangerous for her. But now those days were gone. With time she would try to change her own nature. Taking a break from her sweeping, she began to search through the rice and lentils to pick out any impurities. Soon her sons awoke, their wives got up. They all saw the old woman working, shrivelled with cold, but no one said, 'Amma, why are you wearing yourself out?' Indeed, most likely each one of them was pleased to see her taken down a peg.

From this day on it was Phulmati's rule to work herself to the bone doing the housework and, according to her private policy, remain apart from the others. Her face, which once used to glow with self-respect, was now overcast with deep affliction. Where lightning had flashed there was now the weak glimmer of an oil lamp which could be extinguished by a light puff of wind.

The plan to write a letter of rejection to Murarilal had been carried out, and Kumud's marriage to Dindayal decided. Dindayal was a man of past forty, and of an inferior family, but satisfied with little. He agreed to the marriage without any shilly-shallying. The date was fixed, the groom's party paid its formal visit, and Kumud said farewell to her home.

No one could know how Phulmati felt in her heart, nor could anyone know what Kumud was feeling in hers. But the four brothers were as pleased as though a thorn had been pulled from their hearts. How could the daughter of a noble house open her mouth? If it was written that her fate would be a happy one, she'd be happy; if not, she would suffer unhappiness. God and his will are the last refuge of the helpless. No matter what the defects and vices of the man she married, he was her master to be worshipped. To oppose him was beyond her imagination.

Phulmati interfered in none of the arrangements. What was given to Kumud, what hospitality was offered to the guests, from what houses the gifts came—none of this was any concern of hers. If anyone did ask her advice, she would say, 'Whatever you're doing is fine, why ask me?'

When the bride's palanquin was at the door and Kumud threw her arms around her mother's neck and wept, Phulmati took her daughter into her room and tossed in her lap the hundred and fifty rupees and a few trifling bits of jewellery she'd been able to save. 'Daughter,' she said, 'if I'd had my way, would you have had such a wedding today and would we be saying good-bye like this?'

Until this moment Phulmati had told no one about what happened to her jewellery. She may not have completely understood the fraud her sons had resorted to but at least she knew that she would never have her jewels back, nor anything at all without making the family quarrel even worse. But on this occasion she felt it necessary to justify herself. She could not bear the thought that Kumud would go away thinking her mother had handed over all her jewels to her daughters-in-law, and this is why she had taken her to her room. But Kumud had already understood the trick played on her mother. Taking the rupees and jewellery from her lap, she set them at Phulmati's feet and said, 'Amma, your blessing is equal to thousands and thousands of rupees. Keep these things with you—who knows what troubles you may still have to face?'

Phulmati was about to say something when Umanath came into the room and said, 'What are you doing, Kumud? Come on, be quick about it. The moment's going by.* The groom's people are starting a commotion. Anyway, in two or three months you'll be coming back for a visit, so whatever you have to give or take, get it over with.'

This was like salt on Phulmati's wounds. She said, 'Son, what do I have left to give her? Go, daughter, may God give you a long and happy married life.'

After Kumud said goodbye Phulmati collapsed. The last wish of her life had come to nothing.

A year went by.

Phulmati's room had been the largest and airiest in the house. Several months before she had cleared it out for Bari Bahu and begun to live in a tiny room like some beggar woman. She no longer felt any affection for her sons and their wives. She was now the family maid and had no involvement with anyone in the house or in any of their business. She was alive only because death had not yet come for her. She was not the least bit aware of either joy or sorrow.

Umanath opened his dispensary; there was a feast for his friends, with dancers and other entertainment. Dayanath's printing press was

*The *sait*, or most auspicious moment for the ceremony as prescribed by the priest.

282

started; there were more festivities. Sitanath won his scholarship and set out for England with a great celebration. Kamtanath's eldest son was invested with the sacred thread, and once again there was feasting on a grand scale. But on Phulmati's face there was not even a shadow of happiness.

Then Kamtanath came down with typhoid and was sick for six months and almost died. Soon after Dayanath, to publicize his newspaper, wrote an article that provoked the authorities; he was sentenced to six months in prison. In a criminal proceeding Umanath took a bribe for writing a false report; for this his license to operate the dispensary was revoked. But Phulmati's features never gave any hint of distress. In her life now there was no hope, nothing to interest her, nor even any care. It was as though she were a beast and her life consisted of nothing but two activities—eating and working. The animal is made to work by beating, but it still takes pleasure in eating. Phulmati worked without being told, but she ate as though taking poison. For months she did not oil her hair, nor wash her clothes, and she didn't care, she was devoid of awareness.

The July rains poured down and malaria was rampant. In the skies the clouds were the colour of dust, the dusty ground turned to mud. The damp wind spread ague and fever. The kitchen maid fell ill, so Phulmati soaked and scoured all the household's pots and pans. Then she'd light the cooking fire and set the kettles on it. For her sons had to have their meals right on time. Suddenly she remembered that Kamtanath did not drink tap water. She walked out in the rain to fetch water from the Ganges.

Still lying on his bed, Kamtanath called out, 'Leave it, Amma, I'll fetch the water. The maid's sat around long enough.'

Phulmati looked up at the dust-coloured clouds and said 'You'll get soaked, son, you'll catch cold.'

'You're getting soaked too,' Kamtanath said. 'You don't want to catch cold now.'

Without any expression at all Phulmati said, 'I won't get sick. God's made me immortal.'

Umanath was sitting close by. He was very worried because he'd been getting no income from his dispensary, and in consequence was always trying to keep in the good graces of his elder brother and Bari Bahu. He said, 'Oh, just let her go, brother! She had our wives under her thumb long enough, now let her do her penance.'

The Ganges was so flooded it looked like the sea. On the further side the river bank blended with the horizon. Along the shore only the tips of the trees were visible above the water. The steps that led down to the river were now completely submerged. Holding her pitcher, Phulmati stepped down to the water's edge. She filled the pitcher and was about to start back when her foot slipped, she lost her balance and fell into the water.

For a few seconds she flailed around with her arms and legs, then the waves dragged her under. On the bank a handful of priests yelled out, 'Run, run, the old woman's drowning!' By the time some men came rushing Phulmati had already disappeared in the waves, those heaving waves simply the sight of which set one's heart pounding.

'Who was that old woman?' someone asked.

'Hey, that was Pandit Ayodhyanath's widow.'

'Wasn't Ayodhyanath quite a rich man?'

'Oh he was, but it was written in her fate that she should suffer ill fortune.'

'But all of his sons are grown up now and earning, aren't they?'

'Yes, all of them. But fate is quite another matter . . .'

1932

From *Mānsarovar*, v. 1. Original title, *Betoṅwālī Vidhvā*. Like 'Divided Hearths', with which it makes an interesting contrast, this story is a mini-novel. For all their villainy, the brothers are clearly differentiated and for a brief moment, at least, in one, Sitanath, there is a glimmer of decency; while Kumud offers Phulmati the momentary consolation of her recognition of her mother's goodness. Unusual for Premchand is the occasional personification of the gods in the descriptions of nature, meant, one may suppose, to confer a grander dimension to Phulmati's tragedy.

# The Secret

When he reached the door of Sevashram, Vimal Prakash took his handkerchief from his pocket and brushed away the dust that had fallen on his hair, then with the same handkerchief wiped the dust off his shoes and went inside. He was both founder and director of Sevashram and every morning, on the way back from his stroll, he would stop there to see to business matters.

This morning work had already begun at Sevashram. The teachers were giving the girls their classes, the gardener was watering the flowerbeds, and girls from one class were playing on the green lawn. Their health was of great concern to Vimal.

He paused a moment, pleased as he watched the girls at their ball game, then he went into his office and sat down. After the clerk set yesterday's mail on his desk Vimal opened the letters one by one, skimmed through them and put them down, while his face clouded over with disappointment and worry. He had got no results from the appeals for money he'd had printed in the newspapers. He could not imagine how the institution would be able to continue without help, nor how people could be so ungenerous. He had devoted himself body and soul to this work, donating whatever he possessed to the ashram. What more could people expect of him? He wondered if even now he was not considered worthy of their sympathy and trust.

Still plunged in these concerns he rose and went home, where he deliberated how he might surmount the crisis. The year was not half over and the ashram already owed twelve thousand, which would rise to twenty by the time the year ended. If he raised the girls' fees by one rupee per month the ashram's income would increase by five hundred rupees. And if each girl's fee for the hostel were raised two rupees, that would bring in another five hundred. In this way the ashram's income could be increased by 12,000 a year. But what would happen to his ideal of giving a superior education to the daughters of poor families, charging them only nominal fees? If only he could find a sufficient number of women teachers who would work for nothing more than their room and board! In so vast a country surely there must be twenty or thirty educated ladies willing to do this. He had placed announcements in the newspapers about his need for such teachers but had not so far received a single answer. There was now nothing left to do except to raise the fees.

At this moment a tonga pulled up before his door; a woman stepped out and walked up onto the veranda. Vimal came out from his room to welcome her and, ushering her in, invited her to sit down. The lady was not beautiful, yet there was certainly the glow of breeding and nobility on her features. A slender figure, of average height, pale complexion, smiling, well-dressed—and yet in the way she was attired there was also a hint of poverty.

A visit like this was nothing new for Vimal. Since he had opened the school ladies of good families often came to see him.

'First let me tell you who I am,' the lady said when she was seated. 'My name is Manjula. I saw your notice in the *Leader* a few days ago and have come to offer my help in your project. I had wanted to come several days ago, but couldn't find the opportunity and I didn't want to waste your valuable time by coming in an unsettled state of mind. You might think it flattery when I try to express the veneration I've come to feel towards you for the sacrifices and devotion you show in your service to women. I too have wanted to perform some such service for a very long time, but I haven't been able to do all that I wished to. But with your encouragement it's possible that I too can do something.'

Vimal was among those servants of the Lord who are by nature silent. To hear himself praised was a most severe trial for him and made him feel very much as though he were drowning. For his part, he never praised anyone to their face, so those who were hungry for approval considered him ungenerous. He did commend people behind their backs, but when it came to criticism, he expressed it to their faces and expected the same from others.

Recovering from his embarrassment, he said, 'That would be fine, certainly, and you'll be most welcome. But . . . are you aware of Sevashram's financial situation?'

'When I came here I wasn't concerned with such matters.'

'I was already aware of that. I didn't expect you would be but I merely mentioned it in passing. So then . . . do you live here in Banaras?'

Manjula Devi's home was in Lucknow. She had been educated at the Women's College in Jullunder, was well qualified in English and was also an expert in home economics. And what was most important, in her heart there was a zeal to serve. If a woman like this could assume the burden of Sevashram, Vimal thought, there was no telling what things could be accomplished.

But a question arose in his mind. He asked her, 'Will your husband be living with you?'

The question was commonplace, but it seemed to displease Manjula. She said, 'No, he won't, he'll stay in Lucknow, where he works in a bank for a good salary.'

For Vimal the question became somewhat complicated. Why would a woman whose husband had a good salary want to live apart from him in Banaras?'

But all he said was, 'I see.'

Perhaps guessing his thoughts, Manjula said, 'This must seem a bit peculiar to you. But—is it your opinion of marriage that a wife must live in the shadow of her husband?'

'Absolutely not!' Vimal answered with some passion.

'When I can reduce my needs to a minimum, why should I be a burden on anyone?'

'Quite right.'

'The two of us have had a serious disagreement, and there are several reasons for it. I feel that devotion and worship are the truth of life, he thinks they're ineffective. He doesn't even believe in God. I feel that Hindu civilization is the highest, but he finds nothing in it but defects. How can I get along with a man like that?'

Vimal himself regarded devotion and worship as hypocrisy and could not understand how a woman could leave her husband over a disagreement of this sort. He remembered several cases where a woman, even when her husband abjured his religion, continued to honour her marriage vows. Now here he was confronting a practical demonstration of this problem.

'But doesn't he object?' he asked her.

Proudly Manjula answered, 'I don't care whether he does or not. If a man is free, then so is a woman.'

Then more gently and with some sadness she went on, 'Consider that we've been separated for three years. We live in the same house, but we don't speak to one another. When sometimes he falls ill, I nurse him. If he's in any kind of difficulty, I offer him sincere sympathy. But

287

if I should die he wouldn't care in the least. In fact, he'd be pleased to be rid of me. But he pays my expenses, and therefore . . .'

She choked over her words and for a moment remained silent, staring at the floor. Then, fearing Vimal might think her frivolous and trivial for exposing all the secrets of her private life so gratuitously, she decided it was important to correct any such mistake on his part. And she was able to persuade him that before today no one had ever heard her say such things; she had never even told her mother of her distress. Vimal was the first person she had the courage to say such things to, and the reason was that she knew there was pain in his heart and he could understand a woman's helplessness.

Embarrassed, Vimal said, 'It's too kind of you to imagine I'm like that.'

And he felt trust in Manjula growing in his heart. After a long time a woman had appeared who was able to dare so much for her principles. In his heart he too had been in constant rebellion against society, and Sevashram was actually the outcome of this psychological rebellion. He would gladly hand over Sevashram to a woman like this. Manjula had come, ready for it.

In Manjula's character the desire for self-sacrifice had been excessive. She considered her body the only means for fulfilling this inclination. The power and riches of the world could not give her peace. Mr Mehra, her husband, displeased her merely because like all average people he too loved pleasure and entertainment. For him the point of life was to be swept along by his desires. In accomplishing his selfish aims he could not endure any obstacles such as those presented by religion or conventional morality. If he had been endowed with any generosity and, respecting Manjula's feelings even while disagreeing with her, offered her at least token support, her life might have been happy. But this gentleman had no sympathy at all for his wife, and at every opportunity stood blocking her way, leaving her utterly frustrated, to the point where, not finding a way to develop her feelings, she began to go astray.

If she could have expressed her need in art she might have attained peace, content to find there what she could not in life. But for that she possessed neither the intellect nor the creative power, so that her spirit was always restless, like a bird shut inside a cage. The ego she had suppressed was so strong that she could not become detached from life and do nothing. She wanted to create a free and separate existence for herself. It gave her both pride and pleasure to prove that she too was somebody, not merely a fruit sustained by the tree on which it grew, but someone with her own independent life, her own field of action.

But she discovered when she came out into this world of realities that what she had understood to be the meaning of self-sacrifice was a complete mistake. Now that she worked at Sevashram she came in touch with many people of a certain kind who, if flattered, would be willing to help the school. But Manjula's self-respect would not in any way allow her to accept or practise flattery. Writing them letters to welcome them to Sevashram, going to their homes to invite them to come and inspect it, or going to the railway station to greet them—all these were activities which utterly disgusted her. But she had accepted the burden of administering Sevashram, so she had to go against her heart and, setting the ideal of duty squarely before her, take on all these demeaning tasks, hiding her antipathy as much as she could. But how could she derive any joy and enthusiasm from work which went against her grain? The compromises from which she had tried to escape followed her here in even more repellent forms. Bitterness was gradually colouring her mind, and her spirit of dedicated service beginning to fade.

In contrast, she observed Vimal, on whose face there was never a frown. Ever that same smiling face, the same personality marked by renunciation, the same absorption in his work. He was always ready for the most trifling jobs; if a student or teacher fell ill he was at hand to attend to them. One could only wonder at the inexhaustible store of sympathy he possessed. No suspicion or doubt ever crossed his mind. He had taken one road, and along it he kept moving forward, believing that eventually he would attain his goal. The travellers he met on the way he made his companions, finding happiness in sharing his food with them. He was constantly obliged to worry and flatter, to suffer humiliation, be humble before unworthy persons, and beg for donations; yet he was never depressed or took things ill. There was something in him that leapt up and ran, always the same, despite all the setbacks he endured. There were constant trivial complaints from the women teachers, sometimes they were angry and wanted to leave Sevashram. The washerwoman had done a bad job washing someone's clothes, the servant had splashed water on another's sari, the watchman had yelled at one teacher's dog, another's room had not been swept or the milkman had mixed water with the milk—but what fault was that of the administrators of Sevashram? Yet there was always moaning and whining about just such matters with everybody making a great fuss, and it was up to Vimal, like a servant, to mollify them and cool their anger. The result was that the teachers had great confidence in him, considering him not in the role of a superior but rather as a friend and brother.

But Manjula held herself somewhat aloof from Vimal. She never brought him a complaint, she never sought his advice about anything. Though in his heart he might believe that she considered his involvement in mundane matters hateful and the ruin of his soul, she in fact realized it was in truth a very highly developed form of humanity. Nevertheless, it was difficult for her to break away from the pride she had in her theories about love. But despite her pride, Vimal's chaste and unselfish behaviour attracted her irresistibly to him. He was superior and free from the limitations she had with experience come to attribute to ordinary men. There was not a trace of selfishness in him, he was completely free of conceit. His capacity for sacrifice knew no limits. In Manjula's spiritual life this was the highest ideal of man. But to find Vimal close to this ideal represented a kind of defeat for her. The greatness of an ideal lies in its unattainability—if it becomes readily available why should it still be considered an ideal? By raising the standard of her ideal still higher Manjula hoped to find satisfaction in the thought that Vimal was still very far from attaining it. But Vimal seemed compelled to go on perfectly embodying her faith, like a plank which she seized to keep herself from being carried away by the current; but along with her feet the plank itself was being swept away too and she began to look for something else to hold on to. And finally she found it.

With her sharp eyes she had seen that Vimal was not satisfied with what she had accomplished. Then why did he never complain, why did he never ask her questions about it? With those same sharp eyes she had also guessed that he was not unaffected by her looks and style. So why this coldness and indifference? Did this not prove that he was deceitful or cowardly? When he was so open with others, so sympathetic in the way he treated them, why did he remain so distant with her? Why did he discuss things only superficially with her and where had that candour of their first meeting gone? Perhaps he wanted to demonstrate that he did not care in the least about her, or he might be angry with her only because she did not bow down before the wealthy. Well, he was welcome to his flattering. Manjula would perform her duties but not by violating her self-respect.

One morning she was strolling in the orchard when Vimal came along. After greeting her, he told her that Sevashram's annual festival was near and they would have to begin preparations for it.

Without much interest she said, 'So you have this celebration every year . . .'

'Every year, but this time we're thinking of expanding the activities.'

'I'll do whatever I can to help, though as you know I'm not an expert in such matters.'

'The celebration's success is going to be entirely your responsibility.'

'Mine?'

'Yes. You know, if you want to you can really make something of this institution.'

'I think you're quite mistaken in your expectations where I'm concerned.'

Vimal said confidently, 'Am I mistaken in my expectations or are you in yours? We will find out soon.'

This was the first time Vimal had ever urged her to take on some particular task. Since the day he had confided the care of Sevashram to her hands he had never given her an order. Whenever they met he had not dared and their conversation had always been merely small talk. Perhaps he had concluded that the sacrifice she had already made was more than enough, and to put another burden on her would be oppressive. Or perhaps he saw that if Manjula enjoyed her work here, there would be time enough for him to speak out. When with polite insistence he gave her this order today a new enthusiasm coursed through Manjula. She had never before felt such a personal involvement with Sevashram. Whatever ill feelings she had harboured toward's Vimal were scattered like dust in the wind and she threw herself wholeheartedly into preparations for the festival. She was surprised that she had felt so apathetic about Sevashram up till now. For the whole week she was busy night and day offering hospitality to the guests, scarcely taking time off to eat. Some guests would come by one train, some by another, so that she often had to go to the station at night. In addition to that she had to supervise rehearsals of all sorts of athletic events, not to mention preparing her speech. The reward she got for all this dedication was that, from every point of view, the festival really was a success and brought in several thousands in contributions. But the same day the guests departed she had to welcome yet another one who did not give her a moment's rest: she came down with a fever such as she had never had before. In three days she felt as though she had been suffering years of illness.

Vimal had been frantically engaged in the preparations as well. First he was busy having the tent-awning made and arranging the banquet for the guests. When the celebration was over he had to see that all the rented material securely packed and sent back wherever it had come from. He could not even find time to thank Manjula, and when someone told him that the lady had fallen ill he assumed she must have got a temperature from working too hard, it could not be anything serious. But when he heard that by the fourth day her fever had still not come down and was worse than ever, he came to her in a panic to stand before her and say with a guilty air:

'How are you feeling? Why didn't you send for me?'

Manjula felt as though her fever was suddenly lighter and that the throbbing in her head was easing. She lay there helpless and said, 'Why are you standing? Do please sit down. Otherwise I shall be obliged to get up.'

The look he gave her seemed to say that if it had been in his power he would have taken on all her aches and fever. Then he said emphatically, 'No, no, you must stay in bed, I'll sit down. This is all my fault, I got you into this unhappy situation. Please forgive me. I assigned you work I should have done myself. I'm going immediately to get a doctor. What can I say? I hadn't the least idea of what was happening. I was caught up in quite useless tasks . . .'

And he had just turned to go when Manjula lifted her hand to stop him and said, 'No, no, there's no need of a doctor. You mustn't worry, I'm quite recovered and by tomorrow I'll be able to sit up.'

There were a great many other things rushing through her mind, but she kept them to herself. In her excited state she had no idea what nonsense she might come out with. Until now, because she was a lady, Vimal had kept his eyes lowered in her presence, and of course stayed some distance away. Not because he didn't wish to come closer, but on the contrary, in his simplicity, his decency, he hesitated, fearing that he might offend her. And for her part, she had no intention of coming down from the high throne on which he had placed her. He himself had absolutely no idea of what a pure and great-hearted man he was and for her there was a tremendous charm in preserving the vague image of a virtuous, honest woman flying through the skies forever in the memory of a man like him.

'Yes,' she said light-heartedly, 'why not? Because you are human and I merely a wooden puppet.'

'No, you're a goddess.'

'No, a foolish woman.'

'The things that you've accomplished I couldn't have done in a hundred years.'

'Have you understood why? This is not a woman's victory but her defeat. If with my faults I had been a man instead of a woman I could probably have had only a fourth of this success. It's not my triumph, but the triumph of my womanhood. Beauty is a hollow thing, without reality. It's a deception, a fraud, merely a screen to hide one's weaknesses.'

Vimal responded passionately, 'What are you saying, Manjuladevi? Beauty is the highest truth in the universe. The mahatmas and pandits have done a grievous injustice to the world by declaring beauty a terrible thing.'

Manjula's lovely features sparkled with the light of pride. She had always been unsuccessful in her attempt to view beauty as worthless. And with her faith and devotion she had always regretted that she was good-looking. For a moment this confirmation of her beauty thrilled her, but controlling herself, she said, 'Vimal Babu, please forgive me, but your idolizing of beauty is nothing new. Men always worship beauty. No matter that a few mahatmas and pandits have slandered it, men have usually testified to their adoration for it to the point where they haven't cared about religion. And those pandits and mahatmas, even though they have spat poison on beauty with tongue and pen, they too have worshipped it in their hearts. Whenever beauty has tested them, it's won out over their austerity. Still, what's worthless and untrue will always be worthless and untrue. Its attraction is superficial, only for the eyes. For the wise it has no value. From your mouth at least I don't want to hear any praise of beauty because I regard you as superior to the common run of men and trust you with all my heart.'

Somewhat perplexed, Vimal sat staring at the floor, and kept on staring as though in a state of trance. Then, rising, with his head bowed like one guilty, his steps uncertain, he left her room.

And Manjula did not move.

From that day on all Vimal's enthusiasm and energy suddenly grew cold. It was as though he no longer dared show his face because the veil had been removed from his secret and everybody around was laughing at him. He now came much less regularly to Sevashram, and when he did, he avoided talking with the teachers. He seemed to be hiding his face from everyone. He allowed no opportunity for meeting Manjula, and when she, giving in, came to his house, he made the servant tell her he was not at home while he sat inside, hiding.

And Manjula was unable to understand the secret of how he felt. With his devotion and good will Vimal had attracted her to him, of that there was no doubt. With a woman's profound insight she understood that he had become her worshipper and, on receiving the least encouragement, would be ready to throw himself at her feet. In the life she had led for years there was no love, and even as she took shelter in service and duty she was continually aware of her lack of fulfilment. She would not agree to any moral or religious bond with a man who did not love and trust her. She considered herself independent, and whether society accepted that or not, in this matter her soul knew that she was free.

But the desire to win respect and devotion from Vimal was so strong in her that she could not let this sense of independence find expression. She wanted to maintain the most intimate connection with him, but without sacrificing her self-respect. At the same time she did not want to leave any blemish on his pure and stainless life. She thought that by having him drink merely a tiny drop of medicine she could make him well. And when he was well he would come into the garden of her mind, he would be happy when he saw the blossoms, he would lie down on the green grass and listen to the singing of the birds. That much intimacy with him was what she wanted.

But lamplight can be enjoyed only from a distance. If one touched it one could be burned. Now she realized that the drop of medicine, instead of removing the obstacle, could produce a new illness. Vimal did not possess the power to remain uninvolved. Whatever he wished to have became his own, body and soul, and when he drew away it was as if his link to it was completely broken. She considered this behaviour of his an insult to herself. And she began to be fed up with Sevashram.

She knew that every day he strolled along the riverbank and finally one day she cornered him on his walk and handed him her resignation.

Vimal stared at the ground and said, sounding as though there were a noose around his neck, 'But why this?'

'Because I find that I'm not worthy of this work.'

'But the school is running well, isn't it?'

'Still, I don't want to stay on here.'

'Have I done something wrong?'

'Ask your heart.'

Vimal understood these words in a way that was miles away from what Manjula had intended. The colour left his face, as though the flow of his blood had stopped. He could find no answer. Her decision seemed to allow of no appeal.

Pained, he said, 'As you wish. Take pity on me.'

Softening, Manjula said, 'Then shall I leave? . . .'

294

'As you wish.'

And as though tearing the noose from his throat, he rushed away. Manjula watched him compassionately, as though a ship were sinking before her eyes.

Feeling the whip, Vimal was once again harnessed to the Sevashram wagon. People said that Manjula Devi's husband had fallen ill and so she had to leave. A man committed to his work does not cultivate the illness of love, he has no leisure for writing poems and love letters or sighing deep sighs. Duty lies before him, the desire for progress, the ideal. So Vimal too was preoccupied with his labours. True, from time to time when he was alone he remembered Manjula and his head automatically drooped with shame. He had learned a lesson to last him forever. How stupidly he had acted towards a woman of so many virtues!

Three years passed. That summer Vimal went to Mussoorie for a vacation and was staying at a hotel. One day while he stood near the bandstand listening to the music he caught sight of Manjula sitting on a bench nearby, sparkling with jewels and colours, beside a young man wearing a European suit. They were smiling as they talked to each other, their faces glowing, both of them intoxicated with love. Vimal wondered who the young man could be—he was obviously not her husband. Or was it possible that he was? They might have reconciled. Vimal did not have the courage to approach her.

The next day he went to the cinema hall to see an English show. When he came out during the intermission Manjula appeared again, this time at the cafe. She was dressed completely in an English fashion. The same young man accompanying her yesterday was with her again. Today Vimal was unable to hold back, and before he could give it some thought he was standing before her.

As soon as she saw him Manjula fell silent. She appeared taken completely by surprise, but she quickly regained her poise and said, smiling, 'Hello, Vimal Babu, what are you doing up here?' Then she introduced him and the young man to each other: 'This is Vimal, a great soul, director of Sevashram in Banaras, and this is Mr Khanna, who's just returned from England to enter the Civil Service.'

The two men shook hands.

'Are things going well at Sevashram?' she then asked Vimal. 'I've been reading the annual reports in the newspapers. Where are you staying here?'

Vimal told her, and then Khanna said, 'The show's about to begin again, let's go inside.'

'You go in and watch,' said Manjula. 'I want to talk with Vimal Babu for a bit.'

Khanna's glance at Vimal was full of jealousy before he strode back into the theatre. Vimal and Manjula came outside and sat on the green grass. Vimal's heart swelled with pride. A pleasant feeling of hope spilled over his heart like moonlight.

Her tone grave, Manjula asked him, 'You must think about me sometimes, I suppose? Often I wanted to write to you, but I didn't quite dare. But of course you've been quite happy there? . . .'

This irony did not please Vimal. There she was having a good time but the moment she saw him she became a model of seriousness. He replied drily, 'Yes, everything's been fine. And you've been having a good rest?'

'Rest isn't written in my fate, Vimal Babu,' she answered with some emotion. 'My husband died last year. Whatever property he left me went to pay his debts. I've been caught up in these complications, and my health has suffered too. The doctors advised me to live in the mountains, so since then I've been staying here.'

'And you didn't even write to me about it.'

'As though you didn't have enough troubles on your mind for me to add my own!'

'Still, you should have written to me, as your friend.'

Her voice full of confidence now, Manjula said, 'It isn't your lot in life to get involved in quarrels like that, Vimal Babu. God created you for service and renunciation. That's your field of action. I know, you regard me with compassion, and I can't tell you how much that means to me. One who has never been given love or compassion must be forgiven if she rushes towards them. So you can understand what a great sacrifice I made when I renounced them. But I felt it was my duty. I can bear almost anything but I could not bring down your godliness from its high seat. You're a learned man, and you well know how transient are the pleasures of the world. Don't be tempted by them. You're human, you have desires, you have passions. But you've found your high place by triumphing over them. Guard it well. Spiritual discipline can help you. With such discipline your life will be virtuous and your mind pure.'

Vimal, perfectly aware of what her relationship with Khanna must be, had just now been imagining her engaged in the enjoyment of sexual pleasures. Nevertheless, he sensed a message of genuine sympathy in her advice. Sensual Manjula appeared to him in the form of a goddess: the pride inside him was more powerful than his desire.

With great kindliness he said, 'I'm grateful for the words with which you've honoured me. Tell me, is there any way that I can serve you?'

Manjula stood up and said, 'That you should be favourably disposed towards me is enough.'

At this moment Khanna appeared coming out of the cinema hall.

1936

From *Kafan*. Original title, *'Rahasya'* ('Secret' or 'Mystery').

# Second Marriage

Though our body ages new blood courses through it continually, and the flow of that new blood provides the foundation of our life. In the everlasting order of this earth, in every one of its atoms, in every one of its molecules, the renewal continues to vibrate, like the tones produced by the strings of a sitar.

Ever since he'd remarried, Lala Dangamal felt his youthful spirits reawakened. While his first wife was alive he had spent very little time at home. It had been his custom to pass the hours between dawn and ten or eleven devoted to his puja; then, after taking a meal, he would go to his shop and not return home until one in the morning, dead tired, and go to sleep. If Lila, his wife, were to ask him if he might not come home a little earlier he would get angry and answer, 'Do you expect me to abandon my shop for you, should I stop earning a living? The days when Lakshmi could be satisfied with an offering of water are gone. Now you have to grind your head against her door if you want her to smile.'

And poor Lila would say no more.

It happened that about six months before the time of this story Lila came down with a fever. When Lalaji was about to set out for his shop she became anxious and said, 'Look, I don't feel at all well so do please come home a little earlier.'

Dangamal took off his turban, hung it on the peg, and said, 'If having me hanging around the house makes you feel better, I'll stay back.'

Despairing, Lila said, 'I'm not asking you *not* to go to the shop, I only asked you to come home a little earlier.'

'Do you think I go to the shop just for the fun of it?'

How could she answer that? Her husband's loveless treatment was nothing new. For several years now she had suffered the bitter

298

experience of knowing that she was not appreciated in this house. Though she often reflected on the problem she could not see that she had ever done anything wrong. She even devoted herself more fully to serving her husband than she had before, constantly trying to lighten the burden of his work, constantly trying to please him; and she would never do anything at all contrary to his wishes. If her youthful bloom had faded was that a crime? No one remained young forever. Was it her fault if she was no longer in as good health as she once was? Yet she was being punished without ever being at fault.

The right thing would have been for twenty-five years of living together to have taken by now the form of a deep psychological and spiritual harmony which could have transformed even faults to virtues, or, like a ripened fruit, would have been juicier, sweeter and more beautiful. But Lalaji's businessman's heart weighed every object on a shopkeeper's scales. When an old cow no longer produces calves or milk the best place for her is the cowshed. In his opinion it was enough that Lila continued to be mistress of the house, had enough to eat and lived in comfort. She had the authority to have as much jewellery made as she wanted, to bathe and perform puja as often as she wanted, so long as she stayed away from him. It was a mystery of the complexity of human nature that Dangamal himself kept aspiring precisely for that happiness of which he wished to deprive Lila and which he did not consider necessary for her. He thought her old at forty while he, at forty-five, was still young, full of the madness and joyousness of youth. He now found Lila somehow distasteful, and when the poor woman, aware of the mistakes made by fate, attempted to defend herself against the assaults of nature by taking refuge in lotions and make-up, Lalaji found her aged coquetry all the more disgusting. He would say:

'Hurrah for passion! You're the mother of seven children, your hair has turned gray, your face is wrinkled like wet flannel, but you still crave dyes and rouge and grease! How peculiar women's nature is! Who knows why they go in for all these cosmetics—ask yourself, what more do you want now? Why don't you get it through your head that your youth has flown out of the window and all this artifice isn't going to bring it back?'

But he himself went on dreaming of youth. He resorted to tonics and special foods, had his hair dyed twice a week, and started correspondence with a doctor on the subject of monkey glands.

Seeing him undecided, Lila asked him timidly, 'But can't you please tell me when you'll be coming home?'

Tranquilly Lalaji said, 'How are you feeling now?'

She did not know what to answer. If she told him she was feeling really ill then this fine gentleman might stay home and serve her up constantly with sarcastic comments on how she made him suffer. But if she said she felt fine he might well be freed of any concern and stay out until two in the morning. Caught in this dilemma, she said with some trepidation, 'I was feeling a bit better, now I'm getting a little nauseous—but go, there'll be people waiting for you at the shop. But for God's sake, come back before one or two. The boys will be sleeping and I get uneasy, I worry.'

In a tone of treacly affection, Lalaji said, 'I'll certainly be back by twelve.'

Lila's face clouded over, 'Can't you be back by ten?'

'I can't possibly be home before 11:30.'

'No, half-past ten!'

'Very well—eleven.'

With that promise Lalaji left, but that night at ten a friend invited him to come along to see some dancing girls perform. There was no way he could turn down an invitation like that. When somebody invites you so hospitably what kind of gentleman could fail to accept?

So Lalaji went off to see the dancing girls and only returned home at two. Quietly he woke the servant and went to his room to lie down. Some time earlier Lila, every moment suffering with acute anxiety and worn out with waiting, had fallen asleep.

Finally this unhappy sickly woman took her leave of this world. Lalaji was much grieved over her passing. Friends sent telegrams expressing their sympathy, a daily newspaper offered condolences and printed an exaggerated account of Lila's spiritual and moral virtues. Lalaji thanked all these friends of his most fervently, established five scholarships at a girls' academy in Lila's name, and gave so many funeral banquets in her honour that it was remembered for a very long time in the history of the city.

But hardly a month had passed before Lalaji's friends began to put pressure on him, with the result that after enduring a widower's state for six months he married a second time. After all, what else was the poor fellow to do? One needs a companion to get through life, and at the age he had reached a companion was in a way absolutely indispensable.

Once he had remarried a most surprising transformation came about in Lala Dangamal's life. He was no longer so fond of his shop, and if he did not go to it for weeks on end his business did not suffer. His capacity to enjoy life, which had been weakening day by day, now revived like a drought-stricken tree which turns green again when it is watered and puts out new springs and buds. A new car arrived, new furniture graced the rooms, the servants grew in number, next came a radio, and every day new gifts kept pouring in. Lalaji's geriatric youthfulness became fiercer than any young fellow's, in just the way lightning flashes are more brilliant and fascinating than moonlight. When his friends congratulated him on the change in him he would say:

'My friend, I've stayed young all this time and I always intend to. If old age comes to me I'll disgrace it, set it on a donkey and drive it out of town. I don't know why people always make a connection between youth and old age. Youthfulness has no more to do with age than ethics with religion, money with honesty, or beauty with cosmetics. Can you call today's young people really young? I wouldn't exchange one hour of my life for thousands of their youthful years. There's no excitement in their lives, no zest. What sort of life is theirs?—a stone tied around their necks.'

He constantly elaborated on these ideas to impress them on the screen of his new wife's heart. He was always insisting that Asha, as she was called, accompany him to the cinema, the theatre or on strolls along the river. But for some reason or other Asha had not the slightest inclination to go, and when she did go it was only after much reluctance and procrastination.

One day Lalaji came to her and said, 'Let's take a boat ride on the river.'

It was a rainy day, the river was cresting high, and battalions of clouds, like foreign troops in brilliant uniforms, were advancing in formation across the sky; swings swayed in the orchards, and people walked along the roads singing 'Malhar'* and songs of the twelve seasons.

Asha answered moodily, 'I don't really want to.'

Gently persuasive, Lalaji said, 'What's wrong that you don't crave any sort of amusement? Come along, let's have our ride. I'm telling you the truth, you'll really enjoy the boat.'

'You go along. There are things I have to do.'

'You have people to do those things for you. Why should you bother?'

*'Malhar' is a raga (including many derivatives) for the rainy months, as are the barahmasa, songs describing the various seasons; swings are also associated particularly with the monsoon.

'The Maharaj* doesn't make very good meals. You sit down to eat and leave the table still hungry.'

Asha had been spending most of her free time preparing all sorts of dishes for Lalaji. She had once heard someone say that after a certain age the greatest pleasure in a man's life comes from satisfying his palate.

Lalaji was overwhelmed with delight to think that Asha loved him so much she would give up a boat ride in order to cook for him. For her part Lila had always been ready to go whether she wanted to or not; it was impossible to get rid of her since for no reason at all she would insist and spoil all your fun.

He reproached Asha affectionately, saying, 'You have a very peculiar way of thinking. If for one day the meal has no savour it's no catastrophe, is it? You're spoiling me, you know. Now, if you won't go, neither will I.'

Wriggling like somebody trying to get a noose off from around her neck, Asha said, 'But you're spoiling me too, taking me around everywhere. If this becomes a habit, how's the housework going to get done?'

'I don't give a damn about the housework—not a tinker's damn! I *want to* spoil you and keep you as far as possible from the drudgery of housekeeping. And why do you always address me with the formal '*Aap*'?** I want you to say '*tum*' to me, in fact, say *tu*' to me! Insult me, hit me! You say '*Aap*' as though you were setting me on a throne like a god. I'm not a god in my own house, I just want to be a naughty little boy.'

Forcing a smile, Asha said, 'Very well, I'll say '*tum*' to you. Only aren't we supposed to say '*tum*' to people our own age?—how can we to our elders?'

If his accountant had brought him news that he had lost a hundred thousand rupees he would not have been so stricken with grief as he was by these cruel words of Asha. All his enthusiasm, all his joyousness were chilled. He had been wearing a cap embroidered with flowers tilted at a rakish angle on his head, a saffron scarf of excellent silk around his neck, an embroidered velvet shirt with gold buttons—but all of this finery suddenly seemed utterly ridiculous to him, as though he had been cured of his intoxication by magic.

*A title (in this instance) for a cook.

**Traditionally wives use the formal *Aap* when addressing their husbands and do not call them by name; until now Lalaji has addressed Asha as *tum*; *tu* is the most intimate second person pronoun, reserved, like the French *tu*, for close friends, children, animals and (though not always) the deity.

302

In despair he said, 'Well, are you coming or not?'

'I'm not in the mood.'

'Then shall I not go either?'

'When did I ever stop you?'

'You're saying '*Aap*' again!'

As though summoning up all her inner strength Asha said '*tum*' and blushed with embarrassment.

'Fine,' said Dangamal, 'just keep saying it like that! So then—you won't come? If I tell you to, then you'll have to, won't you?'

'Then I'll go with you—obeying you is my dharma,' she answered, reverting once more to '*Aap*'.

But Lalaji could not order her to come. Words like 'order' and 'dharma' were beginning to trouble him greatly. Annoyed, he was about to leave when Asha suddenly felt sorry for him and finally said '*tum*':

'What time will you be back?'

'Oh—I'm not going.'

'Very well, then I *will* go with you.'

Like a stubborn child who after much crying finally finds his beloved toy and kicks it, Lalaji pouted and said, 'You're not in the mood, so don't go. I'm not insisting.'

'If you don't go you'll be angry.'

Asha went, but without displaying any enthusiasm, and just as she was, wearing her ordinary clothes: no striking sari, no jewels, no make-up, as though she were a widow.

Lalalji began to be greatly vexed by all these things. He had remarried to enjoy the pleasures of youth, as one pours more oil in a flickering lamp to increase its brilliance. If the oil doesn't help, what's the point of pouring it in? He could not understand why her feelings remained so dry and joyless—like a barren tree which, no matter how much you watered it, would not put out any green leaves. He had ordered for her little caskets filled with jewels from everywhere—Delhi, Calcutta, France; and what expensive saris he had set before her. Not one, hundreds! Yet they just lay in a chest to feed the moths. But this was the failing of girls from poor families, he reflected, their outlook was terribly limited. They didn't know how to eat, how to dress up, how to give anything. If they were presented with a treasure they wouldn't know how to spend it.

So Lalaji and Asha had their boat ride, but neither had much fun out of it.

After trying for several months to improve Asha's attitude, Lalaji concluded that she was melancholy by nature. Still, he did not despair:

303

after pouring so much money into this particular business operation how could he renounce his merchant's inclination to derive the maximum profit from it? He devised new forms of entertainment for her. His reasoning was as follows: when something was wrong with the gramophone and it wouldn't play properly or the singer's voice wasn't clear it would have to be fixed, it made no sense to pick it up and put it away somewhere, did it?

Meantime, the elderly cook fell ill and went back to his village, leaving his son in his place, a strange, unsophisticated, rather rustic boy of seventeen or eighteen, a scatterbrain who knew nothing at all about cooking. Every chapati he made was utterly different from every other, though to give a semblance of order the thick ones were put in the middle and the thin ones on the side. The *dal* was sometimes as thin as tea, sometimes as thick as yogurt, and the salting so light that the food was tasteless, at other times so excessive that it tasted bitter as lemons. So Asha washed her hands, betook herself to the kitchen and began to teach the inept lad how to cook. One day she told him, 'You're absolutely useless, Jugal. Have you been out digging or idling all your life that you don't even know how to make a chapati?'

With tears in his eyes Jugal said, 'What does "all my life" mean, Bahuji? I'm just seventeen.'

This started Asha laughing. 'Does it take five or ten years to learn how to make a chapati?' she said.

'If you teach me for a month, Bahuji, then you'll see, you'll be pleased with the fine chapatis I'll make for you. Then—the day I learn I'll ask for a reward from you. And I can already cook vegetables—sort of.'

With an encouraging smile Asha said, ' "Sort of" is right! You'll really have to learn how to cook them—yesterday they were so salty we couldn't eat them, and the spices tasted raw.'

'Where were you when I was cooking the vegetables?'

'Do you think they'd turn out better if I were standing by?'

'If you were standing by I'd keep my wits about me.'

Asha had a good laugh at the boy's simple words. She tried to stop her laughter but it went on as though spilling out of a full bottle that had been overturned. 'And if I don't stay with you?' she said.

'Then I'll go and sit by your door and weep over my fate.'

Asha stopped laughing. 'Why would you weep?' she asked.

'Don't ask, Bahuji, you wouldn't undestand things like that.'

Asha looked at him with questioning eyes. She had of course, quite understood what he meant but pretended not to. 'When your father comes back will you be going away?' she asked.

304

'What else can I do, Bahuji? If you could find some work to give me here then I'd stay. You could have somebody teach me how to drive a car—then I'd be able to take you out for some wonderful rides.' Then, as Asha reached up with a pair of tongs to take down a big pot, he burst out, 'Stop, Bahuji! Put down that pot, what if you stain that beautiful sari?' And he tried to take the tongs from her hand.

'Stay back, you clumsy little fool!' said Asha. 'If you drop it on your foot you'll limp about whining for months.'

Jugal was crestfallen.

Asha smiled and asked him, 'Come now, why are you wearing such a long face?'

Tearfully he answered, 'When you scold me, Bahuji, it breaks my heart. No matter how the master yells at me it doesn't bother me at all. But just to see you giving me a cross look turns my blood cold.'

To console him, she said, 'I wasn't scolding you, I only said I didn't want the pot to fall on your foot, what's wrong with that?'

'But *you* have a hand too. What if it fell out of your hand?'

Lala Dangamal appeared at the kitchen door and said, 'Asha, come here a moment, will you? See how many lovely potted plants I've brought you! We'll have them set before your room. Why are you wearing yourself out working in all this smoke? Tell this fellow to go and bring his father back right away or I'll hire somebody else. There's no shortage of cooks, and after all, no matter how you try, a jackass is never going to get any sense knocked into him. You hear me, Jugal? Write to your father today.'

Asha had set the griddle on the fire and was busy rolling chapatis while Jugal waited to put them on the griddle, so there was no question of her going to inspect the flowerpots. She said, 'Jugal will make a mess of the chapatis.'

Somewhat annoyed, Lalaji said, 'If he does, just throw them out.'

Ignoring him, Asha said, 'He'll learn how to make them in a few days, there's no need to throw them out.'

'Now, you come and tell me where you want the plants set down.'

'I told you, I'll come when I've finished these chapatis.'

'And I'm telling you, leave the chapatis and come.'

'You're making a big fuss over nothing.'

Lalaji was stunned. Never before had Asha answered him so rudely. And it was not just rudeness, he felt some malice in it. Embarrassed, he went away. He was so angry he would have liked to smash the flowerpots and throw the plants into the stove.

In a panic, Jugal said, 'Please go with him, Bahuji, the boss is going to be angry.'

'Don't be silly. Now roast the chapatis quickly or they'll have to be thrown away. And then take some money from me and have some decent clothes made for yourself. You've been going around looking like a beggar. And why is your hair so long, can't you even find a barber?'

Thinking ahead, Jugal said, 'If I spend my pay on clothes, how will I explain it to my father?'

'You nitwit, didn't I tell you I'd pay for them? So take the money.'

Jugal laughed lazily. 'Since *you're* paying to have them made I'll get really nice clothes. A fine muslin shirt and cotton dhoti, a silk scarf and good sandals.'

'But if you had to pay for them yourself?' Asha asked with a sweet smile.

'In that case—why would I have any made at all?'

'You're a sly one, Jugal!'

To display his cleverness further, Jugal said, 'In his own house a man can be satisfied just eating dry bread, but at a banquet he eats only fine delicacies—if he were going to get dry bread there too he wouldn't bother to go to the banquet, would he?'

'I don't know anything about all that—just get yourself a decent homespun shirt and a cap, and here's two annas extra for the barber.'

'Forget it,' said Jugal petulantly, 'I'm not taking your money. If I dress up in fine clothes it will only remind me of you, and if I have cheap ones made I'll feel bad.'

'How selfish you are! You want clothes for nothing and fine clothes in the bargain!'

'When I leave won't you give me a photo of yourself?'

'What will you do with my photograph?'

'I'll put it in my room and always look at it. Oh, and have your picture taken in the sari you were wearing yesterday, and with your pearl necklace too. I don't care for the way you look without jewellery, it's like being naked. . You must have lots of jewellery—why don't you wear it?'

'So you like jewellery, do you?'

'A lot.'

At this moment Lalaji returned in an angry mood and said, 'Haven't you finished those chapatis yet, Jugal? If you can't make any good ones by tomorrow I'm sending you away.'

306

Asha immediately washed her hands and face and very happily went off with Lalaji to have a look at the flowerpots. In her beauty at this moment was the radiance of joy, her words seemed dipped in sugar, and all Lalaji's vexation was annulled.

Asha greedily looked over the flowerpots, 'I won't give up any of them!' she said. 'I want them all set out in front of my room. What lovely plants they are! You must tell me the Hindi name of each one.'

'What will you do with so many?' Lalaji teased her. 'Pick out a dozen that you like and I'll have the rest of them set outside.'

'Oh no you won't! I don't intend to let a single one go.'

'You've become awfully greedy!'

'If I'm greedy, so be it. I won't even let you have one.'

'Oh give me two or three. It was such a lot of trouble to bring them all here.'

'Not a chance, you're not going to get a single one!'

The next day when Asha came out of her room wearing a violet sari and decked in jewels, Lalaji's eyes brightened. He thought that now the magic of his love was surely having some effect. In the past no matter how much he insisted, no matter how much he pleaded, she would not put on any jewellery. She did once in a while wear a necklace, but that too in a casual, careless way. Adorned with jewels today she appeared to be in seventh heaven, she strutted, as though to say, 'See how beautiful I am!'

Lalaji was utterly intoxicated. He wanted all his friends and relatives to come and delight their eyes with the sight of this golden queen and see how happy, how glad, how contented she was. Then those who had opposed his remarrying and expressed their doubts would have their eyes opened to see just how happy he was and what a wonder had been wrought by confidence, passion and experience.

He suggested that they go for a walk in view of the most pleasant weather they were having.

'How can I?' she said. 'I have to go to the kitchen, but I might be free by noon or one. Only then I'll be stuck with all the rest of the household chores. I can't let the whole house go to pot just for the sake of a walk.'

Lalaji caught her hand. 'Oh no, I'm not letting you go into that kitchen today.'

'But the cook is hopeless, there'll be nothing to eat.'

'Then that's his hard luck, he'll be fired today.'

The joy vanished from Asha's face, sadness overwhelmed her. She lay back on a sofa and said, 'I feel some sort of a dull pain in my stomach this morning, I don't know why, but I've never felt anything like it before.'

'How long have you had it?' Lalaji asked anxiously.

'Since last night, but it seemed a little better for a while. Now it's begun again. It's like a steady jabbing.'

Something now occurred to Lalaji that made his heart expand with joy: the Ayurvedic doctor's pills must be having their effect. He must take them regularly, the doctor had said. So why not?—he was the family doctor and his father had been the physician of the Maharaja of Banaras. He knew all the old tried and true prescriptions.

'So you've felt it since last night?' Lalaji said. 'Why didn't you tell me? If you had I'd have asked the doctor to give us a prescription.'

. 'I thought it would go away all by itself. But now it's worse.'

'Where does it hurt? Let me see if there's any swelling.'

Lalaji's hand reached out towards her lap. Asha looked away in embarrassment and said, 'I don't like this nasty mind of yours—I'm at the point of death and all you can think of is fun. Go and get me some medicine.'

Accepting this as a diploma testifying to his virility, Lala Dangamal was more delighted than he'd have been on getting the Victoria Cross. How could he rest until he'd gone forth to broadcast the news? What a fine occasion had come to hand to humiliate all those who out of envy had criticized his marriage, and how quickly!

He went first of all to Pandit Bholanath. Pretending to bewail his bad luck, he said, 'Old man, something terrible's happened: my wife's suffering from a pain in her stomach. She cannot be consoled. She says she's never felt anything like it before.'

Bholanath did not seem particularly sympathetic.

So Lalaji left and went to visit another friend, Lala Phagmal, and told him the bad news in much the same words.

Phagmal was a thorough-going scoundrel. He smiled and said, 'Oh, I know what a wicked old rascal you are!'

Dangamal was positively thrilled. He said, 'Here I am telling you my misfortune and you make a joke out of it. There's not a shred of human kindness in you.'

'I wasn't joking. What's there to joke about? On the one hand there's this tender young girl, on the other you, an old champion in the bouts of love making—you understand me. If this doesn't turn out to be the case, I'll eat my words.'

Lalaji's eyes sparkled. The feeling of youth sprang up in his heart, the glow of youth covered his face. His chest seemed to swell, and when he left his footsteps struck the ground more vigorously and his cap somehow was suddenly canted at a rakish angle. In short, he cut the very figure of a fop.

When Jugal saw Asha sparkling from head to foot he said, 'This is more like it, Bahuji. You should always dress exactly this way. Today I won't let you come close to the stove.'

Shooting glances like arrows from her eyes, Asha said, 'Why these new rules today? You never forbade me before.'

'Things are different today.'

'All right, now tell me what this is all about.'

'I'm afraid you'll be angry.'

'No, no, tell me, I won't be angry.'

'Today . . . you look very beautiful.'

Lala Dangamal had many times praised Asha's youth and beauty; but his praise had always smelled of artificiality. When such words came out of his mouth it was somehow rather like a cripple trying to run. But there was intoxication in these simple words of Jugal, and something that hurt as well. Asha's whole body was trembling. She said:

'You're putting the evil eye on me, Jugal. Why are you staring at me like that?'

'When I leave I'm going to really miss you.'

'You're in the kitchen the whole day—after you finish cooking what do you do? I never get a glimpse of you.'

'The master is there the whole time so I don't come out. Anyway, now he's firing me. We'll see what the Lord has in store for me.'

Asha's expression became severe. 'Who's firing you?'

'The master told me himself he was firing me.'

'Just keep on doing your work, nobody's going to fire you. You're making good chapatis now . . .'

'The master is really furious.'

'Oh, in a few days I'll completely change the way he feels.'

'When he walks with you he looks like your father.'

'You say anything you like, don't you? Careful, better watch your tongue.'

But this thin disguise of dissatisfaction could not hide the secret in her heart: it burst forth from inside her like light.

Just as fearless as before, Jugal said, 'You can shut me up, but everybody says the same thing. If somebody made me marry an old

309

woman of fifty I'd run away from home. I'd either take poison—or else give it to her! So what if I got hanged!'

Asha could not maintain her pretence of anger. He had struck the strings of her heart's *vina* so forcibly that no matter how she tried she could not conceal her anguish. She said, 'Still . . . one must reckon with one's fate.'

'To hell with such a fate!'

'You just watch out, I'll see that you're married off to some old woman!'

'Then I will take poison, you'll see.'

'Why? An old woman will love you better than a young one and serve you better—and she'll put you on the right path.'

'That's what a mother's supposed to do. A wife must do what a wife is meant to.'

'And what is it a wife's supposed to do?'

'You're the master's wife, otherwise I'd tell you just what a wife's supposed to do.'

They heard the sound of the car. Somehow or other the end of Asha's sari had slipped down to her shoulders. Swiftly she drew it back over her head and as she ran towards her room she said, 'After Lalaji eats he'll go out. I'll expect you then'.

From *Mānsarovar*, v. 2. Original title, *Nayā Vivāh* ('New Marriage'). In his listing of his father's short stories Amrit Rai does not cite this one, nor is it mentioned in Madan Gopal's survey of Premchand's work. The objectivity of the narrative and the absence of moralizing suggest that it is a late story.

# Wife into Husband

**M**r Seth hated all things Indian, while to Godavari, his lovely wife, everything foreign was anathema. But patience and humility are the adornments of India's goddesses, so Godavari with a great effort restrained herself when dealing with the foreign clothes her husband brought her, though weeping inwardly over her subservience. Whenever she sat on her terrace to look into the street and saw so many women wearing khaddar* saris, her inner anguish found expression in a deep sigh, and she would feel there could be no more unfortunate woman in the world. She could not do even this much to serve her countrymen! In the evenings, when at Mr Seth's insistence she went to some entertainment or took a stroll, her shoulders drooped with the shame of wearing imported clothes. And when she read in the papers the fiery speeches women had made, her eyes blazed as she forgot for a moment the restrictions that bound her.

It was eight o'clock on the night of Holi. A procession of impassioned women, acting in the cause of independence, halted before Mr Seth's residence and began to prepare bonfires of English clothes. Godavari stood at a window of her room watching the gathering and reining in her sorrow. Out there were those joyous people, intoxicated with freedom, holding their heads high with pride, and here she was, fluttering like a bird in a cage. How could she break these bars? She glanced around the room: everything in it was imported, there was nothing here manufactured in India. Outside they were burning things like these, but here they were stored in boxes, like so much regret stored in her heart. A thought struck her: she would pick up all those things and throw them on the bonfires so that all her regret and weakness could be burned to ash. But fear of her husband's displeasure held her back.

*homespun cloth

Suddenly Mr Seth came into the room. 'Just look at those lunatics burning clothes,' he said. 'If this isn't madness, hysteria, and rebellion all rolled together, you tell me what it is. Someone once said, Indians have no brains and never will. There's always a screw loose somewhere.'*

'You're Indian too,' said Godavari.

Seth lost his temper. 'Yes, but I shall always regret being born in this wretched country. I don't want anyone to call me or consider me Indian. At least in my behaviour and dress, habits, speech and action, I have kept no reminders of my country which would lead anyone to insult me with the name of Indian. Just tell me, when I can buy excellent cloth for eight annas a yard why should I buy coarse sackcloth? In matters like that everyone ought to be completely free to do as he wants. I don't know why the government allows such scoundrels to congregate here. If I had the authority I'd send everyone of them straight to hell. Maybe that would knock some sense into them.'

In a tone full of sarcasm and scorn, Godavari said, 'Don't you care at all about your brothers? Is there any other nation ruled by foreigners? Even the tiniest countries don't want to remain slaves of another people. Isn't it a cause for shame for an Indian to support the government by being unjust to his brothers just for a little personal advantage?'

Mr Seth scowled back at her. 'Only I don't consider them my brothers!'

'But after all, the wages the government pays you come out of *their* pockets.'

'It's no concern of mine whose pockets it comes out of. The *hand* it comes from is my boss's. I don't know what possesses those scoundrels. They say India's a spiritual country. Does 'spiritual' mean going against the Lord's commandments? When everybody knows that nothing can be done against God's wishes, how is it possible that a country as big as India should be subject to the British without Him expressly wishing it? Don't these madmen have enough sense to realize that so long as *He* doesn't want it they can't do the slightest harm to the British?'

'But why then do you work for them? If it's the Lord's will, then you'd get your dinner without having to work for anybody. When you're sick why do you go running for the doctor? The Lord helps them who help themselves.'

'Of course he does,' said Mr Seth. 'But to set fire to your own

*The Indian idiom is close to the English: *koī kal bhī to sīdhā nahīṁ*, 'not even a single screw is straight'.

312

house and burn everything in it such things could hardly please the Lord.'

'So people in this country should just sit back without saying a word?'

'No, they ought to cry, cry the way babies do for their mother's milk.'

Suddenly the bonfires were set ablaze, their flames flew up to hold conversation with the heavens, as though the goddess of independence had put on a robe of fire as she rose to embrace the gods of the sky.

Mr Seth closed the window, for he could not bear the sight of what was happening.

While Godavari stood there like a cow tied to the butcher's stake, suddenly there came the voice of someone singing:

'Look, oh look, when will the homeland's destiny change?'

It was another blow to Godavari's grieving heart. She opened the window and stared down. The Holi fires were still burning and a blind boy was singing to the rhythm of his little tambourine:

'Look, oh look! . . .'

When he came closer to the window, Godavari called to him, 'Oh blind man, stay one minute!'

The blind boy stood there while Godavari opened a little chest. But in it she could find only one pice in change. There were rupee notes, but it was out of the question to give a blind beggar rupee notes. If she could have found a few more coins she would certainly have given them, but there was only the one coin, so worn that the servant had to bring it back from the market because no shopkeeper would accept it. Godavari felt ashamed to give it to the blind boy. For a moment she stood in doubt, holding it in her hand. Then she called him and handed down the coin to him.

'Mataji,*' he said, 'please give me something to eat. I've had nothing to eat all day.'

'You've begged all day and no one gave you anything?'

'What can I do, Mata, nobody gave me a thing to eat.'

'Take this pice and buy yourself some food.'

'I shall eat, Mataji, may God give you happiness. And now I'm going to sleep right here.'

The next day, early in the morning, supporters of the Congress held a public demonstration.

*Mother

313

And Mr Seth brushed his teeth with English tooth powder and an English brush, bathed with English soap, drank imported tea and milk in English cups, and ate English biscuits with English butter. Then, putting on his English suit, he stuck an English cigar in his mouth and came forth from his house, mounted his motorcycle and rode off to see the Flower Show.

Godavari had not been able to sleep all night. The keen torment of despair and defeat afflicted her heart like a scourge and something bitter seemed to have stuck in her throat. She had tried everything any attractive woman could to bring her influence to bear on her husband, but all her blandishments, smiles and sweet talk had absolutely no effect on him.

Not only would he not agree to wear Indian-made clothes, he would never allow Godavari to wear them. It had reached the point where she now swore she would never ask him for anything.

Anger and regret had affected her charitable feelings the way something foul would pollute clean water. She thought, if he couldn't grant her so small a wish, why should she follow all his cues and fulfil his desires like some maidservant? She hadn't sold her soul to him. If today he stole or embezzled, would she be punished for it? It would be on his head, he'd have to pay for it himself.

'As he has authority over his own words and deeds,' she told herself, 'so do I too over mine. Let him slave for the government, flatter them rubbing his nose on their doorstep—what's that to me, should I have to co-operate with him? It's not my fault if I can't respect someone who has no self-respect, who's sold himself out of selfishness. Is he an employee or a slave? There *is* a difference between employment and slavery. An employee does his appointed task according to specified rules, and those rules function for both him and his boss. If the boss insults or abuses him the employee isn't obliged to put up with it. For a slave there are no conditions, his spirit is first enslaved, then his body. When did the government ever tell him not to buy Indian goods? It's even printed on government stamps that you should buy things made in India, so it's clear that there's no government prohibition on things made here. Nevertheless, this fine gentleman, hoping to acquire prestige, wants to outdo the government.'

The night before, Mr Seth, still annoyed, had asked his wife, 'Going to see the Flower Show tomorrow?'

'No,' said Godavari, who was not at all interested.

'It's a fine thing to see, you know.'

'I'm going to a Congress demonstration.'

314

If the roof had fallen in on Mr Seth or his hand had been caught on an electric wire, he could not have been more shocked. With his eyes popping, he had said, 'You're going to a Congress demonstration?'

'I most certainly am.'

'I do *not* want you to go!'

'If you don't have any concern for me, then my dharma does not oblige me to obey every order you give.'

With poison in his eyes, Mr Seth had said, 'Something bad will come of it, I tell you.'

As though exposing her breast to a sword, Godavari had answered, 'Don't worry about it, you're not somebody's god.'

Mr Seth had been furious, he had blustered. Finally, he had turned his face away to lie down. Even next morning, when he was leaving for the Flower Show he did not speak to Godavari.

By the time Godavari arrived several thousand men and women had gathered for the Congress demonstration. The secretary was appealing for donations and a few people were giving what they could. Godavari found a place where other women were standing and began to observe what they were contributing. Most offered only two or four annas apiece—for who among them was rich? Godavari felt in her pocket and took out a rupee, which seemed to her to be sufficient. She was waiting for the basket to come to her, wondering whether to throw it in, when suddenly the same blind boy she'd given the pice to appeared from nowhere and as soon as the basket came his way threw in something. Everyone immediately took notice, curious about what a blind beggar might have. The poor fellow must have got hold of a half-pice somewhere and, though tormented with hunger, gone without food all day. If his singing could have been heard at a party with dancing girls and instruments, money would have rained down on him, but who cared about a blind street singer?

After he had tossed in his pice the boy walked some distance away and began to sing:

'Look, oh look, when will the homeland's destiny change?'

'Look, friends,' said the chairman, 'here is the pice which that poor blind boy threw in the basket. In my eyes this pice is no less valuable than the thousand rupees of some rich man. This is probably everything the boy possesses. When we have the sympathy of such poor folk, then there seems to me to be no doubt as to our victory. Why do paupers like this appear among us? Either because in our society they find no work or, as a result of diseases that come from their poverty, they're no longer capable of work. Or because dependence on charity has left no capacity for work in them. If we do not achieve independence, who is there who can uplift the poor? Listen to what he's singing. How much sacrifice there is in his wounded heart! Can anyone still doubt whose voice this is?' He lifted up the coin. 'Who among you will buy this jewel?'

Godavari was full of curiosity. Could this be the very same coin she'd given him last night? And could he then have gone all night without eating anything at all?

She drew closer to inspect the coin, which had been set upon a table. Her heart began to pound: it was indeed that same worn out coin.

Remembering the blind boy's condition and the sacrifice he had made, Godavari felt her passions rise. In a trembling voice she said, 'Give me the pice, I'll pay five rupees for it.'

The chairman said, 'A sister is offering five rupees for the coin.'

Another voice was heard: 'Ten rupees!'

And a third: 'Twenty!'

Godavari looked at this last bidder. His countenance was radiant with conceit, as though to say, 'Is there anybody here to equal me?' The spirit of competition woke in Godavari. Whatever happened the coin must not fall into this fellow's hands! He thought he had not only offered twenty rupees but also bought the whole world with his donation.

'Forty!' said Godavari.

And immediately that fellow cried out, 'Fifty!'

Thousands of eyes were directed at Godavari, as though to say, 'Only you can salvage our honour!'

Looking at the man, she said in a voice in which a threat could be heard, 'One hundred rupees!'

And immediately the rich man said, 'One hundred twenty.'

At this everyone appeared crestfallen, thinking that surely he had won. They turned to Godavari, desperation in their eyes. But as soon as the words 'One hundred fifty!' came from her lips applause burst out on all sides, as when the spectators at a wrestling match go wild over the victor's triumph.

The man then said, 'One hundred seventy-five.'

'Two hundred!'

Then once again applause. This time her opponent thought it best to retire from the battlefield.

316

Casting a veil of humility over her pride in winning, Godavari stood there while the congratulations rained down on her like flowers.

When people discovered that this lady was the wife of Mr Seth, they felt pity mingle with their joy and envy.

Mr Seth was still enjoying the Flower Show when a police officer conveyed the shocking news to him. He was utterly flabbergasted, and felt as though his body had been drained of all feeling. Then he clenched his fists, ground his teeth, pressed his lips tight together and set out at once for home. Never before had he driven his motorcycle at such speed.

He had hardly set foot in the house before, his eyes shooting sparks, he said to his wife, 'Do you mean to blacken my face?'

Godavari said tranquilly, 'Say something sensible, or do you just intend to go on pouring out insults? If your face is blackened, won't mine be too? If you're ruined, where can I look for help?'

'The whole city's in an uproar,' he said. 'Why did you give away my money?'

In the same quiet way Godavari answered, 'Because I consider it my money too.'

Mr Seth gnashed his teeth. 'Never! You have absolutely no right to spend my money.'

'You're quite mistaken! I have absolutely the same right as you to spend it. Of course, if you people pass a divorce law and then you divorce me, well then I won't have that right any more.'

Mr Seth flung his hat down on the table so violently that it went flying off to the floor. 'I feel pity for your lack of sense,' he said. 'Don't you know what will come of your rebelliousness? I'll be made to answer for it. Since it's obvious that the Congress party is opposing the government, then to help the Congress is to oppose the government.'

'But you haven't opposed the government.'

'But you have!'

'Who'll be punished for it, you or me? If I stole something, would you go to jail?'

'Stealing is one thing, this is something else.'

'So—helping the Congress is worse than stealing or banditry?'

'Oh yes, it's a lot worse if you work for the government.'

'I didn't realize that.'

'If you didn't realize it that just shows your foolishness. You look at the newspapers every day, and still you ask me this! When a Congress man stands up on a platform to give a speech, scores of plain-clothes police officers are hanging around to file a report on him. Lots of informers are always on the tail of Congress ringleaders in order to see what they're up to. They're never that tough on thieves, and that's why there are thousands of robberies and muggings and murders taking place every day which nobody knows anything about, and the police don't give a damn about them. But if they so much as sniff anything political just see how vigilant they become. From the Inspector General down to the constable on the corner they leave no stone unturned. The government's not afraid of thieves, the thief can't hurt the government. The Congress is launching an attack on the government so the government brings all its authority to bear. It's a law of nature!'

When Mr Seth went to his office he was dragging his feet. He had no idea what things were going to be like there today. When he arrived he didn't scold the *chaprasis* as he usually did, nor lord over the clerks, but went silently to a chair and sat down, just as though a sword were dangling over his head. The moment he heard the English Sahib's motorcar the life went right out of him. Every day it was his custom to sit in his room until the Sahib had arrived and gone to his office; then, a half hour later, he would bring the files in to him. But today Mr Seth was standing on the veranda when the Sahib got there; he bowed to greet him, but the Sahib turned his face away.

Still, he did not lose courage. He stepped ahead and drew the curtain, and when the Sahib reached his room Mr Seth turned on the ceiling fan. But he was in a state of high tension wondering when that sword was going to come crashing down on him. As soon as the Sahib sat in his chair Mr Seth made a dash to put the cigar case and matches on the desk.

Then suddenly it seemed that the heavens had split asunder. The Sahib roared, 'You're a traitor!'

Mr Seth stared back at him as though not comprehending what he was talking about, at which the Sahib repeated his accusation.

Mr Seth's blood suddenly heated up. 'It's my opinion,' he said, 'that there's not a more devoted government servant in the country!'

'On the contrary, you're utterly disloyal.'

Mr Seth grew red in the face. 'You're insulting me without any justification.'

'You're an utter scoundrel!'

The redness spread to Mr Seth's eyes. 'You're treating me dishonourably. I'm not accustomed to hearing insults like that.'

318

'Shut up, you bloody fool,' said the Sahib. 'The government doesn't pay you five hundred rupees so you can use your wife to make contributions to the Congress. Absolutely not.'

This was Mr Seth's opportunity to exonerate himself. 'You must believe me,' he said, 'my wife acted completely against my wishes when she gave that money to the Congress. At that moment I'd gone to the Flower Show, where I bought a bouquet from Miss Frank for five rupees. When I came back I learned what had happened.'

'Do you think me an idiot?'

As soon as this thought flashed like a spark in the Sahib's brain, his temper reached boiling point. That any Indian had the nerve to try to make a fool of him! He who was the Emperor of India, to whom great landowners did obeisance, to whose servants great nobles offered rich gifts—that anybody should try to make a fool of him! It was intolerable. He seized a ruler and flourished it.

But Mr Seth was also a sturdy fellow, so though it was his custom always to resort to every kind of flattery, an insult like this was too much. He deflected the ruler with his hand and, advancing towards his boss, punched him in the face so hard that the Sahib saw stars. He had not been prepared for such a counterattack, of course, for it had been his experience that the native was always peaceful, meek and tolerant, particularly when before a Sahib, at which time he would not so much as open his mouth. He fell back in his chair and wiped the blood from his nose. He did not have the courage to take on Mr Seth again, but in his heart he was wondering how he could humiliate him.

Mr Seth retired to his own office and also began to reflect on what had just occurred. He did not regret his action in the least but, on the contrary, felt quite pleased with his daring. What a vile thing, he thought, that he should try to strike me with a ruler! The more you give way to him the more he oppresses you. His wife gallivants with her boyfriends—but he's never had the nerve to speak to her about it, while with me he turns into a tiger! Now he'll go running to the Commissioner and won't give up until he's had me sacked. Godavari's the cause of all this! I've definitely been disgraced. Now we'll be reduced to begging for our food. No one will even ask me for my side of the story, the notice of dismissal will be on its way. Where could I appeal? The Chief Secretary's an Indian, but more English than the English. The Home Member's an Indian too, but the slave of the British—as soon as he hears about Godavari's contribution he'll take to his bed with a fever. I can't expect justice from anybody, the smart thing now is just to get out of here.

He wrote a letter of resignation at once and had it delivered to the Sahib, who scribbled over it, 'Discharged.'

When Mr Seth reached home at noon with his head hanging, Godavari asked him, 'Why've you come home so early?'

Looking distraught, he answered, 'You've accomplished what you set out to. Now you can start bemoaning your fate.'

'What I set out to? Can't you speak more plainly!'

'What happened' (he looked at her menacingly) 'is that I've punched somebody, resigned and come home.'

'Why resign so quickly?'

'What else? Should I stay and be disgraced? The kind of life you've been accustomed to here you'll now have to give up, if not today, then certainly tomorrow.'

'Well, what happened was a good thing. From today you can take part in the Congress movement.'

Mr Seth bit his lip and said, 'You're not the least bit ashamed, and on top of that you rub salt in the wound.'

'Why should I be ashamed? I'm glad your chains have been broken.'

'But have you even thought how we're going to get along?'

'I've thought of everything,' said Godavari. 'I'll manage things and show you. Oh yes, you're going to do whatever I tell you. Until now I've followed all your cues, from now on you'll follow mine. In the past I never complained to you; I ate whatever you gave me to eat, I wore whatever you wanted to wear. If you lived in a palace, I'd live in a palace. If you lived in a hut, so would I. So now you'll live as I do. Whatever I ask you to do, you'll do. Then I'll see if things are working. Dignity isn't found in suits and boots and fancy clothes. Whoever has a pure heart is the one who's great. Until now I was your wife: but starting today, I'm going to be your husband.'

Sethji looked at her affectionately and burst out laughing

1930

From *Mānsarovar*, v. 7. In the context of this story the Hindi title means 'husband [created] out of wife', i.e. wife transformed into husband. One of many stories inspired by Gandhi's call to boycott foreign cloth in the thirties, this comic sketch also makes a case for women's rights. The redemption of the obnoxious Mr Seth is an example of Premchand's fondness for the Gandhian theory of *satyāgraha,* or holding firmly to the truth, one aspect of which is the transformation of human character by exposure to goodness in others.

# Disaffection

It was March, but the barns where grain used to be piled high had become shelters for the farm animals, and in the houses where spring songs once resounded, only weeping could now be heard. During the last monsoon season not a drop of rain had fallen. True, there had been one heavy rain in June; the farmers were ecstatic and sowed for the autumn harvest. But Indradev* seemed to have squandered all his gifts in one shower. Plants sprouted, shot up, and withered. No grass grew in the grazing pastures. Clouds gathered, the thunderheads swelled, it appeared that land and water would be merged together; but they turned out to be clouds not of hope but of sorrow. The farmers prayed constantly, animals were sacrificed to the gods and goddesses, gutters flowed with blood in the hope of water, but Indradev didn't so much as sweat. There were neither plants in the fields nor grass in the pastures nor water in the ponds. Dire misfortune faced them. Wherever you looked the dust was flying. The fearful spectres of poverty and famine were approaching. First, people pawned their cooking pots and jewels, and finally sold them outright. Then it was the turn of the animals, and when there was no other resource for survival the farmers, who would give their lives for the land where they were born, took their children and went away looking for work as labourers. To help those facing starvation the government started work projects here and there; in these places many people gathered in search of any job at all.

One evening Jado Ray came home exhausted, sat down and said to his wife sadly, 'They didn't accept my application.' With that he went into the courtyard and lay down on the ground. His face was yellowed, his innards shrunk. For two days now he hadn't had even a glimpse of

*The god of rain.

anything to eat. The best things in the house—jewels, clothes, oven, pots, whatever there was—all had found their way to their stomachs. The village money-lender, like a chaste wife, averted his eyes when he saw them. Nothing but a loan could help them, and that was what Jado Ray had applied for. But today it had been turned down, and the flickering lamp of hope was extinguished.

Devaki watched her husband with compassion, her eyes flooded with tears. Here he was, tired from running around the whole day, and she had nothing to offer him. Ashamed, she had not even brought water to wash his hands and feet. If he should look at her expectantly while she washed them, what could she give him to eat? For several days now she hadn't seen a speck of grain. But the sorrow she felt at this moment was many times worse than the pain of hunger. A woman is the Lakshmi* of her home, she believes her duty is to feed her family. And though it may be an injustice, the mental anguish she feels over her miserable, forsaken state is something men can never experience.

Suddenly Sadho, her child, woke with a start; longing for sweets, he went to his father and curled himself around him. Since morning the child had eaten just half a roti, and since then got up several times and several times gone back to sleep in tears. A simple child of four, he was unable to see any connection between the rains and sweets. Jado Ray took him in his lap and sorrowfully looked at him. His shoulders drooped and his eyes could not hold in all the sadness in his heart.

The following day this family too left their home and moved on. Just as pride is not inclined to leave a man's spirit or modesty a woman's eye, so too the farmer earning his livelihood by his own toil would not willingly leave home looking for work. Oh but, sinful belly, thou canst accomplish anything! Respect and pride, regret and modesty, these are all shining stars hidden in your dark clouds.

It was morning when the two of them, Jado Ray carrying his son on his back, left their disaster-blighted house. Devaki set on her head the bundle of their old tattered clothes which calamity had spared. Both of them had tears in their eyes, and cried aloud. On the road they met three or four people from the village, but no one even asked them where they were going. There was no sympathy in anybody's heart.

By the time they reached Lalganj the sun was high overhead, looking down on lines of people miles long, but every face shone only with

*Goddess of prosperity

grief and misery. It was the burning sunshine of early May. The wind whistled, blowing gusts of fire. At a time like this countless skeletal bodies not covered by any clothing were caked in dust deep enough to dig, as though the corpses in a burial ground were digging their graves with their own hands. Old and young, men and children, everyone of them laboured with desperation, as hunger and death stared them in the face. In their distress no one had a friend, no one had anyone to wish him well. Pity, sympathy and love are human emotions. But Nature has given us only one emotion and that is self-preservation. Human feelings, like so many hypocritical friends, desert us, but this God-given quality will always be with us.

Eight days went by. It was evening, and work had stopped for the day. Some distance from the workers' encampment there was a mango orchard. There Jado Ray and Devaki sat beneath a tree. The two of them had become so emaciated that they were no longer recognizable. Independent farmers no more, time's revolution had transformed them into labourers.

Jado Ray had set their sleeping child down on the ground. The child had been suffering with fever for several days, and his face, once fair as a lotus, had withered. Devaki shook him gently and said, 'Wake up, son. It's evening.'

Sadho opened his eyes. His fever had gone down. 'Have we come home, Amma?' he asked.

Remembering home, Devaki's eyes brimmed over. 'No, child,' she said, 'but if you're good we *will* go home. Get up and see what a fine orchard this is.'

With his mother's help, Sadho stood up. 'I'm really hungry, Mother,' he said, 'but you have nothing. What are you going to give me to eat?'

Though cut to the heart, Devaki controlled herself and said, 'No, darling, we have everything for you to eat. Your father will be bringing water and in just a little while I'll make you lovely soft rotis.'

Sadho put his head in her lap. 'Amma,' he said, 'if you didn't have me you wouldn't have so much sorrow,' and burst into tears. This was the same ignorant child who a couple of weeks before had thrown tantrums over sweets. What havoc care and sorrow create! Such is the fruit of calamity—what a grief-filled, touching business.

In the meantime several men came along with lanterns, and then wagons loaded with tents and gear for camping. They halted and quickly set up their tents on the spot. There was a commotion all around the orchard. While Devaki was making rotis Sadho slowly got up and, looking at the encampment with wonderment, went over and stood close by.

When padre Mohandas came from his tent he found Sadho standing there. Seeing the longing stamped on the child's face he was flooded with a river of love.

Picking up the child, he brought him into his tent, set him on a cushioned couch, and gave him some biscuits and bananas to eat. In his whole life the child had never tasted such savoury things. The dizzying hunger of fever began to leave him as he ate to his heart's content. Then he moved close to the padre and, looking at him gratefully, asked, 'Will you give me these things every day?'

Smiling at the child's simplicity, the padre said, 'I have much better things than these,' prompting Sadho to say, 'Then I'll come to you every day. Where would my mother get things like these? All she feeds me is rotis.'

Meantime, Devaki had finished cooking. When she called Sadho, he came to her and said, 'The sahib gave me wonderful things to eat. He's a very good man.'

'But I've made you such soft rotis,' Devaki told him. 'Come, I'll feed you.'

'I won't eat now,' said Sadho. 'The sahib said he'd give me all kinds of good things to eat every day. I'm going to live with him now.'

Devaki assumed he was joking. She embraced him and said, 'What do you mean, darling, are you going to forget all about us? See how much I love you!'

Sadho answered in his babyish way, 'But you just give me rotis to eat every day. You don't have anything. The Sahib feeds me bananas and mangoes.' With that, he ran off to the padre's camp again and spent the night there.

Padre Mohandas stopped over for three days. Sadho spent the whole of those three days with him. The padre gave him medicine and his fever abated. When those simple farmers saw this they blessed the padre because the child was healthy again and comfortable, and they prayed for the Lord to keep the padre happy for saving his life.

On the night of the fourth day the padre broke camp and set out. When Devaki got up in the morning there was no trace of Sadho. She thought he must have gone looking for fruit that had fallen from the trees, but after searching for a little while she said to Jado Ray, 'My darling's not here.' Jado Ray said the child must have gone looking for fruit.

But when the sun was up and it was time to set out for work Jado Ray began to worry. 'Stay here,' he told Devaki, 'I'll bring him back right away.'

He searched through all the orchards in the vicinity until finally, when it was past ten, he came back in despair. When Devaki saw that he was alone she burst out sobbing.

Then they both went out looking for their beloved son, with all kinds of ideas running through their minds. Devaki was convinced that the sahib had cast a spell on the child to get him in his power, but Jado doubted this. Still, the child could not go so far alone on an unfamiliar road. They began to follow the marks of the wagon wheels and hoofprints until they came onto a road where they saw traces of many different wheels and hooves. Here they could not make out the particular tracks of the padre's wagon. The hoofprints went towards a thicket and disappeared. Jado Ray and Devaki no longer had any hope. It was noon by now and the two of them were tormented by the sun's heat and overwhelmed with despair. They sat down in the shade of a tree. Devaki wept while Jado tried his best to console her.

When the fierceness of the sun lessened a bit they set out again, only now with hope replaced by desperation. Along with the hoofprints of the horses the dim traces of hope had also disappeared.

It was evening. Here and there herds of cattle could be seen lying about as though lifeless. Grieving, their courage gone, Jado and Devaki stood under a tree where a pair of mynas had built their nest. On this very day their fledgling had been caught in the claws of a bird of prey. All day long they had searched for it and now perched there, disconsolate. But for Jado and Devaki there still remained a glimmer of hope, so they were still in a state of restlessness.

For three days they kept searching for their lost son. They took no food; when they were distressed by thirst they would swallow a few drops of water. Despair kept them going. They felt nothing but grief; whenever they caught sight of the footprints of some child waves of hope and fear surged in their hearts.

But every step seemed to take them further from their cherished goal.

Fourteen years elapsed. During this time everything had changed. Everywhere one saw prosperity worthy of Ram's reign. Indradev no longer showed the cruelty he had before, nor did the land. The grain was piled high, like cresting rivers, the abandoned villages were resettled, labourers had once again become farmers, and the farmers

325

were on the lookout for more land to buy. It was March again, and the barns were piled high with grain. Minstrels and wandering beggars praised the farmers' good fortune. All day and night customers flocked to the goldsmiths' doors until midnight, the tailors had no opportunity to look up from their stitching. Here and there horses neighed at people's doors. The priests of the goddess suffered indigestion from overeating.

Jado Ray's fortunes too have changed. Tile has replaced the thatch on his roof, a pair of fine bullocks is tethered at his door. Now he rides to the market in his covered wagon. His body is no longer so athletic: his stomach in particular shows the effect of his improved circumstances, and his hair has turned white. And Devaki has begun to be numbered among the old women of the village. She is much consulted in practical matters. When she visits a neighbour's house the daughters-in-law of the household tremble with fear. Because of her bitter words and sharp criticism she has great influence in the village. Clothes of soft texture do not appeal to her these days but she is not so indifferent in the matter of jewellery.

They have two children. Madho Singh, their son, helps his father with the farming. The daughter is named Shivgauri. She helps her mother in grinding the grain, and she's a good singer too. She doesn't care much for washing the pots but she's an expert at putting down the mud and cowdung floor in the kitchen. She has never got tired of playing with dolls, and every other day there's a doll's wedding. But they all give careful consideration to thrift. They still remember the Sadho who was lost. They are always talking about him, often with tears in their eyes. There are times when Devaki is troubled all day long by memories of her darling son.

One evening Jado Ray sat on his cot smoking his hooka, as the priest began to ring the temple bell and the bullocks filed home from their day's work with their heads down. It was harvest time, and there were rituals in the temple every day. Shivgauri stood out in the road, caressing the bullocks. As soon as he heard the bell and the clock striking, Jado Ray was about to get up to take the Lord's holy Ganges water* when he saw a young man on a bicycle, scolding the barking dogs as he approached. He threw himself down to touch Jado's feet. Jado scrutinized him, then the two of them embraced each other, while Madho stared in astonishment at the bicycle. Shivgauri ran into the house in tears and said to Devaki, 'Dada's caught a sahib!' Upset,

---

*caranāmrt, lit., 'foot nectar,' water which has been offered to the idol in the temple.

326

Devaki came out of the house. As soon as he saw her the young man fell at her feet. It was Sadho. In tears, she hugged him to her breast. Everyone in the village, men, women and children, gathered around. It was just like a festival.

Sadho said to his mother and father, 'Forgive me, wretch that I am, for whatever offences I've committed. In my ignorance I've gone through a lot of hardships and made you suffer too, but now take me to your hearts.'

Devaki, still crying, said, 'When you left us and ran away we looked for you for three days without eating or drinking, but when finally we gave up in despair we wept for our misfortune. There can't have been a single day since then when we haven't remembered you. An age has gone by while we mourned, but now you've come back! Tell us, son, how did you run away that day and where have you been?'

Shamefaced, Sadho answered, 'Mother, what can I say about myself? I ran away in the middle of the night. That evening I found out where the Padre Sahib would be going and by asking on the way, by noon the next day I caught up with him. At first he advised me to go back home, but when it was clear I wasn't going to agree to that he sent me off to Poona. There were hundreds of boys just like me there. How could I even describe the biscuits and oranges! When I remembered you I used to cry a lot. I was a child then, but when I grew older and got some sense and learned the difference between kinfolk and outsiders I wrung my hands over my ignorance. Night and day I kept remembering. Now through your blessing I've lived to see this auspicious day. I've lived for years among others, I've been an orphan for a long time. Now let me serve you. I'm hungry for love. Give me now the good fortune which for years I didn't have.'

By now most of the village elders had gathered outside Jado Ray's house. One of them, Jagat Singh, said, 'Did you stay so long then with the padres, son? They must have made you a padre* too?'

Sadho bowed his head. 'Yes, that's their custom.'

Jagat Singh looked at Jado Ray. 'This is a very serious matter,' he said.

Sadho said, 'Whatever penance the community prescribes, I'll do it. Whatever offences I've committed against the community I did from ignorance, but I'm ready to take the punishment.'

*i.e., made him a Christian. The community referred to later, in Hindi *birādarī*, is the *jāti*, or caste group, in this case Rajputs, as indicated by the title *'Thākur'*. Having lived with Christians Sadho has automatically lost caste.

Jagat Singh again glanced quickly towards Jado Ray and spoke gravely. 'There's never been anything like this in the Hindu faith. Your mother and father can keep you at home, you're their son, but the community can never share in such a business. Speak, Jado Ray, what do you say, let's hear your opinion too.'

Jado was facing a dilemma. On the one hand there was his affection for his son, on the other he was filled with fear of the community. The son he'd worn his eyes out weeping for now stood before him with tears in his eyes, saying, 'Father, take me to your bosom and I'll be steady as a rock.' What a predicament! How could he explain his feelings to his heartless caste-brothers, what should he do?

But the mother's love welled up: Devaki could not tolerate what was happening. 'I will take my darling home,' she said, 'and keep him close to my heart. I've found him after such a long time. I can't abandon him now.'

Jagat Singh was losing his temper. 'Even if it means you'll be cast out of the community?'

Angry in turn, Devaki answered, 'Yes, even if it means being cast out of the community. Man seeks its protection only for his children's sake. If you lose your son, what use is the community?'

Several of the Thakurs scowled at this and said, 'Thakurain! That's a fine way to show respect for the community! The son can follow any path he chooses and the community won't protest? Can there be a community like that anywhere! We're telling you plainly that if your son lives with you in your house then the community will tell you exactly what *it* can do.'

There had been times when Jagat Singh borrowed money from Jado Ray, so now he said gently, 'Sister! We're not saying you have to cast your son out of the house. He's come back home after so long, we accept that gladly. But attention has to be paid to eating and drinking and the rules regarding defilement. Say, Jado brother, how far will you go in opposing the community?'

His eyes filled with compassion, Jado Ray looked at Sadho. 'You must accept what Jagat brother has said with even more goodness than you've shown to us.' Sadho said with some bitterness, 'What should I accept? To live like an outcast among my own people? To endure disgrace? To have my touch make a clay pot untouchable? I'm never going to put up with it, I'm not such a pitiful creature as that.'

Jado Ray was offended by his son's harsh words. Now that the people of the community were all gathered together he hoped to work out some compromise. As for what went on inside his own house, who was there to see on what terms the boy was living with them? He said angrily, 'But you're going to have to put up with it.'

Sadho could not understand what was behind his father's words; they seemed merely cruel to him. 'I'm your son,' he said. 'I'll go on acting like your son. Love and devotion to you have brought me this far. I've come so I can live at home. If this is not to be then there's nothing left for me but to get out of here as fast as possible. It's pointless to live among those who no longer care for you.'

'My darling,' Devaki said, weeping, 'I'll not let you go now.' Sadho smiled and said, 'Then I'll have to eat from the same dishes as you.'

Looking at him with love and affection, Devaki said, 'I nursed you with milk from my breast, so of course you'll eat from my dishes. You *are* my son.'

Sadho was thrilled by these words. What affection, what a sense of oneness there was in them! 'Mother,' he said, 'when I came it was with the idea that I'd never go away again. But I couldn't bear it if the community cast you out on my account. I couldn't stand having to see the raw pride of these stupid people. So let me go now. Whenever I get the chance I'll come to see you. I will never forget your love. But it would be impossible for me to live in this house eating apart and sitting apart. So forgive me.'

Devaki brought water from the house, and with this she washed Sadho's hands and feet. Then, at a signal from her, Shivgauri timidly approached Sadho, and Madho prostrated himself before him. At first Sadho watched the two of them in consternation, then looking at his mother he smiled and understood. He embraced the two children warmly, and the three of them began to laugh and play together. Their mother watched, scarcely able to contain her pleasure.

After a light meal, Sadho righted his bicycle, bowed his head before his mother and father, and rode away. Away—back to where he had come from in troubled spirits. Devaki was sobbing, Jado's eyes filled with tears, and he felt a twisting in his heart. 'Alas, my dear one,' he thought, 'you're going away from me. Such a worthy and promising son is slipping away from us—and only because our love has not been strong enough.'

1914

From *Mānsarovar*, v. 8. Original title, *Khūn Safed* (*Khūn-e-Safed* in the Urdu version), literally, 'white blood', from an idiom, *khun safed hona*, to lose affection or loyalty. The final phrase of the story is '. . . *isliye ki hamārā khūn safed ho gayā hai*, 'because our blood has become white.' This example of Premchand's early stories—simple in prose, basic in emotions, is also an attack on caste traditions which violate the best natural instincts. And as so often throughout his fiction, it is a woman who embodies both compassion and common sense in sharp contrast to the men around her.

# The Prostitute

The first thing Dayakrishna did when he returned from Calcutta after a six-month absence was to pay a condolence call on his dear friend Singar Singh, whose father had died three months ago. Business had prevented Dayakrishna from coming at that time so he had expressed his sympathy in a letter. But not a single day passed that he did not remember Singar. He needed to stay on in Calcutta for a few more months because his presence there was necessary for carrying out his work in an organized fashion and an absence of even a few days could cause a severe set-back. But when Lila, Singar's wife, wrote to him he felt obliged to return. She had not given any reason, simply asking him to come at once, but from her tone Dayakrishna surmised that there was cause for concern in the situation and it was urgent for him to return.

Singar was the son of a wealthy man, and by nature very carefree, very obstinate, and very fond of idling. Determination and perseverance were utterly alien to him. His mother had died while he was still a child and in raising him his father, neglecting discipline in favour of affection, had protected him from the harsh realities of the world. The boy grew up without the least idea that there was such a thing as hard work. All his wishes were instantly complied with. He soon developed into a young man who had no ideas or principles of his own. Anyone could easily hoodwink him, for it was utterly beyond his capacity to recognize the tricks and wiles of attorneys and accountants. He needed a wise and caring friend who could protect him from the intrigues of selfish people. On his part, Dayakrishna was beholden to him and his family for many favours, and felt obliged in the name of friendship to return.

As soon as he reached home he had a bath and, with the intention of taking his midday meal at Singar's, set out to meet him. By now it was after nine and the day steadily grew warmer.

Hearing of Dayakrishna's arrival Singar immediately came out to meet him. When he saw his friend Dayakrishna was shocked. Singar no longer wore the Sikh's traditional uncut hair; now it was trimmed, curled and parted on one side. In his eyes were no tears nor any other sign of grieving; although he was pale his face wore a smile. He was dressed in a fine silk shirt and velvet shoes, as though he had just come from a party. The words of sympathy on Dayakrishna's lips retreated; words of congratulation now seemed more in order.

As Singar rushed to embrace him he said, 'It's splendid that you've come, my friend, you've been much missed here. But first tell me, did you close down your business in Calcutta or not? If you left everything there disorganized and confused, then you may as well give it all up, for we're not going to let you leave us. How long can you carry on with that austere life style? I must tell you, I've changed my whole outlook. We have parties here every day. I thought, if you're born into this world, why not have a little fun for the short time you have? Otherwise, some day you'll be leaving it full of regret, and you can't take anything with you.'

Dayakrishna stared at him in astonishment. Was this the Singar he knew or a stranger? What a transformation there was in him as soon as his father died!

The two friends went into the drawing room and sat on a sofa. Where earlier Singar's father had simple rugs, bolsters and old-fashioned wardrobes there now were numerous cushioned chairs, divans, rich carpets, silk curtains, big mirrors. The father had been of the hoarding kind, the son was a devotee of spending.

Singar lit a cigar. 'Believe me, I really have missed you, old man,' he said.

'Why are you lying, brother?' Daya protested. 'Months have gone by and you never found time to write to me—and you say you missed me?'

Light-heartedly, Singar said, 'Enough of that, brother, and drink to my health. What else is worthwhile in this life? Consider the time that you spend having fun as the only redeeming feature. For my part, I've given up austerity. Now it's festivities every day!—banquets with friends, boat rides, music, drinking parties. I told myself, for a little while at least let us enjoy this spring and this abundance! Why should we keep sorrow in our hearts? Man comes into the world to enjoy himself, this is the pleasure of living. Anyone who doesn't savour that pleasure lives for nothing. So there it is—let there be a gathering of friends, your lover by your side and a winecup in your hand, I care for nothing more than that.'

331

He opened a cabinet, took out a bottle and filled two glasses. 'This is to drink my health,' he said. 'And I'll drink to yours. Now don't refuse.'

In his whole life Daya had never drunk anything alcoholic. It was not that his was the sort of pious nature that considered drinking a sin; rather it was a fear of addiction that held him back. A mere whiff of liquor would set his heart fluttering. He was afraid now that if he took one sip he would not be able to swallow it. He accepted the glass politely, then set it down, untouched, on the table and said, 'You know I've never taken a drink. Forgive me this time. Perhaps in a few days I could learn the art, but . . . Well, tell me, are you taking any interest in your business or do you just let it get along by itself?'

Singar made a face and said, 'Why bring that up, my friend? One can't spoil one's brief life for the sake of business. We come into the world with nothing, we leave it with nothing. Papa worked himself to the bone making money and when he reached fifty he died. His soul must even now be longing for the pleasures of the world. How much nicer to live poor and happy than to die leaving a pile of money! Better a life free of worry about making money than a life spent worrying about what will happen when you're gone. You set your glass down on the table: come, just drink a little, your eyes will be opened, your heart will be refreshed. Some people take their liquor with soda and ice, but I drink it neat. If you like, I'll have them bring some ice for you.'

Once again Daya asked to be excused, but Singar drank glass after glass. His eyes became red, his speech slurred, he bragged a lot, then he began to sing street songs out of tune, until finally he sank back unconscious in his chair.

Suddenly a curtain at the back of the room was drawn back and Lila signalled to Daya to come. The blood now began to course through his veins a hundred times faster. Indifferent to beauty as his shy, timid nature made him appear, he was in reality strongly drawn to it. Whenever he confronted a beautiful woman he became completely tongue-tied, he blushed and lowered his eyes, yet all the while he longed to throw himself at her feet and offer her his life. His friends called him an old hermit, while women thought him quite sexless and paid him no attention. Once he had made a long lonely train journey to Ceylon sharing the compartment with a young woman, but he had not mustered the courage to address a single word to her. True, if the girl had flirted with him he would have given his life for a tryst with her.

In his shy, inhibited life Lila was the only young woman who

332

understood his feelings and could express her sympathy for him. From the moment he realized this Daya had worshipped her with all his soul and in his inexperienced heart she had come to embody his ideal of womanhood. His thirsty spirit longed not for cooling drinks and nectar but only plain, sweet water. Lila was beautiful, charming, delicate, but that was not what caught his attention. In the parks he had seen women more beautiful, more charming and delicate. The qualities in Lila that attracted him were her compassion and thoughtfulness. In his feelings for her there was nothing except devotion. To carry out whatever she commanded was his deepest desire—this was enough to bring fulfilment to his spirit.

With trembling hands he drew back the curtain, went inside and gazed at her in astonishment. If he were not seeing her here in her own house he would not have recognized her. Her remarkable beauty, youthfulness and exuberance had withered as though someone had sucked the very life out of her. 'What's happened to you, Lila?' he asked in a voice full of pity. 'Are you ill? And you didn't let me know!'

She smiled and said, 'What is that to you? What do you care if I'm ill or well? You'd just go along having a good time. You finally remembered me after six months, then you ask me if I'm ill! Well, the sickness I have will leave me only when it takes my life with it. You've observed the state my husband's in? How can I ever tell you what I feel to see him like that! I live in this house only under compulsion and my life is filled with shame. No one wants me, no one cares about me. When his father died, so did my happy married life. If I try to explain to him I end up feeling like a fool. Night after night he disappears, God knows where. Look at him now, dead drunk. For weeks on end he isn't home long enough for me to say even a few words to him. If he goes on like this for one or two years longer we'll be reduced to beggary.'

'How did he get this way?' Daya asked. 'He was never like this before.'

Her voice full of anguish, Lila replied, 'It's the toll claimed by wealth, what else? The old man killed himself earning money to leave behind for his children. He must have thought he was assuring their security. But I tell you, he bequeathed them the means to destroy themselves, he sowed a poisoned crop. If he hadn't left a fortune perhaps today my husband would be engaged in some kind of work, he might have had some concern for the family, felt a little responsibility, but instead he's withdrawing that fortune from the bank and spending it wildly. I wouldn't be the least bit sorry if I thought that once the money was finished he'd come back on the straight path. But I'm afraid such people are never again fit for anything, they die in prison or the poorhouse.

'Now he's taken up with a prostitute called Madhuri. She's fleecing him, according to her dharma. He's got this wild idea that she's madly in love with him and he's actually proposed to her. I don't know what her response was. I've often felt like going home to my family since I no longer have any sort of relationship with anybody in this house— but I'm afraid that if I did so he'd become all the more unrestrained. I trust nobody except you, that's why I sent for you, hoping you might talk some sense into him. If it turns out that you're unsuccessful, I won't stay with him a minute longer. Well—lunch is ready, you must have something to eat.'

Daya looked towards the drawing room. 'And Singar?'

'He'll be going out at two or three.'

'Won't he mind?'

'I don't care about such things any more. I've decided that whenever he offends me I'll give him a taste of his own medicine. My father was a major in the army, and his blood's flowing in my veins.'

Lila appeared worked up; the fire of rebellion, smouldering in her for months, had suddenly flared up. 'I've suffered so much and borne so much humiliation in this house that I won't feel bad about paying him back any way I can. Until now I've hidden the state of affairs here from my father. If I write to him now, then Singar will know what trouble is. I'm enduring the punishment of being a woman, but there's a limit even to a woman's patience.'

Daya was shocked when he saw the blaze in her eyes, her trembling lips. He felt like someone who, seeing a sick person writhing in pain, wants to run for the doctor. Choking with emotion, he said, 'Right now you must forgive me, Lila. Later perhaps I'll accept your invitation. For my part I assure you that you can consider me your faithful servant. I had no idea of your predicament; if I had I might have figured out some solution by now. Can there be any greater happiness for me than being of some use to you?'

When Dayakrishna left the house he felt as ecstatic as though flying on a plane towards heaven. Today he had found a purpose in life for which he could either live or die. He was a man in whom a woman had placed all her trust. This was a jewel he would not let slip from his hand, even if it cost him his life.

During the next month Dayakrishna did not return to Singar Singh's house, nor was Singar the least bit concerned about it; from their one meeting he had concluded that Daya was not one to take up his new life-style. There was no place for such high-minded people in Singar's world, where only lively, frivolous and corrupt hearts were wanted.

Lila for her part missed him constantly.

But he was no longer the same Dayakrishna. It was as though the magic of sensual living had cast its spell over him. He had sought out Madhuri and begun to frequent her home. No longer Singar's friend, he had become his rival. Both of them worshipped the same idol, but there was a difference in their rituals. Singar regarded Madhuri merely as an object of enjoyment, while for Daya she was to be worshipped because he found contentment only in serving her. Singar considered the pleasure he found with her his by right of purchase; Daya was happy simply for her to accept his adoration. If he perceived any reluctance in Madhuri, Singar treated it as he might treat the disobedience of his favourite mare; while Daya did not consider himself worthy of so much as a glance of pity from her. When Singar gave her some trifling gift, he proudly made a great show of his generosity, as though conferring a great favour. Dayakrishna had little to give her, but whatever he gave was with the devotion of one placing flowers on the altar. In his craving for Madhuri, Singar wanted to keep her in a cage where no one else's glance might fall upon her. Daya, in his unselfish way, found pleasure simply in watching her enjoy herself.

Until now Madhuri's lovers had all been stamped from the same die as Singar: jealous, vain, devoid of tenderness, regarding beauty as a source of sensual fulfillment. Dayakrishna was something quite different—sympathetic, gentle and devoted, as though he wanted to dedicate his life to her. Madhuri had now found something in her life she meant to treat most carefully and hold on to. Expensive jewellery was no longer as valuable in her eyes as the simple amulet given by this saintly man. Jewellery could always be acquired, but if this amulet were lost it might never be found again. Jewels titillated her sensual nature, but in this holy gift there was some divine power which awakened in her a feeling of true affection and purity. Daya never made any display of his love nor harped on the anguish of being apart from her, but Madhuri had complete faith in him, while Singar's declarations of love seemed hollow and meant for show, and she longed for him to be gone. In Daya's restrained words were depth and genuine devotion. To others she had been a mistress, but to Daya the kind of lover in whose heart a storm breaks merely to hear his footsteps. After having been merely an object of lust for others, now at least in the eyes of one human being she was worthy of respect and love.

From the time Singar had heard the news of Daya's meetings with

Madhuri, the flame of jealousy was kindled, he thirsted for his blood. He engaged some disreputable characters to be on the lookout for Daya so they might finish him off wherever they came upon him. He himself began to carry a pistol and keep an eye out for him. Though Dayakrishna was aware of the danger he was in, he still kept his appointed meetings with Madhuri without fail. It seemed as though he didn't care the least bit about his life. But when the scoundrels saw him why would they slink away, or if they had the chance why didn't they assault him?—this was a mystery he didn't understand.

One day Madhuri said to him, 'You mustn't keep coming here, Krishnaji. You don't realize it but you have scores of enemies in this town. I'm afraid something may happen to you at any time.'

It was a frosty winter evening. Madhuri wore a Kashmiri silk shawl as she sat before the fire. At times silvery lightning flashed through the room. Daya realized that tears had come to her eyes, though she turned her face and tried to hide them. With his limited experience he could not fathom why a beautiful young woman, freely enjoying a sensual life-style, should be so shy about showing those tears. Yet, he perceived on her joyous, candid features a tenderness mingled with shame such as he had never seen before—the timid desire and strong affection of a well-born woman—and in her expression truth shone like a sunrise.

'I've never done any person harm,' he said firmly, 'why would anybody be my enemy? I've never got in anyone's way, never picked a fight with anyone. Every beggar comes to the door of one who gives, each one finds his own luck, some get a tiny morsel, some a full plate—why should anybody be envious? If you bestow your favour on a particular one I consider him most fortunate and respect him—why should I be envious?'

In a voice troubled by love Madhuri said, 'No, no, from tomorrow on you mustn't come here any more.'

Daya smiled. 'You can't stop me. You may scold the beggar but not keep him from your door.'

She looked at him with eyes full of affection. 'Are all men as ingenuous as you?'

'But then—what else can I do?'

'Stop coming here.'

'That's not in my power.'

Madhuri reflected a moment. 'Let me say just this—and perhaps you'll agree. Why don't the two of us go away to some other town?'

'Simply because a few people resent me?'

'They don't resent you, they mean to kill you.'

336

Still unmoved, Daya said, 'The day my love wins such a reward, Madhuri, will be a new day in my life. Can there be any death better than that? If it happens I won't be separated from you, I'll live on in your heart and memory.'

Tears in her eyes, she gently tapped his cheek. The love that was in those words pierced her heart like the point of a needle. Such anguish such intoxication—how could she answer that?

'Don't keep saying such things, Krishna,' she said, pity in her voice, 'or else some day—I'm speaking the truth!—I'll drink poison and fall down at your feet. I can't explain what there is in your words that sets me on fire. Now for God's sake don't come any more or you'll see, one day I'll take my life. You don't realize how murderous Singar is; he's lying in wait for you. I'm worn out flattering those thugs of his. And no matter how many times I tell him you're nothing to me, no matter how I slander you and curse you, the cruel man won't believe me. And it wouldn't do to tell you how hard I've tried to convince his *goondas*,* and what dishonour I've suffered at their hands. I've fallen at the feet of men I would consider it a disgrace merely to look at. But when those dogs get a few bones they become all the more bloodthirsty. Now I've had all I can take from them and I beg you to let us go to some place where no one knows us, a place where we can live in peace. With you I'm ready to put up with anything. I won't give up until you decide to do it. I realize that even now you don't trust me, you suspect I might be tricking you somehow.'

'No, Madhuri,' Dayakrishna protested, 'you're being unfair to me. I've never suspected anything of the sort. I don't know why, but from the first day it was somehow clear to me that you were different from your sisters; in you I found the decency and modesty I'd seen in women of good families.'

Staring deep into his eyes, Madhuri said, 'You don't have much talent for the art of lying, Krishna, certainly not enough to deceive a prostitute. I'm neither decent nor modest, nor am I different from my other sisters in this kind of life. I'm a whore, just as corrupt and lustful and deceitful as my sisters, even more so. But unlike other men you didn't come to me for sexual satisfaction and amusement. If you had you wouldn't have remained so controlled even after coming here for all those months. You never boasted, you never tried to intimidate me, and I never expected money from you. You told me all about your real financial situation; nevertheless I gave you not one but many

*Hoodlums

337

opportunities no other man would have let pass. But I couldn't snare you. Whatever other aim you had in coming to me in the first place, it was not sex. Had I thought you so low, so heartless and corrupt, I would not have put up with you. Nonetheless, I began to feel a friendliness towards you. I thought, 'I'm being tested. Until I pass this test I won't be able to have you. And you . . . you're as cruel as you're gentle.'

As she said this Madhuri took Daya's hand and looked at him with eyes full of passion and dedication. 'Now tell me, Krishna,' she went on, 'what did you see in me that attracted you? And careful, no evasions! You're not a man obsessed with physical beauty, I can swear to that.'

Embarrassed, Daya said, 'Beauty is nothing to sneer at, Madhuri! It's the mirror of the soul.'

'There's no shortage of beautiful women here.'

'That's as each man may perceive it. So it must be a fascination left over from one of my previous lives.'

Madhuri frowned. 'You're lying again, your face gives you away.'

Defeated, Daya asked, 'What is the point of asking, Madhuri? I'm afraid you'll begin to hate me. It's possible that the way you see me is not what I am at all.'

She appeared offended; then, as though indifferent, she said, 'In plain words, you don't trust me. One shouldn't put one's trust in prostitutes, after all—how could you not heed the advice of wise men and saints?'

Using its own weapons, her woman's heart had set out to overcome the obstacle.

With the first attack Daya lost courage. 'You're getting angry, Madhuri,' he said. 'I only meant that I was afraid you'd think me guilty of deception. You probably don't know how indebted I am to Singar Singh for all the favours he's done me—the least of them have made me prosper. There was never the slightest bit of hypocrisy in his generosity. So when I returned from Calcutta and saw the way he was living and how his good wife Lila was suffering, well, I figured out a plan to get him out of your clutches. This was the secret of my arrogance; but I failed and found myself caught in the same snare. I've been humbled, so impose any punishment for my deception that you wish.'

Madhuri's pride was shattered. Seething with rage, she said, 'So are you saying you're Lila Devi's lover? Had I known I'd never have let you enter this house. What a snake in the grass you've turned out to be!'

338

She went to the birdcage and pretended to pet the parrot. She could not imagine how she could quell the sudden fire in her heart.

Daya said scornfully, 'I am not Lila's lover, Madhuri, don't slander her. I swear to you now that I've never regarded her in that way. I look at her in the same way as would anybody who sees a fellow creature suffering.'

'It's not a sin to love someone, there's no need for you to prove Lila innocent.'

'I don't want Lila to be accused of anything.'

'Very well, sir, I shall not speak her name. I accept that she's a virtuous wife, and only at her command did you—'

'She's given no command,' he interrupted.

'Aha, so now you're ordering me to be quiet, Krishna! Forgive me. Then you came to me not at her command but by your own wish? *Now* you agree. But tell me next, what are your intentions for the future? And I'll promise—but I can't change the way I'm made. My spirit is weak, my purity was destroyed long ago. Like other precious objects, youth and beauty can be protected by those who are strong. So I ask you, are you ready to take me under your protection? Sheltered by you, with the power of your love, I'm sure I'd be able to resist all the temptations of life. I'll dash this golden palace to pieces, but in exchange I would need the shade of a green tree. Will you offer me that shade? If you can't, then leave me. I'm trapped in my situation. But I promise I'll have nothing more to do with Singar Singh. He'll besiege me, he'll weep, he may have his goondas dishonour me, terrorize me, but for you I can endure anything . . .'

With this she had had her say, but at the same time she glanced indifferently at Dayakrishna, the way a shopkeeper calls out to a customer but also tries to show that he's not at all eager.

Daya did not know what to answer. In a world torn by trouble he had found only a limited place for himself; and now even this tiny space was being taken from him. If he exerted all his energy perhaps he might reclaim it, but there was no room to sit in it; and with this other person beside him there would be no room even to stand. If he persuaded himself that by working like the very devil they might carve out a place for themselves, what would happen to his self-respect? What would people say? Would Lila even want to look at him again? Could he ever confront Singar again? Leaving aside all that, if Lila wanted to consider him fallen, let her; if Singar was jealous and furious with him, let him be so, he didn't give a damn. But what about his own soul? His faith would retreat inside him and flutter like a bird caught

339

in a net, then fly away. Nobility brings the gift of faith with it; in its company we need never doubt. Any doubt would have to be supported by clear proof. But baseness comes already tainted with doubt, challenging belief to be supported by clear—the clearest! —proof.

Humbly he said, 'You know what my situation is?'

'I do.'

'And could you be happy in such circumstances?'

'Why are you asking such a question, Krishna? It pains me. I know and I understand your doubts. I mistakenly thought you knew and understood me too but I see now I was deceived.'

She stood up, as though to leave the room. Quickly taking hold of her hand, he said imploringly, 'You're being unjust to me, Madhuri. Believe me, it's nothing at all like that.'

Still standing, she said objectively, 'You're lying. Even now you can't accept that a woman doesn't take up a profession like mine of her own free will. You think that for a woman to expose her shame for money is something pleasant which she enjoys doing. You find it quite impossible to understand that there can be any womanliness in a prostitute, you can't imagine why she's not constant in her love, or how much she yearns for love or, when by good fortune she finds it, how she clings to it as for her very life. In the bitter salt sea how dear is one drop of sweet water, but how can one who pours sweet water by the pitcherful know it?'

Daya was so bewildered that he could not say a single word. When the doubt hidden in his heart burst forth like a spark what a fearful blaze it created! The deceptive farce he'd played, the imitation of love he'd created, made his remorse all the more agonizing.

Suddenly Madhuri said brutally, 'Why are you still here?'

Swallowing his disgrace, he said, 'Give me a little time to think, Madhuri.'

'To think about what?'

'My duty.'

'I asked no time from you to think about *my* duty. If you're planning on reforming me, forget it. I'm a fallen woman and you're a model of virtue—as long as you feel that way I'm going to treat you the same way I do everybody else. If I'm fallen, then the men who come here to satisfy their lust are no less fallen. You, who are trying to get your hands on your friend's wife by pretending to love a simple woman—if through you I was even to win heaven I'd throw it away.'

Eyes red with anger, Daya said, 'Still the same accusation?'

Madhuri was furious. What was left of her tender feelings for him was swept away in a rising tide of jealousy. Any attack on Lila would not be tolerated, she thought, because Lila was a lady and she herself a prostitute, whose gift of love was automatically unacceptable.

Her voice firm, she said, 'I'm not accusing, I'm stating the truth. I'm not going to avoid the issue through fear of you. Whether you accept it or not, you're crazy about Lila. May she make you happy! I'm quite content with my Singar Singh, I no longer crave salvation. Go and reform yourself first. From now on, be careful! If you ever come here again, even without meaning to, you'll regret it. People such as you cannot reform painted harlots. Only they can who don't let the vanity of doing good works enter their hearts. Where there's love there can't be any kind of discrimination.'

As she said this she rose, walked into an adjoining room and shut the door. Stricken, Dayakrishna lingered there a while, then slowly went downstairs, walking all the while like a man who has no life left in his body.

For two days Dayakrishna did not leave his house. He had never expected Madhuri to treat him the way she did. She loved him, he was sure of that. But a love that was so intolerant, so insensitive to the feelings of others, that so unhesitatingly made false charges of wrongdoing—such a love might be infatuation but not love. He had done well not to fall into her clutches; if he had, God knew what misery awaited him.

But in the very next moment his feelings changed and his heart was filled with tenderness for Madhuri. Then he regreted his narrow and ungenerous words. He had had no reason at all to doubt her. In her situation jealousy was only natural, and in her jealousy there had been no malice, no poison. He accepted that society would slander her, he also accepted that she would not be a virtuous wife. Well, at least Singar would no longer be under her sway; the burden of Daya's indebtedness to him would become lighter, and Lila's life would be happy.

There was a sudden knock on Daya's door; when he opened it he confronted Singar, looking distraught, his hair hanging loose.

Shaking hands, Daya asked, 'Why did you take the trouble to walk here, you could have sent for me.'

Singar stared at him with piercing eyes. 'I came to ask you where Madhuri is. Of course, I know she's most likely in your house.'

'What would I know about where she is? Why would she be in my house?'

'These evasions won't work, do you understand? I'm telling you, I'll kill you if you don't tell me exactly where she's gone.'

'I don't know a thing, believe me. I haven't been out of my house for two days.'

'I was with her last night. This morning I received this letter. I went running to her house, but there was no trace of her there. All that the servants could tell me was that she called a tonga and went off somewhere, nobody was quite sure where. I won't rest until I've searched your house thoroughly.'

And so he did, looking in every corner, in the closets, even under the beds, until, despairing, he said, 'What a crafty, treacherous woman! Just have a look at this letter.'

They both sat on the floor while Daya read the letter.

'Sardar* Sahib, I'm going away for a few days, I have no idea when I'll be back, nor do I know where I'm going. I'm leaving because I've begun to hate this disgraceful, shameless life, and I've come to hate those lewd men for whom I was a plaything in their vile amusement—men among whom you are the foremost. For months you rained gold and silk on me, but I ask you, would you let your sister or wife take part in this market of pleasure for even a thousand times that gold or ten thousand times that silk? Of course not. Those ladies possess something which you hold more precious than all the wealth in the world. But when you came to me, completely drunk, every limb maddened with lust, did it ever occur to you how cruelly you were trampling this woman who does not possess that precious something? Did it ever occur to you how grieved you would be to see your well-born ladies in this situation? Of course not. You have the feelings of those jackals and vultures who when they see a corpse, converge from all directions to tear at it and devour it.

'Understand this: any woman who had it in her power would never offer herself for money. When she does, remember that she has no other refuge, no other support, and that despite this the man is so shameless that he will profit from her situation to satisfy his lust, and along with that so heartless that he will stigmatize her as 'fallen' and is willing to let her die in the same state of misery. Is she not a woman? Does she not have her place in the pure temple of womanhood? But you do not allow her to enter that temple. From her touch the temple deity will be defiled. Well, let this society of men commit whatever outrages it wants. We are helpless, powerless, we have forgotten self-respect, but . . .'

*A way of addressing a Sikh.

342

All at once Singar Singh snatched the letter from Daya's hand and said as he stuffed it in his pocket, 'Why are you reading it with such close attention? There's nothing new in it. It's just all that stuff you taught her, that's what you went there for. I ask you, why were you so jealous of me? I never did you any harm. I spent no less than ten thousand on her this year, whatever was worth anything in my house I threw at her feet. And now she has the audacity to think she's the equal of a real lady. As they say, after the cat's eaten all the mice it goes on a pilgrimage. It's all your doing. What a treacherous tribe they are—they should all be shot! After plundering my house and giving me a bad name all over town now she's giving me advice. There's surely some mystery in all this. She must have got her hands on a new victim. But where can she have run off to? Strike me dead if I don't track her down. Damn her, how she talked of love so that I was completely intoxicated! Of course she's trapped some new victim, if she hasn't you can yank my moustache out.'

Noting Singar's clean-shaven face, Dayakrishna smiled. 'It appears you've already done that.'

This feeble joke seemed to soothe Singar's wounded feelings. He felt a wave of pity as he looked around at Daya's room with its threadbare rug and ramshackle furniture. With his wounded feelings smarting he had at first sought a sarcastic response, but now the wound had cooled and the pain deepened. With the pain, sympathy also woke; so now that the fire had ceased the smoke was gone with it.

He asked, 'Tell me the truth, did you ever make love to her?'

Daya smiled and said, 'I? I merely went to see her beauty.'

'When one sees her beauty the heart loses all control.'

'That's in accord with individual taste.'

'It's like a spell—as soon as you look at her desire strikes your heart like pain.'

'I never felt any pain, I just felt like throwing myself at her feet to worship her.'

'That poetic stuff caused all the trouble. Poor fools like you should marry some simple village girl—and you went to a prostitute for *love*!'

After a pause he added, 'But she *is* treacherous, she is a deceiver.'

'I'm sorry if you expected fidelity from her.'

'You didn't love her—how can I explain it to you?'

A moment later he said, 'But she did say some things in her letter that were true, whether anybody agrees or not. It *is* wrong to treat beauty like something to buy and sell.'

Gently Daya said, 'But when a woman sells her beauty buyers for

343

it come forth. And how many different castes follow the profession.'

'How did the profession get started?'

'From the weakness of women.'

'No, I think men must have started it,' Singar said.

Suddenly he took his watch from his pocket. 'Look, it's already past two and I haven't dined. Dine with me tonight, won't you? We'll talk some more about this. But right now I'm going to look for her. She must be somewhere here in town. She said nothing to anybody in the house. The old woman there—who used to be a prostitute herself—was beating her head and her music master bemoaning his fate. Where in the world could she be hiding?'

He stood up, shook hands with Daya and was about to leave, when Daya asked him, 'You're no longer angry with me, are you?'

Singar said, 'I'm not—and then, I am,' and departed.

For almost two weeks Singar Singh combed the city. He reported Madhuri's disappearance to the police, had a notice printed in the newspapers, and sent his men out on a search for her. But not a trace of her was found. Without Madhuri, his parties lost their fun. Singar's many friends were announced morning and evening and went away disappointed. Singar had no time to gossip with them.

It was the hot weather before the rains. Singar's luxuriously appointed rooms became ovens. There were fans, there were cooling screens of *khas* at the windows, but the heat ignored all attempts to tame it and continued pouring out the fever of its heart.

Singar Singh sat in his private chamber downing glass after glass, but the fire inside him could not be extinguished. This blaze was setting fire to all his heart's superficial rubbish, turning it to ash. It was melting down his long dead capacity for detachment and steadfast contemplation, and driving it violently up to the surface. Madhuri's infidelity had wounded him so deeply that life itself seemed utterly futile to him. She had been the truest thing in his life, both real and beautiful. All the varied lines of his existence had converged on this point, and now that point, like a bubble, had suddenly been destroyed; all those lines, all those tender feelings buzzed around like angry bees whose hive has been destroyed. Now that Madhuri had deceived him there was nothing else to hope for, nothing left in his life—when the mango's juice is gone, the stone is worthless.

Aware of the many days of silence where loud parties had been the custom, Lila was astonished. For several months she had ceased to say anything at all concerning the management of the household; carrying

344

out, without comment, whatever orders came from her husband's quarters had become her life's routine. She seemed to have become completely indifferent, unconcerned with either amusement or adornment.

But this long silence now troubled her melancholy spirits. She wished she might ask him about it, but she could not, lest she lose face. But then, what face did she have to lose?—for she could be respected only when there was someone to ask her opinion. So she had no use for either respect or disgrace. And she wondered why she had been born a woman.

Slowly she drew back the curtain of Singar's room. He was lying on the sofa, silent, like a bird hiding his face in his wings in the still of evening.

She approached him in the beseeching way of a beggar and said, 'I am condemned to silence, but I cannot go on without speaking. Why have there been no parties for such a long time? Are you not well?'

Singar stared at her with sorrowful eyes. 'Lila . . . why haven't you gone to your father's house?'

'Whatever you command, but this is no answer to my question.'

'There's nothing wrong, I'm fine. One doesn't die of such disgrace. Now I'm disgusted with this life of mine. I want to go away for a while. Go back home so I won't worry about you.'

'This is good—you really do worry about me!'

'Take whatever you want with you.'

'I've given up thinking of anything in this house as mine.'

'I'm not speaking from anger, Lila. I don't have any idea of when I'll be back. How can you stay here alone?'

After so many months Lila caught a glimpse of caring in her husband's eyes. She said, 'I married you, not the the goods and possessions in this house. Wherever you live is where I'll live too.'

'All this time living with me has brought you nothing but sorrow.'

She saw one tear in his eye, falling like the moon through the blue sky. She too was moved. After burning for months in the fire of contempt she had found a grain that promised an end of it—how could she reject it? It would not fill her stomach, but it was beyond her power to reject it.

She came very close, sat beside him, and said, 'I'm yours. If you want me to laugh, I'll laugh, if you want me to cry, I'll cry, if you want me with you I'll stay—but if you don't I'll stay anyway. You are my home, my faith, I'm yours in sickness and in health.'

And the next moment her head was resting on Singar's broad chest,

345

his arm was around her waist. Both their faces were bright with joy, tears of joy were in their eyes, and a storm in their hearts was carrying them they knew not where.

After a while Singar said, 'You must have heard, Madhuri's run away somewhere and that crazy Dayakrishna's gone looking for her.'

She could not believe it. 'Dayakrishna!'

'Oh yes, the very next day after she left he went off after her.'

'But he's not that kind of man. And why did she run away?'

'It seems they fell in love with one another. She wanted to live with him but he wouldn't agree.'

Lila sighed. She remembered what Daya had said to her several months ago. His eyes, filled with longing, had begun to trouble her heart.

Suddenly someone violently flung the outer door open and banged at the door of the inner room.

'Arrey!' said Singar in consternation. 'What on earth's happened to you, Krishna?'

Dayakrishna's eyes were red, there was dust on his head and face, and a look so distraught one might have thought him insane.

He shouted, 'Have you heard, Madhuri is no longer in this world!'

And beating his head with both hands he began to sob, as though pouring out his heart and very life through his tears.

From *Mānsarovar*, v. 2, 1933. Original title, *Veśyā*.

# The Funeral Feast

From his sickbed Seth Ramnath cast a despairing look at his wife, Sushila, and said, 'What a wretched man I am, Shila, you've always had to endure suffering with me. When there was nothing in the house you would kill yourself night and day with housework and in looking after the children. Now, when things are a little under control and the days when you could take some rest have finally come, here I am going off and leaving you. Until today I've kept hoping, but now I can hope no longer. Look, Shila, don't cry. Everybody in the world dies, some a few years earlier, some a few years later. The burden of managing the house is yours now. I'm not leaving you much money, but whatever there is will help you get along somehow or other. Why is Raja* crying?'

'He wants something, what else?' Sushila answered, wiping her tears. 'From early morning he's been clamouring for a car. But can you get one for less than five rupees?'

For some time now Sethji had begun to feel a deepened affection for his two children. 'Then order one for him,' he said. 'The poor child has been crying for such a long time. All the longings of my heart have come to nothing. Order some English dolls for Rani too. When she sees other children playing with them she yearns to have them. The wealth I held dearer than life itself has, in the end, all been eaten up by the doctors. Will the children remember that I was their father?— wretched man who loved his wealth more than his son and daughter and never bought anything for them.'

In one's last days, the insubstantiality of the world becomes a harsh reality before one's eyes. Then, regretting what you didn't do and repenting what you did, your heart turns generous and honest.

*'Raja' and 'Rani' are terms of endearment for his son and daughter, Mohan and Revati.

347

Sushila called Mohan and embraced him while she wept. The maternal love, which all this time had suffered within her from her husband's miserliness, now seemed to overflow. But where was the money for a toy car?

Sethji said, 'You'll have your car, child. Take the money from your mother and go with your sister and get a nice little motor car.'

When he saw his mother's tears and understood how his father loved him, Raja's childish obstinacy seemed to dissolve. He said, 'I won't buy it now.'

'Why?' Sethji asked him.

I'll buy it when you're better.

Sethji burst into tears.

Three days later Seth Ramnath died.

While he lives a rich man is a source of sorrow to many, and of pleasure to few. When he dies, the contrary is true. The group of Brahmins in charge of funerals derive one kind of pleasure, the pandits another, and his whole caste community is probably well pleased too because there's one less person who can claim to be their equal—a thorn has been plucked from their hearts. And of course, one musn't forget the man's business partners, who can feel at last that many old scores have been settled, bringing the possibility of consolation after a long, long time.

This was the fifth day after Sethji's death. The great mansion was empty. The children neither cried nor laughed but sat dejectedly close to their widowed mother, who appeared almost lifeless, oppressed by the immense burden of her worries about the future. The little money that remained in the house had been spent on the cremation rites, and now there would be all the customary rituals to pay for. So she wondered how in the world she could manage and somehow get through it all.

Someone was calling at the door. The maid came to announce the arrival of Seth Dhaniram. The two children ran outside. For a brief instant Sushila's hopes rose. Dhaniram was the leader of the community panchayat, so her troubled woman's heart was delighted at his kindness. After all, he was the leader, and if people like him didn't see to the welfare of the helpless, who would? Thanks be to these virtuous people who protect the poor in their misfortune! Thinking this she drew her veil over her face before going out to stand on the veranda, where she found not only Seth Dhaniram but several other people as well.

*The names of Sushila's visitors, though perfectly possible as names, carry a satirical overtone: *dhanī* means rich, Kubera is the Hindu god of riches.

348

'Bahuji,' said Dhaniram, 'only our hearts know the grief we feel at the untimely death of brother Ramnath. How young he still was! But it's God's will . . . But now it's our duty to have trust in the Lord and find a way to go forward. We ought to act so that the honour of the family may be maintained and our brother's soul rest in peace.'

With a sly look at Sushila, Kuberdas said to her, 'Preserving decorum is most important, and it's our duty to see to it. Violating the established rules is unacceptable. How much money do you have, Bahu? I beg your pardon? Did you say *nothing*?'

'How could there be any money in the house, Sethji? The little we had was spent on doctors and medicine.'

'Then a new problem has arisen,' said Dhaniram. 'In a situation like this what should we do, Kuberdas?'

'Whatever may be the case,' said Kuberdas, 'there must be a funeral feast for the community. But of course, it should depend on one's capacity. I'm not saying she ought to borrow. Yet we must not fail to get whatever we can from the family, for we have some obligation towards the dead man. But he will never come again, our relationship with him is severed forever. Therefore everything must be within our means. The Brahmins will certainly insist on a strict observance of tradition.'

'But don't you have anything at all, Bahuji?' Dhaniram asked her. 'Not even two or three thousand?'

'I'm speaking the truth, I have nothing. Would I lie at a time like this?'

'In that case,' Dhaniram said, with a glance of disbelief at Kuberdas, 'you will have to sell this house.'

'Indeed, there's nothing else you can do,' said Kuberdas. 'It would not be good to incur disgrace. What a reputation Ramnath had—he was a pillar of the community. Now—here is a solution. I hold the mortgage for twenty thousand. For this, reckoning discounted interest, I'll get twenty-five thousand. The remainder of whatever the house sells for will be spent on the feast. If anything's left over it will go to the children.'

'How big did you say your mortgage was?' Dhaniram asked him.

'Twenty thousand, at a hundred per cent.'

'But I heard it was somewhat less.'

'It wasn't a verbal agreement, it's written on the mortgage deed. I wouldn't lie for three or four thousand.'

'No, no, did I mean anything like that?' Dhaniram turned to Sushila.

'You heard him, my dear, the panchayat has decided that the house must be sold.'

At this moment Santlal, Sushila's younger brother, appeared on the scene in time to hear this last sentence. 'Why must the house be sold?' he burst out. 'To provide a feast for the caste community? Then they'll all go their way leaving nobody to look after these orphans. You must think about their future too, after all.'

Giving him an angry look, Dhaniram said, 'You have no right at all to interfere in this matter. Thinking only about the future isn't going to do the trick. We have to protect the dead man's reputation after his death. What harm will that do you? But we could be made into a laughing stock. Nothing in the world is more precious than decorum, one would even give one's life for it. If there's no decorum, what's left? If you ask us our advice, that's what we'll say. Our sister's choice lies before her, she can do whatever she wants. It won't be any concern of ours. Come along, Kuberdas, let's go.'

Frightened, Sushila said, 'Don't pay any attention to what my brother said. That's just the way he is. But I won't disregard your advice, you're my elders. You know the state of my affairs. I have no wish to bring grief to my husband's soul—but if his children suffer misfortune, won't his soul be grieved by that? His daughter has to be married, and the boy will need an education. So I can provide a feast for the Brahmins but not for the whole community.

It was as though the two great gentlemen had been slapped. 'What sacrilege! Is there any possible answer to such a statement? The members of the panchayat will never allow themselves to be so dishonoured. People won't laugh at the widow but at the panchayat. How could they tolerate such ridicule? It would be a sin even to look in through the door of a house like this one!'

In tears, Sushila said, 'I'm destitute, I'm ignorant, don't be angry with me. If you people abandon me too how will I ever manage?'

In the meantime two other gentleman had arrived, one very fat, one very thin, with names according to their appearance—Bhimchand and Durbaldas.* Dhaniram briefly described the situation for them. Durbaldas said sympathetically, 'Then why don't we all get together and contribute a few rupees? When the boy comes of age, we'll get our money back. And if we don't, then it's no great matter if we suffer a loss to help a friend.'

Kuberdas frowned. 'You're talking absolute balderdash,' he said. 'With the market the way it is now who has any money to spare?'

*Bhima was the strongest of the five Pandavas in the Mahabharata; *durbal* means weak.

'That's quite true,' Bhimchand confirmed. 'No one's ever seen such a weak market. But in spite of that we must take care of things.'

Kuberdas bristled. He was itching to get his hands on Sushila's house, and such talk might interfere with his selfish designs. All he wanted was to get his money and be done with this business; he did not intend to get entangled in problems with women.

Bhimchand had somehow put him on his guard; but there would definitely have to be a feast. Neglecting this duty would be an offence to society.

Sushila had seen a glimmer of humanity in Durbaldas. Raising humble eyes toward him she said, 'Without people like you I'm nothing at all. You are the master—do whatever you think proper.'

'Surely you must have a bit of jewellery, sister,' he said to her.

'Yes, I have some. Half was sold during his sickness, I have the rest.'

She brought all the jewellery she had and set it down before the members of the panchayat. But it would not fetch more than a mere three thousand.

Durbaldas weighed the little bundle in his hand. 'What good will three thousand do? I'll give three and a half.'

Bhimchand took the bundle and weighed it in hand. 'I say four thousand.'

This gave Kuberdas his opportunity to reintroduce the question of selling the house. 'How much can we do with only four thousand?' he said. 'Offer a feast for the community or fulfil our obligation? It's going to cost the community at least ten thousand. So the house will have to be sold.'

Santlal, tight-lipped, said, 'I ask you again, can you people be so heartless? Have you no pity for these orphaned children? Will you abandon them and make them beggars in the street?'

But nobody paid any attention to his pleading. The matter of the house could no longer be avoided. The market was depressed, one could not expect a return of more than thirty thousand. Twenty-five thousand belonged to Kuberdas. So five thousand would be left over and the jewellery would bring another four thousand. With some frugality feasts could be provided for both the Brahmins and the dead man's own caste community.

Helpless, Sushila brought forth her two children and said, 'You of the panchayat, look at my children's faces! Take everything there is inside my house, but at least leave us the house. I have nothing else in the world. I fall at your feet and beg you: don't sell the house now.'

351

What answer could there be for foolishness such as this? The members of the panchayat themselves did not want to sell the house. They did not feel any hostility towards Sushila and her children; but they had to take this step because there was no other way to offer the caste community a feast. Had the widow at least been able to find a way to provide another five thousand the house could be saved. But that was out of the question for her now, so there was nothing to do but to sell it.

Finally Kuberdas said, 'Look, sister, the market is very low right now. No one would be willing to lend the money. If it's so written in your children's fate, then God will surely devise some other little scheme to help them. As the saying goes, 'Life proposes, death disposes.' So don't worry about your children. The Lord who gave them life is already planning something for their livelihood. But have we failed to make you understand? If even now you don't give up this obstinacy we shall withdraw all our support, and it will become difficult for you to stay here, for people from the city will be pouncing on you.'

There was nothing left now for widow Sushila to do. She would not be able to stay in the village if she fought with the panchayat. Who would make an enemy of the crocodile when he's fallen in the river? She stood up to go into the house, but fell down in a faint on the spot. Until this moment she had held on to some little hope in that, bringing up her children she could forget her widowhood. But now there was darkness all around her.

Seth Ramnath's friends had therefore gained full rights to his house. If one's friends don't have these rights who does? What is a woman, anyway? If she can't understand such serious matters as the propriety of what the community has to do (and do it generously, with pomp and fanfare), then it's pointless to try to tell her anything more. Who would buy the widow's jewellery? Bhimchand had set a price of 4000 rupees for it, but now he realized he'd made a mistake. Durbaldas had valued it at 3000, and therefore he was the one who got hold of it. He and Bhimchand clashed over this matter, but justice was on Durbaldas' side and Bhimchand took a whipping.

Dhaniram observed, 'Look now, Durbaldas, you've made off with the goods. But it's worth a lot more than three thousand. I can't allow such a violation of morality.'

'Come now,' said Kuberdas, 'it's all in the family, it's not going anywhere outside—some day he'll give a banquet for his friends.'

All four good gentlemen laughed. Now that this matter was settled they had time to look into the question of the house. Kuberdas was prepared to accept thirty thousand, but without proper legal proceedings there was the possibility of suspicion being cast on the acquisition. There was no need to risk that, so a broker was summoned. He was a dwarfish, toothless fellow of about seventy named Chokhelal.

'I've been friends with Chokhelalji for three years,' said Kuberdas. 'What a jewel of a man!'

'Look, Chokhelal,' said Bhimchand, 'We have to sell this house. You're an expert agent, so find us a decent buyer.'

'The market situation isn't good,' Kuberdas added, 'but all the same we have to see that Ramnath's children aren't left destitute.' Then he whispered to him, 'Don't go over thirty.'

'Look here, Kuberdas,' said Bhimchand, 'that's not right.'

'Why, what did I do? I only told him to get a good price.'

'You people don't have to tell me that,' said Chokhelal. 'I understand my duty. Ramnath was my friend too. I also know that in having this house built he spent not one pice less than a hundred thousand. But the condition of the market is known to all of you here. At this moment you can't expect more than 25,000 rupees for it. If the right customer comes along then we might get five or ten thousand more; but as things are now, it's going to be difficult to get even twenty-five. It's a case of get what you can for it.'

'25,000 is very little,' said Dhaniram. 'At the very least insist on thirty.'

'Thirty? I'd ask forty if I could, but first let me find the buyer. If you people agree, I'll go for thirty.'

Dhaniram said, 'If it's going to go as cheap as thirty, then why not offer it to Kuberdas? Why should anybody else get such a bargain?'

'If you're agreed on that,' said Kuberdas, 'so be it.'

Dhaniram agreed. Bhimchand was left inwardly seething. The deal was settled. That very day a lawyer wrote out the bill of sale and had it registered. When it was brought to Sushila she sighed and, her eyes brimming with tears, she signed it. Now she was bereft of everything. Like a disloyal friend, this house had stood by her in happy days, but in her time of sorrow it deserted her.

The members of the panchayat sat down in Sushila's courtyard to scribble out their agreement while the hapless widow watched from a window upstairs and wept over her misfortune. When the document was ready, her teardrops rained down upon the paper.

Dhaniram looked up and said, 'Where are those drops of water coming from?'

'My sister is up there crying,' said Santlal. 'She's sealing your document with tears of blood.'

Dhaniram bellowed, '*Arrey*, sister, what are you crying for? This is no time for tears, you should be pleased that the panchayat has gathered in your house today for this auspicious arrangement. Why are you grieving when we're taking care of the affairs of the husband with whom you spent so many days of pleasure and contentment?'

The document was circulated among the community. During the next four or five days the panchayat was kept busy making preparations for the feast. Dhaniram got a commission for providing the ghee, along with the sugar and wheat flour. On the fifth day, early in the morning, the feast for the Brahmins was held, in the evening a second one for the community. The motorcars and buggies lined up at Sushila's door, while inside the guests sat in the traditional rows. The courtyard, sitting room, galleries, veranda, terrace, even the roof, were crowded with visitors, who feasted and sang praises of the panchayat.

'Everybody shares in the cost, of course, but it all has to be properly arranged. You don't often get such tasty things to eat.'

'After Seth Champaram's funeral feast only Ramnath has had one like it.'

'How crisp the *amritis* were!'

'And the *rasgullas* were stuffed with dried fruit.'

'All the credit belongs to the members of the panchayat.'

Dhaniram said humbly, 'It's most kind of all you brothers to say so. We were all close to brother Ramnath. If we didn't see to all the arrangements, who would? I haven't been able to sleep for four days.'

'We're grateful to you! One's friends should be like you.'

'What a wonderful thing! You've preserved Ramnathji's name. The community enjoys this feasting; there is no pleasure in looking at the money.'

The guests went on eating their fill while they eulogized the food, and meantime Sushila sat in her room and thought, 'What selfish people there are in this world! Has everybody in the world turned selfish? There they are, all feasting and rubbing their bellies. Not one of them has even asked whether there's anything left for the orphans!'

A month went by. Sushila was practically down to her last pice. There was no cash left, the jewellery had gone. All that remained now were a

few cooking pots. Meanwhile; quite a few trifling bills had to be paid—
a few rupees to the doctors, some to the tailor, some to the merchants.
To settle these accounts Sushila had to sell what was left of the furniture.
And in a month everything gradually disappeared.

Poor Santlal was an accountant in a shop. From time to time he
would come and give her a few rupees while they scrounged to meet
expenses. The children understood the situation. They didn't bother
their mother, but when some vendor came by the house and they saw
the other children eating fruit or sweets, it was not their mouths but
their eyes which watered. It was heartbreaking to look into such
yearning eyes. These children, who some time ago had scorned dried
fruits and sweets, now longed for the cheapest snacks. Those same
gentlemen who had arranged the feast for the community still walked
past the house, but not one of them looked in.

One evening Sushila lit the fire to make rotis while the children sat
close to the fire, watching with famished eyes and waiting for the *dal* to
cook on the other stove. The girl was eleven, the boy eight.

Getting restless, Mohan said, 'Amma, give me the roti, I'm very
hungry.'

'The dal isn't ready yet,' Sushila said.

'I have a pice,' said Revati. 'I'll go and get him some yogurt.'

'Where did you get it?'

'I found it yesterday in my doll box.'

'Then go, quickly now.'

Revati set off at a run and came back in a few minutes with a little
yogurt in a leaf-dish. Sushila finished making the rotis and gave them
to the children. Selfish like most children, Mohan began at once to eat
the yogurt without offering his sister any.

Sushila watched with bitter eyes. 'Give some to your sister too,' she
said, 'you're eating it all by yourself.'

Mohan was immediately ashamed, the tears came to his eyes.

'No, Amma,' Revati said, 'see how little he has. You eat, Mohan,
and then perhaps you'll fall asleep in a little while. I'll have some of the
dal when it's cooked.'

At that moment they heard two men calling at the door. Revati
went to find out who it was. The men had come to get the house
vacated. Sushila's eyes grew red with anger.

She walked out to the veranda and said, 'My husband's not been
dead a month and you've taken it into your heads to have the house
emptied! You've sold my house that's worth 50,000 for thirty, and
skimmed off 5000 for interest and still you're not satisfied. Say what
you want, I'm not vacating now.'

The agent said humbly, 'Baiji, what choice do I have? I'm only the messenger. You have to give up whatever belongs to somebody else. What's the point of quarrelling about it?'

Sushila herself realized that he was speaking the truth. If she was doomed how long could she expect to survive? Gently she said, 'Tell Sethji to allow me a few day's grace period. But no—don't say anything. Why should I have to feel grateful to anybody for a week or ten days? If it were written in my fate to stay on in this house, I wouldn't be leaving it at all.'

'So it will be empty by tomorrow morning?'

'Yes, yes, that's what I'm saying. But why wait till tomorrow? We'll leave right now. Our things don't amount to such a great deal, after all, so why should Sethji lose a whole night's rent? Go get the keys—or did you bring them?'

'Why be so hasty, Baiji? Just see that it's properly cleared out tomorrow.'

'Why put off the struggle till tomorrow? Munimji, go bring back the key and lock it all up.'

With that Sushila went inside, fed the children, managed to eat something herself, washed the pots, and then sent for an *ekka*.* When it came she loaded on her few belongings, and with a heavy heart bid farewell to that house forever.

When they had had the house built, what hopes were in their hearts! For the house-warming they had feasted several thousand Brahmins. Sushila had run about and worked so hard that afterwards she was sick for a whole month. In this same house their first two sons had died, in it her husband died too. Memories of the dead had purified every brick of it, every single stone was happy with her joy and sorrowful with her grief. Today, this house was no longer hers.

She spent that night at a neighbour's and the following day took a room in a house in a back alley for ten rupees a month.

The hardships suffered by the forsaken family in that room over the next three months are almost impossible to imagine. Poor Santlal, bless him, helped them along with a few rupees. If Sushila had come from a poor family, she might have done menial work in the kitchen or sewn clothes in someone's home; but how could she support herself by doing work her community considered below her caste? If she did, people would say, 'So that's Seth Ramnath's wife!' and she would have

*A one-horse cart

disgraced his name along with her own. There is no escape from the arrayed forces of society.

Sushila's daughter had a few bits of jewellery set aside and they too were sold. When there was hardly enough for bread, where was the rent going to come from? Seth Jhabarmal, the landlord—a respected man of her community who had eaten more than most at the funeral feast— suddenly became anxious. The poor fellow had been patient for such a long time. It was a matter of thirty rupees, and a rupee is not just a few pennies. So great an amount could not be overlooked.

Finally one day Sethji, eyes red with anger, came to Sushila and said, 'If you can't pay the rent, clear out of the house. I have given you every consideration because of the community, but it can no longer go on like this.'

'Sethji, if I had the money I'd pay you first, then spend for myself. You've been so considerate to me so far that I must bow my head at your feet. But for the moment I have no money at all. Do please understand, I'm bringing up the children of a caste-brother. What else can I tell you?'

'Enough of that, I've already heard lots of that kind of talk. The landlord's of the same community, so you think you can suck him dry. If I were some Muslim you'd pay up every month without any fuss, otherwise you'd be thrown out. But I'm of your community, so you think there's no need to pay me. I shouldn't have bothered to even ask you but taken it up with the panchayat.'

At this moment Revati came and stood beside Sushila. Sethji looked her up and down and for some reason or other asked, 'Well , I see this girl has come of age. Has there by chance been any talk of getting her married?'

Revati ran away at once. Sushila, apprehending the glimmer of intimate sentiments in these words, said in a voice charged with emotion, 'There's been no talk of that yet, Sethji. When we can't even pay the rent how can I think of arranging her marriage? And anyway, she's still too young.'

Seth Jhabarmal immediately had recourse to scripture. 'This is the very age for girls to marry,' he said. 'One must never abandon one's prescribed religious duty. No need to talk about the rent—how could I know what a state Ramnath's family was in?'

'Then,' Sushila said carefully, 'do you have a suitable groom in view? You already know, I have nothing to bargain with, no dowry to offer.'

'There'll be no wrangling about the arrangements,' said Seth

Jhabarmal. 'There's a family where the girl can live her whole life in contentment. Her brother can live with her too. His lineage is good, the whole family is well-endowed in every way. The groom's a widower.'

'He must be of the right age,' said Sushila. 'If he's a widower, how old is he?'

'Not much older than the girl, he's forty, but he looks young and vigorous—and a man's appetite decides his age. Anyway, you must understand, this will be the salvation of your family.'

Not concealing her unwillingness, Sushila said, 'I'll think about it and decide. But I'd at least want you to show him to me once.'

'You won't have to go anywhere to have a look, Baiji,' said Sethji. 'He's standing here before you.'

Sushila looked at him with hatred in her eyes. The lust in this old man of fifty! she thought. His chest was drooping down over his navel, and still he was itching to get married. The old villain thought that by tempting her she would hand her daughter over to his embrace. Even if Revati were to die an old maid she would never ruin her life by marrying her to this corpse. But she kept her rage in check. Times had changed, otherwise he would never have dared make such a proposal to people like themselves. She said, 'I thank you for your kindness, Sethji. But I cannot have my daughter marry you.'

'So I suppose you think you'll find a young unmarried man in the community for your daughter?'

'My girl isn't going to marry.'

'And you'll dishonour the name of Ramnath?'

'You're not ashamed to say something like that to me! For the honour of his name I've lost my house, I've lost all our wealth. But I can't drown my daughter in a well.'

'Then hand over the rent!'

'I don't have the money right now.'

Jhabarmal went into the house and flung every single bit of her belongings out into the alley. The pitcher burst, the clay pot broke, the chest of clothes was scattered. Sushila almost indifferently watched this cruel playing out of her misfortunes.

When he had completed the destruction of her home Jhabarmal locked the door and, with a threat of taking her to court to collect his money, went on his way.

Those with power have money, those without it have hearts. With money important deals are made, great palaces are built, there are servants, cars, hunting parties. From the heart comes compassion and tears with it.

Next to Jhabarmal's house a low-caste greengrocer had her shop. She was old, a widow and childless. Though fiery on the outside, she had a tender heart within. She cursed Jhabarmal roundly, picked up all of Sushila's things and brought them into her house. 'Stay in my home, daughter,' she said. 'I remembered my manners, otherwise I would have yanked his moustache out. Death is dancing on his head, he has no family of his own and he's killing himself running after money. Who knows, he thinks he'll take it with him when he dies. You stay in my house, you'll have nothing to worry about here. I live alone and we can share what I have.'

Sushila was frightened. 'Mother,' she said, 'I have absolutely nothing except a couple of pounds of flour. How can I pay you any rent?

The old woman said , 'I'm not Jhabarmal, daughter, any more than I'm Kuberdas. I understand in life there's both sorrow and grief. Don't act stuck-up in the good times, don't worry in the bad. If you can earn just four pice I'll look after your stomach. I saw you at the time when you were living in the mansion and I see you today when you're destitute. I also realise that the kind of nature you had then is the one you have right now. It's my good fortune that you've come into my home. Do you think I'm so blind that I'd ask you to pay rent?'

These simple consoling words lightened the burden on Sushila's heart. She saw that true nobility was to be found among the very poor and low, while compassion in the rich was only another form of arrogance.

Sushila lived with the old woman for six months. Day by day her affection for her grew. And the old woman would bring whatever she could and put it in Sushila's hands; and the two children were as dear to her as her own eyes. Nobody in the neighbourhood had the nerve to look askance at them, the old woman would have raised the very devil. Every month Santlal gave her a little something and with that they managed to get along.

By now it was November and fever was raging. One day while he was playing Mohan suddenly took ill and lay unconscious for three days. His body was so hot that to stand near him one felt as though a flame was coming from him. The old woman ran to exorcists and conjurers, but the fever didn't abate even a little bit. Sushila was afraid it could be typhoid; at the very thought she felt her life dry up in her body.

On the fourth day she said to Revati, 'Darling, you've seen the chief panchayat member's house. Go and tell him that your brother is very sick, could he please send a doctor.'

Revati ran as fast as she could to Kuberdas's house.

Kuberdas said, 'The doctor's fee is sixteen rupees. Will your mother pay it?'

In despair Revati said, 'How can my mother have any money ?'

'Then how in the world can she call my doctor? Where is she anyway? Go and tell her to send for some doctor from the Seva Samiti*, otherwise why doesn't she take him to the charity hospital? What a stupid woman she is, without a pice to her name and she thinks she can give orders to a doctor! She must have thought the head of the panchayat would just hand over the money to pay for it. Why would he, I ask you? The wealth of the community is for religious ceremonies, not to be squandered.'

Revati went home but she could not repeat what she had heard. Why put salt in the wound? So she invented an excuse, telling her mother Kuberdasji was away somewhere.

'Then why didn't you tell his clerk?' Sushila said. 'Did you think you'd find sweets here that you should come running back so quickly?'

At this moment Santlal arrived with a *vaidya*, a practitioner of Ayurvedic medicine.

That day Vaidyaji came; he did not come back the next. After much entreaty the Seva Samiti doctor came twice, then he too could no longer find the time. Mohan's condition worsened every day. During the month that followed the fever refused to come down for a second. Mohan's face had shrunk so much that it was pitiful to see. He would not say a word, and soon he was too weak to turn in bed from one side to the other. While he lay there his skin erupted, his hair began to fall out, his hands and feet became like wood. Santlal came to see him when he could get leave from his job, but this was no help, since there was neither nurse nor medicine.

One evening Mohan's hands turned cold. His mother had already lost hope by then; when she saw the state he was in she began to sob. She had already vowed many times to make offerings to the deity; weeping, her hands folded before her, she walked seven times around Mohan's cot and said, 'Oh Lord, this is the reward of my Karma. Even when I lost everything I was content, holding my child to my breast. But this is a blow I won't be able to bear. Make him well and take me instead! O merciful one, this is the mercy I crave.'

Who can understand the secret of earthly existence? It's not uncommon for a man to steal something and on that same day suffer

*A charitable organization.

360

losses worth twice what he stole. That very night Sushila caught a fever, and at the same time Mohan's fever began to go down. In attending the child she had become weak and thin; once this illness caught her it would not let her go. No one can say whether the deity had been listening to her or not, but her plea was answered to the letter. Fifteen days later Mohan rose from his charpoy and came to his mother; weeping, he lay his head on her breast. Sushila embraced him and while she held him tight she said, 'Why are you crying, son? I'm going to get better. I've nothing more to worry about, God will take care of me. He alone is your protector and your father. Now I'm free of all care and soon I'll be well.'

Mohan said, 'Sister told me you're not going to get better.'

Sushila kissed him and said, 'Sister's silly, let her say it. I'm not leaving you to go anywhere, I'll always be with you. But the day you do anything wrong, the day you steal something, that's the day I'll die.'

Satisfied, Mohan said, 'Then you'll never leave me, Mother?'

'Never, darling, never.'

That night, struck down by sorrow and affliction, the destitute widow entrusted her destitute children to God, and passed on to the other world.

Three years after this event the two children were still living with the old woman. She was more than a mother to them. Every evening after she gave Mohan his dinner, she would take him to school and fetch him when class was over. Revati was now fourteen and did all the housework—grinding spices, cooking and scouring and sweeping. When the old woman went out to sell her vegetables Revati also came to sit with her in the shop.

One day Kuberdas, head of the panchayat, sent for Revati. 'Aren't you ashamed to tend a shop and disgrace your whole caste community?' he asked her. 'I warn you not to be there tomorrow. I've arranged your marriage to Jhabarmalji.'

His wife confirmed this. 'You're grown up now, daughter, so it's no longer proper for you to tend a shop. People are beginning to say all kinds of things. And Seth Jhabarmal would not have agreed to the marriage if we hadn't worked very hard to persuade him. Anyway, just understand, you're going to be a regular queen. He's worth thousands, *hundreds* of thousands. How lucky you are to find such a bridegroom! Your little brother, now, is he going to be made to mind a shop too?'

'What a disgrace for the community!' said Kuberdas.

'It is indeed.'

'What do I know?' said Revati, ashamed. 'Speak to my uncle Santlal about it.'

'Who the devil is he?' Kuberdas burst out angrily. 'A clerk who doesn't earn three pice! Why should I ask him? It's my right to do whatever I think good for the community. I've already taken counsel with the other panchayat members, and all agree with me. If you don't consent we'll begin legal proceedings. You'll be needing money for expenses, so take this and go.'

With that he tossed a twenty-rupee note at Revati. She picked it up and tore it to pieces. Red in the face, she said, 'The community never cared about us when we didn't have a scrap to eat. When my mother died nobody so much as looked in on us. When my brother was sick nobody even asked how he was. I don't give a damn about a community like that.'

As soon as she left, Jhabarmal came out of an adjoining room, looking downcast. Kuberdas's wife said, 'The girl's stuck-up and absolutely shameless.'

'Twenty rupees,' said Jhabarmal. 'Wasted! It's so torn up that it can't be put back together again.'

'Don't you worry,' said Kuberdas. 'I'll take care of her with legal action. There's nowhere she can go.'

'Now you're the only one I can depend on,' said Jhabarmal.

How can the head man of the panchayat say anything untrue? Revati was still a minor, with no mother or father. In such circumstances, the panchayat had full authority over her. It didn't matter whether or not she was willing to accept their oppression. The law could not disregard the authority of the community.

When Santlal heard about what had happened he was enraged. He said, 'Who knows when the Lord will put an end to this community!'

'Can the community force me to accept their authority?' Revati asked him.

'Yes, my dear, the law too is in the hands of the rich.'

'I'll tell them I don't want to live with him.'

'What good will that do? If it was written in your fate, then it's in no one's power to change. Anyway, I'll go to see Kuberdas.'

'No, uncle,' said Revati, 'don't go anywhere. If you believe in fate, then whatever's written in it will be.'

She spent that night at home. Many times she embraced her drowsy brother. When she worried about how Mohan would get on without her she felt her courage weakening. But when she remembered what Jhabarmal looked like, her resolve grew strong.

Early in the morning she went to bathe in the Ganges, as had been her custom for the past several months. This morning it was quite dark, but that was not enough to arouse any suspicion. They suspected something only after eight had struck and she still had not come home.

That afternoon the news spread throughout the community: Seth Ramnath's daughter had drowned in the Ganges, her body had been found.

'Oh well,' said Kuberdas, 'it's just as well. Now the community won't be disgraced.'

Jhabarmal was dejected. 'Now find some other girl for me.'

Meanwhile, Mohan was beating his head and weeping while the old woman held him close and consoled him. 'Why weep for this goddess?' she said. 'Her life was sorrow, nothing but sorrow. Now she's resting in her mother's lap.'

From *Mānsarovar*, v. 4. Original title, *Mṛtak-Bhoj*. Amrit Rai does not list this story in his index of Premchand's short stories, but it is a late one, probably from the early thirties. In it, as so often, Premchand uses the desperate plight of a widow to attack hypocrisy and what he considers the lunacy of strict adherence to religious traditions. In 'Widow With Sons' the obsessive greed of family members is the agent of destruction; in this story the entire community uses its traditions to commit a crime against a helpless individual.

# Desire

Yesterday in our neighbourhood there was a great commotion when a *pan* seller started beating his wife. The poor woman sat there weeping but the heartless wretch felt not the slightest compassion for her. Finally losing her temper, she sprang up and said, 'That's enough, it's not right for you to beat me. From now on I'm through with you. I may have to beg but I won't live in your house.'

With that she picked up an old sari and walked out of the house while her husband stood motionless like an owl watching her. After she'd walked a little way she turned back and opened up the shop's money box to take out a few pice. Perhaps until that moment she still had a grain of feeling left for him, but now the wretch swiftly caught her hand and grabbed the money from her. What heartlessness, what an outrage upon a helpless woman! There had been a day when he would have given his life for her, when he did nothing but wait to see her again. But today he had turned so brutal he didn't even seem to be aware of who she was. The woman put the money down and, without protesting, walked off, nobody knew where.

I* kept watching for hours from my window to see if she might return or if the *pan* seller would try to coax her back. But neither of these things happened. Rather today I learned for the first time the real situation of our women. The shop belonged to both of them, but while the husband spent his time wandering about amusing himself, the woman sat there round the clock, a truly devoted wife. How often did I see her working as late as ten or eleven at night. However much the man cut and trimmed the betel, the woman did even more. But the man is everything, the woman nothing! And whenever he wants, the man can throw the woman out.

My mind was so troubled by this problem that sleep fled from my

*For a reader of the Hindi, verbal endings make it clear that the narrator is a woman.

eyes. Midnight struck and I was still sitting up. The moon shone brightly in the sky; the lord of night sat proudly on his jewel-inlaid throne. Little shreds of cloud would drift slowly near the moon, then lose their shape and break up, as though a white-clad beauty, oppressed and dishonoured by that moon, were departing in tears. This fantasy so disturbed me that I shut the window and went to sit on the bed. My darling lay there deep in sleep. His bright countenance at this moment seemed to me to be rather like the moon—there was the same charming smile which had once gratified my eyes. I could see the same broad chest, where when I lay my head I felt a tender beating and the same strong arms, which when they embraced me stirred up currents of happiness in my heart. But now for such a long time I hadn't seen the bright line of laughter on his face, nor did I feel eager to see it. And for such a long time now I had not laid my head against his chest nor felt his arms embrace me. But why?—had I become someone else or my husband another person?

It had not been such a long time, five years in all—five years since my husband had welcomed me with wide-open eyes and eager lips. I had kept my head modestly bowed, but in my heart what strong desire I felt to look and see the beauty of his face! But compelled by modesty I could not raise my head. Finally gathering courage, I lifted my eyes and, although my glance returned after making only half its journey, still from that half glimpse I felt a happiness I can never forget. The picture is even now engraved on the tablet of my heart. And whenever I recall it I am overcome with joy. In the memory of that happiness there's still the same pleasure, the same thrill.

Now I see that beauty morning, noon, evening, through all eight watches of the day and night I look upon it. But in my heart there is no pleasure. He stands before me and talks to me, and I—I turn back to my crocheting. When he used to leave the house I would go to the door and see him off, and when he turned to smile at me I felt as though I had gained the kingdom of heaven. In the afternoon I would go upstairs and wait for him. When I saw him approaching from afar I would run downstairs like one mad and go to the door to welcome him. But now I'm not even aware of when he's leaving or coming home. Only when he closes the front door behind him do I realize that he's gone out, and when I hear that door open I know he's back. I can't understand whether either of us has become a quite different person.

In the past he was not at home a great deal. When I would hear his voice it was as though lightning shot through me and, enchanted, I

365

would listen to his every little word, watch every little action. My eyes would stay glued to him when he picked up our little boy and fondled him, when he patted the dog's head and made him lie down, when he scolded the old servant as he was leaving, when he filled buckets and watered the plants. But now he stays in the house all day, he laughs in front of me, he talks, and I'm scarcely aware of it. I don't know why.

Then one day he put a bouquet in my hand and smiled. I thought it was a gift of love and was pleased beyond words. It was only a few blossoms and leaves but I could not get enough of looking at them. I held the bouquet for a little while, then put it in a vase on the table. Afterwards I went on doing some work, but I would keep coming back to look at it. How many times I stared at it, how many times I kissed it! If someone had offered me a hundred thousand rupees for it I would not have taken them. Every single petal was a jewel to me. When the bouquet withered I picked it up and put it in a box.

Since that time he's given me innumerable gifts, ornaments each more bejewelled than the other, clothing ever more costly, and he rarely fails to bring me flowers. But I no longer feel that same delight when I get these things. I put them on, look at myself in the mirror and swell with pride, I show them to my friends to make them more envious as I grow more vain—that's all.

A few days ago he gave me this necklace. Everybody is entranced when they see it. I too was thrilled by its beauty and artful construction. Then I opened my jewel box and took out the bouquet. As soon as I held it in my hand lightning coursed through my every nerve and all the strings of my heart were set to trembling. Those dried petals, now faded to yellow, seemed to speak to me, as though words, indistinct, trembling, steeped in passion, came sighing forth from their withered mouths. But that necklace, jewel-studded and glittering, was just a heap of stones and gold without life or consciousness or affection. I kissed the bouquet again, held it to my throat, watered it with my tears, then put it back in the box. All the jewels that filled that box were trivial before this one memento. What was its secret?

Then I remembered an old letter which he had sent me from college. How can I ever forget the happiness which came into my heart, the storm it raised, the river of tears which flowed from my eyes, as I read it through. I had kept this letter in my bridal chest. Now suddenly, struck with an intense desire to reread it, I took it out. As soon as I touched it my hands began to tremble and my heart to pound. I can't tell how long I stood there holding it. It seemed to me that I had become once more what I was when I received this letter. In it was there any poetic expression, any literary analysing of love, any pathetic cry about the pain of separation? There wasn't one word of love in it at all. He had written:

> 'Kamini, you haven't written to me in eight days. Why? If you don't write to me I won't come home for the Holi vacation, do understand this. What do you do all day, anyway? Have you opened my bookcase where the novels are kept or my closet? Why did you open it? You must have thought, 'I won't write, that will shake up this fellow and he may shed some tears.' But it doesn't worry me at all. I go to bed at nine and get up at eight. If I worry about anything it's about not passing my exams. If I do fail, you'll know it.'

How simple this letter was, springing from a naive heart, full of guilelessness, sulky insistence and worry, as though I were completely responsible for him. Could he still threaten me like that today? Not in the least. Only someone who knows the pain of being separated, someone who experiences it could. Now my husband knows that such a threat would have no effect at all on me, that I would laugh and go to sleep, because I know for sure that he'll come home, that he has no other home. Where else could he go?

Since that time how many letters he's written to me. If he leaves town for only a couple of days he's sure to write, and if he goes for ten days or two weeks he writes every day. These letters are filled with carefully chosen words and sentences, carefully chosen ways of addressing me. I read them, sigh, and put them away. Alas! Where has his heart gone? In those lifeless, unfeeling, artificial words of love where is the sense of oneness, the sentiment, the passion, the anger, the fretting? My heart looks for something in them, something unknown, hidden, invisible—but doesn't find it. The letters are perfumed, the stationery elegant. But all their artfulness and decoration look like the artifice and make-up of some woman long past her youth. I never open those letters a second time; I know only too well what's written in them.

It so happened in those days that I was once observing a fast on the occasion of a death in the family. I prayed with head bowed before the image of the goddess. 'I ask you for only one boon, Goddess: let the two of us never be separated; I have no other desire, I want nothing else in the world.'

Four years have gone by since then, and we have rarely been away from each other for even a day. I had asked the goddess for only one boon, and she had granted me a treasury of them. But if I should face the goddess today, I'd say to her, 'Take back all your boons, I don't want a single one of them. I want only to see again that day when the desire of love was in my heart. You gave me everything and yet cheated me of that incomparable happiness which was in desire.' I would pray now to the goddess to give me a day when I might wander by a deserted river bank in a dense forest looking for my beloved. I would say to the waves in the stream, 'Have you seen my dear one?' Let me say to the trees, 'Where has my lover gone?' Will I never know this happiness?

Tonight, at the moment I was thinking these thoughts, a gentle cool breeze began to blow. I was standing at the window with my head leaning outside. The puffs of wind scattered my hair. It felt to me as though my lover were in those sighing breezes. I looked towards the heavens. The rays of the moon, like twinkling stars of silver, were playing hide-and-seek. When I shut my eyes they appeared, when I opened them they vanished. I had the feeling that my lover, sitting among those twinkling stars, was about to descend from the sky. And just then I heard someone in the street singing:

> 'Strange are the lover's renunciations,
>> wondrous the worlds of pain!
> Where have you gone and hidden,
>> squandering love like gold!'*

'Squandering love like gold'—that verse pierced my heart like an arrow. I felt my hair stand on end, a stream of tears flowed from my eyes. It seemed to me as though someone had taken out my heart and brought it to my lover. I let out a scream, and at that very moment my husband woke. He came to me and said, 'You screamed just now! Oh my, are you crying? What's the matter, did you have a nightmare?'

I was sobbing. 'If I'm not to cry, should I laugh?'

He caught my hand and said, 'But why, what's making you cry? Or do you feel like crying for simply no reason at all?'

'You mean you don't know why I'm crying?'

'How can I know what's in your heart?'

'Did you ever try to know?'

'I never had the slightest hint that there could be any reason for you to cry.'

'You're so intelligent and you can still say something like that?'

In consternation my husband said, 'Are you going to explain your riddles?'

'Why, don't you ever cry?'

*Quoted from a poem of Mahadevi Varma

368

'Why would I?'

'Don't you long for something now?'

'All my greatest desires have been fulfilled. Now I want nothing more.'

As he said this he smiled and walked towards me to embrace me. His heartlessness at this moment upset me terribly. I pushed him away and said, 'I don't call this shamming 'love'. Anyone who's never cried can't love. Tears and love flow from the same source.'

At this moment the sound of that singing was heard once more.

> 'Strange are the lover's renunciations,
> wondrous the worlds of pain!
> Where have you gone and hidden,
> squandering love like gold?'

The smile disappeared from my husband's face. I saw him tremble briefly. He appeared to be in the throes of deep emotion. Suddenly his right hand rose up to his chest. He sighed deeply and tears fell from his eyes down his cheeks. Myself in tears I quickly put my head against his chest, re-experiencing that first bliss for which my heart had longed for such a long time. Tonight I heard my husband's heart beating once again, tonight again I knew the passion in his touch.

And till now the words of that verse have kept echoing in my heart—

> 'Where have you gone and hidden,
> squandering love like gold . . .'

1928

From *Mānsarovar,* v. 4. Original title, *Abhilāṣā.*

# The Actress

The curtain fell. In the role of Shakuntala Taradevi had enchanted the audience. When in the course of the play she stood before Dushyanta and addressed him in fiery words expressing intense emotions of regret, anguish and scorn, the spectators, violating theatre conventions, stormed towards the stage and shouted their bravos. Indeed, many of them actually sprang up on the stage and fell at her feet in a rain of flowers and jewels. If at this moment the chariot of Menaka had descended to carry her off, the melée might well have cost the life of a dozen or so of her admirers. The manager quickly appeared to thank these enthusiasts and promised them that the same show would be put on on the following day; with this their frenzy finally subsided.

All this time there was a certain young man standing on the stage who looked as though he might be a prince—tall, impressive, with a complexion like gold, well-built, with the beauty of the gods and a radiant face. When the mob of spectators had made their exit, he asked the manager, 'May I see Taradevi for just a moment?'

'In this theatre that's against the rules,' the manager answered disdainfully.

'Then could I send a note to her?'

'No, sir,' said the manager with the same scornful expression. 'Sorry, our rules don't permit it.'

The young man said nothing more but, disappointed, came down from the stage and was just about to leave when the manager said, 'Wait just a moment. Your card?'

The young man drew a piece of paper from his pocket, wrote something on it, and handed it to the manager, who glanced at it and read: Kunwar Nirmalkant Chaudhuri, OBE. His stern expression softened—Kunwar Nirmalkant, the most influential nobleman and landholder of the city, a gifted writer, skilled in classical music, scholar

370

of a high order, with a yearly earning of eight or ten lakhs, whose donations financed so many institutions—he now stood here as a humble suppliant. The manager, ashamed of his rudeness, said deferentially, 'Do forgive me, I'm afraid I've been very much at fault. I shall take your card to Taradevi at once.'

Signalling him to stop, Kunwar Sahib said, 'No, let it go for now. It could be inconvenient for Taradevi at this moment, it's her time to rest. I'll come back at five tomorrow.'

'I feel certain she would welcome such an inconvenience, I'll be back in a minute.'

But after having disclosed his identity, Kunwar Sahib felt obliged to cloak that indiscretion with restraint, so he thanked the manager courteously and, promising to return on the morrow, took his leave.

In a clean, neat room Tara sat before a table, lost in reflection. The scene of her success last night danced before her eyes. Such days do not come often in a lifetime. How many men had been restless with longing to see her, even fighting with one another, how many of them she had contemptuously pushed away with her feet! Yes, shoved away. But in that crowd only one sublime figure had stood unmoving. What profound passion was in his eyes, what firm resolve! It felt as though those eyes were piercing her heart. Would she see that man again today or not? Impossible to say, but if she caught sight of him this evening she would not let him go without speaking to him.

As she thought about this she looked in her mirror and saw herself fresh as a freshly bloomed lotus. Surely no one could tell that this fresh blossom had already seen thirty-five springs. That glow, that softness, that quickness and sweetness, all could put a girl of twenty to shame. In Tara's heart the flame of love had been rekindled. Almost twenty years before she had had a bitter experience in a love affair and since then led a life such as a widow might lead. How many lovers had wanted to bestow their hearts upon her! But she did not so much as give them a second glance, for in their passion she caught the scent of deception. But oh! today all control was slipping from her grip. Today once more her heart felt that tender anguish of love she had known twenty years before. The pleasing image of a man had possessed her eyes and imprinted itself upon her heart. There was no way she could forget it. Had she simply seen him riding by in a car perhaps he would not have caught her attention. But when she saw him before her ready to offer the gift of love she could not remain unmoved.

371

Suddenly her maid came in and said, 'All the things from last night have been arranged, Baiji, now tell me what I should bring to you.'

'No, no need to bring me any of them,' said Tara. 'But wait—what sort of things are they?'

'Heaps and heaps of things, Baiji, I couldn't begin to count them. There are gold coins, brooches, hairpins, buttons, lockets, rings, just everything. One little box has a gorgeous necklace. I've never seen one like it before. I've put everything in a chest.'

'Very well, bring me that chest'.

When her maid had set the chest on the table a boy brought in a letter and gave it to Tara. She looked at it curiously and read, 'Kunwar Nirmalkant, OBE.' She asked the boy, 'Who gave you this letter? It was the man who wore a silk turban, wasn't it?'

The boy only said , 'Manager Sahib gave it to me,' and dashed away.

The first thing Tara saw in the chest was a little box. She opened it to reveal a beautiful necklace of genuine pearls; beside it was a card. Tara pounced on it and read: 'Kunwar Nirmalkant.' The card slipped from her hand and fell. She jumped up and swiftly crossed several rooms and hallways to come and stand before the manager. He stood up and welcomed her, saying, 'Congratulations on last night's performance.'

Still standing, Tara asked him, 'Is Kunwar Nirmalkant outside? The boy ran off as soon as he gave me the card so I had no chance to speak with him.'

'Kunwar Sahib gave me a note after you'd left last night.'

'Then why didn't you send it to me at once?'

'I thought you might be resting,' the manager answered somewhat fearfully, 'I didn't think it right to bother you. And my dear, to tell the truth, I was afraid that if you met him I might lose you. If I were a woman I would have followed him on the spot. I've never seen such a fine-looking man before. He was the one wearing a silk turban who stood before you. You probably saw him too . . .'

Dreamily Tara answered , 'Oh yes I did. Is he going to come back?'

'Yes, this afternoon at five. He's a most learned man and the most important nobleman of this town.'

'I won't be coming to rehearsal today.'

Kunwar Sahib would surely come. Tara sat before her mirror, while her maid put on her make-up . In this era applying make-up and putting on jewellery is a science. In the past it was just a set of conventions which poets, artists and connoisseurs had, so to speak, established as traditional. Collyrium was considered appropriate for the eyes, henna for the hands, lac for the feet. A particular kind of jewellery was prescribed for every limb. Today that tradition is no longer in vogue. A woman now does her toilette according to her own taste, skill and sense of competition. Her ideal is whatever resources are able to enhance her beauty to the maximum. And in this art Tara was highly skilled. She had been with this theatrical company from the age of fifteen and spent her whole life since playing with the hearts of men. There was no one who could surpass her when it came to knowing how to glance and smile, how to move her body, how to ruffle her hair casually, to absolutely overwhelm their senses. At this moment she was carefully selecting the arrows to draw from her quiver, and when after adorning herself with her weapons she entered the living room it was as though she had taken to herself all the sweetness in the world.

She stood by the table looking at Kunwar Sahib's card, but all the while her ears were straining to catch the sound of his car. She wanted him to arrive at just this moment and find her in this pose, in which he could see displayed all the charms of her figure. Her skill in cosmetics had triumphed over time—who could guess that this restless young woman had already reached the stage when the heart desires tranquillity and, anxious to find sanctuary, has bowed its pride before humility?

Tara Devi did not have to wait long, for Kunwar Sahib may have been even more eager than herself for this meeting. In ten minutes the sound of his car was heard. Tara composed herself. A moment later Kunwar Sahib entered the room. Forgetting her manners, she did not shake hands. Even at this mature age the turmoil and recklessness of love had not diminished. She stood with her head bowed like an embarrassed girl.

Kunwar Sahib's glance, as soon as he came in, fell on her throat where the pearl necklace he had offered her the night before now glittered . Nothing had ever made him so happy, and for a moment he felt as though all the wishes of his life had been fulfilled. He said, 'Forgive me for disturbing you so early in the morning. I imagine this must be your time to rest and enjoy yourself?'

Rearranging her sari, which had slipped from her head, Tara said, 'Can there be anything more delightful than seeing you? And for your gift what can I give you except my sincerest thanks? Now I hope we shall be able to meet from time to time?'

Nirmalkant smiled. 'Not "from time to time": every day! Even if you shouldn't care to see me I shall nevertheless be at your doorstep with my head bowed.'

Smiling in return, Tara replied, 'Yes, at least until that time when you may happen to find some new source of entertainment?'

'For me this is not a matter of entertainment but a question of life and death. Of course, you may think this is only something amusing, but I don't care. If it costs me my life to amuse you I'll consider my life well spent.'

So when the two of them had promised to nurture this love, they enjoyed their breakfast; and after inviting her to dine with him next day Kunwar Sahib took his leave.

During the next month Kunwar Sahib came to her several times each day. Even a moment of separation was intolerable to him. Sometimes they would take a boat out on the river, at other times they would sit on a lawn in the park or engage musicians to play for them. Something new was planned every day . It was now well known throughout the city that Tarabai had snared Kunwar Sahib and he was squandering his wealth with both hands. But for Tara Kunwar Sahib's love was a treasure compared to which all the wealth in the world was insignificant. All she wanted was to see him before her; there was nothing else she wanted.

And yet, even after strolling for a whole month through this bazaar of love, Tara had not found that thing which her soul coveted. Though every day she heard from Kunwar Sahib true and honest words of boundless, incomparable love, the word 'marriage' was never able to find its way among the others; it was as though while suffering thirst she was able to have anything in the market except water. And without water how could this thirst be satisfied? If once it had been slaked, her taste might be directed towards other objects. But for one who is thirsty nothing but water will do. She knew that Kunwar Sahib was willing to give up his life at a mere hint from her, so she wondered why he never uttered that word. Did he want to declare his intention by writing her a letter? Or did he really want her only for his own amusement? That would be a disgrace she could not tolerate; if he asked her she would jump into the fire for him but disgrace like that was not to be borne. A while back she might have spent a few months with some fashionable man-about-town, then left him, making off with his money. But she could not live such a life of shame with the Kunwar Sahib; love must be repaid with love.

In the meantime Kunwar Sahib's relatives were not standing idle and wanted nothing as much as to pry him loose from Tarabai's clutches. Their only hope of succeeding lay in forming a plan to get him married, and they went to work on this at once. They were not really afraid that he would marry this actress, but only feared that he might make over some of his property to her or to any children that came of the liaison.

As a result, pressure was put on the Kunwar Sahib from every quarter, to such an extent that even the European officials urged him to marry. On the day they spoke to him he went to Tarabai in the evening and said, 'Tara, I have something to say to you, and don't refuse.' Tara's heart skipped a beat. 'Say what it is,' she told him. 'What can it be that I can offer you and make my heart grateful for the chance?'

It did not take long for him to say it. Tara accepted and, weeping ecstatically, fell at his feet.

A moment later Tara said, 'I was beginning to despair. You put me to the test for a very long time.'

Kunwar Sahib set his tongue against his teeth, as though he had heard something inappropriate.

'It wasn't like that, Tara. If I'd believed that you'd accept my proposal then probably on that first day I'd have stretched out my hand to ask for your consent, but I didn't consider myself worthy of you. You're a treasure of virtues, while I . . . Well, whatever I am, you know already. I'd decided that for the rest of my life I'd go on worshipping you. Perhaps at times when you were pleased you'd grant me a favour without even my asking. So that was what I longed for, nothing more. If there is anything worthwhile in me it's my love for you. When you give your opinion on literature or music or religion I'm astonished, and I feel ashamed of my own insignificance. For me you're not of this world, but of heaven. I'm surprised that at this instant I haven't gone mad with happiness.'

For some time more Kunwar Sahib went on talking of what he felt. Never before had he spoken so openly.

Tara listened with her head bowed, but her features were marked by a sort of anxiety, mingled with shame. This man was so simple in his heart, so free of deception, so modest and generous!

Suddenly he asked her, 'On which day is the sun going to rise on my good fortune, Tara? Be merciful and don't put it off for long.'

Tara, completely overcome by his simplicity, said in a worried voice, 'What are you going to do about the law?'*

He answered promptly, 'You need not worry about that, Tara, I've already consulted with the lawyers. There's a certain law by which you and I can be joined in a bond of love. It's called a civil marriage. That happy moment can be any day you want—what about it?'

Tara did not look up. She could not speak.

'I'll come early on that morning . Be ready.'

Tara still did not look up. She did not utter a word.

Kunwar Sahib left, but Tara still sat, motionless, leaving him to wonder why this clever woman who played with the hearts of men looked so perplexed.

Only one day remains before the wedding. Tara has been showered with congratulations from every quarter. The men and women of the theatrical troupe have given her gifts according to their capacity, Kunwar Sahib has presented her with a jewel chest, and his three or four of his closest friends have sent various kinds of presents. But Tara's lovely face reflects no pleasure at all. She remains sad and downcast. For four days she had been constantly tormented by one question: could she betray Kunwar Sahib's trust? Could she deceive this god of love who was violating the strictures of his caste for her sake, who had broken relations with his own family, whose heart was as immaculate as a snowflake and vast as a mountain? She could not be so vile, no matter how many young men with whom she had acted out farces of love, no matter how many mad with love of her she had played for fools—never before had she experienced the least misgiving, never had her heart reproached her. Was the reason this that here was a love such as she had never found before?

And then, she wondered if she could make Kunwar Sahib's life happy. Yes, certainly, of this at least she had not the slightest doubt, for there was nothing devotion could not accomplish. But could she deceive nature? Could the brightness of noon be found in the rays of the setting sun? Impossible! That vivacity, that swiftness, that sense of oneness and renunciation and self-confidence, the fusion of which is called youth—where was she to find them? So no matter how much she wanted to she could never make Kunwar Sahib happy. An old mare can never trot with the colts.

Alas, why did she ever let it come to this? She should never have deceived him with her tricks and artificial beauty. After all that had

*Differences in caste make a Hindu marriage out of the question.

happened she could never tell him she was only a painted doll to whom youth had bid farewell long, long ago, leaving only the traces behind.

At twelve that night Tara sat before her table deep in these reflections. The gifts were piled up before her, but she was not aware of them. A few days ago she would have given her life for things like them, she had always craved such things, which could efface the marks of time. Now she had come to hate them. Love is truth, and truth and lies cannot live together.

Tara thought, Why don't I go away from here? To some place where nobody would know her. In a little while, after Kunwar Sahib had married, she could come back and meet him to tell him her whole story. He would be astonished, there was no telling how he'd take it. But for her there was no other road. His days would be spent lamenting, but no matter what pain it caused him she could not deceive her lover. She would be left with the memory of her heavenly love, and all the pain it had given her. She had no right to anything more than that.

Her maid came in and said, 'Come, Baiji, you must be hungry. Come and have a little something to eat, it's past twelve.'

'No,' Tara answered, 'I'm not hungry at all . You go and eat something.'

'Please, don't forget me,' the maid said. 'I'll go with you.'

'Have you any proper clothes set aside?'

'Arrey, Baiji, what have I to do with proper clothes? I'll wear the ones you pass along to me.'

The maid went out. Tara looked at the clock. It really was after twelve. Only six hours more . . . At dawn Kunwar Sahib would come to take her to the temple of marriage. 'Oh Lord,' Tara said, 'why give me now what you denied me so long ? Is this all part of the game you play?'

Tara put on a white sari and removed all her jewellery.* Then she washed her face with soap and warm water and went to stand before her mirror. Where had it gone, that beauty, that radiance which had ravished people's eyes! The outlines of the face were the same, but the glow was gone, and with it the deceptive allure of youth.

Tara found it difficult to stay there any longer. The jewellery and objects of pleasure strewn on the table seemed to mock her. The life she had lived all this time suddenly seemed artificial and intolerable, her cool house equipped with fragrant screens of *khas* and electric fans burned her like an oven.

*Indications of widowhood.

377

Where can I run to? she wondered. If she took a train she would not get away, for early in the morning Kunwar Sahib would send out his men to begin searching for her in every direction. So she must take a road no one would think of.

At this instant Tara's heart was bursting with pride. She felt no sorrow, she felt no despair. She would meet the Kunwar Sahib again, but it would be a reunion without self-interest of any kind. She was taking the road of duty dictated by love, so she was free of sorrow and despair.

Suddenly it occurred to her that when the Kunwar Sahib found that she had gone he might in his grief take some irrevocable and fatal step. The thought terrified her, and for a moment she felt her resolve weaken. Then she sat at her table and began to write a letter.

'Forgive me, my darling,' she wrote. 'I am not worthy to be your slave. You have shown me a kind of love which I could never have hoped to find in this lifetime. That has already become everything for me. As long as I live I shall remain under the spell of your love. It seems to me that in the memory of love there is far more tenderness and bliss than in the enjoyment of it. I shall come back, I shall meet with you again, but only after you have married—that is the one condition of my return.

'Life of my life, don't be angry with me. The jewellery you gave to me I leave behind, like a woman newly widowed, and take with me only that pearl necklace, which was your first gift. And I beg you, please don't try to find me. I am yours and always will be yours.

'Your Tara.'

When she had finished writing Tara set the letter on the table, wound the pearl necklace around her neck, and left her room. From the theatre sounds of music rose. For one brief instant her feet were frozen. Tonight she was breaking the ties of fifteen years. Suddenly she saw the manager coming her way. Her heart began to pound. Quickly she slipped aside and hid in the shelter of a wall. As soon as the manager had gone past she walked out of the building that housed the theatre, through back alleys for some distance, until she found the street that led to the Ganges.

Silence reigned along the river bank. A dozen or so sadhus and sannyasis lay before fires of fragrant incense, and nearby a few pilgrims were sleeping on blankets they had spread on the ground. And like an

378

immense serpent the Ganges coiled its way along beside them. A boatman sat in a small boat moored on the bank. Tara called to him:

'Oh ferryman, will you take the boat across?'

The boatman answered, 'Not so late at night.' But when he heard her offer double fare he picked up the oar, untied the boat and said in his country dialect, 'Where does your ladyship want to go?'

'To the village across the river.'

'At this late hour I won't have any other passengers.'

'No matter, just take me across.'

She stepped into the boat and the boatman shoved off. Slowly it began to drift, like someone wandering in the realm of dreams.

At this moment a moon of the eleventh night* rose over the horizon, sailing forth in its luminous ship, and floated on the ocean of the sky.

1927

---

* i.e., near the full.

From *Mānsarovar*, v. 5. Original title, *Aikṭres.*

# Sacrifice

Anand sat in the upholstered chair, lit a cigar and said: 'Today Vishambhar's made a fool of himself. It's nearing exam time and he's become a volunteer. If he's arrested, that will be the end of the exams. And I'm afraid he'll lose his scholarship as well.'

Rupmani was sitting opposite on a bench, reading a newspaper. Her eyes were on the newspaper but she was listening to Anand. 'Too bad,' she said. 'Didn't you try to talk him out of it?'

Anand frowned. 'When somebody fancies himself another Gandhi, it's not easy to give him advice. On the contrary, *he* was the one advising *me*.'

Rupmani folded up the newspaper and pushed her hair back. 'You didn't tell me. If you had, I might have been able to stop him.'

Annoyed, Anand said, 'Well, nothing's happened as yet, he's probably still at the Congress office—so go and stop him.'

Anand and Vishambhar were both students at the University. The blessings of both Lakshmi and Sarasvati* had fallen to Anand's lot. Vishambhar had not been so lucky. Taking pity on him, the professors had arranged a rather small scholarship for him, and that constituted all his income. A year earlier Rupmani had been their classmate, but this year after an illness she'd quit college. The two young men would meet with her from time to time, Anand to win her heart, Vishambhar for no particular reason at all. If he didn't feel like studying or was depressed he would come and sit with her, perhaps to find some consolation in telling her the tale of his misfortunes. With Anand he didn't feel confident enough to talk very much, especially since Anand never expressed one word of sympathy for him. Instead he would scold him, insult him and treat him like a fool. In an argument Vishambhar could not hold his own against Anand. After all, what does a lamp

*Goddesses respectively of prosperity and learning.

380

count for in comparison to the sun? So Anand dominated him psychologically.

Now, for the first time in his life, Vishambhar had challenged that domination and Anand had come to Rupmani to complain about it. For months Vishambhar, accepting Anand's reasoning, had suppressed his own inclinations; but though overwhelmed by reasoning his heart remained rebellious. Doubtless this year would be ruined, his life as a student might come to an end, in which case these fourteen or fifteen years of hard work would be wasted, and he'd get neither thanks nor profit from it. Was there any point in leaping into the fire? If he stayed at the University he could accomplish a lot for his country there too. Anand, for instance, collected contributions every month and got other students to pledge support for the independence movement. He advised Vishambhar to do the same, and this reasoning had triumphed over his mind for some time but could not win over his own desires.

This morning when Anand went to the college Vishambhar had set out for the Congress office. Returning home, Anand found a letter on his desk:

Dear Anand, I know that what I'm about to do is not in my own interest. But some power I don't understand is drawing me on. I don't want to go, yet I'm going, just as man doesn't want to die, but dies, doesn't want to weep, but weeps. When everyone we're devoted to is taking such terrible risks, there's no other path for me. I can't delude my soul any longer: it's a question of honour, and honour does not allow any compromise.          Your Vishambhar

When he read this Anand felt that he could even now reason with Vishambhar and bring him back. Still in a rage over the boy's folly, he had gone to Rupmani. If Rupmani had flattered him and told him to go after Vishambhar he might have done so . But when she said that *she* could have stopped him he found it intolerable. In his response there had been resentment, harshness and perhaps some jealousy too.

'Fine,' said Rupmani, with pride in the look she gave him, 'I'll go.'

After a moment, suddenly anxious, she asked him, 'Why aren't *you* going?'

She had made the same mistake again. If she'd coaxed and wheedled him he would surely have gone with her. But in her question was the implication that he didn't want to. Vain as he was, he could not go now. As though indifferent, he said, 'It's useless for me to try. Your words will have more of an effect on him. He left this letter on my desk.' He took the letter from his pocket and put it down before

381

Rupmani. 'If he has such grand thoughts about soul and duty and ideals and regards himself as somebody of superior quality I couldn't have any influence on him.'

Because of the sarcasm that was implicit in these words for a moment he did not let Rupmani see his face. She in turn was wounded by his hostility but at the same instant a spark of rebelliousness blazed inside her. She took the letter without hesitation and began to read it, at first only to deliver a counterblow to Anand's antagonism. But as she read it her expression became intense and severe, she grew tense, and the fire of self-dedication came into her eyes.

She set the letter down on Anand's desk and said, 'No, now it would be useless for me to go too.'

Enjoying his victory, Anand said, 'As I have already told you, right now he's obsessed, nobody would be able to influence him. When he's released from jail after a year of hard labour, infected with tuberculosis, or has had his arms and legs broken by the police, then he'll come to his senses. For the moment he's dreaming of cries of victory and adulation.'

Rupmani was staring up at the heavens. In the blue of the sky an image was taking shape: a weak emaciated naked body, dhoti gathered at the knees, head smooth, toothless mouth—the living image of austerity, renunciation, and truth.*

Anand spoke again. 'If I knew that I could save my country with my blood I'd be ready to give it this very minute. But even if a hundred and fifty men like me stepped forward, what would come of it? The only tangible result seems to be throwing away one's life.'

Rupmani was still gazing at that image. It was smiling now, a simple, fascinating smile that had conquered the world.

Anand was saying, 'Fellows who are troubled when exams come around start dreaming up plans for saving the country. But the question they should really face is, if you can't save yourselves how can you save the country? It's easier to get beaten up than to pass your exams.

Rupmani kept her eyes on the skies. The image now wore a severe expression.

As though startled, Anand said, 'By the way, there's a very good film on today. Would you like to see it? We could make it to the first show.'

Bringing herself down from the skies, Rupmani said, 'No, I'm not in the mood.'

Anand gently took her hand. 'Are you feeling all right?'

*A reference to Gandhi

382

She did not try to withdraw her hand. 'Why shouldn't I be feeling all right?'

'Then why not go?'

'I told you, I'm not in the mood.'

'Then I won't go either.'

'It would be better to give the money for the tickets to the Congress.'

'Subtle reasoning! But I agree.'

'Then tomorrow show me the receipt.'

'Don't you trust me even enough for that?'

Anand set out for his hostel. Soon afterwards Rupmani bicycled to the Congress office.

When Rupmani reached the Congress headquarters a group of volunteers was picketing the foreign cloth shops. Vishambhar was not among them, nor was he with another group getting ready to march on to the liquor shops.

Rupmani approached the Congress secretary and asked him if he knew where Vishambhar was.

'The one who was recruited today?' the secretary asked her. 'What a courageous fellow! He's going to work at getting the villages ready. By now he'll have reached the station, he's leaving by the seven o'clock train.'

'Then's he's probably still there?'

The secretary glanced at his watch and answered, 'Yes, you might just find him at the station.'

Rupmani cycled quickly to the station, where she found Vishambhar on the platform. As soon as he saw her he ran to her and said, 'What are you doing here? Weren't you meeting Anand today?'

Looking him up and down, she said, 'Why are you dressed like that? Do you think even wearing shoes is unpatriotic?'

Anxiously he asked her, 'Anand Babu told you, didn't he?'

In a harsh tone she answered, 'Yes, he told me. What in the world were you thinking of? You'll get at least two years.'

His face fell. 'Since you know,' he said, 'why haven't you got a few words to encourage me?'

Her heart ached for him, but she kept up her pose of hostility. 'Do you consider me your friend or enemy?' she asked him.

Vishambhar's eyes filled with tears. 'Why do you ask a question like that, Rupmani? Can't you understand without my having to tell you?'

'Then I tell you: don't go.'

383

'That's not the advice of a friend, Rupmani. I feel sure you're not saying what you really feel. Just think a little—what's my life worth? Even if I got my MA it would mean a job with a salary of a hundred rupees. If I do well at my job and move up in the job I might get to three or four hundred. Instead of that, do you know what I'll get here? My country's complete independence. Even dying for such a cause is far better than living like this. You'd better go now, the train's coming. Tell Anand Babu not to be angry with me.'

Until today Rupmani had always felt sorry for this weak-headed boy. But from this moment he had earned her complete respect. Whatever power there is to draw a heart to sacrifice now moved her heart with such intensity that it seemed as though the circumstances dividing them were annulled. Whatever faults there may have been in Vishambhar had been transformed into things of beauty and suddenly sparkled. She felt herself flying like some bird, looking for shelter in the greatness of his heart.

She stared at him with eager eyes and said, 'Take me with you too!'

Vishambhar felt as though intoxicated. 'You? Anand Babu would never forgive me.'

'I don't belong to Anand!'

'Then—does Anand belong to you?'

Rupmani's eyes blazed with resentment, but she said nothing. Now circumstances seemed to be turning into obstacles again. Why couldn't she be independent the way Vishambhar was? The only daughter of prosperous parents, brought up in luxury, she now felt herself a prisoner. Her soul began to struggle to break the bonds that held her.

The train had arrived, passengers were already getting off and climbing aboard. With tears in her eyes Rupmani said, 'Take me with you?'

'No,' he answered firmly.

'Why?'

'I don't want to answer that.'

'Do you think I'm so spoiled I can't get by in the villages?'

Vishambhar was ashamed. That was actually one important reason, but he said, 'No, it's not about that.'

Then what is it ? Are you afraid my father will disown me?'

'If that's something you're afraid of wouldn't it be worth taking into consideration?'

'I wouldn't care the least bit about that.'

Vishambhar saw the glow of proud resolve on her lovely face. Faced with that resolve he was close to trembling. He said, 'I beg you, Rupmani, please do as I say.'

Silent, she was reflecting.

He went on, 'Give up this idea for my sake.'

She bowed her head and answered, 'If that's your command, Vishambhar, I must accept it. You think I've come to you now on a momentary impulse, ready to throw away my future. But I'll show you, this is no momentary impulse of mine but a firm decision. Go, but listen to what I tell you—let yourself be arrested only when there's been a violation of your self-respect or your principles. I'll pray to God for you.'

The train whistled. Vishambhar climbed aboard and found a seat. While the train pulled out Rupmani stood as though holding the wealth of the world in her lap.

In a corner of her closet Rupmani had a rather tattered photo of Vishambhar. When she came back from the station she took it out, put it in a velvet frame, and set it on her desk. The photograph of Anand was removed.

In the past during college holidays Vishambhar had written to her a few times. After reading his letters only once she had put them aside. Today she took out those letters and read through them again. What pleasure she found in reading them now and how carefully they were put away afterwards in her writing box!

When the newspaper came next day Rupmani seized it greedily. When she read Vishambhar's name she was bursting with pride.

It soon became her routine to go to the Congress office during the day and frequently she took part in the public meetings as well. One after the other her articles of comfort and luxury were discarded. Her silk saris were replaced by coarse homespun ones. She also acquired a spinning wheel* and sat spinning for hours. Day by day her thread became finer; from it she would have kurtas made for Vishambhar.

This was also the time to prepare for the University exams and Anand had absolutely no time to spare. He did visit Rupmani on a few occasions but stayed for only a moment. Perhaps it was her coldness that sent him away so quickly.

A month went by. One evening when Rupmani was about to leave for the Congress office Anand paid a call. Frowning, he said, 'These days it's hard to get a chance to talk to you.'

*The spinning wheel became a Gandhian symbol for the boycotting of foreign cloth during the Independence movement.

385

Rupmani sat down. 'But you have no time to spare from your books. Today I've had no fresh news. I go every day to the Congress office to learn what I can.'

With philosophical indifference, Anand said, 'Vishambhar heard there was a lot of uproar and commotion going on in the village, so he's found the kind of work he's fit for. Here he had to keep his mouth shut, but out there he can thunder all he wants. I admit, though, he has guts.'

The look which Rupmani directed at him said plainly, 'You have no right to talk about him.' Aloud she said, 'If a man has courage, all his defects are cancelled out. I suppose you must have found time to read the Congress bulletins? Vishambhar's been able to arouse the awareness of the villages to such an extent that not a thread of foreign cloth can be sold there and nobody goes to the liquor shops any more. And the good news is that there's no need to picket, and now they're stirring the panchayats to action.'

Anand said casually, 'Then you may take it that their time for being stirred had come anyway.'

Rupmani flared up. 'To do the things he's done is no mean achievement. Yesterday there was to be a huge meeting of the villagers. Everybody in the whole district must have come to it. And I've heard that nowadays no lawsuits are being tried in the courts—the lawyers are all getting cold feet.'

'That's how the Congress has its fun,' Anand said with some bitterness, 'scaring off all the lawyers and zamindars and merchants. There'll be nobody left but peasants and labourers.'

Rupmani realized that he'd come ready to fight. So she too, as though taking up a challenge, answered, 'Then do you want the lawyers and zamindars and merchants to get fat sucking the poor while nobody opens his mouth to protest against a social order that has such injustices? You're an expert in sociology—can such a social order be called in any way ideal? Can there be any development at all of the three basic principles of civilization in such conditions?'

Anand was angry now. 'Education and wealth have always been what counts above everything and always will be, even if their forms are changed.'

'But if even after independence wealth counts above everything and the educated remain just as blindly selfish, then I say it won't matter if we gain independence. The greed of the English capitalists and the devotion of the educated to their own self-interest are oppressing us now. Will the people sacrifice their lives only for the evils we're risking our necks to remove just become national instead of foreign? For me at least the meaning of freedom isn't to have Gobind substituting for John. I want to see the kind of social order where inequality can find no refuge.'

'This is nothing but your own fantasy.'

'Then you haven't read any of the literature about the political agitation.'

'I haven't and I don't intend to.'

'Well, that's no loss for the country anyway.'

'You know, you're not at all the way you used to be. You've been completely transformed!'

At this moment the postman brought in the Congress bulletin and set it down on the desk. Rupmani opened it impatiently. As soon as she saw the first headline her eyes seemed to fill with intoxication. Her throat grew tense in an unaccustomed way and a spiritual glow flashed from her face. She stood up and in great agitation declared, 'Vishambhar's been arrested and sentenced to two years imprisonment.'

As though indifferent, Anand asked, 'What was the charge?'

Rupmani looked at the photograph of Vishambhar with pride in her eyes. 'There was a huge gathering of villagers in Raniganj—that's where he was arrested.'

'I told you before, he'd get two years. He's gone and ruined his life.'

'So you think a person's life is successful only if he earns a degree?' she retorted. 'Do books contain all knowledge and experience? I think the experience of the world and the human character that Vishambhar's going to acquire in those two years is something you couldn't get even in two hundred. If we accept strength of character as the purpose of education, then in the national struggle all our moral strength can't be matched by the struggle to satisfy the stomach. You can accuse us by saying that our primary concern is food, that there can be nothing else for us, we don't have enough courage or strength or endurance or organization, and I accept that. But I won't tolerate having those who give their lives for the sake of the people being called fools. Vishambhar's example will inspire hundreds of thousands to come forward to face the bullets. Do you have the courage to stand up before the people? For the sake of a degree you're ready to hand over your life to the ones who trample you under foot, who regard you as less than a dog. You may consider this a matter of pride for you, but I certainly don't.'

Flaring up, Anand answered, 'So now you're a real revolutionary!'

387

Just as angry, Rupmani said, 'If you smell revolution in straight talk, it's not my fault.'

'Well—I suppose there'll be a meeting today to honour Vishambhar. Will you go?'

'Of course I'll go,' she answered fiercely, 'and I'll speak too. And tomorrow I'll go to Raniganj. The lamp Vishambhar's lit will never go out so long as I live.'

Like a drowning man Anand grasped at a straw. 'Have you asked your mother and father about . . .'

'I'm going to.'

'And will they give their consent?'

'In matters of principle what one's soul commands is the most important thing.'

'So then—this is something new!'

With this Anand got up and left the room without shaking hands. From the faltering sound of his feet it seemed that he was stumbling at every step.

1930

From *Kafan*. Original title, *Ahuti*. Typically understated is Anand's love for Rupmani and his shock on learning that she will marry Vishambhar. It is never clear what in Rupmani and Vishambhar's circumstances presents obstacles to their union—social class, caste, economic status—but it is strongly suggested that her parents would object to it. It is interesting to note that the words 'India' and 'Indian' never appear in this story about the Independence movement of the twenties and thirties.

# Light

After she was widowed Buti's nature turned sour. When she was very angry she would curse her dead husband:

'You passed away, leaving me in this wretched mess! If you were to die so soon God only knows why you had to get married at all. You didn't have any more roasted bhang in the house, so you had to go and get married!'

If she'd wanted she could have married again, as is the custom among Ahirs.* She was not bad-looking, her voice was pleasant. A couple of men were willing to except her, but Buti was reluctant to give up the delusive pleasure of being honoured for her ritual purity. And all her anger fell on Mohan, her older son, who was now sixteen. The other boy, Sohan, still quite young, and her daughter Maina, the youngest, were neither of them yet marriageable. If Buti hadn't been saddled with these three she wouldn't have suffered so much hardship. She could have done only a bit of work and would have been paid with food and clothing. In the past, whenever she wanted she had always been able to get somebody or other to do things for her. But if she did this now, people would say, 'How can she resort to such tricks when she's got three children of her own?' Mohan did his best to lighten her burden. He fed and watered the cows and buffaloes, and did the milking and churning. But Buti was never pleased. Every day she blamed him for one thing or another, and by now Mohan had ceased to pay any attention to her abuse.

Why had her husband left her, dumping the whole burden of running this household on her?—this was her constant complaint. He had destroyed her, poor woman! She no longer had any pleasure in eating, or in dressing up, or in anything at all. Why had she ever come to this house? It was like jumping into an oven. The way of life

*A sub-caste engaged chiefly in raising cattle and selling milk.

demanded by her widowhood and her unsatisfied longing for sensual fulfillment were in constant conflict, and in its fire all the tenderness in her heart was reduced to ash. Her husband had left her nothing. She had possessed pieces of jewellery worth three or four hundred rupees, but one by one they had slipped away from her. In the part of the town where she lived, in her own community, how many women were there who, though older than herself, glittered with jewels, put collyrium around their eyes and drew a broad line of vermillion through the parting in their hair* as though to torment her! Buti was therefore always pleased when one of them was widowed, and fed her children, especially Mohan, with all her spitefulness. She seemed to want to see every woman in the world in her own image, and derived a particular joy in being so ill-tempered. Unable to burn away her frustrated longings, she contented herself with whatever petty satisfactions she could find. So how was it possible for her to hear any gossip about Mohan and not throw it back at him?** Thus it was that one day, as soon as Mohan returned from selling milk in the evening Buti said to him, 'I see you're bent on acting like a bull?'

Mohan looked at her, perplexed. 'What do you mean, "bull"? What's this all about?'

'Weren't you flirting and giggling with that Rupiya behind my back? And yet you ask me what I mean by "bull"? Shame on you! We've no money in the house and you bring *pan* to that one and pay to have her clothes dyed.'

Mohan took a rebellious stance. 'What could I do if she asked me for four pice worth of *pan*? Should I say, "First give me the money, then I'll bring it"? If she gives me her dhoti to get it dyed am I supposed to ask her to pay for it ?'

'So you're our local millionaire! Why couldn't she ask somebody *else*?'

'Who knows, what can I tell you?'

'And now you want to be a dandy. Did you ever bring a pice worth of *pan* into *this* house?'

'Who's here who'd want it?'

'Then as far as you're concerned everybody else in the house is dead?'

'I didn't know you wanted *pan*.'

*Widows traditionally wear white, use no make-up and wear no jewellery.

**The point is made because it is not considered proper for a mother to discuss such matters with her son.

'Is Rupiya the only one in the world who deserves it?'

'Well . . . she's the right age to have fun and dress up.'

Buti was furious. To imply that she was an old woman made a mockery of her widow's way of life. If she was an old woman the virtue she practised meant nothing. Mohan had dealt a cruel blow to her ideal of austerity, on the strength of which she could walk among other women with her head held high. During the five years since her husband died she had wasted her youth for the sake of these children. Five years ago she had still been in the first bloom of her youth. But God chose to burden her with three children, otherwise who could say how much longer she might have been young. If she'd wanted, even now she could paint her lips red, put red lac on her feet and bells on her toes and go around flirting. But she had renounced all that for these children and today Mohan had called her an old woman! Just let that Rupiya come and stand beside her—the girl would look like a mouse. Still—Rupiya *was* young while she herself was old.

'Of course, what else!' she answered Mohan. 'These are the days when I'm to dress in rags and tatters. When your father died I was only two years older than Rupiya. If I'd remarried at that time, all of you would have got what you deserved. You'd be wandering around from one alley to another pan-handling. Well, I'm telling you, if you talk to her again, either you get out of this house or I do.'

Alarmed, Mohan said, 'But Amma, I've already said the word to her.'

'What do you mean?'

'I asked her to marry me.'

'If Rupiya ever shows up in this house I'll take the broom to her and drive her out! This is all her mother's plotting. That pimp is taking my son away from me. Has anyone ever seen such a whore! She just wants to torment me by making Rupiya your concubine*.'

'Amma!' Mohan said, choking with emotion, 'for God's sake be quiet. Why get upset over this? I just thought that in a short time Maina would be going home** and you'd be alone. That is why I thought of bringing Rupiya here. If you don't like it, then I won't.'

'Starting today you'll sleep right here in the courtyard.'

'And just leave the cows and buffaloes outside?'

'Don't worry, nobody's stealing cattle around here.'

---

*saut, i.e. 'co-wife,' here used with abusive intent. Buti means she fears the girl will take control of the house away from her.

**To her future husband's house.

'Do you distrust me so much?'

'Yes, I do!'

'Then I won't sleep here at all.'

'Very well, get out of my house.'

'All right, if that's what you want, I will!'

Maina cooked the evening meal. When Mohan said, 'I'm not hungry,' Buti didn't coax him. His young man's heart could not put up with his mother's harsh domination. It was her house, so let her have it. He'd simply have to look for some new place to live.

Rupiya had filled his hard life with affection. At a time when he was restless with vague desire and his existence had seemed completely empty, she had come into it like a fresh spring, made it blossom so that now it tasted sweet. Whatever he did, his thoughts were always of Rupiya and what he could give her to make her happy. But now how could he possibly go to her? He couldn't tell her that his mother had forbidden him to see her. Think of all they had talked about only yesterday under the banyan tree! Mohan had said to her, 'Rupa, you're so beautiful, hundreds are going to come courting you. What do I have for you in my house?' And Rupiya answered—her words were still playing through his body like music—'I want *you*, Mohan, just you. Even if you got to be the district boss you'd still be just Mohan, if you work as a labourer you'll still be Mohan.' Now he was to go to that same Rupiya and say, 'We can't have anything more to do with one another'?

No, he thought, it can't be. He didn't give a damn about the house. He'd live with Rupiya, apart from his mother. If not in this place, then in some other neighbourhood. Rupiya must be waiting for him right now. How nicely she prepared the *pan* for him!* If his mother ever found out that he'd spent the night at Rupiya's door it could cost him his life. Then let it! His mother had no idea of her good fortune in getting a goddess like Rupiya for her daughter-in-law—who could tell why she had such an aversion to her? The girl liked to chew a little *pan*, she liked to have a little colour in her sari. Nothing more than that!

There was a sound of tinkling bangles. Rupiya was coming, it was she.

She walked over to where he lay and said, 'Have you fallen asleep, Mohan? I've been on the look-out for you for a whole hour. Why didn't you come?'

Mohan pretended he was asleep.

*bira, a special preparation of *pan*, sometimes offered to confirm betrothals.

Rupiya tapped his head. 'Are you sleeping, Mohan?'

Who can describe the fulfilment confirmed by those gentle fingers? Mohan was intoxicated to his very soul. His life seemed to be leaping out to offer itself at Rupiya's feet. The goddess stood before him, ready to grant his wishes. It was as though the universe were dancing and his body had vanished, he was only a sweet sound embraced in the bosom of the universe and dancing with it.

Rupiya said once more, 'Have you really gone to sleep so early?'

'Yes,' Mohan said, 'I was feeling a little drowsy. Why have you come now? If Amma sees us she'll kill me.'

'Why didn't you come tonight?'

'I had a fight with Amma.'

'What did she say?'

'She said, "If you speak to Rupiya it will cost you your life."'

'Did you ask her why she was angry with me?'

'How can I tell you what she said, Rupa? She can't stand anybody having fun eating or dressing up. Now I'll have to stay far away from you.'

'My heart won't accept that!'

'If you talk like this I'll run away with you!'

'Come to me once every day, I don't want anything more than that.'

'And if Amma is angry?'

'Then I understand: you don't love me.'

'If I had my way I'd keep you with me forever.'

At this moment the door of the house creaked. Rupiya ran off.

When Mohan woke the next morning his head felt like a sea overflowing with happiness. Now, it was his custom to scold his little brother Sohan constantly. Sohan was lazy and never offered to help with the chores. This morning he was sitting in the courtyard washing his dhoti with soap. As soon as he saw Mohan he hid the soap and started looking for some avenue of escape.

Mohan smiled and said, 'Has your dhoti got so dirty, Sohan? Why didn't you give it to the dhobi?'

Sohan caught the note of affection in his brother's words. 'The dhobi has to be paid,' he said.

'Then why don't you ask Amma for some money?'

'When does Amma ever give anybody any money?'

'Then take it from me.'

With this, Mohan tossed him a one-anna piece. Sohan was

393

delighted. Brother and mother, both were always scolding him. This morning was the first time after a long time that he tasted the sweetness of affection. He picked up the coin and, leaving his dhoti there, went out to untie the cow.

'It's all right,' Mohan said, 'I'm going to do it.'

Sohan handed the tether to his brother and asked him, 'Shall I bring out the hookah for you?'

This was the first time in his life Sohan had ever shown any good will towards his brother. Now it was Mohan who could not understand the reason for it. He said, 'If there's fire to light it, then bring it.'

Little Maina with her hair loose was sitting in the courtyard making a doll's house. As soon as she caught sight of Mohan she broke up the doll's house and, covering her hair with the edge of her dhoti, started towards the kitchen to pick up the cooking vessels. Mohan asked her:

'What were you playing, Maina?'

Scared, Maina said, 'Nothing.'

'But you make very nice doll's houses. Make one so I can see, won't you?'

Maina's tear-streaked face brightened. What magic there is in a word of love! As soon as it pops out of the mouth it's as though a fragrance is spread and the heart of the one who hears it blossoms. Where there had been fear, trust shines, and a feeling of belonging and affection springs up where there was bitterness. Today Mohan's heart was full of love, and the sweet scent of it had its effect.

Maina sat down again to make a doll's house.

Mohan began to straighten her tangled locks. 'Maina,' he said, 'your doll should be getting married soon. Send out an invitation— and she ought to have some sweets.'

Maina's heart leapt up to the skies. If her brother had asked for water now, she would have brought it right away in a brightly scoured pot.

'Amma wouldn't give the money,' she said. 'The bridegroom's been chosen but how can I send the gifts to his family?'*

'How much will it cost?'

'I'll take one paisa for the sweets and one for the dye. The bridal couple have to have colours, don't they?'

'Then will two paise be enough?'

'Oh yes, give me two paise, brother, then my doll can have a wonderful wedding.'

---

*tika bhejna, sending special gifts to the bridegroom's family.

Mohan held out two paise in his hand. She made a dash for them, he raised his hand, she caught it and pulled it down. He picked her up and held her while she took the coins, then she slipped down and began to dance.Soon after she ran off to invite her little girlfriends to the wedding.

At this moment Buti came along carrying a basket of cow dung. Seeing Mohan standing there, she said in her harsh way, 'You still hanging around? When are you going to milk the buffalo?'

Today Mohan did not fire back with a rebellious answer—as though some stream of tenderness had now opened in his heart. Seeing his mother carrying the heavy basket of cowdung, he took it from her head.

'Leave it, leave it!' Buti said. 'Go milk the buffalo, I'll take the cowdung.'

'Why didn't you call me instead of lifting up such a heavy load?'

Buti's heart was thrilled with affection. 'You go and see to your own work,' she said. 'Why do you keep after me?'

'Taking out the cowdung is my job.'

'And who'll do the milking?'

'I'll do that too.'

'So you're such a great strong fellow that you can do everything?'

'I can do whatever I say I can.'

'Then what will *I* do?'

'Take over some of the children's work, that's your duty.'

'Does anybody ever listen to me!'

Today when Mohan had taken the milk to the market and come back he brought with him *pan*, catechu, betel nut, a small box for the *pan*, and a few sweets.

Buti was furious. 'Did you get some extra money to throw away today?' she said. 'If you waste money at this rate how many days do you think we can get by?'

'I didn't waste a pice, Amma. But I thought before you didn't take *pan*.'

'So now I'm taking *pan*?'

'Of course, what else? Shouldn't somebody with two young sons at least have that little pleasure?'

Somewhere in Buti's harsh dried-up heart a bit of greenness poked its way up with the tiniest new leaf—but with how much life, how much juice in it! She gave one sweet each to Sohan and Maina and was about to give one to Mohan, but he said:

'I brought the sweets for the young ones, Amma.'

'And I suppose you're an old man now?'

'Compared to those kids, yes.'

'But in my eyes *you're* a kid.'

Mohan took the sweet. As soon as Maina got hers she popped it into her mouth and swallowed it, hardly leaving the taste of it on her tongue. Now she looked at Mohan's *laddu* with longing eyes. He broke it in half and gave one piece to her. There was another one still left in the leaf-bag. Buti took it and held it out towards Mohan. 'You've bought so much,' she said. 'Here, take it.'

Mohan put his half of the *laddu* into his mouth and said. 'That one's your share, Amma.'

'The pleasure I get from watching you eat is sweeter than it would taste to me if I ate it.'

She gave him half of the piece and the other half to Sohan. Then she opened the *pan* box and looked in. This was the first time in her life she had enjoyed such a treat. By some luck, she was now getting from her son the prosperity she'd longed for while her husband was alive.* In the box were several small cups, and look, two tiny tongs, and a metal ring above to hang them if you chose. On top was a little tray for placing the *pan*.

As soon as Mohan went out she scoured the box, put the lime and catechu in the cups, cut the betel nut, wet the betel leaf and set everything in the tray. Then she seasoned and folded a leaf and began to chew it, and the taste of this *pan* seemed to smooth away the bitterness of her widowhood. The gladness in her heart turned to generosity in her behaviour. She could no longer stay at home. Her spirit was not so deep that such great good fortune could be swallowed up and hidden in it. Somewhere an old mirror was lying around. She looked at her face in the mirror: there was redness on her lips . . . but it did not come from putting the *pan* in her mouth.

A woman named Dhaniya came along on her way to the well and said, 'Kaki**, give me a bit of rope, the rope for my bucket's broken.'

Yesterday Buti would have answered bluntly, 'I don't provide rope for everybody in the village. If yours is broken, have somebody make you a new one.' Today she smiled and gave Dhaniya a piece of rope and said in a kindly way, 'Has your son's diarrhoea stopped, Dhaniya?'

---

*'*pati ke rāj meṁ . . . larke ke rāj meṁ,*' lit., 'In the kingdom of her husband . . . in the kingdom of her son.'

**Literally, 'aunt'; a common term of affection for older women.

Sadly Dhaniya answered, 'No, Kaki, today he's had it all day. I don't know, may be he's teething .'

'Fill your bucket with water, then I'll go and take a look to see whether it's his teeth or some other trouble. Has anybody put a spell on him?'

'God knows, Kaki, who can say, anyone may have put a spell on him!'

'There's always a great fear of the evil eye striking affectionate children.'

'He crawls right into the lap of anybody who calls him and gives him a kiss. I couldn't tell you how he laughs!'

'Sometimes it's the mother's eye that puts a spell on her child, you know.'

'God forbid, Kaki! Who'd put a spell on her own child?'

'You don't understand things like this. The eye can cast a spell all by itself.'

When Dhaniya came back from the well Buti went with her to have a look at the child.

'You're alone,' she said. 'These days you must have a lot of trouble doing all the work around the house.'

'No, Amma, Rupiya comes and helps with the housework, otherwise by myself it would be the death of me.'

'Rupiya!' Buti was astonished. She had always considered Rupiya nothing more than a butterfly.

'Yes, Kaki. The poor girl is very good-hearted. She sweeps, cleans the whole kitchen and looks after the child. In times of trouble there aren't many who care about you at all, Kaki.'

'She must have had to give up her fancy make-up—or didn't she?'

'Everyone to his own taste, Kaki. No servant could have helped me as much as this girl with her fancy make-up. And I've given her nothing in return. Oh yes, I'll sing her praises as long as I live.'

'You don't know yet what she's really like, Dhaniya. Where does she get money for her *pan*? How come she has saris with a border?'

'I don't mess with those matters, Kaki. Anyway, who doesn't enjoy looking nice? She's at the age to dress up and have good things to eat.'

They reached Dhaniya's house. In the courtyard Rupiya was holding the wailing child in her lap and caressing him.

Dhaniya got him to sleep on his little cot. Buti put her hand on his forehead and gently probed his stomach with a finger. She said they should smear a little asafoetida on his navel. Rupiya began to fan him.

'Give me the fan,' Buti said.

397

'If I wave it will I become an outcaste?' Rupiya answered.

'You must be tired from doing the chores here all day long.'

Dhaniya said, 'You're very kind, Kaki. People around here say you can't speak without being abusive. I was so afraid of you I never came near you.'

Buti smiled. 'Those people didn't lie.'

'Should I believe what I see or what I hear?'

Even now Rupiya had her make-up on, wore a coloured sari and was chewing *pan*. But today it seemed to Buti that there was not only colour in this flower but fragrance as well. She had hated Rupiya; now it was as if that hatred had been washed clean by some holy mantra. What a courteous, modest girl she was! And how sweet was the way in which she talked! These days girls didn't even care about their own children, let alone anybody else's. She'd probably been up all night with Dhaniya's little boy. 'I suppose Mohan must have told her everything last night,' Buti reflected. 'Had it been another girl, she would have turned her face away from me. She would have been spiteful, she would have put on airs. But she acts as though she knew nothing about what I said to Mohan. Maybe Mohan didn't tell her anything after all? Yes, it must be that.'

Today Rupiya struck Buti as very beautiful. And it was certainly true, that if she didn't put on make-up now, when would she? Buti had objected to the make-up only because women who used it were apt to be obsessed with their own pleasure and enjoyment. Even if somebody else's house is on fire they don't give a damn about it, all they care about is giving men a thrill. As though they were advertising their beauty shop and inviting passers-by to stroll in and look around. But self-adornment didn't seem all that bad on people who were so good to others. From it one learned that the beauty of their spirit was just as great as the beauty of their person. And who didn't want their good looks to be praised, who would wish to have it hidden from the eyes of others? Buti's youth had made its farewell bow years before, and still that wish remained. If anybody thought her attractive how glad she'd be. And Rupa was still young.

From that day onwards Rupiya came every day once or twice to Buti's house. Buti insisted that Mohan order a fine sari for the girl. If she came to visit without make up or wearing a plain sari, Buti would say, 'Such an austere appearance isn't suitable for daughters and daughters-in-law. It's right only for old women like me!'

One day Rupa said, 'What do you mean, you're old, Amma! If you just gave men a sign they'd be swarming around like bees. My father would be camping at your door.'

'Go on,' Buti rebuked her gently, 'should I become co-wife beside your mother?'

'But my mother's become very old.'

'And I suppose your father's still a young man?'

'Well, yes, he's made of very good stuff.'

Buti regarded her with eyes full of pleasure. 'Now tell me, shall I have you marry Mohan?'

Rupa was embarrassed. A flush of pink spread over her face.

When Mohan came back that day after selling the milk, Buti said to him, 'Get a bit of money together, Rupa and I have been making plans for you . . .'

1933

From Mānsarovar, v. 1. Original title, 'Jyoti'.

# Divided Hearths

When Bhola Mahto remarried after his first wife died, the bad times began for his son Ragghu. At that time the child was only ten and had spent his days enjoying himself, going around playing stick-ball and the like, but with the arrival of his stepmother he found himself suddenly chained to the grindstone. Panna was a beautiful woman, and beauty and pride go together like a blouse and skirt. She would never put her hand to any hard work, so Ragghu had to set out the cowdung cakes and give the bullocks their fodder, and no one else but he would scour the dirty dishes.

Bhola's feelings had also somehow changed so that now everything about Ragghu displeased him. Following the age-old tradition, he shut his eyes and accepted everything Panna said as the truth. Accordingly, he paid not the slightest attention to Ragghu's complaints, so that eventually Ragghu simply stopped complaining. There was no one to see his tears; not only his father but the whole village became his enemy. 'He's a stubborn kid,' people said, 'he doesn't know how to get along with Panna. The poor woman feeds him and spoils him, and look at the result! Another woman wouldn't even try to look after him, but Panna's so decent and straightforward she keeps on trying.' Everyone hears the grumbling of the strong, while the poor man's supplications go unheeded. So day by day Ragghu's aversion for his stepmother grew stronger and stronger.

Things went on like this for eight years until one day a message from Death arrived with Bhola's name on it. By this time Panna had four children, three sons and a daughter. There was no one now to earn for such a big family, and as for Ragghu, at this point it was not thought necessary for him to worry about them. It was understood that he would marry, his wife would come and set up a separate hearth, and they would live apart.

For Panna everything seemed hopeless, but whatever might happen, she was determined not to stay in Ragghu's house and be dependent on him, she did not intend to end up as a maidservant in a home where he was master. She would not even look at the face of that brat she used to consider her own servant. She was beautiful, not much older than him, still in the bloom of her youth, and she wondered why she shouldn't marry again. If it didn't work out people would laugh, but she didn't care. In her community things were different, after all, she was no Brahmin or Thakur who would be disgraced. That happened only in those high-caste communities where you could do what you wanted in private so long as it was kept hidden from the world outside. So she decided she would set up a new household for the whole world to see and never be beholden to Ragghu.

One evening, a month after Bhola's death, she was lost in such thoughts when suddenly she realized that her children were not in the house. It was time for the bullocks to be coming home and she was afraid one of the little boys might get trampled. There was no one about to watch out for them since Ragghu didn't care a straw what happened to his stepbrothers and never even smiled when they spoke to him. But when she came to the front of the house she saw him sitting with the children around him while he cut up small pieces of sugarcane. Her little girl was holding on to his shoulder, trying to climb up for a ride. Panna couldn't believe her eyes. This was completely unexpected, leading her to wonder if perhaps Ragghu was just trying to show the world how much he cared for them, when all the while a knife was in his thoughts. Like a hunter in ambush, ready to spring, he'd kill them. He was a cobra, a cobra! She said harshly, 'What are you all doing here? Come inside, it's evening, the cattle will be coming by.'

When Ragghu looked at her his eyes were humble. He said, 'But I'm here, Kaki, what is there to fear?'

Kedar, the eldest boy, said, 'Mother, Ragghu Dada's made us a couple of wagons. Look, Khunnu and I will sit on one of them, Lacchman and Jhuniya on the other.'

With this he drew two little wagons from a corner. Each had four wheels, seats, and sides for protection.

Astonished, Panna asked who had made them, and Kedar, annoyed, repeated, 'Ragghu Dada, who else? He got a chisel and an adze from the house and put them together in a flash. They ride good and fast, Mother. Get in, Khunnu, and I'll pull.'

Khunnu sat in the wagon and Kedar began pulling. The wheels

made a grinding sound as though the wagon enjoyed the game too. Lacchman sat in the other wagon and said, 'Dada, pull me!'

Ragghu sat Jhuniya in beside him and pulled the wagon at a run. The boys clapped their hands while Panna watched the astonishing scene and wondered if this was really Ragghu or somebody else.

After a little while the wagons returned. The children went inside the house, describing what their ride felt like. They were all as happy as though they'd flown in a plane.

Khunnu said, 'Mother, all the trees went racing past.' 'And the calves ran away,' said Lacchman. 'And Ragghu Dada pulled both the wagons at the same time,' said Kedar.

Jhuniya was the youngest, with powers of expression limited to her eyes and to jumping around, so she clapped and danced.

'And now, Mother,' Khunnu said, 'we're going to have a cow! Ragghu Dada spoke to Girdhari and Girdhari said he'd bring one tomorrow.'

'She'll give us three seers of milk, Mother,' Kedar said, 'so we'll have lots of milk to drink.'

Meantime Ragghu had come inside. Panna looked at him with disdain. 'So Ragghu,' she asked him, 'is it true you've arranged with Girdhari for a cow?'

As though asking for forgiveness, he answered, 'Yes, I did, he said he'll bring it tomorrow.'

'And where's the money to come from? Have you thought of that?'

'I've thought it all through, Kaki. I got rid of my gold coin. I'm getting 25 rupees for it, and out of that I'll pay 5 on account for the heifer. So you see, she'll really be our cow.'

Panna was stunned. Now her distrustful mind could not but believe in Ragghu's love and goodness. She said, 'But why did you sell your gold coin? Why such a rush to get a heifer right now? When we've put by a little money then we'll get it. It doesn't seem right for you not to have the coin. After such a long time without a cow the children haven't died, have they?'

'This is the time for the children to be getting good things to eat and drink, Kaki,' said Ragghu philosophically. 'If they don't eat well at this age, then when will they? Anyway, I don't like wearing that coin. People must have been thinking, "Oho, his father's dead, so now he thinks he can go around wearing a gold coin."'

Bhola Mahto had died wanting nothing more than to buy a cow; but he hadn't the money, there was no way he could buy one. But now

402

how easily Ragghu had solved the problem! Trusting him for the first time in her life, Panna said, 'When I have jewellery to sell, why sell your coin? Take my necklace.'

'No, Kaki, it looks very good around your neck. For men on the other hand it doesn't matter whether they wear a gold coin or not.'

'Go on, I'm old—what's the use of my wearing a necklace now? You're still a boy, and the coin suited you.'

Ragghu smiled. 'How is it that you've become old so suddenly? Who is there in the village to compare with you?'

Panna was embarrassed by this simple praise. A blush of pleasure coursed through her withered features.

Five years went by. There wasn't another farmer in the village as hard-working, honest and dependable as Ragghu. And he would do nothing that didn't accord with Panna's wishes. He was twenty-three by now, and Panna often reminded him, 'Little brother, send for your bride. How long can she stay wasting away in her father's house? People have started slandering me, they say I won't let you bring your wife home.'

But Ragghu kept putting it off. He would say there wasn't any rush yet. For he'd already heard things about his wife from others and he had no desire to bring a woman such as she was said to be into the house and spoil his peace of mind.

One day Panna finally began to insist. 'So you're not going to bring her home?'

'I told you there wasn't any great rush.'

'Maybe not for you, but there certainly is for me. I intend to send someone for her today.'

'You'll regret it, Kaki. She's got a bad disposition.'

'You've nothing to worry about. When I don't intend to interfere with her with so much as one word is she going to fight with the wind? And she can take over the cooking, then I won't have to do all the work inside and out. I'm sending for her today.'

'If you want to send for her, go ahead. But afterwards don't tell me that instead of making her a proper wife I've turned her into a slave.'

'You don't have to worry! Now go and buy a couple of saris and some sweets.'

Three days later Muliya came from her mother's house. Drums beat at the door, the sweet sound of the shahnais echoed in the skies. The customary cash offerings to the bride were made. In this desert

403

land she was a spring of pure water—fair-skinned, long curving eyelids, a faint rosiness in her cheeks, and a powerful attraction in her eyes: the moment he saw her Ragghu was bewitched.

When she went out early next morning with the pitcher her fair complexion took on the hue of the dawn's golden rays and it was as though Usha, with all her fragrance, her bloom and her intoxication, had come walking by.

Muliya had come from her home already shaped and moulded. She was not going to put up with Panna behaving like a queen with her children roaming around like princes while her husband killed himself with work. And she herself had no intention of slaving for anybody. 'Those children are not even his,' she thought, 'they're hardly brothers. Till such time as they're older they'll stick around Ragghu. But as soon as they're a little grown up they'll start acting big and they won't give a damn about him.

One day she said to Ragghu, 'If you want to slave like this, then go ahead, but I wouldn't stand for it.'

'What can I do?' said Ragghu. 'Those kids aren't old enough to do any work around the house yet.'

'They seem to be from some prince's line and are not your kin in any way. And there's Panna, who's practically starving you to death. I've heard all I can take. I don't intend to stay on here like a slave. I don't get any accounting of the money, I have no idea how much you earn or what she does with it. You assume it stays right here in the house, but just see what kind of pittance you're left with!'

'But if I start handing over the money to you what will people say? Just think about that.'

'Let them say what they want, they don't own me. Remember, when you clean the oven your hands get dirty. So work yourself to death for your brothers if you want, but why should I?'

Ragghu didn't answer. What he'd feared was happening even sooner than he'd expected. If he worked really hard things would turn out all right in six months or a year, but it didn't look as though they could go on like this for that long. As the saying goes, how long can the mother goat pray to save her kid from the sacrificial knife?

One day Panna was drying *mahua* leaves. The monsoon had begun and in the barn the grain was getting wet. She said to Muliya, 'Bahu, stay and watch a bit while I go to the pond to bathe.'

Muliya answered nonchalantly, 'I feel sleepy, you stay here and watch. If you don't bathe one day what will it matter?'

Panna put aside her fresh sari and did not go to bathe that day. Muliya's attack had missed its mark.

Some time later, one evening Panna came home at dark after planting rice, hungry for having eaten nothing all day she was hoping Muliya would have cooked the meal. But she found that the oven was cold, and the children were restless with hunger. Gently she said to Muliya, 'Haven't you lit the oven yet?'

Kedar answered, 'It wasn't lit at noon either, Kaki. Bhabhi didn't cook anything at all.'

'Then what did you all have to eat?'

'Nothing. Khunnu and Lachhman ate last night's leftovers, and I ate some parched grain.'

'And Bahu?'

'She was sleeping, she didn't eat anything.'

Panna lit the fire at once and sat down to cook. She kneaded flour and wept. What misfortune! Burning up all day in the field, and when she came home burning up in front of the oven.

Kedar was fourteen now. He had observed Muliya's attitude and sized up the situation. 'Kaki,' he said, 'Bhabhi doesn't want to live with you.'

Panna was astonished. 'What,' she asked, 'has she told you?'

'She hasn't said anything. But that's what she's got on her mind. So why don't you let her leave? She can live the way she wants, we'll have God with us.'

Biting her tongue, Panna said, 'Shut up, don't even *think* of saying anything like that in front of me! Ragghu isn't your brother, he's your father. If you ever say anything like that to Muliya I'll drink poison.'

The Dussehra holiday was fast approaching. During Dusshera, a fair was held in another village about two miles away. All the village children always went there to celebrate, and Panna too was getting her children ready to go, but where was the money to come from now that Muliya had the key to the strongbox?

Ragghu went to Muliya and said, 'The children are going to the fair so give them each a couple of pice.'

Muliya frowned. 'There's no money in the house,' she said.

'But we just sold the oilseed. Has the money been spent so soon?'

'It has.'

405

'But for what? Do you mean to tell me that on a holiday the children won't be going to the fair?'

'Why don't you tell your stepmother to dig up her money, what's the point of keeping it buried?'

The key was dangling from a peg. Ragghu took it down and was about to open the strongbox when Muliya caught his hand and said, 'Give me the key! If you don't there'll be trouble. We have to pay for food, we have to pay for clothes, and on top of that now we're supposed to give them money for the fair? We don't earn this money so that others can eat and sponge off us.'

Panna said to Ragghu, 'Bhaiya, what money do I have? The children won't be going to the fair.'

'Why not?' said Ragghu, losing his temper. 'The whole village is going but our kids can't go?' With that he freed his hand, took some money from the box and gave it to the children. But when he tried to give the key to Muliya she scowled and threw it out into the yard, then went to lie down.

The children did not go to the fair.

For the next two days Muliya ate nothing and Panna too went hungry. Again and again Ragghu tried to coax first one, then the other, but neither would give in. Finally, in desperation he said to Muliya, 'Say *something*. What is it you want?'

Muliya spoke, addressing the floor:

'I don't want anything. Just send me back home.'

'All right,' Ragghu said. 'Get up and cook something and eat. I'll see that you go home.'

She lifted her eyes and looked at him. When he saw her face he was frightened. That sweetness of hers, that charm, that beauty, everything had disappeared. Her teeth were bared, her eyes bulged, her nostrils were flaring. Staring from eyes as red as burning coals she said, 'Fine—so that's what your stepmother's advised you, she taught you just what to answer! But I'm not that simple. I'll make both of you squirm for this—and what do you think you can do about it?'

'All right, make us squirm. But first have something to eat and drink, then you can do what you like.'

'I won't touch food until I have my own separate hearth. I've put up with a lot but I'm not going to any more.'

Ragghu was stunned; for a moment he could say nothing. He had never so much as dreamed of keeping a home apart. He had seen two or three households in the village break up, and he knew that when their meals were taken separately their hearts were divided too and they became ever more alien to one another. Soon they would lose all sense of kinship and be as distant as anybody else in the village. In his heart Ragghu had resolved that he would not let this catastrophe fall on his family. But as it turned out there was nothing he could do. He thought how he would be disgraced, how people would say that in a year, or even in ten, he couldn't make things work. And then—who was he abandoning? The children he'd cherished and fed, raised like babies, for whom he'd suffered so many hardships—he was to separate from them. Could he throw his loved ones out of the house? He felt completely helpless. His voice trembling, he said:

'Do you want me to part from my brothers? Don't you realize, I won't be able to show my face anywhere!'

'But I can't get along with these people.'

'Then you set up your own hearth. But why do you have to drag me along with you?'

'Do you think I've got any favours in your house? Do you think there's no place for me in the world?'

'Just as you wish, stay wherever you like. I can't separate from my family. The day two ovens are lit in this house it will also break my heart in two. I can't bear such a blow. If there's anything that bothers you I'll take care of it. As for whatever is in the house—you're the mistress of it all, food and drink are in your hands alone. So now what's left to complain about? If there's any kind of work you don't want to do, don't do it. If God had given me the power I wouldn't let you lift so much as a straw. Those tender hands and feet of yours weren't created to do hard work. But what can I do? I have no control over such things. All the same, if there's any work you don't feel like doing, don't. But I beg you, don't tell me to split the family.'

Muliya drew the edge of her sari from her head and moved close to him. She said, 'I'm not afraid of hard work and I don't want others to work and feed me. But I can't stand anyone bossing me. Whatever work your stepmother does, she does it for herself, she does it for her children. She doesn't do me any favours, so why does she lord over me? Of course her children are dear to her, but I have to turn to you for protection. Do you think I can't see that everybody else in the house is taking it easy and the children get milk to drink whenever they want while the one whose strength holds this houseold together is left to go without buttermilk? Does anybody care about *him*? Just look at yourself and see what's happening to you. In ten years you'll be sick, stretched out on a cot. Sit down, why are you standing? Are you going to beat me and run away? I won't compel you to stay with me—or

407

isn't that what the mistress has ordered? I tell you true, you're a hard-hearted man. If I'd known I'd have to put up with such cruel treatment I wouldn't ever have come to this house. Or even if I did I'd never have thought of it as my home. But now I've come to love you, so even if I go home my heart will still be here. And there you are, not caring for me at all.'

These loving words had no effect at all on Ragghu. Just as harshly as before he said, 'Muliya, it can't be. I can't tell you how the very thought of separating hurts me. I couldn't stand the pain of it.'

Muliya laughed and said, 'Then put on bangles and go sit in the women's part of the house and I'll put on a moustache. And I thought you had some brains! But now I can see that you're just a dolt.'

Panna had been standing in the yard listening to their conversation. At this point she could stand no more of it. She came before them and said to Ragghu, 'She's determined to live apart now, so why do you try to force her not to? Keep her with you. God is our master: when Mahto died and we hadn't so much as a leaf to shade us anywhere, in the long run he took care of us. So what have we to fear now? By His mercy the three boys have grown up, so there's nothing to worry about.'

Ragghu looked at her with tears in his eyes. 'Kaki,' he said, 'have you gone crazy? When people keep two hearths, their hearts grow separate too.'

'If she won't agree,' Panna answered, 'what can you do? If this is God's will, then nobody can do anything about it. We've lived together for as many days as fate has written. This now is her desire: so be it. But I can't forget all that you've done for my children. If you hadn't devoted yourself to them who knows what would have happened to them by now, who knows what door they'd be knocking at for scraps to eat or where they'd be wandering around begging. As long as I live I'll sing your praises, and if my hide could serve to make shoes for you I'd gladly give it. Though I may live apart from you, whenever you call I'll come running. Don't ever believe that while we're separated I'll think ill of you. If a day comes when misfortune hits you, that day I'll drink poison and die. May God bless you with money and children! Even as I die every bit of me will keep uttering this blessing. And, if the children are truly their father's, then until they die they'll honour you for your loving care.'

When she had said this Panna went away in tears. Ragghu sat there like a statue, staring at the skies with tears pouring from his eyes.

When she heard what Panna had to say Muliya realized that she had the upper hand. Quickly she stood up, swept the house, lit the oven and went to fetch water from the well. She had had her way.

Among the village women two factions were formed, mothers-in-law versus daughters-in-law, each meeting in their own councils for advice and sympathy from their own kind. A few of the daughters-in-law met Muliya at the well. One asked her, 'I suppose your old woman must have cried a lot today?'

Flushed with victory, Muliya answered, 'After she's been queen of the household so long it can't be any fun to give up her throne. Sister, I don't wish her any ill, but how could we prosper on one man's earnings? This is a time when I too have to eat and drink and get clothes to wear. But no, I'm supposed to kill myself working for her and her children, then when my children come, kill myself working for them. Let her spend her whole life crying.'

One of the women said, 'The old woman wanted you to be her slave for life, destitute and eating scraps.'

Another said, 'Why should anybody kill herself working when even her own children don't care a damn about her, to say nothing of somebody else's. Tomorrow they'll be independent and who'll care about you then? They'll just obey their own wives. It's best to protest right from the beginning, and have no regrets later.'

Muliya took her water and left. She cooked the food and said to Ragghu, 'Go and have your bath, dinner's ready.'

Ragghu seemed not to have heard. With his hand on his head he went on staring towards the door.

'Haven't you heard what I said? Have your bath, dinner is ready.'

'I heard,' said Ragghu, 'am I deaf? If the food's ready go and eat. I'm not hungry.'

Muliya did not ask him again. She went and extinguished the oven fire, took up the food and set it in a hanging pot, covered her face and lay down.

Shortly afterwards Panna came in and said, 'Dinner's ready, so wash come and eat. Bahu must be hungry too.'

'Kaki,' said Ragghu, flaring up, 'are you going to let her stay in the house disgracing me so I can't show my face anywhere? The food isn't important; I'm not eating today, I'll eat tomorrow. But I couldn't stand eating now. Hasn't Kedar come back from school?'

'Not yet but he'll surely be back soon.'

Panna realized that until she fed the children neither she nor

409

Ragghu was going to eat anything. Not only that, she would also have to do battle with Ragghu; she would have to say angry, cutting words, and prove to him that she too wanted to live apart from him. Otherwise he would simply worry himself to death.

Thinking this, she lit a separate oven and began to cook. Meantime, Kedar and Khunnu returned from school. 'Come and eat, children,' said Panna, 'dinner's ready.'

'Shall I call elder brother?' Kedar asked.

'You come and eat,' Panna repeated. 'Bahu has made his dinner separately.'

'Shouldn't I go and ask brother?'

'He'll eat when he feels like it. You sit down and eat. These matters don't concern you. Whoever wants to can eat, whoever doesn't, doesn't have to. If he and his wife want to eat apart, who can change their minds?'

'But why, Amma? Are we going to live apart from them in the house?'

'If that's what they want, we'll live in one house; if they don't, they can put up a wall in the yard.'

Khunnu went to the door and peeped out; before him was a straw hut and there Ragghu lay on a cot smoking his pipe. Khunnu said, 'Brother's out there already smoking his pipe.'

'He'll eat when he feels like it,' Panna said.

Kedar asked, 'Then brother must have scolded sister-in-law, didn't he?'

Muliya was lying in her room listening. She came out and said, 'No, brother didn't, now you come and scold her!'

The colour rushed to Kedar's face. He didn't open his mouth again. The three brothers ate their dinner and came outside. The scorching summer *lu** was gusting and in the mango orchard the village boys and girls were gathering the fruit knocked down by the wind. Kedar said, 'Lots of mangoes are coming down, let's go to the orchard and pick them up.'

Khunnu said, 'But with brother sitting over there? . . .'

'I won't go,' said Lacchman, 'brother'll scold us.'

'But he's living apart from us now,' said Kedar.

'What if somebody beats us,' Lacchman mused, 'does that mean that even then he won't do anything to help us?'

'Don't be silly, why wouldn't he?'

Ragghu saw the three boys standing in the doorway, but he said

*The hot wind of May and June.

410

nothing. Previously, as soon as he came out of the house, he'd scold them, but today he went on sitting motionless. The boys, feeling more daring now, stepped out a little further. Ragghu still did not speak— for how could he? He was thinking, 'Kaki fed them and didn't even ask me. Has a screen come down before her eyes too? What if I called the boys and they didn't come? Anyway, now I wouldn't have the right to punish them. They'll all be running around wild in this hot wind. What if they get sick?' His heart was aching but he could not utter a word. When the boys saw that he kept silent they boldly moved on.

Suddenly Muliya came out and said, 'Are you coming in now or not? She who you're fasting for has had her pleasure feeding the boys, she's eaten too and now she's sleeping peacefully. You know the saying, "If my beloved doesn't care about me, don't call me a happy wife."'

At this moment Ragghu was suffering intensely; Muliya's sharp words added salt to his wounds. Looking at her with sorrowful eyes, he said, 'Things have turned out the way you wanted, so don't start complaining now.'

'But your dinner is all ready to serve.'

'Don't aggravate me. Because of you I've been disgraced. If you don't want to stay with the man you're married to why should anyone else want to flatter me? Go and tell Kaki that the boys have gone to pick mangoes and ask her if I should bring them back.'

Muliya stuck out her thumb and said, '*This* can go to her! You're so damned worried, you go and ask her yourself.'

At this moment Panna came from inside. Ragghu said, 'The boys have gone to the orchard. The *lu* is blowing strong.'

'Who is there to look after them now?' said Panna. 'Let them go to the orchard, let them climb the trees and fall into the pond. What can I do by myself?'

'I'll go fetch them,' said Ragghu.

'If you don't really want to go, why should I tell you to? Had it been up to you to stop them would't you have stopped them? They must have walked right past you.'

Even before Panna had finished speaking Ragghu had shoved his pipe into the corner and started for the orchard. When Ragghu came back from the orchard with the boys he saw that Muliya was still standing at the door of the hut. He said, 'Why haven't you gone and eaten? I'm not hungry now.'

Bristling, Muliya said, 'Sure, why should you be hungry? Your brothers have eaten, so I suppose that was enough to fill your stomach too.'

411

'Don't make me angry, Muliya,' said Ragghu, grinding his teeth. 'If you do there'll be trouble. The food isn't going to run away somewhere. If I miss a meal once I'm not going to die. Do you think that what's happened in the house today is just a trifle? You didn't light the fire in the house, you started a fire in my heart. I was proud enough to think that whatever else happened there could never be a rift in the family—but you finished off all that vain pride of mine. It's fate.'

Muliya said angrily, 'Are you the only one who loves this family? I don't see anybody else moaning and groaning the way you do.'

Ragghu sighed. 'Don't throw salt on my wound, Muliya. You're the only person responsible for all this. If I didn't love this family, who would? I'm the one who's kept them together by sheer hard work. The ones I held in my lap and fed are going to carry on my name. But now I can't even frown at the children I used to scold. If I try to do anything for their welfare people will say I'm swindling my little brothers. Go now, leave me alone, I can't eat anything now.'

Muliya said, 'I'm going to swear an oath to force you to. If you don't want me to, then don't say anything, just come on inside.'

'Look, the food is still fresh. Don't be stubborn.'

'Anyone who won't come in and eat might as well drink my blood.'

Ragghu put his hands over his ears. 'What have you done, Muliya? I was about to come. Go in, I'll eat. It won't matter if I don't bathe and wash but I say this: even if I eat six rotis instead of four, even if you douse me in a tub of ghee, this blot on my soul will never be washed away.'

'Blots and spots, they'll all wash away. It seems this way only in the beginning. Don't you see how the flute of peace is being played over there? Anyway, she agreed that we should live apart. But she doesn't have it so easy now the way she did before, when she got hold of whatever you earned. So why doesn't she start living with us now?'

In a voice that showed his hurt, Ragghu answered, 'That's just what grieves me. I never expected that Kaki would agree to live apart.'

When he sat down and began to eat, it was like taking poison. The bread tasted like chaff, the dal like water, and the water he tried to drink wouldn't go down his throat. He couldn't even look at the milk. After a few bites he stood up, like a mourner at a funeral feast for a loved one.

The evening meal passed in much the same way. However poor his appetite, he fulfilled his promise. All night his mind was troubled. An unknown doubt shadowed his spirit, as though Bhola Mahto were

412

sitting at the door weeping. Several times he woke up suddenly, startled by the feeling that Bhola was staring at him with scorn in his eyes.

He had eaten both of the day's meals, but as though in the house of an enemy. He could not drive the grieving image of Bhola from his mind. At night he couldn't sleep. Whenever he went into the village it was with head down and averted face, as though he had committed the sin of cow slaughter.

Five years passed. Ragghu now had two sons. A wall had been built in the yard, dikes had been set up to divide the fields, and the bullocks had been divided too. By now Kedar was sixteen and had given up studying to work in the fields, while Khunnu grazed the cattle. Only Lacchman was still going to school. Though Panna and Muliya would get angry at the very sight of one another, Muliya's two little boys spent most of their time with Panna. It was Panna who would rub their skin with softening unguents, Panna who applied collyrium to their eyes, Panna who walked about holding them to her bosom. But never once did a word of gratitude come from Muliya's mouth, nor did Panna want one. Whatever she did was without any desire for advantage. Two of her own sons were now earning, her daughter cooked the meals, and she herself saw to whatever work was left over.

Ragghu, on the contrary, was the only one in his family who worked—Ragghu, weak, a near invalid, an old man while still in his youth. He was no more than thirty now, but his hair was a salt-and-pepper gray, his back stooping, and he was worn out with coughing. To see him was to pity him. And farming is a matter of toil and sweat; the kind of work the fields demanded was more than he could give them, so how could his harvest be a good one? He was in debt too, and the thought of this oppressed him even more. What he needed now was some rest. After so many days of constant toil his burden should have been lighter, but Muliya's selfishness and lack of vision had laid waste the fields. If they had all lived together then by now he would have received a pension and would be sitting by the door enjoying his pipe. His brother would have done the work, he'd have given advice. He could be just like Mahto, he could settle disputes, he could go and serve the sadhus and holy men . . . But any chance for all that had slipped away, and day by day the burden of his worries grew worse.

Finally he began to suffer a mild fever. This was the reward for his heartbreak, worry and toil, his doing without. At first he hadn't been concerned, assuming things would get better by themselves. But as he

413

grew weaker, he began to worry about medicine. As for going to doctors or *vaids*, he didn't have the means. And if he had, apart from having to spend the money, would the outcome have been any different? The medicine for a wasting fever was rest and a proper diet. He couldn't get the *vasant-malti* medicine to take nor could he lie about resting and get nourishing food to eat. He got simply weaker and weaker and just ate whatever he was told to eat.

When she had the chance Panna would come and comfort him, but now her children would not speak to him. As for doing anything about medicine, they made a joke of it. Did their brother think that by dividing the family they were storing up bricks of gold? And Muliya had believed that she was going to be weighed down with gold! Tell her one didn't die from sobbing. And lots of moaning and groaning was no good either. A man did as much work as he could, but he didn't give his life for money.

'But what fault is it of Ragghu's?' Panna said to them.

'Go on,' said Kedar, 'I understand it only too well. If I were in my brother's place I'd speak with the stick. The woman had the nerve to be stubborn beyond anything. It's all his doing, and it all worked out just the way it had to.'

At last one day the flickering lamp of Ragghu's life went out and death put an end to all his worries.

At the last he had sent for Kedar. But for Kedar that move threatened the status quo: he feared Ragghu might send him to buy medicine and so he made some excuse not to come.

Muliya's life was plunged in darkness. The ground on which she had constructed the wall of all her schemes now slid away beneath her feet. The prop which had made it possible for her to climb had collapsed. The villagers began to say, 'How quickly God has punished her!' Shamed, she wept continually with her two children. She did not dare show her face to anyone in the village. It seemed to her that everybody was saying, 'She was so proud she didn't think her feet touched the ground. So finally she's got what she deserves!' How could she keep on living in this house? Who could she depend on, who would keep up the farming? Poor Ragghu had been sick, he'd been weak, but so long as he was alive he went on doing his work, even when he felt so weak that at times he would grab his head and sit down to catch his breath before he could begin moving his arms again. The whole harvest was wasting, and there was no one to take charge of it. The stalks of grain lay in the barn, the sugar cane was fast drying up. Alone there was nothing she could do. And then the irrigation was too much work for one man. Where in the world was she going to get three or four labourers? In the village there were not that many, and to get them you had to do a lot of coaxing and plotting. What should she do?

Thirteen days went by while she was in this state, and now the funeral rites were completed. Early next morning Muliya, picking up her two little boys in her arms, went to thresh the grain. When she reached the barn she set the smaller one down beneath a tree on a soft bed of grass and put him to sleep; the other boy sat down near her and she began the threshing. She called out to the bullocks and wept. Had God given them birth for this? So much had happened in so short a time. This time last year the threshing had been going on and she would bring Ragghu a pottage of peas and a bowl of something sweet to drink. Today there was nobody in front of her and nobody behind her. Still, she was not anybody's serving wench! And even now she would not feel any regret for having broken away from Panna.

Suddenly she heard her younger child crying. She looked his way and saw the other boy kissing him and saying, 'Quiet, little brother, quiet!' Gently he moved his hand over the child's mouth, anxiously trying to silence him. When he was unsuccessful he himself lay down beside the child and hugged him affectionately; but failing in this effort he too began to cry.

At this moment Panna came running and picking up the smaller child she caressed it. To Muliya she said, 'Why didn't you bring the children to me, Bahu? *Hai hai!* The poor child was rolling in the dirt. When I'm dead, do what you want, but I'm still alive. When you separated from us the children didn't become separate.'

'You had no free time either, Amma,' said Muliya. 'What was I to do?'

'But why were you in such a hurry to come out here? What if the stalks weren't threshed? Anyway, there are three boys to do it—when shall they come? It was only yesterday that Kedar was saying the grain should be threshed but I told him to water the sugar cane first and thresh later. Threshing can wait for as much as ten days more but if the sugar cane isn't wetted immediately it'll dry up. So the watering was started yesterday and Kedar'll go to the fields until the day after tomorrow. Then the threshing will start. You won't believe it, but ever since his brother died he's been very worried and he asks a hundred times a day, "Bhabhi must be crying a lot, don't you think? Look and see if the children are hungry." If one of your boys is crying he comes running and says, "Look, Amma—what happened, why's he crying?"

415

Yesterday he was crying and said to me, "Amma, if I'd known brother was going to go away so soon I would have given him some help." He gets up from bed as soon as he's wakened. He gets up and starts to work while it's still dark. Yesterday Khunnu said, "First we'll wet down our sugar cane, then we'll do brother's". Kedar scolded him so much for that that afterwards he didn't say another word. Kedar told him, "What do you mean our sugar cane and brother's? If brother hadn't kept us alive, why by now we'd either have died or been out somewhere begging. Today you've turned into a regular expert on sugar cane! It's only because of his goodness that you can sit around acting like a gentleman." Day before yesterday when I went to call them to eat, he was sitting under the awning crying. When I asked him why he said, "Amma, brother died because of grief over this 'separation', otherwise he'd still be alive today. We didn't understand it then, otherwise why would we have quarrelled?"'

At this point Panna directed a significant look at Muliya and went on, 'He's not going to let you live apart, Bahu. He says Ragghu died for you so we too will die for his children.'

Muliya's eyes welled over with tears. Today Panna's words were filled with true anguish, true sympathy and true sincerity. Muliya had never before felt so drawn to him.* And she saw that those from whom she had feared sarcastic and vengeful words had become compassionate and wished her well.

For the first time she now felt ashamed of her selfishness; and for the first time her soul regretted the separation.

Another five years passed. Today Panna was now an old woman and Muliya was mistress of the house. Khunnu and Lacchman were married, but Kedar was still a bachelor. He had decided he wouldn't marry. Several families were interested, several brides had been suggested, but he agreed to none of them. Panna baited the hook, she laid snares, but she couldn't trap him. He would say, 'What happiness is there with women? A woman came into the house, the man's whole outlook changed. After that whatever happens is up to the woman. Parents, brothers and friends, all become alien. When a person like my brother changed what can you expect of others? I've got two brothers given to me by God, what else would I want? I have two boys—my nephews— without marrying, could I ask for anything more?

*Kedar. Muliya has understood that Panna is suggesting marriage between her and her son.

416

What you consider your own *is* your own, what you think belongs to others is theirs.'

One day Panna said to him, 'How will your line be continued?'

'My line is continuing: I think of those two boys as my own.'

'If it's just a matter of how you think, then aren't you going to have to think of Muliya as your wife?'

Annoyed, Kedar said, 'You're mocking me, Amma.'

'What do you mean, mocking? After all, isn't she your sister-in-law?'

'But how could she care in any way for a crude fellow like me?'

'If you just tell me I'll ask her.'

'Oh no, my Amma! You may set her to crying and wailing.'

'But if you want I can just talk with her and sound her out.'

'I don't know,' said Kedar. Then: 'Well, do what you like.'

Panna understood what was in Kedar's mind: the boy had fallen in love with Muliya, but from fear and shyness he had said nothing.

This same day Panna spoke to Muliya. 'What can I do, Bahu? The heart's longings are kept shut up in the heart. If only Kedar's marriage could be settled I'd finally be content.'

'But he's said he's not going to marry,' said Muliya.

'What he says is, if he could find a woman who got along with everyone in the house he'd take her.'

'Where can he find such a woman? You'll have to look around.'

'I've already looked around,' said Panna.

'Really! In what village?'

'I won't tell you yet, but I know that if she marries Kedar the family will be settled and his life will be a success. Though I don't know if the girl will agree or not.'

'Why wouldn't she agree, Amma?' said Muliya. 'Where else could she find such a good-looking bridegroom, so hard-working and decent? He's the incarnation of some sadhu or mahatma—who else stays unmarried because he fears quarrelling and arguments? Tell me where she lives, I'll go persuade her and bring her back.'

'If you wish, then you persuade her. It depends on you alone.'

'I'll go this very day, Amma, I'll fall at her feet and convince her!'

'Then I'll tell you: it's you and no one else.'

Embarrassed, Muliya said, 'You're just making fun of me, Ammaji.'

'What do you mean, making fun of you? He's your husband's younger brother.'

'Why would he care for an old woman like me?'

'But you're the very person he moons about longing for! Apart

417

from you there's nobody who suits him. He's afraid to tell you, but I know what he really feels.'

Muliya's pale body, withered from the grief of widowhood, suddenly flushed pink as a lotus. What she had lost ten years before she had in a way got back in one instant, and with interest. The same charm and exuberance, the same attraction, the same tenderness.

1929

From *Mānsarovar*, v. 1. Original title, *Algyojhā*. Premchand chose this volume to begin the series of collections of his short stories, of which two were published in his lifetime, to be followed by six others, and later by other collections made by his sons.

For two members of a family to set up separate cooking fires is, by village standards, scandalous, equivalent to a complete separation or one of the parties moving away. Many details in the story are taken for granted in the Indian context; for example, when we learn that Ragghu is twenty-three it is understood that he must have been betrothed years before even though his wife has not yet come to live with him. Names are rarely used, titles being preferred; Ragghu's wife is a 'bahu', a daughter-in-law, and is addressed as such by Panna, who, for her part, is called 'Kaki' or 'Amma' by her children and step-son, who in turn refer to Muliya as 'bhabhi', brother's wife. It is important to understand the significance of eating, as much religious as social, in traditional Indian families. In village homes women will not eat until their men have been served, and the maintenance of the hearth is symbolic of all the family relationships. The characters in the story belong to a community in which widows may remarry and marriage to a brother-in-law is permitted.

# PREMCHAND'S
## Novels

## PART II

# Nirmala

PREMCHAND

Translated
and with an Afterword
by Alok Rai

# Contents

# Foreword

P remchand (1880–1936) dominates the landscape of modern Hindi literature like a colossus. He wrote rather deprecatingly about his ordinary, unglamorous life—'a flat, featureless plain... There are a few ditches here and there, but even diligent looking will not reveal any hills, forests, valleys or ruins. People who are fond of wandering in the hills will only be disappointed here.' But it was perhaps just this ordinariness which enabled him to catch the essential rhythm, to crystallize the crucial substance of his social world and his historical moment.

Premchand started out as an Urdu writer in the romantic tradition associated with names likes Abdul Halim Sharar and Ratan Nath Sarshar (author of the famous *Fasaana-i-Azaad)*. However, he soon switched from being a Urdu writer to being one in Hindi—and actually did an abbreviated translation of Sarshar for Hindi readers, *Azaad Katha*. (This shortened version is nearly a thousand pages long!) The move from Urdu to Hindi was a complex one, not least because almost till the end of his days Premchand continued to *write* in Urdu, and only had his writings transliterated (and, alas, sometimes incompetently translated) by anonymous scribes. But it would be fair to say that the switch from Urdu to the still-forming Hindi indicated less a linguistic shift than a need to free himself from the shackles of an established literary tradition. As a consequence, ironically, Premchand has acquired an originary status in the history of modern Urdu literature as well. Thus, he might well be unique in that he stands at the head of not one but of *two* modern literary traditions—Hindi, and Urdu.

Having freed himself from the romantic constraints of the Urdu fiction of the time, Premchand turned his reformist, nationalist pen to writing about aspects of present reality which demanded to be thought about. Thus, he wrote copiously about the evils of his contemporary society—social wrongs which have proved remarkably persistent. The domestic crises of ordinary lives found a sympathetic fabulist in him. In addition to writing memorably about these unglamorous lives, Premchand was a pioneer in making the reality of rural north India available as a subject for the imagination. The very *classic* status of these imaginative forms—stories such as 'Poos ki Raat' and 'Kafan' and 'Thakur ka Kuan', and a novel such as *Godaan*—have made them part of the mental furniture of most educated people in north India. Consequently, one tends to forget the fact that these stories, these ways of thinking and shaping common experiences—rendering them narratable and *therefore* meaningful, meaningful and *therefore* narratable—were once invented, created anew.

It would be fair to say that Premchand was both a creator and a symptom of that great movement of consciousness whose accents can be heard throughout India in the decades around 1900. In this respect, too, Premchand is similar to those other great early-twentieth-century masters who stand at the head of the different linguistic cultures of modern India—figures like Tagore and Karanth and Senapati and Bharati. About these one can legitimately say that they fulfilled, even without presuming to do so, the young Stephen Dedalus's prescription: 'to forge, in the smithy of my soul, the uncreated conscience of my race.'

The manner in which these great originary figures work is by picking up apparently disparate aspects of the life of their times, and endowing them with an unprecedented coherence. In that precise cultural moment, a new cultural subject is born. New continents of experience open up suddenly and become available both to social consciousness and to cultural appropriation. There is a very real sense in which, even without our consent or knowledge, we inhabit the narratives that were invented by these master fabulists, these masters of 'conscience'.

That 'conscience' itself needs to be glossed—because it is both consciousness and also a moral posture, a willingness to take responsibility for matters which have hither to led an ambiguous existence on the edges of social consciousness. That is why these writers remain important, even when we can see through their tricks; even when we can—and who can't?—second-guess them with our far greater sophistication. It is ironic to recall, in this context, something that George Orwell wrote about another great master of a very different kind of 'conscience', Rudyard Kipling: 'vitality and good taste are not the same thing. It needs great vitality even to become a by-word, but to *remain* one... that is genius.'

Among the many aspects of contemporary reality which drew the attention of thinking beings at the turn of the last century, the condition of women was prominent across India. The questions with which *Nirmala* concerns itself dominated the minds of these early-twentieth-century pioneers—the matter of dowry, the many and sometimes flamboyant dangers attendant on the conventional arranged marriage. The durability of many of these questions is indeed remarkable.

*Nirmala* is, in many ways, a classic text of the woman as victim, at least in Hindi. This 1920s melodrama about a young woman who is at the receiving end of rotten social institutions—dowry, and the consequently mismatched marriage with an older man, etc.—was a huge success when it was first published, being perceived as a progressive blow in support of women. The fate of the tender Nirmala, hurrying through her short, unhappy life, lurching from tragedy to tragedy, moved thousands when it was first published—and has continued to do so right down to our own time.

*Nirmala* was first published in *Chand* in twelve monthly instalments, from November 1925 to November 1926: there was no instalment in January 1926. *Nirmala* was published in book form in January 1927: a subtitle described it as a 'revolutionary social novel'. It will immediately be apparent that *Nirmala* built up a furious pace. The first instalment—chapters 1–3—contained varied enough material to sustain a wide constituency of readers. Thus, there are the young girls poised on the edge of matrimony, dreaming strange, troubling dreams; there is the aroused and suddenly articulate wife of chapter 2, slanging it out with her surprised husband and sounding for all the world like a flesh-and-blood version of the liberated but anaemic ladies one imagines as Mahadevi's heroines; and we get a first glimpse of the gluttonous Pandit Moteram who was soon to star in a brilliant series of stories. All this was present in the first instalment itself.

Not surprisingly, the subscription department of *Chand* perked up considerably, and the December 1925 issue carried an advertisement seeking four educated ladies—*sushikshita pracharikaaen*—who would work for the cause of women's education and push *Chand* sales: the two projects are hardly distinguishable. Actual circulation figures are hard to come by, but there is oral testimony that the monthly instalments of *Nirmala* generated a great deal of excitement and anticipation. They were eagerly awaited, eagerly discussed. Even though there was some unpleasantness regarding remuneration, Premchand was sufficiently tempted by the *Chand* readership to continue to write for it, and continued to use the journal as a vehicle for his writings relating to the question of women. From the point of view of the magazine also, *Nirmala* enjoyed a huge success. So much so that Premchand was asked to start another serial as soon as *Nirmala* was, so to speak, done with. This sequel, *Pratigya,* was a pale reworking of an earlier work, *Prema,* and is of no interest here.

Contemporary feminists may well find such texts quaint and sometimes even offensive—and it would be surprising if they didn't—but it would be ungenerous not to concede that it is precisely such texts and their pioneering authors who, assimilating and narrating awkward aspects of their contemporary social reality, have made their modern critics possible. After all, we often disapprove of those on whose shoulders we stand. But, sneering apart, the relevant question for us latter-day readers of *Nirmala* still remains: should we (can we?) continue to read it as it was read when it was first published, seventy years ago—weeping copious tears over the fate of its doomed heroine, raging against the still-present iniquities of an unjust social order, pronouncing anathema upon the poor, pathetic, grotesque Munshi Totaram, her hapless husband?

The critical essay that follows the translated text (see Afterword, 'Hearing Nirmala Silence', pp. 197–211) seeks to offer just such a contemporary reading, informed by current critical practice and current ideological concerns. However, readers may wish to read the Afterword only after they have given the novel a first, unbiased, reading.

# Translator's Note

All translators are perforce required to evolve, for each text, some balance between the poles of exoticism and domestication. There is no need to make heavy weather, theoretical or otherwise, of this necessary labour.

However, the English translator of Indian texts suffers a double jeopardy. Thus, the first reader he must endeavour to satisfy is the Indian reader—from some other linguistic region of this multilingual country. For this reader there are many things that do *not* need to be translated, because they belong to a cultural context with which most Indians are familiar. Not only is the translation of such items unnecessary, it is also inadvisable. The Indian reader of English is notoriously prone to the suspicion that it is not he that is being addressed, but an international reader, somewhere behind his right shoulder. And one way in which this suspicion might be allayed is by *not* translating certain things.

However, these are precisely the things that need to be translated for that hypothetical international reader. And if the situation weren't already complicated enough, it turns out that many of these, in turn, turn out to be untranslatable—they imply too much cultural baggage.

A Glossary has been appended to this translation by way of a compromise. Some readers may find it useful in clarifying textual obscurities. But my fondest hope is that it will tempt some readers at least to engage with the phenomenon of untranslatability itself.

As someone who has tried to teach literature in and through translation, I have always found that it is the experience of *difficulty*, the stuff that 'won't go', so to speak, that is the most interesting. Some of this exists, inevitably, at the nominal level—facts, names, things. But there are other 'things' that aren't things at all, but complex cultural phenomena that are heavy and resistant with alterity—so that a nominal translation is, in fact, a kind of violence. My hope is that a gifted teacher will be able to use such glossary items in order to enable the students to engage not only with a text but also with a culture that is simultaneously understandable— i.e. not exotic—and also different—i.e. not domesticated, common or garden.

# Chapter One

Although there were dozens of people in Babu
Udayabhanulal's household—cousins maternal and
paternal, sons of brothers, sons of sisters—there is little
reason to concern ourselves with them here. He was a good lawyer,
the goddess of wealth smiled on his labours, and providing shelter
to the less fortunate members of his family was neither more nor
less than his duty. We are concerned here only with his two
daughters, the older of whom is called Nirmala, the younger
Krishna. Till but yesterday both were happy playing with dolls.
Nirmala was in her fifteenth year, Krishna in her tenth, yet there
was little difference between their temperaments. Both were
playful, mischievous, full of fun and frolic. Their dolls would
frequently be married off with great extravagance, and they did
their best to avoid doing any work at all. Their mother would
keep calling away, but the two would stay lurking on the terrace
as if unaware altogether as to what the calling might be about.
They quarrelled with their brothers, scolded the servants, and
would dash to the front door at the merest sound of an itinerant
musician. But something has happened today, something that has
suddenly made the older one that much older, the younger one
decidedly younger. Krishna is much the same as ever, but Nirmala
has suddenly become sombre, bashful, and a seeker of solitude.
For the past several months Babu Udayabhanulal has been on the
lookout for a husband for Nirmala. Today his labours have been

crowned with success. A match has been arranged with the elder son of Babu Bhalchandra Sinha, Bhuwan Mohan Sinha. The groom's father has declared he has no demands whatsoever in the matter of a dowry—Babu Udayabhanulal may choose to give or not give anything, just as he pleases. But the members of the baraat must be treated with generous hospitality, he insisted, so as to protect both parties from all possible ridicule. Babu Udayabhanulal was a lawyer all right, but he did not know how to accumulate wealth. The question of the dowry had been a tough nut for him to crack. Thus his relief knew no bounds when the groom's father declared that the dowry was purely optional. He had been apprehensive about all the debts he would have to incur and had even made provisional arrangements with a few moneylenders. His most conservative estimates of the likely cost had been in the region of twenty thousand rupees. He was overjoyed at being relieved of that anxiety.

This same piece of news has made the innocent girl hide her face and take refuge in a lonely corner of the house. There is a strange fear that fills her heart, a nameless dread is gathering in every fibre of her being—for what does the future hold? There is no joy in her heart, no trace of that rapture which expresses itself in the shy glances of maidens and in half smiles that play on their lips, which overcomes their limbs with a deliberate languor. No, there are no aspirations there, no fond expectations, only fears, anxieties and dark imaginings. She is of a tender age.

Krishna understands something of what is going on, but only something. She knows her sister will get all kinds of jewellery, there will be musicians and festivities, guests and dancing—and she is pleased with all that. But she knows also that her sister will part tearfully from all the members of the household, she will leave her home with much weeping and wailing, and Krishna will be left all alone—this she is not too pleased with. But she doesn't understand why all this is happening at all, nor why her mother and father are so keen to drive her sister from their home. It's not as if her sister has said anything unpleasant to anyone, nor quarrelled or anything—so, she thinks, will I too be turned out in this way one day? I too will sit in a corner and weep like my sister, and no one will take pity on me? That is why she too is afraid.

It was evening and Nirmala was sitting by herself on the terrace, staring at the sky with eyes full of longing. If she could, she would have flown away somewhere, far away from all these complications. Normally, the two sisters went out together at that time of day to take the air. If the carriage was not available, they would just stroll in the garden. That is why Krishna was looking for her. Not finding her, she came to the terrace and, seeing her there, said laughingly—Here you are, hiding yourself, and I've been looking for you everywhere! Come, the carriage is ready.

Nirmala replied tonelessly—You go on, I'll stay here.

Krishna—No, my dear sister, you must come today. See how pleasant the breeze is.

Nirmala—I don't feel like going, please.

Krishna's eyes filled with tears. In a quivering voice she said— Why won't you come today? Why won't you speak to me? Why are you hiding yourself in this place and that? I feel afraid sitting alone all by myself. If you won't come, I won't go either. I'll just sit here with you.

Nirmala—And what will you do after I'm gone? Whom will you play with then, whom will you then go out with, tell me?

Krishna—I'll go away with you. I won't stay here by myself.

Nirmala replied smilingly—Amma won't let you go.

Krishna—Then I won't let you go either. Why don't you tell Amma you won't go anywhere?

Nirmala—I'm telling them all right, but who's listening?

Krishna—So isn't this your home too?

Nirmala—It obviously isn't, or else how could I be sent away forcibly?

Krishna—Will I too be turned out this way one day?

Nirmala—So d'you expect to stay here forever? We're girls, we don't really belong anywhere.

Krishna—Will Chandar too be turned out?

Nirmala—Chandar is a boy. Who'll turn him out?

Krishna—Are girls very bad then?

Nirmala—If they weren't bad, would they be thrown out like this?

Krishna—Chandar is such a rascal, but he's allowed to stay. You and I, we never do anything mischievous, do we?

Just then Chandar arrived noisily on the terrace and, seeing Nirmala, announced in a loud voice—So, this is where you're hiding yourself! So, there will be bands playing, and Didi will be decked up as a bride, and be carried away in a palanquin, so!

Chandar was Chandrabhanu Sinha's son. He was three years younger than Nirmala and older than Krishna by two.

Nirmala—I'll report you to Amma if you tease me, Chandar.

Chandar—So why d'you get teased? You'll enjoy the playing of the musicians, won't you? What fun! So, you'll be a bride soon! Say Kishni, you'll enjoy the music too! Such music as you've never heard before!

Krishna—Will it be better than the bands that come wandering by?

Chandar—Better, much, much better, a hundred times, a hundred thousand times better. What d'you know? Listen to one band, and you start thinking it must be the best around. The musicians will be in red uniforms and black hats. And how wonderful they'll look! There'll be fireworks too, rockets will shoot off into the sky and hit the stars and bring red and yellow and green and blue stars crashing down. What fun!

Krishna—Tell me more, little brother.

Chandar—Come for a stroll with me and I'll tell you all. There'll be such wonderful entertainments as you'll never believe possible. There'll be fairies flying about, real fairies I tell you.

Krishna—Let's go then. But you'd better keep your promise or else I'll give you a beating.

Chandrabhanu and Krishna went off for a walk, and Nirmala was left all by herself. She was hurt bitterly by Krishna's going off at this time. Krishna, whom she loved more than life itself, could be so cruel to her. Abandoning her at such a time! It was no big matter, but a grieving heart is like a hurt eye, even the passing breeze causes it pain. Nirmala sat sobbing for a long, long time. Her brother and sister, mother and father, all had turned away from her, forgotten her quite, she might well find herself pining before too long to see just their faces.

The garden was in bloom, pleasant fragrances wafted in. The cool breezes of the month of Chaita were blowing softly. Stars were spangled across the night sky. Lost in her melancholy thoughts, Nirmala fell asleep and was soon wandering in the land of dreams. She saw before her a river in which there rose big waves, and she was sitting on the bank, waiting for a boat. It is evening and the darkness is growing apace like some fearsome beast. She is overwhelmed with anxieties about when and how she will cross the river. She is weeping because she is afraid it will turn to night, and then how will she ever be able to stay in such a place by herself? Suddenly she sees a beautiful boat approach the bank. She leaps up with joy, but as soon as the boat touches the bank and she makes to step onto it, the boatman cries out— 'There's no place for you here!' She pleads with the boatman, falls at his feet, whimpers plaintively, but he keeps repeating, 'There's no place for you here.' In a moment the boat is off again. She starts wailing aloud. Fearful of how she will spend the night on that desolate bank, she leaps into the water in order to clamber onto the boat, when suddenly she hears a voice—'Stop, stop, the river is deep, you'll drown at this rate. That boat is not for you, I'm coming, come sit on my boat and I'll take you across.' Frightened, she looks around her for the source of the voice. In a little while, a small dinghy appears. It has neither sail, nor rudder, nor paddle. Its bottom is leaking, its boards are broken, the boat is full of water and a man is patiently baling it out. She says to him, 'But this is all broken, how will it ever get across?' The boatman replies—'It has been sent for you, come and sit down!' She thinks for a moment—Should I or shouldn't I sit in this boat? In the end she decides she'll take the chance. Better that than spend the night all by herself. Better to drown in the river than be devoured by some fearsome beast. Who knows, the boat might even make it across the river. Thus consoled, she takes courage in both hands and gets onto the boat. For a while the boat moves shakily; but it is taking in water rapidly. She too joins the boatman in baling out the water with both her hands. Try as hard as they will, the water keeps rising, until the boat begins to float out of control—as if about to sink at any moment. Just then, as she raises her hand towards some invisible source of succour, the boat slips away from under her and she loses her footing. She shouts and wakes herself up with the shouting.

She saw her mother standing above her, shaking her by the shoulder.

# Chapter 2

Babu Udayabhanulal's house has been transformed into a veritable marketplace. The goldsmith is hammering away on the verandah, and the tailor's needles are plying busily in one of the inner rooms. The carpenter is making beds under the neem tree outside. A pit is being dug in a shed for the halwai's oven. An entire house is to be readied exclusively for the wedding guests. Arrangements are being made so that each guest has a bed to himself, as well as a table and chair. Personal servants are being recruited at the rate of one for every three guests. The wedding is still a month away but the preparations are in full swing. The hospitality has to be such that it leaves no room whatsoever for complaint . It should be a wedding to remember. One whole set of rooms is crammed full of utensils of all kinds—tea sets of all descriptions, quarter-plates and half-plates and full-plates, huge platters, lotas, glasses. All the numberless relatives who used to spend their days lying around and smoking the hukka are now working away with great eagerness. After all, it may be a long time before they get another such opportunity to demonstrate their usefulness. Where one man is required, five rush. The result is more commotion than work accomplished. There are endless arguments about trivial matters and finally the great Vakil Sahib Udayabhanulal himself has to come and settle the business. One declares that the ghee is bad, the other believes that better is not to be had anywhere, so help me God. A third declares it has a horrible stink, a fourth counters that the man's nose is defective and what does he know about real ghee, anyway? What did you know of ghee before you came to this house, eh? Tempers and voices rise and the Vakil Sahib has to come and pacify them.

It was nine at night. Udayabhanulal was sitting at his desk with the accounts. He made an estimate of likely expenditure practically every day—and was forced to make some change or other every day. His wife was standing there, frowning. After a considerable while Vakil Sahib lifted his head and said—There's no way it can be reduced below ten thousand, and it might go even higher.

Kalyani—In ten days it's gone up from five to ten thousand. At this rate it might even get to a lakh.

Udayabhanu—But what can I do? It won't do to make a laughing stock of oneself. If there's any cause for complaint, people will make unflattering comparisons between our status and the level of hospitality. And besides when the man has not demanded a dowry I'm obliged to make sure the hospitality offered to the wedding guests is of a high order.

Kalyani—Ever since the day Brahma created the world, has anyone ever managed to win the approval of wedding guests? They always manage some pretext or other to find fault and complain. People who don't even get plain rotis at home are transformed into sultans as soon as they become wedding guests. The oil isn't fragrant enough, who knows from what cheap store the soap has been purchased, the servants are disobedient, the hurricane lamps are smoky, the chairs are bug-ridden and the beds sag, the guest-house is poorly ventilated! There are a thousand such complaints. How will you ever answer all of them? If you guard against one set of complaints, they'll find others. Thus, this oil is so fragrant, it's suitable only for prostitutes, we'd like some plain oil, please. This isn't just plain soap we've been provided, rather an occasion for displaying their wealth, as if we didn't know about expensive soaps! O these servants, they're so oppressive, they never leave one alone! And these hurricane lamps, they're so bright they dazzle the eyes; spend a few days with such lamps around and we'll go blind! As for this wretched guest-house where we've been lodged, they'll say, it's like the stricken fortune of an unlucky fellow—constantly buffeted about by the winds. My advice is to stop worrying about pleasing the wedding guests.

Udayabhanu—So what is it you'd have me do?

Kalyani—I'm telling you, make a firm resolve not to spend anything over five thousand. We've got no savings and we'll have to resort to debt—so why should we get in so deep that we won't be able to repay it in our lifetime? After all, I have other children, I have to think about them too.

Udaybhanu—I'm hardly about to drop dead just yet.

Kalyani—Who can tell about living and dying.

Udayabhanu— So this is what you sit and keep planning for?

Kalyani—No need to get angry. Everybody has to die some day, nobody's immortal. Closing one's eyes won't make one's fate go away. I see it every day with my own eyes, the father dies, and the children get knocked about in the streets. So why should a man act foolishly?

Udayabhanu reacted furiously—So I should now take it for granted that my end is near, for thus you have foretold! One hadn't heard of women tiring of the married state so far, but there must be some untold joys in widowhood!

Kalyani—One has only to talk a little plain practical common sense for you to start spouting venom. Isn't it because you know that, after all is said and done, I'm dependent on you, I've nowhere else to go, so I must submit or starve? That's all there is to it. I've only to open my mouth and you fly off the handle, as if I were some servant with no involvement in the family's welfare other than the food I eat and the clothes I wear. The more I yield the more aggressive you become. All kinds of stooges rob you blind, but nobody must say a thing, money may be wasted in all kinds of luxurious ways but not a word must be said, ever. Who's going to pay the price for all these extravagances except my children?

Udayabhanulal—I'm not your slave, am I?

Kalyani—Am I your slave, then?

Udayabhanu—I'm not one of those men who dance to the tune of their women.

Kalyani—Nor am I one of those women who're prepared to put up with being mistreated and never utter a word in protest.

Udayabhanu—I go out and earn the money, I'll spend it any way I please. Nobody has the right to utter a word.

Kalyani—Then manage your own household too! I've no desire to have anything to do with a house in which I'm treated without respect. I have as much right to this home as you. Not one whit less! If you think of yourself as some sort of king, I'm no less a queen in my own eyes. You're welcome to this house of yours, I will not want for a few rotis to feed myself. You can do as you please with your children, feed them or starve them according to your fancy. So long as I don't have to see it happening, I will be spared the pain. Out of sight, out of mind!

Udayabhanu—Do you suppose I'll not be able to run this household without your help? I can look after ten such myself, alone.

Kalyani—You! Mark my words, the whole arrangement will fall apart within a month, to the day!

Even as she said this, Kalyani's face flushed with emotion, she got up impetuously and moved towards the door. The Vakil Sahib was an experienced lawyer, much given to legal hair-splitting in the court, but he knew little about women and their temperaments. This, after all, is one branch of knowledge in which a man remains ignorant even after a lifetime of experience. If he had relented even at this time, held Kalyani's hand and coaxed her to sit down, she might have been persuaded. But this he was unable to do; instead, he fired off one more salvo.

Udayabhanu—It's the thought of your mother's welcome that's making you so arrogant, is it?

Kalyani stopped at the door and stared hard at her husband with bloodshot eyes, then said passionately—There's no reason why I'll be welcomed in my mother's home. And I'm not so down and out as to consent to live on their charity!

Udayabhanu—Where are you off to then?

Kalyani—Who are you to demand that of me? There's room on God's earth for millions of creatures. Should I alone have nowhere to go?

Saying this, Kalyani swept out of the room. Coming out into the courtyard she looked up once at the sky, as if calling upon the stars to bear witness to the heartlessness with which she was being cast out of her own home. It was eleven at night. Quiet reigned over the house. The two sons' beds had been made up in her room as usual. She came to her room and saw that Chandrabhanu was sleeping—but the youngest, Suryabhanu, sat up on seeing his mother and asked lispingly—Where had you gone, Mother?

Kalyani stood where she was and said—Nowhere really, I was with your father.

Suryabhanu—I felt afraid when you were away. Why did you go away, tell me?

Saying this, the child raised both his arms, as if asking to be picked up. Kalyani couldn't restrain herself any longer. Her angry heart overflowed with maternal affection. The tender shoots of affection which had withered in the fierce heat of her anger turned green once again. Her eyes grew moist. She picked the child up and holding him close said—Why didn't you call out to me then?

Suryabhanu—I called out all right, but you didn't hear me. Promise me you won't go away again?

Kalyani—I promise, never again.

Saying this, Kalyani lay down in the bed with Suryabhanu. As soon as he found himself next to his mother, the child was reassured and fell fast asleep. Kalyani was torn between different possibilities—whenever she thought of her husband's words, all she wanted to do was break off all connection with her married home and go away, anywhere. But when she saw her children's faces she was overwhelmed by maternal emotion. Whom could she entrust with her children's care? Who would look after her darlings? Who would feed them with milk and halva in the mornings and bend herself to their routine, so that she might sleep when they did and wake when they needed her? The poor creatures would soon be completely neglected. No, my loved ones, I will not abandon you. For your sake, I'll put up with everything—insult, humiliation, outrage, harsh, cruel words, this and more I will endure for your sake.

Kalyani lay down with the child; but her husband could not sleep. He found it hard to forget hurtful things. What a temper! As if I'm not her husband but her wife! Impossible to say a word. So now I have to submit to being her slave. She alone should live in the house, and all the others, whether relatives or not, should be turned out. She's jealous of them. Keeps wishing me dead so that she might do as she pleases. The darker feelings do find expression, no matter how hard we try to suppress them. I have been noticing this for some time now, she's been saying such hurtful things. She's confident of being welcomed in her mother's house but she'll find out that she isn't welcome there in such a situation, no matter how much they fawn over her right now. When she's there for good, the hard realities of the situation will hit her. She'll come back in tears. What arrogance! She thinks she alone runs this household. If I go away for a few days, they'll realize what it means to be rude to me. Let me break her spirit once and for all. Let her enjoy the pleasures of widowhood. I wonder where she finds the courage to curse me in that way. She seems entirely devoid of love for me, or maybe she supposes I'm so dependent on the household I'll put up with all kinds of cursing rather than move away. That must be it, but I'm not one for staying where I'm no longer wanted. To hell with a home like this, where one has to deal with such people. Is this home at all, or only a special kind of hell? A man returns from the world outside at the end of the day, tired and sorely in need of rest and care and comfort. But here he gets cursed instead. Vows and penances are taken with my death in view! So this is where twenty-five years of conjugal bliss have brought us. I should leave now. When I've made sure her spirit is broken and her temper tamed, I'll come back. Four or five days should prove sufficient. I assure you, you'll rue the day you decided to tangle with me!

Thinking such thoughts Babu Sahib rose, draped his silken wrap round his shoulders, took care to put his card in the spare kurta that he intended to carry with him, took some money, picked up his walking stick and stepped out silently. The servants were fast asleep. The dog woke with a start on hearing his movements and went along with him.

But who could have foreseen the complex fate that was being planned by the Almighty? The heartless puppeteer of life's theatre was sitting in some inaccessible and secret place, working away at his heartless show. Who was to know that what had been intended as a sort of pretence was about to be transformed into reality, mere acting transformed into truth itself.

The contest between night and day had been settled in favour of the night. Its dark forces had established their terror over every aspect of nature. All good things had hid themselves, concealed in darkness, while all that was evil and bad was abroad, flaunting itself. In forests, predators moved about in quest of prey, while in cities other predators prowled in dark alleys.

Babu Udayabhanulal was hurrying towards the Ganga. He

had planned to leave his spare kurta on the river bank and go off to Mirzapur for five days. Seeing his clothes, people would draw the obvious conclusion that he had drowned—his card was in his pocket. There would be no problem with identification. In a flash the news would spread about the entire town. By eight in the morning practically the entire town will be at my door, he thought—then we shall see how capable my lady is!

Deep in these thoughts Babu Sahib was moving along the alley, when he suddenly became conscious of someone walking behind him; at first he didn't give it a second thought. He went on. But every time he turned the man behind turned in the same direction. He realized the man was probably following him and sensed his intentions were no good. Quickly he brought out his pocket torch and turned it on the man's face: he saw a strong fellow with a stout stick on his shoulder. Babu Sahib gave a start of recognition on seeing the man! He was a well known ruffian of the town. Three years earlier he had been charged with dacoity. Udayabhanu had represented the State in the case and the man had been sentenced to three years' imprisonment. Ever since then, he'd been seeking his revenge. He had been released only the day before. Today, quite by chance, he'd seen Babu Sahib alone and realized in a trice that this was a good opportunity to settle scores. He might not get such an opportunity again. He fell behind him immediately and was looking for a suitable moment to strike when Babu Sahib turned the torch on him. Now the rascal slowed down abruptly and said—Know me, Babu Sahib? I'm Matai.

Babu Sahib's tone was severe—Why are you following me in this way?

Matai—Why, can't a man walk where he pleases? Or is this your own private road perhaps?

Babu Sahib had been a wrestler in his youth and was still quite strong. He didn't lack in courage either. Steadying his stick, he said—It seems you aren't satisfied with what you got last time. This time you'll go for seven years.

Matai—Whether I go for seven or fourteen, I won't leave

you alive. Yes, if you're prepared to fall at my feet and swear you'll never again get another man sentenced, I'll let you go. Speak up, are you willing?

Udayabhanu—Are you out of your mind?

Matai—It seems *you* are. Speak up, do you accept my offer? One!

Udayabhanu—Go away or I'll call the police.

Matai—Two!

Udayabhanu—(roaring) Move out of my way, scoundrel!

Matai—Three!

As soon as Matai pronounced 'three' he landed such a blow on Babu Sahib's head that he fell down, unconscious. All he managed to utter was—He's killed me!

Matai came closer and saw that Babu Sahib's head was split open and the blood flowing freely. There was no pulse left in the man. He understood immediately that the deed was done. He took the gold watch off the wrist, the gold buttons from the kurta, the ring from his finger, and went his way as if nothing had happened. Well, he took pity enough to move the corpse to one side.

What a strange turn events had taken, so completely different from what had been planned. O Life, can anything be more meaningless in the whole wide world? Is not life ephemeral like a lamp, extinguished by a passing gust! Even a bubble takes a moment to burst, but life not even that long. What reliance can we place on mere breath, and yet what magnificent edifices of hope we build upon its precarious foundations. We do not even know if we will draw our next breath, but we think far ahead and carry on as though immortal.

# Chapter 3

We will not grieve the hearts of our readers by subjecting them to the widow's wailing and to the weeping of the orphans. The victims of misfortune mourn as they must, and weep and wail and thrash about. There is nothing new in all this. Yes, if you so desire, you may try and imagine Kalyani's anguish as she reviles herself with the thought that she is responsible for her husband's death. Those words which she uttered in a fit of rage have now become arrows lacerating her heart. Had her husband given up his life as he lay groaning in her lap, she would have had the consolation that she had done her duty. There is nothing more soothing to hearts that are afflicted by grief. How buoyed she would have been with the thought that her husband had been happy with her when he went away, that he had loved her till the very end. But Kalyani was denied that satisfaction. She returned repeatedly to the same thought—twenty-five years of her virtuous life had gone to waste. At the very end, she had lost the love of her husband. If only I had not used such harsh words, she thought, he would almost certainly not have left home at that time of night. Who knows what thoughts coursed through his brain then? She tormented herself with thinking about his last moments and wrestled with her exaggerated feelings of guilt night and day. She began to loathe the faces of the very children she would gladly have sacrificed her life for earlier. It is for their sake that I quarrelled with my husband. They are my enemies.

The same house in which there had been crowds of people all day was now completely deserted. The festivities were over. When the provider himself had gone, how could the hangers-on stay much longer? Gradually, within a month, the cousins and nephews had all gone. All those who had boasted of their undying loyalty, even to the death, went without so much as a backward glance. The world was changed utterly. The same children whose happy countenances had commanded a natural affection were now neglected and dishevelled. Where had that radiance gone?

Once her grief had abated the problem of Nirmala's wedding again came into focus. There were some suggestions that the wedding should be postponed for a year. But Kalyani said—After making all these preparations, it would be a pity to let them go to waste by deferring the wedding. After all, the same preparations would have to be made again the next year—and there was little chance of her being able to afford them then. It was better to go ahead with the wedding. After all, no expense is to be incurred by way of dowry. As for the preparations for the wedding-guests, much of all that has been done already—any delay would only mean further loss. Therefore, along with the sad news, Mister Bhalchand was sent this same message. In her letter Kalyani wrote—Take pity on this unfortunate one, this destitute, and rescue her from drowning. My husband had great plans, great hopes, but alas, Providence had other designs altogether. Now my honour rests entirely in your hands. My daughter is already yours. I consider it a matter of pride to treat the wedding guests hospitably, but if some shortcomings should remain I hope you will overlook them in the light of my sorrow. I am confident that you will not allow such an unfortunate as I am now to be disgraced, etc., etc.

Kalyani didn't send this letter in the post. Instead she called the family priest and said to him—I'm sorry to trouble you, but please take this personally and request them very politely on my behalf to bring as few guests as possible. There's no one here now to take care of the arrangements.

The priest Moteram arrived in Lucknow with this message on the third day.

It was evening. Babu Bhalchandra was sprawled in an armchair on the porch, smoking his hukkah in a state of undress. He was a tall, massive man. He seemed like some dark god, or some negro lately recruited from darkest Africa. He was one colour from top to toe—black. His face was so dark that it was difficult to tell where his forehead ended and his hair began. He was one live coal-black image. He suffered inordinately from the heat. Two people were fanning him constantly, but the sweat still kept dripping from his enormous body. He was a high official in the Excise Department. His salary was a full 500 rupees a month, and he extracted huge bribes from contractors. Keeping him happy was all that they were called upon to do. His pleasure was all the law there was, and once that was ensured they could sell water in the name of liquor, or keep their shops open all twenty-four hours of the day. He was so awesome looking that if one were to see him on a moonlit night one would be startled—not merely women and children, even grown men had been known to take fright. A moonlit night was specified because on a dark one he would have been simply invisible, merely merging into the surrounding darkness until only his red eyes remained. Just as a devout Mussalman says his prayers five times a day, so Babu Bhalchandra drank alcohol religiously five times every day. After all, even the qazi is free to accept free liquor. And he, after all, was an official in the relevant government department—he could drink as much as he liked, there were none to stop him, and he reached for the liquor every time he felt thirsty. Just as some colours are sympathetic, and blend harmoniously, so there are others that are violently antipathetic. The red of Babu Bhalchandra's eyes only made the surrounding blackness even more frightening.

The moment Babu Sahib's eyes lighted on Pandit Moteram, he struggled up from his chair and said effusively—Ah, so it's you! You're very welcome! Do come. How very fortunate I am! Is there anyone there? Where have all of them disappeared— Jhagru, Gurdin, Chhakori, Bhavani, Ram Gulam, is there anyone there? All of them couldn't have died at the same time! Come on someone, Ram Gulam, Bhavani, Chhakori, Gurdin, Jhagru. Not a whisper out of any of them, the rascals! I have a dozen servants, but I can't find a single one of them when I need them. God alone knows where they manage to hide themselves. Get a chair for the gentleman here!

Babu Sahib repeated this litany of five names several times, but it did not occur to him to send one of the two servants who were busy fanning him to get a chair for Panditji. After a few minutes a one-eyed servant came in coughing and said—Sarkar, I can't work for such small wages! How long can I live on loans and credit. I'm tired of all this begging.

Bhalchandra—Stop jabbering and go get a chair. The moment he's asked to do something, he starts complaining. Tell me Panditji, is all well where you come from?

Moteram—What can I say—but how can things be well any more? The family is utterly destroyed.

The servant appeared with one broken-down deal box and said—I'm not strong enough to pick up any damn chair.

Panditji sat down embarrassedly on it, hoping all the while that it wouldn't collapse, and placed Kalyani's letter in Babu Bhalchandra's hand.

Bhalchandra—But how could it remain undestroyed after such a mortal blow? What greater misfortune could there possibly be? Babu Udayabhanulal was a long-standing friend of mine. He was a jewel of a man! What a heart he had, what courage (here he wiped his eyes). Losing him, it's as if I've lost my own right hand. Believe me, ever since I heard the news I've no heart left for living, I see only darkness before me now. When I sit down to eat I cannot bear to put a single morsel into my mouth. Every instant it's his image I see before my eyes. I barely touch the food that is set before me and quickly leave the table. I've no desire left to do anything any more. Even a brother's death could not have caused me quite so much grief. No mere man, Babu Udayabhanulal, he was a jewel!

Moteram—Sarkar, there's no rais like him left in the town.

Bhalchandra—I know it well, Panditji, you don't need to tell me. A man like him is one in a million. I knew him better than any other man. In a mere few meetings I had come to respect and even worship him, and I shall continue to think of him in the same way until the end of my days. Please tell the honourable lady that I am truly grieved.

Moteram—No less was expected from you. One rarely meets people as kind and generous as yourself. Who else would have agreed to give a son in marriage and asked for no dowry?

Bhalchandra—O honourable one, one doesn't discuss mundane things like dowry with such a noble soul—a mere connection with him was worth a fortune. I consider myself blessed for that connection alone. What a generous man he was. He cared not a whit for money, he treated it like dirt. It is a terrible custom, simply terrible! If I had my way, I'd shoot all those who give and get dowries—I tell you, I'd shoot them all. No matter what the consequences! I ask you, are you marrying a son or selling him off? If you wish to spend on your son's wedding, feel free to do so, but spend it on the strength of your own resources. Why make the poor girl's father pay? It is baseness, mere baseness! If I had my way, I'd shoot all these rascals.

Moteram—Praise be! God has made you wise. This is the miracle of dharma at work. My mistress desires that the wedding be solemnized on the date originally agreed. As for the rest, she has written it all in the letter. Now you alone can deliver us from the difficulty into which we have been cast by misfortune. Of course, we will provide all the hospitality we can to all the wedding guests you choose to bring with you, but the situation is very different now, sir. There's no one there to take care of things. Please do what you can to ensure that Vakil Sahib's good name is not brought into disrepute.

Bhalchandra kept his eyes closed for one whole minute, then sighed deeply and said—Alas, the God Almighty did not wish that that blessed maiden be married into my family, else why would this calamity have befallen us? All our plans have been dashed to the ground. How elated I used to be at the mere thought that the auspicious day was approaching—but how was I to know that some other plans were being hatched in the Divine Court? The merest remembrance of the departed soul is enough to bring tears to my eyes. Seeing his daughter every day will only reopen a still fresh wound. I could not trust myself to act reasonably in that condition. You may approve or disapprove of it as you will, but once I become attached to someone I find it impossible to forget them even for a moment. Even as things are now, I see his face before my eyes every waking moment. But once his daughter entered my house, I'd find it impossible to continue living. Believe me, my eyes will grow sightless with weeping. I know, I know there's no point in weeping. The dead do not return because one weeps for them. There's nothing to be done except to endure all that happens with fortitude. But what can I do to help my feelings? Merely seeing that orphan girl will break my heart.

Moteram—Do not utter such words, sir. Though the Vakil Sahib is no more, she has you to look up to after all. Now you are like a father to her. She is not the Vakil Sahib's daughter any more, she is yours! After all, everybody doesn't know the sensitive nature of your feelings, they'll merely suppose you chose to break your promise the moment you heard of Vakil Sahib's death. This will bring disrepute to your fair name. Be firm, and go ahead with the wedding ceremonies as planned. After all, there's a lot of wealth even after the master's gone. It is a terrible calamity, but my mistress will leave you and your guests no grounds for complaint as regards hospitality and all that.

Babu Sahib understood right away that Panditji was no mere book-learned pandit; he was an adept in the arts of negotiation. He said—I tell you truly, Panditji, I love that girl even more than I do my own daughter, but when God himself refuses his consent, what can I do? The death is an inauspicious sign which God has sent us, a portent of some impending catastrophe. God is telling us in almost as many words that this wedding is ill-omened. In such a situation, I ask you, how wise is it to go ahead with this wedding? One cannot swallow a fly with cold deliberation. Please explain it kindly to the dear lady—that I am willing to fulfil her every wish, but I'm sure that the consequences of going ahead with this wedding cannot be good. I cannot consent to acting selfishly in this way and hurting the daughter of my dear dear friend.

This last argument reduced Panditji to silence. His opponent had let fly an arrow against which he had no answer. The enemy had used his very weapons, and there was nothing that Pandit Moteram could do in response. He was still casting around for a counter-strategy when Babu Sahib resumed his ritual of calling out to the servants in turn—Where have all of you gone again—Jhagru, Chhakori, Bhavani, Gurudin, Ram Ghulam! Not one of them responds, they must all have died, every single one of them! Have you any thought of providing some water and light refreshments to Panditji? How long can one go on training these fellows? They haven't a trace of intelligence between them. They can see very well there's a visitor who has come a long distance, but what do they care? Come, bring him some water! Panditji, would you like some sharbat or shall I send for some sweets instead?

Moteramji was unwilling to accept any kind of restriction in the matter of sweets. It was his settled opinion that the mere presence of ghee rendered every comestible to a condition of ritual purity. He was extremely fond of rasagullas and besan laddoos but he could well have done without the sharbat. It was against his principles to fill up valuable abdominal space with watery fluids. Thus, he ventured hesitatingly—I am not accustomed to sharbat, but I'll consent to having the sweets.

Bhalchandra—Phalahari?

Moteram—It's all the same to me.

Bhalchandra—That's it, isn't it? This whole business of ritual purity is just so much hypocrisy. I do not care for any of it myself. What, no one's turned up yet? Speak up you rascals, Chhakori, Bhavani, Gurudin, Ram Ghulam!

This time an ancient servant appeared, wracked by a fit of coughing, and said—Sarkar, I pray that I be given my wages. I can't go on working like this. How long can I go on fetching and carrying like this? My legs ache horribly.

Bhalchandra—No matter if they don't do a stroke of work, but they're all very eager about being paid. They need do nothing all day except lie down and cough away, but their pay's mounting up just the same. Go and fetch an anna's worth of fresh sweets from the market, you! On the double, go!

Having commanded the servant, Babu Sahib went inside the house and said to his wife—There's a panditji come from there. He's brought a letter, here, read it.

His wife was called Rangilibai. She was a fair-complexioned woman with a cheerful face. Her youth and beauty were in the process of leaving her, but, like dearly-loved companions who had been with her a full thirty years, they found it difficult to leave her altogether.

Rangilibai was busy making paans. She said—Haven't I made it amply clear that I'm not in favour of this marriage.

Bhalchandra—You've made it clear enough, but I can't bring myself to utter the words. I'm having to make all kinds of excuses.

Rangilibai—Where's the hesitation in telling the plain truth? We just don't want to go ahead with this marriage, that's all. After all, it's not as if we're under some obligation to anyone over this. When we're getting ten thousand in cash somewhere else, why shouldn't we go there? After all, she's no golden girl, is she? If Vakil Sahib had been alive, he would, simply to save his honour, have given fifteen or twenty thousand anyway. But what will we get from there now?

Bhalchandra—But it's not very nice to break our word, after all. People might not actually say anything to our faces, but it will inevitably be perceived as dishonourable. But you clearly won't have it any other way.

Rangilibai packed a paan into her mouth diligently, then opened the letter and began reading carefully. Babu Sahib had very little practice in reading Hindi, and even his wife, who hardly ever read books, could only just about manage to read letters.

She had barely finished the first line when her eyes grew moist, and by the time she finished the letter her eyes were awash with tears. Every word was full of deep sadness, eloquent with humility. Rangilibai's harshness was not really stone-like—it was more like sealing-wax, softened by the mere touch of flame. Kalyani's melancholy letter melted her selfish heart. In a choked voice, she asked—The brahmin is still here, isn't he?

Bhalchandra's heart sank at the sight of his wife's tears. He blamed himself for having needlessly shown her Kalyani's letter. Where was the need for doing that? He had never made such a terrible mistake before. He said hesitatingly—He might be there, though I'd asked him to go off.

Rangili quickly went to the window to look. Pandit Moteram was sitting tight, with all the concentration of a fishing heron, staring in the direction taken by the servant who had gone for the sweets. He squirmed restlessly in his seat. The promise of a mere anna's worth of sweets was lean rations anyway—this waiting on top of that was almost too much for the poor man to bear. Seeing him still sitting, Rangilibai said—He's there, he's still there. Go and tell him we will go ahead with the wedding, of course we will go ahead. Those poor people are in terrible difficulties.

Bhalchandra—You're being childish. I've just told him that the wedding is not acceptable to us any more. I had to put the whole thing in a suitable context. Now if I go and tell him that I've changed my mind, what d'you think he will say? Marriage is a serious matter—it's not a child's game that one can change one's mind about from moment to moment.

Rangili—All right, if you're unwilling to go and say it, send that brahmin to me. I'll explain the whole thing to him in a manner that will persuade him to see it my way without contradicting what you've said to him. You can hardly have any objection to that.

Bhalchandra—You take the rest of the world to be idiots? What difference does it make whether you say it or I do. What's decided is decided—I don't wish to open the matter again. After all, it was you who used to insist you didn't approve of this wedding. It's because of you I had to go back on my word. And now you're changing your mind again. This is monstrously unfair to me. After all, you must show some consideration for my reputation.

Rangili—How was I to know that the widow would become so pathetic? You're the one who used to say that her husband's entire wealth was salted away, and that she only put on a show of poverty in order to get away with giving as little as possible. She's a tricky one, you said. And whatever you said, I believed. One may well hesitate and feel embarrassed about going back on one's word after having been generous. But there should be none in acting generously after having first acted otherwise. If you had said 'yes' and I wished to go and call the whole thing off, your reluctance would have been understandable. But one can legitimately take pride in saying 'yes' after having first said 'no'.

Bhalchandra—You might well think it's a matter of pride, but it seems plain awful to me. And then, how have you decided that what I told you about Vakil Sahib's widow is wrong? By reading that letter? You assume other people are also simple and straightforward like yourself.

Rangili—There seems to be no pretence in this letter. Faked words rarely touch the heart. The stink of falseness never leaves them.

Bhalchandra—You're wrong. False words can touch the heart like truth rarely can. All these writers whose books you spend hours weeping over, do they write the truth, then? Lies, from end to end, pure make-believe. That too is an art.

Rangili—Come on, you want to pretend with me now! Just because I go along with what you say to me, you think you've managed to make a fool of me. But I know you inside out. You want to put all the blame on me and absolve yourself entirely. Tell me, isn't that the truth? While Vakil Sahib was alive, you thought there was no need for any prior agreement regarding the wedding settlement, because he would of himself give whatever was proper;

in fact, without prior bargaining there was always the hope of getting something extra. But now that Vakil Sahib is dead you've started making all kinds of excuses. This isn't humanity, this is petty-mindedness—you had better take the blame for this on your head. Now I'll have nothing whatsoever to do with this wedding business. You may do as you please. I detest hypocrites. Do whatever you do openly, be it good or ill. Speak up, are you in favour of going ahead with the wedding or not?

Bhalchandra—When I am a liar and a hypocrite, why should you bother to ask me at all? But what a judge of people you are. Really, you are quite amazing!

Rangili—You are a tough one, you refuse to be embarrassed even now. But tell me truthfully, haven't I understood you just right?

Bhalchandra—Go away. There might well be some women who can see through men. I used to think that women have very subtle intelligences, but I've lost that faith now. I'll have to accept what the sages have said about women now.

Rangili—Why don't you go and look at your face in the mirror. There's shame written all over your face.

Bhalchandra—Really?

Rangili—Like some conscientious thief might look when caught in the act.

Bhalchandra—Be that as it may, this wedding will not go ahead.

Rangili—I couldn't care less. Marry him where you please. Say, why don't you ask Bhuwan once?

Bhalchandra—All right, we'll leave the decision to him.

Rangili—No hints! Promise?

Bhalchandra—I promise I won't even look in his direction.

By chance Bhuwan Mohan showed up exactly then. Such handsome, well-built, strong young men are rarely to be found in our colleges these days. He resembled his mother almost exactly, the same fair complexion, the same thin rose-pink lips, the same high forehead, the same large eyes—only in his general build did he resemble his father. He looked most attractive in a short jacket and breeches, worn complete with a hat and tie and riding boots. In his hand he carried a hockey stick. There was the swagger of youth in his gait, an air of arrogance in his eyes.

Rangili said to Bhuwan—You're late today? Look, here's a letter from your in-laws. From your mother-in-law in fact. Speak up honestly, it's still morning, too early to start lying. Are you willing to get married there or not?

Bhuwan—I should go ahead with it, mother, but I won't.

Rangili—Why?

Bhuwan—Marry me some place where I get a lot of money. At least a hundred thousand, maybe more. There's no hope of anything there now, is there? Vakil Sahib is no more, and how much d'you suppose the widow has put away?

Rangili—Don't you feel ashamed of talking in this vein?

Bhuwan—What is there to be ashamed of? Money never hurt anybody. And I'll never be able to save a hundred thousand in my whole life. Even if I pass my examinations this year, I won't get to see money for another five years. Then I'll begin to earn a couple of hundred a month. By the time I get to five or six hundred a month, three quarters of my life will be done. There'll never be any opportunity to save anything. I'll never be able to partake of the pleasures of this world. Ah, if only I could marry some rich man's daughter, I'd rest content. I don't ask for too much, just one hundred thousand cash—or else find me some wealthy widow who has only one daughter.

Rangili—No matter what the girl herself is like?

Bhuwan—Money will conceal all her defects. Even if she curses me day and night, I won't complain. After all, who minds being kicked by the cow one is milking?

Babu Sahib's tone was approving—We have great sympathy with those people; we are sincerely grieved that Providence has cast them into such difficulties. But one must always let one's decisions be guided by reason. Even if we try to economize, we will still add up to quite a marriage party. And we can't even be certain of being fed properly when we get there. There can be no other outcome except our being exposed to public ridicule.

Rangili—You're completely alike, father and son. Both of you are eager to sacrifice that poor girl.

Bhuwan—The poor must only enter into relationships with other poor people. To aspire beyond one's status...

Rangili—Go on, you with your status! What makes you so wealthy then? If a poor man should arrive at your doorstep, he will not be offered even a glass of water. And you talk of status!

Saying this, Rangili got up and went off to attend to her kitchen arrangements.

Bhuwan Mohan went off smiling to his room and Babu Sahib came out stroking his moustaches in triumph, eager to tell Moteram of the final decision, but he was nowhere to be seen.

Moteramji had waited awhile for the servant to return from the market, but when he didn't return for a long time Moteram could wait no more. He realized that merely sitting there wouldn't be of much avail, he would actually have to do something about it. If I keep sitting here, trusting to my fate, I will die of starvation. Clearly, you'll never get anything just sitting here. He quietly picked up his stick and stepped out in the direction that the servant had taken. The shops were only a short distance away, and he was soon among them. He found the old fellow sitting calmly at a halwai's, smoking a clay-pipe. As soon as Moteram saw him, he said in a familiar tone of voice—Nothing's ready yet, is it? The master is getting all angry saying that the fellow has gone and got drunk on toddy somewhere. I said—'I'm sure that's not the case, sir. He's an old man, he will take a little time getting to the place and back again.' He's an odd fellow, I wonder how he manages to retain any servants.

The servant—I'm the only one who has stayed with him, and there won't be another. I haven't been paid for a whole year. He starts screaming the moment someone asks to be paid. The poor fellows simply run away. The two servants who were fanning him, they're both government employees—the government gives him two orderlies. That's why they're still with him. But I reason, he and I are two of a kind. I've been with him ten years, I'll last out another one or two the same way.

Moteram—So you're the only one? He calls out a lot of names.

The servant—All of them have come and gone in the last two or three months. But he keeps calling out their names to impress his visitors. Say, can you get me a job somewhere else?

Moteram—Jobs a-plenty, my dear fellow. Where does one find good servants these days? And then you're an experienced hand, you'll have no difficulty finding a job. Is there something fresh cooking here? Babu Saheb asked me, will you be cooking some khichri or should I get the man to make some baatis for you? But I said to him—He's an old man, why trouble him with cooking for me in the evening, I'll go and eat something in the bazaar. You needn't worry. So he said—Well that's all right, you'll find my servant at the shop. So, my dear man, speak up do you have some delicious things ready for me to eat? Your laddoos look fresh. Measure out one seer for me. Should I come up there myself and help you out?

Saying this, Moteramji hauled himself up into the shop and started tasting the man's wares. He gorged himself handsomely, as much as two and a half to three seers. He would interrupt his eating only to shower compliments on the halwai—Sahji, your shop lives up to its reputation in every way. The Banaras fellows can't make rasagullas like yours, though they make good kalakand. But yours isn't bad either. After all, it's not enough merely to add the right ingredients, one must have the art.

Halwai—Have some more, your honour. Have some rabri on my recommendation.

Moteram—I didn't wish to, but if you insist, let me have a pao of it.

Halwai—A pao is hardly enough. Have two at least.

After eating to his heart's content, Panditji took a little stroll in the bazaar and got back to the house around nine. Quiet reigned over the house. A single lantern was burning. He spread out his bedding on the terrace and fell asleep.

He got up the next morning at eight, as was his wont, and saw that the Babu Sahib was taking a stroll. Seeing him awake Babu Sahib greeted him respectfully and said—Maharaj, where had you gone off last night? I waited for you till late in the evening. All the foodstuffs were kept by, awaiting your return. When you didn't come back, they had to be put away. Did you get something to eat or not?

Moteram—I had a little something at the halwai's shop.

Bhalchandra—But how can all those fancy things compare with the simple delights of baati and daal cooked at home? You must have spent at least ten or twelve annas, and still not felt satisfied. But you're my guest, you must let me recompense you for all that you've spent.

Moteram—I ate at that same halwai's shop—the one who sits at the corner of your lane.

Bhalchandra—How much did you have to pay him?

Moteram—I asked him to add it to your account.

Bhalchandra—You should let me know what you had, otherwise the fellow will try and cheat me behind your back. He's a real crook.

Moteram—I had some two and half seers of sweets and half a seer of rabri.

Babu Sahib's eyes opened wide in astonishment, as if he'd heard something quite amazing. His monthly consumption never went up to three seers, and here this fellow had consumed some four rupees' worth on but one occasion! If he stays another day or so I will be bankrupted. What a devil's appetite he has! Three seers! Is there any limit to such eating! He ran into the house in an agitated state and said to Rangili—Have you heard, this fellow ate up three seers of sweets yesterday. A full three seers!

Rangili replied incredulously—Go on, how can he eat three seers. Is he a man or an ox?

Bhalchandra—Three seers is what he owns up to. He must have had full four seers!

Rangili—He must have a devil in his stomach.

Bhalchandra—If he stays today as well, he'll have another six seers for sure.

Rangili—So why should he stay today, let him have his reply and send him on his way. And if he stays, let him know plainly that we don't get our sweets for free. If he wishes to make khichri, he's welcome, otherwise he should be on his way. Let those who so wish, seek deliverance through feeding these gluttons, I have no use for such deliverance.

But Panditji was eager to be off anyway, so Babu Sahib did not have to use his persuasive skills.

Bhalchandra—So, are you ready to leave then?

Moteram—Yes, your honour, I must leave now. I'll get the nine o'clock train, won't I?

Bhalchandra—It would have been nice if you could have stayed another day at least.

Even as he said this, Babu Sahib was afraid the fellow might take him seriously, and so he finished his sentence thus—But of course they must be expecting you back at home.

Moteram—Well, one day is no great matter and in fact I'd intended to have a dip at the Triveni—but if you'll forgive me for saying this, you people don't seem to have the slightest respect for Brahmins. I have devotees who shadow my footsteps in the hope that I might ask them to do something for me. If I should arrive at their doorstep, they consider themselves blessed by fortune, and the whole household, old and young alike, instantly engages itself in providing me service and hospitality. I cannot stay even one moment in a place where I'm not treated with respect. Mark my words, a place where Brahmins are treated with disrespect can never prosper.

Bhalchandra—But Maharaj, surely we are guilty of no such offence!

Moteram—Not guilty! Just this minute you've returned after announcing to your wife that I've consumed a full three seers of sweets. But you haven't really seen real eaters yet—or else you'd know the difference. There are great eaters who can gobble up a full five seers and not even register the fact with a belch. People have to beg me to eat each single sweet, I'm induced with offers of money to eat even more. I'm not some begging Brahmin who awaits your generosity on your doorstep. I'd heard your great name, but little did I know I'd long even for a proper meal. Go away, may the Lord bless your endeavours.

Babu Sahib felt so embarrassed that he couldn't utter a word in his defence. He'd never been shouted at in that fashion. He tried to put up some feeble defence—It wasn't you we were talking about—but the Panditji was not to be mollified. All other insults he could stomach, but not an insult to his appetite. Men can as little suffer a derogation of their appetite as women can of their beauty. Babu Sahib was trying his best to make amends, but he was inhibited by his apprehension that the man might decide to stay. The camouflage had been removed from his stinginess, there was no doubt of that any more. It was essential to do something about it. He had tried his best but was unable to prevent the inevitable. He was kicking himself for having gone inside the house to report on the man's appetite, and for having done so in such a loud voice. And just when the rascal was eavesdropping! But there was little to be gained by feeling sorry now. He wondered what had brought this misfortune upon him. If he goes away in a huff now, he'll certainly malign me upon his return—and I'll stand exposed. I will have to shut him up somehow.

Thinking these dark thoughts he went inside again and said to Rangilibai—The rascal has overheard our entire conversation. He's going away in a huff.

Rangili—When you knew he was standing at the door, why didn't you whisper?

Bhalchandra—Alas, misfortune seeks one out—and it doesn't come singly either. How was I to know he was standing there with his ear to the door?

Rangili—Who knows what unlucky face it was, the very sight of which has brought this misfortune upon us.

Bhalchandra—It was this same rascal, lying out there. If I had known, I wouldn't have looked in his direction at all. Now I'll have to bribe him somehow.

Rangili—Let the man go, how does it matter now, since you don't wish to marry your son into that family anyhow? Let him think what he will!

Bhalchandra—This won't do. Give me ten rupees so that I give him a farewell gift. May the good Lord protect me from having to look at his ill-fated countenance again.

Rangili brought out ten rupees with great reluctance and Babu Sahib went and put them down at Panditji's feet. The Panditji said to himself—Skinflint that you are! You won't forget me easily. And you think you can fool me by offering me ten rupees. Don't delude yourself. I know your kind inside out.

But all he did outwardly was to give his blessings and go his way.

Babu Sahib stood there a long time, lost in thought—I wonder if he still thinks of me as a miser, or have I redeemed my reputation somewhat? Or have these rupees too been a futile offering, a mere waste?

# Chapter 4

K alyani now faced an insurmountable problem. This was her first bitter experience after the death of her husband. What greater misfortune can there be for a poor widow than that she should be saddled with a young, marriageable daughter? Boys can be sent barefoot to school, domestic chores one can do by oneself, one can still survive by eating ordinary, coarse foodstuffs, one can even live in a thatched hut if need be, but one cannot afford to keep a marriageable daughter at home. Kalyani felt so angry at Bhalchandra that she wanted to go personally and blacken his face with her hands, pluck out the hair from his scalp and say to him: You have gone back on your word, you misbegotten bastard. For Pandit Moteram had given her a full and detailed account of all that had transpired there.

She was seething with this anger when Krishna happened to pass by, busy at play, and asked casually—How many days will it be before the baraat comes, mother? Panditji has come back now.

Kalyani—Are you dreaming about the baraat then?

Krishna—That Chandar was saying the baraat would come in two or three days. Won't it, mother?

Kalyani—I've told you once, why d'you keep pestering me?

Krishna—There's going to be a baraat coming to everyone's house, mother, why can't we have one too, please?

Kalyani—Because an awful calamity has struck the fellow who was going to bring a baraat to your house. A huge fire...

Krishna—Really, mother? Then their house must have got destroyed. Where would they be staying then? And where will sister stay?

Kalyani—O you are stupid! You haven't understood a thing. The house didn't really catch fire. He just won't be getting married here now.

Krishna—Why, mother? It was all agreed upon already, wasn't it?

Kalyani—He wanted a lot of money. I didn't have that much to give him.

Krishna—Is he very greedy, mother?

Kalyani—What else? He's a heartless butcher, the traitor.

Krishna—Then it's just as well that sister isn't marrying him. How could she have lived with him? This is something to be happy about, why are you feeling so bad?

Kalyani looked at her daughter with affection in her eyes.

How true her words were. Her innocent words had laid bare the truth of the situation so artlessly. It was truly a matter for joy, not regret, that her daughter was not going to be joined in matrimony to such unworthy people. Who knows how Nirmala would have fared with such people? She would have cursed her ill luck. The merest extra drop of ghee in the daal, or too many left-overs, and her mother-in-law would have thrown a tantrum. But it's the boy himself that's greedy, she thought. It's much better this way, otherwise the poor girl would have had a lifetime of weeping. When Kalyani got up she was feeling better already.

But she had to get her daughter married anyway, and preferably within the year, else she would have to go through all the preparations again. It was no longer important to find a substantial household, nor even a particularly good bridegroom. An unfortunate widow could not even hope for such things! Now all she had to do was somehow shed this burden she had been saddled with, somehow see her daughter through to the other shore—throw her into a well, really. She was beautiful, talented, clever, well-born—no matter. If she doesn't bring a dowry, all her good qualities are just so many disabilities. With a dowry, disabilities are transformed into virtues. The bride herself may be worth nothing, her dowry is all that matters. What a hard destiny it is!

Kalyani herself is far from blameless. Being widowed and helpless doesn't absolve her from blame. She cares much more for her sons than she does for her daughters. Her sons are the prized draught-animals, the first right to the feed is theirs, the cows can have whatever is left over! She owned a house, she had some ready cash, jewellery worth thousands, but she still had to bring up her two sons, see them through their education. Another daughter will be ready to marry in another four or five years. This is why she cannot even think of giving a large sum of money as dowry; after all, the boys must get their due. Something substantial for which they will thank their father.

It was fifteen days since Pandit Moteram had returned from

Lucknow. The very day after returning, he set off again in quest of a potential bridegroom. He had sworn an oath that he would show those Lucknowwallahs there were others in the world besides them. Kalyani awaited his return impatiently. Today she had resolved she would write a letter to him, but she had barely sat down with pen and paper when Pandit Moteram appeared.

Kalyani—Welcome, Panditji, welcome. I was about to write a letter to you. When did you return?

Moteram—I got back this morning, but just then I got an invitation from a rich merchant. I hadn't eaten my fill for some days. So I thought I might as well attend to that while I was about it. I've just returned from the merchant's—there must have been at least 500 Brahmins feasting there.

Kalyani—Did you meet with any success, or was it a wasted journey?

Moteram—No success! How can you even suggest such a thing? I've begun negotiations with full five parties. I've brought their horoscopes. You can select any of those five. Consider this one, his father earns 100 rupees a month in the postal department. The son is still a college-going student. He's confident of getting a job, but there's no wealth in the family. Still, the boy does seem to have good prospects. The family's a respectable one. A mere two thousand rupees will seal the matter. Though they were asking for three.

Kalyani—Does he have any brothers?

Moteram—No, but he has three sisters, all three unmarried. The mother's still alive. Now look at this second one. The boy earns 50 rupees a month in the railways department. He has neither father nor mother. He's extremely good-looking and well-behaved, as well as being a healthy, athletic sort of young fellow. But the family is not respectable; it's rumoured his mother was some kind of masseuse. Some say she was a cook somewhere. His father was a clerk on some estate. There is a small landed estate in the family, but it's heavily mortgaged. You won't have to give anything there. About twenty years old.

Kalyani—I would have said yes if there hadn't been this blot on the family. But one can hardly swallow a fly knowingly.

Moteram—Consider this third fellow. He's the son of a zamindar. The estate's worth about a thousand annually. There's some farming also. The boy's not very educated, but he's clever in matters relating to litigation. He's a widower, his first wife died some two years ago. He has no child by her. Their life-style is not very elevated—they process a lot of their own produce.

Kalyani—Did he want dowry?

Moteram—Don't even ask! They wanted all of four thousand. Look at this fourth one. The man's a lawyer, about 35 years of age. He earns three or four hundred a month. His first wife's dead. He has three sons by her. He owns the house he lives in. And he's also bought some landed property. There's no talk of any dowry here.

Kalyani—What is the family like?

Moteram—Truly excellent, they're reported to be wealthy. Look at this fifth fellow. The father owns a printing press. The boy has studied till the B.A., but he works in the printing press. Age about eighteen. There's no other property except the press—but there's no burden of debt either. The family is neither very good nor very bad. The boy himself is both good-looking and of good character. But it'll take at least a thousand to settle this one, though they started with demanding three. Speak up, now, which bridegroom do you prefer?

Kalyani—Which one do you recommend?

Moteram—I like two of them. One is that chap in the railways, the other is the one with the printing press.

Kalyani—But you said that the first came from a dubious family?

Moteram—Well, there is that problem. Then let's go with the printing press fellow.

Kalyani—But where will we find the one thousand? And one thousand is only your estimate, after all. They might well demand more. And you're perfectly aware of our condition. It is mercy enough if we continue to have food to eat. Where will we find the money? The zamindar sahib wants four thousand, and the post office person also wants two. Let them be. That leaves the lawyer. Well, thirty-five isn't such a great age. Why don't we settle on him?

Moteram—Think it over carefully. I am of course at your service and will go and finalize a deal with whoever you choose. But don't let the one thousand put you off. That printing house boy is a gem. Your daughter will be happy with him. She's beautiful and talented, and he's handsome and well-behaved.

Kalyani—That's what I myself would prefer, but where will I find the money! Who's going to give us that kind of money? Is there some generous soul around? The scroungers have gone after taking all they could get, we don't see any of them now. Instead, they blame me for having turned them out. So why should I reach out for something I know is beyond my grasp? Who doesn't love their own children? And who wouldn't like to see them happy? But what if one is helpless? Put your trust in God and go finalize arrangements with the lawyer fellow. He is rather elderly, but matters of life and death are the prerogative of the Maker. A thirty-five-year-old man is hardly ancient. If the girl is destined to be happy, she'll be happy wherever she goes, and if she's destined to be miserable, she will be miserable, no matter what. My Nirmala is fond of children. She'll love his children as her own. Seek out an auspicious day and go ahead with the betrothal.

# Chapter 5

And so Nirmala was duly married off. She came to her husband's home. The lawyer sahib was called Munshi Totaram. He was a dark, stout man. He wasn't much older than forty, but the hard grind of the legal profession had turned his hair grey. He never had the time to get much exercise, so much so that he scarcely ever went even for a walk. As a consequence of all this he had developed a paunch. Though he was well built, he was constantly nagged by one complaint or another. Dyspepsia and piles were, of course, his constant companions. All in all, he lived a cautious, restricted life. He had three sons. The eldest, Mansaram, was sixteen, the second, Jiyaram, was twelve, and the youngest, Siyaram, was only seven. All three went to English schools. The only other woman in the house was the Vakil Sahib's widowed sister. She was mistress of the house. She was called Rukmini and she was over fifty years of age. There was no one in her in-laws' home that she could have moved in with. So she stayed with her brother on a permanent basis.

Totaram was an adept in the arts of conjugality. Whatever he lacked by way of natural abilities in the matter of making his wife happy, he tried to compensate for by giving her gifts. Though he was normally frugal, he daily brought Nirmala some gift or other. He seemed not to care how much expense he incurred on such things. There might be insufficient milk for the boys, but for Nirmala there were dried fruits, sweets, jams and conserves—she never lacked for anything. He had never in all his life been fond of going out for entertainment, but now, whenever he had a holiday he would take Nirmala out to the cinema, or the circus or the theatre. He would spend a certain amount of his valuable time sitting with her and listen to the gramophone.

But for some reason Nirmala felt hesitant sitting and talking and laughing with Totaram. This might well have been because just such a man had been a father to her, in whose presence she had appeared with her head bowed, feeling awkward and embarrassed about her body. Now someone of his years was her husband. She did not think of him in terms of love but as someone deserving of respect. She would spend a lot of energy trying to avoid meeting him, and the moment she saw him all her natural joyousness vanished.

Vakil Sahib's conjugal arts had taught him that the beloved should be plied constantly with romantic talk. He must declare his passion for her, this was the royal road to her affections. Therefore Vakil Sahib lost no opportunity to exhibit his love for her, but all this only inspired disgust in Nirmala. The very things which in the mouth of a young man would have sent her into raptures, pained her sharply when uttered by the Vakil Sahib. There was no spontaneity in them, no true passion, no exuberance, there was only pretence, and fraud, and dry, unfeeling words. She didn't mind the perfumes and the cosmetics, she didn't mind the entertainments, she didn't mind the dressing-up and the making-up, what she minded was the physical proximity of Totaram. She had no wish to reveal her youth and her beauty to him, because Totaram's weren't the right eyes to savour her charms. She considered him unfit for such appetites. It is the touch of the morning breeze that causes the bud to flower. Both of them, the breeze and the bud, have complementary appetites. But where was Nirmala to find her morning breeze?

By the end of the first month Totaram had made Nirmala his treasurer. Upon his return from the courts he would make over the day's earnings to her, and he imagined Nirmala would be overjoyed at the sight of so much money. Nirmala fulfilled her duties as treasurer with great diligence; she kept meticulous accounts; if there was a shortfall some day, she would ask him the reason. She discussed household matters with him in great detail because this was all she thought him good for. But as soon as he uttered anything even remotely flirtatious and playful, her face fell.

Everytime Nirmala dressed up in all her finery and stood in front of the mirror, admiring her radiant beauty, her heart would fill with longing and desire. She would be consumed with a burning sensation in her heart. She felt like burning the house down. She felt angry with her mother, of course; but her greatest anger was reserved for poor Totaram. This burning resentment was always with her. How could a dashing rider be content with a mere nag, what though walking be her only alternative? Nirmala's situation was that of just such a dashing horseman. She wished to ride in just that way and take pleasure in the very joyous lightning speed of her mount. But what could she hope for from the neighings of the nag, with its anxious, nervous gestures? She might for a few brief moments have been able to forget the truth of her condition, been cheered up by this or that, but Rukmini Devi didn't let her come anywhere near the children, as if she were some wicked witch who would actually devour the little creatures. Rukmini Devi possessed a temperament unique in all the world, it was impossible to divine what could make her happy, or even what annoyed her. The very thing that pleased her on one occasion could infuriate her on another. If Nirmala kept to her room she blamed her for being anti-social, but if she so much as climbed out on to the terrace and chatted with the maids, she would be cursed for being shameless and bringing dishonour to the family name. Why, she'll be dancing in the bazaar next, she declared! Ever since Vakil Sahib began entrusting Nirmala with the money, Rukmini had become determinedly critical of her. Obviously, it seemed to her, the end couldn't be too far away. The boys frequently needed money for something or other. When she controlled the finances she would fob them off with excuses, but now she sent them direct to Nirmala. Nirmala did not approve of the children eating frequently during the day and so would occasionally refuse to indulge them. And this provided Rukmini with an opportunity to deploy her verbal artillery—She's the mistress now, so the children must survive somehow. Poor motherless creatures, who will care for them now? Time was when they would happily devour many rupees' worth of sweets at one time, but now they must beg for pennies. On the other hand, if Nirmala irritatedly gave them whatever they asked, Rukmini would complain in the opposite vein—What's it to her, a mother would have explained to the children that they mustn't have too many sweets. If anything were to happen to the children, I will be the one to be blamed. If this were all, Nirmala might still have resisted retaliating. But the woman simply hounded Nirmala like the secret police. If she went to the terrace, Nirmala was suspected of casting glances at someone; if she spoke to the maid, she would certainly be slandering her, Rukmini. If she sent for something from the market, it was certainly some wasteful luxury. Rukmini was constantly trying to read Nirmala's letters and eavesdropping on her conversations. Nirmala lived in terror of her double-edged sword. So much so that, one day, she said to her husband—Why don't you please speak to your sister, why does she keep after me so.

Totaram reacted sharply—Has she been saying something to you then?

Nirmala—She's always saying something. It's impossible for me to so much as open my mouth without giving her offence. If it's the fact that I'm mistress of the house now that is causing her so much envy, then I request you to entrust the money to her, she's welcome to be the mistress. All I ask is that she let me live in peace.

Even as she said this, Nirmala started to weep. Totaram saw an excellent opportunity to demonstrate his love for Nirmala. He said—I'll deal with her today itself. I'll tell her bluntly that if she can keep her mouth shut she's welcome to stay here; if not, she'd better be on her way. After all, I'll say to her, she's not the mistress of the house, you are. She's there only for your assistance. If, instead of assisting you, she pesters you, there's no further need for her to remain. I'd thought the poor thing is a widow, alone in the world, all she'll do is eat a little food each day and so pass her days. If so many other servants can be supported in this fashion...she is after all my own sister. And then I needed a woman to look after my children, so I asked her to stay. But that doesn't mean that she has a right to rule over you.

Nirmala then said—She is constantly putting the children up to come and demand money from me on one pretext or another. And then they come and bother me endlessly. It's impossible for me to even lie down for a moment's rest. And if I scold them she throws a tantrum and says all kinds of things to me. She thinks I'm jealous of the children. God knows how much I love the children. After all, they're my children. So why would I be jealous of them?

Totaram was livid—If any of the children bothers you, beat him. I can see the boys have become very misbehaved. I'll send Mansaram off to boarding school. As for the other two, I'll fix them myself right away.

Totaram was leaving for the courts just then and so couldn't get started on the chastisement, but as soon as he returned from the day's work he said to Rukmini—Tell me sister, do you wish to continue staying in this house or not? If you wish to continue staying here, you had better learn to keep quiet. What right do you have to make life impossible for others?

Rukmini understood immediately that Nirmala had made her move—but she wasn't one to take such things lying down. For one, she was older, and then she had spent her entire life looking after the house and its inhabitants. Who then would dare to have her turned out? She was shocked by her brother's meanness. She spoke up—So you want me to become a maid then? If I have to live as a maid, I won't be a maid in this house. If it's your wish that someone be allowed to destroy everything in this house, and I should simply stand by and look; see someone straying, and do nothing about it; that I should keep my mouth shut and let some people do what they please and yet be no more than a clay image, then I must vehemently decline. What has happened to you that you are behaving in this fashion? All your wisdom and experience has gone out the window now that that chit of a girl has you in her grip. You've made no attempt to find out what might have happened—all she's done is jerk at your string, and like a faithful puppet you're ready to go to battle, sword in hand.

Totaram—I hear you're constantly finding fault with her, and taunting her about this and that. If you wish to teach her something, you must do so lovingly, with sweet words. Taunts often have completely the opposite effect, and instead of learning, people become resentful.

Rukmini—So that's your wish, that I shouldn't open my mouth about anything—all right, so be it. But don't tell me later that I sat by and did nothing, gave her no sane advice. If she finds my words so unpleasant, then am I out of my mind that I should speak to her? But it's a truth well known that you can no more plough a field with a short-statured bullock than you can expect these young brides to run households. So, I'll be waiting to see how this young one copes.

Just then, Siyaram and Jiyaram came back from school. As soon as they came in they went to their aunt and demanded food.

Rukmini said—Why don't you go and ask your new mother, I'm not allowed to open my mouth any more.

Totaram—If you both so much as dare go anywhere near her rooms, I'll break your legs. Seems you're determined to make mischief.

Jiyaram was a little bolder—All you do is threaten us, why don't you say anything to her? She never gives us any money.

Siyaram supported him in this—She says she'll snip off our ears if we bother her. Doesn't she, Jiya?

Nirmala called out from her room—When did I ever say I'd snip your ears off? Started lying already, have you?

Barely had he heard this than Totaram got hold of Siyaram's

ears and lifted him off the ground. The boy screamed aloud and began crying.

Rukmini ran and snatched the child from Totaram's grasp and said—Let him be, or do you want to kill the child? Shame on you! His ears are all red now. Truly, they say, a new wife makes a man blind. With such portents, I fear the worst for this house.

Nirmala was exulting inwardly over her triumph, but when Munshiji lifted the child up by his ears she couldn't restrain herself. She leapt to his rescue but Rukmini had beaten her to it. Rukmini declared protectively—First you cause all the mischief, and now you pretend to be concerned. When you have sons of your own, then perhaps you'll understand. What can you know of another's pain?

Nirmala—He's standing right here, why don't you ask him what mischief I've caused. All I said was that the boys repeatedly bothered me for money. If I've said a thing beyond that, may I be struck blind.

Totaram—I'm not blind, that I can't see what mischief these boys are up to. All three have become spoilt and wicked. As for the oldest one, I'll pack him off to boarding school right away.

Rukmini—You hadn't thought them wicked so far—so how come your eyes have suddenly become so much sharper?

Totaram—You're the one who has made them wicked and disrespectful.

Rukmini—So now I'm the source of all the trouble! Your home is being ruined because of me! Very well then, I'm leaving. They're your sons, you do with them as you please, kill them off if you will, I won't utter a word.

Saying this she stormed out. Seeing the suffering child, Nirmala was unable to restrain herself and clasped him to her bosom. Picking him up she took him to her room and kissed and cuddled him, but all this only made him cry all the more. His innocent heart was unable to detect in all this affection the maternal love of which fate had deprived him so cruelly. This wasn't love, only pity. This was something over which he had no real claim, only something that was bestowed on him as charity. His father had thrashed him earlier as well, when his mother was alive—but she hadn't clasped him to her bosom and cried. She had merely shown her displeasure by not speaking to him, until he himself forgot his sense of hurt and went running to her. He could understand being punished for mischief; what he couldn't understand was being cuddled after getting a beating. A mother's love can be hard, but that hardness is mixed up with affection. This love on the other hand had pity in it, it didn't have the hardness that is the secret index of a genuine closeness. After all, a healthy limb doesn't get special attention—but when that same limb becomes painful, special precautions are taken to protect it from accidental knocks and shocks. Nirmala's pitiful sobbing merely reminded the child of his motherless condition. He sat weeping a long time in Nirmala's lap, and weeping fell asleep there. Nirmala thought to put him down on the cot so he might sleep comfortably, but in his sleepy condition the boy put his arms around her neck and clung to her as if he were suspended over a deep abyss. Fear and anxiety distorted his little face. Nirmala picked the boy up again, she was unable to put him down on the cot. Holding the child in her arms at that moment was giving her a kind of satisfaction she had not known before. Today for the first time she was assailed by pangs of remorse, without which the path of duty remains forever unclear. She was able to see that path quite clearly now.

# Chapter 6

After this extravagant demonstration of his deep feeling for her that day, Munshi Totaram was confident he had secured an unshakeable hold on Nirmala's affections. Nirmala however, far from being drawn towards him, now ceased talking to him altogether in the casual, light-hearted manner which she had earlier adopted with him occasionally. Instead, she began devoting all her time to the care of the children. Every time he returned home he found her sitting with the children. Sometimes she would be feeding them, at other times helping them put their clothes on. Sometimes she would be playing with them, or telling them a story. Nirmala's thirsting heart, disappointed in the expectation of romantic love, turned to the children as a sort of solace. Spending time with them, taking care of them, laughing and playing with them provided some consolation to her denied maternal longings. Whenever she had to spend time with her husband Nirmala found she was overcome by feelings of awkwardness, and shame and loss of desire, so much so that she found herself wishing to run away. But the honest, simple devotion of the children gladdened her immensely. Initially, Mansaram was a little hesitant about coming near her—but now he too would sometimes come and sit with her. He was roughly the same age as Nirmala, though he was five years behind her in psychological development. Hockey and football constituted the sum of his world, they defined the field of his imagination as well as the whole teeming range of his feelings and desires. He was a handsome, cheerful and somewhat shy young man of slender build—and to him the family home was simply a place where he came in for his meals. For the rest, all his time was spent gadding about all over the place. Listening to him talk about his world of games and sports, for a little while Nirmala was able to forget her own anxieties. She would find herself longing for the days when she herself played with dolls and arranged their weddings—the days which were, alas, recent and still fresh in her memory.

Like many another solitary person, Munshi Totaram was a passionate soul. For a few days he devoted himself to taking Nirmala to all sorts of entertainments. But when he realized all this was unavailing, he returned to his solitary ways. After a whole day's worth of hard mental toil he longed for some light dalliance. But when he entered his garden of delights he found the flowers withered, the plants wilted, and dust swirling about in the flower-beds—and then he longed to ravage that garden altogether. He could not understand why Nirmala was so cold and unfeeling towards him. He tried all he could glean from the marriage manuals but without success. He was at a loss to figure out what he should do next.

He was sitting immersed in these thoughts one day when his classmate Nayansukhram came and sat with him, and after the usual greetings smiled and said—You must be having the time of your life. There's nothing like the embrace of a young wife to restore one's own youthful passion. You're a lucky fellow! Really, there's no better way to bring back one's lost youth than to marry again. Just think how irksome my existence is. My dear wife clings to me relentlessly, but I'm thinking of marrying a second time anyway. So, if you come to know of a likely bride, arrange it for me, please. I promise I'll give you paans made by her own hands by way of commission some day.

Totaram replied in a sombre tone—Beware, don't ever make that mistake, else you'll regret it. Young lasses need young lads, I tell you. You and I are no good for that purpose now. I tell you honestly, I'm sorry I got myself into this mess by marrying again. I'd thought I'd get a few more years to enjoy the pleasures of life—but I've ended up being worse off.

Nayansukhram—What're you saying! There's nothing to

gaining the affections of these wenches—just take them out a few times and praise their looks—and you have them eating out of your hands.

Totaram—I've tried all that. It's no good.

Nayansukhram—So, did you try perfumes, give her flowers, ply her with fancy food?

Totaram—Forget it. I've tried it all. I've tried all there is in the books. It's all bunkum.

Nayansukhram—Well then, I have one piece of advice for you. Get yourself a face-lift. There's a doctor here these days who treats people with an electric current—he can remove all signs of ageing from one's face. Not a wrinkle or gray hair escapes his ministrations. It's pure magic I tell you—making new men from old.

Totaram—How much does he charge?

Nayansukhram—I've heard he charges five hundred rupees!

Totaram—He must be some sort of trickster, I tell you, robbing fools of their money. He must use some oils or other to make one's complexion appear smooth. I've no trust in these sleazy doctors who advertise their wares on the back pages of magazines anyway. If it had been a small sum of money I might have gone along, just for a lark. But five hundred is a lot of money.

Nayansukhram—It's hardly a lot for you. It's only a month's earnings. I tell you, if I had five hundred I'd have gone in for it right away. An hour of youth is worth much much more than a mere five hundred rupees.

Totaram—Go on, tell me some cheaper remedy, some folk medicine or herb that will have the desired effect without demanding as much of me. As for electricity and radium, they'd better be left for the rich. They're welcome to all that.

Nayansukhram—Then prepare to play the part of the young gallant. Throw away this loose, ill-fitting coat of yours and get yourself a tight-fitting achkan made up in fine cloth, and a finely crinkled pair of pyjamas. You'll need a gold chain around your neck, a flashy Jaipuri turban on your head, you'll need surma in your eyes and oil of henna in your hair. And yes, you'll need to flatten your paunch. Get yourself a double-sized cummerbund. It'll be a little uncomfortable all right, but it'll show up the achkan to advantage. As for the hair-dye, I'll get it for you. Commit some hundred-odd ghazals to memory, and remember to recite a couplet or two when you get the chance. Let your talk be suffused with emotion and colour. Let it appear as though you haven't a thought for the cares of this world, that all your attention is focussed on but one object, and that's your beloved. Remain constantly on the lookout for situations in which you demonstrate your courage and manliness. Sometime during the night set up a false racket about thieves, and then single-handed, sword in hand, rise to her rescue. But make sure first that there's no real thief about, else you'll be exposed as a fool and coward. If there's ever a real thief about just stand quiet as a mouse, pretend you aren't there at all, but as soon as he goes away you should leap up sword in hand and demand to know the intruder's whereabouts. Just try this out for a month. And if in that time she doesn't start worshipping the very ground you walk on, demand from me what penalty you like.

Totaram laughed these suggestions off at the time, as was only proper for a worldly-wise fellow like him, but deep down some of the suggestions seemed, well, quite appealing really. And there was little doubt they would, in time, be adopted by him. He began them one at a time so people shouldn't notice too sudden a change. First it was the hair, then the surma for his eyes—and in a month or two he was a changed man. That suggestion about memorizing ghazals was farcical, but there was no harm in bragging about his courage from time to time. From that time he carefully set up situations, each day, in which he might boast about his courageous exploits, until Nirmala began to wonder if he was suffering from some form of clinical delusion. Considering he had been a man who was hypochondriac enough to depend on sundry medicaments even to help himself cope with the barest of bread and lentils, there were good grounds for Nirmala's suspicions of his new-found penchant for bravery. It was obviously too much to expect Nirmala to be impressed by these charades, but she did begin to pity him. Pity instead of anger and loathing. A sane person may deserve anger and loathing, but someone who is so obviously touched in the head deserves only pity. Every so often she would tease him and make fun of him, as people are wont to do with those out of their minds. But she took care to see he didn't actually catch on. She would suppose that the poor fellow was paying for his sins. After all, she thought, all this has become necessary only so that I might forget my misfortunes. But if I can't do anything to alter my fate, why should I torment the poor man?

One evening Totaram returned from his gallivantings at around nine, very much the gallant, and said to Nirmala—I found myself face to face with three rogues today. I'd stepped out in the direction of Shivpur, and it was dark of course. As soon as I got to the road near the rail track, three fellows armed with swords appeared suddenly. Believe me, all three were fearsome dark fellows. And I was all alone with only this walking stick in my hand. And those three against me, armed with swords. I thought then my time was up, but I thought if I had to die anyway I'd at least die a hero. Just then, one of them challenged me—Give up whatever you've got and slip away quietly or else.

I steadied my stick and said—All I have is this one stick, and it's worth at least one man's head.

I'd barely uttered these words when all three fell upon me with their swords. I fended off their blows with my stick. They attacked me furiously, there'd be a loud report, and I would react like lightning to ward off the attack. For some ten minutes those three tried all their skills with their swords and didn't succeed in as much as giving me a scratch. The only pity of it is I didn't have a sword with me. Otherwise not one of them would have survived. But how can I even hope to describe my exploits? My skill and reflexes beggar all description. I amazed even myself with all that agility. When the three of them realized they'd met their match, they sheathed their swords and patted me on the back in congratulation—Brave one, they said, we've never come across a fighter like you. The three of us happily loot villages of more than three hundred inhabitants in broad daylight, but you've worsted us today. We salute you. And with those words they disappeared.

Nirmala replied in all seriousness, albeit with a smile—There must be many sword-marks on this stick?

Munshiji was unprepared for this, but realized he had to say something—I kept foiling them each time. On a couple of occasions, when they did manage to hit my stick, all they gave were glancing strokes incapable of leaving a mark.

He hadn't quite finished saying this when Rukmini Devi burst into the room, wildly excited and panting for breath—Tota, where's Tota. There's a snake in my room. He's somewhere under my bed. I've run away. He must be full two yards long. He's spread his hood and is breathing out poisonous fumes. Come with me please, and bring your stick!

Totaram's face went ashen, he began to shake with fright, but he concealed his feelings and said—Snake, where's the snake? I'm sure you're mistaken. Must be a rope.

Rukmini—I tell you, I've seen it with my own eyes. Why don't you come and see for yourself? Shame on you, a man and afraid!

Munshiji did leave the room but stopped again on the verandah. He was quite unable to move further. His heart beat wildly. A snake is a very irritable creature, he thought, and if he bites me it'll surely be the end of me. What he said was—I'm not afraid. It's only a snake, not a tiger. But a stick's not effective with a snake. Let me go and send someone with a spear.

With these words Munshiji stepped out briskly. Mansaram was sitting at his meal. Munshiji having gone away, he pushed his uneaten food aside, picked up his hockey stick and, rushing into the room, pulled the cot aside. The snake was ready for combat, and instead of slinking away reared itself up with its hood on full display. Mansaram quickly stripped the sheet off the bed and threw it over the snake—and then registered three or four smart blows. The snake struggled and died within the sheet. Then he picked it up on his stick and made to leave. Munshiji was now returning with several people in tow. Seeing Mansaram approach with a dead snake on his stick, Munshiji screamed aloud. But he controlled himself and said—I was hurrying back anyway, why did you rush in and do this? Let someone go and throw it away.

With these words he went bravely and positioned himself at Rukmini's door, and after carefully inspecting the room he stroked his moustaches proudly and said to Nirmala—By the time I could rush back Mansaram had already killed the snake. He's a foolish boy, rushed in with a stick. A snake must always be killed with a spear. That's the trouble with boys. I've killed any number of snakes this way. One must play a snake properly before killing it. Many times, I've simply crushed them to death with my bare hands.

Rukmini was sceptical—Go away, we've all seen how brave you are!

Munshiji was embarrassed—Oh well, at least I'm not asking you for a reward. Go and tell the cook to serve my dinner.

Munshiji went for his meal and Nirmala leaned against the door-frame pensively, thinking to herself—God! Has he really contracted some dreadful illness? Lord, do you wish to make my condition even more pathetic? I can look after him, respect him, devote my entire life to his service, but I cannot do that which I cannot do. It's not in my power to wipe out the difference between our ages. What is it he wants from me? Ah, if only I had figured this out earlier, he wouldn't have had to go to all this trouble and mount this elaborate charade.

# Chapter 7

After that day Nirmala's entire attitude and behaviour began to change. She had decided to sacrifice herself henceforth wholly to familial duty. So far, obsessed with her own despair, she had not given adequate thought to her obligations. There was a furious rage building up within her whose violence had almost taken possession of her entire being. But when her own grief began to abate she realized with a kind of cold clarity that she had no realistic expectation of happiness in her own life. Why then should she ruin herself by going on dreaming of a happiness which she knew to be impossible? After all, she reasoned, not all God's creatures are destined to be happy. I too am one of the unfortunates. I've been chosen by God to carry a burden of misery. It isn't open to me to shed that load. Even if I should wish to shake it off, I won't be able to. What though that burden should cause me to become faint, or break my back, or even if it should become impossible for me to move another step—yet I must keep on keeping on.

One who is sentenced to life imprisonment cannot afford to go on crying. And even if she should, who will heed her? Who will waste their pity on her? She'll cause herself trouble and only stand to increase her suffering by persisting with an endless grief.

When Vakil Sahib got back from the court the next day he found a smiling Nirmala at the door, eager to welcome him upon his return. That flawless vision was enough to satiate his thirsting eyes. After many a long day, today he was favoured with seeing the lotus bloom. There was a large mirror on one of the walls of his room. Normally, there was a curtain in front of that mirror. Today, the curtain was no longer in place. As soon as he stepped into the room he noticed the mirror and was able to see his own face with great clarity. His heart sank at the sight. After a whole day at the courts his face had lost its glow anyway; further, despite the various different tonics and revitalizers he consumed, the wrinkles on his face were only too evident. Despite a tight corset his paunch was thrusting outwards. Nirmala too was clearly visible in the mirror. And what a difference there was between their two countenances! One was a gem-studded palace, the other a broken-down ruin. He was unable to keep his eyes on the mirror. His own palpable inferiority was unbearable to him. He removed himself from his position in front of the mirror, hating himself for the way he looked. There was nothing surprising, after all, in that young and desirable beauty regarding him with disgust. He was unable to keep his gaze fixed on Nirmala's face. Her very beauty had suddenly become a cause of pain and suffering to him.

Nirmala said—What took you so long today? My eyes are weary with looking out for you all day.

Totaram looked in the general direction of the window and said—These cases leave me no time to call my own. There was yet another case to be heard today. But I pleaded a headache and made my escape.

Nirmala—So why d'you take on so many cases? One should work only as much as one can conveniently. There's no point in killing oneself. Don't take on so much work. I'm not greedy about money. If you keep well and healthy, there'll be money enough and to spare.

Totaram—But one can hardly turn away the goddess of wealth.

Nirmala—If this goddess comes bearing gifts of blood and suffering, then it would be better if she didn't come. I'm not at all greedy about money.

Just then Mansaram got back from school. Walking in the hot sun had brought out beads of perspiration on his ruddy, handsome face, and his eyes were glowing. He stood at the door and said— Please, mother, give me something to eat. I have to go out and play.

Nirmala brought him a glass of water and some dried fruits on a plate. When Mansaram started to leave after eating, Nirmala asked him—By what time will you return?

Mansaram—I can't say. There's a hockey match with the whites. The barracks are very far away.

Nirmala—Do come back soon. If the dinner gets cold you'll declare you've lost your appetite.

Mansaram looked at Nirmala with simple affection in his eyes and said—If I should get late, you may suppose that I'm eating somewhere else. There's no need to wait up for me.

After he went away Nirmala said—Earlier he didn't so much as enter the inner rooms and would feel shy talking to me. If he ever needed anything he'd send for it. He's started coming in ever since I made a point of speaking to him.

Totaram declared with some irritation—Why does he come to you when he needs food and drink? Why doesn't he ask my sister?

Nirmala had said what she had said with the intention of earning some praise. She wanted to show Totaram how much she loved his children. And it wasn't even as if this affection was artificial. She felt a genuine fondness for the boys. In fact, in many respects she was herself still a child—she had the same playfulness, the same eagerness, the same innocent love of enjoyment, and being with the children brought these aspects of her being to their full flowering. She was entirely unaware of the envy that normally possesses wives. But she was also unable to read her husband's unexpected frown instead of the anticipated appreciation, and replied innocently—How should I know why they don't go to her; but I can hardly shoo them away when they come to me. And if I did, it would be said I'm jealous of your sons.

Munshiji did not reply to this; but instead of dealing with his clients, he went directly to Mansaram and starting quizzing him on his studies. This was the very first time he had taken so much interest in the education of any of his children. He had never so much as had the time to look up from his work. And then it was nearly forty years since he had last had anything to do with those subjects. Ever since, he hadn't even glanced in their direction. He read nothing except legal books and papers: he never had the time to. But now he decided to examine Mansaram in those very subjects. Mansaram was both clever and hardworking. Even though he was captain of the school 'B' team, he managed to stand first in class. He only had to read a lesson once to master it forever. In his impatience Munshiji was hardly able to come up with such deep and searching questions as might give an intelligent boy some pause, and Mansaram was able to deal with the superficial questions only too easily. In the same way as a swordsman is infuriated to see his opponent evade all his strokes lightly and is driven to striking ever more violently, so Munshiji was maddened by Mansaram's prompt, correct answers. He wanted to ask a question that the boy would not be able to deal with, he desired to find some weakness in his preparation. The questions the boy was able to tackle gave him no joy at all. What he was looking for was something that would flummox the boy. An experienced examiner would have easily spotted and revealed Mansaram's weaknesses. But how was Munshiji going to manage all that on the basis of his forgotten half-century-old learning? Finally, when he could find no other way to vent his anger, he said—I see that you spend whole days wandering about here and there aimlessly. I'm more concerned about your character than I am about your intelligence. And I disapprove strongly of your loafing about in this way.

Mansaram replied fearlessly—All I do is go out for one hour in the evening to play. You can confirm this from both Amma and from Buaji. I'm not fond of loafing about aimlessly. As for the school games, the headmaster himself insists that I come, so I can hardly refuse. But if my going out to play in the evening is not acceptable to you, I'll stop going out from tomorrow.

When Munshiji realized that the conversation was taking an unexpected turn, he said sharply—How am I expected to believe you're not going out somewhere other than to play? I hear complaints.

Mansaram replied angrily—Who has dared to complain against me?

Totaram—How is that to the point? You must know that I would not repeat a false accusation.

Mansaram—If you find anyone who can accuse me to my face that they've seen me loafing about, I'll stop going out altogether.

Totaram—Why should anyone be bothered to do that and earn your enmity? You have gone around with some of your friends and broken the roof-tiles on this man's house. In fact, I've heard this kind of complaint from not one but several people. And there's no reason for me to disbelieve my friends. I desire that you should henceforth live in the school itself.

Mansaram lowered his head and replied—I have no objection to staying there. I'll go whenever you tell me to.

Totaram—Why are you unhappy at the thought of living there? As if it isn't nice staying there. It seems you're horrified at the thought of staying there. What's the matter, what specific problem have you got with staying there?

Mansaram wasn't keen on shifting to the hostel—but when Munshiji voiced that same feeling and asked him the reason for it, he had no way to cover himself except by declaring with apparent cheerfulness—Why should I be unhappy? It's all the same to me whether I'm at home or in the boarding house. There'll be no great problem, and even if there is, I can put up with it. I will go away tomorrow. Of course, if there's no room there, there might be a difficulty.

Munshiji was a lawyer and understood immediately that the boy was searching for some excuse whereby he could get out of going to the hostel and yet evade all his chidings. He said—Why, when there's room for all the other boys, shouldn't there be room for you?

Mansaram—Any number of boys fail to get accommodation

in the hostel and are forced to rent rooms in the city. Recently there was one vacancy in the hostel and fifty applications for that one room.

Vakil Sahib didn't see much point in wasting his time trading arguments with the boy. He merely told Mansaram to prepare himself to leave the next day, ordered the carriage to be brought round, and went off on his evening visits. He had lately taken to going out on pleasure outings every evening: some experienced soul had told him this was the most effective way of ensuring his longevity. After he left Mansaram went inside and informed his aunt Rukmini—Father has told me to move to the school hostel tomorrow, Buaji.

Rukmini was puzzled—But why?

Mansaram—How should I know? He simply declared I was getting spoilt staying at home, loafing about here and there all day.

Rukmini—Didn't you tell him that wasn't true?

Mansaram—Of course I did, but he didn't believe me.

Rukmini—All this must be the doing of your new mother, of course.

Mansaram—No, Buaji, I don't suspect her. She never says anything at all. If I ask her for anything, she gives it to me immediately.

Rukmini—What d'you know of women's wiles—I'm sure this fire is of her making. Wait, let me go ask her.

Rukmini went to Nirmala in a high rage. She could hardly pass up such a wonderful opportunity to accuse Nirmala, upbraid her, chastise her, lacerate her with carefully chosen taunts, make her weep. Nirmala on the other hand held her in respect and deferred to her, didn't talk back. She kept hoping that Buaji would speak words of wisdom, correct her when she made mistakes, and generally oversee everything, but Rukmini was constantly tense and angry with her.

Nirmala got up from her cot and said—Come, Didi, come and sit down.

But Rukmini replied standing upright—Will you not be content until you've driven everyone out of this house?

Nirmala asked hesitatingly—What happened, Didi? I haven't said anything to anyone?

Rukmini—You're throwing Mansaram out of the house, and you can still say you haven't said anything to anyone? Is even this little sharing too much for you to bear?

Nirmala—I swear by your feet, Didi, I know nothing of what you're saying. May I lose my eyes if I've so much as opened my mouth on this subject to anyone.

Rukmini—Why do you swear in vain? Till this day Totaram never said a word to the children. When Mansaram went away to his grandparents for a week he was so anxious he went and fetched the boy back. Now he's turning that same Mansaram out of the house and putting him in the school hostel. If the boy comes to the slightest harm, I'll hold you personally responsible. He's never lived away from the house, he can hardly remember to feed and clothe himself—he stretches out and goes to sleep wherever he happens to find himself. He may be technically a young man, but he's really still a boy. That hostel will be the death of him. Why should anyone there bother with whether he's eaten, or changed, or where he's sleeping? Indeed, when he can't get that attention even at home, how can he expect someone in the hostel to care? I have given you due warning, for the rest it's between you and your conscience.

Having said this much, Rukmini went away.

As soon as Vakil Sahib returned from his evening's outing Nirmala took up the subject with him. She was taking a few English lessons from Mansaram these days—wouldn't those suffer if the boy were sent away? Where would she find another tutor? This was the first that Vakil Sahib was hearing of these lessons. Nirmala had planned to surprise him by talking in English when she had picked up some practice. A little of course she had picked up from her own brothers. But now she was taking regular lessons. Vakil Sahib felt a sharp pang of jealousy when he heard this, and he asked with an angry frown on his face—How long has he been teaching you then? You never told me this.

Nirmala had known him in this mood only once before, when he had beaten Siyaram till the boy was nearly dead. Now she sensed that same mood in an even more ugly form. She said timidly—It doesn't interfere with his studies, I only study with him when he's free. I tell him that if my lessons are interfering with his work, he should go away. Oftentimes, I stop him for ten minutes just when he's leaving to go out and play. I myself want that his work shouldn't suffer.

There was nothing very much the matter, but Vakil Sahib felt overcome by hopelessness and took to his bed, consumed with anxiety. Things had gone far beyond what he had expected. He felt angry with himself for not having taken steps to remove the lad earlier. Now I understand the reason why her ladyship appears so happy these days. The room had never been arranged so carefully earlier, nor had she taken any great care over her appearance, but now I can see all that is changed utterly. He felt angry enough to want to go directly and turn Mansaram out of the house, but experience told him that anger at the present juncture would be ill advised. If the boy grasps anything of what is going on inside my head, it'll be a calamity. He decided he would feel out Nirmala's thoughts on the matter instead. He said—Of course I know that spending a few minutes teaching you will not really harm his studies, but he is a wayward boy, and doing that little gives him an excuse not to do his own work. If he fails in the examination tomorrow, he will directly say—I spent whole days teaching her. I'll employ some Christian woman for you instead. It won't cost a great deal. But you never told me this before. And what could he have taught you anyway? He would simply have dashed off after a little bit of this and that. You'll never learn anything that way.

Nirmala was quick to refute that accusation—No, that's not really true. He used to teach me with great devotion, and there's something about his manner of teaching that makes it very agreeable. You should see him at it some day. I don't think that any old Christian woman could do it that diligently.

Munshiji was pleased at his clever questioning—Does he teach you once a day, or several times?

Nirmala still didn't understand just where these questions were tending. She said—Earlier he used to teach me once in the evening, but lately he's been coming around once more in order to check out my writing. He was saying he's the best student in his class. In fact, he's come first in the recent examination, so why d'you suppose he's not sincere about his studies? I say this particularly because Didi will inevitably suppose it is I who am responsible for this turn of events. And I'll have to suffer her taunts for no reason at all. She was here just a short while back, threatening me.

To himself, Munshiji said—I understand you perfectly. You little chit of a girl, you think you can fool me? You want to achieve your purpose by laying the responsibility on Didi. What he said out loud was—I can't understand why the boy is so terrified at the thought of being sent to boarding school. Other boys might have been pleased at the thought of being with their friends, but this fellow's weeping. Earlier, he'd been working hard at his studies, and that's the reason why he stood first, but lately he's taken to loafing around. If I don't do something about correcting that right away, it will soon be too late. I will employ a 'miss' for you.

The next morning Munshiji emerged from his room fully dressed for the day. Several of his clients were waiting for him in the sitting-room, one of these a Raja Sahib who was worth several thousand rupees annually to Munshiji. But Munshiji left him sitting there, merely promising to be back in ten minutes. He ordered his carriage and went off to see the headmaster of the school. The headmaster was a gentleman, and was courteous and welcoming to Vakil Sahib, but there wasn't a single place available in the hostel. All the rooms were taken. The inspector had issued strict instructions that students from the adjacent rural areas had to be accommodated before city students could be considered.

Therefore, even if a place were to fall vacant, Mansaram was not likely to get it because there were any number of rural applications pending. Munshiji was a lawyer, and was used to dealing day in and day out with people who would, for reasons of avarice, make the impossible possible, the unfeasible eminently feasible. He thought he could achieve his ends by some discreet bribery. He decided he would talk it over with the dealing clerk. But the clerk just laughed off the suggestion—This is not the law-courts, Munshiji, this is a school. If the headmaster gets wind of any of this, he'll lose his shirt and turn Mansaram right out of the school. He might even make a complaint to the senior officers.

Munshiji had no option but to retreat shamefacedly. He returned home around ten feeling deeply frustrated. Just then Mansaram emerged ready to go to school. Munshiji looked at him with cold, baleful eyes, as if he were an enemy, and went inside the house.

After this, for the next ten or twelve days, Vakil Sahib made it his daily business to meet the headmaster of some school or other, morning and evening, and seek to find a hostel place for Mansaram. But there wasn't a single place to be had—and he was told so in plain terms. Now there were only two alternatives remaining—either he could rent separate accommodation and put Mansaram there; or send Mansaram to a school somewhere else. Both these alternatives were easy enough. There were vacant places a-plenty in distant, provincial schools. But of late Munshiji's acute suspicions had been somewhat allayed. Because from that day on, he had never once seen Mansaram entering the inner rooms. Nor even going out to play. Before he went out to school, and after he came back, he kept entirely to his own room. These were hot summer days, and streams of perspiration ran off one even in the open air, but Mansaram, deeply hurt about the charge of loafing about and eager to be absolved of it, never once left his room.

One day Munshiji was eating when Mansaram happened to emerge from his bath. It had been months since Munshiji had seen the boy without his clothes on. What he saw today shocked him to the core. Standing there before him was a mere skeleton. The face was still radiant with the glow of virginity, but his body had wasted away. He asked—Aren't you well? Why have you become so weak?

Mansaram covered himself quickly and said—I'm quite well.

Munshiji—Then why have you become so weak?

Mansaram—I'm not weak. And when was I fat anyway?

Munshiji—Go on, you're a mere shadow of your former self and you say you haven't lost weight? Tell me, Didi, was he always like this?

Rukmini was watering the tulsi in the courtyard—Why should he be any thinner, he's being looked after very well lately, isn't he? I was only a rustic housekeeper, I didn't know how to look after the boys properly. I was ruining them with snacks from roadside vendors. But now there's a clever, educated person who lavishes the utmost attention upon them. So how could he have lost any weight!

Munshiji—Didi, you're being unfair. Who's ever accused you of neglecting the children? In fact, you should yourself take up the tasks that others can't perform. It's hardly proper that you should have no more to do with the running of this house. After all, how can someone who's only a girl look after the boys. That's a job for one such as you.

Rukmini—Till the time I thought it was my job, I did it. But when you yourself have turned stranger to me, why should I insist on my closeness to you and yours? Ask him, when did he last have any milk? Go and check his room out yourself and you'll find the sweetmeats that were sent to him for breakfast are still there, rotting. The lady thinks her job is done when she's provided him the necessary things to eat—why should it be any concern of hers whether the person actually eats them or not? But then, brother, one might be able to raise children in that way if they've never known love and affection. Your sons have always been treated with the utmost love and attention, so how can they be expected to be happy being treated as orphans today? I'm a plain-speaking sort. And anyway, what reason have I got to fear anyone's displeasure? And now I hear you're making arrangements to send the boy off to boarding school. The poor boy doesn't even have the permission to be in his own home any longer. He's afraid to be seen visiting me, but just consider, what private means have I got that I might feed him stealthily?

Just then, having eaten a mere two chapatis, Mansaram got up after having finished his meal. Munshiji asked him sharply— Have you finished eating? You'd sat down to eat a mere one minute ago. So what have you eaten apart from the two chapatis you were served initially?

Mansaram replied hesitatingly—Well, there was daal and vegetables too. My throat hurts if I eat too much, I get acidity.

Munshiji was in a state of deep anxiety when he rose after finishing his meal. If the boy keeps losing weight at this rate he will fall prey to some deadly illness. He was feeling extremely angry with Rukmini right now. She is jealous because she's no longer the mistress of the household. But she doesn't enquire as to why she should have any rights to be the mistress of the household. How can someone who can't do even the simplest accounts be the mistress of such a household? After all, she was the mistress for all of one year—and there wasn't a single pai worth of savings. Roopkala was able to save two hundred to two-fifty on the same earnings. But with Rukmini they barely sufficed for current expenditure. No matter, but an excess of indulgence has spoilt my children. So why do grown-up boys need to be fed by someone anyway? They should be able to look after themselves.

Munshiji spent the whole day wracked by these worries. He even talked about it with a few of his friends. They said—Don't try to obstruct his sports activities. Don't confine him right now, there's less likelihood of his coming under bad influences in the open air than in being cooped up. Preserve him from bad company all right—but not to the extent of forbidding his going out altogether. In fact solitude is greatly destructive of adolescent character.

Now Munshiji realized his own mistake. When he returned home he sought Mansaram out. He'd just got back from school, and without having changed his clothes was lying with a book open in front of him, staring out of the window. His gaze was fixed on a beggar woman with a baby in her arms. And although she was begging, the child was just as pleased as if he were ensconced on a throne. The mere sight of this brought tears to Mansaram's eyes. Isn't that child happier by far than me? What is there in the whole wide world, he thought, that he wouldn't willingly exchange at this moment for his mother's lap? Not even God can create such a thing. Why does he cause children to be born who are destined to be deprived of their mothers? Who is there in the world more unfortunate than I? Who cares what I eat or drink, or whether I live or die? If I should die today, who will grieve? Father now derives pleasure from making me weep, he doesn't even wish to see my face, he's actively taking steps to turn me out of the house! O mother, your much-loved son is accused of being a gadabout and loafer today. That same father to whose care you entrusted your three sons is today accusing me of being a rogue and a vagabond. I'm not fit even to live in this house any longer. Overcome with these thoughts Mansaram broke into tears, sobbing loudly.

Just then, Totaram walked into the room. Mansaram wiped away his tears quickly and stood before him, head bowed. This was perhaps the very first time that Munshiji had stepped into his son's room. Mansaram's heart was beating wildly with anxiety over the new trouble this visit would bring. For an instant, seeing the boy in tears, Munshiji's parental affection was roused from its deep slumber. He asked anxiously—Why are you crying, my son? Has someone said something to you?

Mansaram controlled his gathering tears with some difficulty and said—No, I'm not crying, not at all...

Munshiji—Has your mother said something to you then?

Mansaram—No, she hardly ever speaks to me.

Munshiji—What can I do, my son? I married her in the hope

that I would get a mother for my children, but that hope has been dashed. So, she never speaks to you, does she?

Mansaram—No, she hasn't spoken at all to me the past several months.

Munshiji—She's a strange woman. It's impossible to discover what she wants. Every day she comes up with some new difficulty. She's the one who complained to me that you used to wander about God knows where all day. But how was I to know what was lurking in her heart? So, I inferred you had fallen into bad company and might really be wandering about all day. And how can a father not be upset seeing his own dear son turn into a vagabond? That's the reason I decided to send you to boarding school. That was all there was to it, my son. It's not as if I wanted to put a stop to your athletic activities. It breaks my heart to see you in this condition. It was only yesterday that I discovered I'd made a mistake. Please resume your sports and games by all means, go out morning and evening if you desire. The fresh air can only do you good. And if you ever need anything, let me know directly. You've no need to ask her for anything. Just act as if she isn't present in the house at all. So what if your mother is gone, you still have me.

The boy's innocent heart filled with joy at being treated with paternal affection. He felt as if he was in the presence of God himself. In his despair and his bitterness he had called his father unfeeling and who knows what else, in his heart. Against his stepmother he'd had no complaints. But now he realized how unjust he had been to his god-like father. He was overcome by a surge of filial devotion and fell at his father's feet, weeping, and then wept some more with his head resting there. Munshiji too was overcome with a feeling of deep pity. This was the same son whose absence, even when brief, had filled his heart with impatience; the same son whose courtesy and intelligence and character were widely praised by relatives and strangers alike. How could he have become so hard-hearted in respect of that son? He'd come to think of his own son as his enemy and had decided to send him into exile. Nirmala had become like a wall standing between father and son. In order to pull Nirmala closer to him he had to step back, and every time he did so the distance between father and son grew ever greater. So much so that, today, he was forced to resort to deceit with his own dear son.

Today, after much thought, he has thought of a way in which he hopes to remove Nirmala from her position between them, and bring her around to his other, free, side. In fact he has already started working on that plan. But who knows if he will achieve his desired goal?

From that very day when, despite Nirmala's entreaties and persuasion, Totaram decided to send Mansaram to the hostel, she had stopped taking lessons from Mansaram. She'd even stopped talking to him. She sensed something of what lay behind her husband's distrustful insistence. Really, what a suspicious mind he had! May God protect the honour of such a house. His mind is full of such filthy imaginings. And he supposes that I too am a degenerate creature. Caught up in these thoughts, she spent many days weeping. She asked herself, why does he have such suspicions in his head? What is there in me that strikes him in this fashion? Despite wracking her brain she was unable to think of reasons. So, was her taking lessons from Mansaram, and chatting and joking with him, at the root of his suspicions? Then she would stop taking lessons, she wouldn't so much as speak to Mansaram—no, she wouldn't so much as see his face.

But she found these vows difficult to keep. Talking to Mansaram, joking with him, was strangely exciting and gratifying to her pleasure-loving temperament. Talking with him she felt a deep enjoyment, one she found impossible to describe in words. There was no improper feeling involved in this. She couldn't dream of any sort of illicit relationship with Mansaram. But every person desires the company of his fellows, harbours an indescribable longing for their companionship, and it was this longing which, unknown to her, gave her satisfaction in his company. Now that unsatisfied longing began to burn in Nirmala's heart like a lamp. Lost to all the world, she would wander around as if in quest of some secret thing. She would walk here and there, she would sit still for hours, and yet be unable to concentrate on anything at all. Except that whenever Munshiji happened to come by, she would swiftly suppress her longings in despair and chat with him smilingly about this and that.

The next day, when Munshiji left for the courts, Rukmini made good use of the opportunity to lacerate Nirmala with her taunts—So when you knew that you would have to look after children here why didn't you tell your family members not to marry you off here? You should have been married off where there was no one except the man himself. He would have been pleased with all this careful grooming, this carefully nurtured image—he would have blessed his luck. How will this old man here be taken in by your looks, your demeanour, your winning ways? He married you to provide himself with someone to look after these children, not for sensual pleasures. She kept on tormenting Nirmala in this fashion for long, but Nirmala said nothing at all in response. She would have liked to explain her own conduct but she could not. If she'd said she was only doing what her husband desired, she would be revealing that which should remain private between her and her husband. If, on the other hand, she accepted her own fault in the business and sought to remedy its ill-effects, she was afraid of where the consequences might lead. Normally, she was of a frank and forthright nature, unafraid of speaking the truth, but the delicacy of her present situation forced her to stay quiet. There was no alternative to silence at this juncture. She could see that Mansaram was both withdrawn and sad; she could also see he was getting weaker by the day. But her lips were sealed, her actions banned. Nirmala's embarrassed condition at this moment was that of a thief who has himself been robbed.

# Chapter 8

I t's only when something happens against our expectations that we are grieved by it. Mansaram had never expected that Nirmala, of all people, would accuse him behind his back. Which is why he was in great anguish. Why, he wondered, does she carry tales about me? What does she really want? Could it be simply that I consume her husband's earnings, that her money is spent on my education, my clothes? What she really wants, most likely, is that I shouldn't stay in this house. If I'm not around, she'll be able to save some of her money. She's always seemed very happy with me. Never said a harsh word to me. So was that all a deception? Is it possible? The fowler must tempt birds with grain before he lays nets to ensnare them. Ah! I hadn't realized that under the grain the nets had been laid. All that show of maternal affection was a mere prelude to my expulsion.

All right then, he reasoned with himself, why doesn't she like my staying here? This man who is her husband, is he not also my father? Is the relationship between father and son any less close than that between husband and wife? If I am not envious of the undisputed superiority of her status—she may do as she pleases, I don't utter a word—then why does she wish to deprive me of my father's love? Can she not tolerate someone else getting even a finger's breadth of land in her empire? Even as she lives in her palace, can she not bear even to see me sitting in the modest shade of a tree?

Yes, she must think that once I grow up I'll inherit her husband's property, so it would be best to be rid of me right away. But how am I to reassure her she has nothing to fear on my account? How am I to tell her that I, Mansaram, would rather eat poison and kill myself than do anything to hurt her? Let her know that no matter how many hardships he has to bear himself, Mansaram will never allow himself to become a thorn in her flesh? Though it is, of course, the case that my father is responsible for my birth—and regards me with considerable affection even now. But am I so stupid as not to understand that from the day he married her there is no more place for us in his heart? We may continue to stay here like orphans, but we no longer have any right to be here. It's possible that, out of old habit, our condition here is better than that of the general run of orphans—but orphans is what we are. We became orphans the day our mother died. And whatever little remained to be accomplished, this marriage has rendered complete. As it is, I never had much to do with her. And if she had made her complaint about me to Father at that time, I would not have minded so much. I was prepared for that blow anyway. It's not as if I can't make my own living in the world. But she chose a bad time to strike at me. But then, even wild animals choose to attack just when their quarry is least prepared. That must be the reason why I was treated with such conspicuous generosity. If I was even a little late at mealtimes she would send reminder upon reminder, I was given freshly prepared halvah at breakfast, I was repeatedly asked if I needed money. This is why that hundred-rupee watch was procured for me.

Still, couldn't she think of some other charge to prefer against me, but to accuse me of being a vagabond? After all, when did she ever see me behave like one? She might on the other hand have complained that this fellow doesn't devote time to his studies, or that he is constantly demanding money on some pretext or other. Why did she think of just *that* one complaint? Perhaps because this was the harshest thing she could say about me. She has used her deadliest weapon against me at the very first opportunity, a weapon against which there is no protection. Because she wanted me to lose my place in my father's affections? Keeping me at the boarding school is only an excuse. The real purpose is to remove me from this place unceremoniously. After a month or two my allowance might also be stopped, and who cares if I live or die after that? If I'd known that the inspiration behind this move had come from her, I'd have found some kind of place for myself. I could have found accommodation in some servants' quarters, there would have been places a-plenty on people's verandahs. Still, it's morning now—time to wake up. When there's no more affection left, it's shameless to hang on merely because of the free maintenance one gets. Now this is no longer my home. I was born here and have played here as a child, but now it's no longer mine. Father is no longer my father. I am his son. But he is no longer my father. All the relationships in the world are ultimately founded in affection. And when that's gone, nothing remains. O, mother! Where are you at this hour?

Thinking these thoughts, Mansaram began to weep. The more he dredged up memories of his mother, the more he found himself unable to resist the tears. Several times he called out to his mother as if she were there to listen. Today he felt for the first time what it was to be motherless. He was a self-respecting boy, and he was courageous; but having led a sheltered, protected existence, he was overcome suddenly by a loss of confidence.

It was ten o'clock at night. Munshiji had gone out for dinner. The maid had come twice to summon Mansaram for dinner. The last time Mansaram had said to her in some irritation—I'm not hungry, I won't eat. Stop pestering me time and again!

That was why when Nirmala asked her to go up and summon Mansaram once again she refused—My asking won't bring him here, Bahuji.

Nirmala—Why not? Go and tell him the food is turning cold. Let him come down and eat whatever little he wishes to eat.

Maid—I've said all that and had no effect.

Nirmala—Did you tell him that I was waiting for him?

Maid—No, I didn't try that, tell you the truth.

Nirmala—All right then, go up and tell him I'm sitting here waiting for him. Tell him if he doesn't come down I'll put the food away and go hungry to bed myself. Go this once again,

please, my dear Bhungi (laughing). And if he still refuses to come
down, pick him up and bring him here like a baby.

The maid went up reluctantly but she returned in an instant—
Arre, Bahuji, he is weeping there. Did someone say something
to him?

Nirmala got up with much alarm and staggered a few steps as
if she were a mother who had just heard her child had fallen into
a well. Then she stopped herself and said to the maid—Bhungi,
weeping, did you say? Did you ask him why he was weeping?

Bhungi—I forgot to ask him that, tell you the truth.

He's weeping, she thought. In this still, quiet night, he's sitting
by himself and weeping. Something must have reminded him of
his mother. How can I go and console him? O, how can I? The
merest something arouses suspicion here. You are my witness,
Lord, that I have never ever, even accidentally, said anything to
hurt him. But what am I to do? He must be convinced in his
heart it was I who complained about him to his father. O how
can I make you understand that I have never ever uttered a word
against you? If I should ever malign such a wonderful and blameless
young man, there could be no one worse than me.

Nirmala could see clearly that Mansaram's health was
deteriorating daily: he was getting visibly weaker and the bright
glow of his face was fading fast. The reason for this was also hardly
hidden from her—but it was impossible for her to say anything
about it to her husband. It broke her heart to have to observe all
this and yet be condemned to keeping her mouth shut.
Occasionally, she would feel exasperated that Mansaram was
making so much of such a little matter. After all, even if he had
been called a vagabond by her husband, it didn't actually make
him one, did it? Of course her own situation was entirely
different—the merest whiff of suspicion could destroy her
utterly—but why should he concern himself with such matters?

She felt a powerful desire to go to him and soothe him and
get him to eat something. The poor fellow will remain hungry
all night. And, she told herself, I'm at the root of all this trouble.

Before I came to this house, there was peace all round. The father loved his children dearly, the children loved their father. All these problems have arisen since I came to this house. And where will all this end? God alone knows. The poor fellow is lying all by himself, hungry. Even earlier, he'd only pretended to eat. And then he hardly eats anything anyway—even children of a year or two eat that much.

Nirmala decided to go to him. She decided to go against her husband's wishes. Her heart beat wildly as she made her way up to console him who was, in terms of family relationship, her son.

First she looked in the direction of Rukmini's room. She was sleeping soundly on a full stomach. Then she checked the outer room. All was quiet there. Munshiji had not returned. Having first ascertained all this she arrived in front of Mansaram's door. The door was open, Mansaram was sitting with a book on the table in front of him, head lowered, the very image of grief and anxiety. Nirmala wanted to call out to him but was unable to utter a sound.

When Mansaram raised his head and looked towards the door, he was unable to recognize Nirmala in the dark. He was startled—Who is it?

Nirmala replied in a trembling voice—It is only I. Why aren't you coming down to eat? It's so late now!

Mansaram averted his face and said—I'm not hungry.

Nirmala—Bhungi has reported that to me three times already.

Mansaram—Then you can hear it a fourth time from my lips.

Nirmala—You had nothing in the afternoon either. Why aren't you feeling hungry?

Mansaram replied with bitter laughter—Will there be sufficient food if I did really start feeling hungry?

As he said this, Mansaram tried to close the door to his room—but Nirmala pushed the panel aside and stepped into the room, and, taking Mansaram's hand in her's, said in a gentle voice—Please come and eat a little, for my sake. If you don't eat, then I too will go to bed hungry. Eat just a little, please. Do you want me to remain hungry all night?

Mansaram was plunged in thought. She hasn't eaten either, has been waiting for me all this while. Is she a paragon of affection and concern and caring, or is she a deceiving image of ill-will and envy? The thought of his mother came to his mind. Everytime he had thrown such a tantrum with her, she had come in just this way to cajole him and had refused to leave until she had had her way. He was unable to refuse such entreaty. He said—I am sorry you were put to so much trouble on my account. If I'd known you were hungry because of me, I'd have come and eaten long ago.

Nirmala rebuked him—How could you even suppose that I could eat and go to sleep while you remained hungry? Does the mere fact that I'm your stepmother make me selfish?

Just then Munshiji's cough was heard in one of the outer rooms. It seemed as if he might be coming in the direction of Mansaram's room. Nirmala's face went completely ashen. She got out of the room immediately and, finding no opportunity of making her way to the inner rooms, said in a harsh, loud voice—I'm not some maid-servant that someone should expect me to wait up for them in the kitchen till so late at night. If anyone doesn't wish to eat, they should let me know in good time.

Munshiji saw Nirmala there. Such outrageous behaviour! What did she come here for? He asked her directly—What are you doing here?

Nirmala replied in a harsh, bitter voice—Cursing my luck, that's what I'm doing here. I'm at the root of all mischief, always. So, someone's throwing a tantrum in one corner, someone else is in a temper in another. How many can I appease all at once, and for how long?

Munshiji was a little taken aback—But what is the matter?

Nirmala—He refuses to come down to eat, that's all. Ten times I sent the maid up for him, then I was forced to come myself. It's easy enough for him to say lightly that he's not hungry, but all the blame will fall on me, won't it? The whole world will be ready to put the blame on me. It might well be that he's not hungry, but for the rest of the world it'll be a clear case of the witch not giving him enough to eat.

Munshiji asked Mansaram—Why don't you go down to eat, you? Know what time it is?

Mansaram was still stunned. The things happening before his eyes were so strange that he couldn't make any sense of them at all. How was it possible that eyes which but a moment before had become moist with tears of sincere affection were now suddenly lit with the fires of jealousy? Those lips from which but a moment before nectar had flowed suddenly expelling such poison? He replied in a dazed state—I'm not hungry.

Munshiji scolded him—Why aren't you hungry? And if you weren't hungry, why didn't you say so in the evening? How can you expect someone to stay up through the night in anticipation that you might get hungry? You weren't like this earlier. Since when have you learnt to throw tantrums? Go and eat your dinner.

Mansaram—I can't, I'm not hungry.

Totaram gritted his teeth—All right then, eat when you feel hungry!

And with those words he went inside. Nirmala followed him. Munshiji went inside and lay down while she went to the kitchen in order to wind up and put everything away. Then, having washed her mouth, she had a paan and entered the bedroom smiling. Munshiji asked her—So you've eaten, have you?

Nirmala—I can hardly leave off food and drink because someone's in a temper.

Munshiji—I don't know what the matter is with him. He's dwindling by the day, he spends all his time lying in that room.

Nirmala didn't say a word; she was tossing about on a bottomless ocean of anxiety. What would Mansaram have made of her extraordinary change of mood and manner? Would he not have wondered at the way in which, as soon as his father appeared, her attitude changed entirely? Would he have understood the reason for the change? The poor boy was just about persuaded to come down and eat when this man had turned up. How could she explain all this to him. And could he be expected to understand? What, she thought bitterly, is this misfortune that has befallen me?

Getting up the next morning she busied herself with domestic chores. At nine Bhungi appeared and said to her—Mansa Babu is loading all his books and things on the ekka.

Nirmala was startled—Loading his things on an ekka? Where's he going?

Bhungi—All he said in reply was that he'd stay in the school from now on.

Mansaram had gone to the school directly after getting up and made arrangements with the headmaster for his accommodation there. Initially, the headmaster had said—I have no space here, and there are a number of applications pending longer than yours. But when Mansaram said—If I don't get a place here then I might have to give up my studies, I might not even be able to sit for the examination—the headmaster relented. Mansaram was expected to pass in the first division. All his teachers expected him to add lustre to the school's reputation. So how could the headmaster afford to let go of such a promising pupil? Therefore he agreed to clear a room in his own office for Mansaram. And that is why Mansa had begun loading his things on to an ekka as soon as he got home.

Munshiji asked him—Where's the hurry? You can go away in a couple of days. I'm thinking I should find a good cook who can go with you.

Mansaram—There's a good cook there already.

Munshiji—Take good care of your health. You shouldn't sacrifice your health for the sake of your studies.

Mansaram—No one's allowed to study there after nine, and everyone has to play some game or other regularly.

Munshiji—Why aren't you taking your bedding? What will you sleep on there?

Mansaram—I'm taking a blanket. I don't need anything else.

Munshiji—Why don't you go and eat something while the servant loads your things on to the ekka? You didn't have anything at night either!

Mansaram—I'll eat something there. I've asked the cook to prepare something for me. If I start eating here I'll get late.

Inside, Jiyaram and Siyaram were insisting on going with their brother. Nirmala was trying to cajole the two—They don't allow little boys there, my sons, you have to do all the work there with your own hands...

Just then Rukmini entered and said to her—You have a heart of stone, empress! The boy had nothing to eat at night, and he's leaving the house without having eaten a thing now, and here you are chatting with the boys! You don't know him like I do. Understand that it's not school he's going to—he is exiling himself to the forest, he will never come back. He's not one of those who forgets an injury. It gets engraved in his heart like a line on stone.

Nirmala asked fearfully—But what am I to do, Didi? He refuses to listen to anyone. Please go and call him. He'll come if you call him.

Rukmini—What is the matter anyway, that he's running off like this? He never seemed unhappy at home In fact he didn't like places other than his home. I'm sure you must have said something to him or else complained about him. Why're you planting thorns in this fashion for yourself? I assure you, you'll never be able to live contentedly if you insist on destroying a home in this fashion.

Nirmala replied tearfully—If I've ever said anything to him, may my tongue fall off. Of course, as a step-mother all kinds of blame attaches to me by rights. I beg you, please ask him to come in.

Rukmini asked sharply—Why don't you go and call him? Will it offend your sense of dignity if you do? Would you have held yourself back like this if he'd been your own son?

Nirmala's condition now was that of a wingless bird which sees the snake approaching and wishes desperately to fly, but cannot. It hops up and falls down and flaps about, but it cannot do anything else. She was miserable inside. But she couldn't go out.

Just then the two younger boys entered and declared—Bhaiya has gone away.

Nirmala stood there like a statue, petrified. Gone away? He didn't even come inside the house, didn't even come in to say good-bye to me! Gone away! Such contempt for me! I might well be nothing to him, but there was his aunt! He should at least have come and met her? But of course I was here! How could he step in? I would then have been able to see him, wouldn't I? That's why he went away.

# Chapter 9

The house seemed bereft without Mansaram. Both the younger boys studied in the same school as him. Every day Nirmala would ask the two about Mansaram. She hoped he would at least come home during the holidays, but when the holidays came and went and he did not return, she began to feel very disturbed. She had specially prepared moong laddoos for him. One Monday morning she sent Bhungi to the school with laddoos for him. But Bhungi came back at nine. Mansaram had returned the laddoos untouched.

Nirmala asked—Is his health somewhat better than before?

Bhungi—Far from it, he seems to have become worse.

Nirmala—Doesn't he feel well?

Bhungi—Well, I didn't ask him that, tell you the truth. Yes, but the servant there is a sort of brother-in-law of mine. He was telling me the young master doesn't have much of an appetite. He gets up after a mere two phulkis and then eats nothing else the whole day. He keeps studying the whole time.

Nirmala—Didn't you ask him why he was returning the laddoos?

Bhungi—Well I didn't ask him that, tell you the truth. He just said, take these back, I have no place to put these here. And I brought them back.

Nirmala—Didn't he say anything else? Didn't you ask him why he didn't come home? It was a holiday, after all.

Bhungi—Musn't lie, Bahuji. It didn't occur to me to ask him that. Yes, but he did tell me never to come there again, and never to bring anything for him either—and also asked me to tell you not to send any letters or messages for him. Nor even to send messages with the boys either. And one more thing that I can't bring myself to utter. And then he started to weep.

Nirmala—What was it he said, tell me.

Bhungi—Well, all he said was it was a shame he wasn't dead already, and then he began weeping.

Nirmala let out a deep sigh. She felt as if her heart was breaking. Every fibre of her being screamed in agony. She couldn't keep still and went inside, lay down on her bed and covered her face, and wept bitter tears. 'So he too knows.'

Again and again, the same fatal words began to echo in her consciousness—'So he too knows.' O God, what will happen now? The flame of suspicion in which she had been burning was now a blazing inferno. She had no anxiety for herself. What hope had she of happiness for herself that could have made her anxious for fulfilment? She consoled herself with the thought that she was probably undergoing penance for earlier misdeeds. But is there a creature so shameless that can live for long in such a condition? She had sacrificed her entire life and all its expectations upon the altar of matrimonial duty. Her heart wept but she had to put on a mask of laughter. She had to talk laughingly to the very person whose face she could not bear to see. Who can tell what agonies she had to go through, being embraced by the very body whose touch she abhorred like the cold touch of a snake? She had only one desire in such moments, that the very earth should open and give her refuge! But all this was still confined only within her. She had stopped worrying about herself but the problem had assumed an altogether more terrifying form now. She could not bear to see Mansaram's suffering. The very thought of the effect such an accusation would have on a brave and sensitive boy was enough to make her tremble. No matter what the suspicions she aroused, no matter if she had to commit suicide, she would remain silent no more. She was impatient to go to Mansaram's rescue. She had resolved now to cast aside the veils of modesty and hesitation.

Vakil Sahib always made a point of seeing her once before he left for the courts. It was almost time for him to do that now. Thinking he would appear any moment, Nirmala stationed herself at the door, waiting for him—but what's this? He's going away. Normally he would come to see her and order the carriage while with her. So he won't be coming in today, he would leave from the outer rooms. No, she would not allow this to happen. She said to Bhungi—Go and call the master here. Say I have to tell him something important.

Munshiji was about to leave. As soon as he got the message he came back in, but he didn't quite enter the room—So what's the matter? Tell me quick, because I have an important engagement. A short while back there was a message from the headmaster that Mansaram is running a fever and it would be best if he were treated at home. So I'll go past the school on my way to the courts. Did you want to tell me something special?

It was as if a terrible blow had struck Nirmala. A fierce struggle ensued between her tears and her voice—as if both were determined on asserting their priority and neither was willing to relent. The strangled nature of her voice and the force of her tears were such that it was difficult to say which would emerge victorious if the contest lasted even a moment longer. Finally, however, both emerged simultaneously—but immediately thereafter the stronger asserted itself over the weaker. All she could say was—No, it was nothing special. You're going there anyway.

Munshiji—I asked the boys and they told me he was studying normally yesterday, but who knows what happened to him today?

Nirmala's voice was shaking with agitation—All this is your doing.

Munshiji raised his eyebrows and said—My doing? What wrong did I do?

Nirmala—Ask your own heart.

Munshiji—All I had in mind was that he can't seem to get down to studying at home but he just might in the company of other boys. This wasn't such a bad thing—but what else have I done?

Nirmala—Think hard, is that the reason you sent him away? There wasn't anything else on your mind?

Munshiji hesitated a little, smiling to conceal his sense of weakness, and said—What else could there be? Just ask yourself.

Nirmala—Well, have it your own way. Now please bring him back home with you today. His illness is likely to become worse if he continues to stay there. No one can look after him as well as your sister can at home.

A moment later she added with her head lowered—If you don't wish to bring him back here because of me, then send me away to my mother's home. I will be quite comfortable there.

Munshiji did not respond to this last remark. He left immediately, and in a moment the carriage started for the school.

But what a strange thing the mind is! How strange are its movements, how full of mystery, how impenetrable! How often does it change its appearance. Even fireworks take time changing colours, but the mind is adept in this art, it doesn't take even a fraction of that time. Where there had been parental affection a moment earlier, suspicion reigned once again: Could the whole thing be just a ruse?

# Chapter 10

For two whole days Mansaram remained immersed in deep anxiety. Time and again the memory of his mother came back to him, he went off food altogether and couldn't concentrate on his studies. He became a transformed person. Two days went by and he failed even to do his homework. As a result he was punished by being made to stand on the bench. For the first time in his life he had to suffer this bitter humiliation.

On the third day, still lost in his worries, he consoled himself: Am I the only person to have lost his mother? All step-mothers are like this. So it's not as if something very unusual is happening to me. Now I must simply work twice as hard, like a man—I should do whatever I need to do to keep my parents happy. If I get a scholarship this year, I won't need anything from home anyway. After all, there are so many boys who earn all kinds of distinctions and awards all on their own. Conquering obstacles and acting decisively whenever the opportunity presents itself are the true duties of a man. What's the point of cursing one's fate?

Just then Jiyaram appeared.

Mansaram asked him—How are things at home, Jiya? Our new mother must be very pleased.

Jiyaram—Well I don't know how she's feeling, but she hasn't eaten one proper meal since you came away. She weeps all the time. Except of course when father appears—then she starts to laugh. I put my books together that same evening after you came away. I wanted to come and stay here with you. But that witch Bhungi went and told Ammaji. Father was sitting there, but right in his presence Ammaji came and snatched my books away and said tearfully—If you also go away, then who'll be left in this house? If I'm the reason why all of you are leaving home one by one, I'll leave too. I was feeling irritated anyway, and since Father was no longer there, I said angrily to her—Why should you have to go anywhere? After all this is your house, and you should live in it comfortably. We're the outsiders here, and once we're gone you can have the whole place all to yourself.

Mansaram—That was well said, very well said indeed! This must have made her very angry and she must have gone and complained to Father.

Jiyaram—No, that's not the way things turned out at all. She just sat down on the ground and began to weep right there. I also started to weep, and then she wiped my tears with the corner of her sari and said—Jiya, as God is my witness, I've never said a single word against your brother to your Father. Alas, my fate is accursed and I must put up with it as best I can. Then she said all manner of other things, most of which I couldn't understand. Something to do with Father.

Mansaram asked eagerly—What did she say about Babuji? Do you remember?

Jiyaram—Well, to tell you the truth, I can't really remember any of the things she said. My memory isn't that great, but the sum and substance of what she said was roughly this: that she had had to put up this pretence in order to keep Babuji happy. She was saying all manner of strange things, most of which I couldn't understand. But now I'm convinced it wasn't because of her wishing so that you were sent away.

Mansaram—You are incapable of understanding these moves. These are very deep moves.

Jiyaram—Maybe you think so, but I don't.

Mansaram—How will you understand these things when you can't even understand geometry. How can I ever forget the way in which, that night when she came up to my room to call me for dinner, and very nearly persuaded me too, she switched her tone completely the moment Babuji appeared.

Jiyaram—That's what I too find difficult to understand. Just yesterday, when I got back home from here, she started to ask me questions about you. I told her—He was saying he would never step in this house again. It's not even as if I lied; that's what you *had* said to me. The moment she heard this she started to weep bitterly. I felt a bit sorry I had told her all that. All she repeated again and again was—will he leave this home because of me? Is he so angry with me? Went away and didn't even bother to meet me. Didn't even touch the meal that was ready and waiting for him. Oh! How can I tell you how I'm suffering. Just then Babuji came. She quickly wiped the tears from her eyes and went to him with a smile on her face. This I can't understand. Today she pleaded with me that I should bring you back with me. Today I'll drag you home with me. She's wasted away so much in just two days, you'll feel sorry when you see her. You will come, won't you?

Mansaram did not reply to this. His legs were trembling. Jiyaram ran when he heard the bell for class; but Mansaram lay down on the bench and took a deep, deep breath as if he had not drawn breath a very long time. The words that came from his mouth were heavy with an unbearable agony—O God! But for the honour of his good name, his life seemed meaningless to him. Who can estimate what sadness there was in that deep sigh, what pain, what pity, what pleading! Only now was he beginning to understand the whole, sordid secret, and again and again his grieving heart said just one thing—O God! Such terrible ignominy!

Can a greater misfortune than this even be imagined? Can any greater baseness than this ever be imagined? No father could ever have levelled such a cruel accusation against his own son.

Such a terrible smear on the name of that very person whose good character was held to be a model for his contemporaries, who had never ever allowed impure thoughts to come anywhere near him! Mansaram's heart was fit to break.

The bell rang a second time. The boys went off to their rooms but Mansaram continued to sit with his chin resting on his hands, staring at the ground with unblinking eyes as if his whole world had been swept away in a deluge, and he could no more show his face to anyone ever again. He would be marked absent in school, he might even be fined, but when he had lost his all, such little things could hardly matter any more. If I continue to draw breath even after suffering such ignominy, he thought, then my existence itself is shameful.

In his extreme agony, he burst out—Mother! Where are you now? Your own son, whom you thought so much of, whom you considered the foundation of your own existence, is in such unbearable distress today. His own father has become his mortal enemy. Oh, where are you now?

Then he calmed himself and began to think—But why am I being suspected of this terrible thing. What is the reason for this? What did he see in my behaviour that encouraged him to suspect me thus? He is my father, not my enemy that he should level such an accusation at me. He must certainly have seen or heard something. How much affection he once had for me! He wouldn't even sit down to eat without me, and now that same person has become my enemy—there must be reason for such a transformation.

All right, he considered, on which day exactly was the seed of this suspicion sown? Sending me off to the boarding house came later. That same night he'd come to my room and started to quiz me, his whole attitude had changed that very day. What was it that happened that day, which he found so unacceptable? I'd gone to ask our new mother for something to eat. Babuji was sitting with her at that time. Yes, I remember, his face had flushed with anger then. And from that very day our new mother stopped her lessons with me. If I'd known that my coming and going into the inner rooms, or talking to my new mother, or giving her lessons displeased him, things would not have come to this pass today. And my new mother! What must she be going through?

Mansaram had given no thought to Nirmala's situation thus far. The mere thought of it made his hair stand on end. How will her simple and affectionate heart be able to survive such a terrible blow? Oh, he thought, how deluded I've been. I thought her affection was mere pretence. How was I to know she had had to treat me so badly in order to allay my father's suspicions? Oh! How unjust I've been to her. Her condition must be much worse than mine. I was able to come away here, but where can she escape to? Jiya said she hadn't eaten properly for two whole days. She is crying constantly. I should go and speak to her. Why is she inviting so much misfortune upon herself for a poor unfortunate like me? Why does she ask after me all the time? Sends for me time and again? How am I to tell her— Mother I hold no grudge against you, I have no misgivings with regard to you any more.

She must be weeping even at this moment! What a terrible injustice! What is this that's happening to Babuji? Is this what he married her for? Had he married a mere child in order to murder her this way? Plucked this delicate flower only to trample it in this manner?

How will she ever be saved? How will the glow be restored to her innocent face again? She's being punished in this fashion only because she treated me with affection. This is the reward she gets for her consideration. And shall I continue to sit and see her enduring such manifest cruelty? If not for the sake of my own honour, then certainly for the sake of protecting her I'll have to sacrifice myself. There's no other solution now. Oh! What fond hopes I once had for myself! But I'll have to see them all mingle with the dust now. A pure woman's honour is being put under suspicion—and for my sake! I'll have to give up my life in order to protect her—that is clearly my duty. In this alone there is true courage. Mother, I'll cleanse this black insinuation against your honour with my blood. In this alone lies both your salvation and mine.

He spent the whole day lost in such thoughts. In the evening both his brothers came to persuade him home.

Siyaram—Why don't you come, brother dear? Please come.

Mansaram—I'm not free to come when you ask me to.

Jiyaram—But tomorrow is a Sunday.

Mansaram—But I'm busy on Sunday also.

Jiyaram—Then you'll come tomorrow, won't you?

Mansaram—No, I have to go and see a match tomorrow.

Siyaram—Mother is making moong laddoos. You won't get any if you don't come. We'll eat them all between us, Jiya, we won't give any to him.

Jiyaram—Brother, if you don't come home Mother might come here herself.

Mansaram—Is that right! No, she won't do such a thing. There'll be a lot of trouble if she comes here. Just tell her that I've gone to see a match somewhere.

Jiyaram—So why should I lie? I'll just tell her you're throwing a tantrum. See if I don't bring her with me.

Siya—I'll tell them you didn't go for your classes today. You just spent the day in bed.

Mansaram somehow managed to get rid of the two messengers by promising to come the next day. After the two had left he resigned himself to his anxieties once again. He spent the whole night tossing and turning. He even spent the holiday sitting around, worrying about whether his stepmother would in fact turn up in school. His heart would start beating wildly every time he heard the sound of a carriage. Has she come, then?

There was a small dispensary in the school. A doctor would arrive there for an hour every evening. If people needed medicine, he would dispense them. When he turned up that day, Mansaram went to him and stood there, lost in thought. The doctor knew Mansaram well. He was surprised to see him and said—What have you done to yourself, my dear fellow? You're simply wasting away. You haven't started eating in the bazaar have you? After all, what's the matter with you? Come here to me!

Mansaram only smiled and said—I'm suffering from the disease called life. Do you have a cure for that?

Doctor—I'd like to examine you, please. You've become practically unrecognizable. Saying this, he took Mansaram's hand and examined him carefully—he examined his chest, back, eyes and tongue in turn. Then he said, worried—I'll go and see Vakil Sahib right now. You're suffering from pthisis. All the symptoms point that way.

Mansaram asked eagerly—How many days will it take for it to be all over, Doctor?

Doctor—What are you saying! I'll advise Vakil Sahib to send you to some sanatorium in the hills. God willing, you'll recover in no time at all. The illness is in the first stage right now.

Mansaram—Then it appears it might take another year or two. I can't wait that long. Listen, I don't have any of this pthisis stuff that you think—nor anything else either. There's no need for you to trouble Babuji with any of this. I have a headache right now, give me something for that. And yes, please give me something that brings on sleep too. I haven't slept properly for two whole days.

The doctor opened a medicine cabinet which contained all kinds of poisonous medicines and gave Mansaram a bottle of something. Mansaram asked—This is some kind of poison. If someone were to drink this, would he die?

Doctor—No, he wouldn't die, but his head would probably spin a little.

Mansaram—Isn't there some medicine that could kill someone instantly?

Doctor—There are many such medicines. You see this bottle. If even a drop of this were to be consumed, the person couldn't possibly be saved. He'd be dead in no time at all.

Mansaram—Tell me Doctor, do people who take poison suffer a great deal?

Doctor—Not all poisons cause pain. There are some that kill one in a flash. You see this bottle. If a person takes this, he becomes unconscious, and then never regains consciousness.

Mansaram began to think—Then it's very easy to die. Why are people so afraid, then? Where can I get a bottle like that one? Even if I were to ask the name of the medicine and try and buy it from some chemist, he'd refuse to sell it to me. No matter, I'll find a way of getting it. And I have now found out it's very easy to put an end to one's life.

Mansaram was as happy as if he had won some sort of prize, as if a great load had been lifted off his heart. The cloud of anxiety which had been hovering over his head was all scattered now. After months he felt a burst of energy coursing through his mind. The boys were going to the theatre, they had got the necessary permission from the Inspector. Mansaram accompanied them to the theatre. He was happy like there was no one in the world happier than him. He was rolling with laughter seeing the comic antics in the theatre. He would clap repeatedly and was among the first to call out 'Once more!' He was thrilled listening to the songs and would cry out frequently with joy. The other members of the audience were turning around to look at him. Even the actors were looking in his direction and wondering at this over-appreciative and emotional person. His friends were amazed by his apparent frivolity. He was normally a quiet, serious, reserved sort of young man. Why was he so jovial today, so that there seemed no end to his mirth?

Returning from the theatre at two in the morning, his comic frenzy had not abated. He overturned one student's bed and locked several students' doors from the outside, standing outside awhile and enjoying their loud discomfiture. So much so that the commotion woke up the warden of the hostel and he was forced to upbraid Mansaram for his outrageous conduct. Who knows what terrible struggles must have been going on inside him at that very moment? The cruel impact of suspicion had destroyed utterly his self-respect and his sense of shame. Now he cared nothing at all for the possible humiliation and rejection that his conduct might beget. Because it wasn't really merriment after all—only the heart-rending agony of his hurt soul. After all the boys had gone to sleep he too lay down on his bed, but sleep would not come. He got up after a moment and packed all his books in a suitcase. After all, what was the point in studying if he was about to die? Better death than a life so full of such obstacles, such sufferings!

Still wrestling with these thoughts, he watched the dawn break. He had not slept a wink three nights running. When he got up his legs were trembling and his head was reeling. His eyes were burning and there seemed to be no strength in his limbs. The morning was upon him, but he did not even have the strength to get up and wash his face. Just then he saw Bhungi approach with something tied up in a handkerchief, accompanied by a hostel servant. His blood ran cold. O God! She has come! What'll happen now? Bhungi couldn't have come by herself. The carriage must surely be standing outside? Whereas earlier he did not even have the strength to get up and wash his face, he now leapt up from the bed and ran towards Bhungi and asked her in an agitated voice—Has Ammaji also come with you? When he gathered that she had not come, he regained his composure. Bhungi said to him—Bhaiya, you didn't come yesterday, but Bahuji was waiting for you all day. Why are you cross with her? She keeps saying, I have not complained against him, ever. Today she came weeping to me and said—Take these sweets to him and ask him why he has left his home because of me. Where shall I keep these sweets?

Mansaram replied roughly—You can go to hell with them, you witch! You dare to bring sweets from there! I forbid you ever to come here again. She comes bearing gifts! Go and tell her, it's her home now and may she have joy of it—and that I'm very happy where I am. I eat well and have a wonderful time. Listen you, take care to tell her this in the presence of my father. I'm not afraid of anyone, let them do their worst, so they don't have any regrets. I can remove myself to Allahabad or Lucknow or

Calcutta if that's what they desire. Banaras or any other city, it's all the same to me. What do I have to keep me here anyway?

Bhungi—Please keep the sweets, Bhaiya, otherwise she will kill herself weeping. Believe me, she will kill herself weeping.

Mansaram suppressed his tears and said—Let her die, I don't give a damn! What great happiness has she bestowed on me that I should care? She has destroyed me utterly. Tell her she shouldn't send any messages for me either, I have no use for them.

Bhungi—Bhaiya, you're telling me you eat well and have a wonderful time, but you've become a mere shadow of yourself. You're not even half what you were when you came here.

Mansaram—Your eyes are deceiving you. Just you watch, in a few days I will become like an ox. Oh yes, and tell her also that she should give up all this weeping and wailing. If I ever hear that she's crying and refusing to eat, I promise I'll take bitter revenge. If she's turned me out of the house, let her at least enjoy being there. She expects to fool me with these displays of affection. But I am wise to such women's wiles.

Bhungi went away. Even as he was talking to her, Mansaram began to feel a little cold. The manner in which he had had to suppress his true feelings in order to put on the act was clearly not easy for him. His self-respect was calling upon him to put an early end to this deceitful behaviour; but where will all this end? Will Nirmala be able to withstand such a blow? So far, whenever he had thought of death, he had no thought of anyone else, but today he was forced to realize that another person's life was tied up with his own. Nirmala will inevitably think it was her cruelty that had driven him to take his life. And will her sensitive heart not break under the pain of that realization? Her life is in danger even at this moment. Will she be able to live much longer with the thought that she is a murderess?

Mansaram lay down and pulled the coverlet over himself, but he was still shivering. In a short while he had developed a high fever—and he fell unconscious. He saw all kinds of strange dreams in that comatose condition. Every so often he would wake up with a start—he would open his eyes, and again fall unconscious.

Then, he was startled to hear Vakil Sahib's voice. Yes, it was his voice all right. He threw off the coverlet and got off the bed immediately. He had a strong impulse to give up his life right there in front of him. He thought his father would be truly happy if he were to die right there. Maybe that's why he has come, to see how much longer it is before I die. Vakil Sahib caught hold of his hand to prevent him falling and asked—How are you feeling, Lallu? Why didn't you keep lying? Lie down now, there's no need for you to keep standing.

Mansaram—I'm feeling very well indeed. You put yourself to all this trouble for no reason.

Munshiji did not reply to this. He was shocked to see his son's condition. That healthy boy, whose mere sight used to gladden his heart, had simply withered away. Even in a mere five or six days he had lost so much weight that he was scarcely recognizable. Munshiji lay him down on the bed gently and pulled the coverlet over him. Then he began to think about what he ought to do next. God forbid that he should lose his boy! The mere thought filled him with grief and he sat down on the stool and began to weep bitterly. Mansaram too was crying with his face under the covers. Only a few days back, his father's heart had filled with pride to look at him. But today, even after he had seen his pitiable condition, he was still wondering whether he should take his son home or not. Can't he be treated here? I will sit with him round the clock. And there is a doctor in attendance, so there should be no trouble at all here. He could foresee all kinds of problems with taking his son home. But his greatest fear was that there Nirmala would sit by Mansaram's side all the time, and he would be unable to prevent her—and this was unbearable for him.

Just then, the warden came in and said to him—I think it would be best if you were to take him home with you. You have a carriage, so there should be no difficulty. We won't be able to provide him adequate care here.

Munshiji—Well, I had the same thing in mind when I came here—but he seems to be in a very fragile condition right now. A little carelessness at such a time and he might well pass into delirium.

Warden—There will certainly be some inconvenience in moving him from here, but I'm sure you'll understand that he won't get the kind of care here that he would no doubt get at home. And anyway, it's against the rules to keep sick children in the hostel.

Munshiji—If you like, I can go and get permission from the headmaster. It doesn't seem right to me to move him from here in this condition.

Hearing Munshiji talk about going to the headmaster, the warden thought he was being threatened with higher authority. He replied in some irritation—The headmaster cannot ask me to go against the rules. How can I accept such a great responsibility?

What was he to do now? Would he have to take the boy home with him? He could have used the fear of his condition worsening with moving as an argument in favour of keeping him in the hostel. But there could be no argument in support of putting him in the hospital now. Whoever heard of it would certainly say that the only reason he had dumped his son in the hospital was to avoid having to pay the doctor's fee. Now there was no option except to take the boy home. If the warden had at that point stood out for a bribe, he could easily have collected a few years' worth of his salary in one go, but how could an upright and principled person like him have had the requisite cleverness and cunning? If at this point anyone had suggested the means whereby Munshiji could avoid taking Mansaram home with him, he would have felt deeply obliged—for all his life to come. There wasn't even time enough to think. The warden was right there, pressing him to act promptly. Helpless, Munshiji summoned the two servants and with their assistance made to move Mansaram from his hostel bed. Mansaram was comatose, but he screamed out— What is it? Who is it?

Munshiji—It's only I, my son. I've come to take you home with me. Come, let me pick you up.

Mansaram—Why do you want to take me home? I won't go there.

Munshiji—But you can't stay here, my son, it's against the rules.

Mansaram—But I won't go home—take me somewhere else. Leave me under a tree, in some hut somewhere, anywhere. But not home!

The warden said to Munshiji—Don't pay any heed to what he's saying. He's not in his right mind.

Mansaram—Who's not in his right mind? I'm not in my right mind? Am I abusing someone? Biting someone? Why am I not in my right mind? Let me remain here, and let whatever has to happen, happen here. And if I have to be moved, take me to the hospital, I'll happily remain there. I'll live if I have to, die if I must—but I won't go home under any circumstances.

Upon hearing these words Munshiji again felt emboldened to start pleading with the warden, but the warden was a punctilious man, insistent on the rules. Who will be responsible, he asked, if it turns out to be an infectious disease and some other boy catches it? In the face of that argument, Munshiji's legalistic wiles were of no avail.

Finally, Munshiji asked Mansaram—Why are you so insistent about not going home, my son? You'll have all kinds of comforts there.

Though he had said this, Munshiji was afraid Mansaram might take him at his word and agree to come home. He was looking for some excuse for keeping Mansaram in the hospital even as he tried to lay responsibility for that decision upon the boy's head. This was happening in the presence of the warden; he could be called upon to confirm the fact that Mansaram was going to the hospital at his own insistence. Munshiji himself was entirely blameless in the matter.

Mansaram finally burst out angrily—No, no, a thousand times, no! I will not go home. Take me to the hospital and forbid everyone at home from ever coming to see me there. There's nothing the matter with me, I'm perfectly well. Let go of me, I can walk without support.

He stood up, and like one possessed started to move towards the door, but he stumbled. If Munshiji had not caught hold of him he would have injured himself seriously. With the help of the two servants, Munshiji brought him to the carriage and put him down on the seat.

The carriage started for the hospital. Things had turned out exactly as he had liked—and even in that condition he felt pleased. His son was going to the hospital at his own insistence. Didn't this prove that there were no ties of affection binding him to the home? Didn't that prove Mansaram was blameless? He had been suspecting him without reason.

But in a little while, instead of feeling pleased he began to feel remorse. Instead of taking his dearly-loved son home, he was taking him to the hospital. Even at this time, when his very life was in danger, there was no place in his vast house for his own son. What a cruel irony it was!

But the very next moment a thought entered Munshiji's mind—Could Mansaram have divined his thoughts? Could that be the reason why he was so averse to going home? If that's the case, it's terrible.

The mere thought of that possibility was enough to make Munshiji's hair stand on end. His heart started pounding wildly. If that's also the reason for his fever, then God help us! His condition became truly pathetic then. The little fire that he had lit in order to warm his shivering hands was now threatening to burn his very house down. His heart trembled at the curious mixture of pity and sorrow and regret and anxiety that overcame him now. If this secret weeping could have been heard by others, they would certainly have been moved to tears. If his tears had found a way out, they would have flowed incessantly. He looked once upon his son's wasted face with the loving eyes of a father, then was overcome by grief, and wept and wept and wept.

# Chapter 11

When Munshi Totaram returned from the courts in the evening Nirmala asked him eagerly—Did you see him? How is he now?

But Munshiji noticed immediatedly that there wasn't the merest sign of concern or anxiety on her face. In fact her make-up was if anything rather more elaborate than usual. Normally she never wore a necklace but she was wearing one today. She was always very fond of the jhoomar but today, worn with a fine silk sari, sitting atop her dark lustrous hair, it truly shone like a diadem.

Turning away from her Munshiji said offhandedly—He's ill, what else is there to tell?

Nirmala—But you'd gone to fetch him home?

Munshiji replied to this in some exasperation—He refuses to come, so what am I to do, force him? I tried my best to reason with him—please come home my son, I said—you'll be well looked after there, but the merest mention of home and he lost his temper. He said—I'd rather die here than go home. Finally I had no option but to take him to the hospital.

Rukmini, who had positioned herself on the verandah, said—He was always a stubborn boy. Mark my words, he'll never agree to come here, and he won't get well there either.

Munshiji ventured timidly—If you could go and be with him

for a few days, sister, it would be a blessing. He'll be very happy to see you. Please, my dear sister, please accept my request this once. He'll weep his life away if he's left there all by himself. All he does is cry out to his mother all the time. I'm on my way there right now. Why don't you come with me? He's not well, I tell you. His face has changed beyond recognition. Heaven alone knows what God has in store for us.

Munshiji himself wept as he finished his sentence. But Rukmini was unmoved—I'm willing to go. If my going there would restore my darling boy's health, I'd go despite a thousand difficulties, but I tell you he will not get well. I know him inside out. He's not suffering from any illness but only from the sorrow of being turned out of his own home. It's this sorrow that has taken the form of a fever. So you can try all the medicines you like—the Civil Surgeon himself may try all he likes—but no medicine will be of any avail.

Munshiji—But dear sister, who's turned him out? I only sent him there for the sake of his studies.

Rukmini—Whatever your reason, he's been hurt deeply. It's not as if I have any call to say anything anyway, my opinions don't matter any more. You and your wife are master and mistress of the house now. I'm only a poor unfortunate widow living here on your charity. Why should anyone listen to me or care for me? But I'm forced to speak up sometimes. Mansa will get well only after he returns home—only after he is restored in your affections.

Having said this Rukmini went away. Her ancient eyes had seen a great deal and she could easily penetrate the charades that were being enacted in front of her, but she blamed the innocent Nirmala entirely. She barely checked herself from saying that until this woman remains in this house its fortunes will go from bad to worse. And even though she didn't say so explicitly, Munshiji understood the import of her words in exactly those terms.

After she left he became lost in deep thought. He was feeling so angry with himself that he wanted to dash his head against a wall and give up his life right there. Why had he married a second time? Where was the need? God had blessed him with not one but full three sons. And he was nearly fifty, so why did he re-marry? Was this a snare set by Providence to entrap him? He looked up and saw Nirmala's calm, smiling countenance and promptly went away to the hospital. That smiling face had reassured him deeply. This reassurance had come to him after a long time. After all, could a love-stricken heart have remained calm and unmoved in such circumstances? No, never. That kind of hurt could not be concealed by mere play-acting. He felt a sharp pang of regret for the weakness of his own temperament. He had needlessly harboured suspicions and so caused this turn of events. Even with respect to Mansaram's apparent attitude in the whole business, he was feeling reassured. But in its place a new anxiety had now appeared. Could Mansaram have guessed? Could he be refusing to return home because he has guessed all this? If he has, that is terrible. The mere thought of the possibility shook him to the core. He asked the coachman to drive faster. Today, after many days, the overcast skies clouding his heart finally cleared up, and his long suppressed feelings were eager to burst forth. He leaned out of the window to check whether the coachman had fallen sleep. The horse had never seemed as slow to him as it did now.

He rushed to Mansaram's side as soon as he got to the hospital. He found the doctor standing there, deep in anxiety. Munshiji's heart sank. He couldn't utter a word. With great difficulty he managed to utter this question in a strangled voice—What is the matter, Doctor Sahib?

But before he could say any more he broke down and started to weep—and when there was a second's delay in the doctor's reply to him, he could have died of anxiety. He sat down on the bed and took the boy into his lap and began to sob with grief. Mansaram's body was burning with fever. He opened his eyes once—ah, how terrifying and yet how pathetic that look was! Munshiji embraced his son and asked the doctor—What is his condition, doctor? Why don't you reply?

The doctor's voice was full of doubt—You can see for yourself what his condition is. His fever is 106 degrees—what else can I say? And the fever is still rising. I'm doing what is in my power to do. But it's in God's hands now. I haven't left his side for a minute after you left. I haven't even eaten yet. His condition's so sensitive right now it could turn critical any minute. He's quite unconscious and every so often he has episodes of delirium. Did anyone say something to him at home? He keeps repeating just one thing— Mother, where are you?

The doctor was still saying this when suddenly Mansaram sat up and pushed Munshiji off the bed, uttering in a fevered voice— Who are you threatening? Go on, kill me if you like, kill me now! Can't find a sword to do it with. So, find a length of rope then! I'll put the noose around my neck myself. O Mother, where are you?

And with those words he fell unconscious again.

For a short while Munshiji kept staring at Mansaram's wasted, unconscious face with troubled eyes, then turned to the doctor and taking hold of his hand, said in tones of the utmost, abject pleading—Doctor Sahib, please save my boy. For God's sake, save him or I'll be destroyed. I'm not a rich man, but I'll give you whatever you desire, but save him please! Please call the best doctors, take their opinions, I—I'll pay for everything. I can't bear to see him like this now! O my promising son, my brilliant son!

The doctor replied with genuine feeling in his voice—I tell you honestly, I have done everything I could for him. Now you say you'd like to consult other doctors. I'll send for Doctor Lahiri, Doctor Bhatia and Doctor Mathur right away. I'll send for Vinayak Shastri also—but I warn you against entertaining false hopes. His condition is very serious.

Don't even utter such a thing—Munshiji sobbed. No, God will never treat me with such harshness. Please send off for doctors from Calcutta and Bombay—I'll be your slave for life. All our hopes for the future rest on him. He's the very foundation of my existence. My heart's breaking. Please give him some medicine that restores him to consciousness. Let me hear from his own lips what it is that ails him. O my poor son!

Doctor—Please control yourself. You're a mature man, aren't you? There's nothing to be gained by going on wailing in this fashion and assembling a whole battery of doctors. Just sit quietly and I'll send for some local physicians. Let's see. what they think. But you're fast becoming a patient yourself.

Munshiji—All right doctor. I promise I'll be quiet now, I won't utter a word. Do what you think is best, the child is in your hands now. You alone can save him. All I want is that he should regain consciousness so he can recognize me, understand what I'm saying to him. Isn't there some magic pill that can do this? How I wish I could exchange a few words with him.

'As he was saying this Munshiji once again turned to Mansaram and said feelingly—My son, please open your eyes. How are you feeling now? Here I am sitting by your side, weeping. I have no complaints against you, no suspicions at all.

Doctor—You're incoherent again. Please, sir, you're not a child. You're a mature person, just be patient.

Munshiji—All right doctor, I'll be quiet now. I'm at fault, I know. You may do what you think best. I've left everything to you now. Isn't there some way I can tell him I harbour no suspicions against him? You tell him, doctor, why don't you tell him that his unfortunate father is sitting by his side and weeping. But his heart is clear now. He had some suspicions but they're gone now. Just tell him that much. I don't want anything else. I will sit quiet. I won't open my mouth—but do tell him just this much.

Doctor—For God's sake control yourself or I'll have to ask you to leave. I'm going into my office to write the necessary letters to a few doctors. Just sit quiet here.

Unfeeling doctor! What father could sit by patiently if his son were in such a condition? Munshiji was a sober sort of man normally and knew perfectly well that there was little to be gained by going on in this fashion at such a time—but it was impossible for him to sit quiet in the present situation. If this illness had been due to natural causes, he might well have been patient, even offered consolation to others, sent for the doctors himself, but how could he remain patient with the knowledge that the entire catastrophe was of his own making? Can a father be so heartless? Every fibre of his being was filled with a feeling of remorse. He asked himself, how could I have been so overcome with those terrible feelings? How could I imagine such terrible things without any evidence? So, what should I have done in the situation? What could he have done other than what he did do— this he was unable to work out. The truth is that getting married in the first place was a terrible mistake. Yes, that was the cause of all the trouble.

But then, he thought, it wasn't such an unusual thing I did. After all, all kinds of men and women get married—and spend happy lives together. It was just *that*—happiness—for which I married. Hundreds of people in the neighbourhood have made second and third and fourth, even seventh, marriages, often at ages greater than mine. And they lived happily to the end of their lives. It isn't even as if they all died before their wives. Despite second and third marriages, many of them have become widowers again. If everyone had been reduced to my condition, who would ever have dared marry? My father married in his fifty-fifth year, and when I was born he was full sixty years of age. It's true, things aren't the same now as they were then. Then, wives were illiterate. No matter what the husband was like, they worshipped him. On his part, though, the man consented to overlook a great deal, certainly. After all, when a young man cannot remain contented with an older woman, why should a young woman be any more content with an old man? But then I wasn't such an old man. No one would have placed me any older than forty. But even so it must be admitted that a certain willingness to look the other way is essential if one dares to marry a young woman after one's own youth is past. Women are naturally modest. Of course some of them are brazen hussies, but normally women are much more restrained than men. If they have a properly matched husband, they might laugh and joke with another man, but their affections remain pure. But if they're mismatched then, even if they never look at another man, their heart is invariably sad. In the one case the relationship is a firm, masonry wall, and even a pickaxe can make no difference to it. But the other is a thing of clay and will remain aloft only until someone should happen to strike it.

Lost in these thoughts Munshiji drifted into a brief nap. His emotions were instantly transformed into dreams. And what he encountered therein was his first wife who addressed him thus— What is this you have done, O my lord? That son whom I fed on my very blood, him you have killed in this heartless fashion. Why did you level such a base accusation against such a blameless and ideal son? What is the point in weeping now? You have lost him now. I will snatch him from your cruel hands and take him away with me. You were never so suspicious. So did you wed suspicion along with your new bride? Such a cruel blow to such a sensitive heart! Such a monstrous accusation! Only someone entirely shameless could consent to live after being accused in such a fashion. Not my son, never!

Even as she said this she gathered up her son in her embrace and took him away! Munshiji tried, even through his tears, to retrieve his son from her embrace—but as he stretched his arms out he woke up and saw Doctors Lahiri and Bhatia and half a dozen others standing there.

# Chapter 12

Three days passed and Munshiji still hadn't returned home. Rukmini would go to the hospital twice a day to see how Mansaram was doing. The two boys also went—but how could Nirmala go? She was shackled. She was desperate to find out Mansaram's condition, but when she asked Rukmini all she got in return were taunts; and as for the boys, they could hardly answer her questions coherently. She was eager to go and see him once for herself. She was even worried that suspicion might have weakened Munshiji's paternal affection; and maybe his stinginess was the reason why Mansaram was not being attended to effectively? After all, doctors have no loyalties beyond their fees—the patient can go to hell or heaven for all they care. She had a powerful desire to go to the hospital and hand over a bag containing a thousand rupees and say to the doctor—Please save him, doctor, this is all yours. But she had neither that much money nor courage. If she could only get there somehow, Mansaram would become well again. He was not getting the kind of attention he needed. Else how had the fever not come down in three whole days? But it's not a physical fever at all, it's a mental fever. It'll only go away once the mind is consoled. If she could have spent the night by his side, and Munshiji hadn't let the merest suspicion enter his mind, then perhaps Mansaram could believe that his father bore him no resentment and would get well in no time. But how was all this to be accomplished? Will Munshiji be able to remain contented and happy after seeing her there? Or is he still harbouring those suspicions? When he went from here, it seemed as if he was sorry for the passion that had overcome him. But was it possible that, as soon as she went there,

Munshiji's darkest suspicions would once again flare up and nothing less would satisfy him than the death of his son?

Three days passed as she struggled with these thoughts. No food was cooked, no one ate anything. Some puris would be brought from the market for the boys, while Rukmini and Nirmala would go to bed without eating. They felt no desire to eat.

On the fourth day Jiyaram returned home from school via the hospital. Nirmala asked him—So, son, did you go to the hospital? How is he today? Was he sitting up or not?

Jiyaram replied with tears in his eyes—Ammaji, today he wasn't saying anything at all. He was just thrashing his limbs about on the bed.

The colour drained from Nirmala's face. She asked him anxiously—Was your father there with him?

Jiyaram—Of course he was. He was crying bitterly today.

Nirmala's heart was pounding. She asked—Were the doctors there?

Jiyaram—The doctors were there and talking amongst themselves. The big civil surgeon was saying there was a need to put some fresh blood into the patient's body. Hearing this Father said—Please take as much blood as you want from my body. But the civil surgeon laughed and said—Your blood won't do the trick. We need the blood of someone young. Then he injected something into Bhaiya's arm. It was a big fat needle but Bhaiya didn't so much as utter a sound. I was so afraid I closed my eyes.

Great purposes are formed in moments of passion. Time was when Nirmala had been consumed by fear, but now she became radiant with the glow of resolution. She had decided to give the young blood needed for the transfusion. If her blood could save Mansaram, she would gladly part with the very last drop in her body. She wouldn't be deterred any longer by what people might think. She said to Jiyaram—Go fetch an ekka for me quickly. I'll go to the hospital.

Jiyaram—There'll be many people there at the moment. Just wait for nightfall.

Nirmala—No, go fetch that ekka right now.

Jiyaram—And what if Babuji gets angry?

Nirmala—Let him. Go and fetch that ekka.

Jiyaram—I'll tell him you forced me to get an ekka for you.

Nirmala—Tell him.

While Jiyaram stepped out to fetch the vehicle, Nirmala went in and combed and coiffed her hair carefully, changed her clothes, put on some jewellery, put a paan in her mouth and came to the outer door to await the vehicle.

Rukmini was sitting in her room. Seeing her leave with such elaborate preparation she asked—Where are you off to?

Nirmala—To the hospital.

Rukmini—What will you do there?

Nirmala—Nothing much, what's there for me to do? It's in God's hands now. But I'd like to see him once.

Rukmini—I tell you, don't go there.

Nirmala replied courteously—I'll be back directly. Jiyaram was saying he's doing poorly. I feel restless here—why don't you come with me?

Rukmini—I've already gone and seen him. Suffice it to say that a transfusion of blood is his only hope now. But who'll part with their fresh young blood, and why should they? After all, even that can be very risky.

Nirmala—That's exactly the reason why I'm going. Won't my blood be good enough?

Rukmini—Of course it will, for it's a young person's blood they need. But far better he die and be washed away in the river than that he be saved by your blood.

The vehicle came. Nirmala and Jiyaram went off to the hospital.

Rukmini stood weeping at the door a long time. Today for the first time she felt sorry for Nirmala; if she had had the power she would have kept her back forcibly. She could see in an inarticulate sort of fashion just where this frenzy and passion and sympathy were taking her. Misfortune was beckoning her onward to the path of destruction!

When Nirmala arrived at the hospital the lamps had been lit. The doctors had given their advice and gone away. Mansaram's fever had come down somewhat and he was staring fixedly at the door. He was looking out into the open sky as if awaiting the coming of some divine spirit. He had no sense of his own condition or even of his whereabouts.

Seeing Nirmala standing before him he was startled and sat up suddenly. His lapsed consciousness came right back. The comatose mind suddenly knew everything again. He knew once again everything about his condition, the situation he was in. He stared at Nirmala with wide open eyes, then turned his face away.

Just then Munshiji spoke up in a sharp voice—What has brought you here?

Nirmala was left speechless. How could she tell him what she had come for? A simple enough question, it left her without words. Why had she come? Who could ever have faced such a knotty problem? A member of the family is unwell, she's come to see him, was that such a difficult thing for him to work out and obviate the need for such questioning?

She just stood there, stunned. Listening to the two boys talking about their father's grief and self-recriminations, she had assumed he had shed his suspicions at last. Now she realized that was a mistake. Yes, a grievous mistake. Had she known even tears were ineffective in putting out the flames of his suspicion, she would never have ventured here. She would rather have died of regret and frustration, she would never have stepped out of the house.

Munshiji repeated his question—Why have you come here?

Nirmala replied in a clear voice—Why have you come here?

Munshiji became livid with rage. Nostrils quivering, he leapt off the bed and grabbed Nirmala's hand—There was no need for you to come here. You can come when I ask you to come. Understand?

But, what do we see here! Mansaram, who was barely able even to stir, had got off the bed and stood up, and then fallen at Nirmala's feet with tears in his eyes, saying—O Mother, you have undergone so much trouble for an unfortunate being like myself. I will never ever forget the affection you gave me. I will ask the Almighty for just this one boon, that my next birth should be from your womb, so that I might repay something of what I owe you. God knows I have never thought of you as a stepmother. You have always been a mother in my eyes. You weren't all that much older than me, but you were in the position of a mother to me, and that is exactly how I've always regarded you... But I am faint, and cannot speak any more. Forgive me, Mother. This is our last meeting.

Nirmala held back her tears and said—Why are you talking in this way? You'll be hale and hearty in a couple of days.

Mansaram replied in a weak voice—I've no desire to live any more, nor even the energy to speak further.

Even as he was saying these words, Mansaram lay down on the ground at her feet, all but unconscious. Nirmala looked at her husband fearlessly and asked him—What advice have the doctors given?

Munshiji—They've all gone out of their minds. They say he needs young blood.

Nirmala—If young blood can be arranged for, would that save his life?

Munshiji gave her a sharp look and said—I'm not God, and don't even think that the doctors are gods.

Nirmala—Young blood is not impossible to get.

Munshiji retorted—entirely unaware of the ditch he was walking into—Yes, like the stars.

Nirmala—I'm willing to give my blood. Call the doctor.

Munshiji stood amazed—You!

Nirmala—Yes. Won't my blood do?

Munshiji—You'll give your own blood? No, there's no need for that. There's danger to life in that.

Nirmala—What better way will I find to put my life to some use?

Munshiji looked towards her with tears in her eyes and said—

No, Nirmala, it has now become something infinitely valuable to me. Till this day I'd thought of you merely as an object of my pleasure, today I realize you're worthy of worship. I've been monstrously unjust towards you. Forgive me.

# Chapter 13

Whatever had to happen happened—and nothing that anyone did proved of any avail. The doctor was still in the process of taking blood from Nirmala's body when Mansaram, giving one final proof of his blameless character, bade farewell to this vale of illusion. It was as if he had been tarrying so long only to see Nirmala one last time. How could he leave this world without first having set at rest all suspicions regarding himself. Now his task was done. Munshiji had been reassured in respect of Nirmala's innocence—but only now, when it was already too late, when the traveller had already set his foot in the stirrup and was ready to depart.

The loss of his son transformed Munshiji's life into a burden that had somehow to be borne. After that day, he never smiled again. His life was drained of all meaning. He still went to the courts, but not in order to argue on behalf of clients, only in order to seek diversion for an hour or two before he tired of that and returned home once more. He would sit down to dinner but could hardly bring himself to put a morsel in his mouth. Nirmala would prepare the choicest things, but he never ate more than a few mouthfuls. And even those he could barely keep down! He would go towards Mansaram's room and his heart would break.

Where hopes had once reigned, now there was only darkness. He still had two sons, but when the prized one is gone, what hope is there for the little ones? When the full-grown tree had fallen, what hope was there for saplings? Of course people die, young and old, but his particular sorrow had to do with the fact that he was responsible for his own son's death. Every time that thought crossed his mind, he felt as if his chest had suddenly become too small and his heart would burst.

Nirmala felt truly sympathetic towards her husband. She did her best to keep him happy and would never once refer to matters past. Munshiji felt embarrassed whenever the subject of Mansaram came up between them. He sometimes felt as if he should open his heart out to Nirmala and tell her everything, but a sense of shame held him back. Thus, he could not even procure for himself the relief that one gets by speaking of one's sorrow, by drawing others into sharing one's grief. Instead of being drained away as pus, the toxins continued to enter his bloodstream. And day by day he wasted away.

For the past few days, a kind of friendship had developed between Munshiji and the doctor who had attended on Mansaram. The poor fellow would come by sometimes in order to console Munshiji, and would occasionally drag him out in order to take the air. His wife had come and met Nirmala a few times. Nirmala too had visited their house several times, but every time she returned from there, she would be depressed for days together. Seeing their happy married existence she could hardly help feeling sorry for herself. The doctor earned no more than 200 rupees, but with just that the two of them led a happy life. They had only one maid, and most of the domestic chores had to be done by the mistress. There weren't too many ornaments on her person either, but there was that love between them that reckons not a whit the lack of lucre. Seeing the husband, the wife's face would light up. Seeing her, the husband would be beside himself with joy. Nirmala's house could boast of much more money than their's—her body was laden with ornaments, she never had to do the merest chore around the house—but for all her wealth Nirmala was miserable and Sudha for all her poverty was happy. Sudha had something that Nirmala did not have, something in comparison with which all her wealth seemed worthless, so much so that she felt ashamed of visiting Sudha's house wearing ornaments.

One day, when Nirmala was visiting the doctor's house, Sudha saw her sorrow-laden countenance and asked—You are very melancholy, sister. Is the Vakil Sahib quite well?

Nirmala—What can I say? His condition is worsening daily. I wonder what God has in mind?

Sudha—My husband thinks he needs to go elsewhere for a change of air or he will certainly fall prey to something terrible. He's said as much several times to Vakil Sahib, but he merely replies each time that there's nothing the matter with him, he's very well and has no complaint, thank you. Why don't you try and talk to him today?

Nirmala—If he's willing to disregard the doctor, why will he listen to me?

Even as she was saying this Nirmala's eyes welled up, and the dread that had been gnawing at her for months suddenly burst forth—The signs don't look good to me, sister. Let's see what God intends.

Sudha—You tell him forcefully today to go somewhere for a change of air. A couple of months in another place and many things will have been forgotten. I think even moving to another house might help. After all you won't be able to go out much anywhere. Which month are you in?

Nirmala—The eighth month is nearly done. This anxiety is killing me all the more. I'd never wished for this particular blessing. So why has this misery been inflicted on me? O I am unfortunate! A month before my wedding, my father died. And from that day I've been cursed with ill luck. I'd been betrothed elsewhere—but when my father died those people changed their minds. My poor mother had no option but to marry me off here. Now my younger sister's to get married. Let's see where she ends up.

Sudha—Why did the people where you were first betrothed change their minds?

Nirmala—They alone must answer that. But with Father dead, what hope had they of getting their gold?

Sudha—This is meanness! Where were the people from?

Nirmala—From Lucknow. I don't remember the name now, but he was a big officer in the excise department.

Sudha asked gravely—And what did the son do?

Nirmala—Nothing, he was a student somewhere. Very promising.

Sudha kept looking down at the ground and asked—Didn't he speak to his father? He was a young man, couldn't he have forced his father to come round?

Nirmala—How can I say about that, sister! But who doesn't like to get their hands on some gold? The pandit who went to them as our representative brought back the news that it was the son himself who was responsible for the refusal. The mother was in fact a good woman. She tried her best to persuade her husband and her son—but to no avail.

Sudha—If only I could lay my hands on that son, I'd set him right!

Nirmala—I got what was fated for me. But God knows what poor Krishna will have to go through.

In the evening, after Nirmala had gone, when the doctor sahib returned home, his wife Sudha said to him—What would you call someone who, after being duly betrothed to someone, goes and gets married somewhere else for greed?

Doctor Sinha looked somewhat curiously at his wife and said—That he shouldn't have done such a thing, of course!

Sudha—Wouldn't you say it was the height of meanness—that it was abominable behaviour?

Sinha—Well, I'd have no objection to saying that either!

Sudha—Who's more to blame, d'you think—the groom or the groom's father?

Sinha had still not grasped what lay behind all these questions his wife was firing away at him. He said in a puzzled way—It depends on the situation; if he's dependent on the father, then the father is more to blame.

Sudha—Does a young man then have no moral responsibilities when he's dependent? When he wants a new jacket for himself he can manage to persuade his father despite his initial objection. But can he not insist on being heard by his father in a matter of such great importance? One should say that the groom and his father are both guilty, but the groom is more guilty! The older man thinks, I have to bear the whole cost of this anyway, so whatever I can get from the bride's side is all to the good. But it's the groom's duty, if he hasn't mortgaged his soul entirely, to show some moral courage. If he doesn't do that, then I at any rate would say he's both greedy and a coward. Unfortunately I have just such a man for my husband, and I find I do not have words enough to condemn him!

'But that... that... that situation was altogether different,' Sinha replied stutteringly, 'It had nothing to do with giving and getting. It was something else altogether. The girl's father had died. So what could we do in the situation? And then there was a rumour that there was some defect in the girl. That was a different situation altogether. But who told you this whole story?'

'Why don't you go further and say that the girl was one-eyed, or hunchbacked, or base born, or had loose morals? Why stop at just so much? So, what was this defect then?' Sudha pressed on.

'Well, I didn't see her myself, but I was told that there was some defect,' Sinha replied weakly.

Sudha—Her greatest defect was that her father had died, and she was no longer in a position to bring a big dowry. Why are you ashamed to admit this? After all, I can hardly chop your ears off, can I? And if I do say a few bitter, sarcastic things, you can simply ignore them. And if I should carry on beyond that you can always resort to the stick to discipline me. After all, that's the time-honoured way of keeping women in check. If that girl can be called defective, I'd say the Goddess Lakshmi herself is not free of defect. You were just out of luck, that's all! That's it—you were fated to marry me.

Sinha—Who told you what she was and wasn't? Just as you're convinced on the basis of hearsay, so were we convinced on the basis of what someone said, that's all.

Sudha—I'm not going by hearsay. I've seen her with my own eyes. To cut a long story short, I've never seen such a beautiful woman.

Sinha asked agitatedly—Is she here somewhere? Tell me, where did you see her? Did she come visiting?

Sudha—Yes, she came visiting. And not just once, she's been here many times. I too have visited her home several times. The Vakil Sahib's wife is that same girl whom you forswore because of her defects!

Sinha—Really!

Sudha—Quite! And if she were to find out that you're that self-same great and good man who let her down, she might never step into this house again. There must be no more than a couple of women in this town who are as beautiful, as adept and skilful at household tasks as she is. You think I'm good. But I'm not fit even to be her maid. She has all the wealth and possessions that anyone could want, but if the person's mismatched the rest is of no avail. She is to be admired for her fortitude in consenting to spend her life with that rotten old lawyer. In her position I'd have poisoned myself long ago. She doesn't talk about her grief. She talks and laughs, she dresses up and dons ornaments, but every fibre of her being is forever grieving.

Sinha—She must complain bitterly about Vakil Sahib?

Sudha—Why should she complain? He's her husband, is he not? Now there's no one else for her in the whole wide world but him! He may be old and ailing, but he is her lord. Well born women don't criticize their husbands—that's how bad women behave. She sees his condition and feels resentful, but she never says anything.

Sinha—What possessed the Vakil Sahib to go and get married at his age?

Sudha—If there weren't people like him around, what hope would there be of poor maidens finding husbands? People like you won't give her a second look unless there's a lot of money, so where's the poor creature supposed to go? You've committed a grave injustice and you'll have to do penance for it. God grant that nothing untoward happens to her marriage. But if perchance something happens to Vakil Sahib, the poor woman will be destroyed. She was crying bitterly today. You people are really very cruel. I'll insist on marrying my Sohan to a poor girl.

Doctor Sahib didn't hear that last sentence. He was perturbed with a grave anxiety. The question kept nagging his mind—If anything should happen to Vakil Sahib? Today he saw the awful consequences of his selfish refusal. In truth, he was the one to blame. If he had insisted with his father that he would marry there and not elsewhere, his father couldn't have gone against his wishes and married him off elsewhere, could he?

Just then Sudha said—So would you like to meet Nirmala tomorrow? After all, she too should get a chance to see what you look like. I dare say she won't say anything, but there might be so much reproach in one look of hers that you won't be able to forget it all your life. Speak up—would you like to meet her tomorrow? I'll give her a short account of who you are.

Sinha replied—No, Sudha, I beg you, please—don't ever do such a thing! Otherwise, I promise you, I'll run away from home.

Sudha—Why're you so afraid to partake of the fruit of the thorny tree you yourself planted. Since you were bold enough to wound her, why're you reluctant to see her pain? My father gave you five thousand, didn't he! And you'll get another five or six thousand when you marry off your younger brother. Then you'll be the wealthiest person in the whole world. Eleven thousand is a lot of money. Good God! Eleven whole thousands! It would take a month just to count so much money. And if one's children should take it upon themselves to squander it, it would take them full three generations. Negotiations are going on with someone, aren't there?

This mockery made Doctor Sahib so embarrassed that he was unable to raise his head. He'd lost all his ready wit, his smooth words. He looked ashamed, as if someone had given him a hiding. Just then, there was a call for him. He ran for his life. Today, for the first time, he realized how capable of mockery women can be.

At night in bed Doctor Sinha said to his wife—Nirmala had a sister, didn't she?

Sudha—Yes, she was talking about her just today. Nirmala is already living the life fated for her, but she's very concerned about her sister. Her mother has even less now than she had earlier—so she too will be forced to marry just such an old man.

Sinha—But Nirmala can help her mother.

Sudha replied sharply—You do talk nonsense sometimes. The most Nirmala can do is give her a few hundred rupees—what more? As for Vakil Sahib's condition, you know what it's like. And she herself has a whole long life to live. And then, how can anyone know what the real situation is in their home? For the past six months the poor fellow has been laid up at home. And it isn't as if money falls from the skies. And if he should have ten or twenty thousand, they will be in the bank, not with Nirmala. If our monthly expenditure is two hundred, don't you think their's must be at least four?

Sudha fell asleep, but Doctor Sahib tossed about with anxiety for a long time. Then he thought of something and sat down at his table to write a letter.

# Chapter 14

All three things happened pretty much at the same time—Nirmala gave birth to a daughter, Krishna was betrothed, and Munshi Totaram's house was auctioned off. The birth of a daughter was an ordinary enough event, even though Nirmala thought of it as the most significant event of her life. But the other two events were definitely out of the ordinary. How was it that Krishna was betrothed into such a wealthy family? Her mother had nothing to give by way of dowry; and the old Mr Sinha, who had now retired on his pension, had the reputation of being very greedy. So how did he consent to marrying his son off into such a poor family? People could hardly believe their ears. Then again, the fact that Munshiji's house was auctioned off was very curious. Even if he wasn't thought to be quite a millionaire, Munshiji was certainly reckoned by one and all to be very wealthy. So how come his house had to be auctioned off? The fact of the matter was that Munshiji had borrowed money from a moneylender to buy up the mortgage for some village. He had expected to settle the debt in a year or so, and in another few years he hoped to take possession of the village itself. The landowner of the village would, he had hoped, not be able to keep up with repayments of interest and capital, and in this way he would gain control of the village. This was the assurance on the basis of which he had embarked on the deal. The village was a large one—there was a clear profit of 400–500 rupees per annum. But all his plans came to naught. Despite all his self-promptings, he was quite unable to go to the law courts. The loss of his son had drained him of all motivation to work. Which father can be so heartless as to carry on contentedly after causing his own son's death?

In the event, the moneylender received no interest payments

for a whole year, and despite his repeated urgings Munshiji refused
to go and see him... So much so that, on the last occasion, Munshiji
declared he wasn't the moneylender's slave that he should do his
bidding, let the man do his worst... Finally, the moneylender
decided enough was enough and filed suit. Munshiji never even
went to the hearing. Suddenly, there was a decree against him.
But it wasn't as if he had any money lying around in the house.
And in this short time he'd lost his credit. He couldn't raise the
amount. So finally the house was put on the block. Nirmala was
in the maternity room. When she heard the news her heart sank.
Even though her life was devoid of happiness, she had at least
been free of anxieties in respect of money. If money isn't the most
important thing in life, it is very close to being that. Now this
worry too was added to her other sorrows. She sent word through
her maid that her husband should sell her jewellery and save the
house, but this suggestion was wholly unacceptable to Munshiji.

From that day on, Munshiji was even more immersed in
anxieties. That wealth, for the greater enjoyment of which he
had entered upon his second marriage, was only a memory now.
He was ashamed to be in Nirmala's presence any more. He now
had a sense of the injustice he had done her. As for the birth of a
daughter, that was the final catastrophe.

On the twelfth day Nirmala emerged from the maternity suite
with her newborn infant and went to see her husband. Despite
the many blows, she was happy as can be—happy as if she had no
worries. Clasping her daughter to her bosom she was freed of all
anxiety. Seeing the infant's bright, cheerful eyes her own heart
filled with joy. In this her welling motherhood, all her sorrows,
had been submerged. She hoped to complete her overflowing
happiness by seeing her daughter in her husband's arms—but
Munshiji flinched when he set eyes on the child. His heart didn't
prompt him to reach out and take her in his arms—but he looked
at her once with sad eyes and lowered his head: the child looked
exactly like Mansaram!

Nirmala misread the expression on her husband's face. She

clutched her daughter to herself with a gush of affection as if saying to her husband—If the burden of providing for my daughter oppresses you so much, I'll ensure that after today even her shadow will not be imposed on you ever again. But how could you bear to treat with disrespect this infinitely valuable thing that I have been given after such trials? Holding her daughter close to her, Nirmala betook herself to her room that very instant and wept for long afterwards. She made no effort at all to understand her husband's lack of enthusiasm, else she might not so easily have assumed him guilty of cruelty. After all, she was not crushed by the weight of responsibility, as her husband was. But if she had tried to understand, would it have been too much for her to understand?

Munshiji realized in an instant that he had made a mistake. A mother's heart is so overwhelmed by the rush of present affection that it has no time at all to be anxious about the future and the difficulties it is likely to bring. It finds itself inspired by a magical strength which conquers all possible obstacles. Munshiji rushed inside the house and picked the child up in his arms, proclaiming— I remember now, Mansaram used to look like this—exactly like this!

Nirmala—Didiji was saying the same thing.

Munshiji—The same large eyes and the red lips. God has returned my Mansaram to me in this form. The same forehead, the same mouth, the same hands and feet! Strange are your ways, lord!

Just then Rukmini appeared. Seeing Munshiji there she said— Just look at him, isn't he exactly like Mansaram? He's come back to us. Let anyone contradict this who will, I'll not believe them. Clearly Mansaram! It's been nearly a year anyway.

Munshiji—Just look at her, sister—you can match her feature for feature. Say no more, God has returned my Mansaram to me. (To the child) Say, little one, are you really Mansaram? Don't even think of leaving us ever again, or I'll drag you back. How cruel you were to go away from us. But I brought you back, didn't I? But mark my words now, don't even think of leaving me again. Just look at her, look how she's staring at me!

That very instant Munshiji began constructing an elaborate fantasy for the future based upon his hopes and aspirations. Love of this world was drawing him back yet again. How transitory life is, and yet how long-lived our hopes are! The same Totaram who had tired of life, who used to call out longingly to death morning and night was now thrashing about on the assurance of one thin reed in order to find his way back to the shore again.

But when has such a reed sufficed to reach anyone safely ashore?

# Chapter 15

Nirmala didn't really have time to spare from her numerous domestic troubles, but she couldn't restrain herself when she heard about Krishna's impending wedding. Her mother had been particularly insistent that she come. The biggest attraction for her was the fact that Krishna was marrying into the very same family that she had originally been destined for. The amazing thing was that this time the groom's people had agreed to the match without insisting on any dowry at all. Nirmala had been extremely worried about Krishna's marriage. She was afraid that like herself Krishna would be married off to some mismatched husband. She was very keen on doing something to help her mother, anything so that an appropriate husband could be found for Krishna—but what with her husband having taken to staying at home, and the moneylender's suit, she found herself a little short. Therefore she was greatly relieved when she heard the details of Krishna's impending marriage. She made plans for her departure. Vakil Sahib came to the station to see her off. He had become extremely fond of the little girl. He was reluctant to let go of her and had even consented to accompany Nirmala, but then Nirmala didn't approve of the idea of his parking himself at his mother-in-law's house a whole month before the wedding. Nirmala had not taken her mother into confidence about her own troubles thus far. What was the point in complaining to her and making her grieve over matters that were, so to speak, done? Which is why her mother thought Nirmala led a joyous, happy life. Therefore, when she saw her countenance after all this time, she was shocked to the core. Daughters don't come back from their sasural dwindled and shrunken—and as for Nirmala, she believed Nirmala lacked for nothing by way of wealth and luxury. She had seen any number of young girls— mere crescent moons—returning from their sasurals like regular full moons. She had imagined Nirmala looking radiant, her body filled out, beauty brimming in every limb. The Nirmala she saw was a shadow of her former self. She had neither the vivacity of youth nor the sparkling countenance that commands instant affection. She had none of the charm, the delicacy that distinguishes those who lead easy, luxurious lives. Her face was pale and drawn, her aspect gloomy, her limbs seemed tired—an old woman at just nineteen! After the excitements of their first meeting were done and the two had quietened down somewhat, her mother asked her—Tell me then, don't you get enough to eat? You looked so much better when you lived here. What's the matter with you?

Krishna laughed and said—She was the mistress of the household there, wasn't she? And the mistress has a million things to worry about, so where does she find the time to eat?

Nirmala—I don't think the water suits me there, mother. I feel sluggish there.

Mother—Vakil Sahib will be coming for the wedding, won't

he? I'll ask him why he has reduced my flower-like daughter to this condition. And tell me why you sent me that money. I'd never asked you for anything, had I? I might be poor all right, but I'm not so far gone as to consent to take my daughter's money.

Nirmala was taken aback—Who sent you money? I never sent you any money.

Mother—Don't lie now! Didn't you send me five hundred rupees in bank notes?

Krishna—If she didn't send them, d'you think they dropped from the sky? Your name was clearly written there. And the seal was the same.

Nirmala—I swear I never sent you any money! When did this happen?

Mother—About two months ago. But if you didn't send the money, where did it come from?

Nirmala—How am I to know? But I didn't send the money. My husband has stopped going to the courts ever since his young son died. In fact I was short myself, so how could I find money to send?

Mother—This is most strange. D'you have some other person there close to you in some way? Could Vakil Sahib have sent the money on the sly?

Nirmala—No, mother, that seems unlikely.

Mother—We must find out more about this. But I've spent all the money on Krishna's clothes and jewellery. That's the problem.

Just then some sort of quarrel broke out between the younger boys, and when Krishna went to sort the matter out Nirmala said to her mother—I was very surprised to hear about this marriage. How did it all come about?

Mother—No one here is prepared to believe it could have happened at all. The same people who saw fit to break off a firm engagement, and only for the sake of a little money, were now keen on finalizing a marriage without asking anything at all—it's beyond comprehension. They initiated the proposal. I wrote back stating clearly I had nothing whatever to give them, that a completely dowerless daughter was all I could offer them.

Nirmala—How did they respond to that?

Mother—Shastriji went there with the letter. All he came back and said was that Munshiji didn't want anything now. He was in fact very ashamed at having gone back on his word earlier. I hadn't expected such generosity from Munshiji, but I believe his older son is a very decent person. He's the one who's persuaded his father.

Nirmala—But wasn't he the man who wanted a large dowry earlier?

Mother—Yes, but Shastriji was saying that now the mere mention of dowry is anathema to him. I'm told he even feels sorry about having broken off the earlier match. He'd broken his word for the sake of money and apparently he got a lot of it the next time, but it seems the woman is not greatly to his liking.

Nirmala felt a strong desire to see the man who, after having rejected her, now felt compelled to 'save' her sister. Repentance it might well be, but how many people these days would be willing to do penance in such a fashion? Nirmala grew impatient to talk to the man, to reproach him if only with gentle words, and by showing him her own lovely countenance make him feel even sorrier. At night the two sisters slept in the same room. They exchanged gossip for hours about which girls in the neighbourhood had been married off, which had begotten sons, which had been married off with spectacular display, which husbands had come up to which girls' expectations, and who had brought what ornaments as gifts. Krishna tried time and again to try and ask about her sister's own domestic existence, but Nirmala gave her no chance at all. She knew she would be embarrassed about answering questions that her sister would want to ask. But finally Krishna did manage to ask if Jijaji, her own brother-in-law, would come to the wedding.

Krishna—But he's pleased enough with you now, isn't he? I'd heard widowers were usually excessively fond of their new wives—but he seems to have been quite the opposite. After all, what's he so irritated about all the time?

Nirmala—How can I tell what goes on inside people's heads?

Krishna—I suppose he might be put off by your lack of warmth. You were quite resentful even before you married. You must have said something to him after you got there.

Nirmala—No, that's not the matter Krishna. I swear I don't harbour the slightest feeling of resentment towards him. In fact I do everything for him that I possibly can; if he'd been a god I could hardly have done more than I do already. And he loves me in return. He's constantly looking at my face—but what can he do about something that lies beyond both his own power and mine. He can't become a youth any more than I can become an old woman. He consumes all manner of medicaments and potions in order to become young, and I've forsworn all milk and ghee in order to become an old woman. I hope my thinness will do something to reduce the gap in our ages. But his nourishing substances are of no more avail than my abstinences. And ever since Mansaram died his condition's become even worse.

Krishna—Were you also very fond of Mansaram?

Nirmala—He was just the sort of boy you couldn't help loving. I've never seen such large, lovely eyes. A radiant countenance like a lotus flower. So courageous that if the occasion demanded he'd have leapt into a fire. Krishna, I tell you truthfully, whenever he came and sat next to me I lost all sense of myself. I wished he'd always sit like that with me so I could gaze at him forever. There wasn't even a trace of sinful thoughts in my mind. If I ever regarded him with other than proper emotions, may my eyes lose their sight—but for some reason my heart would overflow with feeling when I found him next to me. That's why I set up that elaborate show of taking lessons, or he wouldn't ever come into the inner rooms. But I do know that if he'd had any sinful intentions, I'd have done anything at all for his sake.

Krishna—Hush, sister. Don't say such things.

Nirmala—True, what I'm saying sounds bad, and perhaps is

bad too. But nothing can change the imperatives of human nature. Speak up yourself—what would you do if you were married off to a fifty-year-old?

Krishna—I'd simply take poison. I couldn't bear to look at his face.

Nirmala—Then you know all there is to know. That boy never so much as raised his eyes to look at me; but these old people are a suspicious lot. He took a dislike to that boy and didn't rest content until he claimed his life. The day Mansa came to know his father harboured suspicions against him, he came down with a high fever which didn't abate till he was dead. O! I can never forget those last few moments. I'd had gone to the hospital, he was lying unconscious with high fever—he didn't have the strength to get up. But the moment he heard my voice he got up with a start, and crying 'Mother, mother' he came and fell at my feet. (Crying) Krishna, at that time I wished I could give up my life for him. He became unconscious as he lay at my feet and never opened his eyes again. The doctor had recommended a transfusion of young blood, and that's the reason I'd gone there, but by the time the doctors could complete the arrangements for the transfusion he was gone.

Krishna—Would a transfusion of fresh blood have saved him?

Nirmala—Who knows? But I do know that I'd have been willing to let him have my very last drop. Even in that condition his face was radiant like a lamp. If he hadn't got up immediately upon seeing me and come running to fall at my feet—if he had only waited until some blood had been transfused, he might well have been saved.

Krishna—So why didn't you force him to lie down that very instant?

Nirmala—You silly fool, you still haven't understood what was going on. By falling down at my feet and showing a mother-and-son relationship between us, he wished to allay his father's suspicions regarding the two of us. That's the only reason why he got up. He gave up his life in order to wipe out the difficulty in which I was trapped, and in that he succeeded. From that day on 'your brother-in-law' became perfectly reasonable. Now I even feel sorry for him. The grief of losing his son will take his life too. Now he's making amends for the injustice he did me by suspecting me in the first place. You'll be frightened looking at his face now. He's truly become an ancient. Even his back has begun to double up a little.

Krishna—Why are old people so suspicious, sister?

Nirmala—Why not go and ask one of them?

Krishna—I think they're perpetually afraid they can't keep a young woman happy. So they're always on the lookout for grounds of suspicion.

Nirmala—You know, so why ask me?

Krishna—But for the same reason he must also be under his wife's thumb. And onlookers must suppose he's deeply in love.

Nirmala—How come you've become so wise so young? But leave all this aside and tell me, d'you like your young man? You've seen his picture?

Krishna—They did send one. Shall I get it for you?

In a flash, Krishna brought the picture and placed it in Nirmala's hand.

Nirmala smiled and said—You're a lucky one!

Krishna—Ammaji also liked him very much.

Nirmala—Go on, speak up, do *you* like him or not? Don't just tell me what other people say.

Krishna (bashfully)—Well, he's not bad to look at, but God alone knows about his temperament. Shastriji was saying though that there are few young men are as upright and courteous as him.

Nirmala—Was your picture sent to them too?

Krishna—Yes, Shastriji himself carried it there.

Nirmala—Did they approve?

Krishna—How can I tell what other people think? But Shastriji said they were very pleased.

Nirmala—All right, now tell me, what would you like as a gift? Speak up now so I can get it ready in time.

Krishna—You can give me what you like. He's very fond of books. Send for some good books.

Nirmala—I'm not asking about him. I want to know what you'd like.

Krishna—But I'm speaking about myself.

Nirmala (looking at the picture)—His clothes all seem to be made of khadi.

Krishna—Yes, he's extremely fond of khadi. I'm told he carries bolts of khadi from village to village in order to sell the stuff. I believe he's also a good speaker.

Nirmala—Then you too will have to wear khadi now. But you detest coarse fabrics!

Krishna—But if he's fond of coarse fabrics, how can I detest them? I've learnt to ply the charkha.

Nirmala—Really, are you able to make yarn?

Krishna—I can, a little. If he's so fond of khadi he must be plying the charkha too. I'd feel so embarrassed if I wasn't able to do it at all.

Talking away into the night the two sisters dropped off to sleep. Around two, when her daughter started to cry, Nirmala awoke. She saw that Krishna's cot was unoccupied and wondered where her sister could have gone at this time of night. Maybe she's gone for a drink of water? But there was a jug of water by the bedside—so, where had she gone? She called out to her a couple of times but there was no sign of her. Nirmala was now really alarmed. All kinds of fears crowded her mind. It occurred to her that she might just have gone inside to her own room. So, when her daughter fell asleep, Nirmala went in and stood at Krishna's door. She was right, Krishna was in her room. The whole household was sleeping and she was busily plying her charkha with possibly more concentration than she had devoted to theatrical entertainments in the past. Nirmala was amazed. She stepped inside and said—What're you up to at this hour, you! This is no time to be plying the charkha.

Krishna was startled and said bashfully, her head lowered—

How come you woke up? I'd left drinking water at your bedside.

Nirmala—I ask you, don't you get time enough during the day for this, that you should be up at the middle of the night with your charkha?

Krishna—But there's no time during the day.

Nirmala—(inspecting the yarn) This looks very fine.

Krishna—Not really. This is coarse. I'd like to make really fine yarn for a turban for him. That'll be my present to him.

Nirmala—That's a very good idea. What could be more valuable for a man like that? All right, get up now—you can make some more tomorrow. If you fall ill at this stage, all will be lost.

Krishna—No, dear sister. You go along and sleep. I'll come presently.

Nirmala didn't try too hard to persuade her—she just went along herself and lay down. But she couldn't get back to sleep. Seeing Krishna's eager excitement and her welling joy, her own heart was overcome by some inarticulate yearning within herself. Oh! How happy Krishna was at this moment. How wonderfully has love suffused her entire being! Then she remembered her own wedding. From the day that the whole process had started she had lost all her spirits, her liveliness. She had sat in her room and cursed her luck and called upon God to take her life rather than deliver her into a life of misery. She had awaited her wedding with the same sense of anticipation that a prisoner awaits an execution—awaited the moment in which she would bid farewell to all her hopes of happiness, awaited the ritual in which, under the marriage canopy, all her hopes would be reduced to ashes in the sacrificial fire.

# Chapter 16

The month passed quickly by. The auspicious day of the wedding arrived. The house filled up with guests. Munshi Totaram came a day in advance and Nirmala's friend Sudha came with him. Nirmala hadn't really tried very hard to persuade her—but she herself seemed keen to come. Nirmala's very particular desire was to meet the older brother of the bridegroom, and if the opportunity presented itself congratulate him on the fact that good sense had at last prevailed.

Sudha laughed and said—But will you be able to speak to him?

Nirmala—Why not? Now it's a different relationship altogether. And if I'm unable to, I can always turn to you.

Sudha—No, you'd better leave me out of it. I can't speak to a male stranger. Who knows what sort of person he is?

Nirmala—He doesn't seem a bad sort—and then it's not as if you're being asked to marry him. All you have to do is talk to him. I'm sure I could have persuaded Doctor Sahib to give you permission to do that.

Sudha—But is there any reason to believe that someone who's generous also has a good character? After all, no man hesitates to stare at another man's wife.

Nirmala—All right, you don't have to speak to him. I'll do the talking and let him stare all he likes. All right?

Just then Krishna came in and sat down. Nirmala smiled and asked her—Tell me truthfully, Krishna, why d'you look so distracted?

Krishna—Your husband's calling for you. You'd better go attend to that first, then you can return to gossiping. He seems angry!

Nirmala—What's the matter? You didn't ask him?

Krishna—He seems to be ailing. He's lost a lot of weight.

Nirmala—So why did'nt you sit down with him and amuse him a little? Why come hurtling here to tell me? Thank the good Lord for his mercy, or you would've got a husband like mine. Sit down and chat with him. You'll discover old people are wonderful talkers. Young people aren't like that.

Krishna—No, sister dear. You'd better go yourself. I can't bear to sit there.

After Nirmala left Sudha said to Krishna—The baaraat must have arrived by now. Why don't they start with the welcoming ritual?

Krishna—How do I know? Shastriji seems to be collecting the necessary materials.

Sudha—I hear the bridegroom's sister-in-law is a very harsh woman.

Krishna—How d'you know?

Sudha—That's what I've heard, so I thought I'd pass on the warning. You'll have to learn to put up with harsh words from time to time.

Krishna—I'm not the quarrelsome sort anyway. And if I don't give her cause to be angry, why will she lose her temper for no reason at all?

Sudha—It's only what I've heard. She quarrels for no reason at all.

Krishna—Well, I do know one thing—that courtesy turns even stone into wax.

Just then there was a sudden uproar—the baaraat had arrived. The two women came and sat down at the window. And in a moment Nirmala too arrived.

She was all eager to see the bridegroom's older brother.

Sudha asked—How will you know which one's the older brother?

Nirmala—Shastriji will be able to tell me. Krishna's father-in-law is the one on the elephant. O, what is Doctor Sahib doing here! There, don't you see him on that horse there?

Sudha—That's him all right.

Nirmala—They must be friends. I doubt that there's any relationship.

Sudha—I'll ask him when I see him. I don't know anything at all.

Nirmala—And the person sitting in the palanquin, he doesn't seem to be the groom's older brother.

Sudha—Not at all. He seems to be all stomach.

Nirmala—Who's that on the second elephant, I can't make him out.

Sudha—No matter, he can't be the groom's elder brother. Don't you see how old he is—must be over forty.

Nirmala—Shastriji must be busy with the preparations for the dvaar-puja or I'd have asked him.

Just then quite by chance the barber arrived. Nirmala had the keys—and her mother had sent word that some money was needed for the welcoming ritual. This barber was the one who had gone with Pandit Moteram when they had taken gifts comprising the tilak.

Nirmala—Is the money needed right now?

Barber—Yes, please. Please let me have it right away.

Nirmala—All right. Tell me, d'you recognize the groom's older brother?

Barber—Of course I do! There he is, right in front.

Nirmala—Where? I can't see him.

Barber—There. He's the one on the horse. That's him.

Nirmala was shocked—What are you saying? The groom's brother is the one on the horse! Do you recognize him or are you just guessing?

Barber—O really. How could I forget so quickly! I've just come from serving refreshments to them.

Nirmala—But that's Doctor Sahib. He's my neighbour.

Barber—That's him, the Doctor Sahib.

Nirmala turned towards Sudha and said—Did you hear what this man is saying?

Sudha stifled her laughter and said—He's lying.

Barber—All right, I'm lying. Can't disagree with my betters. But you'll believe Shastriji, won't you?

Since the barber was a while returning, Pandit Moteram himself came to the courtyard and began to make a noise—Now God alone can protect the honour of this house! The barber's been here an hour already and we still don't have the money.

Nirmala—Just come here a minute, Shastriji. How much d'you need, I'll fetch it right away.

Shastriji came all right, grumbling and panting heavily, then said with a long sigh—This isn't the time to be talking. Get me the money quick.

Nirmala—Just a minute, I'm getting it out. You don't want me to fall over because of the hurry, do you? Now tell me, which one is the groom's older brother?

Shastriji—Ram, Ram, you dragged me all the way here for this little thing? Didn't the barber know?

Nirmala—He was saying it's the man astride the horse.

Shastriji—So who then should he identify? That's him all right.

Barber—I've been telling her all this while, but she refuses to believe me.

Nirmala looked towards Sudha with a look compounded of affection, and love, and mirth, and mock reproach—So, you're the one who's been playing games with me all this while. If I'd known this, I wouldn't have invited you at all. O, you're a deep one all right! You've been playing this elaborate charade with me all these months and never once did you breathe a word of it to me. I couldn't have kept such a thing to myself more than a couple of days.

Sudha—But if you'd discovered this, would you have come to my house at all?

Nirmala—O my God, I've spoken to Doctor Sahib several times in the past. All the blame will fall on you for this. Now, Krishna, d'you see what a wicked thing your sister-in-law is! You'd better be careful with such a devious one!

Krishna—On the contrary, I'll kiss the dust off her feet. I'm grateful I've been blessed with meeting her.

Nirmala—Now I understand. You must have sent the money too. Don't deny it, I'll strike you if you do.

Sudha—It's bad form to insult guests you've invited home.

Nirmala—Just you wait and see in what ways I'm going to get even with you. I'd just sent you a routine, formal invitation— and you came. What will those people be thinking?

Sudha—I've told them what I'm doing.

Nirmala—I'll never come near you again. You could at least have dropped a hint that I should observe purdah with Doctor Sahib.

Sudha—So, where's the harm in his having seen you? If he hadn't seen you how could he have cursed his fate in having lost you? How could he have known the cost he paid for his greed? Now he looks at you but regret is about all he can manage. He doesn't actually say anything out loud, but he feels very sorry for his mistake.

Nirmala—I won't ever visit your house again!

Sudha—You can't get rid of me now. It's not as if I don't know where to find you.

The welcoming ritual was over. The guests were all partaking of refreshments. Munshiji was sitting by the side of Doctor Sinha. Nirmala saw them through the screen on the terrace and was shocked by what she saw. One was the image of youth and health and radiance; but the other... but it's better to say nothing on the subject.

Nirmala had seen Doctor Sahib hundreds of times before, but the thoughts that arose in her on looking at him now were unprecedented. Time and again she wanted to call him and reproach him and upbraid him and hurt him with all manner of taunts—but somehow she restrained herself. The baaraat had gone to the janvaasa. Preparations were going on for the next meal. Nirmala was busy selecting the appropriate serving dishes. Just then the old maidservant came and said to her—My dear, Sudha Rani is calling you. She's waiting in your room.

Nirmala left the serving dishes and went anxiously to see Sudha but stopped as soon as she stepped inside—Doctor Sinha was standing right there.

Sudha said smilingly—There you are, sister. I've brought him before you. Now, you can scold him as much as you like. I'll bar the door and make sure he doesn't run away.

Doctor Sahib replied sombrely—Who's running away. I'm here to take my punishment.

Nirmala said to him with folded hands—Always maintain your kind and generous attitude towards us, that's all I ask. Don't forget us, ever.

# Chapter 17

After Krishna's wedding Sudha went off. But Nirmala stayed on at her mother's house. Vakil Sahib wrote repeatedly but she wouldn't return. She had no desire whatever to go back. There was nothing there to draw her back. She spent the days happily at her mother's, looking after her mother and minding her younger brothers. If Vakil Sahib had come himself to escort her back, she just might have consented; but the young boys of the neighbourhood had given him such a hard time during the wedding that he wasn't too keen on coming back quite so soon. Sudha wrote to her several times—but Nirmala made excuses even to her! Finally one day Sudha took a servant with her as an escort and turned up herself.

After the two had met and embraced, Sudha said—It seems you're afraid to return.

Nirmala—That's true, sister. I came back here full three years after I went off, after my wedding. This time I go, I'll spend the rest of my life there—no more invitations, no more coming away.

Sudha—Why, you can come whenever you want. Vakil Sahib is missing you a lot.

Nirmala—Of course. I'm sure he's staying up nights because he's missing me so much!

Sudha—O you have a heart of stone. One feels sorry seeing the state he's in. He was saying there's no one in the house who takes the slightest interest in him, no son, no little child—so how is he to pass the days? He's been miserable ever since he moved to the new house.

Nirmala—Well, he has two sons, God bless them!

Sudha—He complains about them all the time. Jiyaram pays no heed to what he says to him—and even answers him back in kind. As for the younger one, he's under his brother's influence. The poor man keeps crying in memory of his eldest son all the time!

Nirmala—Jiyaram wasn't naughty earlier, so where did he learn these new tricks? He never refused to listen to me—the merest hint was sufficient.

Sudha—Who knows? It's rumoured he accuses his father of having poisoned his son—he's a murderer, the boy says. He's taunted him several times over his having married you! He says such harsh things that poor Vakil Sahib is reduced to tears. Things got so bad one day that he actually picked up a stone to hit him with.

Nirmala was now seriously worried—That boy's turning out really bad. Whoever told him his father poisoned his brother?

Sudha—Only you can reform him.

Nirmala had a new anxiety now. If this was the way Jiya was turning out—all set to fight with his own father!—then obviously he would be quite ready to quarrel with her. She lay awake a long time worrying about this. She missed Mansaram very keenly that day. Life would have passed so pleasantly with him. As for this boy, if he's like this when his father's still alive, how will he behave once his father's gone? The house is sold already. There must be a pile of outstanding debts, and as for income, it's all but stopped. God alone can help us now! Today for the first time, Nirmala felt anxious about the children. What would happen to her daughter? I'm saddled with this responsibility now, she thought. I didn't really need her. And if she had to be born, she ought to have been born in some lucky person's home. The infant was asleep next to her chest. The mother hugged her daughter even closer, as though someone were trying to snatch her away.

Sudha was in the bed next to Nirmala's. While Nirmala was tossing on a sea of anxieties, Sudha was enjoying the bliss of sleep. Does she worry, Nirmala thought, about what might happen to her child? After all, death comes to young and old alike, so why is Sudha immune to all anxiety? I've never known her melancholy with thoughts of the future.

Just then Sudha awoke. When she saw Nirmala looking in her direction she said—Aren't you asleep yet?

Nirmala—I couldn't get to sleep.

Sudha—Just close your eyes and sleep will come on its own. I'm practically dead to the world within seconds of putting my head on the pillow. Even while he's awake I'm already lost to the world. I don't know why I sleep so much. Probably some illness.

Nirmala—Of course it's a very serious illness. It happens only to the fortunate few. You'd better ask Doctor Sahib to start treating it.

Sudha—So what should I worry about while I lie awake? Sometimes, I miss my mother's home—and on those days it takes me a while to get to sleep.

Nirmala—Don't you miss Doctor Sahib?

Sudha—Never. Why should I miss him? I know he'll have returned after a game of tennis, had his dinner, and be resting soundly.

Nirmala—There, Sohan's got up now. Why should he carry on sleeping once you're awake!

Sudha—Yes, he's got this strange habit. He sleeps when I do and wakes when I wake up. He must have been a holy man in an earlier birth. See that sign on his forehead? He's got the same sign on his arms. Certainly a holy man.

Nirmala—Go on, really holy men don't go applying all those signs and things with sandalwood paste—he must have been a wicked temple-keeper. Say, which temple did you hang about at, you little devil?

Sudha—I'll marry him to your daughter.

Nirmala—Go on! Brothers don't marry sisters!

Sudha—I'll marry them, no matter what. Where else will I find such a pretty girl? Just check sister, is he a little feverish or am I imagining it?

Nirmala felt Sohan's forehead and said—No, his body's warm all right. When did he get this fever? He's drinking his milk all right, isn't he?

Sudha—He was fine when he went to sleep. Maybe he caught a chill. I'll cover him up nicely. He'll be all right by morning.

By the time morning came his condition was much worse. His nose was running and his fever had risen sharply. His eyes were inflamed and his head drooped. He no longer moved his limbs, neither was he smiling and laughing. He just lay silent. It seemed that even the sound of people talking was unpleasant to him. And he had started a small cough. Now Sudha panicked. Nirmala was also of the opinion that Doctor Sahib should be sent for immediately—but her aged mother's opinion was firm—There's no need to send for any doctors and things. It's clear someone's cast an evil eye on the boy. What good would a doctor do in such a case?

Sudha—But Amma, who'd cast an evil eye on him here? He hasn't even left the house.

Mother—It's not always as if someone intends to cast an evil eye. But with some people, their sight itself is inauspicious and an evil eye gets cast anyway, whether they will or no. Sometimes even mothers and fathers end up being the cause of an evil eye.

He hasn't cried even once since he came here. This is exactly what happens to playful children such as him. The day I saw him and his lovable antics I knew something terrible was going to happen. Don't you see his eyes, they aren't focussing here at all? This is the first sign of the evil eye.

The old maid and the neighbour's cook confirmed this assessment. And then Mahngu came and took one look at the child's face and declared—It's a clear case of the evil eye all right, no doubt about it. Just send for a few thin sticks. God willing, the child will be laughing by evening.

Five thin reeds were promptly brought. Mahngu made them all the same size and tied them up with a piece of thread. Then he mumbled something and gently stroked Sohan's head five times with cupped hands. Now the five thin reeds all became of different lengths. The assembled women who saw this strange happening were amazed. Who could now harbour residual doubts about the diagnosis? Once again Mahngu stroked the child's head gently with those reeds. This time they became all the same length once again: just a little difference remained. All this was proof of the fact that only a small part of the malign effect of the evil eye still remained. Mahngu reassured everyone and went away promising to return that evening. The child's condition became even worse during the course of the day. His cough had worsened considerably. Mahngu came in the evening and once again did his bit with the thin pieces of reed. This time all five came out the same length. The women were now reassured. But poor Sohan coughed all through the night. So much so that he lost consciousness several times. Sudha and Nirmala both spent the night sitting by his side. Still, the night passed without anything untoward. Now Nirmala's aged mother thought up something altogether new! Mahngu had been unable to cast off the evil eye, so now it was important to call a maulvi who could blow it away with his magic breath. Sudha was still unable to send word to her husband. The maid wrapped Sohan up in a sheet and carried him off to a mosque so that he could be infused with magic breath; and the ritual was repeated in the evening but poor Sohan's head still drooped. Night came once again and Sudha resolved if it passed safely she would certainly send her husband a telegram in the morning.

But that was not to be. Around midnight the child slipped from their hands. Sudha saw her life's treasure snatched away by death before her very eyes.

The very person whose marriage had been the cause of amusement yesterday was now the cause of tears in everyone's eyes. The same child whose sight filled his mother's bosom with pride had become the cause of insupportable grief. The entire household tried to console Sudha but she found it impossible to reconcile herself to what had happened, impossible to stop her incessant tears. Her greatest regret concerned her anxiety at how she would face her husband. She hadn't even informed him!

A telegram was sent off that very night, and by nine the next morning Doctor Sinha arrived in a car. When Sudha heard the news of his arrival she began to cry even more bitterly. The child's body was washed in advance of the cremation and Doctor Sahib came inside the house on several occasions, but Sudha would not go near him. How could she? How could she bear to face him? Because of her ignorance she was responsible for the jewel of his life having been flung into the river. It broke her heart even to think of going near him. Her husband's eyes had shone with joy every time he saw the child in her lap. The child would make to go into his father's arms. And if she asked him to return him to her the child would cling to his father all the tighter and refuse to come back. Then she would say—He's a selfish one!

So who would she take with her in her arms when she went to see her husband today? Seeing her bare, bereft arms, he might actually break into tears. It seemed easier for her to die rather than confront her husband. She clung to Nirmala's side for fear that she might be forced to meet her husband.

Nirmala said to her—Look sister, whatever had to happen has happened already. So how long will you keep avoiding him? He's leaving tonight, Mother said.

Looking at her through her tear-filled eyes Sudha replied—With what face can I go to him now? I'm afraid my legs might begin to quake so that I'll fall when I see him.

Nirmala—Come, I'll go with you. I'll give you support.

Sudha—You won't run away and abandon me there?

Nirmala—No, I promise I won't.

Sudha—I feel full of fears already. I'm amazed at myself that I've survived being struck by such a terrible blow. He was very fond of Sohan—I wonder what he's going through at this time. I'll hardly be in a position to give him any consolation, I'll break into tears myself. Is he really leaving tonight?

Nirmala—Yes, Mother was saying he hasn't taken any leave.

The two friends went together in the direction of the men's quarters, but at the threshold Sudha asked Nirmala to go back. She entered the room alone.

Doctor Sahib had been worrying about Sudha's condition. He was assailed by all kinds of fears. He was all packed and ready to leave but he didn't feel like leaving. His life seemed totally empty. Time and again he felt resentful against God—if he had to be deprived of this happiness all so quickly, why was it given him in the first place? He had never prayed to God for a child. He could easily have consented to remain childless for his whole life, but being deprived of a child after having been granted one was unbearable. Is a man really only God's plaything? Is that all there is to human existence—a child's playhouse, so that neither its making nor its destruction carries any great significance? But then children too are attached to their playhouses, their paper boats, their wooden horses. And they take special care of their favourite toys. If God is a child, he thought, he's a very strange child.

The mind refuses to accept such a God. The creator of all the worlds cannot be a mere naughty child. We attribute all manner of excellences to him—well beyond the reach of our understanding. But this sort of naughtiness is not among those excellences. Is depriving a bright and lively child of his life merely a form of mischief? Is God responsible for such vicious mischief?

Just then Sudha entered the room noiselessly. Doctor Sahib stood up and coming close to her said—Where have you been, Sudha? I was waiting for you.

The room seemed to swim before Sudha's eyes. Putting her arms around her husband's neck she put her head against his chest and began to weep—but she experienced a strange consolation and a limitless fortitude in being able to weep thus freely. Clasped to her husband's breast she felt a strange strength and energy course through her—as if a poor lamp buffeted by breezes had finally found the refuge of a sheltering hand.

Doctor Sahib held his wife's tear-stained face in both his hands and said—Sudha, why're you allowing yourself to be so melancholy? Sohan did all he'd come here to do, so why then should he linger here? A plant grows when it receives light and air, but becomes strong by having to cope with gusts of wind, so love needs the experience of grief to become strong. There will always be many who are willing to share one's joys and laugh with one, but it's only those who are with us in our moments of grief, those who can weep with us, that are our true friends. What do lovers know of love who haven't had the chance to weep together? Sohan's death has removed any remaining distance there might have been between us. Today we've seen each other in our true character.

Sudha sobbed—I was deceived by appearances. Oh, you weren't even able to see him one last time. God knows where he found so much wisdom in his short life. Every time he saw me crying he'd forget his own pain and smile at me. But on the third day my darling closed his eyes for the last time. I wasn't even able to give him proper medical attention.

As she said this Sudha's tears welled up again. Doctor Sinha clasped her to his bosom and said in an emotion-soaked voice—There's never been a patient, young or old, about whom family members haven't felt they could have given them better medical attention.

Sudha—Nirmala has been a great help to me. I managed to

steal a little sleep from time to time—but not her. She sat up whole nights with him in her arms, walking with him through the small hours. I'll never forget her kindness to me. Are you really leaving today?

Doctor—Yes, I didn't have the time to apply for leave. The civil surgeon was away on a shikar.

Sudha—Is he always away on shikar?

Doctor—Royalty doesn't brook many responsibilities.

Sudha—I won't let you leave today.

Doctor—I'm not that keen on leaving either.

Sudha—So, don't go. Send them a telegram. I'll come back with you. And we'll take Nirmala with us.

When Sudha returned from the outer chambers she was feeling much better. Her husband's loving words had greatly assuaged her sorrow and grief. There is infinite power in the emotion of love, infinite fortitude, and a faith that is boundless.

# Chapter 18

When we are struck by some great misfortune, we not only have to bear the grief associated therewith, we also have to suffer the harsh words and taunts of others. The great world sees a wonderful opportunity to comment on every feature of our lives, an opportunity which it seems to be ever in quest of. Mansaram's death provided people with an invaluable opportunity to say all kinds of unpleasant things. There weren't that many who were in a position to know what had really happened, but it was clear to them anyway that what happened was all due to the evil doings of the stepmother. It was the same story on everyone's lips: God forbid that children should have to suffer the attentions of a stepmother. Let him who wishes to destroy his settled domestic existence, who wishes to expose his children to cruel treatment—let him marry a second time while his children are still around. It has never been known to happen, they say, that the coming of a second wife has failed to destroy a home. The same father who dotes on his children turns into their enemy once the new wife comes—his whole mentality changes. The woman that can treat another's children like her own is yet to be born.

The trouble is people weren't content only with making such comments. There were some who had conceived a very special affection for Jiyaram and Siyaram. They expressed a great deal of sympathy for the two boys—so much so that there were a few women who would remember their mother's sweet and gentle temperament and even start to shed tears. Poor thing! How could she know that so soon after her death her loved ones would be reduced to such a pathetic condition! What chance of their getting milk and butter and such like now! Poor babies!

Jiyaram protested—Of course we do!

But the lady continued—Of course you do—but there's getting and getting, my son. So, you're presented with a whole lot of watery milk and told to drink it if you please—or not. Your poor mother used to send the servant specially to get fresh milk for you. Your faces tell the whole story. A milk-fed countenance is unmistakable—and you simply don't have it any more.

Of course Jiya had no recollection of the milk which his mother had given him, so he could hardly refute that allegation; nor did he remember what he had looked like all those many years ago. So he kept quiet. But it was natural that in time all this 'solicitude' began to produce an effect. Jiyaram was beginning to resent his family. Once Munshiji's house was auctioned and he moved to the newly rented one, he began to be anxious about finding money enough to pay rent. So Nirmala was forced to cut down on the butter. Now that the old income no longer existed, expenses had to be scaled down. Both the man-servants were dismissed. Jiyaram resented these economies bitterly. When Nirmala went away to her mother's, Munshiji cut down on the milk. He had already begun to worry about providing for the future of the new-born girl.

Jiyaram protested angrily—No doubt the savings on milk will suffice to get you a new palace. Why don't you cut out the meals too?

Munshiji—If you're all that fond of milk, why don't you go and get some for yourself. I don't like wasting good money on the watery stuff that's delivered here.

Jiyaram—So I should get the milk now—and what if one of my school-fellows sees me?

Munshiji—So what? Tell him you're off to get fresh milk for yourself. It's nothing to be ashamed of.

Jiyaram—So it isn't. If someone were to see you fetching milk, would you feel embarrassed or not?

Munshiji—Not at all. I've drawn water with these very hands and hauled sacks of grain. My father was no millionaire.

Jiyaram—But my father isn't a poor man. So why should I fetch milk? And why did you dismiss the two servants?

Munshiji—Can't you understand one simple fact, that my income is no longer what it used to be? You don't look quite so naive.

Jiyaram—But why has your income gone down?

Munshiji—When you can't understand such simple things, it's a waste explaining things to you. I'm tired of life, I can't be bothered with taking on fresh cases. And even if I were to, I couldn't actually get around to making the necessary preparation. My heart's not in it any more. I've no desire now except somehow to live out my allotted span. All the rest died with Lallu.

Jiyaram—So who's to blame for that?

Munshiji screamed at him—You fool! It was God's will, that's what. Nobody inflicts that sort of injury on themselves!

Jiyaram—I don't remember God taking such a keen interest in your getting married a second time!

Munshiji could contain himself no longer and screamed back at him with bloodshot eyes—So are you determined to fight with me today? And on the strength of what, may I ask? You don't pay for my upkeep, do you? The day you become capable of doing that, I'll take advice from you. You haven't earned the right to lecture me yet. You better spend another few years practising respect and good manners. You're not my adviser that I must seek your counsel before I do things. I've earned the money and I'll spend it any way I please. You've no right to say anything at all. And if you're ever rude to me in this way again you'll pay a heavy price, I promise you. If I've survived the loss of a gem like Mansaram, your absence won't kill me, so be warned.

But Jiyaram refused to be cowed even by such a sharp tongue-lashing. He carried on—So what is it you desire? That we endure all hardships and never utter a word? I'm afraid I can't live like that. I've seen the price my older brother had to pay for being respectful and well-mannered—and I've no taste for that sort of thing. I can't willingly swallow that kind of poison. So I'll keep a respectful distance from that sort of respect.

Munshiji—Aren't you ashamed to talk in this way?

Jiyaram—Children learn manners from their elders.

Munshiji's temper cooled. He realized that nothing he said was likely to have any effect on Jiyaram. He rose and began pacing up and down. He saw clear portents of a catastrophe looming about his home.

After that, father and son quarrelled about something or other every day. The more Munshiji yielded, the more aggressive Jiyaram became. Until one day Jiyaram went so far as to say to Rukmini— I'll spare him simply because he's my father, though I have friends who'd willingly beat him up in the bazaar at my bidding.

Rukmini duly reported this to Munshiji. Outwardly, Munshiji showed unconcern, but fear awoke in him. He stopped going out in the evenings. A new anxiety had been added to the old ones. He didn't even make the effort to call Nirmala back from her mother's for fear of how the young lout would behave with her. Jiyaram had even hinted at something—Let me see how she dares come back this time. As my name's Jiyaram, I'll humiliate her before she comes anywhere near here. And we'll see what the old man can do.

Munshiji understood that he could do nothing to restrain the young man. If it had been a stranger, he might have resorted to the police and the law to bind him. But what could he do with his own son? Truly is it said that by his own sons is a man finally defeated.

One day Doctor Sinha called Jiyaram to him and thought to have a little talk with him. Jiyaram regarded him with respect and listened to him courteously while he was talking. After he was done, Doctor Sinha asked him what it was that he desired. Jiyaram replied—Shall I tell you plainly? You won't take offence?

Sinha—No, speak up frankly. Let me hear what it is you have on your mind.

Jiyaram—Then listen. Ever since my brother died, I feel angry every time I have to see my father's face. It seems to me he's guilty of murder; and that one day, when he finds the right occasion, he'll murder the two of us brothers that remain. If that weren't his intention, why did he bother to marry a second time?

Doctor Sahib restrained his laughter with some difficulty and said—What need had he to get married in order to kill you? After all, as far as I can see he could quite as easily have murdered you without getting married!

Jiyaram—Never! Earlier, he thought altogether differently— he was devoted to us. Now he doesn't so much as wish to see our faces. His sole desire is to ensure there should be no one in the house except the two of them. He wants to remove us from the path of his future sons—that's what both of them desire most fervently. They inflict all kinds of miseries on us in the hope that we'll go away. That's why he's stopped taking on new cases. But once the two of us are dead you'll see how everything revives once again.

Doctor—But if he wanted to drive you away, couldn't he have made some false accusation and turned you out?

Jiyaram—I've already taken precautions against that sort of thing.

Doctor—What kind of precautions?

Jiyaram—You'll find out when the time comes.

With those words Jiyaram went off. Doctor Sinha tried his best to call out to him—but he didn't once look back.

Several days later Doctor Sinha happened to meet Jiyaram once again. Doctor Sahib was very fond of the cinema—and as for Jiyaram, he lived for nothing else. Doctor Sahib got Jiyaram so involved in talking about the cinema that he brought Jiyaram home with him. It was time to eat, so the two sat down to eat together. Jiyaram found the food very tasty and said—The food at our place is tasteless ever since the cook went away. Buaji makes strictly Vaishnav food. I force myself to eat but I can't actually stand even to look at it.

Doctor—Normally the food here is much better than this. So your Buaji will have nothing to do with either garlic or onions?

Jiyaram—I tell you, all she does is boil the vegetables. And as for my father, he doesn't care a fig if any of us eats or not. That's really why he turned the cook out. But if he doesn't have the money, where does the new jewellery come from?

Doctor—That's not it, Jiyaram. His income has really gone down. You're giving him a lot of trouble.

Jiyaram—I'm giving him trouble? I swear I scarcely ever even talk to him. But he's determined to darken my reputation. He's constantly, pointlessly after me. So much so that he's even started to detest my friends. Tell me, can one survive without friends? I'm not some lout to hang out with disreputable friends—but he's forever going on about my friends. Yesterday I was forced to tell him bluntly—My friends will come and visit me here, like it or not. After all, people can't be pushed around all the time.

Doctor—To tell you frankly, I feel extremely sorry for him. He's at the age when he ought to be taking things easy. He's growing old, and then there's the loss of a young son, and his health isn't too good either. What can such a man do? The little he's actually able to do is a wonder. And if you can't do anything more for him, you could at least be pleasant to him. It's not very difficult, believe me, to make old people happy. Just talking pleasantly to him will gladden his heart. What does it cost you to ask him—Father, how're you feeling today? He sees your rudeness and suffers silently. I tell you truly, he's cried in my presence several times. Let's suppose he made a mistake in getting married. He accepts as much—but why are you shirking your duty? He's your father—you should look after him. You shouldn't say things likely to cause him pain. Why give him cause to think that all of you only exist to consume what he earns, and that there's no one who cares the least bit for him? I'm much older than you, Jiyaram, but I've never once talked back to my father. Even today, when he scolds me, I bow my head and listen to what he has to say. I know whatever he says he's saying for my own good. Who can wish more for one than one's own parents? Who can ever hope to repay all one owes them?

Jiyaram just sat there weeping. He had not lost all his good feelings and had a sharp realization of just how cruel he had been. He had not felt such remorse in a long time. Weeping, he said to Doctor Sahib—I feel thoroughly ashamed of myself. I allowed myself to be led astray. But I can assure you you'll hear no further complaints about me. Please persuade my father to forgive me. I've been truly vicious to him. Tell him to forgive me this once, or I won't be able to bear the disgrace and will go away somewhere and hide—commit suicide even!

Doctor Sahib was thoroughly pleased with his persuasive powers. He embraced Jiyaram warmly and sent him on his way.

By the time Jiyaram arrived back home it was past eleven. Munshiji had just finished eating and come out. Seeing him there he said sharply—Do you know what time it is? It's nearly twelve!

Jiyaram replied with great politeness—I met up with Doctor Sinha and accompanied him to his home. He insisted I sit down and eat with him. That's why I'm late.

Munshiji—You must have gone snivelling to Doctor Sinha, or did you have some other purpose?

At this, a quarter of Jiyaram's politeness evaporated—I'm not in the habit of snivelling.

Munshiji—Not at all. You hardly have a tongue in your head. All those people who tell me about the things you've been saying must surely be inventing them?

Jiyaram—I won't answer for all the other times. But today I said nothing to Doctor Sinha that I wouldn't happily repeat in your presence now.

Munshiji—That's a matter of great happiness. Great, great happiness. Enlightenment has dawned at last.

Another quarter of Jiyaram's politeness disappeared. He raised his head and said—It doesn't quite take enlightenment for someone to become conscious of their mistakes. It's possible to reform oneself without taking recourse to the formulae of enlightenment.

Munshiji—So the louts won't gather now?

Jiyaram—Why do you call people louts without having a shred of evidence against them?

Munshiji—All your friends are louts and rascals. Not one decent fellow among them! I've told you several times not to ask them here—but you haven't heeded my words. I'm telling you for the last time today that if you allow those rascals to gather here even once more, I'll have to take resort to the police.

Another quarter vanished. He retorted—All right then, call the police. Let's see what the police can do. More than half my friends are sons of police officers. But when you yourself are so committed to reforming me, why should I waste my own energies on it?

With these words Jiyaram stalked off to his room, and within minutes one could hear the melodious strains of a harmonium emanating from it.

The carefully nurtured flame of compassion had been extinguished by one thoughtless gust of sarcasm. A little sympathy could have persuaded the horse to move forward again, but the lash of the whip made it act stubborn once more—indeed, made it push backwards out of sheer spite.

# Chapter 19

This time Sudha had to be accompanied by Nirmala. She had wanted to spend a few more days at her mother's place, but how could she leave the bereaved Sudha alone! She had to return. Rukmini said to Bhungi—See how she glows after spending time at her mother's?

Bhungi replied—I tell you, daughters are particularly fond of their mother's cooking.

Rukmini—You're right Bhungi. Only mothers feed their children properly.

Nirmala got the feeling that no one was very pleased with her return. Munshiji tried his best to appear happy but couldn't conceal the anxiety gnawing at his heart. Sudha had named the daughter Asha, or Hope. And she did appear the very image of hope. At the mere sight of her, all cares disappeared. But when Munshiji tried to take her in his arms she started to cry and ran for protection to her mother, as if she didn't so much as recognize her father. Munshiji thought to earn her favour by giving her sweets. There were no servants he could despatch, so he went and asked Siyaram to fetch a couple of annas worth of sweets. Siyaram said bluntly—Nobody sends for sweets for us.

Munshiji replied irritatedly—You're not babies any more!

Jiyaram—So are we grown-ups already then? Just get the sweets here and see for yourself whether we are children or grown-ups! Come on, out with another four annas! Thanks to Asha even our luck might change.

Munshiji—I don't have that much money at the moment. Run along, Siya, and come back quick.

Jiyaram—Siya won't go. He's not a slave. He's as much his father's son as Asha is her father's daughter.

Munshiji—Stop talking nonsense. Aren't you ashamed to compare yourself with a little baby. Go along, Siya, here's the money.

Jiyaram—Don't go, Siya. You're nobody's servant.

Siya was caught in a dilemma. Whom should he listen to? Finally he decided to heed Jiyaram's counsel. The worst his father would do was scold him—while Jiyaram would actually beat him up—and to whom would he appeal then? He said—I won't go.

Munshiji threatened—All right, but don't you dare come to me for anything again.

Munshiji was forced to visit the market himself and get a rupee's worth of sweets. He felt embarrassed asking for two annas' worth. The vendor knew him—and what would he think?

Munshiji came back into the house with the sweets. When Siyaram saw the large container he felt sorry he had disobeyed his father's bidding. How could he go now and ask for sweets? He felt bitterly regretful and began to compare the prospect of Jiyaram's beating against the imagined sweetness of the sweets.

Bhungi brought two plates with sweets and placed them before the boys. Jiyaram scolded her—Take these away!

Bhungi—Why're you getting angry—don't you like sweets?

Jiyaram—These sweets have been brought for Asha, not for us. Take them away or I'll throw them out. We have to beg for pennies, and here's a rupee worth of sweets been purchased.

Bhungi—You have some, Siya Babu, even if he doesn't.

Siya had barely, hesitatingly, reached out for the plate when Jiyaram screamed at him—Don't you dare touch a single sweet or I'll break your arm. Greedy pig!

This frightened Siya and he didn't have the courage to eat

any of the sweets after that. When all this was reported to Nirmala she thought she would mollify the boys. But Munshiji forbade her harshly.

Nirmala protested—But don't you understand? All this anger is directed at me.

Munshiji—He's become insolent, that's all. I restrain myself for fear that people will say they're poor motherless children being ill-treated—or else I'd settle him in a flash.

Nirmala—That's just what I'm afraid of.

Munshiji—But I won't any more—let people say what they will.

Nirmala—They weren't like this earlier.

Munshiji—He has the nerve to say to me—you have grown-up sons, so why did you go and get married! He wasn't even embarrassed saying to me that we'd poisoned Mansaram. He's not my son, he's my enemy!

Jiyaram was standing at the door, listening. He had come with the intention of listening to what the two of them would say in respect of the sweets—but he was unable to restrain himself on hearing Munshiji's last sentence. He said—Why would you set yourself against him if he were not your enemy? What you're saying now, I'd figured out for myself long ago. Mansaram hadn't understood this and he paid the price for it. But it won't work with me. The whole wide world says my older brother was poisoned. So why are you angry when I say it?

Nirmala was stunned! She felt as if someone had heaped burning coals on her. Munshiji tried to scold Jiyaram into silence but he just stood his ground, trading hard words with harsher ones. So much so that even Nirmala lost her temper. This brat, good-for-nothing, has the nerve to stand there and bandy words as if the whole household rests on his shoulders! Frowning, she said—All right, Jiyaram, enough! Now all of us understand what a worthy son you are—now go and sit down outside!

Munshiji had been a little restrained thus far—but seeing Nirmala enter the fray he felt emboldened. He ground his teeth and before Nirmala could prevent him he lunged at Jiyaram to slap him full on the face. Unfortunately she came in the way and the slap fell on her instead. She was shaken—she had not thought there was so much strength in his ancient, dried-up hands. She sat down holding her head. Munshiji's anger flared up even more and he hit out at Jiyaram with his fists—but this time Jiyaram grabbed hold of his arms and pushed him back—Keep your distance! Why are you asking to be humiliated? I'm sparing you because of her, or I'd have dealt with you.

With these words he went out. Munshiji just stood there, shocked. If a divine thunderbolt had struck Jiyaram down at this moment, he would probably have been delighted. He was possessed by all kinds of dark thoughts in respect of the very son whom he had once dandled in his loving arms.

All this time Rukmini had been in her own room. Now she came and said—One mustn't try to strike out at a grown-up son.

Munshiji bit his lip and said—I'll turn him out of the house. I don't care whether he becomes a beggar or a thief!

Rukmini—And who'll be dishonoured by that?

Munshiji—I don't care.

Nirmala—If I'd known my coming back would be the cause of all this, I'd never have returned. Even now it would be best if I were to go away. I can't stay in this house any longer.

Rukmini—He respects you a great deal, believe me. Much worse would have happened today if he didn't.

Nirmala—What worse remains, Didi? I try and be as careful as I can but despite that such things keep happening. I've barely come back home and this has happened. God save us!

No one got up for the evening meal and Munshiji had to eat all by himself. Nirmala was consumed by a new anxiety—how would she get through the rest of her life? If she'd only herself to worry about, it wouldn't have mattered all that much. But now she was burdened by this new cause of anxiety—what did fate have in store for her little daughter?

# Chapter 20

Anxiety drives away sleep. Nirmala lay tossing on her bed. She wanted desperately for sleep to come—but it didn't. She had turned the lamp off and opened the window and put the loudly ticking clock far from her in another room—but still sleep refused to come. She had thought over all the things she had to think about—even her worries were at an end, but sleep still held back. She put the lamp on again and picked up a book. But she had barely read a few pages before she was overcome by sleep. The book lay open.

Just then Jiyaram stepped into the room. His knees were trembling. He looked up and down the room. Nirmala lay sleeping. There was a small metal case in the alcove above her head. Jiyaram stepped noiselessly towards it, picked up the case carefully and left the room quickly. Just then Nirmala opened her eyes. She got up with a shock and rushed to the door. Could this be Jiyaram? Why did he come to my room? Could I have been mistaken? Perhaps he came by way of Didiji's room. What reason could he have had to come here? Perhaps he came in order to talk to me—but what could he want to talk about at this hour? What is he after? She was suddenly afraid.

Munshiji was sleeping up on the terrace. Nirmala was unwilling to sleep there because there was no parapet. She considered going up to wake him—but she ultimately lacked the courage. He was a suspicious man by temperament and might jump to all manner of conclusions. She came back and returned to her book. She would make the necessary enquiries and clarify everything in the morning. Who knows, she thought, I might even have been deceived? It sometimes happens when one is asleep that one imagines things—but the resolve to defer enquiries till the morning did not enable her to get back to sleep.

In the morning when she took his breakfast up to Jiyaram, he was shocked. Bhungi was the one who used to come up every morning—so why had she come today? He felt unable to look her in the face.

Nirmala asked him in full innocence—You'd come to my room last night?

Jiyaram pretended surprise—Me? Why should I come there? Did someone come there?

Nirmala pretended to believe everything he was saying to her—Yes, I felt I saw someone leave my room. I didn't see his face, but from his back I surmised you might have come in for some reason. So how shall we find out who it was? Someone did come, that's for sure.

Jiyaram was eager to prove his innocence—I was away at the theatre last night. And on the way back I stopped at a friend's and spent the night there. I returned just a short while back. There were several other people with me—you can check this up with any of them. Yes, please do—I'm most afraid. If something's lost, I'll be blamed. No thief will be caught, but I'll be blamed. You know Babuji. He'll direct his wrath at me.

Nirmala—But why should you be blamed? Even if something had been stolen, no one could have accused you. After all, one can only steal someone else's things, one can hardly steal something that belongs to one in the first place.

Thus far Nirmala had not noticed her missing metal case. She went into the kitchen to cook—and after Vakil Sahib went to the courts she decided to go and see Sudha. She hadn't seen her for some days now and she wished to consult with her about the night's happenings. She asked Bhungi—Please go and get the jewellery case from my bedroom.

On returning from the room Bhungi said—There's no jewellery case there. Where did you keep it?

Nirmala replied irritatedly—You never manage to find

anything the first time round. How can it be anywhere else? Did you look in the cupboard?

Bhungi—No, truth to tell, I didn't look there.

Nirmala smiled—Then go and look—and come back quick.

Bhungi was back in an instant—There's nothing there either. Now where would you like me to look?

Nirmala got up in a temper—God knows why he gave you eyes! See if I don't come back with it from that same room.

Bhungi trotted along behind her to the bedroom. Nirmala looked in the alcove. She looked in the cupboard. She looked under the bed. Then she opened the big metal box which contained her clothes. But the jewellery case was nowhere to be found. She was puzzled—after all, where could it have gone?

Then suddenly the nocturnal incident flashed before her eyes. Her heart missed a beat. Till now she had been looking for it in a casual sort of way. Now suddenly she was in a fever. She started looking for it in great agitation—but it was nowhere to be found. She looked for it in all the likely places—and then in all the unlikely ones. Such a large metal case could hardly be concealed under the mattress—but she stripped the bed to look there anyway. Every second, her countenance began to droop. She felt as if she was going to die with anxiety. Finally, she struck herself on the chest and began to weep.

Her jewellery is a woman's only wealth. She has no rights to any other part of her husband's wealth. So it is from her jewellery that she derives her strength and her confidence. Nirmala owned full six or seven thousand worth of ornaments. And when she put them on and went out, for that little while her heart was filled with a deep sense of joy. It was almost as if each single piece of jewellery was a shield to protect her against hardship and misfortune. Just last night she had decided she would never live in that house at the mercy of Jiyaram's whims. God forbid that she should ever have to depend on someone else. With these very oars she would somehow manage to row herself and her daughter to the other shore. So what reason did she have to fear? After all, she thought, no one could snatch those ornaments from her. Today these are my ornaments, she thought, but tomorrow they will be my support. How much solace she had derived from that one thought! But today all that wealth had been snatched from her. Now she was truly without support. In the whole wide world she had nothing she could depend upon, no shelter, no refuge. Her hopes for the future had been cut off at the very root and she wept bitterly. God, she cried, were you unable to accept even this little good fortune? An unfortunate like myself has been crippled already, and now you've put out my eyes too. Whom will I turn to, at whose door will I now beg relief? She was wet with perspiration and her eyes were swollen with crying. Nirmala continued to weep with her head bowed and Rukmini tried to console her, but the tears wouldn't stop coming, her grief would not abate.

Jiyaram returned from school at three. When Nirmala heard of his return she got up like one possessed and going up to his room said—Please, I beg you, if you're playing a joke with me, let me have it back. What will you gain by tormenting a poor creature like me?

For a moment Jiyaram was moved. This was his first foray into theft. He had not yet acquired the hardness that derives pleasure from inflicting violence on other people. If at that time he'd had the jewellery box, and had the opportunity to put it back in the alcove, it's likely he would not have let the opportunity pass. But the jewellery box was no longer in his possession. His friends had already delivered it to the jewellery market and sold it off at whatever price they could get. So what other defence did the thief have except more lies—But, Mother, would I play such a joke upon you? You're still looking upon me with suspicious eyes. I've already told you I wasn't even in the house that night—but it seems as if you still can't bring yourself to believe what I'm saying. It's a great pity you regard me as being so despicable.

Nirmala wiped the tears from her eyes and said—No, it's not

that I don't trust you! I'm not accusing you of theft. I just thought you might be playing a practical joke on me.

How could she possibly accuse Jiyaram of theft? After all, what else would the world say other than that false accusations were being levelled against a poor motherless child? I'm the one who's name will be besmirched, she thought.

Jiyaram made as if to reassure her—Come, let me see where it went. Now tell me, which way did the thief come?

Bhungi—Bhaiya, you talk of thieves coming. But even little mouse holes are sufficient for them, and this place has windows everywhere.

Jiyaram—Have you searched the place thoroughly?

Nirmala—I've already looked everywhere in the house. Now where would you suggest?

Jiyaram—Well, you do sleep like a log.

When Munshiji returned home at four he saw Nirmala's condition and said—What's the matter with you? Are you in pain?

And with those words he took Asha into his arms. Nirmala was unable to reply and began weeping again.

Bhungi—This sort of thing has never happened before. I've been in this house all my life. But never has even the smallest thing been stolen. Now the whole world will look upon me with suspicion. Now may the good Lord protect my good name!

Munshiji was unbuttoning his achkan. He did the buttons up again and asked—What happened? Has something been stolen?

Bhungi—All of Bahuji's jewellery has been stolen.

Munshiji—Where was it kept?

Nirmala related the incidents of the night sobbingly, but she didn't mention the bit about seeing someone who looked like Jiyaram leaving her room. Munshiji sighed bitterly and said—God is truly unjust. He strikes at precisely those who are down already. It seems our evil days have come. But where could the thief have come from? No outer door has been forced—and there's no other way anyone could come. I must have committed some terrible sin, that's why I'm being punished in this way! I'd said to you again and again—Don't leave the jewellery case in the alcove. But you refused to heed my words.

Nirmala—How could I have known that such a thing might happen?

Munshiji—You might at least have known that good days are inevitably followed by bad ones. If one wanted to get fresh jewellery made today, that whole lot would cost nothing less than ten thousand rupees. As for our present condition, you know we can barely manage enough to keep the house running, forget about jewellery. I'll go and report it to the police station—but don't entertain hopes of getting anything back.

Nirmala objected—When you know there's nothing to be gained by reporting it to the police, why bother?

Munshiji—Just to be able to do something. It's not possible to suffer such a big loss and do nothing at all.

Nirmala—If there were any chance of getting it back, why would they have been taken in the first place? I wasn't fated to keep them, that's what.

Munshiji—If you're fated to get them, you'll get them back. Or else you've lost them already.

Munshiji got up to leave the room. Nirmala held his hand and said—I implore you, don't go. God forbid but the end result might be even worse than if you didn't go at all.

Munshiji freed his hand and said—You do go on like a child. A loss of ten thousand is not so small that I can simply sit back and do nothing. You don't see me crying, but I know what I'm going through. This has hurt me very deeply.

Munshiji was unable to say more—he felt overcome. But he left the room in a hurry and arrived at the police station. The station officer was very courteous. Munshiji had got him off a bribery charge earlier. Alayar Khan accompanied Munshiji back to the house in order to make the preliminary investigations.

It was evening already. The police officer inspected the house, front and back, carefully. Then he went in and had a good look at Nirmala's room. After that he had a few words on the quiet with some people in the neighbourhood. This done, he said to Munshiji—I assure you, in the name of Allah, this is not the doing of any outsider. I swear to you, if this turns out to be anything other than an inside job, I'll turn in my papers. Tell me, d'you have a servant whom you have reason to suspect?

Munshiji—The only servant we employ these days is a single maid.

Officer—O not that crazy one! This is the doing of someone far more daring, I'm certain.

Munshiji—But who else is there in the house? There are my two sons, my wife and my sister. Which one of these can I suspect?

Officer—By Allah, this is the doing of some member of the household—suspect whomsoever you will! God willing, I'll have this worked out in a few days. I can't assure you that all the missing ornaments will be restored, but I'll certainly catch hold of the thief.

After the police officer went off, Munshiji came in and reported everything he had said to Nirmala.

Nirmala was suddenly afraid—I beg you, please, go and tell the police officer to stop the investigations immediately.

Munshiji—But why?

Nirmala—D'you still need to be told why? Wasn't he saying it was the doing of some member of the family.

Munshiji—Let him rant.

Jiyaram was sitting in his room, praying. He had a distracted look. He had heard people say that the police were able to read people's faces. He was afraid to step outside the house. He was desperate to know what the two were talking about. As soon as the police officer went off and Bhungi stepped outside the room, Jiyaram asked her—So, what was the police officer saying?

Bhungi sidled up to him and said—You know what, the wicked fellow was saying the culprit is certainly a member of the household, it can't be an outsider!

Jiyaram—Didn't my father say something?

Bhungi—Well, not really, he just kept mumbling assent. After all, I, Bhungi, am the only outsider in the house—all the rest are family.

Jiyaram—But I'm also practically an outsider, aren't I?

Bhungi—Why do you say that, Bhaiya?

Jiyaram—My father didn't tell the police officer the names of the people he didn't suspect?

Bhungi—I didn't hear him saying any such thing. The poor police fellow did say though—That Bhungi is a crazy one. She isn't capable of doing this. As for the master, he would have implicated me!

Jiyaram—Well, that clears you. And that leaves only me. Tell me, did you see me in the house that day?

Bhungi—No, truth to tell. You were out to the 'tetar' that day.

Jiyaram—You will swear to that?

Bhungi—Oh it won't come to that. The mistress is getting the investigation stopped.

Jiyaram—Really?

Bhungi—Yes Bhaiya, she was saying repeatedly—Please have the investigation stopped. Let the ornaments go. But the master was not to be stopped.

For five or six days Jiyaram had hardly anything to eat. Sometimes he would take a few morsels, at other times he would say he had no appetite. His face was drained of all colour. He couldn't sleep nights for fear of the police officer. If he had known that things would go so far, he would never have initiated the business in the first place. He had presumed suspicion would fall on some thief. He had imagined himself beyond suspicion—but now it seemed likely that the whole thing was going to blow up in his face. The thorough way in which that miserable inspector was going about the investigation was causing great anxiety to Jiyaram.

When he returned home on the evening of the seventh day he was greatly agitated. Till today, he had entertained some desperate hope of escaping undetected. The stolen goods had not been found till then; but today he'd heard that the stolen ornaments had been located. Any moment now the police officer would arrive with a constable. There was no escape now. If he were to bribe the police officer—and he had the funds to do that—it was still possible that the matter would not be pressed in the courts. But what hope was there of the whole business not becoming known? Even before the stolen ornaments had been found, there was a strong rumour doing the rounds of the city that it was the son who had made off with the family jewels. After the ornaments were found it would be the talk of every little alley. And where would he hide his shame then?

When Munshiji came back from the courts he too was greatly agitated. He sat down on the bed, holding his head in his hands.

Nirmala asked him—Why don't you take off your clothes? You're back later today than on other days.

Munshiji—What's the point? Haven't you heard?

Nirmala—What's the matter? I've heard nothing at all.

Munshiji—The stolen ornaments have been found. Now there's no hope of saving Jiyaram.

Nirmala was not surprised. It was evident from her face that she knew this fact already. She said—I'd warned you not to report the matter to the police.

Munshiji—You suspected Jiyaram?

Nirmala—Of course. I'd seen him leaving my room that night.

Munshiji—Then why didn't you tell me this?

Nirmala—It was not for me to say such a thing. You would certainly have suspected my motives in voicing such a suspicion. Tell me truthfully, would you or wouldn't you?

Munshiji—It's possible, I don't deny that. But even so, you should have said it to me anyway. I wouldn't have made a report to the police. You were very concerned about preserving your own image but gave no thought to the consequences that would follow. I've just come from the police station. Alayar Khan must be on his way here.

Nirmala asked hopelessly—What now?

Munshiji looked up towards the sky and said—As God wills. If I had a couple of thousand to offer to him, it might have been possible to hush the matter up—but you know how things are with us. We're out of luck, that's all there is to it. The sin is mine all right—but on whom is the retribution going to be visited? One son's gone, and the second's reduced to this condition. Foolish he was, and disrespectful, indolent—but he's my son after all. And he'd have come to his senses sometime. This loss will prove unbearable.

Nirmala—If paying some money will help, I can arrange for some.

Munshiji—Can you? How much?

Nirmala—How much will you need?

Munshiji—It'll be impossible to start negotiations at anything below a thousand. I'd charged him one thousand for a case once. He'll get his own back today.

Nirmala—I'll find the money. Go to the police station immediately.

Munshiji took a long time at the police station. He got his chance of talking to the officer by himself after a long wait. And then Alayar Khan was an old crocodile. It wasn't easy to draw him. Even after the matter was settled for five hundred, he accepted the bribe only as a great favour. Still, the job was done. Munshiji told Nirmala on his return—There now, we've made it at last. You provided the money all right, but it was my smooth talking that did the trick in the end. He was persuaded only with the greatest difficulty. An experience never to be forgotten. Has Jiyaram eaten?

Nirmala—No, he hasn't returned after his evening out.

Munshiji—It must be midnight at least.

Nirmala—I've checked several times. His room's dark.

Munshiji—And Siyaram?

Nirmala—He's eaten and gone to bed.

Munshiji—Didn't you ask him where Jiyaram has gone?

Nirmala—He said he didn't tell him.

Munshiji felt suddenly anxious. He woke Siyaram and asked—Didn't Jiyaram say anything to you about when he'd be back? Where's he gone?

Siyaram scratched his head and rubbed his eyes—Didn't say anything to me.

Munshiji—He was fully dressed when he went out?

Siyaram—He was wearing a kurta and a dhoti.

Munshiji—Did he seem happy when he left the house?

Siyaram—He didn't seem particularly happy. He made as if to come inside the house several times but retreated each time without crossing the threshold. He stood on the terrace outside for quite some time. And he was wiping his eyes as he left. He cried often over the last few days.

Munshiji sighed deeply, as if there were little left to live for. He said to Nirmala—I'm sure you did what you did with the best intentions, but even an enemy could not have struck me a more terrible blow than this. If Siyaram's mother had been alive, d'you think she'd have hesitated because of a possible embarrassment? Never.

Nirmala—Why don't you go over to Doctor Sahib's? He might be there. Several boys go there every day. One of them might know something. Despite all my care and caution the blame has finally fallen on me!

Munshiji replied tonelessly, as if to the open window—I'll go there. What else can I do?

When Munshiji stepped out, he found Doctor Sahib standing there. Startled, he asked—Have you been standing here a while?

Doctor—No, I've just arrived. Where are you off to at this hour? It's twelve-thirty.

Munshiji—I was coming to you. Jiyaram still hasn't returned. He isn't at your place?

Doctor Sinha gripped Munshiji's hands in his and was only able to say—Bhai Sahib, you will have to be strong and patient...—when Munshiji fell to the ground as if struck by a bullet.

# Chapter 21

There was a distinct tone of irritation in Rukmini's voice when she said to Nirmala—So, will he go to school barefoot, then?

Nirmala, doing up her daughter's hair, merely said—What can I do? I have no money with me.

Rukmini—You seem to have money enough for new jewellery, but when it comes to the boy's shoes, suddenly there's nothing! Two are gone anyway, do you now want the third to weep his heart out and follow them?

Nirmala took a cold, deep breath—He who has to live will live, and he who has to die will die. I have nothing to do with anyone's living or dying.

There were frequent, daily quarrels between Rukmini and Nirmala nowadays. Ever since the theft of her jewellery, Nirmala's nature had changed entirely. She had begun to grasp at every single paisa. Siyaram might cry as bitterly as he pleased, he wouldn't get a single paisa for sweets. And it wasn't even as if this kind of behaviour was confined to Siyaram—she had the same uncaring attitude towards her own needs. She wouldn't get herself a new dhoti until the last one was reduced to shreds. For months on end she would do without buying oil for her hair. She was fond of eating paan, but for days on end her paandaan remained unattended. So much so that she even neglected to send for milk for her infant daughter. The baby's future had assumed monstrous form and hovered perpetually over her mother's consciousness.

As for Munshiji, he had yielded himself up completely to Nirmala's control. He never interfered in anything she did. For some unknown reason he seemed to defer to her in everything. He went to the courts daily now, without fail. He had not worked so hard even as a young man. His eyesight was failing, and Doctor Sinha had forbidden him from reading at night; his digestion had always been sluggish and was now even worse; he had even begun to develop a little asthma, but even so the poor man worked hard from morning till midnight. Irrespective of whether he felt like working or not, regardless of whether he was well or ill, work he had to all the same. Nirmala felt not the slightest twinge of sympathy for him. An overwhelming anxiety about the future was destroying all her tender emotions. She would fly into a rage every time she heard a beggar's cry. She was unwilling to spend a single paisa.

One day she sent Siyaram to the market to buy some ghee. She didn't trust Bhungi now and so didn't send her to the market any more. Siyaram was not a cautious shopper and had no bargaining skills. And he had to do practically all the shopping. Nirmala would carefully weigh each and every item, and if ever anything was the slightest bit short she would send Siyaram back to the shop. Siyaram spent an enormous amount of time doing just this fetching and returning. As for the shopkeepers, they were reluctant to sell him anything. And today again the same situation arose. Siyaram had, by his lights, shopped around and after much effort bought the best ghee he could find, but Nirmala sniffed it once and declared—It's no good, take it back.

Siyaram replied with manifest annoyance—There isn't better ghee in the market, I've checked all the shops.

Nirmala—So that means I'm lying?

Siyaram—I don't say that, but the shopkeeper won't take it back now. He told me clearly, check it any which way you like here, it's right in front of you—but I won't take it back under any condition. I smelt it and tasted it, then made my purchase. Now how d'you expect me to go back?

Nirmala ground her teeth in rage and said—It's obvious there's animal fat mixed in this ghee, and you expect me to believe the ghee is good. I won't let this ghee into my kitchen—you can do what you please with it, eat it or take it back.

She left the pot there and went into the house. Siyaram felt faint with anger and embarrassment. How could he possibly face going back to the shop? The shopkeeper would tell him bluntly—I won't take it back.

And what would he do then? All the nearby shopkeepers and no doubt some passers-by would stop and stare. He would be shamed in front of all those people. As it was, most shopkeepers in the market were reluctant to sell him goods, and he got no attention at any shop. He'd be shouted at by all. In deep exasperation he said to himself—Let it lie there, I won't go back to the shop.

There's nothing in creation quite so miserable, so pathetic as a motherless child. All the others can forget their sorrows. The child remembered his mother—if my mother had been alive today, would I have been forced to put up with all this? Bhaiya has gone, and so has Jiyaram—so why have I been spared to put up with all this misery? He began to cry. From his anguished heart, with a cold sigh, these words came forth—Why have you forgotten me, Mother—why don't you call me to yourself?

Just then Nirmala came into the room. She had supposed Siyaram would have gone back to the market. Seeing him still sitting there she said angrily—You're still sitting here? When d'you think the food will be cooked?

Siyaram wiped his eyes and said—I'm getting late for school.

Nirmala—So, where's the harm if you're late one day? After all, this is also important work.

Siyaram—There's something or other like this every day. I'm never able to get to school on time. And I get no time to study at home. Nothing is ever bought without several trips to the market. But I'm the one who's scolded and embarrassed there, so what do you care?

Nirmala—Of course, why should I care? I'm your enemy after all, aren't I? If you'd been one of my own I might have cared. But as for me, I wish and pray that you shouldn't get an education. I'm of course full of fault and you're entirely blameless. The fact is, the very name 'stepmother' attracts censure. If a mother gives her child poison, it's nectar; but if I were to give you nectar, it would still be seen as poison. It's because of you people that my life's been ruined, I've spent my entire life weeping, and wondering why God granted me this life at all—but as far as you're concerned my life is all self-indulgence. Of course it gives me great pleasure to torment you. Oh, if only God would ask me but once, I could bring this entire tragedy to an end!

Even as she finished her words, Nirmala's eyes filled with tears. She went indoors. Seeing her tears Siyaram was overcome with fear. It's not that he felt any regret—but he felt anxious about the form his punishment might take. He picked up the pot of ghee and made off for the market with all the tremulous nervousness of a dog entering a new and unfamiliar village. And just like that dog, the merest flicker of his anguish was apparent in every gesture. Even a person of ordinary intelligence could have said he was an orphan.

As he advanced towards the market, at each step his heart beat ever faster with the thought of the battle that lay ahead. He had taken a decision. If the shopkeeper refused to take the ghee back, he would simply leave it there and come away. The shopkeeper would then have to call him back. He had even thought up the words in which he'd scold the shopkeeper. He'd say—So, mister, this is the way in which you make fools of people? You show them the good items and then pack up rotten stuff?

But in spite of this decisiveness his feet were advancing with agonizing slowness! He didn't want the shopkeeper to see him approach the shop; he wished to appear at the shop all of a sudden. So he took an indirect route to the shop.

As soon as he saw him the shopkeeper said—I'd told you I wouldn't take back goods that had been sold. Speak up, did I or didn't I?

Siyaram replied angrily—But you didn't give me the ghee you'd shown me. You showed me one thing, then packed up another—so why won't you take it back? This is highway robbery!

Shopkeeper—If you can get better ghee anywhere in the market, I'll gladly pay a penalty. Pick up the pot and go check out a few other shops.

Siyaram—I don't have the time to do all that. Take your ghee back.

Shopkeeper—That I will not do.

There was a sadhu with a great tuft of hair sitting at the shop and enjoying the goings-on. He came up to Siyaram and took a sniff of the ghee—But the ghee seems excellent, my child.

Emboldened by this the shopkeeper said—The truth is, Babaji, we wouldn't give him inferior stuff anyway. After all, inferior goods shouldn't be passed on to buyers, should they?

Sadhu—Go on child, take the ghee, it's excellent.

Siyaram broke into tears. He had no way now of proving that the ghee was anything other than excellent. He said—But she said the ghee is bad, take it back. I told her the ghee is good.

Sadhu—Who said this?

Shopkeeper—Must be his mother. She's never satisfied with anything. The poor boy has to run to the shops again and again. She's a stepmother after all! If she'd been a real mother she might have cared.

The sadhu looked deeply sympathetic towards Siyaram and was impatient to do something that would bring his misery to an end. He said in a kindly voice—How long has it been since your mother died, child?

Siyaram—This is the sixth year.

Sadhu—You must have been very little then. Strange are your ways, Lord! You have deprived this baby of his mother's love. You do terrible things, God! A six-year-old child left to the tender mercies of a stepmother! Brilliant, God of mercy! Please, Sahji, take pity on this poor boy. Take the ghee back otherwise his mother will not let him back into the house. God willing, your ghee will get sold quickly. And my blessings will be with you.

But the shopkeeper did not return the money. After all, the boy would be forced to come back for the ghee anyway. And who knows how often he'd have to come to the market and fall prey to some cheat. So he gave Siyaram the best ghee he had in his shop. As for Siyaram, he was thinking about how kind the sadhu had been to him. But for his intercession the shopkeeper would never have given him the good ghee.

When Siyaram started for home with the ghee the sadhu fell in with him. And all along the way he spoke gentle words to the boy.

'O my son, my mother too deserted me when I was only three years old. Ever since then it's broken my heart to see poor motherless children.'

Siyaram asked him—Then did your father too marry a second time?

Sadhu—Yes, my son, or else why would I be a sadhu today? Initially my father resisted marrying again. He loved me a great deal. But then suddenly he changed his mind—and remarried. I am a sadhu and shouldn't speak harsh words of anyone—but my stepmother was as unkind as she was beautiful. She'd starve me for days on end and beat me up if I cried. As for my father, his attitude towards me changed entirely. He'd begun to hate the very sight of me. He'd beat me up if ever he heard me cry. Finally, one day, I left home.

Siyaram too had considered the option of leaving home several times. And even now he was thinking the same thing. He asked the sadhu eagerly—Where did you go when you left home?

The sadhu laughed and said—That very day all my sorrows came to an end. Since the day I snapped the ties that bound me to home and freed my mind from fear, I was a liberated soul. I sat the whole day under the bridge. At evening I met up with a holy man. His name was Swami Parmanandji. He was a celibate monk. He took pity on me and gave me shelter. I travelled far and wide in his company. He was a very accomplished yogi. And he taught me the science of yoga. Now I've become so proficient myself that I can see my mother whenever I want. Talk to her even.

Siyaram's eyes opened wide—But your mother's dead!

Sadhu—So what, my son. Yoga has the power to summon up the spirits of the dead at will.

Siyaram—If I learn yoga, can I see my mother?

Sadhu—Of course! Everything is possible with practice. Naturally, you require a good teacher. Yoga offers access to all kinds of powers. You can summon all the riches you want in a fraction of a second. No matter what the illness, you can find a cure for it.

Siyaram—Where is your abode?

Sadhu—My son, I have no fixed abode. I spend my life wandering from place to place. You can go now, son. I have my rituals to attend to.

Siyaram—I'll come with you. I'm reluctant to take leave of you so soon.

Sadhu—No, my son. You're getting late for school.

Siyaram—When will I see you again?

Sadhu—I'll come by sometime. Where's your home, my son?

Siyaram replied happily—Will you come home with me? It's very close by. I'll be greatly honoured.

Siyaram led the way enthusiastically. He was as happy as if he had laid his hands on a bag of gold. Arriving home he said—Come inside for a little while, please.

Sadhu—No, my son. I won't come in now. But I'll come in a day or two. This is your home, isn't it?

Siyaram—What time will you come tomorrow?

Sadhu—I can't tell you definitely. I'll come some time.

The sadhu had gone only a short distance when he met up with another sadhu whose name was Hariharanand.

Parmanand asked him—Where have you been wandering? Did you manage to land anything?

Hariharanand—I've been all over the place. But there's nothing to be found. I thought I'd found a likely one or two, but they merely laughed at me.

Parmanand—It's seems I've found one all right. Let's see if I'm able to trap him.

Hariharanand—You're a great one for boasting. But all the ones you catch take flight after a day or two.

Parmanand—Not this time, I assure you. His mother's dead—and his father's married a second time. His stepmother torments him. He's fed up of home!

Hariharanand—Well, that certainly sounds promising! You've set the trap nicely, I hope?

Parmanand—Wonderfully! This seems the best strategy. First find out which houses in a particular neighbourhood have stepmothers. Those are the houses to go for.

# Chapter 22

Nirmala asked him sharply—Where were you this long? Siyaram replied rudely—I must have fallen asleep along the way!

Nirmala—I'm not implying that, but d'you know what time it is? It's long after ten. The market's hardly any distance at all.

Siyaram—No distance at all. It's really at our doorstep.

Nirmala—What's got into you? Why can't you reply straight? You're carrying on as if you've done me some favour.

Siyaram—Why d'you always talk nonsense? Is it an easy job returning things that have been bought? One has to argue with the shopkeeper for hours. It's lucky there was a holy man there who spoke up in my favour, otherwise he would never have agreed to take it back. I didn't stop anywhere for even a minute—I've come back here directly.

Nirmala—Getting the ghee has taken you till nearly eleven.

Now if you were to go for the wood you'd be gone till evening. Your father's gone away without eating. If you were going to take this long, why didn't you say so before you went out? Now go for the wood directly.

Siyaram was unable to control himself. He replied angrily—Send someone else for the wood! I'm already late for school.

Nirmala—You won't eat?

Siyaram—Won't!

Nirmala—I'm willing to cook. But I can't go and get the wood.

Siyaram—Why can't you send Bhungi?

Nirmala—Haven't you ever seen the kind of shopping she brings back home?

Siyaram—Well I won't go just now.

Nirmala—Don't blame me later.

Siyaram hadn't been to school the past several days. Because of all his shopping errands he had no time to even look at his books. Apart from being shouted at, and being made to stand on the bench or in the corner with a dunce cap, what else could he look forward to there anyway? He used to leave home with his books all right, but he'd take the road out of town and park himself under some shady tree—or watch the soldiers on parade. At three, he would return home. Today he left home—but he didn't feel like sitting somewhere today—and then his intestines were crying out! True, now he couldn't even depend on being fed. Couldn't the food have been cooked by ten? True, Babuji had gone out already. But couldn't a little something have been found for me? If Mother had been alive, he thought, would she have let me leave home in this fashion without my having had a thing to eat? Nobody cares for me any more.

Siyaram felt a great urge to meet the Babaji. He thought—Where'll I find him at this time? Where should I look for him at this hour? The thought of his gentle voice, his encouraging counsel, seemed powerfully attractive to him right now. He said eagerly—O why didn't I go away with him? What's there to keep me at home anyway?

Now, upon leaving home, he went straight to the previous day's ghee shop in the hope that he might meet the Babaji again. But he wasn't there. He stood around a long time then came away.

He had barely got back home when Nirmala came over and said to him—So what kept you today? No food could be cooked in the morning, now are we skipping dinner too? Go and get some vegetables from the market!

Siyaram burst out—I've just come back after a whole day with nothing to eat. You haven't even brought me a glass of water to drink and you're ordering me to go to the market. I won't go, I'm not your servant! After all, what d'you give me but dry rotis. These I'll get anywhere I work. If I have to be a servant, I won't be your servant—so don't bother to cook for me.

Nirmala was left speechless. What's come over the boy today? Other days he used to go off and do as he was told—so why is he being difficult today? But it didn't occur to her even at this point that she should give the boy a little money to buy himself something to eat. She had become so miserly that she said— Helping in the home isn't being a servant. If it were, I too could say I won't cook, and your father could say he won't go to the courts—and where would we be then? If you don't feel like going, say so and I'll send Bhungi. How was I to know you disliked going to the market so much—otherwise no matter if money was wasted on this and that, I wouldn't ask you to go. There, I swear I won't ask you to go again.

Siyaram felt a little shamed but not enough to actually go to the market. In fact he was thinking of the Babaji. He saw the end of all his troubles and the realization of all his hopes in the blessings of that holy man. Under the Baba's protection alone would his meaningless existence acquire point and substance. By sunset he was desperately impatient. He searched the whole market but found not a sign of the Babaji. Without food and drink the whole day, the poor innocent child was the very image of hope and fear as he went up and down the market, into shops and temples, into narrow alleyways, looking for that refuge without which his life had now become unbearable. Once he actually saw a sadhu standing outside a temple. He thought he'd found his man. He was overjoyed and ran up to the sadhu and stood by his side. But it turned out to be quite another holy man. Despondent, he resumed his search.

Gradually the streets emptied of traffic and the doors of houses began to close. Spreading their sacks and cots on city pavements and in the alleys, the vast public of India prepared to savour the pleasures of sleep—but Siyaram did not go back home. He had decided to have no more to do with the place, that home where no one loved him, where he existed merely like some unloved dependant for the sole reason that he had nowhere to go. Even at this time, who in that home could possibly be worrying about his long absence? Babuji must have retired after his dinner and Ammaji must be preparing to sleep. No one could possibly have bothered so much as to look in his room. True, his aunt might be worried about him, might still be waiting up for him. *She* wouldn't eat until his return.

As soon as the thought of his aunt crossed his mind, Siyaram turned his steps homewards. Even if she could do nothing more, she could at least clutch him to her bosom and weep? When he returned, she would at least bring him some water so he might wash his face and hands. Not everyone in the world is born to great good fortune. There are many who do not even get enough to eat—but the ones who run away from home are invariably those deprived of a mother's love.

Siyaram had turned his steps homewards when he happened to see Swami Parmanand coming up the alley towards him.

Siyaram went to him quickly and held his hand. Parmanand was startled and asked—Child, what're you doing here?

Siyaram made up a quick story—I'd come to meet a friend. How far is your camp from this place?

Parmanand—We're leaving this place today, child. We start for Hardwar.

Siyaram was crestfallen—Will you leave today itself?

Parmanand—Yes my child. Now we'll meet next when I return.

There was a catch in Siyaram's throat when he asked—Return?

Parmanand—I'll come back soon, child.

Siyaram's voice sounded broken—I'll come with you.

Parmanand—With me! Will your family allow you to leave like this?

Siyaram—What have I to do with those people?

Siyaram was unable to say anything more. His brimming eyes told the tale of his woebegone existence far more comprehensively than his tongue ever could.

Parmanand took the child into his arms and said—All right, child. If that's your wish, come with me. Enjoy the pleasures of the company of people such as I. God willing, you'll find what you want.

Having hovered over its prey all this while, the predator finally descended on its catch. Now, as to whether the bird will end up in a cage or under the hunter's knife—who can tell?

# Chapter 23

**M**unshiji returned from the courts at five in the evening and directly collapsed on the bed. He was an old man now, and he hadn't eaten a thing all day. His mouth felt dry. Nirmala surmised immediately that he had probably earned nothing all day either. She asked—Got nothing today?

Munshiji—I spent the whole day running around, but not a thing.

Nirmala—What happened in that criminal case?

Munshiji—My client got sentenced.

Nirmala—And in the Pandit's case?

Munshiji—The Pandit lost.

Nirmala—You were very confident there was no case against him?

Munshiji—That's what I thought—and I still say that the claim against him holds no water—but how can I convince someone else?

Nirmala—And in the case regarding the landlord and the lands he claimed were under his own cultivation?

Munshiji—Lost again.

Nirmala—It appears you got up the wrong side of the bed today.

Munshiji was in fact quite unable to carry on working now. He didn't get too many cases for one, and even the ones he did he managed to ruin. But he kept all evidence of failure from Nirmala. On days when he failed to earn, he would borrow a few rupees and hand those over to Nirmala. He had thus borrowed something or other from practically all his friends. But today even that stratagem had proved impossible.

Nirmala was anxious—With you like this, things are going to be difficult indeed. And then your son refuses to go to the market! I feel like getting Bhungi to do everything. He came back with the ghee at eleven. I tried my best to get him to go for the wood but he refused to budge!

Munshiji—So you haven't cooked anything?

Nirmala—Now I understand why you keep losing your cases all the time! Is anyone else able to cook without fuel that I alone should manage it somehow?

Munshiji—So he went away without eating?

Nirmala—What was there in the house that I could feed him?

Munshiji asked fearfully—You didn't give him a little money, then?

Nirmala frowned angrily—Seems it grows on trees in this house?

Munshiji didn't reply to that. He waited a little in the hope that he might get some small refection—but when Nirmala didn't even so much as send for water he lost hope and sloped out. He felt worried at the thought of Siyaram's distress. The whole day's gone by and the poor boy's had nothing to eat. He must be lying in his room. What would have been the great loss if Bhungi had been sent out for the wood this once? What's the point of such careful spending that the household goes hungry? He scrabbled around in his tin box in the hope of finding some small change. He got all the papers out, checked all the various compartments, looked in every corner, but found nothing. If money didn't grow and ripen in Nirmala's box, here it probably didn't even get to flower! But by a happy coincidence, as he was riffling through some papers, a four-anna piece fell out! Munshiji was overjoyed. He'd earned large sums in the past but nothing had given him quite so much joy as today's small coin. Four-anna piece in hand, he stood outside Siyaram's door and called to him. There was no reply. He went inside the room to look. There was no sign of him there—hadn't he come back from school? As soon as he thought of that, he went and asked Bhungi. He learnt the boy had returned from school.

Munshiji asked—Did he have some water to drink?

Bhungi didn't reply. She merely wrinkled her nose and went away.

Munshiji returned slowly to his room and sat down. Today for the first time he felt truly angry with Nirmala—but almost immediately the feeling of anger turned upon himself. Lying on the floor in that darkened room he began to blame himself for having been so unconcerned with the fate of his son. He was tired anyway—and in a little while he fell asleep.

Bhungi came and called out—Babuji, dinner's ready.

Munshiji got up with a start. The lamp had been lit—What time is it, Bhungi? I must've fallen asleep.

Bhungi replied—The kotwali clock struck nine, that's all I can say.

Munshiji—Has Siyaram returned?

Bhungi—He'd be in the house, wouldn't he—if he had?

Munshiji asked in some frustration—I ask you, has he returned or not? Why don't you give me a straight answer? Returned or not?

Bhungi—Well I haven't seen him—so why should I lie?

Munshiji lay back in his bed, saying—Let him return, then I'll come.

Far a full half hour Munshiji lay on his bed staring at the outer door. Then he got up and went out, and turning to the right walked for about two furlongs. Then he came back and asked—Is Siya back?

Someone answered from within—Not yet.

Then Munshiji turned left and went all the way to the end of the lane. No sign of Siyaram anywhere. He came back home and standing at the door called out—Is Siya back?

A voice answered from within—No.

The kotwali clock struck ten.

Munshiji went rapidly in the direction of the Company Park. He thought, it's possible he went there for a stroll and fell asleep on the grass. Getting to the park he looked on every bench, walked all around among the many people lying on the grass. There was no sign of Siyaram. He called out for Siyaram several times but no one answered his call.

Then he thought there might be something on at the school. The school was a little over a mile away. He started for the school but turned back halfway. The market was already shut. No school entertainment could last that long. He was still hoping that Siyaram might have returned. Arriving at his door he called out again—Is Siya back?

The door was closed, and there was no answering voice. He called out again. Bhungi opened the door and said—He isn't back yet.

Munshiji softly beckoned Bhungi to come closer and asked her in a pathetic voice—You know all that goes on in this house. Tell me truthfully, what happened today?

Bhungi—Well, I won't lie, at worst she'll turn me out, what else? But that's no way to treat another's child. Whenever she thinks of something, she packs him off to the market. He spends whole days running to the market. Today when he refused to go for wood, nothing was cooked in the house all day. And then she gets mad if anyone says anything. But if you won't notice anything, how can anyone else point anything out? Come, eat your dinner she's been waiting for you all this while.

Munshiji—Go and tell her I won't be eating tonight.

Munshiji went back to his room and breathed a long, cold sigh. And these pain-soaked words escaped his lips—O God, haven't I been punished enough already? Will you deprive this blind old man of even his stick now?

Nirmala came and said to him—Siyaram still hasn't come back. I kept telling him to stay and eat, I'd cook something for him, but he got up and left without saying anything to me. Who knows where he's roaming? He never listens to anyone. How long can one keep waiting for him? Now you come and eat, I'll put some dinner away for him.

Munshiji gave Nirmala a cold, hard look and said—What time is it now?

Nirmala—Who knows, must be ten.

Munshiji—Not at all, it's midnight.

Nirmala—Midnight? He's never this late. So how long will you wait for him. You didn't have anything in the afternoon either. I've never seen a loafer like this boy.

Munshiji—Yes, he must give you a lot of trouble, isn't it?

Nirmala—See for yourself. It's so late but there's no thought of returning home.

Munshiji—This might well be his last act of mischief.

Nirmala—What things you say! Where can he go anyway? He must've parked himself at some friend's house.

Munshiji—Maybe that's what it is. God grant that that's what it is.

Nirmala—You'd better deal with him sternly when he gets here in the morning.

Munshiji—I will. I certainly will.

Nirmala—Come on and eat now. It's very late.

Munshiji—I'll eat in the morning after having rebuked him strongly. But if he doesn't come back, where will you find another good servant like him!

Nirmala reacted sharply—So, have I driven him away then?

Munshiji—No, of course not. Why would you? After all, he used to work for you. Some devil must have possessed him!

Nirmala said no more. She was afraid the conversation might slip out of control. She went in and didn't even ask him to come to bed. And in a little while Bhungi shut the inner doors too.

Could Munshiji possibly get to sleep? Of his three sons only one remained. And if even he were gone, what would remain in his life except an endless darkness? No one to remember him after he was gone. And what priceless jewels he had lost! Was it surprising that tears streamed down Munshiji's eyes? In that mood of sweeping regret, that enveloping darkness of bitter remorse, only one thin ray of hope kept him this side of a complete breakdown. But when that ray too was gone—who can say what he would go through then? Who can imagine his grief at a moment such as that?

Several times during the night Munshiji dropped off to sleep but awoke with a start each time, imagining he had heard sounds of Siyaram's return.

At daybreak Munshiji was off looking for Siyaram again. He felt ashamed to ask anyone. He felt embarrassed to ask. He expected no sympathy from anyone. Even if they didn't say so to his face, each one of them would think the same thought—now reap what you have sown. For two whole days he went tramping around the school, and fields and markets and parks—for two whole days, without a thing to eat, he kept going.

He returned home at midnight. There was a lantern burning at the door and Nirmala was standing there. As soon as she saw him she said—You didn't tell anyone anything, just went off. Did you find out anything?

Munshiji's eyes were fiery—Get out from my sight or I won't be answerable for what I do! All this is your doing. It's entirely because of you that I've been reduced to this condition. Was this the state of my home six years ago? You've destroyed my well-established home, uprooted my flourishing garden. Now only one stump remains. And you'll rest only when you've destroyed that as well. I didn't bring you to this house to have my whole world destroyed. I wanted to make my happy existence even happier. And this is the price I'm paying. My darling sons who were treated with such indulgence before you came—before my very eyes you began to treat them like servants. And despite seeing it all I remained blind. Go on, get me a little arsenic. That's all that remains now, we might as well get it over with!

Nirmala replied through her tears—I know I'm unfortunate, I hardly need to be told that by you now. God alone knows why I was given this life to live. But how have you concluded that Siyaram will not return?

Moving towards his room Munshiji called out to her—Don't rub salt into my wounds. Go and celebrate the event. All your wishes have been fulfilled.

# Chapter 24

Nirmala wept all night. Such a monstrous accusation! She had seen Jiyaram leaving with the ornaments but kept her mouth shut. Why? Because people would think she was being vindictive by levelling false accusations against the boys. So today she was being blamed because she'd said nothing! Suppose she had stopped Jiyaram at that moment and he'd run away from home because of a feeling of shame—would she not have been blamed then again?

And further, in what way had she maltreated Siyaram? It was only to save money that she sent him to the market. Was it because she wished to save money and buy ornaments for herself? When the earnings had dwindled as they had, what option had she except to watch every paisa and save whatever little she could? And when one couldn't be all that sure even of the young, what sense was there in relying on the longevity of the old? At the time of her daughter's wedding, to whom would she turn for money? And it wasn't as if her daughter's burden was her responsibility alone. She was only trying to save to ease things for her husband. And why just her husband? After his death Siyaram would become head of the household. Would he not then have to bear the expense of his sister's wedding? She'd been exercising all that restraint only to save her husband and son from later difficulties. What else would a daughter's wedding be under such circumstances except a calamity? And now she was attracting further reproach even for such legitimate restraint!

It was afternoon already but even today nothing had been cooked in the house. That eating is part of life—no one thought of that any more. The child kept wandering in and out of the house. Munshiji lay outside as if drained of life. Nirmala was indoors. Every so often the child would go to Siyaram's door and call out to him—but there was no one to answer her call.

In the evening Munshiji came to Nirmala and asked—Do you have some money?

Nirmala was startled—What for?

Munshiji—Answer my question.

Nirmala—Don't you know? You're the provider.

Munshiji—Do you have money or not? If you have some, let me have it. If not, tell me plainly.

Nirmala still refused to let him know plainly. She said—If I had any, it would be in the house somewhere, wouldn't it? I haven't sent any elsewhere.

Munshiji went out. He knew Nirmala had some money—and that was indeed the case. And Nirmala didn't say she didn't; or that she wouldn't give him any. But it was clear from her manner she didn't want to give him any.

At nine in the evening Munshiji came in and said to Rukmini—Sister, I'm going out. Please ask Bhungi to pack a bed-roll and a trunk with some clothes for me.

Rukmini was cooking. She said—Your wife is in the room—why don't you ask her? Where d'you intend to go?

Munshiji—I'm asking you. If I wished to ask her, why would I trouble you? Why're you doing the cooking today?

Rukmini—Who else is there? She has a headache. But where are you going at this hour? Why don't you go in the morning?

Munshiji—Three days have passed in all this hesitation. Let me go and have a look around and see if I can pick up some clue about Siyaram. Some people said he'd been talking to some sadhu. Maybe he talked him into going off somewhere.

Rukmini—By when will you return?

Munshiji—Can't say. Could take a week, could take a month. Who knows?

Rukmini—What day is it today? Have you consulted a pandit about all this?

Munshiji sat down to eat. Nirmala was feeling extremely sorry for him at this time. All her anger had ebbed away. She didn't speak directly to him but woke her daughter up and said to her lovingly—Why don't you go and find out where your father's going? Go on, ask him.

The child looked in at the door and asked in a child's accents—Where are you going, Father?

Munshiji—I'm going far away, my child. I'm going to look for your Bhaiya.

The child replied immediately—I'll come with you.

Munshiji—I'm going really far away. I'll bring something for you. Why don't you come close to me?

The child smiled and hid behind the door but poked her head round the door the next instant and said—I'll come with you.

Munshiji replied in mimicking tones—But I won't take you.

Child—Why not?

Munshiji—Because you won't come to me.

The child came preeningly towards him and sat in his lap. For a while, playing with his daughter, Munshiji forgot the sorrow breaking him up inside.

Having eaten, Munshiji went out again. Nirmala just stood there, looking at him. She wished to say to him—You're going away needlessly. But she couldn't bring herself to say anything. She thought of getting some money out and giving it to him, but she couldn't do it.

Unable to restrain herself, at last she said to Rukmini—Please talk to him, Didi—why is he going away? I know it sounds wrong when I say it, but I can't keep myself from saying this. How will he look for Siya without any sort of base of his own? He's putting himself to trouble needlessly.

Rukmini looked at her with deep compassion in her eyes and went into her room.

Nirmala was holding the baby and hoping that before leaving he might come inside once if only to see the child, perhaps even to meet her—but she waited in vain. Munshiji picked up his bed-roll and trunk and went and sat on the tonga.

Nirmala's heart was breaking. She felt certain she would never meet him again. She went impulsively towards the door, hoping to find Munshiji and ask him to stay—but the tonga had gone already.

# Chapter 25

Many days passed. In fact a whole month went by—but Munshiji didn't come back. Nor did he write. Now Nirmala's constant anxiety was about what would happen if he failed to come back entirely. She wasn't particularly worried about what he might be going through and in what state of health or where he might be knocking about. Her sole concern was with herself and even more with her daughter. How would she run the household? God help them! What would happen to her child? The savings she had effected through relentless meannesses, those savings were dwindling with each passing day. Nirmala resented each petty charge upon those savings as if parting with her very life-blood. Frustrated, she would curse Munshiji. If her daughter cried, she would curse the daughter and call her cruel names. She bitterly resented Rukmini living in the house. When one's heart is burning, one's speech becomes fire-laden. Nirmala was normally soft-spoken but she was now transformed into a harridan. All day long she would utter unpleasantnesses. All the usual softness of her speech seemed lost entirely. There wasn't a touch of sweetness in her now. Bhungi had served them for very many years. She was normally a tolerant sort of being, but this constant nagging got too much for her.

One day she too left. Things got so bad that Nirmala began to loathe even the daughter whom she had loved more than life itself. She would scold on at the slightest pretext and would occasionally beat her. Rukmini would then take the weeping child into her lap and console her with loving words. The poor child had only this refuge left.

The only thing Nirmala liked doing now was talking to Sudha. She kept looking for occasions to visit her. She didn't like to take her daughter on these visits. Earlier, when she had been properly fed and cared for at home, her daughter had gone with her and played happily. But now she'd declare she was hungry the moment she got there. Nirmala would stare at her and ball her fists at her, but the child wouldn't let up her litany of hunger. Which is why Nirmala didn't wish to take her there any more. In Sudha's company she felt she was still a human being. For that duration she was freed of her anxieties. As the alcoholic forgets his anxieties in an alcoholic haze, so Nirmala forgot her's in Sudha's company. Anyone who had only seen her in her own house would have been amazed at the transformation. The harsh, rough-spoken harridan was transformed here into a sweet and fun-loving creature. The normal tendencies of youth would find their normal playful expression at Sudha's. On these visits she came carefully dressed and all made up, determined to keep her tale of woe to herself—she came here to laugh, not to cry.

Perhaps she was not destined to experience even this minimal happiness. Normally, Nirmala visited Sudha during the early part of the afternoon. But one day she was so bored that she landed up in the morning. Sudha had gone down to the river to bathe, and Doctor Sahib was getting dressed for the hospital. The maid was busy with her chores. Nirmala went to her friend's room and sat there contentedly. She thought Sudha must be busy and would show up soon. But after she had waited a few minutes she got an album of pictures down from the shelf and, untying her hair, lay down on the bed to look at the pictures. Just then Doctor Sahib needed to come to Sudha's room—he was looking for his spectacles. He came right into the room. Nirmala had her head towards the door. Seeing him enter she was startled and sat up. She covered her head hastily and stood up. Doctor Sahib made as if to leave the room, then stood near the door and said—Forgive me, Nirmala—I didn't know you were here! I couldn't find my spectacles in my own room—I don't remember where I've put them. I thought they might be here.

Nirmala cast a glance on the alcove above the bedstead and saw the spectacle case there. She reached out and picked it up; then, with her head lowered, awkward and embarrassed, she reached out with them towards Doctor Sahib. Doctor Sahib had seen Nirmala a few times before—but never had such feelings been aroused in him before this. The spark he had kept alive in his heart all these years now burst aflame in this fortuitous gust. When he reached out for the spectacle case his hand was shaking. Even after he had taken the spectacle case he didn't leave the room, but stood there feeling awkward. Suddenly afraid of their being by themselves, Nirmala asked—Has Sudha gone out somewhere?

Doctor Sahib replied with his head bowed—Yes, she's gone down to the river.

But still he didn't leave the room. He just stood there. Nirmala asked again—When will she return?

Doctor Sahib replied again with lowered gaze—Any time now.

But he didn't leave the room. He was gripped by a desperate dilemma. It wasn't the tie of propriety that was holding him back, but only a weak thread of cowardice. Nirmala said again—She must have gone off wandering somewhere else. I'll leave now.

The weak thread of cowardice snapped. A retreating army finds itself possessed of extraordinary energy when it reaches the edge of a river. Doctor Sahib raised his eyes to look fully upon Nirmala and spoke in the accents of love—No, don't go just now, Nirmala. She'll be back soon. Every day you come here for her sake—stay today for mine. Tell me, how long can I continue to burn in this fire? I tell you truly, Nirmala...

Nirmala heard no more. She felt as if the whole earth had begun to spin around her—as if she was being assaulted by thousands of weapons. She quickly pulled down the covering that was hanging on the line and without uttering a word fled the room. Doctor Sahib was left standing there, feeling and looking awkward and embarrassed. He didn't have the courage to ask her to stay.

Just as Nirmala got to the outer door, she saw Sudha alighting from a tonga. As soon as Sudha saw her, she got off quickly and came hurriedly towards her and was about to ask her something—but Nirmala gave her no opportunity, she just shot off like an arrow. Sudha was left standing, bewildered. She could form no idea of what the matter was. But she was troubled. She went in quickly to ask the maid if something had happened. She was determined to discover who was guilty—if the maid or some other servant had insulted Nirmala, she would fire them on the spot. She rushed to her room. But as soon as she entered her room she saw Doctor Sahib sitting on the bed, looking dejected. She asked—Did Nirmala come here?

Scratching his head, Doctor Sahib replied—Well yes, she did.

Sudha—The maid or someone didn't insult her, did they? She didn't say a word to me, just dashed away.

There was a dull, beaten look on Doctor Sahib's face when he replied—No one said anything to her here.

Sudha—But someone has said something! Well, let me find out—but I promise you, once I find the culprit I'll turn him out straightaway.

Doctor Sahib's expression was hangdog—Well I didn't see anyone saying anything to her. Maybe she didn't see you?

Sudha—Don't be absurd! I got off the tonga right in front of her. She looked in my direction but she didn't say a word. Did she come to this room?

Doctor Sahib was dying of apprehension. He said hesitatingly—Well, yes, she came here all right.

Sudha—But she must have gone back when she found you

here. And then some maid must have said something to her. They're lower-caste people you know—so they hardly know how to be polite. Here you, Sundariya, come here at once!

Doctor Sahib—Why d'you call her? She went out from here directly to the front door. She had no time to exchange words with the maids.

Sudha—Then *you* must've said something to her.

Doctor Sahib's heart was beating wildly—What on earth could I have said to her? D'you think I'm that uncivilized?

Sudha—So you saw her coming in here and you kept sitting here nonetheless?

Doctor Sahib—But I wasn't here at all. I was looking for my spectacles in the sitting room and when I didn't find them there I thought they might be here. When I came here I found her sitting here. I wanted to leave immediately but she herself asked me—What is it you need? I replied—Just have a look around, can you see my spectacles anywhere? They were in that alcove above the bedstead. She picked them up and gave them to me. That was all that happened.

Sudha—So she just handed you your spectacles and marched out in a high temper? Really?

Doctor Sahib—She wasn't in a temper at all. As she was leaving I said to her—Why don't you sit awhile. She'll be back any time now. What was I to do if she refused to stay.

Sudha was thoughtful—Well, it doesn't seem to make much sense. I'll go to her and find out what the matter is.

Doctor Sahib—There's no hurry about that. You have the whole day ahead of you.

Sudha got her wrap around her and said—Now my curiosity is aroused—you think I can wait?

Sudha stepped out for Nirmala's house at a fast pace and was there in five minutes. She found Nirmala lying on her bed, weeping bitterly. Her daughter was standing by her side, bewildered, asking her mother why she was crying.

Sudha picked the girl up and said to Nirmala—Tell me

truthfully—what is the matter? Did someone say something to you at my house? I've asked them all, but no one admits to anything.

Wiping her tears, Nirmala said—No, no one said anything to me, really—why would anyone say anything to me?

Sudha—Then why did you decline to speak to me and break into tears the moment you got here?

Nirmala—I'm weeping over my cruel fate, what else!

Sudha—I'll swear some terrible oath if you refuse to tell me!

Nirmala—No, don't do that please—no one said anything to me, so why shall I accuse anyone?

Sudha—Swear on me!

Nirmala—You're being unnecessarily insistent.

Sudha—If you refuse to tell me the truth, Nirmala, I'll infer you have no love for me. Just a shallow pretence of it. I keep nothing from you, and you're treating me like a stranger. I had great faith in you. Now I know that no one's loyal to anyone else.

Sudha's eyes filled with tears. She put the child down on the ground and began to move towards the door! Nirmala got up quickly and held her hand, then said with tears in her eyes—I beg you, please, don't ask me this! You'll feel deeply hurt and I might never be able to show my face to you again. If I hadn't been born unfortunate, why would I have had to live to see such a day. Now I have only one prayer—that I might die soon. If things have come to such a pass, who knows what further degradations are in store for me!

Sudha was sharp enough not to miss the purport of what was being said. She understood that Doctor Sahib had been up to some mischief. The hesitant and awkward manner in which he had spoken, and the way in which he declined to answer pointed questions, his hangdog look—all of it came back to her in a flash. A shiver passed through her from top to toe and without another word she stormed out like an enraged tigress. Nirmala wished to prevent her but she was already gone. In an instant she was on the street and striding in the direction of her home. Nirmala collapsed on the ground and broke into bitter, sobbing tears.

# Chapter 26

Nirmala kept to her bed all day. It seemed as if she had been drained of life. She didn't get up to wash or to eat. By evening she was running a fever. All night long her body remained burning hot. The fever didn't really come down even on the second day—except a little. She just lay in bed staring at the door with a blank gaze. There was nothingness all around—nothingness within and nothingness without. Neither any anxiety, nor any memory, no sorrow even, it was almost as if her mind had died.

Just then Rukmini entered the room carrying her daughter in her arms. Nirmala asked her—Has she been crying a lot?

Rukmini—No, she hasn't even so much as sobbed once. She lay quietly all night—Sudha had sent a little milk for her.

Nirmala—Didn't the milkmaid bring any?

Rukmini—No, she said she wouldn't until the past dues had been paid. How are you feeling now?

Nirmala—There's nothing the matter with me. I was a little warm yesterday, that's all.

Rukmini—Doctor Sahib is in a bad way.

Nirmala asked anxiously—What happened? All is well, I hope?

Rukmini—He is so well he's practically dead. Some say he took poison, others say his heart has failed. God alone knows what happened!

Nirmala breathed a long, cold sigh and said with a catch in her throat—Good God, what will happen to Sudha now? How will she live?

Even as she said this she broke into tears and was sobbing for a long time after. It was only with great difficulty that she was able to get up and get herself ready to go to Sudha's. Her legs were shivering, she needed to support herself against the wall—but she couldn't not go. Who knows what Sudha said to her husband after she went back home? I didn't say anything to her, Nirmala thought, but God alone knows what she made of my words? Oh! What a handsome, kind and well-behaved person has come to such an end! If Nirmala had known her anger would result in such a dreadful consequence, she would readily have suffered in silence and shrugged off Sudha's question lightly and laughingly.

It was breaking her up to think that Doctor Sahib had come to such a sorry end because of her own cruelty. She suffered such excruciating pain that she felt her very heart was on fire. She started for Doctor Sahib's house.

The body was already on its way to the cremation. There was complete silence about the house. All the women had gathered. Sudha was sitting on the ground, weeping. As soon as she saw Nirmala she gave a loud cry and got up and hugged her close. The two wept a long time.

After the other women left and they were by themselves, Nirmala asked—What's all this, sister? What did you go and say to him?

Sudha had asked herself and answered this same question several times in her own mind. And she repeated to Nirmala the same answer that had soothed her own mind—But I could hardly keep quiet, could I? One can hardly help being infuriated by infuriating conduct.

Nirmala—But I never suggested any such thing to you.

Sudha—How could you—of course you couldn't tell me anything. But he, he told me all that had transpired. After that I burst out with all that came into my head. Once he had entertained the evil thought, it was almost as bad as if he'd actually done what he'd thought. Given time and an opportunity the deed *would* have been done. And it's no defence to say one was only suggesting it in jest. In solitary situations the mere fact that certain words are used is enough to show that one's intentions are not good. I never told you this, Nirmala—but several times in the past I'd noticed him stealing looks at you. At those times I'd thought I must be mistaken. But now I know what lay behind those looks and glances! If I'd been more experienced in the ways of the world, I wouldn't have let you visit me in my house. Or at least made sure he never got a chance to look at you. But how was I to know that what men say can be completely different from what they have in mind. Still, whatever God desired has happened. But I don't consider widowhood worse than the kind of married state I discover mine to have been. A poor person is immeasurably better off than a rich person whose wealth threatens his peace of mind like a venomous snake! It's easy to forego a meal altogether, it's far more difficult to eat one that's poisoned!

Just then Doctor Sinha's younger brother and Krishna entered the house—and the house filled once again with the sounds of lamentation.

# Chapter 27

Another month passed. Sudha went away on the third day, escorted by her brother-in-law. Nirmala was left all by herself. Earlier she had been able to amuse herself from time to time by exchanging a few words with Sudha. Now there was little she could do except weep. Her health was deteriorating rapidly. The rent of the house they had been living in proved excessive, so they had to rent something cheaper in a narrow alley. It had one small room and one small courtyard. There was no light, no breeze. The air was fetid. As for food, despite the fact that there was money they went hungry every so often. Who could be bothered to go and get the wherewithal from the shops? And then, without a man in the house, without any sons, why should one undergo the drudgery of cooking every day? And where's the necessity for women to eat every day? One proper meal and they were set for the next two days. As for her daughter, she would make some fresh halvah or rotis for her. So how could her own health possibly remain unaffected? Anxiety, grief, poverty—there was no dearth of causes! She was struck by all the woes and hardships there could possibly be. And she had absolutely refused to take any medicines. What else could she have done anyway? What chance was there of affording medicines on the little money they had? What chance had medicines when they didn't have enough even for food? And so she dwindled from day to day.

One day Rukmini said to her—How long will you go on wasting away like this? One's health is important above all. Come, let's go and see a doctor.

Nirmala replied tonelessly—Isn't it better that those who live only to weep from day to day die quickly?

Rukmini—Death never comes by invitation, though.

Nirmala—It comes uninvited often enough—so won't it come if called? But it will still feel like a long time, sister. Every day counts for a whole year now!

Rukmini—Don't carry on in this fashion! What have you seen so far of the joys of this world?

Nirmala—If such are the joys of this world, then the little that I've seen is already quite sufficient for me. I tell you truthfully, it's only the thought of this daughter which keeps me here, else I'd have gone long ago. God alone knows what this little one is fated to suffer!

And the two women began to weep. Ever since Nirmala became an invalid, confined to her bed, Rukmini had discovered a great capacity for compassion in herself. There is not a trace of resentment in her now. No matter what she is doing, the moment she hears Nirmala call she rushes to her side. She sits for hours by her bedside, telling her stories from the Puranas. She tries hard to cook things that Nirmala might wish to eat. She is beside herself with joy if she ever so much as sees Nirmala laugh—and as for the child, her attentions to her are unceasing. The child's rhythms determine those of her own day, her own sleep and waking. In fact, that child is now the very foundation of her own existence.

After a little while Rukmini said to her—But my dear, why are you so depressed? God willing you will be well in a few days. Come with me to the vaidya today. He's a very nice person.

Nirmala—I'm now at the stage, sister, when no amount of medicine nor any vaidya can do me any good any more. But don't worry about me now. I'll leave my daughter in your charge. If she survives, marry her off into a good family. I couldn't do anything for her—mine is only the guilt of having given birth to her. Keep her unmarried if need be, give her poison if you must, but please don't marry her to an unsuitable husband—this I beg you. I was unable to be of any service to you—I regret this bitterly. I was unable to give happiness to anyone at all. Anyone whose life was at all touched by mine was destroyed utterly. And if my husband should ever return home, please beg him to forgive this unfortunate her many wrongs.

Rukmini was crying as she said—Bahu, you have nothing that you need apologize for. I swear before Almighty God I bear you no ill-will. It's true I've always dealt unfairly with you, and I'll regret that till the end of my days.

Looking up at her timidly, hesitantly, Nirmala ventured—I don't know how to say this, sister—but I can't resist saying it either. My husband has always regarded me with distrusting eyes—but I've never in my whole life felt hostile towards him. Whatever had to happen has happened anyway. So why would I do further wrong and ruin my chances in my next life? I don't know what sins I must have committed in my last life, for which I've been paying such a heavy price in this one. But if I'd committed further misdeeds in this one, imagine my condition then!

Nirmala's breathing was suddenly much faster. She lay on the bed again and looked at her daughter with such a look, a look in which the concentrated essence of her own miserable existence had been distilled—but words can hardly hope to render that.

For three whole days Nirmala lay weeping ceaselessly. She didn't say anything to anyone, she didn't look at anyone, nor did she listen to anyone. She just wept. And who can presume to plumb the depth of her sorrow?

On the fourth day, at sunset, her sad story came to an end. At the same time that birds and animals return to their homes, their nests and hollows, Nirmala's soul, having endured a lifetime of the darts and arrows of clever huntsmen and the claws of predators, and having been buffeted mercilessly by gusts of wind till it could endure no more, flew off to its eternal home.

The entire neighbourhood gathered. The body was brought outside. The question arose as to who would light the funeral pyre. People were still debating the various possibilities when an old wayfarer with a ragged bundle dangling from his shoulder appeared and just stood there. This was Munshi Totaram, come home at last.

# Afterword:
# Hearing Nirmala's Silence

The early 1900s were a time of considerable ideological ferment in India. A sort of damaged modernity seemed available under colonial aegis, a modernity at once embryonic and addled. The story of the encounter between Indian society and colonial (and now postcolonial?) modernity has become a matter of contemporary intellectual concern. Indeed, one may well feel at times that we are still living that ongoing history—along with the other concurrent histories—living simultaneously the *durées* long and short. There has been neither time nor space for a distanced and definitive account of this complex experience, only battlefield reports.

The 'question of women' occupied a prominent place in the nationalist ideological and reform agenda. Suddenly, the proper role and place of women in society—or out of it—became a matter of concern even for the public male world. The available options ranged between the pole of imitation, where we find the feminine equivalent of the ruthlessly caricatured anglicized babu, and the pole of resistance, where women are seen as a last bulwark against an alien and intrusive modernity, as the guardians of the 'inner' worlds.[1]

[1] The appropriate introductory pages in Susie Tharu and K.Lalita;eds., *Women Writing in India* (New Delhi: Oxford University Press, 1994),

Even in the normally placid north Indian plains, the so-called 'Hindi' or 'cow' belt, matters relating to women became increasingly prominent in the nationalist programme. Thus, widow remarriage, the question of women's education, and relatedly, the proper social and public role of women, the matter of dowry and its attendant anomalies—all these were discussed energetically in the many women's magazines that sprang up in the early decades of this century.[2] Mahadevi Verma's *Hamari Shrinkhala ki Kariyan*, although published as a book only in 1942, consisted of a series of stirring and thoughtful essays which she published during the 1930s, agitating and liberating the minds of women and, hopefully, some men too. However, one should perhaps enter a caveat against anachronistic reading here. Yesterday's radicalism starts ossifying into tomorrow's vilified orthodoxy even before it is fully articulated. Thus, Mahadevi Verma's essays might well appear merely tepid to today's radicals. She may well appear inadequately cognizant of the myths of gender—about the essential gentleness of women, etc.—through which also patriarchy works its dread design. The earnest, puffed-sleeved matrons of the early twentieth century, seeking a supportive public role by the side of their men, are no longer the pioneers of liberation but simply deluded dodos, slaves whose dreams of freedom are still marked by the stigmata of slavery. For such readers, there is nothing but infuriation to be had in the writings of this period, with their curious mix of progressive yearnings and conservative inertias. For less activist readers, however, there is a great deal to be learnt about the intricate and difficult pathways by which new ideas gradually reach the public mind, and gain acceptance, and become common

---

vol. I—pp.145–86—discuss these issues and this history with admirable authority. The primary materials which they have assembled, as well as the bibliographical leads which they provide are an excellent starting point for research into these matters.

[2] See Vir Bharat Talwar, 'Feminist Consciousness in Women's Journals in Hindi, 1910–1920', in K. Sangari and S. Vaid, eds., *Recasting Women* (New Delhi: Kali, 1989).

sense. It is educative, and not a little entertaining, to see the bizarre compromises, the vehement phrases and assertions whereby individuals obscure, particularly from themselves, the novelty of their perceptions.

By the 1920s Premchand had become an adept at what might be called the literature of conscience. This is essentially a nineteenth century mode which endeavours to widen the circle of sympathy by including hitherto excluded categories of persons within it. It is reasonable to suppose that Premchand adapted it from the European novelists whom he read and translated. At the heart of this literature of conscience there is what might be called the guilty reader, and the challenge for a pioneer of this kind of literature—such as Premchand unarguably was in the Hindi heartland—is actually to *invent* the guilty reader. However, such an invention requires not only an awareness of social wrong but also, crucially, a sensitivity to the tides and limits of contemporary social consciousness. The implicit contract that binds author and reader is that the writer will not push his reader beyond—or too far beyond—an *acceptable* and, eventually, even *desired* level of moral discomfort. Part of the critical interest for later readers of this literature is, I suppose, to derive the terms, limitations and permissions of this unwritten contract, its complex economy of guilt and vindication, accusation and exoneration, from a sensitive reading of the text in which this contract is, so to speak, in solution.

Essential counterparts of this guilty reader are readers who find in the catalogue of wrongs offered to them a kind of vindication, a dubious moral glow. For these vindicated readers there is at least an acknowledgment of the wrongs that have been done. The memory of infamy is preserved, even if the victims of those infamous deeds are, in history no less than in fiction, long past the reach of recompense. The memorial of acknowledged, recorded truth is the very least that is owed them. There is further, in the act of acknowledgment itself, the expectation that those dark deeds will never be repeated—that acknowledged wrongs are already on their way to being righted. It is just here that the dubiousness of the moral transaction becomes apparent. Because, weeping over the misery of the little chimney-sweeps, the hungry orphans, becomes for the guilty reader too an acceptable and even sufficient form of social action, a form of moral vindication. The writhings of conscience are less strenuous than a reordering of reality. Memorials record the names of Hitler's victims. Apartheid's killers enact the rituals of repentance. Racism lives.

The genre is nevertheless a fertile one, particularly in times when rapid social change allows (and even compels) a degree of exposure which is not given to more settled epochs in which people keep within their social bounds and their ascribed social roles. Dickens' Dombey, taking a train ride through the poorer quarters of the city, or Dostoyevsky's and Balzac's heroes, forced up against the insulted and the injured, become the exemplars of a heightened awareness of social iniquity. This awareness doesn't always lead to generous or moral action—either on the part of the protagonists or on that of the readers. But the literature itself thrives on creating and indulging an awareness of wrong.

The literature of conscience, of the depiction of social injustice, is often characterized by great excess.[3] This, it might be argued, is simply realism. All known societies, past and present (and to come?) *are* characterized by great injustices. However, there is a specific fictional dynamic also at work. The multiplication of wrongs, the lurid representation of real iniquity, gratifies both the vindicated reader—the victim-analogue who finds in the 'excess' a sympathetic recognition of her (sometimes proxy) pain—as well as the guilty reader. For the latter, the intense and luxurious experience of guilt is itself the means of absolution. Still, it seems likely that at least some of the apparent 'excess' of this kind of writing is due, in part, to a fundamental confusion regarding the relation between past wrongs and present rights—indeed, to a presumption that this relation is somehow quantitative and proportional.

[3] The classic study of literary melodrama is Peter Brooks's *The Melodramatic Imagination: Balzac, Henry James, Melodrama and the Mode of Excess* (New Haven: Yale, 1976).

The awareness of wrongs is historically prior to the assertion of rights. The graphic and harrowing depiction of wrongs has been the traditional means whereby societies have been brought to an awareness of the injustices perpetrated under their aegis. One thinks of *Les Miserables* and *Uncle Tom's Cabin*, but instances could be multiplied a hundred-fold. However, it is important to realize that it is the discourse of rights that must be *logically* prior to the discourse of wrongs. Thus, for the wrong even to be perceived as a 'wrong', there has to be a prior if unconscious assent to the notion of a violated right, if only that of equality or fairness. This logical priority has some surprising implications. Thus, two wrongs do not make a right—indeed, even centuries of wrongs cannot *make* a right. But it is the denial of prior right that, so to speak, makes for whole institutions of wrongs.

It has to be some such proportional-quantitative assumption that underlies the vast amount of melodramatic literature in which the discourse of wrongs finds its popular voice. Thus, one of the staples of this kind of writing is the cult of the ennobled poor, of poverty as a spiritually enriching experience: in this realm, worse gets magically transformed into better. And yet we can hardly dare to dismiss a writer like Tolstoy as a purveyor of popular kitsch. Of course, on rational examination the idea appears nonsensical: if poverty were indeed such a powerful school and reservoir of virtue, that would be an argument in favour of having even more poverty, not less. But the very currency of the sentimental idea of some kind of deep link between poverty and spiritual qualities is itself a phenomenon deserving of study. (Involuntary poverty is, of course, entirely different from the voluntary poverty of the monk and the ascetic.)

Similarly, there is the cult of the angelic victim. This fecund genre, particularly in writings dealing with the question of women, may be considered a sub-set of the cult of the ennobled poor. Here also the game consists of representing the woman-victim as being simultaneously damaged and undamaged, wronged but essentially unharmed, both needing salvation and deserving of it.

The fact that such representations are necessarily ambiguous, in the fashion just indicated, interacts curiously with the confusion regarding the proper relation between wrongs and rights. The consequence is a muddled valorization of victimhood which, curiously, works to soften and make manageable the critique of victimizing societies and institutions.

We are now in a position to understand the critical challenge posed by a text like *Nirmala*. At one level the novel is simply absurd, exaggerated, laughable—in the way that Oscar Wilde found Dickens' Little Nell, dying angelically over whole sheaves of pages, irresistibly hilarious. It is possible for sophisticated readers to see *Nirmala* as a sort of nursery gothic, a sentimental tearjerker suitable at best for an innocent age before metafictional knowledge had caused us to be cast out from the garden of naive narration. But that, I suggest, is *not* the only way to relate to such melodramatic narratives.

How then should one 'read' melodrama—as indeed this literature of conscience is frequently described? There is in fact a stubborn terminological problem here. Apart from its specific historical-technical meanings, familiar to students of nineteenth-century Anglo-French theatre, the term 'melodrama' also signals a certain critical contempt, a dismissive and superior attitude. On the rebound from this traditional contempt, the recent years have witnessed a critical move to reclaim this literature— sentimental literature, literature of conscience—as a privileged domain for marginalized and predominantly feminine voices and experiences.[4] This isn't quite the place to chase those hares, and I can only state my intention to avoid both the poles—'male' condescension and feminist celebration. If this is critical androgyny, amen.

---

[4] Joanne Dobson, 'Reclaiming Sentimental Literature', *American Literature*, Vol. 69, No. 2, June 1997. Also see Christine Gledhill, ed., *Home is Where the Heart Is: Studies in Melodrama and the Woman's Film* (London: BFI Books, 1987).

Read for the surface, popular melodrama offers one a privileged glimpse into the world of common sense valuations, the provisional and barely acknowledged reasons and rationalizations by which ordinary people live their strange, ordinary lives. But one may also read melodrama *against* the grain—read it for what is being swamped and disguised in the emotional noise of which it is itself the source.

I would suggest that the form of melodrama is particularly suited to a critical, against-the-grain reading. D.H. Lawrence's critical precept—trust the tale and not the teller—must of course apply to all writing high and low, classical and popular. But in dealing with a popular form such as melodrama, it is both easier and more essential to see through the often absurd and ludicrous surface, the exaggeration and the excess, the teller's special pleading. The power of melodrama—or effectivity, if 'power' seems too grand—is to be found not in the absurd and 'excessive' endings but rather in the feelings that it deploys and brings into play *before* it gets to the ending.

A certain patched-up quality is very much of the essence of melodrama. Melodrama is the tragedy of the weak and the ineffectual. The fervent wordiness of melodramatic speech is also a form of insecurity; its excessive articulation is a thin camouflage for inarticulateness and real-world inconsequence. In thinking of melodrama it is important to bear in mind a necessary ambivalence in speaking about the *subjects* of melodrama: the phrase must connote both the fictional characters who act out its exaggerated and creaky plots, as well as the grateful readers/viewers' who endow those rickety structures with ardent if provisional assent. These 'subjects' live with the consciousness not only of contradiction, which is in the nature of things, but also of inconsistency, which has to do with how one negotiates one's passage through the world.

It follows therefore that the moral conflicts of melodrama must be *sectoral* or segmented moral conflicts. These engage the real emotions of the audience, but there is not, and indeed cannot be, any attempt at an overall resolution, no general solution. In unhappy melodramatic endings, for instance, there is a pointed aversion from pressing on to the stripped-down and bleak certainties of tragedy. The 'tragedy' of these lives is precisely that they are trapped in melodrama, in grooves of rhetoric, in ready-made sets of attitude and response. In happy melodramatic endings the sectoral moral conflicts—between say 'love' and existential authenticity on the one hand, and family values and conservative nostalgias on the other—are arranged in a sort of temporary and fragile equilibrium. The audience of melodrama is forgiving of the obvious falseness because, of course, no other kind of resolution is possible at all. In tragic melodramatic resolutions, on the other hand, the presence of evil, of villainy absolute and external, is the great recourse. The overwhelming and flagrant evil is not merely the trigger of painful difficulty, it is also the unbreachable horizon of explanation. Both kinds of 'resolutions' leave the intrinsic difficulties of the essayed situations undisturbed. Melodramatic resolutions of the problems of melodramatic universes must preserve the possibility of more melodrama. Thus, it is of the essence of the form that in melodrama people kiss and make up over the great and yawning divides. Kiss—and live to fight another day.

The idea of inconsistency provides a useful insight into the matter of melodrama. Right on the surface, there is in *Nirmala* a casual inconsistency of detail which might have been put down merely to hurried or slipshod writing if it did not seem part of a larger aesthetic. For example, in chapter 3 we see Rangilibai, wife of the monstrous Babu Bhalchandra, being accused by her husband of weeping over whole libraries of books. But earlier in the same chapter, we have been told that she rarely read any books at all, but could manage to read letters etc. in Hindi—which, interestingly, was more than her husband could manage. Again, in chapter 13 we are told at the beginning of the chapter that Nirmala did hardly any housework at all—her husband was well off and there was domestic help, etc., but for all that she was far from happy. Far less happy than the happily married Sudha, who had to do all the housework herself. However, later in the same chapter, when Sudha is telling her puzzled—then guilty, and finally tempted—husband about the virtues of Nirmala, she tells him that Nirmala is extraordinarily skilled in all kinds of domestic work.

The point to note is that in this melodramatic universe inconsistency doesn't seem to matter. Indeed, there are other, more serious kinds of apparent inconsistency which might well *be* the secret principle of the aesthetic of melodrama. The novel more or less opens (chapter 2) with the spirited exchange between Kalyani and her husband. The aroused wife accuses her husband of treating her lightly because she is economically dependent on him—as if she were some mere servant with no more involvement in their domestic welfare than the food she eats and the clothes she wears. She storms out of the room in a rush of rhetoric—but there has been no indication in the novel so far, and neither do her later actions indicate, that she is the kind of woman who could have thought or said the sorts of things that she did. Inconsistency is but one way of looking at it. But to my mind the universe of melodrama is *necessarily* disjunctive in this fashion. Here incompatible truths can and *must* be asserted and forced to coexist—but that can happen only *on condition* that they are never pressed home. The pay-off for the reader/audience is the thrill of hearing the truth—their truth—uttered, without having to live through the destabilization that taking it seriously would inevitably imply.

It seems to me therefore that melodrama is a special 'arcadian' sort of form: here all kinds of things might be thought and said without incurring any real risk. Words can be used smoothly, profusely, expressively, because the underlying guarantee of the form is precisely that these words are weightless and cancel each other out.[5]

[5] There appears to be a kind of similarity between this process and Freud's account of the process of mourning in 'Mourning and Melancholia':

It is integral to the form—at least in my understanding of it—that it is characterized by sudden rhetorical shifts. People move smoothly from one set of rhetorical ensembles into another and radically different one, with emotions, words and attitudes firmly in place. This, oddly, serves to capture the hysterical, barely maintained nature of normalcy. This combination of radical ideological instability with total rhetorical certainty in all the positions seems to me the essence of the form. There is a grammatical analogue of all this in the sudden shifts of tense, irksome to the English reader, which produce a kind of narrative *fluctuation:* the reading subject is disconcertingly repositioned, time and time again, without 'adequate' textual preparation, in different consciousnesses, and at variable distances from the action. It takes a little getting used to, this slipping from past tense to historical present, from Godlike distance, through antagonistic observation, to an awkward intimacy with first one and then another character.

Thus, in chapter 13 Nirmala's friend Sudha is confidently taking her husband to task for his cowardice and greed, and even taunts him that he can always resort to the time-honoured means of disciplining her if he so desires: 'If I do say a few bitter, sarcastic things, you can simply ignore them. And if I should carry on beyond that, you can always resort to the stick to discipline me.' But a little later, without batting an eyelid, she declares in praise of her long-suffering friend Nirmala: 'He may be old and ailing, but he is her lord. Well-born women don't criticize their husbands—that's how bad women behave.'

Perhaps the most grotesque instance of this kind of thing occurs right at the end of the novel. Nirmala is at a moment of sheer existential revelation, when the meaning of her miserable life is suddenly clear to her: 'Anyone whose life was at all touched

---

thus, melodrama appears as a form of mourning with formal guarantees—a way of calling unpleasant and difficult things to mind within a framework of immunity. In mourning it is the present and irreversible fact of mortality that provides this enclave of immunity. In the South African Truth and Reconciliation process, of course, the immunity is constitutional.

by mine was destroyed utterly.' But her author—or perhaps it is
the imperatives of the form itself—does not allow her to stay
with this moment of bleak grandeur. She is soon back to mouthing
the appropriate rhetorical platitudes about never having felt
resentful and hostile towards her husband.

It is almost as if melodramatic language has an autonomous
dynamic, and if a character should happen to be in the vicinity of
one of those rhetorical cathexes, their gravitational pull ensures
that the language takes over and says the rest.[6] But that is still a
formalistic account of the matter. The other effect is that of lives
whose bland surfaces conceal violent and often unacknowledged,
and unacknowledgeable—emotions which find expression in such
fortuitous situations. At the level of character, there is the sense
of amorphous, unreconstructed consciousnesses, patched together
with bits and pieces of ideology, fragments of rhetoric.

The problem or phenomenon that I am trying to come to
grips with is particularly acute in the representation of that which
is the unacknowledged but unmistakable subtext of *Nirmala*, i.e.
sexuality. The 'mismatch' between Nirmala and her husband is,
most crucially, a sexual mismatch. The sexual buzz between
Nirmala and her adolescent stepsons, between her and Sudha's
husband—just as much as Totaram's pathetic attempts to win her
favours and her revulsion against his attempts to do so—all this is
what constitutes the substance of the novel. I am convinced that
it is this buzz of sexuality which accounts for much of the novel's
contemporary and subsequent popularity. But it can never be—
*must never be*—acknowledged. In chapter 8, when Nirmala goes
up to her stepson Mansaram's room to persuade him to come
down to dinner, the dialogue is distinctly lover-like. But the motive
force of the scene derives from the fact that this sexuality must be
simultaneously known and not known. The only person who
recognizes the truth, albeit in his perverse, tortured fashion, is
Munshi Totaram—he blunders up the stairs, much to the

[6] Umberto Eco, '*Casablanca*: Cult Movies and Intertextual Collage',
*Travels in Hyperreality* (London: Picador, 1987).

discomfiture of his wife and her stepson. But in this hysterical, melodramatic universe, which rests on this potent combination of knowledge and innocence, Totaram's stubborn and anguished insistence on the underlying truth that, so to speak, generates the ambiguous and therefore delicious condition, makes *him* the villain, the disturber of the melodramatic game.

The melodramatic narrator enters each participating consciousness and reveals the hermetic logic of each marvellously articulate individual: e.g. Nirmala explaining—chapter 24—how she couldn't at any point in her life have done any differently than what she did. She explains that she was really in a situation which would ensue in tragic consequence no matter which route she took: whether she acted or failed to act, spoke up or just kept quiet. All the characters—Mansaram and Totaram, Rukmini and Jiyaram—they all have their passionate, compelling reasons. The helpless individuals are trapped in their individual logics, unable to comprehend let alone affect the larger untenability in which *all* their lives are trapped. The only truths are local, and several incompatible ones are able *and even required* to coexist noisily. It is in this sense that there may well be some peculiar consonance between certain ranges of social experience and the form of melodrama. This excessive, disjunctive form—necessarily excessive, necessarily disjunctive—may well be the appropriate form for lives which rest on a precarious foundation of knowledge and evasion: necessary lying, desperate truth-telling.

It is in this sense also that there might well be some subterranean affinity between melodramatic form and the matter of women. Thus, the form-derived immunity enables the writer to give voice to victimized characters—victims of each other as also of the enveloping circumstance in which they are all trapped. At the same time, the form enables the writer to give credible and even excessive representation to that which works to make these suddenly articulate characters actually voiceless in the real worlds in which they live.

'Melodrama' as a social form, as a ritualized transaction in which guilty and vindicated readers are identified and 'reconciled', has a surprisingly analogical similarity with the 'transactions' in process at the Truth and Reconciliation hearings currently under way in post-apartheid South Africa.[7] Thus, the constitutional frame provides the immunity within which the necessarily acknowledged evil of the past may be named, in deliberate and painful detail—and in being so named, be presumed exorcised. The stating of the truth—as distinct from establishing culpability, degrees of liability, punishment—is intended to be itself the means of effecting reconciliation: between on the one hand the victims (or those who represent them), for they have had their pain acknowledged; and on the other, the perpetrators and beneficiaries of that pain, who in acknowledging that pain are already presumed to have begun the process of repentance and exoneration. Obviously, the most intriguing aspect of the transaction, from my point of view, is the delicate relation between that which is (*and must be*) acknowledged, and that which isn't (*and must never be*) acknowledged. As for the victims (or those who represent them), by not demanding more than this 'reconciliation'—not insisting on 'truth *and justice*' for instance—they already assume a position of moral superiority which, having survived the acknowledged violence, serves retrospectively to mitigate the intensity of the violence and consequently, ironically, mitigates also the guilt of the perpetrators and beneficiaries. It might well be, finally, that the inheritors of past evil—victims, perpetrators, beneficiaries—which *cannot* be undone in any possible present, have no option except to 'reconcile' on the basis of some such melodramatic transaction.

However, while such a strategy of reconciliation might be the only one that is available to societies which have crossed a comprehensively acknowledged threshold of evil—i.e. South

[7] I am grateful to Professor Robert Meister of the University of California at Santa Cruz for having drawn my attention to this dimension of melodramatic phenomena. See his paper 'After Evil: Notes on the Political Culture of National Recovery' (unpublished).

Africa, Bosnia, Rwanda, Pinochet's Chile—the possibility of such reconciliation is precisely what accounts for the radical suspicion of melodrama. After all, it is the avowed purpose of revolutionary ideology to create, through theory and practice, the unreconciled and irreconcilable and implacable victim who seeks not reconciliation but justice. Thus, Franco Moretti, for instance, is critical of melodrama because it tends typically to displace onto nature that which belongs in the domain of society and its institutions: it does not press beyond the fact and *being* of evil to the actual *doing* of evil.[8] That which should attract the liability and culpability of the social is accorded the givenness of nature. However, the grim limit cases of the contemporary world suggest that the term 'history', which is located firmly on the social, *doing* end of the social–natural polarity tends, *beyond a certain magnitude of evil*, to take on the givenness, the remote irreversibility of nature. Ironically, then, once evil crosses a certain threshold, there can be no justice—only perhaps reconciliation. However, these are matters which need independent and not parenthetical consideration. Meanwhile, we must return to our text and its domestic calamities.

What, finally, do we make of Nirmala—and so of *Nirmala*? There is a chilling moment towards the end of the novel: Totaram discovers that it was his second son Jiyaram who stole Nirmala's jewellery and that imminent apprehension by the police is perhaps the reason why he has run away from home, only to die by chapter-end. When Totaram reports his discovery to Nirmala she replies coolly that she has known it all along. Munshiji's anguished question—*Why didn't you say this to me?*—is echoed several times by the reader during the course of the story. Nirmala's silence, her inability to speak, her stubborn refusal to speak up at critical moments, her overwhelming anxiety to *appear* good as distinct from *being and doing* good, her persistent failure to act as a morally responsible person—all this is of course a condemnation of the institutions which have made her what she is, and compel her to

---

[8] Franco Moretti, 'Kindergarten', in *Signs Taken for Wonders* (London: Verso, 1983).

continue to be like that. But Nirmala is actually complicit with the society that has wronged her, perhaps most crucially, by making it impossible for her to perceive the ways in which she has been 'wronged', except externally and superficially. In other words, she is so damaged that she cannot see that deep down at the level of her twisted and unacknowledged instincts she is a damaged person. But one can hardly condemn her society and its institutions without first recognizing the horror of what they have done: they have produced a moral cripple whose very passivity and timidity is pathological and immoral, but who retains through the whole grotesque sequence of events a faint halo of virtue.

Nirmala's aspiration is to a kind of existential virginity, a persistent and dogged refusal to be seduced into action. She must remain unsoiled—*nirmala*, etymologically—even as everything around her gets destroyed precisely because it comes in contact with her—i.e. threatens to 'soil' her. She touches everything through the innocent and youthful vivacity of her being; but she cannot allow herself, finally, to be touched by anything.

Nirmala is a monster of passivity, someone who destroys through her inability (and/or refusal: weapons of the weak) to think and to act, to be a person. She destroys the same 'male' world which has made her what she is, *by the simple and ruthless expedient of insisting on being that which she has been made into.* The true measure of the social violence which Premchand sets out to critique in *Nirmala* is to be found not in the adolescent innocence of Nirmala prior to her traumatic marriage, nor even in the 'innocence' that survives in the form of Nirmala's quest for a condition of passive guiltlessness even as her refusal to act destroys everything around her. It must be located in the monstrous nature of that which is produced as a result of that violence—i.e. Nirmala herself.

# Glossary

*baraat:* the bridegroom's party. According adequate hospitality to the family and friends who comprise this is a major concern of the bride's family.

*lakh:* one hundred thousand, in traditional Indian reckoning.

*rotis:* flat, unleavened bread, cooked on an open fire.

*kurta:* a loose, shirt-like garment which is worn, with regional variations, all over the subcontinent.

*qazi:* a cleric who is trained in Islamic law.

*rais:* a wealthy man, who seems to do little other than consume lavishly. The word has an etymological connection with the word for 'landed estate'.

*dharma:* commonly translated as religion, it is more nearly the necessary order of a sustainable universe.

*rasagullas:* a popular sweet, balls of ricotta-like cheese, swimming in syrup.

*laddoos:* a traditional form of sweet: various substances are packed into round, ball-like shapes.

*sharbat:* a cold drink, made from sundry fruits etc.

*phalahaari:* a truly orthodox Brahmin shuns food cooked by others. Thus, he may be offered fruit—though some will consent to partake of food cooked in such a manner that it regains ritual purity. From people who cannot afford such relatively expensive transformations—often poor and lower-caste—the generous Brahmin accepts the raw materials, *sidha,* which he cooks for himself.

*paan:* the betel leaf, eaten widely across India, in combination with other substances, including the mildly narcotic betel nut.

*khichri:* rice cooked with lentils: a popular form of domestic fast food.

*besan:* chick-pea flour.

*baatis:* a form of unleavened bread—ellipsoid and hard—which is considered rustic.

*halwai:* a maker/seller of traditional Indian sweets.

*seer:* a measure of weight, approximately one kilogram.

*kalakand:* a kind of sweet.

*rabri:* sweetened milk that has been boiled down to a thick consistency.

*pao:* a measure of weight: four paos make a seer.

*daal:* lentils: a staple of the Indian diet. Many varieties, spiced up in a million ways.

*annas:* pre-decimal coinage: sixteen annas made up one rupee.

*achkan:* a tight-fitting long jacket, which generally comes well below the knees.

*ghazal:* a traditional Urdu lyric, often dealing with matters amatory, associated with the great masters—but widely vulgarized, as here.

*surma:* cosmetic, eye-black, powdered antimony.

*tulsi:* Indian basil, commonly grown in the courtyard in traditional Hindu homes. Watering the tulsi is a stereotypical domestic ritual.

*ekka:* a kind of high, horse-drawn carriage.

*moong:* a kind of lentil.

*phulkis:* a kind of roti, lighter and less substantial than some other forms.

*jhoomar:* a kind of ornament, often worn on the side of the head.

*puris:* a variant of the cereal accompaniment of the traditional meal: a cake of unleavened flour, deep-fried, whereupon it swells up dramatically.

*sasural:* husband's home; more precisely, the home of the father-in-law. Interestingly, the bride's own home is called the *maika,* or *mother's* home.

*khadi:* rough, home-spun cotton. Traditional, it was transformed by Gandhi into a potent symbol of anti-colonial resistance. Later histories, other transformations.

*charkha:* a spinning-wheel.

*dwaar-puja:* the beginning of the wedding-ritual proper: the bridegroom is formally welcomed at the entrance to the bride's home.

*tilak:* the gifts which the bride's family sends to the bridegroom's family.

*janvaasa:* the place where the members of the bridegroom's party are housed for the duration of the wedding.

*maulvi:* a Muslim divine.

*dhoti:* a loose, unstitched garment, worn over the lower part of the body.

*paisa:* pre-decimal coinage: four paisas made up one anna, sixty-four a rupee.

*ghee:* clarified butter.

*sadhu:* a Hindu mendicant.

# GABAN
The Stolen Jewels

Translated by Christopher R. King

# Contents

# Translator's Preface and Acknowledgements

Some witty misogynist once joked that translations are like women: if faithful, they are not beautiful, and if beautiful, they are not faithful. Whatever we may think of its underlying viewpoint, this saying points to a fundamental problem that many translators face: since the genius of each language differs, if one tries for too much accuracy, the beauty of the result may suffer, while if one aims for too much beauty the accuracy may diminish. This dilemma, however, seems overstated: one can remain faithful to the meaning and spirit of the original work (though not to sentence construction, word order, etc.—a suspect and ridiculous goal in any case), and also render beautiful the language of its new incarnation. This has been my aim, and it is for the reader who knows both languages to judge how far I have succeeded.

I have also attempted to produce a readable translation, not a definitive, scholarly one. Accordingly, I have not consulted numerous editions, but have used only two: the Hindi version of *Gaban* published in Allahabad by Hans Prakashan in 1962, and the Urdu version published in New Delhi by Diamond Pocket Books (no date given). Although my primary source was the Hindi version, I often used the Urdu version when I got temporarily stuck in the Hindi. (The Urdu version differs by being somewhat shorter—lacking numerous phrases, sentences, and passages appearing in the Hindi version—and by often using a different, more Persianized vocabulary.)

To make my translation readable I have consistently followed certain practices. Chief among these has been the creation of a glossary to explain to Western readers the meaning of Hindi terms difficult or cumbersome to translate. Another major practice has been to usually change the first person to the third person when a character is internalizing his or her thoughts. If the result seemed unclear from time to time, I added some phrase such as 'he thought to himself.' My aim here was to avoid many awkward—at least in English—shifts back and forth between first and third persons, and also many extra quotation marks. Similarly, I have consistently used the past tense to avoid numerous shifts between present and past tense in certain passages.

Premchand has a habit of putting each speaker's name in front of every utterance in almost every conversation. I have usually omitted the speaker's name when it is obvious who is speaking, adding it only when needed for clarity (but using phrases such as 'said Jalpa' or 'Rama asked' rather than only the name). He also has a habit of using extremely short sentences, sometimes in strings. In such cases I have often, though certainly not always, combined them into longer sentences.

In translating idioms and metaphors I have tried to translate as literally as possible whenever it seemed to make sense so as to keep the flavour of the original Hindi, and to add fresh new expressions to the English. For example, in Chapter 2, when Premchand describes Dindayal's behaviour after the death of his sons, I have kept as close to the Hindi as possible: 'He walked as if he were treading on eggs; burned by milk, he even blew on buttermilk before drinking it.' Similarly, in Chapter 8, when Jalpa's anger towards her husband Rama's inaction is described, I have translated the Hindi quite literally: 'It was as if his mouth had been stopped up with curds.' When it comes to dialect, or to bad Hindi—Premchand puts such language almost entirely into the mouths of the Calcutta police—I have made no attempt to reproduce this in English.

In the Hindi edition which I used I found numerous misprints, which I corrected to the obviously intended word or phrase. I found other mistakes, which may be due to editorial sloppiness or to Premchand's own oversights. One of the most amusing of these is the transformation of Rama's mother's name from Jageshwari to Rameshwari partway through the novel. 'Jageshwari' last appears in Chapter 15, while 'Rameshwari' first shows up in Chapter 22 and remains for the rest of the novel! In this case I have used 'Jageshwari' all the way through. Similarly, in much of the novel, Premchand refers to Pundit Indra Bhushan (first introduced in Chapter 15) as 'Vakil Sahab,' but abruptly switches back to 'Pundit' or Punditji' in the portions of the novel (Chapters 29 and 30) describing his last days; I have used 'Vakil Sahab' throughout. In another passage, Rama goes out at a certain time, and returns earlier! I have adjusted these times to make more sense, according to the context of the passage. In another place or two, the amounts of money mentioned do not quite add up, and I have corrected them also.

Finally, I would like to thank those who helped make my translation possible. First, I would like to express my deep appreciation to the unknown reviewer who approved my sample of the first seven chapters. My friends Dr Dhirendra Vajpeyi of the University of Northern Iowa, and Dr Urooj Zaidi of Windsor stood ready to assist me with difficult passages in the Hindi and Urdu versions respectively, though as it turned out I managed to complete the translation without their aid. Perhaps the results would have been improved if I had turned to them more often! My editor at Oxford, Anuradha Roy, generously allowed me substantial extensions of time, and made me feel it was all worthwhile by her comments on the finished product. Lastly, my wife Leela consistently lent me moral support, and patiently listened to many a translated passage and gave me her reactions—usually favourable—to the quality of the English.

# Introduction

Premchand entitled this novel (first published in 1931, though written at least two years earlier) *Gaban* in both the Hindi and Urdu versions. Although the title literally means 'embezzlement,' no embezzlement actually takes place anywhere in the novel. The closest thing to it occurs in Chapter 18:

Rama resolved to deceive Ratan. He knew very well that her impatience was because she thought he'd spent her money. If she knew that she could get her money immediately, then she'd be pacified! Rama wanted to allay her suspicions by showing her a bag filled with money.

Rama's intention is clearly not to steal money from his government office to solve his problems, but only to temporarily 'borrow' it to get one of his most persistent creditors off his back. When his wife Jalpa unwittingly gives this money to the creditor, their friend Ratan, Rama eventually feels obliged to run away since he cannot return the money though he has not spent any of it. Oddly enough, in Chapter 34 Premchand has Rama confess to the police that he has spent three hundred rupees of government money. He has done no such thing!

Whether Premchand intended his title to be taken literally or not, I do not know, but I have chosen to take it more metaphorically. Hence, from one angle, the true 'embezzlement' (a term I take to mean the theft of something which has been entrusted to one) occurs when Ramanath steals Jalpa's jewels from her (Chapter 7), an act which sets off a chain of consequences which entangle the major characters for the rest of the novel. Hence, the subtitle I have chosen: *The Stolen Jewels*.

But why does Rama steal his wife's jewels in the first place? Because his family has gone heavily into debt for his wedding, for which a large part of the expenses has been the jewellery given to Jalpa, and only returning at least some of these jewels to the jeweller will prevent serious trouble. Why is Jalpa not asked to give up her jewels for the family's welfare? Because she has already been unable to accept the fact that she has not received a special necklace, a chandrahar, as part of her wedding present, especially since her husband has greatly exaggerated his family's wealth. And why has it been so difficult for her to accept the absence of this necklace? Because she has been indoctrinated with an inordinate love of jewellery from childhood by her family, relatives, friends, and neighbours.

Therefore, from another point of view, it is jewellery and by extension, the society which exaggerates its importance, who are the actual thieves or embezzlers of the true and natural capacities of people for love, self-sacrifice, and other virtues. Not until Jalpa finally revolts against her upbringing and renounces all her finery, which from her viewpoint has robbed her of her husband, does the course of events begin to change. In describing this internal revolution, Premchand uses language taken straight from the *Upanishads* in the last line of the following paragraph:

At last she gathered them all up one day—velvet slippers, silk socks, all kinds of embroidery, ribbons, pins, combs, mirrors—who could have counted them all. They made a wonderful pile. She'd sink this pile in the Ganges and lead a new life from now on. For the sake of these things she was in her present situation. Today she'd wipe out this tangle of illusions once and for all. Although the thought of throwing away so many beautiful things brought pangs of regret, these few drops of water could not begin to extinguish the raging fire of her remorse and disgust. She spent half the night setting them apart one by one, as if she were preparing for some journey. Yes, it was really a journey for her—from darkness to light, from falsehood to truth.

Jalpa's outer sacrifice is paralleled by an inner one, the sacrifice of her own desire for jewellery and of her own self-indulgence. Once Jalpa renounces the things which have stolen her true nature from her, she gradually becomes an agent of transformation for others—her friend Ratan, her own husband, and Zohra, a Muslim prostitute with whom he has taken up. (Interestingly, just as the Ganges washes away Jalpa's finery, so it also swallows up Zohra at the very end of the novel, for she too is a remnant of Rama's unredeemed past.)

While the corrupting effects of jewellery on the one hand, and renunciation, self-sacrifice, and redemption on the other, are the novel's most important themes, several others—such as the influence of the West, the character of relationships between castes, the position of women, the meaning of marriage and love, the nature of family relationships, and the presence of police corruption—also emerge. I have chosen, however, to comment only on the first two.

The influence of the West, fundamentally ambivalent, appears most emphatically in the character of Vakil Sahab, who extravagantly praises Europe's system of female education:

Until the education of women is widespread, we'll never improve. You probably haven't even gone to Europe. Oh! What freedom, what wealth, what life, what enthusiasm! In a word, one knows it's paradise! And the women are really goddesses! So cheerful, so independent! All this is the prasad of female education!

In a similar way, Ramesh Babu castigates Indian society's craze for jewellery in comparison to Europe's wiser investment of its resources, and heaps scorn on those Indians who wish to copy the English only in superficial things:

And then, is it necessary for us to copy the English in every little thing? We're not English, we're Indian. Eminent Indians have big full-length mirrors in their rooms; you're talking about our mixed-up babus who are obsessed with making themselves caricatures of the English in everything—in dress, in the decoration of rooms, in speech, in drinking tea and alcohol, and in china teacups. But they don't even come close to imitating those things which have made the English English, and because of which they rule the world. Do you too have a longing to become an Englishman in your old age?

The English appear in a bad light, however, for their implicit support of the blatantly corrupt Indian police, and for their ferocious and fatal attack on Devidin's two sons, supporters of the swadeshi movement.

Relationships between castes also display fundamentally ambivalent characteristics. It strains our credulity that both Rama and Jalpa, members of the relatively high-status Kayasth community, soon accept living and eating with Devidin and Jaggo, members of the very low-status Khatik community. Rama's younger brother Gopi, however, displays a much more conventional and believable attitude.

When both of them had gone, Gopi came and said, 'Did Bhaiya live here at this Khatik's place? They certainly seem to be Khatiks.'

'Whether they are Khatiks or Chamars, they're a hundred times better than you or I,' snapped Jalpa. 'They put up a stranger in their own home for six months and gave him food and drink. Would we have had that much courage? For a guest to come here imposes a great burden. If they are lowborn, we are even more lowborn.'

Gopi had washed his hands and face. As he ate his sweets he said, 'No one raises his status by putting someone up. No matter how much merit a Chamar may get from being generous, he'll still be a low-caste Chamar!'

'I consider such a Chamar better than a Brahman pundit who always devours the wealth of others,' said Jalpa.

Jaggo displays concern that first Rama, and later Jalpa, will suffer difficulties from their own caste by eating with her and her husband, but soon becomes reconciled to the situation. In effect, Rama and Jalpa become an adopted son and daughter-in-law, something which seems rather unrealistic for Indian society, but which also seems to express Premchand's genuine outlook.

Finally, I would like to briefly mention several scenes of great beauty or intensity of feeling which strongly affected me and helped convince me that this novel was indeed worth the effort of translation. I hope my readers will share my reactions to these passages, and also find favourites of their own. Among these are: Premchand's soliloquy on the death of Vakil Sahab and his description of Ratan's subsequent remorse (both in Chapter 30); Ratan's angry denunciation of the laws denying widows a share of their husbands' inheritance (Chapter 41); and Rama's confession to Jalpa, Devidin, and Jaggo (near the end of Chapter 48). Let me close with my two personal favourites. First is the scene at the end of Chapter 35 where Ratan is seeing Jalpa off on her trip to Calcutta:

The train arrived, and Gopi entered a compartment and took control. Jalpa's eyes filled with tears. 'Sister, bless me so I can bring him back safely,' she said.

Her faltering heart was seeking for some support, some help, some strength now, and what else could bestow that strength on her except blessings and prayers? These are the everlasting storehouses of that strength and peace which never discourage anyone, which take everyone by the hand, and which ferry everyone across the river of their difficulties.

The engine let out a whistle. The two friends embraced, and Jalpa sat down inside the train.

'Send letters as you go,' said Ratan.

Jalpa nodded.

'If you need me, write immediately. I'll drop everything and come.'

Jalpa gave another nod.

'Don't cry along the way.'

Jalpa laughed. The train moved off.

The second is the scene at the end of Chapter 48 where Jalpa is reflecting on her husband's confession:

Jalpa stood almost motionless on the street for several minutes. How could she stop him? How sad he must be now, how despairing! What had possessed her not to call him to her? Who could know what things would be like in the future or when they might meet again? Never in her three years of married life had her heart been so shaken by love. When she had been concerned just with sensuous pleasure, she had only been able to see the outer surface of love, but now that she had become self-sacrificing, she could see its true form. How delightful it was, how pure, how grand, how glorious! While self-indulgent she had been content just to see the doors of the garden of love. After becoming self-denying she had reached the interior of this garden—what a lovely scene, how sweet-scented, how picturesque, how blooming. Its fragrance, its loveliness, were filled with divinity. When love reaches its highest elevation, it mingles with the divine. Now that she had found this love, Jalpa had no doubts that she would remain a fortunately married woman in this life and the lives to come. This love freed her from the fears of separation, circumstances, and death—and gave her the boon of fearlessness. The whole world and its unlimited abundance seemed trifling in the face of this love.

In conclusion, I would like to quote the Sanskrit mantra from the *Brihadaranyaka Upanishad* which Premchand is almost certainly referring to in the second extract from the novel above:

> *Om asato ma sadgamaya*
> *Tamaso ma jotir gamaya*
> *Mrityo ma amritam gamaya*

It was the rainy season, the month of July. Masses of golden clouds were spread through the sky. A light drizzle was falling intermittently. It was only mid-afternoon but it seemed as if evening had come. In the mango groves girls and their mothers were swinging; three or four on the swings, three or four pushing. Some were singing folk songs, some poetry. In this season, childhood memories awoke in the women. It was as if the soft rain washed away worries from the heart, as if it made even withered minds fresh and green. Everyone was filled with enthusiasm. Green saris echoed the greenery of nature.

Just then a travelling pedlar came and stood near the swings. As soon as he was seen, the swinging stopped and everyone big and small crowded around him. He opened his box and displayed his glittering sparkling wares. There were ornaments of raw pearls, unfinished lace, and gold and silver hemming, coloured socks, beautiful dolls and dolls' ornaments, and children's tops and rattles. Some took one thing, others another. One big-eyed little girl liked the most beautiful among all those sparkling objects—a splendidly coloured chandrahar. 'Mummy,' she said, 'I'll take this necklace.'

The mother asked the pedlar, 'How much is this?' Wiping the necklace with a handkerchief, the pedlar said, 'It cost me twenty annas. The lady can give what she likes.'

'That's very expensive. Its shine will disappear after a very few days.'

Tenderly shaking his head, the pedlar said, 'Beti, in a very few days the child will be married and receive a real chandrahar of her own.'

These warm-hearted words went straight to the mother's heart; the necklace was purchased.

The little girl's joy had no limits; maybe even a diamond necklace would not have given her as much pleasure. Putting it on, she danced and twirled through the whole village. Among her childish treasures, this crystal necklace was the dearest and most precious.

The girl's name was Jalpa, her mother's Manaki.

# 2

The honourable Dindayal lived in a smallish village in Allahabad district. He was not a farmer, but he acted like one, nor was he a landlord, but he acted like one. He was not a sub-inspector of police either, but he acted like one. He was the agent of a landlord, and it was he who held sway in the village. He had four peons, one horse, and several cows and buffaloes. He received a total of five rupees a month as salary, which wasn't even enough for his tobacco expenses. Who knows of the other paths by which his income reached him! Jalpa was his daughter; she had had three brothers before, but now she was alone. If anyone asked her what had happened to her brothers she would say with great simplicity that they had gone to play far away! People said that the agent sahab had had some impoverished fellow beaten so badly that he died; within three years all three of Dindayal's sons had died. From that time on the wretched fellow conducted himself very carefully. He walked as if he were treading on eggs; burned by milk, he even blew on buttermilk before drinking it. Who was left to support the mother and father now!

Whenever Dindayal went to Allahabad he brought back some ornament or other for Jalpa without fail. It never occurred to his practical mind that Jalpa might be more pleased by something else. He considered dolls and toys worthless, so Jalpa played only with ornaments—*these* were her toys. The crystal necklace bought from the pedlar was now her most precious plaything. She had not the faintest desire for a real necklace as yet. Whenever there was a festival or a holiday in the village, she would wear this necklace; no other jewellery seemed any good at all to her.

One day Dindayal brought back a necklace for his wife Manaki in fulfilment of a long-cherished wish. She was entranced with it.

Jalpa didn't like her own necklace any more, and said, 'Father, bring a necklace just like this for me too.'

Dindayal smiled and said, 'I'll bring one, child!'

'When will you bring it?'

'Very soon.'

Jalpa was not satisfied with her father's words. She went to her mother and said, 'Mummy, have a necklace made for me too.'

'That would cost a lot of money, child!'

'You had one made for yourself; why not for me?'

Her mother smiled and said, 'Yours will come from your in-laws.'

The necklace had cost six hundred rupees. It hadn't been easy for Dindayal to get that much money together. It wasn't as if he were some big official. Only once in all these years had an opportunity for getting the necklace come. He doubted whether he'd ever get this much money in his life again.

Jalpa, embarrassed, ran away, but these words had engraved themselves on her heart. Her future in-laws' house was no longer so terrible to her. She'd get a necklace from there, and the people there would love her more than her mother and father did. Whatever her own family couldn't get made would come from her in-laws.

But suppose it didn't come from them? Three other girls had gotten married before her, and not one of them had received a necklace from her in-laws. Suppose it didn't come from her own in-laws either? So wouldn't her mother give her own necklace to her then? Of course she would.

Seven years went by in this way, spent in laughing and playing; and that day, too, came when her long-held yearning was fulfilled.

## 3

Among the people with whom Munshi Dindayal was acquainted was a certain gentleman named Dayanath—a very good and warm-hearted man. He worked in the court, receiving a monthly salary of fifty rupees. Dindayal practically lived at the court, and

Dayanath had dealt with him hundreds of times. He could have collected thousands of rupees from his client but deemed it wrong to take a single paisa. This was not his behaviour just towards Dindayal; it was his nature. It was not that he was a man of very lofty ideals, but he did despise bribery! Perhaps because he had seen its bad results with his own eyes. He had seen some go to jail, others despair of their own children, and still others fall into the clutches of addictions. He had found no example of any one becoming contented from taking bribes. He had the settled conviction that ill-gotten gains lead to ill-doing, nor did he ever forget this.

These days a salary of fifty rupees was nothing much, and taking care of five people on it was very difficult. The boys hankered after good clothes, and the wife jewels, but Dayanath was unmoved. His oldest son abruptly stopped studying after only two months in college. Dayanath told him straight out, 'I can't let everyone else be hungry and naked for the sake of your degree. If you want to study, then make a real effort. Lots of other people have done it, and you can too.' But Ramanath didn't have that much stick-to-itiveness in him. For the last two years he'd been completely idle. He played chess, he strolled about, and he lorded it over his mother and younger brothers. Thanks to his friends, he was able to indulge his predilections. He'd ask for someone's overcoat and go out for a ramble in the evening. He'd wear someone else's pump shoes or strap on another's wrist watch. Sometimes he'd turn himself out in the Banaras fashion, sometimes in the Lucknow manner. If ten of his friends each had a set of clothes made, then he had ten changes of clothing available. This was a completely new use of cooperation. And it was this very youth that Dindayal was pleased to select for Jalpa. Dayanath did not want to arrange the marriage. He didn't have the money or the courage to take up the burden of a new family. But Jageshwari, his wife, got her way through sheer feminine obstinacy, a power before which men are compelled to bow. Jageshwari had been wild to have a daughter-in-law for years. Women she'd known as new brides were now playing with their grandsons, so how was the poor woman supposed to be patient? She'd almost given up hope, and implored God that her wish would somehow come true. When Dindayal sent his message, her eyes nearly popped out of her head. If this prey slipped from her grasp, then who could know how long she'd be on the lookout for another. Why would anyone come to them? They had no money at all, and no property. Who cares about the boy? People look for money. So on this occasion she put forth all her might, and was victorious.

'Bhai,' said Dayanath. 'It seems that you may know what you're doing. I have no such capability myself. To marry off someone who doesn't even concern himself about where his next meal is coming from seems almost immoral to me. And then there's the money to provide for too. We'd need a thousand just to put on a big show, let alone the clothes and jewellery.' And putting his hands on his ears in a gesture of denial, 'No ma'am! I won't accept this burden!'

These arguments had no effect on Jageshwari. 'Dindayal will give some money too.'

'I won't go and ask him.'

'You won't even have to ask. He'll give something on his own. No one gives a second thought to money when it comes to a girl's marriage. Yes indeed! If it's financial resources you need, Dindayal is a dependable fellow. And then, since she's his only remaining child, who's he going to save his money for?'

Dayanath couldn't think up anything to say to this, and merely replied, 'Whether he gives a hundred thousand rupees or none, I won't tell him to give anything or not to give anything. I don't want to take on a debt, and if I have to, then where is the money to come from?'

Jageshwari, tossing this obstacle to the winds, said, 'I'm sure he won't give less than a thousand for the dowry. That's plenty for your big show. Arrange for the ornaments with some jeweller! If he gives a thousand for the dowry, won't he also give a thousand when the bridal party comes to the door? Give *that* money to the jeweller, and if three or four hundred is left to pay, it'll be paid off little by little. Some opportunity or other is bound to come for our boy.'

'It's already come and gone,' said Dayanath scornfully. 'There are no opportunities for someone who can't spare any time from playing chess and strolling around.'

Jageshwari remembered her own marriage. Dayanath too had spent freely in his youth, but as soon as she had appeared, how obsessed he'd become with the worry of earning even a little money. But not even a year had gone by before he became a government servant. 'When our daughter-in-law arrives, he'll come to his senses, you'll see. Remember what you said yourself. Until the yoke is fastened around his neck, it's all fun and games. Once it's there, he'll sober up in a minute. There's no better way to put good-for-nothings on the right track.'

Whenever Dayanath was beaten, he would read the newspaper, as he did now. This was his way of hiding his defeat.

# 4

Munshi Dindayal was one of those men who is courteous with the courteous, but becomes the very devil with the rude. If Dayanath had talked big, if he had spoken of thousands, Dindayal would have played a trick on him that he'd have remembered all his life. But Dayanath's goodness overpowered him. He had thought to give only a thousand, but he handed over a thousand just for the betrothal ceremony. 'If you give a thousand for the betrothal, you'll have to give another thousand at their door,' said Manaki. 'Where will that come from!'

Dindayal took offence at this. 'God is the master,' said he. 'Since they have shown generosity and entrusted me with the boy, then I want to show that we're high-class too and know the value of proper behaviour. If they'd acted high-and-mighty, though, we'd certainly have given them a tongue-lashing.'

Dindayal came up with a thousand, but this, instead of making Dayanath's burden lighter, made it even heavier. Dayanath took to his heels and ran for miles at the thought of interest. He had made a firm resolve to carry out this marriage according to the rule of 'Do the opposite of what's expected' but Dindayal's generosity shattered his self-control. All that pomp and show, those dances and spectacles whose very imagination he'd strangled, now appeared towering before him. The horse tethered in the stable had broken loose, and who could stop him now? It was resolved to celebrate the wedding in a grand manner. Previously he had considered the question of jewels trivial, but now it became the most important of all. Let there be such a charhao that the spectators in the marriage pavilion would be thrilled. Let everyone's eyes be opened. Some three thousand rupees worth of goods was ordered right away. When the jeweller was promised a thousand within a week, he made no objection. He thought to himself that he'd get two thousand straight away, and just six or seven hundred would be left. And these people weren't going anywhere. He'd covered his outlay, so he wouldn't insist on receiving his profit immediately.

Still, there remained the matter of the lack of a necklace. A good inlaid chandrahar could not be had for less than a thousand. Dayanath now set his heart on getting one as long as they'd gone this far; no one would have any excuse to turn up his nose. But Jageshwari did not consent. The game had reversed itself.

'What's it to you?' said Dayanath heatedly. '*You'll* be sitting at home. I'm the one that's going to die of shame when those people wrinkle up their eyebrows and turn up their noses.'

'Where'll you get the money? Have you thought about that?'

'We'll get at least a thousand from them.'

'Are you making a habit of this?'

Abashed, Dayanath said, 'No, no, but won't we get something from them, after all?'

'Whatever we get from them will be spent for their expenses! One doesn't get a good reputation from gathering jewels and ornaments, but from making gifts to Brahmans and giving alms to beggars.'

And thus was the proposal for the necklace rejected.

But never mind how unnecessary Dayanath considered pomp and pageantry; Ramanath regarded them as essential. The marriage procession should proceed so spectacularly that the hulla-baloo would spread through the whole village. First, the bride-groom's conveyance had to be considered. Ramanath held out for a motor-car. His friends encouraged him, and the proposal was accepted. Dayanath was a solitary creature, not on terms of close friendship or familiarity with anyone, while Ramanath was a sociable youth, whose very friends were now taking a leading role in everything. Whatever they did, they did whole-heartedly. Fireworks to be arranged? Then first-class. Dancers? First-class. Singers and musicians? First class, too. Second- or third-class were terms not even mentioned among them. Seeing their extravagance Dayanath got worried, but found himself unable to say a word. What would he have said anyway?

# 5

A drama gets a 'passing mark' when a discriminating audience likes it. The drama of a wedding procession gets a passing mark when passers-by like it. The test of a drama lasts four or five hours, but that of a wedding procession only four or five minutes. All the arranging and decorating, all the scurrying about, all the final touching up, are finished off in five minutes. If 'Wonderful! Wonderful!' comes out of everyone's mouth, then the show has passed, if not, it's failed. Money, effort, worry—all in vain. Dayanath's show passed. It would have been third-class in the city, but it was first-class in the village. Some of the onlookers were becoming intoxicated by hearing the boom-boom tweet-tweet of the instruments, some were goggling at the motor-car, and some were rolling their heads in wonder at the throne of flowers. The fireworks were the central entertainment for everyone. When the rockets hissed upwards and scattered through the sky in red, green, blue and yellow crocus flowers, and when the catharine-wheels went off and a dancing peacock shot forth, people became mesmerized. Wonderful! What skill!

These things had not the slightest attraction for Jalpa. To be sure, she wanted to take a peep at the bridegroom without anyone knowing, but where was the opportunity in such a hurly-burly? At the time of the dwarchar ceremony, her friends dragged her up to the roof, and she saw Ramanath. All her indifference, all her detachment disappeared in a flash. Her face flushed with pride. Love is a storehouse of energy.

After the ceremony, the marriage procession went to the janwasa, and preparations for a meal began. Some people ate puris, while others cooked khichari over a fire of dried cowdung cakes. Dancing and singing started up for the enjoyment of the spectators of these rural festivities.

At ten o'clock the band suddenly started to play again. It

became known that the charhao was coming. During this marriage procession every part of the ceremony was performed with great flourish. The bridegroom is coming for his kaleva? Let the band play. The father-in-law is coming? Let the band play. As soon as the charhao arrived, a great commotion broke out in the bride's house. Men, women, the elderly, the young—all were eager to see the charhao. As soon as the trays of presents reached the marriage pavilion, people left everything and came running to see, and a vigorous pushing and shoving began. Manaki was perishing from thirst, and her throat had dried up, but her thirst fled as soon as the charhao came. Dindayal was lying almost lifeless from hunger and thirst, but sprang to life on hearing the news and came running. Manaki began taking things out one by one to look at and show them. Everybody there was a specialist in this art. The men had had jewellery made and the women had worn it; everyone began to appraise it. How pretty the gold-wire bracelet is; it must weigh about ten tolas. Ha! If it turns out to be a jot under eleven-and-a-half, I've missed my guess. Look at that tiger-face jewel, what workmanship! It makes you want to kiss the craftsman's hands. This, too, won't be less than twelve tolas. Humph! Have you ever seen anything? If this ends up less than sixteen, I'll hide my face. Yes, the stuff is not all that good. Well, look at this comb; the joinery is just right and the work is so exact that one can hardly stop looking. How it glitters. Those are real stones! Where would you find this water in counterfeit stones? What a thing this guluband is! What beautiful flowers it has! And how those diamonds are sparkling in between! Some Bengali goldsmith must have made it. Do those Bengalis have a contract on craftsmanship? Every last craftsman hereabouts is just sitting around uselessly. How can the poor wretches compete with Bengali goldsmiths?

One by one each piece of jewellery was being sized up like this. All at once someone said, 'There's no chandrahar?'

Manaki, pulling a sad face said, 'No, no chandrahar came.'

One woman said, 'Oh! No chandrahar came!'

'Everything else is here,' said Dindayal gravely. 'Only a chandrahar is not.'

'Are we talking about anything else but a chandrahar?' said the same woman mockingly.

Pushing the charhao away, Manaki said, 'The poor girl just doesn't have a chandrahar written in her fate.'

Standing behind the circle of the crowd, like a statue of hope and expectation in the darkness was Jalpa. The names of every other kind of jewellery had come to her ears, but not the name chandrahar. Her heart was pounding. What, there was no chandrahar? Maybe it was under everything else, she kept telling herself. When she learned that there was indeed no chandrahar, she was wounded to the core. It seemed as if there was not a single drop of blood in her body, as if she were going to faint. In this semi-frenzied condition she came into her room and burst into tears. That longing which had sprouted in her heart for seven years, and was by now covered with flowers and foliage, had been struck by a thunderbolt. That luxuriant waving plant was burned and only its ashes were left. All her hopes had been pinned on this very day, and today misfortune had snatched those hopes away. In the frenzy of her disappointment she felt like scratching her face to shreds. If it had lain in her power she would have picked up the charhao and hurled it into a fire. In a niche in her room stood an image of Shiva. She threw it down so hard that it shattered like her hopes. She decided that she would not wear any ornaments; what was the use of wearing them anyway? Let those who were ugly decorate themselves with jewellery, but God had happened to make her beautiful, so she wouldn't look bad even if she didn't wear them. They had brought cheap things, and no one had even questioned what the money had been spent for. If the reckoning had been done properly, twice as many jewels could have been purchased at the same price.

As she was sitting filled with these angry thoughts her three friends came in and stood. They thought that Jalpa had not yet heard any news of the charhao. Jalpa dried her eyes and smiled as soon as she saw them.

Radha smiled back and said, 'Jalpa, it seems as though you must have earned good fortune by carrying out a lot of religious penances; I've *never* seen such a charhao before. Have all your wishes come true, then?'

Raising her long lashes, Jalpa looked at her with such misery in her eyes that it seemed there was now no hope left for her in life. 'Yes, sister, all my wishes have come true!'

None of the three young women was able to guess how filled with unlimited inner pain these words were! All three stared at her with curiosity as if they had not understood her meaning.

Vasanti said, 'I feel like kissing the hand of the craftsman.'

Shahzadi said, 'A charhao ought to be such a thing that people sit up and take notice.'

'Your mother-in-law seems to be very cunning,' said Vasanti. 'She hasn't parted with a single thing.'

Jalpa turned her face away and said, 'That must be it.'

Radha said, 'Everything else is there except a chandrahar.'

Shahzadi said, 'What difference does it make if there's no chandrahar, sister. There's a guluband instead.'

'Yes, what difference does it make if a body is missing one eye,' said Jalpa sarcastically. 'All the other parts are there, so what does it matter if the eyes are there or not!'

Just as we laugh when we hear solemn things from children's mouths, so Radha and Vasanti, hearing these greedy and petulant words from Jalpa's mouth, could not stop their laughter. To be sure, Shahzadi didn't laugh. This craving for ornaments was not a laughing but a crying matter for her. Displaying a feigned sympathy she said, 'What a bunch of yokels they all are for having brought everything but a chandrahar, which is the king of all ornaments. When Lala comes just now I'll ask him where he came up with such a way of doing things—no one acts so senselessly.'

Radha and Vasanti were trembling in their hearts lest Jalpa come to understand that Shahzadi was leading her on. If it had been in their power they would have stopped Shahzadi's mouth; they signalled again and again for her to be quiet, but to Jalpa, however, this sarcasm of Shahzadi seemed to be brimming over with condolences. With tearful eyes she said, 'What good will it do to ask, sister? What had to happen has happened.'

'If you tell me to ask about it, I'll leave him crying,' said Shahzadi. 'When there was no bracelet in my charhao I felt so bitter that I could have given a kick to the whole bunch of jewellery. I didn't sleep a wink until the bracelet was made.'

'So do you know that a chandrahar won't be made for Jalpa?' said Radha.

'If it's going to be made, then it'll be made, but it wasn't made for *this* occasion. It isn't something that costs only five or ten rupees that you can have made whenever you want—it costs hundreds. And then, you don't always find a good craftsman.'

Jalpa's broken heart seemed to revive on hearing Shahzadi's words, and in a voice choked with emotion she said, 'That's just what I think too, sister. If I didn't get it today, then I won't get it later.'

Radha and Vasanti were cursing Shahzadi in their hearts, and threatening her with feigned slaps, but Shahzadi was now thoroughly enjoying the show. 'No, it's not that, Jalli,' she said. 'Everything is possible by insisting on having your way. Keep on reminding your mother-in-law and father-in-law again and again. A great deal can also be done by with your husband by sulking for three or four days. Just understand that your family should get no peace and that they should have this constantly brought to their attention. Let them understand that without your having a chandrahar, there'll be no domestic happiness. If you let up just a little, everything will be spoiled.'

Stifling a laugh, Radha said, 'And if this doesn't work, we'll send for you. Will you get up now, Shahzadi, or are you going to keep on giving advice all night.'

'I'm going. What's the big rush? Oh yes, I remember very well, Jalli, that your mother has a really nice chandrahar. Won't she give it to you?'

Jalpa heaved a long sigh. 'What can I say, sister? I have no hope of that.'

'At least say something once and see what happens. Her days for getting dressed up are long gone,' said Shahzadi.

'I won't say anything.'

'I'll say something.'

'No, no, I beg you. I want to test her mother's love a little.'

Vasanti caught hold of Shahzadi's hand and said, 'Get up now, or you *will* be here all night giving advice.'

Shahzadi got up, but Jalpa stood up and blocked her way. 'No, not now,' she said. 'Sit down, sister, I implore you.'

'I will when these two hags let me sit. Here I'm teaching you tricks and these two are infuriated with me. You're not listening; I'm also a poisonous bitch.'

'You certainly *are* a poisonous bitch,' said Vasanti.

'You've come back after a year at your in-laws too,' said Shahzadi. 'What did you get made to bring with you?'

'And what did you get made in the last three years?' asked Vasanti.

'Forget about me,' said Shahzadi. 'My husband takes no notice of me.'

'Jewellery is worthless compared to love,' said Radha.

'So may your dried-up love be auspicious for you!' said Shahzadi.

Just then Manaki came and said, 'What are the three of you doing sitting here? Come along, people are coming to eat over there.'

The three young women left. Jalpa, seeing the splendour of the chandrahar around her mother's neck began thinking to herself, 'She still hasn't had her fill of jewels.'

# 6

Mahashaya Dayanath returned from the wedding just as dejected as he had been elated in going to celebrate it. Dindayal had given a lot, but all that had been spent for pomp and pageantry and the customary wedding presents. Again and again Dayanath repented of his oversight; why had he spent so much for show and spectacle? There had simply been no need for it. At the very most people would have said that Mahashaya was very miserly. What would have been the harm in hearing that? He hadn't made any contract to show the villagers a spectacle. This had all been Ramanath's rashness. It was he who kept on increasing all the expenses until he had driven his father into bankruptcy. And all the bills could have waited a few days, but the jeweller had not agreed at all. He made Dayanath promise to give a thousand rupees on the seventh day after the wedding, and he had come today on the seventh day. But where was the money to pay him? Dayanath was not in the habit of flattering and wheedling, but today he had done his best to use trickery. He had promised to pay all the money in instalments within six months.

Three months passed. The jeweller, however, was a seasoned

veteran. He deferred payment—and even this was just his good-naturedness—when Dayanath promised to pay the balance in three days or return the things. The third day had come, and now Dayanath couldn't come up with any means to save his honour. Perhaps some more deceitful man might not have been so agitated, and would have kept the moneylenders at bay for months through guile and trickery. But Dayanath was a novice at this.

Jageshwari came and said, 'The food that I made, I don't know how long ago, is getting cold; eat first, and then go sit.'

Dayanath raised his head as though it bore a load of many tons and said, 'You all go and eat. I'm not hungry.'

'Why aren't you hungry? You didn't eat anything last night either. Giving up eating and drinking like this is hardly going to help pay off the moneylender.'

'I'm thinking, what will I tell him today? That I got into a real mess because of the wedding? That our daughter-in-law will give back some of the jewels?'

'You've heard about the state she's in, and yet you can still cherish such a hope? She insists that she won't wear a single piece of jewellery until a chandrahar is made. She's locked up all her jewels in her chest. All she strings around her neck is that glass necklace. I've seen a lot of daughters-in-law but never one like this. Still, it seems pretty bad that her jewels should be snatched away when she's just arrived.'

'You're just sprinkling salt on a burn,' said an irritated Dayanath. 'If it seems like a bad idea, then get out a thousand rupees, give them to me, and I'll go give them to the moneylender. Are you going to give them to me? It seems bad to me myself, but what's to be done? How can we save our necks?'

'Did you arrange your son's wedding, or was it a joke? Everybody goes into debt for weddings; you haven't done anything novel. Who goes into debt for food and clothes? Shouldn't you get some reward from having become a saint? Satyadev is just the same rank as you, and he's built a proper house, bought a zamindari, and must have spent at least five thousand on his daughter's wedding if he spent anything at all!'

'When both boys had left home!'

'Living and dying, that's the way the world goes. Those who

take die, and those who don't take die too. If you wanted to, you could pay off everything in six months.'

Dayanath scowled. 'I can't start doing something in my last days that I never did in my whole life before. Tell our daughter-in-law straight out. What's the need of keeping it secret at all, and how many days can it be kept secret anyway? If not today then tomorrow the whole thing will come out anyway. Just return three or four things, and it'll all turn out fine. Will you speak to her at least once, then?'

'*You* speak to her. *I'm* not saying anything,' said Jageshwari, flaring up.

Just then Ramanath came in carrying a tennis racket. White tennis shirt, white trousers, canvas shoes—this clothing lent an aristocratic dignity to his fair colour and handsome features. He was carrying bracelets of jasmine flowers in his handkerchief whose fragrance was wafting through the air. He was intending to go up the stairs, avoiding his mother's and father's eyes, when Jagsehwari checked him. 'He's the very one who sowed all these thorns, so why not get advice from him? You blew twelve or thirteen hundred rupees on dances and spectacles, so tell us what should be said to the jeweller? With great difficulty we got him to agree to having some of the jewels returned, but who's going to ask her for them? This is all *your* doing!'

Dodging this criticism of himself, Ramanath said, 'What did I spend? Whatever was spent, Father spent. Whatever I spoke in favour of, well yes, I spent that.'

There was a good deal of truth in what Ramanath said. If Dayanath had not been willing, what could Rama have done? Whatever had been done, had been done with his assent. Making accusations against Ramanath could not solve any problems. Dayanath said, 'I'm not blaming you, bhai. *I'm* the one who did it. But we have to get this calamity off our heads somehow or other! The jeweller is demanding payment, and his man is coming tomorrow. What will we say to him? As far as I can see, there's just one way: we'll have to give him as many rupees worth of jewels as we owe him. Even so, he'll kick up a fuss about having them returned, but in his greed for a few rupees he'll go along with it. What's your advice?'

Ramanath said abashedly, 'What advice can I give about this? But I can say this much, that she won't agree happily to this proposal. Mother knows how badly she took there being no chandrahar in the charhao. She's taken a vow not to wear any jewels until one is made for her.'

Jageshwari, seeing support for her side of the argument, said happily, 'That's exactly what I was saying to him.'

Ramanath added, 'All this hullabaloo will spread around and our family secrets will come out.'

Wrinkling his brow, Dayanath replied, 'What's the need of keeping things secret from her? The sooner she understands the real situation the better.'

Ramanath, as young men will, had boasted a lot to Jalpa, making many gross exaggerations. There was the family zamindari, with a profit of several thousand a year; there was money in the bank, with interest coming in. If he were to ask Jalpa to give up some of her jewels now, she'd consider him a complete liar. 'The secret will come out one day,' he said, 'but the result of letting it out so soon will be that she'll begin to think we're low-class. Perhaps she'll even write to her family and then we'll get a bad reputation all over.'

'We never told Dindayal that we were millionaires, did we?'

'So when did you say that we've taken the jewellery on loan and are giving it back in a few days?' asked Ramanath. 'After all, did you put on this whole show to spread your prestige around or for something else?'

'Well then, we'll have to ask for them using some other excuse,' said Dayanath. 'If we don't ask for them, nothing will work out. Tomorrow we either have to give the money or return the jewels. There's no other way.'

Ramanath did not reply. Jageshwari said, 'What other excuse can we make? If we say someone has asked to borrow them, she may not give them to us. And even if she does, how can we return them to her in three or four days?'

Dayanath had a brainwave. 'What if we substituted imitation jewels in place of hers?' But he understood at once that this was a weak ploy, and arguing against himself, said, 'Yes, when the shine wears off later, we'd be put to shame. My brain isn't working at all. All I can think of is that the whole situation should be explained to her. She'll certainly be unhappy for a little while, but the way will be clear for the future.'

It was possible, as Dayanath thought, that after a great fuss Jalpa would calm down, but Rama stood to be disgraced. He wouldn't be able to show his face to her. When she asked what had happened to the zamindari, and what had happened to the money in the bank, what answer could he give? In an indifferent manner he said, 'Nothing will come of this except a little ill-repute. Can't you stall the jeweller for a few months? Then if you want to pay him off, with that much time you can very easily give him a thousand or twelve hundred rupees.'

'How?' asked Dayanath.

'Just like your brother officers do.'

'Rama, that's not possible for me.'

The three of them sat silent for a while. Dayanath had announced his decision. Jageshwari and Rama did not agree, so now the burden of unravelling this knotty problem was on the two of them. Jageshwari too had made a decision of sorts. Dayanath would have to admit his own helplessness and break his own rules. What kind of morality was it that harped on the same old theme of rules when a calamity had fallen upon them? Ramanath was in a real predicament. He knew very well that his father was not about to start doing what he had never done before—taking bribes. He would not hesitate to ask Jalpa for the jewels, and this was exactly what Ramanath did not want. He was repenting, asking himself why he had bragged to Jalpa. Now the whole burden of saving the family honour was on him. Jalpa's wonderful beauty had cast a spell on him from the very first day. He had not been able to contain his joy over his good fortune. Was his family worthy of such a unique beauty? Jalpa's father was a five-rupee-a-month government servant, but she had never used a broom in her own home, had never spread her own bedding, and had never even trimmed her own dhoti, let alone mended tears in it. Dayanath got fifty rupees a month, but here there was only a servant woman for cleaning the kitchen and doing the dishes. All the rest of the work had to be done with their own hands. What could Jalpa know about the difference between the city and the countryside? She'd never had any occasion to live in a city. She'd asked both her husband and mother-in-law with surprise if there were no servants here. There was no shortage of milk and curds in Jalpa's home. Here you couldn't even get milk for the children. What else did Ramanath have to make up for all these short-comings except big talk and sweet words? The house rent was five rupees a month, Ramanath told her it was fifteen. Expenses for the boys' education were barely ten rupees; Ramanath told her forty. At that time he hadn't the slightest suspicion that one day his tissue of lies would be torn to shreds. Falsehood is not far-sighted, but who could have known that the day of reckoning would come so soon? If he hadn't made those boasts, then like Jageshwari, he too could have cast the whole burden on Dayanath and gone merrily on his way. But now he was caught in a net of his own making. What a way for things to turn out!

How many different ways he'd thought of to put things right, but there wasn't one that wouldn't plunge him into some future complications or catch him in a quagmire. All of a sudden a strata-gem occurred to him. His heart gave a leap, but he couldn't bring himself to say what he had thought of. Oh! What a rotten thing! How deceitful, how merciless! Such low cunning towards his own darling! He upbraided himself. If someone had given him a thous-and rupees just then, he would have become his slave for life.

'Have you thought of something?' Dayanath asked.

'Not a thing.'

'We *have* to think of something.'

'You think. I can't think of a thing.'

'Why not ask her for two or three ornaments? You can get them if you want. It's difficult for us.'

'I'm ashamed,' said Ramanath.

'You're a strange one; you won't ask yourself and you won't let me ask, so how is this boat going to keep sailing, after all? If I've said it once I've said it a thousand times—don't put any hope in me. I can't spend my last days in jail. I don't understand what there is to be ashamed of. Who doesn't have bad times like this in his life? Ask your mother.'

Jageshwari seconded him. 'I couldn't stand to see my husband worrying himself to death and me sitting there wearing my jewellery. Otherwise wouldn't I have jewellery now too? All of it disappeared piece by piece. At my wedding not less than five thousand was spent on the charhao, but in only five years everything was sacrificed. Since then I haven't had the good luck to have even a plain ring made.'

'This is not the time to be ashamed,' said Dayanath emphatically. 'We'll *have* to ask her for them!'

Ramanath said shamefacedly, 'I can't *ask* her, but say the word and I'll take them.'

As he said this, his eyes filled with tears of shame and distress from the recognition of his own meanness.

Astonished, Dayanath said, 'You'll take them without telling her?'

'What else did you think I meant,' said Ramanath in a harsh voice.

Dayanath put his hand on his forehead and after a moment said in a hurt voice, 'No, I won't let you do such a thing. I've never deceived *anyone* and I never will. And my own daughter-in-law too! Shame, shame! For something that can be done openly, you want to play these dirty tricks instead? If somehow she should see you doing it, do you understand what she'd think of you? To ask is very much better.'

'So what does it have to do with you? Take the things from me. But when you knew this state of affairs would come, then what was the need of getting all these pieces of jewellery and of bringing this disaster upon us uselessly? It would have been millions of times better to get only as much as we could manage easily. What's the good of a meal that begins to hurt once it's in the stomach? All this time I thought you must have worked out some way out of this. How could I know that you would dump this basket of troubles on to my head? Otherwise I'd never have let you get those things.'

Dayanath, a little ashamed, replied, 'Even so, there was a good deal of carrying on just over the lack of a chandrahar.'

'How could that carrying on have harmed us? If even after all that was done there was still such a fuss, then your purpose wasn't even fulfilled. A bad reputation on the one hand, and on the other this trouble on our heads. I don't want people to know that we're having so many difficulties. After a theft, we could arrange everything.'

Dayanath fell silent. Here he was, listening without a word, while Rama in a frenzy was venting his spleen! At last, when he couldn't bear to hear any more, he got up and went to the library.

This was his unfailing rule. Until he'd read three or four news-papers and magazines, his food wouldn't digest. Once he arrived in this secure fortress, his life was safe from the worries and difficulties of home!

Rama got up and left too, but instead of going to Jalpa's room, he went to his own. He didn't really have a separate room of his own; there was a mardana room where Dayanath chatted with his cronies, the two boys studied, and Rama played chess with his friends. When Rama entered, both boys were playing cards. Gopi was thirteen, Vishvambhar nine, and they were both desperately afraid of their older brother. Rama himself played a great deal of cards and chess too, but let him see his brothers playing and his hands itched to slap them. He could stroll about all day if he liked, but his brothers had no right to go out on a ramble. Dayanath himself never struck the boys, and even played with them when he had the chance. When he saw them flying kites, his boyishness would revive, and he would have three or four goes at bringing down someone's kite. Sometimes he would even play gulli-danda with the children. Hence the boys loved their father as much as they feared Rama.

As soon as they saw him, the boys hid their cards under the floor mat and began to study, waiting for slaps with bowed heads. But Ramanath gave them no slaps this time. Sitting down on a three-legged stool, he said to Gopinath, 'You've seen the bhang shop haven't you? The one at the corner?'

Delighted and relieved Gopinath said, 'Yes, of course I've seen it.'

'Go and bring four paisas worth of majum. And run. Oh yes! Get half a kilo of sweets from the sweet shop too. Take this rupee.'

In about fifteen minutes, Rama went to Jalpa's room with these two delicacies.

# 7

It was ten o'clock at night and Jalpa was lying on the open roof. In the golden May moonlight, the domes, pinnacles, and trees of the city spread out before her like dream pictures. Her eyes were fixed on the moon, and she felt as if she were flying towards it. It seemed to her as if her nose was dry, her eyes burning and her head spinning. As soon as anything came to mind she would forget it, and when she tried hard to remember something nothing would come. Once she remembered her home and began to cry. A moment later she remembered her friends and began to laugh. Suddenly Ramanath, smiling and carrying a small parcel in his hand, appeared and sat down on the charpai.

Jalpa sat up and asked, 'What's in the bundle?'

'Take a guess, then I'll show.'

'It's a golgappa made from laughter.' And she began to laugh.
'Wrong.'

'Is it a bundle of sleep?'

'Wrong.'

'Then it must be a little box of love.'

'Right. Today I'll make you the goddess of flowers.'

Jalpa exploded with laughter. Rama began to array her in jewels made from flowers with great affection. Her tender body began to tingle from the soft cool touch of the flowers. Like the flowers every fibre of her being opened wide with joy.

Rama smiled and said, 'Would you like a little present?'

Jalpa did not answer. Even though she was gazing intently at her husband, she felt embarrassed in this costume. She very much wanted to have a peep at herself in a mirror. A lamp was lit in the room opposite, so she got up, went inside, and stood in front of the mirror. In her rapturous mood it seemed to her that she really was the goddess of flowers. She took up the paandaan, came out, and began making paan.

Rama was now feeling great remorse over his deceitful behaviour. When Jalpa, returning from the room, looked at him with eyes rapturous with love, he turned his face away. He couldn't bring himself to look into those guileless trusting eyes. He thought to himself, 'What a coward I am. Why couldn't I answer Father plainly? Why did I agree to buying all those things? Wasn't it my responsibility to clearly tell Jalpa how things are with us?' His eyes filled with tears. He went and stood near the parapet. In that pure light of love, his impulse to take her jewels seemed like some fearful creature glaring at him. He began to hate himself so much, that for a moment he considered disclosing the whole wretched business; he thought better of it, however. What dreadful results there would be. Even to imagine falling in her estimation was unbearable to him.

Looking at him with love-filled eyes, Jalpa said, 'When my father came to see you and then began to describe you to my mother, I was thinking what you might be like. All kinds of pictures came into my mind!'

Ramanath heaved a deep sigh and did not reply.

'My friends were fascinated when they saw you,' she continued. 'Shahzadi wouldn't move away from the window. She was dying to talk to you. When you went inside, it was she who gave you paan, remember?'

Rama remained silent.

'She was the one who was the most attractive, who had a mole on her cheek, ajii. You looked at her very affectionately, and she nearly sank into the ground from embarrassment. She said to me, "Jiijaa seems very warm-hearted." Her friends teased her a lot, and the poor thing became tearful. Do you remember?'

'I can't remember a thing,' said Rama in a voice like a man drowning in a river.

'Never mind, the next time you go, I'll show you. Did you go to the bazaar today or not?'

Hanging his head, Rama said, 'I didn't have the time today.'

'Go, I'm not going to speak to you any more. You play some trick or other every day. So you'll bring it tomorrow, won't you?'

Ramanath's heart was wrung. She was getting so distressed about that chandrahar! How could she know that misfortune was arranging to plunder all of her possessions? This artless girl for whom he ought to have sacrificed his very life was the very one whose entire treasure he was resolved to snatch away! He became so agitated that it came to his mind to jump from the roof and end his life.

Midnight had passed, and through the shelter of a tree the moon was peeping like a thief. Jalpa was deep in sleep with her arms flung around her husband's neck. Rama got up slowly with a grim resolve in his heart, but the sight of Jalpa, slumbering in the lap of sleep and radiant in her flowers shook him. For a moment he stood lost in looking at her face, smiling in sleep. He didn't have the courage to go into her room, and lay down again.

Jalpa, roused from sleep, asked, 'Where are you going? Is it morning?'

'It's still late night.'

'Then why are you sitting up?'

'It's nothing. I just got up to drink some water.'

Jalpa, becoming amorous, threw her arms around Rama's neck and lulling him to sleep said, 'If you keep on putting a spell on me like this, I'll run away. Who knows why you stare at me like that, or what you're doing. What mantra do you say to make my heart become so restless! Vasanti is right; there's magic in men's eyes.'

'I'm not casting a spell,' said Rama in a broken voice. 'I'm quenching the thirst of my eyes.' They both went to sleep again, the one plunged into rapture, the other drowned in worry.

Three more hours passed, and the nearly-full moon extinguished its lamp. The cool dawn breeze gave its cup of intoxication to nature to drink and danced away. Even the late night bazaar had gone to sleep. Only Rama was still awake. Because of the flood of contradictory arguments in his mind he got up and lay down again and again. Finally, when he heard the sound of four o'clock striking, he rose in a panic and went to Jalpa's room. The jewellery casket was kept in a cupboard. Rama picked it up, and trembling all over went downstairs. His confusion did not allow him the leisure to take out the jewels and select some of them.

Dayanath was sleeping downstairs on the veranda. Rama woke him up gently; confused he asked, 'Who is it?'

Putting his finger to his lips Rama said, 'It's me. I've brought this jewel casket. Please keep it.'

Dayanath, alert now, sat up. Only his eyes had been awake before, but now his wits, too, had awakened. When Rama had spoken of taking the jewels, Dayanath had thought that he was just speaking in the heat of the moment. He had not believed that Rama would make good on what he was saying; he had wanted to remain aloof from these dirty tricks. His inmost soul completely rejected aiding and abetting his son in such sordid work. 'Why did you take it?' he asked.

'Wasn't it *your* order?' asked Rama brazenly.

'You're lying!'

'So shall I put it back?'

Rama's question plunged Dayanath into a terrible dilemma. Abashed, he said, 'How can you put it back now? If she should see you, it would be a disaster. You'd be doing what would make us a laughing-stock. Why are you standing there? Put the casket into my big chest and go lie down. If she wakes up somehow, then we're finished!'

An old cedar chest was kept in Dayanath's room in back of the veranda. Rama put the casket in it and quickly went upstairs. When he reached the roof he stopped and listened; Jalpa was wrapt in the easeful sleep of the hour before dawn.

As soon as Ramanath sat down on the charpai, Jalpa was roused and clung to him. Rama asked, 'What is it? Why did you wake up?'

Gazing around contentedly, Jalpa said, 'Nothing, really. I was having a dream. Why are you sitting up? How late is it?'

Rama lay down and said, 'It's just about morning. What was your dream?'

'It seemed as if some thief took my jewel casket and ran away.'

Rama's heart began to pound with such force that it felt as if a sledgehammer were falling on it! His blood ran cold through fear; he suspected that she must have seen him. He burst out shouting, 'Thief! Thief!'

On the veranda below Dayanath too raised a shout, 'Thief! Thief!'

Jalpa got up in a panic. She rushed into her room and threw open the cupboard. The casket was not there! She fell fainting.

# 8

As soon as morning came Dayanath took the jewels, made his way to the jeweller, and began to bargain. The jeweller had his fifteen hundred, but he was not content to take the sum only in jewels. He could take previously sold jewellery only at a discount, he said. Who takes back something already sold? If they had been taken on approval, it would have been a different matter, but a deal had been made for these things. He advanced such a number of commercial principles, and put the screws to Dayanath in such a way that the poor wretch could think of nothing better than to say 'Yes, yes.' Can a mere office worker overcome a crafty shopkeeper? One thousand five hundred rupees of jewels became two thousand five hundred, and fifty more on top of that. Father and son argued about this for some time, each holding the other to be at fault. They didn't even talk to each other for several days. None the less, news of the theft was kept quiet, for if the police should find out, they both feared that the whole show would be given away. Jalpa was told that her things would never be recovered, so why bring useless troubles on themselves? Jalpa herself thought there was no use making a report when they'd never turn up anyway.

Jalpa loved jewellery perhaps more than anything else in the world, nor was this surprising. When she was an innocent child of three, gold bangles had been made for her. When her grandmother had taken her in her lap to feed her, she had talked only of jewels. 'Your bridegroom will bring very beautiful jewels for you, and you'll strut about.'

Jalpa would ask, 'Will they be gold or silver Grandmother?'

And her grandmother would say, 'They'll be gold, child. Why would he bring silver ones? If he should bring silver ones then fling them in his face.'

Manaki would tease her by saying, 'He won't bring anything but silver ones. Where will he get gold ones?'

Jalpa would begin to cry whereupon everyone—the old grandmother, Manaki, the servant women, the neighbour ladies, and Dindayal—would laugh. For them this was an inexhaustible store of amusement.

When the child grew a little older, she began to perform marriages among her dolls. Charhaos came from the boys; she decked the brides in jewels, sat them in litters and bid them farewell. Sometimes the bride-doll would sulk to get jewels from her bridegroom-doll, and the poor devil would bring them from somewhere or other to please his wife. It was at that very time that the pedlar gave her the chandrahar which she kept in a safe place even now.

When she grew still older, she began to hear conversations about jewels while sitting with older women. In that little world of women they talked of nothing else. Who had had which jewels made, how much they had cost, whether they were first-rate or second-rate, studded with gems or plain, in which girl's wedding how many jewels had been given—on these important subjects there were constant criticisms and counter-criticisms, commentaries and sub-commentaries. No other subject could possibly be so agreeable, so acceptable.

Brought up in this jewellery-saturated world, Jalpa's love of ornaments was only natural. For more than a month after the theft, her condition remained unaltered; she hardly ate or drank, or laughed or talked with anyone. She lay on her bed staring into the empty sky with empty eyes. The whole household tried to reason with her but were defeated as were the neighbour ladies. Her father Dindayal came to console her too, but Jalpa didn't give up her sickness. She no longer had confidence in anyone in the house, so much so, that she was cool even to Rama. She believed that the entire household was neglecting her. Every single one of them was draining her life away. When they had so much wealth, why wouldn't they have new jewels made for her? Those in whom we place our deepest affections are also the very ones with whom we become the angriest. Jalpa was especially furious with Rama. If he would just speak forcefully to his mother and father, then no one could prevent him from getting his way. But was he about to say anything? It was as if his mouth had been stopped up with curds. If he loved her, he wouldn't keep sitting around so unconcerned. He wouldn't be able to sleep at night until he had had everything made. Was his love only feigned? Why would he say anything to his parents anyhow? He would just go on his way. Who was she after all?

She didn't just stay aloof from Rama; if he'd ask her something, she'd let him have a few stinging words. The poor fellow stayed shamefaced; he was being roasted in the fire which he himself had built, the wretch. If he'd known that this would be the result of his vainglorious boasting, he'd have sealed his tongue. Worry and shame crushed his heart. Where he had spent the days from morning to evening in laughter and merriment, in rambles and excursions, now he was stumbling around looking for a job. All his delight had disappeared. Often he grew angry with his father: if he wanted to, he could pay off the whole amount in three or four months, but what did he care! Even if he were to die, his father would not give up his stubborn insistence on not taking bribes. His sincere and ardent heart was smouldering with passion, and when he saw Jalpa's wasted face, he would heave a sad sigh. That pleasant love-dream had dissolved so quickly; would those days ever come again? How could three thousand rupees worth of jewels be made? Even if he were to become a government servant, was an important position likely to come his way? He might not scrape three thousand together even in three lifetimes! He wanted to think up some scheme or other that would make him fantastically rich as soon as possible—if only his name would turn out to be a winner in some lottery! Then he would cover Jalpa with jewels. He'd have a chandrahar made first of all, inlaid with diamonds. If he had known how to make counterfeit notes, he would certainly have churned them out.

One day he had wandered about in search of a job until evening. Thanks to chess, he was acquainted with a great number of prominent people, but fear and embarrassment prevented him from revealing his true situation to any of them. He also knew that his welcome would last just as long as he didn't beg anyone for help. Once he lost his respectability, he could forget about asking them for anything at all. No good-natured person, who would understand everything without having to be told and would arrange some nice position for him, was in sight. He was very depressed today and he felt so angry with his friends that he was ready to scold them one by one, and turn them away from his door with a curse. Just let anyone call him to play a game of chess now, and he'd give them a piece of his mind that they'd remember a long time. When he thought it over a little, however, he realized that in all this he himself was more to blame than his friends. There was not one of his friends to whom he had not boasted and bragged; it was a habit of his. He concealed the true condition of his household as if it were something scandalous, with the inevitable result that despite his numerous friends, he was unemployed. He could not tell anyone of his mental agony, which had become as unbearable as internal suffocation. He came home and sat down with his head hanging.

Jageshwari brought him some water and asked, 'Where have you been all day today? Here, take this and wash your face and hands.'

Rama had just lifted the lota when Jalpa in a waspish mood came and said, 'Take me to my home this instant!'

Rama put the lota down and stared at her as though he had not understood.

'This is hardly the way daughters-in-law take their leave,' said Jageshwari. 'What are you saying, bahu?'

'I'm not that sort of daughter-in-law,' answered Jalpa. 'I go when I feel like it and come when I feel like it, and I'm not afraid of anyone. When no one here even asks after me, then I don't consider anyone my own either. I lie around all day like an orphan and no one even bothers to look in. I'm not a bird whose cage you shut up after giving it water and seeds. I'm a person too. I'm not going to stay in this house another minute. If no one comes with me, I'll go alone. There are no wolves along the way to carry me off, and even if they did, what would it matter? What kind of happiness do I have here anyway?'

Cautiously Rama said, 'After all, you might let us know what's happened?'

'Nothing has happened. I just feel like I don't want to live here.'

Rama said, 'Well, give a little thought to what your family will say if you go like this.'

'I've thought everything over, and I don't want to think about it any more. I'm going to pack my clothes and go by the very next train,' said Jalpa and went upstairs. Rama followed her, thinking that he could calm her down.

Jalpa went to her room and was beginning to fold up her bedding when Rama caught her by the hand and said, 'I swear to you I won't even let you think of going.'

Lifting her eyebrows scornfully Jalpa said, 'I don't care a bit for whatever you swear.'

She wrenched her hand free and began to fold her bedclothes again, while Rama stood sheepishly in a corner. Jalpa fastened up her bedding and then began to clean out her trunk, but not with her previous determination; she opened and shut it repeatedly. The rain had stopped, and only the water caught by the roof was gently dripping.

At last she sat down on the bundle of bedding and said, 'Why did you swear to me?'

A thrill of hope shot through Rama's heart. 'What other way did I have to stop you?' he asked.

'Do you want me to suffocate and die here?'

'Why do you come out with such unfortunate words? I'm ready to go with you; if you won't listen to what I say, you'll force me to take you home. Go, God is the master, but at least ask Father and Mother.'

Oil fell into a dying fire. Jalpa said tormentedly, 'Who are they to me, that I should ask them?'

'Isn't there anyone?'

'No one! If there was, they wouldn't abandon me like this. No one with some money around could bear to see his dear ones suffering. Couldn't your parents have dried my tears? I just lie around here day after day. No one even asks after me. The neighbourhood women come to see me; how can I see them? I won't show my face. Nowhere to come to, nowhere to go to, no one to chit or chat with—can anyone live long like this? I've lost all hope of anything from your parents. After all, there are your two brothers; will they save up something for them, or just give it all to you?'

Rama had a chance to do some bragging again. He was happy to have the opportunity today—after so many days—to please Jalpa once more. 'Your opinion is quite right, dear,' he said. 'It's just as you say. Otherwise two or three thousand would be no big deal for Father. He's got tens of thousands stashed away in the bank; he just goes to the office to amuse himself.'

'But he's a miser from head to toe!'

'If he weren't a miser, where would all that money have come from?'

'I don't care about what other people may have,' said Jalpa. 'There's nothing lacking at our house! You can get bread and lentils there just as well as here. I'll have three or four of my friends, fields and crops, gardens—I'll really enjoy myself.'

'And do you know what kind of shape I'll be in? I'll waste away and die. Only my heart knows how wretched I've been ever since the theft happened. I've told Mother and Father thousands of times if I've told them once; I've hammered away at it, to please have three or four things made. But neither paid me the slightest attention. I don't know why they've turned away from us.'

'When you get a position somewhere, send for me.'

'I'm looking, and I'll get something very soon. After all, I've met thousands of important people so why should it take long? Well, I do want a good posting.'

'I understand which direction the wind is blowing from with these people. Now I can stay here with confidence. Well, haven't you spoken to anyone about a position?'

'I'm ashamed to speak to anyone.'

'What is there to be ashamed of? If you're ashamed, then write a letter.'

Rama gave a start. What a simple method and yet until now this straightforward idea had not occurred to him. 'Yes, you've told me a really good way of doing it,' he said. 'Tomorrow I'll write for sure.'

'First take me home and then write. You'll be back here early tomorrow.'

'So are you really going? Then forget about my writing a letter and getting a position. Do you think I'm going to look for work, or sit around and cry from the pain of your going? No, stop thinking about going just now. No, I tell you I'll run away somewhere. I've seen how things are around this house. Who else is there here besides you whom I'd lie around and rot for? Move away just a little so I can open the bedding.'

Jalpa, moving a little off the bedding, said, 'I'll come back very quickly. As soon as you leave to get me, I'll come.'

'No ma'am,' said Rama, opening up the bundle. 'Excuse me, but I'm not falling into that trap. It won't matter to you; you'll be having a good time with your girl friends, and you won't even ask after me, while here I'll be in danger of dying. You'd never set foot in this house again.'

'You've opened up the bundle I fastened up, otherwise I'd have reached home today feeling very happy,' said Jalpa with gratitude. 'Shahzadi was right when she said men are great magicians. Today I'd really made up my mind to go, so that even if Brahma himself had descended before me I wouldn't have listened to him. But in only two minutes you've spoiled all my plans. You really must write letters tomorrow. We can't get on now without your earning something.'

'I won't wait till tomorrow. I'll go and write two or three letters right now.'

'Have some paan before you go.'

Ramanath had some paan, went to the mardana room, and sat down to write letters. But after thinking a little, he rose abruptly and went out. What can the loving insistence of a woman not bring a man to do!

## 9

Among Rama's acquaintances was a certain Ramesh Babu, head clerk of the Municipal Board. He was over forty, and a connoisseur. When he sat down to play chess, he would play the whole night through and even forget to go to his office, like a bullock unrestrained by his nose-rope in front or his tether behind. His wife had died when he was young and he had not married again. How else could he have borne such a lonely life without some kind of recreation? If he had wanted to he could have made thousands, but he considered earning even a single paisa from bribery to be contemptible. He had a deep affection for Rama; who else was idle enough to play chess with him all night, night after night! The poor fellow had been getting increasingly upset; for several days now he hadn't moved a piece even once. How long could he keep on reading the newspaper? To be sure, Rama had visited once or twice, but he hadn't sat down to play. Each time Ramesh Babu had set out the pieces and caught hold of him to sit him down, but he wouldn't sit. Why would he play chess? His new bride had come. Would he rather gaze at her face or have a romantic *tete-à-tete* with her, or play chess with an old man? Ramesh Babu had thought of inviting Rama over several times, but had let the matter drop after recalling that he wouldn't want to come anyway. What was he to do with himself? Go and see a movie? He had to pass the time somehow or other. He was not particularly fond of movies, but just then he couldn't come up with a better idea. He had just dressed and was about to go out when Rama stepped into the room.

As soon as Ramesh saw him he practically rolled over like a ball and rushed to the door. Seizing Rama by the hand he said, 'Please come in, come in Babu Ramanath Sahab Bahadur. You've completely forgotten this old fellow. Yes, my friend, why would you come these days? You won't have the pleasure of the sweet words of your darling here. Have you found out anything about the theft?'

'Not a thing.'

'It's a very good thing that you didn't make a report at the police station. Otherwise you'd have had to come up with a couple hundred more rupees. Your wife must be feeling very sad?'

'Don't even ask; she's stopped eating and drinking since then. I'm completely fed up. I feel like running away somewhere. Father doesn't listen at all.'

'Does your father have Karun's treasury put aside somewhere? He's just finished spending four or five thousand, so where can he possibly get the money to have jewellery made? It'll cost ten or twenty thousand. Besides, there are the two boys to think about, and then, how much can he rely on the income from his job? How far can fifty rupees go?'

'I'm caught in a real mess. Now it seems that I'll be forced to get a job. I was enjoying life, but now I'm caught willy-nilly in this predicament. Now tell me please, where can I find help to get some kind of service?'

Ramesh took the chess board and pieces from a niche and said, 'Come, play one game, and then we'll think about this problem. It's not as easy as you suppose. You're getting a really good hammering.'

'I don't feel like playing right now. Until this question is dealt with, I won't be in my right mind.'

Placing the chess pieces on the board, Ramesh Babu said, 'Come, sit down. We'll just play one game, and then we'll think about what can be done.'

'I really don't feel like it at all. If I had known I was going to be hit by such bad luck on my first try, I wouldn't have even come close to getting married.'

'Well now, just play three or four moves and you'll want to keep on—and that tangle in your head will loosen up a little.'

The game began. After a few ordinary moves Ramesh Babu struck down one of Rama's rooks.

'Oh, what a mistake!' said Rama.

Ramesh Babu's eyes began to turn red like those of someone drunk. For him chess was no less intoxicating than liquor. 'That was a good move,' he said. 'I'm thinking of a post for you. But the pay is very little, only thirty rupees a month. Right now Khan Sahab, the one with the coloured beard, has it, but he can't manage the work; I've saved his neck more than once. I thought that as long as the work gets done one way or another, let things go on as they are. He has children. He's asked me several times for time off. The position certainly isn't good enough for you, but if you want it, it's yours.'

In the middle of saying this, he slaughtered one of Rama's bishops.

'You're taking away my pieces while you keep me busy talking!' said Rama, making an attempt to replace his bishop. 'That's not fair. Put my bishop back!'

'Look here, friend, don't cheat. I didn't take your bishop by force. Well, do you accept the position?'

'The salary is just thirty.'

'Yes, the salary *is* small, but perhaps it will increase later. My opinion is you should take it.'

'OK, if that's your advice I'll take it.'

'The position is an octroi one. Our Muslim friend was able to have his sons get an MA, and an LLB through this position and two others are studying in college. His girls married into respectable families. Of course, it's necessary to carry out the work with discretion.'

'I don't care about octroi revenue, but bribery is not a good thing.'

'A very bad thing, but what are men with children supposed to do? You can't get by on thirty rupees a month. One hundred fifty is plenty for me; I can even put aside something. But in a home with a lot of people, with boys to educate, with girls to marry off, what can the man of the house do? As long as subordinate officials don't receive a salary which allows them to subsist with dignity, bribery will continue. They eat the same bread and lentils, ghee and milk as anyone else. So why give one person thirty rupees a month and another three hundred?'

Rama's queen was also struck down. Ramesh Babu laughed uproariously.

'If you're going to play quietly, then play,' said Rama indignantly. 'Otherwise I'm going. You keep talking to me and then take all my pieces away.'

'OK, sit down. If I talk now, grab my tongue. Check! So tomorrow turn in an application. You'll likely get the post, but on the day you get it, you'll have to play chess with me the whole night.'

'You'll start complaining after only two losses.'

'The days when you could keep on defeating me are gone, sir. The moon is powerful these days, and I've got a sure-fire mantra now. Who'd have the nerve to beat me now! Check again!'

'I really feel like beating you in the next game and then going, but I'll be late,' said Rama.

'What do you mean late? It's only nine o'clock now. Play, and let your heart's desire be satisfied. Checkmate!'

'OK, there's tomorrow's game. If I don't challenge you to five games tomorrow and beat you each time, then you can say something.'

'Away with you, sir. *You*, beat *me*? Now's the right time if you have the courage!'

'All right, come on. Say whatever you like, but I won't play fewer than five games!'

'Not five, play ten, sir! The night is ours,' said Ramesh Babu. 'Come on, let's eat. Then we can sit down without a care. I'll send word to your home that today you'll sleep here and not to wait up for you.'

Both of them ate and then sat down to play chess again. The first game lasted until eleven, and Ramesh Babu won. The second game, too, fell into his hands. By the time the third game had finished, it was two o'clock.

'I'm getting sleepy now,' said Rama.

'Wash your face then; I've got some ice. I'm not going to let you sleep without playing five games.'

Ramesh Babu was becoming more and more certain that his star was high today, because otherwise it was not easy to defeat Rama three times in a row. He was sure that at present no matter how many games he played victory would be his. When he lost the fourth game however, his confidence left him. Indeed, he became afraid lest he be repeatedly defeated himself. 'We ought to sleep now,' he said.

'Why? You won't finish five games?'

'I have to go to the office tomorrow too.'

Rama didn't insist too much on continuing, and they both went to sleep.

Rama usually didn't get up before eight, and last night he had gone to sleep at three; today he had the right to sleep until ten. Ramesh, according to his usual practice, got up at five, bathed, meditated, went for a walk, and returned by eight. But Rama was still sleeping soundly. Finally, when nine-thirty struck, he woke him up.

'You had no right to wake me up,' said Rama in a temper. 'I was having such a good sleep.'

'Well sir, do you want to submit that application or not?'

'You submit it.'

'And if the Sahab should call for the applicant, should *I* go?'

Rama grunted sleepily and said, 'Do whatever you want. I'm going to sleep.'

He lay down again. Ramesh ate, dressed, and got ready to go to the office. Then Rama got up in a panic, and rubbing his eyes said, 'I'll go too.'

'Well! Wash your face and hands, then, my good fellow!'

'But you're going.'

'No,' said Ramesh, 'I can wait for fifteen or twenty minutes. Get ready.'

'I'm ready. I'll eat when I get back.'

'I'm telling you that I'll wait half an hour.'

Rama washed his face in a minute, ate in five, and then immediately set out for the office with Ramesh.

On the way Ramesh smiled and said, 'Have you thought about what excuse you're going to make at home?'

'I'll tell her Ramesh Babu wouldn't let me go.'

'You'll just get her to say bad things about me, what else? And then you won't be able to come again.'

'I'm not *that* devoted to my wife. So, tell me, won't I have to take my application to the Sahab?'

'And do you think you're going to get a position sitting at home? You'll have to run around for months and months! You'll have to bring dozens of recommendations, and you'll have to wait around morning and night. Is it easy to get a job?'

'Then let me keep clear of a job like that. I'm ashamed to even make an application, let alone start flattering people. I used to die laughing when I thought about a clerk's position, but now this calamity has fallen on my head. The Sahab won't rant and rave at me, will he?'

'He speaks harshly to everyone; people tremble when they go to meet him,' replied Ramesh.

'Then I'm going home. I won't stand for all this.'

'At first everyone gets scared like this, but after you've stuck it out for a while, you get used to it. Your heart is probably pounding for fear of what may happen. When I became a government servant, I was just your age and had been married just three months. On the day my interview was to take place, I was so terrified that I felt as if I was going to my own hanging. But you have no reason to be afraid; I'll fix everything up.'

'You must have been in government service a little over twenty years now, haven't you?'

'A full twenty-five years, sir!' said Ramesh. 'My wife died twenty years ago when I was a ten-rupees-a-month clerk.'

'Why didn't you marry again? You couldn't have been more than twenty-five then.'

Ramesh smiled and said, 'Who feels like eating gur after eating barfi? Who would find a hut pleasant after enjoying the happiness of a palace? Love satiates the soul. You know me now when I've grown old, but I tell you truly that all through my life as a widower, I've never even considered another wife. I've seen many beauties, and several times people have practically besieged me with appeals to marry, but I never had even the desire to. For me, the sweet memories of that love bring back its full living joy.'

Talking like this the two of them reached the office.

# 10

When Rama arrived home from the office it was just about four o'clock. He was still in the office when clouds began to gather in the sky. It was just about to rain, but Rama was so anxious to reach home that he couldn't wait. He hadn't even managed to leave the compound before a downpour began. It was the first rain of June, breaking the heat of the hot season, and he was drenched in a moment. Even so he didn't stop. What did this heavy shower matter, in comparison to the joy of telling the news of his receiving a job? True, the salary was only thirty rupees a month, but after all, it was an octroi revenue position. He was already making mental calculations about how much he would have to save each month to be able to have a chandrahar made for Jalpa. If he could save even fifty or sixty rupees a month, then in five years Jalpa would be loaded down with jewels. He even estimated how much different kinds of ornaments would cost. He didn't stop to take off his wet clothes when he reached home, but went straight to Jalpa's room soaked through as he was.

As soon as Jalpa saw him she asked, 'How did you get so wet? Where did you disappear to last night?'

'I've been really worried about getting a job. I've just come from the office; I've got a position in the Municipal Office.'

Jalpa leaped up and exclaimed, 'Really? What's the pay?'

Rama hesitated to tell her the exact amount. To mention a salary of a mere thirty rupees would be an affront. Who wants to appear contemptible in the eyes of his wife? He said, 'For now I'll get just forty, but it will increase rapidly; it's an octroi revenue position.'

Jalpa had dreamed up some important position for him. 'What can you do with forty? Seventy would have been better,' she said.

'I could have gotten even a hundred-rupee position, but this one will give me a lot of respect and comfort. I'll get over fifty or sixty rupees a month.'

'So you'll take bribes, and cut the throats of poor people?'

Rama laughed and said, 'No darling, it's not a job like that. I'll be getting payments from important bankers and moneylenders who'll give me their throats gladly. I can keep anyone I like standing in the office for the whole day. Every minute is like a gold coin for such people, so they'll flatter me and give me money too, to get their work done as quickly as possible.'

'Well, then it's all right,' said Jalpa, appeased. 'You'll treat poor people fairly.'

'I certainly will.'

'You haven't told Mother? Go tell her and come back. The thing that makes me happiest is that now people will know that I have some rights here too.'

'Yes, I'm going. But I'm going to tell her I'm getting only twenty.'

Jalpa delighted, said, 'Yes sir! But tell her fifteen instead. And it's a waste of time to even mention the extra money from its being an octroi position. They can figure that out for themselves. First of all, I'll have a chandrahar made.'

Just then the postman called out. Rama went to the door and saw that a parcel had come for him, sent by Jalpa's father, Mahashaya Dindayal. Feeling very happy, he took it and went back in. 'This came from your home, see what's in it,' he said, putting it into Jalpa's hands.

Rama bought out the scissors in a flash and opened the parcel. Out came a little box of deodar wood, in which was placed a chandrahar. Rama took it out and laughed as he said, 'God must have heard you; it looks like a very nice one.'

In a choked voice Jalpa said, 'What was Mother thinking of? This is *her* necklace. Send it back as soon as it's time for the post.'

Rama, astonished, said, 'What need is there to send it back? Won't she be angry?'

Jalpa scowled contemptuously and said, 'I don't care. If her majesty gets offended, she can take pleasure in the fact that her husband's alive. I can live quite well without her pity. Only now, after all this time she feels sorry for me. She didn't take pity on me when I was leaving her house. Congratulations to her on her jewellery! I don't want to be obliged to anyone. This is her time of life to dress up and deck herself out. Why should I stand in her way? If you keep on having such good fortune, I'll get lots of jewels. I want to show mother that I'm not hungry for her jewellery.'

'To my way of thinking, you ought to keep the necklace!' said Rama consolingly. Consider how unhappy it will make her to return it. It's a good thing she didn't give it to you when you left, or it would have disappeared with the other jewels too.'

'I won't take it, and that's final.'

'But why?'

'Because that's my wish!'

'There must be some reason for this wish?'

In a choked-up voice Jalpa said, 'This is the reason; Mother is not happy to be giving this. It's quite possible she was crying when she sent it, and there's no doubt she'd be overjoyed to get it back. You should look into the heart of someone who's giving something. If she were to give me just a plain ring with love, then I'd take it with both hands. If she's given this to me by squelching her own feelings, or because she doesn't want to lose her reputation or to be denounced by someone, then has she really given it? Charity is given to beggars. I won't take charity from anyone, even my own mother.'

Seeing Jalpa's hostility towards her mother, Rama could find nothing more to say. Hostility doesn't listen to reason and logic. Rama took the necklace, got up from the charpai and said, 'I'll just show it to Mother and Father. At least we ought to ask them about it.'

Jalpa snatched the necklace from his hand and said, 'Who are they to me that I should ask them? Our only connection is living in the same house. Since they think I'm nothing, then I think they're nothing too.'

She put the necklace back into its container as she spoke and began to sew it up in some cloth for mailing. Timidly, Rama said once more, 'What's the hurry? Send it back in a few days out of consideration for them.'

Jalpa looked at him severely and said, 'I won't have any peace in my mind until I send this back. It'll rankle like a thorn in my heart. As soon as the parcel is ready, off it goes; return it right away.'

In a moment the parcel was ready, and Rama, in an apprehensive mood, took it downstairs.

# 11

When Mahashaya Dayanath learned of Rama's getting a government position, he was delighted. He had not expected him to come to his senses so soon after his marriage. 'It's a good position,' he said. 'If you work honestly, then you'll move on to a really good post. My advice is that you consider other people's money taboo.'

Rama felt like saying outright, 'Keep your advice to yourself, it's not suitable for me.' But he wasn't that brazen.

Dayanath spoke again. 'This position of yours was a thirty-rupees-a-month one. Why are you getting only twenty?'

'Why would they give the full salary to a newcomer? After six months or a year I'll probably get more. There's a lot of work.'

'You're a young man; you shouldn't be frightened of work.'

Rama had a new suit made the next day and bought lots of fashionable things. There was some money left over from the money his father-in-law had given for the wedding, and he borrowed some from friends. He wanted to inspire awe in the whole office by dressing in a thoroughly European style. Nobody would even ask about his salary; the bankers and moneylenders would see his splendor and be intimidated. He knew that a good income depends on just such pomp and show. An ordinary policeman thinks one paisa is plenty, but put a sergeant in his place and no one will have the nerve to show him only one paisa. A tattered beggar thinks that a pinch of food is a lot, but one feels ashamed to give only a rupee to a sadhu wearing an ochre-coloured silk robe. There's a long-standing friendship between alms and appearance.

When Rama turned up on the third day wearing pants and coat, and sporting a hat, his dignity increased still more. The peons all bowed and saluted him. When he came to meet Ramesh Babu and take charge of his work, he saw a Muslim gentleman sitting on the veranda on a torn and dirty carpet with a register spread out on a trunk, and a crowd of business people standing all around him. In front of him was a veritable bazaar of wagons, pushcarts, and horse carriages. Everyone was clamouring for his work to be done quickly. Some were trading insults and abuse, while some of the peons were laughing and joking. Everything was being done in a very disorderly manner. To Rama, sitting on such a ragged, grimy carpet seemed degrading. He went straight to Ramesh Babu and said, 'Do you want to make me sit on that dirty old carpet too? Please have a good table and some chairs sent and tell the peons not to let more than one person at a time see me.' Ramesh Babu smiled, and had the tables and chairs sent; Rama sat on his chair with dignity! The old Muslim munshi laughed to himself at Rama's self-indulgence and thought to himself, 'He's in the first flush of his enthusiasm, obsessed with his new work.' He explained the nature of the work to Rama. And just what did that involve? Merely to balance the accounts for each day's income. There was a printed table to show how much duty should be paid for each kind of goods. Rama understood his work in half an hour. Even though the old munshi had resigned his position of his own free will, he was still feeling sad now that the time had come to go. He had come to sit here for thirty years without a break. Thanks to this place, he had earned both fame and fortune, so why wouldn't he feel sorry to leave? After he had explained the work and was leaving, Rama accompanied him down the stairs. Khan Sahab was pleased by this courtesy. He smiled and said, 'It's an open secret that one has to pay an anna for every receipt! People give it with pleasure. You'll be a rich man, but don't mess things up. Once a practice like this is let slip, it's difficult to establish it again. The peons have a right to a portion of this anna. The previous senior clerk used to take fifty rupees a month, but this one doesn't take a thing.'

Rama, displaying indifference, said, 'It's dirty work; I want to keep my hands clean.'

The old Muslim laughed and said, 'It seems dirty now, but you'll come to enjoy it.'

After seeing off Khan Sahab, Rama returned to his chair and said to a peon, 'Tell these people to please go down below the veranda. And have them come one by one in order. Write down everyone's name in the order they come on a piece of paper.'

One of the merchants who had been standing for two hours said joyfully, 'Yes sir, this will be very good.'

'Whoever has come first should be taken care of first,'

announced Rama. 'The others can wait outside until their number comes. Those who come last of all shouldn't be allowed to make a hullabaloo and get ahead of everybody else while those who get here first stand around gawking.'

Several peons said, 'Yes Babuji, it would be very good if things were managed like this. This kind of free-for-all wastes a lot of time.'

Rama had enough clout to establish this degree of control. His mode of operation began to evoke both praise and criticism among the business community from that very day. Even a big-name college professor could not have earned such renown in his whole life.

After only three or four days of experience Rama knew all the tricks of the trade! He even thought up scams that Khan Sahab hadn't even dreamed of. There were no limits to the chicanery in weighing, counting, and inspecting various goods. When merchants themselves gulped down hundreds of rupees from the same chicanery, why should Rama be contented with only an anna per transaction, half of which was already spoken for by the peons? By weighing and inspecting goods strictly according to the rules, he could make a name for himself, and money too. Why should he let such an opportunity pass, especially when the head clerk was a crony of his! Ramesh Babu was enthralled by the new recruit's adroitness in his work. He gave Rama a slap on the back and said, 'Go by the rules and do what you like; then no one can harm you.'

Rama's income began to grow quickly and along with it his influence. Whenever the withered old veteran clerks of the office had a hankering for cigarettes, paan, tea, or refreshments, they came to Rama; everyone could wash his hands in this flowing Ganges. People began to sing his praises through the whole office. 'He treats money as if it's nothing,' they said. 'What a heart he has! And his tongue is as sweet as his heart. Every vein in his body seems filled with good breeding.' When this was the way things were with the senior clerks, there's no need to ask what it was like with the peons and junior clerks! Before Rama took up office every last person had been just a slave of money, but now both the income and the prestige of these poor fellows increased. Where before they would have given only a tongue-lashing even to cart drivers, now they would grab even their betters by the neck and give them a shove downstairs. Ramanath's authority was beginning to increase.

So far, however, not even one of Jalpa's longings had been fulfilled. On the occasion of Nagpanchami several young women from the neighbourhood came to sing kajli songs with Jalpa. But she didn't stir from her room. In August came the festival of Krishna's birthday. A wealthy merchant lived close by, and the occasion was celebrated with great pomp. An invitation came for mother-in-law and daughter-in-law; Jageshwari went, but Jalpa refused to go. During these three months she had not even once mentioned jewellery to Rama, but this behaviour only intensified her solitary passion. Still more stimulating was an old catalogue which Rama had picked up from somewhere and brought home one day. It contained examples of many different kinds of beautiful ornaments, and the prices were written too. When she was alone, Jalpa would pore over this catalogue, but she would hide it away as soon as she saw Rama; she didn't want to be laughed at for showing her heartfelt desire.

When Rama returned around midnight, he found Jalpa lying on the charpai. Laughing, he remarked, 'There was some very good singing. You made a big mistake by not going.' Jalpa turned her face away and did not reply.

Rama spoke again. 'You must have been upset lying here all by yourself.'

In a cutting tone Jalpa said, 'You say I made a mistake, but I think I did the right thing. Whose reputation would have been dragged through the mud if I had gone?'

Jalpa had not wanted to taunt him, but what he said had provoked her. There was another reason for her resentment too; the whole family had left her alone and gone off to see the festival. If they had any feelings at all, wouldn't they have refused to go?

Rama said shamefacedly, 'There's no question of dragging someone's reputation through the mud. Everyone knows there was a robbery, and to have three or four thousand rupees worth of jewellery made these days, is no easy thing.'

As soon as he uttered the word 'robbery' Rama's heart began to pound. Jalpa stared intently at her husband without moving. Rama feared things would get out of hand from saying any more.

But it seemed to him from her fixed look that she might know the secret of the theft and was not talking openly about it only because of her own mortification. He also recalled the dream which Jalpa had had on the night of the crime. Her gaze stabbed into his soul like an arrow. But then he began to think he had been under a misconception, for there was no other emotion save resentment in that gaze. But why wasn't she speaking? Why had she gone dumb? Her very silence was a calamity. To alleviate his own doubts, and to fathom Jalpa's mind, Rama took a plunge. 'Who could know that as soon as you got out of your bridal sedan this disaster would greet you?'

Jalpa's eyes filled with tears. 'I'm not crying so you'll give me jewels. What was written in my fate has happened, and what is written will happen in the future too. Doesn't time pass for women without jewellery too?'

While these words put a stop to Rama's doubts, the acute suffering hidden in them could not be concealed. In the past three months despite many efforts he had not been able to gather together more than a hundred rupees. Treating the senior clerks with due respect meant having to let money just melt away. But without giving them things to eat and drink, he could not even keep the work going. All of them would become his enemies, and would start thinking of schemes to uproot him. He knew very well that wealth gotten for nothing is not swallowed up by oneself alone. He himself did not waste a single paisa. Like a clever businessman, whatever he spent was only spent to earn more. 'If God wishes, then something will be made in a month or two,' he said reassuringly.

'I'm not one of those women who'd give their lives for jewellery. Still, visiting someone's home like this does make me feel embarrassed.'

Rama's mind surged with remorse. Hopelessness dripped from Jalpa's every word. And who was the cause of this unbounded misery? Was he not also to blame for not once mentioning jewellery in all these three months? If Jalpa had not mentioned the subject out of shame, then did he, Rama, have no other means of drying her tears, of gratifying her, than to remain silent? Every day there was one or another festival in the neighbourhood, every day the women from nearby came to visit, and every day invitations kept arriving. How long could poor Jalpa keep on suppressing her spirit like this, and fretting herself away? Who doesn't enjoy laughing and talking, and who likes to lie around alone like a prisoner? It was because of him that she was enduring this terrible torment.

'Couldn't some ornaments be borrowed from some jeweller?' he thought to himself. He knew several prominent ones. But how could he mention it to them? What if they should refuse? Or it was possible that they might put him off with some excuse. He decided that now was not the right time for borrowing. If somehow he was unable to pay at the promised time, then there would be a useless squabble, and he'd be humiliated. Let him be patient for a little longer.

Suddenly it occurred to him to ask Jalpa's opinion in this matter. Let him see what she said. If she wanted, then some things could be procured from a jeweller on credit, and he would be ready to endure any insults and embarrassments. How anxious he was about jewellery to satisfy Jalpa! 'I'd like to ask your advice about something,' he said. 'Should I ask or not?'

Jalpa was getting sleepy. Closing her eyes she said, 'Let me sleep, bhai; I have to get up in the morning.'

'If you agree, then I'll get some jewellery made on credit. There's no harm in it, is there?'

Jalpa's eyes opened. What a heavy-handed question! It was as if one were to ask a guest to say if one should bring him some food! What bad manners! It could only mean that one didn't want to feed the guest. Rama ought to have brought the things and put them before her. And even if she were to ask repeatedly, he should just say that he'd paid for them and brought them. Then she'd be happy just the same. To ask her advice about this was to sprinkle salt on her wound. She looked at Rama incredulously and said, 'I'm not that keen on jewellery.'

'No, don't say that. What harm can there be in getting a few things from some jeweller? I'll pay it off gradually.'

Jalpa said with conviction, 'No, there's no need to go into debt for me. I'm not some prostitute to snatch and grab things from you and then be on my way. I have to live and die with you. Even if I have to live my whole life without ornaments, I won't tell you to go into debt. Women aren't *that* hungry for jewellery. I'm not one of those who would plunge the whole household into difficulties just to wear jewels. Besides, you said before that your position has a high income, and it didn't look as if you'd have to make special efforts to save.'

'There certainly are savings, and good too, but that'll be when I can save myself from the clerks. All those devils are hell-bent on exploiting me. I didn't know before how many villains I'd have to give offerings to there.'

'So what's the rush now. We'll get them made gradually.'

'Well, if that's your advice, then I'll keep quiet a month or two longer. I'll have a bracelet made first of all.'

Jalpa, overwhelmed with joy, said, 'How are you going to get that much money?'

'I've thought of a way. What kind of bracelet would you like?'

Jalpa could no longer keep up her false restraint. She took out the catalogue of ornaments from the cupboard and began showing Rama. She was as intent on the whole business as if the gold had been bought, the goldsmith had taken his seat, and only the design had yet to be chosen. She liked two designs in the catalogue, and both were really quite pretty. But when Rama saw their prices he fell silent; one was a thousand, the other eight hundred.

'It may not even be possible to have things like this made here, but I'll just make a trip to the jeweller's tomorrow.'

Jalpa closed the catalogue and said in a sympathetic voice, 'Who knows when we'll be able to get so much money together? Oh! They *will* be made, they *will* be made, and if not, who's going to die without jewellery?'

Lost in this perplexity, Rama remained sleepless till late into the night. How very becoming those inlaid bracelets would look on these creamy wrists! Lost in this alluring dream, he never knew when sleep finally came.

## 12

Next day Rama set off for Ramesh Babu's house as soon as morning came. At his place too a tableau had been set up for Krishna's birthday festival. Ramesh Babu himself had no particular fondness for it, but he continued to observe the occasion in memory of his wife, who had celebrated it. When he saw Rama he said, 'Come in, sir. Why didn't you come last night? But who comes to the house of a poor fellow like me? How did you manage to leave Sethji's tableau? It must have been extremely splendid!'

'It wasn't decorated in your fashion. I must say, it was better than in other years. Several kathak dancers and prostitutes came too. I left, but I heard that the singing went on all night.'

'Sethji promised that prostitutes wouldn't be allowed to come, so now what has he gone and done! In the hands of fools like this the Hindu religion will be destroyed. Just the thought of prostitutes is bad enough, let alone allowing them into a temple! Shame, shame! Who knows when these idiots will get some common sense!'

'If there weren't prostitutes, who'd go to look at the tableaus? Not everyone is a yogi and an ascetic like you!'

'If I had the power, I'd use the law to put a stop to this immorality. Well, if you have some free time, come and let's have a game or two.'

'What else have I come for,' said Rama. 'But today you'll have to come with me to a jeweller's, please. Of course I'm familiar with several big firms, but more will happen from your being there.'

'I'm ready to come along. But I'm a real ignoramus in these matters. I never bought anything or had anything made. Do you have to buy something?'

'Who's thinking about buying or selling, I want to haggle a little.'

'I know, you've had a scolding at home.'

'No, not at all. She doesn't even use the word ornament. If I should even ask, she forbids it. But don't I have some obligations too, after all? Not a single thing has been made for her since all her jewels were stolen.'

'I know. It's what one does when one begins to earn. And why wouldn't it be? You're the son of a Kayasth, after all. How much money have you got together?'

'Who's got money? I'll use credit.'

'Don't fall into this craze. Don't go towards the bazaar until you've got money in your hand. Old men make their new wives happy with jewellery. What else have the poor fellows got besides jewellery? Young men have lots of other tricks. Of course, if I wanted to I could arrange for you to get three or four thousand worth of goods, but my friend, debt is a very bad habit.'

'I'll pay everything off in two or three months. If I weren't sure of this, I wouldn't even have mentioned it.'

'So why not be patient for two or three months more? There's no worse sin than debt. Nor is there any worse hardship. Once you lose your fear of debt, I'll see you in the days to come standing in the jeweller's shop. Don't take it the wrong way! I know your income is good. Have faith in your future and do whatever else you want, but don't take a loan. Somehow or other the disease of jewellery has spread through this wretched country. Every year billions of rupees are spent just in buying gold and silver. No other country in the world has so high an expenditure on these metals. So what is it all about? In progressive countries capital is invested in business which provides support to people, and the capital increases. Here capital is spent in decoration, which puts an end to both of those great forces, progress and public philanthropy. Just understand this much; the more fools there are in a country, the more propaganda there'll be for jewellery. At least they stop at piercing noses and ears here, but there are several countries where people even pierce their lips to wear ornaments.'

'Which country is that?' asked Rama with curiosity.

'I don't remember just now, but maybe it's in Africa. It seems surprising to us when we hear of it, but it would be no less surprising to people in other countries to hear of piercing noses and ears. The money which ought to be spent for food goes for presents of jewellery, while children go hungry again and again. It's not right that children shouldn't get milk. It's not right that they shouldn't even get a whiff of ghee in their noses. No one cares if they even see fresh or dry fruits. But the lady of the house will certainly wear her ornaments and the lord of the house will certainly have them made. I see clerks who get ten or twenty rupees a month, who pass their lives like animals in foul-smelling rooms, who can't even get anything for breakfast, but who are still caught up in the craze for jewellery. This custom is bringing about our destruction. I tell you that it's worse than living in slavish dependency on someone else. Even Brahma himself couldn't guess how much we are declining spiritually, morally, physically, economically, and religiously because of this!'

'I suppose there's not a single country where women don't wear jewellery. Isn't wearing jewellery a custom in Europe too?'

'Yes, but your country isn't Europe. People there are wealthy. Let them squander their money—it gives them elegance. We're poor, and we shouldn't waste a single paisa in useless spending.'

Ramesh Babu forgot about chess in this discussion. It was a holiday, and three or four more visitors came; Ramanath slipped quietly away. One thing from their debate sank into his heart; he gave up the idea of taking a loan for jewellery. If somehow he was unable to pay off the amount quickly, he'd get a really bad reputation. He went to the jeweller's market, to be sure, but he didn't have the courage to enter a shop. He decided that he wouldn't even mention jewels for three or four months.

By the time he reached home it was nine o'clock. When Dayanath saw him he asked, 'Where did you go first thing this morning?'

'I just went to see Ramesh Babu.'

'Why don't you go to the library for an hour or two regularly? You waste the day in idle talk. You're of an age to be educated. Even if exams aren't the right way for you, you can still add to your qualifications. At present, when you have to write a simple letter you hide your face in shame. Real education begins after you leave school, and this is what's really useful in our lives too. I've heard some things about you which have made me very unhappy, and I consider it my obligation to explain things to you. I don't ever want even a single paisa of dishonestly earned money to come into my home. I've been working for thirty years. If I'd wanted to I could have piled up thousands of rupees. But I swear to you I've never taken even one paisa wrongly. I can't understand where you got this habit from.'

Displaying a feigned anger, Rama said, 'Who told you? Tell me his name please. I'll tear his moustache out by the roots!'

'Whoever may have told me, it's none of your business. I won't tell you because you'll tear his moustache out. But I do want to ask whether what he said is true or false.'

'Completely false!'

'Completely false?'

'Yes sir, completely false!'

'You don't take any commissions?'

'Commissions aren't bribes. Everybody takes them and takes them openly. People give them on their own without being asked. I don't ask any one for them.'

'Just because everyone takes them openly and people give without being asked doesn't make taking bribes any better.'

'It's not in my power to stop it. Even if I should stop taking it myself, I can't catch hold of the hands of the peons and clerks to make them stop. People who earn only eight or nine rupees a month can't make ends meet if they don't take it. I could stop myself, but I can't stop them.'

'I've explained things to you,' said Dayanath sadly, 'but the power to agree or disagree lies with you.' He left for the office.

Rama felt like telling him outright, 'Why should you find fault with me just because you've decided to renounce all worldly desires? You've always been hard up for money. You couldn't educate your sons, couldn't even give them clothes and shoes to wear. Your boasting would be appropriate if you'd had a happy life along with your good intentions.'

When Rama went inside his mother asked, 'Where did you go today, son? Your father was getting upset about it.'

'No, he wasn't getting upset, but he was giving me advice not to take any commissions. He said it makes your conscience weak and gives you a bad reputation.'

'You didn't ask him, where are all the glorious victories you've won by your great honesty? All our lives we've lived hand to mouth.'

'I wanted to say it, but he would have got angry. He's had to grub for every paisa, and he wants to make me do the same. He doesn't have the sense to take anything for himself. When he saw his tricks weren't working on me, he became very virtuous. But I'm not such an out-and-out idiot. You need common sense to squeeze money out of merchants; it's not fun and games! When someone starts acting like a saint, I think to myself that he's a fool. If he doesn't have the good sense to take anything, what's the wretch going to do? He just will have to wipe away his tears one way or another.'

'Yes, yes, that's just it, son. Someone who knows how to take something for himself will certainly take it. All your father knows is how to sit at home and rattle away about the law. He doesn't say a thing in front of anyone else; it's difficult to get any money out of him.'

When Rama went upstairs to get dressed before going to the office, Jalpa gave him three envelopes to mail. He put them in his pocket, but on the way he opened and read them. What was in them? A long pathetic wail of hardship and pain recited to her three friends. All three were about the same subject; only the emotions were different. 'My life has become a mountain; I can't sleep at night or rest during the day. Sometimes I laugh and joke to please my patidev, but my heart is always crying. I don't visit anyone or let anyone see me. It seems as if this sorrow is going to bring my life to an end. I get promises every day—the money is being gathered, the goldsmith is being arranged, the design is being decided. But it's all just a pack of lies and nothing more.'

Rama put the three letters back in his pocket. He passed by the post office, but didn't drop them off. She still thought he was leading her on. What could he do, how could he make her trust him? If it had been in his power, he'd have put basketsful of jewellery in front of Jalpa right then. He'd have taken her to some big jewellery shop and said, 'Take whatever you want.' What limitless pain, pain which had even lost him her trust! Today he had a real taste of the injury he had caused her in the name of false propriety. If he had known what the results of his play acting would be, perhaps he would have revealed the truth about his boasting. Did he still have room to hesitate in taking a loan in the present situation when Jalpa was being consumed by the intensity of her grief? His heart smote him, and for the first time he sincerely begged God to punish him however he wished, even to take his life, but not to snatch away his Jalpa. Every fibre of his being echoed his plea to God to take pity on his wretched condition.

But at the same time he began to feel angry with Jalpa. Why hadn't she told him all this? Why had she hidden it from him and poured out her heart to her friends?

Goods were being weighed on the office veranda. Bills and coins were piling up on the table while Rama sat plunged in anxiety. Whom should he take advice from? Why had he got married anyway? The whole thing was his fault. When he knew the condition of the household, why hadn't he refused to get married? Today his mind was not on his work. He got up and left early.

As soon as she saw him Jalpa asked, 'You didn't mail my letters, did you?'

'Oh my!' said Rama, making up an excuse, 'I completely forgot them. They're still in my pocket.'

'It's a good thing you forgot. Give them back to me, I'm not going to send them now.'

'Why? I'll send them tomorrow.'

'No, I don't have to send them now. I wrote some things I shouldn't have. If you were to send them off, I'd feel bad. I criticized you very harshly.'

She smiled as she said this.

'You ought to criticize whatever is bad or deceitful or cunning.'

Jalpa asked fearfully, 'Did you read the letters?'

Rama said unhesitatingly, 'Yes. Is it some kind of inexcusable crime?'

In a timid voice Jalpa said, 'Then you must be very angry with me?'

A surge of tears choked her voice. Her head hung down and teardrops from her downcast eyes fell on to the edge of her sari. Bringing her voice under control after a moment, she said, 'I've done something very wrong. Punish me however you like, but please don't be displeased with me. God knows how sad I was after you left with the letters. I don't know how such things could come out of my pen.'

Jalpa knew that Rama was just as worried about jewellery as she was. But usually we exaggerate our sorrow when it comes to telling our friends about our distress. A kind of intimacy is revealed by mentioning things considered secrets. Our friends understand, they don't conceal anything from us, and they are sympathetic to us. This habit of showing intimacy is more prevalent in women.

Rama dried Jalpa's tears and said, 'I'm not displeased with you, darling! There's nothing to be displeased about. When hope is delayed too long it becomes disappointment. Don't I know this much? If you hadn't forbidden me to, I'd certainly have had a couple of things made for you somehow or other. It was a mistake on my part to ask your advice. That was just like asking a guest if he wants food before giving it to him. I didn't give any thought to how people say 'No, no' out of embarrassment even when they want something. God willing, you don't have to wait much longer.'

Looking anxious, Jalpa asked, 'Then you're going to get a loan?'

'Yes, there's no harm in getting a loan. When you don't have to give any interest, a loan is just like cash! The world keeps going through borrowing. Who doesn't borrow? And when there's money in hand people squander it. But if you're saddled with debt, the worry of it keeps you from spending.'

'I don't want to give you a lot of headaches. Now I'll just forget all about even mentioning jewellery.'

'You never mentioned it before either, but that doesn't mean my responsibility has ended. You're unnecessarily afraid of debt. If I sit and wait until I get enough money together, maybe I'll never get enough. This way by borrowing and paying back we'll get three or four things made within a year.'

'But get something small first.'

'Yes, that's just what I'll do.'

When Rama went to the marketplace it had become quite dark. If he went while there was still light, then it was possible that one of his friends might spot him. Most of all, Munshi Dayanath might see him. He wanted to keep this matter a secret.

# 13

Among jewellers, Gangu's shop was famous. Gangu was a Brahman, but very adept in business. There was always a veritable carnival of customers in his shop. His devotion to his calling created confidence in his patrons. One had to worry about being cheated in other shops, but here there was no double-dealing. Gangu smiled as soon as he saw Rama and said, 'Come in sir, come upstairs. It's very good of you to come. Munimji, have some paan brought for him! What's your wish, sir? It seems you're annoyed with me—you never come. You should have mercy on poor fellows like me too now and then.'

Gangu's affability gave courage to Rama. If he hadn't invited him so enthusiastically, Rama might not have had the nerve to enter the shop. He had yet to experience the effect of his good reputation. As he entered the shop, he said, 'What right do poor labourers like us have to come in here, Maharaj? As if we had anything in our pockets!'

'What are you saying, your honour! This is your shop, take whatever you want. We'll settle the prices sooner or later; we don't discriminate among people, Babu Sahab. It's a blessing that you have come to our shop. Should I show you some inlaid work? Perhaps a bracelet or a necklace? We just got some new stuff in from Delhi!'

'Show me an inexpensive necklace.'

'About seven or eight hundred?'

'Oh no, my limit's four hundred.'

'I'll show you both. Take the one you like. We don't play any kind of dirty tricks here, sir. You don't have to worry a bit. Whether it's a five-year-old boy, or a hundred-year-old man, we treat everyone the same. One day we all have to appear before our master, sir!'

A trunk was put in front of them. Gangu took out one necklace after another and began to display them. Rama's eyes opened wide with delight. What dextrous work! How beautifully decorated with precious stones. What lustre! Their sparkle put the lamp to shame. Rama thought to himself that he wouldn't take a loan for more than a hundred, but the four-hundred-rupee necklace didn't appeal to him. He had altogether three hundred rupees in his pocket. He thought to himself that it would be no use to take the necklace if Jalpa might not like it. He should bring her something that would take her breath away as soon as she saw it. How splendid this inlaid necklace would look on her throat. Its thousand bejewelled eyes began to lure him. He stared at it, overpowered, but hadn't the courage to utter a word. How humiliated he would be if somehow Gangu should refuse to give him credit for three hundred rupees. Gangu, divining his uncertainty, said, 'This is something fit for you, sir. Put it in a gloomy home and everything will light up.'

'This is the one I like too, but please understand that I have just three hundred rupees with me.' And Rama's face turned red with shame. His heart began to pound as he looked at Gangu's face.

'Sir, don't even mention money,' said Gangu guilelessly. 'If you say so, I'll send ten thousand worth of stuff with you. This is your store; how could anything be wrong? Tell me, and I'll show you a few more things. We've just received a brand new shishphul. It looks as if the rose has just bloomed. Just seeing it makes one happy. Munimji, just show him the shishphul. And the price isn't that much either; I'll give it to you for two hundred and fifty.'

Rama smiled and said, 'Maharaj, please don't make up things to cheat me; I'm a babe in the woods when it comes to jewellery.'

'Don't talk like that, sir. Please, go show this around the market. If anyone gives you a paisa less than two hundred and fifty for it, I'll give it to you for nothing.'

The shishphul appeared; it was truly a rose on which diamond buds glistened like dewdrops. Rama stared with wide eyes as if something unearthly had materialized before him.

'Two hundred and fifty is the craftsman's reward for his dexterity, sir,' said Gangu. 'Now that's a piece of work.'

'Yes, it's really beautiful, but don't start dunning me for payment right away, friend. I'll pay you as fast as I can without any urging.'

Gangu put both things in handsome velvet cases and gave them to Rama. Then he had Munimji record Rama's name, gave him paan, and took his leave.

There were no bounds to Rama's delight now. It was not a pure delight however, for there was a tinge of unease. It was not the pleasure of a child who has asked for sweets and received them from its mother, but rather of one who has stolen money for them. They certainly taste sugary, but the child's heart is trembling for fear of being beaten on going home. It wasn't that he was particularly worried about paying off six hundred and fifty rupees; given a chance, he could do that in six months. He was afraid that his father would fly into a temper when he heard of the matter. But as he kept going, his eager desire to see Jalpa all decked out in this new finery gradually triumphed over his misgivings. In his hurry to reach home, he left the street and plunged into a narrow lane. The darkness was intense. The sky had already been overcast when he left home, and as soon as he entered the lane raindrops began to fall on his head like buckshot. By the time he could open the umbrella, he was drenched. He began to worry that someone might come in the dark and snatch away the two packages; the continuous rush of the rain made it impossible to hear any other sound. Even murders could happen in these dark lanes. Rama began to repent of having needlessly come this way. It wouldn't have been a disaster to reach home a few minutes later. This untimely downpour was proving an obstacle to his pleasant fantasies. Somehow or other the lane came to an end and he gained the street! Lanterns came into sight. Today he'd had a real experience of how much power light has to create confidence.

When he arrived home, Dayanath was sitting and smoking his hookah. Rama did not enter the room, and was about to go inside, avoiding his father, when Dayanath checked him with 'Where did you go at this hour?'

Rama did not answer him. If he should begin to read out the contents of the newspaper, it could go on for hours. He went straight in. Jalpa was standing in the doorway waiting for him. She immediately took the umbrella from his hand and said, 'My, but you're completely soaked. Why didn't you wait somewhere?'

'Who knows when it might stop? Suppose it rained all night?' he said, and went upstairs. He was certain that Jalpa would be right behind him, but she was sitting downstairs and talking with his younger brothers as if jewels were the farthest thing from her mind, as if she had completely forgotten that Rama had just come from the jeweller's.

Rama changed his clothes and went downstairs, feeling irritable. Just then Dayanath came to eat, and everyone sat down. Jalpa restrained herself, but in the torment of her desire she couldn't eat a thing today. By the time she came upstairs, Rama was lying on the charpai. As soon as he saw her, he said as a prank, 'It was useless to go to the jeweller's today. The necklace was nowhere near ready; I told them to finish it and came back.'

Jalpa's lovely face, which had been sparkling with enthusiasm, fell. 'I knew that,' she said. 'It'll take five or six months to be made, won't it?'

'Certainly not. He was swearing that it will be made very soon.'

'Oh! Give it to me whenever you like!'

Hopelessness lies at the outermost limits of intense longing. Jalpa turned away and started to lie down when Rama burst out laughing. Startled, she realized that he had played a trick on her. 'You're very naughty too!' she said smiling. 'What have you brought?'

'How did you like my little hoax?'

'Men have a habit of doing this, so what's new about what you've done?'

Jalpa was gratified when she saw the two ornaments. Waves of joy began to course through her heart. She wanted to hide her feelings so that Rama wouldn't consider her vain and shallow, but delight thrilled through every part of her body. Smiling eyes, glowing cheeks and open lips—all revealed her secret! She put the necklace around her throat, adorned her hair bun with the shishphul, and intoxicated with joy, said 'I bless you, and may God fulfil all of your heart's desires.'

Today that longing of Jalpa's, which had been the dream of her imaginings and the playground of her hopes from childhood, had been satisfied. Today that craving of hers had been appeased. If her mother Manaki had been there, she would have shown her the new necklace before anyone else, and said to her, 'Congratulations on *your* necklace!'

Pride flooded through Rama. His life seemed like a success to him today. For the first time in his life he tasted the joy of victory.

Jalpa asked, 'Should I go and show Mother?'

Rama said mildly, 'You'll go show Mother? What's so special about them?'

'Now I won't ask you for anything for a whole year. I won't feel easy in my mind until they're paid for.'

Rama said proudly, 'Why worry about money? There's lots of it!'

'Shall I go show these to Mother to see what she'll say?'

'But don't tell her that they're on credit.'

Jalpa scurried downstairs as if a treasure awaited her there.

It was midnight, and Rama was sleeping the sleep of the blessed. Jalpa came out on to the roof and glanced at the sky. It was suffused with clear moonlight—October moonlight in which there is the repose of music, the sweetness of repose, and the passion of sweetness. Jalpa reentered her room, opened her casket, and took out the glass chandrahar which had once made her feel so lucky to wear. But next to the new chandrahar its lustre seemed as dim as the light of the stars next to the clear radiance of the moon. She tore it apart and threw its beads into the lane below in the same way that a devotee consigns earthen vessels to the water once they have been used for worship.

# 14

From that day on Jalpa's love for her husband was marked by a new devotion. When he went to bathe, he found his dhoti set out for him. Soap and oil would be put in the wall niche too. When he got ready to go to the office, Jalpa would bring his clothes and place them before him. Previously he had received paan after asking for it, but now it was practically forced on him. She looked at his face so ceaselessly that it was unnecessary for him to even speak. She even went so far as to fan him when he sat down to eat. Formerly she had prepared food unwillingly and perfunctorily, but now she would go to the kitchen lovingly. She still cooked the same things, but now their taste improved greatly. To Rama the two ornaments he had brought her seemed mere trifles compared to this sweet affection.

The other jewellers learned about Rama's love for ornaments on the very day that he purchased the jewellery from Gangu's store. Whenever he passed that way shopkeepers on both sides would stand up, salaam him, and call out, 'Come over here please, sir, and have some paan. Please have a look at one or two things in our shop.'

Rama's self-restraint increased his reputation still further, so much so that one day a jeweller's agent appeared at the house and proceeded to open his trunk despite Rama's repeated refusals.

To get rid of him Rama said, 'Friend, right now I don't need anything. Why are you wasting my time and yours?'

'At least take a look, sir,' said the agent very courteously. 'If something pleases you, take it, if not, don't. There's no harm in looking! After all, if I didn't visit well-to-do gentlemen like yourself, who would I visit? Others have sold you a lot, and if my luck is in today, then I'll get a little money from you too. Let your wife and mother have a look. Something tells me that my first sale today is going to come from you.'

'Don't even talk about whether the women will like them. If they're good quality, they'll like them immediately. But friend, right now I'm penniless.'

The agent laughed and said, 'How do you expect me to believe what you say, sir! Just tell me and I'm ready to sacrifice five hundred or a thousand for you. We agents take a man's temperament into account, sir. God willing, we'll strike a bargain before I get up to leave.'

The agent took out two things from his chest, one a new-style inlaid bracelet, and the other a pair of ear-rings. Both were extraordinary; they glowed like lamps. It was ten o'clock. Dayanath had gone to the office, and Rama had been about to eat; there was no time to spare. But as soon as he saw these two pieces, he completely forgot about everything, and taking both cases, he went inside. As soon as they saw the two cases in his hands, both women fell upon them and began taking out the things to look at them. Their glittering radiance so enthralled them that they lost all power of judgement.

Rama said, 'Old-fashioned things don't begin to compare with the things made these days.'

'Just seeing those old-fashioned things makes me feel like vomiting,' said Jalpa. 'I don't know how women managed to wear them in those days.'

'So you like both things, do you?' said Rama smiling.

'Why wouldn't I like them? Mother, you take something.'

Jageshwari bowed her head to hide her distress. How could someone whose whole life had been spent in domestic worries ever dream of wearing these jewels! Ah! The poor woman had never had her lifelong yearning gratified. Her husband's income had never been enough for anything to be left over from the expense of bringing up the children. Her penance had begun as soon as she had become mistress of the house, and all her longings had turned to dust one after the other. She averted her gaze from the ornaments; they attracted her so much that she was afraid to look at them, lest her feigned indifference be betrayed. 'What would I do with them, child?' she said. 'My days for getting dressed up have gone by. What have you brought, son, and what are their prices?'

'A jeweller has brought them to show to us; I haven't asked

about prices yet, but they'll be high. I had no intention of buying them, so what was the use of asking about the price?'

'If you didn't intend to buy them, then why did you bring them here?' said Jalpa.

She spoke these words in such an access of emotion that Rama was mortified. There was so much agitation, so much scorn in her voice that he lacked the courage to return the jewels. 'Shall I buy them then?' he asked.

'If Mother hasn't said to buy them, then why get them? Is he letting us have them for nothing?'

'Yes, just suppose that we're getting them free.'

'Do you hear what he says, Mother?' asked Jalpa. 'Go and return them. When we've got ready money, we'll have lots of jewellery.'

Jageshwari, becoming confused, asked, 'Isn't he asking for money now?'

'He'll give them to you on credit,' said Jalpa, 'and he'll charge interest too.'

'Shall I return them?' asked Rama. 'Decide one way or another quickly. If you're going to take them, take them, if not, give them back. Don't get confused and dither.'

This plain talking seemed very harsh to Jalpa just then. She hadn't expected to hear something like this from Rama. Her task was to refuse, while he was supposed to insist on buying them. She looked towards Jageshwari eagerly and said, 'Return them. Who can stand being pestered for payment day and night?'

She was about to close the cases when Jageshwari put on the bracelet, as if wearing it just for a moment would satisfy her longing. Then, ashamed of her frivolous behaviour, she was about to take it off when Rama said, 'You've put it on now Mother, so keep it on. I'm giving it to you as a present.' Jageshwari's eyes became moist. The craving which had never been possible to fulfil was being fulfilled today because of Rama's devotion to her. But how could she place such a heavy burden of debt on her dear son? He was still just an untried youth; what capacity did he have? Who could know whether money would come quickly or slowly? And he didn't even know the prices. If they were high, where would the poor fellow get the money from? How many times would he have to face demands for payment, how many times be humiliated? In a dejected voice she said, 'No son, I put it on just by chance. Take it and give it back.'

Seeing his mother's sad face, Rama's heart trembled with love for her. Couldn't he do even this much for his self-sacrificing mother from fear of debt? Didn't he have a duty to his mother too? 'I'll get lots of money, Mother,' he said, 'don't you worry about it.'

Jageshwari looked towards her daughter-in-law, as if saying, 'See how outrageously he's behaving towards me!'

Jalpa was sitting in a melancholy state of mind. Perhaps she was afraid that her mother-in-law would keep the bracelet. Jageshwari had no doubt that her daughter-in-law did not like her wearing the bracelet. Plucking it off and offering it to Jalpa she said, 'I'm giving this to you as a present from me, daughter; I've already done all the dressing-up that I had to do. Now you put it on and let me have a look!'

Jalpa had not the least doubt that her mother-in-law had plenty of money. She thought that perhaps today Jageshwari's heart had melted with pity and that she'd pay for the bracelet. A moment ago she'd thought that Rama would have to pay, and so despite her own wishes, she'd wanted to return it. But when Jageshwari was going to pay, why should she object? Concealing her true feelings, however, she said, 'If there's no money, then let it be, Mother. What's the hurry now?'

'So are you taking this bracelet?' said Rama with some irritation.

'Mother doesn't agree so what can I do?'

'And these ear-rings, why haven't you kept them?' he asked.

'Go ask how much these things are,' said Jalpa.

'Take them,' said Rama impatiently. 'What's the price to you!'

But when Rama went outside and learned the prices from the agent, he fell silent. The bracelet was seven hundred and the ear-rings one hundred and fifty. His estimate had been three hundred at most for the bracelet and forty or fifty for the ear-rings. He repented that he hadn't asked for the prices to begin with so that now he wouldn't be in the fix of having taken these things into his house. He was ashamed to return them, but whatever happened, he *had* to return them. He couldn't take such a huge burden on his head. 'Those are high prices, friend,' he said to the agent. 'I estimated it would be around three or four hundred.' 'If I were to make the prices a single paisa less, your honour, I couldn't show my face in public,' said the agent, whose name was Charan Das. 'These goods are from Dhani Ram's firm; go and ask. Of course, I get a very small amount as commission which you can give or not as you wish.'

'Well, friend, I can't buy things at these prices just now.'

'Don't say that, sir. This much money has no importance for you. If you should get rid of these things in a couple of months you'd get twice as much for them. Who could be more of a connoisseur than you? These are the sort of things that well-to-do people appreciate. How could country yokels know their value?'

'Eight hundred and fifty is a lot, friend.'

'Don't even think of money, sir. One glimpse of your wife sitting in all her finery will restore all your money!'

Rama was certain that Jalpa would herself hesitate on hearing these prices for the jewellery. He talked no further with the agent. He went inside, let out a loud laugh, and asked, 'What did you think the price of the bracelet was, Mother?'

Jageshwari didn't want to look like a fool by not answering. 'There's really no way to estimate the value of these inlaid things, so whatever is settled on is fine.'

'Well now, you tell us, Jalpa, how much do you think the bracelet would be valued at?'

'Not less than six hundred.'

Rama's whole game was spoiled. He had wanted to scare Jalpa by showing his own misgivings about the price. But there wasn't that much difference between six and seven hundred, and it was possible that Charan Das would agree to six hundred. 'Aren't the stones unfinished?' he asked, feeling a little embarrassed.

'In any case it won't be more than six hundred,' said Jalpa.

'And the ear-rings?'

'One hundred rupees at most.'

'You're mistaken again; he's asking for a hundred and fifty.'

'It's some kind of dodge,' said Jalpa. 'We don't have to accept these prices.'

Rama's stratagem had backfired; Jalpa had not been much

deceived about the prices of these things. And yet, although Rama's financial situation was not hidden from her, there she sat speaking up for seven hundred rupees worth of stuff. How could Rama know that Jalpa, understanding the situation quite differently, had false hopes of receiving the bracelet? There was only one way to save his neck now, and that was for the agent to be unwilling to take six hundred. He said, 'He won't take a paisa less than eight hundred and fifty.'

'So give them back,' said Jalpa.

'I'm ashamed to give them back. Mother, please go to the veranda and tell him we won't give him more than seven hundred. If he accepts, all right, otherwise he can go.'

'Oh yes,' said Jageshwari sarcastically. 'Why not? Let me go talk to the agent!'

'Why don't you tell him? There's nothing to be ashamed of,' said Jalpa.

'I won't be able to give him a straight answer,' said Rama. 'He'll praise me to the skies like this: you're an important man, a rich man, a Rajah. What's a hundred and fifty rupees to you? I'll be sucked in.'

'All right, let's go,' said Jalpa. '*I'll* tell him.'

'Great, that'll take care of everything,' said Jageshwari.

With Rama skulking behind, Jalpa went out on to the veranda and said, 'Oh jeweller! Come here please. Did you come here to rob us, or to sell us some things?'

Charan Das came up to the veranda door and said, 'What's your wish, madam?'

'Did you come to sell us something or to rob us! You're asking seven hundred for the bracelet?'

'It cost seven hundred just to have it made, Your Honour!'

'Fine, take it to those who are ready to sacrifice seven hundred. And you're asking one hundred and fifty for the ear-rings; are you trying to clean us out? We're ready to give six hundred for the bracelet and one hundred for the ear-rings, no more, not one paisa more.'

'Young Mrs, you're being outrageous. How do you get seven hundred from eight hundred and fifty?'

'As you wish. Take your things away.'

'After all this spectacle you want me to take my things back?

Just try them on. If it were only a matter of five or ten rupees, then you wouldn't have changed your tune. I'm not lying to you, young Mrs, when I tell you there's only a very small profit, a paisa on the rupee, on these things. You should understand that out of every paisa come the jewellery shop charges, the cost of bad debts, and various commissions. Now that you know how things are, tell me if I can hope for a little money too. Don't make me come back every morning.'

'I told you, just seven hundred.'

Charan made a grimace as if he'd fallen into a dilemma, and then said, 'Your Honour, it's certainly a loss for me, but it's not possible to put you off. When will I get the money?'

'You'll get it very soon.'

Going inside, Jalpa said, 'After all, he *did* give it to me for seven hundred, didn't he? He took off a hundred and fifty just like that. Now I'm sorry that I didn't offer still less. That's how these people overcharge their customers.'

Rama was alarmed at the prospect of taking on such a heavy burden, but events had grown so out of control, that the burden had fallen on him willy-nilly.

Jalpa, transported with delight, had taken both things upstairs, but Rama was standing with bowed head plunged into worry. When she knew his situation, why hadn't she spurned those things, why hadn't she said forcefully that she wouldn't take them? Why had she been so indecisive? It was going to be hard enough to pay off the six hundred and fifty he already owed; where was so much more going to come from? The fault was really his. He should have driven the agent away from the door.

But he persuaded himself that this was atonement for his own sins. And then, *this* was the very reason that men earned, and not at all from any burning desire to earn a livelihood.

When Rama went upstairs to change clothes after eating, Jalpa was standing in front of the mirror wearing the ear-rings. As soon as she saw him she said, 'Someone's face must have brought me good luck when I got up this morning. I got two things free.'

Astonished, Rama asked, 'Free? How? We won't have to pay for them?'

'Mother's paying, isn't she?'

'Did she say anything about it?'

'If she's giving them to me as presents, then who besides her is going to pay?'

Rama, smiling at her simplicity, said, '*This* is what you thought when you took these things? If Mother were going to give you something, she'd have given it just after your jewellery was stolen. Didn't she have money then?'

'How could I have known,' faltered Jalpa. 'You can still give them back. Just say that the person you got them for didn't like them.'

As she said this, she straightaway took off the ear-rings, tore off the bracelet too, and putting both things back in their cases, offered them to Rama in the same way that a cat playing with a mouse never lets it get beyond its grasp, unable to let go of it even while letting go. She didn't have the courage to stretch out her hands. And wasn't her heart in an exactly similar condition? Her face changed colour. Why was she looking at the ground instead of Rama? Why wasn't she lifting her head? Where was the heartfelt joy that comes from escaping some great misfortune? Her state was exactly like that of a mother after consenting to her child's going abroad. The same helplessness, the same distress, the same affectionate attachment were all appearing on Jalpa's face.

Rama did not have the firm self-control necessary to take the cases from her hands. He was ready to bear everything—to endure the demands for payment, to be humiliated, to skulk around, to burn up with worry. He was not ready to do anything which would break Jalpa's heart, or make her feel wretched. All his knowledge, all his impulses, all his conscience opposed giving her such a shock. In the struggle between love and the force of circumstances, love won.

He smiled and said, 'Let it be. We've got them now, so why return them? Mother will laugh at us too.'

With a contrived trembling in her voice Jalpa said, 'Don't stretch yourself beyond your means. What's the need to take on new troubles?'

In a voice like a drowning man Rama said, 'God is the master!' and immediately went downstairs.

How we destroy the happiness and tranquillity of our lives through momentary embarrassments and allurements! If Jalpa had been able to hold herself steady through the stormy blasts of her cravings, if Rama had not yielded to his embarrassment, if both had had the pure light of love in their hearts, then they wouldn't have strayed off the beaten path and gone towards their ruin.

It was eleven o'clock. It was getting late to go to the office, but Rama was walking as if he were just returning from the last rites of a dear friend.

# 15

Jalpa was no longer the solitary young woman who hid herself away and hung around feeling sad. Now she didn't like sitting at home. Previously she had been helpless, unable to come and go. Now, thanks to the grace of God, she had jewellery. So why should she stay at home denying herself pleasures? Ornaments are not like sweets, whose flavour can be appreciated in solitude. What's the use of locking them up in caskets? At first when an invitation came from the neighbourhood or the Kayasth community, she was sure to go with her mother-in-law. After a few days she didn't need her mother-in-law either, and began to come and go by herself. And then, she wasn't limited by the need to work, either. Her beauty and charm, her attire, her courtesy and conduct, very soon gave her a place of honour among the women of the neighbourhood. Without her, the assembly seemed empty. Her voice was so soft, her speech so sweet, her grace so incomparable, that she seemed to be the queen of her circle of friends. Her coming brought new life into the local female society. Every day there was a gathering somewhere or other. An hour or two of singing and playing, or of gossiping, diverted the young women. Sometimes they met at one person's house, sometimes at another person's. They sang for fifteen days in a row in March. Jalpa's heart was as generous as she was beautiful. The cost of paan usually fell on her! When singers were summoned from time to time, the burden of looking after their well-being was hers. When the women went to bathe in the Ganges from time to time, the cost of the tonga and of the refreshments on the river bank too would fall on her shoulders. Two or three rupees disappeared every day thus. Rama was the ideal husband. If Jalpa were to ask, he would even give up his life at her feet, so what did money matter really? He longed to see her face. This was how Jalpa talked about him every day in her gatherings. When she saw how much honour and respect she had in female society, she could hardly contain her joy.

One day this circle of friends felt compelled to see a film. Every one of them was entranced by the delights there, and they began to go to the cinema every day. Previously Rama had not been fond of the cinema. And if he had been, what would he have done? Now, however, he was earning money, and Jalpa was putting pressure on him, so why wouldn't he go? There were lots of young women at the cinema hall who uncovered their faces and laughed and talked without embarrassment. Their freedom was secretly beginning to work its magic on Jalpa too. As soon as she left home she would uncover her face, but in the cinema, out of embarrassment, she would sit in the section for women in purdah. How much she wished that Rama would sit with her! After all, how was she inferior to those fashionable ladies? Her face and figure were no disgrace to her. She was as well dressed as anyone else, and as good at making conversation. So why should she sit with the women in purdah? Even though Rama was not highly educated, the influences of his place and time had made him broad-minded. At one time he had been such a single-minded devotee of purdah that, when he sometimes took his mother to bathe in the Ganges, he would not even let her talk to the Brahman pandaas. Or if his mother's laughter were to be heard in the men's part of the house, he would come and tell her angrily, 'You have no sense of shame, Mother! People are sitting out there, and here you are laughing,' and Jageshwari would become ashamed. But as he grew older, this attitude of Rama's disappeared. And Jalpa's stunning beauty encouraged him still more. If she had been ugly, coal-black, or boorish, he would have forced her into purdah; he would have been ashamed to be seen sitting or walking with her. But to go on an outing with a matchless beauty like Jalpa brought him pleasure and pride. No other woman could equal Jalpa in features, figure, or dress, in the cultivated society in which they moved. Despite being a country girl, she had adapted to the ways of the city as if she had been born there. Her education in English was a little deficient, but here, too, Rama was bringing her up to standard.

But how was he to break the bonds of purdah? There were so many friends, so many acquaintances of his to be seen sitting in the cinema hall. How they would laugh on seeing him sitting with Jalpa. At last he decided to openly challenge society. He said to Jalpa, 'Today, you and I will sit together at the cinema hall.'

Jalpa's heart began to throb, and her face glowed with ardent delight. 'Really?' she said. 'No, bhai, my friends will never let me get away with it.'

'Nothing will ever come of being afraid like this. What kind of farce is it that women have to hide their faces and sit behind screens!'

Thus the matter was settled. On the first day they both shrank with embarrassment, but from the second day on, their courage blossomed. After a few days the time came when Rama and Jalpa could be seen strolling together in the park in the evening.

Jalpa smiled and said, 'If your father should see us, then what?'

'Then what? Nothing!'

'But I'd just sink into the ground from shame!'

'I'd be embarrassed too, but Father won't come here on his own!'

'And if your mother should see us?'

'Who's afraid of Mother; I'd set her straight with a couple of good arguments.'

In only a few days Jalpa had made her mark on her new circle of friends. She entered into this society much as some skilled speaker first comes on to the stage at an assembly; even learned people, in spite of their wish to belittle him, bow their heads before his splendour. Jalpa, too, 'came, saw, and conquered.' Her beauty had that dignity, that austerity, that splendour, and that brilliance which are the marks of women of good descent. On the very first day one woman gave Jalpa an invitation to tea, which she was unable to refuse, even though she had no desire to go.

When they had both returned from this function, Rama said in a worried voice, 'So we'll have to go to her tea party tomorrow?'

'What could I do? I couldn't even think of refusing.'

'So should I bring a nice sari for you tomorrow morning?'

'Don't I already have saris? What's the use of spending fifty or sixty rupees for such a small occasion?'

'You don't have any really nice saris. Have you seen her sari? I'll bring one just like that for you.'

'I ought to have told her straight out that we had no spare time,' said Jalpa feeling helpless.

'And then we'll have to invite her.'

'What a lot of trouble has fallen on our necks.'

'No trouble at all. It's just that I think that my house is not suitable for this. I'll borrow a table, some chairs, and a tea set from Ramesh, but what can I do about the house?'

'Do we *have* to invite her?' asked Jalpa.

Rama gave no reply to such a graceless remark. He began to worry about a new pair of shoes and a handsome wristwatch for Jalpa. He didn't have a paisa and his expenses were increasing every day. So far, he hadn't even had a chance to give a single paisa to the jewellers. Once Gangu Maharaj had even gestured at him to make a payment. But it was impossible for Jalpa to go to the tea party looking disreputable. No, he couldn't do such an injustice to her. On this occasion her beauty and glamour would make an overwhelming impression. Today everyone would be glittering in their saris, and there would be no shortage of inlaid bracelets and pearl necklaces. But Jalpa, even plainly dressed, was miles ahead of them. None of them came up to the mark in comparison with her. To have secured such a beauty was the fruit of his good deeds in previous lives. After all, these were the days for enjoying the good things of life. If one didn't enjoy oneself while young, what would one have in old age? Even if one had wealth and respect, so what? Once youth passed, what was marriage good for? He became obsessed with bringing the sari and wristwatch. Somehow he got through the night, but the next day he didn't rest until he'd bought the things.

Jalpa flared up. 'I told you that I don't need these. They won't have cost less than a hundred and fifty.'

'A hundred and fifty! I'm not that much of a spendthrift!'

'These things can't be less than a hundred and fifty.'

Jalpa put the watch on her wrist, opened out the sari, and gazed at it spellbound.

'How striking that watch looks on your wrist! I got my money's worth.'

'Tell me the truth. How much did you spend?'

'Shall I tell you? One hundred and thirty-five. Seventy-five for the sari, ten for the shoes and fifty for the watch.'

'So you did spend a hundred and fifty. I just added a little. But how are you going to pay all this off? What a good-for-nothing invitation that bitch has given me! From now on I'm not going out at all.'

Rama was also overwhelmed by the same anxiety, but he didn't dampen Jalpa's delight by displaying his feelings. 'It'll all be paid off,' he said.

'Tell me please where the money's coming from?' asked Jalpa sarcastically. 'We don't save a paisa, so where's the money going to come from? Tell me, now, Father takes care of the household expenses, or we'd know wouldn't we? Do you think I'm just dying for saris and jewellery? Take these things back.'

Rama looked at her lovingly and said, 'Keep these things. I won't bring anything again without asking you first.'

That evening when Jalpa put on the new sari and shoes, strapped the watch on to her wrist, and looked at herself in the mirror, her lovely face was radiant with pride and joy. She might have been sincere when she told Rama to take the things back, but just now she was not prepared to make such a sacrifice. Jalpa and Rama set out towards the cantonment. The woman had only given Jalpa the number of her bungalow, but they found it easily. There was a signboard on the gate—'Indra Bhushan, Advocate, High Court.' Now Rama realized that the woman was Pundit Indra Bhushan's wife. Punditji or Vakil Sahab was one of the best-known lawyers of Kashi. Rama had seen him many times, but how could he have had the good fortune to make the acquaintance of such an important man? Six months ago he would not even have dreamed that one day he would have the honour of being invited to his house, but thanks to Jalpa, this impossible thing had happened today. He was the guest of Kashi's most important lawyer.

Rama had thought that many people would be invited, but nobody else was there besides Vakil Sahab and his wife Ratan. As soon as she saw them Ratan came out on to the veranda, shook hands, took them inside, and introduced them to her husband. Punditji shook hands with his two guests without getting up from his armchair, smiled and said, 'Excuse me, Babu Sahab, my health is not good. Which office are you in here?'

'Yes sir,' said Rama, feeling embarrassed. 'I'm in the Municipal

Office, though only a little while yet. I had an idea of going into the law, but when I saw the situation of the junior lawyers here, I lost courage.'

Rama did not think it improper to lie a little to inflate his own importance. Its effect was bound to be very good. If he said straight out that he was a thirty-rupee-a-month clerk, Vakil Sahab might consider it demeaning to converse with him. 'You did well not to go there,' he said to Rama. 'Where you are now, you'll get a good position after three or four years. Over there it's possible that you might not even get a case for ten years.'

Jalpa was still uncertain whether Ratan was Vakil Sahab's wife or daughter. He was not less than sixty, and the smooth crown of his head gleamed like polished wood amid the surrounding white hairs. His moustache was immaculate, but the furrows on his brow and the wrinkles on his cheeks told of a traveller who was weary of life's journey. As he lay on the armchair he looked as if he had been an invalid for years, though he had a fair complexion which even sixty summers and winters had not been able to change. He had a high nose and forehead, and quite large arrogant eyes. From his face it was evident that he did not like either talking to people or answering their questions. Ratan, on the contrary, was a dark-complexioned, well-built young woman, warm, sociable, and without a trace of pride. Her appearance had none of the hallmarks of beauty; her nose was flat, her face round, and her eyes small. Nevertheless she looked queenly. Next to her Jalpa seemed like a blossom of jasmine near a sunflower.

Tea was brought. Dried fruit, fresh fruit, sweets, ice-cream—everything tastefully arranged on tables. Ratan and Jalpa sat at one table; the other was for Rama and Vakil Sahab. Rama went and sat down, but the older man continued to recline on the armchair.

Rama smiled and said to him, 'Please, you come too.'

The latter, still lying down, smiled and said, 'You go ahead, please, I'll soon be coming too.'

They drank tea and ate fruit, but Rama and Jalpa both hesitated to laugh and joke in front of their host. Old people who are full of life can take pleasure from company, but there are those cold, lifeless individuals who even when young make others into corpses. After much insistence, Vakil Sahab took two sips of tea, and sitting at a distance, watched the goings-on. Thus when

Ratan said to Jalpa, 'Come on, let's take a turn in the garden, and let these two gentlemen have a critical discussion of society and morality,' Jalpa felt as if a noose had been removed from around her neck. Rama, like a caged bird, watched them leave the room and heaved a deep sigh. If he had known this calamity was going to fall on his head here, he wouldn't have dreamed of coming.

Vakil Sahab, screwing up his face, shifted to his other side and said, 'I don't know what's happened to my stomach; I can't digest a thing! Not even milk. I don't know why people are so fond of drinking tea; I'm afraid to even look at it. As soon as I drink it, I feel spasms in my body and sparks in my eyes.'

'You haven't taken any medicine for digestion?'

'I don't have even a shred of faith in medicines,' said Vakil Sahab with aversion. 'You won't find anyone stupider in this world than vaidyas and doctors. None of them has any capacity for diagnosis. The diagnoses of two doctors or two vaidyas will never agree. The symptoms are exactly the same, but one vaidya says it's something wrong with my blood, another something wrong with my bile. One doctor says it's inflammation of the lungs, another a deterioration of the stomach. There you have it; treatment is given by guesswork and patients are slaughtered without mercy. Those doctors would have sent me to damnation by now, but I escaped from their clutches. I've heard a lot of good things about the practice of yoga, but I haven't come across any mahatma from whom I might learn it, and I'm afraid that more harm than good will come from doing anything on the basis of books alone.'

While the two men were refuting the science of hygiene, the two women were having a profound discussion about love.

Ratan smiled and said, You must have been quite surprised when you saw my husband.'

Jalpa had not only been surprised, she had also been deceived. 'This must be Vakil Sahab's second marriage!' she said.

'Yes, we've been married five years now; his first wife died thirty-five years ago. His age was all of twenty-five then. People urged him to marry again, but he had had one son and refused to remarry. He lived alone for thirty years. But when his son died in his prime five years ago, it became indispensable for him to marry again. I had neither mother nor father; my mother's brother brought me up. I can't say whether I captured him or whether I was captivated by his goodness. I think that it was God's wish, but from the time I came here I've been getting fatter and fatter. The doctors tell me that I can't have any children. Sister, it's not that I hanker to have children, but my husband sees how things are with me and feels sad. *I'm* the cause of all his illnesses. If God were to give me a child today, all his illnesses would disappear in a trice. How much I'd like to be thin. I take hot baths in a bathtub, I go walking every day, and I have very little milk or ghee. I eat half of what I used to, I work as hard as I can, but I'm still getting fatter day by day. I simply don't know what to do!'

'He must get angry with you, mustn't he?'

'No, sister, not at all. He's never mentioned it to me even by mistake. He's never uttered a single word which would show his distress, but I know the worry is killing him. I have no power to help him, what can I do? I can spend as much as I like, stay where I like, and he never says a thing. He gives me whatever he earns. I tell him that there's no need for him to practise law now, so why not take it easy? But he can't stand just sitting around at home. All he takes in is a couple of chapatis, and if I really insist, he'll eat three or four grapes. I feel sorry for him and help him as much as I can. After all, it's for me that he's ruining his life.'

'A man like this should be revered like a god. Around here they start preparing for a second marriage before the first wife has died. Living alone for thirty years isn't for everybody.'

'Yes, sister, he *is* like a god. He still cries whenever his first wife is mentioned. I'll show you her picture. His heart's as soft on the inside as he seems stern on the outside. He's arranged for monthly payments to lots of orphans, widows, and poor people. By the way, your bracelet is really pretty.'

'Yes, it was made by a very good craftsman,' said Jalpa.

'I don't know anybody at all here. I don't want to trouble Vakil Sahab about jewellery. I'm afraid to have anything made by an ordinary goldsmith—who knows what they might mix in with the gold. All the jewels of my late co-wife have been kept, but they don't appeal to me. Get Babu Ramanath to have an inlaid bracelet just like yours made for me.'

'Let's see, I'll ask.'

'Your coming today has made me very happy. I just idle around alone the whole day, and I'm perplexed about whom I should visit. I'm not acquainted with anyone nor do I feel like making friends with anyone. I invited a couple of women here and went to their homes too; I wanted to have a sisterly relationship with them. But seeing how they thought and behaved, it seemed good to keep as much distance as possible between us. They both wanted to make a fool of me; they borrowed some money from me and still keep saying they're going to pay it back. It makes me ashamed to say how much they loved all kinds of finery. Why don't you come over for an hour or so every day, sister!'

'Wonderful, what could be nicer than that!'

'I'll send the car.'

'What's the need? I've got legs, haven't I?'

'I can't understand why I don't feel like letting you go. Rama-nathji must have thanked his lucky stars when he got you.'

Jalpa smiled. 'Stars—schmars. He's not thankful at all; he just keeps on scolding me.'

'Really! I don't believe it. Look, here he comes. Ask him to get another bracelet like this one made.'

'Shall we ask Charan Das how long it would take to make another bracelet like this?' said Jalpa to Rama. 'Ratan wants to have one just like it made.'

'Yes, of course he could have it made,' answered Rama readily. 'He can get it done much better than this.'

'How much was the pair?'

'Eight hundred,' replied Jalpa.

'The price doesn't matter, but it must be exactly like this, an exact copy!'

'Yes, yes,' said Rama. 'I'll have it made.'

'But I don't have the money now, bhai,' said Ratan.

A man can't say anything about money in front of women. Can he say that he doesn't have any money at present? He'll die before making this excuse. He'll go into debt, he'll butter up others, but he won't show his helplessness in front of a woman. He considers it contemptible to even mention money. Jalpa knew her husband's financial situation quite well, but if Rama had made some excuse just then, she would have found it very offensive. She was inwardly afraid that her worthy husband might blurt out that he'd have to ask the jeweller first. Her heart was thudding. But when Rama bravely said, 'Yes, yes, don't worry about money. Pay me whenever you like,' she felt happy.

'So when can I hope for it?' asked Ratan.

'Even if I tell the jeweller today, it'll still take at least fifteen days.'

'Please come for tea at my place this coming Sunday,' said Jalpa.

Ratan accepted the invitation gladly, and Rama and Jalpa took their leave. By the time they reached home it was evening, and Ramesh Babu was sitting on the veranda. Jalpa got down from the tonga and went inside, but Rama went over to Ramesh Babu and said, 'Have you been here long?'

'No, I just got here. Did you go to Vakil Sahab's place?'

'Yes, I suffered a loss of three rupees.'

'No matter, you'll get them back. It's not a bad thing to get acquainted with prominent people; important results can come out of it. Invite them over here too some time,' said Ramesh Babu.

'We invited them to tea next Sunday before we left.'

'I'll come too, if you say. You know, don't you, that Vakil Sahab has a brother who's an engineer? I have a brother-in-law who's been sitting around unemployed for a long time. If Vakil Sahab were to give him a recommendation the poor fellow would get a position. You just introduce me and I'll do all the rest. God willing, the Memsahab will be happy with the arrangements for the party. I'll bring a tea set, a painted glass flower vase, and a lamp. Leave the tables and chairs and everything to me. No need for you to bother with coolies or labourers; I'll catch hold of those loafers.'

'Then it'll be a lot of fun,' said Rama. 'I was getting very worried.'

'There's nothing to worry about. I'll put that young brother-in-law of mine to work. I'll tell him to look after everything if he wants a job. Then we'll see how much scurrying around he does.'

'Didn't you arrange a position somewhere for your brother-in-law just two or three months ago?'

'Yes indeed, but there are six more left; seven altogether. Sit down please so we can make a list of important things. There'll be a lot of running around to do from now on if I'm to get everything together. And how many guests will there be?'

'There'll be the Memsahab,' said Rama, 'and maybe Vakil Sahab will come too.'

'You've done very well. If there were lots of people, there'd be too much commotion. It's the Memsahab we have to do business with. What's the good of flattering a lot of idlers?'

The two of them got the list ready. Ramesh Babu began gathering things together the very next day. He had access to many distinguished families, and got together a great many fine things for decoration; the whole house took on a dazzling appearance. Dayanath took part in these preparations too. His task was to decorate things in the proper way. The three of them would argue for hours over questions like which flower pot should be put where, which picture should be hung where, or which carpet should be spread where. These tasks absorbed them before they went to the office, and after they came back. One day a quarrel broke out over where a mirror ought to be put in one of the rooms. Dayanath said there was no need for the mirror in this room and that it should be put in the adjoining room. Ramesh opposed this, while Rama stood silently in uncertainty, unable to say anything one way or the other.

'I've seen hundreds of English drawing rooms,' said Dayanath, 'but never a mirror. The mirror should stay in the dressing room. Putting it here is nonsense.'

'I haven't had the chance to see hundreds of English rooms, but I've certainly seen three or four,' said Ramesh, 'and they all had mirrors. And then, is it necessary for us to copy the English in every little thing? We're not English, we're Indian. Well-to-do Indians have big full-length mirrors in their rooms; you're talking about our mixed-up babus who are obsessed with making themselves caricatures of the English in everything—in dress, in the decoration of rooms, in speech, in drinking tea and alcohol, and in china teacups. But they don't even come close to imitating those things which have made the English English, and because of which they rule the world. Do you too have a longing to become an Englishman in your old age?'

Dayanath considered it very wrong to copy the English, and he also found this tea party displeasing. If there was any satisfaction involved, it was that he would make the acquaintance of three or four important people. He had never worn a coat in his life, and while he drank tea, he wasn't a captive of china tea sets. He didn't object to drinking tea from anything—a katora or katori, a glass, a lota, or a tasla. But just now he was bent on seeing his side of the argument through. 'Well-to-do Indians don't have tables and chairs in their rooms,' he said. 'They use the floor. When you put a table and chairs in the room, you did things English-style. But now, when it comes to the mirror, you're giving the example of Indians. Keep it either Indian or English. As it is now, it's half quail and half partridge! It doesn't look good to wear a coat and pants along with an old-fashioned four-cornered hat!'

Ramesh had thought that Dayanath would be rendered speechless, but when he heard his reply he was thrown into confusion; victory was slipping from his grasp. 'So you've never seen a mirror in an Englishman's room then?' he asked. 'Could you tell us the names of even five or ten such Englishmen? Besides that Kiranta head clerk of yours, you probably haven't even set foot in any Englishman's room. You consider this Christian an ideal example of those with a fancy for English ways, and I agree.'

'That's your language. Call him whatever you like—Kiranta, Chamareshiyan, or worm, but aside from his colour he doesn't fall short of the English in any way. And before him there was a European.'

Ramesh was thinking of a reply to this when a motor-car pulled up at the door. Ratan Bai got out and came on to the veranda! The three men came outside quickly. Rama found Ratan's coming at this time very disagreeable. He was afraid that she might come into the room and reveal his whole pretence. He stepped forward, shook her hand, and said, 'Please come this way. This is my father, and this is my friend Ramesh Babu.' These two worthies, however, neither stretched out their hands nor stirred from the spot, but stood there rather discomfited. Neither did Ratan think it was necessary to shake hands with them. She greeted them from a distance with a namaskar and said to Rama, 'No, I won't sit down. I don't have any spare time right now. I wanted to speak to you.'

As she spoke, they reached the car, and she said in low voice, 'You've told the jeweller, haven't you?'

Rama replied without hesitation. 'Yes, he's making it.'

'The other day I said that I couldn't give you anything just then, but I thought that it might be a bother to you, so I asked for some money. You need eight hundred, don't you?'

Jalpa had said that the bracelet's price was eight hundred. If Rama wished to, he could take that much. But Ratan's simplicity and trust stayed his hands. He couldn't betray the confidence of such a generous, guileless young woman. He didn't hesitate a bit to take three or four annas from each businessman. He knew that all of them too hoodwinked their customers, and to act towards them as he did gave his conscience not the slightest twinge. But to act treacherously towards this goddess would have required a hardened old sinner. Hesitating a little, he said, 'Did Jalpa say the bracelet cost eight hundred? Perhaps she didn't remember. Her bracelet was six hundred. I can have one made for eight hundred if you like.'

'No,' said Ratan. 'I'd like one just like hers. Have one made for six hundred, please.'

She took her bag from the car and took out six one-hundred-rupee notes. 'There was no need to hurry,' said Rama. 'We can settle up when the thing is ready.'

'When I have money it gets spent. That's why I thought I'd dump it on your head. My habit is to do whatever I do as fast as possible. I get all confused by delays.'

She got into the car and vanished like the wind. When Rama went inside to put the money into a trunk, the two old men began to talk.

'Did you see that?' asked Ramesh.

'Yes,' said Dayanath. 'My eyes were open. Now these things are going on at my place too. God save us.'

'That's just the way it is, but these days women like her are useful. If necessary, they can help out some. If you get sick, they can send for the doctor. As for us, even if we should be dying, our wives wouldn't have the nerve to set foot outside the house.'

'I can't stand to see these Western ways, my friend. But what can I do? I'm fond of my children, but sometimes I want to tell Rama straight out to go live somewhere else. That would be like tearing out an eye to get rid of the pain, though. I get angry with those husbands who spoil their wives like this. You'll see, that woman will play Vakil Sahab false one of these days.'

'I don't agree with you there, my dear sir,' said Ramesh. 'Why do you believe that a woman who comes and goes freely is bound to be rotten? She thinks a great deal of Rama, though. Who knows why she gave him that money?'

'It seems to me there's something fishy here. Rama's not pulling a fast one on her, is he?'

Just then Rama came back out and overheard the last sentence. He scowled and said, 'Yes sir, I'm certainly pulling a fast one. I'm deceiving her and extorting money from her. After all, that's my profession!'

'Why are you taking on like that?' asked an embarrassed Dayanath. 'I didn't mean it that way.'

'You've as good as made me into a first-class forger; what else did you mean? Why did such a suspicion enter your mind? What have you seen in me to give rise to this idea of yours? Besides the fact that I dress neatly and move with the times a little, what do you see that's so bad about me? Whatever else I do, I spend what I earn honestly. If the time comes when I have to lie and cheat, I'll take poison and die. Yes, it's true that some people have good sense about spending, and some don't. I have that good sense. If you consider this some kind of fraud, it's your privilege. When you've become so mistrustful of me, I might as well disgrace myself and run away from home. Ramesh Babu is here. You can ask him whatever you like about me. He won't lie out of any consideration for me.'

These statements of Rama's bore enough of the colour of truth to reassure Dayanath. He said, 'The day I come to know that you have taken up this way of doing things, *I'll* disgrace myself and run away. I won't deny that when I saw your expenditure increasing I had my doubts. But I'm content to hear you say that your intentions are pure. I just want my boy's ambitions not to go astray, no matter how poor he might be. I pray to God to keep you on the right path.'

'Well, this little story has come to an end,' said Ramesh, smiling. 'Now tell me, why did she give you money? I was counting; there were six notes—maybe hundred-rupee ones.'

'I swindled her,' said Rama.

'If you play games with me, I'll give you a thrashing. And if you've swindled her out of anything, I'll tan your hide even more, so help me. Swindle away but don't let your reputation be harmed. Don't breathe a word to anyone. I'm not afraid of God; I'll answer whatever he asks. But I am afraid of people. Tell the truth, what did she give you the money for? If you're getting some kind of commission, then cut me in too!'

'She asked me to get an inlaid bracelet made for her.'

'Let's go. I'll get it made by a good jeweller I'm acquainted with. You did badly to take on this trouble. You don't know what women are like; they don't trust anybody. If you spend three or four rupees of your own, they'll think you're robbing them. Yes, maybe you'll add to your good reputation, but a bad reputation is standing by.'

'You're repeating what foolish women say,' said Rama. 'Educated women aren't like that.'

After a little while Rama went inside and said to Jalpa, 'Your friend Ratan came by.'

'Really? Then there must have been a lot of confusion. Nothing was ready here.'

'It's lucky she didn't come inside. She came to give me some money for the bracelet. You probably told her eight hundred. I took six hundred.'

'But I was only joking,' said Jalpa embarrassed.

In this way she absolved herself from any blame, but her mind was in turmoil for a long time. If Rama had taken eight hundred instead, perhaps this turmoil would not have occurred. She was glad for her success, but Rama's prudence had awakened her moral scruples. She was regretting her needless lies. How low Rama must consider her. How dishonourable Ratan must consider her too.

# 16

Nothing special happened at the tea party. Ratan came with the sister of some relative or other, but the Vakil Sahab did not come. Dayanath considered it quite appropriate to withdraw from the house for the duration of the party. True, Ramesh Babu stood on the veranda throughout, but although Rama entreated him several times to take part, he didn't have that much courage.

Jalpa introduced both guests to her mother-in-law. The young women struck her as rather frivolous. Their running all over the house, clattering up to the topmost room, jumping up and down here and there on the roof, and laughing uproariously, seemed like a great hullabaloo to her. According to her sense of morality daughters and daughters-in-law ought to be serious and bashful. It was particularly surprising that even Jalpa joined right in. Ratan didn't even mention the bracelet today.

Rama had not yet had enough time left over from preparing for the party to go to Gangu's shop. He thought that if he were to give six hundred to Gangu, it would be applied to the previous account, and only two hundred and fifty would be left. If six hundred were paid on the new account, then eight hundred and fifty would still be left on the old account. The first approach would give him an excellent opportunity to bolster his credit.

Next day a happy Rama arrived at Gangu's shop and said in a commanding manner, 'How are things, Maharaj? Anything new being made here?'

Gangu was so fed up with Rama's stalling that even the prospect of receiving some money couldn't please him. 'How many things we've made and sold, Sahab!' he said in a complaining tone. 'You've left off coming here. We don't carry on business in this way. Eight months have gone by, and not even a paisa from you.'

'Friend, it makes me ashamed to come empty-handed to your shop! I'm not one of the people whom you have to dun to pay their debts. Put this six hundred rupees on account today and get a nice bracelet ready.'

Gangu took the six hundred, put it into his money chest, and said, 'It'll be made. When will I get the rest of the money?'

'Very soon.'

'Yes, Babuji. Pay off the previous bill.'

Gangu promised to have the bracelet made very quickly, but having struck a bargain with Rama once before, he had learned that he wasn't going to collect his money quickly. The upshot was that Rama plagued him every day, and Gangu fobbed him off just as often. Sometimes the craftsman would fall sick, or sometimes he would go to arrange medical treatment for his wife at his in-laws', or sometimes his sons would become ill. One month passed and the bracelet had not been made. Rama stopped going to the park for fear of Ratan's insistent inquiries, but she also kept watch on the house, and during this month came several times to renew her demands. At last, one July day she said to him, 'If that pig is not going to make it, then why don't you give it to some other jeweller?'

'That bastard has misled me so badly that I don't even want to talk about it. It's too much—every day he says it'll be ready very soon. I made a big mistake when I gave him an advance. It'll be hard to pry it out of him now.'

'Just show me his shop, and I'll collect it from his dead father! Forget his power! We ought to turn such a crook in to the police.'

'Yes, what else?' said Jalpa. 'All these goldsmiths drag their feet, but not like this—gulping down your money and making you run back and forth for something months at a time.'

Rama, scratching his head, said, 'If you'll just be patient for ten more days I'll get the money from him today and give it to some other jeweller.'

'Why won't you show me this scoundrel's shop?' asked Ratan. 'I'll let my whip do the talking.'

'I'm telling you, you'll get your bracelet within ten days.'

'You're stalling yourself. You must have fallen for his flattery. If you'd been harsh with him just once, would he have had the nerve to try this trickery?' asked Ratan.

Finally, with great reluctance, she took her leave. That very evening Gangu gave an unequivocal answer to Rama's pleas: without half the money in advance, the bracelet could not be made, and in addition the previous account had to be paid in full.

Rama felt as though he had been shot. 'But Maharaj,' he said, 'that's no way for a gentleman to behave. It's something for a lady; she gave me an advance for it. Think about it, how can I face her? Have a promissory note written out in my name, and a stamp too; what else will you do?'

'Am I supposed to put honey on the note and lick it? What value is it to me? Loans aren't made for eight months at a time. A month or two is plenty. You're a big shot. What's five or six hundred rupees to you? By the way, the bracelet is ready.'

Rama ground his teeth and said, 'If that was so, why didn't you tell me a month ago? Then I would have made arrangements for the money by now, wouldn't I!'

'How could I know that? You don't understand even this much.'

Rama returned home downcast. Even now, if he had made a clean breast of the whole affair to Jalpa, she would have handed over her bracelet no matter how much it grieved her. But Rama did not have enough courage for this. He couldn't bring himself to give such a blow to her tender heart by telling her the true state of his financial difficulties.

There's no doubt that Rama, who received something over a hundred rupees monthly, could certainly have paid off at least half of what he owed the two jewellers in these eight months if he had known how to practise economy. But since his income was high, so were his expenditures. Whatever he got was spent in outings and recreations, and the jewellers' money was held back in hopes of one lump-sum payment! To make rupees out of cowries—that's merchants' work. Educated people make cowries out of rupees.

Later in the evening, Rama made the rounds of the jewellers once more. He badly wanted to talk another jeweller into something or other, but he didn't succeed anywhere. News travels by wireless in the bazaar.

Rama didn't sleep the whole night. If someone had written him a note for a thousand and given him even five hundred that day, he'd have been contented, but no such person came to mind among any of his acquaintances. He'd boasted and bragged to everyone in his circle, and wined and dined them with an open hand. How could he now disclose his distress without losing face? He regretted having needlessly given the money to Gangu. Bringing charges against him wouldn't work either. If some terrible illness had come along just then, Rama would have welcomed it; at least he'd have received a few days' extension. But not even death comes by invitation. He comes just when we are least prepared. Just let God have a telegram sent from somewhere! But not even the sort of friend who could have sent a false telegram in God's name came to mind. He was tossing and turning in the midst of these anxieties when Jalpa's eyes opened. Rama covered his face with the sheet in a flash, as if he were sleeping without a care in the world. Jalpa slowly drew the sheet aside, and finding him apparently asleep began to gaze at him intently. She soon detected that he was awake, not asleep. Shaking him gently, she said, 'Are you still awake?'

'I don't know why I can't sleep. I was lying here thinking I should go away for a while to earn some money.'

'Will you take me along?'

'How can I travel abroad if I bring you along?'

'So I will be living here alone. I won't stay a minute! But where will you go?'

'I haven't decided yet.'

'So would you really go off and leave me? I won't stand it for a single day. You don't love me; you only pretend to love me.'

'It's only being caught in the clutches of your love that's kept me here; otherwise I'd have gone by now.'

'You're just making it up. If you really cared for me, you wouldn't keep things from me. You're certainly thinking about something important that you're hiding from me. I've noticed for several days that you're drowning in some worry. Why won't you tell me? Where there's no trust, how can there be love?'

'You're deceiving yourself, Jalpa. I've never kept anything from you.'

'So you really love me from your heart?'

'Should I keep telling you this whenever you want?'

'OK, I'm going to ask you a question now. Be on your guard. Why do you love me? Swear you'll tell me the truth.'

'You've asked a very strange and awkward question. If I were to ask you the same question, what would *you* say?'

'I know what I'd say.'

'Tell me.'

'You tell me; I'll tell you too.'

'I don't even know,' said Rama. 'I only know this: you thrill me in every part of my body!'

'Think before you speak. I know very well that I'm not an ideal wife. I haven't even come close to serving you as a wife should. Thanks to the grace of God you haven't had to suffer any difficulties. I don't know anything about housework; whatever I've learned about that, I learned here! So why should you love me? I'm not clever at making conversation, and I'm not that attractive either. Do you know why I'm asking you this?'

'How can I know, bhai. I don't understand a thing.'

'I'm asking so I can make you keep on loving me.'

'I don't know anything about that, Jalpa, but I tell you truly, if you have any shortcomings or faults, I haven't noticed them yet. But what did you see in me? I'm not rich, or educated, or hand-some. Tell me.'

'Shall I tell you? I'm infatuated by your goodness. Why should I hide anything from you now? When I first came here, even though I considered you my husband, I still worried about whether or not you would be pleased by what I said or did. If I had married some other man I would have behaved the same way with him too. This is the usual relationship between husband and wife. But now I wouldn't exchange you even for Krishna who loved the gopis! Still, even now there's something concealed in your heart. You're still keeping something or other from me.'

'This is only your suspicion, Jalpa. I don't hide things from even my friends, let alone the queen of my heart.'

'Look at me when you speak. A man shouldn't lower his eyes.'

Once again it came into Rama's mind to spill out all his troubles, but once again false pride stopped his tongue.

Whenever Jalpa asked him whether or not he was paying off the jewellers, he said that he was giving them a little each month. But today Rama's weakness aroused Jalpa's suspicion. Wishing to dispel her doubts, after a little while she asked, 'Have you finished paying the jewellers yet?'

'There's just a little left now!'

'Do you write down whatever's left?'

'Yes, why shouldn't I? It must be a little less than seven hundred.'

'Why, that's the whole thing! You didn't use Ratan's money, did you?'

Rama had been inwardly trembling lest Jalpa suddenly ask that very question, and now she'd finally asked it. Even then if Rama had taken his courage in both hands and confessed, his difficulties might have come to an end. Jalpa would certainly have been stunned for a moment, and it's possible in a fit of anger and disappointment a few harsh words would have escaped her lips, but then she would have become calm again. By putting their heads together, the two of them would have come up with some expedient or other. If Jalpa had revealed the secret to Ratan, she would have gone along with it. But alas for excessive self-esteem! When Rama heard Jalpa's question, he put on a face as if she had given him a cruel blow.

'Why would I use Ratan's money?' he asked. 'If I wanted to, I could bring three or four thousand worth of stuff today. Workmen *always* have a habit of delaying things! And goldsmiths are famous for being sour-natured. That's all there is to it. In ten days I'll either have her bracelet ready, or give her back her money. But how come you had this suspicion? How could I have possibly spent her money for myself?'

'It's nothing, I was just asking.'

Jalpa soon went to sleep, but Rama fell back into his tangle of difficulties. Where could he get the money from? If he told Ramesh Babu straight out, he'd arrange for him to borrow it from some moneylender. But no, he couldn't tell him under any circumstances. He didn't have the courage.

Early in the morning he ate breakfast and set out for the office. Maybe some kind of arrangement could be made there! He gave no thought to who would carry out this arrangement, just as a patient becomes satisfied by merely going to a vaidya without even knowing whether he will get better! This was exactly Rama's state now. There was nobody but a peon at the office. Rama opened up the register and began to check the numbers. The totals had not been added up for several days, but the chief officer had still signed. When Rama added it up, it came to two and a half thousand. All at once he thought of something new. Why not write two thousand in place of two and a half thousand? Who checked the receipt ledger? Even if the theft should be detected, he could say that he'd made a mistake in adding things up. But he didn't let this thought remain long in his mind. For fear that he might become distracted, he traced the figures in ink with his pencil, put the register in the drawer, and started wandering to and fro.

Goods carts began to come in ones and twos. The drivers saw the Babu Sahab was here today, and thought to themselves that they could pay their tolls quickly and go off duty. For this favour Rama took twice the usual commission, and the drivers paid it gladly, because it was market time, and to wait until twelve or one o'clock for the toll house to give them some time could mean a loss of twenty-four hours. The market closed at ten or eleven o'clock, which would mean waiting until the next day. If prices dropped by even a small fraction of a rupee, theirs could be the responsibility for a loss of hundreds. To give up a few rupees to avoid this couldn't be any great trouble for them.

Rama learned all this for the first time today. After all, he just sat around home in the mornings. If he were to come here instead, he might get five or ten rupees a day, and then this whole dispute would be settled in six months. Even supposing this windfall did not occur every day, he'd get five or ten, if not fifteen, on the average. If he were to get five in the morning, and that much again during the rest of the day, then he'd be free of his debt in five or six months. He opened the drawer and took out the register again; wandering through the maze of its figures no longer seemed so terrible. The new recruit who at first starts at the sound of a rifle, later doesn't panic even in a shower of bullets.

Rama had closed the office and was about to go home and eat, when a pedlar's cart arrived. 'I'll take the toll when I come back,' said Rama. The pedlar began to entreat him; he had something very urgent to do. In the end, the matter was settled for ten rupees. Rama took the toll, put the ten rupees in his pocket, and set out for home. He'd received twenty-five rupees in only two or three hours. If things went at this rate for even a month, he'd reach his goal. He was so happy that he didn't go home to eat. Nor did he order anything from the bazaar. While getting his money changed, he decided not to spend a single rupee. Instead, he sat working till evening and took in four more rupees. When he went home, as the lamps were being lit, a good deal of the load of worry and despondency had lifted from his heart. If this pace lasted for ten days more, he wouldn't be obliged to avoid meeting Ratan.

# 17

Nine days passed and Rama continued to go to the office in the morning and return home when the lamps were lit. Each day he went in the hopes of entrapping some big game, but these hopes remained unfulfilled. Moreover, the sun of good fortune never shone again as it had that first day. None the less, he thought it no small credit to himself that he'd earned a hundred rupees in nine days. He didn't even have a single paisa's worth of paan. And when Jalpa several times suggested going out, he put her off with this and that. Yes, but tomorrow was something else. Tomorrow, when Ratan would ask for her bracelet, what answer could he give? He came home from the office, and sat reflecting on this. Couldn't she agree to wait for one more month? If she'd keep quiet that long, then perhaps he'd be out of debt to her. He was confident that if he plied her with specious reasons, he would make her agree. If she became stubborn, he'd tell her that the jeweller would not return the money.

It was July, and darkness was coming on. Rama was thinking that he might just go and play a few games with Ramesh Babu, but hesitated when he saw the clouds. Just then Ratan arrived. She was not pleased and her face looked severe. She had come from home ready to fight, and intended to throw courtesy and consideration to the winds.

'You've come at a good time,' Jalpa said. 'I'll go out with you myself today. These days his workload doesn't even give him time to lift his head.'

'I have to get back home right away today,' said Ratan harshly. 'I've just come to remind Babuji of tomorrow.'

Rama was inwardly quavering at the sight of her impatient and expectant face. He wanted to please her any way he could. 'Yes indeed,' he answered readily, 'I remember very well. I've just come from the jeweller's shop. I show up there every morning and evening for hours, but those things take a lot of time. Prices depend on workmanship. The price isn't very much for the quality. Two men are working on it, but it probably won't be ready for at least another month. But it will be incomparable; you'll love it.'

Ratan, however, didn't thaw even a little. 'Fine,' she said, flaring up. 'It'll take a month more now will it? This is such workmanship that it won't be finished in even three months! Please tell him to give my money back. Goddesses might wear bracelets made out of expectations; I don't need them.'

'It won't take a month, I'll have it made in a hurry. I just said a month at a guess. There's only a little bit left to be done, now. It took several days to find the precious stones.'

'I don't need to wear a bracelet, bhai. You just give me back my money, that's all. I've seen a lot of goldsmiths! Thanks to your kindness, I could have had three inlaid bracelets by now; I've never seen such cheating anywhere.'

At the word 'cheating,' Rama, enraged, got up. 'It's not cheating; call it my stupidity instead. What need did I have to put myself into such straits? I only gave the money you advanced me to the jeweller to make him happy so he'd work fast. Now you're asking for your money; well, he can't give it back.'

Ratan, looking at him sharply, said 'Why! Why can't he give back the money?'

'Because where is he going to turn around and sell the piece he made for you? It's possible he might sell it after six months or a year. Not everybody likes the same things.'

Ratan scowled and said, 'I don't know anything but that he delayed—so let him suffer. Either give me my bracelet tomorrow, or my money. If you're friends with the jeweller and can't say anything out of your courtesy and consideration for him, then just show me his shop. If for some reason you're ashamed to do that, then tell me his name, and I'll find him. Wonderful! What a good joke! I'll have his shop sold by auction. I'll get him sent to jail. You can't deal with these hoodlums without fighting.'

Rama, shamefaced, stared at the ground. What an unlucky moment it had been when he took the money from Ratan! What a disaster he had unexpectedly brought upon himself.

'That's right,' said Jalpa. 'Why don't you take her to the jeweller's shop? When she sees the thing with her own eyes, she'll feel satisfied.'

'I don't even want to take it now,' said Ratan.

Trembling, Rama said, 'Fine, you'll get your money tomorrow.'

'What time?'

'I'll bring it when I come home from the office.'

'I'll have it all. Don't try to stall by giving me only one or two hundred.'

'You'll get all your money tomorrow,' said Rama, and went into the mardana, where he wrote a note to Ramesh Babu. 'Take this to Ramesh Babu,' he told Gopi. 'Bring back his answer.'

Then he wrote another note and gave it to Vishambhar to take to Manik Das for an answer.

'It's raining,' said Vishambhar.

'So is the whole world going to be flooded? Run!'

'And if I don't find him at home?'

'You'll find him. He doesn't go anywhere at this time of day.'

This was the first time in his life that Rama had asked a friend for a loan. He used all the blandishments and forceful entreaties that he could remember. It was an entirely new experience for him. How many times had letters of the sort he was writing today come to him! How his heart had melted when he had read those letters, but powerless to help, he'd had to make. excuses. Would Ramesh Babu make excuses too? His income was large, his expenses small. If he wanted to, he could make arrangements for the money. Would he be that kind? The two boys had not returned yet, and he started walking back and forth by the door. Ratan's car was still standing where she had left it. Just then she came out, and even though she saw him there, said nothing, got into her car, and drove off.

Where could those two boys have gotten to? They were probably playing somewhere, the little devils. Whatever Ramesh could give would be a windfall. He'd asked for two hundred to no purpose, perhaps Ramesh didn't have that much with him. He had little left after his in-laws snatched his money away. If Manik wanted to, he could give five hundred or a thousand, but he ought to wait and see; his friend would be put to the test today. If these people didn't give him any money today, what did he care? He wasn't anybody's servant to go running if they should summon him to play chess. Rama heard the sound of someone's footsteps and his heart started to pound forcefully. Vishambhar had finally returned. But Manik had written: 'I am very pinched for money these days, and was just about to ask you for something myself.'

Rama tore up the note and threw it away. The self-seeking bastard! If the Sub-Inspector had asked for it, he'd have taken the money and come running as soon as he saw the note. Well, just wait. Manik's stuff would certainly have to have tolls paid on it. He'd get even then.

Just then Gopi returned. Ramesh had written: 'I've made three or four rules in my life and keep them with the greatest strictness. One of them is that I never lend or borrow money from friends. You don't have any experience of this yet, but you will after a while. If friends begin to borrow money, it doesn't take long for ill-will to appear. You are my dear friend. I don't want to make you my enemy, so please forgive me.'

Rama tore up and threw away this note too, and sitting down on a chair stared fixedly at the light. It's doubtful whether he even saw the light. He would have perhaps gazed just as intently at the black, impenetrable cloud masses in the sky!

There's a state of the mind when the eyes are open and see nothing, and when the ears are open and hear nothing.

# 18

Evening had come, and silence had spread throughout the compound of the municipality. The office workers were going one by one, and the sweepers were plying their brooms in the rooms. The peons were putting on their shoes, and the beggars were counting their proceeds of the day. But Rama was sitting in his chair writing in the register.

Today, too, he'd come here early in the morning, but once again he hadn't caught any big game; just the same ten rupees as usual. What means did he have to save his imaginary honour now? Rama resolved to deceive Ratan. He knew very well that her impatience was because she thought he'd spent her money. If she knew that she could get her money immediately, then she'd be pacified! Rama wanted to allay her suspicions by showing her a bag filled with money. He was waiting for the cashier sahab to depart; he had deliberately stayed behind this afternoon. Today's receipts of eight hundred rupees were with him, and he wanted to take them home. The cashier got up right at four o'clock. What need did he have to ask for the day's receipts from Rama? He'd have a holiday from counting rupees. The poor fellow's wrist was aching from sitting all day writing in the ledger and counting money over and over again. When Rama knew that the cashier sahab must have gone some distance, he closed the register and said to the peon, 'Pick up the bag; let's go get these accounts closed.'

'But the cashier babu has gone,' said the peon.

'The cashier has gone!' said Rama opening his eyes wide. 'Why didn't you tell me? How far do you think he's gone by now?'

'As far as the corner of the street maybe?'

'How will he deposit this?'

'Should I go bring him back?'

'Yes sir, go right ahead. Even though I didn't tell you to yet, you'll go and call him back. You're a real calf's uncle, an idiot! Had too much bhang today? Oh well, the money will stay right in this drawer. You'll be responsible.'

'No, Babu Sahab, I won't let the money be kept here. Not every watch keeps the same time. If the money should somehow disappear, then I'd be beaten even though it wouldn't be my fault. And there's not even a suitable lock here.'

'So where should I put this money?'

'Your Honour, take it with you.'

This was exactly what Rama wanted. He had an ekka brought, put the money bag in, and set off for home. As he went he thought that if Ratan could be influenced by threats, he'd have no trouble with her. He could also tell her that there were only three or four days left at most. She'd be reassured by seeing the money in front of her.

Jalpa saw the bag and asked, 'You didn't get the bracelet?'

'It's not ready yet. I thought I'd bring back the money to calm her down.'

'What did you say to the jeweller?'

'What was there to say? He keeps saying in a few days time. Ratan Devi hasn't come yet?'

'She must be coming. She's worried, isn't she?'

When Ratan didn't come by the time the lamps were lit, Rama decided she wouldn't be coming. He put the money in the cupboard and went out for a stroll. But it couldn't have been even ten minutes before Ratan arrived and asked, even as she was coming, 'The bracelet must have come?'

'Yes,' said Jalpa, 'it's come. Put it on! The poor fellow went to the jeweller's several times. The scoundrel *won't* give it to him and plays his usual tricks.'

'What sort of jeweller is it that plays tricks for so many days! If I'd known there'd be such a wrangle about my money, I wouldn't have given it. I don't have either the money or the bracelet.'

Ratan spoke in such a mistrustful way that Jalpa flared up. 'Your money has been put aside,' she said haughtily. 'Take it when you want. This matter is not under my control. The jeweller will give you the bracelet in the end; will you still take it then?'

'Has he promised when he'll give it to me?' asked Ratan.

'What's to be said for his promises? After all he's made hundreds of them.'

'So this means he won't make the thing?'

'Understand what you wish.'

'Then give me back my money; to hell with such a bracelet.'

Jalpa rose with flashing eyes, took the bag from the cupboard, and flung it down before Ratan. 'This is your money,' she said. 'Please take it.'

The reason for Ratan's impatience was exactly what Rama had supposed. She suspected that Rama and Jalpa had spent her money, and this was why she had been dunning them for the bracelet. Seeing the money, her suspicions were calmed. Somewhat shamefacedly she said, 'If he promises to have it done in three or four days, don't worry about the money.'

'I don't expect him to give it to you so soon. When the piece is ready, the money will be asked for.'

'Who knows whether I'll have money then or not. When money comes you see it, when it goes you don't. Who knows how it flies away? What's wrong with your keeping it?'

'Things are the same here,' said Jalpa. 'And to keep someone else's money in your house is dangerous too. If it should get mixed up with other money by accident, someone would have to be punished pointlessly. On the fourth day after my marriage my jewels were stolen. We weren't asleep, but who knows when we dozed off and the thieves did their work. We lost ten thousand.

If such a misfortune were to happen again, and your money was lost, we'd be completely dishonoured.'

'All right, I'll take the money, but look, don't stop being concerned about it. Tell Babuji to keep after that jeweller.'

Ratan left. Jalpa was glad that the burden was lifted from their heads. The most severe injuries in our lives usually come from the hands of our most sincere well-wishers.

When Rama returned from his stroll around half past eight, Jalpa was preparing the meal. As soon as she saw him, she said, 'Ratan came, and I gave her the money.'

The ground shook under Rama's feet. He stared at her in such astonishment that his eyes rolled up towards his forehead. 'What did you say? You gave Ratan the money? Who told you to give it to her?' he said in a panic.

'You brought her money here yourself. As soon as you left she came and asked for the bracelet. I got mad and gave her the money.'

Rama, on his guard now, said, 'She didn't ask for the money!'

'Why wouldn't she? Well, yes, when I gave her the money she started back-tracking—why was I returning it to her? Keep it with you. I told her I didn't keep money from people who have such suspicious natures.'

'For God's sake, don't do anything like this in the future without asking me.'

'So nothing's happened. Go ask her for the money back. But from now on, why give yourself the trouble of bringing money home?'

Rama had become so dispirited that he didn't even have the strength to quarrel with Jalpa. Feeling tearful, he went downstairs and began thinking the whole situation over. It was unjust to get angry with Jalpa. When he had clearly said the money was Ratan's, and had not even given her a hint *not* to give the money to Ratan without asking him, Jalpa was not at fault.

He thought to himself that the problem would not be solved by getting furious and having a row. He needed to calm down and reflect. It was essential to get the money back from Ratan. If he'd been here when Ratan came, how beautifully the whole difficulty would have been smoothed over. What disastrous impulse had come over him to go out for a walk? No one dies from not having a walk for a day. Some hidden power was hell-bent on bringing about his destruction. Ten minutes of absence has spoiled the whole game. Ratan had said to keep the money. If Jalpa had acted with a little intelligence, matters would never have reached such a pass. But again he was starting to think of things that had already happened. The problem was how to get the money back from Ratan! Why not go and say he'd heard that she was angry because her money had been returned, and that in reality he hadn't brought the money for her, but rather had demanded it from the jeweller so he'd finish making the piece and give it to them. It was possible that she'd become ashamed, beg his pardon, and give him the money again. He ought to go there right now.

After deciding this, he glanced at his watch. It was about a quarter to nine and it had grown dark. Ratan wouldn't be able to leave home at this time. Rama got out his cycle and went off to meet her.

Today there was a big celebration at Ratan's bungalow. There was always some kind of festival or banquet or party going on there. Her lonely, silent life made her rush after these things like a thirsty person after water. There was a large crowd of children gathered! A swing was hanging from a mango tree, and the children were swinging in it in the light of electric lamps. Ratan was standing pushing the children in the swing! There was a great uproar. Vakil Sahab, wearing a woolen overcoat even in this weather, was sitting on the veranda smoking a cigar. Rama wanted to go to the swing and talk with Ratan, but seeing Vakil Sahab stand up, he felt too bashful to go over to her. As soon as he saw Rama, Vakil Sahab stretched forth his hand and said, 'Come, Rama Babu, and tell me the news of your Municipal Board.'

Rama sat down on a chair and said, 'Nothing new has happened.'

'When will the motion for the compulsory education of girls pass? Several other Boards have passed it. Until the education of women is widespread, we'll never improve. You probably haven't even gone to Europe. Oh! What freedom, what wealth, what life, what enthusiasm! In a word, one knows it's paradise! And the women are really goddesses! So cheerful, so independent! All this is the prasad of female education!'

Rama, speaking according to the little he knew of conditions in these countries from his reading of newspapers, said, 'But the conduct of women over there is not very good.'

'Nonsense! Each country has its own way of doing things. When you see a young woman and a young man wandering around alone together, you're astonished; you've become so dirty-minded that when you see a man and a woman together you can't stop being suspicious. But where boys and girls study together, this social division becomes relatively unimportant. So many points of sympathy and affection rise among them, that sexual desire plays only a small part. Please grasp that the more independence a country gives to women, the more civilized that country is. To keep women prisoners, or in purdah, or miles away from men means that in our country the general public is so depraved that it doesn't hesitate one bit to insult women. There are literally thousands of subjects such as politics, religion, fine arts, literature, philosophy, history, and science on whose basis young men can build deep friendships with young women. Sexuality is the chief basis of attraction in those countries where people's outlook is parochial. I've lived for a whole year in Europe and America. I've had friendships with lots of beautiful women. I've played with them, even danced with them, but never a word passed my lips that could have made a young woman hang her head in embarrassment. And then, where aren't there good and bad people?'

Rama derived no pleasure from this conversation; he was plunged in worry.

Vakil Sahab spoke again. 'As long as we don't let both women and men freely pursue their own mental development, we'll keep on declining. Don't bind the feet of society with fetters, don't throw chains around its neck. Push for widow remarriage, push hard. But what I don't understand is why the newspapers make such a fuss when a middle-aged man marries a young woman. In Europe old men of eighty marry young women, and elderly women of seventy marry young men. No one says a thing. No one even hears a whisper about it. We want to kill off old people even before they die. None the less, if ever a person needs companionship, it's especially in old age, when he wishes to have some support all the time, when he becomes dependent.'

Rama's attention was fixed on the swing. Just then his greatest desire was to somehow have the chance for a few words with Ratan. But for him to just go there would be against good manners. Finally, after a little while he glanced at the swing and said, 'Where have all these boys come from?'

'Ratan Bai is very fond of children's company,' said Vakil Sahab. 'Who knows how all these boys get here. If you're fond of children, then go on over there.'

This was exactly what Rama wanted, and he reached the swing in a trice. When Ratan saw him, she smiled and said, 'These little devils are leading me around by the nose. None of them ever gets tired of swinging. Come on, you do a little forced labour too, I've got tired.' And she sat down on the nearby brick platform while Rama began to push the swing. When the boys saw a new person, they all became impatient for a turn. Ratan had given them all two turns, but how could the rest of them sit looking on while some of them were having a third turn! Whenever two got off the swing, four more got on. Rama didn't even pretend to like children, but he was trapped; what could he do?

Finally after half an hour of this forced labour he became fed up. His watch showed nine-thirty. But how could he strike up a conversation of any importance? Ratan was so engrossed in the swinging that one might think she had completely forgotten the money.

All at once she came up to the swing and said, 'Babuji, I'll sit while you push, but not from underneath; pump the swing while you stand on it!'

Rama had been afraid of sitting on swings since childhood. Once when some friends forcibly seated him on one, he had become dizzy. But her appeal practically forced him to get on the swing. How could he display his incompetence? Ratan sat down holding two children and began singing a devotional song:

> The swing has been hung from the branch of the kadam tree,
> Oh Radha, Queen, the festival of swings has come.

Rama stood on the swing and began to pump, but his legs were trembling, and his heart was in his throat. Whenever the swing descended, it seemed to him as if something soft was piercing his chest—while Ratan was singing along with the children:

> The swing has been hung from the branch of the kadam tree,
> Oh Radha, Queen, the festival of swings has come.

After a short while Ratan said, 'Push harder please, Sahab. You're hardly moving the swing.'

Ashamed, Rama put more force into it, but the swing didn't go any higher, and he began to get dizzy!

'You don't know how to pump it. Didn't you ever swing before?'

'Yes,' said Rama, shrinking with embarrassment, 'but it's been ten years since I did.'

'So sit down—watch out for these children—and I'll swing you. If you can't reach out and touch that branch up there, tell me.' Rama felt half-dead with fear. 'It's very late now,' he said. 'I'll come again some other time.'

'Ajii, it's not late yet, it's not even ten. Don't panic, the night's hardly begun. Swing a lot and then go, please. And bring Jalpa tomorrow; we'll both swing.'

But Rama got up out of the swing. His face showed terror.

It had seemed to him each time the swing rose that he was going to fall. He wobbled towards his cycle, sat down on it, and fled home.

For some distance he was hardly conscious. His feet kept pushing the pedals by themselves. After going half the distance he came to himself. He turned the cycle around, went a little distance, and then got off and started thinking. What an opportunity he'd let slip because of his embarrassment. He'd come away from there with his tail between his legs. Why hadn't he been able to say a word? Ratan wasn't some sort of monster who would eat him up! Suddenly he remembered that the bag contained eight hundred rupees. When Jalpa had flared up and given Ratan the bag, lock, stock, and barrel, she must not have counted the money in it either; otherwise she would certainly have said something. Heaven forbid that the bag be given to someone else, or that more money be added to what was already there. That would really be a disaster! Then he'd be disgraced. Why not go right now and ask for the excess money back? But it was very late now; he'd have to go again tomorrow.

But even if he got those two hundred rupees back, he'd still be six hundred short. How could he deal with that? He could manage it only if God saw him through this difficulty. If no arrangement had been made by morning, then what? He began to tremble.

There are occasions in our lives when, even though feeling hopeless, we still find some reason to hope. Rama thought that if he visited Gangu once more, he might find him at his shop, and could beg for mercy. It was possible that Gangu might take pity on him. But when he reached the jeweller's market, Gangu's shop was closed. He was just about to return when he saw Charan Das coming. As soon as he saw Rama he said, 'Babuji, you've completely given up coming this way. Tell me, when am I going to get my money?'

'You'll get it very soon, bhai,' said Rama humbly. 'There won't be any delay. Just see, Gangu's got his money, now it's your turn.'

'I know the whole story. If Gangu hadn't been smart enough to take his money, he'd be stamping his feet in frustration like me. It's been going on a whole year. At even twelve per cent interest a year, I'd have earned eighty-four rupees. Come tomorrow and settle up; if not the whole amount, a half or a third—give me something at least. The boss keeps his patience when people pay as well as take. When people turn a deaf ear to him, he begins to suspect that their intentions are bad. So when will you be coming tomorrow, please?'

'Well, bhai, I can't bring the money tomorrow, but I'll come whenever else you say. Couldn't your Sethji arrange for me to have four or five hundred rupees? I'll grease your palm too.'

'What kind of crazy talk is that, Babuji. Sethji won't give you a single paisa. He's behaved very well in not taking legal action against you. I'm forced to hear a lot of things about you behind your back. Do I have to speak to your head clerk?'

'I'm *your* debtor, not the head clerk's!' said Rama, flaring up. 'I haven't lied, I haven't run away from home. Why are you so impatient?'

'A whole year has gone,' said Charan, 'and we haven't received a single paisa. Why wouldn't we be impatient? Consider at least two hundred for tomorrow.'

'I told you I don't have it now.'

'You spend money right and left every day, and still you say you don't have any money! Get some money together tomorrow; our man will certainly come to collect it.'

Rama went off without replying. He'd come here to accomplish something, but had been forced to endure this dunning instead.

He hoped the wretch wouldn't actually send a collector to his father, or he'd really be in the fire. And Jalpa too would realize what a braggart he was.

Although no tears came to Rama's eyes just then, every fibre of his being was weeping. What a big mistake he'd made in concealing the true state of his affairs from Jalpa! She was a sensible woman. If she had known how poor her home was, she would never have let him borrow for her jewellery. She had never directly asked him for anything. It was rather he who had been so obsessed with increasing his own importance. And why hadn't he been more thrifty with his money, especially when taking on such a big financial burden? He should have caught every paisa between his teeth. His total yearly income couldn't be less than a thousand. If he'd been economical he could certainly have paid these two moneylenders—Gangu and Charan—half of what he owed them, but now this disaster had fallen on his head. Why did Jalpa have to go out every day with all the women of the neighbourhood? The tonga driver alone had probably taken hundreds, but it had been considered essential to impress him! The whole bazaar knew that he was only an empty braggart, but not his own wife! How intelligent of him! Why had it been necessary to have curtains for the door? Why had he brought two lamps? Why had he brought the new tape to have the charpais rewoven? As he went along, he added up all the expenses which a man of his means ought to have delayed. A healthy man doesn't worry about what or how much he eats, but when he gets sick he remembers that he ate pakoras yesterday. Victory is an extrovert, defeat an introvert.

'Where did you go?' asked Jalpa. 'Why did you take so long?'

'I had to go to Ratan's bungalow on account of you. You gave her all the money; two hundred of it was mine.'

'How could I know? You didn't say a thing. But none of that money will leave her; she'll send it to you herself.'

'I agree. But I have to produce the government money tomorrow.'

'Take two hundred from me tomorrow. I have it with me.'

Rama didn't believe her. 'You couldn't have that much! Where did you get so much money?'

'What difference does it make to you? I tell you I'll give you two hundred.'

Rama's face lighted up. He began to cherish a few hopes. She'd give him two hundred, he'd take two hundred from Ratan, and he had a hundred himself, so that left around three hundred. But where was that three hundred to come from? No one came to mind from whom he had any hope of getting so much. If Ratan gave back all the money, the whole mess could be straightened out; this was his only remaining basis for hope.

When he lay down after eating, Jalpa asked, 'What thoughts are you lost in today?'

'Thoughts about what? Do I look sad?'

'Yes, as if you're really worried about something, but aren't telling me.'

'If there was something, would I hide it from you?'

'Splendid! Why should you tell *me* the secrets of your heart? After all, the ancient sages have not commanded it.'

'I'm not one of their devotees.'

'I'd know that if I sat in your heart and had a look.'

'You'd see your own image there.'

Jalpa had a terrible dream that night; she shrieked aloud. Startled, Rama asked, 'What is it Jalpa? Are you dreaming?'

Glancing about wildly, Jalpa said, 'My life was in great danger! I don't know what kind of dream I was having.'

'What did you see?'

'What should I tell you? Nothing makes sense. I saw you being arrested and taken away by several policemen. How terrible they appeared!'

Rama's blood dried up. Three or four days ago he would have laughed this dream off. This time he couldn't help being inwardly alarmed, though externally he laughed and said, 'You didn't ask the police why they were taking me away?'

'It seems to be a laughing matter to you, but my heart is trembling.'

A little later Rama began to babble in his sleep. 'Mother, I'm telling you, you won't see my face again; I'm going to drown.'

Jalpa hadn't fallen asleep yet. Frightened, she forcefully shook Rama awake and said, 'You were laughing at me and now you've begun to talk nonsense yourself. My hair stood on end when I heard you. What did you see in your dream?'

Feeling embarrassed Rama said, 'Yes, there's no telling what I was seeing. I don't remember a thing.'

'But why were you threatening mother?' Jalpa asked. 'Tell me truly, what did you see?'

'I don't remember anything,' said Rama, scratching his head. 'I must have started babbling just like that.'

'All right then,' said Jalpa. 'Turn on your side. People talk in their sleep when they lie on their backs.'

Rama turned on his side, but it seemed as if worry and doubt were sitting on his eyes warding off the attack of sleep. He was still awake when two o'clock struck. Suddenly Jalpa got up and draining the contents of the water pot said, 'I'm really very thirsty. Are you *still* awake?'

'Yes, sleep is tired of me. I was thinking about how you came by two hundred rupees. It surprised me.'

'I brought them from my parents' house as I was leaving; I'd put them aside previously.'

'Well, then you're very good at hanging on to money. Why haven't you done that here?'

Smiling, Jalpa said, 'Now that I've got you, I don't worry about money.'

'You're probably cursing your fate!'

'Why would I do that? Let those women whose husbands are idlers, drunkards, hoodlums, or invalids, or whose husbands constantly ridicule them and quarrel with them about every little thing, wail about their fate. If a man is good-natured, a woman will be happy with him even if she has to fast.'

Feeling delighted Rama said, 'So do you find me good-natured?'

'You've turned out to be more than I'd hoped for,' said Jalpa proudly and affectionately. 'I have three friends. Not one of them has a husband like you. One's an M.A., but always ill. The second is a scholar and rich too, but always running after prostitutes. The third is a stay-at-home and a total idler.'

Rama's heart swelled with emotion. How treacherous he had been to this very image of love, this goddess of kindness. If she loved him this much in spite of his many deceptions, how blissful his life would have been if he'd been honest!

# 19

Early next morning Rama sent his man to Ratan. In his letter he
wrote: 'I'm terribly sorry that yesterday Jalpa behaved with you in
a way she shouldn't have. I never intended to return the money to
you. I took the money from the jeweller to put some pressure on
him. You'll get the bracelet for sure in three or four days. Please
send me the money. There were also two hundred rupees of
mine in that bag. Please be so kind as to send them too.'

He left out no possible expression of modesty consistent with
his own self-respect. Until his man returned, he continued to gaze
distractedly along the way he had gone. Sometimes he thought
she'd make excuses, then that she wasn't at home, or that she'd
promise to return the money three or four days later. Everything
depended on Ratan's money. If Ratan flatly refused, then everything would be ruined! Just imagining this made Rama half-dead
with fear. At nine o'clock his man finally returned. Ratan had sent
two hundred rupees to be sure but she hadn't replied to his letter.

Rama looked despairingly toward the sky. Why hadn't she
answered his letter? Didn't she even understand common
courtesy? What a hypocritical woman she was! Last night she had
seemed the very model of benevolence and kindliness, but the
whole time her heart had been filled with revenge! In his worry
about the rest of the money, Rama forgot to bathe and eat.

When the water-carrier came inside, Jalpa asked, 'Is it because
you've had news of some other work that you're just strolling
around? It's going on ten and there's not a trace of the vegetables
you're supposed to bring.'

The Kahar glanced at her angrily and said, 'Do I have four arms
and legs? I was busy. The Babu sent me to bring some money
from the lady.'

'Which lady?'

'The one that comes in the motor-car.'

'So did you bring the money?'

'Why wouldn't I? She lives at the other end of the earth. My
legs are aching from running there and back.'

'All right. Go and get the vegetables right away.'

Off went the Kahar. As soon as Rama came inside with the

money Jalpa said, 'You asked for your money back from Ratan, didn't you? Now you won't be taking any from me.'

'So don't give it to me!' said Rama sadly.

'I *told* you that I'll give you the money. Why did you think of asking for the money so soon? Maybe she thought that you didn't trust her even that much.'

'I didn't ask for the money,' said Rama despondently. 'I just wrote that there were two hundred rupees extra in the bag. She sent them on her own.'

Jalpa laughed and said, 'My money's very lucky, shall I show you? I just kept new rupees. All of them are from this year, see how they glitter! Take a look and your heart will be satisfied!'

Just then someone below called out, 'Babuji, the Seth has sent me for his money.'

Dayanath was just coming inside for his bath when he saw the seth's peon and asked, 'Which seth? Which money? You mean someone in my house hasn't paid for something?'

'The Chote Babu has taken some goods. A whole year has gone by and he hasn't given us even a single paisa. The Sethji said if he just pays when things go wrong, what has he paid? Please make sure that he gives something today.'

Dayanath summoned Rama and said, 'Look here, which seth's man is this? If there's something left to pay, why don't you give it to them straightaway? How much is left to pay?'

Rama didn't have time to say a word before the peon shot out with, 'Seven hundred altogether, Babuji!'

Dayanath's eyes opened so wide they practically reached his forehead. 'Seven hundred! Well, sir, he says seven hundred!'

'I don't know exactly,' said Rama, intentionally stalling for time.

'Why wouldn't you know,' said the peon. 'I have a note with me. You haven't paid a thing for a year. How could it be less?'

Rama shouted at the peon, 'Go back to your shop, I'll come myself.'

'I'm not going unless I get something, Sahab,' said the latter. 'You always put things off just like this, and we have to listen to what you say.'

Rama could stand to be humiliated in front of the whole world, but to be humiliated before his father was as bad as dying. That a man who had never in his life taken a single paisa wrongfully, who would prefer to go hungry rather than borrow for a meal, should have such a shameless and dishonourable son! Rama couldn't wound his father's soul so deeply. He didn't want it revealed to his father that his son was disgracing his name. 'Are you still standing here?' he said to the peon in a harsh voice. 'Get out, or else I'll toss you out on your ear.'

'Give me the money and I'll go. I didn't expect to get sweets at your door!'

'You won't go? Go tell your Lala that I'll file a complaint against him.'

'Why are you saying such shameless things, sir?' said Dayanath, scolding him. 'When you didn't have any money in your pocket, why did you get the thing at all? And when you took it, then pay for it when it's made. You said you'd file a complaint. And if you do file a complaint, what will be left of your reputation? Do you even care about it? Everyone in the city will be pointing fingers at you in scorn, but what do you care! Did you suddenly get this bright idea to load such a burden on your head? Even if it were a wedding or something, it would still be something to discuss. And what kind of woman would see her husband doing something so foolish and not forbid it? After all, did you even think about it when you took on this debt? You don't have such a big income as all that.'

Rama found his father's rebuke very painful. In his opinion his father had no right at all to speak about this subject. He burst out, 'You're getting upset for no reason. If you want me to ask you for money every time, then be so good as to tell me. I'll pay it off little by little from my own salary.'

To himself he thought, 'This is all the result of *your* doing, Father. I'm atoning for *your* sins.'

Seeing father and son arguing back and forth, the peon left silently. Dayanath, fuming, went to take his bath. Rama went upstairs, shame and remorse from his father's scolding radiating from his face. The very disgrace from which he'd fled here and there to save himself, had happened with a vengeance. Even his anxiety about the government money he'd taken had vanished in the face of this humiliation. True borrowers have huge amounts of courage. Your ordinary sensible fellow flies into a panic when he falls into circumstances like Rama's, but tricky fellows don't get rattled. Rama was not yet adroit in this art. If the messenger of Yama, god of death, had come just then to seize his life, he would have jumped out of his skin to bid him welcome. 'What's going to happen to me?' These words were oozing out of every pore of his body. 'What's going to happen to me?' He couldn't utter any other comment about his problem. This question—'What's going to happen to me?'—appeared like an omnipresent fiend glaring at him. These words seemed like innumerable whirlwinds arising in every direction. He was unable to think about them. He could only shut his eyes to them. Tears of distress came to his eyes.

'You said that there was only a little left to pay,' said Jalpa enquiringly.

Rama hung his head and said, 'That bastard was lying; I gave them some money.'

'If you gave them some money, then why would they be pestering you about it? When your income was so small, why did you get any jewellery at all? I never insisted. And even supposing I had said something three or four times, you should still have done things more cautiously. You could have told me a few things too. A man keeps things secret from the whole world, but not from his own wife. You've kept things even from me. If I'd known that your income was so small, would I have been so crazy as to take all the ladies of the neighbourhood out for tonga rides? At the very most I would have felt unhappy from time to time, but at least I wouldn't have had to put up with this dunning from the jeweller. And if you were to file a complaint against him, the seven hundred would become a thousand. How could I know you were playing such a trick on me? I wasn't some prostitute who was filching away your money to feather my own nest. I'm your partner in both good and bad times. In good times you don't have to ask what I have to say if you don't want to, but in bad times, I'll cling to you.'

Not one word came from Rama's mouth. It was time to go to work and there wasn't any time to eat. Rama dressed and left for the office. 'Are you going without eating at all?' asked his mother.

Rama didn't answer her, and was about to leave the house when Jalpa came tearing downstairs and called out to him, 'Why don't you give the two hundred rupees I have to the jeweller?'

Rama had deliberately not asked Jalpa for money as he was

leaving. He had known that if he asked she would give it, but after hearing so much from her, he was not just embarrassed to entreat her for it, he was positively afraid. He didn't on any account want to hear another lecture—even the approaching disasters seemed a little easier to bear. But when Jalpa called to him, a little hope sprang up. He stopped abruptly and said, 'That's a great idea; bring it to me.'

He sat down in the outer room. Jalpa ran upstairs, brought the money, and after rapidly counting it put it in his bag! She thought he wouldn't be able to contain himself for joy after receiving the money, but her hopes went unfulfilled. He still had three hundred rupees to worry about. Where were they to come from? A hungry man wants a full meal; he is not satisfied with four chapatis.

When he reached the street Rama took a tonga and told the driver to go to Georgetown—maybe he'd meet Ratan. If she wanted to she could easily arrange for three hundred rupees. Along the way he kept thinking to himself that today he wouldn't hesitate a bit. After a little while he reached Georgetown, and Ratan's bungalow came into view. She was sitting on the veranda. When Rama saw her, he waved and she waved back. But then he completely lost his nerve. He could not bring himself to go inside. The tonga moved away. If Ratan had invited him in, he would have gone. And if she hadn't been sitting on the veranda, he might still have gone inside. But when he saw her sitting in front, he had been too drowned in his own embarrassment to act.

When the tonga reached Government House, Rama awoke with a start and said, 'Go to the Tolls Office.' The tonga driver turned the horse around.

It was about eleven o'clock when Rama reached the office. His face was drawn, and his heart was pounding. The head clerk, Ramesh Babu, must certainly have inquired about him. He would summon him as soon as he went. He didn't show any favour at all at the office. As he was getting down from the tonga he glanced in the direction of his room, and saw several people standing there looking towards him. He went towards Ramesh Babu's office instead.

'Where have you been till now, sir?' asked Ramesh Babu. 'The cashier sahab has been running all over looking for you! Have you seen the peon?'

'I wasn't at home,' said Rama in a faltering voice. 'I went to Vakil Sahab's. I'm in big trouble.'

'What kind of trouble? Everything's fine at home, isn't it?'

'Yes, everything's fine at home. Yesterday evening there was lots of work here, and I became so involved in it that I lost track of the time. When I finished it and got up to leave, the cashier sahab had gone. I had the day's receipts of eight hundred rupees with me. I began to think where I could keep them. There's no strongbox in my office, so I decided to take them with me. There were five hundred rupees in coins, which I put in the bag, and three hundred in notes, which I put in my pocket, and went home. I had to get a couple of things in the market. When I reached home the notes had disappeared.'

Ramesh Babu stared at Rama in astonishment. 'Three hundred in notes had disappeared?'

'Yes sir, they were in my upper coat pocket.'

'And they didn't knock you down and grab the bag?'

'What can I say, Babuji? I can't begin to tell you what my state of mind has been since then. I've been running around worrying about this ever since. It wasn't possible to make any arrangements.'

'You didn't say anything to your father?'

'You know what he's like. He'd scold me instead of giving me the money.'

'So are you going to keep on worrying?'

'I'll be worrying one way or another until this evening.'

'Then you'd better worry!' said Ramesh, assuming a harsh manner. 'I don't understand how you could be so careless. Not a single paisa has ever fallen from my pocket. Were you walking along the street with your eyes shut or were you drunk? I don't believe what you say. Tell me the truth now, haven't you been spending rather extravagantly? Why did you ask me for money the other day?'

Rama's face turned pale. Pray God the truth wouldn't come out. 'Would I spend government money?' he said, inventing excuses as he went. 'That day I asked you for money because my father had a sudden need. There was no money in the house. When I read your letter to him, he laughed a lot and made other arrangements. I'm astonished myself at how those notes disappeared.'

'If you're embarrassed to ask your father for money, shall I write a letter and ask for you?'

'No, Babuji, for God's sake don't do that, please,' said Rama, putting his hands to his ears in a gesture of disavowal. 'If that's what you want, then please, shoot me instead.'

Ramesh thought for a moment, and then said, 'Are you sure you'll get the money by this evening?'

'Yes, I certainly expect to.'

'Then deposit the money that's in the bag now, but listen, my friend, I'm telling you straight out, if you haven't brought the rest by ten o'clock tomorrow, I won't be responsible. The rules say that I should hand you over to the police this instant, but since you're still just a boy, I'll pardon you. Otherwise, you know that when it comes to government business I don't show any sort of consideration. If my brother or son were in your place, I'd treat them the same way, or rather even more severely. Even so, I'm treating you very leniently. If I had the money, I'd give it to you, but you know my circumstances. I don't have any debt of course, but I don't lend to anyone, and I don't borrow from anyone. It'll be a bad thing if the money doesn't appear tomorrow. Even my friendship won't save you from the clutches of the police. I've done my duty according to my friendship today, or else you'd be in handcuffs right now.'

Handcuffs! This word pierced Rama's chest like an arrow. He trembled from head to foot. His eyes filled with tears as he imagined this calamity. He went very slowly to his chair with his head bowed like a condemned prisoner and sat down, but that terrible word resounded again and again in his heart.

Dark heavy clouds had overspread the sky, and the sun was nowhere to be seen. Was he too shut up in a prison of clouds? Were there handcuffs on his hands too?

## 20

When Rama left the office that evening, Ramesh Babu came running after him and enjoined him to bring him the money the next day. Rama was internally convulsed with anger. You've become the very epitome of righteousness, have you? You damned hypocrite! If you were to be in a fix you'd run around licking other people's boots, but when it comes to me you suddenly become an idealist. These are all toothless threats! When your time comes, may you die slowly!

After walking a little further he began to think he should go to Ratan once more. There was no one else from whom he had any hope of getting money. When he reached her bungalow, she was sitting on a round platform in her garden. Near her sat a Gujarati jeweller who was taking one beautiful ornament after another from his trunk and displaying them. When she saw Rama she was quite pleased. 'Come, Babu Sahab, see what wonderful things Sethji has brought. See how beautiful this necklace is; he says it costs twelve hundred rupees.'

Rama taking the necklace in his hand, looked at it and said, 'Yes, it certainly seems to be a good piece.'

'You're asking a very high price,' said Ratan to the jeweller.

'Madam,' said the jeweller, 'If someone gives you a necklace like this for any less than two thousand, I'll pay any penalty you say. This piece cost me twelve hundred to have made.'

'Don't say that, Sethji,' said Rama smiling. 'You'll have to pay the penalty.'

'Babu Sahab,' said the Gujarati, 'you can get a necklace just like this for even a hundred rupees, and with even more brilliance, but you ought to judge its worth properly. I didn't bargain with you; bargaining is for novices, not for you. We aren't mere tradespeople, Babu Sahab. We observe people's natures, and the lady here has displayed a very noble nature indeed!'

'Bring the price down a little, Sethji,' said Ratan, looking at the necklace in distress. 'You practically swore you would.'

'Don't even mention bringing the price down, madam. This piece is a present for you.'

'OK,' said Ratan. 'Now please tell me something. What's the very least you'll take?'

'Twelve hundred rupees and twelve cowries, your honour,' said the jeweller somewhat maliciously. 'I swear to you I'll sell it for fifteen hundred right here in this city, and what's more, I'll be sure to tell you who bought it.'

As he said this, the jeweller took out the case for the necklace. Ratan was certain that he wouldn't reduce the price now. Like an impatient child Ratan said, 'You're putting away that necklace as if you're afraid the evil eye will fall on it.'

'What am I supposed to do! When the worth of such a piece is not appreciated even in such a distinguished gathering, I feel quite upset.'

Ratan went inside and summoning Rama said, 'Do you think he'll come down a little more?'

'I don't think the thing is worth more than a thousand,' said Rama.

'Ugh, probably! I've got just six hundred rupees with me. If you can manage with four hundred, I'll buy it. He's going to Banaras by the very next train, and he won't agree to credit. Vakil has gone to some meeting, and won't be back before nine or ten o'clock. I'll give the money back to you tomorrow.'

'Believe me, I'm completely broke,' said Rama, feeling very embarrassed. 'I came to ask *you* for some money. I need it very badly. Give me your money and I'll get some nice necklace from around here for you. I'm sure you can get one like this for seven or eight hundred.'

'Go on, you're not going to take me in again. You couldn't get a bracelet made in six months, so where are you going to get a necklace? I've looked around in several shops. Even if such a piece might turn up, or even if it didn't, you'd have to give half again as much around here.'

'So why don't you have him come tomorrow? If he really needs to sell his stuff, he'll stay today.'

'OK,' said Ratan. 'Let's see what he says.'

They both left the room and went back outside. 'Why don't you come tomorrow morning at eight o'clock?' said Rama to the jeweller.

'No, huzur. I have to meet with three or four important people in Banaras tomorrow. If I don't go today, I'll lose a lot.'

'I've got six hundred with me just now,' said Ratan. 'Give me the necklace, please, and take the rest of the money when you get back from Banaras.'

'It wasn't the money,' said the jeweller. 'I usually take it over a month or two. But you can't rely on out-of-province people like me. We're here today and gone tomorrow; who knows when or where we'll return? Give me a thousand now and two hundred later, please.'

'There won't be any deal then,' said Rama.

'That's your privilege,' said the jeweller. 'But I can tell you this much, you won't get a deal like this again.'

'If you've got the money, you can get lots of stuff,' said Rama.

'Sometimes even if you've got the price, you can't find good stuff,' said the jeweller, put the necklace in its case, and began to pack up his trunk as if he didn't intend to remain a moment longer.

Ratan was straining every nerve to listen, like some prisoner standing to hear the judge's decision about his fate. All the affection of her heart, all the passion of that affection, and all the impatience, longing, and effort of that passion, were centred on that necklace as if her very life had hidden itself among the beads, as if the amassed desires of her past and future lives were hovering over it. When she saw the jeweller's trunk closing, she began to writhe like a fish out of water. She opened chests, she opened drawers, but nowhere did she find money.

All at once she heard the sound of an automobile, and looked towards the gate. Vakil Sahab was coming. He stopped the car near the veranda and came towards them. Ratan got off the platform and said, 'You told me you'd be back at nine.'

'We didn't have a quorum there, so what could I do just sitting around? No one really wants to do any work; they all just want to get a good reputation for nothing. Is this some jeweller?'

The jeweller rose and salaamed.

Vakil Sahab said to Ratan, 'Well, did you find anything you liked?'

'Yes, a necklace I like. He's asking twelve hundred for it.'

'Is that all! Look for something else you like. You don't have anything nice for your head.'

'All I want right now is the necklace. Who wears things on their heads these days?'

'Take something and keep it with you; you'll wear it some time. If you don't, you'll see others wearing something like it and say to yourself, "If I had one, I'd wear it too."'

Vakil Sahab loved Ratan like a father, not like a husband. Like an affectionate father at a fair who brings his sons toys after asking them over and over again what they would like, he too would bring toys for Ratan as soon as she said something. What else did he have to please her with besides his wealth? He needed some sort of foundation for his life—a living foundation with whose support he could stand erect in the struggle of life even in his decrepit condition, much as a worshipper needs an image of his deity. Without an image, what will he strew flowers on, what will he bathe with holy Ganges water, what will he give delicious things to? Vakil Sahab needed a wife in exactly the same way. For him, Ratan was merely an embodied figment of his imagination with which he could quench his spiritual thirst. Perhaps without Ratan his life would have been as empty as a face without eyes.

Ratan took the necklace from the case, showed it to Vakil Sahab and said, 'He's asking twelve hundred rupees for it.'

In the eyes of Vakil Sahab the value of money lay in its power to give pleasure. If Ratan liked the necklace, he didn't care what its price turned out to be. He took out his cheque book, and looking towards the jeweller, asked, 'Tell me the truth, now, how much shall I write it for? If there's any difference between its real worth and what you're asking, you'll know.'

The jeweller looked at the necklace as he turned it back and forth, and said hesitatingly, 'Write it for eleven hundred and fifty.' Vakil Sahab wrote the cheque and gave it to him, and he, giving a salaam, departed.

Ratan's face was glowing with joy, now, like spring in all its natural glory. Never before had such pride, such rapture appeared on her face. It was as if she had just received all the riches of the world. She fastened the necklace around her neck and went inside. Vakil Sahab's views and conduct were a curious mixture of the old and the new; he still wouldn't take any food from anyone's hand, even a Brahman's. Today Ratan cooked especially nice dishes for him. How else could she show her gratitude?

Rama sat for a while listening to Vakil Sahab singing his song in praise of Europe. At last, despairing, he left.

# 21

If anyone had wanted to see the very embodiment of the saddest, most hopeless, most worry-consumed being in the whole world just then, he should have looked at the young man pedalling his cycle in front of Alfred Park. If Rama had seen some deadly snake at that moment, he would have welcomed it with open arms and drunk its poison like nectar. Nectar could not protect him now, only poison. Only death could bring an end to his cares. But could death save him from infamy too? As soon as morning came, the news would spread from house to house—he had embezzled government money, and when caught, had taken his life. What good would it be to be free of his worries if even after death he'd bring ridicule and disgrace to his family? But what other recourse did he have?

If he went to Jalpa and related the whole story to her, she'd certainly show him some sympathy. No matter how sad she would be, Jalpa would not hesitate for even an instant to strip off her jewellery and give it to him. By pawning her jewels, he could make good the government money he'd taken. He'd have to reveal his secrets, though; there was no other way.

Rama set out for home with his mind made up. But his pace lacked the quickness which is a sign of mental enthusiasm.

When he arrived home, however, he thought that since he had to do this anyway, what was the hurry? He'd ask her for them whenever he wanted to. He spent some time in casual conversation, ate, and lay down. Suddenly it came to him that there was no reason he couldn't make off with something on the sly. He'd done just that once already to save the family honour. Why couldn't he save his own life in the same way? Perhaps he'd never be able to tell Jalpa by himself how great the disaster was. He'd be lying here till morning at this rate, going back and forth like this. And then he wouldn't have a chance to say anything.

But he began to have misgivings that Jalpa might open her eyes while he was taking something. Then he'd have no other recourse than to go drown himself in the Triveni. Whatever happened, he'd have to make the attempt once. Slowly he moved Jalpa's hand from off his chest and stood up. He had thought that Jalpa would be roused from sleep as soon as her hand was moved, but realized this had only been a misapprehension. Now he had to remove the bunch of keys from the pocket of her jacket. There was no time to be lost. Even in sleep the lower levels of consciousness continue to carry out their work. No matter how deeply a child may be sleeping, it wakes as soon as its mother gets up from the bed.

But when he bent over to take out the keys, he saw that Jalpa was smiling. He drew back his hand abruptly, and in the feeble light of the lamp, gazed at her face, which seemed lost in some pleasant dream. Oh! Was he supposed to betray this guileless creature in such a way? Could he be so treacherous to one for whom he could give up his own life? It was as if Jalpa's artless loving heart was outlined in her lovely face. Ah! What would be her state when she learnt that her jewels had been stolen again? She'd collapse in despair, she'd tear out her hair. How could he endure her agony? What kind of comfort had he ever bestowed on her? If she'd married someone else, she'd have been loaded with jewels by now. A bad fate had brought her to this house where there was no happiness, but rather, even more sorrow.

Just as Rama lay down on the bed again, Jalpa's eyes opened. 'Where have you been?' she asked, looking at his face. 'I was having a really good dream. There was a big garden, and we two were strolling around in it. Suddenly you disappeared God knows where, and a sadhu came and stood in front of me, looking just like one of the gods. "My child, I've come to grant you a boon," he said to me. "Ask whatever you want!" I looked all over for you to find out what I should ask for, but you were nowhere to be seen. I searched through the whole garden, I peered among the trees, but who knows where you had gone. That's it; just then I woke up and I didn't get to ask for my boon!'

'What would you have asked for?' asked Rama smiling.

'Whatever I felt like; why should I tell you?'

'No, tell me. Maybe you asked for a lot of money.'

'Maybe you think money's something important. I don't think it's anything at all.'

'Well, I think living without money is worse than dying. If I could catch some god, I wouldn't let him go without getting a lot of money. I don't want to put up a golden wall, and I have no wish to become a Rockefeller or a Carnegie. I just want enough so that we won't have to suffer from the lack of the ordinary necessities of life. If some god would give me just five hundred thousand, I wouldn't ever ask him for anything again. How many rich men, merchants, and landholders are there even in our poor country who spend five hundred thousand in a year, or even in a month? I'm ready to live seven lifetimes on that amount, but no one gives me even this much. What would you ask for? Really nice jewellery?'

Jalpa frowned. 'Why are you provoking me! Do I dote on jewels more than other women? I've never pestered you for them. If you need them, then take them away today; I'll give them gladly.'

Smiling, Rama said, 'So why don't you tell me what boon you'd ask?'

'I'd ask that my lord and master should keep on loving me forever, and never turn away from me.'

Rama laughed. 'Do you have doubts about that too?'

'Even if you were a god I'd have doubts; you are a man, after all. I never met any woman who didn't have a sad story to tell about the harshness of her husband. For a year or two husbands show lots of affection, and then for no particular reason they seem to lose interest in their wives. Their hearts begin to be fickle. There's no greater calamity than this for a woman. What other boon would I ask for than to be saved from this?'

As she said this, Jalpa threw her arms around her husband's neck, and gazing at him with love-filled eyes, said, 'Tell me truly; do you still want me just like you used to want me? See that you tell me the truth, now! Speak!'

Embracing Jalpa tightly, Rama said, 'Millions of times more than before!'

Jalpa laughed. 'A lie! A total lie! A one hundred per cent lie!'

'You forced me to lie. How'd you find out anyway?'

'I look through my eyes, how else could I find out? You swore we'd be equal partners. But look at you, you keep as quiet as a mouse. If you loved me you'd trust me. How can you even have love without trust? You can't love someone whom you can't tell about the worst that happens to you. Oh yes, you can enjoy yourself with someone like that, play around with her, just like you could if you went to some prostitute. People go to prostitutes to take pleasure, not to say what's in their hearts. That's just the way it is with us. Tell me, yes or no? Why are you looking away? Don't I see that you come home upset about something these days? When we talk about things, I see that your mind is somewhere else. I see that you don't enjoy your food at all either. You pay no attention to whether the dal is thick or thin, whether there are too many or too few vegetables, or whether the rice is cooked enough. You eat as if it's forced labour and then run off in a hurry. How could I not see all this? As if I shouldn't see it! I'm just a plaything; that's how you see me. My work is to give you enjoyment, to play with you, to pleasure you. What should your worries mean to me? But God didn't give me a heart like that. What can I do? When life is passing me by, when I'm just an object of pleasure for you, why should I bury myself in troubles for your sake? That's how I think now.'

Jalpa had never opened her heart to Rama before. He would never have guessed that she was so thoughtful. In reality, he had considered her just a beautiful young woman. Like other men, he too saw his wife in only this aspect. He was entranced by her youthful curves. He had never even tried to look into the essence of her soul. Perhaps he thought she didn't even have a soul. If she hadn't had an abundance of beauty and charm, perhaps he wouldn't even have cared to talk with her. All his attraction to her, all his devotion to her, was based on her appearance. He had thought that this was just what pleased Jalpa. He hadn't wanted to depress her with the weight of his own worries. But today he learned that Jalpa was just as reflective as he was himself. He had an excellent opportunity to blurt out his mental torment just then, but alas for his hesitation and embarrassment! He held his tongue once more. How could he now speak about those matters he had kept hidden for so long? Wouldn't doing so be to assent to Jalpa's accusations? Yes, today the veil of confusion had been lifted from his eyes, and he had learned that trying to create love from sexual enjoyment was only his ignorance.

Lost in these thoughts, Rama finally fell asleep. It was past midnight by then. He had gone to sleep with the intention of rising early in the morning, but when his sleep broke, the sun's rays were streaming into the room to awaken him. He rose quickly, and without even washing his hands and face, dressed, and got ready to go out. He wanted to go to Ramesh Babu's. Now he'd have to tell his story. When Ramesh became acquainted with the whole situation, he'd be prepared to help a little.

Jalpa was preparing the meal. Seeing Rama leaving like this, she gazed at him enquiringly. It was as if worry, fear, indecision, and violence were sitting on his face and glaring out fiercely. For an instant she was nearly beside herself with worry. With a knife in one hand and a bitter gourd in the other, she stood staring towards the door. What was the matter? Why didn't he tell her? Even if she couldn't do anything else, she could offer him sympathy. It occurred to her to call out and ask him what was wrong. She even got up and went to the door, but Rama had already gone far down the street. She noticed that he was walking very quickly, and looking neither left nor right, as if he were obsessed with something. He was tearing along with his head bowed, bumping into passers-by, and paying no attention to all the pushcarts. At last she returned and began cutting up vegetables again, but her mind remained fixed in the direction her husband had gone. What was the matter? Why did he hide so much from her?

When Rama reached Ramesh's house it was past eight o'clock. The Babu Sahab was sitting on his bed meditating. When he saw Rama he gestured him to sit. When his meditation finished after a good half an hour, he said, 'Haven't you even washed your hands and face yet? I don't like this slackness. Whatever else you do or don't do, keep your body clean. What's happened? Have you made some arrangement for the money?'

'It's just because I'm so worried about it that I came to see you.'

'You're a strange one. Are you ashamed to talk to your father? It's not that he won't give you a tongue-lashing, but you'd be freed from this trouble. Tell him everything straight out. Accidents like this happen all the time. What's there to be afraid of? If you don't want to, I'll go tell him.'

'If I were going to tell him, I'd have told him by now. Can't you make some arrangement?'

'Of course I could, but I don't intend to. I don't have any sympathy for someone like you. When you can tell me, why can't you tell him? Mind what I tell you. Go tell him. If he won't give you the money, *then* come to me.'

Rama didn't have the courage to say anything more. How

could people be so harsh in spite of being so close! He got up and left, but nothing came to mind. He was in the same condition as raindrops which fall from the sky into a capricious breeze. He'd walk ten steps forward quickly, then stop to think, then take five or ten steps back. He'd go down this lane and then down that.

Suddenly something occurred to him. Why not write a letter to Jalpa informing her of all his difficulties? He couldn't manage to utter anything from his mouth, but he saw no difficulty in writing something with a pen. He'd write a letter, give it to her, and then go sit in the outer room. What could be simpler than this? He hurried home, and immediately wrote this letter:

My dear one, how shall I tell you about the disaster I'm trapped in? If I can't arrange for three hundred rupees within one hour, there'll be handcuffs on my wrists. I tried hard to get a loan from somebody, but I couldn't find anyone anywhere. If you'd give me one or two of your pieces of jewellery, I could pawn them and take care of things. Whenever I get some money, I'll redeem them. If I hadn't been compelled to do this, I wouldn't have troubled you. For God's sake don't be angry. I'll redeem them quickly ...

He hadn't yet finished the letter when Ramesh Babu came smiling, sat down, and said, 'Have you spoken to him?'

Rama hung his head and said, 'I haven't got the chance yet.'

'So you'll get a chance in a few days? I'm afraid that you'll leave here empty-handed today, and a real disaster will take place!'

'When I've decided to ask him, what's the worry now!'

'If you get a chance today, go see Ratan please. I particularly stressed this the other day, but it seems you forgot.'

'I haven't forgotten, I'm ashamed to tell her.'

'You're afraid to tell your father and Ratan too. If you weren't so bashful with your own people, would we be in this fix today?'

When Ramesh Babu left, Rama thrust the letter in his pocket and went inside determined to give it to Jalpa. Jalpa was about to go visit a woman friend; an invitation had come only a short while before. She was wearing her most beautiful sari. The inlaid bracelet on her arm, and the chandrahar around her neck looked splendid. She was standing before the mirror putting on ear-rings. When she saw Rama she said, 'Where did you go this morning? You didn't even wash your hands and face. You stay away the whole day; you're only home in the mornings and evenings. When you're not here the house seems very empty. Just now I was thinking that if I had to go to my parents' house, should I go or not? I wouldn't enjoy it there at all.'

'You're about to go out somewhere?'

'Sethaniji has invited me, I'll go this afternoon.'

Rama's state just then was something like that of a hunter who sees a doe frolicking with her fawns, puts his levelled rifle back on his shoulder, and becomes entranced in watching the sport of affection and motherly love.

Seeing him staring fixedly at her Jalpa smiled and said, 'Look here, don't give me the evil eye! I'm very afraid of your eyes.'

In a single bound Rama left the real world and reached the world of imagination and poetry. At a time like this when every fibre of Jalpa's body was dancing with joy, was he going to give her his letter and crush her happy fancies? Was he some heartless fowler to draw a knife across the throat of a warbling songbird? Was he some crass lout to tear off a morning flower and trample it beneath his feet? Rama was not that heartless, not that crass. He was incapable of doing such an injury to Jalpa. No matter what calamities might fall on his head, no matter how much disgrace might come to him, no matter if his very life might be ground to bits, he couldn't be so cruel. Lost in devotion, he said, 'I won't give you the evil eye, just clasp you to my heart.' With this one sentence, all worries, all obstacles melted away. He offered himself up as a sacrifice on the altar of the timidity of love. In the face of this disgrace, all the other afflictions of life were insignificant. His condition just now was something like that of a child, who unable to bear the momentary pain of lancing an abscess, forgets all his fears of its bursting and becoming a running sore, and about his being bedridden for years, or perhaps even dying.

When Jalpa started to go downstairs, Rama became so agitated that he hugged her and squeezed her over and over as if he'd never have this good fortune again. Who knew whether this might not be their very last embrace? He clung to her as if he were one of the thousands of silk threads of her clothing. He was like a dying miser clutching the key to his treasury in a fist closing tighter minute by minute. If his fist should be forcibly opened would he not expire on the spot?

All at once Jalpa said, 'Give me a little money, I might need some.'

Startled, Rama said, 'Money! You don't have any money just now?'

'I do, I do, but you're making excuses. Just give me two rupees, I don't need any more!'

And putting her hand in Rama's pocket, she pulled out some money and with it, the letter.

Reaching out, Rama tried to snatch away the letter from her hand, saying, 'Give me that piece of paper, it's a government document.'

'Whose letter is it? Are you going to tell me?'

Jalpa folded it, but then opening the scrap of paper, said, 'This is a government document! What a lie! You wrote it ...'

'Give it to me, why are you giving me so much trouble?'

Rama tried to snatch it again, but Jalpa putting her hands behind her back, said, 'I won't give it back before I read it, that's that. If you keep insisting, I'll tear it up.'

'All right, tear it up.'

'Then I'll read it for sure,' and she took two steps backwards, opened the letter again, and began to read.

Rama made no further attempt to snatch it away. It seemed to him that the sky had split in two and some terrible creature was coming towards him to swallow him up. He tumbled noisily down the stairs and left the house. Where could he hide now? His condition was that of a man who finds himself naked. He was naked even though he was clothed from head to foot. Ah! Everything was out in the open! All his twists and turns were revealed. Everything he'd tried to conceal all these days, which he'd endured so many difficulties to keep hidden, had today smeared itself like soot all over his face. He couldn't bear seeing his ruination with his own eyes. It would be easier to die rather than hear Jalpa's sobbing, his father's upbraiding, and the neighbours' malicious whispering. When he was no longer alive, who would say anything to him! Who would give a damn about him! His whole life was being destroyed for a mere three hundred rupees. But what could he do if it was God's wish? His life wouldn't be worth living after being disgraced in the eyes of his loved ones!

How worthless, how treacherous, how deceitful, how idly

boastful he must appear to Jalpa now! How could he face her?

Wasn't there somewhere in this world where he could begin a new life, where he could avoid everyone and live out his days, where he could hide so that the police could never find him? Where was such a place except in the depths of the Ganges? If he stayed alive, he'd surely be caught within a month or two. What would it be like for him then—he'd be standing in a court, fettered and handcuffed! A group of police would be riding herd on him. Everyone in town would come to watch the show, Jalpa and Ratan too. His father, his relatives, his friends, intimates and strangers, would all be watching the spectacle of his misery with varying emotions. No, he wouldn't defile his honour like that, he wouldn't. Far better to drown himself!

But then something occurred to him; who would look after Jalpa? Dear God, he'd be drowning her along with himself! His father and mother would bear up somehow or other. But who would take care of her? Couldn't he hide himself away some-where? Couldn't he live unknown in some little village far away from the city? It was possible that some day Jalpa would take pity on him, would pardon his offences. It was even possible that he might become wealthy. But it was impossible that he could ever stand before her and look her straight in the eye. There was no telling what state she might be in now. Perhaps she'd understood the purpose of his letter. Perhaps she'd learned something about his situation. Perhaps she'd shown the letter to his mother, and was searching for him in a panic. Perhaps she'd sent the boys to call his father. She must be looking for him everywhere. Pray God no one would come here. Just now he was perhaps more frightened of meeting an acquaintance, than of facing death. He kept looking vigilantly ahead and behind as he hurried along in the burning sun without any idea of where he was going. All at once he started as he heard the whistle of a train. My God, had he come so far? The train was right in front of him. He was seized with an overwhelming desire to take a seat, as if once he'd sat down he'd be freed from all his difficulties, but he had no money in his pocket. There was a ring on his finger. Summoning one of the head coolies he said, 'Can you get this ring sold some-where? I'll give you a rupee. I've got to go by this train. I left home with some money, but it seems I dropped it somewhere. If I go back I'll miss the train and suffer a very big loss.'

The head coolie looked him up and down, took the ring, and went inside the station. Rama paced up and down by the ticket office, staring in the direction the coolie had gone. Ten minutes went by and he was nowhere to be seen. He wouldn't take the ring and disappear, would he? He went inside the station and began to search. He inquired about him from another coolie, who asked, 'What's his name?' Rama bit his tongue. He hadn't even asked his name. What could he say? In the meantime the train blew its whistle again, and Rama became panicky. He realized that the head coolie had tricked him. He entered the train and sat down without any ticket. He decided that he'd say straight out that he had no ticket. Even if he was made to get off, he'd be at least ten or twenty miles away from here.

When the train started, Rama began to feel tearful about his plight. Dear God, he didn't even know whether fate would bring him back or not. When would he ever have happy days again? Those days were gone, gone for good. One day he'd die hiding himself away from the whole world. No one would even shed tears over his dead body. Even his own family would have shed all their tears for him and become resigned by then. Just because of a little embarrassment, he found himself in this situation. If he'd told Jalpa his true state of affairs from the very beginning, he wouldn't have been forced to run away in disgrace today. But how could he have told her without her feeling wretched? Whatever else might be the case, at least he'd kept Jalpa happy for a few days. He hadn't allowed her longings to be killed. Even this little was more than enough for Rama to feel satisfaction now.

The train had not been underway even ten minutes when the door opened and the ticket collector entered. Rama turned pale. The collector would be with him in a moment. He'd be humiliated in front of all these people. His heart began to pound. The closer the ticket collector approached the more rapidly his pulse beat. At last the calamity was upon him. 'Your ticket?' said the official.

Coming to himself a little Rama said, 'My ticket ended up with the head coolie. I gave him some money to bring my ticket, but who knows where he went?'

The collector was not convinced. 'I don't know anything about that,' he said. 'You'll have to get off at the next station. Where are you going?'

'It's a very long trip, I have to go to Calcutta.'

'Please get your ticket at the station ahead, if you don't mind.'

'That's just the problem. I had twenty-five rupees with me. There was a big crowd at the ticket window. I gave the money to the head coolie to bring me a ticket, but he disappeared and never came back. Maybe you know him. He was pretty tall with a pockmarked face.'

'You can put something in writing about this, but you can't travel without a ticket.'

Humbly, Rama said, 'My friend, how can I hide anything from you? I don't have any more money with me. Do whatever you think is suitable.'

'I'm sorry, sir. I'm bound to follow the rules.'

The travellers in the compartment began to whisper among themselves. It was a third-class compartment and most of its occupants were labourers travelling east in search of work. They were enjoying seeing a member of the white-collar species being shamed like this. If the ticket collector had given Rama a good thump and tossed him out, perhaps they would have been even more pleased. Rama had never been so embarrassed. He stood silently with bowed head. This new journey in his life had barely begun. Who knew what other disasters he'd have to experience in the future, or at whose hands he'd have to be deceived? It occurred to him to leap from the train, that to die would be better than to live in this terrible mess. His eyes filled with tears, and putting his head through the open window he began to cry.

All at once an elderly man who had been sitting next to him asked, 'Where are you going in Calcutta, Babuji?'

Thinking that this rustic was making fun of him, Rama flared up. 'What's it to you where I go?'

Paying not the slightest attention to this contempt, the old man said, 'I'm going there too. You and I will go together.' Then he said gently, 'Take the money for the ticket from me. You can pay me back there.'

Rama looked at him carefully now. He was a man of sixty or seventy, so lean that his flesh had practically melted away from his bones. His moustache and hair were shaved. He had no other baggage than one small bundle.

Seeing Rama gazing at him, he spoke again, 'Are you going to get down at Howrah or are you going somewhere else?'

Rama, subdued by a strong sense of gratitude, said, 'Babu, I'll get down at the next stop. After I've made arrangements for money, I'll continue my trip.'

'How much do you need? I'm going there myself. You can give it back when you like. You're not likely to take five or ten rupees from me and then run away. Where's your home?'

'I live right here in Prayag.'

The old man said with loving reverence, 'Blessings on Prayag! Blessings! I've just come from a sacred bath at the Triveni. It's truly a city where the gods live. So how much should I give you?'

Shrinking with embarrassment Rama said, 'Please understand that I won't be able to pay you back while we're travelling.'

'Hey, Babuji,' said the old man unaffectedly, 'you're hardly going to take five or ten rupees from me and disappear. I've seen how the pandaas of Prayag give money to pilgrims without writing anything down. Is ten rupees enough for what you need to do?'

'Yes, that's more than enough,' said Rama, bowing his head.

Rama gave his fare to the ticket collector and thought to himself, 'What a simple, benevolent, honest soul this old man is. How many people among those they call cultivated would come to the rescue of an unknown traveller?' The other passengers too started looking at the old man with veneration.

From the old man's conversation Rama learnt that he was from the Khatik caste, and that he had a vegetable shop in Calcutta. Although originally from Bihar, he had been earning his living in Calcutta for forty years. His name was Devidin, and he had been wanting to go on a pilgrimage for a long time. He was just returning from a journey to the sacred city of Badrinath in the Himalayas.

'You've just come from Badrinath?' asked Rama in surprise. 'The mountain slopes are very steep there.'

'If God is gracious, then everything can happen, Babuji. You just need his grace.'

'You must have children in Calcutta.'

Devidin gave a dry laugh and said, 'All my children are in heaven! I had four sons. Two got married. All of them left, and I'm left sitting by myself, even though all of them were born because of me. The farmer himself harvests the seed he's sown.'

He laughed again. After a little while he said, 'The old woman is still alive. We'll see which of us goes first. She says she'll go first, I say I'll go first; we'll see who wins. If possible, I'll show you myself. She still wears jewellery, sits in the shop wearing gold earrings and a gold necklace. When I said we should go on a pilgrimage, she asked if she was supposed to ruin the business for my pilgrimage. That's the way life is. Whether she dies today or tomorrow, she's not going to leave the shop. There's no one left ahead of us and no one left behind us, there's no one to laugh or cry with us, but she still keeps up the illusion. Even now she keeps wearing one or another piece of jewellery. Who knows when she will get her fill of it. It's the same story in every home. Wherever you look it's the same cry—for God's sake jewellery! For God's sake jewellery! Give up your life running after jewellery; starve the people of your household, sell the things in your home. Sell even your honour—how long shall I go on? Everyone's caught the same disease, the great and the small, the rich and the poor. Where do you work in Calcutta, bhai?'

'This is the first time I'm going,' said Rama. 'I'll see if I can get some job or other.'

'Then stay with me. There's two rooms, a veranda in front, and a little room upstairs. If I sold the house today I'd get ten thousand. I'll let you have one room. You can get your own place when you find some work. I ran away from home fifty years ago and came to Howrah. I've seen both good times and bad times since then. Now I implore God to take me. Oh yes, and to make the old lady an immortal. But no, who'll take her shop, her house, her jewellery?'

Devidin laughed again. He was so jovial, so contented that Rama wondered at him. He laughed at inconsequential things. He laughed where others would cry. Rama had never seen even a young man who laughed like this. He'd told his life story in a very little while. How many jokes he knew too. It seemed as if he'd been an acquaintance of Rama's for years. Rama was obliged in his turn to tell a fabricated story about himself.

'So you've run away from home too?' said Devidin. 'I under-stand. There must have been a family quarrel. Your wife must have said, "I don't have any jewellery, what a wretched fate." Your mother and your wife probably didn't get on well, and you felt even more depressed hearing them squabble.'

'Yes, Babu, that's exactly it. How did you know?'

Devidin laughed and said, 'It's a very powerful magical spell and it's invoked on the skull of a Teli. You don't have any children yet, do you?'

'No, not yet.'

'You must have younger brothers.'

'Yes, Dada,' said Rama, astonished. 'You're right. How did you know?'

Devidin guffawed again. 'It's all a game using spells. Your in-laws are wealthy, I think?'

'Yes Dada. They certainly are.'

'But they're not very bold.'

'You said it, Dada. They've very timid. They haven't even called their daughter home since the wedding.'

'I understand, brother, that's the way of the world. People will steal and beg for their sons, but for daughters there's nothing at all.'

Rama hadn't slept for three days. All day he'd wandered around distractedly in search of money, and all night he'd lain tormented by worry. As he was talking now he began to feel sleepy. His neck bowed and his eyes began to blink. Devidin quickly opened his bundle, took out some cotton matting, and spreading it on the seat said, 'Lie down here, Bhaiya. I'll sit in your place.'

Rama lay down. Devidin looked at him again and again with love-filled eyes as if he were his son just returned from somewhere abroad.

## 22

When Rama had left the room and gone tearing down the stairs, Jalpa had not the slightest suspicion that he was running away from home. She read the letter. She flared up and felt like going and giving Rama a real talking to. Lying and deceiving her like this! But her mood changed in a moment. God forbid that they'd spent government money. Maybe she'd given Ratan government money on that day. As soon as she thought of this, she became angry again. Why had he concealed so much from her? Why had he boasted so much to her? Did he think she didn't even know that there were both rich and poor people in the world? Was every last woman loaded down with jewellery? Was not wearing any jewels a sin? Money for more important things had been used to have jewellery made. You didn't wear jewels at the expense of your stomach and body, or at the expense of committing theft or being dishonourable! Did he think she was so worthless as that?

She thought Rama must be in his room, so she'd go and ask him which jewels he wanted. As she guessed how terrible the situation was fear began to take the place of her anger. She rushed downstairs. She was convinced he must be sitting there waiting for her. But when she entered the room he was nowhere to be seen. His cycle was there, and she peered out of the door immediately. But he was nowhere to be seen on the street either. Where had he gone? Both boys had gone to school. Who could she send to call Rama? An unfamiliar apprehension began to steal into her heart. She dashed back upstairs, took off her necklace and bracelets and bound them up in a handkerchief, went downstairs again, went out on to the street, took a tonga and told the driver, 'Go to the customs office.' She began to repent that she had delayed so long. Why hadn't she taken off her jewellery and given it to Rama right away?

On the way to the office she kept watching attentively left and right. Could he have come so far in such a short time? Perhaps because he was late he'd taken a tonga too today; otherwise she'd surely have met him by now. She asked the driver, 'Tell me, did you see a gentleman going somewhere in a tonga just now?'

'Yes madam,' said the driver. 'I saw a gentleman going in this direction a little while ago.'

Jalpa was somewhat encouraged. She'd arrive just after Rama. Again and again she told the driver to make his horse go faster. It was eleven o'clock by the time she reached the office. Hundreds of people were hurrying here and there. Whom should she ask? How was she to know where he usually sat?

Suddenly a peon appeared. Jalpa summoned him and said, 'Listen, please bring Ramanath Babu here.'

'He's the very person I'm going to fetch,' said the peon. 'Have you just come from his home?'

'Yes, that's just where I've come from. He left home no more than ten minutes ago.'

'He hasn't come here.'

Jalpa was seized with uncertainty. He hadn't come here, she hadn't seen him on the way. Then where had he gone? Her heart began to pound. Her eyes filled with tears. She didn't know anyone else there except the senior clerk, Rama's boss Ramesh. She had never had occasion to speak to him before, but now any bashfulness vanished. Fear suppresses all other emotions. 'Tell the head clerk ... No, I'll come myself,' she said to the peon, 'I have to talk with him.'

The peon, awed by her manner and her dignity, turned around and set off for the head clerk's office. Jalpa followed close on his heels. Ramesh Babu came out as soon as he heard the news of her arrival.

Jalpa stepped forward and said, 'Please excuse me for troubling you, Babu Sahab. He left home fifteen or twenty minutes ago. Hasn't he reached here yet?'

'Well, you're Mrs Ramanath! No, he hasn't reached here yet. But he wasn't in the habit of strolling around during office hours.'

Looking pointedly at the peon, Jalpa addressed Ramesh Babu. 'I have a request to make of you.'

'Come inside and sit down, then. You don't need to keep standing here. I'm surprised he's gone off somewhere. He's probably sitting somewhere playing chess.'

'No, Babuji. I'm worried that he may have gone somewhere else. He wrote a note to me only ten minutes ago.' (She groped in her pocket.) 'Yes, look here's that note. You're well-disposed towards him, he doesn't hide anything from you. Hasn't he lost some government money he was responsible for?'

Surprised, Ramesh said, 'What? Hasn't he told you anything?'

'Not a thing. He's never said one word about this.'

'I just don't understand. He had to get three hundred rupees together today. There were some bank notes which he stuck in his pocket before leaving. Someone pinched the notes while he was in the bazaar.' (Smiling.) 'He doesn't worship some other goddess besides you, does he?'

Jalpa bowed her head in embarrassment. 'If that were one of his shortcomings,' she said, 'then you wouldn't escape this disgrace either. Someone must have taken it from his pocket. He must have said nothing to me out of shame. If he'd told me even a little, I'd have given him some money on the spot without thinking twice about it.'

Ramesh Babu said disbelievingly, 'Is there some money at home?'

'You need three hundred, don't you?' said Jalpa boldly. 'I'll bring it just now.'

'If he comes home, send him here.'

Jalpa went and sat in the tonga again and told the driver to go to the market. She had decided to sell her necklace. In fact, she had several woman friends from whom she could have got money. There is great affection among women. Unlike men, their friendship goes beyond having paan and playing cards together. But she didn't have enough time. When she arrived in the jewel shop area, she began to consider which store she should go to. She was afraid of being cheated. She made a circuit from one end of the market to the other without having the courage to enter any one shop. And time was passing by. At last, seeing an elderly jeweller in one shop, her apprehension diminished. The jeweller was a cunning old rascal; seeing Jalpa's hesitation and vacillation, he understood that he had snared an easy mark.

Showing him the necklace Jalpa asked, 'Can you take this?'

The jeweller, looking at the piece from this side and that, said, 'If I can make a little profit on it, why wouldn't I take it? But it's not a first-rate piece.'

'It's not first-rate because you're buying, but if you were selling, then it would be.'

'You tell me then.'

The jeweller gave it a price of three hundred and fifty, and gradually came to four hundred. Jalpa was already late; she took the money and left without delay. The very necklace which she had bought so eagerly, the craving for which had been implanted in her since childhood, she now sold for half its price without the slightest regret, but rather with a feeling of joyful self-satisfaction. How pleased Rama would be when he found out that she had come up with the money. If he should go to the office, what a good joke it would be, she was thinking as she arrived at the office again. 'What happened? Did you meet him at home?' said Ramesh Babu looking at her.

'What? He hasn't come here yet? I didn't go home.' As she said this she held out a bundle of notes towards Ramesh Babu.

He counted the notes and said, 'That's good, but where is he now? If he wasn't coming, he'd have written me a letter. I was really in great difficulty. You came in the nick of time. I'm pleased to see how sensible you are. You've done your duty like a true goddess.'

When Jalpa returned to the tonga to go home, she felt that she had increased in stature. A strange energy was coursing through her body. She was sure that Rama must be at home sitting and worrying. She'd go and give him a good scolding first of all, and after she'd made him good and sorry, tell him what she'd done. But when she arrived home, Ramanath was nowhere to be seen.

Jageshwari asked, 'Where did you go in this hot sun?'

'I had something to do. He didn't even eat today. There's no telling where he's gone.'

'He must have gone to the office!'

'No,' said Jalpa. 'He didn't go there. I asked a peon there.'

She went upstairs, put the remaining money in her trunk, and began to fan herself. Her body felt aflame from the heat, but her ear was cocked in the direction of the door. She had not the slightest suspicion that Rama had set out for another part of the country.

She didn't become particularly worried until four o'clock, but as the day began to draw to a close her anxiety began to grow. Finally she climbed up to the highest part of the roof, although no one went there because of its dilapidated condition, and ran her eyes all around, but Rama was not to be seen anywhere.

When Rama had not come home by evening, Jalpa began to be alarmed. Where had he gone? He never went out before coming home from the office. If he'd been at the house of some friend, wouldn't he have returned by now? She didn't know whether or not he even had any money in his pocket. Who knew where the poor fellow might have been wandering around all day. She repented again that she hadn't taken off her necklace and given it to him as soon as she'd read his letter. Why had she remained plunged in indecision? The unfortunate fellow must be avoiding home out of shame. Where could he go, whom could he ask for help?

When the lamps were lit she could contain herself no longer. Maybe Ratan would know something. But when she went to her friend's bungalow she learned that Rama had not gone there at all that day.

Jalpa carefully searched through all the parks and grounds where she had often used to ramble with Rama. She returned discouraged around nine o'clock. She had been able to restrain her tears until now, but as soon as she set foot inside and realized that he had not yet come, she sat down and gave way to despair. Now her misgiving that he had fled somewhere became a certainty. Still she had some hope that he might have come and gone while she had been out. She went and asked Jageshwari, 'Did he come home, Mother?'

'He must be sitting somewhere with his cronies shooting the breeze,' said Jageshwari. 'Home is like a hotel to him. He left at ten this morning, and I don't yet know where he is.'

'He comes home from the office before he goes out anywhere. He hasn't come home yet today. If you say so, I'll send Gopi Babu to go and see where he's got to.'

'Where could the boys look for him at this hour? There's no telling about him. Keep a lookout for a little while longer, and then keep his food somewhere. How long are we supposed to wait for him anyway!'

Jalpa gave no answer. She said nothing about what had happened at the office. Jageshwari would have panicked and broken out in a storm of tears. Going upstairs and lying down, she started crying over her misfortune. She became so distressed that she felt as if a spike were rising up through her heart. Over and over she asked herself what was she to do if he didn't come back during the night. Where could anyone look for him until there was some word of where he might have gone? Today for the first time she accepted all this as the fruit of her own actions. It was true that she'd never insisted on having ornaments, but neither had she ever clearly forbidden it. If she hadn't become so distracted after the theft of her jewels, this day would never have come. In her weakened state of mind, Jalpa took the greater portion of the blame upon herself. She'd known that Rama took bribes, that he brought home money by hook or by crook. Nevertheless, she had never forbidden him to do this. Why would she have endangered her own interests thus, stuck her foot out from under her own blanket as it were? Why had she thought up excursions and outings every day? Why hadn't she been able to control her delight when she accepted his presents? Now she was taking the sole responsibility for all this, too, upon herself. Ramanath, overpowered by his love, had done everything just to please her. Young men were like that. Then what had she done to protect him? Why hadn't she understood that one day they'd have to suffer the consequences of spending more than their income? How many things she remembered now from which she ought to have recognized Rama's distress, but to which she had never paid attention.

Jalpa lay drowning in these cares for some time. When the sound of the night watchmen's whistles reached her ears, she rose and went downstairs. 'He hasn't come yet,' she said to Jageshwari. 'Please go and eat.'

Jageshwari was sitting and nodding off. Waking with a start she said, 'Where has he gone?'

'He hasn't come yet.'

'Not come yet! It must be midnight. He didn't say anything at all to you when he was leaving?'

'Nothing at all,' said Jalpa.

'You didn't say anything to him?'

'Well, what could I have said?'

'Should I wake up Lalaji then?'

'What could he do if you woke him up now? Why don't you go eat something?'

'I don't feel like eating anything now. I've never heard tell of such an irresponsible boy. Who knows where he's taken himself off to. At least he could have told us he'd be back at such and such a time.'

Jageshwari lay down again, but Jalpa stayed sitting just as she was for the whole night—a night like a mountain whose every moment dragged by like a year.

# 23

A week went by, but no word of Rama. Some people said one thing, and some said another. Poor Ramesh Babu came several times each day to enquire. All kinds of guesses were being made. The only definite information was that Ramanath had gone in the direction of the railway station at eleven o'clock. Munshi Dayanath's opinion, although he didn't express it in so many words, was that Rama had committed suicide. That's what happened in such circumstances. He'd seen several examples of this with his own eyes. Her mother-in-law and father-in-law laid the whole blame on Jalpa. They said right out that he'd lost his life because of her. She had harassed and plagued him. Just ask her why she kept on dreaming up invitations and outings on such a modest income. No one took pity on Jalpa, no one dried her tears. Only Ramesh Babu praised her promptness and keen intelligence. In Munshi Dayanath's eyes though, her action had no worth. Someone who has started a fire cannot be held guiltless because he comes running with water to put it out.

One day Dayanath returned from the library with his head hanging. Since his face was always habitually gloomy, hanging his head in addition made it clear to even a child that he was badly out of sorts.

'What is it?' asked Jageshwari. 'Did you have an argument with someone?'

'No ma'am. I'm plagued by all these people dunning me for payment. Wherever I go they come running to snatch away my money. There's no telling how many debts he's run up. Today I told them right out I didn't know anything and that I'm not going to give them anything. They can go and ask the Memsahab.'

Just then Jalpa showed up and chanced to overhear these words. Her face had changed so much in the past week that one could hardly recognize her. Her eyes had swollen from repeated crying. Hearing these harsh words from her father-in-law she flared up. 'Yes sir! You please send them straight to me. I'll either give them a talking-to or pay them off.'

'What can you pay them with?' asked Dayanath sharply. 'It

comes to thousands. Why, just one of those jewellers is owed seven hundred. How much have you paid him?'

'His jewels are here, they've only been worn three or four times! If he comes, please send him to me. I'll give his things back to him. If he took five or ten rupees as compensation that would be plenty.'

She was about to go upstairs after saying this when Ratan arrived, embraced her, and asked, 'Haven't you heard anything yet?'

To Jalpa these words seemed to be gushing over with affection and sympathy. Here was someone not even related to her but so concerned, while there were her own mother-in-law and father-in-law who had washed their hands of her and turned away from her. Better strangers than these relatives. Her eyes filling with tears she said, 'No sister, I haven't heard anything yet.'

'How did it happen? You didn't have a quarrel, did you?'

'Not at all, I swear. He didn't even mention to me that he'd lost those bank notes. If he'd even hinted at it, I'd have given him the money. When he hadn't come back by afternoon I went to the office looking for him, and that's when I found out he'd lost some bank notes. I went and paid off the money straight away.'

'I understand,' said Ratan. 'He's fallen in love with someone. You'll find out in a few days. If it doesn't turn out as I said, then I'll pay a fine!'

Jalpa, taken aback, said, 'Have you heard anything?'

'No, I haven't heard anything, but it's my best guess!'

'No, Ratan. I can't believe a word of it. Whatever other faults he has, he doesn't have this one. I have no reason to mistrust him.'

Ratan laughed and said, 'These men are experts in this art. How would you know, you poor thing?'

'If they're experts in this art, then we women are no less expert in judging their hearts,' said Jalpa resolutely. 'I can't agree with you. If he is my husband and master, I'm no less his wife and mistress.'

'All right, let it go. Are you going out somewhere? Come, let me take you somewhere.'

'No, I'm not free just now. And then my family here is determined to finish me off, they won't leave me alive. Where were you thinking of going?'

'Nowhere in particular, just to the bazaar,' said Ratan.

'What are you going to get?'

'I wanted to look at a couple of things in a jewellery shop,' said Ratan. 'I want a bracelet like yours. Your husband finally returned my money after several months; now I can look for myself.'

'What's so special about my bracelet? You can get much better ones in the bazaar.'

'I want one just like it.'

'It'll be hard to find someone to make a copy of it, and then getting it finished will be months of trouble. If you don't have the patience to wait, take mine. I'll get another one made.'

Practically dancing with joy, Ratan said, 'Wow! You're giving me your bracelet, what can I say! I'm so happy that I could let everyone know by beating a drum! It cost six hundred, didn't it?'

'Yes, it did, but I had to waste months in the jeweller's shop. I finally got the inlaid work done by sitting there myself. I'll give it to you out of consideration, to save you all that trouble.'

Jalpa took off her bracelet and placed it on Ratan's wrist. Ratan's face showed a peculiar kind of grave radiance, as if a wretched pauper were receiving something precious. For her it was the ultimate limit of personal joy. In a voice filled with gratitude she said, 'I'm ready to give you whatever you ask. I don't want to take advantage of you. Is it worth any less to you because you gave it to me? Just one thing, though. I can't pay you everything right now. Do you have any objection if I give you two hundred rupees later?'

'No objection at all,' said Jalpa resolutely. 'If you feel like it, don't give me anything at all.'

'No, I've got four hundred rupees with me which I'll give you before I go. If I keep them I'll spend them somewhere else. Money simply never stays put in my hands; what can I do? Until I spend it I feel a little worried, as if I've got a load sitting on my head.'

When Jalpa took out the little bracelet box to give to Ratan, she felt a pang in her heart. How happy Rama had been when he saw this bracelet on her wrist. If he were here today, would it leave her hands like this? And then who could know whether it was even her fate to wear a bracelet or not. She made a great effort to control herself, but tears came anyway.

Ratan saw her tears and said, 'Let it be for now, sister. I'll take it later, what's the hurry.'

Jalpa extended the box towards her and said, 'Why? Just because you saw my tears? I'm giving it out of consideration for you. No, it was even more precious to me than my life. When I see you wearing it I'll be consoled. Do this much for me, don't give it to anyone else.'

'Why would I even think of giving it to anyone else? I'll keep it as a remembrance of you. Today after a very long time my heart's desire has been fulfilled. I'm only sorry that your husband isn't here now. I have a feeling that he'll come back quickly. He's just run away because he's ashamed, nothing else. Vakil Sahab was sorry to hear about it too. People say that lawyers are hard-hearted, but I see that when he hears of someone having even a little difficulty he suffers.'

Jalpa smiled and said, 'Sister, can I ask you something? You won't take it the wrong way, now? Is it possible that you're not really fond of Vakil Sahab?'

For a moment Ratan's pleasure-flushed happy face fell as if someone had reminded her of a long-ago love for whose sake she had left off weeping many years ago. 'I never even thought that I'm a young woman and he's an old man, sister,' she said. 'Whatever love, whatever affection there is in my heart, I've dedicated it all to him. Affection doesn't come from youth or beauty or money, it comes from affection itself. He's working so hard, and in his condition, just for me, who else! Is that a small thing? Will you be going out tomorrow? Tell me should I come in the evening?'

'I won't be going anywhere at all, but you must certainly come. We'll entertain ourselves for a little while. Nothing seems right. I can't keep my mind on a thing. I just don't understand why he was so timid about telling me. That's my fault too. He must have seen something in me, which made him feel he had to keep things from me. What really makes me feel sad is that I never earned his true love. You don't keep secrets from someone you love.'

When Ratan got up to leave, Jalpa noticed that the box with the bracelet was lying on the table. 'Take this with you, sister,' she said. 'Why are you going off and leaving it here?'

'I'll take it. What's the rush just now? I haven't even given you all the money.'

'No, no, take it. I won't agree to your leaving without it.'

But Ratan went downstairs and left anyway, leaving Jalpa standing with the bracelet in her hand.

A little later, Jalpa took five hundred rupees out of her trunk, and going to Dayanath said, 'Please take this money, and have it sent to that jeweller, Charan Das. I'll give you the rest of the money very soon.'

'Where did you get the money?' said he, feeling ashamed.

'I sold the bracelet to Ratan,' replied Jalpa without any embarrassment. Dayanath just stared at her face.

## 24

A month went by. A notice appeared regularly in Prayag's biggest daily newspaper, urging Ramanath to return home, and promising a reward of five hundred rupees to anyone who brought news of him. But no news had yet come from anywhere. Jalpa was wasting away from worry and grief. Seeing her condition, even Dayanath began to take pity on her. At last he wrote Dindayal one day: 'Come and take our daughter-in-law home with you for a while.' As soon as Dindayal received the news, he came rushing over, all flustered. But Jalpa refused to go home.

Taken aback, Dindayal said, 'Do you intend to hang around here and die?'

'If I'm to die like this, who can stop it?' said Jalpa in a solemn voice. 'But I'm not going to die yet, Father, believe me. There's no place for unfortunate people like me at home either.'

'But why on earth won't you come? Both of your friends Shahzadi and Vasanti have come. You'll enjoy yourself laughing and talking with them.'

'I can't bring myself to go and leave Father-in-law and Mother alone here. Since it's written in my fate to cry, I'll cry.'

'What actually happened? I hear that there were debts. Some people say that government money was embezzled.'

'Whoever told you that, told an out-and-out lie.'

'Then why did he leave?'

'I don't know a thing about that. I keep having doubts about that myself.'

'He didn't have a fight with Lala Dayanath, did he?'

'He doesn't even raise his head around Lalaji, or even chew paan, so he's hardly going to have a fight with him. He was fond of roaming around. He must have thought no one would let him go off, so he's just run off by himself.'

'Maybe that's just how it was,' said Dindayal. 'Some people have a craze for gallivanting around all over. Tell me straight out whatever troubles you might have here. Should I send you anything for your expenses?'

'I don't have any troubles, Father,' said Jalpa proudly. 'Thanks to you I don't lack for anything.'

Both Dayanath and Jageshwari tried to persuade her, but she wouldn't agree to go. Then Dayanath snapped, 'Well, it's better than lying around here and crying the whole day.'

'Is it a different world over there?' said Jalpa. 'Will I become different by going there? And why should I be afraid to cry? When I had to laugh I laughed; when I have to cry, I cry. Even if he's gone across the ocean, he'll see me sitting here every moment. He's not here himself, but he's here in every single thing in this house. If I leave here, I'll go crazy with despair.'

Dindayal realized that this proud daughter of his was not going to abandon her insistence on remaining. He got up and went out. When he left in the evening, he held out a fifty-rupee note to Jalpa and said, 'Keep this, you might need it.'

Jalpa shook her head and said, 'I don't need it at all, Father. But yes, I would like you to at least give me your blessing. It might be that your blessing will bring me good.'

Dindayal's eyes filled with tears. Leaving the note on the bed where he had been sitting, he went outside.

The month of September was well under way. Fragments of rainless clouds could be seen scuttling across the sky from time to time. Jalpa would lie on the roof and watch the gambols of these cloud fragments. What other object is more enjoyable for beings tormented by anxiety? Cloud fragments take on many different colours, and fill out into many different shapes. Sometimes they come together in love, sometimes they part in a huff; sometimes they tear along, sometimes they come to a dead stop. Jalpa would think to herself that Ramanath too must be sitting somewhere watching the same cloud-play. This fantasy gave her a strange pleasure. A sort of affection grows for these sky-travelling creatures, very similar to the feeling of kinship a gardener has for plants he has grown himself or a child for the play house he has made himself. Our minds turn inwards in distress. Jalpa now began to fear that God had punished her for her misdeeds. Hadn't Ramanath squeezed money out of others every day, after all? No one gave him that money gladly. But how happy she had been to see this money, for from it had regularly come the ornaments and trinkets she had yearned for. Now she felt incensed whenever she saw those things. They were the root cause of all her griefs. Because of them her husband had had to go to another part of the country. They scratched her eyes like thorns, stabbed her heart like spikes.

At last she gathered them all up one day—velvet slippers, silk socks, all kinds of embroidery, ribbons, pins, combs, mirrors—who could have counted them all. They made a wonderful pile. She'd sink this pile in the Ganges and lead a new life from now on. For the sake of these things she was in her present situation. Today she'd wipe out this tangle of illusions once and for all. Although the thought of throwing away so many beautiful things brought pangs of regret, these few drops of water could not begin to extinguish the raging fire of her remorse and disgust. She spent half the night setting them apart one by one, as if she were preparing for some journey. Yes, it was really a journey for her—from darkness to light, from falsehood to truth. She thought to herself that if God should take pity and let Rama return home, then she'd live so that their expenses would be as little as possible. She wouldn't spend a single paisa unnecessarily. She wouldn't let him bring home even a single paisa over his regular wages. Her new life would begin from today.

Right at four in the morning, when the sounds of people coming and going on the streets began to be heard, Jalpa picked up her bag full of things and set out to bathe in the Ganges. The bag was very heavy; it was difficult to walk even ten steps with it hanging from her hand. Again and again she shifted it from one hand to the other. She was also intent that no one should see her. She had never had occasion to carry such a load before. Horse-cart drivers called to her, but she paid them no attention. When her arms could no longer function, she shifted the bag to her back and started walking again with lengthened steps. She drew the edge of her sari well across her face so that no one would recognize her.

She had nearly reached the bathing ghats when it began to be light. All at once she saw Ratan coming in her car. She attempted to bow her head and hide her face, but Ratan recognized her even at a distance. She stopped her car and asked, 'Where are you going, sister? What's that bag on your back?'

Jalpa thrust the sari aside from her face and said confidently, 'I'm going to bathe in the Ganges.'

'I've just come back from bathing, but let's go, I'll come along with you, I'll take you home and then go home myself. Put the bag in here.'

'No, no,' said Jalpa. 'It's not heavy. Go, you'll be late. I'll keep going.'

But Ratan didn't agree. She got out of the car, took the bag and put it inside. 'What have you put in this? It's really heavy. May I open it and see?'

'There's nothing in it worth your seeing.'

But the bag had no lock. When Ratan opened it and looked, she was astonished. 'Where are you going with these things?'

Jalpa sat down inside the car and said, 'I'm going to sink them in the Ganges.'

Even more astonished, Ratan said, 'In the Ganges! You haven't gone a little mad, have you? Come on, let's go home. We'll leave the bag there and then come back.'

Jalpa said firmly, 'No, Ratan, I'll go after I've thrown these things in the river.'

'But after all, why?'

'First drive on, then I'll tell you.'

'No, first tell me.'

'No, that won't do. First drive on.'

Defeated, Ratan drove the car forward and said, 'All right, now will you tell me?'

Jalpa said reproachfully, 'You of all people ought to have understood. Why are you asking me? What use are these things to me now? Whenever I see them I feel pain and grief. When the one person who enjoyed seeing them has gone, what am I supposed to do with them?'

Ratan heaved a deep sigh, grasped Jalpa by the hand, and said in a trembling voice, 'You're doing a great injustice to your husband, sister. How much delight he must have taken in bringing them to you, and how pleased he must have been seeing how splendid they looked on your arms and legs. Each one of them is a memory of his love. By throwing them into the Ganges you are showing him great disrespect!'

For a moment, Jalpa became lost in thought; she began to feel uncertain. But almost instantly she regained control of herself. 'That's not right, sister. My mind won't be at peace until these things are out of my sight. It's this very love of luxury that's caused this calamity of mine. This is a bundle of misfortunes, not of memories of love. His love is engraved on my heart.'

'Your heart is very hard, Jalpa,' said Ratan. 'I probably couldn't do what you're doing.'

'But for me these things are the real reason for all my troubles.'

After a short silence, she spoke again. 'He's done me a great wrong, sister. I consider that any man who keeps things hidden from his wife does not love her. If I'd been in his place, I wouldn't have run away and abandoned everyone like this. I'd have poured out all the pains of my heart, and I'd have done everything according to his advice. How does this deceit come between man and woman?'

Ratan, smiling grimly, said, 'There are probably very few men who open their hearts to a woman. When you yourself hide things in your heart, why do you have hopes that he won't conceal things from you? Can you honestly say that you didn't conceal things from him?'

'I didn't hide things from him,' said Jalpa with some embarrassment.

'You're telling a lie, a complete lie!' said Ratan forcefully. 'If you'd trusted him, he'd have opened up to you too.'

Jalpa was unable to counter this censure. Now she realized that the beginning of the deceit between her and Rama had come from no one but herself.

They reached the bank of the Ganges and the car stopped. Jalpa began to take the bag, but Ratan pushed aside her hand and said, 'No, I won't let you do it. Just imagine that it's already sunk in the river.'

'How can I possibly imagine that?'

'Show me this much kindness for being like a sister to you.'

'I could wash your feet for being like a sister, but I can't keep these thorns in my heart,' said Jalpa.

'You won't agree no matter what?' said Ratan frowning.

'Yes, no matter what.'

Ratan turned her face away in aversion. Jalpa took the bag, and quickly going down the stairs of the ghat, reached the edge of the river where she lifted the bag and threw it into the water. Her face lit up from her victory over her weakness. She felt more joy and pride than she had ever had when first receiving these things. Among the countless beings performing their devotional ablutions that morning, perhaps no one felt as much inner light as she, as if every particle of her body were suffused with the golden radiance of dawn.

When she had bathed and returned to the car above, Ratan asked, 'Did you toss them in?'

'Yes.'

'You're very ruthless!'

'It's just this ruthlessness that triumphs over one's own heart. If I'd been ruthless some while ago, would this day have ever come?'

The car moved off.

## 25

It had been more than two months since Ramanath's arrival in Calcutta, and he had stayed in Devidin's home all the while. The thought of where the money would come from haunted him constantly like a recurring refrain. He formed all kinds of plans, dreamed up all kinds of things, but he never set foot outside the house. True, when it became quite dark he would go to the neighbourhood reading room without fail. He was always interested in news of his home city and province. He saw the notice that Dayanath had had published in the papers, but gave it no credence. Who knew whether the police might not be practising some deception in order to arrest him? Who could possibly have paid off the money? Impossible!

One day in the same paper Ramanath found a letter published from Jalpa to him. In words filled with insistence and pleading, she urged him to return home. She wrote: 'You have been cleared of all responsibility, no one will say anything to you.' Ramanath became agitated, but then it immediately occurred to him that this too was some deviltry of the police. What proof was there that Jalpa had written this letter? And even if he was to believe that his family had paid off the money, how could he go home? His reputation must have been destroyed everywhere in the city, the police must have put out a written notice. He decided that he wouldn't go. He wouldn't even think of going home until he had at least five thousand in hand. And if the money hadn't been paid off, and the police were searching for him, why then he'd never go home, never!

Devidin's house had two smallish rooms and a veranda below. The shop was on the veranda, food was prepared in one room, and pots and pans kept in the other. There was a small room above and a small open roof; Rama lived in this upper portion of the house. Devidin had no special place for living, sitting or sleeping. After the shop closed at night, this same veranda became a bedroom; both he and his wife slept there. Devidin's work was smoking his chilam and gabbling and gossiping all day; the old woman did all the work of running the shop. She did all the work of bringing things from the market, sending things to the station, and bringing things from the station too. Devidin didn't even recognize the shop's customers. He knew a little old Hindi; he would sit and read the *Ramayana*, *The Parrot and the Mynah*, the *Rasleela*, or *The Story of the Virgin Mary*. After Rama's arrival, he developed a taste for learning English. He would sit from early morning until nine or ten o'clock studying the letters in an English primer with Rama. There would be frequent interruptions for jokes of which Devidin had an unending store. But his wife, Jaggo, didn't like the time Rama spent sitting with him. She had made Rama into her bookkeeper and had him keep her accounts book; she didn't think it worthwhile to hire anyone for such a small amount of work. Previously, she had had her customers do this for her. Rama's staying with them affronted her, but he was so courteous, so ready to be of service, and so devout, that she could not make any open objection. To be sure, by ascribing faults to others and by repeatedly making innuendos to him, she vented her spleen. Rama had declared himself to be a Brahman, and he observed the religious duties of one. By becoming pious and a Brahman he was able to gain the esteem of both husband and wife. He understood the old woman's character and behaviour very well, but what else could he do? He was powerless to brazen it out. Circumstances had robbed him of his self-respect.

One day Ramanath was sitting reading a paper in the reading-room when he suddenly spotted Ratan. From her manner it seemed as if she was searching for someone. Scores of people were sitting reading books and papers. Rama's heart began to pound. He slipped out of the room with averted eyes and bowed head and stood hidden in the darkened veranda at the rear where some old battered trunks and chairs were lying. His soul was burning to meet Ratan and ask her for news of home, but he could not face her because of his shame and embarrassment. Oh! how many things there were to ask! But most important of all was what Jalpa thought of him now. Wasn't she weeping over his cruelty? Wasn't she distressed over his arrogance? Didn't she consider him to be deceitful and dishonest? Hadn't she become thin? And what were people's feelings towards him? Had a search of the house been made? Had a lawsuit been brought against him? He was impatient to know a thousand such things, but how could he show his face? He kept peeping out. When Ratan left and her car had moved off, he felt revived. He didn't go the reading-room for a week, or even set foot out of the house.

Sometimes when he was lying around, Rama became so perturbed that he considered going to the police and telling them the whole story. Whatever was going to happen, would happen. One or two years of imprisonment would be far better than his present life-long captivity. Then he'd make a new entrance into the struggle of life, work more intelligently, and not spend a single bit beyond his earnings. But a moment after thinking like this, he would lose his courage.

Two more months passed in this way, and January arrived. Rama had no winter clothes. He had brought nothing at all from home, nor was he able to have anything made here either. Till now he had made it through the nights somehow or other by spreading a dhoti over himself, but without a quilt or blanket how could he get through the crackling cold of January? The poor wretch lay curled up like a bundle the whole night through. When the cold was particularly bad, he would cover himself with the bedding itself. Devidin gave him an old carpet to spread over himself. This was probably the best covering in the house. This class of people would have only tattered old quilts for spreading, even though they'd wear ten thousand rupees worth of jewels, or spend ten thousand for a wedding. How was anyone supposed to keep warm with this rotten old carpet? But it was better than nothing at all. Rama was too diffident to be able to say anything to Devidin, and Devidin for his part probably didn't want to spend such a lot, or perhaps he simply didn't notice it. When the day began to draw to a close, Rama would shudder as he anticipated the misery of the coming night tearing towards him as if it were the terrible goddess of destruction, Kali. He would get up again and again in the night to throw open the window, and look out to see how much longer morning would be in coming.

One evening as he was going to the reading-room he saw that thousands of beggars had gathered around a large mercantile building. He wondered what was going on, why so many people had collected there. He pushed his way into the crowd to see, and learnt that a wealthy merchant was having blankets given away. The blankets were shoddy, light and thin, but people were falling upon them one by one. It occurred to Rama to take one for himself. Who knew him here? And even if anyone did, so what? If a poor Brahman didn't have the right to accept the gift of a blanket, then who did? But an instant later his self-respect came to life. He stood and stared a little while, and then moved on. Seeing the mark on Rama's forehead, the merchant's bookkeeper took him to be a Brahman. The number of Brahmans among all these beggars was very small. The religious merit of bestowing a gift on a Brahman was much more than ordinary. The bookkeeper was secretly pleased that a sacred Brahman had appeared. Hence when he saw Rama going, he said, 'Punditji, where are you going? Please take a blanket!' Rama almost died of shame. He was only able to utter a few words—'I don't wish to have it.' He moved off again as he said this. The bookkeeper thought that this Brahman god might be leaving because he saw the blankets were shoddy. He had probably never in his whole life met a god with so much self-esteem. Some other Brahman would have buttered him up and insisted on a decent blanket. This ingenuous god who was going off without a word must certainly be some great ascetic soul. He leaped forward, seized Rama by the hand, and said, 'Won't you come, Your Reverence, there's a beautiful blanket kept for you. These others are for beggars.' When Rama saw that he was getting something without even asking for it, that it was being forced on him, he said, 'No, no' twice more, and then accompanied the bookkeeper inside. The latter took him inside the building, seated him, and presented him with a rather good thick blanket. He was so keen to make Rama contented that he even wanted to make him a special religious donation of five rupees, but Rama refused outright to take this. The accumulated conventions of life after life had already been wounded by taking only the blanket; to stretch forth his hand for this donation was impossible for him.

Astonished, the bookkeeper said, 'If you won't agree to take this gift, Sethji will be very grieved.'

Feeling very detached, Rama said, 'I took the blanket when you insisted, but I can't take your donation. I don't need money. The gentleman at the house where I'm staying gives me meals. If I took more, what would I do with it?'

'Sethji won't agree.'

'Please ask his pardon for me.'

'Blessings on your renunciation. It's Brahmans like you who have established the honour of our religion. If you'll please just sit for a while, Sethji must certainly be coming. He'll be very pleased to have the good fortune of seeing you. He's a great devotee of Brahmans. He prays and does homage to them three times a day, Your Reverence. He appears at the bank of the Ganges at three in the morning, and then comes home to worship. At ten o'clock he reads the *Bhagavata Purana*. At midday he takes a meal and then comes here. Around three or four he goes off to pray again and then at eight he comes here again for a little while. At nine o'clock he goes to the temple to hear devotional hymns and after praying again he takes another meal. He'll certainly come in a little while. If you'd sit for a few minutes it would be very good. Where do you live?'

Rama avoided mentioning Prayag and told him that he came from Banaras. At this the bookkeeper's insistence that he stay increased still further, but Rama dreaded lest Sethji should raise some religious topic whereupon he would be unmasked. Promising to come another day, he made his escape.

When he returned from the reading-room at nine o'clock he was afraid that Devidin would see the blanket and ask him where he'd got it. What answer would he give! He'd make up something or other. He'd say that he'd borrowed it from the shop of an acquaintance.

As soon as he saw the blanket Devidin asked, 'Did you get to Seth Karorimal's, Maharaj?'

'Which Seth Karorimal?' asked Rama.

'Well, of course the one who owns the big red building.'

Rama was unable to make up a thing. 'Yes, the bookkeeper wouldn't leave me in peace,' he said. 'He's a very devout soul.'

Devidin smiled as he said, 'A very devout soul! If the land here weren't already firmly in his clutches, it would have been destroyed by now!'

'He acts like a devout soul,' said Rama, 'but God knows what's in his mind. If you don't call someone who reads scriptures and worships all day, and who busies himself with charity and religious observances a pious soul, what do you call him?'

'You should call him a wicked person, a very wicked person. He doesn't show any mercy at all. He has a jute mill. You won't find the kind of cruelty he shows towards the workers in his mill anywhere else. He has people beaten with whips, with whips! He's earned hundreds of thousands by selling ghee adulterated with fat. If one of his servants is even a minute late, he cuts his wages on the spot. By giving away three or four thousand a year, how does he think he can hide his wealth of sins! Really pious Brahmans don't even glance at his door. Was there any other Brahman there besides you?'

Rama shook his head.

'Not one goes there, but greedy and corrupt people do. All of the worshippers like the Seth that I've ever seen get stones in the end. By worshipping stone idols their hearts become stones too. He has three very large pilgrim-houses; the point is he's a hypocrite. Even if a man does nothing else, he ought at least to have mercy in his heart. The hundred religions all have this in common.'

After he had eaten the food kept for him and lain down

spreading the blanket over himself, Rama began to feel intense remorse. He had raked in thousands of rupees from bribes without feeling even a moment's remorse. One got bribes through cleverness, through skill, through exertion, but gifts were the basis of spinelessness, inaction, and hypocrisy. Now he was so wretched that he had to receive his food and clothes through charity. He'd been staying at this house now for two months, but Devidin considered him a guest rather than a beggar; he'd never even felt it was charity. Rama felt such a surge of agitation that he was ready to go to the police station that very instant and spill out his whole tale, and then there'd be an end to this. He'd get two or three years punishment, but his life wouldn't remain in this terrible state of anguish. Why not go and drown himself somewhere? What was the use of living like this? Here he had no home, no background. Instead of making others' burdens lighter, he was looking to others to take care of him. Who was getting any benefit from his life? Damn his life!

Rama made a decision that tomorrow he would fearlessly go and search for work. Whatever was to happen, let it happen.

## 26

Rama was in the middle of washing his face and hands when Devidin arrived with his primer and said, 'Brother, this English of yours is very forbidding. If 's' 'i' 'r' is 'sir', then why is 'p' 'i' 't' 'pit'? If 'b' 'u' 't' is 'but', then why is 'p' 'u' 't' 'put'? It must seem very difficult to you too.'

Rama smiled and said, 'It seemed hard at first, but now it seems easy.'

'On the day I finish this primer, I'll offer Hanuman a laddu or two. Primer (*parai-mar*) means a stranger woman's (*parai*) death (*mar*)! I mean my death. What pleasure would I get from the death of a stranger woman! You have children don't you, brother?'

'Yes, I do!' said Rama, speaking as if there were but as if there might as well not be.

'Has any letter or something come?'

'No!'

'And you haven't written either? My God, you haven't sent a single letter for three months?'

'What sort of letter am I supposed to write until I have some fixed place here?'

'Well, my fine fellow, at least write that you're all right here. You ran away from home, so they must be very worried. Your father and mother are living, aren't they?'

'Yes, certainly.'

'Well then, Bhaiya,' Devidin entreated him almost tearfully, 'Write a letter this very day; do what I say.'

Till now Rama had concealed his true state of affairs. How many times had he wished to say something to Devidin, but whatever he wanted to say always dried up on his lips. He wanted to hear Devidin's assessment, wanted to know what counsel he would give. This time Devidin's good nature defeated him. 'I ran away from home, Dada,' he said.

'I know that,' said Devidin, smiling in his moustache. 'Did you have a quarrel with your father?'

'No!'

'Your mother must have said something?'

'Not that either!'

'Then there must be some kind of trouble with your wife. She must have told you that she wants to live away from your mother and father. You must have said you won't. Or she must have insisted on having jewellery, plagued you about it. Yes?'

Rama, embarrassed, said, 'It was something like that, Dada. She wasn't especially eager for jewellery, but when she got it she liked it and since I was carried away by my love I didn't think about the consequences.'

'You didn't go through any government money, did you?' said Devidin as if the words came out of his mouth by themselves.

Every hair on Rama's body stood on end. His heart pounded. He had wanted to conceal the matter of government money. Devidin's question was like a surprise attack. Rama was like an expert soldier who had wanted to lead his army through mountain passes avoiding the eyes of spies, but this sudden attack had scattered his forces in disorder. The colour left his face. All at once he found himself unable to decide what answer to give.

Divining his state of mind, Devidin said, 'Love is very uncon-

trollable, Bhaiya. Great blunders happen, and you're still a boy.
There are thousands of lawsuits over embezzlement every year.
If you were to investigate them you'd find one reason for all of
them—jewels! I've seen ten or twenty such incidents with my
own eyes. It's just like a disease. The woman says outwardly, "Why
did you bring this? Why did you bring that? Where's the money
coming from?" But inwardly her heart is dancing with joy. A
postal official used to live right here. The poor wretch cut his
throat with a knife. I knew another Muslim gentleman who got
a five-year sentence and died in jail. I knew a third person, a
Brahman pundit, who killed himself by taking opium. It's an
awful disease. But who am I to talk about others? I did three years
in jail myself. It was when I was a young man and this old woman
was in the bloom of youth. When she'd gaze at me, I'd feel as if
she'd sent an arrow into my heart. I was a postman. I distributed
money orders. She was eating out her heart for ear-rings! She'd
say that she wanted only gold ones. Her father was a Chaudhari
and had a dry-fruit shop; he had an inflated opinion of himself. I
was intoxicated with love and I regularly boasted about my
income. Sometimes I bought her garlands of flowers, sometimes
sweets, sometimes perfumes and scented oils. I was a playboy. The
times were good and whatever you asked the shopkeepers for,
you got. Finally I forged a signature on a money order and embezzled the money. Altogether it was thirty rupees. I took her the
ear-rings. She became so happy, so happy that I can't describe it.
But in only a month the theft was detected and I got three years.
When I had done my time and got out, I ran away and came here.
I never went home again. How could I show my face! Of course
I wrote. As soon as this old woman heard the news she came.
Even after all this had happened, her craving for jewellery was
not satisfied. Whenever you look, she's having something or
other made. If she has something made today, then tomorrow
she'll have it broken up and have something else made. The same
old hunk of jewellery keeps on going around like this. She's
found a goldsmith who'll work for peanuts. My advice is to write
a letter home. But what if the police are searching for you? If they
find out where you are, then everything will be ruined. Should I
have someone write a letter and send it?'

'No, Dada!' said Rama vehemently. 'Have mercy. It would do

harm. I'm more afraid of my family than the police.'

'Your family will come as soon as they get news of where you are. They won't make any mention of it to anyone. You don't have to worry about them. The real thing to fear is the police.'

'I'm not afraid of punishment at all,' said Rama. 'I didn't tell you that one day in the reading-room I saw a woman I'm acquainted with. She visits our house a lot. She's a great friend of my wife, and married to an important lawyer. As soon as I saw her I was in a panic. I was so taken aback that I didn't even have the courage to look at her. I got up quietly and went and hid on the back veranda. If I'd talked with her a little then, I'd have learnt all the news from home, and I'm sure that she wouldn't have mentioned our meeting to anyone either, not even to my wife. But I just didn't have the courage. And now, even if I wanted to meet her, I couldn't. I don't have the slightest idea where she's staying.'

'So why don't you write a letter to *her* then?'

'No letter will be written by me.'

'So for how long are you not going to write a letter?'

'Let's see,' said Rama.

'The police must be looking for you.'

Devidin plunged into worry. Rama mistakenly thinking that perhaps fear of the police was making him anxious, said, 'Yes, that keeps on making me uneasy. You can see that I seldom go out during the day. I don't want to drag you down along with myself. I'll leave. Why should I get you tangled up in this? I'm thinking that I'll go somewhere else, go and live in some village where there's not even a whiff of the police.'

'Don't worry about me at all, Bhaiya,' said Devidin, lifting his head proudly. 'I'm not one to be afraid of the police. Having some stranger stay in one's house is not a crime. How am I supposed to know who the police are after? That's the work of the police, for the police to know. I'm not a police informer or spy. I'm not a snitch. You just keep on protecting yourself; we'll see what God does. Oh yes, don't say anything to the old woman or she'll spill the beans.'

Both sat silent for a moment. Both wanted to bring the subject to a close now. All of a sudden Devidin burst out, 'Well, Bhaiya, if you agree I'll go to your home. No one will hear even a whisper about it. I'll go around asking about all the details. I'll meet your father, explain things to your mother, and have a talk with your wife. Then I'll do whatever may seem proper.'

Rama, secretly pleased, said, 'But how will you manage to ask questions, Dada? Won't people say, what's all this to you?'

Devidin guffawed and said, 'Bhaiya, there's nothing easier. Just put a sacred thread around your neck and become a Brahman. Then you can do anything—read palms, explain horoscopes, or tell fortunes. Your mother will come to bring alms. As soon as I see her I'll say, 'Mother, you're having a lot of trouble about a son who's gone far away. Do you have a son who's gone to another country?' As soon as they hear this, the whole house will come to listen. Your wife will come too. I'll look at her hand. I'm a master of those things, brother, don't you worry. We'll see if I earn something to bring back. There's the big February bathing festival too. I'll take a dip in the Triveni where the sacred rivers meet before I come back.'

Rama's eyes sparkled with delight. His mind travelled to the realms of sweet fancies. Jalpa would go running to Ratan. Both of them would ask Devidin all kinds of questions—'Tell us, Babu, where has he gone? He's all right, isn't he? When is he coming home? Does he remember his family sometimes? He hasn't fallen into the clutches of some worthless woman there, has he?' They'd both ask the name of the city where he was, too. If his father had somehow paid off the government money, what a great pleasure that would be. Then there'd only be one worry left.

'So is that advice or not?' said Devidin.

'How will you do it, Dada?' asked Rama. 'It's going to be a lot of trouble for you.'

'I'll have a bath at the February festival too. You don't get religious merit without some trouble. I'm telling you, you come too. I'm going to see all there is to see there. If we see that everything's satisfactory, then you go home without a worry. If anything seems out of whack, then you come back here with me.'

Rama laughed and said, 'What on earth are you saying, Dada! I'll never go in this way. Suppose some policeman should grab me at the station just as I'm getting off the train, why, it would be all over!'

'Why it's a joke, a policeman grabbing you!' said Devidin,

growing serious. 'Just tell me and I'd take him to Allahabad's main police station and stand him up there. And if anyone even looked at me out of the corner of his eyes, I'd twist his moustache for him! There's no way that would happen! I know hundreds of murderers that live right here in Calcutta. They dine as guests of police officers, and even though the police know who they are, they can't do a thing to them. Money has a lot of power, brother!'

Rama gave no answer. A new question had presented itself to him. The things he had considered difficult because of his lack of experience, this old man made easy. And he was no idle boaster. Whatever he said, he was capable of bringing to completion. Could he really go home along with Devidin? If he could get some money here, he could have a new suit made, and go in style. He began to imagine the occasion of his arrival at home wearing a new suit. As soon as they saw him Gopi and Vishvambhar would run inside yelling, 'Our brother has come! Our brother has come!' His father would come out. His mother wouldn't believe it at first, but when his father went to her and said, 'Yes, he's come,' she'd start towards the door, crying. Just then he'd come and fall at her feet. Jalpa wouldn't come; her self-respect would keep her sitting where she was. Rama even began to think up the sentences he would say to bring Jalpa around. Perhaps the money wouldn't even be mentioned. Everyone would be embarrassed to say anything about this subject. When one of our loved ones commits some misdeed, we don't make him feel bad by reviling him. We don't want the least attention given to what happened. We act towards him as if we haven't even the slightest doubt; we forget it all lest he feel he is being dishonoured.

'What are you thinking?' asked Devidin. 'Will you go?'

'Since you are so kind, I'll go,' said Rama in a subdued voice. 'But you'll have to go to my home first and bring back every bit of news. If I'm not satisfied, I'll come back here.'

'Agreed!' said Devidin with conviction.

'There's one more thing,' said Rama, lowering his eyes self-consciously.

'What's that? Tell me!'

'I'll have to have some clothes made.'

'They'll be made.'

'I'll pay you back when I get home.'

'And I'll give you your guru's fee right there too.'

'It's me that has to give you a guru's fee. If I've taught you a few English letters, you won't get any particular benefit from this. But the lessons you've taught me I won't be able to forget my whole life. To praise someone to his face is flattery, but Dada, next to my mother and father I don't love anyone else as much as I do you. You reached out and took my hand in my worst hour, when I was being swept away in the middle of the river. God knows what condition I'd be in by now, which bank I'd have come ashore on!'

'And suppose your father won't let me come into your house?' said Devidin mischievously.

Rama laughed. 'Father will think of you as his older brother; he'll show you so much consideration that you'll get bored. Jalpa will drink the water she's washed your feet in, and look after you so well that you'll become young again.'

'Then the old woman will burn up and die of jealousy,' said Devidin laughing. 'She won't agree, otherwise I'd love for the two of us to take everything—lock, stock, and barrel—go there to Allahabad, and stretch out on our mats to die. I could spend the rest of my days comfortably with you, but this old witch won't leave Calcutta. So it's decided then?'

'Yes, it's decided.'

'When the shop opens let's go and get some cloth, and we'll give it to a tailor today for sewing.'

For a long time after Devidin left Rama sat lost in pleasant dreams. Today he began to frolic unrestrainedly in that very same bottomless and limitless ocean of imagination, whose surging feelings he had never before allowed to take up their abode in his mind, whose depth and breadth and intensity had frightened him so much that he had never let his fickle mind go wandering in their direction for fear of slipping and drowning in them. Now, he had a boat. That trip to the Triveni, the delights of Alfred Park, the joys of Khusro Garden, those gatherings with his friends—all these memories came one after the other and kindled his heart. Ramesh would embrace him as soon as he saw him. His group of friends would ask him, 'Where did you go, pal? Did you travel a lot?' Ratan would come running as soon as she got the news and ask, 'Where did you stay, Babuji? I searched all over Calcutta for you.' And then Jalpa's image came and stood before him.

All of a sudden Devidin came and said, 'It's ten o'clock, Bhaiya. Come on, let's go to the bazaar.'

Rama started and asked, 'It's ten o'clock?'

'Not ten, it's about to strike eleven.'

Rama got ready to go. But when he reached the door he stopped.

'Why, what are you standing there for?' asked Devidin.

'You go. What am I going to do if I go?'

'What are you afraid of?'

'No, it's not that I'm afraid, but what's the use?'

'What am I going to do by myself?' said Devidin. 'What do I know about what kind of cloth you like? Come on and choose what you like. We'll give it to the tailor on the spot.'

'Get whatever you wish. I like everything.'

'What are you afraid of? The police won't do a thing to you. No one will even give you a second look.'

'I'm not afraid, Dada! I just don't want to go.'

'If you're not afraid, then what are you? I'm telling you that no one will say a word to you; I'll take responsibility for that. I mean, it's not as if you're going to lose your life!'

Devidin tried hard to convince him, to reassure him, but Rama would not agree to go. No matter how often he denied he was afraid, he simply didn't have the courage to set foot outside the house. What could Devidin do if some policeman should lay hold of him? Even supposing the policeman was an acquaintance, there was no certainty that he'd allow considerations of friendship to influence him in an official matter. In the end Devidin would be reduced to supplication and flattery, while all the responsibility would fall on Rama's head. If he should be caught, he'd be going to jail instead of Prayag. At last Devidin, baffled, went by himself.

When Devidin returned after an hour, he found Rama walking up and down on the roof. 'Do you have any idea what time it is? It's just about twelve. You're not going to prepare your meal? You're so happy about going home that you've given up eating and drinking?'

'I'll get it ready, Dada. What's the hurry?' said Rama shamefacedly.

·'Take a look at this, I brought some samples. Whatever you like from these I'll take to the tailor.'

Devidin brought out hundreds of samples of wool and silk cloth, and put them before Rama. Not one of them was less than five or six rupees a yard.

Rama, turning the samples this side and that, asked, 'Why did you bring such expensive cloth, Dada? Weren't there any cheaper ones?'

'There were cheaper ones, but the point is they were British.'

'You don't wear English clothes?'

'I haven't bought any for twenty years, nor do I talk about it. The price is higher for Indian-made cloth, but the money stays right here in the country.'

Feeling ashamed Rama said, 'You're very strict about your principles, Dada.'

Devidin's face suddenly brightened. His tranquil eyes sparkled, and his whole body grew taut. Haughtily he said, 'If you live in this country, drink its water and eat its food, and won't even do this much, then a curse on your life! I've given two young sons to this swadeshi movement, Bhaiya. How can I tell you what fine young men they were! Both of them were sent to keep watch on a shop selling foreign cloth. It would have taken a lot of nerve for any customer to go into that shop. Joining their hands in entreaty, beseeching, threatening, shaming, they turned everyone away. The cloth market began to be deserted. All the merchants went to the Commissioner and complained. When he heard what was going on, he became enraged, and sent twenty white soldiers to clear the swadeshi sentinels from the market immediately. These whites told the two brothers to get out, but they didn't budge a fraction of an inch from where they were. A crowd gathered. The whites charged them on horses, but the two of them stood as firm as rocks. Finally, when they couldn't bring things under control in this way, they all began to beat the boys with their bamboo staves. Both heroes took the blows, but didn't stir from their place. When the older brother fell, the younger came and stood in his place. If the two had taken up their own staves, then, Bhaiya, they'd have given those soldiers a good drubbing and chased them away. But for a swadeshi to even lift a hand would have been a big offence against the rules of non-violence, so they didn't even protect their heads. In the end, the younger one too dropped on the spot. People lifted them up and took them to the hospital! That very night both of them departed this life. I swear to you by touching your feet, Bhaiya, that I felt as if my chest had become a yard wide, as if my feet didn't touch the ground. I felt so elated that if God hadn't already taken my other children, I'd have sent them too. When the ritual immersion of their ashes took place, there were a hundred thousand people in attendance. As soon as I'd given my boys to the care of the Ganges, I went straight to the cloth market and stood in the very same place where the dead bodies of the two heroes had fallen. Speak about customers, you couldn't see even the son of a sparrow there. I didn't leave the spot for eight days, except to go home at daybreak for half an hour to bathe and eat a little before going back. On the ninth day the shopkeepers swore that they wouldn't order foreign cloth from then on. After that the watch was lifted. And from that time on, I haven't brought even foreign matches home.'

'Dada,' said Rama wholeheartedly, 'you're a true hero and those two boys were true warriors. Seeing you makes one's eyes pure and sacred.'

Devidin looked at him as if he felt that this fulsome praise were not in the least exaggerated. With the pompous dignity of a martyr he said, 'Whatever these bigwigs do will come to nothing. All they know how to do is complain. They can't do any more than to weep and wail like little girls. These grand patriots can't be at ease without their foreign liquor. If you go take a look at their homes you won't find even a single Indian thing. They'll have ten or twenty kurtas made of coarse homespun cloth for show, but all the other things will be foreign-made. Everyone, great and small, is blindly pursuing the good life. They pretend to work for the betterment of the country. Ha! You're going to better the country! First better yourself. Your work is robbing the poor and enriching foreigners, and this is exactly why you were born in this country. Yes, keep on complaining, and wallow in foreign liquor! Drive foreign cars, enjoy foreign jams and pickles, eat from foreign dishes, take foreign medicines, but keep on whining about the country. The point is, nothing will come from this whining. A mother gives milk to stop the whining of her child, but a tiger doesn't leave its prey. Complain to someone merciful and righteous. What will your threats accomplish? Who is going to pay attention to a threat which has no compassion in it? Once there was a very big meeting here. A certain Sahab Bahadur rose and leaped and bounded around in a fine passion. When he came down from the platform, I asked him, "Sahab, tell me the truth, when you mention self-rule, what sort of picture comes before your eyes? Like the English, you'll draw a big salary too, live in bungalows too, enjoy the mountain air, and travel around wearing English styles. How will the country get better from this kind of self-rule? You and your friends and relations will pass your lives in great ease and comfort, but there will be no benefit to the country!" He wanted to slink away. "You eat five times a day, and good stuff too, while the wretched farmer doesn't even get a single meal of dry parched grain," I said. "The government gives you official positions to suck his blood! Have you ever given him a thought? When you're so crazy about living it up now without even being in power yet, when you do get into power, you'll grind up the poor and swallow them down." '

Rama couldn't bear to hear this censure of respectable society. After all, he was a part of that society too. 'It's not true that educated people don't care about the farmers, Dada,' he said. 'So many of them were or still are farmers themselves. If they believed that farmers could benefit from their sacrifices, and that whatever surplus resulted would be spent on farmers, then they'd cheerfully work for lower salaries. But when they see others gobbling up any surplus, they think if others are to eat it up, then why shouldn't they.'

'So when we get self-rule won't there still be five or ten thousand officers in every province? Won't lawyers still be robbing people? And will the police stop robbing people too?'

For a moment Rama was taken aback. He'd never thought about this himself, but an answer quickly occurred to him. 'Dada, everything will be done by majority vote, then. If the majority says that the office workers' salaries should be reduced, then they'll be reduced. And whatever amount the majority demands for the rural masses, they'll get. The key will remain in the hand of the majority. And even if it takes five or ten years from now, in the future the majority will be the farmers and labourers themselves.'

Devidin, smiling, said, 'Bhaiya, you understand these things too. That's just how I think. God willing, I'll live a little longer. My first question will be whether there'll be a two hundred per cent duty on foreign things and a four hundred per cent duty on automobiles. All right, cook the food now. We'll go give the cloth to the tailor this evening. I'll eat by then too.'

That evening Devidin came and said, 'Let's go, Bhaiya, it's dark now.' Rama was sitting with his head in his hands, sadness spread over his face. 'Dada,' he said, 'I'm not going home.'

Startled, Devidin asked, 'Why? What's happened?'

Rama's eyes filled with tears. 'How can I show my face, Dada! I should have drowned myself!'

As he said this he wept out loud. The anguish which had been lying unconscious till then, revived on receiving these cool drops of water. His tears, as it were, pierced through Rama's whole existence. For fear of these very tears, he had not stirred up his pain, had not attempted to revive it, and by deliberate forgetfulness had wanted to keep it inert, just like some harassed mother fears to wake her child lest he immediately demand to be fed.

# 27

One day a few days later, Rama was returning from the library about eight o'clock when he met several young men on the way, discussing a diagram of a chess problem. This diagram had been published in a local Hindi daily newspaper and a prize of fifty rupees had been promised to the person who solved it. The problem seemed almost insoluble, or at least this seemed evident from the remarks of the young men. It also seemed that many other local chess players had tried their utmost to solve it, but had failed completely. Now Rama remembered that many people had been huddled over a newspaper in the library, making copies of this diagram. Everyone who came had spent three or four minutes looking at the paper; now he realized this was what it had been about.

Rama was not acquainted with any of them, but he was so eager to see the diagram that he couldn't refrain from asking about it. 'Do any of you have a copy of the diagram?' he said.

When they heard this blanket-clad person asking about the diagram, the young men took him for some wandering musician. 'Yes we do,' said one of them coldly. 'But what could you do if you saw it, when some of the best players here are completely baffled. One gentleman who has no equal in chess, is ready to give a hundred rupees of his own to get it solved.'

Another said, 'Why don't you show it to him? Who knows whether this poor fellow might figure it out. Perhaps he's just the person to whom the correct solution might occur.'

There was no kindness in this appeal, but rather sarcasm. The hidden meaning was this: we have no objection to showing it to you, or to your getting an eyeful. But an idiot like you won't even understand it, let alone find a solution!

They went into a shop they frequented, and showed Rama the diagram. He remembered at once having definitely seen the diagram somewhere before, and began to think where that might have been.

One of them said scornfully, 'Surely you must have worked it out?'

Another added, 'If he hasn't yet, he will in a minute!'

And a third said, 'Please, tell us one or two of the moves, won't you?'

Rama, getting excited, said, 'I can't say that I'll solve this, but I did solve a problem like this once, and it's possible I can solve this one too. Please let me have pencil and paper so I can make a copy of it.'

The young men's disbelief grew somewhat less. Rama received pencil and paper. He copied it in a moment, thanked them, and started to leave. All at once he turned around and asked, 'To whom should I send the answer?' One of them answered, 'To the editor of the *Praja-Mitra*.'

When Rama reached home, he began to rack his brains over the diagram, but instead of thinking about the moves of the chess pieces, he thought about where he had seen this diagram before. Like others, he began to look for excuses to avoid making mental efforts, and took a vacation, as it were, on some pretext or other. He sat up half the night with the diagram spread out before him. He had played through many of the most outstanding games of chess, and he remembered all of their board diagrams, but where had he seen this one?

Suddenly it flashed before his eyes like lightning. The lost memory returned. Aha! Rajah Sahab had given him this diagram. Yes, that was right. He had cudgelled his brains for three days before solving it. He'd even copied the diagram and brought it along. So now he remembered every single move, and in a moment the problem was solved. Intoxicated with joy, he pranced around, twirled his moustache in smug satisfaction, gazed at his face in the mirror, and then lay down on the bed. If he kept on getting one chess diagram like this each month, then what couldn't he manage?

Devidin was just lighting the fire when Rama, beaming, came and said, 'Dada, do you know where the office of the *Praja-Mitra* is?'

'Why wouldn't I? Which newspaper around here don't I know about? The editor of the *Praja-Mitra* is a lively young fellow who always has his mouth full of paan. If you go meet him, he talks up a storm, but he's got a lot of courage. He's been to jail twice.'

'Could you go there today, please?'

'Why send me?' said Devidin, looking distressed. 'I can't go.'

'Is it very far?'

'No, it's not far.'

'Then what is it?'

Looking as if he were some sort of criminal, Devidin said, 'It's really nothing, just that the old woman gets angry. I've promised her that I won't get involved in this domestic versus foreign goods dispute or go into any newspaper office. I live off what she gives me, so I have to dance to her tune.'

Rama smiled. 'Dada, you're joking. I have something very important to get done. A chess problem was published in that paper, with a prize of fifty rupees. I've solved it. If my solution is published today I'll get that prize. The undercover police often hang around newspaper offices. That's what I'm afraid of, otherwise I'd go myself. But if you won't go I'll have no alternative but to go myself. It took a lot of effort to solve this problem. I stayed up the whole night.'

'It's not right for you to go there,' said Devidin in a worried tone.

'Then what?' said Rama perplexed. 'Should I send it by post?'

Devidin thought for a moment. 'No, what's the good of sending it by post. If the envelope goes by ordinary post it could end up anywhere, and then your efforts would be wasted. If you register it, it'll get there some time day after tomorrow, and tomorrow is Sunday. If you send it by someone else, he'll make off with the prize. It's also possible that the newspaperman will pull a fast one, publish your answer under his own name, and filch the money.'

'I'll go myself,' said Rama uncertainly.

'I won't let you go. If you should get caught that would be the end of it!'

'I'll get caught for sure one day anyway! How long can I go on hiding?'

'So why are you making such a big fuss before anything has ever happened? Let's see what happens when you do get caught. Bring it, I'll go. I'll make up some excuse or other for the old woman. I'll meet the editor, too; he even lives in the office. Then I'll go wandering around, so I won't be back before ten o'clock.'

'What's the harm in going after ten?' said Rama fearfully.

Devidin stood up. 'If something else should come up before then, nothing would get done today. I'll be back in an hour. The old woman will come late.'

Devidin spread his black blanket around himself, took Rama's envelope, and set out.

Jaggo, his wife, had gone to the market for fruit and vegetables. After half an hour she returned with a small basket on her head, followed by a porter with a larger basket on his head. She was drenched in sweat. As soon as she arrived she asked, 'Where has he gone? Help me get this load down, my neck's broken.'

Rama strode forward and lifted the basket down. It was so heavy that he was hardly able to manage it.

Jaggo asked again, 'Where has he gone?'

Rama fibbed. 'I don't know. He went off this way just now.'

The old woman had the porter put his basket down, sat on the ground, and waving a tattered little fan said, 'He must be having a taste of charas, and look at me, killing myself earning a living while he sits around living it up and smoking that stuff.'

Rama knew that Devidin smoked charas, but to calm the old

woman down said, 'He smokes charas? I haven't seen him do it.'

The old woman moved the back of her sari aside and scratching herself with the handle of the fan said, 'He hasn't given up any kind of intoxication; he'll smoke charas, he'll smoke ganja, he wants liquor, he wants bhang. Yes, he hasn't taken opium yet, or God knows, maybe he does. How can I keep an eye on him every minute? I keep thinking, who knows what's ahead. If you have a little money in hand, even strangers treat you as one of them. But this fine fellow doesn't worry a bit. Sometimes it's going on a pilgrimage, sometimes it's this, sometimes it's that.' Putting her finger on her nose she said, 'I'm plagued to death by him. If God takes me away, then I'll leave his bad company behind, and then his honour will remember me. Then where will he find that Jaggo who worked and worked to let him indulge himself to his heart's content? If he doesn't shed tears of blood then, then tell him that somebody said he would.'

'How much is it?' she said to the porter.

The porter, lighting a bidi said, 'Take a look at the load, Dai; it broke my neck!'

'Yes, yes,' said Jaggo unsympathetically, 'it broke your neck! You're very delicate, aren't you! Take this and come again tomorrow.'

'That's very little,' said the porter. 'I'm not supposed to have a full stomach?' Jaggo gave him two more coins and a few potatoes, sent him off, and started to arrange things in the shop. Suddenly she remembered her accounts. 'Bhaiya,' she said to Rama, 'would you please jot down what I spent today. It was hot as blazes in the bazaar.'

The old woman put her purchases one by one in the shop's display baskets as Rama wrote them down. Potatoes, tomatoes, pumpkins, bananas, spinach, beans, oranges, cauliflowers—she remembered the weight and price of them all. After she had heard Rama read everything out again, she was satisfied. Having earned respite from all her tasks, she filled her chilam, and seating herself on a three-legged stool began to smoke. But from her manner it was apparent that she was smoking to vent her spleen rather than to savour the tobacco. After a moment she spoke. 'If I were another woman I wouldn't put up with him for a moment, not a moment. I keep my nose to the grindstone from early morning, and then slave away sitting in the shop until ten o'clock at night. It's twelve o'clock before I eat and drink. Then after all that, when we have a little money, he wastes whatever I earn in getting intoxicated. I hide it in the most secret place I can find, but he always spots it. And takes it. When I get a few clothes made now and then, it sticks in his craw, and he starts giving me dirty looks. It wasn't written in my fate to enjoy the company of my two boys, so what am I supposed to do? Rip open my chest and die? Even if you ask for it, death doesn't come. If it had been my fate to enjoy myself, would my young sons have died, and would I have had to suffer these torments at the hands of this drunkard? He got carried away by this swadeshi controversy and took the lives of my darlings. Come into this room, Bhaiya, and let me show you their exercise clubs. Both boys could swing them around five hundred times.'

Going into the dark room Rama saw a pair of clubs. They were varnished and were so well kept it was as if someone had just put them down after swinging them.

The old woman gazed at them proudly. 'People said I should give these to the Brahman who carried out the commemoration ceremonies, that every time I saw them I'd keep pining for my sons. But I told them that these clubs are a harmonious pair like my sons. Now *they* are my two darlings.'

Today a boundless respect for the old woman awoke in Rama's heart for the first time. What pure steadfastness! What immense motherly love that had granted life to these two pieces of wood! Rama had thought Jaggo was lost in greed and illusion, ready to sacrifice anything for money, and without any softer feelings. Today he saw how loving, how tender, how wise her heart was. When the old woman looked at his face, her mother's heart for some reason or other suddenly grew impatient to embrace him. Both their hearts were bound together with cords of love. On one side the affection of a son, on the other the devotion of a mother. The hidden feeling of dislike, which had separated them until now, was suddenly removed.

'You've washed your hands and face haven't you, son?' she asked. 'I've brought some very sweet oranges, so have a taste of one.'

'From today I'm going to call you mother,' said Rama, eating the orange.

Two pearl-like tears appeared in the old woman's withered, lustreless, dejected, miserable eyes.

Just then Devidin entered furtively. Flaring up, the old woman asked him, 'Where did Your Highness go riding so early this morning?'

Devi smiled unaffectedly, 'Nowhere. I just went out for a little business.'

'What business? Could I hear about it too, or am I not worthy to hear?'

'I had a stomach ache, I went to the vaidji to get some powder.'

'You're a liar. Just fool those who don't know you. Did you go looking for charas?'

'No, I swear by touching your feet. You're running me down for no good reason.'

'So where did you go then?'

'I *told* you. I ate a bit too much last night, so my stomach swelled up, and something very sweet ...'

'It's a lie, a total lie! Whenever you want to lie, your face clearly tells me that it's some kind of sham. You went out just to look for charas or ganja. I won't believe one word. You keep thinking of getting intoxicated even in your old age, while over here I'm slowly dying. He goes out first thing in the morning and comes back at nine o'clock; looks like he's got some little slut around here!'

Devidin took the broom and began to sweep the shop, but the old woman snatched the broom from his hand. 'Where have you been till now? I won't let you go inside until you tell me.'

Devidin disconcerted, said, 'What's the good of your asking? I went to a newspaper office. Do what you want.'

Giving herself a slap on the forehead, the old woman said, 'So you've caught hold of that craze again? You swore to me that you'd never go near the newspapers again. Tell me, was it *your* mouth, or someone else's?'

'You don't understand what's going on, you just get mad.'

'I understand a lot. The newspaper people stir up trouble, and get poor wretches sent to jail. I've seen it for twenty years. People who hang around those offices get arrested. The police search there every day. Do you want to eat jail bread in your old age?'

Devidin gave an envelope to Ramanath and said, 'This is the

money, Bhaiya. Count it. See, I went to collect this money. If you don't feel like taking all of it, take half.' The old woman, staring in astonishment, said, 'Well, so now you want to drag this poor fellow down with you too? I'll set fire to your money. Don't take it, Bhaiya. You'll be taking your life in your hands if you do. These days you don't meet people who help you for nothing. Everyone shows how greedy they are by cheating people. They'll arrange to have evidence given in court. Throw his money away. Take whatever you need from me.'

When Ramanath told her the whole story, the old woman calmed down. Her raised eyebrows lowered, her harsh expression softened. After driving off the rain showers, the blue sky burst out laughing. Delighted, she said, 'What are you going to bring me with this, son?'

Rama put the envelope in front of her. 'It's all yours, mother,' he said. 'What am I going to do with it?'

'Why don't you send it home? It's been so long since you came and you haven't sent anything.'

'*This* is my home, mother. I don't have any other.'

The old woman's heart, long deprived of affection, thrilled with ecstasy. How many days had her soul thirsted for this filial devotion. All the love gathering up in her wretched heart, like the milk collected in a mother's breast, was impatient to pour itself out.

She counted the notes and said, 'There's fifty here, son! Take fifty more from me. I've kept it in the teapot. Open a tea stall. Put out four or five stools and a table just to the side here. If you sit for a couple of hours morning and evening you'll get by very well. Lots of my customers will take tea from you.'

Devidin said, 'Then I'll take the money for charas from his shop.'

Looking at him with smiling, blissful eyes, she said, 'I'll keep accounts of every paisa. Don't be under any illusions about that.'

Rama went to his room feeling gratified. He had experienced a sort of joy today that he had never experienced at home. The love he received at home was what he ought to have received. The love he received here seemed to have suddenly fallen from the sky.

He took a bath, put the tilak on his forehead, and had just sat down to carry out his pretence of worship when the old woman came and said, 'Son, it's very difficult to cook for you. I've arranged for a Brahman woman to do it; the poor thing is very badly off. She'll cook your meals for you, so you'll eat from her hand. It's not that she lives by all the rules prescribed by her caste, son. She takes loans from me, so that's why she agreed.'

What deep, unlimited motherhood was sparkling in those ancient eyes, and how spotless, how pure! The question of great and small, of caste boundaries, vanished of its own accord. 'When you became my mother,' said Rama, 'all this business of touchability stopped. I'll eat only from your hand.'

'Oh no, son,' said the old woman, biting her tongue. 'I'm not going to take away your dharma. What a difference there is between a Brahman and a Khatik! Whoever heard of such a thing.'

'I'm going to eat in your kitchen. When the mother and father are Khatiks, the son's a Khatik too. Whoever has a great soul is a true Brahman.'

'And what would your own people say if they should hear about this?'

'I'm not worried about what people may hear or say, Mother. People get corrupted from wrongdoing, not from eating or drinking. Food that's given with love is pure. Even the gods eat that kind of food.'

The pride of caste rose up even now in the old woman's heart. 'Son, the Khatiks are not some low caste,' she said. 'We don't take food even from Brahmans. And we don't even take water from Kahars. We won't touch meat or fish. A few of us drink alcohol, but secretly. This husband of mine hasn't given it up at all, son. And some very important temple-goers just gulp it down. But will you like my bread?'

'Bread made with love is nectar, mother, whether it's made from fine wheat or coarse millet,' said Rama, smiling.

When the old woman left there, it was as if her garments were filled with a treasure of joy.

## 28

Ratan had been very concerned about Jalpa from the time Rama had left. She wanted to keep on helping her on any pretext. Nor did she want Jalpa to be punished in any way. If it had been possible to find out Rama's whereabouts by spending some money, she would have been delighted to do so. Her heart was wrung whenever she saw Jalpa's tearful eyes. She wanted to see her looking happy. She had been accustomed to go to Jalpa's house when she became dispirited by her own dark sad home. Laughing and talking there for a while had cheered her up. Now the same misfortune had cast its shadow there too. Previously on going there she had felt that she too was part of the world—that world in which there was life, longing, love and joy. Her own life had already been sacrificed on the altar of a vow, and she honoured that vow with all her might. But does the water kept in a pot by a Shiva-lingam have the same flow, the same waves, the same roar, that a river has? It cools the forehead of Shiva, that's its task, but haven't the flow, the waves, and the roar of the river disappeared from it?

There was no doubt that Ratan was acquainted with the most respectable and prosperous families of the city. But where there was respectability, there was also exaggerated formality, ostentation, envy, and slander. She had also developed an aversion to any contact with any club. There was certainly enjoyment, certainly amusement, but there were also men's eager glances, restless hearts, and lustful words. Though Jalpa's home had no splendour, no wealth, it also had no ostentation, no envy. Rama was young, handsome, and even if he were a voluptuary, Ratan had had no occasion as yet to have any doubt of him in this regard, nor was this even possible with such a beauty as Jalpa around. Fed up with the crookedness and cheating of all the other shopkeepers in life's bazaar, she had taken refuge in this little shop, but now it too had been shattered. Where would she buy the materials of life now, where would she get the real goods?

One day she brought over a gramophone and played it till evening. Another day she bought a basket of fresh fruit and left it. Whenever she came she brought some sort of special gift. Till now she had seldom met Jageshwari, but now she often came and sat with her, and talked about this and that. Sometimes she'd put oil on Jageshwari's head and braid her hair. She began to feel affection for Rama's brothers, Gopi and Vishvambhar, too; now and then she'd take them both around in her car. They would go to her bungalow as soon as they came from school and play there with several other boys. Ratan took great pleasure in their crying, shouting and quarrelling. Even Vakil Sahab began to feel some intimacy with Rama's family. He would ask over and over again, 'Has any letter come from Rama Babu? Have you found out anything? His people aren't having any difficulty, are they?'

One day when Ratan came with a long face and bleary eyes, Jalpa asked her, 'Is something wrong with you today?'

'Nothing's wrong with me,' said Ratan in a dull voice, 'but I had to stay up the whole night. Vakil Sahab has been suffering a lot since last evening. Every winter he has an attack of asthma. The poor man takes emulsions, Sanatoz, and who knows what other sorts of concoctions the whole winter through, but the illness won't let go of his throat. There's a well-known vaidya in Calcutta, and this time we intend to get treatment from him. I'm leaving tomorrow. He doesn't want to take me along, and says there will be a lot of bother there, but my heart won't accept this. At least there ought to be someone who can speak. I've gone there twice, and whenever I've gone I've been sick. There's not the least thing I like there, but it's either look after my own comfort or his sickness. Sister, sometimes I get so fed up that I feel like taking some poison and dying. But God won't do even this much for me. If someone took everything I have to make him well, to root out his sickness, I'd give it cheerfully.'

'Haven't you sent for any vaidya here?' asked Jalpa alarmed.

'I've seen all the vaidyas here, sister. Vaidyas, doctors, I've seen them all!'

'So when will you come back?'

'Nothing is certain. It depends on his sickness. I might come back in a week, or it could take a month or two, who knows? But I won't come back until his sickness is rooted out.'

Fate sat laughing in the starry sky! Jalpa smiled to herself. An illness which has not been ended in youth, is not likely to be ended in middle age. But it was impossible not to have sympathy for Ratan's good intentions. 'God willing, he'll get well soon and come back, sister.'

'If you'd come too it would be a great pleasure,' said Ratan.

'What good would it do even if I could go?' said Jalpa compassionately. 'Here at least I can keep hoping all day that some news will come. There I'd just get more and more worried.'

'My heart says that Rama Babuji is in Calcutta.'

'So please search around for him. If you should somehow learn anything, let me know right away.'

'You don't even have to say that, Jalpa!'

'I know. You'll keep writing won't you?'

'Yes, certainly. If not every day, every other day for sure. But you write back too.'

Jalpa started to prepare some paan. Ratan kept staring at her face expectantly as if she wished to say something and couldn't from embarrassment. When giving Ratan the paan, Jalpa guessing her state of mind, asked, 'What is it, sister? What are you saying?'

'Nothing,' said Ratan. 'I have some money with me; you keep it. If it stays with me, it'll get spent.'

Smiling, Jalpa refused. 'And if I should spend it, then?'

'It's yours, sister,' said Ratan joyfully, 'not some stranger's.'

Jalpa fixed her gaze on the floor, lost in thought and gave no answer. 'You didn't answer, sister,' said Ratan reproachfully, 'and I don't understand why you keep aloof from me. I want there to be no distance between us, but you keep running far away from me. Just suppose I spent fifty or a hundred rupees on you, so what? Sisters don't count every paisa between them like this.'

Looking serious, Jalpa said, 'You won't take it the wrong way if I say something?'

'If it's something bad of course I will.'

'I'm not saying it to hurt your feelings, but it's possible that it will seem bad. Think about it for yourself, is compassion mixed in with this sisterly feeling of yours or not? Are you taking pity on my poverty ...'

Ratan rushed at her, closed her mouth with both hands, and said, 'Enough, let it be. Think what you like, but I never had that feeling in my heart nor could I. If I were hungry, I know that I could tell you, "Sister, I'm hungry, give me something to eat."'

With the same harshness Jalpa said, 'You can say that now when you know that you can feed me with fruits some other time in exchange for rotis or puris from here. But God forbid that a time come when there's not even a piece of roti left in your home; perhaps then you couldn't be so carefree.'

'I wouldn't hesitate to ask you for something even then,' said Ratan resolutely. 'Friendship doesn't take circumstances into consideration. If it does, then don't consider it friendship. When you talk like this, you're shutting my door to you. I had decided in my own mind to spend the days of my life with you, but now you're warning me away from you. Unfortunate people like me can't get love even if they beg for it.'

Ratan's eyes filled with tears as she said this. Jalpa considered herself a sufferer and those who suffer have the freedom to speak the truth unfeelingly. But Ratan's emotional distress was rather more agonizing than hers. Jalpa had some hope of her husband's return. He was young, and as soon as he came Jalpa would forget these wretched days. The sun of her hopes would rise again, and her wishes would blossom again. The future, with all its expectations and desires, was in front of her—immense, brilliant, lovely. What was Ratan's future? Nothing at all, empty darkness!

Wiping her eyes, Jalpa stood up. 'Keep on answering my letters,' she said. 'Keep on giving me money.'

Ratan took a bundle of notes from her purse and put it in front of Jalpa. But there was no pleasure on her face.

Jalpa said simply, 'Did you take it badly?'

'What could I do for you if I took it badly?' said Ratan sulkily.

Jalpa threw her arms around her neck. Her heart was overflowing with affection. She had never felt so much love for Ratan before. Until now she had held aloof from her and envied her, but today she saw Ratan's true character.

She was really an unfortunate woman, and more unfortunate than herself.

A moment later, with tears and laughter mingled together, Ratan took her leave.

# 29

Once in Calcutta, Vakil Sahab made arrangements for a place to stay before anything else; there were no difficulties. Ratan took Maharaj and Timal Kahar along. Both were old servants of Vakil Sahab's and had become almost like members of the family. They found a bungalow outside the city and took three of its rooms; there was no need of more space. The compound had many kinds of plants and flowers, and the place seemed very beautiful. There were a great many other bungalows in the neighbourhood. People from the city came there to take the air and go back refreshed, but Ratan felt torn to pieces there. Those who are with sick people get sick themselves. Those who are sad find even paradise sad.

The trip made Vakil Sahab even weaker. For two or three days his condition was worse than it had been in Prayag, but after a few days of treatment, he became a little better. Ratan would sit near him on a chair from morning until midnight. She didn't even pay any attention to eating or bathing. If Vakil Sahab expressed a desire for her to leave him, she would grieve openly. To calm her, he would try to conceal his true state. She would ask how he was today and he would give a wan smile and say that today he felt very refreshed. If the poor fellow had spent the whole night tossing and turning but Ratan asked whether he had slept, he would say he'd slept a lot. If Ratan put some wholesome food before him, he'd eat it even though he had no appetite. Ratan thought he was getting better. She passed on this information to Dr Kaviraj, who was pleased at the success of his treatment.

One day Vakil Sahab said to Ratan, 'I'm afraid that when I get well I may have to give you some treatment.'

Pleased, Ratan said, 'What could be better? I beg God to give me your illness.'

'Take walks in the evenings. If you want to get sick, then get sick after I get well.'

'Where should I go? I just don't feel like going anywhere at all. Right here seems best to me.'

Suddenly Vakil Sahab remembered Ramanath. 'Go look around the city parks and perhaps you might find Ramanath.'

Ratan remembered her promise. The delightful prospect of finding Rama enlivened her for a moment. If she should meet him sitting somewhere in a park she'd say, 'Tell me, Babuji, now where are you going to run off to?' This imaginary scene brought an elated expression to her face. 'I made a promise to Jalpa that I'd look for him,' she said, 'but I forgot after I came here.'

'Go today,' said Vakil Sahab insistently. 'Not just today, go out every day for a whole hour.'

Looking concerned Ratan said, 'But I'll keep on worrying.'

Vakil Sahab smiled and said, 'About me? I'm getting better.'

'All right,' said Ratan doubtfully, 'I'll go.'

She had begun to have some suspicions of Vakil Sahab's assurances. She saw no signs of his getting better in his bodily manifestations. Why was his face growing paler day by day? Why were his eyes closed all the time? Why was his body wasting away? She was unable to express these doubts to Maharaj and Kahar, and she was embarrassed to ask Dr Kaviraj. If she had met Rama somewhere, she would have asked him. They had been here so long; she would take him to another doctor. She had become somewhat disappointed with this Dr Kaviraj.

When Ratan had gone, Vakil Sahab said to Timal, 'Lift me so I can sit up, Timal. My waist is stiff from so much lying down. And give me a cup of tea. Tea hasn't even shown its face for days. This healthful food is killing me. As soon as I see milk I break out into a fever, but I drink it out of consideration for her. This Kaviraj's treatment doesn't seem to be doing me any good. How does it seem to you?'

Propping up Vakil Sahab with the aid of a pillow, Timal said, 'Babuji, let's see, I was going to say that from the very start. Let's see, I didn't say anything because I was afraid of Bahuji.'

After a silence of several minutes Vakil Sahab said, 'I'm not afraid of death, Timal, not a bit. I don't believe in heaven or hell at all. If people have to be born again according to their essential qualities, then I'm sure I'll be born into some good home. Even so, I don't feel like dying. I think, what will happen when I die!'

'Babuji, let's see, don't say things like that please,' said Timal. 'If God wills, you'll get well. Shall I fetch another doctor? You people have studied English, let's see, you don't believe in anything. Sometimes you should listen to what the villagers say too. Let's see, whether you give them any credit or not, I'm going to bring you an exorcist. The sorcerers and exorcists of Bengal are famous.'

Vakil Sahab turned his face the other way. He had always made fun of the idea of the malevolent effects of evil spirits. He had even given thrashings to several sorcerers. It was his opinion that all this was fraud and trickery, but just now he didn't even have the strength to oppose Timal's suggestion. He turned his face away.

Maharaj brought tea and said, 'Sarkar, I've brought tea.'

Vakil Sahab looked at the cup of tea with hungry eyes and said, 'Take it away, I won't drink it now. If she should find out, she'd be sad. Tell me Maharaj, has my face become a little fresher since I came?'

Maharaj looked towards Timal. He always looked to others' opinions before giving his own. He didn't have the power of thinking for himself. If Timal said, 'You're getting better,' he would confirm it too. If Timal disagreed, then he too felt obliged to disagree. Sensing his uncertainty, Timal said, 'Of course it's fresher, but certainly not as much as it ought to be.'

'Yes, it's somewhat fresher,' said Maharaj, 'but very little.'

Vakil Sahab did not answer. Speaking three or four sentences had tired him out and he lay peacefully inert for five or ten minutes after. Perhaps he had realized his true condition. The shadow of death had fallen on his face, his mind, and his brain. If there was any hope it was only that perhaps the weakness of his mind made his condition seem so wretched. Now and then his inhalations would stop, and it would seem as if he had breathed his last. His mortal agony had begun. Who could know when the obstruction would last a moment longer and bring an end to his life?

In the adjacent park the moonlight had spread a sheet of mist and lay sobbing on the ground. It seemed as if the flowers and bushes, ghosts with bowed heads, torn between hope and fear, put their hands on his chest, touched his cold body, made two tear drops fall, and then looked at him in the same way as before.

Suddenly Vakil Sahab opened his eyes. Two tear drops were irritating both corners of his eyes.

'Timal,' he cried in a feeble voice, 'Has Siddhu come?'

Then, embarrassed by his own question, he smiled and said, 'I thought Siddhu might have come.'

He heaved a deep sigh, fell silent, and closed his eyes.

Siddhu was his son's name; he had died as a young man. His memory was constantly recurring to Vakil Sahab now. Sometimes the boy's childhood appeared before him, sometimes his death came into view—how clear, how full of life these images were. His memory had never been so lifelike, so vivid.

A few minutes later he opened his eyes again and gazed here and there abstractedly. It seemed to him that his mother had come and was asking him how he was.

All of a sudden he said to Timal, 'Come here. Bring me a lawyer. Go quickly, or else she'll be back from her outing.'

Just then the sound of a car horn was heard, and in a moment Ratan arrived. Any thought of summoning a lawyer vanished.

Vakil Sahab, looking pleased, said, 'Where did you go? Did you find out anything about him?'

Putting her hand on his forehead, Ratan said, 'I looked in several places. I didn't see him anywhere. In such a big city one doesn't learn to know the streets quickly, so I wasn't likely to meet him. It's time to take your medicine, isn't it?'

'Bring it, I'll take it,' said Vakil Sahab in a whisper.

Ratan brought forth the medicine and lifting him up gave it to him to drink. She was feeling a little frightened for some reason. An unclear, unknown misgiving was weighing down her heart.

'Should I send a telegram to one of those people?' she asked abruptly.

Vakil Sahab looked at her questioningly. Then grasping her intent on his own he said, 'No, no. There's no need to call anyone. I'm getting better.'

After a moment, making an effort to be alert, he spoke again. 'I want to have my will written out.'

It was as if a cold keen arrow entered Ratan through her foot and came out through her head; as if every joint in her body were loosened, all her limbs disjointed, and every atom of her brain scattered to the winds; as if the earth had gone out from under her, and now she was standing without support, without movement, without life.

'Should I call someone from home?' she said in a choked, tearful, tremulous voice. From whom could she take advice here? There was no one she could call her own.

Now Ratan was feeling impatient for her own relatives and friends, for anyone at all whom she could trust, whose advice she could take. If her family came, they could scurry around and send for some other doctor. What could she do by herself? In the end, what better day for relatives to be of use? It was just in these times of distress that they could render the most service. Then why did Vakil Sahab say not to send for anyone!

She remembered the matter of the will again. Why had that idea occurred to him? The doctor hadn't said anything, had he?

Dear God, what was going to happen? This word, will, with all its associations began to tear apart her heart. She became restless to express her feelings by screaming and crying. She remembered her mother, and a wish came to her to hide her face and cry in the hem of her mother's sari. How much satisfaction it had given her soul as a child to weep into that love-filled hem. How quickly all her distress had been soothed. Ah! Now this support too no longer existed.

Maharaj came and said, 'Sarkar, the food is ready. Shall I serve your thaali?'

Ratan gave him a hard look, and he left quietly without waiting for an answer.

A moment later, however, Ratan felt pity for him. What wrong had he done to come and ask about a meal? Was food something that one could give up? She went into the kitchen and said to him, 'You two eat, Maharaj! I'm not hungry today.'

'Please eat just two chapatis, Sarkar,' pleaded Maharaj.

Ratan was taken aback. There was so much kindness, so much sympathy in his insistence, that she felt a sort of consolation. To think that she had no one of her own here was an oversight. Until now, Maharaj had seen Ratan as a harsh mistress, but today the same mistress was standing in front of him begging for compassion. His better side was touched. Ratan saw a look of keen affection on his weak face.

'Well Maharaj,' she asked, 'Do you think this Kaviraj's treatment is doing Babuji any good?'

Very reluctantly Maharaj repeated the same words he had spoken earlier to Vakil Sahab. 'Something is happening, but not as much as ought to be.'

'Are you trying to fool me too, Maharaj?' said Ratan looking at him disbelievingly.

Maharaj's eyes overflowed with tears. 'God will make everything right, Bahuji,' he said. 'What's there to be alarmed about? We don't have any control.'

'Isn't there any astrologer to be found here?' asked Ratan. 'We could ask him. Having some prayers and scriptures read is good too.'

'I was going to say that before, Bahuji,' said Maharaj with pleasure. 'But you know Babuji's nature, how much these things make him angry.'

'You must certainly bring someone in the morning,' said Ratan firmly.

'The master will take offence.'

'I'm telling you ...'

As she said this she went out of the kitchen into the other room, and sitting down in front of the light began to write a letter to Jalpa.

Sister, I can't tell you what's going to happen. Today I learned that I've fallen into sweet delusions. Babuji had hidden his true condition from me before this, but today it was not in his power to do so. Now I'm the one making excuses. I'm panicking, sister; I feel like taking a little poison and never waking up. The world gives the creator titles—compassionate, kind, the friend of the poor, and who knows how many others. But I say even an enemy could not be more pitiless, more cruel, more harsh than he is. This idea of tendencies from past lives deciding our fate is just something to console our minds. What's the worth of a punishment we know nothing of the reason for? It's a great stick to oppress us, to hammer away on us, and to injure us for some reason or other. I've met with only one flickering lamp along this dark, desolate, thorn-choked path of life. I hid it in the border of my sari, and thanking fate, went singing on my way. But now this light is being snatched away from me! Where will I go in this dark, who will listen to my weeping, who will hold me by my arm?

Pardon me, sister. I didn't have the leisure to find out anything about Babuji. Today I took a turn in several parks, but I didn't learn anything about him anywhere. I'll go again when I have the opportunity.

Give your mother my pranaam.

After writing the letter, Ratan went on to the veranda. A cool breeze was blowing. It was as if nature was lying on the sick bed and heaving sobs.

Just then Vakil Sahab began to breathe very rapidly.

# 30

It was after three o'clock at night. Ratan had been lying in an armchair dozing off and on since midnight, when she suddenly awoke with a start on hearing deep snoring from Vakil Sahab. He was gasping for breath. She sat down at the end of his charpai, lifted his head, and put it on her thigh. She had no idea how late it was, and glanced at the little clock on the table. It was just after three. Four hours were left till morning; Kaviraj would come about nine o'clock. She felt desperate when she realized this. Would this ill-fated night never depart and take its black face away? It seemed as if a whole age had passed.

A few minutes later Vakil Sahab's breath stopped. His whole body was drenched with sweat. He gestured with his hand for Ratan to move away, and putting his head on the pillow closed his eyes again.

All at once, in a feeble voice he said, 'Ratan, it's time to say goodbye now. My offence ...'

He joined his hands together and gazed at her in abject entreaty. He wanted to say something, but no sound came out of his mouth.

Ratan screamed out, 'Timal! Maharaj! Are you both dead?'

Maharaj came and said, 'I had just gone to sleep, Bahuji. Is Babuji ...'

'Don't babble,' Ratan scolded him. 'Go and bring Kaviraj. Tell him to come now.'

Maharaj put on his old overcoat in haste, picked up his staff and set out. Ratan got up and began to light the stove, thinking that perhaps some warmth might be of use. All her panic, all her weakness, all her sorrow had vanished. In their place a powerful self-reliance appeared. Harsh duty aroused her entire being.

When the stove was lit, she began to warm his chest with a flock of cotton. After some fifteen minutes of one application after another, Vakil Sahab's breath became more normal. The noise came under control. Placing both of Ratan's hands on his cheeks, he said, 'You're suffering a lot of stress, darling! How could I know this time would come so fast. I've done you a great wrong, love! Ah, what a great wrong! All my heart's desire remained in my heart. I've destroyed your life—forgive me.'

These were the last words which ever came from his mouth. This was the last formulation of his life, the last tie of affection.

Ratan looked towards the door. There was still no sign of Maharaj. To be sure, Timal was standing there, bottomless darkness before him, but as if he had swooned away in the final agony of his life.

'Timal, would you heat some water?' said Ratan.

Timal standing all the while, said, 'What good is it to heat water, Bahuji? Let him touch the tail of a cow and sprinkle some drops of Ganges water on his face.'

Ratan put her hand on her husband's chest. It was warm. She stared at the door again. Maharaj was nowhere to be seen. Even now she still thought that if Kaviraj came perhaps Vakil Sahab's condition would improve. She was repenting of having brought him there. Perhaps the strain of the trip and the climate had made his illness incurable. She was also regretting having gone out in the evening. Perhaps he'd become cold precisely during her short absence. What else was life but one long repentance!

Was it only one or two things she had to repent for? What comfort had she brought to her husband during these last eight years of his life? He would pore over law books until midnight, while she lay sleeping away. And while he had discussed cases with his clients even during the evening, she had made excursions to the parks and the cinema, and strolled about in the bazaars. What else had she considered him to be but a money-making machine? How much he had wanted her to sit and talk with him, but she had dashed around here and there. She had never tried to move close to his heart, never given him loving looks. She had never lit a lamp in her own house but had wandered around taking pleasure in the lamp-lit homes of others—she had thought of nothing besides her own amusement. A luxurious life and amusement, these had been the two goals of her life. She had been satisfied to calm her burning heart in this way. She had kicked aside her daily bread in a fit of pique because she hadn't received a plate of khir and malai.

Today Ratan became fully acquainted with the love which this departing soul had for her—he had been lost in anxiety about her even just now. For Ratan there had been some pleasure, some interest, some enthusiasm in life. What kind of happiness had there been for him in life? He had taken no pleasure in eating or drinking, nor shown any fondness for fairs and festivals. Was life one long course of austerities, whose chief goal was carrying out one's duty? Couldn't Ratan have made his life happy? Couldn't she have released him for a moment from the cares of his arduous duties? Who could say if this expiring lamp might not have stayed bright some days more with rest and relaxation, but she had never seen herself as having any duties towards her husband. There had always been a rebellion in her inner soul, merely because she had kept asking herself why she had been joined together with him. Had the whole guilt been his? Who was to say whether her poverty-stricken parents, too, had brought her misfortune—were young men the ideal choice for every lady? There were adulterers, hot-tempered brutes, and drunkards among them too. Who could say what her circumstances would have been now if she had married one of them? Ratan was censuring herself with every fibre of her being now. Her head bowed over her husband's cold feet, she began to sob bitterly. All those harsh feelings, which had constantly risen in her heart, all those cutting words she had spoken to him in exasperation, were now stinging her like hundreds of scorpions. Alas! She had behaved like this to a being who had been as deep as the sea. How much tenderness had been in his heart, how much generosity! If she had given him a paan, how pleased he would have been; if she had spoken to him with a smile, how gratified he would have been. But she hadn't done even that much. Her heart was being torn apart by remembering these things one after another. As she bowed her head over his feet she wished with all her might that she could die that very minute. What great affection swelled up in her heart today as her head touched his feet, as if she would have given away the hoarded treasure of an age with no thought of anything in return. Face to face with the supernatural radiance of death, all her internal disaffection, all her ill-temper, all her rebellion, was obliterated.

Vakil Sahab's eyes were open, but there was no sign of any emotion on his face. Even Ratan's frenzied agitation could not kindle his expiring consciousness. He was free from the entanglements of pride and grief; no sorrow for him if someone wept, no happiness if someone laughed!

Timal brought Ganges water in a small ladle and sprinkled it on his face. Today Vakil Sahab made no difficulties. He, who had been the enemy of hypocrisy and tradition, was quiet now, not because he had developed any religious belief, but rather because he no longer had any will. Had he been alive, he would have taken a mouthful of poison rather than be so indifferent.

How peacefully the greatest event of human life takes place. That immense portion of the world, that raging sea of great ambitions, that storehouse of unending efforts, that playground of love and hate, of joy and sorrow, that battlefield of intelligence and strength—no one knows when or how it vanishes, no one. Not even a sob, not even a sigh, not even a wail, comes forth. Who can tell us where a wave of the sea ends? Who knows where a sound is absorbed by the wind? What else is human life but that wave, that sound? Is it any surprise that its completion too is so very quiet, so very invisible? Those who are lovers of the departed ask what substance emanates from the dying. One worshipper of science says it is a subtle radiance which emanates forth. Devotees of the science of imagination say the vital essence may emerge from the eyes, from the mouth, from the crown of the head! Let someone ask them, when a wave is being absorbed, does it flare up? When a sound is vanishing, does it become incarnated? This is merely a rest during that endless journey, not where the journey ends, but where it begins anew.

What an enormous change it is! Someone who couldn't stand the bite of a mosquito, can now be thrust into the earth, or placed on a funeral pyre, and he won't show any displeasure.

Timal glanced at Vakil Sahab's face and said, 'Bahuji, get up and come away from the bed. The master has gone away.'

Then he sat on the ground, and covering his eyes with his hands, burst into tears. Today thirty years of being together had come to an end. The master who had never spoken two words to him, who had never summoned him with the intimate 'tu,' was now leaving him and going away.

Ratan was still waiting for Kaviraj to come. Timal's words struck her like a blow. She rose and put her hand on her husband's chest. After sixty years of restless movement he was now resting. She didn't have the courage to put her hand on his forehead again. As she touched the body and stared at the dead face, she felt indifference mixed with aversion. When her fingers touched the very feet on which she had rested her head and wept, they felt as though they had been slashed with knives! She had never understood how delicate is the thread of life. The thought of death had never entered her mind. And this death had robbed her in front of her eyes!

After a moment Timal said, 'Bahuji, what are you looking at

now? Let's lift him off the bed. What had to happen, has happened.'

He grasped the feet, she the head, and together they laid the body down. Sitting there on the floor, Ratan began to weep, not because now she had no support left in the world, but rather because she had not been able to fulfil her duty to him.

Just then the sound of a car was heard followed by the sound of Kaviraj's footsteps.

Perhaps there was still a dying spark of hope in Ratan's heart! She quickly dried her eyes, adjusted the end of her sari on her head, straightened her dishevelled hair, and standing up, gazed at the door. Dawn had coloured the sky with its golden rays. Was this also the dawn of a new life for Vakil Sahab's soul?

## 31

The corpse was brought to Banaras that very day, and there the cremation took place. A nephew of Vakil Sahab's who lived in Malwa was summoned by a telegram, and he performed the cremation ceremony. Ratan thrilled with horror at the very thought of the funeral pyre; she might have fainted had she gone.

These days Jalpa would spend nearly the whole day with Ratan, who was so distracted by grief that she gave no thought to domestic matters, nor even to eating and drinking. Every day the memory of something or other would set her to weeping for hours. If she had observed even a portion of her obligations to her husband, she would have had some consolation. When she mentioned her neglect of her duty, her harshness, her greediness for finery, she would weep so hard that she would hiccup uncontrollably. She pacified her soul by discussing Vakil Sahab's good qualities. As long as a guardian had been sitting at the door of her life, she had had no concern for dogs and cats, thieves or robbers. But now, because there was no guardian at the door, she remained vigilant—she kept singing the praises of her husband. She and Jalpa never discussed how she was to carry on with her life, which of the servants should be dismissed, or which household expenses should be reduced, as if to be concerned with these would be a lack of devotion to the departed spirit. It also seemed inappropriate to Ratan to eat regular meals, wear clean clothes, or read something to divert her mind. On the day of the shraddh ceremony, she gave all her clothes and ornaments to the officiating Brahman. Of what use were they to her now? On the other hand, she guarded even the smallest possessions of her husband, considering them to be remembrances of him. Her temperament became so gentle that no matter how much damage might occur to something, she didn't get angry. A tea set slipped and fell from Timal's hands, but Ratan didn't even turn a hair. When the very same Timal had broken an inkwell previously, she had scolded him mercilessly and sent him out of the room, but today when much more harm was done, she didn't even open her mouth. It was as if harsher feelings feared to enter her heart lest they be struck down, or perhaps she considered it wrong to allow any thoughts except his praises, or any feelings except grief, into her mind and heart.

Vakil Sahab's nephew's name was Manibhushan, and he was very sociable, cheerful, and competent. In just this one month he had made hundreds of friends. Ratan had no idea of how familiar and informal he had become with all those lawyers and important men who had been acquainted with Vakil Sahab. He began to carry out all the bank business in his own name. Vakil Sahab had twenty thousand rupees deposited in the Allahabad Bank. Manibhushan took control of this, and also began to collect the rent from Vakil Sahab's houses and the village revenues, as if none of this had any connection with Ratan.

One day Timal came and said to Ratan, 'Bahuji, the one who was going has gone, now listen to some news about household affairs too. I've heard that Bhaiyaji has had all the money in the bank put in his name.'

Ratan looked at him so harshly and angrily that he never had the courage to say anything again. That very evening Manibhushan dismissed Timal, charging him with theft. Ratan was not in a position to say anything.

Now only Maharaj was left. Manibhushan plied him with so much bhang that he won him over; Maharaj began to sing his praises. He would say to the maidservant, 'Babuji has a very noble nature. If you bring him some purchases, he never asks how much they cost. He's well-respected in important people's homes.

Bahuji used to split hairs, but this poor fellow says nothing.' The maidservant came into favour as before. She would idle around the outer sitting-room on one pretext or another. Ratan had no inkling of the defences being prepared against her.

One day Manibhushan said to her, 'Kakiji, it seems useless to me now to stay here. I'm thinking of taking you home. Your bahu will take care of you there, the children will amuse you, and the expenses will be less too. If you say so, this bungalow can be sold. We'll get a good price.'

Ratan gave a start as if she had been roused from a faint, or as if someone had shaken her awake. Looking at him disconcertedly, she said, 'Were you saying something to me?'

'Yes, ma'am. I was saying that it's useless for us to live here now. If I were to take you away, how would that be?'

'Yes, that would be all right,' said Ratan sadly.

'If Kakaji wrote a will, then please bring it and I'll take a look.'

'He didn't write a will. And what was the need?' replied Ratan, just as if now she were sitting in the heavens with no concern at all for earthly affairs.

Manibhushan asked again, 'Perhaps he wrote it and put it somewhere?'

'I don't know anything about it. He never mentioned it.'

Secretly pleased, Manibhushan said, 'I'd like to have some memorial built for him.'

'Yes, yes, I'd like that too.'

'You know that the income from the villages is about three thousand a year. That's how much their yearly donation is. I saw their accounts in a book. It's not less than two hundred or two hundred and fifty a month. My advice is to leave all that just as it is.'

'Yes, just that,' said Ratan, pleased.

'So let the income from the villages be put into a religious endowment. The rent from the houses is about two hundred a month. Let a small Sanskrit school in his name be opened from this income.'

'That would be very good.'

'And let this bungalow be sold, and the money be put into the bank.'

'That would be very good,' said Ratan. 'What do I need money for now.'

'We're all ready to serve you. Shall we get rid of the car too? You'll be worrying about all these things from now on, so if we leave, perhaps you'll get some respite in two or three months.'

'What's the hurry now,' said Ratan negligently. 'There's some money in the bank, isn't there?'

'There was some money in the bank, but there've been expenses for a whole month too. There's probably five hundred or a thousand left. It's as if money just flies away in the wind here. I can't stand staying in this city for even a month. We ought to get rid of the car very soon.'

In answer Ratan said the very same thing once again, 'That would be good.' She was in that state of mental frailty when even tiny tasks seem unimaginably huge. Manibhushan's competence defeated her in a way. Even the slight sympathy he showed her at present, she took to mean he was her well-wisher. Grief and remorse had made her mind so fragile and soft that anyone at all could influence it. All her malice and aloofness had been reduced to ashes, and she regarded everyone as one of her own. She had no doubts of anyone, no suspicions of anyone. Perhaps even if some thief had plundered her possessions in front of her, she would have made no outcry.

## 32

After the last of the funeral rites thirteen days after Vakil Sahab's death, Jalpa reduced her visits to Ratan's house. She would only go once a day for an hour or two. At home Munshi Dayanath had had a fever for several days. How could she leave him while he was suffering from his fever? Whenever Munshiji had a touch of fever, he would rave. Sometimes he'd sing, sometimes he'd cry, sometimes he'd see the messengers of Yama, the god of death, dancing before him. He'd set his heart on everyone in the house sitting near him, and on having all his relatives summoned so he could have his final meeting with them because he saw no hope of surviving this illness. Yama himself was standing there in front of them with his aerial vehicle. Jageshwari could manage everything else, but she couldn't stand to hear his nonsense. As soon as he began to weep, she'd leave the room. She questioned the whole business of being plagued by evil spirits.

Munshiji had several files of newspapers in his room; he was addicted to them. When Jalpa began to be restless from sitting there so long, she would start flipping through these files. One day she saw a chess problem in an old paper, for whose solution some gentleman had even offered a prize. She remembered that on the same shelf where Ramanath kept his chess-board and pieces was a notebook in which there were also several such problems. She hastily ran upstairs and took it out. The same problem was in the notebook, and not only the problem but its solution too. Suddenly an idea flashed into Jalpa's mind: how would it be if she had this problem published in some newspaper? Maybe it would catch his eye. The problem was not so easy that it could be quickly solved. When no one in this city was his equal, then the number of people able to solve it could not be large. Whatever else might be, since he had already solved this problem, he'd solve it again as soon as he saw it. Whoever would see it for the first time, would take a day or two to think it over. She would write that whoever found the solution first would receive a prize. It was certainly a gamble. Even if he didn't get the money, at least it was possible that his name would be among those solving it, and she'd learn something of his whereabouts. If nothing happened, then nothing but money would be lost. She'd arrange for a prize of ten rupees. If the prize was small, then no player of any stature would take notice. That would be to Rama's advantage too.

In the midst of this elaborate scheme, she was unable to meet Ratan, but Ratan kept waiting for her the whole day. When she hadn't come by evening, she couldn't bear it. Today she left the house for the first time after her mourning for her husband had begun. There was no excitement anywhere, no life anywhere, as if the whole city were grieving. She loved to drive the car fast, but today she was going even slower than a tonga. Seeing an elderly woman sitting on the side of the street, she stopped the car and gave her four annas. A little farther ahead, two constables were walking with a prisoner in tow. She stopped the car, summoned one of the constables, and giving him a rupee, said, 'Give this prisoner some sweets to eat.' The constable salaamed her and took the rupee, happy in his heart because today he had seen the face of someone blessed with good fortune.

As soon as Jalpa saw her, she said, 'Pardon me, sister. I couldn't come today. Dadaji has had a fever for several days running.'

Ratan at once stepped towards Munshiji's room, asking, 'He's in here, isn't he? Why didn't you tell me?'

Munshiji's fever had subsided somewhat. On seeing Ratan he said, 'I'm very sorry, Deviji, but that's life in this world. Today it's one person's turn, tomorrow another's. This is the fixed movement from life to death. I'm about to go too. I can't be saved. I'm very thirsty; my chest feels as if a hot stove were in it. I'm burning up. There's no one I can call my own, Baiji! All of our relationships in this world are selfish ones. One day a person stretches out his hand and dies. Alas! Alas! I had a son, and he slipped out of my hand too. No one knows where he went. If he were here today he'd give me a mouthful of water. My two other brats don't care at all whether I die or not! They just want to eat and drink three times a day. That's it, they're not good for anything else. When they sit here they both start suffocating. What can I do? This time I'm done for.'

Ratan comforted him. 'This is malaria. You'll be all right in three or four days. It's nothing to get excited about.'

Looking at her dejectedly, Munshiji said, 'Please sit down, Bahuji. You say that if you give me your blessing I might be saved, but I don't have any hope. I'm ready to slap my thighs as a challenge to Yamaraj, the god of death, to fight. I'm going to receive his hospitality now. Where are you going now to save yourself boy! I'll chase him so much that he'll never forget. People say that souls there live just as they do here. There are courts of law just like here, officials, kings, poor people, lectures and newspapers are published. Then what's there to worry about, I'll become a clerk there too! And I'll read the newspapers with pleasure.'

Ratan let out such a laugh that she couldn't keep on standing there. Munshiji wasn't saying these things in jest. His face bore the marks of serious thought. Today Ratan had laughed for the first time in one or two months, and to hide her mirth she went out of the room. Jalpa too came out with her.

Ratan looked at her with guilty eyes and said, 'Who knows what Dadaji must have thought. He probably thinks: "Here I am dying and she feels like laughing." I can't go in there again, or he'll say something again and I won't be able to stop myself from laughing. Just see how ill-timed my laughter was today.'

She began to reproach herself inwardly for her lack of restraint. Jalpa, guessing her state of mind, said, 'I usually feel like laughing at what he says too, sister! Just now his fever is a little lower. When it's higher, he starts saying the silliest things, and then it's hard not to laugh. This morning he was saying, "My stomach has exploded, my stomach has exploded!" He just kept saying it over and over. Neither Mother nor I could understand what he meant. But he kept on repeating it—"My stomach has exploded! My stomach has exploded!" Come, let's go back into the room."

'Won't you come with me?'

'I can't come today, sister.'

'Will you come tomorrow?'

'I can't say. If Dada's condition should improve a little, I'll come.'

'No, bhai, come for sure. I need some advice from you.'

'What advice?'

'Manni says, what's there to do by staying here, let's go home. He says to put up the house for sale.'

Jalpa, suddenly dismayed, seized her hand and said, 'You've given me very bad news, sister! You're going to go off and leave me in this condition? I won't let you go. Tell Manni to sell the house. But until I find out something about him, I won't let go of you. You stayed away for a whole week. For me each moment was like a mountain. I didn't know that I had come to care for you so much. I might die if you go now. No, sister, I'll fall at your feet to beg you to not even mention going away now.'

Ratan's eyes too filled with tears. 'I tell you truly, I couldn't stand it there either. I'll say I don't have to go.' Jalpa, holding her hand, took her to her room upstairs, and putting her arms around her neck, said, 'Swear that you won't go and leave me.'

Ratan embraced her and said, 'Here, I swear I won't go, no matter what happens. What's there for me there? Why should I sell the bungalow? There's two hundred or two hundred fifty from the house rents. It's plenty for both of us to get by. I'll tell Manni today that I'm not going.'

Suddenly she saw the chess pieces and chess problem diagrams on the floor and asked, 'Who were you playing chess with?'

Jalpa told her everything about her scheme to roll the dice of fate on the chess diagrams. She was secretly afraid that her friend would find her proposal worthless, consider it madness, but Ratan was delighted as soon as she heard it. 'Ten rupees is a very small prize,' she said. 'Make it fifty. I'll give the money.'

'But,' said Jalpa doubtfully, 'won't really good players be tempted to compete for a prize that big?'

'It doesn't matter,' said Ratan firmly. 'If Babuji Ramanath sees it, he'll certainly solve it, and I expect that his name would come first. If nothing happens, we'll certainly find out where he is! His address will turn up in the newspaper office. You've certainly thought up a good plan. My heart says it will have good results. I've become convinced of the truth of the heart's urgings. When I went to Calcutta with Vakil Sahab, my heart was telling me that going there wouldn't turn out well.'

'So you have hope?'

'Every hope! I'll bring the money tomorrow morning.'

'Then I'll write the letter today. Whom should I send it to? It should be some well-known newspaper there.'

'The *Praja-Mitra* was mentioned a lot there. You often see people reading it in the libraries.'

'Then I'll write to the *Praja-Mitra*,' said Jalpa. 'But what if they gobble up the money and don't publish the diagram?'

'What would happen? Fifty rupees would be gone. Gobbling up a trifling amount is the mark of someone no better than a dog. But that's not possible. People who go to jail for the welfare of their own country, who endure all kinds of threats, couldn't be that contemptible. If you come with me for half an hour, I'll give you the money right now.'

Half willing, Jalpa said, 'How can I go anywhere now? I'll come tomorrow.'

Just then Munshiji cried out, 'Bahu! Bahu!'

Jalpa darted towards his room. As Ratan was going outside, she saw Jageshwari fanning herself. 'Are you feeling hot, Mother?' she asked. 'I'm shivering with cold. Oh! What's that white stuff all over your feet? Were you grinding flour?'

Looking ashamed Jageshwari said, 'Yes, the vaidya said to feed him bread made with freshly ground flour. Where are you going to get such flour in the bazaar? There's no woman in the neighbourhood to do it on hire. People usually have it ground by female labourers. I'm willing to give an anna for each kilogram, but no one is available.'

'You're using a grindstone?' said Ratan in astonishment.

Smiling abashedly, Jageshwari said, 'It was nothing. A quarter kilogram does for two days. He hardly eats a thing. Jalpa was grinding it, but then I have to sit with her. I can grind away all night, but she can't sit for even a few minutes.'

Ratan went and stood near the hand-mill for a moment, then smiled and sat down on the stool. 'You won't have to grind now, Mother,' she said. 'Bring me a little wheat, and I'll see what I can do.'

Putting her hands to her ears in denial, Jageshwari cried, 'Oh no, Bahu, you're not going to grind anything! Leave here!'

Ratan joined her hands in respectful salutation. 'I've ground flour for a long time, Mother. When I was at home I ground it every day. Bring a little wheat, my Mother.'

'Your hands will ache, you'll get blisters.'

'Nothing will happen, Mother. Please bring some wheat.'

Jageshwari, seizing her hand and trying to make her get up, said, 'There's no wheat in the house. And who's going to bring it from the bazaar this time of day?'

'All right, let it go. I'll take a look in your store-room.'

All the foodstuffs were kept in a room next to the kitchen. Ratan went inside and began poking around the earthen pots. She found some wheat in one of them, and very pleased, said, 'Look Mother, did it turn up or not? You were trying to put me off.'

She took out a little wheat, put it into a basket, and going to the hand-mill began happily grinding away. Jageshwari went to Jalpa and said, 'Bahu, she's sitting at the mill grinding wheat. When I try to make her get up she won't. What will someone say if they see her!'

Jalpa came out of Munshiji's room, and to derive some enjoyment from her mother-in-law's agitation said, 'What disaster have you brought about, Mother! Really, if someone should see this we'll certainly be disgraced! Come on, let me see.'

'What can I do?' said Jageshwari helplessly. 'I tried to persuade her not to, but I failed; she won't listen.'

When Jalpa went and looked, Ratan was absorbed in grinding

the wheat. Her face was glowing with a natural delight. In even this little while beads of perspiration had appeared on her forehead. Her sturdy hands were spinning the hand-mill like a top.

Jalpa laughed and said, 'Hey you, the flour had better be finely ground, or you won't get your money!' Ratan didn't hear her. She smiled uncertainly like deaf people do. Jalpa spoke more loudly. 'Grind the flour very fine, or you won't earn any money!' Ratan laughed too and said, 'I'll grind it just as fine as you tell me to, Bahuji. You should pay me well.'

'Half a paisa per kilo.'

'Half a rupee is the right price!'

'Don't get your hopes up! Half a paisa per kilo is what you'll get.'

'I'll get up when I've ground it all. Why are you standing here?' said Ratan.

'Shall I come, shall I join you too?'

'I feel like singing some hand-mill song!'

'You're going to sing alone?' (To Jageshwari) 'Mother, won't you go sit with Father? I'll come very soon.'

Jalpa sat down by the hand-mill, and the two of them began to sing:

Where have you gone, oh yogi, now that you've bewitched the yogini?

Both of them had sweet voices. The hand-mill, whirling round and round, was doing its work of preparation in accompaniment to their notes. When they would finish a verse and be silent for a moment, the voice of the mill, as if coloured by the echo of their singing, would become even more charming. Both their hearts were full of the natural joy of living just now—there was no burden of grief, no sorrow of separation. They were just like two sparrows twittering away, entranced by the extraordinary splendour of dawn.

# 33

Ramanath's tea-stall had opened, though only at night; it was shut during the day. Even at night it was usually Devidin who minded the shop; still, business was good. On the very first day three rupees came in, and from the second day on, an average of four or five. The tea was so delicious that whoever drank tea there once never went to another stall again. Rama added some things for the customers' enjoyment. When he had accumulated a little money, he bought a handsome table. After the lamp was lit in the evening, the sales of vegetables didn't amount to much, so Rama would take the baskets inside and put the table on the veranda. He'd put a set of playing-cards on the table, and he also began to subscribe to two daily newspapers. The tea-stall thrived. In three or four hours six or seven rupees would come in, and after all the expenses were subtracted, three or four rupees would be left.

In these three or four months of enforced austerity, Rama's craving for a life of pleasure grew even more vehement. He was powerless as long as he had no money in hand. As soon as money began to come, he gave full rein to his craze for trips and outings. He remembered the movies too. Many of the ordinary things of daily life which he'd had to put off getting before, now began to appear without restraint. He bought a beautiful silk sheet for Devidin. Jaggo had recurring headaches, so one day he brought her two little bottles of scented oil. Both of them were gratified. If the old woman would take some load on her head now, he would scold her. 'Kakiji, now that I've begun to earn a little money too, why are you killing yourself? If I see you putting a basket on your head again, I tell you, I'll pick up the shop and throw it away. Then you can give me any punishment you want.' Hearing this son-like scolding the old woman was thrilled. Whenever she brought a load from the market, she would sneak a look to see whether Rama was in the shop or not. If he was sitting there, she'd give some porter one or two paisas to put the load on his head. If he wasn't there she would rush to the shop, quickly lower her burden, and sit at ease, so that Rama would not find her out.

One day a new and much-talked-about drama of Radheshyam's was being put on at the Manorma Theatre, and people were securing their seats a day before. Rama too, was mad to reserve a place. If he couldn't get a ticket for the night performance, he thought, he'd go wild with impatience. Everyone was praising the show highly, and seats were no longer available at even double the price. This eagerness of his thrust aside even fear of the police.

Surely he was not so unfortunate that the police would catch him as soon as he set foot outside the house. If day time was not a good time, then he'd go out at night. But if the police wanted to, couldn't they catch him at night too? But then again, his description was no longer correct. A turban would be more than enough to change the appearance of his face. Persuading himself thus, he left the house at ten o'clock. Devidin had gone somewhere. The old woman asked, 'Where are you going, son?' Rama answered, 'Nowhere in particular, Kaki. I'll be right back.'

Once Rama was on the street, though, his daring began to melt away like snow. At every step he suspected that some constable was approaching. He believed that every policeman, even the lowest chaukidars, knew his description and would recognize his face at a glance. Suddenly the thought occurred to him that undercover plain-clothes policemen roamed around all over the place. Who knew but that the man who was just approaching him might not be some police spy. How attentively he was looking towards him. Wasn't he getting suspicious of someone going along with lowered head like this? Everyone else was looking straight ahead, and then here was someone—Rama—going along somewhere with his head down. To walk along in the midst of this hurly-burly of motor-cars with bowed head was to invite death. Anyone could take such a stroll in a park without being noticed. Here, he ought to look straight ahead. But the man next to him was still staring in his direction; perhaps he *was* from the secret police. To get rid of him, Rama stopped at a shop to have some paan. The man continued on his way, and Rama heaved a sigh of relief.

Now he lifted his head and began to go forward with a stout heart. He knew nothing about their routes at this time, or he would have travelled by tram. He had gone only a short distance when three constables were seen coming towards him. Rama left the street and began to walk along a footpath! What kind of bravery is it to put your fingers into the hole of a snake without rhyme or reason. By great bad luck, the three constables also left the street and took the footpath. (One had to repeatedly dodge here and there to avoid the coming and going of the automobiles.) Rama's heart began to pound. To take another footpath would make things even more suspicious. There was no lane he could slink into either. By now they had come quite near. What was the matter? They were all looking towards him. How stupid he'd been to put on this turban, and how useless it had been. A tiny thing had risen up to undo him. This turban was going to get him caught. He'd put it on to change his appearance, but on the contrary, it had made an even bigger spectacle of him. Yes, the three of them were staring at him. They were talking among themselves too. It seemed to Rama that his legs had no strength. Perhaps they were all comparing him to his official description in their minds. Nothing could save him now. How ashamed his family would be when they got news of his arrest. Jalpa would weep her life away. He wouldn't get less than five years punishment; his life was coming to an end today.

His imagination filled him with such terror that he lost his presence of mind completely. By the time the group of constables reached him, his face was so distorted by fear, his eyes so alarmed, and his gaze so unnatural in searching out other people to avoid the eyes of the police, that it would have been natural for even an ordinary person to be suspicious of him. So how could he escape the practised eyes of these policemen? One of them said to his companions, 'If that man's not a thief, then I'll lose my bet. He looks around just like a thief!' The second said, 'I'm having a few doubts about him myself. You've said it, Pande, he's a real thief.'

The third man was a Muslim; he shouted at Rama, 'Oh sir, oh Mr Turban, come over here, won't you? What's your name?'

'What do you mean by asking my name?' said Rama arrogantly. 'Am I a thief?'

'Not a thief, an honest man. Why won't you give your name?'

Rama hesitated for a moment, then said, 'Hiralal.'

'Where's your home?'

'Home!'

'Yes, your home is just what I'm asking about.'

'Shahjahanpur.'

'Which neighbourhood?'

Rama had never been to Shahjahanpur, nor did he remember any imaginary name to tell his questioner. Losing his courage he said, 'You must be writing up my description.'

'Your description has already been written up,' said the constable threateningly. 'You gave a false name, a false address, and when I asked for your neighbourhood you looked away embarrassed. We've been looking for you for months, and today we found you. Let's get going to the police station.'

He seized Ramanath's hand as he said this. Rama, trying to free his hand, said, 'Bring a warrant, then I'll go. Do you take me for a country bumpkin?'

'Grab his hand,' said the constable to one of his companions. 'You'll see the warrant at the station.'

In cities incidents like this are even more entertaining than conjurers or jugglers, and hundreds of people had gathered. Just then Devidin was returning home after taking some opium, and seeing the crowd he came to have a look too. Seeing three constables dragging Ramanath away, he stepped forward and said, 'Hey! Hey! Corporal, what are you doing? This Punditji is our guest. Where are you taking him off to?'

The three constables were acquainted with Devidin. They stopped, and one of them said, 'He's your guest? Since when?'

Devidin did some calculations in his head and said, 'It must be a little more than four months. I met him in Prayag. That's where he lives too. He came from there with me.'

The Muslim policeman, secretly pleased, said, 'What's his name?'

'Didn't he tell you his name?' asked Devidin, taken aback.

The policeman's suspicions were confirmed. 'It seems that you've met him,' said Pande glaring threateningly. 'Why aren't you telling us his name?'

'Understand, browbeating doesn't work with me, Pande!' said Devidin with ill-founded courage. 'Threats are no good here!'

The Muslim constable, as if he were a mediator, said, 'Old Father, you're getting upset for no good reason. Why won't you tell us his name?'

Looking towards Rama in distress, Devidin said, 'We call him Ramanath. We don't know whether that's his real name or not.'

Glaring at Rama and lifting up his palm as if to strike, Pande said, 'Speak Punditji, what *is* your name? Ramanath or Hiralal? Or both—one for your family, one for your in-laws?'

The third constable addressed the onlookers. 'His name is Ramanath, he says Hiralal. We've proved it.'

The onlookers began to whisper among themselves—it was certainly a suspicious thing.

'It's clear that he gave both a wrong name and address.'

A Marwari gentleman said, 'He's a pickpocket, then?'

A maulvi sahab said, 'He's a wanted criminal.'

Seeing the crowd was with them, the police became even more forceful. Rama now saw that his welfare lay in going quietly along with them. He bowed his head as if he didn't care at all whether a lathi or a sword struck it. Never before had he been so disgraced. Even suffering the rigours of jail could not give rise to this much self-humiliation.

The police station came into sight in a little while. The crowd of spectators diminished to only a few. Rama stared towards it in shame and hope. But there was no trace of Devidin. A sigh escaped from Rama's mouth. Had this support too slipped out of his grasp in this calamity?

## 34

In the office of the police station just then, four men were sitting at a big table. One was the Daroga, rather fair complexioned and an enthusiast of things Western; his large eyes glowed with mildness. Next to him was the Assistant Daroga. He was a Sikh, fond of joking, the very embodiment of liveliness, wheat-coloured in complexion, with a well-built compact body. He wore the long hair and steel bracelets of an orthodox Sikh, but he didn't abstain from cigars. On the other side of the table the Inspector and the Deputy Superintendent were sitting. The Inspector was a middle-aged dark-complexioned man with small cowrie-shaped eyes, heavy cheeks, and very short in stature. The Deputy Superintendent was a tall, lean youth, very thoughtful and taciturn. His long nose and lofty forehead bore witness to his aristocratic descent.

Taking a puff from his cigar, the Deputy said, 'We can't pull it off without an external witness. We'll have to turn one of them into an "approver". There is no alternative.'

Looking towards the Daroga, the Inspector said, 'We didn't leave anything undone, I swear it. We tried all kinds of entrapments and failed. They've all bonded together so strongly that we can't break any of them. We even tried to examine some prospects for external witnesses, but no one would listen to us.'

'We'll have to examine that Marwari again,' said the Deputy. 'Send for his father and threaten him a lot. Maybe that will bring him around.'

'On my honour, that's just what we've been doing since this morning,' said the Inspector. 'The poor father fell at his son's feet, but the boy wouldn't budge.'

For a little while all four sat lost in thought. Finally, the Deputy said in a discouraged tone, 'The case won't go. We'll get a bad name for nothing.'

'Delay things for one more week,' said the Inspector. 'Maybe someone will break.'

After making this decision, both the Inspector and the Deputy left along with the Assistant Daroga. The Daroga had just sent for his hookah when suddenly the Muslim constable appeared and said, 'Darogaji, please arrange for a reward. We've arrested a suspected criminal. He's from Allahabad and his name is Ramanath. At first he gave a false name and residence. He's staying with Devidin Khatik, the one who lives at the corner. If you scold him a little, he'll blab everything he knows.'

'You mean the Devidin whose two sons ...' said the Daroga.

'Yes sir, that's the one.'

In the meantime Ramanath was brought before the Daroga, who looked him over from head to foot as if he was comparing him in his mind to his police description. Then giving him a hard look, he said, 'Well, so this is Ramanath from Allahabad. Well met, brother. You've been giving us trouble for six months. Your police description is so clear that even a blind man could recognize you! When did you come here?'

'Tell the truth about everything, and things won't go hard with you,' the constable advised Rama.

Trying to look cheerful Rama said, 'I'm in your hands now, whether you're lenient or harsh. I was an employee of the Allahabad Municipality. Call it stupidity or bad luck, but I spent three hundred rupees of government duties. I couldn't get enough money together to pay it back on time. Out of shame, I said nothing to my family members, otherwise it wouldn't have been difficult to arrange for that much money. When everything fell apart, I ran away and came here. Every word of this is true.'

'This case is rather interesting,' said the Daroga gravely. 'Did you have a taste for liquor?'

'Put me on oath if ever any liquor touched my mouth.'

'Perhaps he was robbed in the bazaar of love, your honour,' said the constable, making a joke.

Rama smiled and said, 'How would I have time for such cheerful people back there?'

'So did you gamble it away? Or throw it away on jewels for your wife?' said the Daroga.

Rama, ashamed, fell silent. A guilty smile spread over his face.

'That's good,' said the Daroga. 'You'll find especially large ornaments here.'

All of a sudden old Devidin came and stood there.

'What business do you have here?' said the Daroga in a harsh voice.

'I came to give salaams to your honour,' said Devidin. 'Look kindly on this poor wretch, your honour, he's very plain and simple, poor fellow.'

'Watch out, you've been hiding a criminal wanted by the government in your home. Did you come to give him a recommendation?'

'How could I recommend him, your honour? I'm a person of no account.'

'Did you know there's a warrant out on him? He's embezzled government money,' said the Daroga.

'Your honour, it's human to forget and to make mistakes. He's in the days of his youth, he probably spent it—'

As he said this Devidin took out five guineas and put them on the table.

'What's this?' said the Daroga, flaring up.

'It's nothing, your honour,' said Devidin. 'Just for having some paan.'

'You want to bribe me, do you? Look out or I'll have you sent up on the same charge.'

'Please send me, sir. It will save my wife the worry of getting a shroud and wood for my funeral pyre. I'll pray for you as I sit there in jail.'

'If you want to get him released,' said the Daroga, 'then bring fifty guineas here in front of me. Did you know there's a five hundred rupee reward for capturing him!'

'What's a reward like that to you people. This is a poor stranger, who'll remember you as long as he lives.'

'Don't talk nonsense. I didn't come here to earn religious merit.'

'I'm very hard up, your honour. I hardly get any money from the shop.'

'Go and ask for some from your old woman,' said the constable.

'I'm the one who earns the money, brother,' said Devidin. 'You know what happened to my boys. I scraped some money together by practically starving myself, so now I've just come back from a pilgrimage to the seven holy sites, I'm really hard up.'

'Then take your guineas,' said the Daroga. 'Throw him out of here.'

'Whatever you say, that's fine, I'm going. So why are you having me treated so roughly?' said Devidin.

'Put him in custody!' said the Daroga to the constable. 'And tell the Munshi to take down his statement.'

Devidin's lips were trembling with strong feelings. Rama had never seen such agitation on his face, as if some sparrow was beside itself with emotion on seeing crows forcing their way into its nest. He stayed standing at the door of the police station for a minute, then spun around and said something to a constable, then plunged toward the street and left, but returned in an instant and said to the Daroga, 'Your honour, won't you give me a two-hour extension?'

Rama was still standing in the same spot. Seeing so much tender concern, he burst into tears. 'Dada, don't upset yourself now. Let what's written in my fate happen. Even if my own father were here, what more could he do? Until my dying breath, your kindness ...'

Wiping his eyes, Devidin said, 'What are you talking about, Bhaiya? When it comes to money Devidin is not one to turn his back on you. I've lost or won this much money gambling in one day. If I were to sell the house just now, it'd be worth ten thousand. Should I put it on my head and bring it here? Darogaji, don't send my brother into custody now. I'll provide for the money and come back in just a little while.'

When Devidin left, the Daroga said in a voice filled with kindness, 'He's a cunning old man to be sure, but very good-hearted. What did you drug him with?'

'Everyone has pity on the poor,' said Rama.

The Daroga smiled and said, 'Except the police, you should say. I'm not sure that he'll bring fifty guineas.'

'Even if he does bring it, I don't want him to pay such a big penalty. Put me in custody at your pleasure,' said Rama.

'When I'm getting six hundred and fifty instead of five hundred, why should I pass it up? If some other good friend of mine should get the reward for your capture, what's the harm?'

'If I have to do hard labour, then the sooner the better,' said Rama. 'I thought I could live here and escape the attention of the police. Now I know that this apprehension and this twenty-four-hour-a-day fear of being caught are just as deadly as jail itself.'

It seemed that the Daroga had suddenly remembered something he had forgotten. He took out a file from a drawer, flipped back and forth through its pages, then in a mild tone said, 'If I were to tell you some plan by which Devidin's money would be saved and there'd be no blot on your reputation either, how would that be?'

'I have no hope of any such plan,' said Rama in disbelief.

'Well sir,' said the Daroga, 'God has a hundred different ways to play with us. I can arrange it. All you have to do is give testimony in a court case.'

'False testimony?'

'No, completely true testimony. See it like this: it will make a man out of you, you'll escape the clutches of the Municipality, and the government might even give you some financial support. As it is, if your case is sent up, you won't get less than five years punishment. Suppose that this time Devi manages to save you, how long can a nanny-goat look out for her kid, I mean how long can he stop what fate has in store for you? Your life will be ruined. You can understand for yourself what your gains and losses may be. I'm not trying to force your hand.'

The Daroga related the description of a robbery. Rama had read about such cases in the newspapers. 'So I'll have to become an informer and say that I was a partner of these robbers?' said Rama hesitantly. 'That would be false testimony.'

'The case is completely genuine,' said the Daroga. 'You won't be entrapping any innocent people. Only those who ought to, will go to jail. So where's the falsehood then? The people around here are not willing to give testimony out of fear of the robbers. That's all there is to it. I agree that you'll have to tell some lies, but from the standpoint that you'll be beginning a new life, a few lies amount to nothing. Think it over carefully, and give me an answer by evening.'

These words sank deep into Rama's mind. If by lying once he could atone for his previous misdeeds and improve his future too, then what was there to consider? He'd escape going to jail. There was no need for a lot of back-and-forthing. Of course, it ought to be made certain that the Municipality would not make the same accusation against him again, and that he'd get some good position. He knew the police needed him and that they wouldn't refuse any appropriate conditions he might make. Rama spoke as if his soul was caught in some sort of moral crisis. 'I'm afraid that my testimony may implicate some innocent people.'

'I give you my assurance that it won't,' said the Daroga.

'But if the Municipality goes for my jugular tomorrow, who will I call on for help?'

'The Municipality won't have the right to utter even a peep. In criminal cases, the plaintiff is the government itself. When the government pardons you, how can it bring a case against you? A written pardon will be given to you, Sahab.'

'And a job?' said Ramanath.

'The government itself will arrange that. The government wants to keep people like you as its friends. If your testimony is first-rate and you don't get caught in any of the traps of the other side's cross-questioning, then you'll be a made man!'

The Daroga sent for a motor-car and taking Rama along with him set off to meet the Deputy Superintendent Sahab. Why should he delay in displaying his skilful handling of things? He met alone with the Deputy and praised himself to the skies. He'd found out about this man in this way: as soon as he'd seen his face, he'd at once guessed that he was a fugitive, and arrested him on the spot! His guess had turned out to be one hundred per cent right; after all, could his judgement be mistaken? 'I recognized the eyes of a criminal, your honour. He has absconded after embezzling money from the Allahabad Municipality. He's ready to give testimony in the case at hand. The man is educated and looks to be of good family and intelligent.'

'Yes, the fellow appears to be clever,' said the Deputy doubtfully.

'But without a pardon he won't have any confidence in us. If he should ever suspect we're playing a trick on him, he'll go back on us,' said the Daroga.

'That's for sure,' said the Deputy. 'We'll have to have a discussion with the government about him. Telephone the Allahabad police and ask them if there's a case against this fellow. We'll have to tell the government all this.'

The Daroga looked in the telephone directory, dialled the number and began talking.

'What did he say?' asked the Deputy

'He's says there's no case there against a person by that name.'

'I don't understand how that can be, brother,' said the Deputy. 'He didn't change his name, did he?'

'He says no one embezzled any money from the Municipality. There's no such case.'

'That's very surprising. The fellow says that he took the money and ran off. The Municipality says that no one embezzled any money. He's not crazy, is he?'

'I don't understand a thing,' said the Daroga. 'If we tell him there's no charge against him, he'll be gone so fast we won't even see his dust.'

'All right, call and enquire at the Municipality office.'

The Daroga dialled another number, and another question-and-answer session began.

'Was there a clerk named Ramanath in your office?'

'Yes, there was.'

'Did he embezzle some money and abscond?'

'No, he ran away from home, but he didn't embezzle any money. Is he there with you?'

'Yes, we arrested him. He himself says that he embezzled some money. What's going on?'

'You police always have an answer for everything. Use your brains.'

'Our minds aren't working here.'

'Not just there, they don't work anywhere. Listen, Ramanath

made a mistake in adding up the total receipts, panicked, and ran away. We learned later that there was no shortage in the deposit. Do you follow?'

'What can we do now, Khan Sahab!' said the Deputy to the Daroga. 'The bird has flown the coop.'

'How so, your honour? Why should this be told to Ramanath? It's easy, just don't let anyone meet him who could acquaint him with outside news. His family will definitely learn where he is now, and somebody or other will certainly come in search of him. Don't let anyone come to see him. Don't let anything in writing be given to him. Let him be reassured verbally. Let him be told that a report has been given to the Commissioner Sahab for his pardon. We should consult the Inspector Sahab too.'

While the Daroga and the Inspector were conferring with the Deputy Superintendent, Devidin had returned to the police station after an hour. 'The Daroga has gone to the Deputy's,' the constable told him.

'Has the Babuji been taken into custody?' asked Devidin, alarmed.

'No, he took him along.'

Striking his head, Devidin said, 'You can't trust anything that policemen say. I told him I'd be back in an hour with the money, but he didn't have even that much patience. He'll get five hundred from the government; I'm ready to give him six hundred. Yes, in the government it's just doing your duty, what else? They'll send him back to Prayag from there; I'll never even meet him. The old woman will cry herself to death.' And Devidin sat down on the floor right there.

'How long are you going to sit there?' said the constable.

As if stung by an insect, Devidin said, 'I'll go when I've had a word or two with the Daroga. Even if I have to go to jail, I'll certainly scold him, scold him badly. After all, he has children too. Doesn't he fear God even a little? Did you see the Babuji as he was leaving? He was very sad!'

'He wasn't sad at all,' said the constable. 'He was laughing a lot. Both of them got into an automobile and left.'

'Oh yes, he must have been laughing, poor fellow!' said Devidin disbelievingly. 'Even if he was laughing with his face, he must have been crying in his heart.'

Devidin had not been sitting there an hour when all of a sudden Jaggo arrived. Seeing Devidin sitting by the door she said, 'What are you up to here? Where is Bhaiya?'

Devidin, deeply wounded, said, 'They took Bhaiya to the Superintendent. No one knows if we can meet him or if he'll be sent back secretly to Prayag.'

'The Superintendent's more important than the Daroga,' said Jaggo. 'So how could the Daroga say he'd take such and such an amount. Where did they take him?'

'That's just why I'm sitting here: so when he comes I can have a word or two with him.'

'Yes, scold him for sure,' said Jaggo. 'What a shame to his father is a man who's not true to his word. I'll tell him right out, "Do you think you're going to collect some kind of tax from me?"'

'Who's at the shop?'

'I closed it and came here. The poor fellow hasn't even eaten anything yet. He hasn't had a single thing since morning. Let the whole affair go to the devil! He went to get a ticket just for this! If he hadn't gone out of the house this calamity wouldn't have fallen on his head.'

'Suppose they send him to Prayag, then what?' said Devidin.

'Then as soon as a letter comes, we'll go and see him there.'

Wiping tears from his eyes, Devidin said, 'He's going to receive a sentence.'

'If we get the money together, then how's he going to get a sentence? Won't the government take back its own money?'

'No, you little fool, it's not like that. Even if the stolen money is given back, there's no way they'll let him go.'

Jaggo, realizing the grimness of the situation, said, 'Darogaji ...'

She wasn't even able to finish what she was about to say when the Daroga's motor-car pulled up in front of them. The Inspector Sahab was there too. As soon as Rama saw the two of them, he got out of the car, came to them, and looking pleased, said, 'Have you been sitting here long, Dada? Come on, let's go into the room. When did you come, Mother?'

'Speak up, Chaudhuri, have you brought the money?' said the Daroga jokingly.

'When I said I was coming back in a little while, you should have waited for me. Take your money, please.'

'Did you dig it up from somewhere?' asked the Daroga.

'By your grace, I can get five hundred to a thousand or more right now. There's no need to dig in the ground. Come on Bhaiya, the old woman's been standing here quite a while. I've come to pay you off. That was the Inspector Sahab, wasn't it? He used to be in this very station.'

'Well, bhai,' said the Daroga, 'take your money and put it back in that same pot. The advice of my superiors is that we shouldn't let him go. It's not something in my power.'

The Inspector had already gone into the office. The three of them—Devidin, Rama and the Daroga—went into the adjoining room.

When Devidin heard what the Daroga said, he scowled. 'Darogaji,' he said, 'men say what they mean, I know that much. I brought the money as you told me to. You have to keep your promise. To go back on your word after you've said something is the way scum behaves.'

The Daroga ought to have been infuriated after hearing such harsh words, but he didn't mind it at all. He laughed and said, 'Bhai, call me scum, call me a cheat if you want, but we can't let him go. You don't get big game like this every day. I can't put a promise ahead of my promotion.'

Devidin grew hotter hearing the Daroga laugh. 'So what side of your mouth were you speaking from?'

'I spoke out of this side of my mouth, but my mouth doesn't always stay the same. I use this same mouth to abuse someone, and to praise him too.'

Flaring up, Devidin said, 'I hope someone teaches you a lesson by tearing your moustache off!'

'I agree with great pleasure. That was my intention from the first, but I didn't do it out of shame. Now, you've strengthened my heart.'

'Don't laugh, Darogaji. When you laugh my blood boils. I'll say something to the Captain Sahab for sure, even if I have to go to jail. I'm a no-account person, but by your grace I've got connections with very important officers.'

'Oh my dear friend, are you really going to complain against me to the Captain?'

Devidin thought that his threat had worked. 'When you don't listen to what anyone says, when you go back on your word, then others will do what they think best,' he said insolently. 'The Captain's wife comes to our shop every day.'

'Listen, Devi,' said the Daroga. 'If you make any complaint against me to the Captain or his wife, I swear to you that I'll have your house knocked down and thrown away.'

'The day my house is knocked down, that turban and that badge won't stay where they are either, your honour.'

'All right then, shake hands on it! We'll each give the other a couple of blows, that's right!'

'You'll be sorry, sir, I tell you, you'll be sorry.'

Rama could no longer restrain himself. Till now he'd been standing and watching the spectacle of Devidin's anger as abjectly as a wet cat. Letting out a guffaw he said, 'Dada, Darogaji is provoking you. We've settled things so that I'll go free without any giving or taking, and on top of that I'll get a position. The Sahab has given a definite promise. I'll have to stay here now.'

'What's this you're saying, Bhaiya, what are you saying?' said Devidin like a man who has lost his way. 'Have you been tricked by the police? There must be some scheme or other hidden here.'

'I have to give testimony in a case, that's all,' said Rama confidently.

'It must be a phoney case,' said Devidin, shaking his head sceptically.

'No, Dada, it's a completely straightforward matter. I've already asked.'

Devidin's doubts were not pacified. 'I can't say anything more about this, Bhaiya. Just think it over a little before you do anything. If you're worried about my money, then understand that if Devidin cared about money, he'd be a millionaire today. These hands have earned hundreds of rupees every day and thrown it all away. Which case do you have to give testimony in? Do you know anything about it?'

The Daroga giving Rama no opportunity to reply, said, 'It's that robbery case in which several poor people lost their lives. These dacoits created a disturbance through the whole province. Out of fear for them, no one was willing to give evidence.'

'Oh, so he's become an informer?' said Devidin contemptuously. 'So that's it. You'll have to say just what the police teach you, Bhaiya. I'm a man that doesn't understand much, so how could I know the real truth about these things, but if I were told to become an informer, I wouldn't, even if they gave me a lakh of rupees. How can an outsider know who's guilty and who's innocent? Along with three or four criminals there'll certainly be three or four innocent people too.'

'Never,' said the Daroga. 'All of the men who were caught were real dacoits.'

'That's what you say, isn't it?' said Devidin. 'How can I know?'

'Why would we try to implicate innocent people?' said the Daroga. 'Think about that.'

'I've been through all that, Darogaji,' said Devidin. 'It would be better if you would commit them to trial. They'd get a year or two in jail. For the price of one guilty person escaping punishment, you wouldn't have the blood of innocent people on your head.'

'I've thought a lot, Dada,' said Rama timidly. 'I've looked at all the papers. There are no innocent people in this case.'

'Maybe, bhai,' said Devidin sadly. 'Life is very precious too.'

He turned away as he said this. He wasn't able to express his inner feelings any more clearly than this.

Suddenly he remembered something. He turned and said, 'Should I give you some money before I go?'

'What's the need?' said Rama, abashed.

'He'll have to stay right here from today on,' said the Daroga.

'I know that, your honour,' said Devidin in a harsh voice. 'He'll be feasted, he'll have a bungalow to live in, servants, a motor-car. I know all this. No one from outside will be able to meet him, nor will he be able to come and go alone. I've seen all this.'

Devidin left very quickly after he said this, as if he were suffocating there. The Daroga called to him, but he turned away without looking. The pain of defeat was spread over his face. Jaggo asked, 'Isn't Bhaiya coming?'

Devidin, staring at the street said, 'Bhaiya won't be coming now. He didn't become one of us, and now he's the most distant of strangers.'

He left, and the old woman, fuming, followed behind.

# 35

How much delight there is in crying! And how much peace and strength! Anyone who has not sat alone moaning and groaning, weeping and wailing over the memory of someone or the absence of someone, has been deprived of one of the joys of life, worth sacrificing hundreds of laughs for! Ask those that have received this good fortune about the pleasure of this sweet sorrow. After laughing, the mind becomes distressed, the soul disturbed, as if we've grown tired, been defeated. After crying one experiences a new vigour, a new life, a new enthusiasm. When a letter from the office of the *Praja Mitra* reached Jalpa, she read it and burst into tears. Holding the letter in one hand and grasping the doorframe with the other, she wept copiously. Who can say what thoughts made her weep? Perhaps the success of her scheme beyond all her hopes made her soul delirious, took her to the depths of joy, where water is, or to those heights where heat becomes frost. Today, after six months, this happy news had reached her. How long had she been the plaything of treacherous hopes and harsh disappointments? Ah! How many times had the urge to end this life swelled up in her heart! If she had really sacrificed her life, she would never have even seen him! But how hard his heart was. He had sat there for six months without writing a single letter, without even enquiring. Hadn't he understood, after all, that she was likely to weep herself to death from all this? When had he ever cared about her? A man would spend ten or twenty rupees on even his friends and companions. This was not love. Love was a thing of the heart, not of money. As long as there was no trace of Rama, Jalpa had taken the whole blame on her own head. But today, as soon as she had news of him, her heart suddenly hardened. All kinds of reproaches arose. What did he think he was doing sitting there? It was because he was independent, free, not eating someone else's food. If she had gone off like that without saying a word, how would he have behaved towards her? Perhaps he'd have come with a sword and tyrannized her; or perhaps he'd never have looked at her face for the rest of her life. Jalpa opened a complaints office in her innermost heart as she stood there.

All at once Ramesh Babu called out from the doorway, 'Gopi, Gopi, come here please.' Munshiji Dayanath, lying in his room, groaned and said, 'Who is it, bhai? Come into the room! Oh my! It's you, Ramesh Babu! Babuji, I was dying and now I've revived. I just want you to understand that I've got a new lease on life. There's no one ahead or behind. Both boys are good-for-nothings, it means nothing to them whether I live or die. Their mother gets afraid as soon as she sees my face. In a word, it's my poor daughter-in-law who's saved my life. If it weren't for her, I'd have passed on by now.'

Giving false condolences, Ramesh Babu said, 'You've become this sick and I wasn't even informed! Even though I'm here, you're still suffering this much! Your daughter-in-law didn't write me even one note either. You'll have to take leave?'

'I sent a request for leave, but Sahab, I didn't send a doctor's certificate. Where was I going to get sixteen rupees? One day I went to the Civil Surgeon, but he refused to write a letter. You certainly know that he won't do anything without taking a fee. I came back and sent the request. I don't know if it was accepted or not. That's the way it is with doctors. They see that a person is practically dying, but they won't lift a foot without a little present!'

Ramesh Babu, looking worried, said, 'You've told me some very bad news. If your leave is not approved, what will happen?'

'What will happen? I'll just sit at home. If the Head asks, I'll tell him straight out that I went to the Surgeon and he didn't give me leave. After all, why did the government appoint him? Simply to increase the splendour of the chair he sits in? He's willing to see me dismissed, but he won't give me a certificate. The brats have disappeared, and there's no one to even bring you some paan. What can I do!'

Ramesh smiled and said, 'Don't distress yourself over me. I haven't come to take paan, I've come to eat a bellyful of sweets.' (Calling to Jalpa.) 'Bahuji, I've brought some good news for you. Send for some sweets.'

Jalpa placed the paan in front of him and said, 'Tell me the news first, please. Maybe the news you think is fresh has gone stale!'

'I hope that's not so, dear! I've learned where Rama is. He's in Calcutta.'

'I already knew that.'

Munshiji sat bolt upright. It was as if his fever fled and hid itself under the cover of his eagerness. He caught hold of Ramesh's hand and said, 'You've learned he's in Calcutta? Did some letter come?'

'It wasn't a letter,' said Ramesh. 'It was a police inquiry. I told them that there was no charge of any kind against him. How did you find out, Bahuji?'

Jalpa described her scheme, and showed the letter from the office of the *Praja-Mitra* too. There was a receipt for the prize along with the letter which bore Rama's signature.

'It's Rama Babu's signature all right,' said Ramesh. 'It's very clear. It couldn't possibly be forged. I agree with you, Bahuji. Splendid! What a clever piece of work you pulled off! You outwitted everybody. No one thought of it. When we think of it now, it seems such a simple thing. Someone ought to go who can save him, and drag him back here.'

Ratan arrived as this conversation was going on. As soon as Jalpa saw her, she left the room, embraced her, and said, 'Sister, a letter came from Calcutta, he's there.'

'Do you swear by my life?'

'Yes, I'm telling you the truth. Look at the letter, won't you!'

'So go this very day.'

'That's just what I was thinking. Will you come?'

'I'm ready to come,' said Ratan, 'but who will I leave to look after the empty house? Sister, I'm beginning to have some doubts about Manibhushan. His intentions don't seem to be good. There wasn't less than twenty thousand in the bank, but somehow or other it's all been squandered. He says it was all spent for funeral expenses. When I ask for an accounting, he looks at me angrily. He keeps the key to the office with him, and when I ask for it, he puts me off. He's playing some legal trick on me. I'm afraid if I go away and leave him here, he'll sell everything and run off. Potential buyers are coming to look at the bungalow. I'm also thinking that I'll go live peacefully in some village. If the bungalow is sold, I'll have some ready money in hand. If I don't stay here, maybe I won't even see that money. Take Gopi along and leave today. I'll make arrangements for money.'

'Gopinath may not be able to go,' said Jalpa. 'Someone has to look after Dada's medicines too.'

'I'll do that,' said Ratan. 'I'll come every morning, give him his medicine, and leave. I'll look in once every evening too.'

Jalpa smiled and said, 'And who'll sit with him all day?'

'I'll sit with him a little while every day too, but you go this very day. Who knows what condition the poor fellow may be in there. So that's settled, isn't it?'

When Ratan went into Munshiji's room, Ramesh Babu stood up and said, 'Please come in, Deviji. We've learned where Rama Babu is.'

'Half the credit for this is mine,' said Ratan.

'It must have happened according to your advice. Now we have to be concerned about bringing him here.'

'Let Jalpa go and fetch him back, and let her take Gopi along with her. You don't have any objection to this do you, Dadaji?'

Munshi Dayanath did indeed object. If he'd had the strength, he'd have gathered five or ten more people together to keep him company. So why wouldn't he have objected to family members going? But the problem had come upon him so quickly that he was unable to say anything.

Why wouldn't Gopi have been happy on having such a fine opportunity for a trip to Calcutta? Vishvambhar refused to accept defeat in his heart. If the Creator had not made him the younger, this unjust discrimination against him would not have occurred today. How could Gopi possibly be considered more intelligent, for wherever he went, he always lost something or the other before he returned. Yes, Gopi was older, and this divine enactment had rendered him, the younger brother, helpless.

By nine o'clock that night Jalpa was ready to go. She bent her head to her father- and mother-in-law's feet and took their blessing. Vishvambhar was crying; she embraced him lovingly and took her seat in the motor-car. Ratan had come to take her to the station.

As the car drove off, Jalpa said, 'Sister, Calcutta must be a very big city. How will I find out where he is there?'

'First go to the office of the *Praja-Mitra*. You'll find out there. And Gopi Babu is with you, after all.'

'Where will I stay?'

'There are dharmshalas. If not, then stay in a hotel. Look, if you need money, send me a telegram, and I'll send some one way or another. If Babuji comes, it will be a big help for me. This Manibhushan is going to ruin me.'

'Won't the hotel people be roughnecks?' asked Jalpa.

'If they try the least little prank, give them a good thump. Don't even ask. Give them a whack first, and then talk.' (Taking a knife from the waist of her garment). 'Keep this with you, and hide it in your clothes. I keep it with me whenever I go out. It keeps up my courage. You can consider any man who molests a woman to be a coward from head to foot, dirty trash. Once he sees the gleam of your knife and your boldness, he'll be frightened to death. He'll immediately run away with his tail between his legs. But if it should turn out that you are forced to use the knife, don't hesitate for even a moment. Take the knife and plunge it into him. Don't worry a bit about what might or might not happen. What's going to happen will happen.'

Jalpa took the knife, but didn't say a word. Her heart was growing heavy. There were so many things to think about and ask about, that just reflecting on them made her feel uneasy.

The station came into view. The coolies lifted out the luggage. Gopi bought the ticket. Jalpa stood on the station platform like a stone statue, as if she had become unconscious. Before some great test we become silent; all our powers are involved in the preparation for the struggle.

'Be on your guard,' said Ratan to Gopi.

Gopi had been doing physical exercises for several months now. He'd look at his chest as he swung stools. He seemed much the same to those who watched him, but in his own eyes he'd become something more. Perhaps he was even surprised that people did not move out of his way when they saw him coming, or why they didn't get frightened by his shape and size. 'If anyone even lets out a peep, I'll break his bones!' he said conceitedly.

'I know that,' said Ratan smiling. 'Don't go to sleep.'

'I won't doze for even an instant. Sleep won't dare to come!'

The train arrived, and Gopi entered a compartment and took control. Jalpa's eyes filled with tears. 'Sister, bless me so I can bring him back safely,' she said.

Her faltering heart was seeking for some support, some help, some strength now, and what else could bestow that strength on her, except blessings and prayers? These are the everlasting storehouses of that strength and peace which never discourage anyone, which take everyone by the hand, and which ferry everyone across the river of their difficulties.

The engine let out a whistle. The two friends embraced, and Jalpa sat down inside the train.

'Send letters as you go,' said Ratan.

Jalpa nodded.

'If you need me, write immediately. I 'll drop everything and come.'

Jalpa gave another nod.

'Don't cry along the way.'

Jalpa laughed. The train moved off.

# 36

Devidin closed the tea-shop that very day, and all day long roamed around the court where the robbery case was going on and where Ramanath's testimony was being given. Rama's testimony went on for three days continuously and for all three days Devidin neither ate nor slept. Today, as before, the instant he came home he took off his kurta and began to wave a small fan to and fro. It was well into February and a little heat had begun, but not enough to bring out sweat or make a fan necessary. The court officers were wearing winter clothing, but Devidin was soaked in perspiration. His face, where an honest merry old age had resided, had become as angry as if he had just returned from forced labour.

Jaggo brought him some water in a lota and said, 'Shall I put out your chilam for a smoke?' She had shown him this considera-tion for three days now. The old woman had never before asked about bringing his chilam. Devidin understood the significance of this. Looking gently at her he said, 'No, let it be. I won't smoke.'

'Wash your hands and face, there's dust on you.'

'I'll wash them. What's the hurry?'

The old woman was eager to know today's news, but she was afraid lest Devidin get irritable. She wanted to relieve his tiredness, which pleased him. He began to narrate all the events of the day on his own.

'Have some refreshment, won't you. You didn't eat anything this afternoon either. Shall I bring some sweets? Here, give me the fan.'

Devidin gave her the fan, and she began to wave it back and forth. After two or three minutes of sitting with his eyes closed, he said, 'Bhaiya's testimony finished today.'

The old woman's hand stopped. 'Will he come home then from tomorrow?' she asked.

'There's no recess yet,' said Devidin. 'The same declaration has to be made in the Civil Court. And why would he come here again at all. He'll get some nice place to stay at, a horse to ride around on. Oh, but he's a very self-seeking person. He's implicated fifteen innocent people; five or six of them will be hanged, and the others will get ten or twelve years each. It was his declaration that put this case on firm ground. No matter how much he was cross-examined, he didn't hesitate at all; what nerve. Now not one of them will escape. Who acted well and who did not, only God knows, but all of them will be ruined. And he embezzled government money and even ran away from home. We've really been deceived.'

Looking at him with sweet reproach, Jaggo said, 'Our good and evil is with ourselves. The world is self-seeking; who dies for someone else?'

'To give poison to someone who cuts other people's throats for his own self-interest would not even be a sin,' said Devidin in a sharp tone.

Suddenly two persons came and stood before them. One was a fair, handsome boy, not older than fifteen or sixteen. The other was a middle-aged man and from his appearance seemed to be a peon.

'Who are you looking for?' asked Devidin.

The peon said, 'Your name is Devidin, isn't it? I've come from the office of the *Praja-Mitra*. This babu is the brother of that Ramanath who received the chess prize. He came to the office looking for him, and the editor sent him to you. So I'll go now, all right?'

He left as he said this. Devidin surveyed Gopi from head to foot. His features were similar to Rama's. 'Come and sit, son,' he said. 'When did you come from home?'

Gopi considered sitting down at a Khatik's shop to be beneath his dignity. 'I came just today,' he said, continuing to stand. 'My sister-in-law is with me too. I'm staying in a dharmshala.'

'Go and bring the bahu here, won't you,' said Devidin standing up. Rama Babu's room is upstairs, you can stay there comfortably. Why stay at the dharmshala? Don't leave, I'm coming too. There's every kind of convenience here.'

He gave this news to Jaggo, and telling her to sweep out the room, set off to the dharmshala along with Gopi. The old woman quickly swept the room, and brought sweets and curds from a confectioner's shop. She filled an earthen pot with water and placed it upstairs. Then she washed her face and hands, took out a colourful sari, put on jewellery, and fixing herself up, awaited the arrival of the bahu.

Just then a phaeton arrived. The old woman went and helped Jalpa to get out. At first, seeing a vegetable shop, Jalpa hesitated a little, but the loving welcome in the eyes of Jaggo made her hesitation vanish. When they went upstairs together she found everything laid out in its own place as if it were her own home.

Putting water in the lota Jaggo said, 'Bhaiya lived right here in this house, daughter! But now the house has been deserted for fifteen days. Wash your face and hands and have some curds and sugar, won't you daughter! You probably don't know Bhaiya's situation just now, do you?'

Jalpa shook her head and said, 'I don't know anything for certain. I learned from the person who publishes the newspaper that he has been arrested by the police.'

Devidin had come upstairs too. 'They arrested him, no doubt, but now he's become a government witness in a court case. There won't be any case against him now in Prayag and if things work out he'll get government service too.'

'Did he become a government witness because he was afraid of the Prayag case?' said Jalpa proudly. 'There's no case at all against him there. Why would there be one?'

'Wasn't there some affair involving some money?' said Devidin fearfully.

Looking as if she'd been struck, Jalpa said, 'There was nothing to that. As soon as we learnt that he had spent some government funds, we returned the amount. He panicked for nothing and came here. And then he managed to keep so silent that we didn't hear a word from him.'

Devidin's face became as radiant as if he had just been relieved of some torment. 'Well, how could we have known! We tried over and over again to persuade him to write home, and explained how his family would be frantic. But he wouldn't write because of his shame. He mistakenly believed that there had to be a case against him in Prayag. If he had known would he have become a government witness?'

The meaning of 'government witness' was not unknown to Jalpa. Neither was the scorn and dishonour in which it was held by society unknown to her. She knew why government witnesses were created, what kind of temptations were put before them, and how they turned into puppets of the police and strangled their very own friends. If any person becomes ashamed of his evil behaviour and reveals the truth, pushes aside the protection of deceit and trickery, then he is truly a virtuous man, and whatever praise his courage may receive is too little. But the condition is that he be ready to bear the results of what he has done with his companions, that he mount to the gallows laughing and joking. Such a person is a true hero. But if he fears the harshness of punishment, and from the contemptible idea of selfishly saving his own skin turns into a snake in the sleeve and betrays his own companions, then he is cowardly, degraded and heartless. Treachery is just as base among robbers and other enemies of society as it is in any other area. Society never pardons such people, never. Jalpa understood all this very well. But the problem here had become even more tangled. Rama had not disclosed his own misdeeds from fear of punishment. If he'd been truthful about this, at least, despite becoming despicable, he'd have had the virtue of partial truthfulness. Here, other misdeeds had been revealed, which he couldn't possibly have had anything to do with. Suddenly Jalpa did not feel so sure of this. Surely something else had happened which had compelled Rama to become a government witness. Shrinking with embarrassment, she asked, 'Did something ... did something happen here too?'

Aware of her mental distress, Devidin said, 'Nothing at all. He came here with me straight from Prayag. Since he came here, he hasn't gone anywhere. He didn't even go outside. One day he went out and that was it; the police arrested him that very day. He saw a constable coming, got scared because he thought: "He's coming to arrest *me*" and took to his heels. This seemed peculiar to the constable, and he was arrested on suspicion. I got to the police station after they did. At first the Daroga asked for a bribe, but when I returned after getting the money from home, something else had come to light. Who knows what the officers talked about, but they turned him into a government witness. Bhaiya did tell me that he wouldn't have to lie a bit in this affair, and that the police had a genuine case. What objection was there to speaking out the truth? I shut up. What could I do?'

'There's no knowing what kind of narcotic they made him inhale,' said Jaggo. 'Bhaiya wasn't like that. He kept calling me "Mother, Mother" all the time. All kinds of people came to the shop, both men and women. He didn't have the impudence to look at anyone the wrong way.'

'He didn't have any harm in him,' said Devidin. 'I never saw a boy like him. He was deceived.'

After thinking a moment, Jalpa said, 'Has his evidence been given?'

'Yes, it went on for a whole three days. It finished today.'

'So nothing can be done now,' said Jalpa anxiously. 'Will I be able to meet him?'

Devidin smiled at this question of Jalpa's. 'Yes, of course! Go and uncover the whole plot. Upset the whole game. The police are not such stupid asses. These days they don't let anyone meet him. He's closely guarded.'

No more discussion was possible on this question just then. It was not easy to solve such a knotty problem. Jalpa summoned Gopi, who was standing on the edge of the roof watching the passing spectacle of the street. He was as happy as if he were at his in-laws'. He came very slowly and stood by them.

'Wash your hands and face and have something to eat,' said Jalpa. 'You like curds a lot.'

Gopi blushed from shame and went out.

'He won't eat in front of us,' said Devidin smiling. 'We'll both leave. Tell us whatever you need, Bahuji! This is your home. We thought of Bhaiya as our own. Who else is there of ours to sit with us.'

'He would eat what I made with my own hands,' said Jaggo proudly. 'He didn't feel any false pride.'

Jalpa smiled and said, 'Now you won't have to cook, Mother. I'll do the cooking.'

'In our community it's forbidden to eat from the hands of other communities, Bahu,' objected Jaggo. 'Why should I make my community despise me for eating from your hand for even a few days?'

'Our community forbids eating others' food too,' said Jalpa.

'Who's going to come here to see you?' countered Jaggo. 'And then educated people don't even consider these things. Our community is a bunch of idiots.'

'It doesn't feel right that you should cook while I eat,' said Jalpa. 'Whoever makes someone a bahu has to eat food from their hands. Why make them into a bahu if you're not going to eat what they cook?'

Giving Jaggo an approving look, Devidin said, 'Bahu has said something remarkable. Think it over before you give her an answer. Come on, now, let's give these people a chance to rest a little.'

When both of them had gone, Gopi came and said, 'Did Bhaiya live here at this Khatik's place? They certainly seem to be Khatiks.'

'Whether they are Khatiks or Chamars, they're a hundred times better than you or I,' snapped Jalpa. 'They put up a stranger in their own home for six months and gave him food and drink. Would we have had that much courage? For a guest to come here imposes a great burden. If they are lowborn, we are even more lowborn.'

Gopi had washed his hands and face. As he ate his sweets he said, 'No one raises his status by putting someone up. No matter how much merit a Chamar may get from being generous, he'll still be a low-caste Chamar!'

'I consider such a Chamar better than a Brahman pundit who always devours the wealth of others,' said Jalpa.

Gopi went downstairs after his snack. He was very keen to roam around the city. Jalpa didn't feel like eating anything. She had a complicated problem before her—how to get Rama out of this quagmire. Just imagining the scorn and derision awaiting him was a blow to her pride. They would be disgraced in everyone's eyes forever, unable to show their faces to anyone.

And then who would bear the responsibility for the blood of innocent people? No one could know who was guilty and who was innocent among the accused, or how many of them were the victims of enmity and greed. Perhaps three or four of them would even be hanged. On whom would the blame for their murder fall?

Suppose that no one would be blamed, she thought further. Who knew whether anyone could be blamed or not. But for one's own self-interest—Oh! How contemptible! How had he ever agreed to it? Even if he'd been afraid of the Municipality bringing a case against him, it would have meant no more than three or four years of imprisonment. To stoop to such terrible degradation to avoid this!

Even if he learned that the Municipality couldn't do anything to him now, what could possibly be done now? He'd already given his testimony.

Suddenly something pierced her heart like a massive spike. Why couldn't he change his declaration? If he should learn that the Municipality could do nothing to him, perhaps he'd change his declaration on his own. How could he be informed of this? Was it possible somehow or other?

Impatiently, she went downstairs and gesturing for Devidin to come, said, 'Tell me, Dada, couldn't we get even a letter to him? Maybe if we gave the guards a few rupees the letter would reach him.'

Shaking his head Devidin said, 'It's difficult. They put very trustworthy men on guard duty. I went twice, and not one of them would allow me to even stand in front of the gate!'

'What's around that bungalow?'

'In one direction there's another bungalow, in another an orchard of grafted mango trees, and in front the street.'

'He probably comes out in the evening to roam around?'

'Yes, he brings out a chair and sits. One or two police officers stay with him too.'

'If someone should hide in that orchard, how would it be? When he saw Rama alone, he could throw him a letter. He'd surely pick it up.'

'Yes, it's certainly possible,' said Devidin, surprised, 'But how would you meet him alone later?'

When it grew a little darker, Jalpa went along with Devidin to see Ramanath's bungalow. She wrote a letter and put it in the neck of her garment. Again and again she asked Devidin how far they had yet to go. Really! Still so much further to go! The compound there would undoubtedly be lighted. Her heart began to surge with emotion. If she should find Rama sauntering around alone, what would she ask him? She'd wrap up the letter in a handkerchief and throw it in front of him. His expression would be bound to change.

Suddenly a doubt seized her—suppose despite reading her letter he still didn't change his declaration, then what? Who knew whether he even remembered her or not? Suppose he should turn away when he saw her? Her doubts began to frighten her. 'Tell me, Dada, did he ever mention his home?'

'Never,' said Devidin shaking his head. 'He never mentioned it to me. He stayed very sad.'

These words lent even greater force to Jalpa's doubts! They had come some distance out of the wealthy area of the city, and there was dead silence all around. Even the wind was taking a rest now, after blowing hard all day. In the faint light of the moon, the trees and open grounds on the side of the road seemed dejected and lifeless! It began to seem to Jalpa that her efforts would bear no fruit, and that her trip had no purpose. On this endless road, her condition was something like that of an orphan who circles from door to door for a handful of food. He knows that at the next door he'll receive no food, just curses, but he still stretches out his hand, still pleads for more. He has no support from hope; hopelessness itself is his support.

All at once on the right side of the street the light of an electric lamp was visible.

Devidin pointed a finger towards a bungalow and said, '*This* is his bungalow.'

Jalpa looked fearfully towards where he had pointed, but only silence lay around them. No person was there; on the gate was a lock.

'No one's here,' said Jalpa.

Peering inside the gate, Devidin said, 'Yes, maybe they've left this bungalow.'

'They must have gone out somewhere!'

'If they'd gone out, they'd have left a guard at the gate. They've left this bungalow!'

'So let's go back.'

'No,' said Devidin. 'We ought to find out where they've gone.'

On the right side of the bungalow some light showed in the mango grove. Perhaps a Khatik was guarding the grove. Devidin went inside and called out, 'Who's there? Who's leasing this orchard?'

A man appeared out of a dense cluster of mango trees. 'Hey, it's you, Jangli!' said Devidin recognizing him. 'You're leasing this orchard.'

Jangli was a short well-built man. 'Yes, Dada, I'm leasing it,' he said. 'But there's nothing here; I'll even have to pay a fine. How did you happen to come here?'

'No reason, really, I just came by chance. What happened to the fellow who was in the bungalow?'

Jangli looked around and then whispered, 'That informer was detained in it. Everyone left today. I've heard that they'll come back in fifteen or twenty days when the case will be presented again in the High Court. An educated man too, and such a double-crosser. Dada! The testimony he gave was totally false. Who knows if he has any children or not; he wasn't even afraid of God!'

Jalpa was standing right there. Devidin didn't give Jangli a chance to spew out any more poison. 'So they'll come in fifteen or twenty days?' he said. 'Are you sure?'

'Yes, that's just what the guards were saying.'

'Do you know anything about where they went?'

'They went to the site where the incident took place.'

Devidin started to smoke his chilam and Jalpa came out on to the street and began to walk up and down. Her heart had been torn to pieces hearing the scorn heaped on Rama. She felt neither anger nor shame towards him. She was impatient to pull him out of this morass with her own hands. Even if Rama should upbraid her, even if he should spurn her, she was not going to let him fall into this pit of disgrace.

As they were leaving, Jalpa asked, 'You told that man to let us know when they come back, didn't you?'

'Yes, I told him.'

# 37

A month passed. At first, Gopinath roamed around Calcutta for a while, but after only four or five days he got so fed up with the place that he began to repeat the refrain of home, home, home. In the end Jalpa thought it best to send him back. Here in Calcutta he just hid himself away and kept on complaining.

Jalpa went to Rama's bungalow several times. She knew that he hadn't come yet, but she still received a strange satisfaction in making the circuit.

When Jalpa grew tired of reading or lying around, she would go stand in front of the window for a while. One evening while she was standing there, a procession of motor-cars came into view. She became curious about where so many motor-cars were going, and began to look very attentively: there were six of them filled with police officers, and one was full of constables. When her gaze fell on the last car, it was as if a current of electricity coursed through her entire body. She became so obsessed that she flew from the window towards the stairs as if she wanted to stop the car, but in the same instant she realized that by the time she got downstairs all the cars would have gone by. She came back to the window again; Rama's car had come directly in front of her by now, and his eyes were raised towards the window. Jalpa wanted to communicate something with a gesture, but embarrassment stopped her. It seemed as if Rama's car had slowed down. Devidin's voice could be heard too. But the car didn't stop. In an instant it had moved on, though Rama's eyes were still fixed on the window.

Jalpa went to the stairs and said, 'Dada!'

Devidin came to the bottom of the stairs and said, 'Bhaiya has come! What a motor-car that was.'

He came upstairs. 'Did he say something to you?' said Jalpa, her eagerness overcoming her embarrassment.

'What else did he have time to say except "Ram, Ram"? I asked how he was, and he made an encouraging gesture before he moved on. Did you see him or not?'

'Why wouldn't I have seen him?' said Jalpa with bowed head. 'I was standing right at the window.'

'Then he must have seen you too?'

'He was staring through the window at any rate.'

'He must have been perplexed about who it was.'

'Did you find out when the case will be presented?'

'Tomorrow for sure.'

'Tomorrow? So soon? Then whatever has to be done, has to be done today. If he gets my letter somehow or other, then I'll succeed.'

Devidin gazed at her as if to say, 'It won't be as easy to do this as you think.'

'Do you have some doubts that he'll be willing to change his evidence?'

Devidin saw no way out now except to acknowledge his misgivings. 'Yes, Bahuji,' he said. 'I feel very doubtful about it, and what's more, if you ask me it's risky. Even if he does change his disposition he won't escape the clutches of the police. They'll dream up some other charge to catch him, and then bring a new case against him.'

Jalpa gave him a look as if to tell him she was not the least bit frightened by this. Then she said, 'Dada, I'm not taking the responsibility for saving him from the police. I only want to save him from disgrace if that's possible. I can't see so many homes ruined through him. Even if he really were a member of a gang of robbers, I would still want him to stand by his companions, and cheerfully endure whatever fell to his lot. It would never please me to see him betray others and become an informer. But this case is totally fabricated, and I simply can't bear for him to give false testimony to save his own skin. If he won't change his deposition himself, then I'll go to the court myself and bring the whole half-baked affair out into the open, no matter what the results may be. If he leaves me for good, or never looks at my face, I'm willing. But it's just not possible that he should disgrace himself so thoroughly. I've written all this in my letter.'

'Now I'm sure you'll get it all done, Bahu,' said Devidin, gazing at her respectfully. 'When you've made your heart so strong, you'll be able to do everything.'

'Let's leave here at nine o'clock then.'

'Yes, I'm ready.'

# 38

That same Ramanath who had never gone out for fear of the police, who had filled the days of his life by hiding out at Devidin's house like a thief, had now been plunged into a life of luxury fit for a king for the last two months. He had a prettily decorated bungalow to live in, a whole group of servants to attend to him, a motor-car to ride in, and a Kashmiri cook to prepare his food. Important officers stared at his face to see if he had something more to say or if he'd finished. He had become so fastidious that it seemed he was a hereditary nobleman. Luxury had lulled his conscience to sleep. It never occurred to him to ask himself what he was doing or how much innocent blood would be on his hands. Nor was he was ever given the opportunity for solitary thought. At night he would go with officials to the cinema or theatre, and in the evenings on trips in the motor-car. There were always new things to amuse him. His greatest happiness came on the day that the magistrate committed the accused for trial in the Sessions Court. It seemed to him that the sun of his good fortune had risen.

The police knew that there would be no such love feast in the court of the Sessions Judge. By chance, he was Hindustani, and notorious for his impartiality. Police and thieves were equals in his estimation, nor did he show favour or leniency to anyone. This was why the police had considered it important to take Rama on a trip to the sites where the incidents had taken place. They had set up quarters in the richly decorated bungalow of a landowner. They would hunt all day, and at night listen to the gramophone, play cards, or tour the river on barges. It seemed as if some young prince had come out on a hunting trip.

If Rama had any unfulfilled desire in the midst of his luxury, it was that Jalpa could be there too. As long as he had been dependent and poor, it was as if all his capacities for sensuous enjoyment had faded away. Now these cool gusts had revived them. He had become enraptured by the imaginary prospect of receiving a good position as soon as the case was concluded. Then he would go, persuade Jalpa to return with him, and enjoy life's comforts in contentment. Yes, it would be a new kind of life; its standards of behaviour, its principles would be something differ-ent. It would have rigorous self-control and true restraint. Now his life would have some purpose, some ideals. The business of life was not just eating, sleeping, and worrying about money. His aimless life would come to an end along with this case. His feeble will had shown him this new day and was now showing him the dream of a new and perfected life. Such people, like drunkards, make vows every single day, but what is the result of these vows? New temptations keep coming forward and the time for fulfilling the vows keeps being extended. The new day never dawns.

After a month's tour in the countryside, Rama was returning to his bungalow along with his police collaborators. The route went past Devidin's house. He could see his room from some distance away, and involuntarily lifted his gaze upwards. Someone was standing in front of the window. What was Devidin doing standing there just now? He looked more attentively. It was some woman! But where had she come from? Could it be that Devidin was renting the room? He had never done that before.

As the motor-car came nearer, the woman's face came into closer view. Rama stared in astonishment. It was Jalpa! Without a doubt it was Jalpa! But no, no, how could Jalpa have come here? How could she possibly know his whereabouts? Had the old man written a letter to her perhaps? It *was* Jalpa. The Assistant Daroga was driving. 'Sardar Sahab,' said Rama imploringly, 'please stop a moment. I'd like to have a word with Devidin.' The Assistant slowed down a little, but after a little thought he drove ahead.

'You've made me a prisoner!' said Rama angrily.

Grinning with embarrassment, the other said, 'You know how quickly the Deputy Sahab gets hot under the collar.'

After arriving at the bungalow Rama began to think about how he could meet Jalpa. That Jalpa was there he now had no doubt. How could his eyes deceive him? A fiery pain sprang up in his heart; what should he do? How could he go to her? He didn't even remember to change his clothes, but stood for fifteen minutes at the door of his room. No clever scheme occurred to him, and he lay down on his bed in helplessness.

After only a little while, he got up again and went out into the adjacent courtyard. The electric streetlights had come on by now.

A guard was standing at the gate. Just then Rama felt such anger at him that he could have shot him. If he got a good position, he'd tell them off one after the other. He'd get them dismissed; always sticking to him like a devil on his head! Just look at his face! It looks like the hind end of a goat! Oh, what a wonderful turban you have! Just like some basket-carrying coolie! If a dog should bark at you right now, you'd run away with your tail between your legs, but look at you standing here so firmly as if you're protecting the door of some fort!

Another guard came and said, 'The Inspector Sahab has invited you. He's sent for some new gramophone records.'

'I don't have any spare time now,' said Rama furiously.

Then he began to think again. How had Jalpa come here? Had she come by herself or with someone else? That slave driver hadn't given him even a moment to talk with the old man. Jalpa would certainly ask why he had run away. He'd tell her straight out, what else could he have done at the time? But this short time of troubles had solved the question of life, and now they could spend their lives in contentment. As he pondered, it occurred to him that there would be no harm if Jalpa stayed here with him. Outsiders were prohibited from meeting him, but what objection could there be to Jalpa? Right now, however, it wasn't appropriate to raise the question; he'd settle it tomorrow. What a strange creature Devidin was too. He'd come several times before, but today he'd fallen quite silent. At least he could have come and given the news of Jalpa's arrival to him through the constable on guard duty. Then he'd see who wouldn't let Jalpa come! At first this kind of custody had been necessary, but now his test had been completed. Maybe everyone would agree willingly.

The cook brought a thaali of food. There was a single kind of meat. Rama flared up as soon as he saw it. These days he only felt hungry when he saw appetizing food. He wasn't satisfied unless there were chutnies, pickles, and four or five kinds of meat.

'What am I supposed to eat?' he said angrily. 'Your head? Take the thaali away.'

'Your honour,' said the cook fearfully, 'how can I prepare more things so quickly? You came just two hours ago.'

'Is two hours such a short time for you?'

'What can I say to you, your honour?'

'Don't talk nonsense!'

'Your honour ...'

'Don't talk nonsense! Damn!'

The cook said nothing more. He brought a bottle, broke up some ice and put it in a glass, and then moved back and stood silently.

Rama felt angry enough to tear the cook into pieces. He had become very hot-tempered these days.

When the liquor began to course through him, he became even more irate. Looking at the cook with inflamed eyes he said, 'I could grab you by the ear and throw you out if I want. Now! This instant! Do you understand!'

Seeing his anger growing, the cook slunk silently away. Rama took the glass, and gulping down three or four mouthfuls, he went outside and began to stroll around the courtyard. He was obsessed by one overpowering thought; how could he get out of here.

All of a sudden he became aware that outside the wires of the fence there was someone in the cover of the trees. Yes, someone was standing and staring in his direction. Perhaps he was beckoning him to approach. Rama's heart began to thud. Could it be a plot by some conspirators to take his life? He was continuously apprehensive, and hence seldom went outside at night. His instinct for self-preservation urged him to go inside. Just then a motor-car passed by on the street, and in its light Rama saw that the dark shadow was a woman: he could clearly see her sari. Then it seemed to him that she was coming toward him. He began to feel apprehensive again; could it be a man who had changed his dress to deceive him? With each step he took backwards, the apparition moved the same distance towards him until it reached the wires and threw something at him. Rama let out a shriek and jumped back, but it was only an envelope. He calmed down a little. When he looked up again, the apparition had merged into the darkness. Rama bounded forward and picked up the envelope. He felt a mixture of fear and curiosity, but the curiosity was greater than the fear. He concealed the envelope in his pocket, went into his room, shut both doors, and taking the envelope in his hand began to examine it. As soon as he looked at the address, his heart began to tremble with emotion. The writing was Jalpa's.

He opened the envelope in haste—it was Jalpa's writing again. He read the letter in a few seconds, and then heaved a deep sigh. Along with that sigh as if by magic there flew away all his weakness, shame, and self-reproach; all that mental suffering which had been draining away his life-blood; and that terrible load of worry which had oppressed his soul for half a year now. Never before had he felt so much enthusiasm, so much pride, and so much self-confidence. At first he was in a frenzy to go and tell the Daroga that this case was no concern of his. But then he thought that his deposition had been made, and he had already received all the disgrace coming to him, so why should he wash his hands of the results now? But what a dirty trick they had all played on him! And till now they had kept him in the dark. Every last one of them had professed friendship with him, but had kept the real state of affairs concealed from him. Even now they didn't trust him. If he should change his deposition now, he'd learn how hard life could be. If it happened that he didn't get a good position, so what; at least, all their schemes would be reduced to dust and ashes. There would be retribution for this treachery. And even if none of this turned out to be true, he'd still be saved from such a great disgrace. They'd all play some nasty tricks, but what else could they do besides bringing a spurious charge against him? When they couldn't even establish that he'd lived here, what offence could they charge him with? They'd all be put to shame, and wouldn't even be able to show their faces let alone bring a case against him.

But no. They'd played a trick on him, so he'd play the same trick on them. He'd tell them that he'd give evidence if he got a good position today; otherwise he'd tell them straight out that the case was no concern of his. If he didn't do this, then afterwards they'd make him a Daroga and send him to some little police station where he'd rot away. He'd take an inspectorship, and a warrant of appointment should reach him by ten o'clock tomorrow. He went to speak to the Daroga at once, but then stopped. He was aching to meet Jalpa once again. Never before had he felt so much devotion, so much respect for her, as if she were some divine power whom the gods had sent for his protection.

It was ten o'clock. Rama turned off the electric light, came out on to the veranda, and banged the door shut so that it would seem to the guard that he had shut the door from the inside and gone to sleep. He stood for a minute on the darkened veranda. Then he slowly stepped off it, went up to the barbed-wire fence, and began to think how he could get through it. Maybe Jalpa was still in the mango grove, and Devidin would certainly be with her. Only the wire was blocking his way. It was impossible for him to leap over it. He decided to get out by going through the wires. He pulled his clothes tight around him, and thrust his head and shoulders between the wires, but somehow or other his clothes were entangled. When he attempted to free them, his sleeve was caught in the barbs. His dhoti was ensnared too. Now the poor fellow was in an impasse. He couldn't go this way or that. If he were the least bit careless, the barbs would pierce his body.

But he didn't care about clothes now. He stretched his neck still farther forward and came out the other side, giving his clothes a lengthy tear. All his clothes were torn to shreds, and his back bore some scratches too, but even if someone had come and stood right there aiming a rifle at him, he wouldn't have retreated. He threw away his torn kurta on the spot. Even though the shawl around his neck was torn, it was still serviceable. He wrapped it around himself, gathered his dhoti around him, and began to wander around the orchard. It was deathly still. Maybe the Khatik caretaker had gone off to eat. He called Jalpa's name softly two or three times. He didn't hear a sound, but even though he was disappointed, love did not loosen its grip on him. He went under a tree and looked around. He realized that Jalpa had gone. He followed her very footsteps to Devidin's house without the slightest regret. What did he care if someone should find out that he'd slipped out of the bungalow; what could the police do to him? He wasn't a prisoner, he hadn't been ordained to be a slave.

It was midnight. Devidin had returned half an hour ago himself, and was about to eat when he was startled by the sight of a half-naked man. Rama had fastened the shawl around his head to frighten the old man.

'Who is it?' said Devidin fearfully.

Suddenly recognizing Rama, he leaped forward, seized his hand and said, 'You've really got quite a costume there, Bhaiya! What happened to your clothes?'

'When I was going through the fence, they were caught on

the barbs and got torn.'

'Ram, Ram! You didn't get cut?'

'Nothing really, one or two scratches. I went through very carefully.'

'You got Bahu's letter, didn't you?'

'Yes, I got it just before I left. Was she with you too?'

'She wasn't with me,' said Devidin. 'I was with her. Ever since she saw you in the motor-car, she was determined to go.'

'You didn't write any letter to her?'

'I didn't write any letters or notes, Bhaiya. When she came I was surprised myself how she came without knowing a thing. Later on she told me; she sent a chess problem diagram from Prayag and the prize came from there too.'

Rama's eyes opened wide. Jalpa's cleverness astonished him. At the same time a feeling of defeat depressed him somewhat. So he'd lost here too, and badly.

The old woman had gone upstairs. Going to the foot of the stairs, Devidin said, 'Hey, what are you doing? Tell Bahu that a man has come to meet her.'

Devidin grasped Rama's hand again and said, 'Come on, now it's time for you to speak up in court. You've been on the run a long time. You've been arrested without a warrant. Even the police can't arrest you so easily now.'

Rama's joy melted away and he was pierced by shame. What answer could he give to Jalpa's questions? The same fear that had made him flee, had followed on his heels and defeated him in the end. He wouldn't even be able to look Jalpa straight in the eyes. He wrenched his hand away and stood by the stairs in irresolution.

'Why have you stopped?' asked Devidin.

Rama scratched his head and said, 'Go on, I'm coming.'

'Ask him who he is and where he's from,' said the old woman from upstairs.

'He says that he'll say what he has to say to Bahu,' said Devidin, cracking a joke.

'Has he brought a letter?'

'No!'

Everything became quiet. After a moment Devidin asked, 'Shall I tell him to go back?'

Jalpa came to the stairs and said, 'I'm asking you, who is it!'

'He says he's come a long way.'

'Where is he?'

'So who is this standing here?'

'All right, tell him to come upstairs.'

Wrapped in his shawl, partly timid, partly ashamed, partly fearful, Rama went up the stairs. Jalpa recognized him as soon as she saw him. She quickly took two steps backwards, but if Devidin hadn't been there she would have taken two steps forwards.

Never had so much intoxication been in her eyes, never so much unsteadiness in her limbs, never such a glow in her cheeks, and never such a tender quivering in her heart. All her sacrifices had borne fruit.

# 39

The night when those who have been separated meet is the same as the night when travellers make camp—one spent in talking. Both Rama and Jalpa had to tell their stories of the last six months. Rama greatly magnified the description of his difficulties to increase his glory. Jalpa never even mentioned her troubles in her narrative. She was afraid it would cause him grief. Rama, however, took special pleasure in bringing her to tears. How he had come to run away, why he had run away, in what way he had run away—he told his whole epic in heart-rending words, and Jalpa, sobbing away, listened. He was impressed by his own words. Till now he had had to suffer defeat in everything. What had seemed unimaginably difficult to him, Jalpa had shown to be of trifling importance. He could have really spiced up his account of the chess problem, but there too Jalpa had shown him up. So what other means did he have to satisfy his thirst for fame than to make mountains out of the molehills of his sufferings?

'You had to bear all these hardships,' said Jalpa sobbing, 'but you never wrote us a single letter. Why should you have written, what were we to you anyway! Your love was sham! If you cover your eyes, you can't see the mountain in front of you!'

'That wasn't it, Jalpa,' said Rama regretfully. 'Only the heart knows what's happened to it, but it takes some nerve to write too.

When I had to hide my face and run away from home, how could I sit and write the story of my disasters? I thought it over; until I could earn a lot of money, I wouldn't write a word.'

'That was exactly right!' said Jalpa sarcastically, her eyes brimming with tears. 'Men love money the most! And I'm a lover of money. Whether you steal, rob, forge bank notes, give false testimony, get the money any way you can. Hurrah! How well you've understood my nature. As Gosainji the saint said, "Satisfy selfish desires, and everyone will love you!"'

'No, no, dear,' said Rama shamefacedly. 'That wasn't it. I thought to myself, "How can I go home when I'm so down-and-out." I'm telling the truth, I was more afraid of you than anything else. I thought how treacherous, how false, how cowardly you must consider me. Perhaps I felt that if you saw a plateful of money your heart would become a little softer.'

'I might not have even touched that plate,' said Jalpa in a tortured voice. 'Today I've learned how low, how selfish, how greedy you consider me to be! It's no fault of yours, the whole fault is mine. If I were a good woman, why would this day have ever come? Any woman who spends three or four rupees a day, who is determined to wear jewellery worth a thousand or two, when her husband is a thirty-to-forty-a-month employee, is bringing about her and his ruin. If you thought I was so greedy for money, then you did nothing wrong, but I won't jump a second time into the same fire where I was burned once. During these months I've made some atonement for my sins, and I'll keep on doing so for the rest of my life. I don't say that I've had my fill of the pleasures of life, or that I'm tired of clothes and jewellery, or that I hate trips and entertainments. All these desires are much the same as before. If you can fulfil these desires through exertion, through diligence, through industry, then there's nothing to say. But even if you bring a hundred thousand rupees, if it's by making fraudulent schemes, by making your soul filthy, then I'll kick it away. When I learned that you'd become a police witness, I felt so bad that I went to your bungalow right away with Dada. But you had gone away that very day, and just today you've come back. I don't want the blood of so many people on my head. Tell the court clearly that you gave evidence because you were deceived by the police, and that you have nothing to do with this case.'

'I've been thinking about this question ever since I got your letter,' said Rama worriedly, 'but I can't figure out what I should do. I don't have the courage to take back what I've already said.'

'You'll *have* to change your deposition.'

'But after all, how?'

'What's the difficulty? When you know that the Municipality can't bring a case against you, what's there to be afraid of?'

'If it's not fear, shame is something too. It's not in me to say one thing and then turn around and say another from the same mouth. And then I'll get a good position. We'll spend our lives in comfort. I don't have the strength to be knocked around from one alley to the next.'

Jalpa didn't answer. She was thinking how great a proportion of selfishness there was in people.

Rama spoke again, insolently. 'And what if the whole decision doesn't depend on my evidence alone? Even if I change it, the police will stand up somebody else in my place. There's no way the lives of the criminals can be saved. Yes, I'd be beaten for nothing.'

Jalpa glanced at him angrily and said, 'What sort of shameless things are you saying, sir? Are you so far gone that you can cut other people's throats for your own livelihood? I won't stand for this. I'm willing to perform manual labour, to die of hunger. I can let the greatest calamities in the world fall on my head. But I can't accept even the kingdom of paradise by bringing bad fortune to someone else.'

Offended by this idealism, Rama said, 'So do you want me to do coolies' work here?'

'No, I don't want that. But it's far better than eating bread through someone else's blood.'

'Jalpa,' said Rama calmly, 'I'm not as low as you think I am. Everyone feels something bad is bad. I'm also sorry that so many people are suffering at my hands. But circumstances have made me helpless. I don't have the strength to endure any more hard blows. Nor can I quarrel with the police. People hardly follow ideals in this world. Why do you want to make me climb to those heights which I don't have the capacity to reach?'

'Would it be surprising that a person who has the power to commit murder has the power *not* to commit it?' said Jalpa in a cutting tone of voice. 'And who would agree that a person who has the strength to run wouldn't have the strength to stand? When we want to do something, the strength comes by itself. If you decide to change your deposition, then all that you have to say, and the strength to say it, will come by themselves.'

Rama listened with bowed head.

'If you want me to cultivate this evil-doing, then you can say goodbye to me here today,' said Jalpa, growing even more heated. 'I'll go away in disgrace and I won't come to trouble you again. Live happily. I'll fill my stomach by labour and effort. My atonement is not finished yet; that's why this weakness hasn't left us yet. I can see that it won't go until it has destroyed us.'

Rama was cut to the quick. Scratching his head he said, 'I too want to save us from this disaster somehow or other.'

'Then why don't you? If you're ashamed to say anything, then I'll go. That would be best. I'll come along with you and tell your Superintendent Sahab the whole story in plain language.'

All of Rama's perplexities vanished. He didn't want to make himself so abject that his wife would go and plead for him. 'It's not necessary for you to go, Jalpa,' he said. 'I'll let them know.'

'Tell me right out,' said Jalpa with emphasis. 'Are you going to change your deposition or not?'

'I tell you I'll change it,' said Rama as if he'd been forced into a corner.

'Because I say so, or from your own heart?'

'Not because you say so, but from my heart. I hate such things myself. There was just a little hesitation, and you got rid of that.'

Then they talked about other things. How had she learned that Rama had spent the money? How had it been paid off? Had other people heard the news of the embezzlement or had it been kept quiet among the family? What had happened to Ratan? Why had Gopi gone home so fast? Were both boys doing some studying or were they roaming around like vagabonds as before? At last Mother and Father were mentioned. Then plans for their life began to be made. Jalpa said, 'Let's go home, buy a little land from Ratan, and do some farming in comfort.' Rama said, 'It would be much better to open a tea-shop here.' At this a debate began, and in the end Rama had to admit defeat. If they lived here, they couldn't take care of the home, they couldn't educate his brothers, and they couldn't serve Mother and Father. After all, they had some duties towards their family too. Rama was silenced.

# 40

Rama reached his bungalow by daybreak. No one heard or suspected a thing.

After eating breakfast, Rama shaved, dressed, and arrived at the Daroga's quarters. Rama was scowling. The Daroga asked, 'You're well? The servants haven't played any tricks on you, have they?'

Continuing to stand, Rama said, 'Not the servants, *you've* played tricks. Your subordinates, officers, all of you together have made a fool of me.'

Panicking a little, the Daroga said, 'What is this about, after all? Won't you tell me?'

'This is what it's all about. I won't give any testimony in this case now. I have nothing to do with it. You people deceived me, threatened me with a warrant, and forced me to give testimony. Now I know there's no case against me. It was you people's trickery. I no longer wish to give evidence on behalf of the police, and I'll tell this plainly to the Judge Sahab today. I won't have the blood of innocent people on my head!'

The Daroga said angrily, 'You admitted to embezzlement yourself.'

'It was a mistake in addition, not embezzlement. The Municipality didn't bring any case against me.'

'How did you learn that?'

'I'm not going to argue with you about this. I won't give testimony. I'll say right out that the police deceived me and gave me testimony to present. On the date of this incident, I was in Allahabad. The record of my attendance is available in the Municipal Office.'

Attempting to dispel this disaster with laughter, the Daroga said, 'All right, Sahab, the police did indeed deceive you, but as compensation we're willing to give you that reward. You'll get some good position, you'll travel sitting in a motor-car. If you get a position with the secret police, you'll be completely contented. Your honour and influence with the government will be greatly increased. If you do as you intend, you'll wander around in misery. You might get a clerkship in some office, but only with great difficulty. Here the door to your advancement has opened unexpectedly. You'll become an expert, and then one day you'll become Rai Bahadur Munshi Ramanath Deputy Superintendent. We'll have to be obliged to you for your favours. And you are wrong to be angry.'

These temptations had no effect on Rama. 'I'm willing to become a clerk,' he said. 'I don't want your kind of advancement. Let this good fortune be yours.'

Just then the Inspector and the Deputy Superintendent arrived. When he saw Rama, the Inspector proclaimed, 'Our Babu Sahab is already sitting here ready for us. That's the sort of competence that makes one prosper.'

Rama spoke as if he too understood it to be a matter of profit and loss. 'Yes sir, today I'll settle things. I've been guided by your hints all these days. Now I'll go ahead based on what I see with my own eyes.'

The Inspector looked at the Daroga, the Daroga looked at the Deputy, and the Deputy looked at the Inspector. What's he saying? Taken aback, the Inspector said, 'What's the matter? On my honour, you seem to be a little angry.'

'I've decided that I'll change my deposition today,' said Rama. 'I can't shed the blood of innocent people.'

Looking towards him in a kindly manner, the Inspector said, 'You're not shedding the blood of innocent people; you're building the structure of your destiny. On my honour, people very seldom get opportunities like this. What happened today to make you so angry? Do you know anything, Daroga Sahab? None of our men gave him any cheek, did they? If anyone has done anything to offend you, I'll have him shot, on my honour.'

'I'll go and find out right now,' said the Daroga.

'Don't trouble yourself,' said Rama. 'I have no complaints against anyone. I can't destroy my honour for a little personal advantage.'

There was dead silence for a minute. No one could think of

anything to say. The Daroga was thinking up some more trickery, the Inspector another temptation. The Deputy was reflecting on something else entirely. 'Rama Babu,' he said harshly, 'this won't turn out well.'

'It won't turn out well for you,' said Rama, also getting excited, 'but it's the very best thing for me.'

'No,' said the Deputy. 'Nothing could be worse for you. We won't let you go. Our case may be ruined, but we'll give you a lesson that you won't forget for the rest of your life. You'll have to give the same testimony that you gave before. If you make any trouble, if you mix anything up, then we'll treat you differently. You'll be written up in a report and sent off to jail like this.' (Moving his wrists downwards.)

As he said this he glared at Rama as though he would eat him alive. Fear rose up in Rama. These terrible words shook him. If they should bring some fabricated case against him, who would protect him? He had not expected the Deputy, who had acted like the embodiment of tolerance and courtesy, to assume this fearsome appearance all at once, but he wasn't so easily intimidated. 'Are you going to force me to testify?' he said heatedly.

'Yes!' said the Deputy, stamping his foot on the floor, 'I'll force you.'

'That's a fine joke!'

'You think it's a joke to mislead the police! Right now I have two witnesses who can prove that you've been saying seditious things. You'll get sent up for seven years. You'll get calluses on your hands from turning the hand-mill. You won't have those smooth smooth cheeks any more.'

Rama was afraid of jail. His hair stood on end just from imagining life there. He had agreed to give his testimony because of this very fear, and now this fear began to make him cowardly. The Deputy was a master of psychology. He realized how things stood. 'You won't get puris and halwa there,' he said. 'You'll get bread made from flour mixed with dust, broth made from rotten cabbage leaves, and the water from arhar daal to eat and drink. If they put you in solitary confinement for even four months, you won't survive either. You'll die right there. The warder will give you abuse every time he opens his mouth, and beat you with shoes. What do you know about it!'

Rama's face grew pale. It seemed as if his blood was drying up moment by moment. He felt such disgust with his weakness that he burst into tears. 'If that's what you people want,' he said in a trembling voice, 'then so be it! Send me to jail! I'll die for sure? Then my neck will be safe from you. Since you're prepared to go this far to ruin me, then I'm ready to die. Whatever has to be, will be.'

His mind had reached that state of weakness, when the slightest sympathy, the smallest kindness, was far more effective than hundreds of threats. The Inspector quickly perceived the opportunity. 'On my honour, you people don't know this man very well at all,' he said to the Deputy, taking Rama's side. 'It looks like you're intimidating him. Any intelligent person would feel bad about giving evidence this way. It's only natural. Anyone with the least sense of honour will find it displeasing to be a puppet in the hands of the police. If I were in the Babu Sahab's place I'd do the same. But he doesn't mean that he will give evidence against us. You people go about your business. Don't worry about the Babu Sahab, on my honour.'

He took Rama's hand and said, 'Come along with me, Babuji, I'll play some nice records for you.'

Rama freed his hand like a sulky child and said, 'Don't pick on me, Inspector Sahab. Now I have to die in jail.'

Putting his hand on Rama's shoulder, the Inspector said, 'Why do you let such things come out of your mouth, Sahab? May your *enemies* die in jail!'

The Deputy did not intend to leave the smallest loose end untied. Speaking in a severe tone as if he had never been acquainted with Rama, he said to the Inspector, 'Sahab, generally speaking we're ready to extend every courtesy to Babu Sahab, but if he gives testimony against us, or tries to cut us off at the roots, then we'll take our own measures too, we certainly will. We can never let him go.'

At that very moment the government advocate and the barrister got out of their motor-car.

# 41

Ratan kept giving encouragement to Jalpa in her letters, but wrote nothing about herself. Who will tell the story of her own sufferings to someone who is suffering herself? The same Ratan who had never grasped the facts about money, had now in a single month become a beggar even for her daily food. Even though her married life had not been very happy, she had at least never felt the want of anything. Even a rider who makes a journey on a half-dead horse can arrive if the road is good, and servants, money, food, and the like are also there. And if the horse is fast, then don't even bother to ask. Ratan's circumstances were similar. Like the rider, she was slowly making her journey through life. Sometimes she must have become irritable at the horse, and seeing other riders flying by, probably wished that she could go like the wind too. But she hadn't been sad, she hadn't had to bewail her fate. She was like a cow fastened by a thin tether, and absorbed with the bran and oilcake in her trough. Before her are the greenest of meadows in which fragrant grasses are rippling in the wind, but she never breaks the tether to go over there. For her there's no difference between her little tether and a chain of iron. Youth has less desire for love than it does for self-display. The desire for love comes later. Ratan had received all the means for self-display. Her young woman's soul had been possessed by her own adornment and display. Her life had consisted of laughter and pleasure, trips and outings, and eating and drinking, as it does for almost all of humankind. She hadn't had either the wish or the need to venture into deeper waters. Affluence soothes away mental sufferings. She'd had such a variety of ways to make her forget her sorrows—there was the cinema, the theatre, long excursions, cards, pet animals, and music. But humankind has no means to make it forget poverty except to weep, to curse fate, or to become alienated from the world and commit suicide. Ratan's fate had been turned upside down. Her happy dream had been shattered and now the skeleton of poverty was standing and glaring at her.

And it had all been her own doing. Vakil Sahab had been one

of those creatures who never worry about death. Somehow or other he had acquired the false notion that if a man of weak health lives with moderation and watchfulness, he can have a long life. He never had strayed outside the limits of that moderation and watchfulness. So what enmity did death have towards him, that it pursued him so tenaciously without rhyme or reason? The idea of writing his will had occurred to him when he was near death, but Ratan had become so grief-stricken, so fearful on hearing even the mention of a will, that Vakil Sahab had thought it proper to put it off at the time. And from then on he had never regained enough consciousness to have it written.

After his death Ratan had become so alienated that she had lost all good sense about anything. This was the very occasion when she should have been especially watchful. She should have remained as alert as if she had been surrounded by enemies, but she had left everything to Manibhushan. And this very same Manibhushan had gradually plundered her of all her possessions. He devised such schemes and plots that the ingenuous Ratan had not even an inkling of his treacherous behaviour. When the noose had been drawn quite tight, he came to her one day and said, 'The bungalow has to be emptied today. I've sold it.'

'I told you that I wouldn't sell the bungalow now,' said Ratan, a little angrily.

Manibhushan threw off the veil of politeness and said, scowling at her, 'You have a habit of forgetting things. I mentioned it to you in this very room, and you gave your assent. Now that I've sold it, you've begun this song and dance. The bungalow has to be emptied today and you'll have to come along with me.'

'I still want to live right here now.'

'I won't let you live here.'

'I'm not your servant girl.'

'The burden of your care has fallen on me. I'm taking you with me to protect our family traditions.'

Biting her lip, Ratan said, 'I can protect my own traditions by myself. I don't need your help. Without my wishing it, you can't sell a single thing here.'

Manibhushan threw a thunderbolt at her. 'You have no rights whatsoever to either this house or to Kakaji's possessions. They are my possessions. You can only ask me questions about your subsistence.'

Astonished, Ratan said, 'You haven't eaten some bhang, have you?'

'I don't eat so much bhang that I start saying absurd things,' said Manibhushan in a harsh voice. 'You're educated, you were the wife of an important lawyer. You probably know a lot about the law. In joint families a widow has no rights to the possessions of her husband. There was never any family break-up between Kakaji and my father. Kakaji was here and we were in Indore, but that doesn't prove that we had a family split. If Uncle had wanted to give his possessions to you, he would certainly have written some will, and even if something in the will had not been according to the law, we would still have honoured it. The fact that he wrote no will establishes that he didn't want to place any obstacle in the way of the ordinary operation of the law. You'll have to empty the bungalow today. The motor-car and the other things will be auctioned off too. You can come with me or stay here as you wish. A house that rents for nine or ten rupees a month will be plenty for you there. I've arranged for fifty rupees a month for your subsistence. After completing all the financial transactions, there's no more than this to be had.'

Ratan did not answer. For a little while she sat as if she had lost her wits. Then she sent for the motor-car and spent the whole day running from one lawyer to another. Vakil Sahab had had a great many friends among lawyers. All of them expressed regret on hearing of his decease and all were amazed by his not having written a will. There was only one remedy now. That was to try to establish that Vakil Sahab and his brother had split the family. If this could be established, and to do so was very easy, then Ratan would be the mistress of her possessions. If she could not establish this, then she had no recourse.

The unfortunate Ratan returned to the bungalow. She decided that she would not entertain any false hopes for whatever did not belong to her. Not in any way. But who had made such a law? Were women that contemptible, that worthless, that insignificant? Why?

Ratan spent the rest of the day sitting silently plunged in worry. She had thought for so long that she was mistress of this house. What a big mistake it had been. Those who used to gaze at her husband in expectation during his life, had now become the arbiters of her fate! This frightful insult was unbearable to a haughty woman like Ratan. She agreed that the earnings had been Vakil Sahab's, but it was she who had bought that village, and several of the houses in it had been built right in front of her. She had never thought for even a moment that one day this property would be the basis of her subsistence—she simply hadn't been able to be concerned about the future this much. She had experienced the same pleasure in purchasing, improving, and decorating this property that a mother receives in watching her offspring flourish. There was no selfishness in this, just the pride of something connected with herself, the same proprietary tenderness as a mother. But these children which she had taken care of, which she had embraced and sported with, had been snatched from her as soon as her husband's eyes had closed, and now she had no right whatsoever to them. Had she known that this difficult problem would confront her one day, whether she had squandered the money or whether she had given it away, this pain of lost possessions would not have pierced her breast like a spike. Had Vakil Sahab's income been so very big, after all? Couldn't she have gone to Simla during the hot season if she had wanted to? Couldn't she have kept three or four servants if she had wanted to? If she had wanted nothing but jewels, she could have paid for ornaments one by one by selling the houses one by one. But she had never let these things get out of hand. And just to see this fantasy? This dream? What else was it? Now she couldn't even raise her eyes to look at what had been hers only yesterday! How very costly this dream was! Yes, now she was a wretched widow. Until yesterday, she had given alms to others, but today she'd have to beg for them herself. She had no other means of support! She'd been a widow before too; she'd understood herself to be mistress of the house only in error. And now not even this error was left to aid her!

Suddenly her thoughts took a turn in the opposite direction. Why was she thinking of herself as a helpless widow? Was she about to beg at others' doors! Hundreds of thousands of women in this world supported themselves by their own industry and labour. Was she unable to work? Couldn't she sew clothes? Couldn't she open a little shop of some kind? She could teach young boys too. People would laugh to be sure, but why should she care about their laughter? They wouldn't be laughing at her, but at their own society.

When evening came, several people were pushing and shoving in front of the door. Manibhushan arrived and said, 'Kakiji, whatever things you tell me to, I'll have loaded and sent on. I've got a house ready for you.'

'I don't need a thing,' said Ratan. 'And don't you arrange for a house for me. I'm not going to even touch anything I have no rights to. I came here without bringing anything from my home, and I'll go back in the same way.'

'Everything is yours,' said Manibhushan, feeling ashamed. 'How can you say you have no rights. Take a look at that house. It rents for fifteen a month. I think you won't have any discomfort there, and I'll have whatever you say sent there.'

Giving him a scathing look, Ratan said, 'You wasted your time arranging that fifteen-rupee house for me. What will I do with such a big house? A little room you could get for two rupees is enough for me. And there's always the ground to sleep on. The smaller the load of gratitude I have to carry on my head, the better.'

'What do you want, after all?' asked Manibhushan very meekly. 'Tell me, then!'

'I don't want anything,' said Ratan passionately. 'I won't take even a single straw from this house with me. For me, something I have no right to is just like some stranger's thing. I won't become a beggar depending on someone else's mercy. You're the one with the rights to these things; take them. I don't mind at all. Charity can neither be given nor taken forcefully. Thousands of widows in this world are supporting themselves by their own labours. I'm the same. I'll labour like them and if I can't manage it, I'll go drown myself in some ditch. If one can't even take care of one's own stomach, one has no right to keep on living as a burden to others.'

Ratan left the house as she said this and went toward the gate.

Manibhushan, blocking her way, said, 'I won't sell the bungalow if you don't wish me to.'

Ratan looked at him with fiery eyes. Her face was flushed. Checking her rising flood of tears she said, 'I told you, I have nothing to do with anything in this house. I was a hired woman. What connection does a hired woman have with this house? Who knows what hard-hearted wretch made this law? If God exists somewhere, and there is justice where he is, then one day I'll ask that wretch before him, "Weren't there any mothers or sisters in your home? Aren't you ashamed to have dishonoured them?" If my voice had enough power to be heard all over this country, then I'd say to all the women, "Sisters, don't marry into any joint family, and if you do, don't sleep peacefully until you have split your house off from the rest of the family. Don't think that after your husband's gone they'll protect your honour in his home. If your husband doesn't leave you anything, it's all the same whether you live alone, or with his family! You won't be spared from insults or hard labour. If your husband leaves you something, then you can enjoy it only by living alone; if you live with his family, you'll have to give it up. His family is not a bed of flowers for you, but a bed of thorns. It's not a boat to help you cross the sea of life; it's an animal that gulps you down.'"

Evening had come. The dust-laden winds of March were gusting fine grains into the eyes of passers-by. Ratan was walking down the street guarding her shawl. Several women of her acquaintance halted her on the street to question her; several stopped their cars and told her to get in. But their kindness pierced her like an arrow. She hastened to Jalpa's house; today her real life had begun.

# 42

Jalpa and Devidin arrived at the courthouse at ten o'clock sharp. There was a large crowd of spectators; the upper gallery was filled with them, and a great many people were standing on the veranda and in the open ground at the front. Jalpa sat in the upper gallery, while Devidin stood on the veranda.

In the courtroom on one side of the judge stood several police employees, on the other, the record-keeper. Outside the witness-box in front of the judge stood the lawyers for both sides waiting to present their case. The number of the accused was not less than fifteen. All of them were occupying the floor next to the witness-box, manacled and fettered. Some were lying down, some were sitting, and some were talking among themselves. Two were arm-wrestling, while two others were arguing. All of them looked pleased. There was no sign of panic, hopelessness or grief on any face.

Just as eleven was striking, the accusation was presented. First some procedures were discussed, then a couple of police gave evidence. At last Rama was brought to the witness box at three o'clock. A thrill spread through the onlookers. Some came running from the paan shop chewing as they came, others folded up their newspapers and thrust them into their pockets, and everyone pressed forward to fill the courtroom. Jalpa too stood up carefully against the balcony. She wanted Rama to raise his eyes and look at her once, but he was standing with bowed head as if he were afraid to look around. The colour had gone out of his face. He stood, half-frightened, half-confused, as if someone had fastened him there and he had nowhere to escape. Jalpa's heart was thudding as if her fate was being decided.

Rama's deposition began. When she heard the first sentence Jalpa shuddered, the second made her scowl, the third made her face grow pale, and as soon as she heard the fourth she heaved a sigh and sank into the chair behind her. But her heart would not obey, and leaning on the railing she began to give ear to what he was saying again. It was the same police-taught evidence whose gist she had heard from Devidin. There was dead silence in the courtroom. Jalpa coughed several times in the hope that even now Rama might lift his eyes, but his head bowed even more deeply. Who could tell whether he recognized the sound of Jalpa's coughing, or whether his self-disgust had increased. His voice had grown fainter too.

A woman sitting next to Jalpa turned up her nose in contempt. 'I'd like to shoot this bastard. To think that even in this wretched country there are such selfish people like this who don't hesitate to cut the throats of innocent people out of greed for a little money or a job!'

Jalpa did not reply.

A bespectacled woman said despairingly, 'God is the master of this wretched country! May Lalas like this one never have the rule of it! Let them be clerks at most. And for that they're killing their souls. This fellow seems to be some down-and-out no-good person, low status and worthless from head to foot!'

A third woman, smiling at her, asked, 'He's a fashionable man and looks educated too. Well, what would you do with him if you got him?'

'I'd cut off his nose!' said the bespectacled goddess arrogantly. 'That's it, I'd make him noseless and leave him!'

'And do you know what I'd do?'

'No. Maybe you'd shoot him?'

'Nooo! I wouldn't shoot him. I'd stand him up in public and have him given five hundred whacks with a shoe!'

'May he be beaten so hard there won't be a hair left on his head!'

'Don't you feel even a little sorry for him?'

'I have no pity for him. Full punishment for him would be to push him off the top of some high mountain. If this gentleman were in America, he'd be burned alive.'

'Why are you wasting your time saying these nasty things?' said an old woman scolding these young girls. 'He's not worthy of hate, he's worthy of pity. Don't you see how pale his face has become, as if someone were choking him? If his mother or sister could see him, they'd surely burst into tears. This man is not bad at heart. The police have threatened and abused him. It seems as if every word he says is tearing his heart.'

'When a thorn is sticking in your foot, you cry out,' said the bespectacled woman sarcastically.

Jalpa could stay there no longer. Every remark, like a burning spark, raised a blister on her heart. She felt like standing up on the spot and saying. 'This gentleman is speaking total lies, lies from beginning to end, and I can prove it right now.' She suppressed this wild urge with all her might. Her own mind was cursing her for her cowardice. Couldn't she tell them the whole story right now? If that made the police her enemy, let it be so. At least something would come to the attention of the court. Who knows the lives of those wretched fellows might be saved, and the public would know that the testimony was false. But as she was about to speak, her voice died in her throat. Fear of the consequences seized her tongue.

Finally she thought it best to get up and leave.

Seeing her coming down the stairs, Devidin came on to the veranda and in a compassionate voice asked, 'Are you going home, Bahuji?'

Stopping her flow of tears, Jalpa said, 'Yes, I can't stand it here now.'

Coming out of the compound, Devidin said, intending to console her, 'Once the police have intoxicated someone with their promises, he can't be influenced by anything else.'

'That's all for cowards,' said Jalpa with hate.

They continued to walk in silence for some distance. Suddenly Jalpa said, 'Tell me, Dada, can't there be another appeal? Will the judgement on the prisoners be made here and now?'

Devidin understood the intention behind this question. 'No,' he said. 'An appeal is possible in the High Court.'

They walked in silence again for a while. Jalpa stopped under the shade of a tree and said, 'Dada, I want to meet the Judge Sahab today and tell him everything from the beginning. If I give proof, will he agree with what I say?'

Staring at her, Devidin said, 'The Judge Sahab!'

Meeting his eyes, Jalpa said, 'Yes!'

'I can't tell you anything about this, Bahuji,' he said doubtfully. 'That's a matter for the authorities. There's no telling if it will make an impression or fall flat.'

'Can't he say to the police that your evidence is manufactured, false?' said Jalpa.

'He can say it.'

'So shall I meet him today? Will you take me to meet him?'

'Come on, let's go find out, but it's a dangerous affair,' said Devidin.

'How is it dangerous, tell me.'

'Suppose that a case is brought against Bhaiya for giving false testimony and he receives some punishment?'

'So that's nothing. You reap what you sow.'

Surprised at this harshness of Jalpa's, Devidin said, 'There's another thing to worry about. It's what is most to be feared.'

'What's that?' asked Jalpa haughtily.

'The police are great cowards,' said Devidin. 'Their idea of a joke is to insult someone. The Judge Sahab would certainly summon the Police Commissioner to tell him all this. The

Commissioner would think that this woman is ruining the whole show. Let's arrest her. If the judge were an Englishman he'd fearlessly give the police a reprimand. Our Indian brothers are afraid to make a peep in such cases lest a charge of fomenting rebellion be brought against them. That's the thing. The Judge Sahab will certainly give the Police Commissioner an account of all this. What will happen next is not that the case will be dismissed, but rather that the truth will not be allowed to come out. Who knows but they might arrest you? Sometimes when the witness begins to change, or when he's ready to let the cat out of the bag, the police intimidate his family members. Their powers of deception are unlimited.'

Jalpa began to feel afraid. She had no fear of her own arrest, but rather of the police committing some outrage on Rama, and this fear made her timid. She felt as tired now as if she had come from a journey of hundreds of miles. Her courageous resolution melted away like snow.

After going on a little further, she asked Devidin, 'Would it be possible to meet with him now?'

'Who, Bhaiya?' asked Devidin.

'Yes.'

'Not at all. The guard will be made even stricter. They might even leave that bungalow. And even if you could meet him now, what would be the use? There's no way he can change his deposition now. He'd be implicated in perjury.'

After going a little further Jalpa said, 'I think I'll go back to Allahabad. What can I do if I stay here?'

'No, Bahu,' said Devidin looking at her compassionately. 'I won't let you go just now. We wouldn't feel like being at home a moment without you. The old woman would weep her life away. Stay here now and see what the court decision is. I don't think Bhaiya is such a faint-hearted man. Everyone in your caste is devoted to government service, but even if someone gave me a salary of a hundred rupees a month, I wouldn't take a government position. It's different when you earn your own living; a man never gets tired doing this. But after five or six hours in the office, your body starts getting weak, and you start yawning.'

There was no more conversation along the way. Jalpa's heart was not at all willing to accept her defeat. Even though she had lost, she still could not be satisfied to watch this drama like a spectator. She was restless to be included in the drama, and to play her own part. Wouldn't there be another meeting with Rama? There was an ocean of fiery words welling up in her heart, which she wanted to tell him. She had not the slightest compassion for Rama, not a shred of sympathy. 'Congratulations on your wealth and power,' she wanted to say to him. 'Jalpa spurns them, kicks them away. The touch of your bloody hands will bring blisters on my body. I don't consider anyone who sells his soul for money and position to be a man. You're not a man, you're not even an animal, you're a coward! A coward!'

Her lovely face became flushed. Her neck became stiff with pride. He probably thought that when she saw him wearing a tasseled turban riding on a horse, she wouldn't be able to contain herself with joy. She wasn't that low. Forget the horse, even if he flew on the wind, he was still a murderer in her eyes, nothing but a murderer, who had cut the throats of so many men to save his own life! Hadn't she explained it to him again and again? Had it made no impression on him? Oh! So eager for money, so greedy! She was not a beggar in need of his care and protection. Absorbed in these heated feelings, Jalpa reached home.

## 43

A month passed. Jalpa had been upset for several days. Several times near-frenzies came upon her to get the whole story published in some newspaper, to expose the whole sham, to knock down all the castles in the air. But all these excesses of emotion subsided. The hidden strength in the depth of her soul kept her tongue silent. She had ejected Rama from her heart. She felt no anger toward him now, no hatred, not even pity, but only sadness. She might not have wept even if she had received news of his dying. Yes, she would have been sad for a little while, considering it to be a divinely ordained drama, a heartless comedy of the illusory world, a cruel game. That bond of affectionate trust which had been placed on her neck for two or two-and-a-half years had broken, but its mark was still there. During this time she had seen Rama on several occasions passing by her house in a motor-car. His eyes seemed to be searching for someone. There was some shame in those eyes, and an entreaty for forgiveness, but Jalpa never even once raised her eyes towards him. Perhaps even if he had come and fallen at her feet, she still would not have looked in his direction. It was as if his hateful cowardice and great selfishness had torn up her heart. Even so, the mark of that bond of affectionate trust still remained. Now and then that passionately-loved form of Rama's, the sight of which had once made her ecstatic, entered her heart like joyless, dull, faint moon-light amidst spreading darkness, and for a moment her memories wept. And then the curtain of that darkness and silence would fall again. There were no tender memories for her future; only the harsh, arid present, dreadful in form, stood staring at her.

That same Jalpa who had at home given herself airs at every turn, was now the very picture of service, sacrifice, and forbear-ance. Although Jaggo kept on forbidding it, early every morning she would sweep the whole house, clean the cooking utensils and the kitchen, knead the flour, and light the oven. All the old woman would have left to do then, was to bake the rotis. She put all considerations of impurity or untouchability on the shelf. The old woman would keep pushing her into the kitchen and feeding her something or other. A love like that of mother and daughter grew up between them.

All the business of the case had been finished up. All the argu-ments of the lawyers for both sides had been completed. All that was left was to deliver the decision, and today was the appointed date. Taking leave from her household chores very early on this morning, Jalpa was sitting listening intently to the cries of the vendors of the daily papers as if today her future were to be decided. Just then Devidin brought a paper and placed it before her; she fell on the paper and began to read about the decision. And what was the decision but an imaginary story whose chief actor was Rama. The judge praised him again and again. The whole accusation had depended on his deposition.

'Has the decision been published?' asked Devidin.

'Yes, it has been,' said Jalpa as she read.

'Who received punishment?'

'No one got off. One is to be hanged. Five have received ten years each, and nine got five years each. That same Dinesh is to be hanged.'

She put the newspaper down, heaved a long sigh, and said, 'Who knows what will happen to the children and families of these poor fellows!'

Ready for her question, Devidin said, 'I've been finding out about all of them from the very day you told me to. Eight of them have not married yet, and their families are well off; they won't have any difficulties at all! Six of them have married, but their families are well off too. Some of them have trades, some are land-owners, and some have fathers and uncles in service. I've asked several people about them. A subscription has been raised for them here too, and if their families want to take it, it will be given to them. Only Dinesh's family is ruined. There are two small children, his elderly mother, and his wife. He was a teacher in some school here, and lived in a rented home. He's the one who's been destroyed.'

'Were you able to find out anything about his home?' asked Jalpa.

'Yes, it wasn't hard to find out.'

'So when will we go?' said Jalpa entreatingly. 'I'll go along with you. There's time now. Come on, let's have a look.'

'Let me go take a look first,' objected Devidin. 'Just where are you going to go running around with me so thoughtlessly like this?'

Jalpa, having no alternative, restrained herself and said nothing.

Devidin left, and Jalpa began to read the newspaper again, but her attention was fixed on Dinesh. The poor fellow would be hanged. What must have been his state when he heard the order for his hanging. His old mother and wife must have beaten their breasts when they heard this news. The poor fellow was only a schoolmaster after all, and it must have been hard enough to make a living. What other support would there be? Imagining the family's distress, she felt such a burning hatred for Rama that she could no longer continue feeling sad. She flew into a passion. If he were to come now she'd curse him in a way that even he would remember. 'Are you a man? Never. You're an evil demon in human form, an evil demon! You are so beneath contempt that there's no word to express it. You are so base that the lowest of the low spits on you today. Why hasn't someone killed you already? Let those men's lives go, but let no blemish stain your precious name! How did you fall so far! How can someone whose father is so truthful and so honourable, be so greedy and so cowardly!'

Evening came, but Devidin had not returned. Jalpa went and stood at the window again and again, looking here and there, but he was nowhere to be seen. The time dragged on till eight o'clock struck, but he had still not returned. Suddenly a motor-car came and stopped at the door. Rama got out and hailed Jaggo. 'Everything's going well, isn't it Dadi? Where has Dada gone?'

Jaggo looked at him once and then turned away her face. She said only, 'He must have gone, somewhere; I don't know.'

Rama took out four gold bracelets from his pocket, placed them at Jaggo's feet, and said, 'I brought these for you, Dadi. Put them on, they're not too loose, are they?'

Jaggo picked up the bracelets and hurled them to the ground, and glaring at him, said, 'Isn't there room for four bracelets where there's room for so much wickedness? Thanks to God's grace I've worn many bracelets and I still have three or four pounds of gold around. But whatever I've eaten, or worn, has been earned through my own efforts, not through doing wrong to someone else, not through heaping up sins on my head, not through depraving my will. May the womb that gave birth to a bad son like you be burned up. You must have come to give your sinful earnings to your bahu. You must have thought that she'd go wild seeing your platterful of money. You've lived so long with her and yet your greedy eyes still can't understand her. A wicked demon like you isn't worthy of a goddess like her. If you want her to be happy, take your feet back to where they came from; why do you want to shame yourself by appearing before her? If you had come here today wounded or beaten by the police, or if you had received a sentence or been thrown in jail, then she would have worshipped you, washed your feet, and drunk the water. She's one of those women who cannot see evil done to others even if she has to perform physical labour, go hungry, or wear rags. If you were my son, I'd give you poison. Why are you standing here making me angry? Why don't you leave? I haven't taken something from you, have I?'

Rama stood silently listening with bowed head. Then in a wounded tone he said, 'Dadi, I've done something bad and I'll be ashamed of it until my dying breath. But I'm not as low as you think I am. If you knew how harshly the police treated me, you wouldn't call me an evil demon.'

The sounds of their conversation reached Jalpa's ears. She peered down the stairs. Ramanath was standing there with a Banarasi silk turban on his head, a nice silk coat, and gold spectacles on his eyes. In this past month his body had blossomed out, and his complexion had become even fairer. His face had never showed so much lustre before. His last words fell on Jalpa's ears. She swooped forward like a hawk, thundered down the stairs, and launching an attack on him with eyes as piercing as arrows dipped in poison, said, 'If you are so intimidated by harsh treatment and threats, then you are a coward. You have no right to call yourself a man. What was the harsh treatment? May I hear? People have gone laughing to have their heads cut off, have watched their sons dying, have agreed to have their testicles crushed in a vice, but never budged an inch from truth. You're a man too, why did you yield to a threat? Why didn't you stand up, bare your chest, tell them to take aim, but you'd never say what was untrue? Why didn't you bow your head? The soul was put inside the body for the body to protect it, not for the body to destroy it. What reward have you received for your wickedness? Do you know at all?'

'Nothing yet,' said Rama in a subdued voice.

'I'm very happy to hear it!' said Jalpa hissing like a snake. 'May God cause you to get nothing, and disgrace you too! This is my prayer from the bottom of my heart. But no, the police will never wish to make a wax doll like you angry. You'll get a position and perhaps a good one, but you'll never be able to escape from the net you're caught in. Giving false testimony, making a false case, and dealing in evil, these were written in your fate. Go, enjoy your life to the full according to your wish. I told you before and today I'm telling you again, that I have no connection with you. I consider you dead. That's enough, go. I'm a woman, but if some-one wanted to get me to do something wicked by threatening me, if I couldn't kill him, then I'd cut my own throat. Don't you even have as much courage as a woman?'

Whining as abjectly as a beggar, Rama said, 'Won't you listen to any of my explanations?'

'No!' said Jalpa proudly.

'So shall I leave in disgrace?'

'As you wish!'

'You won't forgive me?'

'Never! Not in any way!'

Rama stood for a moment with bowed head, then slowly coming down from the veranda, said to Jaggo, 'Dadi, when Dada comes tell him to meet me for a little while. I'll come whenever he says.'

Jaggo softening a little, said, 'Come here tomorrow.'

Getting into the car, Rama said, 'I won't come here any more, Dadi!'

When the car had gone, Jalpa in a censorious mood, said, 'He came to show off the car, as if he had bought it!'

Jaggo scolded her. 'You shouldn't have been so unrestrained, Bahu! A man can't think of anything to say when his heart is wounded.'

'He's not one to feel shame, Dadi!' said Jalpa harshly. 'He's sold his soul for this comfort. Why should he ever give it up? You didn't ask him what he wanted to meet Dada for. If he'd been here he would have given him such a tongue-lashing that he'd have remembered his mother's milk!'

'If I'd been in your place, Bahu, I wouldn't have said such things,' said Jaggo reproachfully. 'You have a very hard heart. If it had been another man would he have listened so silently? I was trembling all over for fear that he would give you a blow with his fist. But he *is* a very meek fellow!'

'They don't call that meekness, Dadi,' said Jalpa with the same harshness. 'It's shamelessness.'

'Did Bhaiya come here?' said Devidin, arriving. 'I saw him in the motor-car along the way.'

'Yes, he did come,' said Jaggo. 'He said he wanted to meet you.'

'I'll meet him,' said Devidin sadly. 'Did you talk with him at all?'

'What talk?' said Jaggo regretfully. 'First I worshipped him, then when I shut up, Bahu put a garland of flowers around his neck.'

Jalpa lowered her head and said, 'A man must endure the results of what he does.'

'He came to meet us expecting us to receive him as our own,' said Jaggo.

'No one went to invite him,' said Jalpa. 'Did you find out anything about Dinesh, Dada?'

'Yes, everything,' said Devidin. 'His home is in Howrah. I know the address and everything.'

'Shall we go now or some time tomorrow?' said Jalpa, feeling some misgivings.

'Whatever you wish. If you like we can go right now; I'm ready.'

'You must be tired,' said Jalpa.

'I don't get tired doing things like this, daughter.'

It was eight o'clock, and there was a continuous crush of motor vehicles on the street.

The footpaths on both sides of the street were full of women and men walking along all dressed up, laughing and talking. How engrossed in enjoyment the world is, thought Jalpa to herself. Whoever has to die for it, let him die, but the world will stubbornly persist in its ways. Everyone sits in his own little house of earth; if the whole country is washed away, no matter, as long as his house is saved, and there is no obstacle to his own welfare. Jalpa's innocent heart would have rejoiced to see the market-place closed. She would have been glad to see everyone with bowed heads, scowling, frenzied, and with faces red from their inner anger. She didn't know that the fall of such small fry as Dinesh didn't make even a ripple in this sea of people, let alone a noise.

## 44

When Rama left in the motor-car he couldn't think of a thing. He had no idea of where he was going. Familiar routes had become unfamiliar to him. He was not angry at Jalpa, not in the least, nor was he angry at Jaggo. He was angry with his own weakness, his own greed, and his own cowardice. Surrounded by the influence of the police, his sense of moral propriety had been corrupted. The enormity of the injustice he was perpetrating had only occurred to him on the day when Jalpa first admonished him. But subsequently no doubts had arisen in his mind, for the police officers had diverted his thoughts by building up high hopes for him. They'd tell him, 'Sir, don't worry about your wife at all. When you go to meet her with an inlaid necklace, and show her a plateful of money, all of your Begum Sahab's anger will vanish. You'll go to some nice place in our province and spend your life in ease. How is she going to be angry!' and they'd give him numerous examples they'd seen with their own eyes. Rama became confused. And then he hadn't had a chance to meet Jalpa again. The police made a deep impression on him. Today he'd gone to give Jalpa the good news of his victory with an inlaid necklace in his pocket. He knew she'd surely be pleased to see it. And just tomorrow he would be receiving a letter of appointment from the Police Commissioner under the signature of the Home Secretary of the United Provinces. After many outings for three or four days, he'd set out for home. He wanted to take Devidin and Jaggo along with him too; how could he forget their beneficence? He had gone to Jalpa with these resolves in mind, much as some devotee might go with offerings of flowers and food to attend on a deity. But the deity, rather than granting a boon, had spurned his tray of flowers, and trampled on his food. He hadn't had a chance to say anything. Coming out from the poisonous atmosphere of the police today, he was able to breathe pure air, and his good sense awakened. Now that he could see his baseness in its true form, how hideous, how fiendish an image it was. He didn't have the courage to gaze at himself. He thought to himself that he'd go to the judge right now and tell him the whole story. If the police became his enemies, if he was thrown in jail to rot, so what. He'd reveal the whole deception. Wouldn't the judge be able to change his decision? The accused were still in custody. The police would grind their teeth, and make a great fuss; maybe they'd even eat him alive. Eat him alive! It was this very weakness which had blackened his name.

Jalpa's furious image came before his eyes again. Oh, how enraged she had been! If he'd known how angry she'd be, he'd have changed his deposition even if the world had turned topsy-turvy. They'd really tricked him, the policemen. If the judge didn't listen to anything and didn't acquit the accused, then Jalpa would never look at him again. How could he face her? What would he do for the rest of his life? And for whom?

He stopped the car and looked around. He had no inkling of where he was. All at once he saw a watchman, and asked for the address of the judge's house. The watchman laughed and said. 'Your honour has come very far out of the way. It's at least six or seven miles from here; he lives over by Chowringhee.'

Rama asked the way to Chowringhee and set off again. It was nine o'clock. He thought to himself that if he didn't meet the Judge Sahab, the whole game would be spoiled. He wouldn't go away until he met him. If he listened, everything would be fine; if not, he'd speak with the High Court judges tomorrow. Would anyone listen? If not, he'd get the whole thing published in the newspapers, and then everyone's eyes would be opened.

The motor-car was going at thirty miles an hour; he'd reach Chowringhee in ten minutes. There was still the same hustle and bustle here, but Rama kept driving through all the uproar. Suddenly a policeman flashed a red light at him. He stopped, stuck out his head, and saw that it was that same Daroga!

'Haven't you gone to the bungalow yet?' asked the Daroga. 'Don't drive so fast; you'll have an accident. Tell me, did you meet your Begum Sahab? I thought she'd be with you. She must have been really happy.'

Rama felt such rage that he wanted to tear out the other's moustache by its roots, but quickly inventing a story he said, 'Yes sir, she was very happy! Extremely happy!'

'I told you so, didn't I! That's just the medicine for a woman's anger. You were trembling when you left.'

'That was my stupidity.'

'Let's go, I'll come with you. We'll play a game of cards and get a little drunk. The Deputy Sahab and the Inspector Sahab will come too, and we'll send for Zohra. We'll have a good time for a while. Why don't you have Mrs. Ramanath come stay at the bungalow? She's staying at that Khatik's house now.'

'There's something important I've got to go the other way for just now. You take the car. I'll come on foot.'

The Daroga got into the car and said, 'No, Sahab. I'm not in a hurry. Go wherever you like. I won't interfere in the least.'

'But I'm not going to the bungalow now,' said Rama getting a little huffy.

'I'm getting the picture,' said the Daroga smiling, 'but I won't interfere in the least. That same Begam Sahab of yours ...'

'No sir,' said Rama interrupting. 'that's not where I have to go.'

'So is there some other target? There'll be no small goings-on at the bungalow today. Everything you need to amuse yourself will be there.'

Suddenly glaring at the other furiously, Rama said, 'Do you think I'm that corrupt? I'm not so low as that.'

'All right, sahab,' said the Daroga a little shamefaced. 'My offence, pardon me. I won't ever be so rude again. But don't think you're out of danger yet. I'm not going to let you go anywhere that I don't feel completely confident about. You don't know how many enemies you have. I'm saying this for your own good.'

Biting his lips in vexation, Rama said, 'It would be better if you didn't concern yourself with what's good for me. You people have destroyed me and you still won't get off my back. Let me die in my own way. I'm fed up with this slavery. I don't want to become a little child following its mother around. You want your car; take it gladly. I've had to sacrifice fifteen men to ride in a motor-car and live in a bungalow, and my heart isn't that strong. Take the car please.'

He got out of the car as he said this and walked quickly ahead. The Daroga called out to him several times, 'Please listen, listen to what I have to say,' but he didn't even turn around to look. Walking a little further ahead, he took a turn; it was the very street where the judge's bungalow was. He didn't meet anyone on the street. Rama walked first on the footpath on this side of the street, then on the other side reading the numbers as he went. He stopped abruptly on seeing one number. He stood for a moment, looking to see if anyone would come out so he could ask if the Sahab was there or not. He didn't have the courage to go in. It occurred to him that if the judge should ask him why he had given false testimony, he wouldn't know what answer to give. To say that the police had forced him to give testimony, that they had tempted him, and had threatened to beat him, was a shameful thing. What answer did he have if the judge asked where his common sense had gone when he had brought so much disgrace on his head and stooped so low as to take the lives of so many men just to save himself from a two- or three-year sentence? He'd be forced to feel ashamed, and he'd look like a fool. He turned back; he didn't have the capacity to face such shame. Shame has always defeated heroes. Those who don't even fear death, don't have the courage to stand before shame. To jump into a fire, or to stand in front of a sword is much easier in comparison. To avoid shame and preserve honour, great kingdoms have been destroyed, rivers of blood have flowed, and lives have been utterly consumed. This same shame drove Rama's feet to turn back today; probably even a jail sentence didn't frighten him as much.

# 45

Rama went to sleep at midnight, so he didn't wake up until nine o'clock the next morning. He was dreaming—Dinesh was going to the gallows. All at once a woman with a sword ran to the gallows and cut the rope, and a commotion broke out all over. The woman was Jalpa; no one dared to approach her. Then she leaped forward and struck at Rama. He sat up in a panic and saw that the Daroga and the Inspector were standing in his room, while the Deputy was lying back in the armchair, smoking a cigar.

'You slept a lot today, Sahab!' said the Daroga. 'When did you get back yesterday?'

Rama sat down in a chair and said, 'I got back after a little while. This case will be appealed to the High Court, won't it?'

'What appeal?' said the Inspector. 'It'll just be the observance of a formality. You've made the case so strong that no one can shake it even if he tries. On my honour, you've worked a miracle. You don't have to worry about anything from that side. True, until the decision is made it's appropriate to look after your safety, and this is why arrangements have been made for guarding you again. As soon as the High Court makes its decision, you'll have your position.'

Puffing out a cloud of smoke from his cigar, the Deputy said, 'The Commissioner Sahab has given you this Departmental Order, which you should have no doubts about. Look, here's the name of the Home Secretary of the United Provinces. As soon as you show this D.O. there, it'll get you some very good post.'

'The Commissioner Sahab is very pleased with you, on my honour,' said the Inspector.

'Very pleased,' said the Deputy. 'He'll also write a separate letter directly to the United Provinces. Your fortune is made.'

As he said this, he handed the D.O. to Rama. Rama opened the envelope, took a look, and without any warning tore it into bits. The three men stared at him in astonishment.

'Did you have a lot to drink last night?' said the Daroga. 'This won't be to your advantage.'

'On my honour,' said the Inspector, 'if the Commissioner Sahab finds out, he'll be extremely displeased.'

'I don't understand this at all,' said the Deputy. 'What do you mean by this?'

'It means that I don't need this D.O., nor do I want a position. I'm leaving here today,' said Rama.

'You can't go anywhere until the High Court gives its decision,' said the Deputy.

'Why?'

'It's the Commissioner Sahab's order,' said the Deputy.

'I'm not anyone's slave.'

'Babu Ramanath,' said the Inspector, 'why are you spoiling a game that's completely arranged? Whatever was to happen, has happened. In five or ten days the High Court's decision will be confirmed. What's best for you is to happily accept the reward you're getting and spend your life in comfort. If God wishes, some day you too will reach some high office. What advantage is there to you in making police officers angry and enduring the miseries of jail? On my honour, if these officers withdraw their favour even a little bit, you'll drop out of sight. On my honour, just one hint would bring you a ten-year sentence. What can you be thinking of? We don't want to play those nasty tricks on you, but yes, if you want to force us to be harsh with you, then we'll have to be harsh. Don't think jail is easy, please. May God take you to hell rather than send you to jail. Violence and abuse are ordinary punishments there. If you're forced into solitary confinement, then death has come for you. On my honour, jail is worse than hell.'

'This poor fellow is helpless against his Begum Sahab,' said the Daroga. 'Maybe she's plotting against his life. He's cowed by her ill-will.'

'What happened?' said the Inspector. 'You gave her that necklace yesterday, didn't you? Even then she didn't agree?'

Rama took the necklace out of his coat pocket and put it on the table. 'That necklace is here,' he said.

'Well, she didn't accept it,' said the Inspector.

'She's some proud lady,' said the Deputy.

'We'll have to give her a little beating too,' said the Inspector.

'That will depend on the Babu Sahab's manners and courtesy,' said the Daroga. 'If you don't force our hand without rhyme or reason, we won't go after you.'

'We ought to take a recognizance from that Khatik too,' said the Deputy.

A new problem confronted Rama now, far more complicated and far more terrible than before. It was possible that he would have sacrificed himself on the altar of duty and readied himself for a three- or four-year jail sentence. Perhaps he might even now have decided to surrender himself, but there was no way he could find the courage to thrust Jalpa into danger along with himself. He had been so intimidated by being in the clutches of the police that now he couldn't see any way of extracting himself honourably. He saw that he couldn't overcome his opponents in this struggle. All the fire went out of him. Feeling powerless, he said, 'What is it you people want from me, after all?'

The Inspector looked at the Daroga and winked as if to say, 'We've got him!' He said, 'Nothing more than this, that you continue to be our guest, and that you leave here after the High Court settles the case, because after that we'll no longer be responsible for your protection. If you want to get some certificate, you'll get it; but the choice of taking it or not is entirely yours. If you're smart you'll take it and profit from it; if not you'll be knocked around here and there—the proverb that sin brings no pleasure will come true for you. We don't want any more than this from you then. On my honour, everything you might want will be made available to you here; but until the case is over, you can't be free.'

'Will I be able to go on trips?' asked Rama dejectedly, 'or not even that?'

'No sir!' said the Inspector as if giving an aphorism.

'You were given that freedom,' said the Daroga, giving a commentary on the aphorism, 'but you used it wrongly. Until it's certain that you can use it appropriately, you'll be deprived of this privilege.'

The Daroga looked towards the Inspector as if he wanted praise for this commentary, which he received to his delight.

The three officers took their leave and Rama, lighting a cigar, began to ponder on this forbidding situation.

## 46

Another month went by, and the date for the presentation of the case in the High Court was fixed. The same timidity and sycophancy as before came into Rama's habits and he danced to the officers' tunes. He drank more than before too; it was as if sensuality had him in its grip. From time to time a prostitute, Zohra, would come to his room, and he would listen to her sing with great pleasure.

One day he said to her longingly, 'I'm afraid that I might fall in love with you, and what else could the result be but that I'd spend the rest of my life feeling sad. What hope could there be of your being faithful!'

Zohra, secretly pleased, gazed at him with her big bright eyes and said, 'Yes, Sahab, what would I know about being faithful? I'm a prostitute after all.'

'Can there be any doubt about it?' queried Rama.

'No, not at all. You people bring us hearts brimful of love, but we don't place any value on this. That's the way it is, isn't it?'

'Not a doubt.'

'Forgive me, please, but you're taking the men's side. The

truth is that you people come to us to divert yourselves, just to console yourselves, just to enjoy yourselves. When you're not looking for faithfulness at all, why would you receive it? But I do know this much, that if the world should learn how many of us were disillusioned by men's faithlessness and lost our peace of mind, its eyes would open wide. It's our mistake if we want faithfulness from promiscuous people; it's like looking for meat in a hawk's nest. If a thirsty man runs towards a dried-up well, I don't think it's the well's fault.'

When Zohra left that night, she gave welcome news to the Daroga. 'Today His Excellency enjoyed himself a lot. If God wishes it, in three or four days he won't even mention his wife's name.'

Pleased, the Daroga said, 'That's just why I sent for you. It would really be a pleasure if his wife left this place. Then we wouldn't have anything to worry about. It seems that people from the independence movement have met with that woman. They're all devils of the same sort.'

Zohra's comings and goings increased to the point where Rama fell into his own trap. He wanted to establish his credibility in the officers' view by displaying his love for Zohra. Just as children burst into tears during a game, so his pretence of love became a passion of love. Now Zohra appeared faithful, and a veritable goddess of love to him. True, she wasn't as beautiful as Jalpa, but cleverer in conversation, more deft in manners, more cunning in the art of being charming. Completely new plans began to grow in his heart.

One day he said to her, 'Zohra, the time of parting is coming. I'll have to leave here in three or four days. Will you still remember me then?'

'I won't let you go,' said Zohra. 'Take some good position here. Then you and I can live in comfort.'

'Are you saying that from your heart, Zohra?' said Rama almost obsessed. 'See here, swear on my head that you won't deceive me.'

'If that's what you're afraid of, then arrange a temporary marriage. If those words provoke you, then marry me. Call some pundits. What more can I do to prove my love?'

Rama became almost delirious on receiving this proof of sincere love. And the hypnotic effect of these words was all the greater for having come from Zohra's mouth. This lovely woman, to whom very prominent men were devoted, was ready to make such a big sacrifice for him! Isn't whoever finds lumps of gold in a mine where others have found only sand extremely fortunate? For several days a struggle had been going on in Rama's mind. How dull, how difficult his life with Jalpa would be. Her righteousness and truthfulness would tug him at every step and his life would become one long penance—a never-ending striving. A virtuous life had never been his ideal. He too, like ordinary men, wanted to have a life of luxury and enjoyment. His temperament, much attracted to sensual pleasure, was now drawn strongly away from Jalpa towards Zohra. He began to remember examples of devoted prostitutes, and along with this came instances of the fickle behaviour of wives. He decided it was all a delusion. People were neither virtuous nor vicious from birth: everything depended on circumstances.

Zohra came and went every day, making yet another knot in their ties of affection. In such a situation, even a disciplined youth would have been shaken, let alone a pleasure-loving one like Rama. He had not yet been able to lose his way wandering around here and there because, as soon as his wings had been fledged, he had been netted and put in a cage. Even after being out of this cage for some days, he hadn't found the courage to fly. Now a new vision was before him. This was not some little cage of clay, but rather a garden of flowers waving in the wind, where the pleasures of freedom existed even in captivity. Why shouldn't he enjoy the delights of sporting in this garden!

## 47

The more Rama was caught in Zohra's love-snare, the fewer became the doubts of the group of police officials towards him. His confinement was gradually relaxed to the point where one day the Deputy took Rama with him on an evening trip in the motorcar. When the car passed in front of Devidin's shop, Rama drew his head inside so that no one might see him. He was eager to know if Jalpa was there or if she had left, but he couldn't bring himself to stick out his head. He still understood in his heart that the way he had taken was not a very good one, but despite knowing this, he didn't want to leave it. Had he seen Devidin he would have bowed his head in shame; he would have been unable to prove his side of things by any argument. He thought to himself that the best course for him was to stop meeting him altogether. Aside from Devidin, Jaggo, and Jalpa, he was not acquainted with anybody in this city whose criticism or scorn he feared.

The car was turning here and there as it went in the direction of the Howrah bridge, when all at once Rama saw a woman coming towards them from the steps down to the river carrying a pitcher of Ganges water on her head. Her clothes were quite dirty and she was so wasted that her neck was pressed down by the weight of her burden. Her gait seemed rather similar to Jalpa's. What would Jalpa be doing here, he thought to himself. But in an instant the car had moved forward and Rama caught sight of the woman's face. His heart nearly stopped. It was Jalpa! Hiding his head to one side of the window he looked intently. There was no doubt that it was Jalpa, but how frail, as if she were an elderly widow. There was no longer that loveliness, that charm, that liveliness, that pride. Rama was not heartless; his eyes filled with tears. Jalpa in this state while he was still alive? Surely Devidin must have turned her out and she'd become a servant to support herself. No, Devidin was not so inhuman. Jalpa herself must have refused to be dependent on him. She was certainly a haughty woman. How was he to find out what was going on?

The car had gone far ahead. All of Rama's playfulness, all of his enjoyment had vanished. That ill-clothed sorrowful image of Jalpa stood before his eyes. Whom should he talk to? What should he say? Who was one of his own here? If he even mentioned her name to the police, they'd all get a nasty shock and would stop his leaving home again. Oh! What a look of deep sorrow had been spread over her face, what hopelessness there had been in her eyes! Ah, how many sorrowful sighs coming from a burning heart there seemed to be in her sunken eyes, as if they had never seen laughter, as if they had withered before their buds had ever blossomed.

After a while Zohra came, mincing, smiling, and swaying, but today Rama was harsh and cutting even to her.

'Are you remembering someone today?' she asked.

She threw her round, soft, butter-smooth arms around his neck as she said this, and drew him toward her. Rama made not the slightest effort on his part, but kept his head bowed towards his heart as if that was its support now.

In a voice dripping with tenderness she asked, 'Tell me the truth, why are you so sad today? Tell me everything. Are you mad at me for something?'

In a voice shaking with emotion Rama said, 'No Zohra. I'll always be obliged to you for the kindness you've shown a poor wretch like me. You took care of me when the shattered boat of my life was sinking. Those were the most fortunate days of my life and I'll always worship their memory in my heart. But difficulty draws unfortunate people towards itself over and over again. Even the ties of love can't prevent them from being pulled in that direction. The circumstances in which I saw Jalpa today are piercing my heart like spears. She was walking along dressed in torn and dirty clothes, and carrying Ganges water in a pitcher. My heart was shattered to see her in such a state. I've never felt so much grief in my life. I can't say anything about what's happening to her.'

'She was at the home of that wealthy old Khatik?' asked Zohra.

'Yes, she was, but I can't say why she left there. The Deputy Sahab was with me. I couldn't ask her a thing in front of him. I know she'd have turned away if she had seen me, and that perhaps she considers me contemptible, but at least I would have known why she's in this plight now. Zohra, whatever you may be thinking about me in your heart, I'm drowned in the thought that you love me. And at least we expect sympathy from those who love us. There's not a single other person to whom I could tell the state of my heart. Even though you were sent to make me stray off the path, you took pity on me. Maybe you thought it wasn't proper to kick a man who was down. If today you and I should quarrel for some reason, and tomorrow you saw me in distress, would you feel no sympathy for me at all? If you saw me starving, would you treat me with less kindness than a man would a dog? I would hope not. Even if sadness or indifference might enter where love has once lived, it's not possible for violent feelings to do so. Won't you show me even a little sympathy? If you want to, Zohra, you can find out everything about Jalpa, where she is, what she's doing, what she thinks of me in her heart, why she doesn't go home, and how long she intends to stay. If you can somehow persuade Jalpa to go to Prayag, Zohra, I'll be your slave for life. I can't bear to see her in this condition. Maybe I'll escape from here this very night. I don't have the slightest fear of what might happen to me. I'm not brave, I'm a very weak man, and my spirit is always defeated by danger, but even my shamelessness can't endure this wound.'

Zohra was a prostitute and she was well acquainted with all kinds of men, good and bad; she had a sense of discrimination about them. She saw a big difference between this young man from a different province and other individuals! At first she had come here as a slave to money, but after three or four days she found herself attached to Rama. Mature women cannot be indifferent to affection. Rama might have every fault, but he also had affection. This was the first man she had met in her life who had opened his heart to her, who had not hidden anything from her; she didn't want to lose this jewel. She didn't feel the slightest jealousy while listening to what he said; on the contrary, a self-interested sympathy was evoked. By pleasing this young man, so guileless concerning love, she could make him her slave for good. She had no fears about Jalpa. No matter how beautiful she might be, Zohra could make her pale with envy through her own skill in the arts and her own fine manners. She had left more than one great beauty of the Kayasth community weeping in her wake before this. So how could Jalpa be considered noteworthy?

'So why do you feel so much grief for her, darling?' said Zohra, trying to raise his spirits. 'Zohra is ready to do anything for you. I'll find out about Jalpa tomorrow, and if she wants to stay here I'll arrange everything for her comfort, and if she wants to go I'll send her by rail.'

Very humbly, Rama said, 'If I could meet her once, the burden would be lifted from my heart.'

'That's not easy, darling,' said Zohra growing worried. 'Who will let you leave here?'

'Tell me some plan.'

'I'll leave her in a park and come here. You go there with the Deputy Sahab and meet her on some pretext. I can't come up with anything else.'

Rama was about to say something when the Daroga called out, 'May I join your private conference too?'

The two of them quickly recovered themselves and opened the door. In came the Daroga smiling, and sitting next to Zohra said, 'How can it be so quiet here today! Is the treasury empty today? Zohra, fill a goblet with your henna-dyed hands today. Ramanath, dear brother, don't be angry!'

'Let it be, now, Darogaji,' said Rama sourly. 'You seem to be a little drunk.'

The Daroga seized Zohra's hand and said, 'Enough, one goblet Zohra! And another thing, today accept me as your guest and treat me with hospitality!'

'Darogaji,' said Rama, feeling very ill-disposed to his visitor, 'please leave now. I can't stomach this.'

'Do you have written authority?' said the Daroga looking at him glassy-eyed.

'Yes sir,' said Rama, bursting into a rage. 'I have written authority.'

'Well, your authority is rejected!'

'I tell you, leave here.'

'Well! You're telling me to leave? That's about as impossible as a frog catching a cold. Why not. Come on, Zohra, leave him here to babble.'

He grabbed Zohra's hand and lifted her to her feet as he said this.

Rama wrenched his hand away and said, 'I've told you, leave here. Zohra can't go just now. If she should go, I'll drink your blood, hers and yours, both of you. Zohra is mine, and as long as I'm here no one can even look in her direction.'

He grasped the Daroga's hand as he said this, thrust him out the door, and shutting it forcefully, fastened the iron bolt. The Daroga was a strong man, but his intoxication had weakened him. Standing outside on the veranda he began to hurl abuse and kick the door.

'Tell me and I'll go shove that wretch off the veranda,' said Rama. 'Devil's spawn!'

'Let him blather away. He'll go off by himself.'

'He's gone!'

'You did very well to throw that pig out,' said Zohra, looking delighted. 'He would have taken me off and harassed me. Would you really have hit him?'

'I would have killed him. I wasn't myself then. Who knows where I got so much strength from.'

'And suppose he doesn't let me come any more from tomorrow?'

'If he says even the slightest unpleasant thing meanwhile, I'll shoot him. Look over there, there's a pistol on the shelf. You're mine now, Zohra! I'm completely devoted to you, everything I have is at your feet, and I can't be satisfied till I have the same from you. You're mine, and I'm yours. No third woman or man has any right to come between us—not till I die.'

Zohra's eyes were sparkling. 'Don't say such things, darling,' she said, putting her arms around his neck.

# 48

For the whole day Rama wandered around in the jungles of emotional turmoil. Sometimes the pitch-dark mountain passes of despair came before him, sometimes the joyfully rippling greenery of hope. Zohra must have left him too! She'd gone making immense promises. What need did she have to do that? She'd come and say they hadn't met. She wouldn't deceive him, would she? If she went and told the whole story to the Deputy Sahab then disaster would befall poor Jalpa without any warning. Could Zohra's nature be so base? Never, for if she were so faithless, so deceitful, then this world wasn't worth staying in. Then the earlier one could die disgraced, the better. No, Zohra wouldn't deceive him. He remembered those days when Jalpa would feel his pockets and take out the money as soon as he came from the office. Now that same Jalpa had turned into a paragon of truthfulness. Then she had been a thing for love; now she was an object for adoration. Jalpa! He was not worthy of her. He couldn't reach the heights where she wanted to take him. Even if he could, he might get dizzy and plunge downwards. Nevertheless, he'd bow his head down to her feet. He knew that she had cast him out of her heart, that she was alienated from him, and that she would feel no sorrow if he sank, or joy if he swam. But perhaps even now if she had news of his dying or being caught in some terrible crisis, tears would come to her eyes. She might come to see his dead body. Yes! He'd hardly be dead before he wouldn't seem so low in her view.

Rama was now extremely remorseful about the error he had committed through failing to act according to what Jalpa had told him. If he'd changed his deposition to the judge during the court session according to her instructions, if he hadn't been frightened by threats, if he'd strengthened his courage, then he wouldn't be in this situation. Now he believed he would have endured every difficulty with Jalpa by his side. Wearing the armour of her belief in him, of her love for him, he would have been invincible. Even if he had been hanged, he'd have climbed the gallows laughing and joking.

But whatever mistakes he had made previously, this time he was suffering these hardships not through some mistake but for Jalpa's sake. If he had to endure captivity, it was much better to do so laughing and grinning than weeping and snivelling. After all, what else could he do to build up the confidence of the police officials in him? Those bastards would torment Jalpa, insult her, bring a false case against her, and get her sentenced. His situation would become even more unbearable. He was weak, and so he could stand all their insults, but Jalpa might give up her life.

Today he had learned that he couldn't leave Jalpa; giving up Zohra seemed almost impossible too. Could he keep both of these beautiful women pleased? Would Jalpa agree to live with him under these conditions? Never. She might never forgive him. Even if she should learn that he was going through these torments for her alone, she wouldn't forgive him. She'd say, 'Why did you stain your soul for me? I can take care of myself.'

He remained plunged in these perplexities the whole day. His eyes were glued to the street. The time for bathing came and went, the time for eating came and went, but he paid no heed to anything else. He attempted to divert himself with a newspaper, he sat down with a novel, but he couldn't apply his mind to anything. Nor did the Daroga come today. He was either ashamed of last night's incident or offended by it, or perhaps he had gone out somewhere. Rama didn't even ask anybody about it.

Like all weak men, Rama too was embarrassed by yesterday's lapse. When he sat alone, he felt bad about his condition—why was his tendency towards a life of sensuality so strong? He wasn't so devoid of conscience that his downward progress pleased him, but as soon as other people came, or a bottle of liquor appeared, or Zohra sat before him, all his knowledge of religious and moral duty was vitiated along with his conscience.

It was ten o'clock in the evening, but Zohra was nowhere to be seen, and the gate was shut. Rama no longer expected her to come, but even so he remained alert. What was going on? Hadn't she even met Jalpa, or hadn't she even gone? If she didn't come by tomorrow, he intended to send someone to her home. He dozed off a few times, and by then it was morning. The same distress began again. He ought to send someone to her house to summon her; at least he'd know whether she was at home or not.

He went to the Daroga and said, 'You weren't in your right senses last night.'

'That wasn't it,' said the Daroga, concealing his spite. 'I was only teasing you.'

'Zohra didn't come home last night. Please send someone to find out what's going on. I hope she's not angry.'

'She'll come by herself if she wants to,' said the Daroga dejectedly. 'There's no need to send anyone.'

Rama did not insist a second time. He understood that his excellency was out of sorts. He went quietly away. Whom should he say something to now? It seemed shameful to talk with everyone about this. People would think that this gentleman had turned out to be a really dissolute fellow. At least he had a little intimacy with the Daroga.

He didn't see Zohra for a week, and lost all hope of her coming. In the end she'd proven to be treacherous, Rama thought. It had been a big mistake to expect anything from her. Or was it possible that a police official might have forbidden her coming? At least she could have written him a letter. How she had deceived him! He'd poured out his heart to her for nothing. If she should say anything to these policemen, he'd be caught in a tangled mess of his own making. But Zohra couldn't be treacherous; his own inner soul bore witness to that. Otherwise she would never have agreed to what he'd asked her to do. To be sure, she'd tried to arouse him in the first few days, but then her behaviour had begun to change all on its own. Why had she said to him again and again with tearful eyes, 'You won't forget me, will you, Babuji?' Memories of many such longing things that she had expressed recurred to him and drove out suspicions of her deceit from his heart. Surely something unanticipated had happened. When he sat by himself he would often remember Zohra and weep like a child. He came to have an aversion to liquor. The Daroga would come, the Inspector would come, but Rama found it disagreeable to sit with them for even five or ten minutes. He didn't want anyone to tease him or to speak with him. He would scold the cook when he came to call him to eat. He had not the slightest wish to wander about or go on an outing. No one here was sympathetic to him, no one was his friend; he found solace only in sitting here by himself and repressing his feelings. Even his memories held no pleasure for him now. No, it was as if even those memories had been erased from his heart. A sort of indifference settled over his spirits.

It was eight o'clock on the seventh day. A very good new film was to begin showing today, a love story. When the Daroga came and told Rama about it, he got ready to go. He was just changing his clothes when Zohra arrived. Rama gave her one angry glance, and then began to comb his hair before the mirror. He didn't say a word. To be sure, he was a little surprised to see her appearance so plain and unadorned. She was wearing only a white sari and there was not a single piece of jewellery on her. Her lips were faded, and in place of the usual flirtatiousness, her face was gleaming with passionate seriousness.

She stood for a minute, and then going up to Rama said, 'Are you angry with me? Without even asking, and me not to blame?'

Rama didn't answer, but began to put on his shoes. Seizing his hand Zohra said, 'Are you displeased because I didn't come for so long?'

'Even if you hadn't come now, what right would I have had to say anything?' asked Rama coldly. 'You went out of your own kindness.'

As he said this, he realized that he was wronging her, and he gazed at her ashamed.

'This is a good joke!' said Zohra smiling. 'You yourself

entrusted me to do something, and now that I've done it and come back, you're getting mad. Did you think it would be so easy that it could all be done in the twinkling of an eye? You sent me to receive a boon from that goddess who is like a flower on the outside, but a rock on the inside, who is so strong even though she's so delicate.'

'Where is she? What is she doing?' asked Rama dejectedly.

'She's at Dinesh's home, the same one who was sentenced to be hanged. He has two children and there's his wife and his mother. All day long she amuses the children, brings water from the river for the old woman, does all the household tasks, and goes around collecting funds for them from important people. There was no property and no money in Dinesh's household, and his family was in great distress. They had no supporter to encourage them, and every last one of their friends turned their backs on them. They had gone without food several times; Jalpa saved their lives by going.'

All of Rama's dejection vanished. He left off putting on his shoes, sat down on the chair, and said, 'Why are you standing? Tell me everything from the beginning; you started in the middle. Don't leave out a single thing. How did you reach her to start with? How did you find out where she was?'

'It was nothing,' said Zohra. 'First of all I went to that Devidin Khatik. He gave me Dinesh's address. I went there as fast as I could.'

'Did you call her when you got there? Wasn't she startled when she saw you? She must certainly have flared up!'

'I didn't look like this,' said Zohra smiling. 'I went home from Devidin's and dressed to play the part of a Brahmo Samaj lady. I don't know what it is about me that lets others know right away who I am or what I am. When I see other Brahmo ladies no one even looks in their direction. But when my dress is the same, when I'm not wearing anything flashy or any excessive jewellery, everybody still stares at me. I can't hide what I really am. I was afraid that Jalpa would see right through me, so I cleaned my teeth thoroughly so there wasn't even a trace of paan. I went there looking as if I were some lady college-teacher. I disguised myself so well that no one, let alone Jalpa, could guess who I was; the curtain was drawn. I told Dinesh's mother that I was studying in a university here, and that my home was in Munger in Bihar. I took sweets for the children; I went to play the part of a sympathizer, and in my opinion I played it very well. Both of these poor women started crying, and I wasn't able to control myself either. I promised to keep on visiting them from time to time. Just then Jalpa arrived bringing water from the Ganges. Speaking in Bengali I asked Dinesh's mother, "Is she a water-carrier from the Kahar caste?" She replied, "No, she's come like you to share our grief. Her husband's a clerk in some office. I don't know anything else. She comes every morning and takes the children to play. I used to bring water from the river myself; she put a stop to that and brings it herself. She's given us our lives back. There was no one else around to help us. The children were suffering badly. I don't know what good karma brought us this gift."

'There's a small park in front of their house, and children from all over the neighbourhood play there. It was evening, and Jalpa Devi took both children along with her to the park. The grandmother gave each child one sweet from those I had brought, and they both began to leap and dance around. Seeing how happy they were, I felt like crying. Eating the sweets, they left with Jalpa. Once the children were playing in the park I began to talk with her.'

Rama pulled his chair closer and leaned forward. 'How did you begin?' he asked.

'I was just telling you. I asked her, "Jalpa Devi, where do you live? After hearing those two women sing your praises, I've fallen in love with you."'

'You used those words!'

'Yes, I thought I'd make a little joke. She looked at me surprised and said, "You don't seem to be a Bengali. No Bengali speaks such clear Hindi." I said, "I live in Munger and I spend a lot of time with Muslim women there. I feel like meeting you sometimes. Where do you live? I could come for an hour or so now and then. By sitting with you a while I too will learn some compassion!"

'Looking embarrassed, Jalpa said, "You're making fun of me. Why, you're studying in college and I'm just an uneducated village woman. But I'd become civilized by associating with you. Come here whenever you like; you can think of this as my home."

'I said, "Your lord and master has given you a lot of freedom.

He must be a man of very liberal opinions. Which office does he work in?"

'Jalpa looked at her nails and said, "He's a candidate for a police post."

'"He's a policeman and he gives you the freedom to come here?" I asked with surprise.

'Jalpa did not seem to be prepared for this sort of question. A little startled, she said, "He doesn't say anything to me ... I didn't tell him about coming here ... He seldom comes home. He lives right there with the police."

'She had given three answers at once. Even so, she was having misgivings about their credibility. She stared in another direction looking a little disconcerted.

'"Is there any way by saying something to your husband that you could arrange a meeting for me with that informer who gave evidence against the prisoners?" I asked her.'

Rama's eyes opened wide and his heart began to thump.

'When Jalpa heard this,' Zohra said, 'she looked at me piercingly and asked, "What would you gain by meeting him?"

'I said, "Can you arrange a meeting or not? I want to ask him what he got by incriminating so many men. I'd like to see what answer he gives."

'Jalpa's face grew stern. "He could say that he did it for his own benefit!" she said. "Everyone thinks about his own benefit. I did too. When no one asks hundreds of policemen this question, why would he be asked? There's nothing to gain from it."

'I said, "Well, suppose your husband had turned informer like this, what would you have done?"

'She looked at me in a frightened way and said, "Why do you ask me this question? Why don't you look for the answer in your own heart?"

'I said, "I'd never speak to him or look at his face again."

'Reflecting deeply, Jalpa said, "Maybe I'd see it that way—or maybe I wouldn't—I can't say. After all, police officers have women folk in their homes too. Why don't they say something to their men? It's possible that my heart may become like theirs, just as theirs have become like their men's."

'By now it had become dark  Jalpa Devi said, "I'm getting late and the children are with me. Please come meet me again tomorrow if it's possible. I get a lot of pleasure from your conversation."

'As I started to leave, she spoke again to me as she was leaving herself. "Please come for sure. I'll meet you right here. I'll wait for you regularly."

'But after only ten steps more she stopped again and said, "I didn't even ask your name. I haven't got my fill of talking with you yet. If you're not getting late then come and let's gossip away a little longer."

'That was just what I wanted. I told her my name was Zohra.'

'Really!' exclaimed Rama.

'Yes, what was the harm. At first even Jalpa was a little surprised, but it didn't matter. She understood that I was probably a Bengali Muslim. We both went back to that house; who knows how we could even sit in that little wooden box. There wasn't even space for a sesame seed. Clay pots here, water there, a bed over here, bedding over there. The dampness and bad smell practically tear your nose apart. The food was ready; Dinesh's wife was washing the pots and pans. Jalpa made her get up. "Go feed the children and put them to bed," she said. "I'll do the washing up." And she started to scour them herself. Seeing this service had such an effect on my heart that I sat down on the spot and began to wash the pots which had been scoured. Jalpa told me to leave off, but I didn't. I kept on washing the pots. Then she moved the water container to one side and said, "I won't give you any water. Get up now. I'm ashamed. I beg you to leave; you've been punished for coming here. You must never have had to do such work in your whole life." I said, "Nor you either. When you're doing it, what's the harm in my doing it?"

'"It's different for me," she said.

'"Why?" I asked. "Whatever it is for you, it's the same for me. Why don't you have a servant?"

'"Servants ask for eight rupees a month," she said.

'"I'll give you eight rupees each month," said I.

'Jalpa gave me a look full of true love, true joy, and true blessing. That look! Ah! How pure it was, how purifying! How low, how hateful my life seemed to me then compared to this disinterested service of hers. I can't describe how much pleasure I received from washing those pots and pans.

'When I got up after washing them, she was sitting and pressing the feet of the old woman. I stood silently. "If you're going to be late, then go and come again tomorrow," she said to me.

'"No," said I. "I'll take you home and leave from there."

'In fact we left there after nine o'clock. On the way I said, "Jalpa, you're really a goddess."

'"Zohra, don't say that," she blurted out. "I'm not performing services, I'm doing penance for my sins. I feel very sad. There's probably not a more unfortunate woman in the whole world than me."

'I asked as if I didn't know, "I don't understand what you mean."

'Staring straight ahead she said, "You'll understand some day. My penance won't be finished in this life. It will take several lives for that."

'"You're perplexing me, sister!" I said. "I don't understand a thing. I won't let go of you until you explain yourself."

'Jalpa heaved a sigh and said, "Zohra, what's easier, to keep something to oneself, or to burden others with it?"

'In an injured tone I said, "All right, if you don't have that much confidence in me during our first meeting, I won't find fault with you, but sooner or later you'll have to confide in me. I won't leave you."

'The two of us walked some distance in silence. All at once Jalpa said in a trembling voice, "Zohra, if just now you learned who I am, you might turn away from me in hatred and run far away from even my shadow."

'I don't know what magic there was in those words but I felt a thrill all through my being. This was a cry from a heart filled with grief and shame and it brought the outlines of my ruined life straight before me. My eyes filled with tears. I felt like ending my acting and revealing who I was. I can't say why being with her affected me like this. I've made duffers out of many a police officer and many a cunning rogue, but in front of her I was as timid as a wet cat. Somehow or other I curbed my feelings.

'When I spoke my voice was choked too. "You're wrong, Devi. Perhaps I'll fall at your feet then. To be ashamed of one's defects or the defects of those close to one is the action of a true-hearted person."

' "But what good would it do you to know my situation? Just consider me to be a poor wretched woman who takes pleasure in spending time with poor wretches like herself."

'She put me off like this again and again, but I wouldn't let go. Finally she let it out.'

'Not like that, you'll have to tell me everything,' said Rama.

'How can I tell you a story that might go on half the night? It'll take hours,' said Zohra. 'When I'd kept after her a long time, she finally told me, "I'm the unlucky wife of that informer who has caused such suffering to those prisoners." And she burst into tears. Then bringing her voice under control she said, "We live in Allahabad. Something happened which forced him to run away. He just fled and came here without saying a thing to anybody. After several months we learned he was here." '

'There's a story behind that too,' said Rama. 'Nobody else but Jalpa could have thought of it.'

'I learned all that the next day,' said Zohra. 'Now I'm thoroughly acquainted with the very core of your being. Jalpa is my friend. It's hardly likely that she's hidden anything from me.

' "Zohra," she said to me, "I'm trapped in a terrible predicament. On one side is the life of a man and the ruin of several families; on the other is my own destruction. I can save all these prisoners' lives today if I wish. I can give the court proof of a sort which will remove all credibility from the informer's testimony, but I won't be able to save the informer from punishment. Sister, I'm suffering the torments of hell from this dilemma that's fallen on me. I can't let these people die, and I can't toss Rama into the fire!" She burst into tears as she said this and continued, "Sister, I'll die before any harm comes to him from me. I'll see what the decision is. I can't say what action I'll take then. Maybe I'll tell the whole story right there in the High Court, or maybe I'll take poison and die."

'Just then we reached Devidin's house and took our leave of each other. Jalpa earnestly insisted that I return at the same time the next day, because she had no leisure for conversation all day long, but was only free in the evenings. She wanted to raise at least enough money to save Dinesh's family from any distress. She'd already raised over two hundred rupees and I too gave five rupees. Once or twice I mentioned that she should stay out of these disputes and go home, but I tell you plainly that I never emphasized it. Whenever I hinted at it, she'd make a face as if to say she didn't even want to hear of it and I never was able to finish saying it. There's something to be considered, shall I tell you?'

'What's that?' said Rama as if his attention was elsewhere.

'If I speak to the Deputy Sahab, he'll have Jalpa taken to Allahabad. She won't suffer any inconvenience. There'll be two women to escort her to the station while chatting with her. The train will be ready and they'll see that she's seated in it. Or you think up some other arrangement.'

Rama looked her in the eye. 'Would that be proper?'

'No, it wouldn't,' said Zohra looking ashamed.

Hastily putting on his shoes, Rama asked, 'She's staying at Devidin's house, isn't she?'

'Then you're going right now?' said Zohra, getting up and standing in front of him.

'Yes, Zohra, I'm going right now. I'll just have a few words with her and then go where I ought to have gone long ago.'

'But think a little about the result.'

'I've thought it all through,' said Rama. 'At most it'll be three or four years of imprisonment for the offence of giving false evidence. Enough, let me leave! Don't forget that we may meet again, Zohra!'

Rama came down from the veranda into the courtyard and was outside the gate in an instant. 'Has Your Honour informed the Darogaji?' said the watchman.

'There's no need to,' said Rama.

'I'll just go ask him. Why are you taking away my living, Your Honour?'

Rama did not answer, but went quickly out into the street. Zohra stood motionless, looking at him with sorrowful eyes. She had never felt such a love—such an apprehensive love—for him before, like some heroic young woman watching her beloved set out for the battlefield unable to contain herself for pride.

The watchman rushed to tell the Daroga. That poor fellow had lain down after eating. He rushed out in a panic and ran after Rama. 'Babu Sahab,' he cried out, 'just listen please, stop for a moment, what's the use of this? May I know where you're going?'

In the end the wretched man tripped and fell. Rama came back, lifted him up, and asked, 'You didn't hurt yourself, did you?'

'It's nothing really,' said the Daroga. 'I just stumbled a little. Where are you going just now, after all? Please think about what the consequences of this will be.'

'I'm coming back in an hour. Jalpa may have incited the other side to file a petition with the High Court. I'm going to straighten her out.'

'How did you learn about this?'

'Zohra heard it somewhere and came to tell me,' said Rama.

'She's a very treacherous woman! A woman like that ought to have her head cut off.'

'That's just why I'm going. Either I'll send her to the station right now or I'll deal with her so severely that even she'll remember. There's not much time to talk with her. Please let me out of this captivity for the night.'

'I'll come too, wait a little.'

'No, you'll spoil the whole thing. I'll be back very soon.'

The Daroga was rendered speechless. He stood in thought for a minute, and then went back and set off towards the police station talking to Zohra. For his part Rama quickened his pace, took a tonga and arrived at Devidin's house.

Jalpa had returned from Dinesh's home and was sitting and chatting with Jaggo and Devidin. These days she ate just once a day. Just then Rama called out from below. Devidin recognized his voice and said, 'Perhaps it's Bhaiya.'

'Ask him what he's come here for,' said Jalpa. 'Go there where he is.'

'No, daughter,' said Devidin. 'I'll just ask him what he has to say. How did he get permission to go out at this time?'

'It must be to give me a lecture, what else!' said Jalpa. 'But don't hope for anything!'

Devidin opened the door. 'Dada, you must be surprised to see me here at this time,' said Rama coming inside. 'I got permission to come for an hour. I have to beg your pardon for the many bad things I've done. Is Jalpa upstairs?'

'Yes, she is,' said Devidin. 'She's just come. Sit down. I'll bring you something to eat.'

'No, I've already eaten,' said Rama. 'I just want to say a few things to Jalpa.'

'If she doesn't agree, you'll be needlessly humiliated,' said Devidin. 'She's not a woman to do what she's told.'

'Will she talk a little while with me, or doesn't she even want to see my face? Please go and ask.'

'What's there to ask?' said Devidin. 'They're both just sitting there. Go on. It's still your house just like it was before.'

'No, Dada, ask her. I won't go just like that.'

Devidin went upstairs and said, 'He wants to say something to you, Bahu!'

Jalpa hung her head and said, 'So why doesn't he say it? Have I locked up his tongue?' She said this so loudly that Rama could hear her even from downstairs. What harshness! It was as if all her eagerness to meet him had fled. 'If she doesn't want to speak with me, I won't force myself on her,' said Rama standing below all the while. 'I've decided to tell the Judge Sahab about the whole rotten mess. That's the reason I've come this time. It's because of me Jalpa has had all these troubles. I'm sorry that my good sense was clouded over. Selfishness made me blind. Love of my own life and fear of suffering robbed me of my understanding. Some evil spirit had me in its grip, but her actions have pacified it. I'll probably have to enjoy the government's hospitality for three or four years. I'm not afraid, and if I live we'll meet again. If not forgive my weakness and forget me. You too, Devidin Dada and Dadi, please pardon my faults. I won't forget your kindness until my dying breath. If I return alive, perhaps I'll be able to do something for you. My life has been completely ruined, both in this world and the next. I also have to tell you that it was I myself who stole her jewellery. There was no money to give the jeweller, so it was necessary to give back the jewellery. That's why I had to take such a wicked action. I'm still suffering the consequences today and I'll probably be suffering them till the day I die. If she'd been told the whole story straight out right then, even though she would have taken it badly, this calamity wouldn't have come upon us. I deceived you too, Dada. I'm not a Brahman, I'm a Kayasth. I played a trick on a godlike person like you. Who knows what my punishment will be for this. Pardon me for everything. That's all, that's what I came to say.'

Rama stepped down from the veranda and strode off quickly. Jalpa came down from the room above, but by the time she reached the lower storey Rama was nowhere to be seen. Stepping off the veranda she asked Devidin, 'Where has he gone, Dada?'

'I didn't see a thing, Bahu. My eyes were filled with tears,' said Devidin. 'You won't find him now. He was practically running when he left.'

Jalpa stood almost motionless on the street for several minutes. How could she stop him? How sad he must be now, how despairing! What had possessed her not to call him to her? Who could know what things would be like in the future or when they might meet again? Never in her three years of married life had her heart been so shaken by love. When she had been concerned just with sensuous pleasure, she had only been able to see the outer surface of love, but now that she had become self-sacrificing, she could see its true form. How delightful it was, how pure, how grand, how glorious! While self-indulgent, she had been content just to see the doors of the garden of love. After becoming self-denying she had reached the interior of this garden—what a lovely scene, how sweet-scented, how picturesque, how blooming. Its fragrance, its loveliness, were filled with divinity. When love reaches its highest elevation, it mingles with the divine. Now that she had found this love, Jalpa had no doubts that she would remain a fortunately married woman in this life and in the lives to come. This love freed her from the fears of separation, circumstances, and death—and gave her the boon of fearlessness. The whole world and its unlimited abundance seemed trifling in the face of this love.

Just then Zohra arrived. Seeing Jalpa standing on the footpath, she said, 'What are you standing here for, sister? I couldn't come earlier today. Come on, I have to tell you a lot of things today.'

They both went upstairs.

## 49

Was the Daroga likely to have any peace of mind? He waited an hour for Rama after his departure, and then went to Devidin's house on horseback. There he learned that Rama had left more than half an hour before. He returned to the police station, but there was no word of Rama here. He began to feel that Devidin had deceived him. He must have hidden Rama somewhere. He drove his motorcycle as fast as he could back to Devidin's and began to threaten him. 'If you don't believe me, search the house; what else can you do?' said Devidin. 'It's not even very big—one room downstairs, one upstairs.'

'Why won't you tell me where he's gone?' said the Daroga, getting off his motorcycle.

'If I knew anything I'd tell you, Sahab!' said Devidin. 'He came here, quarrelled with his wife, and left.'

'When is she going to Allahabad?'

'Babuji Rama didn't say anything about her going to Allahabad. She's not leaving here until the High Court makes its decision.'

'I'm not convinced of what you're saying,' said the Daroga.

He went into the downstairs room as he said this and scrutinized every single thing. Then he went upstairs and was startled to see the three women. It came to Zohra's mind to be mischievous, so she pulled the edge of her sari far over her face and hid her hands. The Daroga was suspicious. Maybe that rascal Rama had changed into this costume and was sitting right here!

'Who's this third woman?' he asked Devidin.

'I don't know her. She comes to meet Rama's wife from time to time.'

'Watch out if you try to fool *me!* You're trying to hide a culprit by dressing him up in a sari! Which one of these is Jalpa Devi? Tell her to please go downstairs. Let the other woman stay.'

When Jalpa withdrew, the Daroga went up to Zohra and said, 'Well, you rascal, pulling these stunts on me! You left me saying one thing and when you got here you started having fun. All your anger vanished into thin air. Now take off this disguise and come along with me. It's getting late.'

He removed the sari from Zohra's head as he said this. She let out a guffaw. The Daroga looked as if he had slipped and fallen into an ocean of amazement. 'Oh! It's you Zohra?' he said. 'What are you doing here?'

'I'm carrying out my duty.'

'Where did Ramanath go? You must certainly know.'

'He had gone well before I got here. Then I sat here and talked about things with Jalpa Devi.'

'All right, please come along with me. We have to find out where he is.'

'He hasn't reached the bungalow yet?' asked Zohra with feigned curiosity.

'No! There's no telling where he's got to.'

On the way the Daroga asked, 'When is Jalpa leaving?'

'I taught her a good lesson,' said Zohra. 'There's no need to visit her anymore. She'll probably come around now. Ramanath scolded her badly, and she's become frightened by his threats.'

'Are you sure she won't be up to any mischief now?'

'Yes, that's just what I think.'

'So where did he go?' said the Daroga.

'I can't say.'

'I'll have to report him. It's important to inform the Inspector Sahab and the Deputy Sahab. He hadn't drunk too much, had he?'

'Well, he was drunk,' said Zohra.

'Then he must have collapsed somewhere. He's been a great nuisance. I'm just going over to the police station. Shall I drop you at your house?'

'That's very kind of you.'

The Daroga seated Zohra on his motorcycle and in a little while let her off at the door of her house. But even in this short time, his mind had shifted. 'I don't feel like going now, Zohra!' he said. 'Come on, let's have some chitchat today. I haven't had a kind look from you in days.'

Zohra took one step up the stairs and said, 'Go inform the Inspector Sahab first. This is no time for chitchat.'

'No, I won't go now,' said the Daroga getting off his motorcycle. 'We'll see about it in the morning. I'm coming too.'

'You don't listen. Maybe the Deputy Sahab is coming. He sent word to me today.'

'You aren't playing a trick on me, are you Zohra? Look here, it's not nice to be so ungrateful.'

Zohra went up the stairs, shut the door, and putting her head out the upstairs window, said, 'Aadaab arz!'

# 50

The Daroga went home to bed about eleven o'clock. When he woke up it was eight o'clock. He had just got up when he was called to the phone. It was the Deputy Sahab. 'This Ramanath has made a big mess. We'll have to keep him someplace else, and send all his stuff to the Commissioner Sahab. Did he spend the night at the bungalow?'

'No sir,' said the Daroga. 'He made some excuse last night and went off to his wife.'

'Why did you let him go?' said the Deputy. 'We're afraid that he's told everything to the judge. The case will have to be tried again. You've made a very grave blunder. All our efforts have been ruined. You should have stopped him by force.'

'Has he gone to the Judge Sahab then?' asked the Daroga.

'Yes, Sahab, that's just where he went, and the judge has over-turned the case. He'll have the case heard again, and Rama will change his declaration. There's no doubt of it now. And it's all your bungling. We'll all be swept away in this flood. Zohra betrayed us too.'

The Daroga immediately took Rama's things and left for the Police Commissioner's bungalow. He was feeling so angry at Rama that he could have swallowed him feet and all! How often had he explained things to the bastard, how much regard he had shown him, but he had still acted treacherously. Zohra was in the thick of the plot too. Scolding his wife had been nothing but a pretext. He'd settle Zohra Begum's hash this very day. Where could she go? He'd have some words with Devidin too.

It's not even necessary to mention the commotion that went on for a week among the police. They went round and round day and night in anxiety about the case. They were even more worried about themselves, and the Daroga was in the biggest panic of all. He couldn't see any hope of saving himself. Both the Inspector and the Deputy threw all the responsibility on his head and completely distanced themselves from him.

The rumour that the case would be heard again began to spread through the whole city. This event was completely unprecedented in the history of English law; nothing like it had ever happened before. The lawyers had legal wrangles over it. Could the Judge Sahab even do something like this? But he was unyielding. The police made great efforts, and the Police Commissioner even went so far as to say the whole Police Department would have its reputation ruined. But the judge paid no heed to any of this. To be responsible for ruining the lives of fifteen people on the basis of false testimony was intolerable to his soul. He gave notice to both the High Court and the government.

The police now scurried back and forth night and day searching for Rama, but somehow or other Rama had hidden himself away without a trace.

Government officials carried on a correspondence for weeks. Reams and reams of paper were covered with ink. The newspapers took up a steady critical commentary on the matter. One journalist met Jalpa and published her account of things. Another published Zohra's. Their descriptions revealed all the secrets of the police. Zohra revealed that she had received fifty rupees a day to divert Ramanath and to see that he had no opportunity to think and reflect. The police ground their teeth when they read these accounts. Both Zohra and Jalpa had dropped out of sight or the police would certainly have given them a taste of their merry pranks.

Finally after two months a decision was made, and a member of the Civil Service was appointed to the case. The deliberations were begun in a bungalow outside the city where, it was hoped, there would not be too large a crowd. Nevertheless a crowd of ten or twelve thousand people gathered there every day. The police went head over heels trying to make one of the accused turn informer, but their efforts bore no fruit. If the Daroga wanted, he could have produced new witnesses; but he was so distressed by the selfishness of his superior officers, that he did nothing but watch the whole spectacle from a distance. When superiors get all the glory, and subordinates all the disgrace, what interest could the Daroga have in racking his brains in anxiety for new witnesses? His superiors saddled him with all the blame in this matter: it was because of *his* carelessness that Rama had escaped their clutches; if he had been kept under strict surveillance, how could Jalpa have written a letter to him, and how could he have met her at night?

Under these circumstances what else was there to do except

dismiss the case? The tables were turned, and the misfortune intended for others fell on the heads of the police. The Daroga was demoted, and the Assistant Daroga was given an undesirable transfer to the tarai.

Half the city turned out to welcome the accused on the day of their release. Even though the police released them at ten o'clock at night, the spectators had assembled. They dragged Jalpa along too, and Devidin came as well, far behind. Flowers rained down on her and the skies echoed with cries of 'Victory to Jalpa Devi!'

But Ramanath's trials were not yet over. It was determined to bring charges of perjury against him.

# 51

The case began at ten o'clock sharp in the very same bungalow. The August showers had begun. Calcutta was becoming a swamp, but an enormous multitude of spectators was standing in the open area in front of the bungalow; Dinesh's wife and mother were among the women. Ten or fifteen minutes before the hearing began, Jalpa and Zohra arrived in closed vehicles; they received permission to enter the courtroom.

The police began to give their evidence. The Deputy Superintendent, the Inspector, the Daroga, the Assistant Daroga—all gave declarations. The lawyers from both sides cross-questioned them but there was nothing noteworthy in these proceedings. The formalities were being duly observed. After this came Ramanath's declaration, but it contained nothing special either. He gave a complete description of his life during the past year, concealing nothing. On being questioned by the lawyers, he said, 'Jalpa's self-sacrifice, devotion, and true love opened my eyes, and even more than this, Zohra's kindness and sincerity. I consider it my good fortune to have received light from the very direction where others receive darkness. In the midst of poison I received nectar.'

After this came declarations for the defence from Devidin, Jalpa, and Zohra. The lawyers questioned them too, but truthful testimony can hardly be discredited. Zohra's declaration made a particularly strong impression. She saw that the soul she had been sent to fasten in chains, was writhing with pain and needed his wounds dressed, not chains. He needed a helping hand, not the shock of a blow. 'When I saw his faith, his unshakable confidence in Jalpa Devi, I forgot about myself,' she said. 'I felt ashamed of my meanness and my selfish blindness. It dawned on me then how wretched, how degraded my life was, and when I met Jalpa and saw her disinterested service and her ardent penance, the lacklustre ideas of my mind melted away too. I came to hate my voluptuous life, and I decided that I too would take refuge in the shelter of her sari.'

But even more remarkable was Jalpa's declaration. Tears came to the eyes of the spectators as they listened. These were her final words: 'My husband is guiltless, not only in the eyes of God, but in the eyes of the law too. It was written in his fate that he would have to atone for my obsession with a life of luxury, and he did so. He fled from the market-place hiding his head in shame. If he transgressed against me at all, it was in constantly contriving ways to fulfil my wishes. He never hesitated to take the greatest of burdens on himself to please me, to keep me happy. He forgot that the luxurious lifestyle doesn't know how to be satisfied. He encouraged me where it would have been proper to stop me, and even now I'm sure that only the threat of action against me has stopped his mouth. If there is any offender, it's me, for whom he's had to suffer so many difficulties. I agree that I forced him to change his declaration. If I believed that he had taken part in those robberies, I'd have been the first to censure him. I couldn't bear for him to build his own prosperity on the corpses of innocent people. On the days when those robberies occurred my husband was in Prayag. If the court desires it can verify this by telephone. If necessary, a declaration can be taken from officers of the Municipal Board. In circumstances like this my duty could be no other than what I did.'

'Was any report requested from Prayag concerning this matter?' the court asked the government lawyer for the prosecution.

'Yes sir,' said the lawyer, 'but we are not disputing this matter.'

'It is clearly established from this that the accused had no part in the robberies,' said the lawyer for the defence. 'There only remains the matter of why he became an informer.'

'For his own selfish ends, what else?' said the prosecuting lawyer.

'And I tell you that he was deceived, and when he learned that the fear which had made him agree to be a puppet in the hands of the police was his own misapprehension, he was threatened by them,' said the defending lawyer.

No witnesses for the defence remained now, and the prosecuting lawyer began the debate. 'Your Honour, today an accusation has been presented to you of a kind that fortunately very seldom occurs. You are familiar with the Janakpur robberies. In several villages in the vicinity of Janakpur robberies took place constantly, and the police began to search for the robbers. For months police officers took their lives in their hands as they tried to discover the bandits. At last their efforts succeeded and they received information of the bandits' whereabouts. They were all found sitting inside a single house, and the police captured them all simultaneously. But you know how difficult it is to produce proof for the courts in such matters. The public is so frightened of these people that for fear of life it's not prepared to give testimony. This goes so far that even those whose homes were robbed vanished when their time to testify came.

'My honourable listeners, just when the police were caught in this tangle, along comes a young man and claims to be the leader of these robbers. He gives such a vivid, such an authoritative description of them that the police are taken in. Finding such a person at such a time seems like divine aid to the police. The young man had fled from Allahabad and reached here half-starving. Meeting with such a favourable opportunity to make his fortune, he decided to realize his selfish objectives. He had not the slightest fear of any punishment for turning informer, for he had confidence in receiving some good position through the recommendations of the police. The police treated him with great respect and hospitality and made him their agent. It was very likely that the police would have dropped the case against these culprits and released them for lack of any evidence, but falling victim to this young man's trickery they decided to proceed with the accusation. Whatever his other qualities may be, there's no denying the keenness of his powers of invention. He gave such an accurate description of the robberies that not a single link in the chain of events was missing. He conjured up everything from the first bud to the last fruit. The police went ahead with their case.

'But it seems that in the meanwhile he got an even better opportunity to improve his lot! It's quite possible that organizations which oppose the government may have offered enticements to him, and that these enticements suggested a new way to fulfil his selfish aims by which fame, wealth, public applause, and the pride of patriotism would be his. He can do anything for his own self-interest, whether cutting somebody's throat, or donning the garb of a sadhu. This is the distinguishing mark of his life. We're glad that his judgement finally got the better of him, whether or not he'll get any benefit from it. It's just as objectionable for the police to punish the innocent as it is for them to release the guilty. They don't start such cases just to show their skilfulness. Nor is the government so devoid of legal principles that it would be beguiled by the police into proceeding with a groundless case. But who is responsible for the bad reputation the police have acquired through the trickery of this young man, and for the thousands of rupees of government money spent? Such a person ought to receive an exemplary punishment so that no one will have the courage to play such tricks again. A person who creates such a world of falsehood should not remain free but have his access to cheat society cut off. The most suitable place for him just now is one where he will have an opportunity to reflect deeply for some days. Perhaps he will undergo an inner awakening in the solitude there. You should consider only whether or not he deceived the police. There no longer remains any doubt that he did deceive them. If threats were made, he could have retracted his deposition after the first court session during the second session with the judge. But even then he did not do so. This makes it clear that his accusations of police threats are false. Whatever he did, he did of his own free will. If such a person does not receive punishment, then he'll be bold enough to carry out his wicked acts again, and his violent tendencies will become even stronger.'

Next the lawyer for the defence gave his rebuttal. 'This case is unprecedented not only in the history of English law, but perhaps also in the worldwide history of law. Ramanath is an ordinary young man, and his education too is very ordinary. He's not a man of lofty opinions. He's an employee of the Allahabad Municipal Office, where his work is to collect duties on produce. He takes bribes from merchants according to the usual custom, and he spends extravagantly without paying attention to his income. Finally one day when there's a mistake in the total he fears that he's misspent some of it. He panics so much that he runs away from home without saying a word to anyone. His office then becomes suspicious of him, and his accounts are checked. It becomes apparent that he hasn't embezzled anything, but has only made a mistake in his accounts.'

Then mentioning how Ramanath fell into the clutches of the police, how he became an informer, and how he gave testimony, he said, 'Now a new change comes into Ramanath's life, a change which turns a pleasure-loving promotion-greedy youth into a devout and conscientious one. His wife Jalpa, whom it is no exaggeration to call a goddess, comes here from Prayag in search of him, and when she learns that Rama has become a police informer in a lawsuit, she comes to meet him secretly. Rama is staying comfortably in his bungalow, and a sentry is on guard at the gate. Jalpa does not succeed in meeting her husband, so she writes a letter, throws it in front of him, and goes off to Devidin's house. Rama reads this letter, and the curtain falls from his eyes. He secretly goes to meet Jalpa. She tells him the whole story, and urges him strongly to change his declaration. Rama at first expresses misgivings but later agrees and returns to his bungalow. There he tells the police officers straight out that he's going to change his declaration. The officers offer him many inducements, but when these have no effect on Rama and when he learns that there's no embezzlement case against him, they threaten him with arresting Jalpa. Rama's courage breaks. He knows the police can do whatever they want, so he changes his plans and reaffirms his previous declaration in the judge's court session. The defence did not cross-question Rama in the lower court. In the higher court he was cross-questioned, but even though he had nothing to do with this case, he answered the questions in such a way that even the judge could not doubt his testimony and the accused were sentenced. The police began to show even more regard to

Ramanath. They gave him a letter of recommendation, and may have even recommended him to the government of the U.P.'

'Then Jalpa Devi resolved to take care of the children of Dinesh, the accused sentenced to hang. She took care of the necessities of life for them by asking for contributions all over the place, she did their housework with her own hands, and took their children to play.'

'One day while taking a trip in a motor-car, Ramanath sees Jalpa with a water jar on her head. His sense of self-respect is awakened. Zohra has been appointed by police officials for Ramanath's amusement. Moved by seeing the young man's mental agony, she goes off with the intention of bringing him all the news about Jalpa. She meets Jalpa at Dinesh's house, and when she sees Jalpa's self-sacrifice, service, and devoted labour, this prostitute's heart is so influenced that she becomes ashamed of her own life and a feeling of sisterhood grows up between the two of them. After a whole week she goes to Ramanath and tells him the entire story. He immediately leaves his quarters and after a few words with Jalpa goes straight to the judge's bungalow. Whatever happened after that is here before us.

'I don't say that he didn't give false testimony, but if you take note of the circumstances and the temptations, the degree of this offence is greatly reduced. If the result of this false testimony had been that an innocent person had been punished, it would be a different matter. On this occasion, the lives of fifteen young men were saved. Is he still a perjurer? He himself has admitted to his perjury. Should he be punished for this? His simplicity and goodness so enchanted even a prostitute that instead of diverting and misleading him, she became a light on his way. Does Jalpa Devi's conscientiousness deserve to be punished? It is Jalpa and no other who is the heroine of this drama. Her true devotion, her unaffected love, her devoutness, her adoration of her husband, her selflessness, her dedication to service—which of her virtues shall we praise! She has bestowed the gift of freedom from fear on fifteen families. She knew how bright her worldly prospects would become by siding with the police, and how many of life's worries this would free her from. It was possible that she, too, might have had a motor-car, servants, a fine house, and costly jewellery. Are these joys of no value to the heart of a beautiful young woman? But she prepares to bear great suffering. Will she be rewarded for her devotion to righteousness by being forced to stumble down the path of life deprived of her husband? Isn't so much devotion, so much sacrifice, so much deliberation—in an ordinary woman who hasn't received any higher education— an indication of some divine impulse? Is it of no importance that a fallen woman became her companion in such activities? I, for one, consider it important. Accusations like this don't present themselves every day. Perhaps you will never again have an opportunity to hear one like this. You are sitting here to make a decision about an accusation but outside this court is another greater court where your judgement will be weighed. Your decision about Jalpa will be made with an impartiality which that greater court will accept—a court that is not concerned with those niceties of the law in which we get entangled, in whose complexities we are caught, so that we usually stray from the path, and usually fail to distinguish the good from the bad and the bad from the good. If you determine anyone to be a criminal for telling the truth after repenting for lying, for passing his life in difficult circumstances after spurning a life of ease and pleasure then you will not be presenting the world with a very high ideal of justice.'

In giving his rebuttal, the prosecuting lawyer said, 'Righteousness and ideals are things worthy of great respect in their rightful places, but a man who knowingly gave false testimony has surely committed a crime, and ought to be punished for it. It's true that he didn't embezzle anything in Prayag and that he was merely under a misapprehension about this. But in such conditions an honest person was obliged to clear himself when he was arrested. Why did he deceive the police by giving false testimony out of fear of punishment? This is something to consider. If you think that he did something improper, then you should certainly punish him.'

Now it was the time for the decision of the court to be heard. Everyone had grown sympathetic to Rama, but they were also convinced that he would receive a sentence. It remained to be seen what that sentence would be. People drew closer together in great eagerness to hear the decision, pulled their chairs more forward, and even stopped their whispering.

'The only matter of concern is this: to protect himself, a young man sought the support of the police, and when he learned the very fear for which he was seeking support was totally baseless, he retracted his deposition. If Ramanath had been a truthful person, why would he have taken refuge with the police? But there is no doubt that the police suggested this means of protecting himself by giving false testimony and tempted him with it. I am unable to agree that the proposal to give testimony in this affair originated in his own mind. He was tempted, and he agreed from fear of punishment. Moreover, he must certainly have been assured that the people against whom he was being prepared to give testimony were really criminals, because Ramanath is as devoted to the law as he is fearful of punishment. He is not one of those professional witnesses who don't even hesitate to incriminate innocent people for their own selfish reasons. If this were not so, then he would never have agreed to his wife's insistence on changing his deposition. It's true that he learned there was no case of embezzlement against him after the first court session and that he could have retracted his deposition in the subsequent judge's court. He certainly expressed this intention at that time, but the threats of the police overcame him. It was natural for the police to threaten him on this occasion to save their reputation, because they had no doubt about the accused being criminals. Ramanath succumbed to threats, which certainly demonstrates his weakness, but is excusable given the circumstances. I therefore acquit Ramanath.'

## 52

For happiness and peace, can any place be better than the banks of the Ganges on a cool, pleasant, brisk April evening by a grove of dhaak trees bending to the wind, with cows and sheep tied up beneath them, with the leafy vines of pumpkins and bottle-gourds rippling on the thatched roofs of clay huts, and no turmoil and tumult? Below, the golden Ganges, sparkling in red, black and green veils, singing in deep voices, here rushing forward and there shrinking back, here volatile and there solemn, flows on into endless darkness as if she is going forward into the anxiety-ridden, struggle-filled, darkling future while playing the multi-coloured games of childhood memories in the lap of pleasure. Here, near Prayag, Devi and Rama had come and taken refuge.

Three years had passed. Devidin had purchased land, planted an orchard, bought cows and buffaloes, and was experiencing happiness, satisfaction, and peace in disinterested action and unceasing effort. That paleness, those wrinkles, were no longer on his face, but instead a new vigor, a new lustre, were shining forth.

It was dusk, and the cows and buffaloes had returned from the grazing ground. Jaggo fastened them to their stakes, brought a little hay, and placed it before them. Just then Devidin and Gopi arrived in an ox-cart loaded with grain stalks. Dayanath had cleared away the ground beneath the banyan tree, and there the stalks were unloaded; this was the threshing-floor of the little settlement. Dayanath had been dismissed from his position and was now Devidin's assistant. Even now he had the same fondness for newspapers; several papers came every day, and in the evenings when he had leisure, Munshiji would read them out loud and explain their meaning. Among his listeners were usually several people from the nearby villages, forming a little daily assembly.

Rama had become so attached to this life that he wouldn't have dreamed of moving back to the city even if he'd received the superintendentship of a police station or the inspectorship of the customs office itself. Early every morning he would rise to bathe in the Ganges, and after some exercise he would drink some milk, and as the sun rose he would take out his chest of medicines and sit down. He had studied several books on Ayurvedic medicine and gave out remedies for minor illnesses. A number of patients came each day, and his reputation grew steadily. As soon as he had a respite from this work, he would walk around his garden where various vegetables had been planted along with fruit trees and flowering trees, and medicinal roots and herbs. Just now the garden produced only vegetables, but a good yield of limes, guavas, jujubes, oranges, mangoes, bananas, myrobalans, jackfruits, wood apples, and other fruits was expected in three or four years.

Devidin unfastened the bullocks from the carts, tied them to their stakes, and said to Dayanath, 'Hasn't Bhaiya come back yet?'

Gathering up the grain stalks, Dayanath said, 'He hasn't come back yet. I don't have hopes of her getting well now. Times have changed. How happily she used to live. She had a carriage, a motor-car, a bungalow, and dozens of servants. Now she's come to this. Everything was available; Vakil Sahab left a fine estate, but his relatives gobbled it up.'

'Bhaiya used to say that if she'd gone to court she'd have got everything,' said Devidin, 'but she says she won't lie in court. She's a very high-minded woman.'

All at once Jageshwari came out of a large hut carrying an infant in her embrace, and putting the child on Dayanath's lap, said to Devidin, 'Bhaiya, please go take a look at Ratan. Who knows how things are going with her? Zohra and Jalpa are both crying. Now where has that child got to?'

'Let's go see, Lala,' said Devidin to Dayanath.

'What good will it do for him to go?' said Jageshwari. 'He's frightened to death by seeing a sick person.'

Devidin went to Ratan's little room—where she was lying on a bamboo bed. Her body had wasted away. Her face which had been as radiant as a sunflower had faded and become pale. Those colours which had given her living picture a throbbing vitality had fled; only her form had been left behind. It was as if that melodious, life-giving music, flooded with beauty and joy, had been absorbed into the heavens, and only its faint, sad echo remained. Zohra was bent over her, watching her with a gaze that combined tenderness, distress, despair, and longing. For a whole year she had not known the difference between day and night in her devoted service to Ratan. How could she not feel gratitude for the love Ratan had showed her, for the sisterly affection she unreservedly maintained for her in an atmosphere of distrust and exile? Ratan bestowed that sympathy on her that she did not receive even from Jalpa. Sorrow and arduous labour had brought them together, and their souls were joined. This intimate love was a new experience for her, one she had never even imagined. In this friendship her deprived heart found both the love of a husband and the affection of a son.

Devidin looked towards Ratan's face with anxious eyes, and then taking her pulse asked, 'How long has it been since she stopped speaking?'

'She was speaking just now,' said Jalpa, wiping her eyes. 'All of a sudden her eyes rolled up and she became unconscious. Haven't you brought the vaidya yet?'

'He has no remedy for her,' said Devidin, and taking a few ashes passed his hand over Ratan's head, muttered something, and applied a pinch to her forehead. 'Open your eyes, Ratan beti,' he called to her.

'My motor-car came, didn't it?' said Ratan, opening her eyes and looking around disconcertedly. 'Where has that man gone? Tell him to bring it a little later. Zohra, today I'll take a stroll through my garden. We'll both have a swing.'

Zohra began to cry again, nor could Jalpa stem the flow of tears either. Ratan stared at the ceiling for a moment, and then as if her memory had suddenly awakened, she asked with a sad smile, 'Was I dreaming, Dada?'

A curtain of blackness fell across the blood-red sky, and at the same time death drew his curtain across the life of Ratan!

When Ramanath returned with the vaidya later that evening, the silence of death reigned. The sorrow of Ratan's death was not that sorrow which makes us wail and groan, but rather that sorrow which makes us weep silently, whose memory never leaves us, and whose load never lifts from our hearts.

After Ratan's passing, Zohra was left alone. The two of them had slept together, sat together, and worked together. Now that she was alone Zohra took no pleasure in any task. Sometimes she would go to the bank of the river to remember Ratan and weep, and sometimes go and stand for hours among the mango seedlings which the two of them had planted, as if she had become a widow. Jalpa did not have much leisure from tending the child and preparing food to spend a lot of time with her, and when she did Zohra would begin to weep whenever Ratan was mentioned.

It was August and war had broken out between earth and water. The armies of the latter had descended on the vehicle of the wind and were raining down shafts from the heavens. Its land forces were wreaking havoc on the earth. The Ganges was gulping down villages and towns. Village after village was washed away. Zohra watched the spectacle from the river bank. She had never before experienced how huge the slender-limbed Ganges could become. Her waves thundered in frenzy, hands of foam were leaping out of their mouths, and changing their stances like cunning fencers. Now they would move forward a step, then fall back, and then leap forward after turning around in a circle. Now a hut would come sweeping by, rolling as it went, as if some drunkard was running; now a tree would go swimming by with its branches and leaves dripping and rising like some stone-age creature. Cows and buffaloes, beds and seats passed before one's eyes like enchanted pictures.

Suddenly a boat came into view. Several men and women were clinging to rather than sitting in it, as the craft sometimes rose and sometimes fell. It seemed about to turn topsy-turvy at any time, but how wonderful their courage! All of them were still calling out, 'Victory to Mother Ganges!' The women were still singing songs in praise of the river. And who might be watching this life and death struggle? People were standing on both sides, standing and repressing their feelings in this tense situation. When the boat rolled to one side or the other, their hearts would leap into their mouths. Attempts were made to throw ropes, but every rope fell short. All at once the boat turned over and all those living beings sank into the waves. For a moment a few men and women were seen to go down and come up again, but then they vanished from view. Only one whitish thing was moving towards the bank. A strong current brought it within twenty yards of the edge. From close up it became apparent that it was a woman. Zohra, Jalpa, and Rama were all standing there. A child could be seen in the woman's embrace. The three of them were in great distress to pull the two victims out, but it was not easy to swim the twenty yards towards them. Moreover, Rama was not very skilful at swimming; once he was swept off his feet by the force of the waves, there would be no stopping anywhere before the Bay of Bengal.

'I'm going,' said Zohra.

'I'm ready to go,' said Rama shamefacedly, 'but I doubt I can even reach there. How fast it's going!'

Taking a step into the water Zohra said, 'No, I'll bring them out very soon.'

She went into the water up to her waist. 'Why are you risking your life uselessly?' said Rama becoming alarmed. 'Perhaps there's a steep drop. I was about to go.'

Making a gesture of refusal with her hands, Zohra said, 'No, no. Swear you won't come. I'll bring them back very soon. I know how to swim.'

'It's just a dead body,' said Jalpa.

'Maybe there's still life,' said Rama.

'Good!' said Jalpa. 'Then Zohra can swim out and bring them back whenever she has the courage.'

Looking anxiously towards Zohra Rama said, 'Yes, she knows something about swimming. May God see that she returns. I'm ashamed of my own cowardice.'

'What's there to be ashamed of?' said Jalpa brazenly. 'What's the good of putting your own life in danger for a dead body? If she were alive, then I'd tell you myself to go bring her.'

'Who can know from here whether she's alive or not?' said Rama reproaching himself. 'It's true, a man with children becomes a coward. I stood here and Zohra went.'

Without warning a powerful wave came and pushed the corpse back into the main current. Zohra had reached the body and was about to seize hold and pull it when the wave moved it away. Zohra herself was washed some little distance into the flow of the river by its force. She recovered herself, but a second wave gave her a blow.

Distraught, Rama leaped into the water and called out with all his might, 'Zohra! Zohra! I'm coming.'

But Zohra no longer had the strength to struggle with the waves. She was being swept away with great speed by the current, close to the corpse. Her hands and feet stopped moving.

Suddenly a surge came and swallowed them both up. After a moment Zohra's dark hair could be seen. Just for an instant! This was their last glimpse of her, and then she was no longer visible.

Rama made about a hundred yards, thrashing his arms and legs mightily, but the impetuous flow of the waves exhausted him in even this short distance. Where to go now? There was no trace of Zohra anywhere. His last glimpse of her was still before his eyes.

Jalpa was standing on the bank crying out, so distressed that she too hurled herself into the water. Rama was now unable to keep going. One force pulled him forward, another backward. In the force ahead was affection, despair, and sacrifice; in that behind was duty, love, and obligation. Obligation stopped him, and he turned back.

Rama and Jalpa stood up to their knees in the water for several minutes staring in the direction where Zohra had disappeared. Rama was speechless from self-reproach, Jalpa from sorrow and shame.

At last Rama said, 'Why are you standing in the water? You'll catch a cold.'

Jalpa came out of the water and stood on the bank, but said not a word—the shock of death had defeated her. This event today had once again demonstrated before her very eyes how uncertain life was. She had feared for Ratan's life well before her death; it had been apparent that she would be a guest in this world only a short while longer. But Zohra's death had been like a thunderbolt! Just a few minutes ago the three of them had happily set out to watch the play of the waters. Who had suspected that they would have to watch such a terrible play of death?

In these last three years Zohra had enchanted everyone with her service, self-sacrifice, and straightforward nature. What other means did she have to wipe out her past, to wash out her former stains? All her lustful desires, all her passions, had dissolved in her service. In Calcutta she had been an object of sensuous pleasure and amusement. A respectable man would probably not have even let her enter his home. Here everyone had treated her something like a beloved spouse. Dayanath and Jageshwari had been pacified by telling them that she was Devidin's widowed sister. In Calcutta, Zohra had begged Jalpa just to let her live with her. She had come to hate her own life. Jalpa's trustful nobility had put her on the path to self-purification, and Ratan's pure disinterested life had continually encouraged her.

After a little while Rama too came out of the water and set out for home plunged in grief. But he and Jalpa would often come and sit on the river bank and gaze for hours towards the place where Zohra had drowned. For several days they continued to hope that perhaps Zohra had survived, and that she would come back from somewhere or other. But very gradually this feeble hope was swallowed up in sorrow. Still, even now Zohra's form would revolve before their eyes. The seedlings she had planted, the cat she had cared for, the clothes she had sewn, her room—all these were her memorials, and whenever Rama went near them, Zohra's likeness would stand before his eyes.

# Glossary

*Translator's Note:* This glossary is meant for non-Hindi-speaking Western readers who may not be acquainted with most of the Hindi terms I have not translated. The glossary also includes two or three lesser-known place names, and some English words used in an unfamiliar way.

In numerous cases, I have shamelessly borrowed definitions from R.S. McGregor's *The Oxford Hindi-English Dictionary* (Delhi, 1993), though frequently modifying or supplementing them. In other cases I have used my own definitions.

I have deliberately not attempted to give a systematic scholarly transliteration of any of the Hindi terms, knowing that Indian or Western readers familiar with Hindi do not need it, and that Western readers not familiar with Hindi probably do not want it.

| | |
|---|---|
| aadaab arz | Muslim expression of courtesy appropriate for both arrivals and departures; in its one occurrence in the novel it is used ironically |
| ajii | Expression used to call someone's attention without using his or her name |
| anna | Obsolete (as of 1957) coin equal to one-sixteenth of a rupee |
| approver | Accused person who testifies against others in turn for immunity from punishment, and for monetary or other rewards |
| arhar dal | Type of pulse or lentil |
| babu | Title of respectful address; also, in a transferred sense, a clerk or government servant |
| babu sahib | A still more respectful variant of babu |
| babuji | Another still more respectful variant of babu |
| bahu | Term of reference and of address for a daughter-in-law or for a young bride or wife |
| bahuji | More respectful variant of bahu |
| baiji | Respectful term of address for a woman |

| | |
|---|---|
| barfi | Usually rectangular sweet made from thickened milk and sugar, sometimes with the addition of nuts, etc. |
| begum | Title of Turkish origin for a lady of rank, or a queen; more loosely, a respectful or sometimes ironic term of reference or address for a woman, especially a wife |
| begum sahab | More elaborate version of begum |
| beti | Literally, daughter; also an affectionate term of address from an older person to a younger woman |
| *Bhagavata Purana* | Sanskrit work of 18,000 stanzas dealing with aspects of ancient Indian mythology, legend, history, and theology, especially known for its treatment of the childhood and youth of Krishna |
| bhai | Term of address meaning 'friend' or 'brother' |
| bhaiya | Term of address and reference meaning 'friend' or 'brother'; in this novel it is the term which Devidin usually uses to address or to refer to Ramanath, and becomes something very like a proper name |
| bhang | The hemp plant, especially its crushed or ground leaves, eaten or mixed into drinks for its narcotic effects |
| bidi | Hand-rolled Indian cigarette made from a twist of tobacco rolled up in a tobacco leaf |
| Brahmo Samaj | Religious movement founded in Calcutta by Ram Mohun Roy in 1828 to reform Hinduism from within |
| Chamar | A very numerous community of very low ranking in the Hindu caste system, traditionally associated with leatherwork |
| Chamar-eshiyan | Low or base person. (My own theory is that this word is a combination of 'camar' and 'Christian.') |
| chandrahar | Special kind of necklace made of circular and semi-circular pieces of precious materials |
| chapati | Thin, soft, round, unleavened baked wheat cake; a staple item in the north Indian diet |
| charas | Sticky or waxy gum or resin found on the hemp plant, smoked like ganja, and like ganja more intoxicating than bhang |
| charhao | Collection of jewellery or clothes given as a present by the bridegroom to the bride |
| charpai | Four-legged bed consisting of a wooden frame and a loosely woven mesh of fabric or heavy twine |
| chaudari | Honorific title; also a term for the headman of a village, or the leader of a community |
| chowkidar | Watchman, guard, or local policeman |

| | |
|---|---|
| chilam | Clay bowl with or without a stem in which tobacco, etc. is smoked |
| chote babu | The junior or younger babu; in its only occurrence in the novel it refers to Ramanath as opposed to his father |
| daal | Split lentils or pulses; raw, or cooked and spiced |
| dada | Elder brother or paternal grandfather; also a respectful term of address or reference for an older man. It may also be used to address non-relatives as a sign of affection and respect; Ramanath frequently addresses Devidin in this way |
| dadi | Paternal grandmother; also a respectful form of address to an older woman. It may also be used to address non-relatives as a sign of affection and respect; Ramanath frequently addresses Jaggo in this way |
| dai | Elder sister or mother |
| daroga | Police inspector or superintendent; the police officer in charge of a police station |
| darogaji | Respectful term of address or reference for daroga |
| deodar | Species of deciduous tree; deodar pine or cedar (*Cedrus deodara*) |
| devi | Literally, 'goddess' or 'lady'; a respectful term of address or reference for a woman |
| deviji | A still more respectful from of devi |
| dhaak | Species of deciduous tree; *butea frondosa* |
| dharma | An almost untranslatable Hindu term including: moral or religious duty, the proper performance of one's social and religious role, fulfilling prescribed customary religious observances, religion, way of life, etc. |
| dharmshala | Rest-house for travellers and pilgrims, built as an act of religious merit |
| dhoti | Garment worn around the lower body consisting of a single piece of cloth, one end of which passes between the legs and is tucked in behind |
| dwarchar | Marriage rite performed at the door of the bride's house |
| ekka | One-horse vehicle |
| ganja | Buds or flowers of the hemp plant, usually smoked like tobacco in a chilam and like charas more intoxicating than bhang |
| golgappa | Very small pastry of wheat flour, made in the form of a hollow sphere, and filled with a savoury liquid; a popular street snack |
| gopi | Wife of a cowherd; specifically, any of those in love |

|  | with the legendary deity Krishna as described in the *Bhagavata Purana* |
|---|---|
| gulli-danda | Children's game in which a smaller stick is lifted and hurled with a larger stick |
| guluband | Type of close-fitting necklace |
| gur | Unrefined dark reddish-brown sugar made by boiling down sugarcane juice |
| halwa | Soft sweet made with ghee (clarified butter), sugar or syrup, and spices combined with a basic ingredient which may be semolina, carrots, etc. |
| huzur | Old-fashioned term of address for a person of high social standing, meaning something like 'Your Highness'; often used jokingly or ironically |
| Jalli | Affectionate nickname for the novel's female character, Jalpa |
| janwasa | Living quarters of the bridegroom's party at a wedding |
| jiijaa | Term of reference for an older sister's husband |
| kadam | Species of tree (*Nauelea cadamba*) |
| Kahar | Community of low rank in the Hindu caste system whose traditional tasks included fetching water and carrying palanquins |
| kajli | Special type of song sung in Savan (July–August), the fifth month of the Hindu calendar |
| kakaji | Term of reference and address for a father's younger brother, or more generally, for an elder male relative. It may also be used to address non-relatives as a sign of affection and respect; Ramanath occasionally addresses Devidin in this way. Manibhushan also uses this term to refer to Vakil Sahab |
| kakiji | Term of reference and address for a father's younger brother's wife, or more generally, for an elder female relative. It may also be used to address non-relatives as a sign of affection and respect; Ramanath occasionally addresses Jaggo in this way. Manibhushan also uses this term to address Ratan on occasion |
| kaleva | Particular meal taken by the bridegroom and his party in the bride's house |
| Karun | Legendary person of fabulous wealth |
| Kashi | Alternative name for Banaras or Varanasi |
| kathak | Particular style of north Indian dance |
| katora | Shallow metal cup or bowl used in cooking, and for serving meals on a thaali |

| | |
|---|---|
| katori | Smaller version of a katora |
| Kayasth | Community of medium rank in the Hindu caste system associated with Muslim culture and language, whose traditional occupation was writing; under British rule, disproportionately represented in government service |
| Khatik | Community of low rank in the Hindu caste system, traditionally sellers of fruits and vegetables, and also distillers of alcoholic beverages |
| Khatri | Hindu community of merchants and traders; of medium rank in the caste system |
| khichari | Mixture of rice and lentils cooked together with ghee (clarified butter) and spices |
| khir | Liquid sweet of rice, milk, and spices; often eaten on special occasions |
| Kiranta | Derogatory term for a Christian |
| kurta | Long-sleeved, collarless garment worn over a lower garment by men |
| laddu | Large round sweet whose basic ingredients are usually chick-pea flour or thickened milk, sugar, and spices |
| lala | Respectful term of reference, especially for members of the Kayasth and various business communities such as bankers, merchants, tradesmen, scholars, and clerks. Also a respectful term of reference and address for a father, a father-in-law, or a brother-in-law |
| lathi | Long staff, usually of bamboo |
| lingam | Phallic image, one of the most common forms in which the great Hindu god Shiva is worshipped |
| lota | Small round pot, usually made copper or brass for water or other drinkable fluids |
| maharaj | Literally, great king or emperor; often used as a term of address to a brahman (especially as a cook) or to a superior |
| mahashaya | Gentleman; also a respectful term of reference or address meaning something like 'Sir' |
| mahatma | Literally 'great soul'; a saint or saintly person used ironically in the text |
| majum | Spiced sweet or drink made with bhang |
| malai | Cream, clotted cream, or the skimming from boiled milk |
| mardana | The men's or public part of a house |
| Marwari | Hindu business community from the region of Marwar in Rajasthan |

| | |
|---|---|
| maulvi sahab | Respectful term of reference or address for a scholar or teacher, especially of Muslim law, Persian, or Arabic |
| memsahab | Term of reference for a European woman; also a humorous or ironic term for a wife; in this novel it is used to refer to both Ratan and Jalpa |
| munshi | Title of respect for an educated man; also, a writer or a teacher or tutor, especially of Persian or Urdu |
| Nagpanchami | Hindu festival falling on the fifth day of the light half of the month of Savan (July–August) when women worship snakes to obtain blessings for their children |
| namaskar | Formal expression of courtesy among Hindus, appropriate for both arrival and departure |
| nayab daroga | Assistant daroga |
| paan | Popular Indian concoction of areca-nut, lime, spices, and various other ingredients wrapped in a betel leaf and slowly chewed in the mouth as a sort of combination of snack and digestive aid |
| paandaan | Container for holding the ingredients of paan |
| paisa | Money; also, historically, one-fourth of an anna or one sixty-fourth of a rupee, and now, one-hundredth of a rupee |
| pakora | Small piece of vegetable, fruit, or even meat, dipped in a spicy batter of chick-pea flour and deep-fried |
| pandaa | Community of Brahmans whose traditional duties involve superintending places of pilgrimage or temples, and serving as registrars for genealogies |
| patidev | Literally, 'husband-god'; a traditional respectful term for husband |
| pranaam | Formal respectful greeting |
| prasad | Food offered to someone of higher spiritual status, or more frequently, to the image of a deity, and then, its nature having changed by contact with something higher, eaten by the worshipper or shared with friends and family |
| Prayag | A variant name for Allahabad |
| puri | Round, soft, unleavened, deep-fried wheat cake; regarded as more special than a chapati |
| Ram Ram | The repeated name of Rama, hero of the *Ramayana*, used as a greeting among Hindus |
| rai bahadur | High-ranking title given to Indians during British rule |
| ramayana | The epic poem whose earliest version is in Sanskrit, glorifying the deeds of the deity Rama |

rasleela        Folk dance drama of north India based on scenes from the life of Krishna. In its one occurrence in the novel, it seems to refer to a written version of such a drama

roti            Generic term for several kinds of bread-cake, including chapatis and puris

sadhu           Wandering holy man or ascetic

sahab           Title for a prominent person, an officer, or (historically) a European used as both a term of reference and address; roughly translatable as 'sir'

sahab bahadur   During British rule, a title for a European official or for an Indian receiving British patronage

sardar sahab    Respectful term of address or reference for a Sikh

sarkar          Term of address meaning something like 'Sir' or 'Your honour'

seth            Title of respect used as both a term of reference and address for merchants, bankers, etc.

sethaniji       Similar title for the wife of a seth

sethji          A still more respectful variant of seth

shishphul       Woman's head ornament

shraddh         Hindu ceremony benefiting and honouring deceased relatives in which libations and offerings of food are made to the deceased and food and gifts are given to the officiating Brahmans and to relatives

swadeshi        Literally, belonging to one's own country; historically, the name of a movement to ban the importation of foreign goods, especially cloth, into India

tarai           Low-lying land, especially that at the foot of the Himalayas. In the context of the novel, the Assistant Daroga's transfer to the tarai represents a hardship assignment to an undesirable location because of its isolation and unhealthy climate

tasla           Brass or iron vessel with steep sides used to boil rice, knead dough, etc.

*The Parrot*    The title of a collection of stories well-known in India
*and the Mynah*

Teli            Community of low rank in the Hindu caste system whose traditional occupation was oil-milling and oil-selling; also a pejorative, implying an unclean or dirty person

thaali          Flat metal plate with a vertical rim widely used to serve meals in north India

tilak           Sectarian mark made (with saffron, sandalwood, etc.)

|         | on the forehead. In the one occurrence of this word in the novel, Ramanath puts a tilak on his forehead to maintain his pretence of being a Brahman |
|---------|---|
| tola    | Measure of weight, approximately equal to thirteen grams |
| tonga   | Horse-carriage; usually drawn by a single horse |
| Triveni | The conjunction of three sacred rivers—the Ganges, the Jumna, and the mythical subterranean Saraswati—at Prayag (Allahabad), and one of the holiest sites of Hinduism |
| tu      | The most informal of the Hindi pronouns for 'you': used to express great intimacy between equals, or to express social distance between master and servant, parent and child, etc. |
| *Upanishads* | Collective title for some of the oldest mystical sacred writings of Hinduism |
| vaidji  | Respectful term of address or reference for a vaidya |
| vaidya  | Ayurvedic doctor |
| vakil   | Lawyer, pleader, or advocate |
| zamindari | Landed estate; the whole system of collecting land revenue through zamindars (landholders or landowners who played the role of tax-farmers) |

# *Appendix*
### *The Aim of Literature*[1]

Gentlemen, this conference is a landmark in our literary history. To date, our conferences and associations have usually only discussed language and language propaganda. So much so that the first [modern] literature available in Hindi and Urdu was written not with the aim of moulding ideas and feelings but only in order to create the language. That, too, was an important task. Until it acquires a stable, fixed form, where will a language find the capacity to express thoughts and feelings? We would be ungrateful if we did not feel thankful towards those language 'pioneers' who cleared our path by creating the Hindustani language. They have done a great thing for our national community.

Language is a means, not an end. Now that our language has acquired a stable form we should move on and turn our attention to the content and the aim for which that foundational work was started in the first place. The language in which works like *Bagh-o bahar* and *Baital pacchisi* initially marked the peak of service to literature has now become a suitable medium for enquiry into scholarly and scientific matters. This conference marks the clear recognition of this fact.

[1] 'Sahitya ka uddeshya', Presidential speech given at the first Progressive Writers' Conference, Lucknow, 9 April 1936, in Premchand, *Kuch vichar*, Allahabad, Sarasvati Press, 1982, pp. 5–25.

# Appendix

Language is both for ordinary conversation and for writing. The language of ordinary conversation existed also at the time of Mir Amman and Lallujilal, but the language in which they took their first, tentative steps was the written language, and that is literature. Ordinary conversation serves to impress our ideas upon our friends and close ones, to draw out our feelings of joy and sadness. Writers do the same thing with their pens. True, their audience is much wider, and if their words contain some truth their works continue to influence the hearts for centuries.

I do not mean to say, however, that anything that is written is literature. We call literature a work which expresses some truth, whose language is mature, polished and beautiful, and which has the ability to leave an impression on the heart and mind. In literature, this power emerges in full when it is the truths and experiences of life that find expression. Although we once used to be impressed by stories of magical adventures, ghost tales and romances of parted lovers, now they hardly hold any interest for us. Undoubtedly a writer who knows human nature can describe the truths of life even in tales of magic and in love stories about princes and princesses, but this confirms the dictum that in order for literature to exert any influence it necessarily has to mirror the truths of life. Then you can turn it any way you want—even the tale of a cock–sparrow or the rose and the nightingale can come handy.

There have been many definitions of literature, but in my opinion the best definition for it is—'the criticism of life'. Whether in the form of an essay or a poem, literature should criticize and explain life.

The age that we have just crossed had no concern for life. Our literary people would use their imagination to conjure magical worlds, whether it was *Fasana e-'Ajaib, Bostan-e Khyal* or *Chandrakanta Santati*.[2] The aim of those tales was simply to entertain and satisfy our taste for the wondrous. That literature should have anything to do with life was beyond imagination. A story is a story, life is life—the two were considered opposites. Similarly, poets were tainted by individualism. The satisfaction of desire was their ideal of love, the satisfaction of the

---

[2] *Fasana-e 'Ajaib* (1824), by Mirza Rajab 'Ali Beg Surur (1787–1867), *Bostan-e khyal* (1882–91) and *Chandrakanta Santati*, the multi-volume sequel by Devkinandan Khatri and his son Durgaprasad Khatri of *Chandrakanta* (1892), were all popular examples of narratives of wonder and adventure.

eyes, their ideal of beauty. Poetry circles would display their fireworks and talents in order to express these erotic feelings. A new wordplay, a new fancy was enough to earn praises, however distant they might have been from objective reality. Fanciful images involving *ashiyana* (nest) and *qafas* (cage), *barq* (lightning) and *khirman* (heapstack) were used with such skill to illustrate the various states of despair and suffering of the lover separated from his beloved that the listeners would have to clasp their bosoms. And just how popular this kind of poetry is still today, is something you and I know very well.

There is no doubt that the aim of poetry and of literature is to sharpen our perceptions, but human life is not just confined to love between man and woman. Can a literature whose themes are confined to the emotional states of love and the pain of separation and despair that spring from it, a literature which believes that escaping from the problems of the world is the meaning of life, answer our needs for thoughts and feelings? The mental and emotional states of love are only a part of human life, and if literature remains largely confined to them it brings little honour to the community and the age it belongs to, and their taste.

Whether in Hindi or Urdu, poetry was pretty much in the same condition. It is not easy to remain uninfluenced by the popular literary and poetic taste of one's age. And everybody longs for praise and appreciation. For poets, poetry was their means of livelihood, and who but the wealthy elites could appreciate poetry? Our poets never had the chance to confront ordinary life nor could they be influenced by its truths, and they were all, rich and poor, victims of a general intellectual crisis, which meant that no mental and intellectual life was left.

We cannot blame the literary people of that period for this. Literature is but a mirror of its age. The same feelings and thoughts which animate people's hearts also come to dominate literature. In that decadent age, people either made love or became engrossed in spiritual matters and asceticism. And when literature comes to be seen through the filter of the world's transience, when each and every word is coloured with despair and filled with moanings about the iniquity of the times or reflects erotic feeling, you can rest assured that the national community will be trapped in inertia and decadence and will have no strength of purpose and struggle left. It will have blinded itself to high ideals and will lose its ability to see and understand the world.

Appendix

However, our literary tastes are changing rapidly. Nowadays literature is not just meant for relaxation, it has a further aim apart from entertainment. It no longer only tells stories of happy and unhappy lovers, but it ponders on the problems of life and solves them too. It no longer seeks inspiration and vigour from wondrous and stupefying tales, or allure in alliteration, but concerns itself with issues affecting society and individuals. Currently, good literature is judged by the sharpness of its perception, which stirs our feelings and thoughts into motion.

The aims of ethics and of literature are the same—the difference is only in their manner of teaching. Ethics tries to mould intelligence and character through arguments and preaching, while the chosen field of literature are mental and emotional states. Whatever we see in our lives and whatever experiences and blows we encounter, once they reach the imagination they inspire literary creativity. The sharper a poet or a writer is, the more attractive and of high order the literary work will be. A literature which brings no challenge to our tastes, which does not provide us with mental and spiritual satisfaction, which does not awaken strength and dynamism within us, which fails to raise from slumber our sense of beauty, and which does not produce in us true determination and true resolve to overcome difficulties—such a literature is of no use to us today and it is not even worthy of the name.

In earlier times, religion kept society in check. Religious imperatives were the basis for the spiritual and ethical civility of man, and religion used either fear or reward—virtue or sin as its instrument. Now literature has taken this task upon itself, and its instrument is the love of beauty. Literature tries to awaken in man this love for beauty. There is no human being who does not have a perception of beauty. And the more developed and active this tendency is in a writer, the more influential his or her work will be. By contemplating nature and sharpening perception, the writer's sense of beauty becomes so acute that anything ugly, uncivilized and lacking in humanness becomes unbearable to him and he will attack it with words and feelings. In other words, one could say that the writer weaves a cloak of humanness, divineness and civility. It is the duty of a writer to support and defend those who are in some way oppressed, suffering or deprived, whether they be individuals or groups. He pleads justice on their behalf and considers himself successful when through his efforts the court's sense of justice and beauty is awakened.

However, unlike an ordinary lawyer, a writer cannot plead for the innocence of his clients using just any kinds of arguments, fair or unfair. A writer cannot employ exaggeration, nor can he spin tales. In the courtroom of society, the writer knows, such methods fail to make any impression. Society can change its heart only when he does not shy an inch from the truth, otherwise the jury will form a bad opinion and will decide against him. A writer writes stories, but keeping in mind reality. A writer shapes images, but so that they may be alive and expressive. A writer surveys human nature with sharp eyes, studies psychology and tries to have characters who behave in every situation as if they were made of flesh and blood. Thanks to natural empathy and love of beauty, a writer can reach even the most subtle areas which human beings are usually unable to reach because of their humanity.

The tendency towards depicting reality is growing so much in modern literature that stories nowadays try not to go beyond the limits of direct experience. We are not content to think that characters resemble real human beings in their psychological makeup, but we want to be sure that they really are human beings and that the writer has succeeded, as much as possible, in writing their life story. Because we no longer believe in characters created from fantasy, their acts and thoughts fail to impress us. We want to rest assured that what the writer has created is based on actual experiences and that he himself is speaking through his characters. That is why some critics call literature the psychological history of a writer.

The same event or situation does not leave the same impression on everyone. Every person has a different mentality and point of view. A writer's ability lies in having the reader agree with his own mentality or way of looking at things. Herein lies an author's success. At the same time, we also expect every writer to awaken our senses and broaden our mental horizon thanks to his wide knowledge and breadth of ideas—his vision should be subtle, deep and wide enough so as to give us spiritual pleasure and strength.

In every individual, whatever stage of self-reform he or she may be at, lies the potential to reach a better state. But we are affected by our weaknesses as by diseases. Just as physical health is our natural state and sickness is its opposite, in the same way mental and moral health are also our natural states, and we are unhappy about our mental and moral deficiencies in the same way as a sick person is unhappy about his sickness. And just as a patient keeps searching for a cure, we, too, strive to get rid of our weaknesses in order to become better human beings. We go in search of holy men and *faqirs*, perform religious rituals, sit at the feet of our elders, listen to the sermons of wise men, or study literature. It is our lowly tastes and our lack of love that are responsible for all our weaknesses. How can weaknesses persist where there is true love for beauty and wide-ranging love? Love is the real spiritual food, and all weaknesses stem from not getting this food or from getting it in a polluted form. The writer or artist produces within us this experience of beauty and the warm spirit of love. One sentence, one word, one hint and we feel lit up inside. But until the artist himself is drunk with love for beauty and his own soul is lit up by this light, how can he bestow it upon us?

The question is: what is beauty? This seems like a meaningless question at first sight, because we have no doubt in our minds as to what beauty is. We have seen the sun rise and set, we have seen the glow of dawn and sunset, we have seen fragrant flowers, birds chirping sweetly, brooks gurgling gently, springs dancing—this is beauty.

Why do we feel happy inside when we see these things? Because of the harmony of colour and sound. Music bewitches us because of the harmony between musical instruments. We ourselves have been created by different elements coming together in equal measure, and therefore our soul is constantly yearning for that harmony and balance. Literature expresses an artist's spiritual harmony in a visible form. And harmony creates beauty, it does not destroy it. It strengthens within us feelings of loyalty, truthfulness, sympathy, love for justice and equality. And wherever these feelings exist we find strength and life; wherever they are absent we find division, opposition, self-interest, hatred, enmity and death. This alienation and conflict are signs of a life contrary to nature, just as sickness is a sign of an unnatural way of life. How can narrow-mindedness and self-interest possibly exist where affinity with life and equality exist? When our soul is nurtured in the free atmosphere of nature, the germs of baseness and wickedness die of their own accord, exposed to the light and the air. It is by setting oneself apart from life that all these mental and emotional diseases are created. Literature makes our lives natural and free. In other words, it is thanks to literature that our minds are refined. This is the main aim of literature.

# Appendix

The 'Progressive Writers' Association'—this name sounds wrong to me. A writer or artist is naturally progressive. Were this not his nature, he would probably not be an artist. A writer is someone who feels something lacking, both within and also outside himself. It is to remedy this lack that his soul is restless. A writer feels that the individual and society are not in the happy and carefree state he or she would like to see them in. This is why he chafes under the present mental and social conditions. He wants to put an end to these unpleasant conditions so that the world can become a better place to live and to die. This pain, this feeling keeps his brain and heart active. His heart, laden with pain, cannot bear to see any group suffering under the constraint of rules and conventions. Why cannot we find the needful to free that group from slavery and poverty? The more acutely a writer feels this pain, the greater the force and truth his work will produce. How a writer manages to control the intensity with which his perceptions are expressed is the secret of his craft. It is perhaps necessary to emphasize this special quality here because not every writer or author has the same understanding of progress *(unnati)*. What one community considers to be progress, another may well consider decadence, and for this reason the writer does not want to subject his art to any objective. To the writer, art means the expression of mental dispositions, whatever good or bad effect they may have on an individual or society.

What I mean by progress, is the condition which produces in us the resolve and energy to act, that which makes us realize the unhappy state we are in, the internal and external causes which have brought us to this wretched and lifeless state, and that which makes us strive to remove them.

To me, poetic ideas have no meaning if they make the impermanence of the world have a stronger hold over our hearts (our monthly journals are filled with these ideas) and if they do not arouse within us dynamism and zeal. If we tell the story of two young lovers in a way that makes no impact on our love of beauty and only makes us weep for them because they are apart, what movement have we brought to the mind and taste? Perhaps once people did get sentimental about them, but nowadays these stories are useless. The time for this sentimental art is gone. Nowadays we need an art which carries a message of action. Now, I also say with Mister Iqbal:

Ramz-e hayat joi juz dar tapish nayabi
radakuljum armidan nang ast ab-e ju ra.
Ba ashiyan na nashinam ze lazzat-e parvaz
gahe bashakh-e gulam gahe bar lab-e juyam.

[If you are searching for the water of life you will not find it but amid struggle.
For a river, to go and rest in the ocean is shameful. I never sit in the nest to
enjoy flying, I am sometimes on a rose branch, sometimes on the bank of a
river.]

In other words, egotism, giving prominence to our individual point
of view, is what pulls us down towards inertia, decadence and indifference, and this kind of art is useless for us, both as individuals and as a
community.

I have no hesitation in saying that I weigh art on the same scales of
usefulness as I do with other things. Undoubtedly, the aim of art is to
strengthen our sense of beauty, and art is the key to our spiritual
happiness, but there is no mental and spiritual happiness one can
achieve through taste which does not also have a useful aspect. Happiness is naturally allied with usefulness, and a useful thing can give us
both pleasure and pain.

A glowing sky at sunset is undoubtedly the most beautiful spectacle,
but the same glow in the sky, if seen during the monsoon, will not give
us any pleasure. During the monsoon we want to see black rainclouds.
When we see flowers we feel happy, because we look forward to their
fruit. We get spiritual pleasure from tuning our life in accordance with
nature because our life is enhanced and developed by it. It is nature's
course to grow and develop, and the feelings, perceptions and ideas
that give us pleasure enhance this growth and development. An artist
is someone who prepares the condition for development by creating
beauty through art.

But beauty, too, like any other element, is not neutral and objective,
it is relative. A thing which will give pleasure to a wealthy man may be
a source of displeasure to somebody else. Whereas a rich man enjoys
perfect bliss by sitting in a garden full of fragrant flowers and listening
to the birds chirping, a sensible man may be repulsed by the same
display of opulence.

Since the beginning of life, fraternity, equality, civility and love
have been a golden dream for idealists. Religious prophets have always
tried, albeit unsuccessfully, to make this dream come true by means of

religious, moral and spiritual rules. Buddha, Jesus, Muhammad and all the other prophets and religious founders have tried to build equality on ethical foundations, but no one has been successful, and perhaps the difference between rich and poor is more cruelly evident now than ever before.

'It is stupid to try what has been tried before'; according to this saying, if we try now to reach the high goal of equality by holding on to religion and ethics we will not be successful. Should we therefore forget this dream as if it were the product of an excitable mind? But then there will be no ideal left to guide man towards progress and fulfilment. In that case it would be better for humankind to stop living. We must consider that the ideal which mankind has pursued and cultivated from the beginning of civilization and for which it has made so many sacrifices, the ideal thanks to which religions came into being, is an imperishable truth and we must step onto the path of progress. We need to create a new association that will be comprehensive and in which equality, no longer based only on moral obligations, will acquire a concrete shape. This is the ideal that our literature must set for itself.

We will have to change the standard of beauty. So far this standard has been based on wealth and love of pleasure. Our artist wanted to hold on to rich people: his existence depended on their appreciation, and it was the aim of art to give expression to their joys and sorrows, their hopes and disappointments and the competitiveness among them. The artist fixed his gaze on the women's inner quarters and on palaces and bungalows. Mud huts and ruins were not worthy of his attention. He considered them beyond the pale of humanity. And if he ever mentioned them, it was to deride them. It was to laugh at the villagers' rustic clothes and behaviour; their uncorrect pronunciation of Urdu words and their misuse of verbal expressions were the butt of his unremitting sarcasm. That they too are human beings and have hearts and aspirations, this was beyond the imagination of art.

Art was, and still is, a byword for the narrow worship of sensuous beauty for well-turned phrases and composed emotions. It has had no ideal, no high goal for life: its loftiest imagining is to stay away from devotion, detachment, and spiritual and worldly matters. This has been the highest aim in life for our artists. Their vision is not yet ample enough that they may see the highest form of beauty in the midst of life's struggle. They cannot acknowledge that beauty exists also in starving and naked people. For them, beauty lies in a beautiful woman, not in the poor and ungainly mother who is toiling hard after putting her baby to sleep on the hay. If our artists have decided that beauty definitely dwells in painted lips, cheeks and eyebrows, how can it have anything to do with tangled hair, cracked lips and sunken cheeks?

But this is a defect of narrow vision. When their view of beauty opens up wide, they will see that while painted lips and cheeks hide heartlessness and pride in one's beauty, the tears of those faded lips and sunken cheeks contain the spirit of renunciation, faith and forbearance though there is no sophistication, prettiness or showiness in them.

Our art is crazy after the love for youth, and yet does not know that youth does not mean reciting poetry with one hand on one's heart, protesting against the cruelty of one's beloved or despairing for her beauteous pride and her coquettishness. Youth means idealism, self-renunciation and the desire to confront troubles with courage. Our art must say with Iqbal:

Az dast-e junun-e man jibril zabun said-e
Yazdan bakamand avar ai himmat-e mardana.

[Jibrail is a weak prey in my crazed hands. O manly courage, why didn't you catch God himself with your bow?]

or

Chun mauj saz-e vajudam ze sail beparvast
guman mabar ki daran bahr sahila juyam.

[ Like a wave, the boat of my life cares not for the tide, Do not think that in this sea I am looking for the shore.]

This condition will arise once beauty becomes for us so wide as to encompass the whole creation within its bounds. Beauty will not be confined to some particular category, its flight will not be restricted within a four-walled garden, but it will soar into the sky surrounding the entire earth. Then we will no longer endure base taste and we will endeavour to uproot it completely. When we are no longer able to accept a system in which thousands of people are slaves to a few oppressors, then, not content with creating something on paper, we will create a system that will not be the enemy of beauty, taste, self-respect and humanity.

The goal of the poet is not just to excite a literary gathering and provide means for entertainment—please, do not make him stoop so low. His goal is not the truth that follows patriotism and politics, but the truth that leads ahead holding high its beacon.

We often complain that our society has no place for writers, that is for Indian writers. In civilized countries, a writer is a respected member of society, and the cream of society and the members of the cabinet consider themselves lucky to interact with them. But India is still in the Middle Ages. If a writer chooses to support himself by pleading with the wealthy and remains ignorant and indifferent to the movements, activities and revolutions that are taking place in society, if he continues to live happily or sadly in a world of his own making, then it is no injustice if there is no place for him in this world. But once a favourable disposition becomes the only requirement needed to become a writer, just as no education is needed to become a mahatma and spiritual greatness is enough, you will see that writers will also emerge in their thousands just as there are now mahatmas at every step.

There is no doubt that one is born, not made, a writer; but if we can increase this gift with education and curiosity we will surely be doing a better service to literature. Aristotle and the other philosophers have laid down strict rules for becoming a writer; and principles and regulations have been set for a writer's intellectual, moral, spiritual and emotional education and refinement. But nowadays in Hindi, to have a disposition is considered enough to become a writer, and there is no sense that one needs to prepare for it in various ways. Even if a writer is completely ignorant of politics, sociology or psychology, he can still be a writer.

The ideal that we have nowadays set for a writer requires that all these disciplines be necessarily part. Literature is no longer limited to individualism or egotism, but tends to turn more and more towards the psychological and the social. Now literature does not view the individual as separate from society, on the contrary it sees the individual as an indissoluble part of society! Not so that the individual should rule over society and make literature a means for pursuing his self-interests, as if eternal enmity existed between him and society, but because the individual's existence is dependent on the existence of society, outside of which his value is next to nothing.

Those of us who have been given the highest education and the highest intellectual powers have consequently greater responsibility towards society. I will not consider worthy of respect the 'intellectual capitalist' who, after having acquired high education at the expence of the society, uses it simply for his own self-interest. To draw personal advantage from society is something that no writer will ever want to do. The duty of that intellectual capitalist should be to consider the welfare of society even worthier of attention than his own, and to try with his knowledge and ability to bring to society as much benefit as possible. Whatever branch of literature he may devote himself to, he should be acquainted with that branch in particular, and generally with all others.

If we read the reports of international literary conferences we notice that there is no scientific, social, historical or psychological question which has not been discussed. When, conversely, we look at the limitations of our own knowledge in India, we feel ashamed at our ignorance. [In India] we think that in order to write literature, a quick mind and a fast pen are enough. But this idea has been the cause of our literary decadence. We will have to raise the standard of our literature, so that it can serve society more usefully and so that society may give it the position it rightly deserves; our literature will discuss and assess every aspect of life, and we will no longer be satisfied with eating the leftovers of other languages and literatures. We will ourselves increase the capital of our literature.

We should choose topics fitting our tastes and disposition and become fully competent in them. This is of course difficult, given the economic condition in which we live, but our ideal should remain high. Even if we do not reach the top of the mountain, we will reach the middle, which is always better than staying at the bottom. With the light of love shining within us and the ideal of service before us, there is no difficulty we cannot surmount.

In the temple of literature there is no place for those who hold wealth and fame dear. Literature only needs worshippers who accept that service is what makes their life meaningful, whose hearts bleed with pain and burn with love. Our honour is in our own hands. If we serve society truthfully, honour, prestige and fame will themselves come and kiss our feet. And why should we be obsessed with honour and prestige after all? Why should we feel despondent if we do not get them? The spiritual happiness that accrues from service is our true reward; why should we feel the desire to show off in front of society?

# Appendix

Why should we yearn with the desire to live more comfortably than others do? Why should we count ourselves among the wealthy? We are soldiers brandishing the flag of society, and our goal in life is to live simply and keep our gaze high. A true artist cannot love a life of self-interest, he does not need appearances to feel content inside, in fact he hates them. He believes, with Iqbal, that:

> Mardum-e azadam aguna rayaram ki mara
> Mitavan kusthav yak julal-e digaran.

[I am free and modest enough that others can kill me with a cup of water.]

Our association has entered the field of action with these principles in mind. It does not want literature to remain dependent upon sensuality and eroticism. It aspires to make literature the messenger of action and effort. Our association has no contention about language. Once our ideal becomes wider, language will naturally become simpler. Inner beauty (*bhav-saundarya*) can afford to be indifferent to artificial adornments. The writer who looks up to wealthy patrons adopts a sumptuous creative style, a writer who belongs to ordinary people (*jansadharan*) will write in the language of ordinary people. Our aim is to create in the country an atmosphere in which the kind of literature we aspire to will be able to grow and prosper. We want our association to be established at literary centres and regular discussions to take place there about trends in creative literature: there should be debates, guidelines, critical exchanges. Only then will such an atmosphere be created. Only then will a new era begin for literature.

We want associations to be established in each province and in each language which will be able to spread our message in every language. It is a mistake to think that this plan of ours is a new one. No, collective feelings have already been present in the hearts of the 'servants of literature' in our country. In each and every language of India, the seeds of this idea have already been sown, by nature and by circumstances, and here and there the seedlings have already started sprouting. To water them and strengthen their aim is our goal.

We literary people lack strength of action. This is a bitter truth, but we cannot shut our eyes in front of it. So far the aim we had set for literature did not require any action. In fact, the absence of action was a good thing, because often action brings along partisanship and narrowness. If a religious person becomes proud of his or her piety, it would be better if they believed in 'eat drink and be merry'. Such bohemians can be the rightful recipients of God's mercy, while someone who takes pride in his or her piety cannot.

In any case, as long as the aim of literature was only to provide entertainment, to put us to sleep by singing lullabies and make us shed a few tears in order to lighten our hearts, it had no need for action. It was like a mad lover whose sorrow was felt by others; but in our mind literature is not only a plaything for entertainment and sensual enjoyment. The only literature that will pass our test is that which contains high thinking, a sense of freedom, the essence of beauty, the soul of creativity and the light that emanates from the truths of life, a literature which instils in us dynamism and restlessness, not sleep; because to go on sleeping now would be a sign of death.

Translated by
FRANCESCA ORSINI